Child & Adolescent Development

A Chronological Approach

Danuta Bukatko

CENGAGE Learning™

Australia • Brazil • Japan • Korea • Mexico • Singapore • Spain • United Kingdom • United States

CENGAGE Learning™

Child & Adolescent Development
A Chronological Approach
Danuta Bukatko

Executive Editors:
Maureen Staudt
Michael Stranz

Senior Project Development Manager:
Linda deStefano

Marketing Specialist:
Courtney Sheldon

Senior Production/Manufacturing Manager:
Donna M. Brown

PreMedia Manager:
Joel Brennecke

Sr. Rights Acquisition Account Manager:
Todd Osborne

Cover Image:
Getty Images*

*Unless otherwise noted, all cover images used by Custom Solutions, a part of Cengage Learning, have been supplied courtesy of Getty Images with the exception of the Earthview cover image, which has been supplied by the National Aeronautics and Space Administration (NASA).

Printed in the United States of America

Child and Adolescent Development: A Chronological Approach, 1st Edition
Danuta Bukatko

This book contains select works from existing Cengage Learning resources and was produced by Cengage Learning Custom Solutions for collegiate use. As such, those adopting and/or contributing to this work are responsible for editorial content accuracy, continuity and completeness.

ISBN-13: 978-0-495-83063-4

ISBN-10: 0-495-83063-1

Cengage Learning
5191 Natorp Boulevard
Mason, Ohio 45040
USA

Cengage Learning is a leading provider of customized learning solutions with office locations around the globe, including Singapore, the United Kingdom, Australia, Mexico, Brazil, and Japan. Locate your local office at: **international.cengage.com/region.**

Cengage Learning products are represented in Canada by Nelson Education, Ltd.
For your lifelong learning solutions, visit **www.cengage.com/custom.**
Visit our corporate website at **www.cengage.com.**

Child and Adolescent Development

A Chronological Approach

Accessible and Engaging: Tying Theory and Practice Together

INFANCY (AGES 0–2) PART THREE

PHYSICAL DEVELOPMENT 5

KEY THEMES in Physical Development

2 **NATURE & NURTURE** How do nature and nurture interact in physical development in infancy?

SOCIOCULTURAL INFLUENCE How does the sociocultural context influence physical development in infancy?

CONTINUITY/DISCONTINUITY Is physical development during infancy continuous or discontinuous?

INTERACTION AMONG DOMAINS How does physical development during infancy interact with other domains of development?

RISK/RESILIENCE What factors promote risk or resilience in physical development during infancy?

1 Marc knew he had to dress the baby quickly. It had been a hectic morning. His wife's car hadn't started, and they had to arrange for her to get a ride to work. Now he and their three-month-old daughter, Abbie, had to step up the pace to get to daycare. Marc hastily pulled out a sweatshirt and pants from the baby's dresser, grateful that Abbie was in a good mood and didn't seem to mind the rapid tempo of the morning's routine. "Here you go, honey. Let's get these pants on you. Here are your pants from Aunt Rose. Bloooie pants!" Abbie responded with a gleeful s[...] and a few kicks. But as he lifted the waistband over Abbie's diaper, he could see that he had a problem. Worn only once before, these pants now barely covered the middle of Abbie's little calf. "Well, little girl, you sure look funny like that. We're going to have to start all over again." Looking at the picture of a younger, newborn Abbie that stood on the dresser, he couldn't help but notice the remarkable changes that his daughter had gone through in only three short months.

149

1 Each chapter begins with an engaging vignette and
2 a reminder of the recurring five **"Key Themes"** or big-picture questions that developmental psychologists seek to answer.

3 **Research Applied to Parenting/Education, Atypical Development,** and **Controversy: Thinking It Over** features bring the study of child development to life and encourage students to think critically about the everyday applications of research.

4 CONTEXTS OF DEVELOPMENT 16

4 **Contexts of Development** chapters discuss development issues in the broader context of family, peers, and the community at large.

Student-Centered Approach

A range of study and review tools are available in every chapter.

5 Marginal Glossary
Key terms are defined on appropriate pages within the chapter.

KEY THEME
NATURE & NURTURE

5 **basic (primary) emotion** Emotion, such as joy, sadness, or surprise, that appears early in infancy and seems to have a biological foundation.

Emotional Expression in Infancy Even infants only a few days or weeks old are capable of producing the facial expressions associated with several emotions, including interest, distress, disgust, joy, sadness, anger, and surprise (Field et al., 1982; Izard, 1978; Izard et al., 1995). By seven months of age, the infant has added expressions of fear to his repertoire (Izard et al., 1980). The fact that these discrete facial expressions appear so early in infancy, before much learning can have taken place, provides strong support for the idea that emotional expressions are to some extent biologically determined. These emotions are often called **basic (or primary) emotions.**

Although even the earliest displays of basic emotions are usually readily recognized by adults, their form and the conditions that elicit them may change over the first few months. Two important emotional expressions in infancy, smiling and crying, demonstrate these changes. The smile is one of the most captivating and irresistible infant behaviors. In the newborn this behavior occurs primarily during the state of REM sleep, when dreaming is thought to occur, in bursts of several smiles in succession (Emde & Koenig, 1969). The mouth stretches sideways and up, producing a simple

490 PART FIVE ■ CHAPTER 13 CONTEXTS O...

6 CHAPTER RECAP

Summary of Developmental Themes

SOCIOCULTURAL INFLUENCE

How do sociocultural factors influence the contexts of development in middle childhood?

Culture has been shown to influence parenting demands, especially in the degree to which children are expected to be compliant and helpful in order to help the family survive.

RISK/RESILIENCE

What contextual factors promote risk or resilience in middle childhood?

Divorce and single parenthood can put children at risk, but the practice of effective parenting overrides the effects that these variations in family structure might have. Children can be at risk for negative developmental outcomes if they experience poor peer relationships. However, research has identified several ways in which success with peers can be promoted. For example, fostering prosocial behaviors, good social skills, and effective social-information processing can help children in their interactions with peers. Certain characteristics of schools can promote or discourage academic achievement. Children thrive when they experience smooth transitions to school, have small classes, and interact with teachers who encourage autonomy and initiative.

Chapter Review

THE FAMILY IN MIDDLE CHILDHOOD

In what ways do parenting strategies vary across different cultural groups?

Cultures vary in the degree to which children must contribute to the family's subsistence, do chores, and obey their parents. In some cultures, parents demand a very high degree of compliance, whereas in others, the empha... sis in parent-child interactions is sociability.

Assistance with sources of stress, such as help with child care and counseling, can be helpful in alleviating some of the stresses that single parents face.

What does the research indicate about the impact of having gay or lesbian parents?

KEY TERMS AND CONCEPTS

collaborative learning (p. 477)
cooperative learning (p. 477)
cultural compatibility hypothesis (p. 478)
sociometric nomination (p. 459)
sociometric rating scale (p. 459)

6 Chapter Recap
Appearing at the end of each chapter, the Chapter Recap includes:

- a **Summary of Developmental Themes**
- a general **Chapter Review**
- a **Key Terms and Concepts** list reinforcing important takeaways from the chapter.

7 PATHWAYS: CONNECTING THE STORY OF DEVELOPMENT

	INFANCY (0–2 YEARS)	EARLY CHILDHOOD (2–6 YEARS)
Physical Development	• Evidences rapid gains in height and weight, with faster rates of growth in the head region and regions nearer the center of the body • Shows period of rapid brain development, including formation and pruning of synapses • Shows basic learning capabilities in the form of habituation, operant and classical conditioning, and imitation • Shows improvements in visual accommodation, saccadic movements, acuity, and vergence • Attracted first to external features of objects and to movement, and later to internal features of objects • Localizes sounds • Recognizes melodic rhythms and other features of music • Shows sensitivity to smells, tastes, and tactile stimuli	• Shows advances in gross motor skills such as running, jumping, and skipping • Evidences slower but regular increases in size • Shows evidence of implicit learning
Cognitive/ Language Development	• Attends to increasingly complex patterns including those with facelike organization • Responsive to biological motion • Shows signs of depth perception • Shows intermodal perception • Develops *means-ends behavior* • Attains the *object concept* • Shows sensitivity to changes in number • Relies on egocentric and landmark cues to locate objects • Classifies objects according to physical similarities, as well as thematic and simple taxonomic relations • Distinguishes between animate and inanimate objects • Shows recognition memory for simple stimuli	• Shows gains in ability to make perceptual discriminations • Can classify according to basic-level concepts • Understands the meaning of simple number terms, and eventually the basic principles of counting • Displays good intuitions about mathematical operations such as addition and forming fractions • Uses landmark cues to negotiate spatial environments • Uses geometric cues to aid spatial location • Begins to be able to read maps • Realizes that others can have different visual perspectives • Develops a *theory of mind* • Shows elementary planning activities • Displays knowledge of scripts

7 Pathways: The Development Story
Appearing at the end of the infancy, early childhood, middle childhood, and adolescence chapters, this chart provides an at-a-glance summary of the physical, cognitive, and socioemotional milestones across development.

Learning and Teaching Resources

FOR STUDENTS

Student Study Guide

This print guide includes many resources for practice and review including learning objectives, chapter reviews, key terms, and multiple-choice questions.

Online Learning Center

The textbook website includes study aids such as ace quizzes, interactive flashcards, tutorials, and animations. Additionally, it offers critical thinking practice through the "What Do You Think?" and "See for Yourself" features.

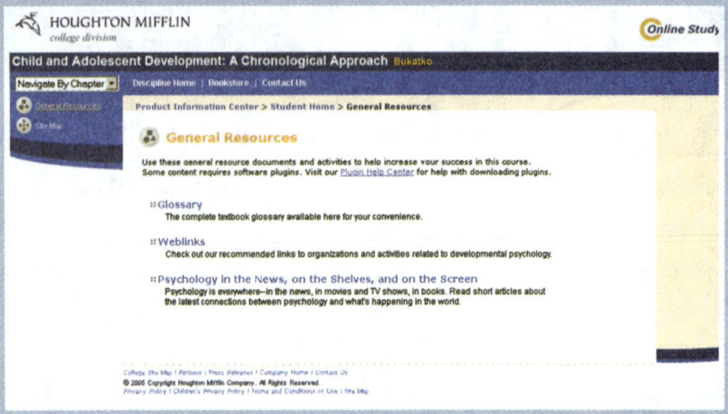

Student CD-ROM

For self-study and practice, this CD-ROM offers video clips, overviews, animations, quizzing, and glossary terms.

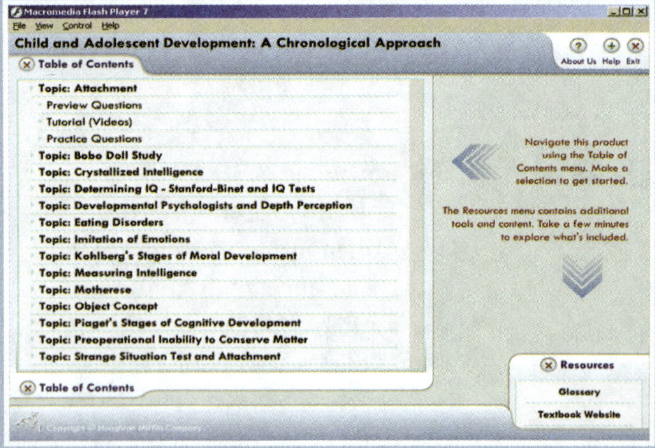

FOR INSTRUCTORS

Online Teaching Center

This instructor website offers many tools including Powerpoint presentations, Classroom Response Systems (clickers), art and tables from the textbook, and a downloadable *Instructor's Resource Manual.*

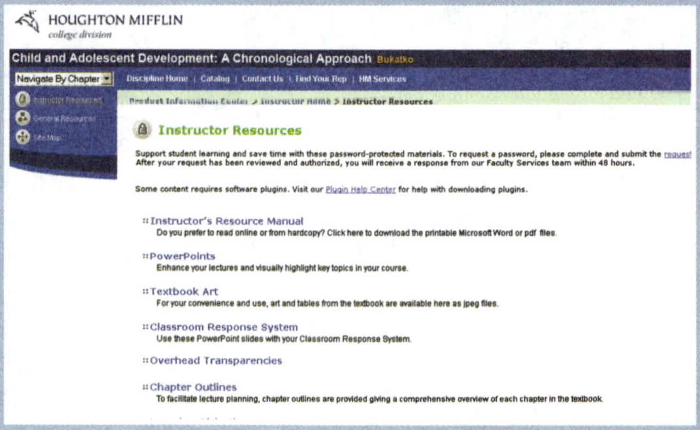

Blackboard®/WebCT®

These courses allow instructors to utilize, customize, and administer all instructor resources developed specifically for this text.

HM Testing

HM Testing (powered by Diploma) is a flexible test-editing program with a comprehensive grade-book function for easy administration and tracking. The test bank includes over 1,600 multiple-choice questions and 80 essay questions keyed to learning objectives.

Child Development Psych in Film

Contains twelve clips from Universal Studio films illustrating concepts in developmental psychology such as cognitive development, moral reasoning, parenting styles, and adolescent development. Clips from films like Parenthood, *Snow Falling on Cedars, Sixteen Candles,* and many others are combined with commentary and discussion questions.

Brief Contents

Features

Controversy: Thinking It Over

Research Applied to Parenting

Research Applied to Education

Atypical Development

Pathways: Connecting the Story of Development

Contents

13 CONTEXTS OF DEVELOPMENT 448

PART SIX ADOLESCENCE (AGES 12–18) 495

14 PHYSICAL AND COGNITIVE DEVELOPMENT 495

15 SOCIAL AND EMOTIONAL DEVELOPMENT 530

16 CONTEXTS OF DEVELOPMENT 551

Preface

Most of us who teach a course in child development know that we tend to fall into one of two camps: those who teach the course from a topical perspective, treating each content area in development as a discrete entity, and those who teach a chronologically-based course, following children's growth from one age to the next. There are a lot of reasons for taking one approach versus the other, some of which may be driven by the particular teaching philosophies of the instructor, and some of which may be motivated by the needs of the students enrolled in our courses. I myself had always been a "topical" person, believing that describing language, or cognitive, or emotional development was better done in one focused stream, unbroken by interruptions about other developments also taking place at a given age. What I learned from writing this book is that there is distinct and genuine value in telling the story of development chronologically. The various content areas of development—the biological, cognitive, and socioemotional spheres—do, after all, interact with each other during each phase of the child's growth. What better way to appreciate that fact than to consider them together in the context of a particular chronological time period? Perhaps even more important, considering child development from a chronological perspective exposes the possibility that certain developmental tasks might be more important at some times than others. Indeed, the challenges mastered by the toddler are very much different from those faced by a preadolescent. Such potentially significant concepts might be overlooked if one's focus is solely on a topic rather than a developmental time period.

Regardless of which tactic the instructor takes—topical or chronological—many of the issues in teaching are similar. How do we get our students to learn so much material? How can we help them to make sense of the vast storehouse of information that keeps accumulating in our journals and books? Are there some themes or concepts that seem especially important for our students to appreciate above all others, and most important, to remember once they leave our courses? These were the very questions that motivated the first topical child development book Marvin Daehler and I co-authored almost twenty years ago, and they remained the issues that concerned me when I began this chronological text. Our answer to these dilemmas for the topical text was to organize the book around a set of fundamental themes or recurring questions. I believe that using a small set of organizing themes helps to frame the "big picture" for a chronological text as well.

There are several other considerations that are also important to me as an author. As a teacher, I have always been committed to helping students think scientifically about developmental psychology. Part of that process means that students should reflect on how the theories and data that comprise the field of developmental psychology challenge or affirm any intuitions they may have about children. It also means that students need to develop a critical stance toward what they read. Throughout their learning, students should also appreciate the historically important knowledge base upon which contemporary developmental psychology has been built. My commitments to these principles are reflected here in several ways: relying heavily on theories and empirical studies in telling the story of child development, encouraging students to think about competing ideas, and attempting to provide a balance of classic studies in developmental psychology with recent findings from the research literature.

Finally, I am deeply committed to the idea that knowledge gained from science can have important implications for the way we parent, teach, and create social policy pertaining to children. My students seem to insist on this principle, and judging from various movements to link research to practice among researchers, there is growing momentum to do precisely this in the field of psychology. I sincerely hope readers will find that this textbook helps them in their work with children, whatever form that may take.

A Chronological Approach

Childhood is divided in this textbook into four major periods: infancy (birth to 2 years), early childhood (2 to 6 years), middle childhood (6 to 11 years), and adolescence (12 to 18 years). These seemed to be the natural ways in which to partition the first eighteen years of life given children's major accomplishments and the circumstances in which they develop. Within each time frame, the child's attainments in the physical, cognitive, and socioemotional domains are discussed along with the forces that seem to be responsible for them. In addition, for each time frame beyond infancy, I have included a chapter on the context of development in recognition of the fact that as they mature, children find themselves in different social, cultural, and educational situations, and are thus subject to new and powerful influences.

Key Themes

The following five themes are highlighted throughout the discussion of child development:

Nature & Nurture

- How do nature and nurture interact in development?

Sociocultural Influence

- How does the sociocultural context influence development?

Continuity/Discontinuity

- Is development continuous or discontinuous?

Interaction Among Domains

- How do the various domains of development interact?

Risk/Resilience

- What factors promote risk or resilience in development?

By drawing out these themes, I hope that readers are stimulated to think about the process of development, or why development proceeds as it does. These **Key Themes** are designed to help students discern the importance and interrelatedness of various facts, and as vehicles for instructors to encourage critical analysis among students. In addition, some of the themes—**Risk/Resilience**, in particular—may help students to appreciate the ramifications of theory and research for applied issues such as parenting practices, education, and social policy for children.

Within each chapter, some or all of the five developmental themes serve to organize and provide coherence for the material. The themes are highlighted for students in several ways.

1. The themes most immediately relevant to a chapter are listed at its start.
2. Indicators in the margins of the chapter point to discussions of each key theme.
3. Each chapter closes with a brief synopsis of how the key themes are illustrated in the domain explored by the chapter.

Students and instructors may, of course, find additional instances of the five themes. They may also locate new and additional themes. This process is certainly in keeping with the goal of setting in motion a search on the part of readers for integration and coherence in the vast material that constitutes the scientific study of child development.

Features and Study Tools

The chapter outlines, **For Your Review** lists (bulleted recaps at the end of major sections), margin and end-of-text glossaries, and **Chapter Recap** (including a **Summary of Developmental Themes,** a general **Chapter Review,** and a **Key Terms and Concepts** list) all serve to underscore important themes, terms, and concepts. I hope that students will actively utilize these aids to reinforce what they have learned in the chapter body. In addition, several strategies are intended to make the material in this text more accessible to students: vignettes to open the chapter, the Research Applied to Parenting/Education feature, the liberal use of examples throughout the text, and an extensive program of illustrations accompanied by instructive captions.

Research Applied to Parenting/ Education

Designed to identify some of the implications of research that extend beyond the laboratory, this feature is intended to help students think about questions and concerns that typically affect parents and teachers in their interactions with children. The **Research Applied to Parenting/Education** feature addresses such topics as the steps parents might take to reduce the risk of sudden infant death syndrome and the strategies teachers might follow to promote gender equity in the classroom. Each topic covered in this feature is introduced with a continuation of the chapter-opening vignette and is followed by a set of points that, based on our current knowledge, leads to positive consequences for children and their development. These points, of course, should not be considered the final word on the subject, but they will help readers to understand how research has led to practical benefits for children, parents, and teachers. For a complete list of topics covered in this feature, see page viii.

Atypical Development

By including an **Atypical Development** feature within each chapter, I hope to emphasize that the same processes that help to explain normal development can also help us understand development that is different from the norm. The reverse applies as well: that understanding atypical development can illuminate the factors that guide more typical child development. Thus, such topics as attention deficit hyperactivity disorder, autism, and language impairment are included in this feature. A complete list of topics appears on page viii.

Controversy: Thinking It Over

Controversy: Thinking It Over boxes continue to serve as the foundation for debate and extended discussion in the classroom. They are organized in a three-question framework to better promote critical thinking and a deeper appreciation of all sides of a theoretical debate:

1. What Is the Controversy?
2. What Are the Opposing Arguments?
3. What Answers Exist/What Questions Remain?

A complete list of topics appears on page viii.

Pathways Charts

Appearing at the end of the infancy, early childhood, middle childhood, and adolescence chapters, these charts provide an at-a-glance summary of the physical, cognitive, and socio-emotional milestones across development. The adolescence **Pathways** collects all the charts in one place, providing a complete and convenient reference and review tool.

Teaching and Learning Support Package

Many useful materials have been developed to support the study of *Child and Adolescent Development* and enhance the teaching and learning experience.

For the Instructor

Instructor's Resource Manual

The *Instructor's Resource Manual*, written by Lora Harpster, Salt Lake Community College, contains a complete set of chapter outlines and learning objectives, as well as lecture topics, classroom exercises, demonstrations, and handouts. It also features recommended readings, videos, and Internet sites.

Test Bank

The *Test Bank*, written by Ashley E. Murphy, University of Minnesota, includes over 1,600 multiple-choice items. Each is accompanied by a key that provides the learning objective, the text page number on which the answer can be found, type of question (Fact, Concept, or Application), and correct answer. To encourage students to think critically, we include a set of essay questions in each chapter (over 80 in the entire test bank).

HM Testing CD-ROM

HM Testing (powered by Diploma) is a flexible testing program that allows instructors to create, edit, customize, and deliver multiple types of tests via print, network server, or the web on either Macintosh or Windows platforms. The test bank contains over 1,600 multiple-choice and 80 essay questions. The test bank Word files are also included on the CD-ROM for easy reference.

PowerPoint Presentations

A comprehensive set of *PowerPoint Presentations* accompanies this text and consists of lecture sequences, tables, and figures from the main text. The slides are available on the *Online Teaching Center.*

Classroom Response System

Classroom Response System (CRS) content, available on the *Online Teaching Center,* allows instructors to perform "on-the-spot" assessments, deliver quick quizzes, gauge students' understanding of a particular question or concept, conduct anonymous polling for class discussion purposes, and take their class roster easily. Students receive immediate feedback on how well they understand concepts covered in the text and where they need to improve. Answer slides provide the correct answer and explanation of why the answer is correct.

Online Teaching Center

The *Online Teaching Center* is a comprehensive gallery of online resources that provides one central place to access all teaching preparation tools. It includes the complete *Instructor's Resource Manual, PowerPoint Presentations,* CRS content, video guides, downloadable PDFs of the overhead transparencies, and selected art from the textbook. It can be found by following the links at **college.hmco.com/pic/bukatkoCAD1e.**

Content for Course Management Software

Blackboard and *WebCT* course cartridges are available, allowing instructors to use text-specific material to create an online course on their own campus course management system. The cartridges feature all of the content described on the *Online Teaching* and *Study Centers* as well as *HM Testing.*

Developmental Psych in Film DVD

This DVD contains twelve clips from Universal Studio films, illustrating concepts in developmental psychology such as cognitive development, moral reasoning, parenting styles, and adolescent development. Clips from films such as *Parenthood, Snow Falling on Cedars, Sixteen Candles,* and many others are combined with commentary and discussion questions to help bring developmental psychology alive for students and demonstrate its relevance to contemporary life and culture. Teaching tips are correlated to specific text chapters and concepts on the *Online Teaching Center.*

Lecture Starter Video and Guide

The *Lecture Starter Video* contains a series of high-interest, concise segments that instructors can use to begin a class meeting or change to a new topic. The accompanying guide briefly describes each segment, indicates concepts that can be addressed using each segment, and offers suggestions on how to use each segment.

Online Teaching Tools

Links to useful and practical information on online teaching tools can be found on the *Child and Adolescent Development* website, including a link to useful print resources such as *Teaching Online: A Practical Guide* (0-618-00042-9).

For the Student

Student CD-ROM

This brand new CD-ROM comes packaged with the textbook and contains videos and animations illustrating key concepts and classic and contemporary studies in child development (such as eating disorders and the Bobo doll study). It also offers supportive pedagogy that helps students test their comprehension of these key concepts.

Study Guide

The *Study Guide*, written by Karen L. Yanowitz, Arkansas State University, contains the same set of learning objectives that appear in the *Instructor's Resource Manual* and the *Test Bank*. Each chapter also contains a detailed study outline, a key terms section, and a self-quiz consisting of thirty multiple-choice questions. An answer key tells students not only which response is correct but also why each of the other choices is incorrect.

Online Study Center

The student website contains study aids such as self-tests (Ace Quizzes), flashcards, chapter outlines, learning objectives, and **See For Yourself** and **What Do You Think?** activities. All web resources are keyed to the textbook and can be found by following the links at **college.hmco.com/pic/bukatkoCAD1e.**

Child Development in Context: Voices and Perspectives

The innovative reader *Child Development in Context: Voices and Perspectives*, by David N. Sattler, Geoffrey P. Kramer, Virginia Shabatay, and Douglas A. Bernstein, features personal narratives taken from popular and literary authors covering concepts, issues, and topics related to child development. Concept guides, critical-thinking questions, and research questions promote analysis of the articles. Featured authors include Brian Hall, Anne Lamott, Frank McCourt, Annie Dillard, Russell Baker, Richard Rodriguez, and Nora Ephron.

ACKNOWLEDGMENTS

My students at Holy Cross continue to serve as the primary inspiration for my work on this text. They often come to courses on child development with a genuine concern for the well-being of children. Many have jobs or do volunteer work with children, and often they plan on careers in pediatrics, child psychology, social work, speech and language pathology, education, or other fields involving children. Their need to know about how to make a difference with children continues to underlie my motivation as a teacher and an author.

I would also like to thank Holy Cross for providing the resources and the time to work on a project such as this one. A sabbatical leave, a dedicated staff, and technical assistance are just a few of the practical things Holy Cross was able to offer by way of support and I am very grateful.

I want to especially acknowledge the contributions of Marvin Daehler at the University of Massachusetts to the content of this text. Marv wrote the earlier versions of some of the chapters that appear in this book, and although I take full responsibility for any shortcomings that may be reflected here, Marv deserves thanks for providing a solid base upon which I was able to build.

I appreciate the insightful comments and criticisms provided by the reviewers of this text. Their classroom experiences have provided a broader perspective than my own, and this book becomes stronger because of their valued input. I would like to express thanks to the following reviewers:

Kristine Anthis, *Southern Connecticut State University*

Kate Byerwalter, *Grand Rapids Community College*

Donna Gray, *Irvine Valley College*

June Millovich, *Saddleback College*

John Prange, *Irvine Valley College*

Penny Skemp, *Mira Costa College*

Dennis Thompson, *Georgia State University*

Laura Walker, *Brigham Young University*

Several members of the Houghton Mifflin team deserve my sincerest thanks. I use the word "team" because this project has truly been a cooperative effort. Jane Potter, sponsoring editor, has shown exceptional enthusiasm and support for this project, as well as an array of fresh ideas about how to deliver an appealing and high quality text. Rita Lombard, senior development editor, has continued to be a friend and coach *par excellence*, infusing this project with her expert and insightful guidance. Her creativity is especially evident in many places in this book from the design elements to the special features. Aileen Mason, senior project editor, has overseen the production of this text with the greatest of patience as well as all of the attention to details that is required by a project of this scope. Ann Schroeder and Maria Sas did an outstanding job of capturing visually the concepts being conveyed in the photos and artwork. Thanks go to Henry Rachlin, designer, who gave this text a wonderful vibrant look; and to Sue Gleason, Lisa Goodman, and Sandra Cannon for their comprehensive copyediting, proofreading, and indexing; and to Lynne Blaszak, senior media producer, Dustin Brandt associate media producer, and Carolyn Nichols, senior editor, for their creative input into the technology resources accompanying the text. Special thanks to Amy Whitaker, marketing manager, and Sam Abrams, marketing assistant, who have provided unfailing support in their efforts to promote the text. I appreciate very much all of their outstanding contributions.

Lastly, I would like to thank my husband and son, Don and Nick, for their patience, encouragement, and unconditional support.

Danuta Bukatko

THEMES AND THEORIES 1

Andrew had spent an enormous amount of time carefully aligning the beams, braces, and other equipment at just the right locations on his building project. It looked great! He was fascinated by how he could make the crane swing up and down, and how it would lift and drop the small metal pieces with the magnet. But six-year-old Andrew was so absorbed in his play that he failed to notice his one-year-old sister, Heather, rapidly crawling toward these shiny, eye-catching objects. Benjamin, at fourteen, was the oldest child in the family and had been placed in charge of watching both Andrew and Heather as their parents prepared dinner in the kitchen. Unfortunately, he had also become distracted by the challenging new computer game he had just borrowed from his friend.

As she crawled within reach of Andrew's construction set, Heather grabbed the truck on which the crane was mounted and pulled it sharply, pitching beams, equipment, and everything else into a chaotic heap. For one brief instant, Andrew froze in horror as he observed the devastation his little sister had just wrought.

Then came the almost reflexive, inevitable shriek at the top of his lungs: "HEATHER! GET OUTTA HERE!" as he simultaneously swung his arm in Heather's direction in an uncontrollable burst of emotion. Andrew's shout was more than enough to produce a wail from Heather, but the sting across her back from Andrew's hand didn't help, either. Benjamin, startled by the uproar, anticipated the melee about to begin and raced to the kitchen, knowing full well that his mother and father were the only ones who would be able to reinstate tranquility after this unfortunate exchange between his little brother and sister.

Although the specifics may be very different, this type of exchange between siblings is probably not uncommon in families and households around the world. And it serves to introduce some of the issues central to this book. For example, consider the developmental differences displayed by Heather, Andrew, and Benjamin during this interaction. Heather, only one year of age, does not move about or handle objects in the same way as her older siblings. Perhaps even more important, Heather seems to have very little appreciation for the consequences her impulsive reach might have on both Andrew and the construction set. Her six-year-old brother displays far greater physical dexterity and more sophisticated planning and thinking about the toys that are part of his play. Andrew also has excellent verbal skills with which to express his thoughts and emotions, although he still has some difficulty regulating the latter. Yet Andrew's reasoning about his world pales in comparison with that of his older brother, Benjamin, who is captivated by a complex computer game. Moreover, at the age of fourteen, Benjamin has been given increased responsibility, such as looking after both younger siblings. Although he is not always as careful and conscientious in this task as his mother and father might like, his parents feel reasonably assured that, if things are not going well, Benjamin knows where to seek assistance.

Children undergo enormous changes in motor, cognitive, social, and emotional capabilities as they progress from birth through adolescence. Our goal in this book is to describe and try to explain those changes.

How did these enormous developmental differences come about? That is a primary question addressed in this book. But there are other matters of interest in the sequence of events described here. How should their parents now deal with the conflict in order to bring about peace between Heather and Andrew? How would you? How should his parents respond to the angry outburst from Andrew? How might they have encouraged Benjamin to take his baby-sitting responsibilities more seriously?

When we think about trying to understand how children develop and become competent individuals in interactions with one another and their physical environment, common sense seems like the place to start. For generations, common sense provided the parenting wisdom by which caregivers understood and reared children. For example, when Heather, Andrew, and Benjamin could not get along with one another, their parents often spanked the child whom they thought might be at fault. They followed a commonly accepted approach to dealing with conflict, a method that seems to be shared in many cultures. As an illustration, among the proverbs expressed by the Ovambo of southwest Africa is the saying, "A cranky child has not been spanked," and Korean parents may say, "Treat the child you love with the rod; treat the child you hate with another cake." Proverbs like these, which promote physical discipline for children, can be found in many cultures around the world (for instance, see Palacios, 1996).

Although common sense is extremely important in child rearing, in some circumstances it may yield unexpected and perhaps even undesirable consequences. For example, is physical punishment the best way to prevent unacceptable behaviors in children? Caregivers in many societies believe spanking is an effective method of dealing with angry outbursts like that displayed by Andrew. However, researchers have found that the children of parents who routinely resort to physical punishment often initiate more aggressive acts than do the children of parents who rely on alternative methods of disciplining undesirable conduct (Bandura & Walters, 1959; Dodge, Pettit, & Bates, 1994). This relationship has been observed in Native American (McCord, 1977) and British working-class homes (Farrington, 1991), as well as in families in the United States, Australia, Finland, Poland, and Israel (Eron, Huesmann, & Zelli, 1991). In other words, under some circumstances, physical punishment appears to encourage rather than discourage aggressive actions and may escalate into increasingly coercive interactions between parent and child. Thus the commonsense practice of disciplining by physical punishment, a practice supported by various cultural proverbs and recommendations, may need to be examined more closely. This is precisely the point at which the need for the scientific study of children and their development enters.

WHAT IS DEVELOPMENT?

Development, as we use the term, means all the physical and psychological changes a human being undergoes in a lifetime, from the moment of conception until death. The study of human development is, above all, the study of change (Overton, 2006). From the very moment of birth, changes are swift and impressive. Within a few short months, the newborn who looked so helpless (we will see that the true state of affairs is otherwise) comes to control his or her own body, to locomote, and to master simple tasks, such as self-feeding. In the years that follow, the child begins to understand and speak a language, engages in more and more complex thinking, displays a distinct personality, and develops the skills necessary to interact with other people as part of a social network. The range and complexity of every young person's achievements in the first two decades of life can only be called extraordinary.

development Physical and psychological changes in the individual over a lifetime.

One of the goals of this book is to give you an overview of the most significant changes in behavior and thinking processes that occur in this time span. In the pages that follow, we *describe* the growing child's accomplishments in many domains of development. For example, we detail the basic physical and mental capabilities in infants and children and examine the social and emotional skills children acquire as they reach out to form relationships with their family members, peers, and others. We tell this story from a chronological perspective, starting with the amazing capabilities and achievements of *infancy* (from birth to two years), and moving through the important developmental accomplishments of *early childhood* (about two to six years), *middle childhood* (about six to eleven years), and *adolescence* (about twelve to eighteen years).

A second important goal is to help you appreciate just why children develop in the specific ways they do. In other words, we also try to *explain* developmental outcomes in children. How do the genetic blueprints inherited from parents shape the growing child? What is the role of the environment? How does the society or culture in which the child lives influence development? Does the child play a passive or an active role in his or her own development? We are repeatedly concerned with some other questions about development. Do the changes that take place occur gradually or suddenly? Do all children follow a common developmental pathway, and if not, what factors explain these individual differences? And how do the many facets of development influence one another? As you may imagine, although we often seek simple answers to these questions, they are neither simple nor always obvious (Horowitz, 2000).

Developmental psychology is the discipline concerned with the scientific study of changes in human behaviors and mental activities as they occur over a lifetime. *Developmental psychologists* rely on research to learn about growth and change in children. This approach has its limitations: researchers have not studied every important aspect of child development, and sometimes studies do not point to clear, unambiguous answers about the nature of development. Indeed, psychologists often disagree on the conclusions they draw from a given set of data. Nonetheless, scientific fact-finding has the advantage of being verifiable and is also more objective and systematic than personal interpretations of children's behavior. As you read about development in the chapters that follow, the controversies as well as the unequivocal conclusions, try to use them to sharpen your own skills of critical analysis.

An essential ingredient of the scientific process is the construction of a **theory**, a set of ideas or propositions that helps to organize or explain observable phenomena. More than a personal opinion or casual hypothesis, a scientific theory is firmly grounded in the information collected by researchers. For many students, theories seem far less interesting than the vast assortment of intellectual, linguistic, social, physical, and other behaviors and capabilities that undergo change with time. However, by describing children's accomplishments in a systematic, integrated way, theories *organize* or make sense of the enormous amount of information researchers have gleaned. Theories of development also help to *explain* our observations. Is your neighbor's little boy shy because he inherited this trait, or did his social experiences encourage him to become this way? Did your niece's precocious mathematical skills develop from her experience with her home computer, or does she just have a natural flair for numbers? Was Andrew's angry reaction to his baby sister a biological response or something he had learned? Psychologists are interested in understanding the factors that contribute to the emergence of behavioral skills and capacities, and their theories are ways of articulating ideas about what causes various behaviors to develop in individual children.

A good theory goes beyond description and explanation, however. It leads to *predictions* about behavior, predictions that are clear and easily tested. If shyness results from social experiences, for example, the withdrawn four-year-old should profit from a training program that teaches social skills. If, on the other hand, shyness is a stable, unchangeable personality trait, even extensive training in sociability may have very little impact. Explaining and predicting behavior are not only gratifying but also essential for translating ideas into applications—creating meaningful

developmental psychology Systematic and scientific study of changes in human behaviors and mental activities over time.

theory Set of ideas or propositions that helps to organize or explain observable phenomena.

social policy Programs and plans established by local, regional, or national public and private organizations and agencies designed to achieve a particular social purpose or goal.

programs and ways to assist parents, teachers, and others who work to enhance and promote the development of children. For example, when a theory proposes that adults are an important source of imitative learning and that parents who display aggressive behavior provide a model for responding to a frustrating situation, we can begin to understand why common proverbs like "Spare the rod and spoil the child" sometimes need to be reevaluated.

The knowledge that developmental psychologists acquire through their research can also address many concerns about social policy. **Social policies** are programs and plans established by local, regional, or national organizations and agencies. These are often government programs, but businesses, private foundations, and other groups attempt to implement social policies that are designed to achieve a particular purpose with respect to the members of a society as well. The goals of many of these policies are geared toward alleviating social problems. Social policies may, for example, be concerned with increasing the effectiveness of education for children, improving their health, reducing teenage pregnancy, eliminating child abuse, reducing low birth weight and infant deaths, preventing young people from smoking cigarettes, encouraging parents to enforce the use of seat belts, promoting self-esteem, and a host of other goals. Research can help identify social problems that limit or interfere with children's development and can assist policymakers in establishing programs to reduce or eliminate the factors that hinder psychological health and competence in children. At the same time, research may shed further light on the mechanisms and processes that underlie behavior. You will have the opportunity to consider many social policies that bear on children in the chapters that follow.

In this chapter, our discussion focuses on several broad theories, and some of their historical antecedents, which have influenced explanations of children's behavior. No single theory is sufficient to provide a full explanation of all behavior. Some theories strive to make sense of intellectual and cognitive development; others focus on social, emotional, personality, or some other aspect of development. Theories also vary in the extent to which they present formalized, testable ideas. Thus some are more useful than others in providing explanations for behavior that can be rigorously evaluated. And they often disagree in their answers to the fundamental questions of development. Before we examine specific theories, let's consider a cluster of basic questions that all theories of development must address.

For • Your • Review

- What is development?
- What is developmental psychology?
- What role do theories play in the scientific process?
- What role does developmental psychology play in the formation of social policy?

Five Major Themes in Developmental Psychology

As you read about different aspects of child development—language acquisition, peer relationships, motor skills, emergence of self-worth, and many others—you will find that certain questions about development surface again and again. We call these questions *themes in development.* Various theories provide different answers to these questions. Good theories, grounded in careful research, help us to think about and understand these major themes. What are these key questions?

HOW DO NATURE AND NURTURE INTERACT IN DEVELOPMENT?

We have all heard expressions like "He inherited a good set of genes" or "She had a great upbringing" to explain some trait or behavior. These explanations offer two very different answers to a basic question that has, since the beginnings of psychology, fueled a controversy among theorists, which continues to rage even today. Dubbed the **nature-nurture debate**, the dispute centers on whether the child's development is the result of genetic endowment or environmental influences.

Do children typically crawl at nine months and walk at twelve months of age as part of some inborn, unfolding program or because they have learned these motor responses? Do they readily acquire language because their environment demands it or because they are genetically predisposed to do so? Are boys more aggressive than girls because of cultural conditioning or biological factors? In some areas, such as the development of intelligence and the emergence of gender roles, the debate over nature versus nurture has been particularly heated.

Why all the uproar about such a question? One reason is that the answer has major implications for children's developmental outcomes, for parenting practices, for the organization of schooling, and for other practical applications concerning research. If, for example, experiments support the view that intelligence is guided largely by heredity, providing children with rich learning experiences may have minimal impact on their eventual levels of intellectual skill. If, on the other hand, research and theory more convincingly show that intellectual development is shaped primarily by environmental events, it becomes vital to provide children with experiences designed to optimize their intellectual growth. Answers to this type of question are likely to have an impact on social policy by affecting how funds are allocated to health, educational, and many other programs.

Psychologists now recognize that both nature and nurture are essential to all aspects of behavior and that these two forces combine to mold what the child becomes. Thus the controversy has shifted away from identifying *which* of these two factors is critical in any given situation. Instead, the question is *how* heredity and environment *interact* to fashion the behaviors we see in children and eventually in adults.

There is an important implication in this idea that nature and nurture are intimately interwoven: *children are active players in the process of development.* That active role may be evident at two different levels. The first begins with certain attributes and qualities that children possess and exhibit, perhaps because of inborn qualities of personality or behavioral style. By virtue of being placid or active, fearful or curious, children elicit reactions from others. Thus children are not simply passive recipients of the environment or blank slates on which it writes. Their own capacities and efforts to become immersed in, to get "mixed up" with, their physical and social world often modify what happens to them and can affect their development in profound ways. A second, perhaps more fundamental, way in which children contribute to their own development is through actively constructing and organizing ways of thinking, feeling, and communicating to assist them in making sense of their world. Children formulate these conceptualizations to help them respond to and understand the rich array of physical and social events they experience.

HOW DOES THE SOCIOCULTURAL CONTEXT INFLUENCE DEVELOPMENT?

Development is influenced by more than just the immediate environment of the family. Children grow up within a larger social community: the *sociocultural context.* The sociocultural context includes unique customs, values, and beliefs about the proper way to rear children and the ultimate goals for their development. Think back to your family and the cultural standards and values that determined how you were reared. Were you allowed to be assertive and speak your mind, or were you

nature-nurture debate Ongoing theoretical controversy over whether development is the result of the child's genetic endowment or environmental influences.

Children grow up in many different cultures and social settings. This Malaysian American family, celebrating the Chinese New Year at their home in San Francisco, has adopted some customs and values from American culture, yet maintained many traditions and practices brought with them from their native country. Various sociocultural contexts provide the backdrop in which specific parenting practices are carried out. Researchers must consider these different kinds of experiences to fully understand development.

expected to be compliant toward adults and never challenge them? Were you encouraged to fend for yourself, or were caregivers, relatives, and even cultural institutions, such as the school, church, or some other agency, expected to assist with your needs throughout childhood, adolescence, and perhaps even into your early adult years? How was your development affected by your family's economic status and educational attainments? by your gender and ethnic identity?

Sociocultural factors affect everything from the kinds of child-rearing practices parents engage in to the level of health care and education children receive; they affect, for example, children's physical well-being, social standing, sense of self-esteem, "personality," and emotional expressiveness. As you explore the various domains of development, you will come to appreciate that many developmental outcomes are heavily influenced by the sociocultural context.

Is Development Continuous or Discontinuous?

Everyone agrees that children's behaviors and abilities change, sometimes in dramatic ways. However, there is less consensus on how best to explain these changes. On the one hand, development can be viewed as a *continuous* process in which new attainments in thinking, language, and social behavior are characterized by gradual, steady, small, *quantitative* advances. For example, substantial progress in reasoning or problem solving may stem from the ability to remember more and more pieces of information. Or, as neural coordination and muscle strength gradually increase, the infant may advance from crawling to walking—a progression that, by anyone's account, has substantial consequences for both child and caregiver. Thus, even though at two given points in time the child's ability to think or locomote may look very different, the transformation may arise from gradual, quantitative improvements in the speed, efficiency, or strength with which mental or physical processes are carried out, rather than from a dramatic reorganization of some underlying capacity.

Alternatively, some theories see development as *discontinuous*. They explain development in terms of the child's progress through a series of **stages**, or periods during which innovative developmental accomplishments abruptly surface, presumably because some fundamental reorganizations in thinking or other capacities underlying behavior have taken place. In this view, development undergoes rapid transitions as one stage ends and a new one begins, followed by relatively stable periods during which the child's behaviors and abilities change very little (see Figure 1.1). Abrupt or

stage Developmental period during which the organization of thought and behavior is qualitatively different from that of an earlier or later period.

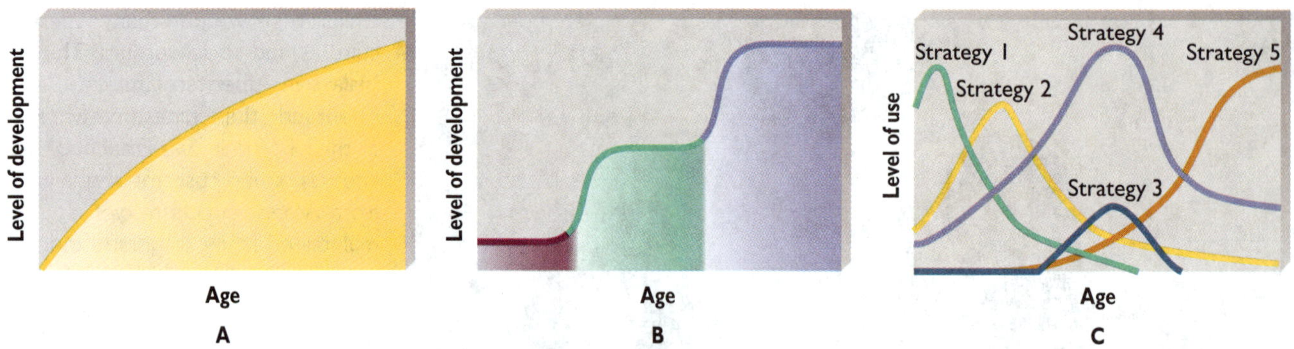

FIGURE 1.1

Development as a Continuous Versus a Discontinuous Process

Children display many changes in their abilities and behaviors throughout development. According to some, the best way to explain these changes is in terms of the gradual acquisition of the structures and processes that underlie growth (A). Others believe that development undergoes a series of stagelike transformations during which underlying structures and processes exhibit rapid reorganization followed by a period of relative stability (B). However, other approaches suggest that, at any given time, children may exhibit multiple ways of demonstrating some ability or capacity, as is evident in the "overlapping waves" (Siegler, 1998) depiction of development (C). According to this view, the ability or capacity displayed by children will depend on a variety of situational and developmental factors.

rapid changes resulting in a dramatic reorganization in how children perceive, think, feel, or behave are interpreted as *qualitative* advances in development. From this perspective, children establish new ways of thinking—for instance, during the early school years—that change problem solving, moral judgment, interactions with peers, and other activities. In adolescence they move to yet another level of thinking that influences these various domains of behavior in still different ways.

When we try to discern if development is continuous or discontinous, it is important to remember that there is considerable variability in individual children's skills that can complicate how we decide between these two points of view. Many ways of behaving and thinking are available to children at any given time. Which one will be expressed depends on a variety of circumstances. Robert Siegler (1996, 1998) has suggested that different strategies or ways of responding can best be described as "overlapping waves," because they often coexist in the child's repertoire. Some methods of responding may be exhibited more frequently at younger ages and others at older ages. Although some strategies may be lost as the child gains more experience and as others are freshly formulated, at any particular time children are likely to be able to use several competing approaches for responding to a situation. For example, when young children demonstrate the ability to add two numbers, say 4 plus 3, they may do so using several different strategies, such as counting from 1, counting beginning with the larger of the pair of numbers, comparing the problem to another whose answer is already known, or directly retrieving the information from memory. Which specific strategy is employed will depend on how much experience the child has had with the problem, how familiar he or she is with each of the numbers, how quickly the answer must be determined, and how much effort is required to carry out the strategy, among other things. Thus to conclude that a child has moved into a stage or phase in which he or she is able to carry out addition profoundly underestimates the variety of competencies he or she can draw on to demonstrate that capacity.

Few, if any, aspects of human growth appear to mimic the dramatic transformations found in the life cycle of an insect as it changes from egg to larva to pupa and finally to adult—periods in which a stable physical organization is followed by rapid reorganization and emergence of a new point in the life cycle. Yet, over the months and years, children do become quite different. Whether these changes are best understood as quantitative or qualitative advances are points of frequent disagreement among theories of development.

An important developmental theme is that the various domains of development interact with each other. For example, children who interact with each other as they work at a computer are not only enhancing their social skills, but also advancing their thinking abilities.

How Do the Various Domains of Development Interact?

Many times the child's development in one domain will have a direct bearing on her attainments in other domains. Consider just one example: how a child's physical growth might influence her social and emotional development. A child who has become taller than her peers may experience very different interactions with adults and peers than a child who is small for his age. The taller child might be given more responsibilities by a teacher or be asked by peers to lead the group more frequently. These opportunities may instill a sense of worth and offer occasions to practice social skills that are less frequently available to the smaller child. As these social skills are exercised and become more refined and advanced, the taller child may receive still more opportunities that promote social and even cognitive development. Our ultimate aim is to understand the child as a whole individual, not just as someone who undergoes, for example, physical, perceptual, emotional, cognitive, or social development. To do so, we must keep in mind that no single component of development unfolds in isolation from the rest.

What Factors Promote Risk or Resilience in Development?

Human development may proceed along many different paths and at quite different rates from one individual to another. One especially important reason that differences emerge is that individual children are exposed to various kinds and levels of benefits and risks during their development. For example, *risk* may be a consequence of genetic or biological complications, as well as rearing or cultural events, that promote development in less than optimal ways. An accidental head injury; exposure to a disease, such as AIDS; being reared by an abusive parent; experiencing parents' divorce; attending an unstimulating daycare center; or exposure to the devastating consequences of war are just a few of the many factors that can affect the course of development and may limit healthy progress. Individual children, because of their genetic or biological makeup, or because of other resources available in their environment, respond to these risks in different ways. *Resilient* children, those who seem able to most effectively resist the negative consequences of risk, tend to have a constellation of individual qualities that include a relatively relaxed, self-confident character that permits them to adapt and to respond intelligently in difficult situations and circumstances. In addition, they are likely to have the benefits of a close, encouraging relationship with at least one member of their family and with others beyond the family, such as a teacher or close

FIGURE 1.2
Five Major Themes in Developmental Psychology

Throughout this book, we repeatedly consider these themes and the ways developmental psychologists attempt to answer these questions. Charts like this one will appear in every chapter.

Key Themes in Development

- **Nature & Nurture**
  How do nature and nurture interact in development?
- **Sociocultural Influence**
  How does the sociocultural context influence development?
- **Continuity/Discontinuity**
  Is development continuous or discontinuous?
- **Interaction Among Domains**
  How do the various domains of development interact?
- **Risk/Resilience**
  What factors promote risk or resilience in development?

friend, through their membership in some supportive agency or organization, such as a club or church (Luthar, Cicchetti, & Becker, 2000; Masten & Coatsworth, 1998; Runyan et al., 1998; Rutter, 1990; Werner, 1995).

Several points about risk and resilience are important to note. First, most researchers recognize that, when children are said to be at risk, it is usually not because of a single factor, such as poverty, exposure to disease, or attendance at a school with few resources. Rather, risk factors tend to occur in clusters. Thus understanding child development requires an awareness of the many layers of influence that have an impact on children's lives, from family settings, to neighborhoods, to the larger society (Sameroff, 2005). Second, some researchers feel that the term *resilience* should be restricted to instances in which children are able to overcome some adversity, and that other terms (such as *promotive factors* or *assets*) are more appropriate when we are describing positive factors in development, regardless of risk (Wright & Masten, 2005). Finally, a discussion of risk and resilience usually has strong implications for interventions that might improve the lives of children who experience hardship. Thus these topics are of special interest to developmental psychologists involved in education, clinical issues, and other applied fields.

In the discussions that follow concerning various historical contributions to developmental psychology and the major theoretical approaches still important in the field today, it will be apparent that answers pertaining to the themes often differ. These five developmental themes, summarized in Figure 1.2, will have an important influence on our discussion of developmental psychology throughout this book. Perhaps one of the best ways to review them is to take a few minutes to consider your stand on each of the themes.

FOR • YOUR • REVIEW

- Can you think of ways that nature and nurture might interact in the process of child development? Can you think of examples of how children play active roles in their own development?
- How and to what extent do you feel that society's concerns, values, and resources affect an individual's development?
- Do you find it easier to understand development in terms of continuous or discontinuous, stagelike change?
- To what extent do you think advances or difficulties in one domain affect the child's development in other domains?
- Can you think of examples of factors that might put children's development at risk?

THE STUDY OF THE CHILD: HISTORICAL PERSPECTIVES

Human development became a focus of serious study comparatively late in the history of science, having its origins only a little over one hundred years ago. Despite its relatively short history, however, developmental psychology has grown at an astonishing rate in the last several decades and is a thriving modern-day field of study. Each year hundreds of books and thousands of articles about children's growth are published for professionals interested in specific theoretical issues and for parents or teachers. Scientists and laypersons, however, have not always had such a focused and conscious desire to understand the process of child development. In fact, societal attitudes toward childhood as a concept have shifted considerably over the last several centuries.

THE CONCEPT OF CHILDHOOD

Contemporary society views childhood as a separate, distinct, and unique period, a special time when individuals are to be protected, nurtured, loved, and kept free of most adult responsibilities and obligations. Child labor laws try to ensure that children are not abused in the work world, and the institution of public education signals a willingness to devote significant resources to their academic training. But childhood was not always viewed in this way (Borstelmann, 1983).

Children in Medieval and Renaissance Times From the Middle Ages through premodern times, European society's attitudes toward children differed strikingly from those of our contemporary society. Although their basic needs to be fed and clothed were tended to, children were not coddled or protected in the same way infants in our society are. As soon as they were physically able, usually at age seven or so, children were incorporated into the adult world of work; they harvested grain, learned craft skills, and otherwise contributed to the local economy. In medieval times, Western European children did not have special clothes, toys, or games. Once they were old enough to shed swaddling clothes, they wore adult fashions and pursued adult pastimes, such as archery, chess, and even gambling (Ariès, 1962).

In certain respects, however, premodern European society regarded children as vulnerable, fragile, and unable to assume the full responsibilities of adulthood. Medical writings alluded to the special illnesses of young children, and laws prohibited marriages of children under age twelve (Kroll, 1977). Religious movements of this era proclaimed the innocence of children and urged that they be educated. Children's souls, as well as adults', must be saved, said clerics, and they held that parents were morally responsible for their children's spiritual well-being. Parents recognized that children were also a financial responsibility and helped them set up their own households as they approached adulthood and marriage (Pollock, 1983; Shahar, 1990). Thus, even though medieval children were incorporated quickly into the adult world, they were recognized both as different from adults and as possessing special needs.

A noticeable shift in attitudes toward children occurred in Europe during the sixteenth century. In 1545 English physician and lawyer Thomas Phayre published the first book on pediatrics. In addition, the advent of the printing press during that century made possible the wide distribution of other manuals on the care of infants and children. The first grammar schools were established to educate upper-class boys in economics and politics. Upper-class girls attended convent schools or received private instruction intended to cultivate modesty

In many regions of the world, children spend much of their time engaged in physical labor. This girl, helping to harvest rice in Cambodia, very likely had little opportunity to learn to read or write. Historically, and in some cultures yet today, attitudes about childhood differ greatly from those held in recent times in most Western societies.

In premodern Europe, children often dressed like adults and participated in many adult activities. At the same time, though, children were seen as fragile and in need of protection.

and obedience, as well as other skills thought to be useful in their future roles as wives and mothers (Shahar, 1990).

Probably one of the most significant social changes occurred as a result of the transition from agrarian to trade-based economies in the sixteenth and seventeenth centuries, and the subsequent growth of industrialization in the eighteenth century. As people relocated from farms to towns and as the production of goods shifted outside the home, the primary role of the family in Western society changed from ensuring economic survival to the nurturing of children (Hareven, 1985). Closeness and emotional attachment increasingly became the hallmarks of parent-child relations.

The Age of Enlightenment The impact of these sweeping social changes was consolidated by the writings of several key thinkers who shaped the popular understanding of childhood. In the seventeenth and eighteenth centuries, two philosophers proposed important but distinctly different ideas about the nature and education of children. In his famous treatise *An Essay Concerning Human Understanding* (1961), originally published in 1690, the British philosopher John Locke (1632–1704) described his views on the acquisition of human knowledge. Virtually no information is inborn, according to Locke. The newborn's mind is a *tabula rasa*, literally a "blank slate," on which perceptual experiences are imprinted. Locke's philosophy of **empiricism**, the idea that environmental experiences shape the individual, foreshadowed the modern-day psychological school of behaviorism. Locke believed that rewards and punishments from others, imitation, and the associations the child forms between stimuli are key elements in the formation of the mind.

In a second work, *Some Thoughts Concerning Education* (1693/1964), Locke expounded further on his philosophy of training children:

> The great mistake I have observed in people's breeding their children … is that the mind has not been made obedient to discipline and pliant to reason when it was most tender, most easy to be bowed. … He that is not used to submit his will to the reason of others when he is young, will scarce hearken to submit to his own reason when he is of an age to make use of it.

Locke further argued in support of the importance of early experiences and proper training but also that child rearing and education should proceed through the use of reason rather than harsh discipline. In his view, parents must find a balance between being overly indulgent and overly restrictive as they manage their child's behavior. As we will see, many of these same themes resound in contemporary research on good parenting and represent a contrast to the strict disciplinary stance of Western society before the eighteenth century.

The second influential philosopher of the Enlightenment was Jean Jacques Rousseau (1712–1778), a French thinker who embraced the ideal of the child as a "noble savage." According to Rousseau, children are born with a propensity to act on impulses, but not necessarily with the aim of wrongdoing. They require the gentle guidance of adult authority to bring their natural instincts and tendencies in line with the social order. In *Émile* (1762/1895), Rousseau set forth these beliefs about child rearing:

> Never command him to do anything whatever, not the least thing in the world. Never allow him even to imagine that you assume to have any authority over him. Let him know merely that he is weak and that you are strong; that by virtue of his condition and your own he is necessarily at your mercy.

empiricism Theory that environmental experiences shape the individual; more specifically, that all knowledge is derived from sensory experiences.

> ... Do not give your scholar any sort of verbal lesson, for he is to be taught only by experience. Inflict on him no species of punishment, for he does not know what it is to be in fault.

Rousseau emphasized the dynamic relationship between the curious and energetic child and the demands of his or her social environment as represented by adults. Adults should not stifle the child's natural development and spirit through domination. Contemporary theories that acknowledge the active role of the child in the process of development have distinct roots in Rousseau's writings.

Rousseau also advanced some radical ideas about education. Children, he held, should not be forced to learn by rote the vast amounts of information that adults perceive as important. Instead, teachers should capitalize on the natural curiosity of children and allow them to discover on their own the myriad facts and phenomena that make up the world. Rousseau's ideas on the nature of education would be incorporated in the twentieth-century writings of Jean Piaget.

Both Locke and Rousseau emphasized the notion of the child as a developing, as opposed to a static, being. Both challenged the supposition that children are merely passive subjects of adult authority, and both advanced the idea that children should be treated with reason and respect. Having been elevated by the efforts of these worthy thinkers to an object of intellectual interest, the child was now ready to become the subject of scientific study.

THE ORIGINS OF DEVELOPMENTAL PSYCHOLOGY

By the mid- to late 1800s, scholars in the natural sciences, especially biology, saw in the study of children an opportunity to support their emerging theories about the origins of human beings and their behaviors. Charles Darwin, for example, hypothesized that the similarities between the behaviors of humans and those of other species were the result of common evolutionary ancestors. Similarly, Wilhelm Preyer, another biologist, was initially interested in the physiology of embryological development but soon extended his investigations to behavioral development after birth. In the United States and Europe, key researchers who participated in the birth of psychology as an academic discipline also began to show an interest in studying children. By the beginning of the twentieth century, developmental psychology was established as a legitimate area of psychological inquiry.

The Baby Biographers: Charles Darwin and Wilhelm Preyer One of the first records of the close scrutiny of a child for the purpose of scientific understanding comes from the writings of Charles Darwin. Eager to uncover important clues about the origins of the human species, Darwin undertook to record in great detail his infant son's behaviors during the first three years of life. Darwin documented the presence of early reflexes, such as sucking, as well as the emergence of voluntary motor movements, language, and emotions, such as fear, anger, and affection. When he saw similarities, he linked the behaviors of the young child to those of other species, such as when, for example, he concluded that the infant's comprehension of simple words was not unlike the ability of "lower animals" to understand words spoken by humans (Darwin, 1877).

In 1882 the German biologist Wilhelm Preyer published *The Mind of the Child* (1882/1888–1889), a work that described in great detail the development of his son Axel during the first three years of life. Preyer wrote meticulously of his son's sensory development, motor accomplishments, language production, and memory, even noting indications of an emerging concept of self. Although Preyer followed in the footsteps of several previous "baby biographers," including Darwin, he was the first to insist that observations of children be conducted systematically, recorded immediately and unobtrusively, and repeated several times each day. By advocating the application of scientific techniques to the study of children, the baby biographers,

G. Stanley Hall is considered to be the founder of modern child psychology.

Preyer in particular, set in motion the beginnings of the child development movement in the United States.

G. Stanley Hall: The Founder of Modern Child Psychology The psychologist perhaps most responsible for launching the new discipline of child study in the United States was G. Stanley Hall, who, in 1878, became the first American to obtain a Ph.D. in psychology. Hall is also known for founding the first psychological journal in the United States in 1887 and, in 1891, the first journal of developmental psychology, *Pedagogical Seminary* (now called the *The Journal of Genetic Psychology*). In addition, he founded and served as the first president of the American Psychological Association (APA).

As the first American to study in Europe with the pioneer psychologist Wilhelm Wundt, G. Stanley Hall returned to the United States in 1880 with an interest in studying the "content of children's minds." Adopting the questionnaire method he had learned about in Germany, he had teachers ask about 200 kindergarten-age children questions like "Have you ever seen a cow?" or "What are bricks made of?" The percentages of children who gave particular answers were tabulated, and comparisons were made between the responses of boys and girls, city children and country children, and children of different ethnic backgrounds (Hall, 1891). For the first time, researchers were collecting data to compare groups of children, in contrast to previous approaches that had emphasized the detailed examination of individual children.

Alfred Binet: The Study of Individual Differences The French psychologist Alfred Binet is known primarily as the developer of the first formal assessment scale of intelligence. Binet was a pioneer in the study of **individual differences**, those unique characteristics that distinguish one person from others in the larger group.

Binet's original interest lay in the general features of children's thinking, including memory and reasoning about numbers. To that end, he closely scrutinized the behaviors of his two daughters as they progressed from toddlerhood to the teenage years. He noted, in particular, how one daughter, Madeleine, was serious and reflective as she tried to solve problems, whereas the other daughter, Alice, was more impulsive and temperamental (Fancher, 1998). His studies of children's thinking had two significant outcomes: first, they demonstrated that a description of individual differences contributed to the understanding of human development, and second, they provided the basis for more formal tests of children's mental abilities (Cairns & Cairns, 2006). In response to a request from the Ministry of Public Instruction in Paris for a tool to screen for students with learning problems, Binet and another colleague, Theodore Simon, developed a series of tasks to systematically measure motor skills, vocabulary, problem solving, and a wide range of other higher-order thought processes (Binet & Simon, 1905). This instrument could identify patterns in mental capabilities that were unique to each child.

The idea of mental testing caught on very quickly in the United States, especially among clinicians, school psychologists, and other professionals concerned with the practical side of dealing with children. For the first time, it was legitimate, even important, to consider variation in mental abilities from person to person.

James Mark Baldwin: Developmental Theorist Considered the founder of academic psychology in Canada (Hoff, 1992), James Mark Baldwin established a laboratory at the University of Toronto devoted to the systematic study of movement patterns, handedness, and color vision in infants (Cairns, 1992). Soon, however, his interests shifted away from gathering empirical data. He became one of the most important developmental theorists of the early twentieth century.

individual differences Unique characteristics that distinguish a person from other members of a larger group.

One of Baldwin's most important propositions was that development is a dynamic and hierarchical process, such that "every genetic change ushers in a real advance, a progression on the part of nature to a higher mode of reality" (Baldwin, 1930, p. 86). Baldwin applied these ideas to the domain of cognitive development by suggesting that mental advances occur in a stagelike sequence in which the earliest thought is prelogical but gives way to logical and eventually hyperlogical or formal reasoning—ideas that today are often linked to Piaget.

Baldwin is also recognized for his unique perspective on social development and the formation of personality. Instead of characterizing the child as a passive recipient of the behaviors and beliefs endorsed by the larger society, he described the child's emerging self as a product of continual reciprocal interactions between the child and others. The proposition that development results from a mutual dynamic between the child and others took a long time to catch on among psychologists, but this idea, so popular today, is actually almost a century old (Cairns & Ornstein, 1979).

By the start of the 1900s, the foundations of developmental psychology as a scientifically based discipline were firmly established. Psychologists were well poised to begin the study of differences among groups of children, individual differences among children, and the hypotheses generated by emerging theories of development.

Sigmund Freud: The Importance of Early Experience During the early decades of the twentieth century, Sigmund Freud's theory also became extremely influential, particularly with respect to explaining emotional and personality development. Freud proposed in his psychosexual theory of development that many aspects of the individual's personality originate in an early and broad form of childhood sexuality. The fuel that powers human behavior, according to Freud, is a set of biological instincts. The psychological tension induced by these instincts, called *libido* or *libidinal energy*, gradually builds and requires eventual discharge. Under many circumstances, this energy is reduced as rapidly as possible. Sometimes, however, tensions like those associated with hunger or pain in infants cannot be eliminated immediately. Because of these delays, mental structures and behavioral responses eventually organize into more satisfactory ways of decreasing tension. For example, behavioral acts might include calling out to the caregiver as a signal to be fed or eventually learning to feed oneself, responses that normally lead to a reduction in libidinal urges by effective, rational, and socially acceptable means.

The locus of tension and the optimal ways to reduce needs change with age. Freud identified five stages of psychosexual development, periods during which libidinal energy is usually associated with a specific area of the body. During the *oral stage*, lasting until about one year of age, libidinal energy is focused around the mouth and is reduced through sucking, chewing, eating, and biting. Throughout the subsequent *anal stage*, from about one to three years of age, this energy is centered on the anal region and is lessened by satisfactorily expelling body wastes. The *phallic stage*, typically bridging the period between three and five years of age, is characterized as a time of desire for the opposite-sex parent and of other forms of immature gratification surrounding the genitals. A relatively long *latency* period lasts from about five years of age to adolescence and is a time in which libidinal energy is submerged or expressed, for example, through a more culturally acceptable focus on the acquisition of social or intellectual skills. During the final stage, the *genital stage*, which occurs in adolescence and continues throughout adulthood, mature forms of genital satisfaction are theorized to be an important source of tension reduction.

Freud believed that the individual's progression through these stages is greatly influenced by maturation. However, the environment also plays a critical role. Lack of opportunity to meet needs adequately or to express them during a stage could lead to negative consequences in the way the child relates to others and to feelings of low self-worth. For example, the infant whose sucking efforts are not gratified may become *fixated*; that is, preoccupied with actions associated with the mouth for the rest of his or her life. A child whose toilet training is too lax may become messy, disorderly, or wasteful, whereas one whose toilet training is too strict may display a possessive, retentive (frugal and stingy) personality or show an excessive concern with cleanliness and orderliness in later adulthood.

Freud's view of development has been criticized extensively for its overemphasis on libidinal gratification, as well as for its cultural and gender limitations. So, too, has his method for arriving at his theory: asking adults to reflect on their earliest experiences. As a consequence, his contributions have often been discounted. Nevertheless, for Freud, as for many developmental psychologists today, events that occur during the earliest years of development and that involve interactions with the family were of paramount importance in understanding and explaining behavior throughout the later years of an individual's life.

THE CONTINUED GROWTH OF DEVELOPMENTAL PSYCHOLOGY IN THE TWENTIETH CENTURY

From the beginning of the twentieth century to the mid-1940s, psychologists interested in development increasingly concentrated their efforts on gathering descriptive information about children. At what ages do most children achieve the milestones of motor development, such as sitting, crawling, and walking? When do children develop emotions, such as fear and anger? What are children's beliefs about punishment, friendship, and morality? It was during this era of intensive fact gathering that many *norms* of development—that is, the ages at which most children are able to accomplish a given developmental task—were established. For example, Arnold Gesell established the norms of motor development for the first five years of life, guidelines that are still useful to psychologists, pediatricians, and other professionals who work with children in diagnosing developmental problems or delays (Gesell & Thompson, 1934, 1938).

Over the years, questions about norms gave way to research on the variables that might be related to specific aspects of development or cause it to occur in the way it does. For example, is maturation or experience responsible for the sequence of motor behaviors most children display? Even almost seventy years ago, researchers found that the answer was not simple. Myrtle McGraw (1935, 1939), in her classic studies of the twins Johnny and Jimmy, reported that training Johnny (but not Jimmy) to reach for objects, crawl, and swim during infancy accelerated motor development, but only when he was already showing signs of physiological maturity. Similarly, does the predictable sequence of language development occur because of biological influences or learning? What factors lead to the emergence of emotional ties children form with caregivers? Researchers today continue to ask questions like these, recognizing more and more the complexities of the influences on child development.

In her classic studies of a pair of twins, Myrtle McGraw found that both maturation and experience contributed to motor skill development.

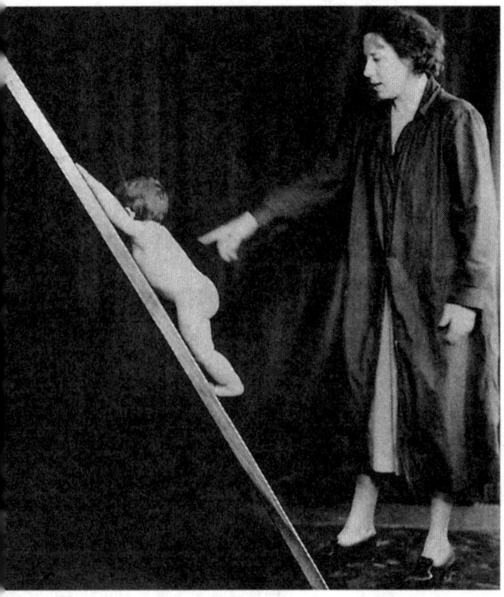

The first half of the twentieth century also saw the founding of a number of major institutes or research centers that attracted bright young scholars who dedicated their lives to the scientific study of children. A further sign of the professionalization of the discipline was the formation of the Society for Research in Child Development (SRCD) in 1933 for scientists who wished to share their growing knowledge of child behavior and development. Today the membership of this society numbers about 5,000 (SRCD, 2002) and includes developmental researchers, practitioners, and professionals working in such settings as colleges, universities, research institutes, and hospitals.

Scholars now approach child development from an assortment of disciplines, including anthropology, sociology, education, medicine, biology, and several subareas of psychology (such as neuropsychology, comparative psychology, and clinical psychology), as well as the specialized area of developmental psychology. Each discipline has its own biases, as defined by the questions each asks about development and the methodological approaches it employs to answer those questions.

Nonetheless, our pooled knowledge gives us a better understanding of development than we might expect from a field that officially began only a century ago.

FOR • YOUR • REVIEW

- How have views of childhood changed from medieval and Renaissance times to today?
- What were John Locke's and Jean Jacques Rousseau's views of childhood?
- How did Charles Darwin, Wilhelm Preyer, G. Stanley Hall, Alfred Binet, and James Mark Baldwin contribute to developmental psychology?
- What was Sigmund Freud's psychosexual theory of development?
- What emphases emerged in research on children during the first half of the twentieth century?

THEORIES OF DEVELOPMENT

A number of major theories influence our understanding of development today. We introduce them and briefly highlight some of the major concepts and principles associated with each in the sections that follow. However, their contributions will be a major part of our discussion in later chapters as well. In considering these theories in this first chapter, we focus in particular on where each stands with respect to the major themes in developmental psychology.

LEARNING THEORY APPROACHES

Learning theorists study how principles of learning cause the individual to change and develop. **Learning**, the relatively permanent change in behavior that results from experience, undoubtedly contributes to why the infant smiles as her mother approaches, the three-year-old says a polite "Thank you" on receiving his grandmother's present, the five-year-old displays newfound skill in tying her shoes, and the adolescent expresses a clear preference about the most fashionable item of clothing to wear.

In the extreme view, some learning theorists believe, as John B. Watson did, that learning mechanisms can be exploited to create virtually any type of person.

> Give me a dozen healthy infants, well-formed, and my own specified world to bring them up in and I'll guarantee to take any one at random and train him to become any type of specialist I might select—doctor, lawyer, artist, merchant-chief, and yes, even beggar-man and thief, regardless of his talents, penchants, tendencies, abilities, vocations, and race of his ancestors. (Watson, 1930, p. 104)

Although present-day supporters of learning theory seldom take such a radical position, they are in agreement that basic principles of learning can have a powerful influence on child development (Bijou, 1989; Gewirtz & Peláez-Nogueras, 1992; Schlinger, 1992).

Behavior Analysis **Behavior analysis** is a theoretical account of development that relies on several basic principles of learning to explain developmental changes in behavior. Behavior analysis sprang from the radical learning position introduced by John B. Watson and was extended in more recent years by B. F. Skinner (1953, 1974) and others. Nearly a century ago, the Russian physiologist Ivan Pavlov observed that dogs would often begin to salivate at the sound of a bell or some other arbitrary stimulus when the stimulus had previously been accompanied by food. In this type of learning, called *classical conditioning*, a neutral stimulus begins to elicit a response

learning Relatively permanent change in behavior as a result of such experiences as exploration, observation, and practice.

behavior analysis Learning theory perspective that explains the development of behavior according to the principles of classical and operant conditioning.

after being repeatedly paired with another stimulus that already elicits that response. We learn certain behaviors and emotions as a result of classical conditioning. For example, children and adults may become anxious on entering a dental office because of its association with previous painful treatments performed by the dentist.

To understand a second basic principle of learning, consider two babies who smile as their caregivers approach. With one baby, the caregiver stops, says "Hi, baby!" and briefly rocks the cradle. With the other baby, the caregiver walks on past, preoccupied. Which baby is more likely to repeat his smiling response when the caregiver nears again? If you reasoned that the first is more likely than the second because the behavior was followed by a positive event (attention or approval), which often increases the frequency of a behavior, you know something about the principle of operant conditioning. *Operant conditioning* (also called *instrumental conditioning*) refers to the process by which the frequency of a behavior changes depending on response consequences in the form of a desirable or undesirable outcome. Behavior analysts have used this principle to account for the emergence of such straightforward behaviors as the one-year-old's waving good-bye to far more sophisticated skills involving memory, language, social interaction, and complex problem solving.

Operant and classical conditioning have been shown to have enormous potential to change behavior. *Behavior modification*, sometimes called *applied behavior analysis*, involves the systematic application of operant conditioning to modify human activity. To illustrate, Jason Stricker and his colleagues (Stricker et al., 2001) investigated whether thumb sucking could be reduced in children who engaged in such activity at an age when it is no longer considered appropriate. They identified a seven-year-old child with attention deficit hyperactivity disorder (ADHD) who often sucked his thumb while watching television and in other situations. Would consistent feedback to the child help him become aware of this activity and reduce this behavior? To test this possibility, the researchers attached two small transmitters to the child, one to his wrist and a second to his shirt, just below his mouth. When the child raised his hand to his mouth to engage in thumb sucking, bringing the wrist and shirt transmitter close to each other, the transmitters triggered a nearby device that began to produce a beeping tone. The researchers recorded the percentage of time the child engaged in thumb sucking during ten-minute sessions of television viewing over a number of weeks. During a baseline period, the child did not wear the transmitters. In other sessions, he wore transmitters that were either

Social learning theory emphasizes the important role that observation of another person plays in learning. This young boy is acquiring new behaviors by watching his mother and imitating what she does. Social learning provides a mechanism by which many desirable social customs and actions become part of the child's repertoire.

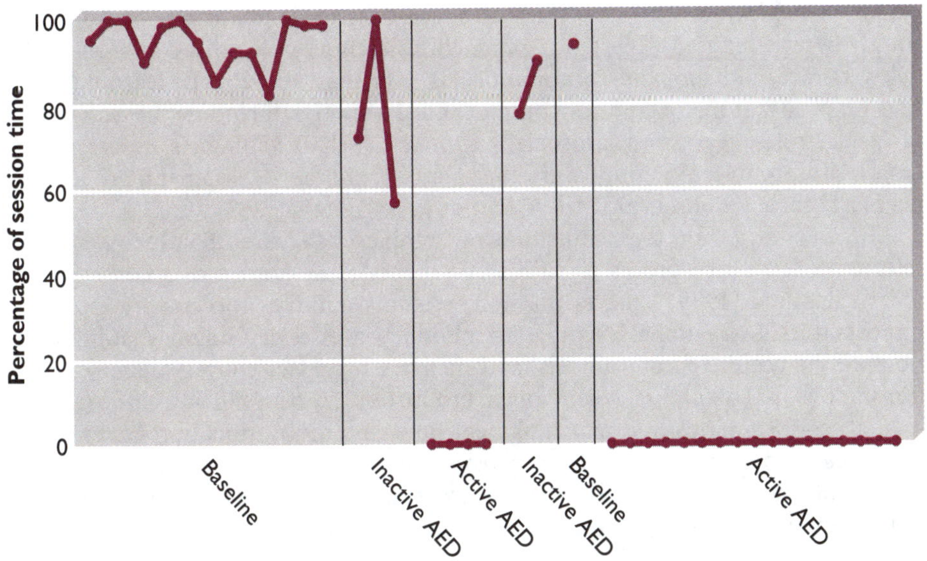

FIGURE 1.3

A Behavioral Approach to Reducing Thumb Sucking in Children

The seven-year-old child observed in this study often sucked his thumb. During the baseline period sessions in which he was simply observed watching television, he engaged in this activity a high percentage of the time. Next, a set of transmitters, called an "awareness enhancement device" (AED), was attached to the child. When the device did not activate a beeping tone (Inactive AED), he continued to display such behavior frequently. However, when the tone was activated whenever the child sucked his thumb (Active AED), the practice ceased. As predicted by behavorial theories, response consequences can have a powerful effect on behavior.

Source: Stricker et al. (2001).

activated or not activated to provide feedback. The findings of this experiment are shown in Figure 1.3. The results clearly demonstrate the elimination of the thumb sucking when the transmitters produced feedback about the activity. The feedback may have helped the child become aware of his thumb sucking; in addition, the sound may have been annoying enough to yield the change in his behavior.

Applied behavior analysis has become a powerful approach used by teachers, therapists, and caregivers to bring about changes in behavior ranging from the elimination of temper tantrums and other disruptive responses to encouraging healthy diets and safe driving habits. Even some of its detractors have suggested that behavior analysis may have done more to benefit human welfare than any other psychological theory (Hebb, 1980). For this reason alone, learning theory has appealed to many in their efforts to understand development. Yet behavior analysis has drawn extensive criticism. Its critics, including some learning theorists, remain unconvinced that a behavior can be understood without taking into account the child's feelings and reasons for engaging in that behavior. In other words, mental, emotional, and motivational factors also play a prominent role in how a child interprets and responds to stimulation. Among various learning perspectives, social learning theory attempts to incorporate these factors into its explanation of behavior and development.

Social Learning Theory **Social learning theory** emphasizes the importance of learning through observation and imitation of the behaviors displayed by others. Social learning theorists start with the assumption that whether an individual will be friendly, outgoing, confident, and honest rather than shy and perhaps hostile and untrustworthy depends largely on the socialization practices of parents and caregivers throughout that person's childhood. Although operant and classical conditioning play a substantial role, social learning theorists underscore **observational learning**, the acquisition of behaviors from listening to and watching other people, as a particularly important means of acquiring new behaviors. The two-year-old who stands before a mirror pretending to shave in imitation of his father is displaying observational learning. Similarly, you may have witnessed the embarrassment of a parent whose three-year-old has uttered a profanity, a behavior probably acquired by the same process.

According to Albert Bandura, psychology's best-known spokesperson for social learning, a society could never effectively convey complex language, social and moral customs, or other achievements to its younger members without relying extensively on observational learning. Bandura (1965) notes that significant learning occurs, often completely without error, through the act of watching and imitating another

social learning theory Theoretical approach emphasizing the importance of learning through observation and imitation of behaviors modeled by others.

observational learning Learning that takes place by simply observing another person's behavior.

person, a *model.* For example, girls in one region of Guatemala learn to weave simply by watching an expert, an approach to learning new skills common to the fields, homes, and shops of communities all over the world. Social learning theorists propose that many kinds of complex social activities, including the acquisition of gender roles, aggression, prosocial responses (such as willingness to assist others), resistance to temptation, and other facets of moral development, are learned primarily through observing others (Bandura & Walters, 1963).

In accounting for the acquisition of complex behaviors, Bandura has often referred to cognitive processes within his theory, now known as *social cognitive theory.* Bandura (1989) believes that four sets of cognitive processes are especially important in observational learning. Attentional processes determine what information will be acquired from models, and memory processes convert these observations into stored mental representations. Production processes then transform these mental representations into matching behaviors, and motivational processes define which behaviors are likely to be performed. As each of these processes becomes more sophisticated, observational and other forms of learning become increasingly refined and proficient, and the child becomes more effective in regulating his or her own behavior (Grusec, 1992).

Learning Theory and Themes in Development What stance do behavior analysts and social cognitive theorists take on the five major developmental themes we introduced at the beginning of this chapter? Keep in mind that, as our discussions of behavior analysis and social cognitive theory suggest, not all learning theorists share the same views about the prime determinants of development.

- ***Nature & Nurture*** Behavior analysts believe that biological and genetic factors may limit the kinds of responses that can be performed and help to define which events are reinforcing or punishing. But ultimately it is the environment that controls behavior. For behaviorists, a child's functioning is the outcome of a history of behaviors and their associated consequences. In social cognitive theory, biological factors and the environment are believed to play a mutual, interactive role in contributing to development (Bandura, 1989). In keeping with their strong experiential emphasis, behaviorists believe the child's role in development is passive. Skinner claimed that "a person does not act upon the world, the world acts upon him" (1971, p. 211). According to Skinner, psychologists should abolish references to unobservable mental or cognitive constructs, such as motives, goals, needs, or thoughts, in their explanations of behavior. Bandura's social cognitive theory differs from behavior analysis by embracing mental and motivational constructs and processes for interpreting and understanding others as well as the self. Social cognitive theory therefore confers a much more active status on the child than does behavior analysis.
- ***Sociocultural Influence*** Behaviorists believe that, although societies differ in the responses viewed as desirable or unacceptable, the mechanisms of learning are universal for individuals in all cultures. Rewards and punishments delivered in the immediate environment are the key to understanding development. Social learning theorists give sociocultural context more emphasis than behaviorists do by pointing out, for example, that advances in communication technology (such as television) expand the opportunity for children and adults to acquire many novel skills and patterns of behavior through observational learning.
- ***Continuity/Discontinuity*** Both behavior analysts and social learning theorists consider development to be continuous rather than stagelike. Any departure from this pattern would stem from abrupt shifts in environmental circumstances, such as when the child enters school or the adolescent enters the work environment.
- ***Interaction Among Domains*** Whereas behavior analysts explain development in all domains in terms of the basic principles of learning, social cognitive theorists stress that learning is linked to the child's physical, cognitive, and social

development. Thus this latter perspective acknowledges the interaction among different domains of development by recognizing that the child's learning is a consequence of what he or she feels, believes, and thinks.

- *Risk/Resilience* The general principles of learning apply to all individuals, whatever their situation, and can account for both risk and recovery from risk. It is important to analyze the unique kinds of experiences each person receives; for example, the specific models to which she or he is exposed or the particular behaviors rewarded by others in the environment.

PIAGET'S COGNITIVE-DEVELOPMENTAL THEORY

Jean Piaget's keen observations and insights concerning the behavior of children laid the groundwork for his theory of cognitive development. Piaget's ideas about how thinking develops have influenced psychologists, educators, and many others in their attempts to understand children.

According to **cognitive-developmental theory**, behavior reflects the emergence of various cognitive *structures*, organized units or patterns of thinking, that influence how the child interprets experience. Cognitive-developmental theories tend to share the fundamental assumption that normal children display common intellectual, emotional, and social capacities despite widely varying experiences. Most three- and four-year-olds around the world, for example, believe that a gallon of water, when poured from one container to another of a different shape, changes in amount, an error children rarely make once they reach seven or eight years of age. Cognitive-developmental theorists explain this profound change in reasoning in terms of children's acquiring new ways of understanding their world.

The most extensive and best-known cognitive-developmental theory was put forward by Jean Piaget. His vigorous defense of physical and mental *action* as the basis for cognitive development (Beilin & Fireman, 1999) and his belief that intellectual capacities undergo *qualitative* reorganization at different stages of development have had a monumental impact, not only on developmental psychologists, but also on educators and other professionals working with children.

Piaget's Theory Piaget's vision of human development was based on two overriding assumptions about intelligence: (1) it is a form of biological adaptation, and (2) it becomes organized as the individual interacts with the external world (Piaget, 1971). **Adaptation** is a tendency to adjust or become more attuned to the conditions imposed by the environment. **Organization** refers to a tendency for intellectual structures and processes to become more systematic and coherent. Just as arms, eyes, lungs, heart, and other physical structures assemble and take shape to carry out biological functions, so do mental structures array themselves in ever more powerful patterns to support more complex thought. These changes, however, depend on the opportunity to look and touch, handle and play with, and construct and order the rich assortment of experiences stemming from action on the environment. From the abundant encounters provided in commonplace physical and social experiences, the child confronts unexpected and puzzling outcomes that ultimately lead to reorganizations in thought.

The basic mental structure in Piaget's theory is a **scheme**, a coordinated and systematic pattern of action or way of reasoning. A scheme is a kind of template for acting or thinking applied to similar classes of objects or situations. The infant who sucks at her mother's breast, at her favorite pacifier, and at her thumb is exercising a scheme of sucking. The six-year-old who realizes that his eight Matchbox cars can be stored in an equal number of boxes regardless of how they are scattered about the floor is also exercising a scheme, this time one concerned with number. The infant's schemes are limited to patterns of action applied to objects: sucking, grasping, shaking, and so forth. The older child's schemes will often involve mental processes and be far more complex as he or she reasons about such things as classes of objects, number, or spatial relations, and, by adolescence, the meaning of life and the origins of the universe. For Piaget, earlier schemes set the stage for constructing new and more sophisticated schemes.

Piaget believed that schemes change through two complementary processes. The first, **assimilation**, refers to the process of interpreting an experience in terms

cognitive-developmental theory Theoretical orientation, most frequently associated with Piaget, emphasizing the active construction of psychological structures to interpret experience.

adaptation In Piagetian theory, the inborn tendency to adjust or become more attuned to conditions imposed by the environment; takes place through assimilation and accommodation.

organization In Piagetian theory, the inborn tendency for structures and processes to become more systematic and coherent.

scheme In Piagetian theory, the mental structure underlying a coordinated and systematic pattern of behaviors or thinking applied across similar objects or situations.

assimilation In Piagetian theory, a component of adaptation; process of interpreting an experience in terms of current ways (schemes) of understanding things.

of current ways of understanding things. The second, **accommodation**, refers to the modifications in behavior and thinking that take place when the old ways of understanding, the old schemes, no longer fit. To illustrate these two processes, consider the infant's first experience with sucking a pacifier. Upon feeling it in the mouth, the infant engages the already formed scheme for sucking on the mother's breast. In other words, this new experience is *assimilated* into the pre-existing scheme. But the shape and taste of the pacifier are not the same as the mother's breast. The child's scheme must *accommodate* to this new encounter. In a similar manner throughout development, the child's intellectual capacities become reshaped and reorganized as the child attempts to adjust—that is, accommodate—to new experiences.

For Piaget, assimilation and accommodation are complementary aspects of all psychological activity, processes engaged in a constant tug of war in the never-ending goal of acquiring understanding (Valsiner, 2006). Fortunately, adaptation in the form of newer and more complex schemes is the result of this continuous dynamic. The outcome of adaptation is a more effective fitting together of the many pieces of knowledge that make up the child's understanding. The process by which assimilation and accommodation bring about more organized and powerful schemes for thinking is called **equilibration**. Each new experience can cause imbalance, which can be corrected only by modification of the child's schemes. In trying to make sense of his or her world, the child develops more adaptive ways of thinking.

During some periods of development, schemes may undergo rapid and substantial modification and reorganization. The more effective levels of knowledge that emerge from these restructurings are the basis for different stages in Piaget's theory of development. Piaget proposed that development proceeds through four stages: *sensorimotor, preoperational, concrete,* and *formal.* Much more will be said about each of these stages as we progress through this book; however, Table 1.1 briefly identifies them. Each higher stage is defined by the appearance of a qualitatively different level of thinking, an increasingly more sophisticated form of knowledge through which the child displays greater intellectual balance for responding to the environment. However, each new stage does not suddenly appear full-blown; it arises from the integration and incorporation of earlier ways of thinking.

Piaget's wide range of observations, his frequently surprising findings about what infants and children can and cannot do, and his theoretical explanations and

Table 1.1 Piaget's Stages of Cognitive Development

Stage	Emerging Cognitive Structure (schemes)	Typical Achievements and Behaviors
Sensorimotor (birth until 1½–2 years)	Sensory and motor actions, initially reflexes, quickly differentiate by means of accommodation and co-ordinate to form adaptive ways of acting on the environment.	Infants suck, grasp, look, reach, and so forth, responses that become organized into complex activities such as hand-eye coordination, knowledge of space and objects and eventually rudimentary symbols designed to solve problems and understand the physical world.
Preoperational (1½–7 years)	Symbols stand for or represent objects and events, but communication and thought remain relatively inflexible.	Children begin to acquire language and mental representations, but thought remains unidimensional and oriented around the self.
Concrete Operational (7–11 years)	Cognitive operations permit logical reasoning about concrete objects, events, and relationships.	Children are no longer fooled by appearance, and they can reason more systematically with respect to classes, number and other characteristics of their physical and social world.
Formal Operational (11 years and above)	Operations can be performed on operations. Thought becomes abstract, and all possible outcomes can be considered.	Adolescents and adults are able to reason about hypothetical outcomes. Abstract issues (e.g., religion, morality, alternative lifestyles) are systematically evaluated.

assumptions have sparked a wealth of research on cognitive, social, and moral development. Many researchers applaud his innovative conceptualizations concerning development. For example, Piaget vigorously embraced the notion of children as active participants in their own development, a viewpoint that others have widely adopted (Siegler & Ellis, 1996). However, the central concept of qualitative differences in thinking between children and adults, and particularly of stagelike transformations, has been less favorably received (Fischer & Bidell, 2006; Thelen & Smith, 1994). We will say more about these issues in the chapters to come.

Piaget's Theory and Themes in Development How does Piaget's theory address the five major themes of development?

- *Nature & Nurture* Piaget theorized that a number of biologically based factors contribute to cognitive development. Among them is maturation, the gradual unfolding over time of genetic programs for development. Another factor is the child's inherent tendency to act, physically or mentally, on the environment. Nevertheless, for Piaget, development is clearly the product of the interaction of these factors with experience. In Piaget's theory, knowledge is *constructed*; that is, created and formed by the continuous revision and reorganization of intellectual structures in conjunction with experience. Piaget's constructivist model depicts a mind actively engaged in knowing and understanding its environment.
- *Sociocultural Influence* For Piaget, children develop in much the same way in all cultures around the world because of their similar biological makeup and the common physical and social world to which all humans must adapt. Different cultural or educational opportunities, however, can affect the speed and ultimate level of achievement in cognitive development.
- *Continuity/Discontinuity* Although recognizing continuous changes, Piaget's theory focuses on the ways schemes undergo reorganization and change to form distinctive stages in development. In his later writings and conversations, Piaget began to downplay the importance of stages (Piaget, 1971; Vuyk, 1981). He believed that an overemphasis on stages had led to too much concern with describing periods of intellectual stability or equilibrium when, in fact, cognition is always undergoing development. Cognitive development, he eventually concluded, is more like a spiral in which change constantly occurs, although sometimes at faster rates than at other times (Beilin, 1989).
- *Interaction Among Domains* Piaget's theory has implications for many domains of development. For example, his ideas about cognitive development have been used to explain changes in communication, moral thinking, and aspects of *social cognition*, such as how children understand the thoughts, intentions, feelings, and views of others. Nevertheless, Piaget has been criticized for paying relatively little attention to how social and emotional domains influence cognitive development.
- *Risk/Resilience* Piaget placed very little emphasis on individual differences in development. His goal was to identify the principles that applied to cognitive and other aspects of development in all children. However, in his emphasis on providing children with environmental experiences that match their biological readiness to learn, Piaget does suggest some factors that might put children at risk.

INFORMATION-PROCESSING APPROACHES

Computer information processing as a metaphor for human thinking has generated so many models and theories that it is difficult to single out any one approach as a prototype (Klahr & MacWhinney, 1998). However, one common thread evident in any **information-processing** point of view is the notion that humans, like computers, have a *limited capacity* for taking in and operating on the vast amount of

accommodation In Piagetian theory, a component of adaptation; process of modification in thinking (schemes) that takes place when old ways of understanding something no longer fit.

equilibration In Piagetian theory, an innate self-regulatory process that, through accommodation and assimilation, results in more organized and powerful schemes for adapting to the environment. information processing Theoretical approach that views humans as having a limited ability to process information, much like computers.

information processing Theoretical approach that views humans as having a limited ability to process information, much like computers.

information available to them. Thus changes in cognitive structures (for example, short- and long-term memory) and processes (for instance, strategies, rules, and plans associated with attending, remembering, and decision making) are an essential component in explaining how older children might process information more fully and effectively than younger children.

What sets an information-processing theory apart from many other theories is its detailed effort to explain exactly how the child comes to identify the letters of the alphabet, remember the multiplication tables, recall the main ideas of a story, give a classmate directions to his or her home, or decide whether it is safe to cross the street. For example, how does a six-year-old solve addition problems? She may have practiced this activity over and over, and learned the answer to each particular problem by rote over many months of exposure to them. Or she may rely on some kind of strategy that permits her to consistently arrive at the correct answer. For example, she could start with the first number of the addition problem and then add one unit the number of times indicated by the second number. Thus, for the problem 3 + 5, she may begin at 3 and add 1 to it the necessary five times to arrive at the correct answer.

How could we tell whether one child was engaging in the first procedure, retrieving information from long-term rote memory, and another child, the second procedure of utilizing a rule to determine the answer? One clue could come from the length of time it takes to solve various addition problems. If a child is using the first technique, she can be expected to solve each problem in about the same length of time. If she uses the second technique, however, she will likely take somewhat longer to answer a problem in which the second number is very large than when it is very small. We may also see the child producing other observable behaviors, such as holding up three fingers to begin with and counting off additional fingers to arrive at the correct answer.

As this example illustrates, information-processing theorists frequently attempt to describe the rules, strategies, and procedures that children employ to complete a task and that help them to remember, make inferences, and solve problems. Why has this approach become popular in developmental psychology? One reason is disenchantment with learning, Piagetian, and other perspectives for explaining behavior. For instance, although learning theories attempt to identify which abilities are learned, they have offered few insights into how the child's mind changes with age in learning these abilities. Piaget's cognitive-developmental theory is concerned with this issue, but his explanations have been difficult to translate into ideas about how the mind actually functions. Moreover, the information-processing approach can be extended to account for development in many other domains, including language acquisition, peer relationships, and even social and personality development. Not surprisingly, given their breadth of application, information-processing approaches are discussed further in a number of the chapters that follow.

Information-Processing Approaches and Themes in Development Because of the wide variety of information-processing models theorized to account for changes in cognitive development, we can draw only broad conclusions concerning their positions on the various themes in development.

- ***Nature & Nurture*** Information-processing models have said little about nature and nurture. Some basic capacities to perceive and process information are assumed at or before birth, and the system may be attuned to respond in certain ways, for example, to language and other kinds of information. The environment has an obvious impact on development because it provides input for processing by the mind. The implicit assumption in most models is that basic cognitive structures and processes interact with experience to produce changes in the system. Children, of course, react to the environment, but they also initiate and construct strategies and procedures that assist in processing information more effectively. From this perspective, children take an increasingly active role in controlling their own learning and development.

- *Sociocultural Influence* As in the case of learning theory, the sociocultural context of development has been largely ignored by information-processing theorists. This is probably because researchers have typically focused on identifying how the mind operates on specific problems rather than on how the mind is affected by the kinds of problems a culture presents to it.
- *Continuity/Discontinuity* In most information-processing models, cognitive development is theorized to undergo quantitative rather than qualitative changes. For example, children retain increasing numbers of items in both short-term and long-term memory, and interpret information and apply various strategies more efficiently and effectively with development. Similarly, the acquisition of new strategies for storing and retrieving information, new rules for problem solving, and new ways of thinking about and processing information are interpreted as shifts in ability that come about because of relatively small, continuous improvements in the capacity to process information.
- *Interaction Among Domains* A notable limitation of many information-processing models is their failure to consider emotional, motivational, and other domains of behavior. How social factors, such as instructions, modeling, and the cultural context of learning, lead to developmental changes in processing information is also rarely spelled out (Klahr, 1989). However, as already noted, information-processing approaches have been extended to other domains of development, including language and social and personality development.
- *Risk/Resilience* Many information-processing theories pay little heed to the factors that might result in risks in development. However, their potential to explain such differences in terms of variations in rules, strategies, and other procedures for processing information is considerable.

Erikson's Psychosocial Approach

For the most part, the theoretical models we have examined so far have been concerned with learning and cognitive development. With *psychosocial* models, we shift to a substantially greater focus on emotions and personality. At one time, Freud's theory of personality was extremely influential in explaining emotional and personality development. However, Erik Erikson's theory has gained far greater attention in recent years. Like Freud, Erikson theorized that personality development progresses through stages. During each stage, the child must resolve conflicts between needs or feelings and external obstacles that are unique to that particular time in the life span. The satisfactory resolution of these conflicts leads to a healthy personality and a productive lifestyle. But, in contrast to Freud, Erikson included several additional stages during adulthood, and he gave socialization and society far greater importance in his theory.

Erik Erikson outlined eight stages of personality development. His psychosocial theory emphasized that at each stage, individuals must successfully adapt to new forms of demands placed on them by society. He also stressed that cultures frequently differ in how they help individuals negotiate those demands.

Psychosocial Theory In his classic work *Childhood and Society* (1950), Erikson outlined eight stages of development, as summarized in Table 1.2. During the first stage, Erikson theorized that *incorporation*, or taking in, is the primary mode for acting adaptively toward the world. In Erikson's view, this mode of activity extends beyond the mouth and includes other senses, such as looking and hearing, and motor systems, such as reaching and grasping, systems designed to expand the infant's resources for absorbing and responding to reality. Each subsequent stage identified another important mode for adapting to the environment.

Society, according to Erikson, plays a critical role in shaping and forming reality for the child. Communities create their own demands and set their own criteria for socializing the child. In one society, an infant may be permitted to

Table 1.2 Erikson's Stages of Psychosocial Development

Stage	Adaptive Mode	Significant Events and Outcomes
Basic Trust Versus Mistrust (birth to 1 year)	Incorporation—to take in (and give in return)	Babies must find consistency, predictability, and reliability in their caregivers' behaviors to gain a sense of trust and hope.
Autonomy Versus Shame and Doubt (1–3 years)	Control—to hold on and to let go	The child begins to explore and make choices in order to understand what is manageable and socially acceptable.
Initiative Versus Guilt (3–6 years)	Intrusion—to go after	The child begins to make plans, set goals, and persist in both physical and social exchanges to gain a sense of purpose and remain enthusiastic even in the face of inevitable frustration.
Industry Versus Inferiority (6 years to puberty)	Construction—to build things and relationships	The child acquires skills and performs "work" in the form of becoming educated and supporting the family in order to feel competent and attain a sense of achievement.
Identity Versus Identity Confusion (puberty to adulthood)	Integration—to be oneself (or not be oneself)	The adolescent attempts to discover his or her identity and place in society by trying out many roles in order to answer the question, "Who am I?"
Intimacy Versus Isolation (young adulthood)	Solidarity—to lose and find oneself in another	Having achieved a sense of identity, the young adult can now share himself or herself with another to avoid a sense of isolation, self-absorption, and the absence of love.
Generativity Versus Stagnation (middle adulthood)	Productivity—to make and to take care of	The adult produces things and ideas through work and creates and cares for the next generation to gain a sense of fulfillment and caring.
Integrity Versus Despair (old age)	Acceptance—to be (by having been) and to face not being	The older adult reviews and evaluates his or her life and accepts its worth, even if he or she not reached all goals, to achieve a sense of wisdom.

breast-feed whenever hungry over a period of several years, whereas infants in another society may be nursed or bottle-fed on a rigid schedule and weaned within the first year of life. In another example, the timing and severity of toilet training, as well as the means by which caregivers initiate it, may differ vastly from one society to another. Cultures differ in the requirements imposed on the child, yet each child must adapt to his own culture's regulations. Thus Erikson's **psychosocial theory of development** highlights the child's composite need to initiate adaptive modes of functioning while meeting the variety of demands framed by the society in which she lives.

Erikson theorized that the individual confronts a specific crisis as society imposes new demands in each stage. The resolution of each crisis may or may not be successful, but triumphs at earlier stages lay the groundwork for the negotiation of later stages. Moreover, each society has evolved ways to help individuals meet their needs. Caregiving practices, educational programs, social organizations, occupational training, and moral and ethical support are examples of cultural systems established to foster healthy, productive psychosocial development.

A common theme underlying the various features of Erikson's theory is the search for **identity**, or the acceptance of both self and one's society. At each stage, this search is manifested in a specific way. The need to develop a feeling of trust for

psychosocial theory of development Erikson's theory that personality develops through eight stages of adaptive functioning to meet the demands framed by society.

identity In Eriksonian psychosocial theory, the acceptance of both self and society, a concept that must be achieved at every stage but is especially important during adolescence.

a caregiver, acquire a sense of autonomy, initiate exchanges with the world, and learn and become competent in school and other settings are examples of how the infant and child discovers who and what she or he is and will become. During adolescence, the individual confronts the issue of identity directly. But the answer to "Who am I?" is elaborated and made clearer as the individual progresses through each psychosocial stage.

In summary, Erikson's views of personality development highlighted the practices society uses to encourage and promote healthy social and personality development. However, he painted development with a broad brush; consequently, his theory is frequently criticized for its vagueness. Still, just as Piaget identified meaningful issues in cognitive development, Erikson—regardless of the precision of his specific formulations—had a flair for targeting crucial issues in social and personality development.

Psychosocial Theory and Themes in Development Our discussion of Erikson's theory has already focused on a number of themes in development, but let's consider them once more.

- *Nature & Nurture* A biological contribution to behavior, extended from Freud's theory, is evident in Erikson's positions. Yet psychosocial theory must be considered interactionist, given the momentous role the presence and absence of appropriate socializing experiences play in resolving conflicts that arise at every stage. At the same time, in Erikson's theory, the emphasis on establishing an identity for self within society suggests an active role for the child in development.
- *Sociocultural Influence* The broader sociocultural context in which caregivers encourage children to master, explore, and engage in their physical and social environments, especially during the early years of life, plays a critical role in Erikson's theory of development. For Erikson, the sociocultural context is a key factor in understanding an individual's personality and social relationships.
- *Continuity/Discontinuity* Erikson identified eight stages in personality development. The successful negotiation of earlier stages lays the groundwork for continued psychological growth. The individual unable to work through a crisis at one time, however, may still effectively resolve it at a later stage.
- *Interaction Among Domains* Erikson links social, emotional, and cognitive development together in the individual's efforts to achieve identity. For example, a sense of trust emerges from taking in through the senses as well as the motor system; a sense of industry reflects intellectual competence as well as the ability to interact effectively with others; and discovering one's identity requires the integration of all of one's psychological skills and competencies.
- *Risk/Resilience* The psychosocial stages are common to every individual in every culture. However, the success with which each stage is negotiated can vary dramatically from one individual to another and from one society to another. Although not specifically focused on risk factors in development, Erikson's theory offers many insights into how and why risks and resilience might come about.

CONTEXTUAL APPROACHES

Psychologists have long recognized that children live in vastly different circumstances and that these differences can have a dramatic influence on development. Some children grow up in households with a single parent, others with two parents, and still others with grandparents and perhaps aunts and uncles; children in foster care, on the other hand, may be shuffled frequently from one family to another. In addition, siblings within the same family may receive quite different experiences as a function of being the eldest or youngest, or of being singled out for certain kinds of treatment and expectations by family members. Number of siblings, economic

Contextual approaches to development give recognition to the dramatic impact that broad sociocultural factors can have on children's lives. These children in Ethiopia attend an overcrowded school with few educational resources, a setting far different from classrooms in most Western countries. Schooling and work, family structure, economic resources, and many other social contexts vary tremendously for children living in different cultures. Researchers need to consider these types of broad factors affecting children's lives in order to fully understand development.

resources, space and privacy, independence, and emotional atmosphere are among the vast assortment of factors that vary in the immediate surroundings of children.

Differences in the contexts of development extend far beyond a child's immediate family, however. Physical surroundings, access to schools, job opportunities, technological innovations, natural disasters, political systems, and war, as well as the cultural dictates of the community, influence the way children are reared. Some of these circumstances will be more supportive of development than others. Apart from the physical and sociocultural contexts in which each child lives is still another factor: the innate and species-specific predispositions, the biological context that equips the child to learn and develop.

Developmental theories usually focus on immediate experience, defined narrowly in terms of contemporary circumstances and recent events, and how it affects development. Yet culture, the historical legacy of earlier generations of a given social group, as well as the evolutionary pressures that have shaped humans to exist in their natural environment, are also major factors affecting growth. Put another way, the transformation from infant to child to adult takes place within a complex, multidirectional system of influences (Gottlieb, Wahlsten, & Lickliter, 2006). **Contextual models**, sometimes called *systems views*, are concerned with understanding this broad range of biological, physical, and sociocultural settings, and how they affect development.

Ecological Systems Theory The most extensive description of the context in which development proceeds has been put forth in the **ecological systems theory** proposed by Urie Bronfenbrenner (1989, 1995). Ecological theories in general stress the need to understand development in terms of the everyday environment in which children are reared, a concern that is seldom the focus of many other theories. Commenting on the state of developmental psychology several decades ago, Bronfenbrenner claimed that "much of contemporary developmental psychology is the science of the strange behavior of children in strange situations with strange adults for the briefest possible periods of time" (Bronfenbrenner, 1977, p. 513). Development, Bronfenbrenner believes, must be studied not only in the laboratory, as it had been, but also in the homes, schools, neighborhoods, and communities in which it takes place.

One of Bronfenbrenner's major theoretical contributions has been his comprehensive portrait of the environment—the ecological forces and systems that exist at several different but interrelated levels—and the bidirectional and reciprocal

contextual models Theories of development that are concerned with the effects of a broad range of biological, physical, and sociocultural settings on the process of development.

ecological systems theory Bronfenbrenner's theory that development is influenced by experiences arising from broader social and cultural systems as well as a child's immediate surroundings.

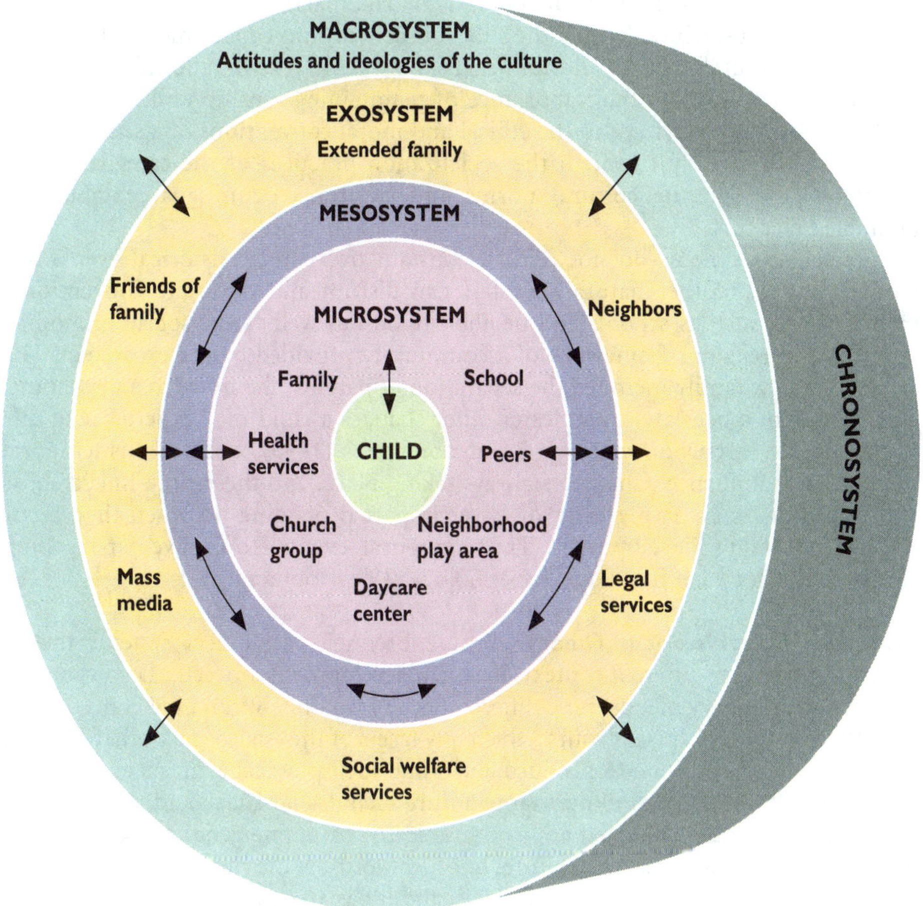

FIGURE 1.4

Bronfenbrenner's Ecological Model

At the core of Bronfenbrenner's ecological model is the child's biological and psychological makeup, based on individual genetic and developmental history. This makeup continues to be affected and modified by the child's immediate physical and social environment (microsystem), as well as interactions among the systems within this environment (mesosystem). Other broader social, political, and economic conditions (exosystem) influence the structure and availability of microsystems and the manner in which they affect the child. Social, political, and economic conditions are themselves influenced by the general beliefs and attitudes (macrosystem) shared by members of the society, and all of these systems are affected by changes that occur over time (chronosystem).

Source: Adapted from Garabino (1982).

relationships that exist among them. These levels are shown in Figure 1.4. At the center is the child's biological and psychological makeup, including her cognitive capacities and socioemotional and motivational propensities (such as temperament and personality) for responding to and acting on the environment. Settings with the most immediate and direct impact on an individual's biological and psychological qualities make up the **microsystem**. These settings include the home and members of the household, social and educational circumstances (including classmates, teachers, and classroom resources), and neighborhoods (including physical layout, friends, and acquaintances).

The **mesosystem** includes the many interrelationships among the various settings within the microsystem. For example, opportunities and expectations within the family, such as access to books and learning to read or an emphasis on acquiring basic academic and socialization skills, may critically influence the child's experiences and success in another microsystem, the school. As another example, a child of divorced parents living in separate neighborhoods may undergo frequent moves between the two homes. Such a living arrangement may have repercussions for the range and kinds of friendships the child can establish with peers.

Social, economic, political, religious, and other settings can affect development either directly or indirectly through their impact on those who care for the child. These wider contexts make up the **exosystem**. In many countries today, for example, the child seldom is part of either parent's work environment. Nevertheless, the parent who encounters a difficult problem at work may bring frustrations home and express them through angry exchanges with members of the family. Urban renewal planned at city hall may have dramatic consequences for children and their interactions with peers, hopefully for the better, but perhaps not always with that effect. Skirmishes between rival villages or countries may bring poverty if the family breadwinner is killed in fighting.

microsystem In Bronfenbrenner's ecological systems theory, the immediate environment provided in such settings as the home, school, workplace, and neighborhood.

mesosystem In Bronfenbrenner's ecological systems theory, the environment provided by the interrelationships among the various settings of the microsystem.

exosystem In Bronfenbrenner's ecological systems theory, environmental settings that indirectly affect the child by influencing the various microsystems forming the child's immediate environment.

The broadest context is the **macrosystem**. The macrosystem includes the spiritual and religious values, legal and political practices, and ceremonies and customs shared by a cultural group. Cultural beliefs about child rearing, the role of schools and family in education, the importance of maintaining kinship affiliations, tolerance for different lifestyles, and the ethical and moral conventions of a society affect the child both directly (through the socialization practices of the caregivers) and indirectly (through the cultural norms and strictures defining acceptable and desirable behavior).

These four systems do not remain constant over time. Historical events like famines, wars, or other natural disasters can disrupt and devastate conventional microsystems, such as schools and neighborhoods, as well as the social, economic, political, and religious framework of a community provided by the exosystem. The arrival of a new family member, the separation of parents, the move to a new home, and the loss of a peer are examples of other changes a child may experience at different times. The **chronosystem** is Bronfenbrenner's (1995) term for this temporal dimension of influence. Change is always taking place, and these time-linked shifts and transitions may have greater or lesser impact depending on when they occur during the child's development. Thus temporal events, too, have far-reaching consequences for each individual's psychological development.

Vygotsky's Sociohistorical Theory Bronfenbrenner's ecological systems theory highlights the many different contexts in which development proceeds. Lev Vygotsky's sociohistorical theory blends these different levels into one overarching concept: culture. What is culture? It is, of course, the many facets of the environment that humans have created and continue to produce, including such physical artifacts as tools and furnishings. But, even more important, culture includes language and the practices, values, and beliefs accumulated and communicated from one generation to the next through that language system. Culture, in other words, is the human-generated, historical accumulation of one's surroundings, and it has an enormous influence on the way children are reared. Vygotsky's **sociohistorical theory** emphasizes the unique collective wisdom compiled by a culture and transmitted to the child through ongoing, daily interactions with the more knowledgeable members of that society.

A central tenet of Vygotsky's sociohistorical theory is that, as children become exposed to and participate in their community, they begin to internalize and adopt, often with the guidance of a skilled partner, such as a parent or teacher, the culturally based, more mature and effective methods of thinking about and solving problems (Wertsch, 1985; Wertsch & Tulviste, 1992). For example, in sitting down with and reading to the child, the caregiver demonstrates how important this activity is, so that eventually the child comes to value it in her own behavior. Vygotsky believed that language is an especially important tool in this dialogue, because it, too, is internalized by the child to affect thinking and problem solving.

One quality that permeates both ecological systems theory and sociohistorical views of development is the seamless alloy that embodies development as the child is affected by and, in turn, actively influences his or her surroundings (Sameroff, 1994). Development is dynamic, a never-ending *transaction* involving continuing, reciprocal exchanges: people and settings transform the child, who in turn affects the people and settings surrounding him, which further reshape the child in an endless progression.

Lev Vygotsky's sociohistorical theory emphasizes that the cultural experiences to which children are exposed become an indispensable part of their development. This Maya Indian father in Guatemala is teaching his young child how to make bricks. In doing so, the parent is transmitting important information to his offspring. By becoming aware of how communities transmit knowledge to their young members, we can begin to appreciate how culture influences attitudes, beliefs, and values, as well as cognitive development.

Consider the baby born with low birth weight. Such an infant often displays a sharp, shrill cry and has difficulty nursing. Because of these factors and the baby's fragile appearance, a mother who might otherwise feel confident may become anxious and uncertain about her caregiving abilities. Her apprehensions may translate into inconsistent behaviors, to which the baby, in turn, responds with irregular patterns of feeding and sleeping. These difficulties further reduce the mother's confidence in her abilities and enjoyment of her baby, leading to fewer social interactions and less positive stimulation for the infant. As a consequence, achievements in other areas of development, such as language acquisition, may be delayed. But what factor, precisely, caused these delays? To answer this question, we might point to the child's low birth weight or the mother's avoidance of her infant. However, these explanations fall far short of capturing the many complex elements that contributed to the mother's behaviors and the child's development. The importance of these complex transactions becomes especially apparent when psychologists and others attempt to modify the course of development. The mother who has avoided her low-birth-weight infant because of a widening gulf of anxious reactions brought about by disappointments and unhappy exchanges will need more than simply to be told to start talking to her child to encourage his language development. She may need to gain a greater understanding of the typical problems such babies face, receive support and reinforcement for her efforts to initiate confident caregiving skills, and acquire richer insights into how development is affected by experiences, only some of which she can control.

Dynamic Systems Theory It should be evident by now that contextual theories champion the importance of many interacting events to account for development. **Dynamic systems theory** captures this idea and at the same time stresses the emergence over time of more advanced, complex behaviors from these many interactions (Lewis, 2000). Of particular interest in this theoretical orientation is the notion that development reflects more than an accumulation of past events; it is, instead, the product of reorganizations that arise from the interactions of various levels of the system that could not be observed or expected from each component level by itself. One outcome of this reorganization is a stable, more adaptive way of responding (Novak, 1996; Thelen & Smith, 1994, 2006). When the right combinations of elements are present, new, sometimes unexpected, capacities emerge.

One of the more important implications of dynamic systems theory is that development is not controlled or regulated by any one particular factor, for example, by the brain, the genes, child-rearing practices, or any other specific influence. Instead, these various components are parts of a process that induces more organized and advanced behaviors or ways of thinking. Perhaps one of the best examples illustrating a dynamic systems view is learning to walk. As Thelen and Smith indicate, "Learning to walk is less a prescribed, logically inevitable process than a confluence of available states within particular contextual opportunities" (1994, p. 72). In more concrete terms, learning to walk results from a necessary combination of inherited human anatomical and neural systems, opportunities to exercise muscles, the desire to move around more effectively, the availability of acceptable surfaces and other supportive physical environments, and parenting that fosters exploration and sensorimotor development. Walking begins when the right blend of these comes together (see Figure 1.5). So, too, do new accomplishments in perception, language, cognition, and social behavior.

Ethological Theory Development is influenced by yet one more broad context: the biological history and constraints that have been a part of human evolution. In the nineteenth century, Darwin and other biologists concluded that adaptive traits—those that improved the likelihood of survival and thus ensured a greater number of offspring for further reproduction—were more likely to be found in succeeding generations of a species. Darwin hypothesized that, through *evolution*, the descent of living species from earlier species of animals, humans inherited biological traits

macrosystem In Bronfenbrenner's ecological systems theory, major historical events and the broad values, practices, and customs shared by a culture.

chronosystem In Bronfenbrenner's ecological systems theory, the constantly changing temporal component of the environment that can influence development.

sociohistorical theory Vygotsky's developmental theory emphasizing the importance of cultural tools, symbols, and ways of thinking that the child acquires from more knowledgeable members of the community.

dynamic systems theory Theoretical orientation that explains development as the emerging organization arising from the interaction of many different processes.

FIGURE 1.5
A Dynamic Systems Model of Walking
According to dynamic systems theory, development arises from the interactions of several systems, each of which displays variability but which, under the right conditions, result in new, more organized patterns of behavior. For example, walking may emerge when the child's physical development, muscle strength, environment, motivation, and encouragement from parents all come together.

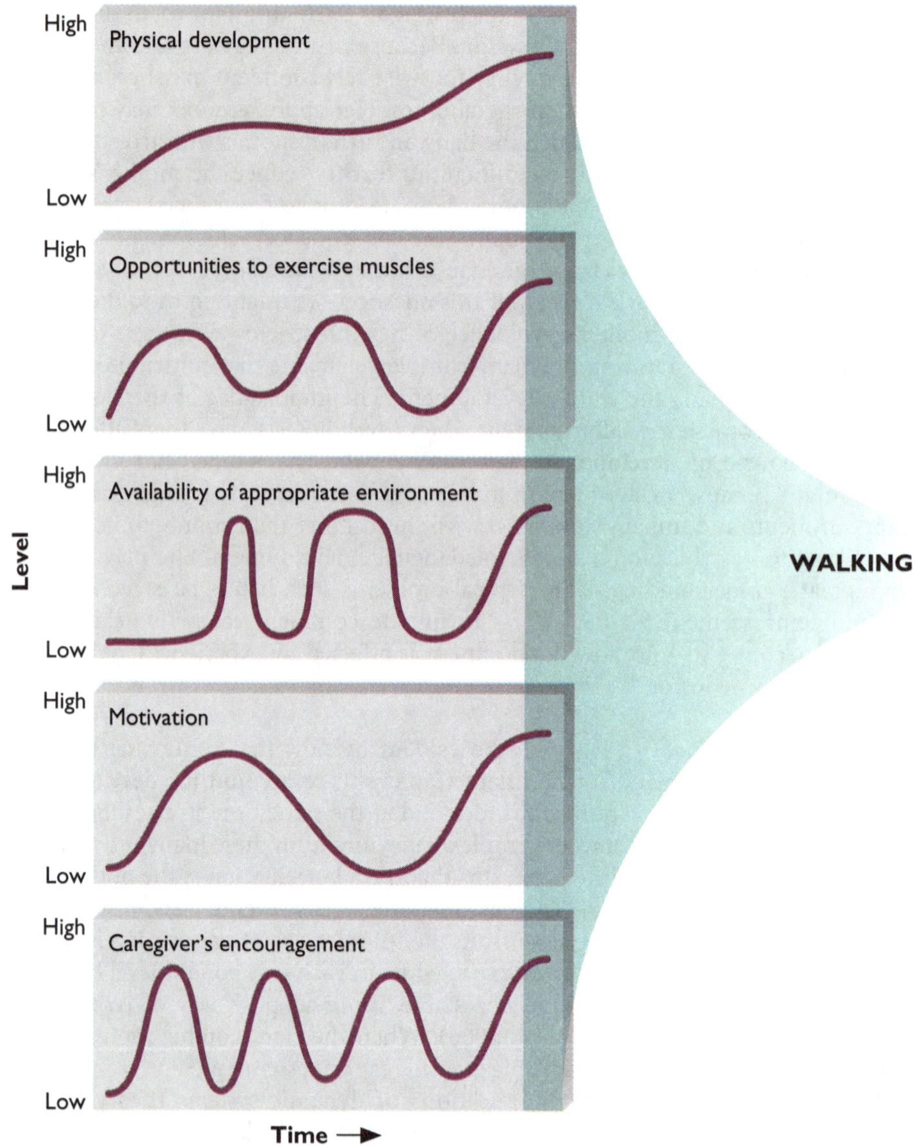

and capacities that improved their rate of survival. **Ethology** is the discipline specifically concerned with understanding how adaptive behaviors evolved and what functions they still serve for the continuation of the species.

Ethological theory surfaced in the 1930s when European zoologists, such as Konrad Lorenz (1963/1966) and Nikolaas Tinbergen (1951), investigated aggressive actions and the courtship and mating rituals of such species as the mallard duck and stickleback fish. Their observations led to explanations that took into account the *mutual* interchange between the inherited, biological bases of behavior and the environment in which that behavior was exhibited (Hinde, 1989). Ethological studies propose answers to questions like the following: Why do babies cry or smile? Why might the ten-year-old fight or be friendly? Ethologists point out the adaptive value of such activities for the individual in the specific environment in which he or she is growing up.

Ethological theory proposes that human infants, as well as the offspring of other species of animals, begin life with a set of innate, *species-specific* behaviors common to all members. In human babies, these include reflexes, such as sucking and grasping, and may also include more complex activities, such as babbling, smiling, and orienting to interesting sensory events—behaviors exhibited by normal infants around the world. These species-specific behaviors help infants meet their needs

ethology Theoretical orientation and discipline concerned with the evolutionary origins of behavior and its adaptive and survival value in animals, including humans.

either directly, as in the case of sucking as a means of ingesting food, or indirectly, as in the case of smiling, a behavior that attracts caregivers and encourages them to provide support.

Besides innate behaviors, the young of many species are predisposed to certain kinds of learning that are not easily reversed, learning that may occur only during limited *sensitive* or *critical* periods in development. A **sensitive period** occurs when an organism is highly responsive or vulnerable to specific kinds of environmental stimulation. One of the best-known examples is found in various species of birds, including geese. Usually, shortly after hatching, the gosling begins to follow and prefers being near a particular object. Normally, that stimulus will be another goose, its mother. In displaying this tendency, the gosling not only learns about its species more generally but also increases the likelihood of being fed and protected. This form of learning that takes place during a brief interval early in life and is difficult to modify once established is known as **imprinting**.

Do other animals show imprinting? Mammals, such as horses and sheep, do. What about human infants? John Bowlby's (1969) theory of attachment suggests that they do, at least to some degree. Bowlby noted that the crying, babbling, and smiling behaviors of young infants signal needs and elicit supportive and protective responses from adults. These behaviors, along with following and talking in older infants, become organized and integrated with social and emotional reactions of caregivers to form the basis for attachment, a mutual system of physical, social, and emotional stimulation and support between caregiver and young. Many experts believe that the failure to form this strong emotional bond with a caregiver in infancy is linked to serious emotional and other problems that occur later in childhood, an issue that will be discussed more fully in later chapters.

Konrad Lorenz, an ethologist, is being followed by young geese that have imprinted to him. Imprinting in young animals typically occurs to other members of the same species who, under normal circumstances, are present shortly after hatching or the birth of an animal. One question posed by ethologists is whether human infants also show some form of imprinting.

Contextual Theories and Themes in Development Contextual models generally agree on many of the themes in development, and where differences exist, they are most often found in ethological theories.

- *Nature & Nurture* Contextual theories differ widely in their emphasis on nature and nurture, but all recognize the importance of both to development. For ethologists, however, behaviors are closely linked to nature because they have helped, or continue to help, humans survive. Contextual models, even those having an ethological focus, tend to view the child as actively engaged with the environment. In calling for their caregivers, exploring and playing, and seeking out playmates, infants and children elicit reactions from the adults and peers around them. Both individual and environment change in highly interdependent ways, and the relationship between the two is *bidirectional*, each influencing the other (Bell, 1968).
- *Sociocultural Influence* Perhaps more than any other theoretical orientation, contextual theories are concerned with the ways broad sociocultural patterns affect development. Contextual approaches often search for evidence of how the larger social systems and settings in which children are reared affect their behavior and shape their minds.
- *Continuity/Discontinuity* Most contextual models place little emphasis on qualitative changes in development. Instead, such models describe the continuous ebb and flow of interactions that transpire throughout development to produce incremental change. However, ethologists often emphasize that particular periods in development are critical for establishing certain competencies. For example, infancy is considered a crucial time for forming emotional ties with caregivers.
- *Interaction Among Domains* Not surprisingly, most contextual models are typically concerned with the entire fabric of human growth and claim substantial interactions among cognitive, linguistic, social, and other domains. Ethological theorists especially focus on the interrelationship between biological and other aspects of development.

sensitive period Brief period during which specific kinds of experiences have significant positive or negative consequences for development and behavior; also called *critical period*.

imprinting Form of learning, difficult to reverse, during a sensitive period in development in which an organism tends to stay near a particular stimulus.

- ***Risk/Resilience*** Aside from ethological theories, contextual perspectives focus on the unique configuration of circumstances that foster cognitive, linguistic, social, and personality development. Given the immense number of factors potentially affecting the child, individual differences are often an important aspect to be explained by such theories, including factors that promote risk and resilience. In their emphasis on the multiple layers of influences on child development and on the transactions that occur between child and caregiver, contextual theories capture the complexities involved in any discussion of risk and resilience.

FOR • YOUR • REVIEW

- What is learning? What are some of its basic mechanisms? How do behavior analysis and social learning theory differ in explaining what takes place during learning?
- What are the primary factors underlying change in Piaget's theory of cognitive development? How do schemes, assimilation, accommodation, and equilibration help to explain the increasingly adaptive and organized nature of cognition?
- What characteristics distinguish information-processing approaches from other theories of development?
- What is the focus of Erikson's theory of psychosocial development?
- What common assumptions underlie various contextual approaches to development—for example, Bronfenbrenner's ecological systems theory, Vygotsky's sociohistorical theory, dynamic systems theory, and ethological theory? How do they differ?

What Develops?

All theories of development, of course, are ultimately concerned with the simple question: What develops? As you have seen in this chapter, the answers differ. For learning theorists, what develops is a set of responses. For Piaget, it is a set of cognitive structures. For information-processing enthusiasts, it is mental structures and strategies for responding. For psychosocial theorists, it is identity. For most contextual theorists, it is a pattern of mutually supportive individual and cultural relationships. For ethologists, it is adaptive behaviors.

Theories, by giving us models for observing and interpreting behavior, have had an enormous influence on the way we view children and their development. Why so many different theories? The reason is that each brings an important perspective to our understanding of development. Some remind us of the importance of emotions, others of cognitive structures. Some keep us honest about the role of our biological nature; others perform the same service for the culture in which we are born and reared. Various theories enrich and broaden our understanding of development. We will frequently draw on their contributions for interpreting the many behaviors of children. We hope that you will, too.

As we have introduced developmental theories, we have also discussed their positions on five major themes of development. Table 1.3 summarizes these positions for the major theories introduced in this chapter. As you read further, you may find yourself revising your own stand on the five themes. We trace their presence throughout the remainder of this book with marginal cues placed beside important research and discussions that bear on each theme. Beginning with the chapter titled "Genetics and Heredity," we also open each chapter with a list of the most relevant themes discussed in it and conclude by summarizing how the themes have applied to the developmental domain under discussion.

Table 1.3 The Main Developmental Theories and Where They Stand on the Five Themes of Development

Theme	Learning Theory Approaches	Piaget's Theory	Information-Processing Approaches	Erikson's Psychosocial Theory	Contextual Approaches
How do nature and nurture interact in development?	Emphasis on the role of the environment.	Emphasis on interaction of nature and nurture. Maturation sets limits on how rapidly development proceeds, but experience is necessary for the formation of cognitive structures.	Structures and processes presumably have an inherent emphasis, but experience is likely to be important for their operation.	Stress on an interactional position that recognizes societal demands as well as the child's biological makeup.	Major emphasis on the interaction of biological structures and environmental experiences.
How does the sociocultural context influence development?	Sociocultural factors determine which behaviors are reinforced, punished, or available from models, but the principles of learning are considered to be universal.	Cognitive structures underlying thought are universal.	Rules, strategies, and procedures acquired to perform tasks might differ from one culture to another, but these differences have received little attention.	Sociocultural context is a major component.	Culture is a critical determinant of behavior, although ethological principles are presumed to apply in all cultures.
Is development continuous or discontinuous?	Continuous. Development consists of the acquisition of a greater number of learned responses.	Discontinuous. Development proceeds in four qualitatively different stages.	Usually continuous. Development consists of the acquisition of more effective structures and processes for performing tasks.	Discontinuous. Development proceeds through eight stages.	Continuous. Development involves transactions between the child and the environment.
How do the various domains of development interact?	Universal learning processes work in many domains, but learning itself is highly situational.	Cognitive development has implications for social and moral development.	Usually concerned only with cognition, but have also been used to understand social and emotional relationship.	Failure to progress through stages may disrupt progress in many domains besides personality development.	Because of the strong interdependence between child and environment, all aspects of development are closely related.
What factors promote risk or resilience in development?	Risk and resilience can be understood in terms of reinforcements, punishments, and the types of models to which the child is exposed.	Does not place an emphasis on risk and resilience, but suggests that risks can occur if environmental experiences matching the child's biological readiness are not supplied.	Little explicit consideration of risk and resilience, although the potential is there.	Not specifically focused on risk and resilience, but failure to negotiate the stages can result in risk.	Focus on multiple factors that influence development as well as on role of child-caregiver transactions provides excellent starting point for examining risk and resilience.

CHAPTER RECAP

Summary of Developmental Themes

NATURE & NURTURE

What roles do nature and nurture play in development?

This issue is concerned with how genetic and experiential variables interact to influence behavior. One implication of this interaction is that children play an active role in the process of development.

SOCIOCULTURAL INFLUENCE

How does the sociocultural context influence development?

Children grow up in a social environment and cultural community that can have a tremendous impact on the behaviors that are displayed.

CONTINUITY/DISCONTINUITY

Is development continuous or discontinuous?

Changes in behavior may stem from quantitative, incremental developmental advances or qualitative reorganization. Children's behavior also may be influenced by multiple strategies or ways of responding.

INTERACTION AMONG DOMAINS

How do the various domains of development interact?

Developmental psychologists are concerned with the "whole" child; thus they are interested in how skills and capacities acquired in some area affect other aspects of behavior.

RISK/RESILIENCE

What factors promote risk or resilience in development?

Certain biological or environmental factors may be associated with a course of development that is less than optimal. Other factors may protect the child from the impact of these risks. Developmental psychologists are interested in identifying the complexities of risk and resilience so that appropriate interventions can be designed.

Chapter Review

WHAT IS DEVELOPMENT?

What is development?

Development refers to all of the physical and psychological changes a human being undergoes from conception until death.

What is developmental psychology?

Developmental psychology is the discipline concerned with the scientific study of changes in human behaviors and mental processes over a lifetime.

What role do theories play in the scientific process?

Theories serve to organize information gathered by researchers, explain observations, and predict behaviors that should occur in future observations.

What role does developmental psychology play in the formation of social policy?

The information gathered in research should be helpful in suggesting specific actions for *social policy*, plans by government or private agencies to alleviate social problems.

THE STUDY OF THE CHILD: HISTORICAL PERSPECTIVES

How have views of childhood changed from medieval and Renaissance times to today?

In medieval and premodern times, although recognized as vulnerable, children quickly became a part of adult society. By the seventeenth and eighteenth centuries, children were viewed as worthy of special attention in terms of parenting and education. By the beginning of the twentieth century, children became the objects of scientific study.

What were John Locke's and Jean Jacques Rousseau's views of childhood?

Philosophers, such as John Locke, emphasized *empiricism*, the view that experience shapes the development of the individual, whereas others, such as Jean Jacques Rousseau, wrote about the curious and active nature of the child.

How did Charles Darwin, Wilhelm Preyer, G. Stanley Hall, Alfred Binet, and James Mark Baldwin contribute to developmental psychology?

Baby biographers, such as Charles Darwin and Wilhelm Preyer, carried out the first systematic observations of individual children. G. Stanley Hall introduced the questionnaire method for studying large groups of children. Alfred Binet initiated the movement to study *individual differences* in children's behavior and abilities. Theorist James Mark Baldwin viewed the child as a participant in his or her own cognitive and social development.

What was Sigmund Freud's psychosexual theory of development?

Freud emphasized the importance of early experience on development and posited a series of psychosexual stages that children must successfully negotiate in order to demonstrate normal personality development.

What emphases emerged in research on children during the first half of the twentieth century?

For much of the first half of the twentieth century, work was carried out on gathering descriptive information about children. Arnold Gesell and others focused on establishing norms of behavior. Subsequently, research began to be initiated to investigate the variables that might cause development.

THEORIES OF DEVELOPMENT

What is learning? What are some of its basic mechanisms? How do behavior analysis and social learning theory differ in explaining what takes place during learning?

Learning is the permanent change in behavior that results from experience. *Behavior analysis* relies on two basic forms of learning, classical and operant conditioning, to bring about behavioral change. *Social learning theory*, as outlined by Albert Bandura, adds *observational learning* as an important mechanism by which behavior is continuously modified and changed.

What are the primary factors underlying change in Piaget's theory of cognitive development? How do schemes, assimilation, accommodation, and equilibration help to explain the increasingly adaptive and organized nature of cognition?

Jean Piaget's *cognitive-developmental theory* highlights the child's construction of *schemes* or patterns of acting on and thinking about the world. Through *assimilation* and *accommodation*, a child's schemes actively adapt to the demands of the environment by becoming more organized, conceptual, and logical. These regulatory processes of *adaptation* and *organization* result in *equilibration*. Cognitive development progresses through a series of qualitatively different stages according to Piaget's theory.

What characteristics distinguish information-processing approaches from other theories of development?

Information-processing models use the computer as a metaphor in accounting for cognitive development. Developmental differences in cognitive structures and processes, such as rules, strategies, and procedures, account for changes in attention, memory, thinking, and problem solving.

What is the focus of Erikson's theory of psychosocial development?

Erikson's *psychosocial theory of development* focuses on the sociocultural context in which behavioral needs are met. Personality development proceeds through a series of stages in which self and societal demands are resolved to construct one's *identity*. Individuals who successfully negotiate these demands become contributing members of society.

What common assumptions underlie various contextual approaches to development—for example, Bronfenbrenner's ecological systems theory, Vygotsky's sociohistorical theory, dynamic systems theory, and ethological theory? How do they differ?

Contextual models view human development from a broader framework involving multiple, bidirectionally interacting levels of influence. *Ecological systems theory* looks beyond the immediate experiences of family, peers, and friends, and considers the broader sociocultural contexts in which development proceeds. In particular, processes within the *microsystem*, *mesosystem*, *exosystem*, *macrosystem*, and *chronosystem* are considered. Vygotsky's *sociohistorical theory* views culture as the historical legacy of a community and emphasizes the social interactions by which this heritage is transferred from others and adopted by the child to become part of his or her way of thinking. *Dynamic systems theory* proposes that new, complex, and sometimes qualitatively different behaviors arise from the interaction of events at many different levels in the system. *Ethology* pays special attention to the biological, evolutionary heritage each individual brings to the world as the basis for species-specific behaviors found to be adaptive in interacting with the environment. Ethologists pay special attention to experiences that occur within *sensitive periods* in development and to mechanisms of learning like *imprinting*.

Key Terms and Concepts

accommodation (p. 23)
adaptation (p. 20)
assimilation (p. 20)
behavior analysis (p. 17)
chronosystem (p. 31)
cognitive-developmental theory (p. 20)
contextual models (p. 28)
development (p. 3)
developmental psychology (p. 4)
dynamic systems theory (p. 31)
ecological systems theory (p. 28)
empiricism (p. 12)
equilibration (p. 23)
ethology (p. 32)
exosystem (p. 29)
identity (p. 26)
imprinting (p. 33)
individual differences (p. 14)
information processing (p. 23)
learning (p. 17)
macrosystem (p. 31)
mesosystem (p. 29)
microsystem (p. 29)
nature-nurture debate (p. 6)
observational learning (p. 19)
organization (p. 20)
psychosocial theory of development (p. 26)
scheme (p. 20)
sensitive period (p. 33)
social learning theory (p. 19)
social policy (p. 4)
sociohistorical theory (p. 31)
stage (p. 7)
theory (p. 4)

STUDYING CHILD DEVELOPMENT

2

To me, research is discovery: an odyssey of surprises, confirmations, and unexpected twists and turns that contribute to the excitement of a research career. ... The excitement of a research career is that the story told by the data is always more interesting than the one you expect to confirm. In this sense, human behavior is far more interesting and provocative than even the most thoughtful theories allow, and this means that the scientist must be instructed by the lessons revealed by unexpected research findings—while maintaining humility about her or his capacity to predict the next turn in the road. (Thompson, 1996, p. 69)

These words, written by developmental researcher Ross Thompson, reveal the genuine enthusiasm of the scientist for the task of systematically observing and making sense of human behavior. Like investigators in many disciplines, developmental psychologists are firmly committed to the idea that theories and hypotheses, such as those described in the chapter titled "Themes and Theories," should be thoroughly and systematically tested using sound principles of science. But, as Thompson suggests, researchers must be prepared to modify or even cast off theories if their observations suggest other truths. At first glance, this outcome may seem discouraging. But, as many researchers can attest, great rewards lie in the simple notion of discovering something new.

Part of the reason that researchers get drawn into the enterprise of developmental psychology is that they are captivated by and want to understand the fascinating, complex, and oftentimes surprising array of behaviors children display. Moreover, there is the sheer fun of being a "child watcher." As even the most casual of observers can confirm, children are simply delightful subjects of study. Research can also make a real difference in the lives of children. For example, newborn nurseries for premature infants now contain rocking chairs so that parents and nurses can rock and stimulate babies previously confined to isolettes. Bilingual education programs capitalize on the ease with which young children master the complexities of language. Clinical interventions help shy children master the social skills that help them to establish positive peer relationships. The benefits of each of these approaches have been revealed through the systematic study of the child.

Collecting data about children, then, is an essential and rewarding aspect of scientific developmental psychology, and being well grounded in research techniques is important for students of the discipline. With this principle in mind, we devote this chapter to methodological issues in developmental psychology. We hope that, by alerting you to important issues in the research process, we will better equip you to think critically about the findings of the numerous studies you will encounter in subsequent chapters.

Research Methods in Developmental Psychology

Like their colleagues in all the sciences, researchers in child development seek to gather data that are objective, measurable, and capable of being replicated in controlled studies by other researchers. Their studies, in other words, are based on the **scientific method**. Frequently they initiate research to evaluate the predictions of a specific theory (for instance, is cognitive development stagelike, as Piaget suggests?). The scientific method dictates that theories must be revised or elaborated as new observations confirm or refute them. The process of scientific fact-finding involves a constant cycle of theorizing, empirical testing of the resulting hypotheses, and revision (or even outright rejection) of theories as new data come in. Alternatively, investigators may formulate a research question to determine an application of theory to a real-world situation (for instance, can early intervention programs for preschoolers boost IQ scores?). Regardless of the motivation, the general principles of good science are as important to research in child development as they are to any other research arena. Although many of the methods child development researchers use are the very same techniques psychologists routinely employ in other specialized areas, some methodological approaches are particularly useful in studying changes in behavior or mental processes that occur over time.

Measuring Attributes and Behaviors

All researchers are interested in identifying relationships among **variables**, those factors in a given situation that have no fixed or constant value. In child development studies, the variables are individual attributes, experiences, or behaviors that differ from one time to the next or from one person to another. Ultimately, researchers

scientific method Use of objective, measurable, and repeatable techniques to gather information.

variable Factor having no fixed or constant value in a given situation.

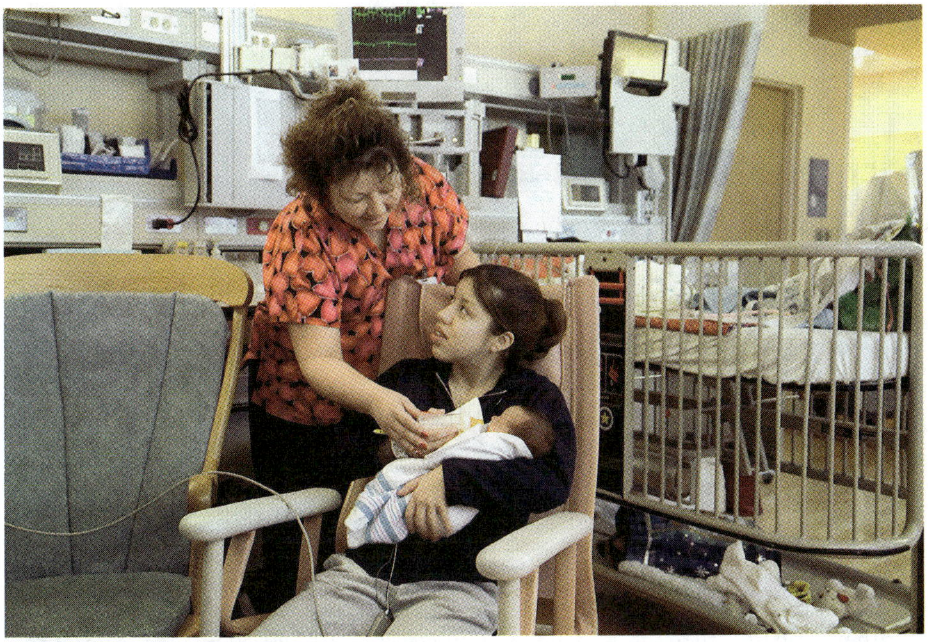

The scientific study of child development has resulted in changes in how children are treated in real-life settings. For example, because of research on the kinds of experiences that benefit premature infants, caregivers are now encouraged to touch and sensitively interact with their preterm babies.

are interested in determining the causal relationships among variables; that is, they wish to identify those variables directly responsible for the occurrence of other variables. Does watching television cause children to behave aggressively? Do withdrawn children have academic problems once they enroll in school? Does the way a parent interacts with a toddler raise or lower the child's later intelligence? In posing each of these questions, researchers are hypothesizing that some attribute or experience of the child is causally related to another attribute or behavior.

The first problem the researcher faces is that of **operationally defining**, or specifying in measurable terms, the variables under study. Take the case of aggression. This term can be defined as parental ratings of a child's physical hostility, the child's own reports of his or her level of violent behavior, or the number of hits and kicks recorded by an observer of the child's behavior. The key point is that variables must be defined in terms of precise measurement procedures that other researchers can use if they wish to repeat the study.

The measurement of variables must also be valid and reliable. **Validity** refers to how well an assessment procedure actually measures the variable under study. Parental reports of physical violence, for example, or even the child's own self-reports may not be the best indicators of aggression. Parents may not want a researcher to know about their child's misbehavior, or they may lack complete knowledge of how their child behaves outside the home. Children's own reports may not be very accurate because the children may wish to present themselves to adults in a certain way. If a trained observer records the number of hits or kicks the child displays during a school day, the resulting measurement of aggression is likely to be valid.

Reliability is the degree to which the same results will be obtained consistently if the measure is administered repeatedly or if several observers are viewing the same behavior episodes. In the first case, suppose a child takes an intelligence test one time, then two weeks later takes the test again. If the test has high *test-retest reliability*, she should obtain similar scores on the two testing occasions. In the second case, two or more observers viewing a child's behavior should agree about what they are seeing (for example, did the child smile in the presence of a stranger?); if they do agree, the test has high *inter-rater reliability*. Both types of reliability are calculated mathematically and are usually reported by researchers in their published

operational definition Specification of variables in terms of measurable properties.

validity Degree to which an assessment procedure actually measures the variable under consideration.

reliability Degree to which a measure will yield the same results if administered repeatedly.

reports of experiments; both are very important factors in good scientific research. Measurements of behavior that fluctuate dramatically from one observation time to another or from one observer to another are virtually useless as data.

METHODS OF COLLECTING DATA

What is the best way for researchers in developmental psychology to gather information about children? Should they simply watch children as they go about their routines in natural settings? Should children be brought into the researcher's laboratory to be observed? Should the researcher ask the child questions about the topic under study? Each approach offers advantages and disadvantages, and the choice of research tactic will often depend on the nature of the investigator's questions. If we are interested in exploring children's spontaneous tendencies to behave aggressively as they play (for instance, do boys play more aggressively than girls?), we will probably find a *naturalistic approach* most appropriate. If we want to see whether children's behavior is influenced by the presence of an aggressive model, we might use a *structured observation* to systematically expose some children to this manipulation in a laboratory setting. If we want to examine how children understand aggression, its antecedents, and its consequences, we might adopt another strategy, such as a *structured interview* or a *questionnaire.* Sometimes researchers combine two or more of these data collection methods within a study or series of studies.

Naturalistic Observation Researchers have no better way to see how children really behave than to observe them in natural settings: in their home, on the playground, at school, and in other places that are part of their everyday life. After all, the ultimate goal of developmental psychology is to describe and explain changes in behavior that actually occur. **Naturalistic observations** do not involve the manipulation of variables; researchers simply observe and record behaviors of interest from the natural series of events that unfolds in a real-world setting.

A study by Herbert Ginsburg and his colleagues (Ginsburg, Pappas, & Seo, 2001), for example, used naturalistic observations to assess the degree to which preschool-age children used mathematical concepts in their spontaneous free-play activities.

In naturalistic observations, researchers observe and record children's behaviors in real-life settings such as playgrounds, schools, or homes.

naturalistic observation Study in which observations of naturally occurring behavior are made in real-life settings.

The study was conducted in four daycare centers that enrolled children from different ethnic and social class backgrounds. Each of the eighty children in the study was videotaped for fifteen minutes during free-play time. Then raters coded the videotapes for the presence of six types of mathematical activities: classification, dynamics (or transformation of objects), enumeration, magnitude comparison, spatial relations, and pattern and shape exploration. The results showed that children spent almost half of the observation period engaged in some form of mathematical activity. Furthermore, there were no gender or social class differences in the tendency to use mathematical concepts in free play.

Several methodological issues are especially relevant to naturalistic observations. First, as researchers code the stream of activities they observe, they need to use clear operational definitions of the behaviors of interest. Ginsburg and his colleagues did so by specifying the elements that constituted each particular form of mathematical activity. For example, enumeration was defined as counting, use of one-to-one correspondence, estimation of quantity, or any statement of number words. Second, researchers must be aware that children (and others) might react to the presence of an observer by behaving in atypical or "unnatural" ways. To reduce such **participant reactivity**, children in this study were acclimated to the video camera and cordless microphone they wore before the recordings began. Finally, to minimize the effects of **observer bias**, the possibility that the researcher would interpret ongoing events to be consistent with his or her prior hypotheses, pairs of independent observers coded thirty of the eighty children to ensure the reliability of the findings. Researchers usually require that at least one of the observers is unfamiliar with the purposes of the study.

An important advantage of naturalistic observations is that researchers can see the events and behaviors that precede the target behaviors they are recording; they can also note the consequences of those same target behaviors. In this way, they may be able to discern important relationships in sequences of events. Moreover, naturalistic observations give researchers powerful insights into which variables are important to study in the first place, insights they may not derive solely by observing children in the laboratory. For example, a laboratory study might not reveal the high level of unguided engagement preschoolers have with mathematical concepts. Often the trends or phenomena identified in such preliminary studies become the focus of more intensive, controlled laboratory experiments. Naturalistic observations also have the distinct advantage of examining real-life behaviors as opposed to behaviors that may emerge only in response to some contrived laboratory manipulation.

Some cautions regarding this method are in order, however. A wide range of variables may influence the behaviors under observation, and it is not always possible to control them. Cause-and-effect relationships, therefore, cannot be deduced. Do preschoolers evidence mathematical thinking because they are in a "school" environment or because certain kinds of toys or materials are available to them? Or do none of these environmental circumstances matter? Answering questions like these requires the systematic manipulation of variables, a tactic that is part of other research approaches.

Structured Observation Researchers cannot always depend on a child to display behaviors of scientific interest to them during observation. Researchers who observe a child in the home, school, or other natural setting may simply not be present when vocalization, sharing, aggression, or other behaviors that they wish to study occur. Therefore, developmental psychologists may choose to observe behaviors in a more structured setting, usually the laboratory, in which they devise situations to elicit behaviors of interest to them. **Structured observations** are the record of specific behaviors the child displays in a situation that the experimenter constructs. Structured observations, like naturalistic observations, are a way to collect data by looking at and recording the child's behaviors, but this form of looking takes place under highly controlled conditions.

participant reactivity Tendency of individuals who know they are under observation to alter natural behavior.

observer bias Tendency of researchers to interpret ongoing events as being consistent with their research hypotheses.

structured observation Study in which behaviors are recorded as they occur within a situation constructed by the experimenter, usually in the laboratory.

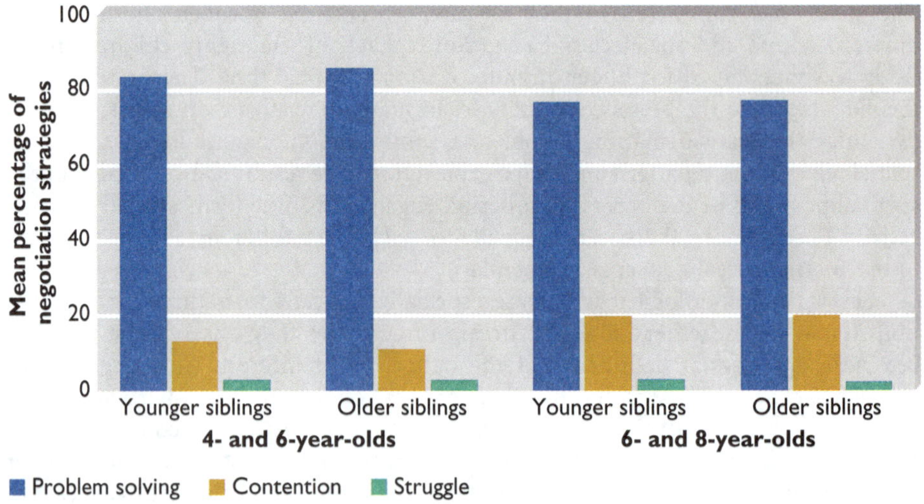

FIGURE 2.1

A Structured Observation

What happens when siblings are instructed to divide up desirable toys? Ram and Ross (2001) structured a laboratory task in which children had to decide which of six toys each sibling would get. Their negotiation strategies were coded as problem solving (attempts to satisfy each child in the pair), contention (attempts to satisfy one's own desire), and struggle (withdrawing from the negotiation or using an aggressive strategy). The results show that the predominant strategy used by both older and younger children was problem solving.

Source: Adapted from Ram & Ross (2001).

A study of the ways in which siblings resolve potential conflicts illustrates how structured observations are typically conducted (Ram & Ross, 2001). Pairs of siblings ages four and six years and six and eight years, respectively, were brought to a laboratory. First, each child was escorted to a private room and asked to rate the quality of his or her relationship with the sibling. Each child was also asked to indicate how much he or she liked six toys that the siblings could later take home. Next, the siblings were reunited and instructed to divide up the toys between themselves. The researchers were interested in the types of negotiation strategies these children used. A portion of the results is shown in Figure 2.1. As the graph shows, the most prevalent strategy was "problem solving," attempting to achieve a solution that satisfied both children. Least frequent was a class of behaviors the researchers called "struggle," the display of some form of overt conflict.

Although these researchers could have attempted to conduct their study of sibling interactions through naturalistic observations in the children's homes, they might have had to wait a long time for the targeted interactions to take place spontaneously. Furthermore, by conducting this study in a laboratory, the researchers were able to keep tight control over the instructions the children received and the specific toys they had to divide between themselves.

At the same time, structured observations may have limitations, especially if they are conducted in a laboratory setting. Children may not react in the same ways in the research room as they do in real life. They may be reticent to display negative behaviors, such as lack of cooperation with a brother or sister, in front of the researcher, or they may show heightened distress or shyness because of the unfamiliar setting. One solution to this problem is to confirm the results of laboratory studies by conducting similar studies in children's natural environments.

Structured observations can focus on a variety of types of behaviors. Like many structured observations, the study by Ram and Ross focused on children's overt actions, in this case their physical and verbal behaviors. Researchers often record other behaviors, such as the number of errors children make in a problem-solving task, the kinds of memory strategies they display, or the amount of time they take to learn a specified task. When structured observations are conducted in the laboratory, it is also possible for researchers to obtain *physiological measures*, the shifts in heart rate, brain wave activity, or respiration rate that can indicate the child's reaction to changes in stimuli. Physiological measures are especially useful in examining the behavior of infants, because the range of overt responses that very young children usually display is more limited than that of older children.

The Interview and the Questionnaire Sometimes the best way to glean information about what children know or how they behave is not simply to observe them but to ask them directly. Researchers have found that talking with children about their conceptions of friendship, gender roles, problem-solving skills—in fact, almost anything in the child's world—has yielded a wealth of material for analysis.

Many investigators use the technique of **structured interviews**, studies in which each participant is asked the same sequence of questions. For example, the goal of study conducted by Mary Levitt and her colleagues (Levitt, Guacci-Franco, & Levitt, 1993) was to explore the sources of social support for seven-, ten-, and fourteen-year-old children from different ethnic backgrounds. More than 300 African American, Anglo American, and Hispanic American children were interviewed about the people most important in their life. Each child was questioned by an interviewer of the same cultural background as the child, to maximize the child's comfort with the session and the accuracy of his or her responses. Examples of the standard questions employed in this study include "Are there people who make you feel better when something bothers you or you are not sure about something?" and "Are there people who like to be with you and do fun things with you?" The results showed that, for all children, regardless of ethnic background, the family was an important source of social support. Moreover, members of the extended family (such as grandparents, aunts, and uncles) played an increasing role during middle childhood, whereas peers assumed a significant support role during adolescence.

Structured interviews provide a useful way to obtain information on what children know, how they feel, and how they interpret their world.

structured interview Standardized set of questions administered orally to participants.

Another "asking" technique that researchers use with children is to obtain written responses to a standard set of items in a **questionnaire**. Because questionnaires can be administered to large numbers of children at the same time, researchers can use this method to obtain a large set of data very quickly. Questionnaires can also be scored quickly, particularly if the items ask participants to pick from a set of multiple-choice items or to rate items on a numerical scale. Children, however, may have difficulty understanding the items and may not be able to answer accurately without guidance from an adult. Under those conditions, oral interviews with individual children may provide more reliable and valid information about how children think and feel.

Researchers who use interviews and questionnaires to collect data from children must be careful, though. Sometimes young respondents, like their adult counterparts, will try to present themselves in the most favorable light or answer questions in the way they think the researcher expects them to. In the study of children's sources of social support, for example, participants may have said that they talked with their parents when they had problems because they knew this was the expected response. To prompt participants to answer as honestly as possible, researchers try not to react positively or negatively as the participant responds and also try to explain, before the start of the interview or questionnaire, the importance of answering truthfully.

Another way to collect data by interview is the **clinical method**, a flexible, open-ended technique in which the investigator may modify the questions in reaction to the child's response. A notable example was Jean Piaget's use of the clinical method to explore age-related changes in children's thinking capabilities. Consider the following segment, in which Piaget (1929) questions a six-year-old boy about the sun:

Piaget: *How did the sun begin?*

Child: *It was when life began.*

Piaget: *Has there always been a sun?*

Child: *No.*

Piaget: *How did it begin?*

Child: *Because it knew that life had begun.*

Piaget: *What is it made of?*

Child: *Of fire ...*

Piaget: *Where did the fire come from?*

Child: *From the sky.*

Piaget: *How was the fire made in the sky?*

Child: *It was lighted with a match.* (p. 258)

Note how Piaget follows the child's line of thinking with each question he asks. The format of the interview changes with an older boy, age nine years.

Piaget: *How did the sun start?*

Child: *With heat.*

Piaget: *What heat?*

Child: *From the fire.*

Piaget: *Where is the fire?*

Child: *In heaven.*

questionnaire Set of standardized questions administered to participants in written form.

clinical method Flexible, open-ended interview method in which questions are modified in reaction to the child's responses.

Piaget: *How did it start?*

Child: *God lit it with wood and coal.*

Piaget: *Where did he get the wood and coal?*

Child: *He made it.* (p. 265)

Piaget gained some enormous insights into the thinking processes of children by using the probing, interactive questions typical of the clinical method. Having the flexibility to follow the child's train of thought rather than sticking to a rigid protocol of predetermined questions allows the researcher to gather fresh insights. The weakness of this approach, however, lies precisely in this flexibility. Because the questions asked of different participants are likely to vary, systematic comparisons of their answers are difficult to make. Moreover, the researcher may be tied to a theoretical orientation that biases the formulation of questions and the interpretation of answers. Nonetheless, the clinical method can be a valuable research tool, particularly in exploring the way children think and reason.

The Meta-Analytic Study Sometimes researchers do not actually collect empirical data themselves but instead make a statistical analysis of a body of previously published research on a specific topic that allows them to draw some general conclusions. Instead of looking or asking, they "crunch" data; that is, they combine the results of numerous studies to assess whether the central variable common to all has an important effect. This technique, called **meta-analysis**, is particularly useful when the results of studies in the same area are inconsistent or conflict with one another.

A good example of meta-analysis is a study conducted by Janet Hyde and her colleagues to assess the existence of sex differences in children's mathematical skills (Hyde, Fennema, & Lamon, 1990). Many researchers have concluded that boys perform better than girls on tests of mathematical skill, particularly after age twelve or thirteen (Halpern, 1986; Maccoby & Jacklin, 1974). Such observations have spawned numerous debates about the origins of this sex difference. Is mathematical skill biologically given, or is it learned through experiences in the environment? The answer to this question has important educational implications for male and female students. Hyde and her colleagues collected one hundred studies conducted from 1967 through 1987 that examined the question of sex differences in mathematics performance. (This body of studies represented the participation of more than 3 million participants!) For each study, a statistical measure representing *effect size* was computed, a mathematical way of expressing the size of the difference in male and female scores. Hyde and her colleagues (1990) found that the average difference between males and females across all studies was small, leading the researchers to conclude that sex differences in mathematical ability are not large enough to be of great scientific significance.

Conducting a meta-analysis requires the careful transcription of hundreds of statistical figures, a powerful computer, and a good deal of computational skill. Because the researcher taking this approach did not design the original studies, she or he cannot always be sure that the central variables have been defined in identical ways across studies. Moreover, studies that do not present their data in the form necessary for analysis may have to be eliminated from the pool; potentially valuable information may thus be lost. Despite these difficulties, the meta-analytic approach allows researchers to draw conclusions based on a large corpus of research, not just individual studies, and thereby to profit from an accumulated body of knowledge. This technique has recently become increasingly popular in developmental research and has provoked the reevaluation of more than one traditional notion about children.

From our discussion it should be clear that there is no single right way to study children. Researchers must consider their overall goals and their available resources

meta-analysis Statistical examination of a body of research studies to assess the effect of the common central variable.

Table 2.1 Advantages and Disadvantages of Information-Gathering Approaches

Approach	Description	Advantages	Disadvantages
Naturalistic Observations	Observations of behaviors as they occur in children's real-life environments.	Can note antecedents and consequences of behaviors; see real-life behaviors.	Possibility of participant reactivity and observer bias; less control over variables; cause-and-effect relationships difficult to establish.
Structured Observations	Observations of behaviors in situations constructed by the experimenter.	More control over conditions that elicit behaviors.	Children may not react as they would in real life.
Interviews and Questionnaires	Asking children (or parents) about what they know or how they behave.	Quick way to assess children's knowledge or reports of their behaviors.	Children may not always respond truthfully or accurately: systematic comparisons of responses may be difficult; theoretical orientation of researcher may bias questions and interpretations of answers.
Meta-Analytic Studies	Statistical analysis of other researcher's findings to look for the size of a variable's effects.	Pools a large body of research findings to sort out conflicting findings; no participants are observed.	Requires careful mathematical computation; variables may not have been defined identically across all studies.

as they make decisions about how to construct a research study. Table 2.1 summarizes the advantages and disadvantages of the four general types of data collection just described.

RESEARCH DESIGNS

Besides formulating their hypotheses, identifying the variables, and choosing a method of gathering information about children, investigators must select the research design they will use as part of their study. The *research design* is the overall conceptual approach that defines whether the variables will be manipulated, how many children will be studied, and the precise sequence of events as the study proceeds. Research designs may be fairly complex, and an investigator might choose more than one design for each part of a large study. Generally, however, researchers select from one of three study types: correlational designs, experimental designs, and case studies or single-case designs.

correlational study Study that assesses whether changes in one variable are accompanied by systematic changes in another variable.

positive correlation Relationship in which changes in one variable are accompanied by systematic changes in another variable in the same direction.

negative correlation Relationship in which changes in one variable are accompanied by systematic changes in another variable in the opposite direction.

correlation coefficient (*r*) Statistical measure, ranging from +1.00 to –1.00, that summarizes the strength and direction of the relationship between two variables; does not provide information about causation.

The Correlational Design Studies in which the researcher looks for systematic relationships among variables use the correlational design and are called **correlational studies.** Instead of manipulating the variables, in this design the investigator obtains measures of two or more characteristics of the participants and sees whether changes in one variable are accompanied by changes in the other. Some variables show a **positive correlation**; that is, as the values of one variable change, scores on the other variable change in the same direction. For example, if a positive correlation exists between children's television viewing and their aggression, as the number of hours of TV viewing increases, the number of aggressive acts committed increases as well. A **negative correlation** indicates that, as scores on one variable change, scores on the other variable change in the opposite direction. Thus, using our example, a negative relationship exists if aggression decreases as TV viewing increases.

The statistic used to describe the strength of a relationship between two variables is called the **correlation coefficient**, or ***r***. Correlation coefficients may range from +1.00 (perfectly positively correlated) to –1.00 (perfectly negatively correlated).

As the correlation coefficient approaches 0.00 (which signifies no relationship), the relationship between the two variables becomes weaker. A rule of thumb is that correlations of .70 or higher usually signify strong relationships, whereas those below .20 represent weak relationships. In most cases, values falling in between indicate a moderate relationship between two variables.

We can use a portion of a study conducted by Carol MacKinnon-Lewis and her colleagues (MacKinnon-Lewis et al., 1994) to illustrate the key features of correlational research. One objective of these investigators was to see if relationships existed between boys' aggressive behaviors and several family variables, such as the number of negative life events the child had experienced. The latter included experiences such as a parent leaving home or a divorce between parents. The investigators found a statistically significant correlation of $r = .40$ between the number of negative life events reported by boys and the number of fights they started with peers. Thus, the more stress the boys experienced within the family, the more fights they initiated in school. In contrast, the number of negative life events experienced by boys correlated $r = .04$ with the mothers' tendency to judge their sons as having hostile intentions in interactions with others, suggesting no relationship between those two variables.

Because researchers do not actively manipulate the variables in correlational studies, they must be cautious about making statements about cause and effect when strong relationships are found. In the previous study, for example, do negative life events cause boys to be aggressive? Or does their aggression contribute to stress and negative events within the family? Still another possibility is that some third factor not measured by the researchers influences both variables. Perhaps, for example, the child's father is aggressive, and that factor influences both the son's aggression and the number of negative life events in the family.

Despite these limitations on interpretation, correlational studies are often a useful first step in exploring which variables might be causally related to one another. In addition, in many instances experimenters are unable to manipulate the variables that are the suspected causes of certain behavior. In the preceding study, for example, it would be impossible to systematically vary the number of negative life events experienced by boys. In such cases, correlational studies represent the only approach available to understanding the influences on child development.

The Experimental Design The **experimental design** involves the manipulation of one or more **independent variables**—the variables that are manipulated or controlled by the investigator, often because they are the suspected cause of a behavior—to observe the effects on the **dependent variable**, the suspected outcome. One major goal of this type of study is to control for as many factors as possible that can influence the outcome, aside from the independent variables. Experimental studies are frequently conducted in laboratory situations, in which it is possible to ensure that all participants are exposed to the same environmental conditions and the same task instructions. In addition, **random assignment** of participants to different treatment groups (in which one group is usually a *control group* that receives no treatment) helps to avoid any systematic variation aside from that precipitated by the independent variables. As a consequence, one distinct advantage of the experimental study design is that cause-and-effect relationships among variables can be identified.

To illustrate the experimental design, consider the following questions: Do adolescents engage in more risk-taking behaviors when they are with a group of peers than when they are alone? Moreover, in risk-taking situations, are adolescents more influenced by being with their peers than are older individuals? In one portion of a study reported by Margo Gardner and Laurence Steinberg (Gardner & Steinberg, 2005), adolescents (ages thirteen to sixteen), young adults (ages eighteen to twenty-two), and older adults (over age twenty-four) were asked to play a computer game of "Chicken." The game required participants to "drive" a car as close to an abruptly appearing wall without crashing, with the appearance of the wall signaled by a

experimental design Research method in which one or more independent variables are manipulated to determine the effect on other, dependent variables.

independent variable Variable manipulated by the experimenter; the suspected cause.

dependent variable Behavior that is measured; suspected effect of an experimental manipulation.

random assignment Use of principles of chance to assign participants to treatment and control groups; avoids systematic bias.

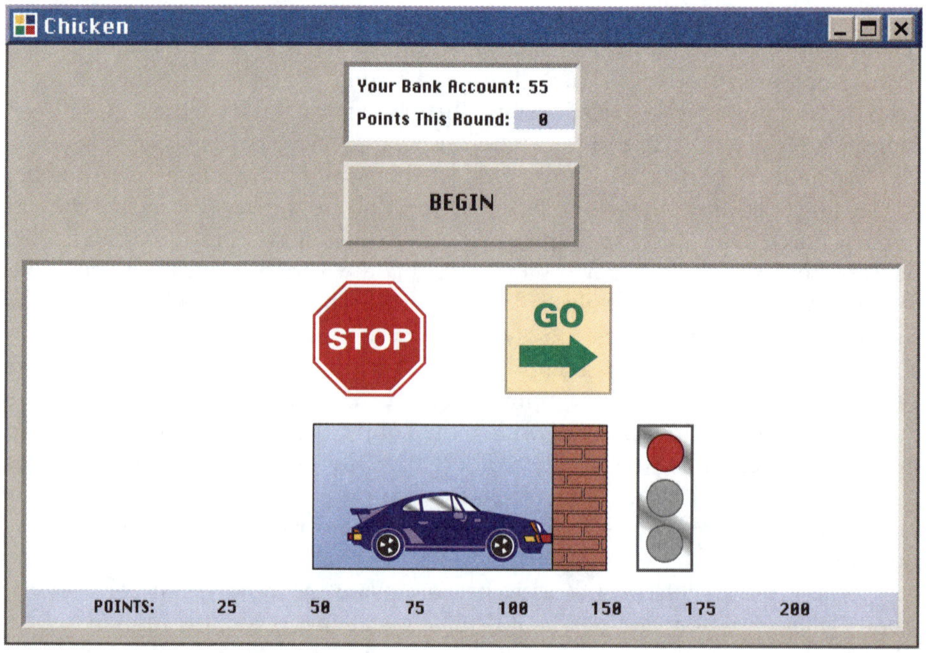

FIGURE 2.2

Assessing Adolescents' Risk Taking

To assess the influence of peers' presence on adolescents' risk-taking behaviors, Gardner and Steinberg (2005) asked participants to play a computer driving game. The goal of the game was to drive the car as close to a wall as possible without crashing, in order to obtain points. Yellow and red lights flashed on the screen before the wall appeared. Here, the car crashed because the driver kept the car moving when the red light appeared.

Source: Gardner & Steinberg (2005).

yellow and then a red warning light (see Figure 2.2). Although points could be won by driving after the yellow light signal appeared, the risk of crashing into the wall was also greater. In this experiment, there were two independent variables—age of the participants and the test situation—whether the game was played alone or in the presence of two familiar peers. The dependent variable was the number of risk-taking behaviors displayed during the computer game. Risk taking was defined as the length of time participants moved the cars after the yellow warning light flashed on the screen. It also included the number of times a car was restarted and moved after the yellow light appeared.

On the surface, it may seem that the design of this study was relatively straightforward. However, individuals could vary their risk taking while playing "Chicken" for any number of reasons, such as the speed of car or the predictability of the warning signals and the appearance of the wall. Therefore, it was important for the researchers to control for as many variables as possible, such that only the independent variable changed across conditions. Under such circumstances, the experimenter can be more confident that the independent variable is causing changes in the dependent variable. The experimenters took steps to address these issues. The speed of the car was kept constant across all experimental conditions, for example, and the warning signals and wall were presented at varied, predetermined times across the fifteen trials for each participant. The results of this experiment, shown in Figure 2.3, indicated that adolescents displayed significantly more risky behaviors when they were with their peers than when they were alone. In addition, the effect of the peer group on risky driving was much greater for the adolescents than for the other two age groups.

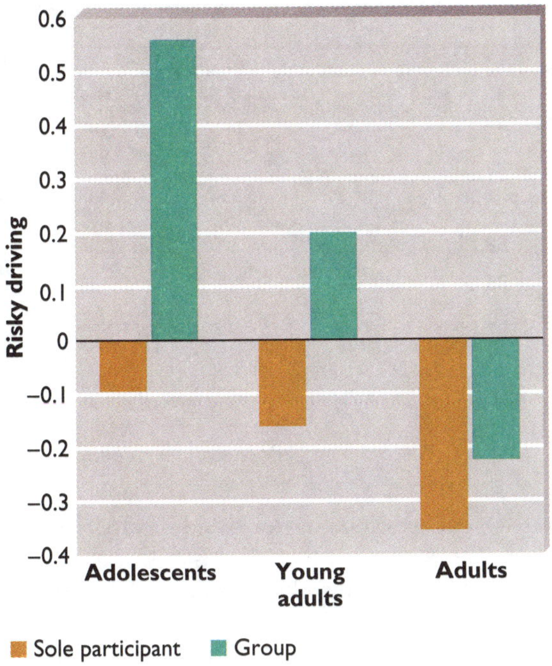

FIGURE 2.3

An Experimental Study

This graph shows the results of an experiment assessing adolescents', young adults', and adults' risk-taking behaviors in the computer driving game. The independent variables were the participants' age and the context of the game, playing alone or with two other peers present. The dependent variable was the amount of risk taking (a higher score represents greater risk taking). The results show that adolescents are more likely to take risks in the presence of peers than when they are alone and that the effect of peers is magnified for this age group compared with the others.

Source: Gardner & Steinberg (2005).

The experimental approach has been the traditional design choice for many developmental psychologists because of the "clean" answers it provides about the causes of developmental phenomena. Yet it has also been criticized for providing a narrow portrait of child development. Development in the real world is likely to be caused by many variables; few changes are likely to be the result of a single or even a few independent variables. In that sense, experimental studies typically fail to capture the complexities of age-related changes. Moreover, we have already mentioned that children may not react normally when they are brought into the laboratory setting, where most experiments are conducted. Children may "clam up" because they are shy about being in unfamiliar surroundings with strangers and mechanical equipment. Or they may rush through the experimental task just to get it over with.

In recognition of these problems, many researchers have tried to achieve a more homelike feeling in their laboratories, with comfortable couches, chairs, tables, and rugs instead of sterile, bare-walled rooms filled with equipment. Another tactic has been to conduct **field experiments**, in which the experimental manipulations are actually carried out in a natural setting, such as the child's home or school. In one such field experiment, Grover Whitehurst and his colleagues (Whitehurst et al., 1994) randomly assigned children attending preschool to one of three experimental conditions, to see if the type of reading experiences they had influenced their language skills. For six weeks, a ten-minute period was allocated each day to one of the following conditions: (1) school reading, in which the teacher read a book and concurrently asked children numerous questions about the story and promoted discussion; (2) school plus home reading, in which teachers read to children in the same special manner, but parents were also trained to read to children at home using an active discussion approach; and (3) control, in which children engaged in ten minutes of teacher-supervised play. The groups were formed such that no more than five children participated in each at any single time. The results, displayed in Figure 2.4, showed that, at the end of six weeks, children in both reading groups scored significantly higher on a test of vocabulary compared with the control group and that the school-plus-home reading group scored higher than the school reading group. In the follow-up phase six months later, both reading groups continued to show advantages over the control group in language skills. Because the only known variation in the children's experiences was systematically introduced by the researchers in their manipulation of the independent variable (the type of reading

field experiment Study in which the experimental manipulations are carried out in a natural setting.

FIGURE 2.4

A Field Experiment

The data from Whitehurst et al.'s (1994) field study show that children who had special reading experiences at school and at school plus home received higher scores on a test of vocabulary on a posttest (six weeks after the program began) and a follow-up test (six months later) compared with the control group. A field experiment employs many of the features of an experiment but is conducted in a natural setting.

Source: Adapted from Whitehurst et al. (1994).

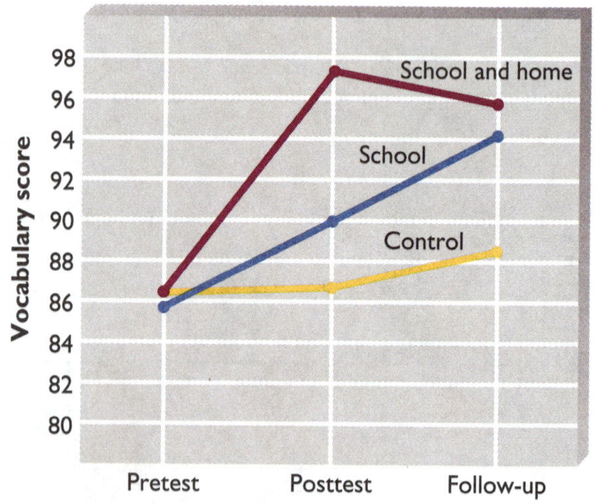

group to which children were exposed), changes in behavior could be attributed to type of reading program. In addition, the natural setting of this field experiment minimized the problems associated with bringing children into the artificial surroundings of a laboratory.

In some instances, it is not possible for the researcher to randomly assign participants to treatment groups, because of logistical or ethical difficulties. In these cases, the researcher may take advantage of the natural separation of participants into different groups. **Quasi-experiments** are studies in which researchers investigate the effects of independent variables that they do not manipulate themselves but that occur as a result of children's natural experiences. Suppose a researcher wanted to investigate the effects of a longer school year on children's academic skills. One way to make sure that it is the length of the school year that influences performance, rather than the initial characteristics of the children, is to randomly assign children to two groups, one with a longer school year and one with a regular school year. That way, children with greater and lesser abilities, for example, would be equally likely to appear in both groups. However, it would be unethical, and also logistically very difficult, to assign children to different schools in this way. Julie Frazier and Frederick Morrison (1998) learned of one elementary school that was extending its school year from 180 to 210 days and took the opportunity to assess the impact on the achievement of kindergartners in mathematics, reading, general knowledge, and vocabulary. The researchers found that children with additional time in school during the year showed greater gains in achievement, especially in mathematics, compared with students who attended a school with a regular 180-day calendar.

The results of quasi-experimental designs must be interpreted with caution. The children who experienced an extended school year may have differed in systematic ways from children who had a regular academic year, ways that could have accounted for their better performance. For example, the former group may have had parents who were very concerned with academic achievement and spent more time teaching them at home. The investigators took great care to try to make the two groups equivalent at the outset of the study by matching them on intelligence test scores, medical history, parents' occupations, parents' expectations about school, and several other dimensions. Could other competing explanations for the outcomes be ruled out? Because the schools were in the same district, their curricula were equivalent. Most revealing, though, was the pattern of exactly at what time gains in achievement were made. Through the winter, when the two school programs still had an equivalent number of days, the students in both groups showed similar patterns of growth in achievement. However, it was during the summer, after the extended days occurred, that student achievement patterns diverged. Thus researchers who conduct quasi-experimental studies must be very concerned with ruling out alternative explanations for their findings. Despite these methodological difficulties, quasi-experimental studies offer a way to address important questions about

quasi-experiment Study in which researchers investigate the effects of independent variables that they do not manipulate themselves but that occur as a result of participants' natural experiences.

the complex influences on child development, questions that often have powerful real-world implications.

Case Studies and the Single-Case Design Some notable discoveries about developmental processes have come from the in-depth examination of a single child or just a few children. At times, psychologists make an intensive description of an individual child, much as the baby biographers did. Freud and Piaget both relied heavily on such **case studies** of individuals to formulate their broad theories of personality and cognitive development, respectively. Case studies can be particularly revealing when researchers discover a child with an unusual ability or disability, or an uncommon past history. The details of a child's background, cognitive skills, or behaviors can, in some cases, provide important insights about the process of development or even a critical test of a theory. For example, researchers (Fletcher-Flinn & Thompson, 2000) reported the case of a three-and-a-half-year-old child who was able to read at the level of an eight-and-a-half-year-old. Did this precocious reader focus on the sounds made by each letter in a word, a process that many reading specialists say is essential to skilled reading? Extensive tests and observations indicated that this child had little awareness of the correspondence between individual letters and their sounds, a finding that suggests that successful reading may not depend on phonics skills for all children. Although case studies can provide a rich picture of a given aspect of development, they must also be interpreted with caution. The observations reported in case studies can be subjective in nature and thus vulnerable to the phenomenon of observer bias that was discussed earlier in this chapter.

In other instances, researchers introduce experimental treatments to one or a few children and note any changes in their behavior over time. The emphasis is on the systematic collection of data, rather than on providing a detailed narrative, as is often done in case studies. Frequently the purpose of these **single-case designs** is to evaluate a clinical treatment for a problem behavior or an educational program designed to increase or decrease specific activities in the child.

Suppose we wish to evaluate the effectiveness of a treatment for stuttering in children. One team of researchers selected four boys, ages ten to eleven years, who had difficulty with stuttering (Gagnon & Ladouceur, 1992). Their first step was to record the percentage of stuttered syllables each boy spoke during the baseline period prior to the start of the treatment. Next, the treatment began. During two one-hour sessions per week, each boy received instruction on how to recognize stuttering and how to regulate breathing during stuttering. Special speaking exercises and parent information sessions were also introduced. Finally, the participants' speech was assessed at one month and six months following the end of treatment. Figure 2.5 shows the decline in percentage of stuttered syllables among the children from baseline through follow-up periods. Was the treatment effective? The fact that all four participants showed similar declines in stuttering and that the stuttering remained low during follow-up several months later suggests that it was.

Single-case designs do not require large groups of children or the random assignment of participants to groups. Each participant essentially serves as his or her own control by experiencing all conditions in the experiment over a period of time. As with any study involving only one or a few individuals, however, researchers' ability to generalize to a larger group of children may be limited. Perhaps the child or children they selected for the study were particularly responsive to the treatment, a treatment that might not work as well for other children. In addition, the researcher must be aware of any other circumstances concurrent with the treatment that may have actually produced the behavior changes. For example, did the children in the stuttering study mature neurologically, and did that maturation cause the reduction in speech problems? The fact that the treatment started at different times for each of the four children and was immediately followed by a decrease in stuttering suggests that the treatment and not some other factor caused the changes.

case study In-depth description of psychological characteristics and behaviors of an individual, often in the form of a narrative.

single-case design Study that follows only one or a few participants over a period of time, with an emphasis on systematic collection of data.

FIGURE 2.5
A Single-Case Design

In this example of a single-case design, four boys with stuttering problems were observed during a baseline period. Next, a program to treat their speech problems was begun. The graph shows that the percentage of stuttered syllables declined dramatically following the onset of treatment and remained low during the follow-up period. Because the four children showed similar patterns of behavior change, and because the behavior change was maintained long after the treatment ended, the researchers concluded that their treatment was effective.

Source: Gagnon & Ladouceur (1992).

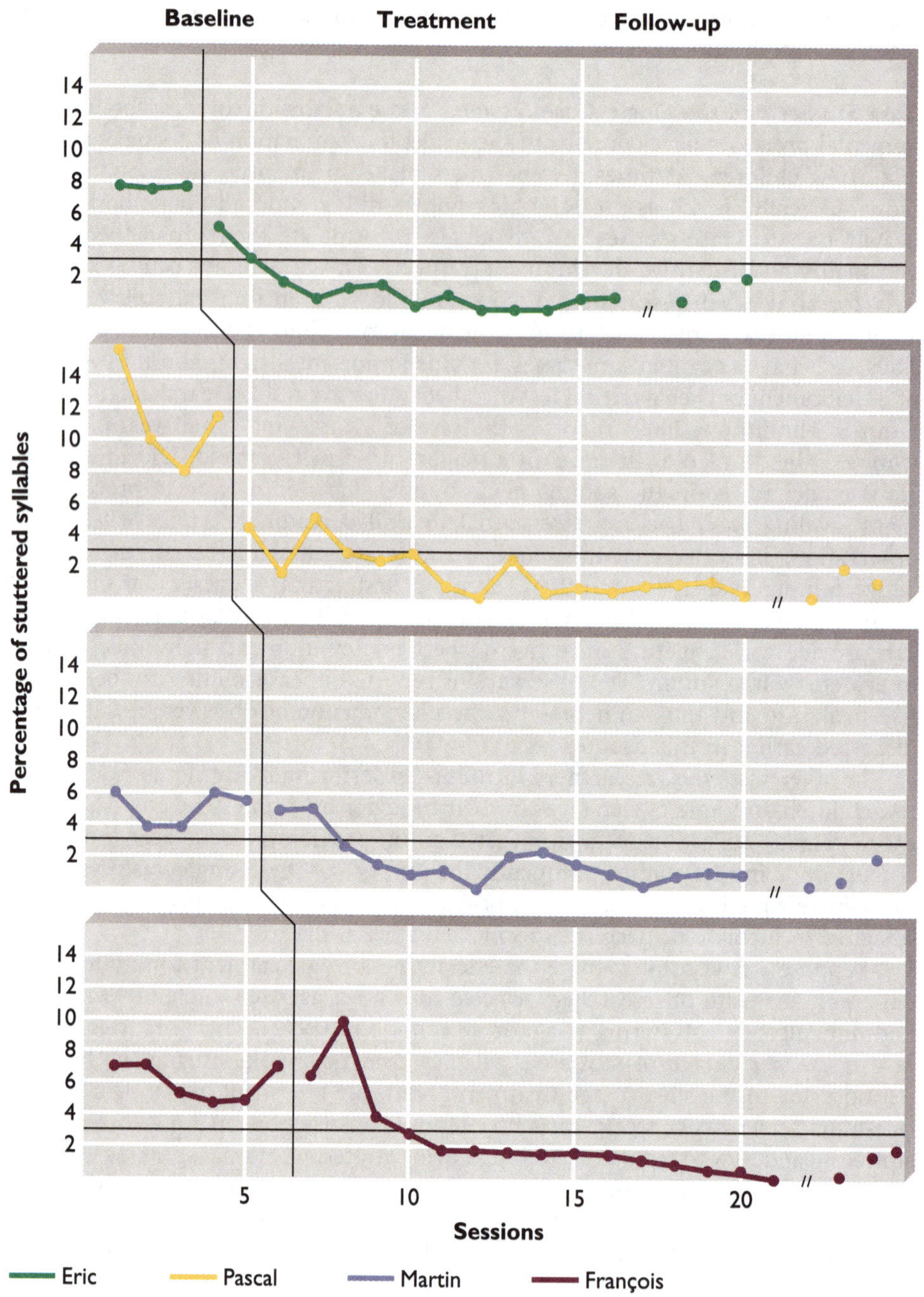

Table 2.2 presents an overview of the strengths and weaknesses of case studies and single-case designs, as well as other research designs that we have examined briefly here.

FOR ◆ YOUR ◆ REVIEW

- What issues must researchers pay attention to when they measure attributes and behaviors?
- What four information-gathering techniques do developmental researchers generally have available to them? What are the advantages and disadvantages of each technique?
- What are the different research designs that researchers might employ to study child development? What are the strengths and weaknesses of each design?

Table 2.2 Strengths and Weaknesses of Research Designs

Design	Description	Strengths	Weaknesses
Correlational Design	Researcher sees if changes in one variable are accompanied by systematic changes in another variable.	Useful when conditions do not permit the manipulation of variables.	Cannot determine cause-and-effect relationships.
Experimental Design	Researcher manipulates one or more independent variables to observe the effects on the dependent variable(s).	Can isolate cause-and-effect relationships.	May not yield information about real-life behaviors.
Field Experiment	Experiment conducted in a real-life, naturalistic setting.	Can isolate cause-and-effect relationships; behaviors are observed in natural settings.	Less control over treatment conditions.
Quasi-Experiment	Assignment of participants to groups is determined by their natural experiences.	Takes advantage of natural separation of children into groups.	Factors other than independent variables may be causing results.
Case Study/Single-Case Design	In-depth observation of one or a few children over a period of time.	Does not require large pool of participants.	Can be vulnerable to observer bias; ability to generalize to the larger population may be limited.

Special Issues in Developmental Research

Because of the nature of the questions that developmental researchers ask, certain research strategies take on special significance. How does some aspect of development change with age? How do individual children display transitions in how they think or behave? How do nature and nurture interact to result in a specific developmental outcome? To answer questions like these, researchers turn to an array of strategies that are especially useful when questions about child development are involved.

Strategies for Assessing Developmental Change

The developmental researcher faces a problem unique to this field: how to record the changes in behavior that occur over time. For the most part, the investigator has two choices: to observe individual children repeatedly over time or to select children of different ages to participate in one study at a given time. Each approach has its strengths and limitations, and each has contributed substantially to our understanding of child development.

The Longitudinal Study **Longitudinal studies** assess the same sample of participants repeatedly at various points in time, usually over a span of years. This approach has the longest historical tradition in developmental psychology. The early baby biographies were in essence longitudinal observations, and several major longitudinal projects that were initiated in the early 1900s continued for decades. One of the most famous is Lewis Terman's study of intellectually gifted children, begun in 1921 (Terman, 1925; Terman & Oden, 1959).

Terman identified 952 children aged two to fourteen years who had scored 140 or above on a standardized test of intelligence. He was interested in answering several questions about these exceptionally bright children. Would they become extraordinarily successful later in life? Did they possess any specific cluster of common personality traits? Did they adapt well socially? The sample was followed until most participants reached sixty years of age, and a wealth of information was collected over this long span of time. One finding was that many individuals in this sample had highly successful careers in science, academics, business, and other professions. In addition,

longitudinal study Research in which the same participants are repeatedly tested over a period of time, usually years.

Longitudinal studies assess the same individuals over a span of years, sometimes ranging from infancy through adolescence. This strategy for assessing developmental change allows researchers to identify the stability of many human characteristics.

contrary to many popular stereotypes, high intelligence was associated with greater physical and mental health and adaptive social functioning later in life.

Longitudinal research is costly and requires a substantial research effort. Participants followed over a period of years often move or become unavailable for other reasons; just keeping track of them requires constant and careful recordkeeping. In addition, one might raise questions about the characteristics of the people who remain in the study: perhaps they are less mobile, or perhaps those who agree to participate in a thirty-year study have unique qualities that can affect the interpretation of the project's results (for instance, they may be less energetic or be more curious about themselves and more introspective). Another difficulty lies in the fact that participants who are tested repeatedly often get better at the tests, not because of any changes in their abilities, but because the tests become more familiar over time. Participants who take a test of spatial skill again and again may improve due to practice with the test and not as a result of any developmental change in their abilities. If the researcher attempts to avert this outcome by designing a different version of the same test, the problem then becomes whether the two tests are similar enough!

One of the biggest methodological drawbacks of longitudinal research is the possibility of an **age-history confound**. Suppose a researcher began a twenty-year longitudinal study in 1970 and found that individuals' gender-role beliefs became less stereotyped as the years progressed; that is, participants were less likely to believe that females are dependent, passive, and emotional, and that males are independent, aggressive, and logical. Are these shifts in attitude associated with development? Or did some historical factor, such as the women's movement, bring about the changes in beliefs? Because participants age as cultural and historical events occur, it is often difficult to decide which factor has affected the results of a longitudinal study. Moreover, consider a twenty-year longitudinal study begun in the 1940s versus a similar study begun in the 1990s. Many of the factors that are likely to influence children's development today—television, daycare, and computers, to name a few—probably would not have been included in studies begun five decades ago.

age-history confound In longitudinal studies, the co-occurrence of historical factors with changes in age; affects the ability to interpret results.

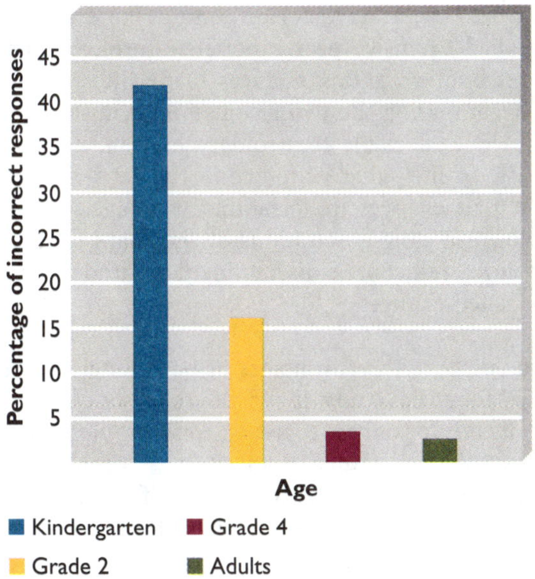

FIGURE 2.6
A Cross-Sectional Study
In this example of a cross-sectional study, children of different ages were asked two progressively misleading questions about each of several portions of a video clip they watched. Kindergarten children made significantly more incorrect responses to the second set of misleading questions. Cross-sectional studies allow researchers to examine age differences in performance quickly and efficiently.
Source: Data from Cassell, Roebers, & Bjorklund (1996).

Despite all these difficulties, the longitudinal approach has distinct advantages that no other research tactic offers; in fact, certain research questions in child development can *only* be answered longitudinally. If a researcher is interested in identifying the *stability* of human characteristics—that is, how likely it is that early attributes will be maintained later in development—the longitudinal approach is the method of choice. Only by observing the same person over time can we answer such questions as "Do passive infants become shy adults?" or "Do early experiences with peers affect the child's ability to form friendships in adolescence?" For researchers interested in understanding the process of development and the factors that precede and follow specific developmental phenomena, particularly with respect to individual differences, the longitudinal strategy remains a powerful one.

The Cross-Sectional Study Possibly the most widely used strategy for studying developmental differences is the **cross-sectional study**, in which children of varying ages are examined at the same point in time. Cross-sectional studies take less time to complete and are usually more economical than longitudinal studies.

A good example of cross-sectional research is the investigation by William Cassel and his colleagues (Cassel, Roebers, & Bjorklund, 1996) of children's responses to repeated questions about a past event. Children from kindergarten and second and fourth grades, as well as adults, watched a video of two children fighting over a bicycle. One week later, participants were asked to recall what they saw. In one portion of the experiment, they were also asked two increasingly misleading questions about each of several segments in the videotaped episode. Figure 2.6 shows the results: kindergartners gave significantly more incorrect responses to the second set of misleading questions compared with the other age groups.

The cross-sectional approach allowed the researchers to make a rapid assessment of the children's performance without waiting for them to grow several years older. They were, however, unable to draw conclusions about individual children and about how characteristics observable at one age might be related to characteristics at another age. Would the children who were most resistant to misleading suggestions also resist those suggestions years later? The cross-sectional approach does not provide answers to these kinds of questions. Most cross-sectional studies involve pooling the scores of individual participants such that the average performance of an entire group of children of a specified age is reported; the average scores of two or more groups of children are then compared. The result is that information about individuals is not the focus of data analysis in this type of study.

Another difficulty with cross-sectional designs is that cohort effects may interfere with our ability to draw clear conclusions. **Cohort effects** are all the characteristics

cross-sectional study Study in which individuals of different ages are examined at the same point in time.

cohort effect All the characteristics shared by individuals growing up in a specific social and historical context.

shared by children growing up in a specific social and historical context. For example, many of today's five-year-olds have had extensive peer experience through their enrollment in daycare and other preschool programs, whereas many fifteen-year-olds probably have not. A researcher comparing the two groups might mistakenly conclude that younger children are more sociable than older children, but the differential exposure to agemates early in life—that is, the cohort effect—may be responsible for the findings, rather than changes in sociability with age. Cross-sectional studies are a quick means of providing descriptions of age changes in all sorts of behaviors. Where they sometimes fall short is in helping us to understand the processes underlying those age-related changes.

The Sequential Study One way to combine the advantages of both longitudinal and cross-sectional approaches is the **sequential study**, in which groups of children of different ages are followed repeatedly but for only a few years. For example, David Cole and his colleagues (Cole et al., 2001) examined changes in children's self-concepts from the elementary to the high school years. Two groups of children—a group of third-graders and a group of sixth-graders—were followed for a period of six years. Every six months, the children took a battery of tests assessing several aspects of self-confidence, such as academic competence, social acceptance, and physical appearance. Thus, by the end of the study, data were available for children in the third through eleventh grades.

Figure 2.7 shows the results for academic competence. Both boys and girls showed gains in this domain from third through sixth grade but evidenced a decline

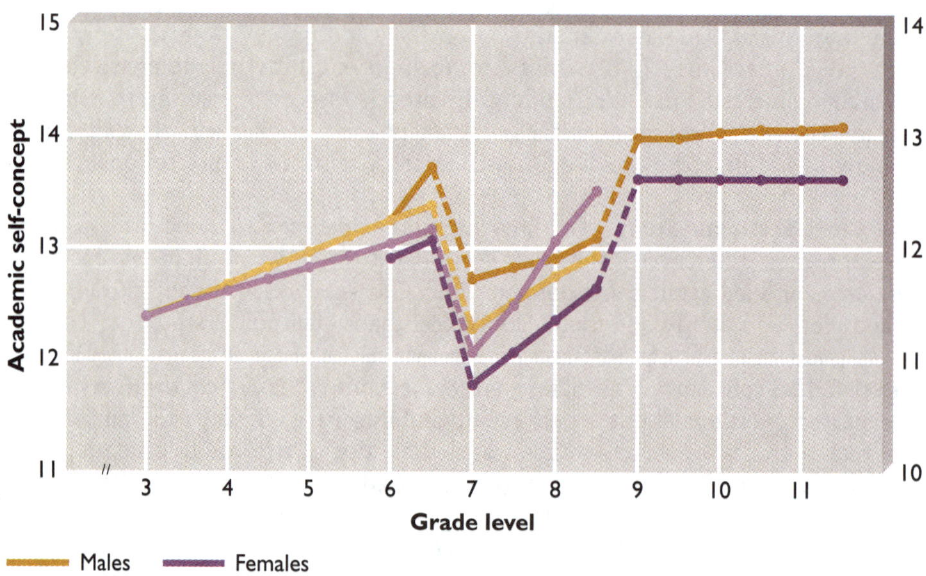

FIGURE 2.7

A Sequential Study

Age differences in behavior patterns over time can be assessed with sequential studies. In a study of children's self-concepts from elementary school through high school, Cole and his colleagues (Cole et al., 2001) assessed two groups of children over a period of six years. The first was a group of third-graders. The data in the graph show changes in their academic self-concept from third through eighth grade (based on a test with the scale shown on the left y-axis). The second group was in the sixth grade at the start of the study. The data in the graph show changes in their self-concepts from sixth through eleventh grade (based on a test for older children with the scale shown on the right y-axis). Thus information about a nine-year age span was obtained in six years.

Source: Adapted from Cole et al. (2001).

sequential study Study that examines groups of individuals of different ages over a period of time; usually shorter than a longitudinal study.

in seventh grade, followed by increases in successive years. (Note that both groups of children were measured in sixth, seventh, and eighth grades.) Because subsets of the children were assessed repeatedly, information about the stability of self-concept for individual children was available, just as it would have been in a longitudinal study. The benefit of the sequential design was that it allowed information about a nine-year span to be obtained in six years.

Although most developmental researchers still prefer to conduct cross-sectional studies because of their expediency, the sequential study provides a convenient way to reap the advantages of both cross-sectional and longitudinal approaches to studying developmental change.

The Microgenetic Study Longitudinal, cross-sectional, and sequential studies may not reveal a complete picture of development. When researchers use these methods, they tend to focus on average differences in performance from one time to the next or from one age group to another. But this approach usually does not tell us much about the precise processes that change as the child develops. A key feature of the **microgenetic approach** is examining a child's performance while she is engaged in a specific task, making note of any changes in behaviors that occur from trial to trial. Through this close analysis of the child's progress from one level of understanding to another, we can glean important details about development and have a better sense of the mechanisms that are responsible for change (Siegler, 1997; Siegler & Crowley, 1991).

An experiment conducted by Robert Siegler and Elsbeth Stern (1998) illustrates this method. These researchers were interested in second-graders' tactics as they solved arithmetic problems that involved the principle of inversion—for example, 35 + 8 – 8. Here, it is possible to use a shortcut to arrive at the answer—the quantity (8 – 8) can be quickly discounted because the result is 0. Only children who did not know the inversion principle were selected to participate. In solving these problems, what kinds of strategies would children use? With repeated practice with these problems, would they eventually learn the inversion principle? Several strategies for solving inversion problems were defined by the researchers:

- *Computation.* Adding all of the numbers
- *Negation.* Adding the first two numbers but then answering without subtracting the third number
- *Unconscious shortcut.* A quick answer, with a vague reference to computation or negation in the child's explanation but no evidence of actually computing the second and third numbers (in other words, the child uses the inversion principle but cannot explain it)
- *Computation shortcut.* Actual computation, but then an explanation that the shortcut would work (the child does not use the inversion principle but can explain it)
- *Shortcut.* A quick answer, no evidence of computation, and an explanation of the inversion principle

The strategies in this list were presumed to increase in sophistication from top to bottom. In the experiment, one group of children received twenty inversion problems, and a second group received ten inversion problems and ten standard problems (for example, 35 + 8 – 2) over a total of six practice sessions. After each individual problem was completed, the researcher asked the child how he or she figured out the problem. The researchers noted the child's numerical answer, the time it took to solve the problem, the explanation the child provided, and any other behaviors that occurred during the trial. Figure 2.8 shows a portion of the results for children who received blocks of twenty inversion problems.

In the graph, trial 0 represents each child's first use of the best strategy, the shortcut (thus 100 percent of the children are represented at this point). Notice that, three trials before trial 0, on trial –3, 87 percent of the children were using the unconscious shortcut, but very few were using computation or any other strategy.

microgenetic study A research approach in which close observations are made of the individual child's behavior from one trial to the next.

FIGURE 2.8

A Microgenetic Analysis of Children's Strategy Use

In Siegler and Stern's (1998) experiment, children were closely observed as they solved a series of problems involving the inversion principle. The best strategy to use was a shortcut (for example, 8 − 8 = 0). Trial 0 on this graph represents the point at which each child began to use this strategy. Notice that on previous trials (for example, Trial −3), many children were using an unconscious shortcut, as opposed to computation, to solve the problems. (Note that in this particular portion of the study none of the children used negation.) A microgenetic approach allows researchers to understand more of the details of the process of development.

Source: Siegler & Stern (1998).

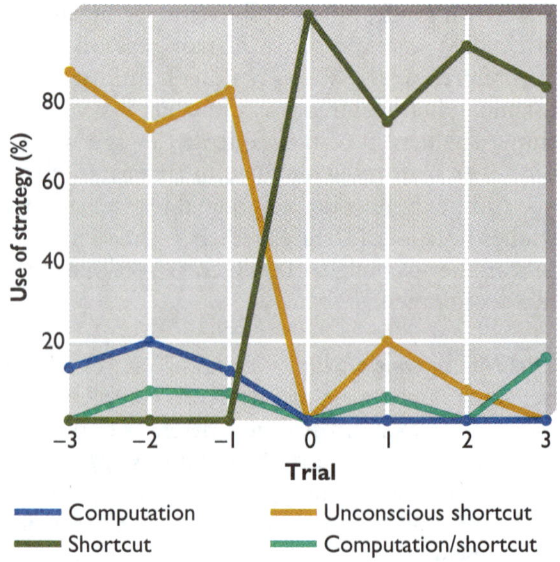

This pattern suggests that, right before children discover the actual shortcut, they use it without being fully aware of it or able to verbalize it. This pattern of results, by the way, did not emerge for children who had mixed sets of inversion and standard problems. Instead, they relied more on computation shortcuts right before they discovered the inversion principle.

As you can see, fine-grained analyses of trial-to-trial changes in children's responses can provide rich information—in this case, about the way their thought processes change. However, this approach requires careful planning and the selection of tasks that are likely to reveal developmental change, as well as concentrated efforts at close observation. Despite these challenges, the microgenetic approach is increasingly becoming part of the arsenal of methods used to study developmental change.

It should be obvious that no single research approach represents the perfect way to study development. Table 2.3 summarizes the relative benefits of each of the research strategies for assessing developmental change.

Table 2.3 Strategies for Assessing Developmental Change

Approach	Description	Advantages	Disadvantages
Longitudinal Study	Repeated testing of the same group of children over an extended period of time	Can examine the stability of characteristics.	Requires a significant investment of time and resources; problems with participant attrition; can have age-history confound.
Cross-Sectional Study	Comparison of children of different ages at the same point in time	Requires less time; less costly than longitudinal study.	Cannot study individual patterns of development or the stability of traits; subject to cohort effects.
Sequential Study	Observation of children of two or more different ages over a shorter period of time than in longitudinal studies	Combines the advantages of both longitudinal and cross-sectional approaches; can obtain information about stability of traits in a short period of time.	Has same problems as longitudinal studies, but to a lesser degree.
Microgenetic Study	Close observation of children's trial-by-trial performance as they are engaged with a task	Permits the identification of the precise processes that change with development.	Requires careful selection of tasks that will reveal developmental changes, as well as close, careful observations.

Cross-Cultural Studies of Development

Some of the most fundamental questions about the nature of development concern the universality of the various features of psychological growth. Do all children learn language in the same way, regardless of the specific language they acquire? Does children's thinking develop in a universal sequence? Are certain emotions common to all children regardless of attitudes about the appropriateness of crying, smiling, or feeling angry in the larger social group in which they live?

If psychological development does display universal features, this circumstance has far-reaching implications. It could imply, on the one hand, that a child's behavior is largely shaped by biological factors and, more specifically, by the genes that govern the unfolding of some human behaviors. Variations in aspects of psychological development across cultures, on the other hand, imply that the differences in the child's experiences weigh heavily in bringing about those behaviors. **Cross-cultural studies**, which compare children from different cultural groups on one or more behaviors or patterns of abilities, can be extremely useful in answering questions like these.

Take, for example, the development of play. One hypothesis put forward by Piaget is that there is a general progression in early childhood from *exploratory play*, in which the toddler throws, manipulates, and otherwise learns about the functions of objects, to *symbolic play*, in which he or she pretends with objects—for example, sipping from an empty cup or using a block as a telephone. Marc Bornstein and his colleagues (1999) recorded and coded the naturally occurring play behaviors of twenty-month-old children and their mothers in two countries, the United States and Argentina. Mother-child pairs were provided with the same set of eight toys and were told to play as they normally would for ten minutes. These researchers found that, despite being the same age, children in the United States engaged in more exploratory play with their mothers, whereas Argentine children engaged in more symbolic play. Moreover, mothers' play behaviors were strongly related to children's patterns of play. Thus there were clear cultural differences, perhaps linked to the different social goals in the two groups. Exploratory play patterns, which involve manipulating and combining objects, are consistent with the emphasis on individual achievement, independence, and self-reliance in the United States. On the other hand, symbolic play patterns among Argentine mothers and their children often included social behaviors, such as feeding or putting a doll to sleep. These social behaviors are compatible with the orientation of Argentine society toward the larger, collective group. Thus the transition from one form of play to another may be less influenced by universal processes, as suggested by Piaget, than by culture-specific experiences.

Cross-cultural studies allow researchers to explore the extent to which children's behaviors are universal or specific to a given culture. For example, are the emotions expressed by these Thai girls interpreted in common ways across cultures?

Cross-cultural studies can present unique challenges to the researcher. If children from two cultural backgrounds are being compared, the researcher must make sure the tasks are well understood and have equivalent forms despite differences in language or in the kinds of activities the children are used to doing. For example, children in some cultures may never have seen a photograph or a two-dimensional drawing. Asking these children to categorize objects in pictorial form may put them at an unfair disadvantage if they are to be compared with children who have extensive experience with two-dimensional representations. Moreover, if the researcher is an outsider to the cultural group being observed, he or she may provoke atypical reactions from the individuals under study. Parent-child interactions, peer play, and many other behaviors may not occur as they would in the natural course of events, because of the presence of an outside observer. Cross-cultural researchers must thus pay special attention to the possibility of *participant reactivity*.

cross-cultural study Study that compares individuals in different cultural contexts.

For some researchers, cross-cultural studies play a different sort of role, in that they provide a way of understanding human development as it is shaped and formed by the unique contexts in which it occurs. From this perspective, a researcher may try to avoid imposing the values and concepts of his or her own culture on another, trying instead to discover the particular beliefs, values, and modes of thinking in the group under study. The goal is not to compare cultures in order to document similarities and differences; rather, it is to study cultures in an in-depth fashion in order to describe behaviors and underlying meaning systems *within* that culture (Miller, 1999; Saarni, 1998; Shweder et al., 2006; Super & Harkness, 1997). A research approach that is often used to achieve these goals is **ethnography**, a set of methods that includes observations of behaviors within the natural environment and interviews with individuals about values and practices within the culture. Ethnographers often live within a particular culture as *participant-observers*, immersing themselves over an extended period of time in the daily routines and practices of a culture (Weisner, 1996). Using these methods, researchers have obtained rich descriptions of what it means to be a child in cultures as diverse as the Gusii tribe of western Kenya (LeVine et al., 1994), Samoa (Ochs, 1988), and the poor neighborhoods of Brazil (Scheper-Hughes, 1992).

The cross-cultural approach has benefits in terms of understanding human development as it occurs not only in other countries but also in our own society, in which cultural diversity is increasingly becoming a characteristic of the population. Consider some statistics. In Canada, approximately 16 percent of children age fourteen years and under come from non-Caucasian background cultures (Statistics Canada, 2005). In the United States, over 40 percent of children under age eighteen are African American, Hispanic, Native American, or Asian (U.S. Bureau of the Census, 2005). By the year 2010, the majority of children under eighteen will have these ethnic heritages in several states, including Hawaii, California, Texas, New York, and New Mexico (McLoyd, 1998). Thus, in order to capture the elements of human development in the broadest and most meaningful sense, researchers will have to study concepts that are relevant and indigenous to these cultures. Individual autonomy and competition may be valued goals of socialization in middle-class Caucasian culture, for example, but they have less relevance in African American or Native American cultures (McLoyd, 1998). Cross-cultural studies can provide important insights into almost all aspects of child development. For this reason, we draw on available cross-cultural work as we discuss each aspect of the growth of children.

FOR • YOUR • REVIEW

- What four research tactics allow researchers to address questions about developmental change? What are the strengths and weaknesses of each tactic?
- What functions do different types of cross-cultural studies serve in developmental research?

ETHICAL ISSUES IN DEVELOPMENTAL RESEARCH

All psychologists are bound by professional ethics to treat the participants under study humanely and fairly. In general, researchers try to minimize the risk of any physical or emotional harm that might come to participants from taking part in research and to maximize the benefits that will accrue from the findings of their work. The American Psychological Association has drawn up the following specific guidelines for the use of human participants. First, participants must give **informed consent** before participating in a research project; that is, they must be told the purposes of the study and be informed of

ethnography Set of methods, including observations and interviews, used by researchers to describe the behaviors and underlying meaning systems within a given culture.

informed consent Participant's formal acknowledgment that he or she understands the purposes, procedures, and risks of a study, and agrees to participate in it.

any potential risks to their well-being, and then they must formally agree to participate. Second, participants have the right to decline to participate or to stop participation, even in the middle of the experiment. Third, if participants cannot be told the true purpose of the experiment (sometimes knowing the experimenter's objective will influence how participants behave), they must be *debriefed* at the conclusion of the study. When participants are **debriefed**, they are told the true objective of the study and the reasons for any deception on the part of the experimenter. Finally, data collected from participants must be kept confidential. Names of participants must not be revealed, and care must be taken to protect their anonymity. To ensure that experimenters comply with these guidelines, virtually all research institutions in the United States are required to have review boards that evaluate any potential risks to participants and the researchers' compliance with ethical practice.

The same ethical guidelines apply to using children as participants in research, but frequently the implementation of these guidelines becomes a difficult matter. Who provides informed consent in the case of an infant or a young toddler, for example? (The parents do.) Is it proper to deceive children about the purposes of a study if they cannot understand the debriefing? (In general, it is a good idea to avoid any kind of deception with children, such as telling them you are interested in how quickly they learn a game when you are really interested in whether they will be altruistic with their play partner.) Are some subjects of study taboo, such as asking children about their concepts of death, suicide, or other frightening topics that might affect them emotionally? (Such studies, if conducted, must be planned very carefully and conducted only by trained professionals.) What about cases in which treatments are suspected to have beneficial outcomes for children? Can the control group properly have the treatment withheld? For example, if we suspect that children's participation in an early intervention preschool program will have real benefits for them, should children in the control group be kept out of it? (One solution to this thorny problem is to offer the control group the beneficial treatment as soon as possible after the conclusion of the study, although this is not always a satisfactory compromise. The control group still has to wait for a beneficial treatment or intervention.)

Many researchers assume that children's vulnerability to risk as they participate in psychological experiments decreases as they grow older. Because infants and young children have more limited cognitive skills and emotional coping strategies, they are viewed as less able to protect themselves and to understand their rights during participation in research. This assumption certainly has some logical basis and, in fact, is confirmed by research showing that second-graders have difficulty understanding the concept of confidentiality, as well as the contents of a debriefing statement (Hurley & Underwood, 2002). Some types of research, however, may actually pose a greater threat to older children. As Ross Thompson (1990) has pointed out, older children are developing a self-concept and a more elaborate understanding of the ways others evaluate them. Older children may thus be more susceptible to psychological harm than younger children when the researcher compares their performance with that of others or when they think teachers or parents may learn about their performance. In addition, older children may be more sensitive to research results that reflect negatively on their family or sociocultural group. These situations require awareness on the part of the researcher of the subtle ways children can be adversely affected by the research enterprise.

Table 2.4 sets forth the ethical guidelines on using children as participants in research established by the Society for Research in Child Development (1996). Probably the overriding guiding principle is that children should not be subjected to any physical or mental harm and should be treated with all possible respect. In fact, because children are frequently unable to voice their concerns and have less power than adults do, developmental researchers must be especially sensitive to their comfort and well-being.

debriefing Providing research participants with a statement of the true goals of a study after initially deceiving them or omitting information about its purposes.

CONTROVERSY: THINKING IT OVER

Should Researchers Reveal Information They Learn About Participants in Their Studies?

Researchers often study issues that are sensitive but that can have important consequences for the well-being of children. For example, a researcher might be interested in finding out the factors that predict the emergence of eating disorders in adolescents or the consequences of parental drug abuse for the child. However, research that can be very illuminating about the nature of childhood problems often raises difficult ethical dilemmas (Fisher, 1994).

What Is the Controversy?

Suppose the researcher discovers that a particular child has a serious eating disorder or that a young child has ingested harmful illegal drugs kept by the parents in the home. What are the ethical obligations of the researcher in such situations? Should the concerns about the welfare of individual children override any potential benefits of the research for children in general? Furthermore, should the identities of children with serious problems be revealed to parents, school personnel, or others responsible for their well-being, at the risk of violating children's trust that data will be kept confidential?

What Are the Opposing Arguments?

Ethical guidelines state that researchers who discover that a child is at risk must take steps to make sure that the child obtains appropriate assistance. Such action is based on the concept of "jeopardy" outlined by the Society for Research in Child Development and referred to in Table 2.4. The idea is that ethical concerns about the welfare of particular children should be a primary concern and override any potential benefits of the research for children in general. Also implicit in the concept of jeopardy is the notion that, in some circumstances, confidentiality must be broken to protect the best interests of the child.

However, as a consequence of such actions, the child may drop out of the study in order to receive some form of treatment or intervention. If several children in the study drop out, the opportunity to complete the research project could be lost, along with the potential benefits of the results of the study for a

Table 2.4 Ethical Guidelines in Conducting Research with Children

- *Nonharmful procedures.* The investigator may not use any procedures that could impose physical or psychological harm on the child. In addition, the investigator should use the least stressful research operation whenever possible. If the investigator is in doubt about the possible harmful effects of the research, he or she should consult with others. If the child will be unavoidably exposed to stress in research that might provide some diagnostic or therapeutic benefits to the child, the study should be reviewed by an institutional review board.
- *Informed consent.* The investigator should inform the child of all features of the research that might affect his or her willingness to participate and should answer all questions in a way the child can comprehend. The child has the right to discontinue participation at any time.
- *Parental consent.* Informed consent should be obtained in writing from the child's parents or from other adults who have responsibility for the child. The adult has the right to know all features of the research that might affect the child's willingness to participate and can refuse consent.
- *Deception.* If the research necessitates concealment or deception about the nature of the study, the investigator should make sure the child understands the reasons for the deception after the study is concluded.
- *Confidentiality.* All information about participants in research must be kept confidential.
- *Jeopardy.* If, during research, the investigator learns of information concerning a jeopardy to the child's well-being, the investigator must discuss the information with the parents or guardians and experts to arrange for assistance to the child.
- *Informing participants.* The investigator should clarify any misconceptions that may have arisen on the part of the child during the study. The investigator should also report general findings to participants in terms they can understand.

Source: Adapted from the ethical standards set by the Society for Research in Child Development (1996).

larger group of children (Beauchamp et al., 1982). Some researchers believe that the benefits of a well-conducted study can override the obligation to help a particular child for whom a problem has been revealed.

What Answers Exist? What Questions Remain?

In some cases, researchers may have a legal obligation to enforce the principle of jeopardy. A federal law, the Child Abuse Prevention and Treatment Act enacted in 1974, resulted in the creation of mandatory reporting procedures for suspected cases of child abuse and neglect in every state. In many states, researchers are included among individuals who are required to report. Thus a researcher who discovers that a child has been abused or neglected, as in the preceding example of a child who has ingested parents' illegal drugs, may be required by law to report the case to the proper authorities. The fact that the child might drop out of the study or that confidentiality is broken is simply a necessary consequence.

In other cases, the issue may be more difficult to resolve. Research can be of help, though, in supplying information on how children themselves feel when such ethical dilemmas arise. Celia Fisher and her colleagues (Fisher et al., 1996) asked adolescents to judge what researchers should do if they discover that a child has a substance abuse problem, has been physically or sexually abused, displays a life-threatening behavior, or engages in delinquent behaviors. Most adolescents favored reporting instances of child abuse or threats of suicide to a responsible adult. For less severe problems, such as cigarette smoking and nonviolent delinquent acts, adolescents were more inclined to say that the researcher should do nothing. In cases like the latter, rather than reporting children to parents or authorities, researchers might decide to urge children to seek assistance on their own.

Other questions remain. Does the age of the child matter in such ethical decisions? Should these decisions be handled differently with adolescents than with younger children? How can research help us to address questions such as these?

FOR YOUR REVIEW

- What ethical guidelines apply to the participation of children in research?
- What ethical concepts should guide researchers who discover that children in their research projects may be experiencing some form of risk in their lives?

CHAPTER RECAP

Chapter Review

RESEARCH METHODS IN DEVELOPMENTAL PSYCHOLOGY

What issues must researchers pay attention to when they measure attributes and behaviors?

Like other scientists, developmental psychologists are concerned with using sound methodologies to glean information about children. The *scientific method* is used not only to test theories but also to gather information that can have applications in the lives of children. Researchers need to be concerned with *operationally defining* the *variables* in the study. That is, the variables must be specified in measurable terms. Variables must be *valid*; that is, they must actually measure the concept under consideration. Variables must also be *reliable*; that is, obtained consistently from one time to another or from one observer to another.

What four information-gathering techniques do developmental researchers generally have available to them? What are the advantages and disadvantages of each technique?

Naturalistic observations involve the systematic recording of behaviors as they occur in children's everyday environments.

Two special concerns in this approach are *participant reactivity*, the chance that children will react to the presence of an observer by behaving in atypical ways, and *observer bias*, the possibility that the researcher will interpret observations to be consistent with his or her hypotheses.

Structured observations, usually conducted in the laboratory, allow the experimenter more control over situations that accompany children's behaviors. Researchers can measure children's overt behaviors or obtain physiological measures, such as heart rate or brain wave activity. One limitation of this approach is that children may not act as they would in a natural context.

Researchers can employ *structured interviews* or *questionnaires* if they are interested in children's own reports of what they know or how they behave. Alternatively, they can use a more open-ended technique, the *clinical method*. Researchers need to be aware that children may not always answer questions truthfully and that systematic comparisons and unbiased interpretations by the researcher may be difficult to obtain, especially with the clinical method.

Meta-analysis permits investigators to analyze the results of a large body of published research to draw general conclusions about behavior.

What are the different research designs that researchers might employ to study child development? What are the strengths and weaknesses of each design?

In *correlational studies*, the investigator attempts to see whether changes in one variable are accompanied by changes in another variable. Researchers may observe a *positive correlation*, in which increases in one variable are accompanied by increases in another, or a *negative correlation*, in which increases in one variable are accompanied by decreases in the other. The statistic used to assess the degree of relationship is the *correlation coefficient* (*r*). One caution about this design is that cause-and-effect conclusions cannot be drawn.

In the *experimental design*, the researcher manipulates one or more *independent variables* to see if they have an effect on the *dependent variable*. *Random assignment* of participants to different treatment groups helps ensure that only the independent variable varies from one group to the other. Therefore, cause-and-effect relationships among variables can be identified. Variations on this technique are *field experiments*, in which the experimental manipulations are carried out in a natural setting, and *quasi-experiments*, in which the assignment of participants to experimental groups is determined by the participants' natural experiences. Because of this circumstance, researchers conducting quasi-experiments must be concerned with ruling out alternative explanations for their findings.

In *case studies* or the *single-case design*, the researcher intensively studies one or a few individuals over a period of time. The former usually involves a detailed narrative description, whereas the latter involves the systematic collection of data. The ability to generalize to a larger population may be limited with these approaches.

Special Issues in Developmental Research

What four research tactics allow researchers to address questions about developmental change? What are the strengths and weaknesses of each approach?

Longitudinal studies test the same participants repeatedly over an extended period of time. This approach requires a significant investment of time, may involve attrition of participants, and could be vulnerable to the *age-history confound*. It is the only method that allows researchers to examine the stability of traits.

Cross-sectional studies examine participants of different ages at the same time. Although this approach requires less time and fewer resources than the longitudinal approach, it is vulnerable to *cohort effects*.

Sequential studies examine children of two or more ages over a period of time, usually shorter than that used in longitudinal studies. This approach combines the advantages of the cross-sectional and longitudinal approaches but is also vulnerable to the problems associated with each.

Microgenetic studies require the close observation of children as they perform some task, in order to identify the specific processes that change with development. They require careful planning and the selection of tasks that will reveal developmental change, as well as intensive efforts at observation.

What functions do different types of cross-cultural studies serve in developmental research?

Cross-cultural studies, which compare individuals from different cultural groups, can be especially helpful in answering questions about universals in development. Researchers must make sure that tasks are comparable across cultural groups, however.

An important methodological tool, especially for those who wish to learn about the meaning systems within a culture, is *ethnography*, the use of observations and interviews by a researcher who acts as a participant-observer.

Ethical Issues in Developmental Research

What ethical guidelines apply to the participation of children in research?

Participants in research must be asked to provide *informed consent*, given the chance to decline participation, be *debriefed* if there has been any deception, and receive assurance that their data will be kept confidential.

What ethical concepts should guide researchers who discover that children in their research projects may be experiencing some form of risk in their lives?

Researchers should always be most concerned with the welfare of the child. In some cases, this concern may mean that confidentiality may have to be broken or that the child will have to drop out of the study to receive an intervention.

KEY TERMS AND CONCEPTS

age-history confound (p. 56)
case study (p. 53)
clinical method (p. 46)
cohort effect (p. 57)
correlation coefficient (*r*) (p. 48)
correlational study (p. 48)
cross-cultural study (p. 61)
cross-sectional study (p. 57)
debriefing (p. 63)
dependent variable (p. 49)
ethnography (p. 62)
experimental design (p. 49)
field experiment (p. 51)
independent variable (p. 49)
informed consent (p. 62)
longitudinal study (p. 55)
meta-analysis (p. 47)
microgenetic study (p. 59)
naturalistic observation (p. 42)
negative correlation (p. 48)
observer bias (p. 43)
operational definition (p. 41)
participant reactivity (p. 43)
positive correlation (p. 48)
quasi-experiment (p. 52)
questionnaire (p. 46)
random assignment (p. 49)
reliability (p. 41)
scientific method (p. 40)
sequential study (p. 58)
single-case design (p. 53)
structured interview (p. 45)
structured observation (p. 43)
validity (p. 41)
variable (p. 40)

GENETICS AND HEREDITY 3

Michelle and Derek flopped down on the couch after a long evening of teacher conferences. They had coordinated the night so that Michelle visited all of Alison's fourth-grade teachers and Derek saw Keesha's sixth-grade teachers. Now they were ready to compare notes. "Keesha's doing just great," Derek reported. "Her teachers all say she's conscientious, responsible, and very meticulous about her work. No complaints whatsoever. In fact, she seems to be a real star in math and science. How's Alison doing?" Michelle looked at him and smiled, knowing that what she was about to say would not be a surprise to her husband. Since their daughters had been toddlers, both parents had noticed just how different their two little girls were. Keesha was so absorbed and focused on whatever she was doing and always cautious about trying new things. Alison, on the other hand, was a real free and creative spirit, willing to try anything and concerned less with the details of a task than with getting it done as quickly as possible. Michelle responded, "Well, Alison's going to have to get extra help in math, but her teacher says her poems

NATURE & NURTURE How do nature and nurture interact in development?

RISK/RESILIENCE What factors promote risk or resilience in development?

and stories are very creative. In fact, she's putting one of her poems up in the showcase by the school office. She's just got to buckle down and make sure she gets all of her homework done, though. Especially in math." Michelle and Derek prided themselves on being accepting of their girls' individual strengths and weaknesses—setting high expectations but respecting their individuality, too. But for both parents it was still a puzzle: how could two children growing up in the same house with the same family be so different?

Parents of more than one child are aware of similarities among them. However, they often take particular notice of the differences; for example, by pointing out how one child "takes after" perhaps his mother and another after her father. What are the mechanisms by which such resemblances and differences come about? Although we may grant the contribution of nature to eye color, gender, height, and many other physical traits, heredity's role in other characteristics, such as whether we are contented or quick-tempered, prone to alcoholism, likely to suffer depression, bright and quick-witted, active or more sedentary, is far less certain. Is Alison more impulsive and Keesha more cautious because these qualities developed as a result of their different genetic endowments or because their parents and others encouraged them to develop in these ways? Or did their individuality come about for more complex reasons—perhaps because Keesha and Alison actively pursued different paths of responding to their daily experiences as a result of their unique genetic makeup?

In this chapter, we examine hereditary contributions to development. Major advances in our understanding of the basic biological units of inheritance and their effects on behavior help us to better appreciate the mutual, interactive relationship between nature and nurture. Experiences mold, modify, and enhance biological predispositions, and in a similar manner, genetic endowment influences, perhaps even actively promotes, selection and preference for certain kinds of environments. Our goal is to understand just how such complex interactions evolve.

We begin with a brief overview of the principles of heredity. The blueprint for development is replicated in nearly every cell of our body. This blueprint includes genetic instructions that distinguish us from other species of plants and animals. Regardless of the language we speak, the work we do, the color of our skin, or how friendly we are, we share a genetic underpinning that makes each of us a human being. This biological inheritance also contributes to our individuality. With the exception of identical twins, each of us begins with a different set of genetic instructions. But even for identical twins, in whom genetic makeup is the same, the influence of distinctive experiences ensures that each of us is a unique individual, different from everyone else.

In this chapter, we also examine several examples of hereditary variations that pose problems for development. As researchers learn more about the ways in which genetic influences occur, we can design environments to help minimize the restrictions imposed by certain hereditary conditions. We consider, too, how genetic counseling assists parents in deciding whether to have children or how to prepare for a child who is likely to experience developmental problems.

Most psychological development, of course, cannot be linked to simple genetic instructions. Intelligence, temperament, and personality, along with susceptibility to various diseases and conditions, are the outcome of complex interactions between genetic and environmental events. In the final section of this chapter, we consider research involving identical and fraternal twins, siblings, adopted children, and other family relationships to help us understand the complex tapestry that genetic and environmental factors weave for cognitive, social-emotional, and personality development (Gottlieb, Wahlsten, & Lickliter, 2006; Rutter, 2002).

PRINCIPLES OF HEREDITARY TRANSMISSION

KEY THEME
NATURE & NURTURE

Whether we have freckles, blond hair, or a certain type of personality can be influenced by genetic factors, but none of these characteristics is bestowed directly on us at conception. We must make a distinction between what our genetic makeup consists of and the kind of individual we eventually become. In other words, we must distinguish between the **genotype**, a person's constant, inherited genetic endowment, and the **phenotype**, his or her observable, measurable features, characteristics, and behaviors. A given phenotype is the product of complex interactions involving the genotype and the many events that are part of an individual's experience.

Modern theories of the genotype can be traced to a series of experiments reported in 1866 by Gregor Mendel, an Austrian monk. From his observations of the characteristics of successive generations of peas, Mendel theorized that hereditary characteristics are determined by pairs of particles called *factors* (later termed **genes**, the specialized sequences of molecules that form the genotype). He also proposed that the information provided by the two members of a pair of genes is not always identical. These different forms of a gene are today known as **alleles**. Sometimes many possible alternative versions exist for a particular gene.

Mendel also outlined the basic principle by which genes are transferred from one generation to another. He concluded that offspring randomly receive one member of every pair of genes from the mother and one from the father. This is possible because the parents' **gametes**, or sex cells (egg and sperm), carry only one member of each pair of genes. Thus, when egg and sperm combine during fertilization, a new pair of genes, one member of the pair inherited from each parent, is reestablished in the offspring. That individual, in turn, may transmit either member of this new pair to subsequent children. Thus genetic information is passed on from one generation to the next.

At about the same time Mendel's research was published, biologists discovered **chromosomes**, long, threadlike structures in the nucleus of nearly every cell in the body. In the early 1900s, several researchers independently hypothesized that genes are located on chromosomes. Yet another major breakthrough occurred in 1953 when James Watson and Francis Crick deciphered the structure of chromosomes and, in so doing, proposed a powerfully elegant way by which genes are duplicated during cell division. By 1956, researchers had documented the existence of forty-six chromosomes in normal human body cells. Today, some fifty years after Watson and Crick's monumental discovery, the mapping of the sequence of the **human genome**—the nearly 3 billion chemical base pairs that make up every human's biological inheritance—is complete (National Human Genome Research Institute, 2003).

THE BUILDING BLOCKS OF HEREDITY

How could hereditary factors play a part in the differences displayed by Keesha and Alison or in a child's remarkable musical ability or in yet another's mental retardation? To understand the genotype and its effects on appearance, behavior, personality, or intellectual ability, we must consider genetic mechanisms at many different levels.

To begin with, every living organism is composed of cells—in the case of mature humans, trillions of cells. As Figure 3.1 indicates, within the nucleus of nearly all cells are the chromosomes that carry genetic information critical to the cells' functioning. Genes, regions within the strands of chromosomes, determine the production of specific proteins in the cell. The genes, in turn, are made up of various arrangements of four different chemical building blocks called **nucleotides**, which contain one of four nitrogen-based molecules (*adenine*, *thymine*, *cytosine*, or *guanine*). The nucleotides pair together in one of only two ways to form the rungs of a remarkably long, spiral staircaselike structure called **DNA**, or **deoxyribonucleic acid** (see Figure 3.1). An average of about 1,000 nucleotide pairs makes up each gene, although some genes have substantially more pairings (National Research

genotype Total genetic endowment inherited by an individual.

phenotype Observable and measurable characteristics and traits of an individual; a product of the interaction of the genotype with the environment.

gene Large segment of nucleotides within a chromosome that codes for the production of proteins and enzymes. These proteins and enzymes underlie traits and characteristics inherited from one generation to the next.

allele Alternate form of a specific gene; provides a genetic basis for many individual differences.

gamete Sperm cell in males, egg cell in females, normally containing only twenty-three chromosomes.

chromosome Threadlike structure of DNA, located in the nucleus of cells, which forms a collection of genes. A human body cell normally contains forty-six chromosomes.

human genome Entire inventory of nucleotide base pairs that compose the genes and chromosomes of humans.

nucleotide Repeating basic building block of DNA consisting of nitrogen-based molecules of adenine, thymine, cytosine, and guanine.

deoxyribonucleic acid (DNA) Long, spiral staircaselike sequence of molecules created by nucleotides identified with the blueprint for genetic inheritance.

1. The **human body** has about 10 trillion cells. Proteins determine the structure and function of each cell.

2. Most **cells** contain a nucleus. Located within the nucleus are forty-six chromosomes that carry the instructions that signal the cell to manufacture various proteins.

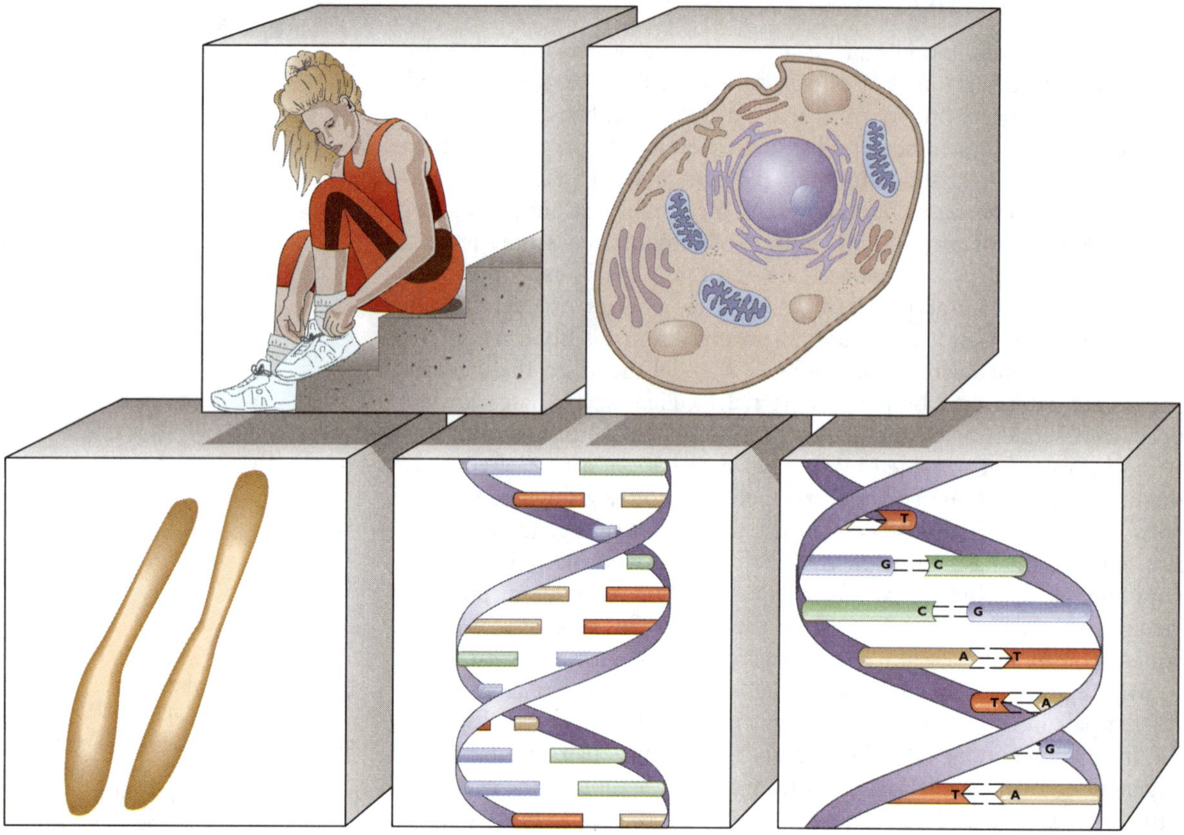

3. A **chromosome** is a long thin strand of DNA organized as a coiled double helix. A full set of forty-six chromosomes in humans is believed to contain somewhere between 26,000 and 38,000 genes, far fewer than had been believed before the human genome was mapped.

4. A **gene** can be made up of thousands of nucleotide pairs. Each gene typically has information designed to specify the production of one or more particular proteins.

5. **Nucleotides**, composed of four different kinds of chemical building blocks—adenine (A), thymine (T), cytosine (C), and guanine (G)—are the smallest genetic unit and are paired in specific combinations. Nearly 3 billion pairs of nucleotides make up the total complement of DNA in humans.

FIGURE 3.1

The Building Blocks of Heredity

Hereditary contributions to development can be observed at many levels. This figure depicts five major levels. Nearly every cell in the human body carries the genetic blueprint for development in the chromosomes. Specific regions on each chromosome, the genes, regulate protein production. Looked at in even more detail, the human genome consists of chemical molecules that are the building blocks for the genes. Each of these different levels of the individual's biological makeup can offer insights into the mechanisms by which the genotype affects the phenotype, the observable expression of traits and behaviors.

Source: Adapted from Isensee (1986).

Council, 1988). Genes differ from one another in number and sequence of nucleotide pairings, and in their location on the chemical spiral staircases, or chains of DNA, that we call the chromosomes.

Just as Mendel theorized, hereditary attributes are, in most cases, influenced by pairs of genes or, more specifically, the two allelic forms of the pair. One member of the pair is located on a chromosome inherited from the mother; the other, on a similar, or *homologous,* chromosome acquired from the father. Figure 3.2 shows a

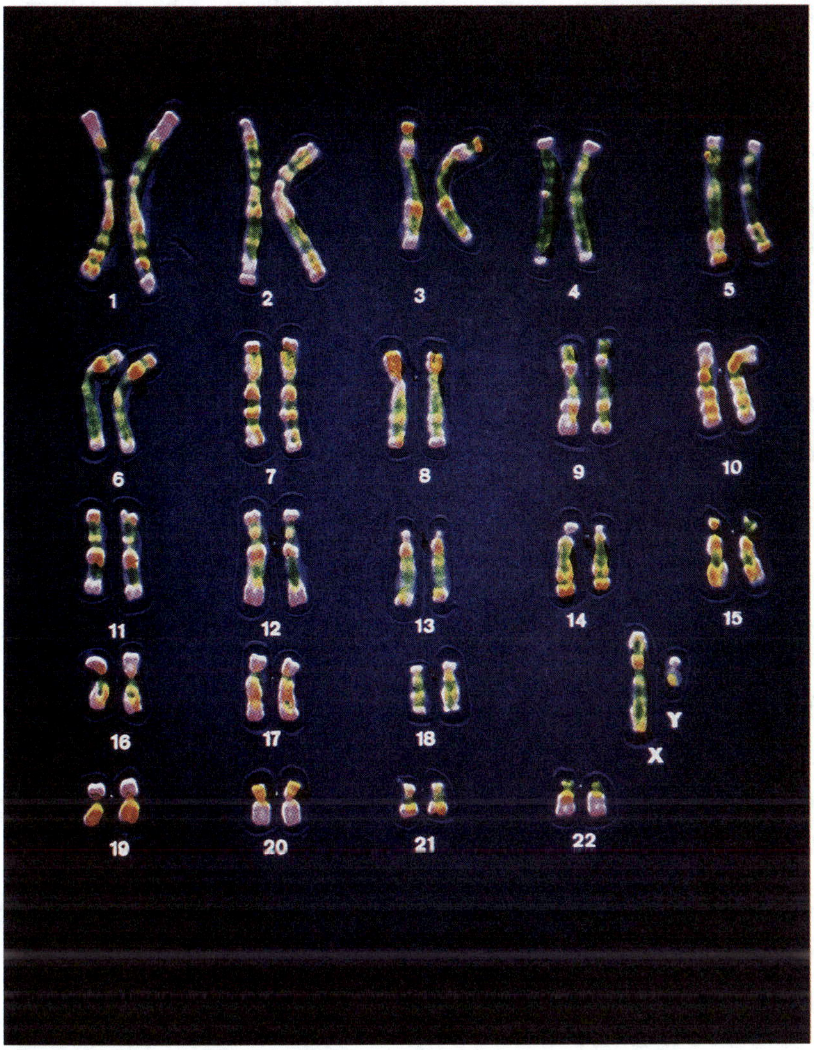

FIGURE 3.2
Chromosomes in the Normal Human Male
This karyotype depicts the twenty-two homologous pairs of autosomes and the two sex chromosomes in the normal human male. In females, the twenty-third pair of chromosomes consists of an XX pair instead of an XY pair.

karyotype, or photomicrograph of the forty-six chromosomes that humans (in this case, a male) normally possess.

As can be seen in Figure 3.2, the homologous sets of chromosomes that are not genetically involved in the determination of sex, called **autosomes**, can be arranged in pairs and numbered from 1 to 22 on the basis of their size. The remaining two chromosomes specify the genetic sex of an individual and differ for males and females. In females this pair consists of **X chromosomes**; both are relatively large and similar in size. The normal male has one X chromosome and a much smaller **Y chromosome**. The Y chromosome is believed to carry only a few dozen genes, in sharp contrast to the 2,000 to 3,000 genes estimated to be on the X chromosome (Jegalian & Lahn, 2001).

Cell Division and Chromosome Duplication

Each of us began life as a single cell created when a sperm cell, normally containing twenty-three chromosomes, from the father united with an ovum (egg), normally containing an additional twenty-three chromosomes, from the mother. The developmental processes started by this fertilized egg cell, called a **zygote**, are more fully described in the chapter titled "The Prenatal Period and Birth." Remarkably, however, nearly every one of the millions of different cells in the newborn, whether specialized for bone or skin, heart or brain, or in some other way, contains the same genetic blueprint established in the initial zygote.

karyotype Pictorial representation of an individual's chromosomes.

autosome One of twenty-two pairs of homologous chromosomes. The two members of each pair are similar in size, shape, and genetic function. The two sex chromosomes are excluded from this class.

X chromosome Larger of the two sex chromosomes associated with genetic determination of sex. Normally females have two X chromosomes and males, only one.

Y chromosome Smaller of the two sex chromosomes associated with genetic determination of sex. Normally males have one Y chromosome and females, none.

zygote Fertilized egg cell.

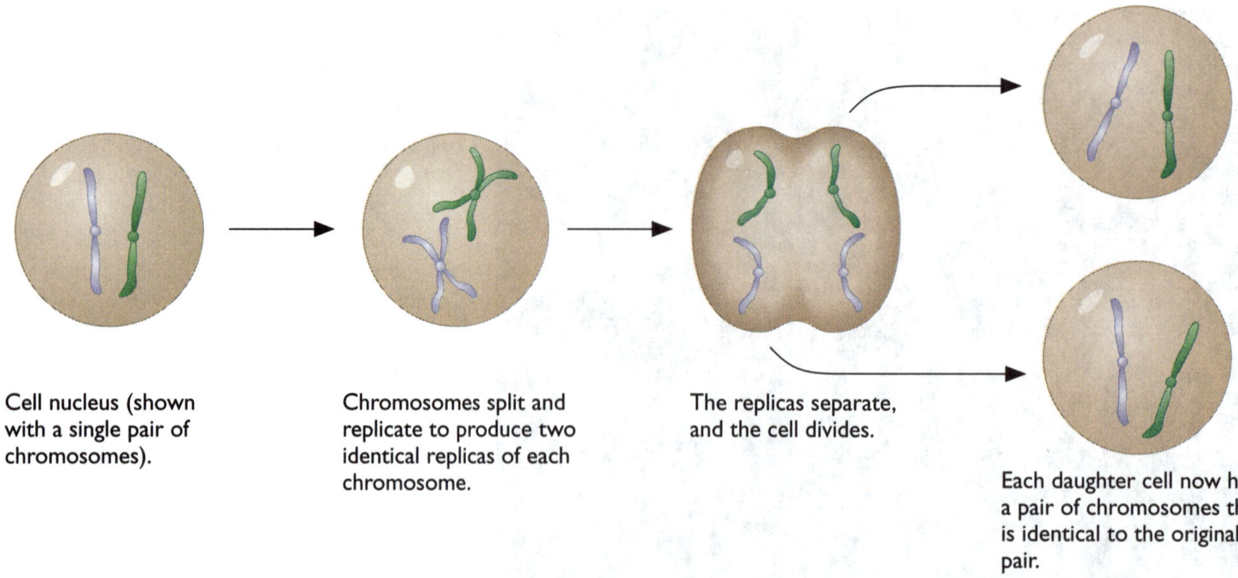

FIGURE 3.3

The Process of Mitosis

The process of mitotic cell division generates nearly all the cells of the body except the gametes. During mitosis, each chromosome replicates to form two chromosomes with identical genetic blueprints. As the cell divides, one member of each identical pair becomes a member of each daughter cell. In this manner, complete genetic endowment is replicated in nearly every cell of the body.

How does this extraordinary duplication of DNA from one cell to another and from one generation to the next take place? Most cells divide through the process called **mitosis**. During mitosis, genetic material in the nucleus of the cell is reproduced such that a full complement of DNA becomes available to each new cell. Even before cell division occurs, the chemical bonds linking the nucleotides that form the rungs of the DNA ladder weaken. The pairs of nucleotides separate as though they were being unzipped from each other. At the same time, additional nucleotides are manufactured in the cell and attach to the separated nucleotides. Because each nucleotide can combine with only one other type, the two newly formed strands of DNA are rebuilt exactly as in their original sequence. The two newly formed copies of DNA eventually separate completely, so that one becomes a member of each of the two new daughter cells, as depicted in Figure 3.3.

The process of cell division associated with the gametes (the sex cells) is called **meiosis**. Meiosis, which results in twenty-three chromosomes in the egg and sperm cells, actually involves *two* successive generations of cell divisions. In the first stage, each of the forty-six chromosomes begins to replicate in much the same way as mitosis begins. However, before the identical replicas split apart, the cell divides, so that each daughter cell receives only one chromosome from each of the twenty-three pairs, as pictured in Figure 3.4. In the second stage, the replicas of the twenty-three chromosomes completely separate, and the cell divides once more, each cell again receiving one of the replicas. Thus, from these two successive divisions, four cells are produced, each with twenty-three chromosomes.

Random segregation of the twenty-three homologous chromosome pairs in the first stage of meiosis yields more than 8 million possible combinations of gametes with one or more different sets of chromosomes. Along with an equivalent number of possible unique arrangements from a mate, mother and father together have a gene pool of about 64 trillion different combinations from which their offspring may derive. But the potential for genetic variability is actually far greater because of the phenomenon known as **crossing over**, a key part of the first stage of meiosis. Before homologous chromosome pairs separate in the first cell division, they

mitosis Process of cell division that takes place in most cells of the human body and results in a full complement of identical material in the forty-six chromosomes in each cell.

meiosis Process of cell division that forms the gametes; normally results in twenty-three chromosomes in each human egg and sperm cell rather than the full complement of forty-six.

crossing over Process during the first stage of meiosis when genetic material is exchanged between autosomes.

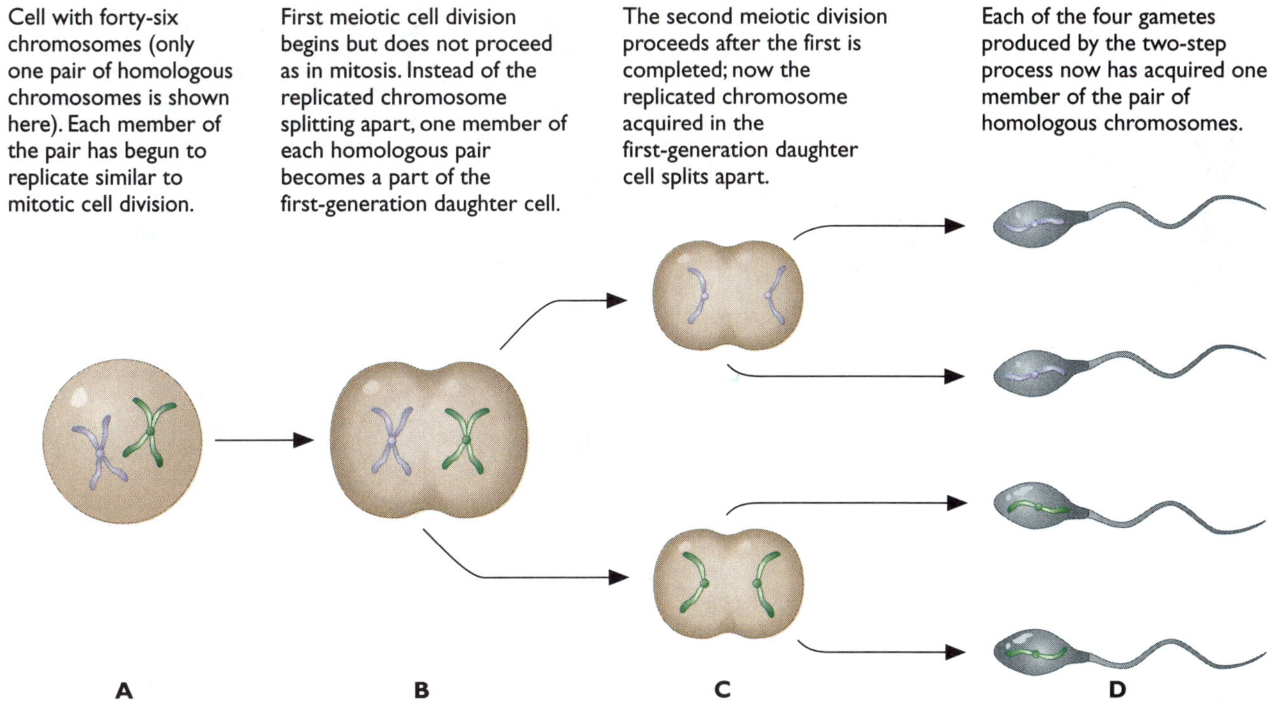

FIGURE 3.4

The Process of Meiosis for Sperm Cells

As meiosis begins (A), DNA replicates as in mitotic cell division. However, before the replicated arms split apart, one member of each pair of homologous chromosomes moves to become part of each first-generation daughter cell (B). Once the first generation of daughter cells is established, DNA replicas split as part of the second meiotic division (C). This one replica of one member pair of homologous chromosomes is contributed to each second-generation daughter cell (D). From these two successive divisions, four cells, each with twenty-three chromosomes, are produced.

mysteriously align, and segments of DNA transfer, or cross over, from one member to the other member of the pair, as shown in Figure 3.5. The genetic variability ensured by crossing over makes it virtually impossible for two individuals to have the same genetic makeup, even siblings, unless the two are identical twins.

GENE EXPRESSION

We have briefly described key structures of inheritance—nucleotides, genes, and chromosomes—and the way these are replicated in cells of the body, including gametes. But how does the genotype affect the phenotype? In other words, how does the underlying genetic blueprint promote the appearance of blue eyes, baldness, and dark skin or such complex traits as shyness, schizophrenia, and intelligent problem solving? The answer begins with the alleles, the specific form a particular gene may take.

We have already learned that each of us typically inherits two genes that code for a particular protein in the cell, one from our mother and the other from our father. These may be identical—that is, have the same allelic form—or they may differ. When both have the same allelic form, a person's genotype is said to be **homozygous** for whatever characteristic that gene affects. For example, three different alleles exist for the gene that governs blood type: A, B, and O. When both inherited alleles are A, both B, or both O, a person has a homozygous genotype for blood type. But, if an individual inherits two different alleles of the gene for blood type, let's say A and B, that person's genotype is **heterozygous**.

The consequences of a homozygous genotype are usually straightforward: the child's phenotype will be influenced by whatever characteristics are specified by that

homozygous Genotype in which two alleles of a gene are identical, thus having the same effects on a trait.

heterozygous Genotype in which two alleles of a gene are different. The effects on a trait will depend on how the two alleles interact.

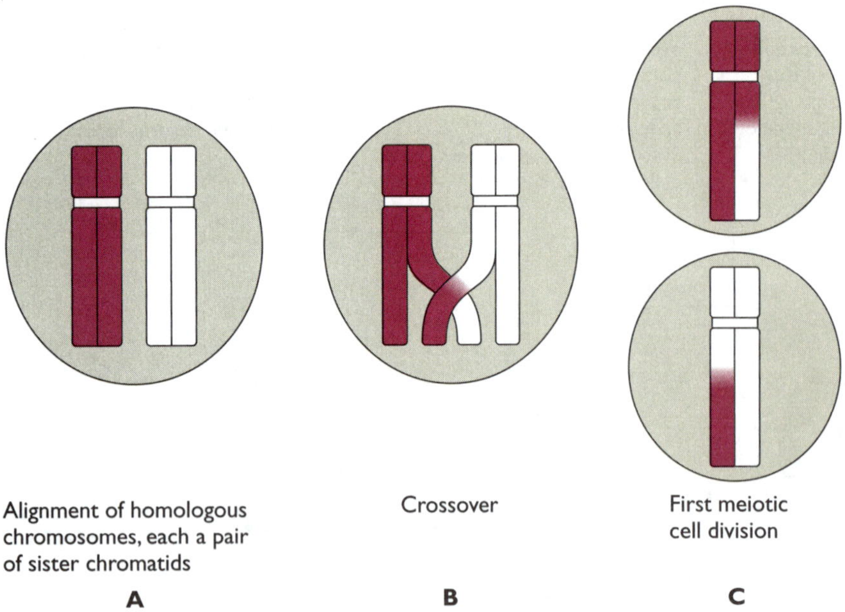

FIGURE 3.5

Crossing Over: The Exchange of Genetic Material Between Chromosomes

In the process known as crossing over, genetic material is exchanged between homologous pairs of chromosomes during the first stage of meiotic cell division. (A) Initially, autosomes that have begun DNA replication align with each other. (B) Genetic material between homologous chromosomes is exchanged. (C) One member of each homologous pair of chromosomes randomly segregates or relocates to two different regions of the parent cell, and the first generation of cell division in meiosis takes place.

particular allelic form. But the effects of a heterozygous genotype depend on how the alleles influence each other. When a child's phenotype shows the effects of only one of the two allelic forms, the one whose characteristics are observed is **dominant**; the allelic form whose influence is not evident in the phenotype is **recessive**. For example, a person who inherits both an A and an O allele for blood type will be classified as having Type A; the allele for Type A is dominant, and the allele for Type O is recessive.

Cystic fibrosis, the most common autosomal recessive disorder in Western Europe (McGinness & Kaback, 2002) and a leading cause of childhood death among Caucasian children, provides another example of a dominant-recessive relationship between alleles. The shortened lifespan typically stems from a thickening of the mucus lining the respiratory tract, which interferes with breathing. Most Caucasian children inherit a gene pair that does not include the allelic form that codes for cystic fibrosis; they have a homozygous genotype that contributes to normal development. About one in twenty-five people of Caucasian ancestry, however, has a heterozygous genotype in which one gene is normal and the other carries the genetic information that results in cystic fibrosis. The normal allele is *dominant*. Thus someone who is heterozygous for this condition can lead an ordinary, productive life. But a child of a mother and father each of whom has a heterozygous genotype might inherit two alleles coding for cystic fibrosis (see Figure 3.6). In the latter condition, the two recessive alleles are no longer masked by a normal gene; this child (about 1 in every 2,500 Caucasian children) will suffer from cystic fibrosis. Medical researchers today are actively investigating the potential for *gene therapy*, the replacement of the gene that codes for a disorder, to reduce and even eliminate the devastating consequences of cystic fibrosis and other inherited diseases (Human Genome Project Information, 2006).

In some circumstances, the child's phenotype will reflect the influence of *both* allelic forms if they differ. When the characteristics of both alleles are observed, they exhibit **codominance**. For example, a child with Type AB blood has inherited a gene for Type A blood from one parent and another gene for Type B blood from the other parent.

Table 3.1 summarizes a number of traits and characteristics associated with dominant-recessive patterns. But we must be cautious when drawing inferences about these relationships. Many traits are **polygenic**; that is, determined by several genes, sometimes located on different sets of chromosomes. For example, eye color, although largely governed by the dominant-recessive relationship between allelic forms of a single gene, is affected by other genes as well.

dominant allele Allele whose characteristics are reflected in the phenotype even when part of a heterozygous genotype. Its genetic characteristics tend to mask the characteristics of other alleles.

recessive allele Allele whose characteristics do not tend to be expressed when part of a heterozygous genotype. Its genetic characteristics tend to be masked by other alleles.

codominance Condition in which individual, unblended characteristics of two alleles are reflected in the phenotype.

polygenic Phenotypic characteristic influenced by two or more genes.

genomic imprinting Instances of genetic transmission in which the expression of a gene is determined by whether the particular allelic form has been inherited from the mother or the father.

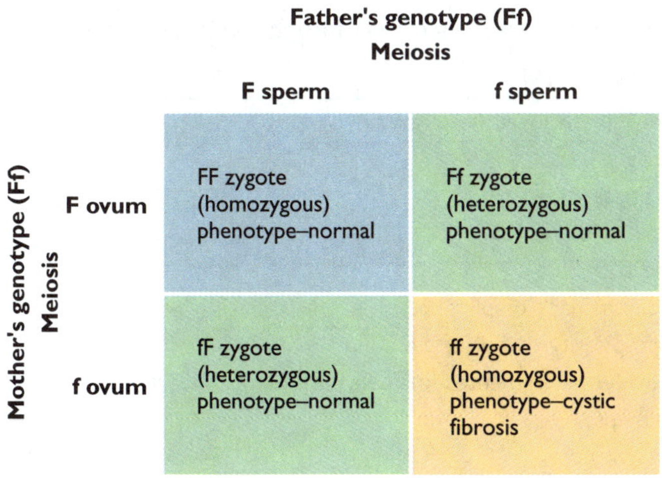

FIGURE 3.6

The Pattern of Inheritance for Cystic Fibrosis

The inheritance of cystic fibrosis is one of many traits that are influenced by a single pair of genes. In this figure, F symbolizes a normal allele and f represents the allele for cystic fibrosis. When parents with heterozygous genotype for this disease have children, their offspring may inherit a homozygous genotype with normal alleles (FF), a heterozygous genotype with one normal and one abnormal allele (Ff or fF), or a homozygous genotype with two abnormal alleles (ff). Because the normal allele dominates, children with a heterozygous genotype will not exhibit cystic fibrosis. When both alleles carry genetic information for the disease, however, cystic fibrosis will occur.

GENE FUNCTIONING AND REGULATION OF DEVELOPMENT

How do genes influence the development of a phenotype? A major new field of study called *proteomics* has emerged to attempt to answer precisely that question (Ezzell, 2000). We can give only a brief glimpse into this rapidly evolving area. Although exceptions exist, genetic information is typically conveyed from the DNA in the cell's nucleus to the organic and inorganic substances in other parts of the cell. This process is performed by *messenger ribonucleic acid*, or *mRNA*, a molecule somewhat similar to DNA; mRNA replicates some segment of the DNA. This copy is transported outside the nucleus of the cell, where it can then initiate a series of events that produce proteins to give the cell its unique ability to function. It is important to remember that the genes do not directly cause appearance, behavior, or any other phenotypic expression. Instead, our appearance and behavior are, in part, the end result of an extensive chain of biochemical processes started by the instructions provided by the DNA.

Many mysteries remain concerning exactly how genes influence development. For example, humans are believed to have between 20,000 and 25,000 *structural genes* that code for the production of proteins that govern the physiological functions of a cell (Ensembl Human, 2006; International Human Genome Sequencing Consortium, 2004). Yet structural genes account for only 1 to 2 percent of the nearly 3 billion base pairs estimated to make up the human genome (Pennisi, 2001). Some of the remaining DNA consists of other types of genes that start and stop or modify the functioning of structural genes. But large stretches of DNA are made up of repeat sequences of base pairs or of other patterns that seem to have simply replicated themselves, and their functions, if any, remain unknown.

KEY THEME
NATURE & NURTURE
RISK/RESILIENCE

Other new discoveries are continuing to be made about genes and how they influence development. For example, sometimes it matters whether a particular gene has been inherited from the mother or the father. This phenomenon, called **genomic imprinting**, is best illustrated by the *Prader-Willi* and *Angelman syndromes*, estimated to affect about 1 in 10,000 persons. Individuals with Prader-Willi syndrome display, among other physical and behavioral characteristics, short stature, obesity, and mild to moderate mental retardation. In contrast, individuals with Angelman syndrome display marionettelike disturbances in gait, epilepsy, and more severe learning difficulties, including minimal or no speech. Prader-Willi syndrome stems from the absence of a particular gene or set of genes on chromosome 15 inherited from the father and the inability of the mother's genetic material on the homologous chromosome to compensate for this loss. In contrast, Angelman syndrome arises from the absence of that same gene or set of genes inherited from

TABLE 3.1 Alleles of Genes That Display a Dominant and Recessive Pattern of Phenotypic Expression

Dominant Traits	Recessive Traits
Brown eyes	Gray, green, blue, hazel eyes
Curly hair	Straight hair
Normal hair growth	Baldness
Dark hair	Light or blond hair
Nonred hair (blond, brunette)	Red hair
Normal skin coloring	Albinism (lack of pigment)
Immunity to poison ivy	Susceptibility to poison ivy
Normal skin	Xeroderma pigmentosum (heavy freckling and skin cancers)
Thick lips	Thin lips
Roman nose	Straight nose
Earlobe free	Earlobe attached
Cheek dimples	No dimples
Extra, fused, or short digits	Normal digits
Second toe longer than big toe	Big toe longer than second toe
Double-jointedness	Normal joints
Normal color vision	Red-green colorblindness
Farsightedness	Normal vision
Normal vision	Congenital eye cataracts
Retinoblastoma (cancer of the eye)	Normal eye development
Normal hearing	Congenital deafness
Type A blood	Type O blood
Type B Blood	Type O blood
Rh-positive blood	Rh-negative blood
Normal blood clotting	Hemophilia
Normal metabolism	Phenylketonuria
Normal blood cells	Sickle cell anemia
Familial hypercholesterolemia (error of fat metabolism)	Normal cholesterol level at birth
Wilms tumor (cancer of the kidney)	Normal kidney
Huntington's disease	Normal brain and body maturation
Normal respiratory and gastrointestinal functioning	Cystic fibrosis
Normal neural and physical development	Tay-Sachs disease

the mother and the inability of the father's genetic material to compensate for the loss (Everman & Cassidy, 2000; Lombroso, 2000). Susceptibility to certain cancers, growth disorders, and some types of diabetes are also known to occur as a result of genomic imprinting.

Substantial progress in understanding genetic influences has been made in recent years. However, important questions still exist concerning the effects of the human genome on a wide range of complex human behaviors of interest to psychologists. In the section that follows, we highlight additional examples of several specific gene mutations and chromosomal disturbances that can have profound repercussions for development. Keep in mind that serious consequences associated with gene and chromosomal deviations affect a relatively small number of individuals. Nevertheless, the consequences often reverberate and extend well beyond those individuals, to their family and others within the community.

FOR • YOUR • REVIEW

- What roles do genotype and the environment play in determining a phenotype?
- What is the human genome? How do the nucleus of the cell, chromosomes and DNA, genes, and nucleotides play a role in genetic influences on development?
- How many autosomes exist in the human karyotype? Of what importance are the X and Y chromosomes?
- What is the difference between mitosis and meiosis, and what is the impact of the phenomenon of crossing over?
- How do homozygous and heterozygous genes and the presence of dominant, recessive, and codominant allelic forms account for the inheritance patterns associated with various phenotypes? What are polygenic traits?
- How do genes regulate the development of the phenotype? What is genomic imprinting?

GENE AND CHROMOSOMAL ABNORMALITIES

KEY THEME
RISK/RESILIENCE

Changes in the structure of genes, or **mutations**, introduce genetic diversity among individuals. Mutations occur surprisingly often; perhaps as many as half of all human conceptions occur with some kind of genetic or chromosomal change (Plomin et al., 2001). Most mutations are lethal, resulting in loss of the zygote through spontaneous abortion very soon after conception, often before a woman even knows she is pregnant. A small number of other mutations will have little impact on development. However, some can have enduring, often negative, consequences for an individual and his or her quality of life, consequences that may be passed on from one generation to the next. In fact, more than 5 percent of all diseases observed in individuals before the age of twenty-five are at least in part the result of some type of genetic or chromosomal anomaly (Rimoin et al., 2002). Moreover, birth defects and genetically based diseases contribute to a disproportionately high number of hospitalizations and medical expenses in the United States (Yoon et al., 1997). Globally, almost 8 million children are born with genetically linked birth defects (Christianson, Howson, & Modell, 2006). We consider here the consequences of just a few of the more than 1,400 gene and chromosome anomalies that have been identified as influencing physical and behavioral development (Peltonen & McKusick, 2001).

GENE VARIATIONS

An estimated 100,000 infants are born each year in the United States alone with some kind of problem caused by a single dominant or recessive gene. For about 20,000 of these babies, the problem is significant (Knowles, 1985). Table 3.2 lists a few of the more serious of these. In many cases, the effects are evident at birth (*congenital*), but the consequences of some are not observed until childhood or even late adulthood. We will discuss several dominant and recessive disorders to illustrate their effects on development, the interventions and treatments available for them, and the insights they provide concerning the genotype's contribution to intellectual and behavioral capacities.

mutation Sudden change in molecular structure of a gene; may occur spontaneously or be caused by an environmental event such as radiation.

TABLE 3.2 Some Inherited Gene Syndromes

Syndrome	Estimated Frequency (live births in U.S.)	Gene Located on Chromosome	Phenotype, Treatment, and Prognosis
Autosomal Recessive Syndromes			
Huntington's Disease	1 in 10,000–20,000	4	Personality changes, depression, gradual loss of motor control and memory caused by massive neuronal cell death that often begins in mid-adulthood. Thus affected individuals may transmit the disease to another generation of offspring before becoming aware of the disease. In some individuals, symptoms may begin earlier and be more severe if the dominant gene is transmitted by the father, another example of genomic imprinting.
Marfan Syndrome	1 in 10,000–20,000	15	Tall, lean, long limbed, with gaunt face (some believe Abraham Lincoln had syndrome). Frequent eye and heart defects. Cardiac failure in young adulthood common. Suicide second most common cause of death. Associated with increased paternal age.
Neurofibromatosis Type 1	1 in 3,500	17	Symptoms range from a few pale brown spots on skin to severe tumors affecting peripheral nervous system and distorting appearance. Minimal intellectual deficits in about 40% of cases. Other forms of neurofibromatosis are associated with genes located on other chromosomes.
Williams Syndrome	1 in 10,000	7	See text.
Autosomal Recessive Syndromes			
Albinism	1 in 10,000–20,000. Several forms. Most common occurs in about 1 in 15,000 African Americans, 1 in 40,000 Caucasians, but much more frequently among some Native American tribes (1 in 200 among Hopi and Navajo, 1 in 132 among San Blas Indians of Panama).	11 (also 15)	Affected individuals lack pigment *melanin*. Extreme sensitivity to sunlight and visual problems.
Cystic Fibrosis	Most common genetic disease in Caucasian populations in U.S., especially those of Northern European descent, affecting about 1 in 2,500. Less common among African American and Asian American populations.	7	Respiratory tract becomes clogged with mucus; lungs likely to become infected. Death often in young adulthood, but individuals may have children. Prognosis for females poorer than for males. Pulmonary therapy to remove mucus accumulation in lungs helps delay effects.

TABLE 3.2 Some Inherited Gene Syndromes *(continued)*

Syndrome	Estimated Frequency (live births in U.S.)	Gene Located on Chromosome	Phenotype, Treatment, and Prognosis
Autosomal Recessive Syndromes			
Galactosemia	1 in 60,000	9	Mental retardation, cataracts, cirrhosis of the liver caused by accumulation of galactose in body tissues because of absence of enzyme to convert this sugar to glucose. Heterozygous individuals have half the normal enzyme activity, enough for normal development. Galactose-free diet is only treatment, although many still display learning and behavioral problems.
Gaucher Disease	1 in 600 Ashkenazic Jews. Others, rarer forms found in all populations.	1	Enlarged spleen contributing to pain, cardiac failure, and failure to thrive. Frequent bone fractures, bruising, and bleeding. Limited treatment available.
Phenylketonuria	1 in 15,000. Somewhat higher rate of incidence in Caucasian than in Asian or African American populations.	12	See text.
Sickle Cell Disease	1 in 400 African Americans. Also frequently found in malaria-prone regions of world.	11	See text.
Tay-Sachs Disease	1 in 3,600 Ashkenazic Jews. Very rare in other populations.	15	Signs of mental retardation, blindness, deafness, and paralysis begin 1 to 6 months after birth. No treatment available. Death normally occurs by 3 or 4 years of age.
ß–Thalassemia (Cooley's anemia)	1 in 800–3,600 in populations of Greek and Italian descent. Much less frequent in other populations.	11	Severe anemia beginning within 2 to 3 months of birth, stunted growth, increased susceptibility to infections. Death usually occurs in 20s or 30s.
Sex-Linked Syndromes			
Colorblindness (red-green)	About 1 in 100 males of Caucasian descent see no red or green. About 1 in 15 Caucasian males experience some decrease in sensitivity to red or green colors.	X	If completely red-green colorblind, lack either green-sensitive or red-sensitive pigment for distinguishing these colors and see them as yellow. If decreased sensitivity to red or greens, reds are perceived as reddish browns, bright greens as tan, and olive greens as brown.
Duchenne Muscular Dystrophy	1 in 3,500 males. Most common of many different forms of muscular dystrophy. Several forms, including Duchenne, are X linked.	X	Progressive muscle weakness and muscle fiber loss. Mental retardation in about ⅓ of cases. No cure, and few live long enough to reproduce. Responsible gene located on short arm of X chromosome; appears to be massive in number of nucleotide pairs.

(continued)

TABLE 3.2 Some Inherited Gene Syndromes *(continued)*

Syndrome	Estimated Frequency (live births in U.S.)	Gene Located on Chromosome	Phenotype, Treatment, and Prognosis
Sex-Linked Syndromes			
Fragile X Syndrome	1 in 4,000 males; 1 in 8,000 females.	X	See text.
Hemophilia A	1 in 10,000 Caucasian male births for the most common form.	X	Failure of blood to clot. Several different forms; not all are sex linked. Queen Victoria of England was carrier for the most common form. Potential for bleeding to death, but administration of clot-inducing drugs and blood transfusions reduces hazard.

Sources: Adapted from Beaudet et al. (2001), Committee on Genetics (1996), Laskari, Smith, & Graham (1999), McKusick & Amberger (2002), Scriver et al. (2001).

The smiling face of this girl with Williams syndrome epitomizes one of the behavioral characteristics common to such children, a strong orientation to initiating and maintaining social relationships. Their unusual pattern of strengths and weaknesses in various areas of cognition and language as well as their inquisitiveness about other people are of considerable interest to those who study child development. Such observations support the view that some aspects of development may be domain specific rather than more broadly determined by intelligence or personality.

Williams Syndrome: Discordances in Language, Cognition, and Social Behavior About 1 in 10,000 children is born with **Williams syndrome**, caused by the deletion of a small number of genes on chromosome 7. The syndrome is autosomal dominant, although most occurrences are the result of a mutation. Children with Williams syndrome possess a distinctive set of facial features, including a short, upturned nose and full lips. They also display curvatures of the knee and hip that produce an unusual postural appearance and gait, and they often have heart and kidney abnormalities.

Individuals with Williams syndrome are typically mildly to moderately retarded. Perhaps most puzzling, however, is their strikingly uneven profile of cognitive and social strengths and weaknesses. For example, as young children they seem especially preoccupied with the faces of adults and show relatively few social inhibitions, even among strangers (Mervis, 2003). When young, they are also extremely sensitive to certain sounds, such as those made by a drill or vacuum cleaner, or the loud noises produced by fireworks or the bursting of a balloon. Their ability to acquire language is initially slow and may never reach a high level of grammatical complexity. However, children with Williams syndrome accumulate a surprisingly large vocabulary that permits them to engage in relatively sophisticated, although somewhat stereotyped, verbal interactions (Moldavsky, Lev, & Lerman-Sagie, 2001). Complementing these verbal abilities tend to be some rather uncommon abilities with respect to creating and imitating music (Levitin & Bellugi, 1998). For example, some, after having heard a musical selection only once and regardless of the language in which it may have been sung, are able to reproduce the piece with extraordinary skill. Despite these strengths, children with Williams syndrome show poor visual and spatial abilities, poor planning and problem solving, and little competence in acquiring numerical skills.

Individuals with Williams syndrome have become of special interest to developmental, cognitive, and social psychologists because of their unusual, and quite uneven, profile of intellectual and behavioral strengths and weaknesses. As is shown later in this text, many cognitive abilities may be modular; that is, they may undergo relatively specific patterns of development that are distinct from other abilities. In addition, when we discuss the nature of intelligence in later chapters, you will see that extensive debate occurs about whether it is best to view intelligence as a general capacity or as a set of more specific abilities. The observations of children with Williams syndrome are relevant to both of these issues. They show, in particular, that genes may have highly targeted consequences for intellectual, social, and other developmental capacities.

Sickle Cell Disease: A Problem Arising out of Adaptive Circumstance **Sickle cell disease** is a genetic disorder whose incidence is extremely high in many regions of West Africa and around the Mediterranean basin. Sickle cell disease is also found in about 1 out of every 400 African Americans (Ashley-Koch, Yang, & Olney, 2000) and in high numbers of Greek Americans and others whose ancestors came from regions in which malaria commonly occurs. The defect introduces a change in a single amino acid in hemoglobin, the molecule that permits the red blood cells to carry oxygen. As a result, red blood cells become crescent shaped rather than round.

Sickle-shaped cells are ineffective in transporting oxygen; they also survive for a much shorter duration than normal red blood cells, and the bone marrow has difficulty replacing them. The consequences are often anemia, jaundice, low resistance to infection, and susceptibility to stroke, severe pain, and damage to various organs when the distorted cells block small blood vessels. Blood transfusions can help to alleviate the more serious problems, and research in both Europe and the United States raises the possibility that bone marrow transplants can provide a cure (Davis & Roberts, 1996). Despite their physical limitations, elementary school children with sickle cell disease appear quite similar to unaffected peers in terms of emotional well-being and view themselves no differently in terms of social satisfaction, competencies, and feelings of depression. Still, children with sickle cell disease, especially girls, tend to be somewhat less popular in the classroom and boys somewhat less aggressive, perhaps because of their more limited energy and slower physical development (Noll et al., 1996).

About one in every twelve African Americans is a carrier of the sickle cell gene. These individuals, who possess a heterozygous genotype, have the **sickle cell trait**. They manufacture a relatively small proportion of cells with abnormal hemoglobin. Few of these individuals show symptoms of sickle cell disease; most live normal lives. But insufficient oxygen, which may occur in high-altitude regions, when flying in unpressurized airplane cabins, or after strenuous exercise, can trigger sickling of red blood cells in those who have the trait. Nevertheless, carriers of the sickle cell gene are more resistant to malaria than are individuals who have normal

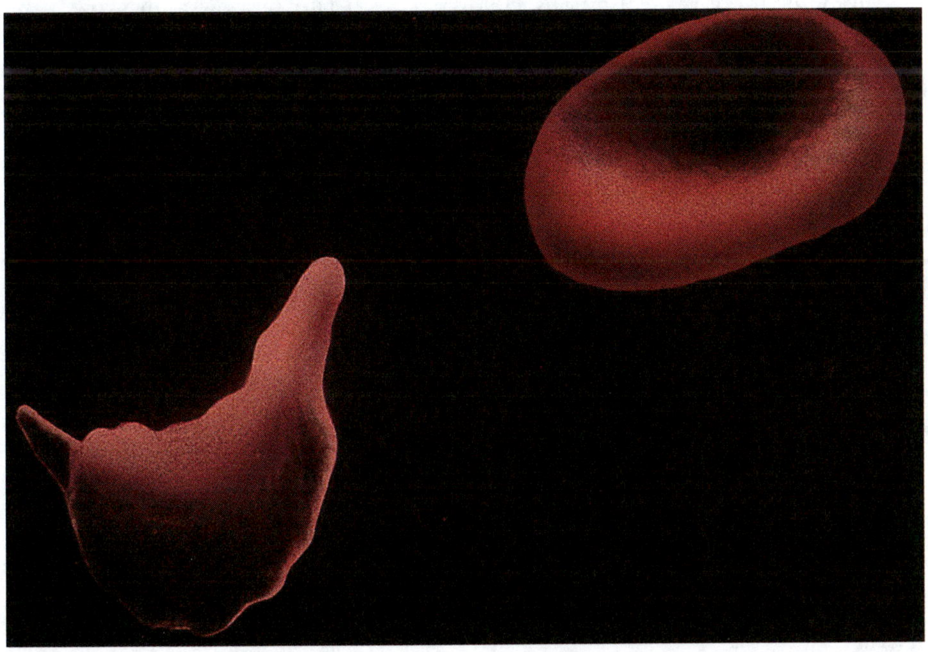

Individuals who suffer from sickle cell anemia, a genetically inherited disorder, have a large proportion of crescent-shaped red blood cells like the one shown at the bottom left. A normal red blood cell (upper right) is round and doughnut-shaped. Sickle-shaped cells are ineffective in transporting oxygen and may cause damage to various organs and pain by blocking small blood vessels.

Williams syndrome Dominant genetic disorder involving the deletion of a set of genes, which results in affected individuals' typically having a strong social orientation, good musical ability, and some unusual linguistic capabilities; accompanied by mental retardation and severe deficits in numerical and spatial ability.

sickle cell disease Genetic blood disorder common in regions of Africa and other areas where malaria is found and among descendants of the people of these regions. Abnormal blood cells carry insufficient oxygen.

sickle cell trait Symptoms shown by those possessing a heterozygous genotype for sickle cell anemia.

hemoglobin—an adaptive feature that accounts for the high incidence and persistence of the trait in regions where malaria is present.

Phenylketonuria: A Genetic Problem Modifiable by Diet **Phenylketonuria (PKU)**, a recessive metabolic disorder, provides a good illustration of how changing the child's environment—in this case, diet—can reduce a disorder's more harmful consequences. An infant with PKU appears normal at birth. However, retardation sets in soon thereafter and becomes severe by four years of age if the condition is untreated. The child may also have convulsions, hyperactivity, and other behavioral problems. In this condition, *phenylalanine*, an amino acid in milk and high-protein foods, such as meat, cannot be metabolized normally by the liver. As a result, phenylalanine and other metabolic products accumulate in the blood, and the nervous system becomes deprived of needed nutrients. Fortunately, screening using blood samples collected a day or two after birth can detect elevated levels of phenylalanine. An infant identified as having PKU can then be placed on a diet low in phenylalanine to prevent its more serious effects. Experts agree that the diet must be started relatively early, within the first few weeks after birth, and continued at least through adolescence, to ensure nearly normal mental development (Phenylketonuria, 2000). Here, then, is an excellent example illustrating that genes, by themselves, do not necessarily cause particular developmental outcomes; environmental factors interact with the genotype to yield a specific phenotype.

KEY THEME
NATURE & NURTURE

Even though the more serious consequences of phenylketonuria can be prevented, a completely normal prognosis for these children cannot be guaranteed. The diet is difficult to maintain; it requires a careful balance between excessive phenylalanine to prevent neural damage and sufficient nutrients. Weekly blood tests may be necessary to keep metabolite concentrations within an acceptable range, a regimen for which child, parents, and testing centers may be ill prepared. The bland and unappetizing diet can be a source of conflict between child and caregiver as well, creating management problems within households attempting to lead relatively normal lives (Phenylketonuria, 2000).

Even under optimal conditions, children with PKU may show some growth and intellectual deficiencies. For example, these children seem to have difficulty in planning and problem-solving tasks in which working memory or sustained attention is required to inhibit well-learned, simpler reactions in order to master new, more complex responses (Diamond et al., 1997; Ris et al., 1994). Moreover, individuals with PKU who successfully reach adulthood still need to be concerned about their diet. For example, children born to mothers who continue to display elevated levels of phenylalanine during pregnancy show increased risk for heart defects and mental retardation (Platt et al., 2000; Rouse et al., 2000). If a mother returns to a low-phenylalanine diet before or early in her pregnancy, the risks can be reduced substantially. Although dietary modifications are helpful, it remains unclear whether this intervention completely eliminates some negative consequences of PKU.

Sex-Linked Syndromes As already indicated, only a few dozen genes may be located on the Y chromosome, whereas the X chromosome carries many. This imbalance has substantial implications for a number of phenotypes said to be *sex linked* because the gene associated with them is carried only on the X chromosome. Hemophilia, red-green colorblindness, and Duchenne muscular dystrophy (see Table 3.2) are sex linked because they are inherited via specific genes on the X chromosome. Thus they occur much more frequently in males than in females.

As with genes for autosomes, those that are sex linked often have a dominant-recessive relationship. Females, who inherit two genes for sex-linked traits, one on each X chromosome, are much less likely to display the deleterious effects associated with an abnormal recessive gene than are males, who, if they inherit the damaging allele, have no second, normal allele to mask its effects. Hemophilia, a condition in

phenylketonuria (PKU) Recessive genetic disorder in which phenylalanine, an amino acid, fails to be metabolized. Unless dietary changes are made to reduce intake of phenylalanine, severe mental retardation occurs.

which blood does not clot normally, is a good example because it is nearly always associated with a defective gene on the X chromosome. Because the allele for hemophilia is recessive, daughters who inherit it typically do not exhibit hemophilia; the condition is averted by an ordinary gene on the second X chromosome that promotes normal blood clotting. A female can, however, be a carrier. If she possesses a heterozygous genotype for hemophilia, the X chromosome with the abnormal allele has a fifty-fifty chance of being transmitted to either her son or her daughter. When a son inherits the abnormal allele, he will exhibit hemophilia because the Y chromosome does not contain genetic information to counter the allele's effects. If a daughter inherits the abnormal allele, she will be a carrier who may then transmit it to her sons and daughters, as has occurred in several interrelated royal families of Europe.

Fragile X Syndrome: A Sex-Linked Contributor to Mental Retardation Geneticists have identified a structural irregularity that consists of a pinched or constricted site near the end of the long arm of the X chromosome in some individuals (see Figure 3.7). This anomaly, termed **fragile X syndrome**, may be the most frequently inherited source of mental retardation associated with a specific gene (Moldavsky et al., 2001). Males with fragile X syndrome commonly have a long, narrow face; large or prominent ears; and large testes. Cardiac defects and relaxed ligaments (permitting, for example, hyperextension of finger joints) are also frequent components of the disorder. Behavioral attributes include poor eye contact and limited responsiveness to external stimulation, as well as hand flapping, hand biting, and other unusual mannerisms, such as mimicry. Females who possess a heterozygous genotype often show, to a much lesser extent, some of the physical characteristics of the disorder. Many of these women display a normal or nearly normal level of intelligence, although, as with other sex-linked gene disorders, they are carriers for the syndrome.

FIGURE 3.7

Chromosome Illustrating Fragile X Syndrome

Fragile X syndrome is one of the most frequently occurring genetic causes of mental retardation. This photo micrograph illustrates the pinched or constricted portion of one of the pair of X chromosomes in a heterozygous female and the X chromosomes in an affected male.

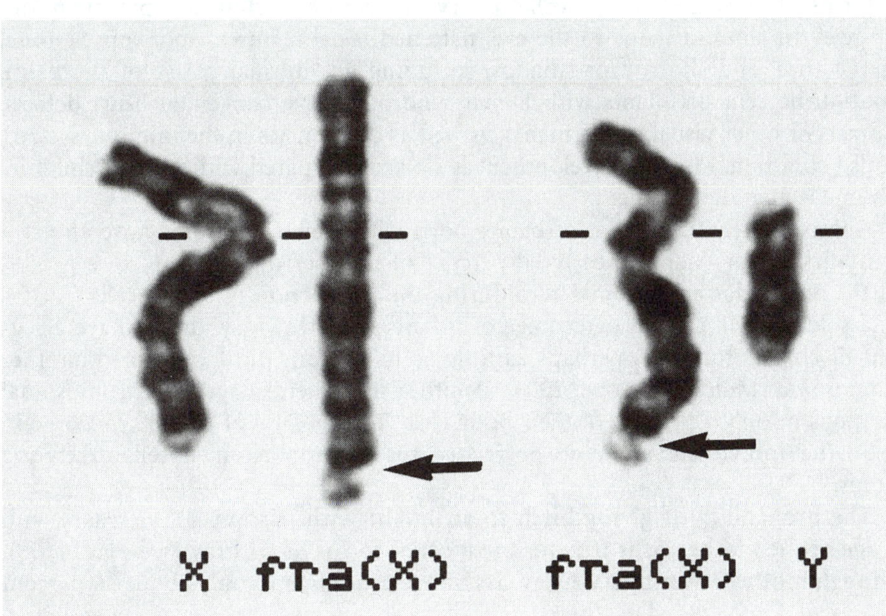

fragile X syndrome Disorder associated with a pinched region of the X chromosome; a leading genetic cause of mental retardation in males.

An unusual feature of fragile X syndrome is that its severity seems to increase as the abnormal gene is passed on from one generation to the next, a phenomenon termed *anticipation*. This progression begins when one set of three nucleotides, which repeats between 5 and 50 times in the normal gene, for some reason expands to 50 to 200 repetitions. Once this expansion begins, the gene seems to become unstable for subsequent offspring, so that more copies of the three nucleotides are spewed out, as though the replication process has difficulty turning off (Eliez & Reiss, 2000). The inheritance of this unchecked expansion is accompanied by a spectrum of learning difficulties ranging from mild to severe mental retardation. Thus the size of the abnormal segment of the gene, along with the severity of the disorder, appears to increase as it is passed from a grandfather, in whom the initial amplification may occur (even if he shows no evidence of the disorder), to a daughter (who may be minimally affected because she has an additional X chromosome to compensate for the disorder), to a grandson (who now displays full-blown fragile X syndrome).

CHROMOSOME VARIATIONS

Mutations in specific genes are only one of several sources of variation in the human genome. Occasionally, whole sections of a chromosome are deleted, duplicated, or relocated to another chromosome, or an extra chromosome is transmitted to daughter cells during cell division. When this happens, normal development is often disrupted. Perhaps as many as half of all conceptions that result in spontaneous abortion include such chromosomal abnormalities (Schreck, & Silverman, 2002; Jacobs & Hassold, 1995). If the child survives, structural aberrations of the chromosomes are often associated with mental retardation and severe physical deformations.

Human embryonic growth virtually never proceeds when a complete pair or even a member of one pair of autosomes is missing. **Trisomy**, the inheritance of an extra chromosome, also very often results in the loss of the zygote or miscarriage in early pregnancy (Jacobs & Hassold, 1995). However, three copies of chromosomes 13, 18, and 21 may be observed in surviving human newborns. Of these, trisomy 21, or Down syndrome, occurs most frequently. Even with this syndrome, however, fewer than 25 percent of conceptions survive to birth (Tolmie, 2002).

Trisomy 21 (Down Syndrome) Trisomy 21, or **Down syndrome**, is one of the most common genetic causes of mental retardation, arising in about 1 out of every 800 live births (Tolmie, 2002). Physically observable features include an epicanthal fold that gives an almond shape to the eye, flattened facial features, poor muscle tone, short stature, and short, broad hands, including an unusual crease of the palm. About 40 percent of infants with Down syndrome have congenital heart defects. Cataracts or other visual impairments, as well as deficiencies in the immune system, are also common. Physical development is slowed compared with normal children, as is intellectual development.

Approximately 95 percent of babies born with Down syndrome have an extra twenty-first chromosome. Nearly 90 percent of these errors originate in egg cells, and the remainder arise from errors during the production of sperm cells (Jacobs & Hassold, 1995). A small percentage of infants with Down syndrome have a segment of chromosome 21, perhaps as little as its bottom third, shifted to another chromosome (Moldavsky et al., 2001). Another small percentage has chromosomal deviations in only a portion of their body cells. The severity of Down syndrome in these latter individuals seems to be related to the proportion of cells exhibiting trisomy.

The probability of giving birth to an infant with trisomy 21 increases with the age of the mother, as is true for most other forms of trisomy (see Figure 3.8). Although mothers over thirty-five years of age give birth to only about 16 percent

trisomy Inheritance of an extra chromosome.

Down syndrome Disorder resulting from an extra chromosomal material on pair number twenty-one; associated with mental retardation and distinct physical features.

This 13-year-old boy with trisomy 21, or Down syndrome, has learned to read. He has made considerable progress in academic subjects as is evident from his contribution to this geography project. By being provided with an enriching environment, many with Down syndrome are able to accomplish levels of skill that permit them to engage in meaningful work and be active members of their community.

of all babies, they bear more than half of infants with Down syndrome. To explain these findings, experts have often proposed an "older egg" hypothesis. According to this view, the ova, which begin the first phases in meiosis even before the mother's own birth, change with age, either due to the passage of time or perhaps because of increased exposure to potentially hazardous biological and environmental conditions. These older egg cells, released during ovulation in the later childbearing years, are then more susceptible to chromosomal errors while undergoing the final steps of meiosis. Other researchers have proposed a

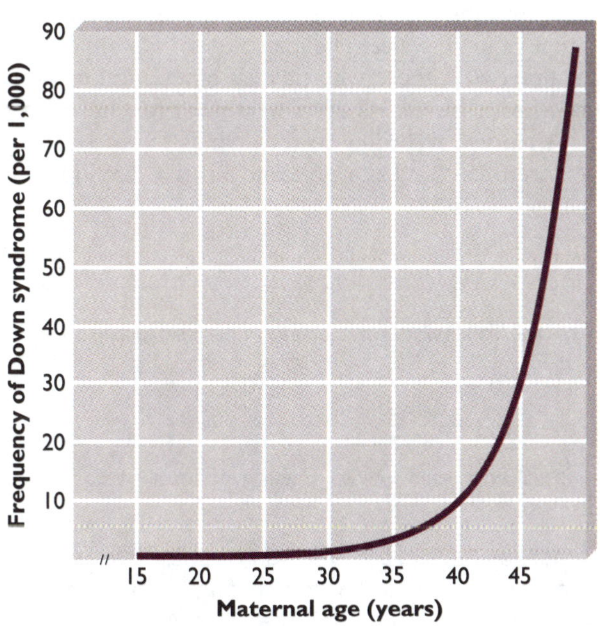

FIGURE 3.8

Relationship Between Maternal Age and the Incidence of Down Syndrome

The incidence of Down syndrome increases dramatically as a function of the mother's age. One in every 1,500 babies born to a mother age twenty-one has Down syndrome. For forty-nine-year-old mothers, the incidence is much higher: one in every ten babies has Down syndrome. Several different explanations have been offered to account for these findings.

Source: Data from Epstein (2001).

"relaxed selection" hypothesis to account for the increased frequency of Down syndrome in older mothers. According to this view, older mothers are less likely than younger mothers to spontaneously abort a zygote with trisomy 21. Still another view is that egg cells containing the extra chromosome are unlikely to be selected during ovulation. However, as they become a proportionally larger pool of the available ova over time, the possibility that one is released during ovulation increases (Tolmie, 2002). New research suggests that the age of the father is also a factor in the incidence of Down syndrome. According to an analysis of date from 70,000 births in Denmark, fathers who were age 50 years or older were three times more likely to have a Down syndrome child than fathers age 29 years or younger (Zhu et al., 2005).

KEY THEME
RISK/RESILIENCE

Thanks to better medical and physical care, the majority of individuals born with Down syndrome may be expected to live more than fifty years (Tolmie, 2002). Many show considerable proficiency in reading and writing. But we still have much to discover about Down syndrome. For example, individuals with trisomy 21 who survive beyond age forty frequently develop the abnormal brain cells and show some of the same behavioral symptoms found in adults who acquire Alzheimer's disease (Janicki & Dalton, 2000). Alzheimer's disease is characterized by memory and speech disturbances, personality changes, and increasing loss of intellectual functioning, typically in individuals between fifty and seventy-five years of age. At least one form of Alzheimer's disease is thought to be inherited, and, not surprisingly, the responsible gene appears to be located on chromosome 21.

Sex Chromosome Syndromes As we have already noted, males normally have an X and a Y sex chromosome, and females have two X chromosomes. However, variations in the number of sex chromosomes as a result of errors during meiosis can occur in humans. For example, an individual may inherit only a single X, an extra chromosome (XXX, XXY, XYY), and, on rare occasions, even pairs of extra chromosomes (for example, XXXX, XXYY, XXXY). Table 3.3 describes several of these variations in more detail.

When it was first discovered that some humans possess an extra sex chromosome, these individuals were typically thought to display intellectual deficits, along with an assortment of abnormal and socially unacceptable behaviors. For example, in the 1960s some researchers claimed that an extra Y chromosome contributed to more aggressive and antisocial behavior. Males with an XYY chromosomal makeup do tend to be taller than other males and display some learning difficulties, but they actually show a nearly normal range of intelligence. The majority of individuals who have this chromosomal pattern, along with those who possess other combinations of sex chromosome patterns, lead normal lives. What matters most for individuals put at risk by sex chromosome variations, according to research, is the presence of a stable and supportive family environment that can promote positive development (Bender et al., 1995).

KEY THEME
NATURE & NURTURE
RISK/RESILIENCE

FOR • YOUR • REVIEW

- What is the basis for each of the following genetically influenced disorders?

  Williams syndrome   Sickle cell disease and sickle cell trait

  Phenylketonuria   Fragile X syndrome

- What phenotypes are associated with each? Why is each of interest to developmental psychologists?
- What variations in the chromosomal makeup of an individual are possible? What is the most common example of chromosomal trisomy? What are examples of chromosomal variation associated with the sex chromosomes?

TABLE 3.3 Examples of Observed Sex Chromosome Syndromes

Disorder	Estimated Frequency (live births in U.S.)	Phenotype	Prognosis
45, XO (Turner syndrome)	1 in 2,500 females (more than 90% are spontaneously aborted); 80% of cases involve the absence of the paternal X chromosome.	Short stature, usually normal psychomotor development but limited development of secondary sexual characteristics. Failure to menstruate and sterility due to underdeveloped ovaries. About 50% have webbed, short neck. Near-average range of intelligence but serious deficiencies in spatial ability and directional sense.	Increased stature and sexual development, including menstruation but not fertility, can be induced through administration of estrogen and other hormones. In vitro fertilization permits carrying of child when adult.
47, XXX (Triple-X syndrome)	1 in 1,200 females; 90% have received two copies of maternal X chromosome.	Not generally distinguishable. Some evidence of delay in speech and language development, lack of coordination, poor academic performance, and immature behavior. Sexual development usually normal. Tendency for tall stature.	Many are essentially normal, but substantial proportion have language, cognitive, and social-emotional problems.
47, XXY (Klinefelter syndrome)	1 in 600 males (increased risk among older mothers); 56% received two maternal chromosomes, 44% two paternal sex chromosomes.	Tend to be tall, beardless, with feminine body contour, high-pitched voice. Some evidence for poor auditory short-term memory and difficulty with reading. Testes underdeveloped, individuals usually sterile.	Many with normal IQ, but about 20% may have occasional mild to moderate retardation.
47, XYY (XXY syndrome)	1 in 1,000 males	Above-average height, some have learning disabilities, but near-average range of intelligence.	Most lead normal lives and have offspring with a normal number of chromosomes. Higher proportion than normal incarcerated, but crimes no more violent than those of XY men.

Sources: Adapted from Beaudet et al. (2001), Jacobs & Hassold (1995), McGinniss & Kaback (2002), McKusick & Amberger (2002), Allanson & Graham (2002).

GENETIC COUNSELING

Advances in detecting gene and chromosomal defects, as well as in understanding the biochemical and metabolic consequences of various inherited disorders, have led to a rapidly expanding medical and guidance specialty called **genetic counseling**. Obtaining a family history to summarize the occurrence of various diseases among ancestors and other relatives is usually the first step. If warranted, *parental* **genetic screening** may be carried out. For example, chromosomal abnormalities, as well as dominant and recessive genes associated with all of the disorders listed in Tables 3.2 and 3.3 (and many more not listed in these tables), can be detected through parental screening. Thus genetic counselors can provide prospective parents with estimates of the likelihood of bearing a child with a specific problem, although parental screening, of course, does not identify new mutations that may arise in offspring. Prospective parents can then use this information to decide whether, for example, adoption or other new reproductive technologies, such as those discussed in the chapter titled "The Prenatal Period and Birth," may be a better choice than bearing their own children.

genetic counseling Medical and counseling specialty concerned with determining and communicating the likelihood that prospective parents will give birth to a baby with a genetic disorder.

genetic screening Systematic search using a variety of tests to detect developmental risk due to genetic anomalies.

There are many reasons for carrying out such tests. For example, prenatal testing is often recommended for women who are older than thirty-five because of their increased risk for Down syndrome; when a genetic disorder has been reported in the family history; if parents are members of an ethnic group at risk for a specific genetic disease; or if delayed or unusual development of the fetus occurs during pregnancy (Cuniff & Committee on Genetics, 2004). The finding of a serious inherited disorder may lead to a decision to terminate the pregnancy if religious and ethical values allow such a choice. However, prenatal screening tests, along with neonatal screening carried out shortly after birth, can serve another important purpose: that of suggesting therapy and treatment designed to prevent or minimize the more devastating consequences of some metabolic disorders (Erbe & Levy, 2002).

PRENATAL DIAGNOSIS

Procedures now exist that can be performed prenatally to detect hundreds of genetically and environmentally induced defects in fetal development. Some of these procedures provide unequivocal answers about the presence or absence of a problem. Other, often less invasive, procedures provide estimates of increased likelihood of the presence of some defect. If they are suggestive of a developmental disability, they are followed by more conclusive diagnostic tests. One of the best-known definitive tests is **amniocentesis**, in which a small amount of amniotic fluid is withdrawn via a syringe inserted (under the guidance of an ultrasound image) in the woman's abdominal wall. Cells in the amniotic fluid are extracted and submitted to biochemical and chromosomal examination (see Figure 3.9). Amniocentesis is an especially effective

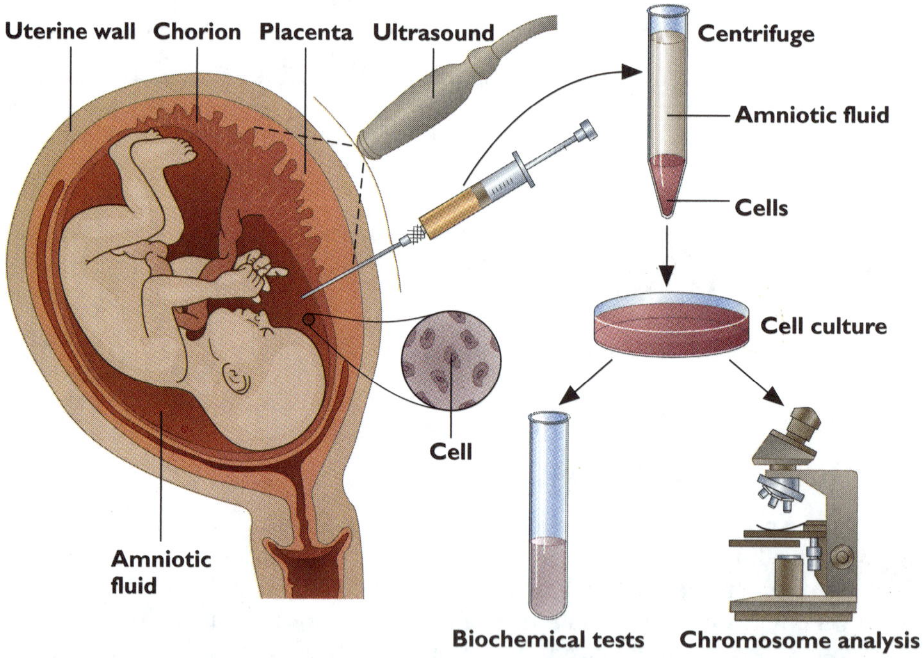

FIGURE 3.9
The Process of Amniocentesis
In this prenatal screening procedure, a needle is inserted into the amniotic fluid surrounding the fetus. A small amount is withdrawn, and cells shed by the fetus are separated from the fluid by centrifuge. The cells are cultured and submitted to various biochemical and other tests to determine whether chromosomal, genetic, or other developmental defects exist.

Source: Adapted from Knowles (1985).

amniocentesis Method of sampling the fluid surrounding the developing fetus through insertion of a needle; used to diagnose fetal genetic and developmental disorders.

procedure for detecting chromosomal variations, and it provides information about some metabolic problems as well. The test is usually performed between the thirteenth and eighteenth weeks of pregnancy. However, researchers are studying whether it can be safely carried out a few weeks earlier. Even when amniocentesis is performed later in pregnancy, the possibility of some increased risk exists from infections and spontaneous abortion (Elias, Simpson, & Shulman, 2002; Tongsong et al., 1998).

Another test that provides much the same information as amniocentesis but that can be carried out somewhat earlier in pregnancy (between ten and twelve weeks) is **chorionic villus sampling**. In this diagnostic procedure, a small sample of hairlike projections (*villi*) from the chorion, the outer wall of the membrane in which the fetus develops and that attaches to the woman's uterus, is removed by suction through a thin tube inserted through the vagina and cervix or, in some cases, through the abdominal wall. Information gained at this earlier time can reduce uncertainty and anxiety about the possibility of a developmental disability (Caccia et al., 1991). However, chorionic villus sampling, in contrast to amniocentesis, does not provide information about possible neural tube defects, the procedure is somewhat more difficult to carry out unless performed by skilled technicians, and some researchers report a slightly increased risk of miscarriage and limb malformations (Elias, Simpson, & Shulman, 2002; Hsieh et al., 1995).

In **fetal blood sampling**, blood is withdrawn directly from the umbilical cord of the fetus for biochemical and chromosomal examination. This particular procedure, normally carried out from about the eighteenth week of pregnancy onward, permits the detection of various chromosomal and genetic errors, and is especially useful in evaluating disorders associated with the blood. Although relatively safe, the procedure does appear to be slightly more risky than other invasive tests (Elias, Simpson, & Shulman, 2002).

Because of the possible increase in risk and their relatively high cost, amniocentesis, chorionic villus sampling, and fetal blood sampling are normally performed only when there is some reason to believe that fetal abnormalities may occur. Other, less

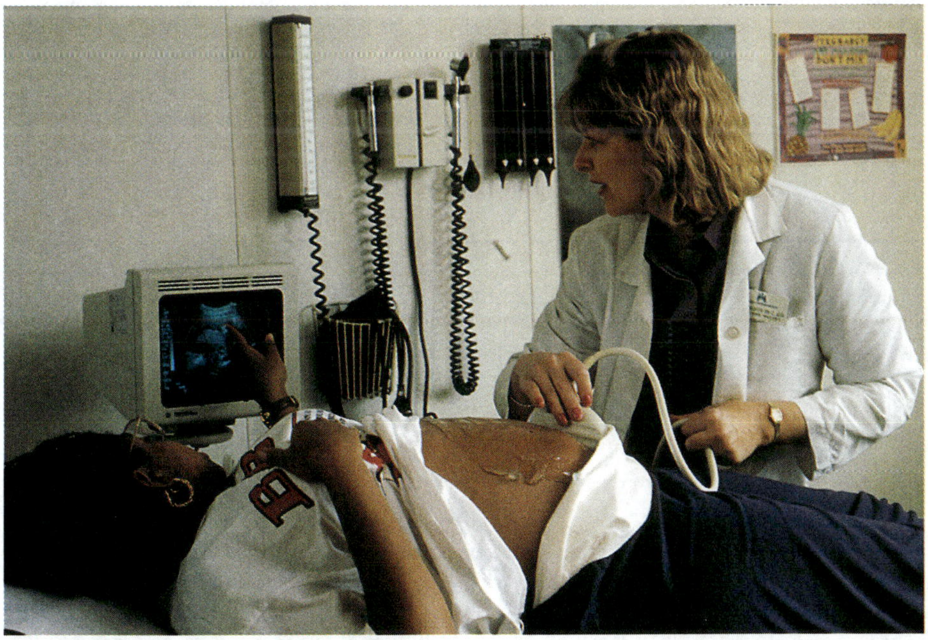

The use of ultrasound to provide a visual image of the developing fetus has become a common practice in medical facilities around the world. Prospective parents are often thrilled by this opportunity to obtain a glimpse of the fetus. The use of ultrasound can also be important for obtaining a more accurate assessment of the age of the fetus. It provides assistance in carrying out other tests to determine if development is proceeding normally and, in some case, permits surgical procedures designed to improve the likelihood of a healthy newborn.

chorionic villus sampling Method of sampling fetal chorionic cells; used to diagnose embryonic genetic and developmental disorders.

fetal blood sampling Method of withdrawing blood from the umbilical cord of the fetus; used to diagnose genetic disorders, especially those that affect the blood.

invasive procedures also exist. For example, several types of **maternal blood screening** tests, such as the *alpha fetoprotein test* and the more extensive and accurate *triple screen test,* can be carried out at around fifteen to twenty weeks of gestational age to provide evidence of increased risk for Down syndrome, neural tube defects, and certain kidney and other problems. Scientists have also begun to examine fragments of fetal DNA that circulate in the mother's blood stream for indicators of genetic problems (Kaiser, 2005). Certainly the most widespread of the noninvasive diagnostic procedures, however, is **ultrasonography**, often called *ultrasound.* Ultrasound is now used routinely in many countries to help determine whether fetal growth is proceeding normally. Sound waves, reflecting at different rates from tissues of varying density, are represented on video monitors and even printed to form a picture of the fetus. The picture can reveal such problems as microcephaly (small head size), cardiac malformations, cleft lip and palate, and other physical disabilities (Dooley, 1999; Grandjean et al., 1999). And in combination with a blood test, ultrasonography can be used to detect Down syndrome as early as 11 weeks prenatally (Malone et al., 2005).

Ultrasonography is widely used to assist in carrying out other prenatal diagnostic tests, to verify the age of the fetus (interpretation of maternal and fetal blood tests are often highly dependent on an accurate assessment of age), and to monitor lifesaving operations that may on rare occasions be performed on the fetus within the womb (Harrison, 1996). Although not universally recommended in the United States because of its limits as a diagnostic tool, ultrasound has become a popular tool for informing specialists and parents about the course of prenatal development.

Ethical and Social Issues

The major prenatal diagnostic tests are summarized in Table 3.4. At the same time that they offer important information, their availability also raises a number of ethical and social issues. Note, for example, that many of these tests are carried out relatively late in pregnancy, and prospective parents may have to wait several weeks longer before they learn the results. This waiting period can create enormous apprehension, especially among those who have reason to believe that a problem

Table 3.4 Prenatal Screening Tests

Prenatal Test	When Usually Administered (gestational age)	Typical Waiting Period for Results	Other Comments
Amniocentesis	13–18 weeks	About 2 weeks	Can be administered in weeks 11–14 but normally is not because the available supply of amniotic fluid is more limited.
Chorionic Villus Sampling	10–12 weeks	24–48 hours	Possibly a slightly greater risk than associated with amniocentesis, including limb deformities.
Fetal Blood Sampling	18 weeks or later	24–48 hours	Possibly somewhat greater risk than associated with amniocentesis.
Maternal Blood Screening	15–20 weeks	One week	Not definitive but provides information about increased risk for Down syndrome and neural tube and some metabolic defects.
Ultrasonography	About 6 weeks and later	None	Provides picture of growing fetus. Not definitive for identifying many disorders. Little evidence of any risk. Often used to accompany other test procedures.

may exist. Moreover, some expectant women feel almost coerced into using these technological advances to learn more about their pregnancies even when there is little to suggest a genetic problem (Henifin, 1993; Wertz & Fletcher, 1993). Some would say these tests are overused. Yet a physician who fails to at least offer prenatal diagnosis in circumstances in which it can be informative runs legal risks for incompetent obstetric practice (Wertz & Fletcher, 1998).

Prospective parents have choices regarding whether or not to have such tests performed. In many cases those about to become parents would like to know about possible problems, if for no other reason than to effectively prepare for and address them even before birth. In fact, a substantial number of expectant women who learn that the fetus carries some abnormality still elect to continue the pregnancy, especially if the problem is less severe and possibilities exist for prenatal or postnatal therapy (Pride et al., 1993). On the other hand, in some countries such tests may not be available. And, even when they are, not everyone takes advantage of them. For example, women of African American or Hispanic ethnic identity, at least in some areas of the United States, are far less likely to undergo prenatal testing than Caucasian or Asian women (Kuppermann, Gates, & Washington, 1996).

Another issue concerns access to the results of these tests. For example, might insurance companies or other health organizations drop coverage if they become aware of results that indicate expensive medical treatment in the future? And, finally, there is the issue of sex preselection.

Controversy: Thinking It Over

Should Sex Preselection Be Permitted?

At one time in medieval Germany, couples placed a hammer under their bed if they wished to conceive a boy; in Denmark they chose a pair of scissors for that location if they desired a girl (Golden, 1998). In China and India, where abortion is more widely practiced, evidence already exists that sex selection has been exercised; a disproportionate number of males have been born in these countries in recent years. As a consequence, China and India, as well as some other countries, have passed laws forbidding the use of prenatal tests solely to determine the sex of the fetus and to influence the course of pregnancy when the fetus is male or female (Wertz & Fletcher, 1998).

What Is the Controversy?

Although many adamantly oppose the use of a procedure that leads to the selective abortion of a healthy fetus on the basis of sex, *preselection*, the effort to tilt the probability toward having either a male or a female conception, may be far less objectionable. In fact, in 1996 40 percent of individuals in the United States already supported the unrestricted availability of sex preselection if an effective procedure became available (Wertz & Fletcher, 1998).

We are, in fact, at the point at which this possibility exists. Previous efforts have focused on the timing or technique involved in procreation to increase conception of a male or female. These attempts have generally failed to provide a reliable method of conceiving a boy or a girl. However, in 1998 a new, far more effective procedure was reported, at least for promoting the conception of females (Fackelmann, 1998). This new procedure is based on the difference in the amount of DNA found in the X and Y chromosomes. With the help of a dye that attaches to the DNA and glows when exposed to the light of a laser, sperm cells carrying an X chromosome, which contain about 2.8 percent more DNA than sperm cells carrying a Y chromosome, shine more brightly. By introducing lopsided distributions of cells carrying the X chromosome into the uterus during periods when a woman might become pregnant, these specialists claim to have attained markedly higher numbers of successful pregnancies resulting in girls, a procedure that could also be expected to be successful in

maternal blood screening Tests performed on a woman's blood to determine whether the fetus she is carrying has an increased risk for some types of chromosomal and metabolic disorders.

ultrasonography Method of using sound wave reflections to obtain a representation of the developing fetus; used to estimate gestational age and detect fetal physical abnormalities.

skewing the odds toward boys. Other techniques associated with assisted reproduction (see the chapter titled "The Prenatal Period and Birth") can also be used to increase the likelihood of, or even virtually guarantee, a boy or a girl.

What Are the Opposing Arguments?

Proponents of sex preselection claim that parents in most Western countries do not show a strong preference for having a boy or a girl first; but family balancing, having one boy and one girl, is frequently seen as the ideal family complement (Silver, 1998). Having the opportunity to rear children of both sexes is also often viewed as a desirable experience for parents. For other couples, sex preselection may serve to prevent a sex-linked genetic disease from being passed on to their offspring.

Opponents of sex preselection are concerned that, even in countries in which no strong preference exists for rearing either boys or girls, the practice supports the potential for sexual bias or increased sexism, a potential that may become more visible once a choice is available to prospective parents (Fackelmann, 1998). A second argument is that determining a conception on the basis of sex is but the first step in the emergence of a "preference mentality." This mentality can ultimately lead to preselection on the basis of other desired traits and attributes, intended to create "perfect" children and essentially treating children as a commodity (Darnovsky, 2004). Thus the potential for discrimination against those who do not meet the ethnic, cultural, or community ideal may increase substantially.

What Answers Exist? What Questions Remain?

The American College of Obstetricians and Gynecologists (2002) currently supports the notion that sex preselection is ethical and justified in cases in which it will prevent sex-linked genetic disorders in offspring. In the United States, the public also seems to be in support of this position. Opinion is much more divided, however, with respect to sex preselection for other purposes. Recent advertisements have appeared in the United States that target some ethnic groups and emphasize, "Choose the sex of your next baby" and "Desire a son?" Declarations in favor of sex preselection for the purpose of family balancing and even for selecting the sex of a child in a first pregnancy have been made by individuals associated with organizations such as the American Society for Reproductive Medicine, established to deal with these kinds of issues (Kolata, 2001; Sachs, 2001). Perhaps to help address the controversy, psychologists need to conduct research on the following questions in order for the public to gauge whether regulations should be considered: To what extent do preferences for boys versus girls exist? What social and cultural factors promote them? Does raising offspring of both sexes in a balanced family lead to different outcomes for children? Does it result in more successful and effective parenting? Given advances in sex preselection, are we nearing a time when professionals will be recruited to help create "designer" children with respect to other traits? Could such efforts actually contribute to harmful effects by lessening genetic diversity in humans? What other kinds of psychological research might be conducted to help answer whether a need exists for regulation of sex and other kinds of trait preselection?

behavior genetics Study of how characteristics and behaviors of individuals, such as intelligence and personality, are influenced by the interaction between genotype and experience.

heritability Proportion of variability in the phenotype that is estimated to be accounted for by genetic influences within a known environmental range.

identical twins Two individuals who originate from a single zygote (one egg fertilized by one sperm), which early in cell division separates to form two separate cell masses. Also called *monozygotic twins*.

fraternal twins Siblings who share the same womb at the same time but originate from two different eggs fertilized by two different sperm cells. Also called *dizygotic twins*.

FOR • YOUR • REVIEW

- What are the major diagnostic tests for prenatal development? What are their limitations and their advantages?
- What ethical and social issues emerge from the use of prenatal diagnostic tests?
- What is sex preselection, and what are arguments for and against its practice?

DEVELOPMENTAL AND BEHAVIORAL GENETICS

As our previous discussion indicates, chromosomal errors and particular genes can have drastic, often devastating, effects on physical, intellectual, and social development. Yet similarities observed among relatives—the wry sense of humor in a mother and daughter or the musical talent of a grandfather and his grandchildren—are not likely to be linked to a single, isolated gene. Might these attributes and behaviors reflect a contribution from many genes? Or are these phenotypic resemblances primarily the result of experiences shared by kin? Researchers engaged in **behavior genetics** attempt to learn to what extent the diversity of human traits, abilities, and behaviors stems from combinations of genes versus experience. Behavioral geneticists are helping to show that the entire realm of human behavior is influenced by nature and nurture in a variety of complex, sometimes surprising, ways (Plomin et al., 2001; Rutter et al., 1999a, 1999b).

KEY THEME
NATURE & NURTURE

THE METHODS OF BEHAVIORAL GENETICISTS

Behavior geneticists have available to them a number of different methods. A major goal of many of these studies is to provide an estimate of the heritability of various traits and behaviors. **Heritability** refers to the extent to which the variability in a sample of individuals on some characteristic, such as shyness or assertiveness, is a result of genetic differences among those individuals. Of course, the variability that is not accounted for by the genotype must then be a result of the environmental circumstances those individuals have had the opportunity to experience. Thus, although research on heritability was initially designed to provide answers about the contribution of the genotype, it also helps to shed light on the role of experience in development (Plomin et al., 2001).

Selective Breeding Studies When studying the fruit fly or the mouse, behavior geneticists can use *selective breeding* experiments to learn whether certain phenotypic expressions can be increased or decreased in offspring. Members of a species that display a specific attribute are bred to each other, usually over many generations. If the attribute is inherited, subsequent generations of offspring can be expected to display it more and more frequently or strongly. For example, after thirty generations of selective breeding in which either highly active mice were bred only to each other or mice showing only a low level of activity were bred to each other, researchers observed no overlap in terms of the amount of activity displayed by members of the two groups (DeFries, Gervais, & Thomas, 1978). Those bred for high activity were thirty times more active; they would run the equivalent of a football field during two three-minute test periods compared to the other mice, which would not even run the equivalent of a first down (Plomin et al., 2001). Selective breeding in various species of animals has revealed genetic contributions to many different attributes, including aggressiveness, emotionality, maze learning, and sex drive (Plomin et al., 2001).

Family Resemblance Studies Selective breeding, of course, cannot be used to examine human behavior. Instead, behavior geneticists gain information about hereditary and environmental influences on human behavior by examining resemblances among family members. These studies investigate similarities among *identical* and *fraternal twins*, siblings, and other members of families who are genetically different from one another to varying degrees. **Identical**, or *monozygotic*, **twins** come from the same zygote: a single egg fertilized by a single sperm. A cell division early in development creates two separate embryos from this zygote, and the twins are genetically identical. **Fraternal**, or *dizygotic*, **twins** come from two different zygotes, each created from a separate egg and a separate sperm. Fraternal twins are no more genetically similar than siblings born at different times, each averaging about half of their genes in common. However, they do share some of their prenatal environment

If you were given their names, would you be able to tell these twins apart once they moved and were no longer seated side by side? Virtually everyone would have a great deal of difficulty with such an assignment unless they could constantly keep an eye on at least one of them as he moved about. Because their genetic makeup is the same, identical or monozygotic twins typically look very much alike and display very similar traits and behaviors as can be seen here. Twin studies provide important information about the contributions of heredity and environment to development.

and, by virtue of being the same age, may share other experiences to a greater extent than siblings born at different times.

If identical twins resemble each other more than fraternal twins in intelligence or shyness, one potential explanation for this similarity is their common genotype. The degree of resemblance is usually estimated from one of two statistical measures: concordance rate or correlation coefficient. The **concordance rate** is the percentage of pairs of twins in which both members display a specific attribute when one twin is identified as having it. Concordance rate is used when measuring characteristics that are either present or absent, such as schizophrenia or depression. If both members of every twin pair have a particular trait, the concordance rate will be 100 percent. If only one member of every pair of twins has some particular trait and the other does not, the concordance rate will be 0 percent. When attributes vary on a continuous scale, such that they can be measured in terms of amount or degree, resemblances are estimated from a *correlation coefficient.* This statistic helps to determine whether variables such as intelligence or shyness, which have some quantitative value, are more similar for identical than for fraternal twins or more similar among siblings than among unrelated children.

Adoption Studies Identical twins may resemble each other more than fraternal twins do because identical twins share the same genotype. However, another explanation for any greater resemblance may be that identical twins share more similar experiences. One way to potentially reduce the effects of similarity in experience is to study biologically related family members who have been adopted or reared apart from each other. If an attribute is influenced by genetic factors, children should still resemble their biological siblings, parents, or other family members more than their adoptive relatives. On the other hand, if the environment is the primary determinant of an attribute, separated children can be expected to resemble their adoptive parents or other adopted siblings more closely than their biological parents or siblings.

Adoption studies, just as in the case of twin studies, pose many challenges for evaluating hereditary and environmental influences (Rutter et al., 1999a). For example, in the past, adopted children were often placed in a home similar to that of their biological parents. Under these circumstances, the relative contributions of family environment and heredity to an attribute are extremely difficult to distinguish. In addition, information on the biological family has not always been readily available in the case of adoption. Nevertheless, a number of large-scale investigations of genotype-environment effects involving twins, adopted children, siblings, half-siblings, and unrelated children in blended families are currently under way (Bouchard, 1997; Plomin, DeFries, & Fulker, 1988; Reiss et al., 2000). These and other studies are just beginning to illuminate the complex interactions and correlations that exist between heredity and experience, intricate relationships that we must consider more fully as well.

Conceptualizing the Interaction Between Genotype and Environment

KEY THEME
NATURE & NURTURE

How a genotype influences development depends to a great extent on the environment. Likewise, how an environment affects behavior often depends on the geno type. These conditional relationships are the basis for complex *interactions* between heredity and experience; the influence of one on the other is not constant across individuals or environmental circumstances, or even during different periods of development (Collins et al., 2000; Rutter & Silberg, 2002).

Range of Reaction The interactive relationship between genotype and environment can be conceptualized in terms of the concept of **range of reaction,** the idea that, depending on environmental conditions, a broad range of phenotypes may be expressed as a function of the genotype (Turkheimer, Goldsmith, & Gottesman,

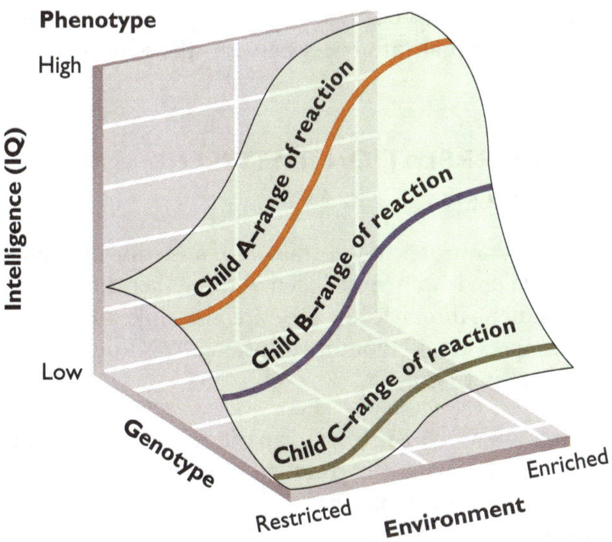

FIGURE 3.10

The Concept of Range of Reaction for Intellectual Performance

As the product of the interaction between genotype and the environment, the phenotype for any attribute shows a broad range of reaction. For example, the intelligence score of any child, even one who is born with the potential for high intellectual ability, is likely to be limited when the environment is severely restricted. An enriched environment will benefit all children, although perhaps those with greater intellectual potential (Child A or B) more than a child with less intellectual potential (Child C).

Source: Adapted from Turkheimer, Goldsmith, & Gottesmane (1995).

1995). Figure 3.10 illustrates this concept for intellectual performance. Consider a child with Down syndrome (represented, for example, by child C in Figure 3.10). Transferring this child from an unstimulating institutional setting (a restricted environment) and engaging him in supportive learning activities (more enriched environments) very likely will help him to achieve a much higher level of cognitive functioning (Feuerstein, Rand, & Rynders, 1988). The performances of children with other genotypes (as represented by child A and child B in Figure 3.10) can be affected, too, perhaps even more greatly, depending on whether they are reared in deprived or stimulating conditions.

Canalization The principle of **canalization**, a kind of "channeling" of development, suggests yet another way to think about genotype-environment relationships. A highly canalized attribute is one influenced primarily by the genotype; experiential factors can have an impact on the course of development, but only under extreme conditions (Waddington, 1971). Imagine an emerging capacity as something like water flowing through terrain in which channels of varying depths have been cut. The channels help to steer the flow in one of several possible directions. However, the channels are so deeply cut by the genotype that only extreme environmental pressures can change the course of some phenotypes.

For example, various aspects of early motor development tend to emerge on a fairly regular basis during infancy. Presumably the genotype has carved a relatively deep course for their appearance. However, as you will soon learn, the emergence of early motor skills is not completely protected from disturbances in experience. Other aspects of early development, including some aspects of language acquisition and certain social behaviors, such as smiling, may also be highly canalized.

Gilbert Gottlieb (1991) has extended these ideas, proposing that the channeling process may come about not only through the genotype but also from early experiential influences. Exposure to certain types of stimulation during a critical period may steer development just as hereditary information can. As an example, Gottlieb looks to the early experiences of mallard ducklings. If prevented from hearing their own vocalizations and instead exposed to a chicken's call early in development, the ducklings later show a preference for the chicken's call rather than for sounds produced by members of their own species.

Gottlieb (2000) has argued that the genome itself is not isolated from the influences of the environment. A classic example is evident in some reptiles—the temperature during incubation determines the sex of the offspring, a feature you might have thought was determined solely by genetics. As we learn more about how genetic information is transcribed into proteins, we may discover other ways in which events both within and outside the organism change how the genetic transcription

concordance rate Percentage of pairs of twins in which both members have a specific trait identified in one twin.

range of reaction Range of phenotypic differences possible as a result of different environments interacting with a specific genotype.

canalization Concept that the development of some attributes is governed primarily by the genotype and that only extreme environmental conditions will alter the phenotypic pattern for these attributes.

process takes place. In other words, we may begin to more fully appreciate that development is the outcome of bidirectional influences between the genotype and levels of experience.

Key Theme
Nature & Nurture

Conceptualizing the Correlation Between Genotype and Environment

The task of determining what proportion of various traits derives from the genes and what proportion comes from the environment is laden with further difficulties. Not only do genotype and environment interact, but they are also linked or *correlated* with each other in several complex ways (Plomin & Rutter, 1998; Rutter et al., 1999a; Scarr, 1992; Scarr & McCartney, 1983).

Passive Links One correlation between genotype and experience arises from the tendency for parents to establish a child-rearing environment in harmony with their own interests and preferences. Assume, for example, that sociability has some genetic basis. Sociable parents may transmit this orientation to their children either through their genes, through the social environment created in their home, or through both mechanisms. This kind of correlation between genotype and environment is labeled as *passive*, because it has been created for the child by the parents.

Evocative Links Another type of correlation between genotype and environment, termed *evocative* or *reactive*, occurs when aspects of the environment, particularly other people, support or encourage behaviors that may have a genetic component; that is, other people's behavior occurs in response to or is evoked by the child's genotype. For example, an active preschooler is likely to prompt teachers to provide large-muscle toys to dissipate some of her energy. A ten-year-old's eagerness to read may encourage a teacher to offer additional opportunities for learning. A sociable child is more likely to attract the attention of peers than a shy or passive child. Thus attributes that have a biological basis are likely to evoke patterns of behavior from others that complement the child's genetic tendencies.

Active, Niche-Picking Links In yet another type of correlation between genotype and environment, termed *active*, the child may be attracted by and eagerly seek out experiences more compatible with his or her genotype. Bright children could prefer to exercise their intellect and to play with peers who are also bright. The athletic child may find little pleasure in practicing the piano but spend countless hours skateboarding and playing basketball. Thus any genetic basis for various traits and activities influences the kind of environment a child attempts to create and experience. Sandra Scarr and Kathleen McCartney (1983) described this kind of linkage as **niche picking,** to emphasize that children and adults selectively construct and engage environments responsive to their genetic orientations.

Scarr and McCartney (1983; Scarr, 1992) believe that the strength of passive, evocative, and active correlations between genotype and environment changes with development. The experiences infants receive are often determined for them by their caregivers. Thus initial correlations between genotype and environment are more likely to be influenced by passive factors. As children gain greater independence and control of their environment, however, others around them are likely to notice and support their individual differences, and niche picking becomes an increasingly important factor as children have the opportunity to choose their own interests and activities.

An important implication of these changing relationships is that children within the same family may become less similar to one another as they grow older and become freer of the common environment their parents provide. Older siblings can select niches befitting their individual genotypes more easily than can younger children. When Sandra Scarr and Richard Weinberg (1977) studied adopted children, they obtained support for this prediction. During early and

niche picking Tendency to actively select an environment compatible with a genotype.

middle childhood, adopted but biologically unrelated children in the same family showed similarities in intelligence, personality, and other traits. Perhaps these resemblances came about both as a result of adoption procedures that encouraged the placement of children in homes somewhat like their biological home and from the common family environment the adopted children now shared. As adopted siblings neared the end of adolescence, however, they no longer exhibited similarities in intelligence, personality, or other traits; the passive influence of the common environment established by the adoptive parents had become supplanted by active niche picking.

The notion of niche picking provides us with an even more startling prediction. When identical twins are reared apart, they may, with increasing age, actually come to resemble each other more, and perhaps as much as identical twins reared together! This greater correspondence would emerge as others react to their similar behaviors and as opportunities arise for the twins to make more choices. In the Minnesota Study of Twins Reared Apart, pairs of identical twins, separated as infants and having no interactions with each other until well into adulthood, revealed remarkable similarities not only in gait, posture, gestures, and such habits as straightening eyeglasses, but also in storytelling skill, spontaneous giggling, phobic tendencies, hobbies, and interests, resemblances rarely observed between fraternal twins reared apart and usually not considered to have a strong genetic basis (Bouchard, 1984; Bouchard et al., 1990; Lykken et al., 1992). Furthermore, identical twins reared apart showed as high a correlation on many intellectual tasks and personality variables as those reared together. These results suggest that niche picking can be a powerful means of maintaining behaviors supported by the genotype.

Niche picking, the tendency for an individual to seek out and become attracted to activities that are compatible with his or her genotype, is an important aspect of the interaction between nature and nurture. Because of her talent at painting, this young person may be drawn to a future career or avocation involving art. She is also likely to pursue additional training and opportunities to become even more skilled as an artist.

HEREDITARY AND ENVIRONMENTAL INFLUENCES ON BEHAVIOR

Research findings involving studies of family resemblances, adopted children, and identical and fraternal twins can be, and often are, interpreted in many different ways precisely because of the complex interactions and relationships that genotype and environment share in shaping behavior. These interpretations sometimes have powerful implications for intervention and social policy (Baumrind, 1993; Jackson, 1993; Scarr, 1992, 1993). Should families or communities, for example, expend resources for educational and mental health efforts if a substantial biological basis for behavior exists? Or does this kind of question, concerned with *how much* heredity contributes to variations in the human phenotype, fail to recognize that educational and social opportunities are essential to maximize competencies, even where genetic contributions are considerable?

KEY THEME
NATURE & NURTURE

Consider the following: about 90 percent of the variability in height among individuals reared in a typical community is believed to be a consequence of genetic factors. However, even though height is strongly influenced by the genotype, its average increase among young adult males in Japan since the end of World War II has been about three and a half inches (Angoff, 1988). Clearly, changes in the environment have had a profound impact on a characteristic that receives a significant contribution from the genes. Environmental factors can surely be expected to have an impact on other inherited characteristics as well (Collins et al., 2000; Rutter, 2002).

Intelligence Despite their many limitations, most studies have relied on IQ tests to measure the contributions of genotype and environment to intelligence. Table 3.5 summarizes correlations on IQ test scores among individuals who share different genetic relationships with one another. Environmental contributions are

Table 3.5 Correlation in IQ as a Function of Genetically Related and Unrelated Individuals Living Together and Apart

Relationship	Raised	Observed
Monozygotic twins	Together	0.85
Monozygotic twins	Apart	0.74
Dizygotic twins	Together	0.59
Siblings	Together	0.46
Siblings	Apart	0.24
Midparent/child	Together	0.50
Single parent/child	Together	0.41
Single parent/child	Apart	0.24
Adopting parent/child	Together	0.20

Note: The data are based on a meta-analysis of 212 IQ correlations reported in various studies. In the case of twins and siblings, the heritability estimates are increased by an unspecified amount because of the common evironmental contribution from the prenatal environment shared simultaneously by twins and sequentially by siblings. "Midparent" refers to the mean of the IQ scores of both parents.

Source: From B. Devlin, S. E. Feinberg, D. P. Resnick, & K. Roeder (Eds.), *Intelligence, genes, and success: Scientists respond to* The Bell Curve, pp. 45–70. Copyright © 1997. Used by permission of Springer-Verlag and the author.

revealed by findings that individuals reared together show somewhat higher correlations for intelligence scores than those with the same genetic relationship reared apart. Nevertheless, the impact of the genotype on intelligence is also evident. The correlations for IQ increase as the similarity in genotypes rises.

We can make sense of several additional findings by considering correlations between genotype and environment. For example, IQ scores for younger adopted children reared together are positively correlated (about .20), as indicated in Table 3.5. However, they are much closer to .00 for adolescents. Moreover, intelligence has been found to be highly correlated in infancy and early childhood for *both* identical and fraternal twins and, with increasing age, to become *even greater* for identical twins but to decline to the level reported in Table 3.5 for fraternal (dizygotic) twins (Fischbein, 1981; Wilson, 1986). These findings probably reflect the impact of passive links (the similar rearing environment created by the parents) on intelligence early in childhood and more opportunity for niche picking later in development.

KEY THEME
NATURE & NURTURE

Identical twins, however, do not always become more similar as they grow older. As twins who have been reared together become older, fraternal, and to some extent identical, twins become more dissimilar on many aspects of intelligence tests (McCartney, Harris, & Bernieri, 1990). Perhaps they actively attempt to establish a *unique* niche in the family and community, efforts that may also be encouraged by parents of the twins (Schachter, 1982).

Despite the evidence that the heritability of intelligence is high, a classic investigation by Marie Skodak and Harold Skeels (1949) illustrates the substantial impact experience still has. One hundred children born to mentally retarded mothers, most of whom were from low socioeconomic backgrounds, were adopted before six months of age into homes that were economically and educationally well above average. These children displayed above-average intelligence throughout childhood and adolescence, and substantially higher IQs than their biological parents, an outcome reflecting the contribution of environmental factors. Nevertheless, the children's IQs were still correlated with those of their biological mothers, indicating a hereditary contribution to these scores as well.

Temperament and Personality Genetic influences typically account for 20 to 50 percent of the variability in personality differences within a population (Plomin et al., 2001; Saudino, 1997). **Temperament**, an early-appearing constellation of personality traits, has been of particular interest in terms of possible genetic influences. A number of broad qualities characterize temperament. One of these is *sociability*, the tendency to be shy or inhibited and somewhat fearful of new experiences versus outgoing and uninhibited, characteristics that are likely precursors to introversion and extroversion, respectively, in older children and adults. Another trait is *emotionality*, the ease with which an individual becomes distressed, upset, or angry and the intensity with which these emotions are expressed. A third trait is *activity*, as evidenced by the tempo and vigor with which behaviors are performed. Identical twins consistently show higher correlations on these characteristics (typically between .40 and .60) than fraternal twins (typically between .10 and .30), suggesting an inherited component (Emde et al., 1992; Goldsmith, Buss, & Lemery, 1997; Robinson et al., 1992). Perhaps inherited differences in physiological reactivity underlie these differences. For example, with respect to sociability, young children who remain aloof and are reluctant to play with novel toys display increased heart rate and muscle tension in unfamiliar situations compared with children who are more outgoing and spontaneous (Kagan, 1994).

KEY THEME
NATURE & NURTURE

Does the environment also play some important role in temperament and other personality differences? Studies comparing the personalities of unrelated children in the same household report that the correlations are fairly low and often approach zero, especially in later childhood and adolescence (Plomin et al., 2001). *Shared environment*, the kinds of experiences children in a home or community have in common and that are assumed to foster similarity in children within the same family, simply does not have much effect for many aspects of personality. In contrast, *nonshared environment*, the experiences unique to individual children as they interact with parents, peers, and others, can play a powerful role in development, one that tends to make children in the family different rather than similar (Goldsmith, Buss, & Lemery, 1997; Plomin et al., 2001).

How can this be? One possibility is that peers, as well as genes, play a pivotal role in determining the differences in personality and social adjustment displayed by children reared in the same family (Collins et al., 2000; Harris, 2000; Vandell, 2000). Perhaps, too, parents actually do treat their children differently, even though they claim not to. Although mothers and fathers typically do not report much differential treatment, siblings frequently express another take on the matter. Observations of how parents interact with their sons and daughters seem to provide some ammunition in support of the children's perceptions. For example, the toys with which boys and girls are encouraged to play may differ considerably in some families (Lytton & Romney, 1991). And siblings do sometimes perceive that they are being treated unequally by their parents, a factor that can be related to a decline in the quality of their relationships with one another (Kowal & Kramer, 1997).

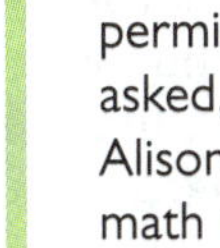

RESEARCH APPLIED TO PARENTING

Treating Siblings Fairly

The girls woke up the next morning and started to prepare for school. As Keesha came down the stairs for breakfast, she asked, "Mom, can I have Stacy over after school? We want to practice gymnastics. Can she come over? Please?" Michelle answered without hesitating, "Of course, dear. Just be sure she has her parents' permission, OK?" Alison heard this exchange as she came out of her room and asked, "Can I have a friend over, too?" Michelle stiffened a little. She knew that Alison needed time for her homework after school, especially in light of what her math teacher had said the night before. "Alison, I'd love for you to have a friend over, but we really have to focus on your homework. After school today, let's lay out a plan so you can get your work done and then have some fun. But today is not a good day to have someone over." "That is so unfair!" Alison snapped back angrily. "How come she gets to have a friend over and I can't?" "Oh, boy!" thought Michelle to herself. "I'm going to have to figure out a way to handle this one!"

temperament Stable, early-appearing constellation of individual personality attributes believed to have a hereditary basis; includes sociability, emotionality, and activity level.

Should parents treat their children differently or in the same way? The answer is far from clear. For example, historically, identical twins were often dressed alike and treated almost as if they were one and the same individual. Today parents are advised to recognize their twins' individuality by encouraging them to gain unique experiences and to "pick out" their own niche in the family and community. As a consequence, they may be treated differently by parents and others. Other siblings, of course, share only about half of their genes and are quite distinct in physical appearance, personality, intellectual ability, and other characteristics. Parents may react to these differences in each child's characteristics. When is differential treatment a good thing? When is it a source of conflict? Research indicates that parents might consider some of these points when confronting this matter.

1. *Expect siblings to kindle different reactions from others.* Because all children, with the exception of identical twins, are born with different genotypes, they are likely to evoke distinctive kinds of responses from family members, teachers, peers, and others. These responses can, in turn, serve to magnify existing differences in the behaviors of siblings.
2. *Assume that siblings will actively search out ways to be different from one another.* Children very likely will engage in niche picking to set themselves apart from others within the family—a process called *sibling deidentification* (Feinberg & Hetherington, 2000). Whether it stems from biology or experience, the opportunity to find one's niche within the family, as well as the larger community, is an important aspect of development for all children.
3. *Anticipate that siblings will experience family events in different ways and will need to be treated differently in some circumstances.* Siblings within the same family—by virtue of their birth order, spacing, and unique events such as an illness, the death of a grandparent, or a move to a new neighborhood—will necessarily receive unique experiences because of their specific developmental status. In fact, distinct socialization practices for children of different ages is the norm, because treatment by caregivers could otherwise be developmentally inappropriate. Younger children typically need more nurturance and care; older children, increased independence and greater responsibility. Caregivers recognize that differential treatment is sometimes necessary (Dunn & McGuire, 1994). Children as young as five years of age notice these differences. Younger children would prefer being the oldest in the family; that is, in their eyes, older siblings seem to have higher status (McHale et al., 1995). Furthermore, children and adolescents perceive greater differential treatment of same-sex siblings than of brother-sister dyads by parents (McHale et al., 2000). Stress within the family may magnify these differences (Crouter, McHale, & Tucker, 1999). Children do not always find differential treatment to be unfair. In fact, when children experience differential treatment on the part of their parents but feel it is justified—that is, equitable even though not equal—sibling relationships are generally positive (Kowal & Kramer, 1997).
4. *Treat siblings impartially when possible and appropriate.* Impartial treatment of siblings by parents, to the extent that it is appropriate, is associated with less conflict among siblings and between children and their parents (Brody & Stoneman, 1994; McHale et al., 1995). In other words, parents who maintain a balance between socialization practices that are equitable within the limits of age-appropriate differences have children who interact effectively and in constructive ways with others, including their siblings. Differences in parenting arising from the individual needs of children can have positive consequences, but only as long as these differences do not reflect a form of parental "favoritism."

Parents with more than one child often want to treat each one of them equally but need to fine-tune their parenting efforts to the needs and age-appropriate activities of individual children. Fine motor skills demonstrated by the older sibling may permit her to color or carry out other activities that are beyond the capacity of her younger sibling, who, as shown here, has found her own way to keep busy. By providing individual support and avoiding "favoritism," parents seem to help siblings learn to appreciate others' abilities.

KEY THEME
NATURE & NURTURE

Behavioral and Personality Disorders Table 3.6 summarizes the concordance rate for identical and fraternal twins for a variety of behavioral and personality disorders. None of these findings indicates 100 percent concordance even in identical twins, despite the identity of their genetic makeup. Thus environmental factors play an important role in the manifestation of each of these problems. In fact, concordance measures for *conduct disorders* (fighting and aggressive behavior, failure to accept parental discipline) in both identical and fraternal twins are relatively high, suggesting that environmental factors contribute substantially to their appearance in both groups.

KEY THEME
RISK/RESILIENCE

The genetic contribution to *bipolar disorder*, a disorder characterized by rapid and wide mood swings between feverish activity and withdrawn, depressed behaviors, appears to be substantial. Family studies reveal that children of a parent with bipolar disorder are at far greater risk for displaying the illness than children without such a parent. Research on adoptees provides further evidence that genotype plays a role; the risk for adopted children whose biological parents have the illness is about three times greater than for adopted children whose biological parents do not have it (Rutter et al., 1999b). Recent work on *autism*, a disorder characterized by a lack of social communication (and more fully described later in this text), also reveals an ample hereditary contribution (Rutter et al., 1999b).

Table 3.6 The Genetic Basis of Selected Behavioral and Personality Disorders: Twin Data

Evidence for the genetic basics of behavioral and personality disorders is often supported by studies of twins. For these disorders, the likelihood that both members of a pair will display the disorder, if exhibited by one, is greater when the pair are identical twins rather than fraternal twins. However, environmental factors may contribute to high concordance rates for both identical and fraternal twins, as is likely for conduct disorders.

Twin Concordances	Identical Twins	Fraternal Twins
Conduct disorder	.85	.70
Bipolar disorder	.65	.20
Autism	.65	.10
Unipolar depression	.45	.20
Alcoholism—males	.40	.20
Schizophrenia	.40	.10
Alcoholism—females	.30	.25

Source: Data from Plomin (1994).

Alcoholism, although not linked to a single gene, shows a modest genetic component. In fact, more recent studies now put the concordance rate at over .50 for identical twins and over .30 for fraternal twins who are male, somewhat higher than shown in Table 3.6 for the general population (Kendler et al., 1997; McGue, 1999). *Schizophrenia*, a form of psychopathology that includes disturbances in thoughts and emotions, such as delusions and hallucinations, also exhibits some genetic contribution. As the biological relationship to someone diagnosed as having schizophrenia increases, an individual's risk for the same diagnosis rises. When one twin has schizophrenia, the other twin is about three times more likely to display schizophrenia if identical than if fraternal. Adoption studies further confirm a role for the genotype: schizophrenia is far more prevalent among adopted children who are the biological offspring of a schizophrenic parent than among those of a nonschizophrenic parent (Gottesman & Shields, 1982). At the present time, no single gene seems to be responsible for the findings; instead, polygenic contributions are more likely.

Recent behavioral genetic research raises the possibility that the *same* genes could have some role in different manifestations of psychopathology, including anxiety and depression or aggressive behavior and antisocial behavior (Eley, 1997). These "general" genes, in other words, may contribute to wide variations in characteristics and behaviors that are often problematic for the individual.

Other Characteristics A host of other characteristics, including empathy, reading disabilities, sexual orientation, obesity, onset of pubertal development, susceptibility to various illnesses such as heart disease and cancer, and a propensity to be physically aggressive, have a genetic linkage (Brendgen et al., 2005; Castles et al., 1999; LeVay & Hamer, 1994; Mustanski et al., 2004; Pèrusse & Chagnon, 1997; Plomin, Owen, & McGuffin, 1994). In addition, how individuals perceive their family environment also appears to be influenced by the genotype (Hur & Bouchard, 1995; Plomin et al., 1994), as does the way caregivers parent and how children adjust to that parenting (Neiderhiser et al., 1999). The influence of the genotype affects the entire breadth of human behavior, although the precise mechanisms by which it does so remain to be revealed.

FOR • YOUR • REVIEW

- What methods do behavior geneticists use to investigate the extent to which behavior is influenced by combinations of genes and experiences? Why are identical and fraternal twins—as well as adopted children—important in work designed to evaluate the heritability of behavior?
- How do concordance rate and correlation differ as measures in investigating genetic and environmental contributions to development?
- How are conceptualizations of the interaction between genotype and environment advanced by notions of range of reaction and canalization?
- How do passive, evocative, and active niche-picking correlations between the genotype and experience differ from one another?
- To what extent are behavioral phenotypes, such as intelligence, personality and temperament, personality disorders, and other characteristics, influenced by heredity?
- To what extent are shared and nonshared environments important in accounting for similarities and differences in children's behavior?
- Why might parents treat siblings differently, and how do children interpret these differential treatments?

CHAPTER RECAP

Summary of Developmental Themes

NATURE & NURTURE

How do nature and nurture interact in development?

The phenotype, the observable behaviors and characteristics of an individual, is the product of a complex interaction between genotype and environment. Environment includes biological contexts, such as the foods we eat, but more frequently we consider it to be the experiences provided by caregivers and others. The relationship between genotype and environment is complicated by their interaction with each other and by passive, reactive, and niche-picking correlations. As a consequence, experiential factors are tightly interwoven with genotype to produce the range and variety of behaviors and characteristics an individual displays. Both genotype and environment are indispensable to development.

Researchers recognize the child's active efforts to seek out environments that support and maintain behavioral orientations and preferences influenced by hereditary factors. As the child achieves greater control over the environment, he or she has increasing opportunities to find a niche. In other words, behaviors, activities, and skills that the child displays not only are a consequence of imposed social and physical experiences, but also reflect the selective efforts of the child to discover interesting, challenging, and supportive environments. Inherited and environmentally imposed influences may be met with eager support or active resistance to determine each child's unique life history.

RISK/RESILIENCE

What factors promote risk or resilience in development?

Individual differences are pervasive in intellectual, temperamental, and a host of other cognitive, social, and emotional aspects of development. Hereditary and environmental factors determine these differences. Alleles of genes contribute to the wide range of physical, cognitive, emotional, and social adaptations displayed by individuals. These individual differences are not produced solely by genes; they are also the product of a rich medley of physical, social, and cultural contexts in which each individual matures. A distinctive combination of genes and experiences promotes both the risk and the resilience we observe in human abilities and behavior.

Chapter Review

PRINCIPLES OF HEREDITARY TRANSMISSION

What roles do genotype and the environment play in determining a phenotype?

The genetic endowment inherited by an individual is the *genotype*. A *phenotype* refers to the traits and behaviors displayed by an individual. The phenotype is the result of the complex interactions between genotype and the experiences provided in the environment.

What is the human genome? How do the nucleus of the cell, chromosomes and DNA, genes, and nucleotides play a role in genetic influences on development?

The entire inventory of nucleotide base pairs that compose the genes and chromosomes in humans is called the *human genome*. The structures associated with the principles of heredity must be examined at several different levels. An individual's body is composed of trillions of cells. Twenty-three pairs of *chromosomes* (a total of forty-six), consisting of *deoxyribonucleic acid*, or *DNA*, are located in the nucleus of most cells in the human body. The central unit of hereditary information is the *gene*, a segment of a chromosome. *Nucleotides* are two different sets of pairs of repeating molecules that form the biochemical building blocks for the genes and the basic structure of the chromosomes.

How many autosomes exist in the human karyotype? Of what importance are the X and Y chromosomes?

The human *karyotype* consists of twenty-two pairs of *autosomes*. Males and females differ in the composition of the twenty-third pair of chromsomes. In females, both members of the pair normally are *X chromosomes*. In males, one is normally an X chromosome, and the other is a *Y chromosome*.

What is the difference between mitosis and meiosis, and what is the impact of the phenomenon of crossing over?

Cell division in the human body takes place in two different ways. *Mitosis* is the process of cell division by which the forty-six chromosomes are duplicated in the body cells. The *gametes*, or sperm and egg cells, are formed by *meiosis*, a process of a cell division that results in twenty-three chromosomes in each of these cells. The random process by which a member of each of the twenty-three pairs of chromosomes is selected for the gametes, combined with *crossing over* during meiosis, ensures that every individual, with the exception of identical twins, has a unique hereditary blueprint. Once the gametes combine, the fertilized egg cell is called a *zygote*.

How do homozygous and heterozygous genes and the presence of dominant, recessive, and codominant allelic forms account for the inheritance patterns associated with various phenotypes? What are polygenic traits?

Variants of genes on the twenty-three pairs of chromosomes, or *alleles*, often interact with one another to establish probabilities of inheritance for particular traits characteristics. A *dominant* allele will reflect its characteristics even when it is part of a *heterozygous genotype*, in which two alleles of a gene are different. A *recessive* allele is expressed only when it is part of a *homozygous* genotype, in which two alleles of a gene are the same. *Codominance* refers to the condition in which unblended characteristics of two alleles are reflected in the phenotype. Many human traits, however, are *polygenic*; that is, they are influenced by two or more genes.

How do genes regulate the development of the phenotype? What is genomic imprinting?

Genetic information coded in DNA is sent by mRNA to regions outside of the cell nucleus. This process sets in motion the production of proteins that result in different cell functions. *Genomic imprinting* refers to instances of genetic transmission in which the parental source, mother or father, determines gene expression.

GENE AND CHROMOSOMAL ABNORMALITIES

What is the basis for each of the following genetically influenced disorders?

Williams syndrome	Sickle cell disease and sickle cell trait
Phenylketonuria	Fragile X syndrome

What phenotypes are associated with each? Why is each of interest to developmental psychologists?

Mutations, or spontaneous changes in the molecular structures of genes, can have wide-ranging influences on development, from almost no consequence to death. Some genetic or chromosomal problems are passed from one generation to the next. *Williams syndrome* is caused by deletion of a small number of genes on chromosome 7. The phenotypic features include a short, upturned nose; full lips; and curvature of the knee and hips. Children with Williams syndrome display uneven developmental profiles; they often have a large vocabulary, unusual skill in music, and great attention to social stimuli, but poor spatial, numerical, and problem-solving skills.

Phenylketonuria (PKU) results from the presence of two recessive genes for the trait. Untreated children with PKU may exhibit convulsions, severe mental retardation, and hyperactivity. Early intervention with a modified diet can prevent the symptoms from manifesting themselves.

Sickle cell disease results from the presence of two recessive genes that cause the red blood cells to become less efficient in transporting oxygen. The result can be anemia, jaundice, infection, and vulnerability to stroke, organ damage, and pain. An individual with *sickle cell trait* has only one of the recessive alleles but may still show symptoms under conditions of low oxygen. The presence of this allele provides protection against malaria.

Fragile X syndrome results from constriction in the X chromosome and is said to be sex linked. The phenotype will typically have a long, narrow face, large ears, and large testes. Fragile X is the most frequently inherited source of mental retardation associated with a single gene.

What variations in the chromosomal makeup of an individual are possible? What is the most common example of chromosomal trisomy? What are examples of chromosomal variation associated with the sex chromosomes?

Presence of only one chromosome on the autosomes does not eventuate in human growth and development, but the presence of extra chromosomal material, or *trisomy*, can occur. The most common disorder contributing to mental retardation is trisomy 21 (Down syndrome), associated with inheritance of an extra chromosome. Variations in number of sex chromosomes also occur but do not always contribute to behavioral or other developmental problems, especially if a supportive environment is available. Some of the patterns that can occur are XO, XXX, and XYY.

GENETIC COUNSELING

What are the major diagnostic tests for prenatal development? What are their limitations and their advantages?

Genetic counseling provides prospective parents with information on the probability of having children affected by birth defects. *Genetic screening* involves the use of systematic tests on parents or fetus to locate risks due to genetics. *Amniocentesis* is effective for diagnosing chromosomal and metabolic disorders but carries some risk of infection and spontaneous abortion. *Chorionic villus sampling* can be done earlier in pregnancy but cannot diagnose neural tube defects, requires more medical skill, and is associated with a slightly elevated risk of miscarriage. *Fetal blood sampling* can detect chromosomal and genetic errors and blood disorders but carries somewhat elevated risks. *Maternal blood screening* can detect neural tube defects and Down syndrome. *Ultrasonography* can detect many physical abnormalities but cannot detect many other developmental disorders.

What ethical and social issues emerge from the use of prenatal diagnostic tests?

Controversial ethical and social issues include whether to have the tests in the first place, decisions made once the results of the tests are known, and the opportunity to carry out sex preselection.

What is sex preselection, and what are arguments for and against its practice?

Sex preselection refers to techniques that increase the likelihood that either a girl or a boy will be conceived. This technique allows for family balancing, may lead to a desirable parenting experience, and may prevent passing on sex-linked traits. Opponents argue that the practice may support sex bias and may lead to a "preference mentality" whereby children would be selected for other traits as well.

Developmental and Behavioral Genetics

What methods do behavior geneticists use to investigate the extent to which behavior is influenced by combinations of genes and experiences? Why are identical and fraternal twins—as well as adopted children—important in work designed to evaluate the heritability of behavior?

Behavior genetics is a method of attempting to determine the relative contribution of heredity and environment to traits and behaviors that are often the result of combinations of genes. To determine contributions from combinations of genes, behavioral geneticists frequently engage in selective breeding with lower organisms or compare findings among various family members, such as *identical twins, fraternal twins*, siblings, and adopted children, because these groups differ in the extent to which they share a common genotype. *Heritability* refers to the extent to which the variability on some characteristic in a sample of individuals is accounted for by genetic differences among those individuals.

How do concordance rate and correlation differ as measures in investigating genetic and environmental contributions to development?

The *concordance rate* refers to the percentage of pairs of twins who display the same characteristics. The correlation coefficient is a statistic that measures the degree of relationship between pairs of individuals of varying levels of biological relationship to one another.

How are conceptualizations of the interaction between genotype and environment advanced by notions of range of reaction and canalization?

The concept of *range of reaction* highlights the fact that a trait or behavior influenced by a person's genotype may be unique to a particular kind of environment. The principle of *canalization* emphasizes that some traits and characteristics are highly determined by the genotype or, conversely, that some environments may have a powerful influence on how these are displayed.

How do passive, evocative, and active niche-picking correlations between the genotype and experience differ from one another?

Correlations between genotype and environment may be *passive*, in that caregivers with specific genotypes are likely to provide environments supportive of their children's genotypes; *evocative*, in that parents, peers, and others are likely to react in ways that accommodate genetic inclinations; and *active*, in that children may attempt to find or create environments that support their individual genetic propensities; that is, engage in *niche picking*.

To what extent are behavorial phenotypes, such as intelligence, personality and temperament, personality disorders, and other characteristics, influenced by heredity?

Intelligence, *temperament* and other personality variables, social adjustment and behavioral disorders, and other traits and characteristics often display considerable heritability, suggesting that the genotype contributes substantially to variability among children for many aspects of development.

To what extent are shared and nonshared environments important in accounting for similarities and differences in children's behavior?

The shared environment provided by the family increases similarity among siblings, often to a limited extent. However, the nonshared environment that children within the same family experience contributes substantially to individual differences among children.

Why might parents treat siblings differently, and how do children interpret these differential treatments?

Different inherited characteristic among children may lead parents to treat them differently. Siblings perceive differential treatment from their parents, but when the differential treatment is interpreted as equitable, even if not equal, positive relationships between siblings are fostered.

Key Terms and Concepts

allele (p. 71)
amniocentesis (p. 90)
autosome (p. 73)
behavior genetics (p. 94)
canalization (p. 97)
chorionic villus sampling (p. 91)
chromosome (p. 71)
codominance (p. 76)
concordance rate (p. 97)
crossing over (p. 74)
deoxyribonucleic acid (DNA) (p. 71)
dominant allele (p. 76)
Down syndrome (p. 86)
fetal blood sampling (p. 91)
fragile X syndrome (p. 85)
fraternal twins (p. 94)
gamete (p. 71)
gene (p. 71)
genetic counseling (p. 89)
genetic screening (p. 89)
genomic imprinting (p. 76)
genotype (p. 71)
heritability (p. 94)
heterozygous (p. 75)
homozygous (p. 75)
human genome (p. 71)
identical twins (p. 94)
karyotype (p. 73)
maternal blood screening (p. 93)
meiosis (p. 74)
mitosis (p. 74)
mutation (p. 79)
niche picking (p. 98)
nucleotide (p. 71)
phenotype (p. 71)
phenylketonuria (PKU) (p. 85)
polygenic (p. 76)
range of reaction (p. 97)
recessive allele (p. 76)
sickle cell disease (p. 83)
sickle cell trait (p. 83)
temperament (p. 101)
trisomy (p. 86)
ultrasonography (p. 93)
Williams syndrome (p. 83)
X chromosome (p. 73)
Y chromosome (p. 73)
zygote (p. 73)

The Prenatal Period and Birth

4

She was expecting. It was great news. But this time her concerns outweighed the joy. Carole was already caring for two little ones, both under the age of five, and also working full time to provide income to help ends meet. Her job paid only a little more than minimum wage—never enough, even when added to her husband's paycheck. However, neither she nor her husband had gone to college. Nor did either have the kinds of skills to obtain a really high-paying job. It would be a struggle to provide for another child.

Although only four weeks into her pregnancy, Carole knew the embryo was undergoing rapid developmental changes and would continue to do so for many more weeks. She avoided alcohol as soon as she learned of her pregnancy. She had stopped smoking even before her first child was born. But was there enough money for prenatal care? Did she need to make modifications in her diet or adjustments in her work to ensure that her unborn child would have a healthy start? Would her persistent anxieties take a toll as well? She wanted the best for this new addition to the family. But she wasn't completely sure if she would be able to make that happen.

Key Themes in The Prenatal Period and Birth

Nature & Nurture How do nature and nurture interact during prenatal development and birth?

Sociocultural Influence How does the sociocultural context influence prenatal development and birth?

Continuity/Discontinuity Is development before and after birth continuous or discontinuous?

Risk/Resilience What factors promote risk or resilience during prenatal development and birth?

Most women experience both pride and apprehension when they learn they are pregnant. Those feelings are often influenced by a multitude of social and cultural views and ideas about pregnancy. Although societies differ enormously in their specific beliefs, anthropologists report that expectant women around the world are often urged to avoid certain activities and to carry out various rituals for the sake of their unborn. In Western cultures, admonitions about pregnancy exist as well; obstetricians may advise a pregnant woman to stop smoking, avoid alcohol, and let someone else clean the cat's litterbox, and they may recommend taking supplements containing folic acid and other nutrients.

Fortunately, the mysteries surrounding this remarkable time are beginning to become clearer. Our discussion of prenatal development will open with a brief description of the amazing sequence of events taking place between conception and birth. At no other time does growth take place so rapidly or do so many physical changes occur in a matter of weeks, days, and even hours. Some cultures, such as the Chinese, tacitly acknowledge these dramatic events by pronouncing the baby one year old at birth. In the typical nine months of confinement to the womb, the fetus indeed undergoes an epic journey.

Although fetal growth proceeds in a highly protected environment, we are also discovering the ways in which drugs, diseases, and other factors affect prenatal development. We summarize our current understanding of these influences and then consider the birth process, another point at which the influences on development can be significant.

The Stages of Prenatal Development

Three major overlapping periods define the life of a human organism. **Prenatal development** is launched from the moment of conception and continues until the beginning of labor. All but the first few days of this period are spent within the confines of the womb. **The perinatal period** dawns at about the seventh month of pregnancy and extends until twenty-eight days after birth. This phase is associated with the impending birth, the social and physical setting for delivery, and the baby's first adjustments to his or her new world. Among the events included in the perinatal period are the medical and obstetrical practices associated with delivery, and the preparations and care provided by parents and others to assist in the transition from the womb to life outside. The **postnatal period** begins after birth. The child's environment now includes the broader physical and social world afforded by caregivers and others responsible for the infant's continued growth.

Prenatal development is further divided into three stages based on key biological events that take place. The **germinal period**, also known as the *period of the zygote*, encompasses the first ten to fourteen days following conception. Cell division and migration of the newly fertilized egg, culminating with its implantation in the uterine wall, characterize the germinal period. The second stage, the **embryonic period**, continues from about two to eight weeks after conception. The formation of structures and organs associated with the nervous, circulatory, respiratory, and most other systems mark the embryonic period. The final stage, the **fetal period**, lasts from about eight weeks after conception until birth. This period is distinguished by substantial physical growth, in which organs and systems are refined in preparation for functioning outside the womb.

prenatal development Period in development from conception to the onset of labor.

perinatal period Period beginning about the seventh month of pregnancy and continuing until about four weeks after birth.

postnatal period Period in development following birth.

germinal period Period lasting about ten to fourteen days following conception before the fertilized egg becomes implanted in the uterine wall. Also called *period of the zygote*.

embryonic period Period of prenatal development during which major biological organs and systems form; begins about the tenth to fourteenth day after conception and ends about the eighth week after conception.

fetal period Period of prenatal development, from about the eighth week after conception to birth, marked by rapid growth and preparation of body systems for functioning in the postnatal environment.

Another way to describe the period of 39 weeks that constitutes a full-term human pregnancy is in terms of three roughly equal time periods, or *trimesters*. The first trimester is the first 12 weeks, the second trimester encompasses weeks 13 to 27, and the third trimester occurs from week 28 to birth. You can see that partitioning the prenatal period in terms of trimesters does not neatly correspond to the germinal, embryonic, and fetal periods that we have just finished describing. However, this system has a long-standing tradition of use within the healthcare community.

FERTILIZATION

Even before her own birth, Carole, like most other human females, had formed approximately 2 million primitive egg cells in her ovaries. Their numbers, however, declined with development; by puberty, perhaps only 30,000 remained. Of this abundant supply, about 400 mature and are released for potential fertilization during the childbearing years (Moore & Persaud, 2003). In contrast, male sperm production begins only at puberty, when an incredible 100 to 300 million sperm may be formed daily.

The opportunity for human conception begins about the fourteenth day after the start of the menstrual period. At this time, a capsule-like *follicle* housing a primitive egg cell in one of the ovaries begins to mature. As it matures and changes position, the follicle eventually ruptures and discharges its valuable contents from the ovary. After being expelled, the egg cell, or *ovum*, is normally carried into the Fallopian tube. This organ serves as a conduit for the egg, which moves toward the uterus at the leisurely rate of about one-sixteenth inch per hour. The Fallopian tube provides a receptive environment for fertilization if sperm are present. If unfertilized, the ovum survives only about twenty-four hours.

Sperm reach the Fallopian tube by maneuvering from the vagina through the cervix and uterus. Sperm can migrate several inches an hour with the assistance of their taillike appendages. From 300 to 500 typically negotiate the six- or more hour trip into the Fallopian tube; these usually survive about forty-eight hours.

If an ovum is present, sperm seem attracted to it, possibly because they detect its scent-like chemical cues (Spehr et al., 2003; Roberts, 1991). The egg also prepares for fertilization in the presence of sperm. Cells initially surrounding the ovum loosen their protective grip, permitting the egg to be penetrated. As soon as one sperm cell breaks through the egg's protective linings, enzymes rapidly transform its outer membrane to prevent others from invading (Moore & Persaud, 2003).

Human development begins with the penetration of the egg by a single sperm as shown here (egg and sperm are magnified greatly). Although the egg is the body's largest cell and the sperm the smallest, each contributes twenty-three chromosomes to form the hereditary basis for the development of a new living entity.

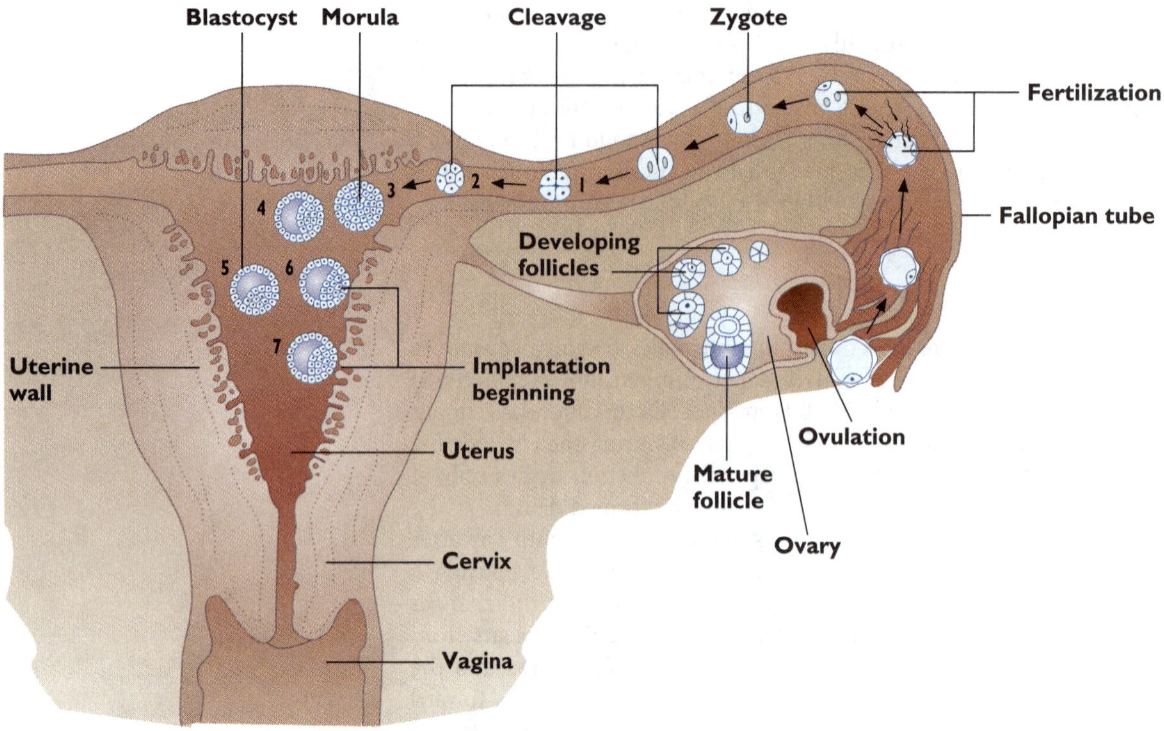

FIGURE 4.1

Fertilization and the Germinal Period

During the early development of the human embryo, an egg cell is released from a maturing follicle within the ovary, and fertilization takes place in the Fallopian tube, transforming the egg cell or ovum into a zygote. Cleavage and multiplication of cells proceeds as the zygote migrates toward the uterus. Differentiation of the zygote begins within the uterus, becoming a solid sixteen-cell sphere know as the *morula*, then a differentiated set of cells known as the *blastocyst*, which prepares for implantation in the uterine wall. Once implanted, it taps a vital source of nutriments to sustain further development. (The numbers indicate days following fertilization.)

Genetic material from egg and sperm quickly mix to establish a normal complement of forty-six chromosomes. The egg, the body's largest cell, barely visible to the naked eye, weighs about 100,000 times more than the sperm, the body's smallest cell. Despite the enormous difference in size, both contribute equivalent amounts of genetic material to the zygote.

The Germinal Period

After fertilization, the zygote continues to migrate down the Fallopian tube (see Figure 4.1). Within twenty-four to thirty hours after conception, the single cell divides into two cells, the first of a series of mitotic divisions called *cleavages*. At roughly twenty-hour intervals these cells divide again to form four, then eight, then sixteen cells. During the cleavages, the zygote remains about the same size; thus individual cells become smaller and smaller.

After three days, about the time the zygote is ready to enter the uterus, it has become a solid sphere of sixteen cells called a *morula*. Each cell is alike in its capacity to generate a separate, identical organism. About the fourth day after conception, however, the cells begin to segregate and carry out specific functions. One group forms a spherical outer cellular layer that eventually becomes various membranes providing nutritive support for the embryo. A second, inner group of cells organizes into a mass that will develop into the embryo. This differentiated group of cells is now called a *blastocyst* (Sadler, 2004).

About the sixth day after conception, the blastocyst begins the process of attaching to the uterine wall to tap a critical new supply of nutrients. By about the tenth to fourteenth day after conception, the implantation process is completed. In preparing for this event, the blastocyst began secreting hormones and other substances to inhibit menstruation, or the shedding of the uterine lining, and to keep the woman's immune system from rejecting the foreign object. One of these hormones eventually becomes detectable in the woman's urine as a marker in pregnancy tests. If the zygote fails to attach to the uterine wall, it is expelled; the frequency of such events is unknown because a woman seldom realizes that a potential pregnancy has terminated.

THE EMBRYONIC PERIOD

The embryonic period, which begins with the implantation of the blastocyst in the uterine wall and continues until about the eighth week after conception, is marked by the rapid differentiation of cells to form most of the organs and systems within the body. This differentiation, known as *organogenesis*, is achieved by the production and migration of specialized cells having distinctive functions.

Formation of Body Organs and Systems The first step in the formation of various body organs and systems involves the migration of unspecialized embryonic cells to establish a three-layered embryo. The three layers serve as the foundation for all tissues and organs in the body. The *endoderm*, or inner layer, will give rise to many of the linings of internal organs, such as lungs, the gastrointestinal tract, the liver, the pancreas, the bladder, and some glands. The *mesoderm*, or middle layer, eventually develops into skeleton and muscles, the urogenital system, the lymph and cardiovascular systems, and other connective tissues. The *ectoderm*, or outer layer, will form skin, hair, and nails, but its earliest derivatives will be the central nervous system and nerves.

How, by simply migrating to a layered configuration, do undifferentiated cells come to establish a highly distinctive set of organs and systems? Understanding this process remains one of the most important issues in prenatal development. The immediate environment surrounding a cell appears to play a major role. Although at first unspecialized, a cell's potential becomes constrained by its association with neighboring tissues, which secrete proteins called *paracrines*. The cells responding to paracrines may then activate or suppress genetic activity responsible for specialized functions (Gilbert, 2003). Thus, cells are induced by their surroundings to take on certain forms and functions. For example, if cells from the ectodermal layer are removed and placed in a culture so that they grow in isolation from other cell layers, they form epidermal, or skinlike tissues. If placed with a layer of mesodermal cells, however, a nervous system will emerge (Abel, 1989). Cells also seem to be sensitive to the density of cells around them, releasing biochemical signals that slow down cell proliferation when an organ seems to have grown enough (Lien et al., 2006).

KEY THEME
NATURE & NURTURE

Because the embryonic period is the major time for development of organs and systems, many possibilities for disruption exist. However, under normal conditions, the sequence of primary changes in prenatal development proceeds in a fairly regular pattern.

Early Brain and Nervous System Development About the fifteenth day after conception, a small group of cells at one end of the ectoderm starts to grow rapidly. The growth creates a reference point for the cephalic (head) and caudal (tail) regions of the embryo, and helps to distinguish left from right side. The cells induce the development of the *neural tube*, which in turn initiates the formation of the spinal cord, nerves, and eventually the brain.

Rapid changes in the neural tube begin about the third week. At first, the neural tube is open at both ends. The tube begins closing in the brain region and, a few days later, in the caudal region. Its failure to knit shut at either end can have drastic consequences for development. In *anencephaly*, a condition in which the cephalic region of the neural tube does not close, the cerebral hemispheres fail to

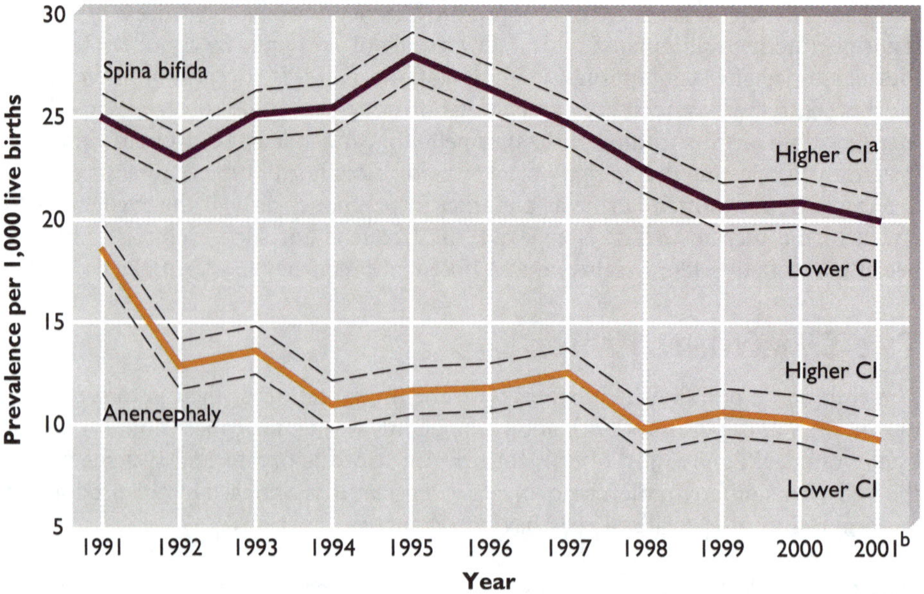

Note: Excludes data for Maryland, New Mexico, and New York, which did not require reporting for spina bifida and anencephaly for certain years.
[a]95% confidence interval. [b]Data for 2001 are preliminary.

FIGURE 4.2

Decline in Neural Tube Defects Associated with the Increased Use of Folic Acid Supplements

Rates of neural tube defects have dropped substantially in the United States since 1991. During this same period, the use of folic acid supplements by women in their childbearing years increased, in part because of government recommendations, as well as regulations requiring that all enriched cereal grain products be fortified with folic acid. These factors very likely contributed to the substantial decline in NTDs.

Source: Mathews, Honein, & Erickson (2002).

develop, and most of the cortex is missing at birth. Newborns with such a condition survive only a short time.

Spina bifida is a condition that arises when the caudal region of the neural tube fails to close. The resulting cleft in the vertebral column permits spinal nerves to grow outside the protective vertebrae. In more serious cases, the infant may be paralyzed and lack sensation in the legs. Surgery often must be performed. Sometimes it can be done even before birth to keep the condition from getting worse. But lost capacities cannot be restored, and malformations in brain development and impaired intellectual development may accompany spina bifida (Northrup & Volcik, 2000).

KEY THEME
NATURE & NURTURE

The frequency of both neural tube defects, now about 1 in every 1,000 births in the United States, has declined sharply over the last twenty years (Mathews, Honein, & Erickson, 2002). This decline, as illustrated in Figure 4.2, appears to be the consequence of two factors. A better understanding of the benefits of nutritional supplements taken early in pregnancy, particularly folic acid and other components of the vitamin B complex, has helped to prevent neural tube defects in the first place. In the United States, as well as in other countries such as Chile and Mexico, declines in spina bifida and anencephaly have been noted after efforts have been made to fortify grain products with folic acid (López-Camelo et al., 2005; Martinez de Villarreal et al., 2002; Mathews, Honein, & Erickson, 2002; Williams et al., 2005). In addition, in the case of more serious neural tube defects, such as anencephaly, the pregnancy is often not carried to term (Limb & Holmes, 1994).

The second month after conception is marked by continued rapid development of the head and brain. Nerve cells show an explosive increase in number; estimates are that as many as 250,000 neurons are generated every minute during the prenatal period (Dowling, 1998). Neurons also undergo extensive migration once the neural tube closes; they soon make contact with one another. The region of the head greatly enlarges relative to the rest of the embryo to account for about half of total body length. The embryo is still tiny; it is less than one and a half inches long and weighs only about half an ounce. However, nearly all organs are established by this time, and the embryo is recognizably human.

One of the most striking milestones is reached about the sixth week after conception, when the nervous system begins to function. Now, irregular and faint brain wave activity can be recorded. Soon, if the head or upper body is touched, the embryo exhibits reflex movements. In a few more weeks muscles may flex, but it will still be some time before the woman is able to feel any movement.

THE FETAL PERIOD

The change from embryo to fetus is signaled by the emergence of bone tissue at about the eighth week after conception. Organ differentiation continues, particularly in the reproductive system and the brain. However, the fetal period is best known for growth in size and the genesis of processes that help organs and systems to function. One positive consequence is that the fetus becomes much less susceptible to many potentially damaging environmental factors.

During the third month after conception, the fetus increases to about three and a half inches in length and about one and a half ounces in weight. Its movements become more pronounced. At nine weeks, the fetus opens and closes its lips, wrinkles its forehead, raises and lowers its eyebrows, and turns its head. By the end of twelve weeks, the behaviors have become more coordinated. The fetus can, for example, display sucking and the basic motions of breathing and swallowing. Fingers will bend if the arm is touched, and the thumb can be opposed to fingers, an indication that peripheral muscles and nerves are functioning in increasingly sophisticated ways (Samuels & Samuels, 1996).

The Second Trimester In the second of the three trimesters into which prenatal development is sometimes divided, the fetus's body grows more rapidly than at any other time. By the end of the fourth month, the fetus is about eight to ten inches long, although it still weighs only about six ounces. During the sixth month, the fetus rapidly starts to gain weight, expanding to about one and a half pounds and reaching a length of about fourteen inches.

By the middle of the second trimester, fetal movements known as *quickening* become unmistakable to the woman. The fetus stretches and squirms as well. Near the end of this trimester, brain wave patterns begin to look like those observed in the newborn. Should birth occur at this time, there is some chance of survival if specialized medical facilities are available.

The Third Trimester The final months add finishing touches to the astonishing progression in prenatal development. The cerebral hemispheres, the regions of the brain most heavily involved in complex mental processing, grow rapidly, folding and developing fissures to give them a wrinkled appearance. *Myelin*, which helps to insulate and speed the transmission of neuronal impulses, begins to form and surround some nerve fibers. Brain wave patterns indicating different stages of sleep and wakefulness can also be observed. The sense organs are developed sufficiently to enable the fetus to smell and taste, as well as to hear, see, and feel. The fetus continues to gain weight rapidly (nearly half a pound per week), although growth slows in the weeks just preceding birth. Control of body temperature and rhythmic respiratory activity remain problematic if birth occurs at the beginning of the third trimester. Nevertheless, **viability**, or the fetus's ability to survive outside the womb, dramatically improves over the course of these three months.

viability Ability of the baby to survive outside the mother's womb.

The onset of birth can be expected when the fetus reaches a **gestational age** of about 274 days. Gestational age, commonly employed in the medical profession to gauge prenatal growth, is derived from the date of onset of the woman's last menstrual period before conception. This method of calculation makes the embryo or fetus about fifteen days older than determining age from the date of conception (Reece et al., 1995). The average gestational period has declined in the last ten years and is now 39 weeks (Davidoff et al., 2006). In addition, as any parent knows, variability in the timing of birth is the norm. Gestational age appears to be a few days shorter for Japanese and African American babies compared to Caucasian babies, for infants born to mothers younger than nineteen or older than thirty-four years, and for second and later children compared with firstborns (Mittendorf et al., 1990, 1993).

Assisted Reproduction

For many prospective parents, conceiving and having a baby proceeds as a normal part of the process of establishing a family. However, for many men and women, the opportunities to become a parent are limited or require special consideration. For example, an estimated 6 million couples in the United States have difficulty conceiving (Centers for Disease Control and Prevention, 2005a). Other couples who may be carriers of genetic diseases (see the chapter titled "Genetics and Heredity") wish to avoid the risk of passing these disorders to their offspring. For these couples, recent advances in the field of reproductive technology have opened up many alternatives, in addition to adoption, in their efforts to become parents; these advances also are dramatically affecting traditional notions about what it means to be a mother or father.

If a male is infertile or carries a genetic disorder, for example, couples may elect *artificial insemination by donor* (see Table 4.1). In this procedure, a donor, who is usually anonymous and is often selected because of similarity in physical and other characteristics to a prospective father, contributes sperm which are then artificially provided to the mother when ovulation occurs. If a female is infertile, a carrier of a genetic disease, or unable to complete a pregnancy for various reasons, options may include one or a combination of new reproductive technologies involving *egg donation, fertility drugs, gamete intrafallopian transfer (GIFT), in vitro fertilization (IVF)*, or *surrogacy*. Surrogate motherhood has sometimes been termed the "renting" of another woman's womb, but this concept can be misleading because, in many cases, the surrogate mother may donate an egg for prenatal development, as well as her womb. The surrogate in that case is the biological mother as well as the bearer of the child who has been conceived by artificial insemination using the prospective

Table 4.1 Examples of New Technologies Associated with Assisted Reproduction

Artificial Insemination by Donor	Sperm from a donor (often anonymous) are artificially provided to a woman during ovulation.
Egg Donation	An egg is harvested from a donor, fertilized, and inserted in another woman's uterus.
Fertility Drugs	Drugs given to stimulate the development and release of egg cells from the ovary to increase the likelihood of conception by traditional means or to increase the harvest of eggs for other assisted reproduction technologies.
Gamete Intrafallopian Transfer (GIFT)	Surgical insertion of both sperm and eggs in the Fallopian tube, where fertilization normally occurs. Zygote intrafallopian transfer (ZIFT) is similar except that fertilization occurs in vitro and the zygote is inserted in the Fallopian tube.
In Vitro Fertilization (IVF)	Eggs harvested from the ovaries and fertilized in a petri dish for subsequent implantation into a woman's uterus.
Surrogacy	A contractual arrangement in which a woman carries a pregnancy to term and in which the pregnancy involves either the surrogate's egg and sperm donated by the father or a couple's zygote established through in vitro fertilization.

father's sperm. Alternatively, with in vitro fertilization, eggs can be removed from a woman's ovaries, fertilized in a laboratory dish with the prospective father's sperm, and transferred to another woman's uterus. In this situation, the biological and social mothers may be one and the same except during the gestational period, when the surrogate mother's womb is used. Furthermore, a woman who cannot or chooses not to conceive in the traditional way might undergo in vitro fertilization and carry her own or another woman's fertilized egg during her pregnancy.

Legal, medical, and social controversies swirl around the technologies associated with assisted reproduction (Collins, 1995; Wright, 1998). For one thing, those who offer artificial insemination, apart from fertility clinics, are not always licensed, nor are they required to receive special training. Thus the competence of the practitioners, the safety of their various activities, and the frequency of this practice are unknown (Guinan, 1995). In addition, whereas adopted children are often informed of their status, children born as a result of new reproductive technologies may not know about their biological history. And, even if told, for example, that their legal and biological fathers may be two different individuals, these offspring typically are unable to obtain further information, because doctors who draw on sperm banks are not required to keep records linking donors and recipients (Guinan, 1995). In some other countries, such as England and Sweden, however, legislation has been enacted to permit individuals to obtain such information (Daniels & Taylor, 1993). Legal debates can also erupt over who is the rightful father or mother when, for example, a surrogate mother resolves to keep the child she has carried to term.

Medical concerns are linked to the use of fertility drugs because they increase the rate of multiple pregnancies to perhaps as much as 40 percent, compared with 3 percent in the general population without the use of such drugs (Centers for Disease Control and Prevention, 2005). Multiple pregnancies, especially when they involve more than two fetuses, increase risks both to the woman and to her offspring. Evidence exists, too, that single children born to mothers who receive assisted reproduction, even with various factors such as maternal age controlled, tend to be of lower birth weight and are at increased risk for birth defects (Dhont et al., 1999; Hansen et al., 2005; Tough et al., 2000). Controversies further extend to the costly medical procedures associated with assisted reproduction. The fee for assisted reproductive technologies in the United States can be $10,000 or more per treatment, and must be added to the increased costs of delivering multiple children and infants at risk (Katz, Nachtigall, & Showstack, 2002). Should insurance companies be mandated to pay expenses accompanying the repeated efforts that are often required to conceive?

The desire to have their own children is a powerful motive for many couples. This is evident from the large number of fertility clinics—perhaps as many as 400 operating in the United States alone and probably 20 or so more in Canada (Centers for Disease Control and Prevention, 2005a; Nemeth, 1997). In Western societies, about 1 in every 100 conceptions involving first-born children may be completed by means of in vitro fertilization (Van Balen, 1998). Studies conducted in Europe, the United States, and Taiwan reveal that children conceived by means of assisted reproduction show few emotional, behavioral, or other problems during their development (Hahn & DiPietro, 2001; Van Balen, 1998). For example, Susan Golombok and her colleagues (Golombok et al., 1995; Golombok, MacCallum, & Goodman, 2001; Golombok et al., 2002) have followed samples of children from the United Kingdom who were conceived by in vitro fertilization or donor insemination and who are now entering into adolescence. They found no differences between these children and children who were conceived without assistance on scales evaluating ability to function in school, peer relationships, and self-esteem. Parents, especially mothers, of these children are sometimes reported to display greater warmth and more concern than other parents, perhaps an indication of their commitment to and the value they place on their children (Hahn & DiPietro, 2001). The general conclusion from research is that the risks to children born to parents who have been assisted in their reproductive efforts are low and that their development is similar to that found in the larger population of children.

gestational age Age of fetus derived from onset of mother's last menstrual period.

FOR • YOUR • REVIEW

- What constitutes the prenatal, perinatal, and postnatal periods of development?
- What are the major changes that take place following conception during the germinal, embryonic, and fetal periods of prenatal development?
- When are the major organs and systems of the body established? What is the course of brain and nervous system development in the embryo and fetus?
- How can various kinds of assisted reproduction help those couples who have difficulty conceiving or are concerned about the inheritance of genetic disorders in their offspring? What are some of the medical and legal issues associated with various forms of assisted reproduction?

Environmental Factors Influencing Prenatal Development

We can readily imagine that a host of events must occur, and at the right times, for prenatal development to proceed normally. What kinds of environmental support do embryo and fetus receive in their liquid, somewhat buoyant, surroundings, and how well protected are they from intrusions that can disrupt their development?

Support Within the Womb

The embryo and fetus are sustained by a number of major structures, including the placenta, the umbilical cord, and the amniotic sac. The **placenta**, formed by cells from both the blastocyst and the uterine lining, produces essential hormones for the fetus. Just as important, it serves as the exchange site at which oxygen and nutrients are absorbed from the woman's circulatory system, and at which carbon dioxide and waste products are excreted from the embryo's circulatory system. The transfer takes place through a network of intermingling, blood-rich capillaries originating in the woman's and the fetus's circulatory systems. Thus blood is not normally exchanged between a woman and her fetus. Although blood cells are too large to cross the membranes separating the two systems, smaller molecules of oxygen, carbon dioxide, nutrients, and hormones can traverse the barrier. So can some chemicals, drugs, and diseases that interfere with fetal development, as we will see shortly.

The **umbilical cord** is the conduit to and from the placenta for the blood of the fetus. The fetus lives in the womb surrounded by the fluid-filled **amniotic sac.** Amniotic fluid helps to stabilize temperature, insulates the fetus from bumps and shocks, and contains substances necessary for the development of the lungs. The fluid is constantly recirculated and renewed as the fetus ingests nutrients and urinates.

placenta Support organ formed by cells from both blastocyst and uterine lining; serves as exchange site for oxygen, nutrients, and waste products.

umbilical cord Conduit of blood vessels through which oxygen, nutrients, and waste products are transported between placenta and embryo.

amniotic sac Fluid-filled, transparent protective membrane surrounding the fetus.

teratogen Any environmental agent that can cause deviations in prenatal development. Consequences may range from behavioral problems to death.

Principles of Teratology

Most fetuses negotiate the average thirty-eight-week period from conception to birth as healthy, vigorous newborns. Yet, as we discuss in the chapter titled "Genetics and Heredity," genetic factors can modify normal progress. So, too, can environmental factors. The study of disabilities and problems that arise from environmental influences during the prenatal period is called *teratology*. Environmental agents that cause disruptions in normal development are known as **teratogens.**

The fact that external agents can upset the course of prenatal development in humans was first appreciated in 1941 when McAllister Gregg, an ophthalmologist, confirmed that rubella, commonly called German measles, causes visual anomalies in the fetus. During this same decade, many infants born to women exposed to the atomic bomb were reported to have birth defects. This finding, along with studies involving animals, implicated radiation as a teratogen (Warkany & Schraffenberger, 1947). The import of these early observations became more fully appreciated when researchers documented that women who had taken a presumably harmless antinausea drug called *thalidomide* frequently bore infants with severe arm and leg malformations (McBride, 1961).

Key Themes
Nature & Nurture
Risk/Resilience

The widely publicized thalidomide tragedy made it abundantly clear that environmental agents can seriously harm human embryos without adversely affecting the woman or others during postnatal development (Wilson, 1977). In fact, the embryo may be susceptible to virtually any substance if exposure to it is sufficiently concentrated (Samuels & Samuels, 1996). A number of broad generalizations have emerged from research on teratogens since the 1960s (Abel, 1989; Friedman & Hanson, 2002; Vorhees, 1986). These principles help to explain the sometimes-bewildering array of adverse consequences that specific drugs, diseases, and other agents can have on development.

- ***The Principle of Susceptibility: Individuals within species, as well as species themselves, show major differences in susceptibility to different teratogens.*** Thalidomide provides a good example of this principle. Scientists knew that extremely large amounts of the drug caused abnormal fetal development in rats (Cohen, 1966). However, the doses given to pregnant women in Europe and Canada, where thalidomide was available as an over-the-counter preparation to reduce morning sickness and anxiety, were considerably smaller. For reasons unknown, the embryos of humans between twenty and thirty-five days after conception are extremely sensitive to small amounts of thalidomide. More than 10,000 babies were born without limbs or with limb defects and intellectual retardation. The genotype of an individual woman and her fetus may also affect susceptibility. Some fetuses were exposed to thalidomide during this sensitive period, yet at birth these babies showed no ill effects from the drug (Kajii, Kida, & Takahashi, 1973).

- ***The Principle of Critical or Sensitive Periods: The extent to which a teratogen affects the fetus depends on the stage of development during which exposure occurs.*** Figure 4.3 shows that many human organs and systems are most sensitive to toxic agents during the third to eighth week after conception, when they are still being formed. However, vulnerability to teratogens exists throughout much of prenatal development. In fact, the brain continues to undergo substantial neural differentiation, migration, and growth during the second and third trimesters of pregnancy, as well as after birth. As a consequence, exposure to teratogens throughout prenatal development may have especially important behavioral consequences.

Key Theme
Continuity/Discontinuity

- ***The Principle of Access: The accessibility of a given teratogen to a fetus or an embryo influences the extent of its damage.*** Many factors determine when and to what extent an embryo or a fetus is exposed to a teratogen. At one level, cultural and social practices may prevent a pregnant woman from using or encourage her to use drugs, prevent her from being inoculated or encourage her to be inoculated for certain diseases, or prevent her from being exposed to or encourage her to be exposed to chemicals and other toxins. For example, use of cocaine may be socially approved in one segment of a culture and avoided in another. However, even when a teratogen is present, it must still gain access to the uterine environment; for example, through a woman's inhaling, ingesting, or injecting a drug intravenously. How a woman has been exposed to the agent, the way she metabolizes it, and how it is transported to the womb influence whether a teratogen reaches a sufficient threshold to have some effect.

Key Theme
Sociocultural Influence

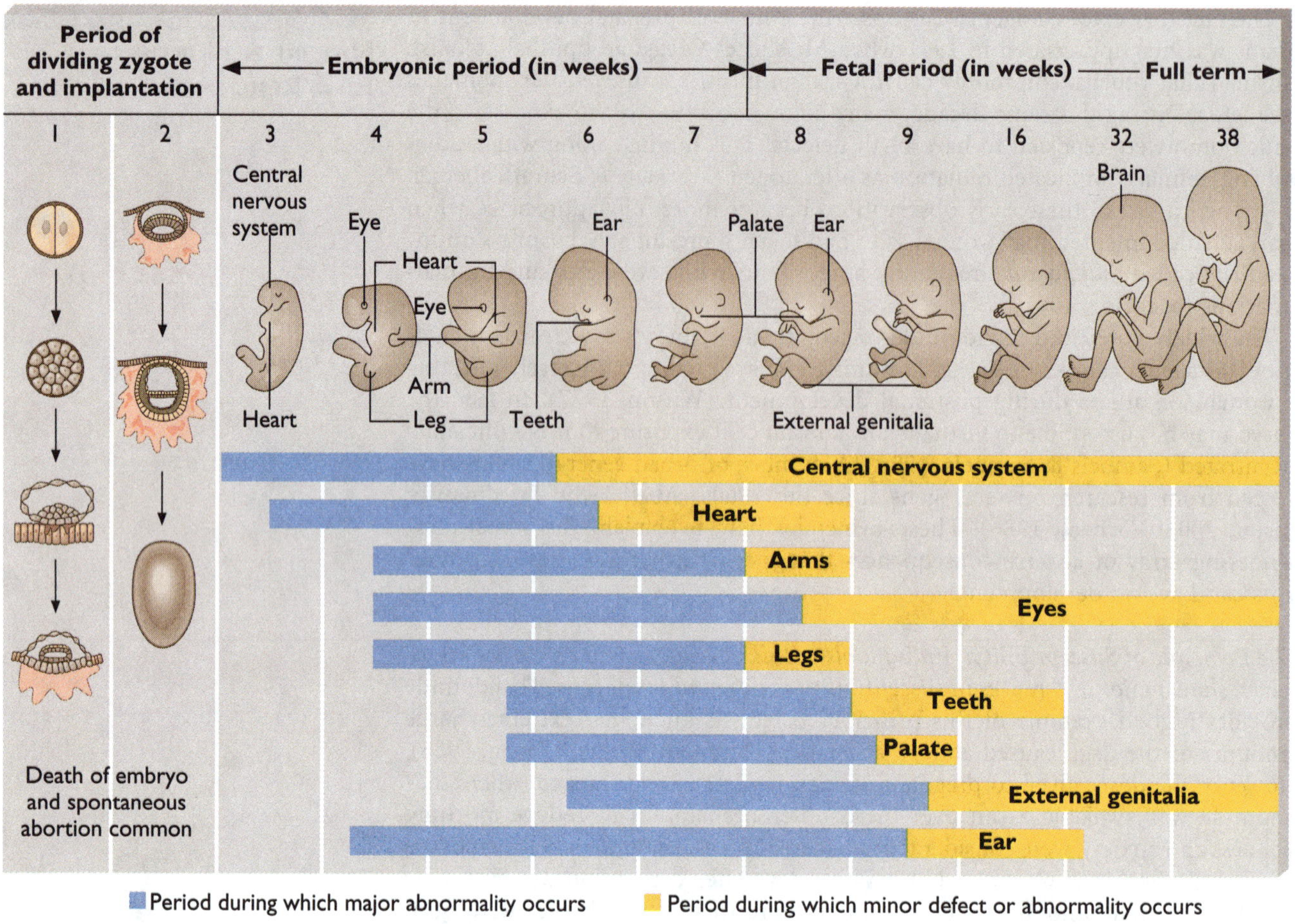

FIGURE 4.3

Sensitive Periods in Prenatal Development

During prenatal development, organs and systems undergo periods in which they are more or less sensitive to teratogenic influences, environmental agents that can cause deviations in development. The potential for major structural defects (blue-colored sections) is usually greatest during the embryonic period, when many organs are forming. However, many regions of the body, including the central nervous system, continue to have some susceptibility to teratogens (yellow-colored sections) during the fetal period.

Source: Moore & Persaud (1998).

- ***The Principle of Dose-Response Relationships: The amount of exposure to or the dosage level of a given teratogen influences the extent of its damage.*** The severity of a teratogen often is related to level of dosage. The more a woman smokes, for example, the greater the likelihood that her baby will be of low birth weight. The concentration of a toxic agent reaching the fetus, however, cannot always be determined from the woman's exposure to it. The severity of an illness a woman experiences—for example, rubella—does not always predict the effect of the disease on the fetus.
- ***The Principle of Teratogenic Response: Teratogens do not show uniform effects on prenatal development.*** Teratogens may cause death or disrupt development of specific organs and systems. They may also have behavioral consequences, impairing sensorimotor, cognitive, social, and emotional development. The principles of species and individual differences, as well as the timing, duration, and intensity of exposure to the teratogen, govern the effect a specific teratogen will have on prenatal development. Alcohol, for example, can cause congenital defects during the embryonic period but may interfere with prenatal weight gain and contribute to postnatal behavioral problems during the second and third trimesters of pregnancy (Abel, 1989). One other important implication of this principle is that very different

fetal alcohol syndrome (FAS)
Cluster of fetal abnormalities stemming from mother's consumption of alcohol; includes growth retardation, defects in facial features, and intellectual retardation.

teratogenic agents can produce a similar pattern of disabilities. Thus efforts to pinpoint why a baby was born with a given anomaly are not always successful.

- ***The Principle of Interference with Specific Mechanisms: Teratogens affect prenatal development by interfering with biochemical processes that regulate the differentiation, migration, or basic functions of cells.*** This principle helps to differentiate folk beliefs from scientific explanations of fetal anomalies. A woman's looking at a frightening visual stimulus, for example, has no direct consequence for the fetus. However, hormonal imbalances induced by chronic levels of stress may have an impact on development.

- ***The Principle of Developmental Delay and "Sleeper Effects": Some teratogens may delay development temporarily with no long-term negative consequences; others may cause developmental problems only late in development.*** Although some teratogenic effects can be observed at birth and are permanent and irreversible, others may be nullified, especially when a supportive caregiving environment is provided. However, the effects of teratogens on later development are probably substantially underestimated because many produce "sleeper effects." These are consequences that go unnoticed at birth but seed problems that become apparent in childhood and even later. For example, women treated with *diethylstilbestrol (DES)*, a hormone administered from the 1940s through the 1960s to prevent miscarriages, gave birth to daughters who showed a high rate of genital tract cancers and sons who displayed a high incidence of abnormalities of the testes when they reached adulthood.

Drugs as Teratogens

Key Theme
Risk/Resilience

Now that we have considered general principles involving teratogens, we can examine the effects that specific environmental agents have on the embryo or fetus. A number of substances that expectant women may use, either as medicine or as mood-altering devices, frequently become part of the intrauterine world. We focus on their consequences for both embryonic and fetal development.

Alcohol Because alcohol readily crosses the placenta, its concentration in the fetus is likely to be similar to that in the woman (Teratology Society, 2005). Moreover, because it lacks some enzymes to effectively degrade alcohol, the fetus may be exposed to it for a longer period of time (Reece et al., 1995). Among pregnant women in the Western world, alcohol is more widely used than any other teratogen and, according to some experts, is the single most frequent cause of mental retardation in industrialized countries (Reece et al., 1995). Current data indicate that about 10 percent of pregnant women have consumed alcohol and 2 percent used it frequently (Centers for Disease Control and Prevention, 2004a).

This young Swedish girl, displaying features often associated with fetal alcohol syndrome, was born to a mother who was an alcoholic. Physical characteristics, including microencephaly (small head size), eyes widely set apart, and flat thin upper lip are often accompanied by delayed physical growth and mental retardation.

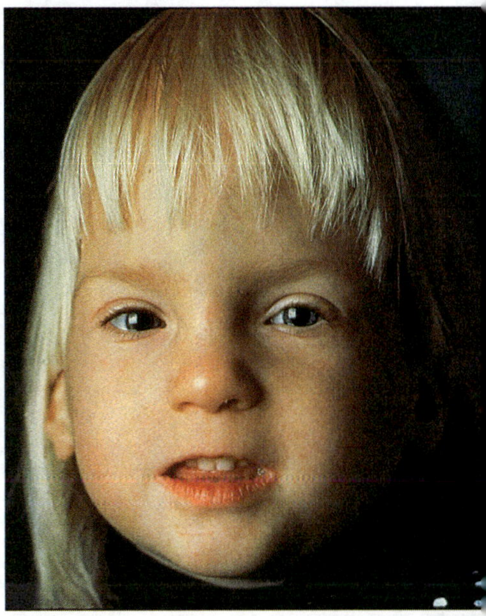

Widespread recognition of the dangers of alcohol emerged in the early 1970s, when three sets of characteristics were observed in a number of babies born to alcoholic women (Jones & Smith, 1973). These included prenatal and postnatal growth retardation, microcephaly, and abnormal facial features, as well as mental retardation and other behavioral problems, such as hyperactivity and poor motor coordination, suggestive of central nervous system dysfunction. This constellation of deficits, known as **fetal alcohol syndrome (FAS)**, appears in as many as 6 percent of infants born to alcoholic mothers (Day & Richardson, 1994). *Alcohol-related neurodevelopmental disabilities (ARND)* have been identified in many other children prenatally exposed to alcohol. These children exhibit retardation or learning difficulties, along with other behavioral problems (Mattson et al., 1997; Stratton, Howe, & Battaglia, 1996). Perhaps as many as 1 in every 100 births in the United States displays FAS or ARND (Sampson et al., 1997).

Binge drinking, usually identified as five or more drinks within a short time, even if it takes place infrequently, can be especially hazardous because it exposes the fetus to highly concentrated levels of alcohol (Chasnoff, 1986; Streissguth et al., 1994). However, even limited alcohol consumption, some researchers report, is linked to an increase in spontaneous abortions and to reduced alertness, less vigorous body activity, more tremors, and slower learning in newborns compared with babies of women who do not drink (Jacobson & Jacobson, 1996; Streissguth et al., 1994). Work by Anne Streissguth and her colleagues shows that prenatal exposure to relatively moderate amounts of alcohol contributes to measurable deficits in attention and school performance, small declines in IQ, and more frequent behavioral problems in children and adolescents (Bookstein et al., 1996; Streissguth et al., 1994; Streissguth et al., 1999). For example, these children and adolescents tended to be more impulsive and had difficulty organizing their work, especially under stress. Moreover, the tendency to display neurocognitive deficits was related to the amount of prenatal alcohol exposure, an example of the dose-related principle, and was especially evident when the woman engaged in occasional binge drinking. Nevertheless, there was no clear threshold at which negative consequences began to appear. As a result, Streissguth et al. (1999) concluded that even small amounts of alcohol can be harmful.

How does alcohol produce such effects? One way is by directly modifying cell functioning. Examination of infants with fetal alcohol syndrome who died shortly after birth reveals structural changes in the brain caused by delays and errors in the way neurons migrate to form the cortex, or outer layer, of the brain (Clarren et al., 1978). Alcohol consumption has also been linked to delayed growth of the frontal cortex and to changes in the functioning of the hippocampus, which is involved in memory (Savage et al., 2002; Wass, Persutte, & Hobbins, 2001). The metabolism of alcohol also requires substantial amounts of oxygen, so less oxygen may be available for normal cell functions. These findings provide further justification for the American Academy of Pediatrics' recommendation of complete abstinence, because "there is no known safe amount of alcohol consumption during pregnancy" (American Academy of Pediatrics, 2000).

Cigarette Smoking About 13 percent of women in the United States smoke during pregnancy, a percentage that has been declining in recent years. The percentage is higher among Caucasian (14 percent) and African American women (9 percent) than among Hispanic women (4 percent) (National Institute on Drug Abuse, 2003). It may also be far higher in other countries in which less effort has been directed toward publicizing the negative health consequences of smoking.

No evidence exists to indicate that smoking during pregnancy causes major congenital defects. However, nicotine and some other of the more than 2,500 chemicals found in tobacco smoke do have serious consequences for fetal and infant mortality, birth weight, and possibly postnatal development (American College of Obstetricians and Gynecologists, 1994). Spontaneous abortions, stillbirths, and neonatal deaths increase in pregnant women who smoke (Streissguth et al., 1994). The most consistent finding from studies of babies born to smokers compared with nonsmokers, however, is their smaller size (Ernst, Moolchan, & Robinson, 2001; Secker-Walker et al., 1997). The more and the longer a woman smokes during pregnancy, the lower her baby's average weight at birth, even when equated for length of gestation, because babies of women who smoke are also likely to be born a few days early (Pollard, 2000; Shah & Bracken, 2000). Every cigarette smoked on a daily basis by a mother during the last trimester of pregnancy reduces the baby's weight by about one ounce (Bernstein et al., 2005).

As with alcohol consumption, a reduction in oxygen may account for these effects. Smoking increases carbon monoxide, which displaces oxygen, in the red blood cells of both woman and fetus. Nicotine also reduces blood flow to the placenta. Moreover, a fetus's heart rate goes up when a woman smokes, a reaction that may take place to maintain adequate oxygen (Samuels & Samuels, 1996). Babies of women who use tobacco have larger placentas and more frequent placental abnormalities than babies of the same weight born to nonsmoking women (Meyer &

Tonascia, 1977; Weinberger & Weiss, 1988). Nicotine may also interfere with metabolic activity important to cell regulation and differentiation.

The long-term behavioral consequences of prenatal exposure to smoke are less well understood. Some researchers have failed to find evidence of poorer performance on cognitive, academic, or other tasks for children exposed to smoke prenatally (Ernst et al., 2001). However, other researchers have reported that infants born to smokers display poorer learning (Martin et al., 1977), a higher-pitched cry (Nugent et al., 1996), and reduced visual and auditory alertness (Franco et al., 1999). Moreover, studies carried out in the United States, the Netherlands, and New Zealand reveal a small but significant increase in behavioral problems in children and adolescents whose mothers smoked during pregnancy (Fergusson, Woodward, & Horwood, 1998; Orlebeke, Knol, & Verhulst, 1999; Weitzman, Gortmaker, & Sobel, 1992). Although efforts to control other factors potentially contributing to these observations have often been undertaken, genetic, family differences, continued passive exposure to smoke from a caregiver or others in the family, and transmission of smoking-related substances during breastfeeding cannot be eliminated as possible causal contributors to these outcomes (American Academy of Pediatrics, 2001; Becker et al., 1999; Orlebeke et al., 1999). Once the child is born, passive exposure to environmental tobacco smoke created by others in the child's household is associated with significantly increased health risks, such as sudden infant death and other respiratory problems (American Academy of Pediatrics, 1997; Brown, 2001).

Prescription and Over-the-Counter Drugs Legal drugs in addition to alcohol and tobacco can be hazardous for fetal development. Some are known teratogens (see Table 4.2), but knowledge of the effects of many remains perilously limited. Aspirin, for example, has been demonstrated to impair behavioral competence in the offspring of lower animals. One well-controlled study found that aspirin may also be associated with lower IQ in early childhood (Streissguth et al., 1984). Certainly, large doses of aspirin, but also of alternative pain relievers such as acetaminophen, may increase risk to the fetus (Reece et al., 1995).

Caffeine, too, has been implicated in birth defects in animals, although studies have failed to reveal any consistent link in humans. However, babies born to mothers who consume higher amounts of caffeine tend to have lower birth weight than babies of mothers who drink less coffee (Eskenazi et al., 1999). Caffeine also has a behavioral impact on the fetus. Lawrence Devoe and his colleagues (1993) used ultrasound to record biweekly two-hour observations of fetal activity during the final ten weeks of pregnancy in ten heavy-caffeine consumers (more than 500 milligrams, or five cups of coffee, daily) and ten low-caffeine consumers (less than 200 milligrams, or two cups of coffee, daily). Fetuses exhibited considerably more arousal (defined by irregular heart rate and breathing activity, frequent body movements, and rapid eye movements) when exposed to the higher amounts of caffeine. The more highly aroused infants may have consumed more energy, a factor that could contribute to their lower birth weight. However, the long-term implications of this difference in activity remain unknown.

Perhaps an even greater concern is the number of prescription and over-the-counter drugs consumed during pregnancy. Most expectant women use at least one medication, and the average is more than three (Buitendijk & Bracken, 1991). Little is known about the effects of many of these products, and even less is known about the interactive consequences when multiple drugs are used. In addition, as new drugs are developed, their impact as potential teratogens needs to be considered. The case of Accutane, a prescription medication used to treat acne, provides a vivid example. When first introduced as a treatment, Accutane taken by pregnant women resulted in a very high rate of physical deformities in the children who were born. Between 25 and 35 percent showed such irregularities as facial deformities, heart problems, and impairment of the nervous system (Lammer et al., 1985). Because the consequences of Accutane exposure for the embryo and fetus are so severe, the U.S. Food and Drug Administration has

Table 4.2 Prescription and Other Frequently Used Drugs and Their Effects on Prenatal Development

Drug	Description and Known or Suspected Effects
Alcohol	See text.
Amniopterin	Anticancer agent. Facial defects and a number of other congenital malformations as well as mental retardation (Hanson, 1997).
Amphetamines	Stimulants for the central nervous system, some types frequently used for weight control. Readily cross placental barrier. Fetal intrauterine growth retardation often reported but may be a result of accompanying malnutrition or multiple-drug use. Increased amounts and duration of exposure prenatally found to be correlated with aggressive behavior in 8-year-olds (Billing et al., 1994).
Antibiotics (streptomycin, tetracycline)	Streptomycin associated with hearing loss. Tetracycline associated with staining of baby's teeth if exposure occurs during second or third trimester (Friedman & Polifka, 1996).
Aspirin	Possibility of increased bleeding in both mother and infant (Hanson, 1997). See text for other complications that can arise.
Barbiturates (pentobarbital, phenobarbital, secobarbital)	Sedatives and anxiety reducers. Considerable evidence of neurobiological and behavioral complications in rats. Readily cross human placenta; concentrations in fetus may be greater than in woman. Newborns may show withdrawal symptoms (Friedman & Polifka, 1996). No consistent evidence of long-term effects in humans.
Benzodiazepines (chlordiazepoxide, diazepam)	Tranquilizers. Not shown to have teratogenic effects, although newborns may display withdrawl symptoms with diazepam (Friedman & Polifka, 1996).
Caffeine	See text.
Hydantoins (Anticonvulsants)	Treatment for epilepsy. Produce *fetal hydantoin syndrome,* including heart defects, cleft lip or palate, decreased head size, and mental retardation. Controversy continues over whether effects are entirely caused by drug or by conditions associated with the mother, including her epilepsy (Hanson, 1986).
Lithium	Treatment for bipolar disorder. Crosses placenta freely. Known to be teratogenic in premammalian animals. Strong suggestive evidence of increased cardiovascular defects in human infants. Behavioral effects unknown. Administration at time of delivery markedly reduces infant responsivity (Friedman & Polifka, 1996).
Retinoids	Antiacne medicine. Effects similar to large amounts of vitamin A.
Sex Hormones (androgens, estrogens, progestins)	Contained in birth control pills, fertility drugs, and other drugs to prevent miscarriages. Continued use of birth control pills during pregnancy associated with heart and circulatory disorders. Behavioral and personality implications suspected. Masculinization of female embryo from exposure to high doses of androgens or progestins.
Thalidomide	Reduces morning sickness and anxiety. Deformities of the limbs, depending on time of exposure, often accompanied by mental retardation (Friedman & Polifka, 1996).
Tobacco	See text.
Tricyclics (imipramine, desimipramine)	Antidepressants. Some tricyclics cross the placenta. Studies with rats reveal developmental and behavioral disturbances. Studies with humans reveal no consistent findings (Friedman & Polifka, 1996).
Vitamins	Large amounts of vitamin A known to cause major birth defects. Excessive amounts of other vitamins may also cause prenatal malformations (Reece et al., 1995).

Note: This listing is not meant to be exhaustive, and other drugs may have teratogenic effects. No drug should be taken during pregnancy without consultation with a qualified physician.

recently issued a public health advisory to minimize pregnant women's exposure to this drug (Food and Drug Administration, 2005). In general, expectant women are usually advised to take *no* drugs during pregnancy, including over-the-counter remedies, or to take them only under the close supervision of their physician.

Illegal Drugs The effects of illegal drugs, such as marijuana, heroin, and cocaine, on prenatal development are even more difficult to untangle than the effects of prescription and over-the-counter medications. Drug users are rarely certain of the contents or concentrations of the drugs they consume. Wide variation in frequency of use, the possibility of interactions from exposure to multiple drugs, poor nutritional status, inadequate or no prenatal care, and potential psychological and physiological differences both before and after taking such drugs compound the problem of isolating their teratogenic effects. The lifestyle of many illegal-drug users can be described as essentially chaotic (Chasnoff, 1992), so that conclusions about the impact of the drug itself are often difficult to make.

Research with animals has shown that the psychoactive ingredients associated with marijuana cross the placenta and are stored in the amniotic fluid (Harbison & Mantilla-Plata, 1972). They may also be transferred postnatally through the mother's milk (Dalterio & Bartke, 1979). Still, efforts to determine the effects of marijuana on human fetal and postnatal development reveal few consistent findings (Zuckerman & Bresnahan, 1991). As with tobacco, fetal weight and size appear to be reduced. Length of gestation may also be shorter for heavy marijuana users, a finding consistent with giving marijuana to speed labor, a practice carried out at one time in Europe.

A higher-pitched cry, visual problems, lower scores on memory and verbal tasks, and more restless sleep patterns in early childhood are reported with prenatal exposure to marijuana (Dahl et al., 1995; Fried, Watkinson, & Gray, 1998; Lester & Dreher, 1989). However, social and economic differences in the backgrounds of the children could also account for these findings. In fact, in some cultures, such as Jamaica, marijuana use correlates positively with neonatal test performance (Dreher, Nugent, & Hudgins, 1994).

KEY THEME
SOCIOCULTURAL INFLUENCE

The effects of heroin and morphine became a public concern as early as the late 1800s, when doctors reported withdrawal symptoms in newborns whose mothers used these substances (Zagon & McLaughlin, 1984). By the early 1900s, heroin and morphine were known to be transmitted through the placenta, as well as through the mother's milk. Today, an estimated 9,000 infants born in the United States each year are exposed to heroin or methadone, a pharmacologically similar product (Sprauve, 1996). Often given under regulated conditions as a heroin substitute, methadone's effects on fetal development are just as powerful as heroin's. So, too, may be the effects of a newer synthetic form of heroin, OxyContin, a prescribed painkiller that has recently achieved the status of widely sought-after street drug.

Although congenital defects have not been positively linked to heroin and methadone, stillbirths and infant deaths are more frequent, and lower birth weight is common (American College of Obstetricians and Gynecologists, 1994). About 60 to 70 percent of infants born to heroin- and methadone-addicted women also undergo withdrawal symptoms, such as diarrhea, sweating, a distinctively high-pitched cry, tremors, and irritability (Sprauve, 1996). Developmental difficulties continue to be observed in infants and children exposed to heroin and methadone. However, high-quality caregiving can play a powerful role in lessening the negative impact of prenatal exposure to heroin in children, at least for those who do not experience neurological damage (Ornoy et al., 1996).

Each year in the United States alone, more than 200,000 infants are estimated to be born to mothers who use illegal drugs (National Institute on Drug Abuse, 1995). However, probably none of these drugs has received more widespread attention than cocaine. Cocaine in its many forms—including crack, an especially potent and addictive variation—readily crosses the placenta. Once it reaches the fetus, it stays longer than in adults, because the immature organs of the fetus have difficulty breaking it down. Cocaine also can continue to influence the baby after birth through the mother's milk.

Dire effects for the fetus and subsequently for postnatal development as a result of exposure to cocaine have been widely publicized (Chavkin, 2001; Frank et al., 2001). Indeed, evidence exists that cocaine may be associated with prematurity and low birth weight (Bendersky & Lewis, 1999), as well as with attentional, motor, and some early neurobehavioral difficulties (Eyler et al., 1998; Fried et al., 1998; Singer, Arendt, et al., 1999; Stanwood & Levitt, 2001). However, these observed relationships can often be explained by other factors known to interfere with development. In fact, a detailed review of the results of a number of well-controlled studies by Deborah Frank and her colleagues concluded that exposure to cocaine for those undergoing a normal gestational period is *not* a factor that leads to poor physical growth or delayed acquisition of motor skills, lowered cognitive abilities, or behavioral, attentional, or affective disturbances in young children (Frank et al., 2001).

The primary position of Deborah Frank and her colleagues, and a common thread of agreement emerging among researchers, is that other risk factors regularly associated with the use of cocaine—such as increased exposure to tobacco and alcohol, poor nutrition, diminished parental responsiveness, abuse and neglect, social isolation of the family, and the increased stress typically accompanying poverty—play a *far more important* role in negative outcomes for development during early childhood than does cocaine itself (Bendersky & Lewis, 1999; Frank et al., 2001; Miller & Boudreaux, 1999). Thus the prognosis for children subjected to cocaine and other illegal drugs in utero should and does improve substantially when interventions are undertaken to reduce or eliminate these other risk factors (Butz et al., 2001; Field et al., 1998; Kilbride et al., 2000). In other words, although the potential for negative consequences of prenatal exposure to cocaine cannot be ruled out, intervention at other levels appears to be the key to improving the developmental outlook for children exposed to this and other drugs. So, too, may be the need to educate the public, as well as professionals, about the known consequences for development of exposure to cocaine.

CONTROVERSY: THINKING IT OVER

Should a Drug-Abusing Expectant Woman Be Charged with Child Abuse?

Consider the circumstances surrounding the prosecution of Cornelia Whitner of South Carolina. Her son was born with cocaine in his system. In 1992 Cornelia pled guilty to a charge of child neglect after admitting to the use of cocaine in her third trimester of pregnancy. She was sentenced to eight years in prison.

What Is the Controversy?

Although the conviction of Cornelia Whitner has since been overturned, the issues surrounding this and similar cases deeply divide law enforcement, medical, and service agencies in the United States, Canada, and many Western European countries (Capron, 1998; Peak & Del Papa, 1993). Since the mid-1980s, more than 200 American women in thirty states have been prosecuted on charges of child abuse and neglect, delivery of drugs to a minor, or assault with a deadly weapon for allegedly harming their offspring through prenatal exposure to cocaine or other illegal drugs (Paltrow et al., 2000). Court cases with policy implications for whether a woman can or should be arrested if she exposes a fetus to illegal drugs are continuing to be debated at the highest judicial levels, including the U.S. Supreme Court (Greenhouse, 2000; Paltrow et al., 2000). Is this an effective way to reduce the likelihood of drug use and any of its accompanying risks for the fetus?

What Are the Opposing Arguments?

Some say that a concerned society should impose criminal or other charges on a pregnant woman who uses a drug that may be dangerous to the fetus. A number of jurisdictions in the United States and provinces in Canada have implemented laws permitting a newborn to be removed from a parent on the grounds of child abuse or neglect because of drug exposure during pregnancy. In some cases, the woman has been ordered to be confined to a drug treatment facility during pregnancy. After all, anyone found to provide such illegal substances to a child would certainly expect to face criminal or other charges. Are the circumstances that much different in the case of a pregnant woman and her fetus?

Others believe the situation is vastly different and further claim that criminal charges, imprisonment, or mandatory treatment are counterproductive (Beckett, 1995; Farr, 1995). Legislation specifically targeted at pregnant drug users might actually drive prospective mothers, out of fear of being prosecuted, away from the care and treatment needed for both themselves and their fetuses. Moreover, the tendency to rely on criminal procedures could limit the resources available for the implementation of innovative, well-funded public health efforts for treating addiction and its consequences for the fetus (Chavkin, 2001).

What Answers Exist? What Questions Remain?

At the present time, no research has been carried out on whether threats of criminal procedures or other forms of punishment dissuade a woman from using drugs during her pregnancy. If studies with this or other populations demonstrate that these kinds of actions are effective in reducing drug use, perhaps greater justification would exist for the extension of this approach to expectant women. But, given the recent findings that the negative consequences for the fetus often stem less from the illegal drugs themselves than from the myriad other factors associated with drug use, would such actions be helpful? In other words, are poor nutrition and a host of other social and economic factors, as well as the chaotic lifestyle that often accompanies drug use and over which a woman may not always have control, the primary culprits in impaired fetal development? If so, then intervention must take place at the public health level. And do your views about how to address this issue change given that alcohol and tobacco have been shown to have more serious consequences for fetal development than many illegal drugs (Bendersky & Lewis, 1999; Frank et al., 2001; Miller & Boudreaux, 1999; Streissguth et al., 1999)? If laws are introduced to protect the fetus from illegal drugs, should these laws not also be extended and applied to those who use readily available, heavily advertised, and common drugs that are known to have even more serious teratogenic effects? Research has begun to shed light on some of these issues by providing knowledge about the effects of exposure to drugs on fetal development. What other kinds of developmental research would be useful in helping to resolve these competing views? Are there alternatives that might be proposed to help solve a very complex problem: ensuring an optimal start for every child at birth?

Diseases as Teratogens

Key Theme
Risk/Resilience

Somewhere between 2 and 8 percent of babies born to American women are exposed to one or more diseases or other forms of illness during pregnancy (Landry, 2004). Fortunately, most babies are unaffected. Moreover, significant progress has been made in eliminating the potentially negative fetal consequences of several diseases, such as mumps and rubella (German measles), at least in some countries. Recently, for example, the Centers for Disease Control have declared that rubella has been virtually eliminated in the United States (Centers for Disease Control and Prevention, 2005b). Unfortunately, rubella, a highly preventable illness, continues to be a major cause of fetal malformations and death worldwide, because vaccination programs are limited in some regions of the world. Other diseases, some of which are described in Table 4.3, continue to pose risks for the fetus in even the most medically advanced countries. Their impact on the fetus can be serious, sometimes devastating, even when a woman is completely unaware of illness.

Toxoplasmosis Toxoplasmosis is caused by a parasite found in many mammals and birds; about 22 percent of adults in the United States have been exposed to it (Centers for Disease Control and Prevention, 2004b). However, the disease is found with greater frequency in some European countries, including France and Austria, and in tropical regions. Humans occasionally contract the disease by touching cat feces containing the parasite or, even more frequently, by eating raw or partially infected cooked meat, especially pork and lamb. Children and adults are often unaware of their exposure, because the infection may have no symptoms or cause only a minor fever or rash.

Infections early in pregnancy can have devastating consequences; fortunately, risk of transmission to the fetus at this time is lowest (Foulon et al., 1999). Growth retardation, jaundice, accumulation of fluid in the brain, and visual and central nervous system damage are the most frequent teratogenic outcomes. Some infants show no symptoms at birth; only later may mental retardation, neuromuscular abnormalities, impaired vision, and other eye problems become apparent. Research carried out in Europe indicates that early treatment with antibiotics can help reduce some of its more devastating consequences (Foulon et al., 1999).

Cytomegalovirus Cytomegalovirus (CMV), a member of the herpes family of viruses, causes swelling of the salivary glands and mononucleosislike symptoms in adults. It is the single most frequent infection found in newborns today, affecting 1 to 2 of every 100 babies. As many as 10 percent of infected infants can be expected to sustain some congenital damage (Friedman & Hanson, 2002). No effective treatment exists.

KEY THEME
SOCIOCULTURAL INFLUENCE

CMV is most frequently reported in Asia, Africa, and lower socioeconomic groups, in which up to 85 percent of the population may be infected. Yet 45 to 55 percent of middle- and high-income groups in Europe and the United States are infected as well (Hagay et al., 1996). Transmission occurs through various body fluids. CMV can be passed easily between children playing together, for example, in daycare centers and in family daycare settings (Bale et al., 1999) and from child to adult through physical contact.

Fortunately, the aftermath of contracting the virus in early childhood is generally not serious. Infection can occur within the womb, during birth, and through breast-feeding with more severe consequences (Adler, 1992; Stagno & Cloud, 1994). The negative outcomes are typically greatest for the fetus if a woman contracts the disease for the first time during her pregnancy (Guerra et al., 2000). Growth retardation, jaundice, skin disorders, and small head size are common consequences. About one-third of infants showing these characteristics at birth will die in early infancy; a large percentage of those who survive will be mentally retarded. About half of infants sustaining congenital damage from CMV show no symptoms at birth, but many will subsequently display progressive loss of hearing or other, subtler defects, including minimal brain dysfunction, visual or dental abnormalities, or motor and neural problems (Pass, 1987; Landry, 2004).

Sexually Transmitted and Other Diseases Several diseases identified as teratogenic are transmitted primarily through sexual contact, and the infection and its symptoms are usually concentrated in the genitourinary tract (see Table 4.3). Syphilis and certain strains of herpes simplex, for example, are virtually always contracted from infected sexual partners. On the other hand, some diseases, such as acquired immunodeficiency syndrome (AIDS) and hepatitis B, can be acquired through exposure to infected blood as well.

Table 4.3 Diseases and Maternal Conditions That May Affect Prenatal Development

Disease	Physical and Behavioral Consequences for the Fetus
Sexually Transmitted Diseases	
Acquired Immunodeficiency Syndrome (AIDS)	See text.
Chlamydia	Nearly always transmitted to infant during delivery via infected birth canal. Estimated 100,000 (of 155,000 exposed in the United States) become infected. Often causes eye infection in infant and some increased risk of pneumonia. Other adverse effects suspected (McGregor & French, 1991).
Gonorrhea	If acquired prenatally, may cause premature birth (Reece et al., 1995). Most frequently contracted during delivery through infected birth canal and may then attack eyes. In the United States and many other countries, silver nitrate eye drops are administered to all newborns to prevent blindness.
Hepatitis B	Associated with premature birth, low birth weight, increased neonatal death, and liver disorders (Pass, 1987). Most frequently contracted during delivery through birth canal or postnatally.
Herpes Simplex	Of its two forms, only one is transmitted primarily through sexual activity. Both forms, however, can be transmitted to the fetus, causing severe damage to the central nervous system (Pass, 1987). Most infections occur during delivery through birth canal containing active herpes lesions. The majority of infants will die or suffer central nervous system damage (Nahmias, Keyserling & Kernick, 1983). If known to carry the virus, woman may need to be tested frequently during pregnancy to determine if the disease is in its active, contagious state because symptoms may not be present even when active. If the disease is active, cesarean delivery is used to avoid infecting the baby.
Syphilis	Damage to fetus does not begin until about 18 weeks after conception. May then cause death, mental retardation, and other congenital defects (Reece et al., 1995). Infected newborns may not show signs of disease until early childhood.
Other Diseases	
Cytomegalovirus	See text.
Influenza	Some forms linked to increased heart and central nervous system abnormalities, as well as spontaneous abortions (Reece et al., 1995).
Mumps	Increased risk of spontaneous abortion and stillbirth.
Rubella	Increased risk of spontaneous abortion and stillbirth. Growth retardation, cataracts, hearing impairment, heart defects, mental retardation also common, especially if exposure occurs in the first or second month of pregnancy.
Toxoplasmosis	See text.
Varicella-zoster (chicken pox)	Skin and muscle defects, intrauterine growth retardation, limb reduction.
Other Maternal Conditions	
Diabetes	Risk of congenital malformations and death to fetus two to three times higher than for babies born to nondiabetic women (Coustan & Felig, 1988). Excessive size at birth also common. Effects are likely to be a consequence of metabolic disturbances rather than of insulin. Rapid advances in care have helped reduce risks substantially for diabetic women.
Hypertension (chronic)	Probability of miscarriage or infant death increased.
Obesity	Increased risk of diabetes and large-for-gestational-age babies (Lu et al., 2001).

(continued)

Table 4.3 Diseases and Maternal Conditions That May Affect Prenatal Development *(continued)*

Disease	Physical and Behavioral Consequences for the Fetus
Pregnancy-Induced Hypertension	5%–10% of expectant women experience significant increase in blood pressure, often accompanied by *edema* (swelling of face and extremities as a result of water retention), rapid weight gain, and protein in urine during later months of pregnancy. Condition is also known as *pre-eclampsia* (or *eclampsia,* if severe) and *toxemia.* Under severe conditions, woman may suffer seizures and coma. The fetus is at increased risk for death, brain damage, and lower birth weight. Adequate protein consumption helps minimize problems. Drugs used to treat high blood pressure may be just as hazardous to fetus as the condition itself.
Rh Incompatibility	Blood containing a certain protein is Rh positive; Rh negative if it lacks that protein. Hereditary factors determine which type the individual possesses. If fetus's blood is Rh positive, it can cause formation of antibodies in blood of woman who is Rh negative. These antibodies can cross the placental barrier to destroy red blood cells of fetus. May result in miscarriage or stillbirth, jaundice, anemia, heart defects, or mental retardation. Likelihood of birth defects increases with succeeding pregnancies because antibodies are usually not present until after birth of first Rh-positive child. A vaccine (Rhogam) can be administered to the mother within 3 days after childbirth, miscarriage, or abortion to prevent antibody formation.

Sexually transmitted diseases (STDs) can interfere with reproduction in a number of ways. They may compromise the woman's health (AIDS, gonorrhea, hepatitis B, herpes simplex, syphilis), scar or disturb reproductive organs so that conception and normal pregnancy cannot proceed (chlamydia, gonorrhea), directly infect the fetus (AIDS, herpes simplex, syphilis), or interfere with healthy postnatal development (AIDS, hepatitis B, herpes simplex, syphilis) (Lee, 1988). In recent years, the frequency of STDs has risen rapidly in populations around the world. None, however, has had as dramatic an impact as AIDS.

Of the estimated 16,000 children having human immunodeficiency virus type 1 (HIV-1) in the United States and the more than 1.1 million children currently living with the disease worldwide, most were infected prenatally, during birth, or shortly after birth through an infected mother's breast milk (Burgess, 2001; Lindegren, Steinberg, & Byers, 2000). Prior to 1995, about 25 percent of infants born to HIV-positive women could be expected to eventually acquire AIDS. However, as can be seen in Figure 4.4, new medical treatments have reduced the transmission rate by more than one-third, at least in countries in which expensive drugs such as zidovudine are available (Lindegren et al., 2000).

Of those infants who do become infected with HIV, about 20 percent show rapid progression to AIDS and death in early childhood. However, with new advances in treatment, about two-thirds live more than five years; the average length of survival in Western countries is now greater than nine years; and about 25 percent of children do not show severe symptoms of AIDS until after ten years (Barnhart et al., 1996; Brown, Lourie, & Pao, 2000; European Collaborative Study, 2001). Children receiving medication for HIV also show substantial benefits in terms of maintaining more normal levels of cognitive functioning throughout much of their childhood (Brown et al., 2000). Thus the negative course of the disease can be slowed for cognitive and other aspects of development (Tardieu et al., 1995). Unfortunately, however, for many children around the world, limited medical services, poverty, and the absence of social support will adversely affect their development while living with the disease.

KEY THEME
NATURE & NURTURE
RISK/RESILIENCE

Environmental Hazards as Teratogens

Radiation was one of the earliest confirmed teratogens, and it can cause genetic mutations as well. Radiation's effects include spontaneous abortion, small head size,

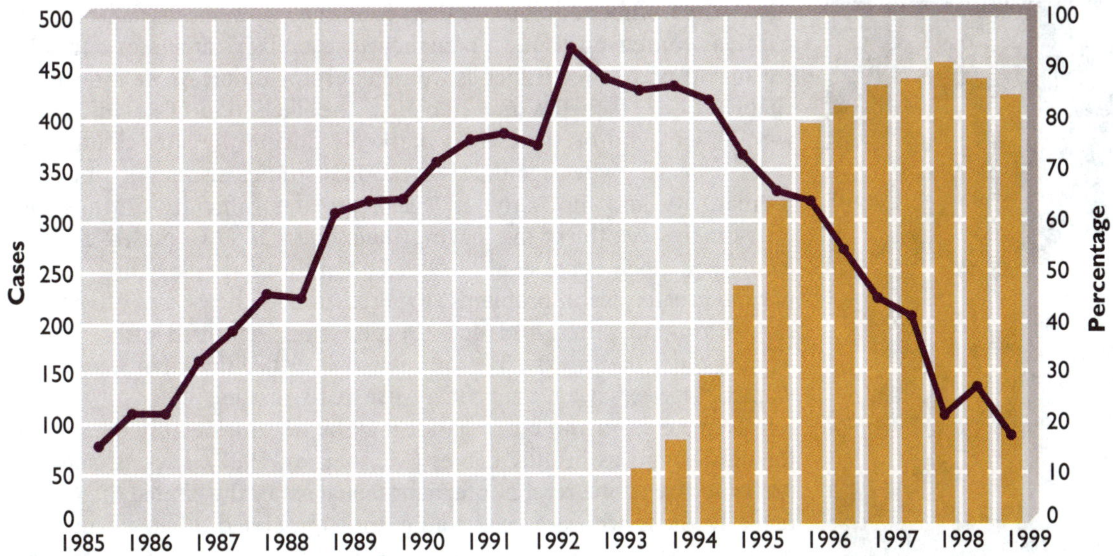

FIGURE 4.4

Decline in HIV/AIDS Transmitted to Offspring via HIV-Infected Women

The transmission of HIV/AIDS infection to infants and children via HIV-infected women has declined dramatically in the United States in recent years. The data from thirty-two reporting states reveal that introducing treatment with zidovudine (represented by the shaded bars as the percentage of women receiving treatment with the drug) has been as important factor in reducing the number of cases of infants and children reported with HIV/AIDS. Unfortunately, about 90% of the approximately 1.1 million children around the world with HIV/AIDS are born in sub-Saharan Africa, where this method of treatment is often too expensive or unavailable.

Source: Lindgren, Steinberg, & Byers (2000).

and other defects associated with the skeleton, genitals, and sensory organs. Even low doses of radiation have been linked to increased risks of cancer and neural damage; pregnant women are urged to avoid unnecessary x-rays and other circumstances in which exposure might occur.

Chemicals and other elements in the environment pose another significant source of potential risks. Known teratogens include lead, mercury, and polychlorinated biphenyls, or PCBs (a synthetic hydrocarbon once used in transformers, hydraulic fluid, and other industrial equipment), as well as many elements found in paints, dyes and coloring agents, solvents, oven cleaners, pesticides, herbicides, food additives, artificial sweeteners, and cosmetic products (Hubbs-Tait et al., 2005; Needleman & Bellinger, 1994). Careless handling and disposal of such elements and their excessive production and use are one problem. They pervade the foods we eat and the air we breathe. Mercury, for example, can occur in especially high concentrations in large predatory fish such as swordfish and tuna (Hubbs-Tait et al., 2005); the U. S. Food and Drug Administration recommends that pregnant and nursing mothers as well as young children avoid consuming these fish (U.S. Department of Health and Human Services, 2004). In addition, many women of childbearing age are exposed in the workplace to hazardous substances such as lead, formaldehyde, and carbon monoxide.

Women's Conditions and Prenatal Development

Key Theme
Risk/Resilience

In addition to teratogens, a number of health conditions are associated with increased risk during pregnancy. Several of these conditions (diabetes, pregnancy-induced and chronic hypertension, Rh incompatibility) and their consequences for the fetus are summarized in Table 4.3. Additional factors influencing the prenatal environment include the age of the woman, her nutritional status, and her emotional state.

Teenage mothers give birth to nearly 500,000 babies in the United States each year. Many of them will be unmarried teens who have received little or no prenatal care, factors that increase the risk for delivering less healthy babies.

Age The number of older mothers is on the rise in industrialized countries as women postpone pregnancy to establish careers or for other reasons. Is pregnancy riskier as women become older? As we show in the chapter titled "Genetics and Heredity," the likelihood of having a child with Down syndrome increases markedly during the later childbearing years, especially after age thirty-five. Some studies also report increased prematurity and mortality, as well as greater difficulty during labor, for women over thirty-five having their first child (Gilbert, Nesbitt, & Danielsen, 1999; Reece et al., 1995). The findings are likely due, in large part, to greater health problems (hypertension, diabetes, and others) that can accompany increased age. Despite these elevated risks, healthy women older than thirty-five routinely deliver healthy infants, just as do women between twenty and thirty-five years of age.

Teenagers, on the other hand, may be at considerably greater risk for delivering less healthy babies (McAnarney, 1987). Lack of adequate prenatal care is one reason; pregnant teenagers in the United States, particularly those who are very young and unmarried, often do not seek medical services. Another reason pregnancy at these early ages poses more problems is the complicated nutritional needs of adolescents; many teenagers are still growing themselves. Although the rate of births to teenagers has declined steadily throughout the 1990s in the United States (Hoyert et al., 2001), it is still substantially higher than in other industrialized nations and double or even triple that in most Western European countries. In any given year, about one in twenty-five teenagers is likely to bear a child; this translates into slightly over 400,000 births per year to teens (National Center for Health Statistics, 2005).

Nutrition What foods are needed for the health of the woman and her fetus? The seemingly obvious but important answer is a well-balanced diet. Extreme malnutrition during prenatal development can be especially detrimental. During World War II, famines occurred in parts of Holland and in Leningrad in the former Soviet Union. When the malnutrition occurred during the first few months of pregnancy, death, premature birth, and nervous system defects were especially frequent. When famine occurred later in prenatal development, retardation in fetal growth and low birth weights were more likely (Antonov, 1947). Although not everyone agrees about the guidelines, women of normal weight for their height are typically advised to gain about twenty-five to thirty-five pounds during pregnancy.

Diets must be not only sufficient in number of calories but also balanced with respect to adequate protein, vitamins, and other nutrients. In fact, intake of many nutrients should be increased during pregnancy, as Table 4.4 indicates. Fortunately, unless deficiencies are so severe that malformations and deficits in neuron formation cannot be overcome, many cognitive problems associated with prenatal undernutrition and the lowered birth weight that often accompanies it may still be reversed when adequate nourishment and stimulation are provided following birth (Pollitt, 1996).

Key Theme
Sociocultural Influence

Stress Cultural beliefs about potentially harmful consequences of frightening or stressful events on fetal development are pervasive, and many societies encourage a calm atmosphere for pregnant women (Samuels & Samuels, 1996). In studies in which researchers have carefully measured anxiety, family conflict, positive and negative life events, and the availability of physical and social support for the woman, stress has been linked to greater complications during both pregnancy and birth. Anxiety appears to lengthen labor, increase the need for more anesthesia during delivery, and produce more birthing complications. High stress, particularly early in pregnancy, seems to contribute to a shorter length of gestation and therefore to more frequent preterm births and more infants with lower birth weight (Glynn et al., 2001; Wadhwa et al., 1993). In addition, fatigue associated

Table 4.4 Nutritional Need Differences Between Nonpregnant and Pregnant Women 24 Years of Age

Nutrient	Nonpregnant	Pregnant	Percentage Increase	Dietary Sources
Folic acid	180 mcg	400 mcg	+ 122	Leafy vegetables, liver
Vitamin D	5 µg	10 µg	+ 100	Fortified dairy products
Iron	15 mg	30 mg	+ 100	Meats, eggs, grains
Calcium	800 mg	1200 mg	+ 50	Dairy products
Phosphorus	800 mg	1200 mg	+ 50	Meats
Pyridoxine	1.6 mg	2.2 mg	+ 38	Meats, liver, enriched grains
Thiamin	1.1 mg	1.5 mg	+ 36	Enriched grains, pork
Zinc	12 mg	15 mg	+ 25	Meats, seafood, eggs
Riboflavin	1.3 mg	1.6 mg	+ 23	Meats, liver, enriched grains
Protein	50 g	60 g	+ 20	Meats, fish, poultry, dairy
Iodine	150 mcg	175 mcg	+ 17	Iodized salt, seafood
Vitamin C	60 mg	70 mg	+ 17	Citrus fruits, tomatoes
Energy	2200 kcal	2500 kcal	+ 14	Proteins, fats, carbohydrates
Magnesium	280 mg	320 mg	+ 14	Seafood, legumes, grains
Niacin	15 mg	17 mg	+ 13	Meats, nuts, legumes
Vitamin B-12	2.0 mcg	2.2 mcg	+ 10	Animal proteins
Vitamin A	800 µg	800 µg	0	Dark green, yellow, or orange fruits and vegetables, liver

Source: Reece et al. (1995).

with long hours at work, especially work that involves prolonged standing, increases preterm birth and health problems for a pregnant woman (Gabbe & Turner, 1997; Luke et al., 1999). Stress also may indirectly affect prenatal development by leading a woman to increase smoking, consume more alcohol, or engage in other activities known to have negative effects on the fetus (McAnarney & Stevens-Simon, 1990).

The social support a pregnant woman receives from family and friends is an important factor that can lessen the consequences of stress during pregnancy (Feldman et al., 2000). Among women who experience a variety of life changes before and during pregnancy, those with strong social and personal assistance—for example, those who can obtain a ride to work, get help when sick, or borrow needed money—have far fewer complications than women without such resources (Norbeck & Tilden, 1983). In fact, women who receive as little as twenty minutes of psychosocial support addressing their concerns and offering encouragement during regular prenatal visits have babies who weigh more than the babies of women who do not receive this benefit (Rothberg & Lits, 1991). How well a family functions during stressful times may be a more important predictor of complications during and after pregnancy than how many stressful events are actually experienced (Smilkstein et al., 1984).

After learning about the many teratogens and other factors that can affect prenatal development, we may be surprised that babies manage to be born healthy at all. But they do so every day. We should wonder, rather, at the rich complexity of prenatal development and appreciate more deeply that it proceeds normally so much of the time. Ninety to ninety-five percent of babies born in the United States are healthy and fully prepared to adapt to their new environment. Knowledge of teratogens allows prospective parents as well as others in the community to maximize the chances that all infants will be equipped to enter the world with as many resources as possible.

FOR • YOUR • REVIEW

- What kinds of supportive functions do the placenta, umbilical cord, and amniotic sac provide for the embryo and the fetus?
- What are teratogens? What principles apply to how teratogens have their effects?
- How do alcohol, cigarette smoke, prescription and over-the-counter drugs, and illegal drugs affect prenatal development?
- What kinds of risks exist for the embryo and fetus exposed to rubella, toxoplasmosis, cytomegalovirus, and sexually transmitted diseases?
- What maternal conditions affect the well-being of the fetus and embryo?

Birth and the Perinatal Environment

Key Theme
Sociocultural Influence

Societies vary enormously in the techniques and rituals that accompany the transition from fetus to newborn. Some interpret pregnancy and birth as natural and healthy; others, as an illness requiring medical care and attention (Newton, 1955). The !Kung, a hunting-and-gathering people living in the Kalahari Desert of Africa, build no huts or facilities for birthing. They view birth as part of the natural order of events, requiring no special intervention (Shostak, 1981). In contrast, pregnancy and childbirth in the United States and many other countries throughout much of the twentieth century has been regarded more as an illness to be managed by professionally trained medical personnel (Dye, 1986). In 1900 fewer than 5 percent of babies were born in hospitals in the United States. Today about 99 percent of all babies in the United States are born in hospitals (Declercq, 1993; Hosmer, 2001).

Preparing for Childbirth

With the shift from childbirth at home to childbirth in the hospital came an increase in the use of medication during delivery. Concerns about the impact of these medications, along with reports of unmedicated but seemingly pain-free delivery by women in other cultures, prodded professionals and expectant parents alike to reconsider how best to prepare for the birth of a baby. After observing one woman who reported a pain-free delivery, Grantley Dick-Read, a medical practitioner in Great Britain, concluded that difficult childbirth was fostered largely by the tension and anxiety in which Western civilization cloaked the event. Dick-Read (1959) proposed that women be taught methods of physical relaxation, given information about the process of childbirth, and encouraged to cultivate a cooperative relationship with their doctor to foster a more natural childbirth experience. Others, including Fernand Lamaze (1970), adopted similar ideas, adding procedures to divert thoughts from pain and encouraging breathing activities to support the labor process.

In recent years, **prepared** (or **natural**) **childbirth**, which involves practicing procedures designed to minimize pain and reduce the need for medication during delivery, has become a popular alternative for prospective mothers. Women who attend classes and adhere to the recommendations of Lamaze and other childbirth education programs (including the National Childbirth Trust in the United Kingdom) generally require fewer and lower amounts of drugs during delivery than women who have not participated in prepared childbirth. Women who attend childbirth classes may experience no less pain, but relaxation techniques and an additional element frequently promoted in these programs—the assistance of a coach or trainer, sometimes the father—seem to help counter the discomfort and lead to a more positive evaluation of childbirth (Waldenström, 1999).

prepared (natural) childbirth Type of childbirth that involves practicing procedures during pregnancy and childbirth that are designed to minimize pain and reduce the need for medication during delivery.

Societies differ enormously in their approach to the birth of a baby. In the United States, most births occur in hospitals. In contrast, more than four of every five births in the Trobriand Islands (part of Papua New Guinea) take place in villages where a midwife is in charge.

Research Applied to Parenting

Nurturing and Caring During Labor

Carole knew the signs of the onset of labor; after all, she had already gone through two deliveries. Birthing had proceeded smoothly for her other two children despite her anxieties about the whole process, especially the first time. Maybe it helped to have her husband participate with her in childbirth classes. During those pregnancies she had learned about the various options, ranging from massage to hypnosis to traditional medication, even delivering the baby in water, an alternative the birthing center offered for those who wished to do so. One other thing had been extremely helpful: the presence of a ***doula,*** another woman to accompany her throughout the entire period of labor. Carole was not certain about some of the other alternatives for making the delivery easier and more comfortable. But of one thing she was very sure: she would have a doula with her throughout the birthing process this time as well.

In addition to exhilaration, most women delivering a baby go through a lot of hard work and some, perhaps considerable, discomfort. It can be a very anxious time. Human birth differs from that of other species of mammals in that it typically requires some form of assistance (Rosenberg & Trevathen, 2001). In many cultures, the help comes from friends and relatives or from midwives, just as it did in the United States many decades ago. With the relocation of childbirth to hospitals, however, women became isolated from family and friends, and a more private and impersonal procedure emerged. Perhaps with that change something very important was lost. Research has helped to identify this loss and has led to alternatives in birthing practices that may benefit both men and women as they become new parents.

1. ***Include a partner or some other trusted companion in preparing for and assisting during childbirth.*** Studies carried out in Botswana, Guatemala,

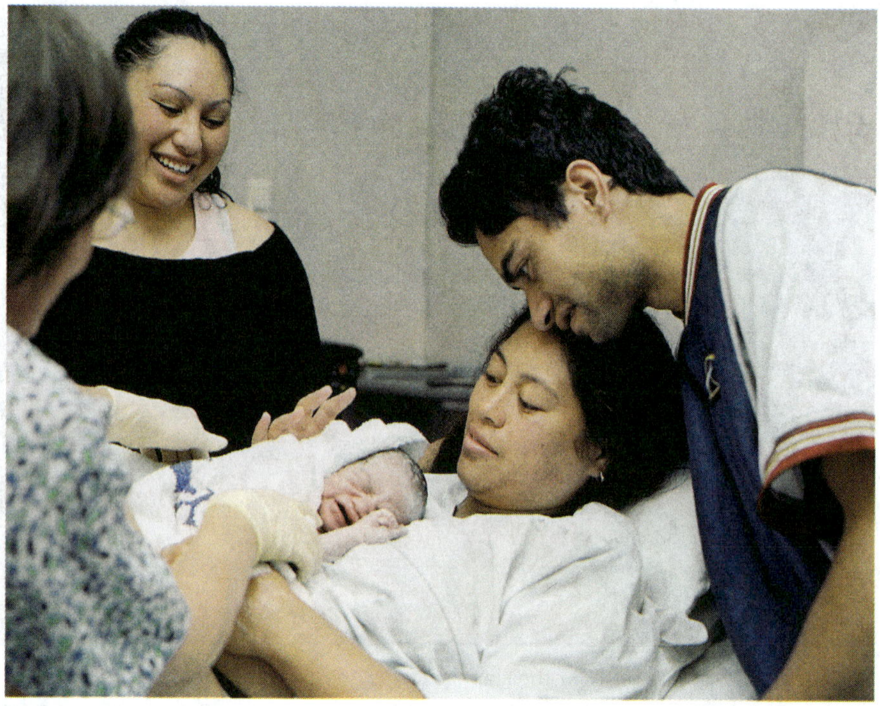

Today, fathers, and sometimes other friends and family members, are encouraged to furnish social and emotional support to women who are about to deliver a baby. When such support is provided by a trusted companion, labor is shorter, fewer drugs are required, and babies are born exhibiting less distress.

several European countries, and the United States demonstrate that having a continuously supportive companion during delivery is helpful to women and their newborns (Kayne, Greulich, & Albers, 2001; Madi et al., 1999; Scott, Berkowitz, & Klaus, 1999). For example, in the Guatamalan studies, first-time mothers were assigned a doula, a woman experienced with delivery who stayed with the mother to provide emotional support, increase her physical comfort, inform her about what was happening during labor, and advocate for her needs (Klaus & Kennell, 1982). Women given these personal attendants spent a far shorter time in labor, required drugs or forceps less frequently, and delivered babies who showed less fetal distress and difficulty breathing than women who received only routine nursing care. Sometimes fathers or other partners are actively encouraged to take on some of these functions as well and can be very effective (Cunningham, 1993), although a doula may be able to provide a more balanced and informative perspective on the sequence of unfolding events.

2. ***Consider what type of practitioner might be most beneficial during childbirth.*** Of course, fathers or other partners who assist in labor are not likely to be experts in the process. Midwives, nurses, or others far more experienced in childbirth, whose additional primary function is to provide personal assistance while managing labor, have received positive evaluations as well. Compared with physicians, midwives who oversee birthing produce, for example, lower rates of deliveries undergoing cesarean birth or other surgical procedures, less use of medication by the mother, and greater satisfaction with care (Butler et al., 1993; Oakley et al., 1996; Sakala, 1993). Whereas about 5 percent of births in the United States are now accompanied by midwives, this figure is nearly 75 percent in many European countries (Alan Guttmacher Institute, 1993).

3. ***Explore the different alternatives available to assist in delivering a baby.*** The positive outcomes achieved by midwives appear to stem from an attitude that inspires women to not just deliver babies but also draw on their own inner resources, as well as their support networks, for giving birth. For example, midwives are likely to suggest greater flexibility in positioning and moving about during labor, perhaps even soaking in a tub. Standing, squatting, or sitting in special chairs, or even hanging from a bar, are increasingly being offered as alternatives to the traditional recumbent position for delivery. These choices can increase a woman's comfort through the natural benefits of gravity and thus reduce stress for both mother and baby. In fact, in non-Western cultures, these alternative positions for childbirth are the norm (Rosenberg & Trevathen, 2001).

LABOR AND DELIVERY

When labor begins, the wet, warm, and supportive world within the uterus undergoes a rapid transformation, and the fetus must adjust to an earthshaking series of changes. During normal birth, the fetus begins to be subjected to increasingly stronger pressure. Because the birth canal is typically smaller than the size of the head, pressure—as great as thirty pounds of force—will probably cause the head to become somewhat elongated and misshapen (Trevathen, 1987). This is possible because the cerebral plates are not yet knitted together, allowing them to slide up and over one another. At times the fetus may experience brief disruptions in oxygen as the flow of blood in the umbilical cord is temporarily obstructed. And then the infant emerges head first into a strange, new

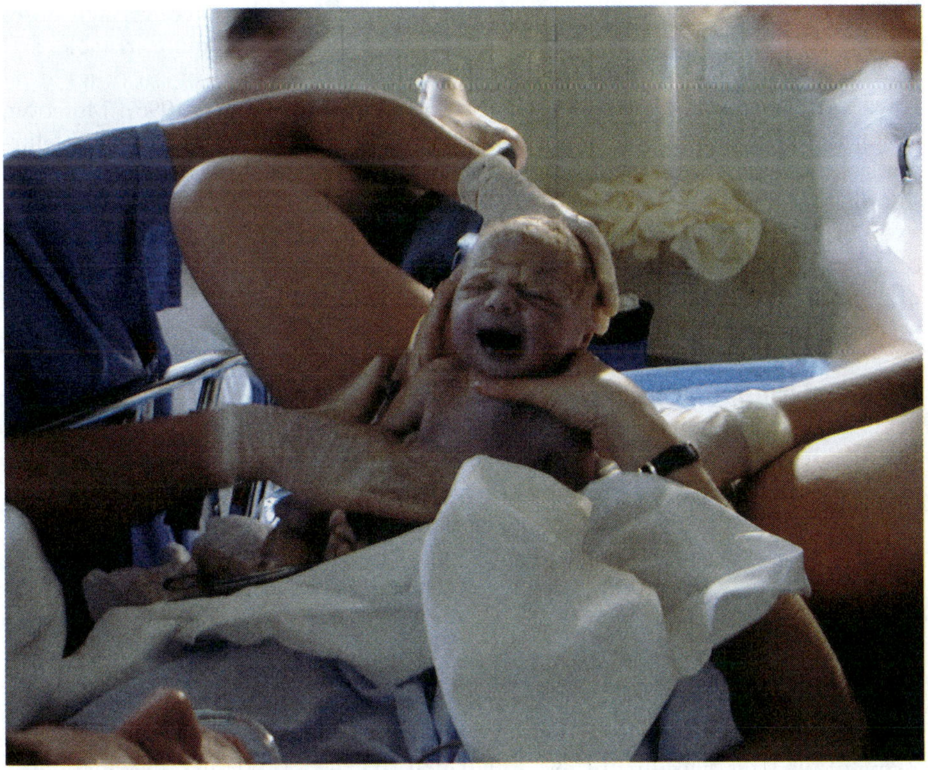

This woman, who has just given birth, now has the opportunity to see and hold her infant for the first time. In contrast to earlier practices, parents in most hospital settings today are allowed ample time to become acquainted with their newborns immediately after birth.

world, one drier, possibly colder, and often much brighter and noisier. Within minutes the new arrival must begin to take in oxygen. The baby must also soon learn to coordinate sucking, swallowing, and breathing to obtain sufficient nutrients.

Labor is a complicated, interactive process involving the fetus, the placenta, and the woman. What brings about its onset? The answer begins with the hypothalamus, pituitary, and adrenal glands of the fetus. When these become mature enough, they help to produce a cascading sequence of hormones and other events, including some in the placenta, that are especially important in initiating labor (Nathanielsz, 1996). In fact, measurement of one hormone in the placenta as early as the sixteenth to twentieth week of pregnancy can predict whether a delivery will occur somewhat before, somewhat after, or about the time of the anticipated due date (Smith, 1999).

The first of the three traditional stages of labor (see Figure 4.5) begins with brief, mild contractions perhaps ten to fifteen minutes apart. These contractions become increasingly frequent and serve to alter the shape of the cervix, preparing it for the fetus's descent and entry into the narrow birth canal. Near the end of the first stage, which on average lasts about eleven hours for firstborns and about seven hours for later-borns, dilation of the cervix proceeds rapidly to allow passage through the birth canal. The second stage consists of the continued descent and the birth of the baby. This stage usually requires a little less than an hour for firstborns and about twenty minutes for later-borns. It also normally includes several reorientations of both the head and shoulders to permit delivery through the tight-fitting passageway (Rosenberg & Trevathen, 2001). In the third stage, which lasts about fifteen minutes, the placenta is expelled. These durations are, however, averages; enormous variation exists from one woman to another.

Medication During Childbirth In Western societies, births are often accompanied by some form of medication. Anesthesia blocks the transmission of pain, analgesics lessen feelings of discomfort, and sedatives help the woman to relax. All of these drugs readily pass through the placenta and enter the fetus's circulatory system. Critics of the routine use of drugs point out that babies whose mothers receive high doses during labor are less attentive and responsive to caregivers, are more irritable, and gain weight more slowly than babies exposed to small amounts or no drugs at all (Brazelton, Nugent, & Lester, 1987; Emory, Schlackman, & Fiano, 1996). Moreover, some behavioral differences may persist well beyond infancy. Heavy use of drugs during labor has been associated, for example, with an increased incidence of learning disorders among school-age children (Brackbill, McManus, & Woodward, 1985).

Developmental differences between babies born to medicated and nonmedicated women, however, are not consistent. Some experts believe the negative effects of exposure to drugs at birth have been markedly overstated and occur only when medications are used excessively (Kraemer et al., 1985). Thus women need not experience unreasonable pain or feel guilty if drugs are administered. Efforts to make the birth process gentler, such as by reducing illumination and noise or by delivering the baby under water, have also been proposed (Daniels, 1989; LeBoyer, 1975), although the advantages of these practices for either women or infants have not been documented. The use of other complementary and alternative medical procedures, such as acupuncture and various relaxation techniques, also remain unproven with respect to benefits to mother or newborn (Allaire, 2001). However, as we have already discussed, providing a network of social support does help.

KEY THEME
RISK/RESILIENCE

Cesarean Birth A *cesarean birth* is the delivery of a baby through a surgical incision in the woman's abdomen and uterus. Cesarean births are recommended, for example, when labor fails to progress normally, when the baby's head is very large, or when birth is *breech* (foot or rump first) rather than head first. Concerns about stress on the fetus that might lead to increased risk of brain damage, vaginal infections that might be transmitted to the baby, and expensive malpractice suits (should things go awry during vaginal delivery) have led to more than a fivefold increase in the frequency of cesarean sections in the past thirty years in the United States. Today slightly over 27 percent of deliveries in the United States are cesarean rather than vaginal (Centers for Disease Control and Prevention, 2005c).

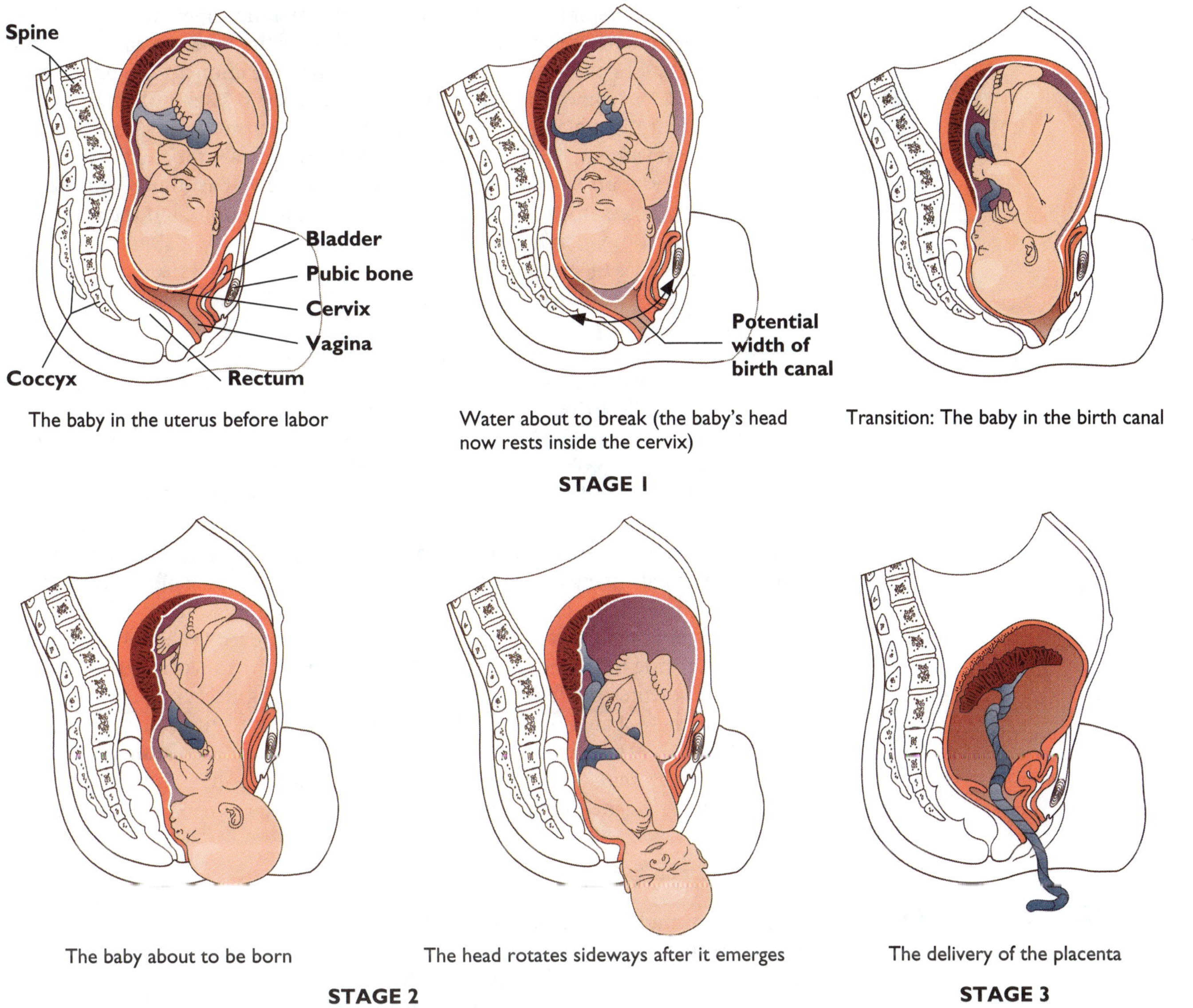

FIGURE 4.5

The Three Stages of Childbirth

In the first state of labor the cervix, the neck of the uterus, dilates and thins to open a passage through the birth canal. The amniotic fluid, if not already lost, helps by exerting firm, even pressure on the cervix. When the pressure becomes too great, the sac containing the amniotic fluid will rupture, a process known as "breaking the water." The head of the fetus will soon enter the birth canal, and the second stage of labor begins. During the second stage of labor, each contraction continues to push the fetus farther along the approximately four inches of birth canal. During a normal delivery, the head emerges first (known as *crowning*), much as though pushing through the neck of a tight turtleneck sweater. The orientation of the head toward the mother's back is one of the reasons birthing for humans often needs the assistance of others (Rosenberg & Trevathen, 2001). Once the head has emerged, shoulders twist around in the birth canal, and the head turns sideways to permit delivery of the rest of the body. In the final stages of labor, the placenta is delivered.

Women who undergo cesarean section face an increased risk of infection and a longer hospital stay than women who give birth vaginally. Moreover, cesarean babies are likely to be exposed to greater maternal medication. Other concerns center on the different experiences that both mother and infant receive under such circumstances. For example, when cesarean babies are delivered before labor begins, they do not have a misshapen head and appear perfectly healthy. However, they have substantially lower levels of two stress hormones, adrenaline and noradrenaline, known to facilitate respiration by helping to keep the lungs open and clear. These hormones also enhance cell metabolism, circulation of the blood to the brain, and activity level, factors that help the infant make the transition to his or her new environment and become responsive to caregivers. Thus cesarean babies generally tend to have more trouble breathing, are less active, sleep more, and cry less than other babies (Trevathen, 1987). Mothers, too, tend to evaluate their experience of a cesarean delivery, especially if unplanned, less positively than those who deliver vaginally. Nevertheless, the quality of mother-infant interactions and the psychosocial functioning of the infants a year after their birth appear quite similar regardless of type of delivery, suggesting that there are few long-term negative consequences of cesarean births (DiMatteo et al., 1996; Durik, Hyde, & Clark, 2000).

Birth Trauma The increase in the frequency of cesarean sections in the United States has come about partly because of concerns about birth trauma, or injuries sustained at birth. A potentially serious consequence is *anoxia*, or deprivation of oxygen. Anoxia can result from, for example, damage to or lengthy compression of the umbilical cord or head during birth, problems associated with the placenta, or failure of the baby to begin regular breathing after birth. If oxygen deprivation lasts more than a few minutes, severe damage to the central nervous system, including *cerebral palsy*, can result.

Fortunately, brief periods of anoxia have few long-lasting effects. Furthermore, an adequate postnatal caregiving environment can help to counter potentially negative outcomes for infants experiencing periods without oxygen (Sameroff & Chandler, 1975). Concerns about anoxia and other birth traumas have led to the widespread use of **fetal monitoring devices** during labor. Most of these devices record fetal heartbeat to determine whether the fetus is undergoing stress during delivery. However, some experts argue that reliance on medically sophisticated equipment promotes interventions that only exacerbate the difficulty of delivery. In fact, by focusing on a supportive context to reduce anxiety, less birth trauma will occur than that which the technology was designed to prevent (Hafner-Eaton & Pearce, 1994; Sakala, 1993).

Low Birth Weight

KEY THEME
Risk/Resilience

KEY THEME
Sociocultural Influence

As infant and childhood diseases have come under greater control in recent decades, the treatment and prevention of low-birth-weight infants (those weighing less than 2,500 grams, or five and a half pounds) has gained increased attention. Mortality rate declines rapidly as birth weight increases to near-normal levels. The United States has a higher proportion of infants born with low birth weight than many other developed countries, a major reason why its infant mortality rate is also higher than in many other industrialized countries (see Figure 4.6).

Babies with low birth weight fall into two major groups: those born preterm (less than thirty-five weeks' conceptual age), whose development has generally proceeded normally but has been cut short by early delivery, and those born near their expected arrival date but *small for gestational age (SGA)*; that is, displaying intrauterine growth retardation. Thus low-birth-weight infants compose a heterogeneous group, perhaps needing separate types of medical treatment and intervention, and facing different developmental outcomes. Congenital anomalies are somewhat more frequent in SGA infants, for example, whereas respiratory distress is more likely among infants who are born preterm.

Caring for Infants with Low Birth Weight In general, infants born with low birth weight face numerous obstacles, not only in terms of survival but also throughout subsequent development (Agustines et al., 2000; Chan et al., 2000). Cerebral palsy, seizure disorders, and neurological difficulties that include hemorrhaging associated with regions of the brain, respiratory difficulties, and eye disorders are some examples of the problems observed. These difficulties are found especially frequently among infants born with *very low birth weight* (less than 1,500 grams, or 3 pounds and 3 ounces) and even more so among those with *extremely low birth weight* (less than

fetal monitoring device Medical device used to monitor fetal heartbeat during delivery.

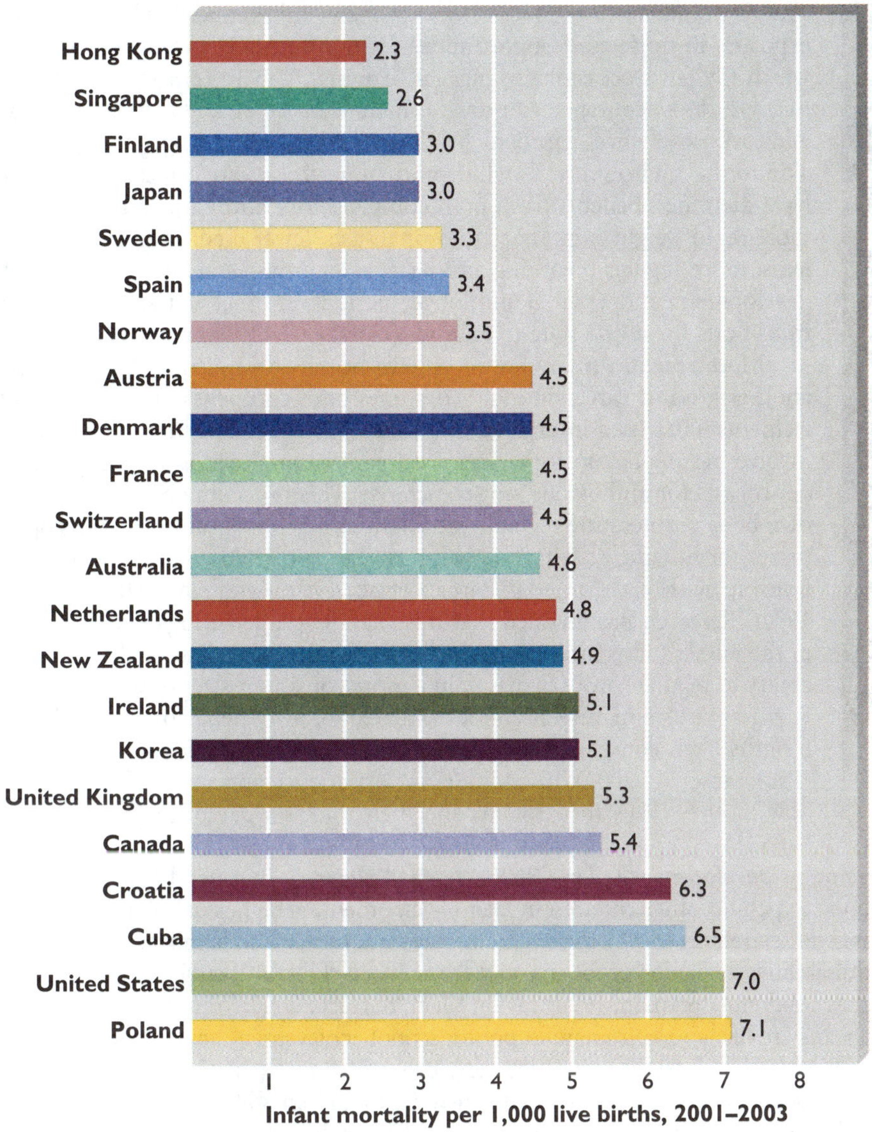

FIGURE 4.6

Infant Mortality in Selected Developed Countries

The infant mortality rate (deaths before one year of age per thousand live births) is a measure that provides an indication of the overall health of a nation. A number of countries have a lower infant mortality rate than the United States.

Source: Data from United Nations, *Population and Vital Statistics Report* (2005).

1,000 grams, or 2 pounds and 2 ounces) or who are born at less than twenty-seven weeks' gestational age. In addition to these problems, all low-birth-weight and premature infants face the major task of maintaining physiological stability and achieving regular cycles of activity involving sleep and wakefulness. To deal with these problems, premature infants spend much of their time in an isolette, a small plexiglass chamber that carefully controls temperature and air flow with the aid of a respirator. They may be fed with a stomach tube and are often given painful heel pricks and other interventions to monitor the effects of medication and treatment.

KEY THEME
NATURE & NURTURE

The types of experiences that premature infants have typically received have been of considerable concern in terms of their social and psychological consequences for development. At one time parents were either excluded completely from neonatal intensive care units (NICUs), the specialized medical facilities designed to care for low-birth-weight infants (called *special care baby units* in Great Britain), or were given little opportunity to see or care for their newborns. However, that policy has changed substantially as evidence emerged showing the importance of appropriate stimulation for postnatal development (Ramey, Bryant, & Suarez, 1987; Thoman, 1993). NICUs and parents now sometimes provide *compensatory stimulation*, experience to duplicate what the baby would have gained while still in the womb. For instance, the baby might be exposed to oscillating devices or waterbeds to simulate the movements the fetus experiences prenatally; muffled recordings of a human voice, a heartbeat, or other

The opportunity to interact with each other shortly after birth has consequences for both mother and child. For children born with low birthweight, these occasions may be more difficult to arrange. Nevertheless, research reveals that encouraging parents to engage in these kinds of experiences is beneficial to children.

sounds to match those usually heard in the womb; reduced light and reduced exposure to noise; and opportunities for nonnutritive sucking, an activity in which the fetus occasionally engages (Thoman, 1993). Caregivers and others may also be encouraged to provide suitable *enriching stimulation:* visual and auditory experiences, prudent handling, and social and body contact more akin to the environment to which normal newborns are exposed. Researchers have identified benefits from both compensatory and enriching stimulation: more rapid weight gain, shorter hospital stays, fewer medical and eating problems, more regular breathing and heart rate, improvements in sensorimotor development, more stable and longer periods in quiet states, and smoother transitions from one state to another (Gorski, 1991; Thoman, 1993).

More recently, many hospitals have begun to implement *kangaroo care,* another kind of caregiving that combines both compensatory and enriching elements. First used in Bogotá, Colombia, about a decade ago, kangaroo care involves resting the unclothed premature infant on the mother's body between her breasts for an hour or longer each day. This procedure helps the mother's own body temperature regulate the infant's body temperature, permits opportunity for nursing activity, and helps mother and child establish a social relationship with each other (Charpak et al., 1997; Ludington-Hoe & Swinth, 1996). Research has revealed that this experience, given to premature infants in the NICU for as little as an hour a day for fourteen days, facilitates infants' ability to regulate arousal, maintain a more consistent sleep-wake pattern, and engage in more mature attentional and exploratory behaviors as much as six months later, compared with premature infants not receiving kangaroo care (Feldman et al., 2002). In addition, the experience appears to positively affect how mothers view their infants and their role as a parent (Neu, 1999).

Promoting Development in Low-Birth-Weight Children In general, low-birth-weight infants lag behind other children in later development. A higher proportion, especially those with extremely low birth weight, display visuomotor and language deficits, learning disabilities, behavior problems, and fewer social skills, and suffer more peer rejection as children (Bregman, 1998; Taylor, Klein, & Hack, 2000; Vohr et al., 2000). These problems are likely to culminate in poorer school achievement and the need for more special education intervention (Klebanov, Brooks-Gunn, & McCormick, 1994; Saigal et al., 2000). Fortunately, many low-birth-weight children still do surprisingly well, as revealed by an analysis of data from more than eighty studies conducted in North America, Europe, Australia, and New Zealand (Aylward et al., 1989). Indeed, the enormous, although justified, concern about the development of some of these children often overshadows the fact that the ones who display severe disabilities represent only a small proportion of all very low-birth-weight children (McCormick, 1997).

KEY THEME
NATURE & NURTURE

As we have begun to see in other examples of children with special needs, one very important factor contributing to positive developmental outcomes appears to be the support and encouragement of parents. Providing parents with opportunities to engage in suitable caregiving in the hospital setting, instructing them to recognize the specific needs of their infant and what behaviors to expect, and extending the emotional support of professional staff and other parents are types of assistance that have proven beneficial to low-birth-weight children (Achenbach et al., 1993; McCormick et al., 1993; Ramey et al., 1992). For example, Jeanne Brooks-Gunn and her colleagues (1993) found that low-birth-weight children who participated in educational daycare programs, and whose families received regular home visits and joined in frequent parent group meetings, were able to maintain higher levels of performance on cognitive tests than children in families for whom these resources were unavailable (see Figure 4.7).

Parenting a low-birth-weight infant, especially one who shows medical complications, can be very stressful (Taylor et al., 2001). Despite the continuing demands and increased burdens that are often a part of such child rearing, mothers of very low-birth-weight children report levels of satisfaction and positive feelings with respect to their parenting that are similar to those of mothers of normal-birth-weight children by the time their offspring reach three years of age (Singer,

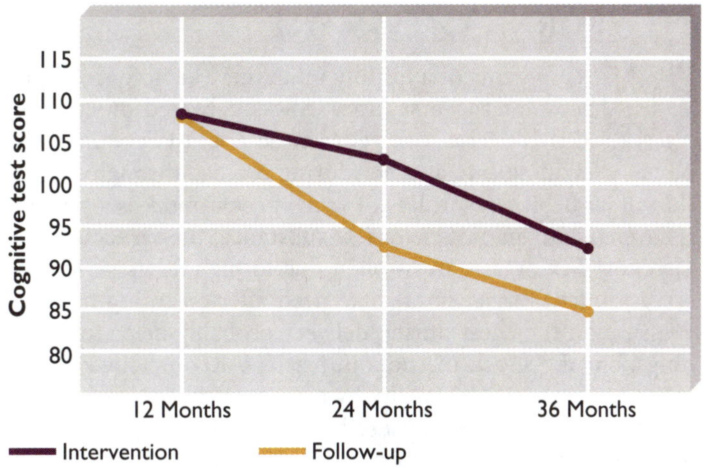

FIGURE 4.7

Low-Birth-Weight Children's Cognitive Development as a Function of Intervention

In a large-scale study investigating the effects of providing home visits and educational child care for low-birth-weight infants and their families, Brooks-Gunn and her colleagues found that performance on measures of intellectual development was substantially better for those who received the intervention than for those who did not. Although some decline in scores occurred even for the group receiving intervention, it was far less than for those who did not receive the intervention. Both groups performed similarly at the youngest age (twelve months), perhaps because tests measuring cognitive skills often are not very sensitive to differences at that age.

Source: Brooks-Gunn et al. (1993).

Salvator, et al., 1999). Moreover, the caregivers of children born with extremely low birth weight are as enthusiastic and supportive of making every effort to provide the best medical care possible for these children as are parents of children born with normal birth weight (Streiner et al., 2001). In bringing up a low-birth-weight child, however, providing family- and child-oriented services appears to be especially important in helping to reduce stress, especially for those mothers who are less educated and may have fewer other resources available (Klebanov, Brooks-Gunn, & McCormick, 2001).

Attempts to reduce complications associated with low birth weight have proceeded on two fronts. Improved medical care in NICUs and supportive caregiving have permitted more low-birth-weight, especially extremely low-birth-weight, infants to survive and develop normally. These positive findings reflect more effective treatment (for instance, for respiratory distress) and management of the NICU (as in reductions in bright light, loud noise, and sleep interruptions), designed to reduce stress in individuals who are among the least capable of responding to stress (Als et al., 1994; Bregman, 1998). Yet, despite the increased number of survivors, the proportion of children showing neurological or cognitive problems has remained stable (Lorenz et al., 1997; O'Shea al., 1997; Piecuch, Leonard, & Cooper, 1998; Stevenson et al., 1998). Thus a second major assault on the problem has been in the form of prevention. Researchers have catalogued a long list of demographic, medical, and behavioral factors associated low birth weight; for example, inadequate prenatal care and nutrition, heavy smoking, and drug use. Because many of these factors are preventable, educational programs targeted toward pregnant women at high risk, including teenagers, have become increasingly important. These programs can reduce the incidence of low birth weight, especially when offered consistently and early in the course of pregnancy (Fangman al., 1994; Seitz & Apfel, 1994). Indeed, future progress in addressing the problems that accompany low birth weight is likely to be as closely tied to improved and more widespread programs of prevention as to new medical advances.

FOR • YOUR • REVIEW

- What are the benefits of prepared childbirth and a supportive relationship with another individual for both parent and newborn child?
- What are the stages of delivery? How does medication during delivery affect the newborn?
- What are the benefits and disadvantages of cesarean births for mother and child? Why is this procedure often carried out?
- How do premature and small-for-gestational-age infants differ? What are the factors that increase the likelihood of low birth weight? What practices help children born with low birth weight?

Newborn Assessment

Even parents of a healthy infant may be in for a surprise when they see their baby for the first time. Unless delivered by cesarean section, the baby is likely to have a flattened nose and a large, distorted head from the skull bones' overriding one another during passage through the narrow birth canal. The skin of all babies, regardless of racial background, is a pale pinkish color and often is covered with an oily, cheeselike substance (the *vernix caseosa*) that protects against infection. Sex organs are swollen due to high levels of sex hormones.

An infant's most immediate need after emerging from the womb is breathing. Pressure on the chest during delivery probably helps to clear the baby's fluid-filled lungs, but the shock of cool air, perhaps accompanied by jiggling, a slap, or some other less-than-gentle activity by a birth attendant, makes the first breath more like a gasp, quickly followed by a reflexive cry. The umbilical cord may continue to pulse for several minutes after birth; in many societies the cord is not cut until after it ceases to do so (Trevathen, 1987).

The second major task the baby must accomplish upon entering the world is regulating body temperature. Babies lose body heat about four times more rapidly than adults because of their lower fat reserve and relatively large body surface (Bruck, 1962). As a consequence, newborns, although they can effectively maintain their temperature when held close to a caregiver's body, are often quickly placed under heaters.

Newborns typically weigh five and a half to ten pounds, and measure eighteen to twenty-two inches in length. Many procedures for evaluating their health have become available in recent years, but one that is routinely administered is the *Apgar Scale* (Apgar, 1953). Typically assessed at both one and five minutes after birth, the Apgar measures five vital signs: heart rate, respiratory effort, muscle tone, reflex responsivity, and color. Each vital sign is scored 0, 1, or 2 based on the criteria described in Table 4.5. In the United States, 90 percent of infants receive a total score of 7 or better; those who score lower than 4 are considered to be at risk.

Key Theme
Risk/Resilience

A more extensive measure, developed by T. Berry Brazelton (1973) and given several days after birth, is the *Neonatal Behavioral Assessment Scale (NBAS)*. The NBAS evaluates, for example, the baby's ability to interact with the tester, responsiveness to objects in the environment, reflex motor capacities, and ability to control functions such as breathing and temperature. Newborn performance on the NBAS

Table 4.5 The Apgar Scoring System

The Apgar Scale is used at and shortly after birth to diagnose the physical condition of a newborn. The ratings for each vital sign are added for a total score ranging from 0 to 10. An infant who scores less than 4 is considered to be at risk.

	Ratings		
Vital Sign	*0*	*1*	*2*
Heart rate	Absent	Slow (below 100)	Over 100
Respiratory effort	Absent	Slow, irregular	Good, crying
Muscle tone	Flaccid	Some flexion of extremities	Active motion
Reflex responsivity	No response	Grimace	Vigorous cry
Color	Blue, pale	Body pink, extremities blue	Completely pink

Source: Adapted from Apgar, 1953. From V. Apgar, "A Proposal for a New Method of Evaluation of the Newborn Infant," *Anesthesia and Analgesia: Current Researches*, 32, 260–267. Copyright © 1953. Used by permission of Lippincott Williams & Wilkins. www.anesthesia-analgesia.org

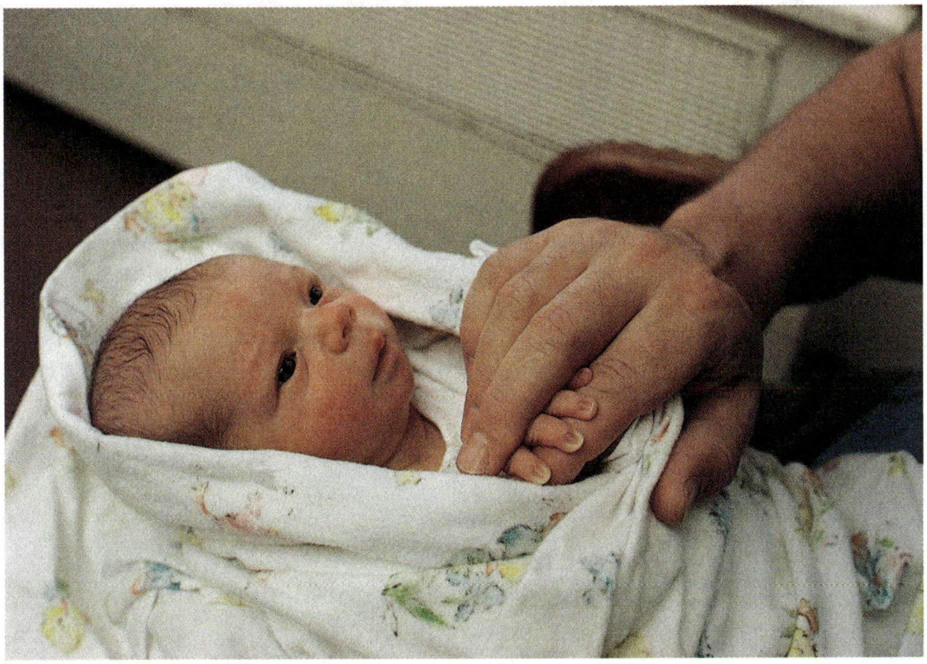

This two-day-old baby, holding her father's hand, has entered a world in which new forms of physical and social stimulation can be experienced. Although newborns and young infants spend much of their time sleeping, this infant is engaged in alert inactivity, a time in which she may be learning much about her environment.

has been used to assess neurological condition and can indicate whether certain prenatal or perinatal conditions, as well as intervention programs, have had an effect (Korner, 1987; Tronick, 1987). An NBAS score can also predict later developmental outcomes. Babies who score poorly on the scale continue to be somewhat less responsive to caregivers in the first few months after birth (Vaughn et al., 1980). In general, however, the predictive validity of the NBAS (along with other infant tests) for long-term development is only modest at best (Brazelton, Nugent, & Lester, 1987). Nevertheless, parents who observe while examiners give the NBAS or who are trained to give it themselves seem to become more responsive to and effective in interactions with their infants (Worobey, 1985).

As these last two chapters have shown, there are many events in the period from conception to birth that lay important foundations for development. By the time the infant takes its first breath and utters its first cry, many of the first steps in his or her developmental story have already been taken.

FOR • YOUR • REVIEW

- What are the first tasks for the newborn following birth?
- Why are scores on the Apgar Scale and the Neonatal Behavioral Assessment Scale important?

Chapter Recap

Summary of Developmental Themes

Nature & Nurture

How do nature and nurture interact during prenatal development and birth?

Prenatal development is the product of complex interactions involving genetic instructions inherited from parents and the expectant woman's physical and emotional conditions, as well as exposure to drugs, diseases, hazardous chemicals, and medications before and during pregnancy and during labor. We have seen, for example, that differentiation of organs and systems in the embryo typically obeys principles established by biochemical and physiological processes. Yet these processes do not operate in a vacuum. Teratogens and various intrauterine conditions can radically alter the normal developmental path. Thus events in the life of the woman may change the immediate environment within her womb, with drastic consequences for the fetus. The reactions, attitudes, and availability of the newborn's caregivers and the stimulation they provide are other major sources of potential influence on the baby's development.

Sociocultural Influence

How does the sociocultural context influence prenatal development and birth?

The immediate internal environment of the fetus and the perinatal environment provided for the newborn can be influenced dramatically by the larger social, economic, and cultural settings in which pregnancy and birth take place. The woman's actions during pregnancy are often modified or regulated by a network of expectations, advice, and resources within the culture in which she lives. An expec-tant woman in one community, for example, may have access to medical and other kinds of care that provide a more or less healthy environment for the fetus than a woman in another community may have. Industrial or government units may legislate controls on chemical pollution in one country and ignore them in another. Scientific and technological advances in prenatal testing, birthing practices, and newborn care may be available in one region of the world but not in another; even when available, however, not all parents may have the economic resources or the desire to use them.

Continuity/Discontinuity

Is development before and after birth continuous or discontinuous?

When the zygote attaches to the uterine wall and taps a new source of nourishment, its course of development changes dramatically. Once the various organs and systems are formed and become less susceptible to environmental disruptions, the fetus achieves a vastly different status. The process of birth itself is a major transition. Such spectacular changes fit with discontinuous or stagelike descriptions of development. So do the marked shifts in vulnerability to teratogens observed during prenatal development. Underlying the progressions, however, are biochemical and physiological processes governing cell proliferation, differentiation, and the emergence and functioning of biological systems, which can be seen as continuous. Many dramatic changes are essentially the product of modest accumulative modifications in the multifaceted, complex environment that promotes development.

Risk/Resilience

What factors promote risk or resilience during prenatal development and birth?

Newborns everywhere undergo many common gestational experiences; however, differences in development arise because the fetus is not immune to the influences of the larger world. Because of exposure to teratogens and other maternal conditions, babies will differ in their physical and behavioral qualities, and their ability to cope with and adapt to their new environment. Greater knowledge of and sensitivity to those differences by caregivers, whether exhibited by a newborn with special needs, such as one with low birth weight, or by an infant who falls within the typical range for newborns, can help to ensure success for the continued development of every child.

Chapter Review

The Stages of Prenatal Development

What constitutes the prenatal, perinatal, and postnatal periods of development?

Prenatal development is the period that extends from conception to birth. The *perinatal period* extends from about the seventh month of pregnancy until twenty-eight days after birth. The *postnatal period* is the time that follows birth.

What are the major changes that take place following conception during the germinal, embryonic, and fetal periods of prenatal development?

During the *germinal period*, about the first ten to fourteen days after conception, the zygote migrates from the Fallopian tube to the uterus, becomes multicelled, and implants itself in the uterine wall to gain access to a new source of nutrients obtained from the mother. The *embryonic period* begins after implantation and continues until about the eighth week after conception. The embryonic period is marked by development of the placenta and other supportive structures within the uterine environment and by the differentiation of cells into tissues that form the major organs and systems of the embryo. The *fetal period*, beginning in about the eighth week after conception and lasting until birth, is marked by substantial growth and by refinement of organs and systems. By the last trimester, the ability of the fetus to survive on its own (*viability*) improves. For human infants, birth typically occurs at 274 days *gestational age*.

When are the major organs and systems of the body established? What is the course of brain and nervous system development in the embryo and fetus?

The major body organs and systems, including the brain and nervous system, differentiate during the embryonic phase. Neurons continue to form and migrate during the fetal period. Brain activity, sensory reactions, and movement are exhibited by the fetus.

How can various kinds of assisted reproduction help those couples who have difficulty conceiving or are concerned about the inheritance of genetic disorders in their offspring? What are some of the medical and legal issues associated with various forms of assisted reproduction?

Among the assisted reproduction technologies are artificial insemination by donor, egg donation, fertility drugs, gamete intrafallopian transfer, in vitro fertilization, and maternal surrogacy. Some of the issues raised by these technologies include the competence of the practitioners, the fact that children born with these methods may not know about their biological heritage, and the increased risk of multiple pregnancies.

ENVIRONMENTAL FACTORS INFLUENCING PRENATAL DEVELOPMENT

What kinds of supportive functions do the placenta, umbilical cord, and amniotic sac provide for the embryo and the fetus?

The *placenta* serves as the major organ for transfer of nutrients from the mother's circulatory system and for expelling waste products from the fetus. The *umbilical cord* connects the fetus to the placenta. The *amniotic sac* provides a fluid-filled, protective surrounding in which development of the fetus occurs.

What are teratogens? What principles apply to how teratogens have their effects?

During both embryonic and fetal development, *teratogens*, or environmental agents harmful to the organism, can disrupt development and interfere with later behavior. The effects of teratogens differ depending on the genetic susceptibility of the embryo or fetus, how the teratogen reaches the prenatal environment, its level of dosage and manner of exposure, and where it interferes with cellular activity. A teratogen's effects also differ depending on the time at which exposure occurs during prenatal development. Not all the consequences are observed immediately; they may not even be evident until well into the postnatal years.

How do alcohol, cigarette smoke, prescription and over-the-counter drugs, and illegal drugs affect prenatal development?

Many different drugs are able to cross the placental barrier and can have teratogenic effects. Among those known to have the greatest impact on fetal development are alcohol, which can result in *fetal alcohol syndrome (FAS)*, and cigarette smoke, which is associated with low birth weight. The effects of prescription and over-the-counter drugs on prenatal development are not always well known but can include low birth weight and lower IQ. Teratogenic effects, such as cognitive impairment, are linked to the use of illegal drugs. However, their effects are often confounded with other factors known to have significant negative consequences for the fetus. These factors include lack of proper nutrition, poor health of the mother, absence of medical care, lack of emotional and social support, and high levels of stress.

What kinds of risks exist for the embryo and fetus exposed to rubella, toxoplasmosis, cytomegalovirus, and sexually transmitted diseases?

Diseases can have serious repercussions on both prenatal and postnatal development. Rubella is associated visual, auditory, and heart defects, as well as mental retardation. Toxoplasmosis can cause visual problems and intellectual impairment. Cytomegalovirus is also associated with mental retardation, as well as sensory or motor problems. Sexually transmitted diseases are associated with low birth weight, visual defects, mental retardation, and in the most serious cases, death.

What maternal conditions affect the well-being of the fetus and embryo?

Less positive outcomes in prenatal development are possible if the mother is either very young or in the late childbearing years; has poor nutrition, a high level of stress, or lack of social support; or suffers from certain conditions, such as diabetes, obesity, and pregnancy-induced hypertension.

BIRTH AND THE PERINATAL ENVIRONMENT

What are the benefits of prepared childbirth and a supportive relationship with another individual for both parent and newborn child?

Prepared (natural) childbirth may reduce the need for medication during delivery and often leads women to give more positive evaluations of childbirth. The presence of someone familiar with the birth process but continuously present to provide emotional support and information to the mother, appears to have benefits for both mother and newborn.

What are the stages of delivery? How does medication during delivery affect the newborn?

Childbirth proceeds through three stages. In the first and longest stage, labor helps to initiate preparation of the birth canal. Passage of the fetus through the birth canal makes up the second stage. During the third stage, the placenta is delivered. Labor appears to be initiated by hormones produced by the fetus and the placenta. Newborns whose mothers receive medication during delivery may show less responsiveness, greater irritability, and slower weight gain.

What are the benefits and disadvantages of cesarean birth for mother and child? Why is this procedure often carried out?

Cesarean deliveries are relatively common in the United States, despite their greater expense, greater recovery time for the mother, and the risk of exposure to medication to the newborn. Babies delivered via cesarean birth may also show greater initial breathing problems. The large number of cesarean births in the United States may stem, in part, from the extensive use of *fetal monitoring devices,* which signal fetal distress during delivery. Fetal distress is linked to concerns about the long-term negative consequences of birth trauma, such as exposure to oxygen deprivation.

How do premature and small-for-gestational-age infants differ? What are the factors that increase the likelihood of low birth weight? What practices help children born with low birth weight?

Premature infants are born before thirty-five weeks' conceptual age. Babies who are small for gestational age are born near their due date but show growth retardation. Risk factors for low birth weight include inadequate prenatal care, poor nutrition, smoking, and drug use. Compensatory and enrichment programs for low-birth-weight infants increase early weight gains and other developmental outcomes.

Newborn Assessment

What are the first tasks for the newborn following birth?

Respiration and maintenance of body temperature are two immediate critical goals for the newborn.

Why are scores on the Apgar Scale and the Neonatal Behavioral Assessment Scale important?

Tests given to the newborn shortly after birth, such as the Apgar Scale and the Neonatal Behavioral Assessment Scale, provide some indication of the baby's physiological state and ability to interact with caregivers and respond to stimulation.

Key Terms and Concepts

amniotic sac (p. 118)
embryonic period (p. 110)
fetal alcohol syndrome (FAS) (p. 120)
fetal monitoring device (p. 140)
fetal period (p. 110)
germinal period (p. 110)
gestational age (p. 117)
perinatal period (p. 110)
placenta (p. 118)
postnatal period (p. 110)
prenatal development (p. 110)
prepared (natural) childbirth (p. 134)
teratogen (p. 118)
umbilical cord (p. 118)
viability (p. 115)

PHYSICAL DEVELOPMENT 5

Marc knew he had to dress the baby quickly. It had been a hectic morning. His wife's car hadn't started, and they had to arrange for her to get a ride to work. Now he and their three-month-old daughter, Abbie, had to step up the pace to get to daycare. Marc hastily pulled out a sweatshirt and pants from the baby's dresser, grateful that Abbie was in a good mood and didn't seem to mind the rapid tempo of the morning's routine. "Here you go, honey. Let's get these pants on you. Here are your blue pants from Aunt Rose. Bloooie pants!" Abbie responded with a gleeful smile and a few kicks. But as he lifted the waistband over Abbie's diaper, he could see that he had a problem. Worn only once before, these pants now barely covered the middle of Abbie's little calf. "Well, little girl, you sure look funny like that. We're going to have to start all over again." Looking at the picture of a younger, newborn Abbie that stood on the dresser, he couldn't help but notice the remarkable changes that his daughter had gone through in only three short months.

KEY THEMES in Physical Development

NATURE & NURTURE How do nature and nurture interact in physical development in infancy?

SOCIOCULTURAL INFLUENCE How does the sociocultural context influence physical development in infancy?

CONTINUITY/DISCONTINUITY Is physical development during infancy continuous or discontinuous?

INTERACTION AMONG DOMAINS How does physical development during infancy interact with other domains of development?

RISK/RESILIENCE What factors promote risk or resilience in physical development during infancy?

Physical growth and advances in motor skills are among the most readily apparent signs of development in infancy. Many first-time parents are astonished at just how quickly infants outgrow their newly purchased clothes, sometimes literally overnight! And they are likely to be equally astonished that, in the course of only a few months, the young infant who could barely control his head when picked up becomes an active, mobile explorer. These transformations are accompanied by less obvious, but no less revolutionary, changes in the brain.

The growth of the body, the development of the brain, and the acquisition of physical skills affect virtually every behavior displayed by the child and are, in turn, influenced by the social, emotional, and cognitive demands made on her as growth occurs. Consider how newfound motor coordinations may, for example, dramatically awaken cognition. The six-month-old who begins to reach for and grasp objects acquires a novel and powerful means of gaining information about the world and, at the same time, a new way to control and influence her environment. By the same token, the reactions of others to changing stature and accomplishments can arouse a child's pride and promote renewed efforts, or they can lead to discouragement and apprehension. For example, when children begin to crawl, they may confront new barriers and repeated choruses of "No, don't do that." How these freshly imposed limits, inspired by burgeoning physical and mental capacities, are faced and resolved can affect many other aspects of solving problems or building relationships with others.

How do body, brain, and motor skills develop during infancy? To what extent do parenting, culture, or other environmental events influence their course? And what basic capacities does the infant possess to learn and to derive information from the senses—vision, audition, taste, touch, and smell? In this chapter we explore the basic physical capacities of the infant, as well as the rapid and important changes that take place in this sphere during the first two years.

The infant's achievements in the domain of motor development often have profound consequences for other areas of development. Consider this infant's acquisition of the ability to reach for objects. He is now equipped to explore the textures and shapes of objects, and in some cases, their tastes. By reaching, he is also able to make requests for objects, thereby gaining a stronger sense of control over events in his life.

Body Growth and Development

There is probably no more obvious indicator of development than change in a child's physical size. We tend to use the words *grow* and *develop* interchangeably in describing the physical transformations of childhood, but they do not refer to the same processes. Strictly speaking, *growth* is the increase in size of the body or its organs, whereas *development* refers not only to changes in size but also to the orderly patterns, such as growth spurts, and the more complicated levels of functioning that often accompany increases in height and weight.

Norms of Growth

By recording information about the height and weight of large numbers of children from diverse populations, we can determine whether a particular child's individual growth falls within the range expected for his or her chronological age and ethnic background. These **norms**, quantitative measures that provide typical values and variations in height and weight for children, have become an essential reference for attempting to answer questions about how biological and experiential factors influence growth.

Length and Height The most rapid increase in body length occurs during the fourth month of prenatal development, when the fetus grows about 1.5 millimeters a day. The fetus continues to grow rapidly, albeit at a somewhat slower rate, during the remaining prenatal weeks. The newborn maintains a high rate of growth for several months following birth. In fact, if growth rate during the first six months after birth were sustained, the average ten-year-old would be about one hundred feet tall (McCall, 1979)! Girls can be expected to reach approximately half their adult height a little before two years of age and boys a little after two years of age (Fredriks et al., 2000).

Individual children, of course, may differ enormously in their growth rate, and their growth sometimes occurs in sudden spurts. One remarkable fact revealed by research is that growth of one-quarter to one half inch can occasionally occur virtually overnight in infants and toddlers (Lampl, Veldhuis, & Johnson, 1992). Marc, in this chapter's opening vignette, may have actually been an unwitting witness to just such an event.

Weight In contrast to that of height, the maximum rate of increase in weight takes place shortly after birth. In their first few days, newborns typically lose excess body fluids and shed 5 to 10 percent of their birth weight. They then usually make rapid weight gains, normally doubling their birth weight in about five months and nearly tripling it by the end of the first year (Pinyerd, 1992). To give you a sense of just how fast this process takes place, if the gains for the first six months were sustained, the average ten-year-old would weigh in at about 240,000 tons (McCall, 1979).

Patterns in Body Growth

Specific organs and systems of the body often develop at rates different from that for the body as a whole. The most dramatic example is probably head size. Two months after conception, the head constitutes nearly 50 percent of total body length. By birth, however, head size represents only about 25 percent, and by adulthood only about 12 to 13 percent of total body length, as Figure 5.1 shows. The central nervous system, along with the head, undergoes an early and extremely rapid increase in weight. Other organs—for example, the muscles and the respiratory and digestive systems—follow a pattern similar to overall weight change: substantial gains during the first two years.

Directionality of Growth Growth generally follows the principle of **cephalocaudal development** (*cephalocaudal* combines the Greek words for "head" and "tail"). This principle describes the tendency for systems and parts of the body near the

norm Quantitative measure that provides typical values and variations in such characteristics as height and weight for children.

cephalocaudal development Pattern in which organs, systems, and motor movements near the head tend to develop earlier than those near the feet.

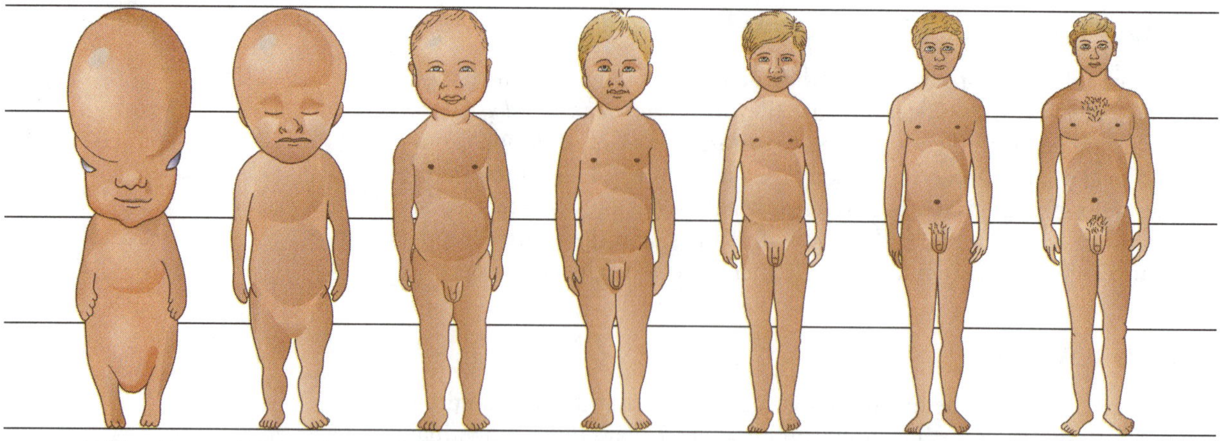

FIGURE 5.1

Changes in Body Proportions during Prenatal and Postnatal Growth

The size of the human head in proportion to the rest of the body shows striking changes over the course of prenatal to adult development. Two months after conception, the head takes up about half of the entire length of the body. By adulthood, the head makes up only about 12 to 13 percent of total body length. The head's tendency to grow more rapidly than regions of the body near the "tail" demonstrates patterns of cephalocaudal development.

Source: Adapted from Robbins et al. (1928).

head to mature sooner than those more distant from the head. Body growth also tends to reflect a pattern of **proximodistal development**. This principle points up the fact that regions nearer the trunk of the body tend to grow and become more differentiated earlier than those more peripheral to the body.

Individual and Group Differences Children show substantial deviations from the norm in their rates of physical growth and development. Individual variations in size are already noticeable at birth; for example, boys tend to be slightly longer and heavier than girls at this time (Copper et al., 1993). Variability in growth occurs among ethnic and cultural groups as well. For example, although individual differences account for much of the variability in size, American infants of African heritage tend to weigh slightly less than American infants of European heritage at birth, even when social class, gestational age, and other factors known to affect birth weight are equated (Goldenberg et al., 1991).

FOR • YOUR • REVIEW

- What are norms for growth? How do they provide information about whether physical growth is proceeding normally?
- What patterns of growth are observed during infancy? How do they differ for various parts of the body? How do they differ among individuals and ethnic groups?

The Brain and Nervous System

In no other time before now has the brain and its influence on the development of human behavior received more attention. Major advances in the field of *cognitive neuroscience*, the study of neural and other structures and systems of the brain associated with behavior, have produced insights and generated widespread interest among psychologists, parents, and the public about the relationship

proximodistal development Pattern in which organs and systems of the body near the middle tend to develop earlier than those near the periphery.

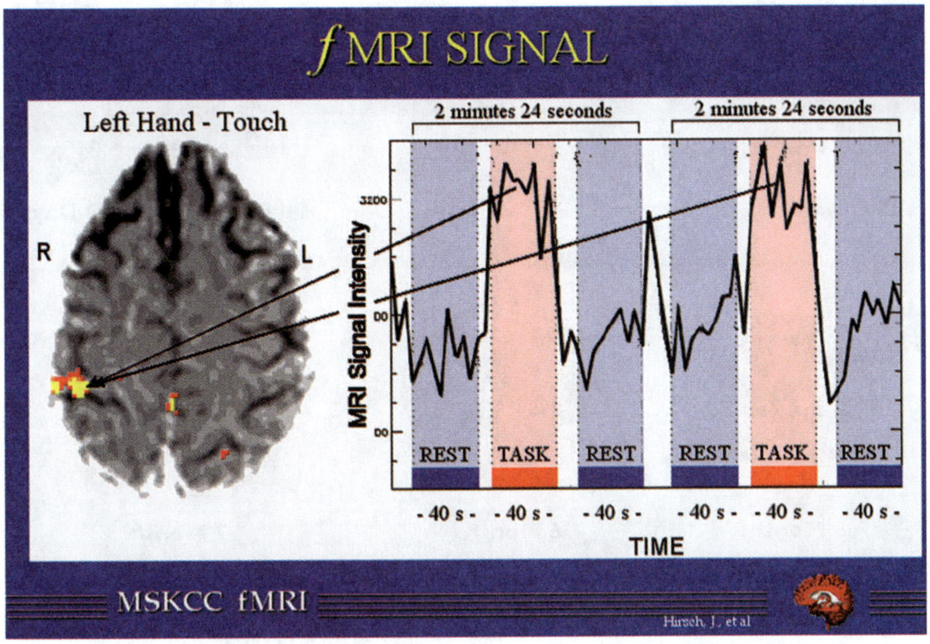

Cognitive neuroscientists employ many newer methods to understand how the brain functions as it processes information. One procedure involves functional magnetic resource imaging (fMRI). In this procedure, information about blood flow and the availability of oxygen to various regions of the brain, an indicator of neural activation, is measured. Here, while the left hand is receiving tactile stimulation, one section of the brain (the right post central gyrus) shows activation, as indicated by the bright yellow and red coloration in that region. When the hand was not being touched (rest periods), the intensity of the fMRI signal was much less. This and other emerging technologies hold great promise for learning which specific areas of the brain are involved in various kinds of cognitive processing.

between the brain and behavior. In large part, much of this enthusiasm has been spurred by the emergence of fascinating new technologies for studying the brain (Thompson & Nelson, 2001). Among these innovative procedures are *positron emission tomography* (PET scans), *functional magnetic resonance imaging* (fMRI), and the recording of *event-related potentials* (ERP). These techniques measure metabolic activity, blood flow, and electrical events, respectively, and provide clues about which areas of the brain are functioning when an individual is engaged in motor, sensory, linguistic, emotional, and other information processing. At the present time, PET scans have limited utility for studying normal infants and children because they require injection of a radioactive substance. However, fMRI (which measures cerebral blood flow) and ERP (which is a measure of electrical activity generated by the synchronous firing of neurons) are among the more widely available noninvasive procedures that hold considerable promise for investigating normal and abnormal brain development (Casey, Thomas, & McCandless, 2001; Nelson & Monk, 2001). Theoretical and practical questions about the importance of early experience and the possibility of critical periods for receiving certain kinds of stimulation have further fueled enthusiasm for studying the brain (Bruer, 1999). We summarize here a few of the major developmental changes that take place in the brain during the child's first two years.

The Developing Brain

Even before birth, brain growth is rapid. As Figure 5.2 shows, the size of the brain swiftly increases, from about 4 percent of its adult weight at five months after conception to about 25 percent at birth (Spreen, Risser, & Edgell, 1995). The *brainstem*

FIGURE 5.2
The Developing Human Brain

During prenatal development, the human brain shows dramatic increases in size, and the cerebral cortex takes on a convoluted pattern to increase surface area. During the last trimester of prenatal development, the brain takes on an adult-like shape, and by birth most of the neurons have formed. The brain's weight increases most dramatically from about the fifth prenatal month until the infant is about two-and-a-half years of age. The drawings have been made to a common scale; however, the first five have been enlarged to a common size to show details.

Source: Adapted from Cowan (1979).

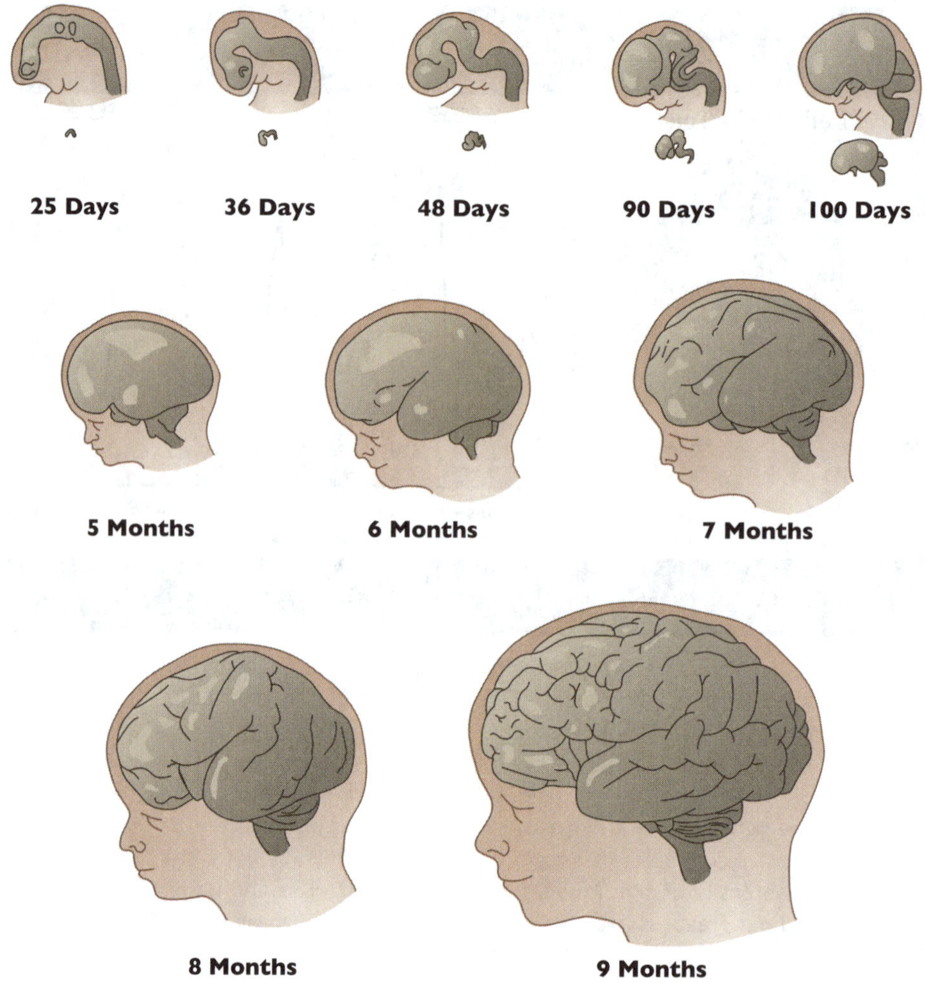

and *midbrain* (see Figure 5.3), which are involved in basic reflexes and sensory processing, as well as such essential biological functions as digestion, elimination, and respiration, are fairly well established at birth (Joseph, 2000). In contrast, neural changes in the *cortex*, the part of the brain most closely linked to sensation, motor responses, thinking, planning, and problem solving, continue to take place well after birth. Within the cortex, regions associated with sensory and motor functions tend to be among the earliest to mature. The frontal cortex, the region of the brain most directly involved in higher levels of cognition, tends to be among the latest.

With development, several important changes occur in **neurons**, the cells that carry electrochemical messages. These changes include *proliferation, migration,* and *differentiation.* Parts of many neurons also become surrounded by **myelin**, a sheath of fatty material that serves to insulate and speed neural impulses by about tenfold. An estimated ten times more **glial cells** (from the Greek word for "glue") than neurons also form within the brain. Glial cells establish a scaffolding for neuron migration, provide the material from which myelin develops, facilitate the transfer of nutrients to neurons, and instruct the neurons to form synapses with other neurons (Ullian et al., 2001).

neuron Nerve cell within the central nervous system that is electrochemically designed to transmit messages between cells.

myelin Sheath of fatty cells that insulates and speeds neural impulses by about tenfold.

glial cell Brain cell that provides the material from which myelin is created, nourishes neurons, and provides a scaffolding for neuron migration.

Neuron Proliferation The production of new nerve cells is known as *neuron proliferation.* Neuron production in humans begins near the end of the first month of prenatal development, shortly after the neural tube closes, and much of it, at least in the cerebral cortex, is completed by the sixth month of prenatal development. Thus, at a very early age, a finite but very large number—certainly well over 100 billion—of young neurons have formed (Nelson, 1999a; Nelson, Thomas, & de Haan, 2006).

Neuron Migration Shortly after their formation, neurons move, or *migrate*, from the neural tube where they were produced to other locations. In some regions of

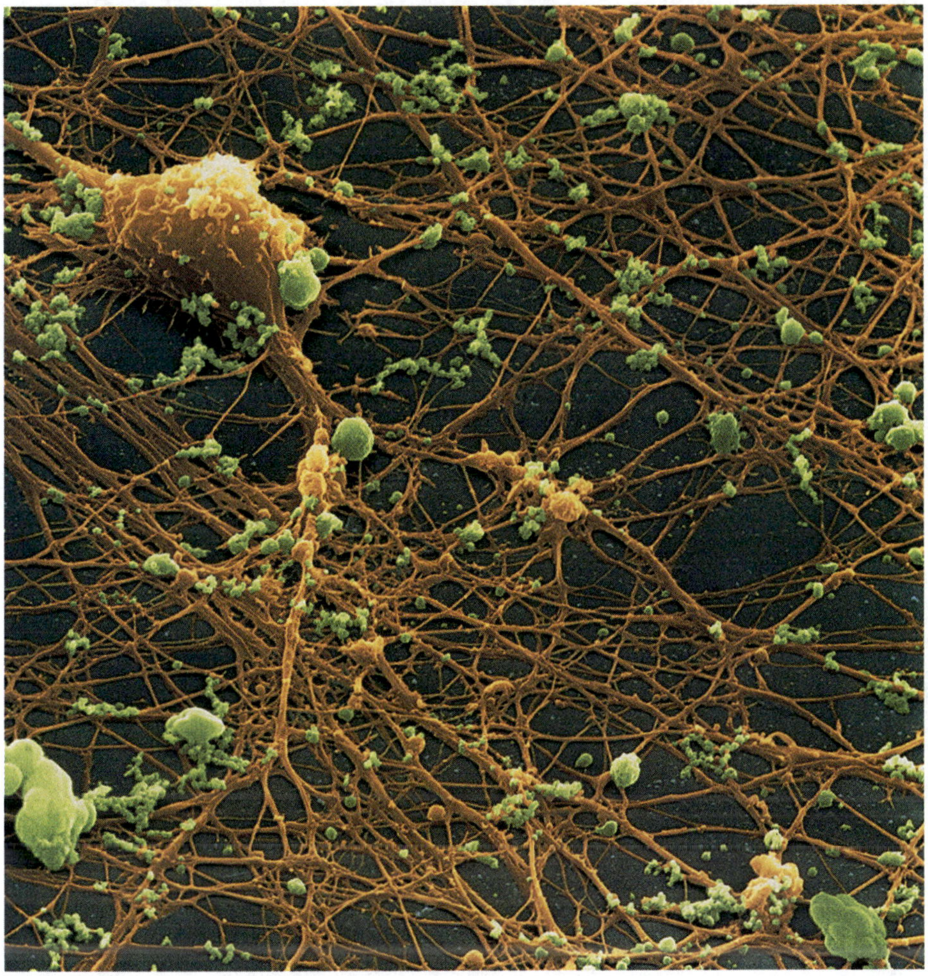

This color-enhanced photo, taken with a scanning electron microscope, shows a neuron. Neurons carry the electrochemical messages that are the basis for behavior. Even before birth, massive numbers of neurons are manufactured and migrate to various regions of the brain, where they begin to establish connections with other neurons.

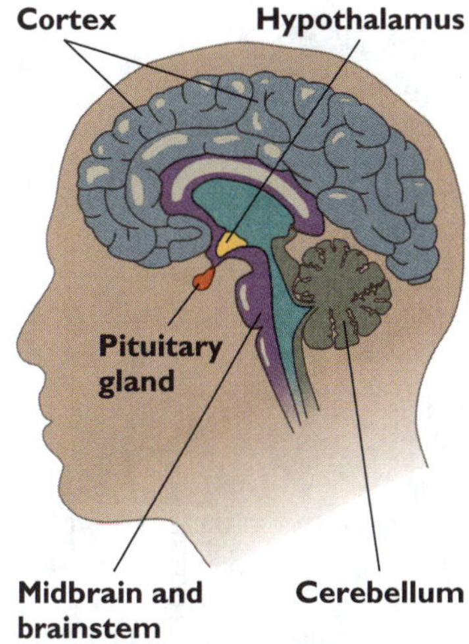

FIGURE 5.3

Cross-Section of the Human Brain

Certain regions of the brain are closely associated with specific functions. The overarching cortex is essential for most of behavior and includes regions associated with processing sensory and motor information, as well as areas heavily involved in thinking, planning, and problem solving. The early-developing midbrain and brainstem are important to basic biological functioning. The cerebellum is centrally involved in coordination and control of voluntary movements. Both the hypothalamus and pituitary glands are believed to play a major role in the regulation of physical growth.

the brain this movement occurs passively, so that, as additional neurons are born, older neurons are pushed farther to the outside of that portion of the brain. This type of growth takes place, for example, in the hypothalamus, the brainstem, and the cerebellum. However, for many other regions of the brain, such as the cerebral cortex, the neurons may migrate a great distance, passing through levels of older neurons that already have reached their final destination. These regions of the brain are formed by an *inside-out* pattern of development in which layers of nerve cells nearer the outer surface are younger than layers deeper in the cortex (Nelson et al., 2006). Under these circumstances, how do neurons know where to migrate and when to stop migrating? Both neurochemical and mechanical information probably play a role. Young neurons attach to and maneuver along the surfaces of fibers of glial cells radiating to the region of their destination, detaching from their guide, as shown in Figure 5.4, at programmed locations. Both the production and the migration of large numbers of neurons in the cortex occur in waves, especially during the seventh and eleventh weeks of gestational age (Spreen et al., 1995). However, some teratogens, including mercury and alcohol, are known to interfere with the onset and path of neuron migration. In fact, developmental defects ranging from mental retardation to behavioral disorders have been linked to interference in the migratory patterns of nerve cells (Gressens, 2000).

KEY THEME
RISK/RESILIENCE

Neuron Differentiation Whereas neuron proliferation and migration take place prenatally for the most part, *neuron differentiation*—the process of enlarging,

FIGURE 5.4

The Migration of Neurons via Glial Fiber

Wrapping themselves around glial fibers, neurons climb in spiral fashion to a particular layer in the cortex of the brain. Because the cortex of the brain develops in an inside-out pattern, earlier waves of neurons need to progress across shorter distances, and their migration may be completed within a day. However, later waves of neurons pass through earlier layers of the cortex and migrate across a greater distance, so that their journey may require several weeks. Some teratogens can interfere with this migratory pattern and, if the disruption is severe, result in a variety of developmental defects.

Source: Adapted from Kunzig (1998).

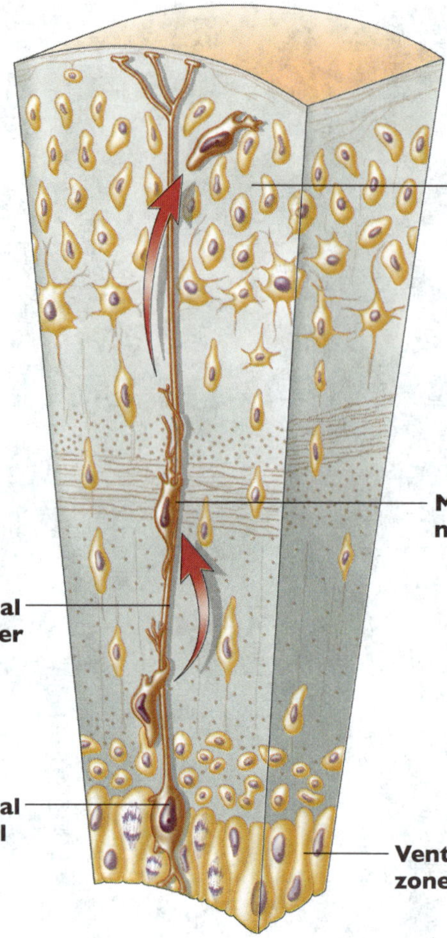

forming synapses with other neurons, and beginning to function—flourishes postnatally. Neural differentiation, along with the growth of glial cells and other tissues, including myelin, contributes to the substantial postnatal increase in the size of the brain.

KEY THEME
NATURE & NURTURE

Some aspects of neuron differentiation proceed without external stimulation. Ex perience, however, plays a major role in the selection, maintenance, and strengthening of connections among many neurons (Nelson et al., 2006). Scientists knew this even decades ago when classic work investigating the effects of vision on brain development in cats illustrated this complex relationship (Hubel & Wiesel, 1979). By the time a kitten's eyes open, neurons in the visual receptor areas of the cerebral cortex have already established some connections and can respond, for example, to sensory information from either eye or to visual patterns with a broad range of characteristics. But the neurons become far more selective and tuned to particular kinds of sensory information as the kitten experiences specific forms of visual stimulation. If the kitten is exposed only to dark-light transitions in the visual field that are horizontal, for example, neurons begin to respond only to those patterns; likewise, exposure only to dark-light transitions that are vertical produces neurons sensitive only to that orientation.

Without stimulation and the opportunity to function, neurons are unlikely to establish or maintain many connections with other neurons; their synaptic density becomes substantially reduced. For example, in the visual cortex the total number of synapses rises meteorically in the first few months after birth, but then the connections show a small decline from about eight months of age to the late preschool years, followed by a more substantial decline between about four and ten years. These dramatic changes in the visual cortex can be seen in Figure 5.5. Neurons may even die if no synapses are formed with other neurons. In fact, one theory holds that massive cell death, perhaps as great as 50 to 75 percent of neurons, occurs

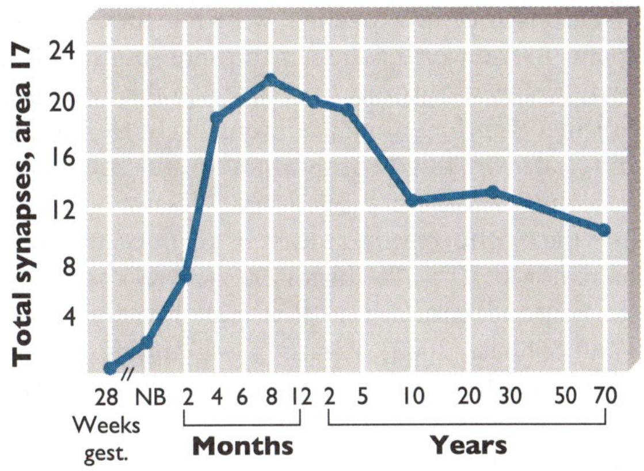

FIGURE 5.5

Estimated Number of Synapses for Neurons in the Human Visual Cortex as a Function of Age

Differentiation of the neurons in the human visual cortex proceeds rapidly shortly after birth and reaches a peak before the end of the first year. The number of synapses ($\times 10^{11}$), connections of dendrites to other neurons, then declines to about half of the original peak number over the lifespan. The rapid increment is associated with visual stimulation after birth and accompanies significant improvements in visual abilities before a year of age. The number of synapses reflects an initial overproduction; those that become functional are then likely to be maintained over the remaining years. Other regions of the cortex may show a similar pattern of rapid increase and then decline in number of synapses, although perhaps at different periods in development.

Source: Adapted from Huttenlocher (1994).

during normal development in the brains of some animals and perhaps in some regions of the human brain, although probably not in the cerebral cortex (Huttenlocher, 1994). Thus the typical infant is genetically equipped with the capacity for neurons to generate many synaptic connections, perhaps far more than a person will ever need. That surplus provides the opportunity for a rich variety of experiences to affect development; it also means that, if damage or destruction occurs to some synapses early in life, others may replace them.

PLASTICITY IN BRAIN DEVELOPMENT

Because of the unspecialized nature of young neurons, the immature brain displays substantial **plasticity**, or the ability, within limits, of alternate regions of the cerebral cortex to take on specialized sensory, linguistic, and other information processing (Johnson, 2000). Infants or children who suffer damage to regions of the cerebral cortex that process speech, for example, are often able to recover because neurons in other parts of the cortex take on this function. On the other hand, although considerable plasticity is retained by some regions of the mature adult brain (Thompson & Nelson, 2001), the prognosis for recovery of language in adults after an accident or a stroke is usually much poorer because the remaining neurons in various regions of the brain have become dedicated to processing certain kinds of experiences.

William Greenough and his colleagues contend that neurons in human and other mammalian brains exhibit two different kinds of plasticity (Greenough, Black, & Wallace, 1987). Some neurons are sensitive to *experience-expectant* information. As a result of a long evolutionary process, these neurons begin to grow and differentiate rapidly at about the time they can be expected to receive the kinds of stimulation important to their functioning. In many mammals, for example, parts of the visual cortex involved in depth or pattern perception develop quite rapidly shortly before and after the eyes open or, in the case of humans, shortly before and after birth. Research with lower animals indicates that visual deprivation during these periods—being reared in the dark or without patterned light, for example—results in the permanent loss of some kinds of depth and pattern vision, losses that do not occur when equivalent lengths of deprivation occur during other periods.

Other neurons are sensitive to *experience-dependent* information. Many opportunities for learning occur at unpredictable times during development. Each person learns different and unique things, even into old age. The distinctive perceptual features forming the image of a neighbor or the attributes defining the concept of democracy are unique representations registered within an individual's neural system. Here, then, is a form of plasticity that implicates neural differentiation as a critical aspect of brain functioning throughout a person's lifetime.

How do neurons form connections with one another as a result of experiences in the environment? A now-familiar mantra among contemporary neuroscientists is

plasticity Capacity of immature systems, including regions of the brain and the individual neurons within those regions, to take on different functions as a result of experience.

KEY THEME
NATURE & NURTURE

"Neurons that fire together wire together." As the organism encounters particular events in the world, whether they are sounds, visual stimuli, or other forms of stimulation, specific groups of neurons in the brain become activated. Each time neurons fire in synchrony, they are more likely to maintain connections with one another. Implicated in this process is an amino acid called *glutamate*, which is involved in communication among neurons. When neurons fire out of synchrony, however, they lose their connections, at least in part because the receptors for glutamate are altered or removed. Thus the history of activity that neurons have with one another shapes the neuronal connections that remain versus those that are lost (Heynen et al., 2003; Penn & Shatz, 2002). Clearly, these findings from the laboratories of neuroscientists have important implications for the role of early experience in infancy.

Brain Lateralization

One of the brain's most obvious physical characteristics is its two mirrorlike structures, a left and a right hemisphere. By and large, sensory information and motor responses on the left side of the body in humans are processed by the right hemisphere, and those on the right side of the body are processed by the left hemisphere. In addition, in most adults the left hemisphere is especially involved in language functioning, whereas the right hemisphere is more typically engaged in processing certain types of spatial, emotional, or other nonverbal information. But these differences are by no means absolute. For example, speech is controlled primarily by the left hemisphere in about 98 percent of right-handed adults but in only about 60 percent of left-handed adults (Caplan & Gould, 2003).

Does hemispheric specialization already exist at birth, or does the brain show progressive **lateralization**, the process by which one hemisphere comes to dominate the other in terms of a particular function? Based on research on left-hemisphere damage in children, Eric Lenneberg (1967) proposed that, at least until age two, both hemispheres are capable of carrying out language functions equally well and that lateralization increases only gradually until adolescence. Other researchers, however, suggest that lateralization actually begins much earlier (Kinsbourne & Hiscock, 1983), perhaps as a consequence of exposure to fetal testosterone (Geschwind & Galaburda, 1987; McManus & Bryden, 1991). For example, some physical differences in the two hemispheres already exist at birth (Kosslyn et al., 1999). Perhaps such brain asymmetries contribute to the observation that most infants lie with the head oriented to the right rather than to the left, an orientation that later predicts hand preference (Michel, 1988). Even before three months of age, most babies more actively use and hold objects longer in the right hand than in the left (Hawn & Harris, 1983). Most dramatic is evidence from ultrasound images of fifteen-week-old fetuses: 90 percent were observed to suck their right thumb, a preference that was linked consistently to handedness at ten to twelve years of age (Hepper, Wells, & Lynch, 2005).

lateralization Process by which one hemisphere of the brain comes to dominate the other; for example, processing of language in the left hemisphere or of spatial information in the right hemisphere.

FOR • YOUR • REVIEW

- What are the major methodological procedures that have permitted advances in the study of the developing brain?
- Which regions of the brain develop earliest and latest? To what functions do those regions contribute?
- What developmental changes occur in neurons? How do myelin and glial cells contribute to neuronal development?
- When does the plasticity of the brain decline? What is the difference between experience-expectant and experience-dependent information?
- What evidence exists for brain lateralization in infancy?

MOTOR SKILL DEVELOPMENT

During postnatal development, cartilage continues to be transformed into bone, and bones elongate and increase in number to become scaffolding to support the body in new physical orientations. As the brain and nervous system mature, neural commands begin to coordinate thickened and enlarged muscles, permitting more powerful and refined motor activities. Infants begin to roll from side to back, reach for objects, and eventually crawl, stand up, and walk. Two complementary patterns are evident in the emergence of motor activity: *differentiation*, the enrichment of global and relatively diffuse actions with more refined and skilled ones, and *integration*, the increasingly coordinated actions of muscles and sensory systems. Throughout infancy, motor skills become more efficient, coordinated, deliberate, or automatic as the task requires.

For child development theorist Jean Piaget, sensorimotor activity was essential to understand, for it served as the prototype and first stage in the construction of knowledge. Contemporary child development researchers, too, recognize that the acquisition, coordination, and integration of basic motor skills are not only interesting topics of study in their own right but also can give us important insights into early cognitive and perceptual development.

THE FIRST ACTIONS: REFLEXES

At first glance, newborns seem helpless and incompetent. Babies eat, sleep, and cry; their diapers always seem to need changing. Yet a more careful look reveals that infants enter their new world with surprisingly adept abilities, among them a set of **reflexes**, involuntary reactions to touch, light, sound, and other kinds of stimulation, some of which are exhibited even prenatally.

Reflexes are among the building blocks that soon give rise to voluntary movements and the acquisition of *developmental milestones*—significant achievements in motor skills. Along with breathing and swallowing, *primitive reflexes*, such as rooting and sucking (see Table 5.1), provide nourishment for the infant's survival. Among our evolutionary ancestors, other reflexes, such as the Moro and palmar reflexes,

Among the reflexes that babies display is the swimming reflex. When young infants are placed in water, breathing is suspended, and they engage in swimlike movements with their arms and legs.

reflex Involuntary reaction to touch, light, sound, and other kinds of stimulation.

Table 5.1 Typical Reflexes Observed in Newborns and Infants

Considerable variability exists among infants in their reflexes and the ages at which they can be elicited (Touwen, 1974). The presence or absence of any single reflex provides only one among many indicators of healthy or atypical development.

Name of Reflex	Testing Procedure	Response	Developmental Course	Significance
Primitive Reflexes				
Palmar or Hand Grasp	Place finger in hand.	Hand grasps object.	Birth to about 4 months	Absence may signal neurological defects; persistence could interfere with voluntary grasping.
Rooting	Stroke corner of mouth lightly.	Head and tongue move toward stimulus.	Birth to about 5 months	Mouth is brought to stimulus to permit sucking.
Sucking	Place finger in mouth or on lips.	Sucking begins.	Birth to about 6 months	Ensures intake of potential nutrients.
Moro	(1) Sit child up, allow head to drop about 20 degrees backward, or (2) make a loud noise, or (3) lower baby rapidly.	Baby extends arms outward, hands open; then brings hands to midline, hands clenched, spine straightened.	Birth to about 5–7 months	Absence may signal neurological defects; persistence could interfere with acquisition of sitting.
Babinski	Stroke bottom of foot.	Toes fan and then curl.	Birth to about 1 year	Absence may signal neurological defects.
Asymmetric Tonic Neck Reflex	Place baby on back, arms and legs extended, and rotate head 90 degrees.	Arm on face side extends, arm on back side of head flexes.	About 1 month to 4 months	Absence may signal neurological defects; persistence could prevent rolling over, coordination.
Postural Reflexes				
Stepping	Hold baby under arms, upright, learning forward.	Makes walk-like stepping movements.	Birth to about 3 months	Absence may signal neurological defects.
Labyrinthine	(1) Place baby on back. (2) Place baby on stomach.	Extends arms and legs. Flexes arms and legs.	Birth to about 4 months	Absence may signal neurological defects.
Swimming	Place baby in water.	Holds breath involuntarily; arms and legs move as if trying to swim.	Birth to about 4–6 months	Absence may signal neurological defects.
Placing	Hold baby under arms, upright, top of foot touching bottom edge of table.	Lifts foot and places on top of table.	Birth through 12 months	Absence may signal neurological defects.
Landau Reaction	Place baby on stomach, hold under chest.	Lifts head, eventually other parts of body, above chest.	Head at 2 months, other parts of body later	Absence may signal neurological defects; inadequate muscle tone for motor development.
Body Righting	Rotate hips or shoulder.	Rotates remainder of body.	4 months to more than 12 months	Absence may signal neurological defects; difficulty in gaining postural control and walking.

helped to protect newborns from danger. *Postural reflexes*, including stepping, swimming, and body righting (which are surprisingly similar to later voluntary movements), appear to be designed to maintain a specific orientation to the environment. If primitive or postural reflexes are absent, are too strong or too weak, display unequal strength when normally elicited from either side of the body, or continue to be exhibited beyond certain ages, a pediatrician may begin to suspect cerebral palsy or some other neurological impairment and developmental difficulties for the baby (Blasco, 1994).

MOTOR MILESTONES

Reflexes are often viewed as fixed responses to a stimulus. However, many early motor behaviors that young infants soon produce consist of coordinated actions. For example, babies exhibit **rhythmical stereotypies**, repeated sequences of motions performed with no apparent goal. Rubbing one foot against the other, rocking back and forth, bouncing up and down, swaying side to side, striking or banging objects, mouthing and tonguing, and shaking and nodding the head are just a few of the movements that exercise bones, joints, and muscles. Stereotypies, along with early reflexes, appear to be the bits and pieces of the primitive melody of behavior that eventually are recruited and integrated into organized voluntary motor skills and activities (Thelen, 1996).

Many more organized goal-directed voluntary actions emerge during the first year, as infants gradually gain neuromotor control of their heads, arms, and legs. Some of these actions—grasping, crawling, and walking, for example—are motor milestones: once mastered, new worlds open up to the infant. Moreover, they lead caregivers to respond in different ways: childproofing the home to prevent accidents, allowing greater independence, expecting more mature behavior. Most gains in infant movement illustrate progress in coordinating (1) *postural control*, the ability to maintain an upright orientation to the environment; (2) *locomotion*, the ability to maneuver through space; and (3) *manual control*, the ability to manipulate objects (Keogh & Sugden, 1985). Table 5.2 contains a summary of the young child's major achievements in motor development.

KEY THEME
INTERACTION AMONG DOMAINS

Postural Control Keeping the head upright and stable at about two to three months of age represents one of the first milestones in infant motor development. This achievement is followed by mastery of other significant postural skills, such as maintaining an upright sitting position, moving to a standing position, and standing without assistance. The milestones, built on various postural reflexes among other things, often reflect a *cephalocaudal* progression. Head control, for example, precedes control of the trunk, and command of the legs is the last to develop. The integration of postural skills is also important. For example, the ability to keep the head upright while sitting or while standing on a stable surface is one thing; the ability to do this when being carried about or during self-movement requires integration of far more information to retain motor control.

Locomotion No one doubts that a monumental achievement in infancy is the ability to move about the environment. One early milestone in locomotion is the capacity to roll over. Then comes success at initiating forward motion, a skill marked by considerable variation (Adolph, Vereijken, & Denny, 1998; Freedland & Bertenthal, 1994). Some infants use arms to pull and legs to push, others use only arms or legs, and still others scoot forward while sitting. *Crawling*, locomotion with stomach touching the floor, may soon give way to *creeping*, locomotion on hands and knees—and then again it may not. The varieties of forward motion invented by babies often generate lively discussions among caregivers.

Once babies are able to pull themselves upright, they often *cruise*; that is, move by holding onto furniture or other objects to help maintain their balance while stepping sideways (Barela, Jeka, & Clark, 1999). Forward walking while holding onto

rhythmical stereotypy Repeated sequence of movements, such as leg kicking, hand waving, or head banging, that has no apparent goal.

Table 5.2 Milestones of Motor Development

This table describes the sequence of motor skill development that takes place during infancy. Children often show individual differences in the exact ages at which they display the various developmental achievements outlined here. Nonetheless, successful attainment of these milestones is often used as one indicator of healthy development.

2 Months	• Holds head steadily when held upright • Lifts head up
3 Months	• Holds head steady while being carried • Rolls over • Raised head and chest
4 Months	• Grasps cube
6 Months	• Sits without support • Stands while holding onto something
7 Months	• Rolls from back to stomach • Attempts to crawl and/or creep
8 Months	• Achieves sitting position without help • Pulls to standing
9 Months	• Walks while holding furniture (cruises) • Demonstrates neat pincer grasp • Bangs two objects held in hands
10 Months	• Walks with help • Plays pat-a-cake
11 Months	• Stands alone • Turns pages of book
12 Months	• Walks alone • Drinks from cup
14 Months	• Builds tower using two cubes • Scribbles
15 Months	• Walks sideways and backward • Attempts to use spoon and fork
17 Months	• Walks up steps
18 Months	• Begins to run
20 Months	• Kicks ball forward • Throws ball overhead

someone's hand typically follows. By about twelve months of age, about half of American babies and infants in many other countries walk alone. Skill in walking continues to be refined throughout infancy and early childhood. The infant's steps become longer and show less side-to-side motion, while the toes point more forward, refinements that are linked with opportunities to practice walking (Adolph, Vereijken, & Shrout, 2003).

Prewalking and walking skills likely depend on the growth of higher brain centers. But even before independent walking, many of the components of this ability are evident. For example, when babies six months of age are placed on a treadmill and held so they do not have to support their full weight, they display alternating stepping similar to that involved in walking (Thelen & Ulrich, 1991). Even six-week-olds produce surprisingly coordinated leg movements when lying on their backs (Thelen, Skala, & Kelso, 1987). However, even though the coordinated action pattern underlying these abilities may be available much earlier, the task constraints of maintaining upright posture, lifting the leg against gravity, moving forward, and other factors delay the onset of walking.

Manual Control Generally speaking, infants show an ability to control arms and legs much sooner than areas more distant, such as fingers and toes, an example of the principle of *proximodistal development*. However, in the weeks that follow birth, infants make enormous progress in reaching. Moving the hand to the mouth appears to be among the earliest goal actions (Lew & Butterworth, 1997; Rochat, 1993). Newborns also display *prereaching* in their attempts to contact objects that catch their attention. These early efforts are neither accurate nor coordinated with grasping. Still, movements show speeding up, slowing down, and changes in direction, just as in later, more accurate reaches (Rönnqvist & von Hofsten, 1994; von Hofsten & Rönnqvist, 1993). Systematic reaching for objects begins at about three months of age. By about five to six months, infants display mature, *ballistic* reaches to rapidly and accurately retrieve an object in the visual field. In gaining mastery over this response, babies engage in a series of submovements, not always perfectly executed but often quickly corrected to meet the goal of obtaining the target (Berthier, 1996; Berthier & Robin, 1998), and will even intercept a target moving past their line of sight (Robin, Berthier, & Clifton, 1996). The ability to see their own hands is not necessary in early reaching; however, infants eventually make greater use of visual cues to help them retrieve an object (Clifton et al., 1993; McCarty et al., 2001; Robin, Berthier, & Clifton, 1996).

When first attempting to reach, very young infants typically keep their hands closed in fistlike fashion. By about four months of age, infants awkwardly pick up an object by grasping it with the palm of the hand. Over the next few months, they shift from using the inner palm to using opposing thumb and fingertips, a progression that culminates in a neat *pincer grasp* at about nine months of age.

Another important component of motor skill is increased coordination between the two hands. Very young infants often attempt to grasp objects with both hands, but once babies gain an ensemble of skills, including head control and postural balance while sitting by themselves and when leaning forward, one-handed reaches and more consistent, stable reaching become a part of their repertoire (Rochat & Goubet, 1995; Spencer et al., 2000). Increased coordination is further reflected in the appearance of complementary hand orientations, such as holding a toy dump truck in one hand while using the other hand to fill it with sand. This *functional asymmetry* emerges at about five to six months of age but becomes especially refined as the child enters the second year and begins to display self-help and advanced motor tasks requiring sophisticated use of both arms and hands.

A major motor milestone that babies around a year of age typically reach is that of walking. Although this baby is not quite old enough to walk independently, infants show surprisingly coordinated leg movements well before this milestone is reached. Do you think this kind of practice might also help her to begin walking earlier? Although we typically think of the onset of walking as primarily the result of maturation, cross-cultural research suggests that, in communities in which a great deal of opportunity is provided to acquire this ability, children begin to walk at somewhat earlier ages.

DETERMINANTS OF MOTOR DEVELOPMENT

Are the emergence, refinement, and integration of motor skills primarily dependent on genetic or maturational factors? Or are they the consequence of practice, cultural, or other experiential factors? Many pioneers in developmental psychology advocated a strong maturational theory to explain the orderly acquisition of motor skills. But we now recognize that these changes are better understood in terms of the confluence of both biological and experiential factors.

KEY THEME
NATURE & NURTURE

Biological Contributions One of the strongest arguments in support of a genetic or maturational basis for the development of motor skills is their tendency to be displayed at predictable times and in similar ways in normal children. Moreover, the onset of such skills as sitting and walking shows greater concordance for identical than for fraternal twins. Greater similarity in gross motor activities, such as running, jumping, and throwing, is found in children who are more closely related biologically (Malina, 1980). Even intellectually and physically disabled babies attain major milestones in an orderly manner, although at a later age than other children. For example, blind children, who show substantial delays in acquiring postural, locomotion, and manual coordination skills, eventually acquire them nonetheless (Tröster & Brambring, 1993).

In the Navajo culture babies are often swaddled for most of the day. Wayne Dennis's research with Hopi infants who were also cared for in this way suggests that this baby, despite the lack of opportunity to practice sitting up, crawling, and standing alone, will begin to walk about the same time as an infant who has not been swaddled.

Experiential Contributions Could experiential variables also play a role in motor development? With respect to the acquisition of expert motor skill, the answer is most certainly yes. However, it may be true for attaining basic developmental milestones as well. Lack of opportunity to engage in physical activity seriously interferes with reaching developmental milestones. For example, babies who spent most of their first year in an orphanage lying in cribs and receiving few other forms of stimulation typically did not walk before age three or four (Dennis, 1960). When special programs encourage blind infants to acquire self-initiated movement, they do so at ages more comparable to their sighted peers (Fraiberg, 1977).

Several investigators in the 1930s conducted studies with sets of twins to test the role of experience in motor skill development. Typically, one twin received extensive training in, say, handling blocks, climbing stairs, or roller skating; the other twin did not (Gesell & Thompson, 1934; Hilgard, 1932; McGraw, 1935). When given a chance to acquire the skills, the untrained twin often rapidly achieved the same level of skill displayed by the trained twin. In another early study, Wayne and Marsena Dennis investigated child-rearing practices among the Hopi Indians (Dennis & Dennis, 1940). Some Hopi Indian mothers followed the tribal tradition of tightly swaddling their babies in a cradleboard; the mother would strap the board to her back for all but about an hour a day during her waking hours for the first six to twelve months of her child's life. These Hopi babies had little opportunity to practice sitting up, crawling, and walking. Other Hopi mothers reared infants without swaddling. The researchers found that swaddling had little bearing on when infants initiated walking, an observation reconfirmed in a later study of the effects of Hopi rearing customs (Harriman & Lukosius, 1982).

What can we conclude from these investigations? Perhaps that the typical range of daily activities and experiences in which infants and children are engaged is sufficient to promote normal locomotor development. But consider other findings. Infants from one to seven weeks of age, given a few minutes of daily practice with the placing and stepping reflexes, retain them and begin walking earlier than infants who receive no special training or whose legs are passively moved back and forth (Zelazo, 1983). Moreover, practice in sitting helps infants acquire these skills (Zelazo et al., 1993).

Esther Thelen and her colleagues (Thelen & Smith, 1994, 2006) have applied a far broader perspective to the role of experience in motor development. Thelen has argued that all complex motor skills require the assembling and reassembling of multiple processes involving, among other things, motivation, elements of the nervous system that regulate posture and balance, increased bone and muscle strength, and changes in body proportions. These assemblages are further constrained by the biodynamics of the human body, as well as the situational context. However, when the right improvisation of components exists, infants display mastery of motor skills or advance to new levels of competence. Neither biological nor experiential factors alone are responsible. Instead, motor development is a dynamic system; its multiple components become "tuned" into sequences of more effective, self-organized actions over time (Lockman & Thelen, 1993).

Key Theme
Sociocultural Influence

Cross-Cultural Differences

Given the multiple processes involved, it should not be surprising to learn that ethnic and cultural differences in motor development exist as well. At birth and throughout their first year, African American babies, as well as infants among the Wolof of Senegal, the Gusii of Kenya, the Yoruba of Nigeria, the Bantu of South

Africa, and the Ganda of Uganda, typically outperform Caucasian infants on a variety of motor skills (Lester & Brazelton, 1982; Werner, 1972). Parents in a fairly prosperous rural community in Kenya made extensive efforts to teach their infants to sit or walk (Super, 1976). In fact, their language, as in some other regions of East Africa, contained distinctive words to denote the specialized training. The more caregivers promoted specific motor skills, the earlier their children tended to display them. For example, 93 percent of one group of caregivers said they taught their babies to crawl, and babies in this group began crawling at about five and a half months of age. In contrast, only 13 percent of the caregivers in a nearby group expressed support for teaching their infants to crawl, and these babies did not crawl until about eight months of age.

Many factors could contribute to the cultural differences, but one finding strongly implicates child-rearing efforts. Advanced motor development in this part of Kenya was limited to sitting, standing, and walking, skills considered culturally important. Other milestones not taught or valued, such as head control or the ability to roll over, were acquired later than they are by American infants. A similar observation comes from Jamaica. Some mothers in that country perform special stretching and massaging exercises to encourage their infants to sit and walk alone (Hopkins & Westra, 1990). Children of these mothers sit by themselves and walk earlier than other children.

We cannot be certain whether training focused on particular skills or more general experiences are responsible for cultural differences. Children in East Africa, for example, spend more time in an upright position, seated on a caregiver's lap or riding on her back, than children in the United States (Super, 1976). The activities may strengthen trunk and leg muscles to aid the earlier appearance of sitting, standing, and walking. However, gains achieved from training in one of two particular skills, such as stepping or sitting, do not appear to generalize to the other (Zelazo, 1998; Zelazo et al., 1993). And infants who become increasingly proficient in crawling up and down a slope have to relearn how to go up and down the same slope when they start to walk (Adolph, 1997).

Children of the Ache of Eastern Paraguay are significantly delayed in acquiring a host of motor skills. For example, walking is not exhibited until twenty one to twenty-three months of age. This small band, which engages in hunting and gathering, does not encourage the acquisition of motor skills in infants. When families migrate to the forests, the women closely supervise their children younger than three years, preventing them from venturing more than a yard or so into the uncleared vegetation (Kaplan & Dove, 1987). For the Ache, keeping infants close by may be crucial for their continued survival, but it gives little opportunity for infants to practice motor skills. Because the Ache have been relatively isolated and the total population at times quite small, genetic factors cannot be ruled out as contributing to the delay, but cultural concerns and efforts to either promote or discourage the acquisition of motor skills appear to have a significant effect on their development.

FOR • YOUR • REVIEW

- How do primitive and postural reflexes differ? What purpose do they serve for the infant?
- When are rhythmical stereotypies exhibited?
- What are the major milestones associated with the development of postural control, locomotion, and manual control? How do the principles of cephalocaudal and proxomodistal development apply to the emergence of the major motor milestones?
- What factors contribute to motor development? How do cultural practices influence their acquisition?

SLEEP

Infants display a wide variety of behavioral states: regular and irregular sleep, drowsiness, alert inactivity, alert activity, and crying. Each of these has distinctive features. Crying or distress usually begins with whimpering but swiftly shifts to full-scale cries, often accompanied by thrashing of arms and legs. During alert activity, the infant also exhibits vigorous, diffuse motor activity, but such exertions are not accompanied by signs of distress. During alert inactivity, the baby is relatively quiet, at least in terms of motor activity, but actively engages in visual scanning of the environment. In this state, the baby appears to be most responsive to sensory stimulation and may be learning a great deal. But it is sleep that is usually of greatest concern to parents, especially in the first few months when the adults in the household are often awakened by the child's cries, sometimes several times in a night. Fortunately, part of the process of physical development includes changes in sleep patterns that bring the cycles of infants and caregivers into greater alignment with one another.

PATTERNS OF SLEEP

Babies sleep a lot. Although individual differences are great, newborns average sixteen to seventeen hours of sleep a day. Sleep and wake cycles are extremely short, and babies are easily disrupted by external stimulation. As the weeks pass, infants gradually sleep less, but for longer periods; by about three to five weeks of age, a pattern begins to emerge in which the longest sleep periods take place at night (Thompson, 1982). But naps during the day continue to be a regular occurrence all the way through the preschool years. In fact, in some cultures, such naps are never eliminated.

The development of sleep patterns differs substantially across various cultures. In most industrialized countries, parents eagerly look forward to having their infants adopt a routine that matches their own. A significant milestone is reached when the baby of three or four months finally sleeps through the night. In some cultures, such as the Kipsigi of rural Kenya, however, infants are permitted more flexibility and will not sleep through the night until much older (Super & Harkness, 1982).

Like adults, infants (even before they are born) display two distinct sleep states (Groome et al., 1997). During active or REM *(rapid eye movement)* sleep, eye movements and muscle jerks are frequent, and breathing and heart rate are irregular. During quiet sleep *(NREM)*, eye and muscle movements are few, and physiological activity is more regular. The proportion of time spent in the two states, however, shifts dramatically with development. About eight in sixteen hours of sleep is spent in REM sleep as a newborn, but only about two in seven hours of sleep as an adult.

Active or REM sleep has been linked to dreaming, but it is not clear whether young infants dream. However, REM sleep is believed to be important for normal brain activity (Roffwarg, Muzio, & Dement, 1966). *Autostimulation theory* proposes that REM sleep provides powerful stimulation to the central nervous system, which in adults is interpreted as sensory and motor activity associated with dreaming. According to this theory, stimulation during REM sleep compensates for the relatively brief number of hours each day that the infant is awake. Infants kept awake for relatively lengthy periods of time show reduced amounts of REM sleep, and premature infants, whose wakeful periods are even shorter, show more REM sleep than full-term babies (Halpern, MacLean, & Baumeister, 1995). If autostimulation theory is correct, it is a further demonstration of how important stimulation is for development, even at those times when a large amount of sleep is essential as well.

SLEEPING ARRANGEMENTS

KEY THEME
SOCIOCULTURAL INFLUENCE

Where should infants sleep? The answer is actually very controversial. Historically, and in most cultures today (such as Japan), an infant and mother sleeping together—or *co-sleeping*—is the norm (Latz, Wolf, & Lozoff, 1999). In fact, Mayan mothers view putting very young children in a separate room at night as almost equivalent to child neglect (Morrelli et al., 1992). However, American mothers typically justify such a practice, especially after the baby is a few months old, as a way to encourage self-reliance and independence. Decisions about sleeping arrangements are deeply ingrained in cultural beliefs concerning the values of closeness and interdependence, and of privacy and self-reliance. This being said, co-sleeping has become more common in American households. In one recent national study, 47 percent of mothers report sharing a bed with their infants either "sometimes" or "frequently" (Willinger et al., 2003).

What does research reveal about the risks or benefits of co-sleeping practices? James McKenna and his colleagues contend that, in co-sleeping arrangements, mothers and infants engage in greater synchronized sleep, breathing, and arousal patterns that serve to protect infants from apnea, irregular patterns of temporary cessations in breathing. Those breathing cessations, in turn, can be related to tragic, unexplained deaths in infants (McKenna & McDade, 2005; Mosko, Richard, & McKenna, 1997). However, other research suggests that co-sleeping can actually put the infant at risk for death, especially if infants are younger than 11 weeks of age (Tappin, Ecob, & Brooke, 2005). Co-sleeping is especially hazardous on a couch or if the parent smokes, consumes alcohol, or uses other drugs (Hauck & Hunt, 2000). In response to this growing body of research, the American Academy of Pediatrics does not recommend bed sharing with infants (American Academy of Pediatrics, 2005). A far safer alternative to bed sharing for those who wish to be in close contact appears to be having the baby sleep within arm's length but in an infant crib.

RESEARCH APPLIED TO PARENTING

Reducing Sudden Infant Death Syndrome

At the end of what had been a busy and tiring day, Marc and Linda looked forward to feeding and bathing Abbie, playing with her a bit, and then putting her to bed. Today, especially, they really needed some time to themselves. Fortunately, their daughter cooperated. Almost as soon as she had been placed on her back in her crib, Abbie quieted down and closed her eyes. Linda was compulsive, though, about bedtime routines—there would be no rushing now. She checked to make sure that there were no stuffed animals tucked in the corners and that the bumper pads were securely fastened at each end of the crib. Even the remotest possibility that anything bad might happen to Abbie was simply unthinkable.

The abrupt, unexplained death of an infant less than one year of age who stops breathing during sleep is known as **sudden infant death syndrome (SIDS)**. These deaths, most frequently reported in babies about two to four months of age, are particularly tragic because they occur with no identifiable warnings. The highest incidence appears to occur at a time when basic automatic respiratory reflexes governed by the brainstem begin to be supplemented by voluntary, cortex-regulated breathing essential for vocalization and the emergence of speech.

SIDS, once known as *crib death* or *cot death*, claimed the lives of between 1 and 2 of every 1,000 babies born in the United States in recent decades. Much higher rates had been reported in some other countries, such as New Zealand (Mitchell et al., 1997). It continues to be the third leading cause of infant mortality in the United States and in most Western countries. Only congenital malformations and low birth weight or prematurity contribute to more deaths among infants (Hoyert, Kung, & Smith, 2005). Although researchers still do not know what causes SIDS, specific steps that parents can take are now known to reduce its risk of occurring.

1. *"Back to Sleep."* Up until the 1990s, parents were often advised to place their infants in a prone position (on their stomach) when ready for sleep. However, studies conducted around the world (Australia, Britain, New Zealand, the Netherlands, Norway, Sweden, and many other countries, including the United States) suggest that, when parents stop this practice, the incidence of

sudden infant death syndrome (SIDS) Sudden, unexplained death of an infant or a toddler as a result of cessation of breathing during sleep.

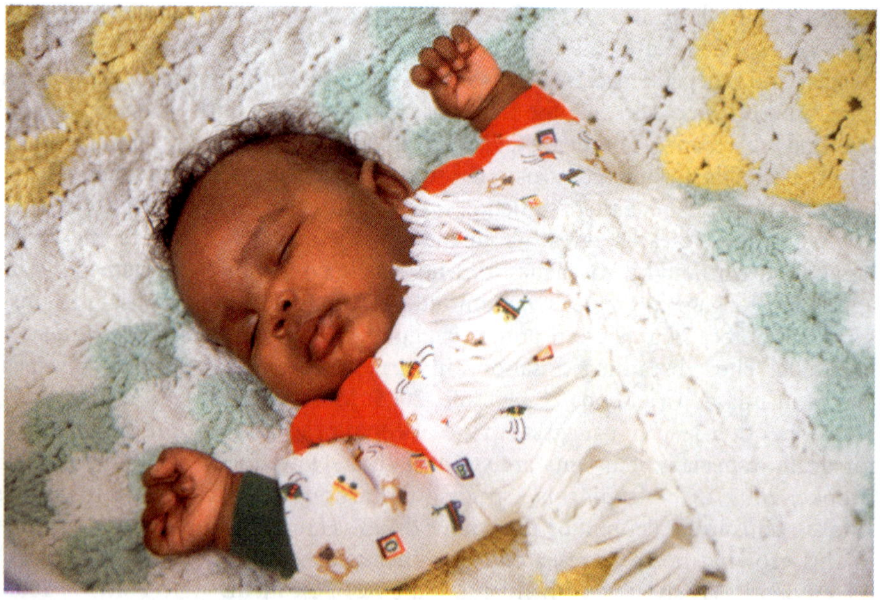

Placing infants on their backs in preparation for sleep appears to have reduced the frequency of sudden infant death syndrome (SIDS). The decline in SIDS associated with this practice is reported in many countries, including the United States, where pediatricians in the 1990s launched a "back to sleep" campaign.

SIDS declines (Hauck & Hunt, 2000). Thus in 1994 pediatricians initiated a "Back to Sleep" campaign to encourage parents to place healthy infants on their back to sleep. This single change has been estimated to reduce the incidence of SIDS as much as 80 percent in some nations and greater than 50 percent in the United States (Hauk, 2001; Kochanek et al., 2004).

2. ***Eliminate exposure to cigarette smoke and other drugs.*** Numerous studies have confirmed that a mother's smoking or use of other drugs during pregnancy is associated with a greater likelihood of SIDS (Mitchell & Milerad, 1999). However, exposure even to passive smoke after birth (from mother, father, or other live-in adults) increases the risk as well.
3. ***Provide firm bedding.*** The incidence of SIDS in Australia and New Zealand had been among the highest in the world. In these countries, less firm bedding (use of wool or of bark from the ti tree) appears to have contributed to the risk of SIDS for infants sleeping prone, perhaps because of a tendency for this softer bedding to trap carbon dioxide.
4. ***Avoid overheating.*** High room temperature and high body temperature because of excessive bedding or clothing are also known to increase the incidence of SIDS (Guntheroth & Spiers, 2001). Adequate ventilation also helps to prevent overheating of the infant, as well as to disperse carbon dioxide.
5. ***Have the infant use a pacifier during sleep.*** Although the mechanism is not yet understood, use of a pacifier is associated with a significant drop, sometimes as much as 90 percent, in the incidence of SIDS. Pacifier use should start at about one month of age when breastfeeding has been well-established and discontinued at twelve months of age because of its association with ear infections and dental complications (Hauk, Omojokun, & Siadaty, 2005).

SIDS is associated with a number of other factors, including the colder months of the year, economically depressed neighborhoods, having a cold, being male, being a later-born or one of a multiple birth, and low birth weight. In addition to susceptibility to the buildup of carbon dioxide and increased temperature, other characteristics that are hypothesized to play a role in causing

SIDS include a deficit in arousal and anomalies associated with heart rate (Hauck & Hunt, 2000). Parents may have little control over some of these factors. Unfortunately, efforts to educate everyone about a better sleeping position or use of firmer bedding have not reached all caregivers (Brenner et al., 1998; Kemp et al., 1998). The rate of placing infants on their stomach is higher than average among African American families, younger mothers, and low-income families, and in some regions of the United States, in daycare centers where infants are put to sleep during nap periods (Moon & Biliter, 2000; Willinger et al., 2000). As more and more parents turn to daycare centers, family daycare providers, or other family members (such as grandparents or siblings) to care for their young infants, it is vital that these alternative caregivers also be informed about the importance of infants' being placed on their back for naps and during other sleep periods (Flick et al., 2001; Moon, Patel, & McDermott Shaefer, 2000). Research indicates that babies accustomed to sleeping on their back are particularly susceptible to increased risk of SIDS if placed prone or on their side (because of the possibility of rolling into a prone position) (Hauck & Hunt, 2000; Mitchell et al., 1999).

Although the benefits far outweigh the drawbacks, one unintended outcome of having infants sleep on their back has been more frequent reports of misshapen heads, particularly flattening of the back of the head (Najarian, 1999). The problem, not normally serious, can be substantially reduced by varying head position each time the baby is placed for sleep and giving the infant plenty of experience on his or her stomach during periods when awake and under the watchful eye of a parent. Adequate "tummy time" also helps to strengthen the shoulders and arms, and minimizes possible delays in achieving various milestones of motor development associated with the upper body (American Academy of Pediatrics, 2000).

FOR • YOUR • REVIEW

- What states do newborns display?
- What kinds of sleep patterns are found in newborns?
- Why does controversy exist concerning the sleeping arrangements for young infants?
- What factors are associated with SIDS? What steps can caretakers take to reduce the likelihood of SIDS?

BASIC LEARNING PROCESSES

Infants come into the world remarkably well prepared to adapt to the environment. A fundamental ability evident right from birth is the capacity to learn. Learning helps children respond to the demands of their physical and social world, achieve goals, and solve problems. Infants learn, for example, that a stove can be hot, that hitting a sibling will make their parents angry, and that the sound that will make the family dog arrive is the dog's name. What are the basic forms of learning? How early do these important capacities appear? We consider here four basic forms of learning: *habituation*, *classical conditioning*, *operant conditioning*, and *imitation*.

HABITUATION

The gradual decline in intensity, frequency, or duration of a response to the repeated occurrence of a stimulus is known as **habituation**. Even newborns display habituation. For example, they may show less arousal—that is, reductions in heart rate or fewer searching eye movements—as they are shown a colorful toy or hear the same bell

habituation Gradual decline in the intensity, frequency, or duration of a response over repeated or lengthy occurrences of the same stimulus.

ringing over and over. Habituation is thus a simple, adaptive form of learning to ignore things that offer little new information and that, in a sense, have become boring.

The finding that, once babies have habituated to an event, they often display a renewed response to a change in the stimulus indicates that habituation is a form of learning rather than merely fatigue or an inability to continue responding. For example, if touched on the leg instead of the arm or exposed to a sound other than the ringing of a bell, they may become aroused once again. The return of a response is an example of **recovery from habituation** (sometimes called **dishabituation**) and suggests that the baby perceives the new stimulus as different from the old one.

Low-birth-weight, brain-damaged, and younger babies tend to habituate less rapidly than older, more mature infants (Krafchuk, Tronick, & Clifton, 1983; Rovee-Collier, 1987). In fact, as we will see in the next chapter, an infant's rapid habituation and recovery from habituation to new stimuli are associated with greater cognitive capacities in later childhood. In addition, researchers have been able to capitalize on habituation responses in order to study a vast array of infants' cognitive and social abilities.

Classical Conditioning

As we learned in the chapter titled "Themes and Theories," in *classical conditioning* a neutral event paired with a stimulus that triggers an inborn reaction can begin to elicit a response similar to the one initiated by the original stimulus. Consider a nipple placed in a newborn's mouth; it tends to elicit sucking. The nipple is an **unconditioned stimulus (UCS)**; the sucking response is an **unconditioned response (UCR)**. After a series of trials in which a neutral stimulus—say, a distinctive odor—is paired with the nipple (the UCS), the odor may also begin to elicit sucking even when the nipple is not present. The odor has become a **conditioned stimulus (CS)**, and the sucking response it initiates, a **conditioned response (CR)**. Table 5.3 summarizes the sequence of steps in classical conditioning for this and other typical examples.

Table 5.3 Examples of Classical Conditioning

Classical conditioning is learning in which a neutral event (conditioned stimulus), through its association with a cue (unconditioned stimulus) that naturally elicits a reflexlike response (unconditioned response), comes to elicit the same response (conditioned response).

	Step 1 (Stimulus ↘ Response)	Step 2 (Stimulus ↘ Response)	Step 3 (Stimulus ↘ Response)
General Principle	UCS ↘ UCR	CS + UCS ↘ UCR	CS ↘ CR
Example 1	Nipple ↘ Sucking	Odor + Nipple ↘ Sucking	Odor ↘ Sucking
Example 2	Injection Needle ↘ Fear	Doctor + Injection Needle ↘ Fear	Doctor ↘ Fear

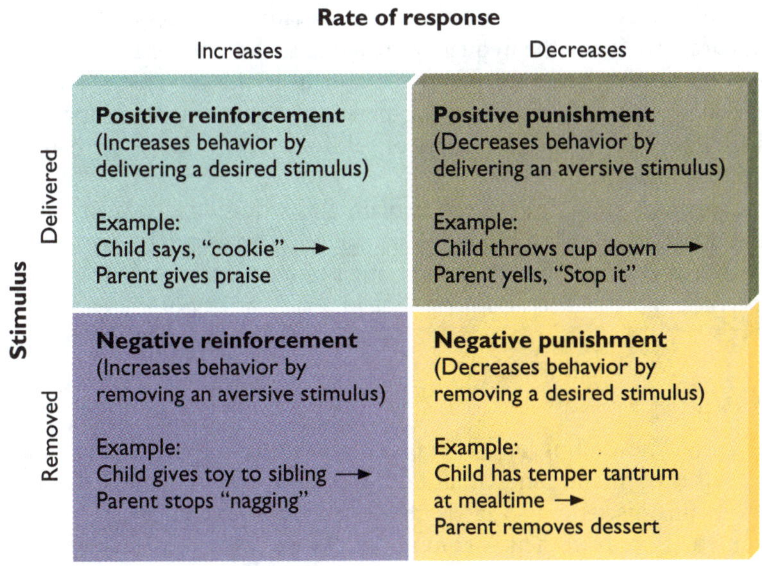

FIGURE 5.6

Positive and Negative Reinforcement and Punishment

Reinforcement leads to an increase in the rate of responding; punishment leads to a decrease in the rate of responding. *Positive* refers to the presentation of a stimulus following a response; *negative* refers to the removal of a stimulus following a response.

Infants display classical conditioning within hours of birth. Elliot Blass and his colleagues (Blass, Ganchrow, & Steiner, 1984) paired a tactile stimulus, stroking of the newborn's forehead (CS), with the delivery of a sugar solution to the mouth (UCS) that elicited sucking (UCR). Newborns learned to orient and initiate sucking (CR) with stroking of the forehead (CS) alone. Thus important associations, particularly those surrounding feeding activity, can be acquired through classical conditioning shortly after birth. But some types of classical conditioning are difficult for infants to learn. For example, researchers have not been able to successfully condition infants younger than three or four weeks to respond to aversive stimuli, such as foot withdrawal at loud noises or a painful prick. Perhaps the youngest infants lack the motor and neural abilities needed to escape noxious events; they must depend on caregivers for protection until they acquire simple locomotor skills for avoiding aversive stimuli (Rovee-Collier, 1987). As infants become older, classical conditioning occurs more rapidly and involves a broader range of stimuli.

OPERANT CONDITIONING

In *operant* (or *instrumental*) *conditioning*, the frequency of spontaneous, sometimes novel behaviors changes as a result of positive and negative consequences. Put another way, behaviors tend to increase when followed by rewards (**positive reinforcement**) or the removal of aversive events (**negative reinforcement**) and to decrease when followed by the loss of rewards (**negative punishment**) or an aversive outcome (**positive punishment**). The term *positive* in this context indicates that, when a behavior occurs, it causes a stimulus event that either increases the rate of the response (reinforcement) or decreases it (punishment). The term *negative* in this context indicates that, when a behavior occurs, it leads to the removal of a stimulus that either increases the rate of the response (reinforcement) or decreases it (punishment). Figure 5.6 summarizes these relationships and provides examples of positive and negative reinforcement and punishment.

Operant conditioning can be observed in infants within the first few hours of birth. For example, newborns will either increase or decrease pressure during sucking when the availability of milk, a positive reinforcer, is contingent on an increase or a decrease in pressure (Sameroff, 1972). And as with classical conditioning, operant conditioning seems to work best with behaviors important to infants, such as searching for (head turning, mouthing) and obtaining (sucking) food or other stimuli that are comforting. In other words, babies seem to be biologically prepared to learn about some things that are especially important for them.

recovery from habituation (dishabituation) Renewed response to a change in a stimulus, which indicates that the infant has detected that change.

unconditioned stimulus (UCS) Stimulus that, without prior training, elicits a reflexlike response (unconditioned response).

unconditioned response (UCR) Response that is automatically elicited by the unconditioned stimulus (UCS).

conditioned stimulus (CS) Neutral stimulus that begins to elicit a response similar to the unconditioned stimulus (UCS) with which it has been paired.

conditioned response (CR) Learned response that is exhibited to a previously neutral stimulus (CS) as a result of pairing the CS with an unconditioned stimulus (UCS).

positive reinforcement Occurrence of a stimulus that strengthens a preceding response. Also known as a *reward*.

negative reinforcement Removal of an aversive stimulus, which strengthens a preceding response.

negative punishment Removal or loss of a desired stimulus or reward, which weakens or decreases the frequency of a preceding response.

positive punishment Occurrence of an aversive stimulus that serves to weaken or decrease the frequency of a preceding response.

Visual and auditory events can be especially powerful reinforcers for infants. Babies will work hard, modifying the frequency or rate of sucking, vocalizing, smiling, and other behaviors under their control, to see and hear things. These kinds of stimulation, of course, typically occur in the presence of parents, grandparents, neighbors, and siblings who, as major sources of reinforcers, encourage the baby to become responsive to them.

Classical and operant conditioning can explain the acquisition of many other behaviors throughout infancy and childhood. Through repeated associations of events and from positive outcomes, including the reinforcing actions of caregivers or "instructors," children become more skilled and proficient in a rich variety of endeavors.

IMITATION

Habituation, classical conditioning, and operant conditioning are the basis for mastering many vital tasks of infancy and childhood. However, one element that seems to be missing from this discussion so far is children's active role in observing and interpreting events that occur in their surroundings. As we saw in the chapter titled "Themes and Theories," social learning theorists have considered observational learning an important means by which children acquire many complex social and cognitive skills (Bandura, 1977b). Individuals often learn behaviors important to the community by observing the activities of others, who in turn provide further guidance. Imitation has become an increasingly important element in explaining learning throughout development.

When does imitation become possible? How important is this ability in the learning of infants and children? Andrew Meltzoff and M. Keith Moore (1999) argue that even newborns and very young infants imitate a variety of responses, including tongue protrusion, mouth opening, and possibly even facial expressions portraying such emotions as happiness, sadness, and surprise (Field et al., 1982). Although some investigators have been unable to replicate these results, many others, including the authors of one study involving infants from Nepal (see Figure 5.7), report amazing imitative competence in neonates (Reissland, 1988).

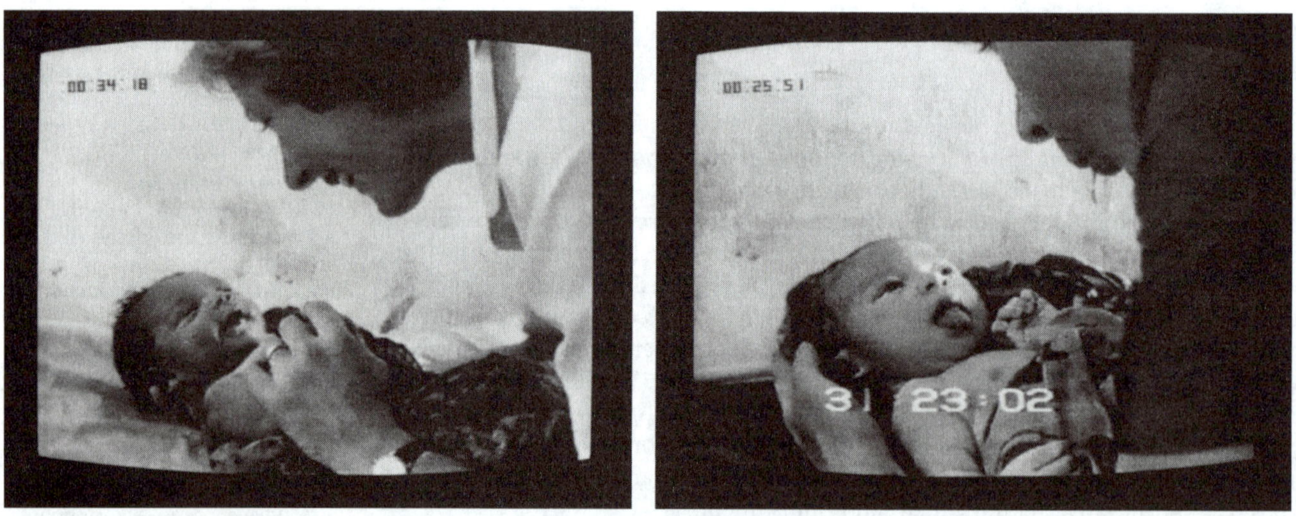

FIGURE 5.7

Facial Imitation in Newborns

Within an hour after birth, babies in Nepal showed different responses when an experimenter used pursed versus widened lip movements. On the left, the baby broadens his lips in response to widened lips by the model. On the right, the baby exposes his tongue in response to pursed lips by the model. The findings support the highly controversial position that even newborns are capable of imitating facial gestures.

More controversial, though, is what the imitative behaviors mean. Piaget (1962), for example, claimed that infants younger than eight to twelve months could imitate someone else's behavior, but only when able to see themselves making these responses. Because babies cannot view their own face, imitative facial gestures would be impossible, according to Piaget, until after about one year of age, when symbolic capacities emerge. From this perspective, then, facial gestures are stereotyped, rigid responses triggered by or tethered, so to speak, to limited forms of stimulation. For example, perhaps tongue protrusion by a model arouses the infant, which in turn promotes a sucking response that naturally invokes tongue protrusion from the infant (Karmiloff-Smith, 1995). Alternatively, perhaps this behavior reflects an active effort to explore an interesting object available in the infant's visual field (Jones, 1996). In either case, infants could be responding to just one or two types of stimuli and producing a kind of reflexive motor activity that is not really a form of imitation (Anisfeld, 1996).

Meltzoff and Moore (1999) counter that very young infants imitate a variety of responses, modify their imitations to increasingly match the modeled behavior over time, and exhibit their imitations primarily to other people and not to inanimate objects. These arguments contradict the view that such behaviors are simply a fixed pattern of reflexive actions. They propose instead that infants imitate in order to continue interacting with others. In fact, babies as young as six weeks will imitate behaviors of a model up to twenty-four hours later. The infant produces these imitative actions, according to Meltzoff and Moore, to help determine whether the model is the same person seen earlier; that is, as a way to help to identify and communicate with the model. If this interpretation is correct, imitation has an important social-communicative function and signals one of the earliest games babies play to learn about others in their surroundings.

Between six and twelve months of age, infants clearly display far more frequent and precise imitations, matching a wide range of modeled behaviors (Kaye & Marcus, 1981; Meltzoff & Moore, 1999). Piaget and others (McCall, Parke, & Kavanaugh, 1977) believed that **deferred imitation**, the ability to imitate well after some activity has been demonstrated, was not possible until about eighteen to twenty-four months of age. Piaget held that deferred imitation, along with pretend play and the emergence of language, provides one of the first major pieces of evidence for symbolic capacities (see the next chapter). However, as we have already seen, Meltzoff and Moore observed infants as young as six weeks reproducing a model's behavior a day after seeing it.

Other research confirms that deferred imitation can be observed far earlier than Piaget claimed. For example, six-month-olds will remove a mitten from a puppet's hand, shake it, and try to put it back on the puppet after observing this sequence of actions performed by a model twenty-four hours earlier (Barr, Dowden, & Hayne, 1996). Moreover, toddlers as young as fourteen months who see a peer pulling, pushing, poking, and inserting toys in the laboratory or at a daycare center will reproduce the behaviors in their own home as much as two days later when given the same toys and will imitate other novel behaviors as much as a week later (Meltzoff & Moore, 1999). The capacity for deferred imitation, then, appears to emerge much sooner than previously assumed. In fact, the results accord well with research on memory (discussed in the next chapter) showing that infants younger than one year can recognize stimuli hours and even days later.

The findings of imitation at very young ages provide clear and compelling evidence that infants, as well as older children, learn many new behaviors by observing others. In fact, fourteen- to eighteen-month-olds are more likely to imitate an adult's action that is accompanied by the verbal expression "There!"—indicating it was intentional—than an action accompanied by the verbal expression "Whoops!"—implying a mistake (Carpenter, Akhtar, & Tomasello, 1998). This finding suggests that very young children are capable of selectively imitating the deliberate actions of others, an important achievement for learning the more important social and cultural skills valued by other members of the community.

deferred imitation Ability to imitate a model's behavior hours, days, and even weeks after observation.

FOR • YOUR • REVIEW

- What are the basic principles of habituation, classical conditioning, and operant conditioning? What does recovery from habituation tell us about the habituation process?
- What are an unconditioned stimulus, an unconditioned response, a conditioned stimulus, and a conditioned response?
- How do positive reinforcement, negative reinforcement, negative punishment, and positive punishment affect behavior?
- Why is imitation an important component of learning theory? What evidence exists for imitation in early infancy? What is the significance of deferred imitation?

Sensory Capacities

Although various kinds of learning contribute to mastering new behaviors and enriching each individual's skills and competencies, these depend on other basic processes, including sensation and perception. What exactly do infants sense and perceive?

Sensation refers to the basic units of information recorded by a sensory receptor and the brain. **Perception** refers to the process of organizing and interpreting sensations. Sensations consist of, for example, registering different regions of brightness or of *contours*, the transitions in dark-light shading that signal borders and edges of elements in a visual array. With respect to auditory input, sensation refers to such abilities as discriminating a difference in the intensity or frequency of a sound. Perception, on the other hand, takes place when the infant recognizes his mother's face by sight or interprets a sequence of sounds as a familiar lullaby. Thus sensations are typically thought to be the building blocks; perception, the order and meaning imposed on those basic elements. In this chapter, we emphasize the infant's sensory capacities; in the next, we consider perception.

Two broad observations about the research in this area are worth making at the outset. First, vision has been studied far more than any other sensory domain. To some extent, this bias reflects the widespread view that sight provides the major source of information for humans. Vision, however, has also been easier to study than hearing, smell, and other senses. Second, knowledge of sensory (and perceptual) development in newborns and young infants has expanded far more rapidly than knowledge of their development in older infants and children. The disparity reflects the efforts of researchers to uncover the earliest appearance of sensory and perceptual capacities and the finding that many important changes in these domains occur in the first few months after birth.

Measuring Infant Sensory and Perceptual Capacities

How can we possibly know what babies see, hear, or smell when they are unable to tell us about it in words? Researchers have devised ingenious techniques, some quite simple, to help answer this question. Most of these procedures are based on measures of **attention**; that is, alertness or arousal focused on a specific aspect of the environment. For example, when infants display attentional preferences by looking longer at one thing than at another, they are communicating that they perceive differences between visual arrays. Not only have the techniques described below revealed much about infants' sensory abilities, but they have also been enormously powerful in helping us to understand the perceptual and cognitive capacities of infants.

sensation Basic information in the external world that is processed by the sensory receptors.

perception Process of organizing and interpreting sensory information.

attention State of alertness or arousal that allows the individual to focus on a selected aspect of the environment.

Preferential Behaviors In 1958 Robert Fantz placed babies on their back in an enclosed, criblike chamber. Through a peephole, he and his colleagues observed how long the babies gazed at different visual stimuli inserted in the top of the brightly illuminated chamber. Observers were able to determine where the infants were looking because the reflection of the stimulus could be seen on the cornea, the outer surface of the babies' eyes, as they looked at the objects. Using this method, Fantz (1961) found that one- to six-month-olds attended to disks decorated with bull's-eyes, stripes, newsprint, or facelike figures far longer than to solid-colored circles.

The simple methodology encouraged many researchers to study the visual capacities of infants by observing their preferential looking. The procedure has some limitations, however. What can we conclude, for example, when the infant attends to both members of a pair of stimuli for the same length of time? Is the baby unable to discriminate the two, or does she prefer to look at one just as much as the other? Nor can we be certain about what features the infant is processing when gazing at a stimulus.

Despite the limitations, babies often show preferences in what they attend to, and this simple procedure has proven enormously useful in assessing whether they prefer a human face over equally complex patterns; features such as edges, corners, or movement within a visual array; and other patterns or characteristics of visual information. By using special photographic techniques involving infrared lights and appropriate film, researchers can pinpoint specific regions and aspects of a figure at which the baby looks, and how she or he inspects a stimulus. Such procedures have revealed, for example, which features of a human face infants are most likely to scan, as Figure 5.8 shows.

Habituation *Habituation* of attention, the simple form of learning described earlier, is another technique that capitalizes on the infant's tendency to prefer looking at some things more than others. Babies shown the same stimulus for relatively lengthy periods or over a series of trials pay less and less attention to it. A change in the stimulus, however, may elicit *recovery from habituation*, or, if the habituated stimulus is paired with one that is dissimilar, the infant may show a preference for the new one, both indicators that the child has perceived a difference.

To illustrate the use of a habituation procedure, consider a recent study conducted by Maria Hernandez-Reif and her colleagues (2003). These researchers were interested in newborns' ability to notice differences in temperature. In the experiment, a small plastic tube with either cold (68° F/20° C) or warm (76° F/24° C) water was placed in the newborn's hand until he or she grasped it reflexively. The experimenter noted how long the newborn held the tube until he or she dropped it. The same temperature vial was repeatedly placed in the infant's hand until, over

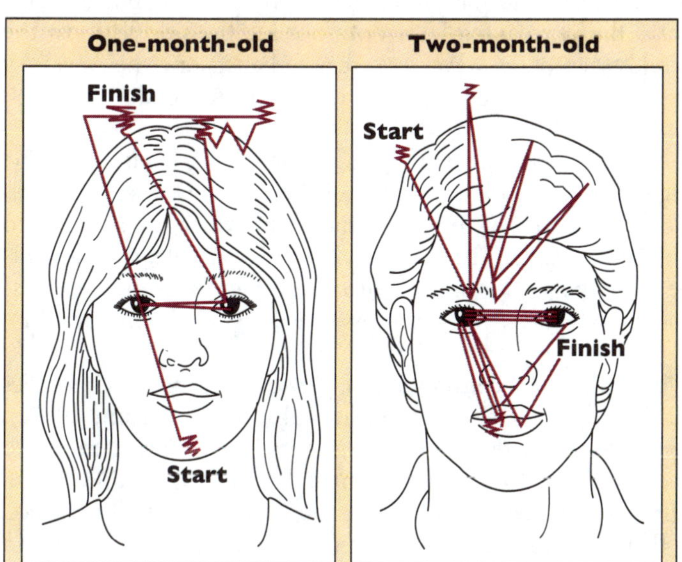

FIGURE 5.8
Visual Scanning
Using specialized techniques, researchers can often pinpoint the specific features in a visual stimulus at which infants are looking. Here the typical patterns of scanning these facelike stimuli by a one- and a two-month-old have been recorded. Note how the younger infant's gaze tends to be directed to the outer or external regions of the facial stimulus—that is, hair and chin. The older infant's gaze is more frequently directed to inner features, such as the eyes and mouth.
Source: Adapted from Salapatek (1975).

trials, the length of holding time declined to a criterion level. Would holding time increase when a tube of a different temperature was placed in the hand? The answer was yes. If infants had been presented with the cold tube, they showed an increase in holding when the warm tube was placed in their hand. If they had experienced the warm tube on habituation trials, they showed an increase in holding with the cold tube. (You might want to consider your answer to the following question, though: What could the researchers conclude if the infants showed no difference in responding when the new temperature was presented to them?) You can probably see why the habituation procedure, although simple in its design, has yielded extraordinary insights into the capacities of even very young infants.

Operant Conditioning More complex forms of learning, such as operant conditioning, can be used to further test an infant's ability to process sensory cues. To receive milk and other tangible rewards, such as interesting visual and auditory stimuli, babies will learn to suck faster or slower, turn their head, look, and perform other behaviors that indicate that they discriminate the arrays.

Operant conditioning procedures figure prominently in research on auditory perception. One procedure, established by Peter Eimas and his colleagues (1971), has proven especially informative. Babies are given a special nipple designed to record their rate of sucking. A baby who sucks energetically or at a rapid rate may be rewarded by hearing some pleasant sound; for example, the consonant-vowel pairing *pa*. After hearing *pa* repeatedly, the rate of sucking typically declines as the infant habituates to the stimulus. What will the baby do when a different sound, such as *ba*, is introduced? Infants as young as one month begin to suck at a high rate again in order to keep hearing *ba*. They can discriminate the new consonant-vowel pair from *pa*; they are already able to distinguish some important sounds that occur in language.

In addition to behavioral methods—preferential looking, habituation, and operant conditioning—physiological measures, such as heart rate or the neurological activity of the brain and even the firing of individual neurons, can be recorded to clarify the sensory and perceptual abilities of infants (de Haan & Nelson, 1997; Teller, 1998). Fortunately, the results of the various methods often complement one another in providing information about what infants are processing.

VISION

The visual system of the newborn and young infant is not yet fully developed. The center of the retina (the *fovea*), the optic nerve, the visual cortex, and other parts of the visual apparatus all continue to mature in the weeks following birth (Hainline, 1998). Consequently, the very young baby does not see the world in just the same way as an older child or adult. However, contrary to beliefs once held even by those in the medical community, the newborn infant is far from blind.

Visuomotor Skills The eye includes a lens designed to refract, or bend, light. The lens focuses visual images onto the *retina*, the back of the eye that houses the *rods*, which are responsive to the intensity of light, and the *cones*, which are sensitive to different wavelengths of light. The lens of the human eye is variable; small, involuntary muscles change its shape so that images of objects viewed at different distances are brought into focus on the retina, a process called **visual accommodation**. When the lens works effectively, we can see things clearly.

Newborns display limited visual accommodation. However, the process improves rapidly to nearly adultlike levels by about three months of age (Aslin, 1987a). Improvements in the physical characteristics of the eye and in paying attention to visual information may contribute to the developmental change (Hainline, 1998). In addition, the *pupillary reflex*, which controls the amount of light entering the eye, is sluggish during the first few months after birth, further reducing the ability to focus (Aslin, 1987a). As a result, infants are unable to see details of stimuli. However,

visual accommodation Visuomotor process by which small involuntary muscles change the shape of the lens of the eye so that images of objects seen at different distances are brought into focus on the retina.

they discriminate best those patterns and objects about eight to twenty inches away, the typical distance of a caregiver's face when holding or feeding the baby.

Eye movements are another essential part of looking. **Saccades**, rapid movements of the eye to inspect an object or to look at something in the periphery of the visual field, are produced within hours of birth (Lewis, Maurer, & Kay, 1978). At first, the saccades are initiated slowly and cover only small distances; neonates must launch a sequence of them to "catch up" to a peripheral target (Aslin, 1993). Saccades typically become more accurate, however, during the first three to four months and continue to improve in accuracy throughout childhood (Fioravanti et al., 1995).

Humans exhibit another pattern of eye movements, **smooth visual pursuit**, which consists of maintaining fixation on a slowly moving target almost as though the eyes were locked onto it. Newborns display only brief periods of smooth pursuit, but its execution continues to improve through six to eight months of age (von Hofsten & Rosander, 1997), when it begins to appear adultlike. The development of both saccadic and smooth visual pursuit eye movements is closely linked to the improving capacity of infants to sustain attention to visual arrays (Richards & Holley, 1999).

In looking for an object, both eyes normally move together in the same direction. Sometimes, however, the eyes must rotate in opposite directions, turning toward each other as, for example, when a person tries to see a fly that has landed on his or her nose. This response, called **vergence**, occurs when fixations shift between far and near objects; otherwise, we would see double images. Vergence occurs irregularly in infants younger than two months, especially when objects are not static and move to different depths (Hainline & Riddell, 1995; Thorn et al., 1994). For example, young babies' eyes may fail to rotate far enough toward each other to converge on a visual target.

Acuity How well are young infants able to see, despite their immature visuomotor skills? This question concerns **visual acuity**. One common test of visual acuity, the *Snellen test*, is based on identifying letters or other symbols on a chart twenty feet away. Babies, of course, cannot name letters, so other procedures are used to test their visual acuity. Several methods have been devised, but one that has proven reasonably good relies on *preferential looking*. As an array of, say, black and white stripes appears more frequently (the stripes become narrower), the pattern becomes more difficult to see, and the stimulus eventually appears gray. Infants unable to detect the stripes quickly lose interest, preferring to attend instead to a pattern they can still detect. By pairing stimuli with different frequencies of stripes and observing preferential looking, researchers can gauge the visual acuity of infants.

Two key findings emerge from the many investigations of visual acuity and *contrast sensitivity*, another more complex measure of visual capacity that takes into consideration ability to discriminate when illumination, orientation, and other aspects of contour also vary. First, even newborns detect contours, although their acuity and sensitivity to contrast is estimated to be about forty times poorer than in children or adults, as suggested in Figure 5.9 (Maurer et al. 1999). Second, acuity and contrast sensitivity improve rapidly during the first six months after birth and continue to improve at a slower rate for several years thereafter (Adoh & Woodhouse, 1994; Tschopp et al., 1999). The gain, especially during early infancy, is owed to enhanced visuomotor skills and neural pathways for vision, changes in the shape and physical characteristics of the eye, and greater efficiency in the functioning of visual receptors in the retina.

Color Perception Can babies see colors? The answer is yes, at least after a few months of age. Although very young infants may not see a full range of colors, perception of several hues is possible. For example, shortly after birth babies can detect red hues, especially if they are highly saturated; that is, contain relatively few wavelengths of other light (Adams & Courage, 1998). Detection of other hues, especially blue, comes later and is thought to become adultlike by three months of age (Kellman & Arterberry, 2006; Teller, 1998).

saccades Rapid eye movement to inspect an object or view a stimulus in the periphery of the visual field.

smooth visual pursuit Consistent, unbroken tracking by the eyes that serves to maintain focus on a moving visual target.

vergence Ability of the eyes to rotate in opposite directions to fixate on objects at different distances; improves rapidly during first few months after birth.

visual acuity Ability to make fine discriminations among elements in a visual array by detecting contours, transitions in light patterns that signal borders and edges.

FIGURE 5.9
What the Two-Month-Old Sees
Although adults with normal vision would see a clear image of this individual, the two-month-old would perceive the same individual in far less detail as suggested by the photo on the right. Acuity in young infants, however, rapidly improves and typically approaches a normal level sometime between about six and twelve months of age.

ATYPICAL DEVELOPMENT

Visual Problems in Infancy

KEY THEME
RISK/RESILIENCE

How important is visual sensory stimulation during infancy and early childhood for the development of the normal capacity to see? Earlier in this chapter, we describe research carried out on young kittens suggesting that early perceptual stimulation was essential for the growth of neurons in the visual receptor areas of the cortex. Although experimental procedures cannot be carried out on human infants, several naturally occurring problems in infancy suggest similar consequences for the development of human visual abilities.

Approximately 1 in every 10,000 babies is born with *cataracts*, a clouding of part or all of the lens of the eye that impairs the capacity to see patterned stimulation (Sireteanu, 1999). If uncorrected, the baby's visual acuity, as well as other visual abilities, can be seriously impaired. Moreover, if the cataract is located in only one eye, the normal eye will actively suppress whatever responsiveness exists in the affected eye. The result is a lack of improvement in acuity in the affected eye, as well as impairment in depth perception because of the loss of binocular vision. Fortunately, cataracts are often relatively easy to detect. They can be surgically removed if medical resources are available, and substitute contact lenses can be implanted so that visual input will be focused on the retina. When such procedures are followed early in infancy, acuity in the affected eye or eyes improves rapidly, even after only an hour of patterned visual experience, and continues to improve rapidly with an outcome of normal visual development (Maurer et al., 1999).

Perhaps an even more frequent visual problem, affecting as many as 5 percent of infants and young children, is *amblyopia*, a condition sometimes called "lazy eye." Amblyopia refers to the failure of vision to develop in one eye, again because of suppression of visual input by the other eye. A common cause of amblyopia is *strabismus*, or the inability of the two eyes to display vergence. In many circumstances, strabismus is also relatively easy to detect; the eyes appear misaligned, or the child appears "cross-eyed" because muscles controlling the directionality of one of the eyes may be too strong or too weak. When strabismus is corrected early, normal depth perception and vision again become possible, as the two eyes begin to work together. However, for some infants and young children, the complementary functioning of the two eyes may go awry even without visible evidence of strabismus if, for example, the ability of one eye to focus is better than the other. A child with amblyopia displays the progressive loss of depth perception that vergence provides (Banks, Aslin, & Letson, 1975), and the weaker eye may become functionally blind. Fortunately, many procedures are available to correct such conditions, including patching the stronger eye for a period of time to strengthen the weaker one. If not performed early, preferably in toddlers and especially before the end of the preschool years, the loss of visual capacities can be permanent. However, parents, and sometimes even pediatricians, may not always be aware of these visual problems. Thus caregivers need to take the initiative in ensuring that their infants' and toddlers' vision is evaluated by experts who can conduct relatively simple tests for amblyopia; adequate perceptual stimulation early in development is an essential ingredient to the emergence of normal visual capacities.

AUDITION

Just as opinion once held that newborns are blind, so did it assert that newborns are deaf (Spears & Hohle, 1967). However, the fetus is listening well before birth. Brain wave patterns, heart rate changes, and activity level observed on ultrasound scans reveal responses to vibroacoustic stimulation (Kisilevsky, Hains, & Low, 1999; Kisilevsky & Muir, 1991). Low-frequency sounds, the kind that are produced in human speech, are detected by the fetus sometimes as early as twenty-three weeks of age (Kisilevsky & Low, 1998; Lecanuet, 1998). Sensitivity to a wide range of sounds at lower and lower intensities increases dramatically during the remainder of the prenatal period (Hepper & Shahidullah, 1994).

Persuasive evidence that fetuses hear also comes from several studies indicating that newborns prefer to listen to the sounds they heard before birth. Anthony DeCasper and Melanie Spence (1986) asked expectant women to read aloud a passage from Dr. Seuss's *The Cat in the Hat*. Women read the passage twice a day during the last six weeks of pregnancy; their fetuses were exposed to the story for a total of about three and a half hours before birth. Two or three days after birth, the babies listened to either the same passage or a new story while outfitted with a special pacifier that recorded rate of sucking. Depending on the rate of sucking, the recording of the story would turn on or off. When newborns heard *The Cat in the Hat*, they changed their rate of sucking to listen to it but did not do so for the new story. Some kind of learning about the Dr. Seuss story apparently took place prenatally.

What precisely does the fetus hear, and what is it learning from these exposures? We are not really sure. As newborns, infants prefer to listen to their mother's voice rather than the voice of a stranger (DeCasper & Fifer, 1980), especially the lower-frequency sounds associated with their mother's voice (Spence & Freeman, 1996). Because the mother's body tissue and bones are very good conductors of sound, the newborn already has had considerable exposure to characteristics of the mother's speech (Lecanuet, 1998). However, the fetus can also learn something about the cadence of sound as well. After expectant women in France repeatedly recited a rhyme from the thirty-third to thirty-seventh week of their gestation period, changes in fetal heart rate in response to the rhyme revealed that the fetus differentiated it from another novel rhyme even when recited by someone else (DeCasper et al., 1994).

Hearing Little research exists on exactly how well babies hear immediately after birth. Physiological measures taken from the auditory brainstem suggest that responsivity is nearly adultlike for some frequencies, especially those in the middle range, of sounds that humans can detect (Sininger, Doyle, & Moore, 1999). However, work using attentional and behavioral measures with older infants reveals marked improvement in most auditory skills throughout the first few months. Certainly by about six months of age, babies are able to detect and discriminate numerous features of sound, such as its frequency and intensity, almost as well as do adults (Saffran, Werker, & Werner, 2006).

Not all babies, however, are able to hear at birth. Deafness and other hearing disabilities strike an estimated 1 to 3 out of every 1,000 infants born in the United States (Stein, 1999). That translates into perhaps as many as 20,000 infants each year who are hearing impaired. Lower rates are found in some Western European nations, such as France (Baille et al., 1996), but higher rates are found in many other regions of the world. New screening techniques—for example, physiological measurements of neural activity in the auditory brainstem—can be used with infants to detect the possibility of hearing loss. Auditory screening is often administered to those infants born at risk in families with a history of hearing impairment or to those exposed to cytomegalovirus and other diseases or drugs known to affect hearing. However, auditory screening of infants is not universal in many countries, including the United States and the United Kingdom, despite the known benefits of early intervention (Joint Committee on Infant Hearing, 2000; Kennedy, 2000). In fact, congenital hearing impairment is detected in only about half of the infants who have the impairment in the United States during the first year of life (Eilers & Berlin, 1995).

Sound Localization Shortly after birth, babies display **sound localization**, the ability to locate a sound in space by turning their head or eyes in the direction of the sound. This early ability, which may be reflexive, declines during the first two months and then reemerges at about four months of age in the form of a more deliberate search for sound (Field et al., 1980). Ability to locate the precise position from which a sound originates improves markedly throughout infancy and into early childhood (Ashmead, Clifton, & Perris, 1987; Morrongiello, Fenwick, & Chance, 1990). By six to eight months of age, infants also begin to appreciate the distance from which a sound emanates. At this age, babies hearing a sound in the dark produced by an object beyond their reach are less likely to attempt to retrieve it than an object producing a sound that is within their reach (Clifton, Perris, & Bullinger, 1991).

Smell, Taste, Touch, and Sensitivity to Pain

Developmental researchers have given far less attention to smell, taste, and the cutaneous senses—the receptor systems of the skin responsible for perceiving touch, pressure, pain, and temperature—than to vision or hearing. Each of these senses also functions shortly after birth and furnishes crucial adaptive and survival cues for the baby. Smell, for example, may be critical for determining what is edible and may also be involved in early attachment to the caregiver.

Smell Facial expressions, changes in rate of respiration and blood flow in the brain, and approach-avoidance activities involving head turning are just a few of the responses indicating that newborns detect odors. Do babies turn up their noses at the unpleasant smell of rotten eggs? Can they detect the food-related smells of fish, butter, banana, or vanilla? They most certainly can (Steiner, 1979). In fact, at 3- to 4- days of age, infants show a preference for the smell of human breast milk as opposed to formula milk, even when they have been bottle-fed from birth (Marlier & Schaal, 2005). Moreover, newborns become increasingly sensitive to many smells during the first few days of life (Marlier, Schaal, & Soussignan, 1998).

sound localization Ability to determine a sound's point of origin.

Parent-infant recognition occurs by odor among many species of animals. Can human infants identify their caregivers this way as well? Again, the answer is yes. By five days of age infants turned their heads longer in the direction of a breast pad that had been worn by the mother than to an unused one. By six days of age, infants also preferred a pad obtained from their own mother to one from an unfamiliar mother (MacFarlane, 1975). By the same token, can family members identify their infants on the basis of odor? Indeed, within the first few days of birth and after brief contact, not only mothers but also fathers, grandmothers, and aunts can recognize newborn kin by their smell alone. In other words, humans may inherit some family olfactory signature about which they are sensitive or learn very quickly (Porter, Balogh, & Makin, 1988).

Taste Receptors for the basic tastes of sweet, sour, salty, and bitter, located mostly on the tongue, develop well before birth; the fetus may already taste as it swallows amniotic fluid. Facial expressions and rate of sucking reveal more clearly that newborns can discriminate tastes (see Figure 5.10). Sweet stimuli, for example, elicit a relaxed facial expression resembling a smile; sour stimuli produce lip pursing or a puckered expression; and bitter stimuli elicit mouth opening as though expressing disgust (Steiner, 1979).

Innate preferences for some tastes may help infants to meet nutritional needs and protect them from harmful or dangerous substances. And there may be a genetic basis

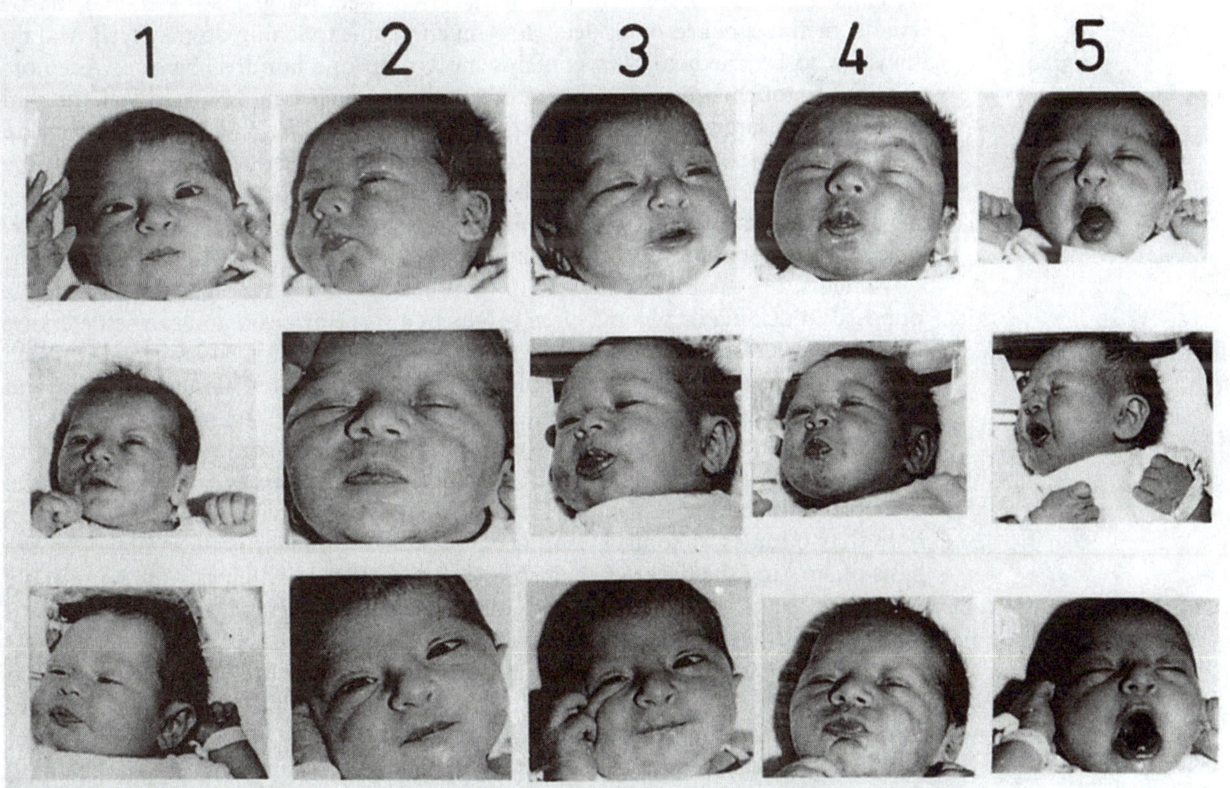

FIGURE 5.10
Discriminating Tastes
Babies produce different facial expressions depending on what they taste. The first column shows the resting faces of three newborns. Column 2 shows the same babies after they received distilled water—their expressions show very little change. After sweet stimulation, the babies' facial expressions are more positive and relaxed, resembling a smile or licking of the upper lip, as shown in column 3. However, their mouths become more pursed after sour stimulation (column 4) and more arch-shaped after bitter stimulation (column 5).

KEY THEME
NATURE & NURTURE

for individual sensitivity to certain tastes, such as bitterness and sweetness (Mennella, Pepino, & Reed, 2005). Preferences can, however, be modified by early experience. For example, babies fed sweeter fluids in the first few months after birth ingest more sweet water at six months of age than babies not given this experience (Beauchamp & Moran, 1982). The desire for salt in a specific food may also be established early in infancy (Beauchamp & Cowart, 1990; Sullivan & Birch, 1990). Infants can detect flavors from their mother's milk as well—for example, garlic, alcohol, and vanilla—an ability that might familiarize them to the foods common to their family and culture (Mennella & Beauchamp, 1996). In fact, early exposure even to unpleasant tastes can make them more tolerable to infants. Julia Mennella and her colleagues exposed infants to Enfamil, a common milk-based formula, or Nutramigen, an unpleasant-tasting protein-based formula used to treat colic, starting at two weeks of age. Seven months later, all infants were given Enfamil, Nutramigen, and Alimentum, a novel unpleasant-tasting protein-based formula. Videotapes of each group of infants showed that those exposed early to the unpleasant-tasting formula were more accepting of both Nutramigen and Alimentum; they drank more and were more relaxed and happy as the formula was given to them (Mennella, Griffin, & Beauchamp, 2004).

Although learning appears to be important in the emergence of odor and taste preferences, we should emphasize one more thing. Until about two years of age, children will put just about anything into their mouth. Thus among the most important things they must learn is what *not* to taste (Rozin, 1990).

Touch and Temperature Infants are usually kissed, hugged, stroked, and maybe even sometimes poked or tickled. How much of this touching do they feel? And do they like to be touched? Skin contains more than one hundred types of receptors sensitive to touch, pressure, temperature, and pain (Reisman, 1987). In fact, the skin is the body's largest organ, and its sensory receptors are the earliest to develop prenatally. As we saw in the chapter titled "The Prenatal Period and Birth," even the fetus responds to touch. We have already noted in this chapter as well that, in the newborn, tactile stimulation can elicit a variety of reflexes. Clearly, then, even newborns can feel sensations on their skin.

Infants, for the most part, like to be touched. Touching, especially stroking as opposed to tickling or poking, often results in a smile or a coo and can settle crying (Pelaez-Nogueras et al. 1997). And for infants born at risk because of low birth weight, massage therapy—the application of long strokes along the body and limbs—has been shown to accelerate weight gain (Field, 2001).

As with smell, the touch system illustrates the sensory communication that can facilitate social interactions between infant and caregiver. Just as caregivers recognize their babies by odor shortly after birth, so can they recognize them by touch. After only sixty minutes of contact, mothers and fathers can identify their infants on the basis of stroking the backs of the babies' hands (Bader & Phillips, 1999; Kaitz et al., 1992; Kaitz et al., 1994). This ability may be adaptive in encouraging caregivers to be responsive to their offspring.

A difficult problem for newborns, particularly premature infants, is regulation of body temperature (Moffat & Hackel, 1985). Cooling awakens babies, makes them more restless, and increases their oxygen consumption, responses that facilitate heat production. Because many newborns are unable to sweat or pant, exposure to high temperatures produces reddening of the skin, less activity, and more sleep, events that decrease heat production and assist heat loss (Harpin, Chellappah, & Rutter, 1983). When warm, babies also assume a sunbathing position, extending their extremities, perhaps a good clue for a caregiver who is trying to decide whether a baby is too warm (Reisman, 1987).

Sensitivity to Pain Heel pricks, circumcision, and other medical procedures involving newborns and young infants have come under increasing scrutiny in recent years because of concerns about the pain they may cause. Historically, newborns experiencing such invasive procedures were rarely given pain reduction medication (Ramenghi et al., 1996), and even major operations on very young infants were carried out with little or no effort to diminish pain. Why was this the case? The answer is that newborns were believed to have neither the neurological capacity to experience pain nor the ability to remember it. An additional concern was the potential negative side effects of pain medication on an immature organism.

Today we know that brain centers involved in the detection of pain are well developed prenatally and that behavioral responses (such as crying and facial expressions) consistent with the discomfort associated with pain are readily displayed by preterm and full-term newborns (Anand et al., 2001). Moreover, evidence has been gathered to suggest that exposure to painful circumstances early in infancy can lead to lasting changes in the endocrine and immune systems, and to continued behavioral sensitivity to pain later in development (Porter, Grunau, & Anand, 1999; Taddio et al., 1995). Medications may be an important part of efforts to manage pain, but offering sucrose or the opportunity to engage in nonnutritive sucking and even exposure to music during minor operations can work, too. All of these strategies have been shown to have comforting effects for infants in painful situations (Anand et al., 2001; Joyce, Keck, & Gerkensmeyer, 2001).

FOR • YOUR • REVIEW

- What is the difference between sensation and perception?
- How are attention and other behavioral and physiological measures used to investigate infant sensory and perceptual capacities?
- What limitations exist in infant visual accommodation, saccadic eye movements, smooth visual pursuit, vergence, and other visuomotor capacities? How quickly do these achieve adultlike ability?
- What kinds of visual problems are found among infants? Why is the correction of these problems important in infancy or early childhood?
- What is infants' ability to perceive color?
- What are the basic auditory capacities of the infant? How does sound localization develop?
- Can newborns and very young infants discriminate smells, tastes, touch, and temperature differences? Can they feel pain?

CHAPTER RECAP

Summary of Developmental Themes

NATURE & NURTURE

How do nature and nurture interact in physical development in infancy?

Physical growth, brain development, and the acquisition of motor skills are the products of complex systems influenced by both biology and experience. For example, biological processes, both genetic and hormonal, augment the proliferation and migration of neurons, events associated with physical growth and the development of motor skills. At the same time, environmental factors can have a potent effect on the way brain wiring proceeds. Experiences such as practice and training can also encourage the acquisition of motor skills.

Babies seem to be intrinsically motivated to exercise rudimentary motor skills. Once a child attains locomotion or other skills, she or he provokes new reactions from caregivers which may include encouragement or restrictions of the types of behaviors the child displays.

We cannot help but be impressed by the remarkably adaptive resources immediately available to infants for gaining knowledge of their environment. The basic mechanisms of learning—habituation, classical and operant conditioning, and imitation—are ready to influence behavior at or shortly after birth. A newborn's sense organs are sufficiently developed to provide rudimentary capacities to see, hear, feel, taste, and smell, and often function even before birth. We have also seen, however, that sensory capacities improve substantially as a result of experiential fine-tuning. Thus the environment plays an early and powerful role in determining which capacities are acquired and maintained.

Sociocultural Influence

How does the sociocultural context influence physical development in infancy?

Physical growth and motor skill development are embedded within settings, resources, and beliefs promoted by the society in which the child lives. For example, the extent to which a culture encourages specific skills, such as the acquisition of motor milestones, affects infants' efforts to achieve these behaviors.

Continuity/Discontinuity

Is physical development during infancy continuous or discontinuous?

Physical development, brain development, and the acquisition of motor skills show spurts at certain times in development. These patterns often give rise to conceptions of stagelike development. But even dramatic changes, such as those exhibited in attaining motor milestones in infancy, are grounded in processes undergoing continuous transformations. Small, incremental changes in the relative strength of muscles, for example, may initiate substantive dynamic reorganizations in complex systems of behavior. Basic learning processes also emphasize continuity as a basis for development.

Interaction Among Domains

How does physical development during infancy interact with other domains of development?

Improvements in the execution and coordination of motor skills have dramatic influences on the responses and expectations of caregivers and others. For example, once capable of walking, the child has a greater ability to initiate independence and to explore the environment, enhancing cognitive development. At the same time, parents may become more restrictive, a dynamic that can have social and emotional repercussions.

Learning plays a substantial role in almost every aspect of development. The child learns cognitive and social skills, acceptable ways to express thoughts and feelings, and numerous other behaviors. Gains in sensory capacities are substantially influenced by physiological and neural advances.

Risk/Resilience

What factors promote risk or resilience in physical development during infancy?

Variations in physical or motor development may arise from biological or experiential factors that can limit or augment development. The differences can significantly influence the child and the reactions of others, as precocious or delayed skill acquisition demonstrates. Of particular concern here is that the infant receive appropriate sensory and other environmental experiences during the time that neuronal differentiation is taking place. Infants not treated for cataracts, for example, may experience permanent loss of vision later in development.

Chapter Review

Body Growth and Development

What are norms for growth? How do they provide information about whether physical growth is proceeding normally?

The term *grow* essentially applies to the increase in size of the body or its organs. *Grow* and *develop* are often used interchangeably; however, the latter refers not only to changes in size but also to any orderly pattern of change. *Norms* derived from measurements carried out on a large sample of individuals within a population provide an estimate of the range of what is considered typical in development.

What patterns of growth are observed during infancy? How do they differ for various parts of the body? How do they differ among individuals and ethnic groups?

Growth norms reveal rapid height and weight gains just before and after birth, and much slower but regular increases in size beginning at about two years of age. Some regions of the body—for example, the head—show faster rates of growth early in life than other regions, a phenomenon called *cephalocaudal development*. Regions nearer the center of the body also tend to develop somewhat sooner than regions more peripheral, a reflection of the principle of *proximodistal development*. Boys tend to be larger than girls in early infancy, and infants from some ethnic groups tend to be larger than others.

The Brain and Nervous System

What are the major methodological procedures that have permitted advances in the study of the developing brain?

New methodologies to investigate the brain, including positron emission tomography (PET), functional magnetic resonance imaging (fMRI), and recording of event-related potentials, have recently promoted widespread attention to the brain and its development.

Which regions of the brain develop earliest and latest? To what functions do those regions contribute?

The brainstem and midbrain, which control essential biological functions, are fairly well established at birth. The cortex, the portion of the brain that controls thinking, planning, and voluntary responses, develops after birth. The sensory and motor regions of the cortex develop earliest; the frontal cortex develops later.

What developmental changes occur in neurons? How do myelin and glial cells contribute to neuronal development?

The three major changes that *neurons* undergo are proliferation (production of neurons), migration (movement of neurons to their final destination), and differentiation (formation of synapses with other neurons). *Myelin* speeds neural impulses, and *glial cells* nourish and provide scaffolding for migrating neurons.

When does the plasticity of the brain decline? What is the difference between experience-expectant and experience-dependent information?

Plasticity of the brain is apparent in infancy and declines toward the end of childhood, although considerable plasticity is still evident in mature adult brains. Neuron differentiation may proceed at critical or sensitive times for experience-expectant information but occurs throughout development for experience-dependent information. An important principle underlying the development of neural connections is repeated episodes of firing in synchrony.

What evidence exists for brain lateralization in infancy?

Infants display behaviors suggestive of hemispheric specialization, or *lateralization*, at birth. They lie with head oriented in one direction, hold objects in preferred hands, and show preferences in the direction in which they turn to localize a sound.

Motor Skill Development

How do primitive and postural reflexes differ? What purpose do they serve for the infant?

Reflexes, involuntary responses to stimulation controlled by subcortical processes, are among the earliest motor actions displayed in newborns. Primitive reflexes (such as rooting and sucking) help to increase the likelihood of survival, whereas postural reflexes (such as stepping and swimming) help the infant to maintain a specific orientation in his or her environment.

When are rhythmical stereotypies exhibited?

Rhythmical stereotypies, repeated motor actions with no apparent goal, are among the earliest organized motor behaviors displayed by infants.

What are the major milestones associated with the development of postural control, locomotion, and manual control? How do the principles of cephalocaudal and proximodistal development apply to the emergence of the major motor milestones?

Postural control includes keeping the head upright and balanced, maintaining an upright sitting position, and standing with, and later without, assistance. Locomotor skills include rolling over, crawling or creeping, cruising, and walking. Manual control includes prereaching, ballistic reaching, and a shift from reach with hands formed in a fist to use of a pincer grasp. The cephalocaudal principle highlights the fact that regions nearer the head tend to undergo more rapid development than regions farther away from the head. The proximodistal principle is illustrated by the fact that arms and legs come under the infant's control before fingers and toes.

What factors contribute to motor development? How do cultural practices influence their acquisition?

Genetic preadaptation may contribute to the emergence of motor skills, but research indicates that experience can be important as well. Some societies promote the acquisition of basic motor skills, such as crawling and walking, and as a consequence, such skills often appear somewhat earlier among infants and very young children in those societies.

Sleep

What states do newborns display?

Newborns display regular and irregular sleep, drowsiness, alert inactivity, alert activity, and crying. Alert inactivity is the state in which the infant appears to be most able to profit from experience.

What kinds of sleep patterns are found in newborns?

Newborns sleep for about two-thirds of the day, but in short sleep-wake cycles. A relatively large proportion of the infant's time involves REM sleep, a state that may provide him or her with stimulation even while asleep.

Why does controversy exist concerning the sleeping arrangements for young infants?

Some cultures encourage the practice of co-sleeping. In addition, some researchers hypothesize that co-sleeping may help to prevent such problems as apnea in infants. These practices stand in contrast to the general belief in our culture that sleeping in one's own room promotes self-reliance and independence. In addition, the medical community currently advises against co-sleeping. One compromise is to have the infant sleep in a crib in the caregiver's room.

What factors are associated with SIDS? What steps can caretakers take to reduce the likelihood of SIDS?

The risk of *sudden infant death syndrome*, or *SIDS*, is highest at age two to four months. SIDS is also associated with the colder months, poverty, low birth weight, having a cold, being a male, and being a later-born or multiple-birth child. To reduce the risk of SIDS, caregivers should place the infant to sleep on the back, provide a pacifier, eliminate exposure to cigarette smoke and co-sleeping, remove soft bedding materials, and provide adequate ventilation in the child's room.

Basic Learning Processes

What are the basic principles of habituation, classical conditioning, and operant conditioning? What does recovery from habituation tell us about the habituation process?

Habituation refers to the gradual decline in responding as a result of repeated exposure to an event, a basic form of learning that helps in orienting to new information in the environment. Increased attention to new information following habituation indicates *recovery from habituation (dishabituation)*. This response suggests that infants are able to distinguish between familiar and new events. *Classical conditioning* involves the pairing of a neutral stimulus with one that naturally elicits a response. The neutral stimulus then begins to elicit the response as well. *Operant conditioning* involves the delivery or removal of a reinforcing or punishing stimulus so that behaviors preceding the stimulus increase or decrease.

What are an unconditioned stimulus, an unconditioned response, a conditioned stimulus, and a conditioned response?

The *unconditioned stimulus (UCS)* is the stimulus that elicits a reflexlike response. No training is required to obtain it. The *unconditioned response (UCR)* is the reaction that results from the presentation of the UCS. The *conditioned stimulus (CS)* is a neutral stimulus that begins to elicit a response similar to the UCS with which it has been paired. The *conditioned response (CR)* is the resulting learned response to the CS.

How do positive reinforcement, negative reinforcement, negative punishment, and positive punishment affect behavior?

Reinforcement increases the future likelihood of a behavior through the occurrence of a reward (*positive reinforcement*) or the removal of an aversive stimulus (*negative reinforcement*). Punishment results in the decrease of a future behavior through the removal of a desired stimulus (*negative punishment*) or the application of an aversive stimulus (*positive punishment*).

Why is imitation an important component of learning theory? What evidence exists for imitation in early infancy? What is the significance of deferred imitation?

Imitation is often the means by which infants and children learn the social and cultural behaviors that are important to their community. Research shows that newborns and young infants imitate behaviors such as tongue protrusion, mouth opening, and facial expressions of emotion. *Deferred imitation* refers to the infant's ability to reproduce a model's behavior at a later time. Its presence suggests a capacity for symbolic thinking.

Sensory Capacities

What is the difference between sensation and perception?

Sensation refers to the receipt of information by the sensory receptors (eyes, ears) and the brain. *Perception* refers to the organization and interpretation of that information.

How are attention and other behavioral and physiological measures used to investigate infant sensory and perceptual capacities?

Researchers rely on measures of *attention*, habituation and recovery from habituation, and learning, as well as measures of heart rate and neurological activity of the brain, to study infant sensory and perceptual capacities.

What limitations exist in infant visual accommodation, saccadic eye movements, smooth visual pursuit, vergence, and other visuomotor capacities? How quickly do these achieve adultlike ability?

The infant's *visual accommodation* response, the ability to focus at different distances, is initially limited but improves by three months of age. *Saccades*, rapid eye movements to inspect objects, are initially slow and cover small distances. Improvements are seen in the first three to four months and throughout childhood. *Smooth visual pursuit*, maintaining fixation on a moving target, is displayed for only brief periods by newborns but become adultlike by six to eight months. *Vergence*, the ability of the eyes to rotate in opposite directions, is irregular prior to two months. *Visual acuity*, a measure of how well infants can see, improves rapidly in the first six months.

What kinds of visual problems are found among infants? Why is the correction of these problems important in infancy or early childhood?

Among the problems infants may display are cataracts, the clouding of the lens, and amblyopia, the failure of vision to develop in one eye. Early treatment is important because visual input may influence the kinds of neural connections that are made. If treatment is delayed, visual capacities may be permanently lost.

What is infants' ability to perceive color?

Color vision is limited prior to the age of three months. Initially infants detect primarily red hues but see the full range of colors in successive weeks.

What are the basic auditory capacities of the infant? How does sound localization develop?

Infants are sensitive to different frequencies and intensities of sound by six months of age. Their *sound localization* skills start out as reflexive but by four months of age become more deliberate and precise.

Can newborns and very young infants discriminate smells, tastes, touch, and temperature differences? Can they feel pain?

Newborns and young infants are responsive to different smells, including the smell of their caregivers. They can discriminate tastes such as sweet, sour, and bitter. Newborns respond to tactile stimulation and changes in temperature, and show through their behavioral responses that they feel pain.

KEY TERMS AND CONCEPTS

attention (p. 174)
cephalocaudal development (p. 151)
conditioned response (CR) (p. 171)
conditioned stimulus (CS) (p. 171)
deferred imitation (p. 173)
glial cell (p. 154)
habituation (p. 169)
lateralization (p. 158)
myelin (p. 154)
negative punishment (p. 171)
negative reinforcement (p. 171)
neuron (p. 154)
norm (p. 151)
perception (p. 174)
plasticity (p. 157)
positive punishment (p. 171)
positive reinforcement (p. 171)
proximodistal development (p. 152)
recovery from habituation (dishabituation) (p. 171)
reflex (p. 159)
rhythmical stereotypy (p. 161)
saccades (p. 177)
sensation (p. 174)
smooth visual pursuit (p. 177)
sound localization (p. 180)
sudden infant death syndrome (SIDS) (p. 167)
unconditioned response (UCR) (p. 171)
unconditioned stimulus (UCS) (p. 171)
vergence (p. 177)
visual accommodation (p. 176)
visual acuity (p. 177)

6 Perception, Cognition, and Language

The apartment had suddenly grown quiet. The three other babies and their mothers who had been helping to celebrate Chad's first birthday had departed. Only Tanya, Chad's mother, remained with him as the light faded at the end of the day. Picking up the torn gift wrappings, Tanya reflected on the events of the past year. She thought back to her first glimpse of Chad. She had counted his toes and fingers to make sure they were all there. She had wondered aloud, as she first held him, "What do you see? Do you recognize me? What do you hear? Do you like my songs? What are you thinking?" Tanya had vowed to be a good mother, to help Chad learn. She couldn't afford the colorful playland that had beckoned to him at the toy store. But she had picked up some nice secondhand toys and books at a neighbor's yard sale and looked forward to showing them to Chad when the novelty of his new birthday gifts wore off. She wasn't sure if playing with him would make him smarter. She knew, though, that she loved those moments when he seemed to be captivated by her songs and stories about the world.

KEY THEMES in Perception, Cognition, and Language

NATURE & NURTURE How do nature and nurture interact in perception, cognition, and language development in infancy?

SOCIOCULTURAL INFLUENCE How does the sociocultural context influence perception, cognition, and language development in infancy?

CONTINUITY/DISCONTINUITY Are perception, cognition, and language development during infancy continuous or discontinuous?

RISK/RESILIENCE What factors promote risk or resilience in perception, cognition, and language development during infancy?

As you saw in the last chapter, newborns are already engaging in the lifelong process of learning. Their vision, hearing, and other sensory capacities provide enormous amounts of information. But how do infants organize that information? Do they think? What can they remember? How do they embark on the extraordinary but essential process of communicating with others? And, as Tanya wondered, what part do the infant's early experiences play in later development?

These are precisely the kinds of questions psychologists have often asked. Why? Because perception, cognition, and language are fundamental processes by which children come to understand their world. *Perception*, the interpretation of sensory information from visual, auditory, and other receptors, is the vehicle by which we glean information about the world in the first place. **Cognition** refers to those thought processes and mental activities that include attention, memory, concept formation, and problem solving. Remarkably, as you will see in this chapter, there is good evidence that many elements of cognitive processing are present early in infancy. We will also consider the views of two major theorists—Piaget and Vygotsky—in their conceptualizations of cognition in infancy. Finally, we will examine the major milestones in the acquisition of language skills in infancy, a feat that marks the entrance of the child into the world of human communication. All of these processes—perception, cognition, and language—serve as the essential foundation for the more complex aspects of development to be described in the rest of the chapters that follow.

PERCEPTION

Tanya's queries about whether Chad could see or hear as she first held her son are the kinds of questions many parents pose to their newborns even as they seem to provide their own answers by vocalizing, making funny facial expressions, touching, caressing, and rocking the baby. Still, the uncertainty remains: what exactly do infants *perceive* when, for example, caregivers interact with them or when shiny new toys are given to them?

Is the world of the newborn a "great blooming, buzzing confusion" caused by a barrage of unorganized sensations, a view proposed by William James (1890) more than a century ago? If so, the young infant would not apprehend objects or meaningful events at first but would acquire the ability to do so only from learning, over a lengthy period of time, which pattern of basic sensory features is associated with a particular perceptual array (Gordon & Slater, 1998). Perhaps, then, as a result of repeated experience with distinctive sensory input, the infant comes to recognize the human face or to perceive how far away an object is located or to hear a sequence of sounds as a lullaby. According to this viewpoint, perceptual development is a *constructive* process; that is, one of imposing sense and order on the multisensory external world.

James and Eleanor Gibson and many of their students offer a strikingly different opinion of the early perceptual capacities of infants (Pick, 1992). For them, babies come into the world well equipped to respond to the structure and organization of many stimuli and readily perceive the patterns afforded by objects and other sensory events. Some theorists go even further. According to the *nativist* position, the newborn from very early on has, for example, a set of *core principles* and mechanisms to process complex visual cues signifying objects and three-dimensional

cognition Processes involved in thinking and mental activity, such as attention, memory, and problem solving.

space, and to interpret other sensory input (Spelke & Newport, 1998). Of course, even within this framework, experience provides ever greater opportunity to refine knowledge about which properties processed by the senses are stable and important, and which can be ignored as relatively uninformative.

Visual Perception

Because newborns have limited motor skills, we are often tempted to assume that their sensory systems—their eyes, ears, nose, mouth, and skin—must be passive, too, that receptors merely await stimulation. But Eleanor and James Gibson convincingly argue that perceiving is an active process (Gibson, 1966). "We don't simply see, we look" (Gibson, 1988, p. 5). Even neonates actively mobilize sensory receptors to respond to stimulation flowing from their bustling environment, skills that become apparent when we examine their visual perceptual abilities.

Perception of Pattern and Form Few questions fascinate psychologists more than when and how infants recognize patterns and other configurations of visual arrays. Are babies born with the ability to perceive objects as wholes? Some researchers think so. Others have argued the more traditional view: that this capacity is acquired only through extensive visual experience and that infants become aware of or construct perceptions of integrated, holistic, and meaningful visual figures through repeated opportunities to process contours, angles, shading, and other primary sensory features.

Key Theme
Nature & Nurture

As we have already learned, very young infants detect contours of visual stimuli. They also respond to movement associated with contours. Does that necessarily mean that they see a unitary object or pattern? Perhaps not, but evidence suggests that, by two or three months of age, babies are likely to see the whole. Furthermore, infants now additionally inspect and analyze the components of complex stimuli, scanning a variety of their visual properties and carrying out a much more deliberate, organized search (Bronson, 1994). A good example of this developmental change is demonstrated by the **externality effect**: infants younger than about two months of age typically focus on the outer contours of a complex stimulus as if caught by this sensory feature, so that little systematic exploration of its internal characteristics takes place. However, older infants tend to scan its internal features as well (Maurer, 1983; Salapatek, 1975). We saw an illustration of the externality effect in the previous chapter's discussion of preferential looking. Babies younger than two months tend to fixate on the outer contours of the face, such as hair or the chin line; older infants much more frequently inspect internal features, such as the eyes or mouth (see Figure 5.8).

Other experiments provide further evidence that babies perceive entire forms and patterns at least within a few months after birth but continue to show improvement in form perception throughout infancy (Kellman & Arterberry, 1998). One especially convincing illustration involves subjective, or gradient-free, contours. Look at the Kanizsa figure shown in Figure 6.1. You should see a highly visible triangle appearing to stand "above" three black, disklike figures at each of its corners. But closer inspection will reveal that the brain subjectively assumes the triangular form; no contour is present to mark its edges. Infants, perhaps when as young as one or two months and certainly by three to four months, perceive subjective figures, too, a powerful demonstration that perception of form is not always based on a detectable contour (Ghim, 1990; Treiber & Wilcox, 1980).

externality effect Tendency for infants younger than two months to focus on the external features of a complex stimulus and explore the internal features less systematically.

Perception of Faces Some perceptual patterns are especially significant to the infant. One is the human face. Do even newborns recognize faces, perhaps the faces of their caregivers? Based on the discussion so far, it should not be surprising to learn that, by about two months of age, infants do assign great importance to the

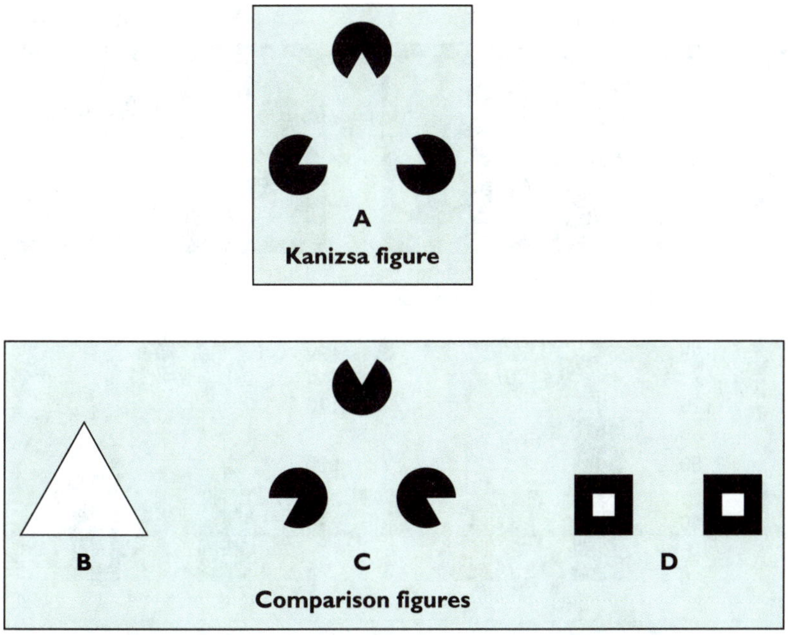

FIGURE 6.1
Infants' Subjective Perception of Form

Infants, as well as adults, perceive the subjective triangular figure (A) even though no contour is present to define it. After becoming habituated to the Kanizsa figure, babies are shown other figures, including a standard triangle formed by visible contours (B), the indented circular figures rotated to eliminate the subjective triangle (C), or a completely different array of stimuli (D). Infants show the least recovery from habituation to the traditional triangle (B), suggesting that they perceived the triangular shape produced by the Kanizsa figure.

Source: Adapted from Trieber & Wilcox (1980).

face, attending to it more than to other, equally complex arrays. But an even earlier, perhaps innate preference also makes evolutionary sense, because faces are a vital source of information for social and emotional relationships.

Some researchers have found evidence that newborns prefer, at least for moving configurations, a facelike image—two eyelike representations above a mouthlike feature—to other arrangements of the same components (Johnson et al., 1991). Mark Johnson and his colleagues (Johnson, 1992; M. H. Johnson et al., 2000) suggest that this inborn preference arises from a fairly primitive subcortical visual system that functions in newborns. Within about two months of age, this primitive system is supplanted by a more sophisticated cortical visual system that explores and discriminates faces from other, equally complex stimuli (Mondloch et al., 1999). The primitive system helps to ensure, however, that the infant gets off to the right start by preferring this extremely important perceptual array. Moreover, newborns display preferences for certain kinds of faces. Alan Slater and his colleagues (Slater et al., 1998) showed babies between one and six days of age pairs of female faces that had been judged by adults as attractive and unattractive. These infants gazed at the attractive faces longer than the unattractive faces. By five months of age, they also prefer looking at pictures of faces with larger eyes, just as do adults (Geldart, Maurer, & Carney, 1999).

On the other hand, infants' early preferences for faces may be simply a manifestation of their general tendency to prefer stimuli with certain kinds of configurations—in this case, stimuli with a top-heavy arrangement of features. In a series of three experiments, Viola Cassia and her colleagues recorded the looking times of

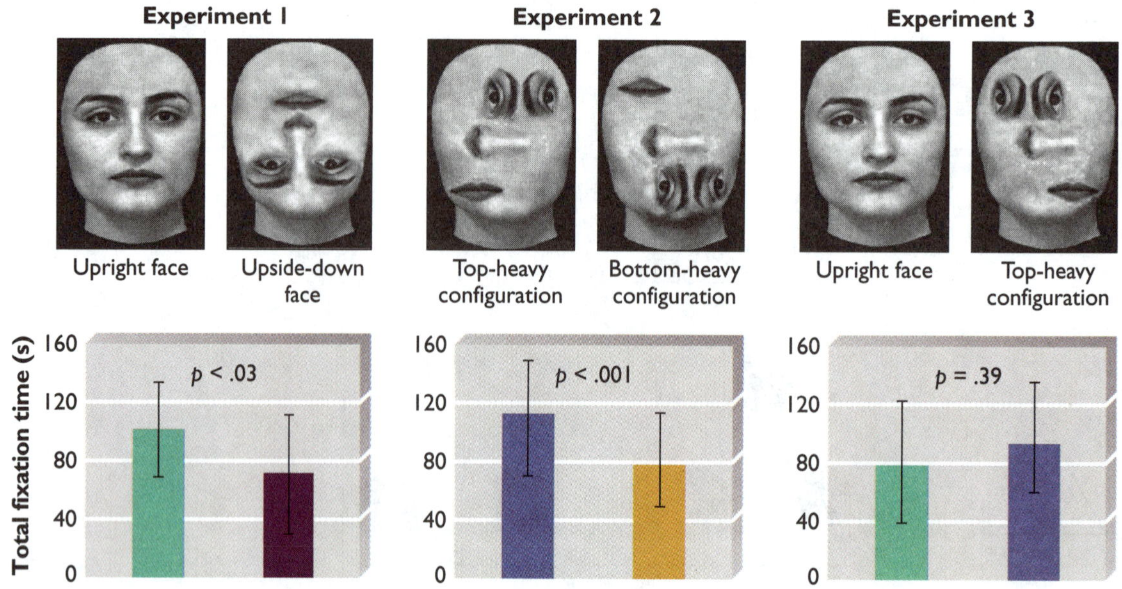

FIGURE 6.2

Newborn Attention to Facelike Stimuli

Is there a newborn tendency to look at human faces? Or are there other properties of facelike stimuli that capture their attention? To answer this question, Cassia and colleagues (2004) presented newborns with pairs of stimuli that varied in a number of ways. Looking times for each of the pairs are provided along the bottom of the figure. In experiment 1, newborns looked significantly longer at the human face. In experiment 2, they preferred the top-heavy configuration on the left. In experiment 3, there was no significant preference between a correctly configured human face and a top-heavy stimulus that contained the elements of a face. The results argue against an inborn face preference and instead support the idea that infants prefer stimuli that have a greater number of features at the top.

Source: Cassia, Turati, & Simion (2004).

newborns as they viewed pairs of facelike stimuli (see Figure 6.2). Newborns showed consistently greater interest in stimuli for which features clustered at the top and showed no specific preference for a correctly ordered human face when it was paired with another top-heavy, but rearranged, facelike stimulus. The researchers concluded that general perceptual preferences were at work rather than a specific tendency to prefer human faces (Cassia, Turati, & Simion, 2004).

When does a baby discriminate his or her mother's face from that of another person? Perhaps within days after birth (Bushnell, Sai, & Mullin, 1989). However, as you might guess, this recognition is based on outer elements, such as hairline or head contours, rather than on a full appreciation of a mother's facial features (Pascalis et al., 1995). By six months of age, differences in brain wave patterns are evident when a baby looks at her mother's face compared with a stranger's face (de Haan & Nelson, 1997). The safest conclusion is that infants are attracted to and identify significant aspects of the human face early in their development and make rapid strides in perceiving and recognizing this important social stimulus.

Perception of Objects Much of the visual environment is made up of objects and their surfaces. How does a baby perceive a rattle apart from the table on which it lies or the family dog as distinct from the floor on which it sits? James J. Gibson (1979) argued that the dynamic flow of visual information provided by kinetic cues is essential to this capacity.

Research carried out by Philip Kellman, Elizabeth Spelke, and others supports Gibson's position regarding the importance of kinetic information for perceiving objects, even in infants as young as three months of age (Kellman, 1996; Kellman & Spelke, 1983). Kellman, Spelke, and their colleagues initiated similar studies

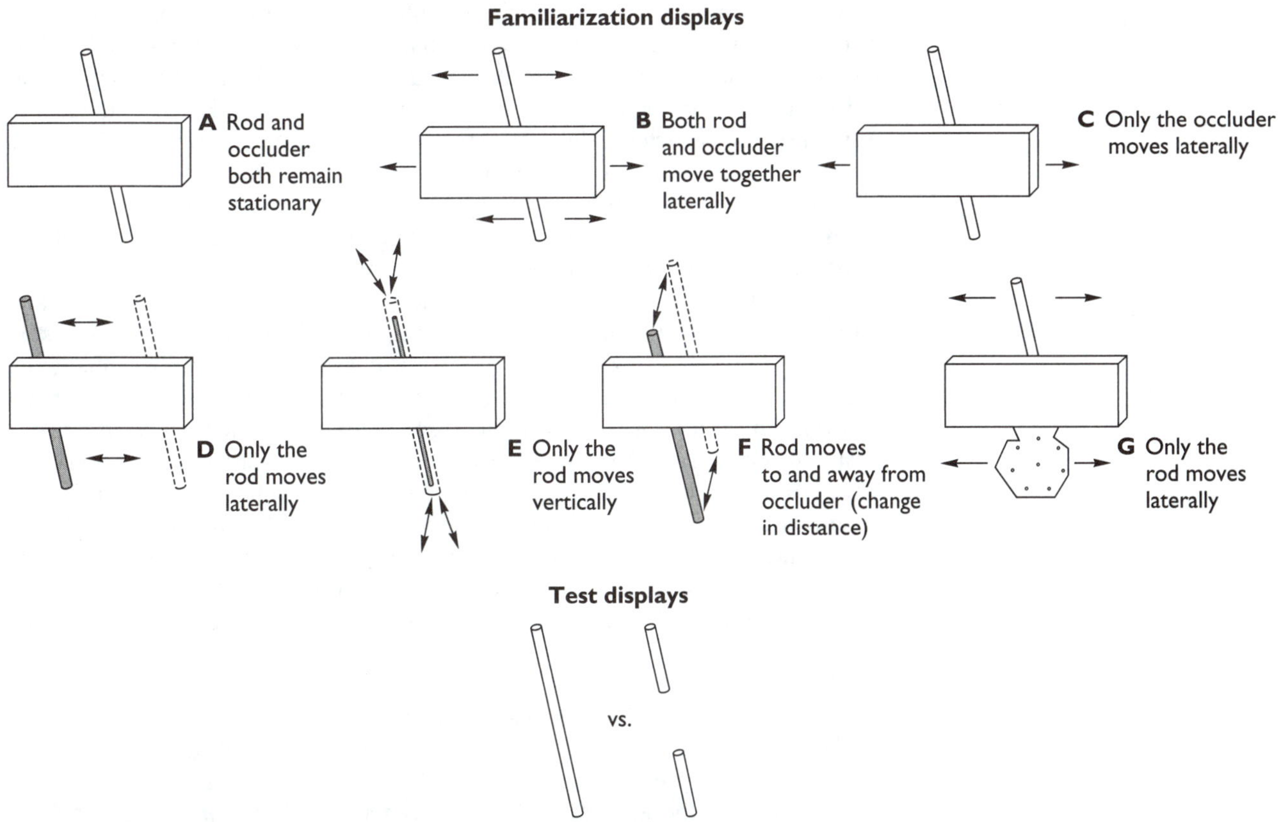

FIGURE 6.3

Inference of Unity and Coherence

Under some conditions, four-month-olds respond as if they perceived an occluded rod as a single complete figure. Infants are habituated to one of the seven familiarization displays shown here and are then presented with the test displays. After viewing conditions A, B, and C, infants respond to the complete rod in the test display as novel, indicating they perceived the rod in A, B, and C as being broken. When shown conditions D, E, F, or G, however, infants appear to perceive the rod as a connected whole, showing less attention to the complete rod than to the broken rod in the test display. The results indicate that young infants are able to infer unity and coherence for objects. Research suggests newborns do not make these perceptual inferences.

Source: Adapted from Spelke (1985).

investigating how a variety of movements associated with an occluded rod influences the infant's inferences about the unity of that rod. Figure 6.3 illustrates some of the variations that infants were shown. Babies interpreted the rod as complete and unbroken as long as its two protruding ends appeared to move together in the same direction and independently of the block during habituation trials, even if the two visible ends were of quite different shapes (Kellman & Banks, 1998). If neither the rod nor the block moved, or if the rod and block shifted together in the same direction, or if only the occluding block moved during habituation trials, the infants did not "fill in" the unseen portion of the rod; they treated the stimulus as two short pieces separated by an intervening space. By about six months of age or older, infants are more likely to infer a unitary rod when its ends move together in a different direction—for example, when it rotates behind an occluder (Eizenman & Bertenthal, 1998).

Kinetic cues associated with viewing three-dimensional arrays are not the only way for infants to infer object unity (Mareschal & Johnson, 2002). A recent set of studies involved two-dimensional computer-generated figures in which a rectangular surface was displayed on a textured background and appeared to bisect the end projections of a rodlike element, much like the stimuli appearing in Figure 6.3. When the end projections were misaligned so that they did not appear to project toward one another, the infants did not infer their unity as part of a single occluded rod (S. P. Johnson et al., 2000). Thus characteristics of the occluded form, as well as its movement in the textured background, contributed to its perception of connectedness. According to Scott Johnson (2004), infants build their understanding of the unity of obstructed objects by integrating information about its motion and the position and orientation of its elements, a process that takes time.

Amy Needham (2001) and her colleagues (Needham & Baillargeon, 1998; Needham & Modi, 2000) have argued for yet one other important factor in object perception for infants, especially when perception takes place in a relatively cluttered environment in which many contours and surfaces are intermingled. Such a condition might exist, for example, when the infant is able to see a pacifier stuck among numerous toys in a box or among kitchen utensils in a drawer. Needham suggests that, in these circumstances, having viewed or manipulated the object as a separate entity at an earlier time is critical. Because the infant has memory for the segmented visual display on the basis of experience with it, he or she is able to perceive it in other contexts. Needham's work, then, points out the role that the infant's emerging cognitive capacities might play in the very young infant's perception. In other words, perceiving an object may stem not only from processing features and characteristics of the external sensory environment but also from what the infant brings to the perceptual task in the form of memory of having interacted with it before.

Biological Motion The role of kinetic cues, and of motion in general, for early infant perceptual development is demonstrated in yet another phenomenon known as *biological motion*. Bennett Bertenthal (1993) and his colleagues (Proffitt & Bertenthal, 1990) carried out a series of studies in which infants were shown points of light moving as though attached to the head and major joints of a person walking. Adults who observe this pattern readily interpret the light movement as though it is someone walking. In other conditions, the pattern of lights was inverted, or an equivalent amount of motion was shown but with the lights scrambled so that the motion did not simulate the appearance of a person walking. Using attentional and habituation measures, these experiments demonstrated that, by the time infants have reached three to five months of age, the "walker" has taken on special meaning to them compared with other patterns of light motion. These findings show just how prepared the human infant is to derive information from motion cues (Kellman & Arterberry, 1998).

Depth Perception In addition to seeing to the left and right and above and below, babies see depth or distance. Yet visual images are recorded on the retina in twos. When and how do we acquire the ability of depth perception? One source of information is *binocular vision*. Sensory information differs slightly for each eye. The ability to fuse the two distinct images to perceive a single object is called **stereopsis,** a capacity that improves markedly during the first four months after birth. Stereopsis provides clues to depth as effectively for six-month-olds as for adults (Fox et al., 1980; Held, Birch, & Gwiazda, 1980).

Still other sources of information about depth and distance are available to infants. A classic series of studies involving the visual cliff suggests that kinetic cues are among them. The **visual cliff** consists of a large sheet of glass bisected by a relatively narrow plank. A patterned surface is placed immediately under the glass on one side, but much farther below it on the other side. Richard Walk (1968) found that an infant old enough to crawl could usually be coaxed to cross the shallow side but was much less likely to crawl over the deep side. The kinetic cues provided by his own head and body movements signaled depth; the babies showed the same response regardless of whether they could use one or both eyes.

Even babies too young to crawl react to the shallow and deep sides of the visual cliff differently. When placed face down on the glass surface, two- to three-month-olds become quieter, are less fussy, and show a greater decrease in heart rate on the deep side than on the shallow side (Campos, Langer, & Krowitz, 1970). Such reactions

stereopsis The ability to fuse the two distinct images from the eyes to perceive a single object.

visual cliff Experimental apparatus used to test depth perception, in which the surface on one side of a glass-covered table is made to appear far below the surface on the other side.

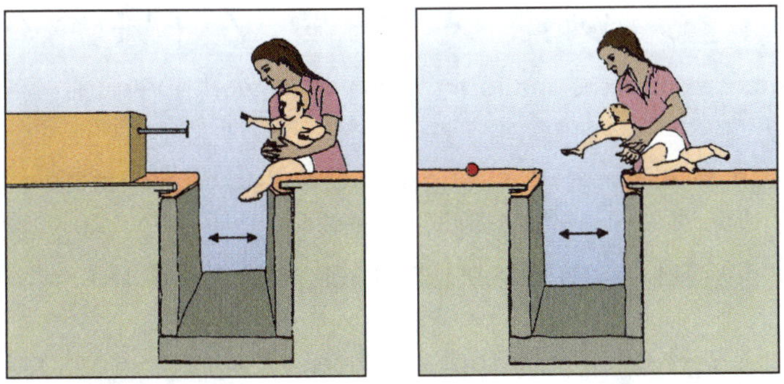

FIGURE 6.4

Avoiding a Risky Fall

Although infants at a very young age can perceive depth, their understanding of its consequences has to be relearned to fit the postural limitations associated with different motor skills. An infant may resist leaning too far to reach an attractive object located across a gap when sitting (A). However, that infant may readily try to crawl across a gap of a similar width and would fall if not caught by the experimenter (B). Similarly, in learning to locomote down an inclined plane, the child seems to have to relearn that he or she will fall down a steep slope that he or she can successfully negotiate when crawling. Coordinating perceptual information with permissible actions has to be relearned with each motor milestone in development.

Source: Adolph (2000), p. 292.

suggest that infants have not yet associated anxiety or fear with depth and find the visual information provided by the deep side more interesting than that on the shallow side. In fact, depth cues may already influence attention at birth, because newborns prefer looking at three-dimensional objects to looking at two-dimensional figures (Slater, Rose, & Morison, 1984).

Surprisingly, however, learning to avoid a drop-off occurs relatively independently when babies are acquiring the ability to sit, crawl, and walk. Karen Adolph has observed infants as they attempt to either reach across or crawl over a gap, and as they attempt to negotiate crawling or walking down a steeply inclined surface (Adolph, 1997, 2000). Whereas infants may avoid reaching across a gap that would cause them to lose their balance and fall from their seated position, they may readily attempt to crawl across a gap that is far too wide for them to avoid falling (see Figure 6.4). Similarly, even though they may have learned to safely crawl down an inclined plane, they seem to have to relearn the dangers of that same slope when beginning to walk. Although infants may perceive depth, awareness of the risks accompanying it does not transfer to the acquisition of later postural and motor milestones. Instead, infants need to learn to coordinate their perception of depth with safe actions for negotiating their surroundings as each new kind of postural and motor ability is acquired.

Finally, other cues, collectively described as *pictorial*, signal depth in photos or two-dimensional arrays. Pictorial cues include relative size (near objects appear larger), shadows, interposition of surfaces (one surface hides another), and linear perspective (lines converging toward a horizon), as well as the surface contour cues depicted in Figure 6.5. Infants begin to use many of these cues to identify nearer configurations by about five to seven months of age (Kellman & Arterberry, 1998; Sen, Yonas, & Knill, 2001; Yonas & Owsley, 1987). Thus infants respond very early to an abundant array of cues signaling depth and the three-dimensionality of objects.

FIGURE 6.5

Surface Contour as a Cue Implying Depth

Objects with certain kinds of markings can produce the illusion of depth in a two-dimensional array. One end of one of the cylinders in each pair shown here appears to be closer than the other, depending on the pattern of surface contours. When shown these two-dimensional arrays, infants seven months of age also process this kind of pictorial depth cue; they are more likely to reach toward the end of the cylinder that looks closer. Five-month-olds do not consistently reach to the apparently closer end; these surface cues do not yet provide a source of information about depth for them. These and other findings indicate that infants begin to use a variety of pictorial cues to interpret depth in the layout of two-dimensional visual arrays at around five to seven months of age.

Source: Sen, Yonas, & Knill (2001), p. 168.

FOR • YOUR • REVIEW

- How early do infants see patterns and forms in the visual world? What is the externality effect?
- What is the developmental course of infant perception of faces? When can an infant distinguish the faces of caregivers from the faces of others?
- How early and using what kinds of cues do infants perceive objects in their world?
- What is meant by the perception of biological motion?
- How early and using what kinds of cues do infants perceive depth? What evidence exists to indicate that its perception does not always produce appropriate responses to the dangers associated with depth?
- Why do developmental psychologists no longer believe the infant's visual world is simply a "blooming, buzzing confusion"?

AUDITORY PERCEPTION

We saw in the previous chapter that newborn infants can hear; in fact, we saw evidence of auditory abilities even in the prenatal period. But how does the infant organize the variety of sounds that come her way—the chimes of the dining room clock or the melody played when the mobile above her crib turns? As Tanya wondered, does Chad like the songs she sings to him throughout the day, especially before bedtime?

Patterns of Sound In every culture that has been observed, caregivers sing to their infants (Trehub, Unyk, & Trainor, 1993). Can babies distinguish music from noise? Might they even have a preference for some kinds of music? Two- and three-month-olds do recognize changes in tempo, the rate at which sounds occur (Baruch & Drake, 1997), and in intervals between brief bursts of sound that denote simple rhythmic change (Demany, McKenzie, & Vurpillot, 1977). Between six months and one year of age, they also begin to distinguish between more complex rhythms and patterns of sounds (Clarkson, 1996; Morrongiello, 1984). For example, at eight months of age babies recognize changes in short (six-note) melodies, including a transposition in key and the shift to either a higher or a lower frequency of a single note in a sequence (Trehub, Bull, & Thorpe, 1984; Trehub, Thorpe, & Morrongiello, 1985). Surprisingly, under some circumstances eight-month-olds can keep track of absolute pitch better than adults can (Saffran & Griepentrog, 2001).

In addition to detecting differences between sound patterns, infants show clear preferences for certain auditory events. Perhaps because of its voice quality or tempo, they prefer to listen to a song or lullaby directed by an adult to another infant over the same song or lullaby by the adult singing alone (Trainor, 1996). In fact, four-and-a-half- to six-month-olds can boast of some budding capacities as music critics. Carol Krumhansl and Peter Jusczyk (1990) chose short passages of Mozart minuets and introduced brief pauses at locations judged by adults to be either natural or awkward places for musical phrases to end. Babies preferred looking at a loudspeaker that played natural versions of the music to a speaker that played unnatural versions. Other research has shown that infants prefer the original passages of Mozart minuets over versions in which the intervals between sequences of notes have been altered to create a more dissonant, less pleasing sound, as heard by adults (Trainor & Heinmiller, 1998). In addition, after hearing two Mozart sonatas daily over several weeks' time, seven-month-olds can distinguish these from other Mozart sonatas, even when tested two weeks later (Saffran, Loman, & Robertson, 2000).

Babies are indeed sensitive to rhythmic and melodic contour. Brain hemisphere asymmetries in responsiveness to melodic changes (a left-ear/right-hemisphere advantage) are found in many young infants, just as they are observed in adults

(Balaban, Anderson, & Wisniewski, 1998). Moreover, the ability to detect satisfying musical phrasings may be important not only for appreciating music but also for the phrasing and sound rhythms that commonly underlie speech.

Speech Research on infants' hearing abilities has often been conducted to answer another question: How soon do babies perceive human speech? Practically right from birth, it seems. Two- to six-month-old infants show a distinct preference for human speech over nonspeech sounds by listening to it longer (Vouloumanos & Werker, 2004). And the language areas of the brain show greater activation when infants only a few days old listen to speech as opposed to nonspeech sounds (Peña et al., 2003). Most important for our understanding of language development, however, infants respond in specific ways to small acoustic variations in human speech that distinguish one word or part of a word from another.

The smallest unit of sound that affects the meaning of a word is called a **phoneme**. Phonemes are surprisingly complicated bursts of acoustic energy. For example, a difference of less than one-fiftieth of a second in the onset or transition of a frequency of sound is enough for adults to discriminate the distinctive phonemes */p/*, */b/*, and */t/* in the sounds *pa*, *ba*, and *ta*. (Linguists use slashes to identify the phonemes of a language.) Are infants able to hear the differences? Indeed they are. In fact, before six months of age babies distinguish all the important sounds in any of the hundreds of languages spoken around the world (Werker & Desjardins, 1995).

From these findings, some who study language acquisition argue that babies are born with a "speech module," an innate capacity to detect and process the subtle and complicated sounds that make up human language (Fodor, 1983). The complexity of language acquisition, according to this view, requires a specialized ability because the cognitive skills of infants and young children are so limited. An alternative view is that phoneme discrimination hinges on broader, more general auditory capacities, capacities not limited to processing speech sounds or even necessarily unique to humans but that infants are able to exploit quite early in development.

KEY THEME
NATURE & NURTURE

What evidence exists for either of these positions? Certain research findings contribute to the view that speech perception involves special language-oriented mechanisms. These are based on the concept of **categorical perception**, the classification of sounds as the same even when they differ on some continuous physical dimension, except when on opposite sides of a critical juncture. For example, the English consonants */b/* and */p/* in the sounds *ba* and *pa* differ only in voice onset time (VOT), the period during which the vocal chords begin to vibrate relative to the release of air by the vocal apparatus. Small changes in VOT are typically not heard as more or less like *ba* or *pa*. Instead, English speakers hear only *ba* as long as VOT continues to fall on one side of the categorical boundary and only *pa* when it falls on the other side. But if the difference in VOT crosses a critical point, the phoneme boundary, the two sounds are readily distinguishable. Infants as young as one month already demonstrate categorical perception for many different speech sounds (Aslin, 1987b; Kuhl, 1987). These findings imply that there might be something special (and innate) about how speech signals are processed.

However, many researchers remain uncertain about whether babies are born with a special sensory mode for speech (Saffran, Werker, & Werner, 2006). For one thing, categorical perception can be observed with some sounds other than those found in speech. For another, monkeys, and even chinchillas, also distinguish speech sounds categorically (Kuhl & Miller, 1978; Kuhl & Padden, 1983), a finding that further argues against a specialized innate human ability to process phonemes.

INTERMODAL PERCEPTION

We have considered the development of seeing, hearing, and other senses in isolation from one another, but, of course, most objects and events bombard us with multiple sensory inputs. The sight of a cup provides information about how to shape the mouth to drink from it. The toddler who hears his mother's voice from

phoneme Smallest unit of sound that changes the meanings of words.

categorical perception Inability to distinguish among sounds that vary on some basic physical dimension except when those sounds lie at opposite sides of a critical juncture point on that dimension.

another room expects to see her when he walks into that room. We often perceive these experiences as integrated and coordinated, and draw perceptual inferences because of the typical relationships observed from multimodal stimulation. Sometimes, of course, we can be fooled by all these correlated experiences: a good ventriloquist really does make the dummy appear to be talking!

How does the capacity to integrate several sensory inputs, referred to as **intermodal perception**, begin, and how important is it for development? One traditional view is that input received via the various senses is initially *unimodal*; that is, the senses function separately and independently. Only after repeated multimodal experiences, this argument runs, do babies come to recognize the correlations among various sensory inputs. Thus intermodal perception involves, for example, learning that, when objects are shaken, some rattle and make a noise, but others do not; that material that feels soft can also look soft; and that a square-looking peg will not fit into a round-looking hole. According to this viewpoint, intermodal perception stems from *integration* or *enrichment* through the repeated association of sensations from two or more modalities. Alternatively, from a more Piagetian perspective, it is the outcome of constructing multisensory schemes from correlated sensory experiences (Lickliter & Bahrick, 2000).

KEY THEME
NATURE & NURTURE

But others have suggested that some intermodal perception is already possible at birth (Gibson, 1982; Gibson, 1979). According to this perspective, a primitive unity exists among the senses in early infancy, and with development and experience, **perceptual differentiation**, the ability to distinguish information coming through each particular sensory modality, occurs. A related aspect of this point of view is that important sensory information is often *amodal*; that is, not tied to a particular sensory modality but shared across two or more of them. Examples of amodal characteristics of sensory input are *temporal synchrony*; that is, the correlated onset and offset of stimulation that can occur between two or more sensory modalities (such as hearing someone begin and stop speaking while simultaneously seeing their lips start and stop), and tempo and rhythm, common components of both auditory and visual experience.

Some researchers believe that the ability to process amodal properties is especially important for early perceptual development (Bahrick & Lickliter, 2000; Lewkowicz, 2000). For example, Lorraine Bahrick and Robert Lickliter (2000) suggest that the redundancy of different perceptual cues that contribute to temporal synchrony attracts the infant's attention. As a consequence of this attentional bias, infants begin to learn about arbitrarily correlated properties and qualities of objects and events, such as the voice that belongs to a particular parent, the bark that signifies the family's pet dog, or the verbal label for a particular color. Some go so far as to claim that this kind of learning begins very shortly after birth (Slater et al., 1999). But regardless of how early it begins, this perspective emphasizes that intermodal properties cannot be ignored as important components in perceptual development very early in infancy.

Sight and Sound To determine whether infants link visual and auditory events, Elizabeth Spelke (1976) developed a simple procedure in which four-month-olds could look at either of two films shown side by side. At the same time, the infants could hear a soundtrack coming from a speaker located between the two viewing screens. The soundtrack matched events in one of the two films; for example, an unfamiliar woman engaged in a game of peekaboo or someone playing a percussion instrument. Would infants pay more attention to the film synchronized with the soundtrack? Spelke found this to be the case, at least when the percussion sounds could be heard.

Before four months of age, infants can also infer that a sound made by one object versus multiple objects hitting a surface should match up to visual arrays containing one object versus multiple objects (Bahrick, 2002). Five-month-olds even link sounds such as an auto or a train coming or going with concordant visual progressions of approaching and retreating movement (Pickens, 1994; Walker-Andrews & Lennon, 1985).

Experience may have permitted three- to five-month-olds to learn about these relationships. However, other research suggests that newborns quickly master the

intermodal perception Coordination of sensory information to perceive or make inferences about the characteristics of an object.

perceptual differentiation Process postulated by Eleanor and James Gibson in which experience contributes to the ability to make increasingly finer perceptual discriminations and to distinguish stimulation arising from each sensory modality.

association between a sound and a visible toy. After seeing a toy presented in several different locations and making a particular sound for brief periods of time, neonates displayed increased attention if the sound originated apart from the toy or if it accompanied a different toy (Morrongiello, Fenwick, & Chance, 1998). Thus even newborns possess some kind of amodal process that guides and unifies sensory information from separate senses, such as hearing and vision (Kellman & Arterberry, 1998).

Intermodal perception in infants extends to social and linguistic information as well. For example, three-and-a-half-month-olds are likely to look at that parent, seated to one side, whose voice is coming from a speaker centered in front of the baby (Spelke & Owsley, 1979). By six months of age, babies hearing a strange male or female voice recite a nursery rhyme look longer at a face of the same sex than at a face of the opposite sex (Walker-Andrews et al., 1991). In addition, babies are able to match the maturity of a face with its voice; they look more at the face of an adult or a child, depending on who is heard talking from a central speaker (Bahrick, Netto, & Hernandez-Reif, 1998). By two months of age, babies also recognize auditory-visual correspondence in people who are speaking, attending more to facial expressions articulating vowel sounds that match than to facial expressions that do not match what they hear (Patterson & Werker, 2003).

Sight and Touch By six months of age, infants who explore an object with their hands alone can also recognize it by sight alone (Pineau & Streri, 1990; Rose, Gottfried, & Bridger, 1981; Ruff & Kohler, 1978). But coordination of some visual and tactile information exists much earlier, when the mouth is used to explore objects. In one experiment, one-month-olds showed greater visual attention to a hard, rigid object or a soft, deformable object, depending on which they had been given time to suck (Gibson & Walker, 1984). Other research reveals that infants five months of age exhibit intermodal perception between proprioceptive (or internal body cues) and visual cues. Infants showed differential visual attention to point light displays (similar to those used in studying sensitivity to biological motion) depending on whether those displays mirrored the motion produced by the movement of their own hidden legs or the movement of the legs of another infant (Schmuckler & Fairhall, 2001).

Babies can even be surprised by a discrepancy between vision and touch. Emily Bushnell (1981) showed infants a solid object within a box. Its location was distorted by mirrors. When babies reached for it, they touched another object that differed in size, shape, and texture. Infants younger than nine months failed to investigate the novel object actively or to search for the one they could see, but older infants did both. Thus there is substantial evidence that infants before a year of age make inferences about their world based on intermodal perception.

FOR • YOUR • REVIEW

- What sound patterns do infants prefer to listen to?
- What arguments exist for or against the view that infants possess an innate capacity to detect phonemes?
- How does intermodal perception develop?
- What evidence exists to show that infants recognize the correlation between visual and auditory information as well as visual and tactile cues?

COGNITION

Tanya wondered aloud what one-year-old Chad was thinking. Does it even make sense to use the word *thinking* when we are describing an infant? Are we attributing too much competence to a child who is so young and who has so much growing yet to do? Perhaps infants do not think in the same ways as older children and adults, but Piaget and Vygotsky, two preeminent theorists in developmental psychology, saw the roots of complex thought in infancy. Even more compelling evidence for "thinking" in infants comes from recent studies of how they react to disappearing objects and how they behave in simple problem-solving situations.

PIAGET'S THEORY AND INFANCY

As we saw in the chapter titled "Themes and Theories," one of the most important beliefs espoused by Piaget is that children actively construct their knowledge of the world, incorporating new information into existing knowledge structures, or *schemes*, through *assimilation*. As a result, schemes are modified or expanded through the process of *accommodation*. To Piaget, this process clearly begins in infancy. For example, the young infant may attempt to grasp a new, round squeeze toy, relying on a pre-existing scheme for grasping objects. As a consequence, that scheme becomes altered to include information about grasping round objects. The outcome is greater *equilibrium* or balance among the pieces of knowledge that make up the child's understanding. Thus what a child can understand or mentally grasp at any given point in time is heavily influenced by what the child already knows or understands. At the same time, the child's schemes are constantly transformed, as equilibrium is continually disrupted by the never-ending flow of information from the surrounding world.

KEY THEME
CONTINUITY/DISCONTINUITY

Piaget maintained that thought processes become reorganized into distinct stages at several points in development. Although the schemes in early stages lay the foundation for later knowledge structures, their reorganization is so thorough that schemes in one stage bear little resemblance to those in other stages. According to Piaget, the child progresses through the *sensorimotor*, *preoperational*, *concrete operational*, and *formal operational* stages, reflecting major transitions in thought in which early, action-based schemes evolve into symbolic, then logical, and finally abstract mental structures.

Piaget claimed that all children progress through the stages of cognitive development in an invariable sequence in which no stage is skipped. In addition, each stage contains a period of formation and a period of attainment. When the child begins a new stage, his schemes are somewhat unstable and loosely organized. By the end of the stage, his schemes are well formed and well organized. Even though Piaget provided age norms for the acquisition of each stage, he believed that, because cognitive development is the result of maturational factors working in concert with environmental experiences, some children may reach a stage more quickly or more slowly, depending on the opportunities for learning that their environment has provided. Ultimately, though, the evolution of thought shows a universal regularity, according to Piaget. The foundations for this course of cognitive growth are laid down during the sensorimotor stage.

The Sensorimotor Stage (Birth to Two Years) The most striking characteristic of human thinking during the **sensorimotor stage** is its solid basis in action. Each time the child reaches for an object, sucks on a nipple, or crawls along the floor, she is obtaining varied feedback about her body and its relationship to the environment, which becomes part of her internal schemes. At first, the infant's movements are reflexive, not deliberate or planned. As the child passes through each of the six substages of the sensorimotor period, outlined in Table 6.1, her actions become increasingly goal directed and aimed at solving problems. Moreover, she is able to distinguish self from environment and learns about the properties of objects in that environment and how they are related to one another.

A significant accomplishment of the sensorimotor stage is the infant's progression toward **means-ends behavior**, the deliberate use of an action to accomplish some goal. During the early substages of sensorimotor development, the infant often

sensorimotor stage In Piagetian theory, the first stage of cognitive development, from birth to approximately two years of age, in which thought is based primarily on action.

means-ends behavior Deliberate behavior employed to attain a goal.

Table 6.1 The Six Substages of Piaget's Sensorimotor Stage

Substage	Major Features	Object Concept
Reflexive Activity (Birth–1 month)	Formation and modification of early schemes based on reflexes such as sucking, looking, and grasping	No attempt to locate objects that have disappeared
Primary Circular Reactions (1–4 months)	Repetition of behaviors that produce interesting results centered on own body (e.g., Lucienne accidentally, then repeatedly, touches her quilt)	No attempt to locate objects that have disappeared
Secondary Circular Reactions (4–8 months)	Repetition of behaviors that produce interesting results in the external world (e g., Lucienne accidentally, then repeatedly, kicks the dolls in her bassinet)	Search for objects that have dropped from view or are partially hidden
Coordination of Secondary Schemes (8–12 months)	Combination of actions to achieve a goal (e.g., Lucienne pulls a doll to make her bassinet hood sway)	Search for completely hidden objects
Tertiary Circular Reactions (12–18 months)	Experimentation with different actions to achieve the same goal or observe the outcomes (e.g., Laurent drops a case of soap, then a piece of bread)	Ability to follow visible displacements of an object
Invention of New Means Through Mental Combinations (18–24 months)	Thinking through of potential solutions to problems and imitation of absent models (e.g., Jacqueline imitates her playmate's tantrum)	Ability to follow invisible displacements of an object

initiates actions accidentally rather than purposefully. When Piaget's daughter Lucienne was almost four months old, she was observed to shake her bassinet

> by moving her legs violently (bending and unbending them, etc.), which makes the cloth dolls swing from the hood. Lucienne looks at them, smiling, and recommences at once. (Piaget, 1952b, pp. 157–158)

Lucienne repeated her kicking to make the dolls shake in what Piaget calls a *circular reaction*, the repetition of a motor act to experience the pleasure it brings. Her first kick, however, was totally accidental. Several months afterward, when Lucienne was eight months old, Piaget placed a new doll over the hood of her bassinet. This time her behavior revealed a greater degree of intentionality.

> She looks at it for a long time, touches it, then feels it by touching its feet, clothes, head, etc. She then ventures to grasp it, which makes the hood sway. She then pulls the doll while watching the effects of this movement. (Piaget, 1952b, p. 256)

Throughout the first two years, the child increasingly uses actions as a means to obtain some end or goal. He also experiments with new means to reach the same goal, as Piaget's son Laurent did when he successively dropped a soap case and then a piece of bread to investigate how objects fall.

A second aspect of sensorimotor development is the child's gradual separation of self from the external environment. Initially, the child derives pleasure from actions that center on her own body. At three months of age, Lucienne "strikes her quilt with her right hand; she scratches it while carefully watching what she is doing, then lets it go, grasps it again, etc." (Piaget, 1952b, p. 92). The circular reaction, in this case, was repeated because of the satisfying sensations it brought to Lucienne's hand. Weeks later, in the episode of the swinging dolls, Lucienne's

A significant attainment in infancy is the understanding of object permanence. Children under three to four months of age act as if a hidden or obstructed object no longer exists. By age eight months, though, children will remove a barrier to look for a hidden object.

kicking in the bassinet produced a gratifying result in the external environment. In general, the child becomes less centered on the self and more oriented to the external world.

The completion of the sensorimotor stage and the beginning of the next stage is signaled by the child's display of *deferred imitation*, the ability to imitate a model that is no longer present. At age sixteen months, Piaget's daughter Jacqueline was playing with a boy who suddenly had a dramatic temper tantrum. The next day, the normally well-behaved Jacqueline mimicked the little boy's behaviors with remarkable accuracy. To do so, she must have had the ability to *represent* the boy's overt behaviors in internal form and to draw on that representation hours later. This ability to represent events and objects internally marks the beginning of a major transition in thought.

The Object Concept An important accomplishment of the sensorimotor stage is the attainment of the **object concept**, or *object permanence*. Infants who possess the object concept realize that objects continue to exist even though they are not within immediate sight or within reach to be acted on. Up to three months of age, the saying "Out of sight, out of mind" characterizes the child's understanding of objects. At about four months of age, he will lift a cloth from a partially covered object or show some reaction, such as surprise or puzzlement, when an object disappears. At about eight months of age, he will search for an object that has completely disappeared; for example, when it has been covered entirely by a cloth. In the last two phases of the attainment of the object concept, he will be able to follow visible and then invisible displacements of the object. In the first instance, the twelve-month-old will follow and find a toy that has been moved from under one cloth to another, as long as the movement is performed while he is watching. In the second instance, the eighteen-month-old can find an object moved from location A to location B, even if the displacement from A to B is done while he is not looking. Thus Piaget believed that the object concept emerges late in the first year of life and does not become fully elaborated until the second year.

object concept Realization that objects exist even when they are not within view. Also called *object permanence*.

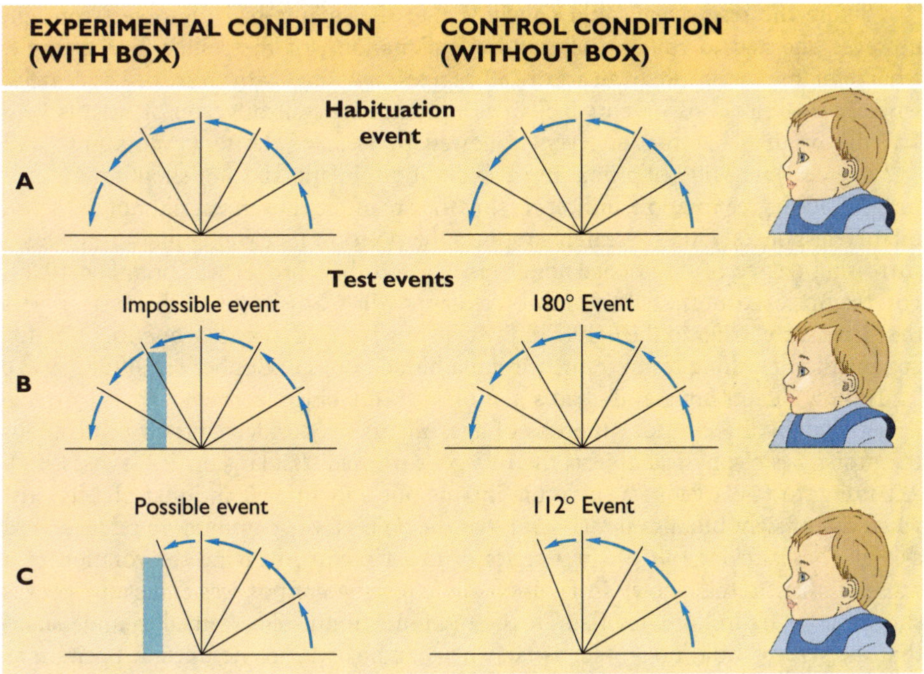

FIGURE 6.6

Do Infants Have an Object Concept?

In Baillargeon's experiment, infants were habituated to a screen rotating 180 degrees (A). Next, infants in the impossible-event condition saw the screen appearing to pass through the location of a box (B, on left), whereas infants in the *possible-event* condition saw the screen stop at the location of the box (C, on left). Infants in the *impossible-event* condition looked significantly longer at this event, suggesting that they were puzzled by what they saw and therefore had an object concept. The control conditions (shown at right) were included to make sure the infants were not responding to the arc of the screen's movement.

Source: Adapted from Baillargeon (1987a).

Not all researchers think that the object concept is a relatively late accomplishment in infancy. Renée Baillargeon (1987a) believes she has obtained evidence showing that infants as young as four months of age have a rudimentary understanding of the continuing existence of objects. She conducted a unique experiment in which infants behaved as if they understood that an object continued to exist even when it was concealed by a screen. Figure 6.6 shows the phases of this experiment. At first, infants observed a screen that rotated back and forth 180 degrees over repeated trials. As you might expect, they eventually showed habituation of fixation to this display. Next, a box was placed behind the screen. Initially, when the screen was still flat against the table, the box was visible, but as the screen rotated away from the child, it hid the box from view. In the possible-event condition, the screen stopped moving at the point where it hit the box. In the impossible-event condition, the box was surreptitiously removed and the screen passed through the space the box would have occupied. As you already know, infants in a habituation experiment should look longer at the novel event, in this case, the screen that rotated only 112 degrees. However, these infants looked significantly longer at the impossible event, apparently drawn in by the fact that the screen was moving through the space where the object should have been. Because infants are presumed to look longer at the stimulus display that goes against their internal knowledge, this procedure is often called the *violation-of-expectation* method.

Before the researcher could conclude that the infants had the object concept, however, she had to rule out alternative explanations for the results. For example, what if infants simply prefer an arc of 180 degrees compared with an arc of 112 degrees, whether there is a box or not? Baillargeon included a control group of infants who saw the original habituation event followed by each of the test events (180 and 112 degrees) but without a box. In this condition, infants did not show preferences for the 180-degree rotation, indicating that the arc of the movement did not influence infants' responses. Other research supports the position that young infants possess a surprising degree of knowledge about objects and their properties (Bremner, 1998). For example, six-and-a-half-month-old infants will reach in the dark for an object they have seen earlier in the light. Simply reaching is a much easier sequence of motor actions than reaching for and uncovering a hidden object (Goubet & Clifton, 1998). Thus these infants apparently had some form of the object concept.

In fact, by three to four months of age, infants may understand far more about the properties of physical objects than Piaget surmised (Baillargeon & DeVos, 1991). According to Baillargeon, such young infants not only understand that objects exist when out of sight but also understand that the objects' size continues to be preserved as well (Baillargeon, 1987b). In a series of experiments involving the rotation of a screen similar to that shown in Figure 6.6, the rectangular box was either upright (as shown in the figure) or lying flat. Three- and four-month-olds seemed to understand that the screen could not rotate as far when the box was in the upright position as it could when lying down. Moreover, if the object was something that could be squeezed, such as a ball of gauze the infants had previously played with, they were not surprised by the continued rotation of the screen in front of it. They did show surprise when the screen seemed to rotate past the position of a hard and rigid box. Apparently, young infants quickly move beyond simply understanding that an object exists under a cover or behind a barrier; they also develop ideas about physical properties of objects, such as their height and rigidity (Baillargeon, 1995).

Similarly, experiments by Elizabeth Spelke and her colleagues show that infants seem to appreciate the concept of *solidity*, the fact that one object cannot pass through the space occupied by another object. In one study, represented in Figure 6.7, two-and-a-half-month-old infants saw a ball roll across a ramp and behind a screen for several trials. Next they saw the ball roll as a partially visible box blocked its path. When the screen was removed, infants viewed the ball either resting in front of the box or at the end of the ramp. Infants looked significantly longer at the impossible result, the ball at the end of the ramp, suggesting to Spelke that infants recognize the concept of solidity. Some of Spelke's other experiments imply that young infants also understand the principle of *continuity*, the idea that objects move continuously in time and space (Spelke et al., 1992).

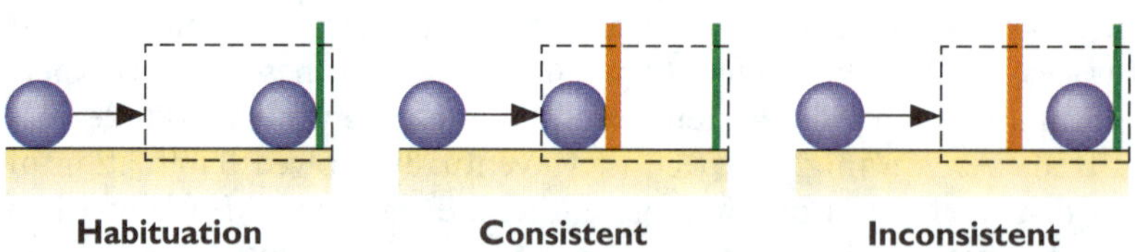

FIGURE 6.7

Infants' Concepts of Solidity

In an experiment conducted by Elizabeth Spelke and her colleagues, two-and-a-half-month-old infants were habituated to the scene on the left, a ball rolling across a ramp. In the test phase, infants saw events that were either consistent or inconsistent with the principle that one object cannot pass through the space occupied by another. The infants looked longer at the inconsistent event, leading Spelke and her colleagues to postulate that this early knowledge about objects is innate.

Source: Spelke et al. (1992).

KEY THEME
NATURE & NURTURE

The Core Knowledge Hypothesis The results of the violation-of-expectation experiments have led some contemporary researchers to formulate the **core knowledge hypothesis**, the idea that young infants possess innate knowledge concerning important fundamental properties of objects (Baillargeon, 2001; Spelke & Hespos, 2001). The implication is that even young infants possess a startling degree of competence as they encounter items and events in the world. Core knowledge becomes elaborated with experience, according to these theorists, but the infant starts out with much more capability than Piaget presumed. There are some problematic findings for those in this camp, however. For example, Neil Berthier and his colleagues (Berthier et al., 2000) had two- and three-year-olds participate in a task similar to the one shown in Figure 6.7. In this case, however, the researchers asked the children to retrieve the ball from behind one of several doors positioned in front or in back of the wall. Children under age three performed poorly; they did not open the door right in front of the wall. If infants have early knowledge of the concept of solidity and can represent hidden objects, why would children several years older fail to locate the object? At the very least, the findings suggest that a great deal of knowledge about the locations and properties of objects develops in infancy and beyond (Butler, Berthier, & Clifton, 2002; Keen & Berthier, 2004).

The contrasting point of view is that infants' performance in violation-of-expectation tasks is due not to innate core knowledge but rather to perceptual and memory processes that detect more broadly that "something is different" or "something is familiar" (Bogartz, Shinskey, & Schilling, 2000). It is wrong, say the critics, to imbue young infants with more advanced or specialized cognitive and representational skills about the properties of objects than is warranted (Haith, 1998; Smith, 1999b). Rather, it is better to assume that basic, general cognitive processes are responsible for the behaviors we observe. Knowledge about objects is built, say many of these theorists, through rapid advances in attention and memory abilities, as well as the child's experiences in the world. Experts hope that well-designed experiments that rule out competing explanations will help to resolve this controversy (Aslin, 2000; Cohen & Cashon, 2006).

Even if young infants do have some form of object concept, why do they fail to retrieve a covered object prior to eight months of age? One possibility is that infants do not yet have the skill to solve means-ends tasks; that is, to develop and execute a plan to reach for and uncover the hidden object. However, seven-month-old infants will pull down a transparent screen to reach for an object behind it; they do not make this response when the screen is opaque (Shinskey & Munakata, 2001). A means-ends deficit cannot account for such results, as, under some circumstances, we see that infants can put into action a sequence of steps in order to obtain a visible object. Yuko Munakata and her colleagues hypothesize that infants' representations of hidden objects are weaker than for visible objects and thus make search tasks more demanding (Munakata et al., 1997). As infants have more experiences in the world, however, and the neural networks that underlie representations of objects become strengthened, children become more successful in retrieving hidden objects (Munakata, 2001, 2006).

The A-Not-B Error A common error that occurs when the child is about seven to nine months of age is the A$\overline{\text{B}}$, or **A-not-B error**. In this task, an object is hidden in location A, found by the infant, and then, in full view of the infant, moved to location B. Piaget observed that the child would mistakenly but persistently search for the object in location A. He hypothesized that the infant's incomplete knowledge of the object concept leads to this error, in large part because the sensorimotor scheme for searching in location A still controls the child's thought. Researchers, however, have generated several alternative hypotheses about the reasons for the A-not-B error.

For one thing, memory difficulties may play a role. Eight- to twelve-month-old infants are less likely to make the A$\overline{\text{B}}$ error when they can search for the object at B immediately, as opposed to after a delay. In addition, when watching infants make the A$\overline{\text{B}}$ error, Adele Diamond noticed that, even though some infants mistakenly reached for A, they actually looked at B, the correct location of the hidden toy (see

core knowledge hypothesis The idea that infants possess innate knowledge of certain properties of objects.

A-not-B error Error that an infant makes when an object is hidden in location A, found by the infant, and then, in full view of the infant, moved to location B. Piaget observed that the child will mistakenly but persistently search for the object in location A.

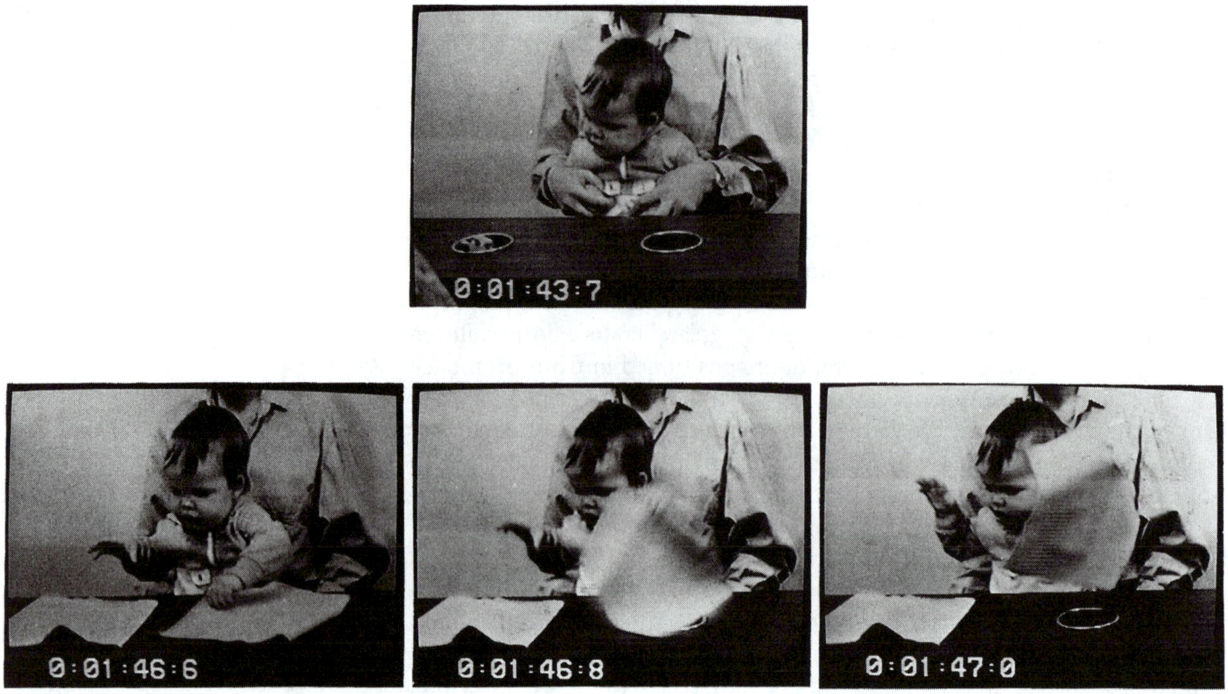

FIGURE 6.8
Alternative Explanations for the A$\overline{B}$ Error
A toy has been hidden first in the right well (location A), then is placed in the well on the left (location B), as shown in the first photograph. The next three photographs show that after the object is hidden, the infant reaches for location A even though he looks persistently at location B. The looking behavior suggests that he has the object concept when there are visible displacements of the object. Diamond (1991) believes that one reason infants reach for the incorrect location is because they fail to inhibit motor responses.

Figure 6.8) (Diamond, 1985). They behaved as though they knew the correct location of the toy but could not stop themselves from reaching to A. In other studies, adult monkeys, which normally perform successfully on the A$\overline{B}$ task, make mistakes identical to those of seven-to-nine-month-old human infants when lesions are made in very specific areas of their frontal cortex; these are the brain areas that control the inhibition of responses (Diamond & Goldman-Rakic, 1989). Diamond (1991) proposes that infants have the object concept well before age seven months but, due to the physical immaturity of this special cortical area, they cannot suppress their tendency to reach for location A. Lending support to this hypothesis are data showing that infants who are successful in the A$\overline{B}$ task display more powerful brain electrical activity from the same frontal region of the cortex (Bell & Fox, 1992). Moreover, when infants' responses to the A$\overline{B}$ situation are assessed using the habituation procedure rather than using the child's motor response, they look longer at an impossible event (a toy moves from A to B and is then found at A) than at a possible event (a toy moves from A to B and is found at B) (Ahmed & Ruffman, 1998). Thus infants seem to know the correct location of the transposed object but do not show this knowledge when tasks require reaching.

Another account of the A$\overline{B}$ error states that infants may not be able to efficiently update their representation of the object's location after it is moved to B; in fact, they perform better when the A and B locations are covered with distinctive shapes and colors (Bremner & Bryant, 2001). Perhaps the most comprehensive description comes from a dynamic systems perspective. In this view, the infant's errors arise from competing tendencies of different strengths: the strong memory of the object at A and a deteriorating plan to look at location B in the face of few perceptual cues (Smith et al., 1999; Spencer, Smith, & Thelen, 2001). Any of several factors can improve performance: better memory for spatial locations, stronger perceptual cues about the object's location, or heightened attention to the events in the task. As you can see, we now have several alternatives to Piaget's notion that the object concept relies on an internal, sensorimotor-based scheme, all of them emphasizing changes in the ability of infants to process information.

Early Spatial Reasoning From early infancy onward, children organize the objects in their world according to relationships in space. Where does the infant find her shoes or an enticing snack? Usually she has developed a mental picture of her home and other familiar physical spaces to guide her search for missing objects or to reach a desired location. As he did for many other areas of cognitive development, Piaget set forth some of the first hypotheses about the child's concepts of space, ideas that researchers have subsequently modified or enriched.

During infancy, Piaget (1954) stated, the child's knowledge of space is based on her sensorimotor activities within that space. For example, the child searches for objects by using *egocentric* frames of reference. In other words, if a ball disappears under a couch or chair, the infant represents its location in relation to her own body ("to the left of my arm") rather than in relation to some other external object ("to the left of the door"). Only with the advent of symbolic ability at the end of the sensorimotor stage are children able to use frames of reference external to the self.

Many researchers have confirmed that infants, in the absence of environmental cues, indeed rely on the positions of their own body in space to locate objects. For example, in one study, nine-month-olds readily learned to locate an item hidden under one of two covers situated to either their left or their right. Shifted to the opposite side of the table, however, they looked in the wrong location because of their egocentric responding (Bremner & Bryant, 1977). When the investigator made the covers of the two hiding locations of distinctively different colors, infants were able to locate the hidden toy even when they were moved to a different position around the table (Bremner, 1978).

Toward the end of the first year, children quite literally reach out into the world for cues denoting spatial relationships. Infants slightly under nine months of age use landmarks denoting the physical locations of objects to find them in larger spatial environments. When playing peekaboo, for example, infants in one study were assisted in locating a face when different-colored lanterns were positioned by the correct window. These cues helped, even if their own positions were shifted (Lew, Bremner, & Lefkovitch, 2000). Thus infants are not as egocentric as Piaget claimed when other external information is available to assist them in finding objects. Moreover, it is likely that the infant's growing ability to locomote toward the end of the first year—to crawl and walk around in his environment—is connected in some way to advances in spatial reasoning (Newcombe & Huttenlocher, 2006).

FOR • YOUR • REVIEW

- What are the infant's chief accomplishments during the sensorimotor stage according to Piaget? What is the primary basis for thought in this stage?
- What is the object concept? What are the stages of acquisition of this concept according to Piaget?
- What is the core knowledge hypothesis? What research findings support this position on infants' conceptual knowledge? What are the criticisms of this point of view?
- What is the A-not-B error? How does Piaget account for this error? What are some other explanations for the occurrence of this behavior in infants?
- What principles guide infants' spatial understanding according to Piaget? Does research support his point of view?

Concepts

Aside from learning about the properties of single objects, as in the object concept, children also quickly learn about relationships that can exist among sets of objects. Sometimes objects resemble one another perceptually; they seem to "go together" because they are the same color or shape. At other times, the relationships among objects can be more complex. The perceptual similarities may be less obvious; moreover, some sets can be embedded within others. Cocker spaniels and Great Danes, two different-looking dogs, can be classified together in the group "dogs," and both breeds fit into a larger category of "animals." In each case, we are describing children's **concepts**, the organization of information on the basis of some general or abstract principle.

As one psychologist put it, "Concepts and categories serve as the building blocks for human thought and behavior" (Medin, 1989). Concepts allow us to group isolated pieces of information on the basis of common themes or properties. The result is greater efficiency in cognitive processing. Suppose someone tells you, "A quarf is an animal." Without even seeing one, you already know many of the quarf's properties: it breathes, eats, locomotes, and so on. Because concepts are linked to one of the most powerful human capabilities—language—as well as to other aspects of cognition, understanding how different kinds of concepts develop is an important concern of developmental psychologists. Many modern-day accounts of concept development arose out of attempts to test or expand the groundbreaking ideas of Piaget about how children understand classes of objects. Today's research findings are quite clear. Already in infancy, we see progress in how children think conceptually.

Early Classification Skills One of the earliest signs of classification skills in young children occurs toward the end of the first year, when children begin to group perceptually similar objects together. Susan Sugarman (1982, 1983) carefully watched the behaviors of one- to three-year-olds as they played with successive sets of stimuli that could be grouped into two classes, such as plates and square blocks, or dolls and boats. Even the youngest children displayed a spontaneous tendency to group similar-looking objects together by pointing consecutively to items that were alike. With the habituation paradigm, it has also been possible to show that three- and four-month-old infants respond to different classes of items, such as dogs versus cats or horses, on the basis of perceptual similarity (Oakes, Coppage, & Dingel, 1997; Quinn, Eimas, & Rosenkranz, 1993). But what is especially important to the emergence of more fully developed concepts is that as infants get older, they notice the *correlations* among perceptual features—that wings typically go with beaks, for example, or that long ears consistently accompany small, puffy tails (Younger, 2003).

Between ages one and three, children experience a rapid growth in classification skills. One important way in which we see changes is in terms of the bases they use for grouping objects together. For example, at fourteen months of age, infants successively touch objects that appear in common contexts, such as "kitchen things" and "bathroom things" (Mandler, Fivush, & Reznick, 1987). Two-year-olds will match items on the basis of *thematic relations*, clustering items that function together or complement one another, such as a baby bottle and a baby (Markman & Hutchinson, 1984). They will also occasionally classify items *taxonomically*, grouping objects that may not look alike on the basis of some abstract principle, such as a banana with an apple (Ross, 1980). Taxonomic classification is easier for young children when they hear that objects from the same category share the same label even though they may not look very much alike (for instance, a panther and a tabby house cat are both called "cats") or when their similarities are pointed out in some other way (Deák & Bauer, 1996; Nazzi & Gopnik, 2001).

In fact, mothers often provide varied information of this sort to their young children about objects and their membership in categories, saying such things as "That's a desk. That's a desk, too." Or they point sequentially to objects that come from the same conceptual group (Gelman et al., 1998). As children encounter new

concepts Definition of a set of information on the basis of some general or abstract principle.

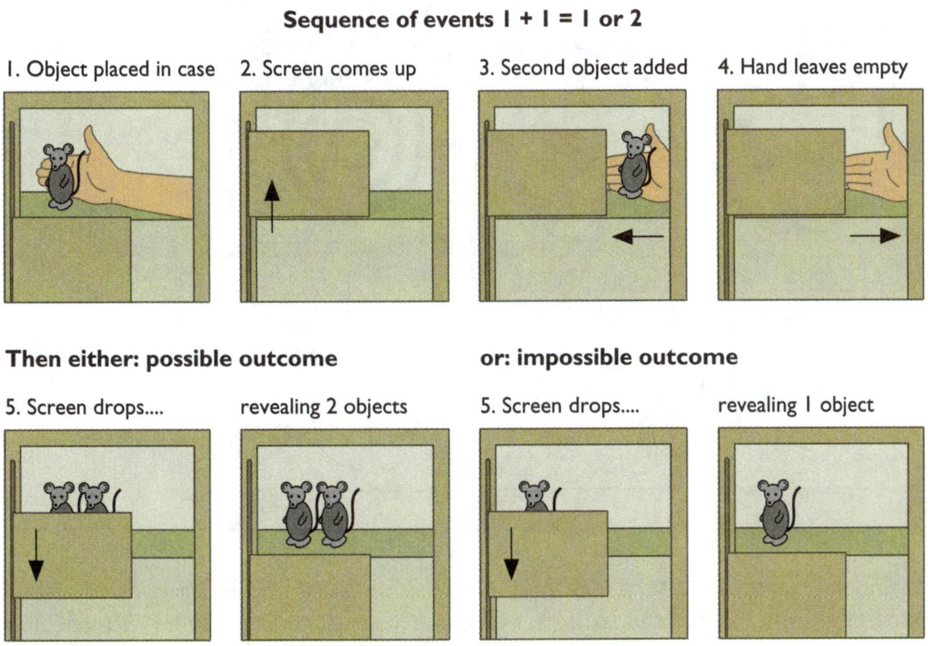

FIGURE 6.9
Can Infants Add?
This figure shows the sequence of events used in Wynn's (1992a) experiments with five-month-olds. Infants first saw a hand place a mouse doll in the display. Next, a screen rotated up to hide the doll. A hand appeared with a second doll, placing it behind the screen and leaving the display empty-handed. During the test, the screen dropped down and revealed either two dolls (possible event) or one doll (impossible event). Infants looked longer at the impossible event, suggesting they knew something about the additive properties of numbers.

Source: Adapted from Wynn (1992a).

instances of a category, they incorporate information about those examples into their prior knowledge about the category (Carmichael & Hayes, 2001). And, as children grow older, they become capable of using a wider range of relations to classify objects so that their exclusive reliance on shared perceptual features lessens.

Infants' Responses to Number Another kind of conceptual understanding has to do with numbers. When and how do children begin to understand that some sets of objects have "more" than others? When do they begin to appreciate that "2" is different from "4" and that the objects themselves do not matter when numerical entities are being compared? Thanks to a growing body of research, we now know that infants demonstrate sensitivity to basic aspects of numerical relationships. Habituation studies show that newborns can detect differences in small numeric sets, such as two versus three (Antell & Keating, 1983), and that six-month-olds differentiate between eight and sixteen dots (Xu & Spelke, 2000). Infants even seem to understand something about additive properties of numbers. In one experiment, five-month-old infants watched as a toy was placed in a case and then was hidden by a screen. The infants watched as a second, identical toy was placed behind the screen (see Figure 6.9). When the screen was removed and only one toy remained—an impossible outcome if the infants appreciated that there should still be two toys—they showed surprise and looked longer than they did when two toys were visible (Wynn, 1992a). Other researchers have confirmed that, before age six months, babies show numerical competencies that likely serve as the foundation for more complex reasoning about quantities (Canfield & Smith, 1996; Simon, Hespos, & Rochat, 1995).

KEY THEME
NATURE & NURTURE

But what exactly is the nature of those competencies? The preceding findings raise several interesting questions about the processes that underlie infants' behaviors. First, is sensitivity to number another example of innate core knowledge? To some researchers, the answer is yes, especially because infants only five months old appear to be sensitive to addition and subtraction events (Wynn, 1998). Others disagree and point out that the infants in these experiments might be responding on the basis of changes in the visual display other than number. For example, when stimulus items change in number, they also change in the amount of contour, or exterior boundary length, that they contain; two mouse dolls have more total "outline" than one mouse doll. In a study in which the stimuli varied either in contour length or in number, infants responded on the basis of contour length rather than

FIGURE 6.10
Infant Recognition Memory

Fagan tested infant recognition memory by using visual stimuli in a paired-comparison procedure. For each row, one of the stimuli was presented repeatedly until habituation occurred. Then one of the other stimuli in the row was paired with the familiar stimulus to see if infants preferred the novel item. Infants only a few months old looked longer at novel items up to fourteen days after the initial familiarization.

Source: Adapted from Fagan (1974).

number (Clearfield & Mix, 1999). Similarly, infants respond to changes in surface area of stimuli as opposed to their number (Clearfield & Mix, 2001). Thus it may be more accurate to say that infants respond on the basis of the *amount* of things rather than the *number* of things (Mix, Huttenlocher, & Levine, 2002).

Memory

Few cognitive skills are as basic as the ability to store information encountered at a given time for potential retrieval seconds, minutes, days, or even years later. It is hard to imagine how any other cognitive activity, such as problem solving or concept formation, could take place without the ability to draw on previously experienced information. How could we classify dogs, horses, and giraffes into the category "animals" without remembering the shared features of each? In one way or another, memory is a crucial element in most of our thinking. How early can we demonstrate the presence of memory? How long do the memories of young infants last? How much information are infants capable of retaining through memory? Before we begin to answer these questions, we need to consider some of the distinctions researchers have made concerning different types of memory.

One contrast is the difference between recognition and recall memory. Tasks that measure **recognition memory** require participants to indicate somehow that they have experienced a picture, word, or other stimulus before. In other words, there has to be some behavioral response to the experimenter's question "Have you encountered this item on previous trials of this experiment?" In **recall memory**, participants must reproduce previously presented stimuli. For example, they might be asked to generate a series of actions they had previously witnessed ("Can you show me how we fed the fish before?") or, among older children who can speak, to say a list of words or numbers they had heard previously. Another contrast is sometimes made between explicit and implicit memory. **Explicit memory** refers to recollection of a past event or experience, such as hearing a story being read or viewing a picture of a female face in a laboratory experiment. Explicit memory is a conscious process and can be demonstrated via either recognition or recall. **Implicit memory** refers to nonconscious recollections of how to do something behaviorally, such as learning to use a spoon to eat cereal or, among older children, learning how to ride a bike. The child may have little awareness of all of the small improvements that have taken place in those skills over time. For the most part, the research described below concerns the development of explicit memory.

recognition memory Ability to identify whether a stimulus has previously been encountered.

recall memory Ability to reproduce stimuli that one has previously encountered.

explicit memory Conscious recollection of a past event or experience.

implicit memory Nonconscious recollections of how to do something behaviorally.

How Can We Study Infant Memory? A big obstacle to studying infant memory, of course, is that infants do not speak. How, then, can researchers determine anything about their memory capabilities? Two techniques used to study infant perception, *habituation* and *operant conditioning*, have been fruitful in studies of infant memory, especially recognition memory. In addition, researchers have developed several other ingenious procedures to shed light on early memory that involves recall.

Much of the earliest research on infant memory was conducted by Joseph Fagan, who used the habituation procedure to study recognition. First, a visual stimulus, such as a photograph of a human face or a geometric figure (some examples are shown in Figure 6.10), is presented to the infant for a predetermined period of time. On a subsequent trial, the same stimulus is paired with a completely new item, and the time the infant spends looking at each picture is recorded. In this *paired-comparison procedure*, infants typically look longer at the novel stimulus than at the familiar one, suggesting that they remember the familiar item. Using this basic approach, Fagan (1974) demonstrated, for example, that five- to six-month-olds familiarized with black-and-white photos of human faces for only a few minutes retain information about them for surprisingly long periods of time. When the recognition test occurred three hours or up to fourteen days after the initial familiarization, infants showed consistently longer visual fixations to the novel stimulus. You will probably agree that this is an impressive level of performance for infants only a few months old!

Carolyn Rovee-Collier and her colleagues have used a different technique, relying on operant conditioning to demonstrate infants' early memory capabilities (Rovee-Collier & Hayne, 1987; Rovee-Collier & Shyi, 1992). As shown in Figure 6.11, an infant lies in a crib with a ribbon running from his ankle to an overhead mobile. Within a few minutes, the infant recognizes the contingency between his foot kicks and the movement of the mobile; his rate of kicking increases dramatically. Suppose, however, that the mobile is removed from the crib for two weeks. When the mobile is reintroduced, does the infant remember that this is the object that he can move with a foot kick? The answer is yes: three-month-olds vigorously kicked when the

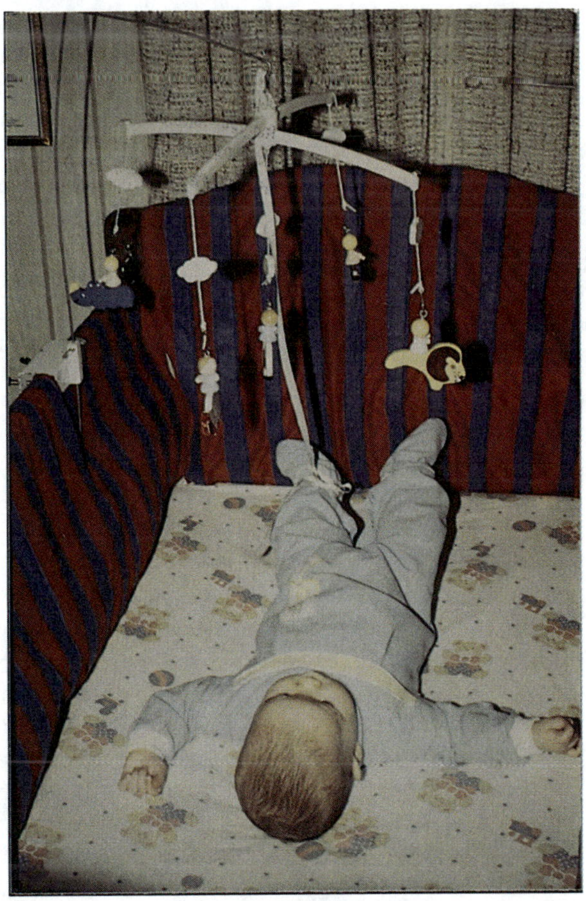

FIGURE 6.11

Using Operant Conditioning to Study Early Memory

Infants in Rovee-Collier's studies had a ribbon attached between their feet and an interesting mobile overhead. Infants quickly learned that kicking made the mobile move. When the mobile was removed and then reintroduced after a delay interval, infants showed that they "remembered" it by vigorously kicking again.

Source: Stricker et al. (2001).

familiar mobile was replaced over the crib but did not kick as much when a brand-new mobile was put in the same position (Enright et al., 1983).

Studying infant recall requires different procedures. In the previous chapter, you learned about a technique called *deferred imitation*, in which infants are shown a unique sequence of actions and then observed to see whether they imitate those behaviors at a later time. For example, in Andrew Meltzoff's studies, infants typically see the experimenter pull the square ends off a dumbbell or push a button on a box with a stick. When tested as long as four months later, a substantial number of fourteen-month-olds remembered the specific action sequences (Meltzoff, 1995). Similarly, Patricia Bauer and her colleagues have used a method they call **elicited imitation**, in which older infants and preschoolers must repeat a sequence of actions demonstrated by the experimenter. One sequence used in these studies is "making a gong." Children watch as the researcher shows three distinct steps to an event they have never seen before: (1) putting a bar across two posts; (2) hanging a plate from the bar; and (3) hitting the plate with a mallet. Then, weeks or even months later, the children return to the laboratory and are asked to repeat the sequence of actions with the array of parts they see on the table. In other words, they must initially imitate and then later recall a correctly ordered set of behaviors. Bauer's studies show that, by the time most children start their second year, they need to see the sequence only once in order to remember it one month later. By twenty months of age, memories for the sequence can last for as long as twelve months (Bauer, 2002; Bauer et al., 2000). These studies provide dramatic evidence for the presence of recall memory well before children have fully developed their language skills.

Infant Memory Capabilities At just how young an age do infants display memory? One experiment involving recognition memory shows that even newborns can retain information for at least a twenty-four-hour period (Swain, Zelazo, & Clifton, 1993). On the first day of the study, newborns heard a tape of a word, either *beagle* or *tinder*, which was repeated during the experimental session while an observer recorded the number of head turns the infants made toward the sound. As you would expect with the habituation procedure, the number of head turns declined over the session. One day later, one group of infants heard the same word again, whereas a second, experimental group heard a new word. Infants in the first group made fewer head turns toward the stimulus word and more head turns away from it than infants in the second group. Evidently, they remembered some very specific properties of the auditory stimulus for the duration of several hours. Thus recognition memory is evident right from the child's earliest hours after birth.

Early memories are easily disrupted, however, by changes in the context of the task. Suppose an infant in an operant conditioning experiment learns the original contingency between a foot kick and the movement of the mobile when she is in a playpen lined with a yellow cloth with green squares. Twenty-four hours later, the mobile is reintroduced, but this time the cloth liner is blue with red stripes. Now the infant does not show a memory for the previous day's events; she does not kick nearly as much as she did at the end of training the previous day (Rovee-Collier et al., 1992). Infants six months of age and under encode very detailed and specific information about an event, even when that information is not the central focus of attention. Put another way, infants will show evidence of memory only when the conditions during training and memory testing are as similar as possible (Hayne & Rovee-Collier, 1995). By the latter portion of the first year, however, infants are more likely to disregard differences in contextual cues when they are tested for memory, perhaps because their memories are more robust (Hartshorn et al., 1998). More broadly speaking, they can remember things that are learned in one place and tested in another (Rovee-Collier, 1999).

There are several other important developmental changes in both recognition and recall in the first two years. First, as infants mature, they store information more rapidly. Whether they are participating in a habituation, operant conditioning, deferred imitation, or elicited imitation experiment, they need fewer trials to "study" the items they are supposed to remember (Bauer, 2004; Courage & Howe, 2004;

elicited imitation Method in which older infants and preschoolers must repeat a sequence of actions demonstrated by the experimenter.

Hayne, 2004). In experiments using deferred imitation of a three-part sequence of actions, for example, six-month-olds typically need six exposures to the sequence in order to remember, whereas fourteen-month-olds need only one (Barr et al., 1996; Meltzoff, 1995). Second, infants can retain information for longer and longer periods of time. In deferred and elicited imitation tasks, the general finding is that six-month-olds can retain information over a twenty-four hour period, nine-month-olds for up to five weeks, and twenty-month-olds for as long as twelve months (Bauer, 2004). Finally, as infants grow older, they remember a greater amount of information. Whereas the majority of six-month-olds typically enact one segment of a three-part sequence in imitation tasks, nine-month-olds can reproduce more than one (Bauer, 2004). Using the habituation task, Susan Rose and her colleagues similarly found that, at five to seven months of age, infants had trouble recognizing a string of three or four different objects that were presented as part of one memory trial but that, by twelve months of age, almost half of infants were successful (Rose, Feldman, & Jankowski, 2001b).

KEY THEME
INTERACTION AMONG DOMAINS

Brain Development and Memory Ultimately, any account of memory developm ent will have to be connected to changes in the structures or processes that occur in the brain. Neuroscientists have been actively exploring brain functioning in both animals and humans to try to establish the underlying substrates of different cognitive processes, including memory. Fruitful approaches have included studying the memory performance of animals that have had different portions of the brain lesioned (or damaged), "scanning" the brain to measure metabolism and blood flow, and recording the electrical activity of the brain while individuals perform memory tasks.

We have already noted that even very young infants show a robust preference for novel stimuli, indicating their recognition memory for "old" items they have seen before. Infant monkeys show similar patterns of behavior; however, when their hippocampus is removed at fifteen days of age, preferences for novelty disappear (Bachevalier, Brickson, & Hagger, 1993). As Figure 6.12 shows, the hippocampus is a brain structure located below the cerebral cortex that has long been known to be involved in memory functioning. Apparently, the hippocampus, which is a part of the *limbic system*, is an early-developing structure that is necessary for the display of fundamental memory processes such as recognition (Nelson, Thomas, & de Haan, 2006).

Toward the latter part of the first year, portions of the temporal and prefrontal lobes of the brain (see Figure 6.12) begin to mature, as is revealed by *positron emission tomography*, or PET scans. PET scans allow neuroscientists to measure, among other things, the glucose activity in different portions of the brain. Interestingly, the levels of glucose metabolism in the temporal lobes of monkeys begin to look adult-like at four months of age, the age at which they begin to reach for a novel object after a short delay (Bachevalier, Hagger, & Mishkin, 1991). Similarly, glucose metabolism in the prefrontal lobes begins to appear mature in one-year-old human infants (Chugani, 1994). This is also the age at which infants correctly search for objects in the A-not-B task and at which they can locate objects after a delay (Nelson, 1995).

Researchers have also begun to record the electrical activity of the brain on-line while infants participate in memory tasks. In one study, five-month-old infants heard a succession of one hundred identical stimuli, either a click or a tone. The next day, fifty of the "old" stimuli were presented with fifty "new" ones (for instance, a tone if a click had originally been heard). Electrical firing patterns of the brain were more pronounced for familiar than for unfamiliar stimuli. Brain waves also had less variable onset times for familiar stimuli on the second day compared with the first day (Thomas & Lykins, 1995). Put another way, physiological responses were more consistent and prominent for the stimuli that had been put into memory.

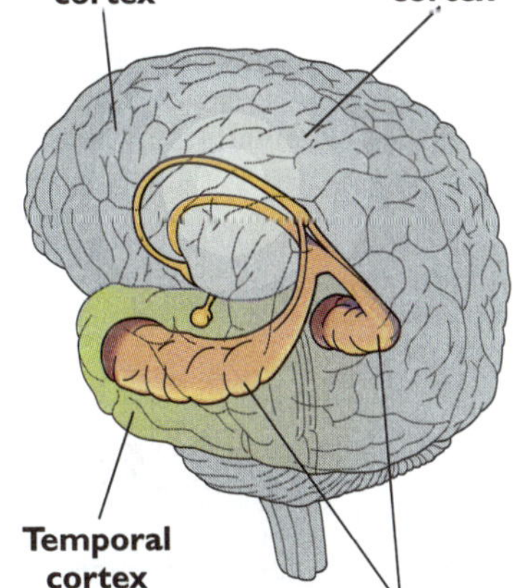

FIGURE 6.12
The Brain and Memory Development
Several regions of the brain are implicated in memory development. The hippocampus matures early, and part of its function may be to direct recognition memory. Portions of the temporal and prefrontal cortex mature later in the first year and apparently are involved in more demanding memory tasks.

PROBLEM SOLVING

One of the most powerful and uniquely human cognitive skills is the ability to solve problems. Whether you are completing an analogy, computing an arithmetic solution, or testing a scientific hypothesis, problem solving typically involves several steps or phases. Often you start with planning the steps to the solution of the problem, considering both the information you have at the start and the final goal. Clearly, you must attend to the portions of the problem that are relevant to its solution. You will probably select from a number of strategies to help you achieve your goal (for example, count on your fingers or use a calculator). In many cases, you must rely on your understanding of what different symbols in the problem (such as "+" or "=") represent. Frequently you must draw on a body of information from memory and examine relationships among several pieces of that information. Once you have the solution, you will often apply this new knowledge to similar contexts. Given the number of steps involved and the complex, intertwined relationships among them, you can see why problem solving is considered to be an example of what is called "higher-order thinking."

What are the earliest instances of problem-solving activity in humans? Piaget's descriptions of the development of means-ends behavior during the sensorimotor stage of development suggest that infants show the beginnings of problem solving. Other researchers have confirmed that infants are capable of solving problems, combining several subgoals to reach an interesting toy. In an experiment conducted by Peter Willatts (1990), twelve-month-olds saw a barrier in front of a cloth on which was placed a string attached to a toy (similar to what is depicted in Figure 6.13). To get the toy, infants had to remove the barrier, pull the cloth, and then pull the string. In a control condition, the toy was not attached to the string. Infants in the first group tended to remove the barrier without playing with it, quickly pulled the cloth, and grasped the string to reach the toy. Their behavior suggested that

FIGURE 6.13

Transfer of Problem Solutions Among Infants

Even one-year-olds can transfer the solution of one problem to another when the goal sequences are similar. Each of these problems requires the child to bypass a barrier, pull the cloth, and grab the string to obtain the toy. Infants who were successful in solving one of these problems could typically solve the others, even though the problems were not perceptually identical.

Source: Chen, Sanchez, & Campbell (1997).

reaching the attractive toy was of utmost interest. In contrast, infants in the control group played with the barrier, were slower to reach for the cloth, and frequently did not grasp the string, probably because they recognized that the barrier, cloth, and string could not help to bring the toy closer. Willatts (1990) concluded that infants are capable of putting together several subgoals with the deliberate intent of reaching a goal. Similarly, in another experiment, a group of ten-month-olds was observed as they were encouraged either to throw a ball into a plastic tub or to fit the ball into a tube. Infants reached for the ball faster in the first instance, suggesting that they were planning their actions in accordance with the ultimate goal (Claxton, Keen, & McCarty, 2003).

Problem-solving among infants can even start to take on some complex qualities. There are some circumstances in which very young children can discern the similarities across problems and *transfer* that knowledge from one problem to another. When problem-solving situations look perceptually different but share similar goal sequences—for example, remove a barrier, pull the correct cloth, and pull the correct string to reach a toy, as shown in Figure 6.13—infants who are one year of age show the ability to transfer the solution to other problems once they have been successful with the first (Chen, Sanchez, & Campbell, 1997). Most would agree that these are sophisticated skills considering the young age of these children.

FOR • YOUR • REVIEW

- What changes have researchers observed in classification skills during infancy?
- What kinds of numerical competencies do infants display?
- What are the major features of recognition memory in infancy?
- What do studies employing the elicited imitation technique tell us about recall memory in infancy?
- What major changes in the brain accompany developmental improvements in memory?
- When do infants first evidence the ability to engage in problem solving and transfer?

VYGOTSKY'S SOCIOCULTURAL THEORY AND INFANCY

KEY THEME
SOCIOCULTURAL INFLUENCE

Piaget assumed that cognitive processes function in similar ways across cultures, that the nature and development of thinking have universal qualities. Standing in sharp contrast to these claims are the theoretical ideas of the prominent Russian psychologist Lev Vygotsky (1978). As we saw in the chapter titled "Themes and Theories," Vygotsky wrote that the child's cognitive growth must be understood in the context of the culture in which he or she lives. Vygotsky believed that, in their formal and informal exchanges with children, caregivers, peers, and tutors cultivate in them the particular skills and abilities their cultural group values. Gradually, regulation and guidance of the child's behavior by others is replaced by internalized self-regulation. Lev Vygotsky made such *social activity* the cornerstone of his theory, which, like Piaget's, has had enormous impact on the field of developmental psychology.

The concept of **scaffolding** is a way of thinking about the social relationship involved in learning from another person (Wood, Bruner, & Ross, 1976). A scaffold is a temporary structure that gives the support necessary to accomplish a task. An effective caregiver or teacher provides such a structure in problem-solving situations, perhaps by defining the activity to be accomplished, demonstrating supporting skills and techniques in which the learner is still deficient, and motivating the beginner to complete the task. The collaboration advances the knowledge and

scaffolding Temporary aid provided by one person to encourage, support, and assist a lesser-skilled person in carrying out a task or completing a problem. The model provides knowledge and skills that are learned and gradually transferred to the learner.

abilities of the apprentice, as illustrated by the following study of an infant learning to label objects. Anat Ninio and Jerome Bruner (1978) visited the child in his home every two weeks from age eight months to two years. One commonly shared activity they observed was reading from a picture book, with the boy's mother providing the scaffold for the child to learn more about his language.

> The mother's (often quite unconscious) approach is exquisitely tuned. When the child responds to her "Look!" by looking, she follows immediately with a query. When the child responds to the query with a gesture or a smile, she supplies a label. But as soon as the child shows the ability to vocalize in a way that might indicate a label, she raises the ante. She withholds the label and repeats the query until the child vocalizes, and then she gives the label if the child does not have it fully or correctly.
>
> Later, when the child has learned to respond with shorter vocalizations that correspond to words, she no longer accepts an indifferent vocalization. When the child begins producing a recognizable, constant label for an object, she holds out for it. Finally, the child produces appropriate words at the appropriate place in the dialogue. Even then the mother remains tuned to the developing pattern, helping her child recognize labels and make them increasingly accurate. (Bruner, 1981, pp. 49–50)

Cognitive development, as you can see, takes place in a distinctly social context, resulting from the child's collaboration with and internalization of social exchanges with parents, peers, and, later, teachers (Rogoff, 1998). An important ingredient in the process of guided participation is the establishment of **intersubjectivity**, the mutual attention and shared communication that take place between two individuals, in this case, between expert and learner. We will see evidence of intersubjectivity in this chapter when we discuss how episodes of *joint attention* contribute to language acquisition. Intersubjectivity is also undoubtedly related to many of the aspects of emotional and cognitive development to be discussed in upcoming chapters. Infants show the early beginnings of participating in shared attention and communication in the first few months of life in such simple routines as the game of peekaboo (Rochat & Striano, 1999). By twelve months, they seem to know that, when an adult looks at a toy, they should follow the adult's eyes—in particular, in order to view the same object (Brooks & Meltzoff, 2002). Those moments when infant and caregiver share the same psychological space seem to provide especially rich contexts for development.

FOR • YOUR • REVIEW

- What are the central elements of Vygotsky's sociocultural theory as they apply to infancy?
- What is the significance of the phenomenon of intersubjectivity?

Language

Aside from walking, there are few accomplishments that parents focus on more than their baby's first use of language. The child's first words are typically recorded in the baby book with great excitement and perhaps are captured as quickly as possible with a camcorder. E-mails documenting the event fly to family and friends. Aside from denoting the infant's emerging and expected maturity, language means that the infant now has a way to participate in human interactions in a dramatically new way. She can express what she wants or needs with methods other than crying or making a facial expression. Language truly marks a significant turning point in the child's life.

A baby's contact with language is—initially, at least—noticeably one-sided. Although she may gurgle or coo, most of her experience is as a listener. Among her

intersubjectivity Mutual attention and shared communication that take place between two individuals.

first tasks is to learn to identify the myriad sounds that make up her native language. In other words, she must distinguish specific sounds in the stream of spoken language, note the regularities in how they are combined, recognize which combinations constitute words, and eventually, when she makes the transition from listener to speaker, form the consonant-vowel combinations that are the building blocks of words and sentences. The fundamental sound units and the rules for combining them in a given language make up that language's **phonology**. If you have studied a foreign language, you will recognize that some sounds appear only in certain languages, such as the prolonged nasal *ñ* sound in Spanish and the French vowel that is spoken as though *e* and *u* are combined. Furthermore, each language has its own rules for combining sounds. In English, for example, the *sr* combination does not occur, whereas *sl* and *st* appear frequently. An important task for the child is to absorb the sounds and combinations of sounds that are acceptable in her native language and, eventually, to detect which of these sounds form words.

Another basic language skill that the child must master is linking the combinations of sounds he hears to the objects, people, events, or relationships they label. **Semantics** refers to the meanings of words (sometimes called the *lexicon*) or combinations of words. For example, *cookie* is an arbitrary grouping of sounds, but speakers of English use it to refer to a specific class of objects. The child thus attaches words to conceptual groups, learning when it is appropriate to use them and when it is not (for example, *cookie* does not refer to all objects or edible goods found in the bakery). The child also learns that some words describe actions (*eat*), whereas others describe relationships (*under* or *over*) or modify objects (*chocolate cookie*). Mapping combinations of sounds to their referents (that is, the things to which words refer) is a central element of language acquisition.

PHONOLOGY

What does it take to learn a language? The infant's first steps consist of attending to the sounds of speech as a special type of auditory stimulation, deciphering the units of sound that occur in her language, and discerning which clusters of sounds constitute words, clauses, and phrases. Thus, during much of the infant's first year, the emphasis is on phonological development, both in receiving messages from others and in being able to produce them on his own.

Early Responses to Human Speech As we discussed earlier in this chapter, the basic building blocks of spoken language are called *phonemes*, the smallest units of sound that change the meanings of words. In the words *pat* and *bat*, for example, the phonemes */p/* and */b/* make a big difference in the meaning of the word. Recall also that infants as young as one month can discriminate different phonemes and do so categorically, ignoring small acoustic variations in a sound unless the sound pattern crosses a phonemic boundary. At two months of age, infants add to their repertoire the ability to discriminate vowels (Marean, Werner, & Kuhl, 1992).

Remarkably, young infants show an ability to detect phonemes and vowel sounds from a variety of languages. However, by six to ten months of age, infants show a decline in the ability to distinguish those basic sounds that do not appear in their native language (Kuhl et al., 1992; Polka & Werker, 1994; Werker & Tees, 1984). In one study, six- to eight-month-olds reared in an English-speaking environment could readily discriminate among phonemes used only in Hindi, whereas eleven- to thirteen-month-olds had more difficulty with this task (Werker & Lalonde, 1988). Adults can regain such lost discriminations only with considerable practice or under highly restricted listening conditions (Werker, 1989). Thus it does not appear that we completely lose the capacity to make these discriminations. Instead, toward the end of the first year of exposure to speech, our auditory and perhaps our attentional and cognitive functioning undergo a reorganization that limits our sensitivity to the sounds not utilized in the language we hear (Lalonde & Werker, 1995). At the same time, early phonemic competencies for the native language become even stronger.

KEY THEME
NATURE & NURTURE

phonology Fundamental sound units and combinations of units in a given language.

semantics Meanings of words or combinations of words.

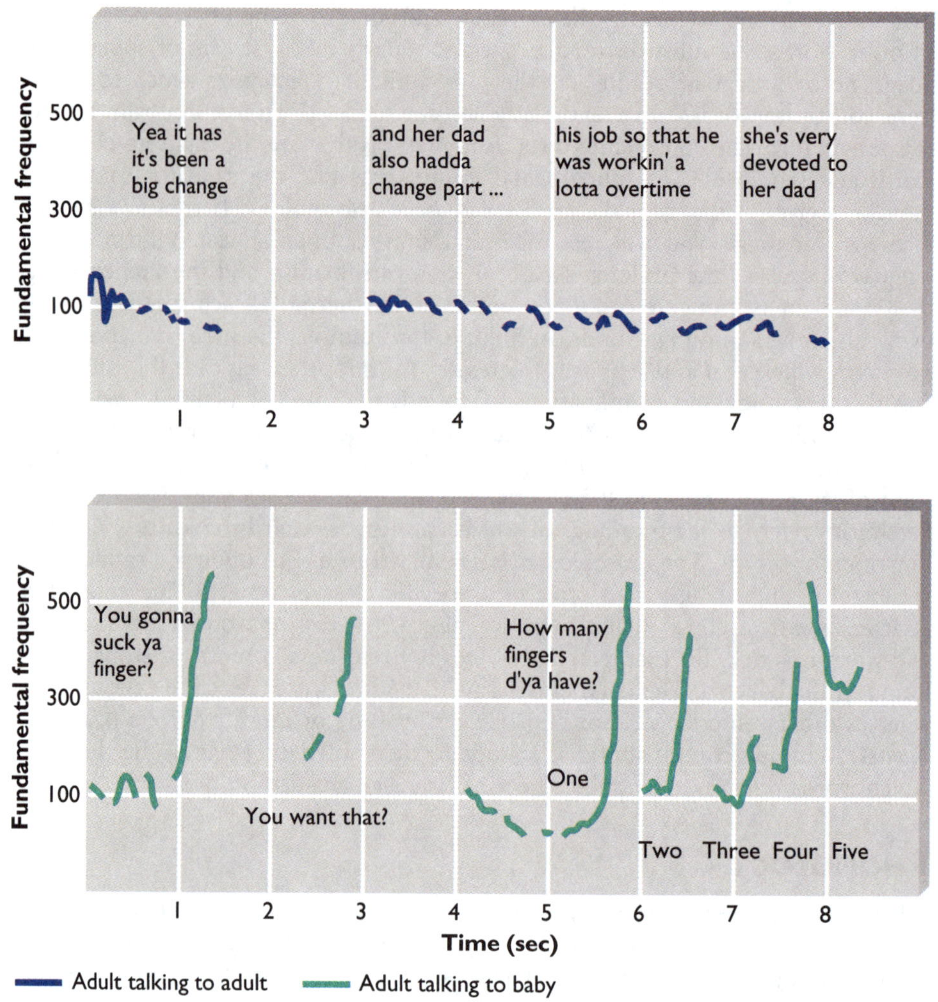

FIGURE 6.14

The Acoustical Properties of Maternal Speech to Infants

These two samples of maternal speech show the special acoustical qualities that make speech to infants (bottom) distinct from speech to adults (top). The vertical axis represents fundamental frequency, a measure of auditory pitch. Note the frequent use of modulation of pitch and the predominance of high pitch in maternal speech to infants. Babies seem to be especially responsive to the qualities of this type of speech.

Source: Adapted from Fenald (1985).

One recent study showed that between 6 and 12 months of age, American infants improved in their discrimination between the English phonemes /ra/ and /la/, whereas the performance of Japanese infants declined (Kuhl et al. 2006).

Infants also show an early sensitivity to **prosody**, the patterns of intonation, stress, and rhythm that communicate meaning. One example of a prosodic feature is the pattern of intonation that distinguishes questions from declarative statements. When you raise your voice at the end of a question, you are signaling a different communicative intent than when you let your voice fall at the end of a declarative sentence. Researchers have found that infants prefer the prosodic features associated with the high-pitched, exaggerated, musical speech, often called "baby talk," which mothers typically direct to their young children. Figure 6.14 illustrates some of the acoustical properties of **motherese**, or **parentese**, as this form of communication is called. In one study, Anne Fernald (1985) trained four-month-olds to turn their heads to activate a loudspeaker positioned on either side of them. The infants were more likely to

prosody Patterns of intonation, stress, and rhythm that communicate meaning in speech.

motherese (parentese) Simple, repetitive, high-pitched speech of caregivers to young children; includes many questions.

make this response if their "reward" was a female stranger's voice speaking as the woman would speak to a baby than if she was using normal adult speech. Other research has shown that it is the positive affective tone of "baby talk" that infants are particularly attracted to (Singh, Morgan, & Best, 2002). In light of these preferences, it seems fitting that mothers from cultures as diverse as France, Italy, Germany, Britain, Japan, China, and the Xhosa tribe of southern Africa have been found to raise their pitch when they speak to their young infants (Fernald, 1991; Papoušek, 1992).

Infants' sensitivity to the prosodic features of speech prepares them for the more complex aspects of language learning that lie before them. As early as two days of age, they show a clear preference for hearing a stream of speech from their native language as opposed to a foreign language (Moon, Cooper, & Fifer, 1993). Sometime between six and nine months of age, infants begin to show a preference for listening to unfamiliar isolated words from their native language. For example, American infants prefer unfamiliar English words over Dutch words. At ten months of age, they also prefer words with a strong-weak stress pattern (for instance, *crossing* versus *across*), which are more common in English (Jusczyk, Cutler, & Redanz, 1993; Jusczyk, Friederici, et al., 1993). Young infants thus seem to be especially tuned in to the rhythmic properties that distinguish one language from another (Nazzi, Bertoncini, & Mehler, 1998).

Finding Words in Others' Speech Perhaps most impressive is the finding that, between about six and eight months of age, infants show that they can detect the beginnings and endings of specific words in a stream of their native speech, a skill that should strike you as remarkable if you have ever tried to detect the presence of particular words when listening to someone speak a foreign language. To explore this ability, Sven Mattys and Peter Jusczyk (Mattys & Jusczyk, 2001) first familiarized infants with a single word, such as *dice*. Next, infants heard the target word within a passage, such as "Two dice can be rolled without difficulty," or they heard the same sound pattern but across two different words, as in "Wired ice no longer surprises anyone." Infants showed a clear preference for the first type of correctly segmented passage, probably using rhythmic cues, as well as noting the different acoustic properties that phonemes have at the beginnings versus the ends of words (for instance, /d/ sounds slightly different at the beginning than at the end of a word). Words starting with vowels, though, are much harder for infants to locate in speech segments than words starting with consonants. Only sixteen-month-olds could locate words such as *ice* or *eel*.

The infant's capacity to extract information about the probability that one sound will follow another, a phenomenon called *statistical learning*, may be an important part of her ability to detect words in the speech stream (Saffron, 2001). In one experiment, researchers exposed eight-month-olds to an unbroken stream of sounds, such as *tibudopabikudaropigolatupabikuti*, for two minutes. In this example, every instance of *pa* was followed by *bi*. On the other hand, *pi* was followed by *go* only one-third of the time. When later presented with *pabiku* versis *pigola*, infants showed a clear attentional preference for *pigola*, suggesting that they were sensitive to the chances that one sound would follow another (Saffran, Aslin, & Newport, 1996).

KEY THEME
NATURE & NURTURE

Studies show that several factors can help infants find words in a stream of speech. One is the use of parentese. Hearing new words spoken in the melodic rhyth m of parentese helps infants to distinguish those words from parts of words; hearing words spoken in regular adult tones makes the task more difficult (Thiessen, Hill, & Saffran, 2005). A second factor is the presence of the infant's name. In one recent study, when six-month-olds heard new words immediately after their own name (for example, "Emma's *cup* is here"), recognition for those words was greater than when they followed another novel word ("Autumn's *bike* is here"). Familiar words, such as one's own name, may thus help call out new words from the stream of speech and act as an important tool in language acquisition (Bortfeld et al., 2005).

Once infants can locate words, the pathway is prepared for the next critical aspect of learning a language, namely, learning the meanings of words. Word recognition skills improve dramatically in the second year, especially as infants begin to use their knowledge of word meanings to decipher the sounds they hear. At eighteen months of age, for example, toddlers need to hear only the very first portion of a word, such as *daw* in *doggie*, in order to look at the picture the word represents (Fernald, Swingley, & Pinto, 2001). This relationship between meaning and sound is one example of how the various facets of language are, in fact, very much interrelated.

Cooing and Babbling: Prelinguistic Speech Well before the child utters her first word, she produces sounds that increasingly resemble the language spoken in her environment. At birth, the infant's vocal capabilities are limited to crying and a few other brief sounds, such as grunts, sighs, or clicks. Between six and eight weeks, a new type of vocalization, **cooing**, emerges. These brief, vowel-like utterances are sometimes accompanied by consonants, usually those produced in the back of the mouth, such as */g/* or */k/*. Infants coo when they are in a comfortable state or when a parent has made some attempt to communicate, either with speech or with coos of his or her own. In the weeks that follow, the infant's vocalizations become longer and begin to include consonants formed at the front of the mouth, as in */m/* or */b/*.

The next significant accomplishment is the emergence of **babbling**, the production of consonant-vowel combinations such as *da* or *ba*. Most children begin to babble at about three to six months and refine their skills in the succeeding months. To many listeners, the infant's babbling sounds like active experimentation with the production of different sounds. These vocalizations are especially likely to occur in the context of mutually coordinated caregiver-child interactions (Hsu & Fogel, 2001), and they are often accompanied by such facial expressions as smiles or frowns (Yale et al., 1999), perhaps to emphasize the child's communicative intent. At about seven months, the infant will repeat well-formed syllables, such as *baba* or *dada*, a phenomenon called **canonical babbling**. It is almost as if the infant is trying to say words. At nine or ten months, the child's babbling includes more numerous and complex consonant-vowel combinations, as well as variations in intonation (Davis et al., 2000).

KEY THEME
Interaction Among Domains

The changes in children's productive capabilities are linked to physiological changes in their vocal apparatus and central nervous system that occur during the first year. In the months after birth, the infant's larynx descends farther into the neck, the oral cavity grows, and the baby can place her tongue in different positions in her mouth (not just forward and backward as at birth). At the same time, the cortex of the brain replaces the brainstem in controlling many of the child's behaviors. In general, early reflexlike vocalizations, such as cries, fade as more controlled voluntary utterances, such as coos and babbles, enter the child's repertoire (Stark, 1986).

KEY THEME
Nature & Nurture

The fact that most infants, regardless of their culture, begin to coo and babble at similar ages suggests that biological factors direct the onset of these behaviors. Even deaf children vocalize with coos and babbles in the first few months of life (Stoel-Gammon & Otomo, 1986), and both deaf and hearing children exposed to sign language make repetitive, rhythmic hand gestures akin to babbling, prior to full-fledged signing (Petitto et al., 2001; Petitto & Marentette, 1991; Takei, 2001). The fact that the right side of the mouth opens wider than the left when children babble probably also signals the role of the left hemisphere in this process (Holowka & Petitto, 2002). Nature thus plays a prominent role in the emergence of the child's utterances. But even at this early stage of language development, the form the child's vocalizations take is influenced by the language spoken around her. Studies have shown identifiable differences in babbling among infants from varying cultures. One group of researchers conducted a spectral analysis of the vowel sounds made by ten-month-olds in Paris, London, Algiers, and Hong Kong. The procedure involved translating the acoustic properties of speech into a visual representation of the intensity, onset, and pattern of vocalization. Infants from different countries varied in the average frequencies of the sounds they produced; the differences paralleled those of adult speakers from the same countries (Boysson-Bardies et al., 1989). Thus the child's linguistic environment has a distinct effect on his own speech before he can speak true words.

cooing Vowel-like utterances that characterize the infant's first attempts to vocalize.

babbling Consonant-vowel utterances that characterize the infant's first attempts to vocalize.

canonical babbling Repetition of simple consonant-vowel combinations in well-formed syllables.

protodeclarative communication Use of a gesture to call attention to an object or event.

protoimperative communication Use of a gesture to issue a command or request.

Later Phonological Development At around one year of age, some of the child's babbles begin to sound like words, a major achievement that is discussed in greater detail below. From the perspective of phonology, though, the infant's ability to make different sounds is still somewhat restricted. Infants say a limited number of consonants and vowels, usually the same ones that appear in their babbles (Ingram, 1999). Some sounds, such as */m/* and */b/*, are more common than others, such as */l/* and */r/* (Leonard, Newhoff, & Meselam, 1980). As the child's ability to speak improves, she adds consonants to the ends of words (such as *bite* instead of *bi*), although not consistently (Sternberger, 1992). Perhaps the best characterization of this phase is that infants say words, and sometimes change them, in accordance with the sounds they are capable of articulating.

Once children enter a period of rapid vocabulary acquisition, between eighteen months and two years of age, the range of sounds they produce expands. And they link those sounds in the intonation patterns, or vocal melody, that characterize their native language (Snow, 2006). Certain kinds of errors are common, though, and may persist until children are in preschool or even elementary school. They might replace a *k* sound with a *t* to say *tootie* instead of *cookie* or substitute *w* for *r* in the word *rabbit*. Or children might delete a syllable that is unstressed, for example, saying *nana* for *banana*, or use reduplication, calling a bottle *baba* (Vihman, 1998).

FIRST WORDS

Typically at about one year of age, children say their first words, perhaps *cookie*, *Mama*, or *Dada*. Certainly the uttering of first words is a major accomplishment, marking the visible entry of the child into the world of spoken, shared communication. The child's comprehension and production of words also signal a new focus in the mastery of language: semantic development.

Gesture as a Communication Tool Late in the first year, before or as they speak their first words, many children begin to use such gestures as pointing, showing, or giving as a means to communicate with other people (Bates, Camaioni, & Volterra, 1975). Carlotta, a ten-month-old infant observed by Elizabeth Bates and her colleagues, provides some good examples of several kinds of nonverbal communication that seem to express meaning. In one observation, Carlotta held up her toy and extended her arm in a showing motion to an adult. Here she was using a **protodeclarative communication** that, much as a declarative sentence does, called the adult's attention to the object. Another time, Carlotta pointed to the kitchen sink and said, "Ha!" a **protoimperative communication** intended to get the adult to do something (Bates, 1979). Often children's gestures are accompanied by direct eye contact with the communication's recipient. As children get older, they may add a vocalization to the gesture for added emphasis (Messinger & Fogel, 1998), much as Carlotta did when asking for water. Children may also repeat their communications if the messages are not understood. This constellation of behaviors and the context in which they occur suggest that children use gestures as a purposeful means to an end (Scoville, 1983).

Linda Acredolo and Susan Goodwyn (1988) found that a child between eleven and twenty-four months of age uses gestures not just to show or request but also to symbolize objects or events. The child may signify a flower, for example, by making a sniffing gesture or the desire to go outside with a knob-turning motion. A significant number of children's gestures re-create the functions of objects rather than their forms or shapes. For example, participants in the study would put their fist to one ear to signify a telephone or wave their hands to represent a butterfly.

Late in the first year, many young children use gestures to communicate, either to call an adult's attention to an object or to get an adult to do something. Gestures typically drop out of the child's repertoire, though, as spoken language develops.

Acredolo and Goodwyn believe a strong relationship exists between the development of symbolic gestures and verbal abilities because both appear at approximately the same point in development, with gestures usually preceding words by a few weeks (Acredolo & Goodwyn, 1988; Goodwyn & Acredolo, 1993). In fact, researchers have reported a tight correspondence between gestures for specific objects and the words that are produced for them several weeks later (Iverson & Goldin-Meadow, 2005). Recognizing that one thing can symbolize another represents a major cognitive advance, one that is essential for the use of both gestures and spoken language. Gestures, however, may be easier for the child to produce than the complex coordination required for a verbal utterance. During their second year, infants begin to combine two distinct ideas with a gesture plus a word, for example, by pointing to a box and saying "open." These communications are the precursors of the more complex spoken speech the child will soon start to use at age two years (Goldin-Meadow, 2006).

By the middle of the second year, children are less likely to use gestures as their sole means of communication. Gestures unaccompanied by verbalization are less useful when the "listener" is out of view, and they are usually correctly understood by only a limited number of adults. Parents also probably tend to encourage the child's verbalizations more than they do the use of gestures (Acredolo & Goodwyn, 1990a). So oriented do hearing children become to words as a means of expression that, by two years of age, they are much more likely to learn new names for objects as opposed to new gestures to represent them (Namy & Waxman, 1998).

All of this is not meant to say that children stop using gestures entirely. In fact, quite the contrary is true. Both adults and children tend to use gestures as an accompaniment to their speech, giving emphasis to what they are saying or elaborating on a concept visually. Children begin to use gesture in these new ways as their speech gets more complex, at ages two and three (Mayberry & Nicoladis, 2000). Even blind children gesture while they speak to others, suggesting that this behavior is not merely an imitation of the communication styles of adults (Iverson & Goldin-Meadow, 2001). Rather, gesture seems to be very much intertwined with the communicative process.

The One-Word Stage From about twelve to twenty months of age, most children speak only one word at a time. Children's first words are most frequently **nominals**,

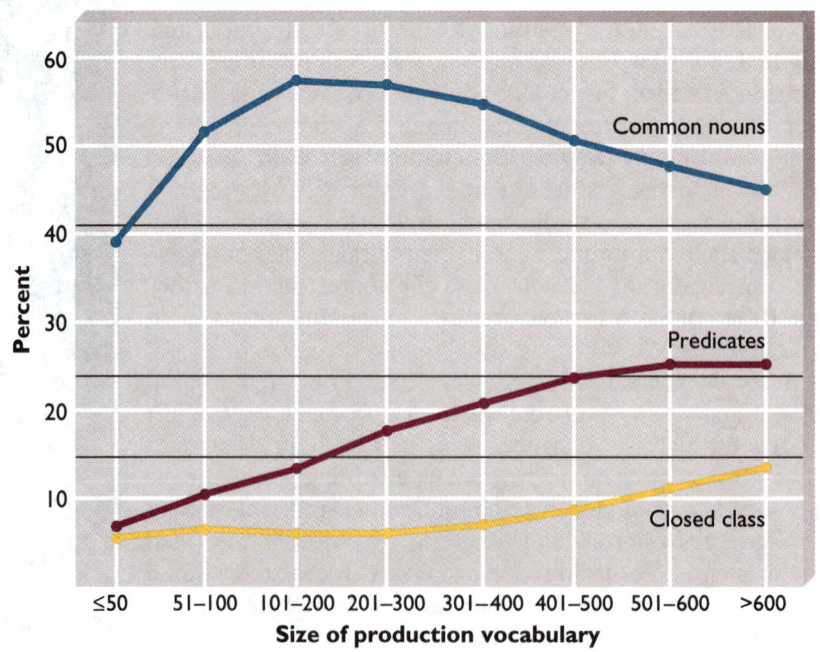

FIGURE 6.15

Changes in the Proportion of Word Types in Children's Vocabularies

As children's vocabularies grow from only a few words to several hundred (the horizontal axis on the graph), the proportion of nouns rises and remains high. The proportion of other types of words children learn, such as predicates (verbs and adjectives) and closed-class words (prepositions, conjunctions, and other relational words), remains lower. The children in this study ranged in age from sixteen to thirty months.

Source: Bates et al. (1994).

labels for objects, people, or events, although action words (*give*), modifiers (*dirty*), and personal-social words (*please*) also occur (Bates et al., 1994; Nelson, 1973). Children's early words usually refer to people or objects important in their lives, such as parents and other relatives, pets, and familiar objects. Children are also more likely to acquire labels for dynamic objects (*clock*, *car*, *ball*) or those they can use (*cup*, *cookie*) than for items that are stationary (*wall*, *window*). Figure 6.15 shows how the proportion of word types changes in the vocabularies of children between one and two and a half years of age.

Children acquire their first ten words slowly; the typical child adds about one to three words to his or her repertoire each month (Barrett, 1989). From about age eighteen months onward, however, many children show a virtual explosion in the acquisition of new words. This remarkable period in language development is called the **vocabulary spurt** (Barrett, 1985; Bloom, 1973). In one longitudinal study of vocabulary growth in one- to two-year-olds, some learned to say as many as twenty new words, mostly nouns, during each week of the vocabulary spurt (Goldfield & Reznick, 1990). Figure 6.16 shows the rapid rate of vocabulary growth for three children in the middle of their spurt. Within the same period, children also typically show a spurt in the number of words they understand (Reznick & Goldfield, 1992). When rapid vocabulary growth first begins, children also show a temporary increase in the number of errors they make in naming objects, forgetting words they recently learned. The influx of new words may temporarily interfere with knowledge that has been recently stored, a finding that is perhaps to be expected at this transitional time in language development (Dapretto & Bjork, 2000; Gershkoff-Stowe, 2001; Gershkoff-Stowe & Smith, 1997).

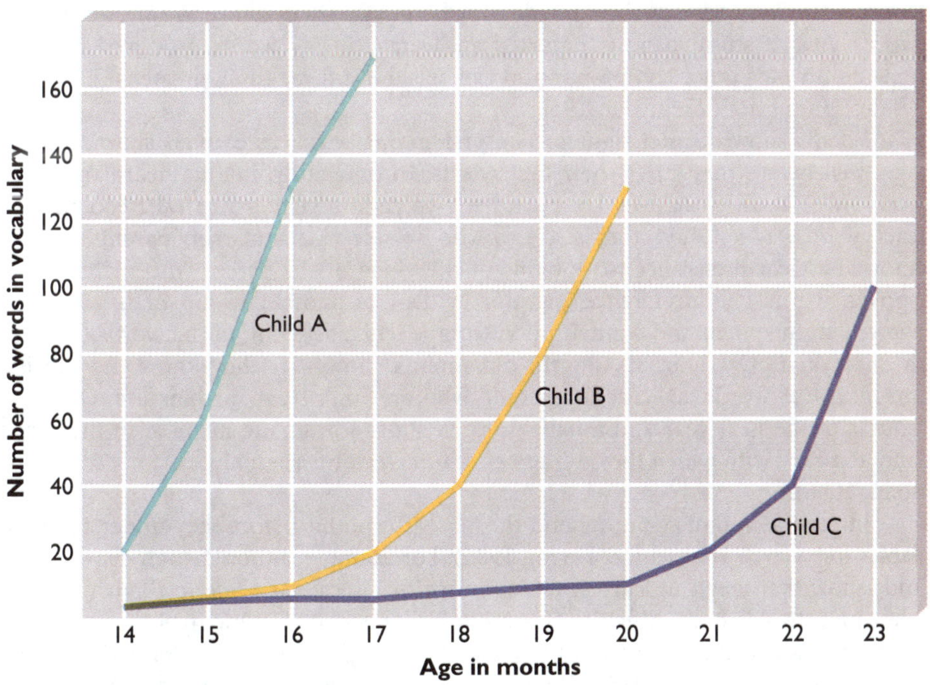

FIGURE 6.16

The Vocabulary Spurt in Three Young Children

Many children show a vocabulary spurt, a sharp rise in the number of new words they learn, as they approach two years of age. However, children may begin their spurts at different ages, as the graph clearly shows. Child A showed an early spurt, beginning at fifteen months. Child B's spurt began at the more typical age of eighteen months. Child C showed a late spurt at twenty-one months.

Source: Adapted from Goldfield & Reznick (1990).

nominal Word that labels objects, people, or events; the first type of word most children produce.

vocabulary spurt Period of rapid word acquisition that typically occurs early in language development.

Some of the child's first words are bound to a specific context; that is, the child uses the word to label objects in limited situations. Lois Bloom (1973) observed that one nine-month-old used the word *car* only when she was looking out the living room window at cars moving on the street. She did not say "car" to refer to parked cars, pictures of cars, or cars she was sitting in. This type of utterance, used when the child applies a label to a narrower class of objects than the term signifies, is called an **underextension**. Over time, the child begins to use single words more flexibly in a wider variety of contexts (Barrett, 1986). Children may also show **overextension**, applying a label to a broader category than the term signifies. For example, a toddler may call a horse or a cow "doggie." The child often applies the same word to objects that look alike perceptually (Clark, 1973). At other times, the child may misuse a word when objects share functions, such as calling a rolling quarter a "ball" (Bowerman, 1978). As with underextensions, the child's use of overextensions declines after the second year.

Most noticeable at this phase of language learning is the child's intense desire to communicate her thoughts, feelings, and desires. Even though her language skills are limited to one or at most two words at a time, the young child is enormously eager to find ways of talking about favorite people, toys, and objects (Bloom, 1998; Dromi, 1999).

Comprehension Versus Production If you have ever tried to learn a new language, you undoubtedly found it easier to understand what another speaker was saying than to produce a sentence in the new language yourself. An important point to remember about children's early language is that their **receptive language**, what they comprehend, far exceeds their **productive language**, their ability to say and use the words. In one study, parents reported an average of 5.7 words produced by their ten-month-olds but a comprehension average about three times greater, 17.9 words (Bates, Bretherton, & Snyder, 1988).

Infants show distinct signs of comprehending words as early as six months of age, well before they utter their first words. In one study, infants heard the word *mommy* or *daddy* produced by a synthetic voice in a gender-neutral frequency. As each word was repeated, they also saw side-by-side videos of their parents. Infants showed a clear preference for looking at the video of the parent who matched the spoken word. This preference was not evident in another group of infants who viewed strange men and women on videotape while listening to the words (Tincoff & Jusczyk, 1999). Thus six-month-old infants show that they know the specific meanings of words, at least for people who are important in their life. Over the course of the next year and a half, children show a dramatic increase in the speed and accuracy with which they understand spoken words (Fernald, Perfors, & Marchman, 2006).

In general, infants comprehend the labels for nouns before they understand the labels for verbs (Tomasello & Farrar, 1986). For example, although eighteen-month-olds show that they can learn what it means for a Lego car to *neem* ("push"), fourteen-month-olds have difficulty (Casasola & Cohen, 2000). One hypothesis for this delay in understanding verbs has to do with the notion that many verbs denote the actions or motions of objects. Thus, in order to understand a verb, the child has to first understand something about the object involved and the actions and motions it is capable of (Kersten, 1998). In fact, when young children are learning new verbs (such as "This one is *spogging*"), they often attend to how objects look as much as to what they do (Kersten & Smith, 2002).

That young children understand so much of what is said to them means they have acquired some important information about language before they actually speak. They know that people, objects, and events have names. They know that specific patterns of sounds represent objects and events in their environment. Most importantly, they begin to appreciate the usefulness of language as a means of expressing ideas, needs, and feelings.

underextension Application of a label to a narrower class of objects than the term signifies.

overextension Tendency to apply a label to a broader category than the term actually signifies.

receptive language Ability to comprehend spoken speech.

productive language Meaningful language spoken or otherwise produced by an individual.

referential style Type of early language production in which the child uses mostly nominals.

expressive style Type of early language production in which the child uses many social words.

Individual and Cultural Differences in Language Development Although children show many common trends in the way they acquire language, they also show significant individual differences in rates and types of language production. You may have heard a family member or friend report that her child said virtually nothing for two or three years and then began speaking in complete sentences. Although such dramatic variations in language milestones are not frequent, children sometimes show unique patterns in their linguistic accomplishments, patterns that still lead to the attainment of normal language by later childhood.

One example of wide individual variation is the age at which children say their first word. Some children produce their first distinguishable word as early as nine months, whereas others may not do so until sixteen months (Barrett, 1989). Similarly, some children show good pronunciation, whereas others have difficulty making certain sounds, consistently substituting *t* for *k* or *b* for *v*, for example (Smith, 1988). In addition, not all children display the vocabulary spurt (Acredolo & Goodwyn, 1990b), or they may start their spurt at different ages, as Figure 6.16 indicates. The results of a study of more than 1,800 children underscore just how variable the size of children's vocabularies can be: at sixteen months of age, some children spoke 10 or fewer words, whereas others spoke as many as 180 words (Fenson et al., 1994).

Children may also differ in the content of their one-word speech. Most one-year-olds tend to use nominals predominantly, displaying what Katherine Nelson (1973) termed a **referential style**. Other children show a different pattern: rather than naming objects, they frequently use words that have social functions, such as *hello* or *please*, thus displaying an **expressive style**. Expressive children use words to direct or comment on the behavior of other people. According to some research, referential children tend to have a larger vocabulary and show more rapid advances in language development, at least in the early stages (Bates et al., 1988; Nelson, 1973).

How do we explain these individual differences in the rates and styles with which children acquire language? There are several hypotheses. Perhaps individual differences result from differences in the neurological structures that control language or from inborn differences in temperament. For example, referential children tend to have a long attention span, smile and laugh a lot, and be easily soothed (Dixon & Shore, 1997). Children who are more advanced in language comprehension and production show a similar profile (Dixon & Smith, 2000). This style might allow them to profit from incoming information about the names of objects. Another possibility is that parents influence the rate and form of children's vocabulary development. Some parents, for example, may spend a great deal of time encouraging their infants to speak, focusing especially on labeling objects. Others may be more relaxed about letting the infant proceed at his or her own pace. Researchers have confirmed that the overall amount and variety of speech that parents produce for their infants is related to the acceleration of vocabulary growth (Hoff & Naigles, 2002; Huttenlocher et al., 1991).

Cultural differences in how children speak in the one-word stage bolster the idea that what children hear others say influences what they themselves say. Unlike American children, Korean toddlers show a "verb spurt" before a "noun spurt" (Choi, 1998; Choi & Gopnik, 1995); similarly, Mandarin-speaking toddlers utter more verbs than nouns as they and their mothers play with toys (Tardif, 1996; Tardif, Gelman, & Xu, 1999). Mothers from both Asian groups pepper their speech with many more verbs and action sequences, saying things such as "What are you doing?" and "You put the car in the garage." American mothers, in contrast, use far more nouns (for instance, "That's a ball") and ask questions that require a nominal as an answer (such as "What is it?").

Chinese mothers use more verbs and action sequences in their speech to children than American mothers. It is interesting to note that Chinese-speaking toddlers use more verbs than nouns in their early speech. Thus the form of early speech is influenced by the sociocultural context in which the child lives.

ATYPICAL DEVELOPMENT

Developmental Delay

We have emphasized in this text that it is not unusual to observe individual variations in the ages at which children achieve milestones in motor development, and as we have just seen, in cognitive and language development as well. When children deviate noticeably from those milestones in one or more areas, however, they are said to have a **developmental delay.** About 5 percent of children under age three years display developmental delays. The causes can be a genetic disorder, low birth weight, exposure to disease, or an environment that does not support the child's progress. Typically, the first identification is made by the child's pediatrician during regular medical checkups. The physician may recommend a developmental screening to identify the degree and specific areas of delay. Federal legislation, the Individuals with Disabilities Education Act (IDEA) Amendments of 1997, requires early identification of developmental delays as well as provision of appropriate services from educational and social systems within the community (American Academy of Pediatrics, 2001). The idea is that early diagnosis and treatment can result in better outcomes for each child.

What kinds of assessment tools are used to perform a screening? A variety of measures are available, including the Denver Developmental Screening Test, the Peabody Picture Vocabulary Test, and an assortment of questionnaires that ask parents to report their children's behaviors. Sometimes, an early childhood specialist will use an infant intelligence test. Most tests of infant intelligence are based on norms for behaviors that are expected to occur in the first year or two of life. Because the infant's accomplishments tend to be in the domains of motor, language, and socioemotional development, these areas appear most frequently on the various tests.

One widely used test is the *Bayley Scales of Infant and Toddler Development*, designed by Nancy Bayley (2005) to predict later childhood competence. The test consists of several scales. The Cognitive and Language scales assess the young child's sensory and perceptual skills, memory, learning, acquisition of the object concept, and linguistic skill. The Motor Scale measures the child's ability to control and coordinate the body, from large motor skills to finer manipulation of the hands and fingers. Table 6.2 shows some sample items from each scale. Designed for infants from one through forty-two months of age, the test yields a *developmental index* for both the mental and the motor scale. In other words, the infant's scores are compared with the scores for the standardization sample (the large sample of normal infants whose performance was assessed at the time the test was developed) and are expressed in terms of how much they deviate from the average scores of that sample. The Bayley scales also contain a Behavior Rating Scale to assess the infant's interests, emotions, and general level of activity compared with the standardization sample.

If a child has been identified as having a developmental delay, he or she is referred to a local early intervention program. Here, a multidisciplinary team—often a pediatrician, psychologist, social worker, physical therapist, occupational therapist, nutritionist, and speech and language specialist, among others—develops an *individual family service plan* to help the child achieve the most positive outcomes. Parental support and involvement are often cornerstones of successful early intervention programs. More will be said about the impact of early intervention programs on child development in upcoming chapters.

developmental delay The condition children are said to have when they deviate noticeably from motor, cognitive, or language milestones in one or more areas.

Table 6.2 Sample Items from the Bayley Scales of Infant and Toddler Development

Age	Cognitive/Language Scales	Motor Scale
2 months	Turns head to sound Plays with rattle Reacts to disappearance of face	Holds head erect and steady for 15 seconds Turns from side to back Sits with support
6 months	Lifts cup by handle Looks for fallen spoon Looks at pictures in book	Sits alone for 30 seconds Turns from back to stomach Grasps foot with hands
12 months	Builds tower of 2 cubes Turns pages of book	Walks with help Throws ball Grasps pencil in middle
17–19 months	Imitates crayon stroke Identifies objects in photograph	Stands alone on right foot Walks up stairs with help
23–25 months	Matches pictures Uses pronoun(s) Imitates a 2-word sentence	Laces 3 beads Jumps distance of 4 inches Walks on tiptoe for 4 steps
38–42 months	Names 4 colors Uses past tense Identifies gender	Copies circle Hops twice on 1 foot Walks down stairs, alternating feet

Source: Bayley Scales of Infant and Toddler Development. Copyright © 2005 by The Psychological Corporation, a Harcourt Assessment Company. Reproduced by permission. All rights reserved. "Bayley Scales of Infant Development" is a registered trademark of The Psychological Corporation.

LANGUAGE IN THE CONTEXT OF SOCIAL INTERACTIONS

KEY THEME
NATURE & NURTURE

Many researchers of child language hold as a central tenet that language is a social activity, one that arises from the desire to communicate with others and that is nurtured in social interactive contexts. Although these researchers acknowledge that there may be innate predispositions of the young human organism to learn language, they emphasize the role that experiences with more mature, expert speakers play in fostering linguistic skill.

Parentese and Language Development Children need models whose speech does not exceed their processing abilities. Many qualities of parental speech directed at children are well suited to the child's emerging receptive and productive skills, providing a *scaffolding*, or framework, from which the child can learn. Most parents present a scaled-down version of spoken language as they interact with their young offspring, a version that contains simple, well-formed sentences and is punctuated by exaggerated intonation, high pitch, and clear pauses between segments of speech (Newport, 1977). Caregivers describe concrete events taking place in the present and often refer to objects with diminutives, such as *kitty* or *doggie*. They also include repetitions of what the child has said, as well as many questions. Questions in particular serve to facilitate the occurrence of **turn taking**, the alternating vocalization by parent and child. Some questions are also used as **turnabouts**, elements of conversation that explicitly request a response

turn taking Alternating vocalization by parent and child.

turnabout Element of conversation that requests a response from the child.

from the child, as in "You like that, don't you?" or "What did you say?" Also, parents often follow the child's verbalization with a **recast**, repeating what the child has said but correcting any errors. **Expansions**—more elaborate verbal forms—may be added, too. Thus, when a child says, "Ball fall," his mother might reply, "Yes, the red ball [expansion] fell [recast]." Recasts and expansions provide children with cues that their verbalization needs improvement and a model for how to improve. Children, in fact, often imitate and retain their parents' recasts (Farrar, 1992; Saxton, 1997).

The following exchange between one seven-month-old, Ann, and her mother illustrates several of these concepts (Snow, 1977).

Mother	Ann
Ghhhhh ghhhhh ghhhhh ghhhhh Grrrrr grrrrr grrrrr grrrrr	
	(protest cry)
Oh, you don't feel like it, do you?	
	aaaaa aaaaa aaaaa
No, I wasn't making that noise. *I wasn't going* aaaaa aaaaa.	
	aaaaa aaaaa
Yes, that's right.	

Notable in the exchange is the mother's pattern of waiting for her child's vocalization to end before she begins her response, an example of turn taking. If the child had spoken actual words, a real conversation would have taken place. The mother also repeated the child's vowel-like sound but embedded it in more elaborate speech. By the time the infant reaches eighteen months, the mother's tendency to expand or explain her utterances becomes even more pronounced, as in the following brief episode (Snow, 1977):

Mother	Ann
	(blowing noises)
That's a bit rude.	
	Mouth.
Mouth, that's right.	
	Face.
Face, yes, mouth is in your face. *What else have you got in your face?*	
	Face. (closing eyes)
You're making a face, aren't you?	

According to Snow (1984), two general principles operate during caregiver-child interactions. First, parents generally interpret their infants' behaviors as attempts to communicate, even when that interpretation may not seem warranted to an objective observer. Second, children actively seek relationships among objects, events, and people in their world and the vocal behaviors of their caregivers. The result of these two tendencies is that parents are motivated to converse with their children and children have a mechanism for learning language.

Parentese may serve a number of functions in the child's growing competence with language. First, this form of speech may assist the child's acquisition of word meaning. Mothers tend to say the names for objects more loudly than other words in their speech to infants, and often they place the object label in the last position in their sentence, as in "Do you see the *rattle*?" (Messer, 1981). Mothers also tend to highlight new words by raising their pitch as they say them (Fernald & Mazzie, 1991) or moving an object as they label it (Gogate, Bahrick, & Watson, 2000). Second, the intonations of motherese may

recast Repetition of a child's utterance along with grammatical corrections.

expansion Repetition of a child's utterance along with more complex forms.

facilitate the child's acquisition of phonology and *syntax*, the rules concerning how words can be combined to express particular meanings. In one recent study, for example, researchers found that, the more exaggerated a mother's speech (by lengthening the vowels between consonants), the more likely an infant was to successfully discriminate speech sounds (Liu, Kuhl, & Tsao, 2003). Another study demonstrated that seven- to ten-month-olds oriented more frequently to motherese that contained pauses at clausal boundaries (for example, "Cinderella lived in a great big house/but it was sort of dark. ...") than to motherese that was interrupted within clauses (for example, "Cinderella lived in a great big house but it was/sort of dark. ..."). Infants did not show these differential preferences in response to regular adult speech (Kemler Nelson et al., 1989). Infants show a similar sensitivity to even smaller grammatical units, the phrases and even the words within a sentence, but only when sentences are spoken in motherese (Jusczyk et al., 1992; Myers et al., 1996; Nazzi et al., 2000). The prosodic features of motherese may thus assist the infant in identifying phonologically and syntactically relevant elements of language. Finally, exposure to motherese may provide lessons in conversational turn taking, one aspect of pragmatics that governs speech in interactions with others.

KEY THEME
RISK/RESILIENCE

Are there any other effects of interactions with caregivers on child language development? Researchers have observed that, the more mothers talk with their children, the more words their children acquire (Huttenlocher et al., 1991; Olson, Bayles, & Bates, 1986). It is not just *how much* mothers talk to their children that makes a difference, however; *how* they talk also matters. When mothers use many directives to control their children's behaviors and are generally intrusive, language development is slowed. When mothers (or teachers) use questions, expansions, and conversational turn taking to elicit language from children or follow the children's vocalizations with a response, language development proceeds more rapidly (Hoff-Ginsberg, 1986; Nelson, 1973; Tamis-LeMonda, Bornstein, & Baumwell, 2001; Valdez-Menchaca & Whitehurst, 1992).

KEY THEME
SOCIOCULTURAL CONTEXT

As important as motherese may seem, it is not a universal phenomenon. Although features of motherese have been observed in many languages and even among deaf mothers signing to their deaf infants (Gleason & Weintraub, 1978; Masataka, 1996), mothers in some cultures adopt a distinctly different style in talking with their infants. Consider the following two examples of maternal speech, one American and the other Japanese, as observed by Anne Fernald and Hiromi Morikawa (1993):

AMERICAN MOTHER: *That's a car. See the car? You like it? It's got nice wheels.*

JAPANESE MOTHER: *Here! It's a vroom vroom. I give it to you. Now you give it to me. Give me. Yes! Thank you.*

Whereas American mothers tend to name objects and focus on the exchange of information, Japanese mothers rarely name objects, using them instead to engage their infants in social routines. Perhaps it is not surprising, then, that American infants use substantially more nouns in their speech at nineteen months of age. Similarly, other researchers have noted that Japanese mothers ask fewer questions but use more nonsense sounds and songs than American mothers (Bornstein et al., 1992; Toda, Fogel, & Kawai, 1990). Thus mothers may have different agendas as they speak with their children, and their style of speech may subtly shape the children's utterances.

Another example of variation in the use of motherese can be found in the Kaluli society of Papua New Guinea. In this culture, talking with others is a highly valued social skill, yet few adult verbalizations are directed to infants. Infants may be called by their name, but until they pass their first year, little else is said to them. When mothers do begin to talk to their babies, their speech contains few of the elements of motherese. Turn taking, repetitions, and elaborations are absent; usually mothers simply make directive statements that require no response from the child. Nevertheless, Kaluli children become proficient users of their language within developmental norms (Schieffelin & Ochs, 1983). Joint linguistic interactions between caregiver and child thus may not be essential to the emergence of language.

Linguistic exchanges with other interaction partners—fathers, siblings, peers, and others—may uniquely influence the child's eventual level of linguistic skill. For example, when fifteen-month-olds "converse" with their father, they experience more communication breakdowns than when they talk with their mother. Fathers more often request clarification, change the topic, or do not acknowledge the child's utterance after they fail to understand what she or he said (Tomasello, Conti-Ramsden, & Ewert, 1990). Thus, in communicating with fathers, children are challenged to make adjustments to maintain the interaction. Children also learn language by overhearing it on educational television (Wright et al., 2001), in conversations between mother and older siblings (Ashima-Takane, Goodz, & Derevensky, 1996), or even between two strangers (Akhtar, Jipson, & Callanan, 2001). Children are normally exposed to a rich and varied range of linguistic stimuli from different sources in the environment; many theorists believe this fact ensures that children will learn the details of linguistic structures that may not be present in the verbalizations of a single conversation partner, such as the mother (Gleitman, Newport, & Gleitman, 1984; Wexler, 1982).

Joint Attention and Language Development One of the most remarkable observations made in recent years is that young language learners are able to use subtle social cues to figure out which objects new words are labeling. Suppose an adult says, "Let's find the *gazzer*" and looks at an object, rejects it, and excitedly picks up another object without naming it. The infant assumes the second object is the *gazzer* (Tomasello, Strosberg, & Akhtar, 1996). Or suppose an adult and an infant are playing with several unfamiliar, unnamed objects; then the adult introduces a new object, saying, "Look, I see a *modi*!" without pointing to any object. Again, the infant assumes the newest object is the *modi* (Akhtar, Carpenter, & Tomasello, 1996). These studies demonstrate that infants have an impressive ability to interpret social cues in deciding how labels and objects match up. They also show that episodes of **joint attention**, those times in which child and caregiver share the same "psychological space," are important contexts for language acquisition. Many parents and infants tend to spend substantial time in these moments of mutual engagement. For example, parents of infants tend to label many objects, often in the context of joint book reading or the child's manifest interest in a particular object or person in her surroundings (Ninio & Bruner, 1978). A typical scenario goes like this: The infant turns his head, points, and maybe even coos as the family dog enters the room. The mother also turns and looks, and says "Doggie." These are precisely the conditions under which infants seem to remember the words that name objects (Masur, 1982).

Researchers have found that the amount of time infants spend in joint attention with their caregivers, whether in book reading or other contexts, is a strong predictor of their early language skills (Carpenter, Nagell, & Tomasello, 1998). According to Paul Bloom (2000), this evidence indicates that the child is actively seeking to find out what is on the minds of the adults with whom she is interacting—what their words refer to and what they are intending to communicate.

RESEARCH APPLIED TO PARENTING

Reading to Children

It was only a couple of months later that Chad began to say a few different words. But after that, his vocabulary expanded rapidly, and he started stringing words together. As she prepared her son's bed, Tanya marveled at the progress Chad was making. This was her favorite time of day. Every night, just before Chad was put to bed, Tanya would pull him up in her lap and take a picture book from the shelf. At first, she just pointed to and named things in the book, often encouraging Chad to participate by asking, "What's that?" As his vocabulary increased, Tanya elaborated on his answers and asked other questions: "What does the doggie say?" "Woof-woof!" squealed Chad, enjoying the ritual perhaps every bit as much as, maybe even more than, his mother.

The research findings discussed earlier show that how and how often parents speak to children can influence language development. One context in which mothers' speech tends to be particularly lavish is during book reading. Erika Hoff-Ginsberg (1991) found that, when mothers and two-year-olds were

joint attention Episodes in which the child and another individual share the same "psychological space" as they encounter experiences in the world.

reading books, mothers showed the greatest diversity in the vocabulary they used, the greatest complexity of syntax, and the highest rate of replies to their children compared with other contexts, such as mealtime or toy play. Other research has shown that the amount of time parents spent reading stories to their twenty-four-month-olds predicted the children's language ability up to two years later (Crain-Thoreson & Dale, 1992). As a result of such findings, many child development experts encourage parents to read to their young children.

Grover Whitehurst and his colleagues have developed a program called *dialogic reading* to stimulate language development in preschool children at risk for academic failure, but the general principles can be applied by any parent interested in promoting his or her child's language development. Here is some advice the researchers have developed for parents:

1. ***Ask what questions (such as "What is this?") to stimulate the child to speak.*** Avoid yes/no questions that require only brief answers.
2. ***Follow the child's answer with a question.*** Ask, for example, what shape or color an object has or what it is used for.
3. ***Repeat the child's utterance in the form of a recast.*** For example, follow "Cow" with "Yes, that's right, it's a cow." This gives the child feedback that she is correct.
4. ***If the child does not have an answer, provide a model and ask him to repeat.*** For example, say "That's a bottle. Can you say 'bottle'?"
5. ***Be generous with praise and encouragement.*** Make comments such as "Good talking" or "Nice job."
6. ***Be responsive to the child's interests.*** When the child expresses an interest in a picture or part of the story, follow her interest with encouragement to talk.
7. ***Have fun.*** Do not pressure the child; take turns with the child, and even make the activity a game.

Dialogic reading has been shown to increase language skills in children from different social classes when used by daycare teachers as well as parents (Arnold & Whitehurst, 1994). Of course, children learn language skills in many other contexts, such as mealtime conversations (Snow, 1993). Thus children whose parents do not read to them often are not necessarily fated to have poor language skills (Scarborough & Dobrich, 1993). Nonetheless, reading to children, even when they are as young as 8 months old, leads to desirable outcomes in language development (DeBaryshe, 1993; Karrass & Braungart-Rieker, 2005).

FOR ◆ YOUR ◆ REVIEW

- ◆ What kinds of phonological skills and preferences have researchers observed in infants?
- ◆ What are some of the features of infants' early vocalizations?
- ◆ How do infants use gestures as communication tools?
- ◆ What are the important features of children's language during the one-word stage?
- ◆ What are some of the individual and cultural variations in language acquisition that have been observed by researchers?
- ◆ Which features of social interactions help to explain language in infants? What parental activities can promote infants' language skills?

Chapter Recap

Summary of Developmental Themes

Nature & Nurture

How do nature and nurture interact in perception, cognition, and language development in infancy?

There are several indicators that, for humans, nature sets early predispositions to perceive, think, and develop language in certain ways. For example, young infants seem to understand the principle of solidity, the idea that one object cannot pass through the space occupied by another object. Although not everyone agrees, some researchers see a part for nature here. Infants also show an early sensitivity to phonemes and prosody in language. However, many of these abilities also seem to be nurtured within the context of interactions with caregivers.

Sociocultural Influence

How does the sociocultural context influence perception, cognition, and language development in infancy?

Piaget's theory emphasizes the universal cognitive attainments of all children, regardless of their cultural background. However, research has shown that the sociocultural context, the cornerstone of Vygotsky's theory, cannot be ignored. For example, cultures vary in the extent to which caregivers use parentese with their infants, a factor that may influence the rate of language acquisition.

Continuity/Discontinuity

Are perception, cognition, and language development during infancy continuous or discontinuous?

Piaget stressed stagelike attainments in thinking. However, others who have empirically reevaluated his work and who have studied perception and language make claims for more continuous changes in their focus on the underlying basic processes that contribute to development.

Risk/Resilience

What factors promote risk or resilience in perception, cognition, and language development during infancy?

One domain in which children frequently show striking differences is in the rate at which they achieve language milestones. The type of speech they experience from caregivers has been shown to predict advances versus delays in the acquisition of language.

Chapter Review

Perception

How early do infants see patterns and forms in the visual world? What is the externality effect?

Newborns do not examine visual patterns systematically and are often attracted to external features that show high contrast (the *externality effect*) or movement. Within a few months, they engage in more systematic exploration of visual arrays. Their perception of the unity and coherence of objects is enhanced by kinetic cues and prior experience with the stimuli.

What is the developmental course of infant perception of faces? When can an infant distinguish the faces of caregivers from the faces of others?

Some research suggests that a preference for facelike forms shows up as early as the newborn period. Infants show a clear preference for faces over other complex forms by two months of age. According to some evidence, infants can distinguish the caregiver's face a few days after birth.

How early and using what kinds of cues do infants perceive objects in their world?

Infants perceive objects as entities by at least three months of age. Kinetic cues seem to provide especially important information about the integrity of objects.

What is meant by the perception of biological motion?

In some experiments, the only visual information provided is points of light attached to the joints of a moving organism. Infants seem to distinguish these stimuli as different and unique as compared with random motions of points of light.

How early and using what kinds of cues do infants perceive depth? What evidence exists to indicate that its perception does not always produce appropriate responses to the dangers associated with depth?

Depth information is provided to infants by kinetic cues, the differential flow of optic information that derives from self-induced movement or as a result of movement among arrays in the visual field. It is also provided by *stereopsis*, fusing the two images delivered by each eye into a single image. At about five to seven months of age, infants begin to process depth provided by pictorial cues. Infants also show recognition of depth cues when they are placed on an apparatus called the *visual cliff*.

Why do developmental psychologists no longer believe the infant's visual world is simply a "blooming, buzzing confusion?"

Young infants do not respond to all visual stimuli with equal likelihood right from birth. The fact that they have preferences for some stimuli over others suggests that they are not bombarded with an array of visual information. In addition, perceptual development proceeds in an organized manner. For example, young infants tend to scan only the exteriors of stimuli and begin to explore the interiors of stimuli only as they mature.

What sound patterns do infants prefer to listen to?

Infants show a preference for listening to human speech and to songs delivered in a child-oriented style. They also prefer musical patterns that conform to acceptable phrasing.

What arguments exist for or against the view that infants possess an innate capacity to detect phonemes?

Young infants can detect *phonemes*, the basic unit of sound used to differentiate the meaning of words in languages. They also respond to them *categorically*. However, by the end of the first year, as a result of exposure to only a subset of these sounds, they often discriminate only those phonemes heard in their own language.

How does intermodal perception develop?

Intermodal perception is the ability to integrate information arising from more than one sensory modality. One current position holds that intermodal perception is possible at birth and that *perceptual differentiation*, the ability to identify information coming from specific senses, arises with experience. Some amodal properties of stimulation, such as temporal synchrony, may be highly salient to young infants and assist in their acquiring an understanding of the correlations that exist among the various sensory properties of objects and events.

What evidence exists to show that infants recognize the correlation between visual and auditory information as well as visual and tactile cues?

Infants will look at film sequences that correspond in tempo to sound tracks and at the face of the caregiver whose voice they hear on a speaker, indicating a recognition that certain sights go with particular sounds. Infants also show visual recognition of items they had previously put in their mouths, showing awareness of the correlation between visual and tactile cues.

Cognition

What are the infant's chief accomplishments during the sensorimotor stage according to Piaget? What is the primary basis for thought in this stage?

The chief feature of the *sensorimotor stage* is that thought *(cognition)* is based on action. Children develop *means-ends behavior*, separate the self from the external environment, and attain the *object concept*. The end of this stage is signaled by the child's ability to engage in deferred imitation, a form of representation skill.

What is the object concept? What are the stages of acquisition of this concept according to Piaget?

The *object concept* refers to the child's understanding that objects continue to exist even if they are not in view. Piaget described the following stages in the acquisition of object concept: up to three months, the infant will not search for a covered object; at about four months, the child will search for a partially covered object; at about eight months, the child will search for a completely covered object; at about twelve months, the child can follow visible displacements of the object; and at about eighteen months, the child can follow invisible displacements of an object.

What is the core knowledge hypothesis? What research findings support this position on infants' conceptual knowledge? What are the criticisms of this point of view?

The *core knowledge hypothesis* asserts that young infants possess early knowledge about the properties of objects, such as their solidity and the fact that they move in continuous paths. Supporting experiments show that infants look longer when impossible events, such as a ball rolling through a path occupied by a box, take place. However, other studies show that much older children have difficulty predicting the specific location of a ball rolling down an obstructed track.

What is the A-not-B error? How does Piaget account for this error? What are some other explanations for the occurrence of this behavior in infants?

The *A-not-B error* occurs when infants about seven to nine months of age see an object hidden in location A and then moved to location B. The typical response is to look for the object in location A. Piaget believes that the error occurs because infants are still guided by the sensorimotor scheme to look in location A. Others suggest that memory problems, the failure to inhibit the response to reach for location A, or the failure to update the representation of the events are responsible.

What principles guide infants' spatial understanding according to Piaget? Does research support his point of view?

Infants respond to spatial tasks based on egocentric frames of reference, according to Piaget. They determine an object's location in relation to their own body rather than in relation to some external object. Researchers have confirmed that, in the absence of strong external cues, infants do use egocentric frames of reference. However, when strong cues, such as color cues or distinctive landmarks, are made available, infants do not respond on an egocentric basis.

What changes have researchers observed in classification skills during infancy?

At age one year, infants classify objects on the basis of shared perceptual features. By age two, children classify on the basis of thematic relations and, to some extent, on the basis of taxonomic relations. These are all manifestations of infants' ability to understand and use *concepts*.

What kinds of numerical competencies do infants display?

Infants age six months and younger have been shown to detect differences in number with small-size sets. They also seem to detect the addition or subtraction of items to a set of stimuli.

What are the major features of recognition memory in infancy?

Infants are capable of recognizing stimuli after brief exposure to them and for long periods of time—even two weeks. *Recognition memory* can be disrupted in young infants, though, by changes in the context of the event. Even newborns have been shown to be capable of recognition memory. Recognition is one form of *explicit* (as opposed to *implicit*) *memory*.

What do studies employing the elicited imitation technique tell us about recall memory in infancy?

In *elicited imitation*, children must repeat a sequence of actions to which they had previously been exposed. By two years of age, children can remember a three-part sequence for a month or more after only one viewing of it, suggesting that they are capable of *recall*.

What major changes in the brain accompany developmental improvements in memory?

Changes in the temporal and prefrontal lobes seem to correspond to developmental improvements in memory.

When do infants first evidence the ability to engage in problem solving and transfer?

Children show evidence of problem solving by age twelve months, when they will perform several behaviors in sequence in order to achieve a goal. Once successful in a simple problem-solving task, they can transfer the solution to other situations which have the same goal sequence.

What are the central elements of Vygotsky's sociocultural theory as they apply to infancy?

Vygotsky stated that, in order to understand development, it is vital to understand the cultural context in which the child lives. He emphasized the concept of *scaffolding*, the temporary support for problem solving provided to the child by caregivers and teachers. For the infant, this could involve the caregiver's defining the problem, demonstrating a solution, and providing motivation to succeed. As the infant becomes more competent, this support is withdrawn.

What is the significance of the phenomenon of intersubjectivity?

Intersubjectivity refers to the mutual attention and shared communication that take place between child and caregiver. These may be opportune times for children to learn language and also to develop emotionally and cognitively.

LANGUAGE

What kinds of phonological skills and preferences have researchers observed in infants?

Newborns show a tendency to respond to language as a unique auditory stimulus. Young infants detect phonemes and vowel sounds from a variety of languages but show a decline in this ability by the second half of the first year. Infants show an early sensitivity to the *prosody*, patterns of intonation, stress, and rhythm that mothers around the world include in their speech to young children. Children's sensitivity to rhythmic properties of language helps them to differentiate their native language from others and possibly to detect the presence of specific words in a stream of speech. The focus of language development during infancy is on mastering *phonology* and some aspects of *semantics*.

What are some of the features of infants' early vocalizations?

Infants typically *coo* at six to eight weeks, *babble* at three to six months, and produce syllablelike *canonical babbling* at seven months.

How do infants use gestures as communication tools?

They might use a *protodeclarative communication* to call attention to an object or a *protoimperative communication* to make a request. Sometimes children's gestures symbolize objects; later in development, gestures may accompany verbalization in order to elaborate a point.

What are the important features of children's language during the one-word stage?

By one year of age, most children are speaking one-word utterances, usually *nominals*, or nouns. At about eighteen months or so, children may show a particularly rapid phase of growth in word acquisition called the *vocabulary spurt*.

At the earlier stages of word learning, children may restrict their use of some words to particular contexts (*underextension*) or apply them to too broad a category (*overextension*). Children comprehend word meanings much earlier than they are able to produce words. Their *receptive language* exceeds their *productive language*. Labels for verbs are harder for children to understand than labels for nouns.

What are some of the individual and cultural variations in language acquisition that have been observed by researchers?

Some children's early speech is *referential*; it includes mostly nominals. Other children are *expressive*; they use words with social functions. Fairly substantial individual differences also occur for the rate of language acquisition. Culture, too, can have an influence on the types of words children produce in the early stages of acquisition. For example, children from some Asian cultures learn verbs before they learn nouns. Despite these variations, the patterns of language development across children are so regular that they are used as one way to assess the possibility of *developmental delay*.

Which features of social interactions help to explain language in infants? What parental activities can promote infants' language skills?

Several characteristics of caregiver-child speech, called *motherese* or *parentese*, facilitate development. Specific techniques include *turn taking*, *turnabouts*, *recasts*, and *expansions*. The amount and content of maternal speech to children, especially in episodes of *joint attention*, predict the rate and form of children's language acquisition. Reading to children is an excellent way to promote language skills.

Key Terms and Concepts

A-not-B error (p. 205)
babbling (p. 220)
canonical babbling (p. 220)
categorical perception (p. 197)
cognition (p. 189)
concepts (p. 208)
cooing (p. 220)
core knowledge hypothesis (p. 205)
developmental delay (p. 226)
elicited imitation (p. 212)
expansion (p. 227)
explicit memory (p. 210)
expressive style (p. 224)
externality effect (p. 190)
implicit memory (p. 210)
intermodal perception (p. 198)
intersubjectivity (p. 216)
joint attention (p. 230)
means-ends behavior (p. 200)
motherese (parentese) (p. 218)
nominal (p. 223)
object concept (p. 202)
overextension (p. 224)
perceptual differentiation (p. 198)
phoneme (p. 197)
phonology (p. 217)
productive language (p. 224)
prosody (p. 218)
protodeclarative communication (p. 220)
protoimperative communication (p. 220)
recall memory (p. 210)
recast (p. 227)
receptive language (p. 224)
recognition memory (p. 210)
referential style (p. 224)
scaffolding (p. 215)
semantics (p. 217)
sensorimotor stage (p. 200)
stereopsis (p. 194)
turn taking (p. 227)
turnabout (p. 227)
underextension (p. 224)
visual cliff (p. 194)
vocabulary spurt (p. 223)

7 Social and Emotional Development

It's a quiet time on Sunday morning, just after a big breakfast, and Cindy admires her eight-month-old son Michael as he sits in his infant seat. He is looking at her so intently, raising his eyebrows a bit and scanning her face, gurgling contentedly. Suddenly the phone rings. Michael falls silent and opens his eyes wide. Cindy raises her eyebrows into two big arches and opens her mouth, making an exaggerated "Oohh" sound, suggesting surprise. Her baby eyes her with fascination, chortles, then smiles broadly. Cindy smiles back, chuckles, and says, "Must be Grandma calling to see how you are. Let me answer the phone, okay, honey?" She touches Michael affectionately under the chin as she gets up to reach for the phone. The baby lets out a shriek of delight and smiles again. Cindy can't help but laugh at the antics of her young son.

KEY THEMES in Social and Emotional Development

NATURE & NURTURE How do nature and nurture interact in social and emotional development in infancy?

SOCIOCULTURAL INFLUENCE How does the sociocultural context influence social and emotional development in infancy?

CONTINUITY/DISCONTINUITY Are social and emotional development in infancy continuous or discontinuous?

INTERACTION AMONG DOMAINS How do social and emotional development during infancy interact with other domains of development?

RISK/RESILIENCE What factors promote risk or resilience in social and emotional development during infancy?

This scene, in all its simplicity, is a typical one in many families. Babies and caregivers revel in each other's company, and although the infant cannot yet speak, he participates fully in the interaction in nonverbal ways. In this case, the communication relies less on language than on both overt and subtle nuances in facial expressions and sounds that communicate emotional states. Some have characterized the back-and-forth nature of this exchange as a well-choreographed "waltz" wherein each partner looks to the other for cues about what to do next, so that the interaction proceeds smoothly and enjoyably. The episode underscores that, even in the first year of life, infants are distinctly social beings, able to initiate as well as respond in the dynamic social exchanges that are emblematic of humans in so many cultures.

In this chapter, we focus on the social and emotional worlds of human infants. We see how infants convey and understand emotions as personal expressions of moods or feeling states. Given the social dimension of emotions, we will also investigate the role they play in the child's relationships with others, specifically in the special "attachments" that emerge between child and caregivers. What is the psychological significance of these early emotional bonds, and how do they influence the child's later development? Finally, we will take a brief glimpse at other dimensions of the infant's growing social competence—in particular, her understanding of "self," other individuals, and social groups.

EMOTIONS IN INFANCY

The interaction between Cindy and her infant suggests that emotions play a key role in social exchanges between infants and adults. This may not always be the case, as illustrated by the Gusii of Kenya. The Gusii culture places great emphasis on suppressing intense emotions, probably to maintain harmony in the small, tribal living units characteristic of that group. Consequently, mothers maintain a bland, neutral expression when interacting with their infants and try to inhibit strong shows of emotion in their children (Dixon et al., 1981). These differing cultural norms are reflected in the parenting styles of each culture and the behaviors children eventually display. At the same time, however, research with young infants in many other cultures suggests that emotions are an integral part of the social lives of infants and their caregivers.

KEY THEME
SOCIOCULTURAL INFLUENCE

Do infants exhibit the full range of emotions that we see in adults, or does a developmental progression occur in the types of emotions children display? Do children change in their ability to understand emotions in themselves and others, to read facial expressions and interpret them, to know the circumstances that lead positive and negative emotions to arise, and to appreciate the consequences of different emotions? These are just a few of the questions with which we begin.

WHAT ARE EMOTIONS?

Emotions are a complex set of behaviors produced in response to some external or internal event, or elicitor, which serve to motivate and direct thoughts and actions.

emotion Complex behavior involving physiological, expressive, and experiential components produced in response to some internal or external event.

Emotions include several components. First, they have a *physiological* component, involving changes in autonomic nervous system activities, such as respiration and heart rate. Fear or anxiety, for example, may be accompanied by more rapid breathing, increased heart rate and blood pressure, and perspiration. Second, emotions include an *expressive* component, usually a facial display that signals the emotion. Smiles, grimaces, cries, and laughter overtly express a person's emotional state. Third, emotions have an *experiential* component, the subjective feeling or cognitive judgment of having an emotion (Izard, Kagan, & Zajonc, 1984; Sroufe, 1996).

KEY THEME
INTERACTION AMONG DOMAINS

Given the complex nature of emotions, measuring them becomes an important issue for researchers because all three dimensions—physiological, expressive, and experiential—must be considered. One approach is to record changes in physiological functions, such as heart rate (acceleration or deceleration), heart rate variability (the individual's basic heart rate pattern), or electroencephalogram (EEG) patterns showing brain activity as affective stimuli are presented (Fox, 1991; Fox & Davidson, 1986). Newer technologies, such as *positron emission tomography (PET)* and *functional magnetic resonance imaging (fMRI)*, are also being used to track the activities of the brain as emotions are being experienced (Cacioppo & Gardner, 1999). Another strategy is to conduct fine-grained analyses of the child's facial expressions or vocalizations. Tiny movements of the muscles in the brow, eye, and mouth regions produce the facial configurations associated with joy, sadness, anger, and other emotions (Izard & Dougherty, 1982). Similarly, the frequency, loudness, duration, and sound patterns of the child's vocalizations indicate emotion (Papoušek, Papoušek, & Koester, 1986). Often, facial expressions, body movements, and vocalizations function as an ensemble of emotion indicators; for example, a facial expression of anger, raising arms upward, and crying combine to signal "pick me up" (Weinberg & Tronick, 1994). Finally, as the child grows older, her interpretations of her own and others' emotions can be assessed through the use of self-report measures ("Tell me how often you felt cheerful in the last week") and tasks requiring the child to label, match, or produce emotional expressions ("Tell me how the person in this picture feels" or "Show me the person who feels sad").

Although each methodological approach has helped to illuminate aspects of the child's emotional life, researchers must be cautious when interpreting their data. When physiological changes, such as decelerated heart rate, occur as the infant watches a lively segment of "Sesame Street," is he experiencing interest or surprise? The emotion that corresponds to a specific reaction of the nervous system is not always clear. Likewise, when the infant shows an overt emotional expression, such as crying, is he signaling an internal emotional state of sadness or fear? Despite these methodological difficulties, researchers have learned a good deal about emotional development in the last two decades.

Theoretical Perspectives on Emotional Development

Are human emotions biologically based, preprogrammed responses to specific environmental stimuli, or are they the products of the myriad learning experiences that accumulate over the course of infancy and childhood? Do emotions function in neat, discrete packages—anger being separate from sadness and fear? Or are different emotions simply points on a continuum of positive or negative arousal? These are some of the questions addressed by contemporary perspectives on emotion.

KEY THEME
NATURE & NURTURE

Biologically Based Explanations The main champions of a strong biological view of emotions are Paul Ekman and Carroll Izard. After studying people in various cultures, Ekman (1972, 1973) concluded that there are universal facial expressions for certain basic emotions that are interpreted in similar ways across cultures. Ekman showed photographs of six faces, each depicting a particular emotion—happiness, sadness, anger, fear, surprise, or disgust—to participants in the United States, Japan,

Chile, Brazil, and Argentina. As they looked at each photograph, participants were asked to identify the emotion displayed. Ekman (1972) found a high degree of accuracy across cultures as to which emotions were represented. A recent meta-analysis of ninety-seven studies confirms what Ekman first reported—that individuals from a wide variety of cultures correctly recognize fundamental emotions, showing the highest degree of accuracy for happiness (Elfenbein & Ambady, 2002).

Similarly, Izard believes that, because certain emotional expressions are displayed by very young infants, they are necessarily innate and have distinct adaptive value (Izard, 1978; Izard & Malatesta, 1987). When the newborn infant tastes a bitter substance, such as quinine, for example, she will pull up her upper lip, wrinkle her nose, and squint her eyes, indicating she has detected the unpleasant stimulus. No learning is necessary to produce this reaction of disgust. The caregiver observing this signal might respond by removing a potentially harmful substance from the baby's mouth, thereby ensuring her well-being. The experience of emotion, Izard states, is the automatic product of the internal sensory feedback the individual receives from making the facial expression; wrinkling the face produces the feeling of disgust. Izard also maintains that, once an emotion is activated, it in turn motivates the individual to act. The experience of disgust, in other words, may lead the baby to spit out the distasteful substance. According to Izard and his colleagues, infants show a small set of discrete emotions, such as joy, anger, and fear, that function independently of one another. With development, these emotions become more interrelated and connected to cognition (Ackerman, Abe, & Izard, 1998). Furthermore, different patterns of expressing emotions eventually become organized as personality traits that can vary across individuals (Izard & Ackerman, 2000).

KEY THEME
INTERACTION AMONG DOMAINS

Both Ekman and Izard acknowledge that learning may play a role in emotional development, especially as children learn to control and regulate their emotions. They maintain, however, that the role of biological factors is paramount and that emotions originate in the genetic blueprints with which the child begins life.

A Cognitive-Socialization Explanation Michael Lewis and Linda Michalson (1983) have provided an alternative account of the emotional life of the child, one that emphasizes the cognitive activities involved in emotional experiences. According to these theorists, an environmental event does not directly produce an emotional expression. Instead, the child relies on cognitive processes to assess the event, how it compares with past events, and the social rules surrounding the event. Suppose, for example, the child encounters a barking dog. Whether he cries with fear or smiles at the noisy animal depends on his past experiences with dogs (has he ever been bitten?) and on what parents and others have instructed him to believe about animals ("Barking dogs will bite—stay away!" or "Some dogs get excited when they want to play—it's okay"). Cognitive processes thus act as *mediators*, or mental events that bridge the gap between environmental stimuli and the response the individual ultimately expresses. This conceptualization accounts for individual differences in emotional reactions when the same event produces different responses from two people.

KEY THEME
INTERACTION AMONG DOMAINS

According to Lewis and Michalson, socialization plays an important role in shaping the time and the manner in which emotions are displayed. Children in our culture learn that it is appropriate to feel happy at birthday parties and sad when a friend's grandmother dies, and that a smiling face and a sad face should be made under these respective circumstances. Socialization also guides the way emotions are managed. Young children in many cultures, for example, learn to inhibit expressions of fear and anger. Finally, socialization directs the way children label and interpret emotions. When the young child cries due to a physical injury and the parent says, "That hurts, doesn't it?" the interpretation provides pain as the reason for the tears. When crying is the response to the collapse of a tower of toy blocks, the parent may provide a different interpretation for the child, such as "That's frustrating." These kinds of communications serve as an important vehicle by which children learn how to interpret their own emotional states.

KEY THEME
NATURE & NURTURE

KEY THEME
NATURE & NURTURE

Emotion as Part of a Social Context For social-contextual theorists, such as Joseph Campos and Carol Saarni (Campos et al., 1994; Saarni, 1999; Saarni, Mumme, & Campos, 1998), emotions are deeply and inextricably intertwined with the social environment. Children's understanding of their own and others' emotions and how they regulate their emotional states arise from the crossroads of personal goals and social interactions with others. What the child wants and desires, as well as the reactions of those in the social environment, create the "mix" for experiences of emotions. Emotions serve to motivate the individual toward particular social actions. For example, the emotion of "pride" can be the outcome of glowing comments from the parents after a child produces a colorful drawing. For that same child, the experience of pride will likely motivate her to share a newly crafted picture with a visiting grandmother. Emotions also arise when the emotions of others are observed (a mother shows great fear at the sound of thunder) or when one remembers emotional experiences from the past.

Rather than describing discrete emotions, such as joy or fear, contextual theorists emphasize the positive or negative tone of emotions and their intensity. Emotions are not conceptualized as *entities* but instead are viewed as *processes* embedded in social interactions (Barrett, 1998). In other words, it is of paramount importance to understand how they work or function. According to this perspective, considerable attention is necessarily given to the process of socialization and to the role of culture. How do families help children to regulate their emotions, to control, for example, angry outbursts or overt expressions of fear? How do different cultures conceptualize emotions, and what emotional styles do they emphasize: being expressive or more restrained, for example? These are the types of research questions that are motivated by this important perspective on emotional development.

FOR • YOUR • REVIEW

- What are the three components of emotions?
- What are the different ways in which researchers measure emotions?
- What are the main ways in which biological, cognitive-socialization, and social-contextual theories of emotion differ from one another?

EARLY EMOTIONAL DEVELOPMENT

Much of the groundwork for emotional development occurs during the first year or so of life. Parents and young infants frequently rely on nonverbal signals laden with emotional overtones to communicate with one another, as we saw with Cindy and Michael at the start of this chapter. Just what behaviors are infants capable of showing and "reading"?

Emotional Expression in Infancy Even infants only a few days or weeks old are capable of producing the facial expressions associated with several emotions, including interest, distress, disgust, joy, sadness, anger, and surprise (Field et al., 1982; Izard, 1978; Izard et al., 1995). By seven months of age, the infant has added expressions of fear to his repertoire (Izard et al., 1980). The fact that these discrete facial expressions appear so early in infancy, before much learning can have taken place, provides strong support for the idea that emotional expressions are to some extent biologically determined. These emotions are often called **basic** (or **primary**) **emotions**.

KEY THEME
NATURE & NURTURE

basic (primary) emotion Emotion, such as joy, sadness, or surprise, that appears early in infancy and seems to have a biological foundation.

Although even the earliest displays of basic emotions are usually readily recognized by adults, their form and the conditions that elicit them may change over the first few months. Two important emotional expressions in infancy, smiling and crying, demonstrate these changes. The smile is one of the most captivating and irresistible infant behaviors. In the newborn this behavior occurs primarily during the state of REM sleep, when dreaming is thought to occur, in bursts of several smiles in succession (Emde & Koenig, 1969). The mouth stretches sideways and up, producing a simple version of the smile. Although many hypotheses attempt to explain why very young infants produce this facial gesture (including the popular but mistaken notion that "gas" is responsible), the most consistent finding is that neonates smile when they experience a shift in physiological arousal state, such as when they fall asleep or become drowsy (Wolff, 1987). At approximately two weeks of age, the form of the smile changes. After the initial broadening of the lips, the corners of the lips retract even farther (with the mouth often opening), the cheek muscles contract, and the skin around the eyes wrinkles (Messinger, Fogel, & Dickson, 1999). Now the infant smiles during states of wakefulness, sometimes in response to familiar voices and sounds, sweet tastes, and pleasant food odors (Fogel, 1982; Steiner, 1979). By three months of age, smiles increase in frequency, and full-blown smiles—with open mouth and cheeks raised—become increasingly reserved for interactions in which the infant looks at a smiling mother (Messinger, Fogel, & Dickson, 2001). Because the "social smile" plays a substantial role in initiating and maintaining interactions between the infant and significant adults in her life, it is considered an important milestone in infant development. The shift from smiling as a reflexlike behavior to a controlled, voluntary response parallels the increasing maturation of the cerebral cortex, which is responsible for higher-order mental processes and deliberate, goal-directed behaviors.

Crying is another common way in which infants express emotion. Newborn babies cry for a variety of reasons, but primarily because they are hungry, cold, wet, in pain, or disturbed out of their sleep. The nature of the baby's distress is often reflected in the type of cry she emits. In an extensive study of eighteen infants observed in their home, Peter Wolff (1969) identified three patterns of crying. The first is the *basic* (or hungry) *cry*, a rhythmical sequence consisting of a vocalization, a pause, an intake of air, and another pause. The second is the *angry cry*, in which extra air is forced through the vocal cords during the vocalization segment of the basic cry. Finally, in the *pain cry*, the infant produces a long vocalization followed by an even longer silence as he holds his breath and then gasps.

Like smiling, crying is a response that promotes contact between the infant and the caregiver. Mothers usually react to their young infants' cries promptly, especially an angry or a pain cry, and when they do, infants actually cry less in succeeding weeks and months (Bell & Ainsworth, 1972; Wolff, 1969). Usually the first order of business is to make sure the infant's physical needs are met. Other effective techniques for soothing the crying infant include providing a pacifier, swaddling with a blanket, and tapping some part of his body, that is, providing some form of rhythmic or continuous stimulation (Brackbill, 1975). Picking up the baby and holding her on one's shoulder is also soothing, probably because this act provides the infant with a broad range of stimulation that distracts her from crying (Korner, 1972).

By the time the infant is about two months of age, the causes of crying are no longer purely physiological. An infant might cry when the caregiver puts him down in his crib or when a favorite toy is removed from his grasp. At about this time, a new type of cry emerges: the *fussy* or *irregular cry*, which varies in intensity, is less rhythmical, and seems to function as a demand for particular objects or actions. At eight months of age, the infant will pause in crying to see if the mother or other adults are receiving the message (Bruner, 1983). As the infant gains more voluntary control over his vocalizations, crying patterns become even more varied and controlled, and are displayed in a wider range of situations to signal an assortment of messages. Individual differences in the crying patterns of some infants are useful in diagnosing developmental abnormalities. Malnourished infants, for example, display more variability in the pitch of their cries, whereas children who have suffered oxygen deprivation produce shorter, higher-pitched cries (Michelsson, Sirvio, & Wasz-Hockert, 1977; Zeskind, 1981).

Recognizing Others' Emotions Besides producing expressions themselves, infants are capable of discriminating and responding to emotional displays in others. Several remarkable studies conducted by Tiffany Field and her colleagues suggest that three-day-old infants are capable of imitating the facial expressions for happiness, surprise, and sadness when an adult models these expressions (Field et al., 1982, 1983).

Infants widened their eyes and opened their mouth on "surprise" trials, drew back their lips on "happiness" trials, and tightened their mouth and furrowed their brow on "sadness" trials (see Figure 7.1). Although some researchers offer alternative explanations for these findings, many believe that infants have an early sensitivity to emotional expressions in others. In addition, researchers have shown that, by three to four months of age, infants are able to distinguish among several expressions, particularly happiness when it is juxtaposed with anger, surprise, or sadness (LaBarbera et al., 1976; Young-Browne, Rosenfeld, & Horowitz, 1977). Interestingly, infants tend to look less at sad faces and more at angry ones (Montague & Walker-Andrews, 2001).

Do infants derive meaning from the facial expressions they observe in others, or do they simply respond to changes in isolated facial features that contribute to these expressions (such as the upward curve of the mouth in a smile)? In the latter half of the first year, a phenomenon called **social referencing** suggests an infant's ability to interpret facial expressions. If infants are placed in an unfamiliar situation or encounter a strange object and are uncertain how to respond, they often will look to their caregivers for cues. The facial expression the caregiver displays typically will influence the infant's own emotional response and subsequent actions. For example, in one study, twelve-month-olds were placed on the shallow side of the visual cliff apparatus, which is used to assess the perception of depth. They were coaxed to move toward the place on the cliff where the surface appears to drop off. At this point, half of the participants' mothers posed a happy expression and the other half exhibited fear. Of the infants whose mothers smiled, 74 percent crossed the deep side of the cliff. In contrast, none of the infants whose mothers showed fear crossed the deep side. Moreover, these babies tended to produce fearful expressions on their own face (Sorce et al., 1985). Thus the infants not only "read" the expression they saw on their mothers' faces but also correctly interpreted its message.

KEY THEME
INTERACTION AMONG DOMAINS

Social referencing is a clear sign of the distinctly *interactive* nature of emotions. It is also a sign that infants begin to appreciate the referential nature of communication as well as the intentions of others. When infants in one study heard an experimenter say "Eew!" in a strong negative tone while looking at a toy, they were less likely to approach it than if she said "Nice!" However, if the experimenter made any of these comments while out of view, infants did not make use of the emotional tones in her messages (Moses et al., 2001). At twelve months of age, infants even pick up on similar emotional cues provided by an adult actress on television (Mumme & Fernald, 2003). Infants seem to appreciate that, by expressing emotions—but specifically in a social context—individuals intend to communicate something about objects, people, or events. In that sense, social referencing is linked to advances in cognition. It is probably also an early indication of the child's internalization of the views and values of parents, a process that will continue throughout the early years of childhood (Desrochers et al., 1994; Kochanska, 1994).

Emotions as Regulators of Social Interactions Given infants' ability to express and identify emotions in the context of interactions with others, developmental psychologists now recognize that emotions serve an important function in regulating and modulating early social exchanges. This dynamic process begins at about two or three months of age, when the infant looks into the adult's eyes and produces a "social smile" or a cry, to which the adult responds. The adult vocalization or facial expression, in turn, often precipitates another emotional response from the infant. Such episodes of reciprocal, mutually engaging cycles of caregiver-child behaviors are called **interactive synchrony**. These symmetrical interactions increase noticeably over the first six months of life (Hsu & Fogel, 2003). During the child's first year, interactive synchrony characterizes about 30 percent of face-to-face interactions between infant and caregiver (Tronick & Cohn, 1989).

social referencing Looking to another individual for emotional cues in interpreting a strange or ambiguous event.

interactive synchrony Reciprocal, mutually engaging cycles of caregiver-child behaviors.

At about three months, primary caregivers typically assume the major responsibility for guiding interactions, producing repetitions of exaggerated faces and vocalizations to which the infant pays rapt attention (Stern, 1974). Infants without

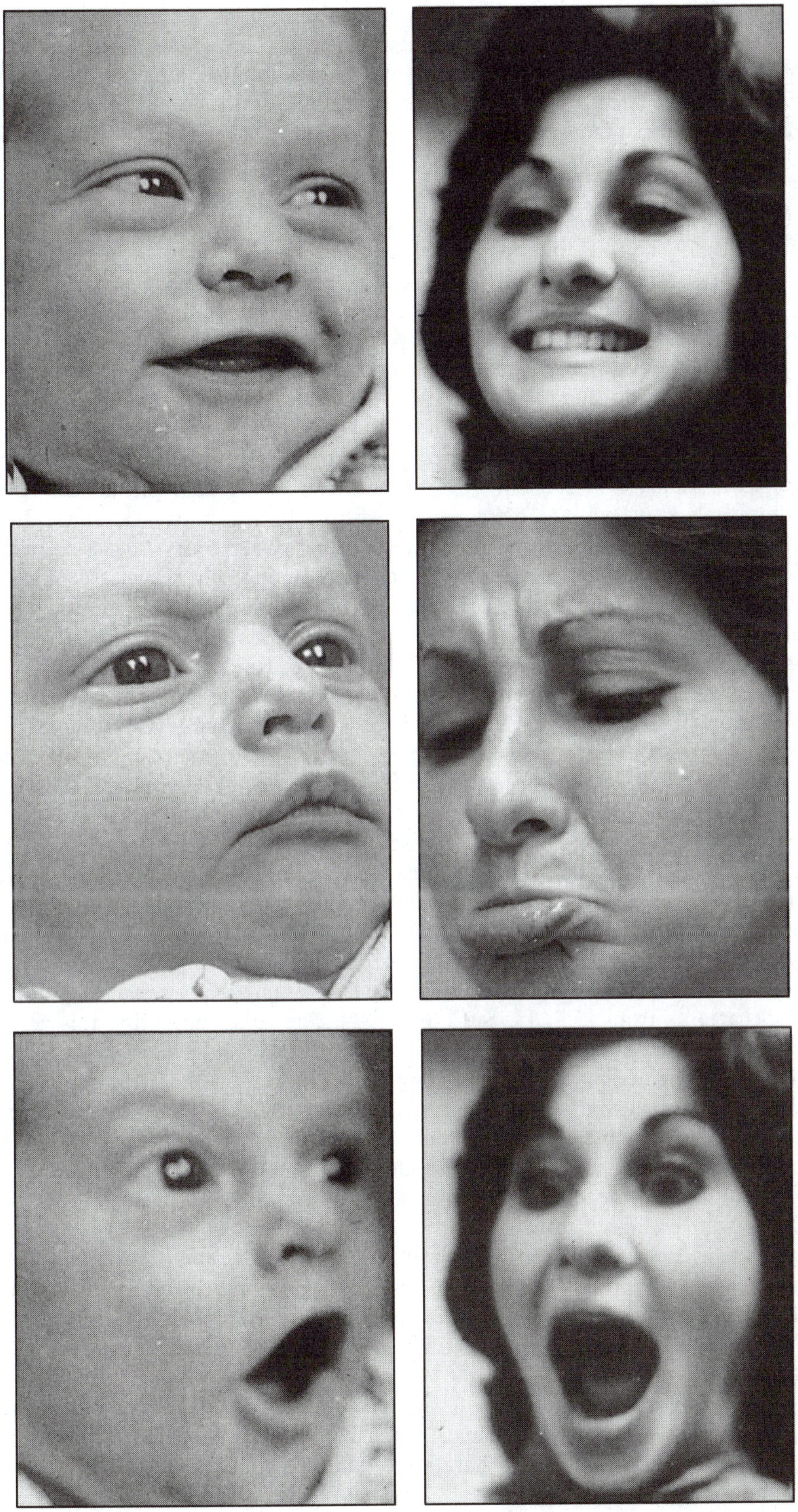

FIGURE 7.1

Infants' Imitation of Facial Expressions

According to some research, three-day-old infants are capable of imitating expressions for happiness (top), sadness (middle), and surprise (bottom) when they were modeled by an adult. These emotions are categorized as *basic emotions*.

doubt notice and react to their mother's expressive displays. They especially attend when the mother's actions are contingent on their own behaviors; that is, when the mother's smile or vocalization directly follows the infant's behavior (Bigelow & DeCoste, 2003). When mothers do not return a smile, however, but show a *still-face* or a neutral pose, infants respond with a quizzical or sober look, avert their gaze, and touch themselves or some nearby object (Toda & Fogel, 1993; Tronick et al., 1978). By about six to nine months of age, infants more clearly take the initiative; their displays of positive affect now more often precede their mother's (Cohn & Tronick, 1987). Thus, throughout early infancy, the child becomes an increasingly active partner in an emotionally toned, interactive "duet" with the caregiver.

But what about the other 70 percent of the time, when infant-caregiver interactions are *asynchronous*, or uncoordinated with each other? Edward Tronick and his colleagues believe that these episodes, which constitute the majority of infant-caregiver relations, play an equally important part in normal emotional development. A common occurrence after a sequence in which infant and caregiver are not coordinated is the infant's attempt to repair the "interactive error." When the mother looks sad, for example, the infant's subsequent gaze aversion or crying encourages the mother to modify her own behavior, and frequently she does (Cohn & Tronick, 1983). If the mother has made a still-face and then reverts back to a responsive social interaction style, the infant shows greater ability to rebound emotionally (Haley & Stansbury, 2003). Thus episodes of asynchrony give infants opportunities to learn about the rules of interaction and, in cases in which they are able to repair an interaction, give them a sense of mastery or control over their environment (Tronick & Cohn, 1989).

KEY THEME
RISK/RESILIENCE

Affective exchanges between infant and caregiver lay the groundwork for social behavior and emotional dispositions at later ages. Researchers have observed that depressed mothers tend to be less positive in face-to-face interactions with their infants (Campbell, Cohn, & Meyers, 1995). Perhaps as a consequence, infants of clinically depressed mothers express a good deal of negative affect in face-to-face interactions (Cohn et al., 1986). They tend to express more sadness and anger, and their negative affect extends to other adults who are not depressed (Field, 1995; Field et al., 1988; Pickens & Field, 1993). These infants also show brain wave patterns similar to those of depressed adults (Dawson, 1994; Field et al., 1995). Thus the dominance of negative emotions during early mother-child interactions culminates in a general mood or background emotional state that apparently pervades the child's own behaviors (Tronick, Ricks, & Cohn, 1982). The child may bring this general affective tone to new situations; for example, an anxious child is likely to interpret a new event as frightening, whereas a happy child may react with curiosity.

Finally, the nature of the affective exchanges between mother and child influences the strength of the emotional bond, or *attachment*, between them. Infants who attempt to elicit responses from their mother by smiling, vocalizing, or crying at six months of age are more likely to have healthy attachments at age one year than children who withdraw from such interactions (Tronick et al., 1982); depressed mothers tend to have children with poorer-quality attachments (Teti et al., 1995). As is discussed later in this chapter, healthy attachments, in turn, are correlated with many other positive developmental outcomes in social and cognitive functioning. Hence the tone of these early interactions is a crucial facet of child development.

Regulating One's Own Emotions An important developmental accomplishment is the child's ability to regulate or manage his or her own emotions. Behaviors such as calming down after getting angry have important repercussions for the child's social relationships and perhaps even mental health (Cicchetti, Ackerman, & Izard, 1995). In fact, much of the development of emotion that we have described—expressing, recognizing, and understanding emotions, as well as socialization experiences regarding emotions—culminates in the ability to regulate one's affective state (Denham, 1998).

Emotion regulation has its earliest roots in infancy. In general, infants rely on caregivers to help them regulate their emotions through carrying, rocking, or soft vocalizations (Jahromi, Putnam, & Stifter, 2004). Distraction also helps, at least in the short run (Harman, Rothbart, & Posner, 1997). Even young babies, however, make some attempts to regulate their own affective states, whether it be by sucking on a pacifier, by looking away if they become too aroused, or even by falling asleep (Kopp, 1989; Walden & Smith, 1997). Sometimes, specific emotions seem to be linked to specific regulatory behaviors. For example, infants who experience fear when seeing an unpredictable mechanical toy withdraw from the stimulus or look at the mother. In contrast, when frustrated and angered by the removal of an attractive toy, infants distract themselves or try to approach the toy (Buss & Goldsmith, 1998).

FOR • YOUR • REVIEW

- What are some of the basic emotions that researchers have observed in young infants?
- What are some of the changes in crying and smiling that occur during infancy?
- Why is the emergence of social referencing so significant in the course of emotional development?
- What are the dynamics of interactive synchrony between infant and caregiver? What is the significance of these types of interactions for the infant's development?
- What strategies do infants typically use to regulate their emotional states?

TEMPERAMENT

Emotions are not just transitory states of feeling and expression; often we discern a child's more enduring emotional mood and describe her personality as "cheerful" or "hostile," "easygoing" or "irritable." As we saw in the chapter titled "Genetics and Heredity," researchers have found that infants and children vary in **temperament**, a style of behavioral functioning that encompasses the intensity of expression of moods, distractibility, adaptability, and persistence. Individual differences among infants in these qualities often remain relatively stable over time and across different situations (Rothbart & Bates, 2006).

Patterns of Temperament Stella Chess and Alexander Thomas (1982, 1990, 1991) have offered one conceptualization of temperament, identifying three basic patterns that many children display:

- The *easy* child generally has positive moods, regular body functions, a low to moderate energy level in responses, and a positive approach to new situations. This child establishes regular feeding and sleeping schedules right from early infancy and adapts quickly to new routines, people, and places.
- The *difficult* child is often in a negative mood, has irregular body functions, shows high-intensity reactions, withdraws from new stimuli, and is slow to adapt to new situations. The difficult child sleeps and eats on an unpredictable schedule, cries a good deal (and loudly), and has trouble adjusting to new routines.
- The *slow-to-warm-up* child is somewhat negative in mood, has a low level of activity and intensity of reaction, and withdraws from new stimuli. However, with repeated exposure to new experiences, she or he begins to show interest and involvement.

Chess and Thomas (1991) note that children with different temperaments will evoke different patterns of reactions from their parents, teachers, and peers. "Easy" children usually elicit the most positive reactions from others, whereas children from the other two temperament categories typically draw more negative reactions.

temperament Stable, early-appearing constellation of individual personality attributes believed to have a hereditary basis; includes sociability, emotionality, and activity level.

Later in life, children with "easy" temperaments may adjust more readily to important transitions, such as the start of school or making new friends. An important dimension of development, say Chess and Thomas, is the "goodness of fit" between the child's temperament and the demands placed on the child by the environment, specifically by parents, teachers, peers, and others.

Other researchers have proposed alternative descriptions of temperament types. For example, Jerome Kagan and his colleagues (Kagan, 1994; Kagan, Reznick, & Snidman, 1988) noted that some infants tend to show wariness and fearfulness when they encounter unfamiliar people, objects, or events, and others react with interest, spontaneity, and sociability. Longitudinal studies show that both the first group, called *inhibited*, and the second, called *uninhibited*, tend to maintain their distinctive style from infancy through adolescence.

Mary Rothbart and her colleagues (Rothbart, 1986; Rothbart, Derryberry, & Posner, 1994) have offered another increasingly popular description of temperament. Infants are thought to differ in terms of *reactivity*, or how easily the child becomes aroused in response to events in the environment. Some children react quickly and intensely, whereas others are slower to react and are generally calmer. A second dimension of temperament in this model is the ability to *regulate the self*, to adjust one's level of arousal and to soothe oneself. Some children are better able than others to shift their attention or to inhibit behaviors in order to bring themselves back to a calm state.

KEY THEME
SOCIOCULTURAL INFLUENCE

One caution about categorizing infant styles concerns the cross-cultural dimensions of temperament. Although the preceding categories may capture individual differences in the emotional styles of Western infants, they do not necessarily apply to children from other cultures. For example, when Japanese mothers were asked to describe the behavioral styles of their infants, the "easy/difficult" dimension appeared in their responses, but so did unique qualities such as "self-assertiveness" (for instance, a tendency to like pleasant sounds, enjoy exercising the body, and feed quickly) (Shwalb, Shwalb, & Shoji, 1994). Cultural differences in parental expectations regarding children's temperament may, in turn, lead to differences in parenting styles that circle back to influence the child's general style of emotional responding to people and objects.

KEY THEME
NATURE & NURTURE

Biological Bases of Temperament There are good reasons to believe that individual differences in temperament are rooted in biology. For example, children in Kagan's two temperament categories show different profiles of physiological responsiveness. Inhibited children show more pronounced cardiac reactions, a greater rise in blood pressure when changing from a sitting to a standing position, and more tension in skeletal muscles compared with uninhibited children. Kagan and his colleagues postulate that differential responsiveness in the limbic system, the portion of the brain below the cortex that controls emotions, may lie at the root of temperament differences (Kagan, Snidman, & Arcus, 1993).

Infants who are prone to be irritable also show distinct patterns of brain wave functioning. In one study, infants were observed as they saw and heard novel stimuli; their level of motor activity and emotional responses were of particular interest. Then, when the infants were nine months of age, patterns of EEG activity were measured. Compared with other infants in the study, active, irritable children who were hard to soothe at four months of age showed greater brain wave activity in the right frontal lobe, the portion of the brain thought to be involved in the expression and processing of emotions (Tucker, 1981). These same infants at twenty-four months of age tended to be fearful and inhibited (Calkins, Fox, & Marshall, 1995).

Stephen Porges and his associates (Porges, Doussard-Roosevelt, & Maiti, 1994) have focused on *cardiac vagal tone* as a physiological component of temperament. This measure assesses the degree to which the heart is influenced by the vagus nerve, one of the principal nerves in the autonomic nervous system originating in the brainstem. Infants who show high baseline cardiac vagal tone tend to be reactive; they respond both positively and negatively in stressful situations compared with infants with low cardiac vagal tone (Gunnar et al., 1995; Huffman et al., 1998; Stifter, Fox, & Porges, 1989). In addition, infants who show declines in vagal tone while a series of novel stimuli are presented are more attentive and easier to soothe (Huffman et al., 1998). Perhaps these infants are better able to regulate their emotional states. It is interesting to note that these two patterns of physiological responding—reactivity and self-regulation—correspond to the two major dimensions of temperament proposed by Mary Rothbart.

If individuals differ in the way their bodies tend to react emotionally, then it is logical to presume that genetics plays a role in temperament. As we noted in the chapter titled "Genetics and Heredity," studies comparing identical and fraternal twins, and parents and children, on dimensions of temperament suggest that they have a genetic component. Even so, most researchers of temperament agree that biology only sets in place certain predispositions. Any explanation of a child's personality development most certainly needs to include the complex interplay between initial behavior patterns and environmental experiences (Kagan & Fox, 2006; Rothbart & Bates, 2006).

KEY THEME
RISK/RESILIENCE

Temperament and Later Development Does early temperament forecast any of the child's characteristics later in life? It appears so. For example, the extent to which an infant tends to show negative emotions at three months of age predicts poorer cognitive abilities for that child at age four years, even when factors such as the mother's responsiveness are ruled out as influences on the child (Lewis, 1993). In the domain of social development, infants who tend to express anger and frustration score higher on measures of aggression at age six to seven years than children who express less anger as infants (Rothbart, Ahadi, & Hershey, 1994). It seems that the relatively stable emotional style a particular child displays early in life may have a far-reaching impact on both cognitive and social functioning later on. According to some researchers, early temperament styles are likely to have a strong relationship to adult personality types (Rothbart, Ahadi, & Evans, 2000).

FOR • YOUR • REVIEW

- What are the different ways in which child temperament has been characterized?
- What is the evidence for a biological basis for temperament?
- How is temperament in infancy related to later development?

ATTACHMENT

One of the most widely discussed and actively researched aspects of emotional and social development is **attachment**, the strong emotional bond that emerges between infant and caregivers. The concept of attachment occupies a prominent place in developmental psychology because of its link with successful cognitive, social, and emotional development throughout childhood.

How does attachment emerge between infant and caregiver? In what ways is this emotional bond expressed? What roles do the caregiver and infant play in its formation? What is the significance of attachment in the later development of the child? Do we observe the same patterns of attachment among children across cultures? We begin by examining the course of attachment in infancy and then explore the answers to these questions.

THE ORIGINS OF ATTACHMENT: THEORETICAL PERSPECTIVES

What forces govern the emergence of attachment? Historically, there have been two important perspectives on this question: learning theory and ethological theory.

attachment Strong emotional bond that emerges between infant and caregiver.

KEY THEME
NATURE & NURTURE

Learning Theory Learning theorists believe that certain basic drives, such as hunger, are satisfied by **primary reinforcers**, rewards that gratify biological needs. In the case of the young infant, an important primary reinforcer is food. Other rewards, called **secondary reinforcers**, acquire their reinforcing qualities from their association with primary reinforcers. Because they are connected repeatedly with the reduction of the hunger drive, mothers acquire secondary reinforcing properties. Eventually the mother's presence in contexts outside feeding is rewarding to the infant.

Is the activity of feeding related to the emergence of infant-mother attachments, as learning theorists predict? Evidently not, according to a series of classic experiments conducted by Harry Harlow and his associates (Harlow & Zimmerman, 1959). These investigators separated infant monkeys from their mothers and provided them instead with extended contact with two surrogate mothers, one a figure made of wire mesh and the other a figure covered with terry cloth. The wire surrogate was equipped for feeding half of the monkeys; the terry-cloth surrogate fed the other half. The infant monkeys lived with both their surrogates for at least 165 days, during which time several observations of the monkeys' behaviors were made. One measure was the number of hours per day spent with each surrogate. As Figure 7.2 shows, infant monkeys preferred the cloth "mother" regardless of which surrogate was providing nourishment. In a subsequent test of attachment, when a frightening stimulus, such as a mechanical spider, was introduced into the monkeys' cage, the monkeys chose the cloth mother to run and cling to, even if they had been fed by the wire mother.

Harlow's findings challenged the view that attachments are based on the mother's acquisition of secondary-drive characteristics. The fact that the infant monkeys

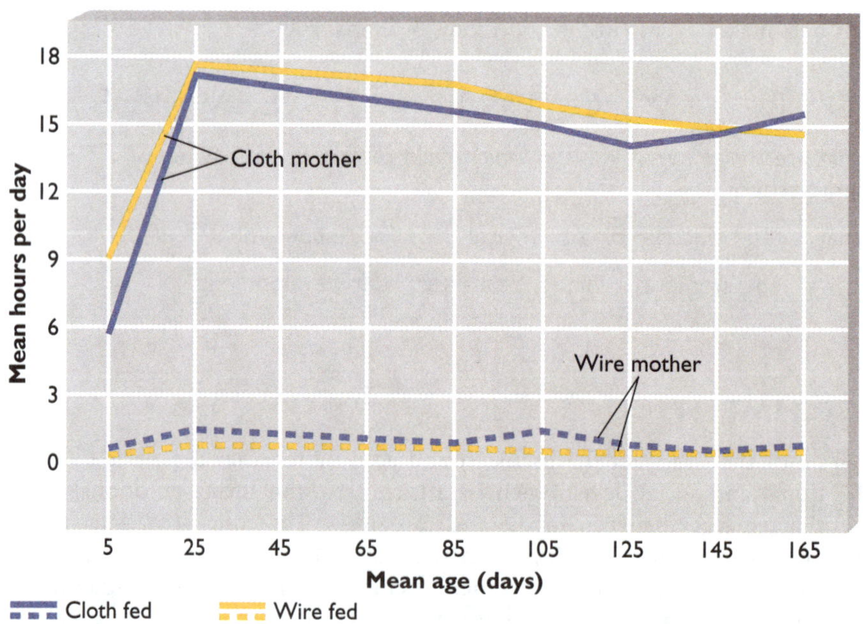

FIGURE 7.2

Forming Attachments: The "Cloth Mother" and "Wire Mother" Experiment

In Harlow's research, infant monkeys spent more time with a cloth surrogate mother than with a wire surrogate mother, regardless of which one fed them. This graph shows how much time infant monkeys spent with each surrogate as a function of feeding conditions.

Source: Reprinted with permission from Harlow, H. F., & Zimmerman, R. R., "Affectional Responses in the Infant Monkey," *Science, 130*, 421–432. Copyright 1959 American Association for the Advancement of Science.

primary reinforcer Reward that gratifies biological need or drives.

secondary reinforcer Object or person that attains rewarding value because of its association with a primary reinforcer.

did not seek out the surrogate that fed them under either normal or stressful conditions led Harlow to conclude that "contact comfort," the security provided by a physically soothing object, played a greater role in attachment than the simple act of feeding.

Harlow's experiments showed that infant monkeys reared with surrogate mothers preferred the cloth mother even when the wire mother provided nourishment. Here, the infant monkey is actually nursing from the wire mother but still maintains contact with the cloth mother. These findings challenge the hypothesis that attachment arises from the caregiver's association with feeding the child.

The Ethological View Proponents of the ethological position state that attachments occur as a result of the infant's innate tendency to signal the caregiver and the caregiver's corresponding predisposition to react to these signals. As a result, infant and caregiver are brought together, a bond is forged between them, and the survival of the infant is ensured. In other words, attachment is an adaptive, biologically programmed response system that is activated early in the infant's development and follows many of the principles of *imprinting* described in the chapter titled "Themes and Theories."

The principal spokesperson for this perspective, John Bowlby (1958, 1969), initially was concerned with the detrimental effects of institutionalization on infants and young children. Scientists in the late 1940s had reported that children who spent extended periods of time in hospitals and orphanages during their early years often showed serious developmental problems, including profound withdrawal from social interactions, intellectual impairments, and in some cases, physical delays (Skodak & Skeels, 1949; Spitz, 1946a). Bowlby proposed that the cause lay in the lack of a close emotional bond between child and primary caregiver.

Bowlby (1969) maintained that attachments develop in a fixed sequence.

- In the first two months, infants emit *signaling behaviors*, such as crying and smiling, that bring the caregiver physically close to the infant. Infants emit these signals indiscriminately, but as caregivers respond, stable patterns of interaction emerge.
- Between two and six months of age, smiles and cries become increasingly restricted to the presence of the caregiver, usually the mother.
- From six to twelve months of age, clearer signs of the infant's strong attachment to the caregiver develop. At this point, most infants become visibly upset at the mother's departure, a phenomenon called **separation anxiety**, and also show signs of **reunion behavior**, happily greeting the mother on her return. Once they are able to move about, infants will ensure nearness to their mother by approaching and clinging to them. About the same time, they also display **stranger anxiety**, a wariness or fear at the approach of someone unfamiliar.
- The final phase of attachment occurs at about three years of age, when the relationship between mother and child becomes more of a partnership and the child comes to appreciate the mother's feelings, motives, and goals.

The regularity with which infants show this sequence of behaviors and the adaptive function they serve, says Bowlby, suggests its biological and evolutionary basis.

According to Bowlby, infants become attached to those who respond consistently and appropriately to their signaling behaviors. Thus Bowlby saw the maladaptive development of institutionalized infants as a consequence of the absence of the dynamic, contingent interaction between child and caregiver. Although institutional settings met children's basic physical needs, they often did so at the convenience of the caregiver's schedule rather than in response to the child's behaviors. Modern-day studies of infants growing up in orphanages in Romania echo these important themes. In one recent report, for example, less than 20 percent of 95 infants raised in an institutional setting showed signs of healthy attachments. An important predictor of those healthy emotional relationships was the quality of caregiving in the institution; that is, the emotional involvement, sensitivity, and responsiveness of the adults who worked in the orphanage (Zeanah et al., 2005). Bowlby's general scheme concerning the origins and course of attachment has framed literally hundreds of investigations of the development of attachment.

separation anxiety Distress that the infant shows when the primary caregiver leaves the immediate environment.

reunion behavior The child's style of greeting a caregiver after a separation.

stranger anxiety Fear or distress that an infant shows at the approach of an unfamiliar person.

The Developmental Course of Attachment

For the most part, research has confirmed the sequence of behaviors outlined by Bowlby in the emergence of attachment. Infants can discriminate their mother's face from those of strangers at two days of age and their mother's voice and odors a few days after that (DeCasper & Fifer, 1980; Field et al., 1984; MacFarlane, 1975). However, they emit their signals to anyone who is available. By about seven months of age, these indiscriminate behaviors give way to attachments to specific people, most notably the mother or primary caregiver. Stranger anxiety becomes full blown, and separation anxiety is usually manifested as well. In the months that follow, children show evidence of multiple attachments to fathers, substitute caregivers, and grandparents (Schaffer & Emerson, 1964).

Key Theme
Interaction Among Domains

At age two years, most children continue to show strong attachments, but by three years some of the manifestations of this bond begin to change. Separation distress diminishes for most children, probably due to advances in cognition. For example, children begin to appreciate the fact that, even though the caregiver may depart for several hours, she always returns (Marvin, 1977). The impact of repeated experience with separation and reunion episodes may extend to a more general understanding that negative emotional experiences often yield to strong positive affect, that distress can be followed by stability (Schore, 1994). As children develop insights into the perspectives of others and as their communication skills improve, they can better understand the reasons for temporary separations and can express their emotions in ways other than crying or clinging.

Measuring Attachment The **Strange Situation**, developed by Mary Ainsworth and her associates, is a standardized test frequently employed to measure the quality of the child's emotional ties to her mother (Ainsworth et al., 1978). Table 7.1 shows the eight episodes that comprise this measure, which is administered in a laboratory setting.

On the basis of her extensive observations of the patterns of behaviors shown by infants, Ainsworth (Ainsworth et al., 1978) distinguished three patterns of attachment: secure attachment and two categories of insecure attachment: avoidant and ambivalent attachment. Other researchers have identified still a third type of insecure attachment called disorganized/disoriented attachment. These attachment categories are described as follows:

- **Secure attachment.** Children in this group show many clear signs of attachment by displaying stranger anxiety and separation protest, and by greeting the mother enthusiastically upon her return. They also use the mother as a **secure base** for exploration, exploring their new surroundings but looking or moving back to the mother as though to "check in" with her. They obviously feel comfortable in the presence of the mother and distressed and apprehensive in her absence.
- **Avoidant attachment.** Infants in this category are less distressed when the mother leaves and less enthusiastic in greeting her when she returns. They tend to avoid or ignore her, playing in isolation even when she is present in the room. All of these behaviors, according to Ainsworth, constitute a form of insecure attachment.
- **Ambivalent (or resistant) attachment.** Tension characterizes the behaviors these children show toward their mothers. Although they display noticeable proximity-seeking behaviors when the mother is in the room, sometimes clinging excessively to her, they also show angry, rejecting behavior when she returns, even hitting or pushing her away. Some children in this category are extremely passive, showing limited exploratory play except for bouts of crying that are used as signals to be picked up and held. These children, too, are considered insecurely attached.
- **Disorganized/disoriented attachment.** Children in this attachment category show fear of their caregivers, confused facial expressions, and an assortment of avoidant

Strange Situation Standardized test that assesses the quality of infant-caregiver attachment.

secure attachment Attachment category defined by the infant's distress at separation from the caregiver and enthusiastic greeting upon his or her return. The infant also displays stranger anxiety and uses the caregiver as a secure base for exploration.

secure base An attachment behavior in which the infant explores the environment but periodically checks back with the caregiver.

avoidant attachment Insecure attachment in which the infant shows little separation anxiety and does not pay much attention to the caregiver's return.

ambivalent (resistant) attachment Insecure attachment in which the infant shows separation protest but also distress upon the caregiver's return.

disorganized/disoriented attachment Infant-caregiver relations categorized by the infant's fear of the caregiver, confused facial expressions, and a combination of avoidant and ambivalent attachment behaviors.

Table 7.1 The Episodes of the Strange Situation

Episode*	Persons Present	Action	Attachment Behaviors Assessed
1	Caregiver, baby, observer	Observer introduces mother and baby to experimental room and leaves.	
2	Caregiver, baby	Baby explores and plays while caregiver is passive.	Secure base
3	Stranger, caregiver, baby	Stranger enters room, converses with caregiver, and approaches baby.	Stranger anxiety
4	Stranger, baby	Caregiver leaves room unobtrusively.	Separation anxiety
5	Caregiver, baby	Caregiver returns and greets baby.	Reunion behavior
6	Baby	Caregiver leaves room, saying, "Bye-bye."	Separation anxiety
7	Stranger, baby	Stranger enters and orients to baby.	Stranger anxiety
8	Caregiver, baby	Caregiver returns and greets baby.	Reunion behavior

*Each episode except the first lasts for about three minutes.

Source: Adapted from Ainsworth et al. (1978).

and ambivalent attachment behaviors in the Strange Situation (Main & Solomon, 1986). These behaviors are accompanied by physiological signs of stress (Hertsgaard et al., 1996).

In the United States, about 65 percent of infants are typically categorized as securely attached, about 20 percent as avoidantly attached, and about 10 percent as ambivalently attached (van IJzendoorn & Sagi, 1999). Other data suggest that perhaps as many as 15 percent of infants show signs of disorganized attachments (Lyons-Ruth & Jacobvitz, 1999).

Another way to measure attachment is the *Q-sort.* In this method, mother and infant are observed for a specified period of time, after which the observer sorts through a series of ninety cards containing descriptions of the mother-infant relationship. Several piles are created, from "least characteristic" to "most characteristic" of the child. The child's attachment score is based on the extent to which these ratings correlate with the characteristics of a securely attached child, as defined by a panel of experts on childhood attachment (Waters & Deane, 1985). The use of the Q-sort has permitted researchers to study attachment in a broader range of contexts and in a wider age range of children than has the Strange Situation (Thompson, 2006).

KEY THEME
NATURE & NURTURE

The Antecedents of Secure Attachment How do secure, high-quality attachments develop? Landmark research by Mary Ainsworth and her colleagues (Ainsworth, Bell, & Stayton, 1971, 1972, 1974) suggests that the mother's style of interacting with her infant and her responsivity to the baby's signals are key factors.

Ainsworth and her associates visited the homes of twenty-six infants and their mothers for about four hours every three weeks during the entire first year of the infants' lives. When they were about one year old, the infants were brought to the laboratory to be tested in the Strange Situation and were classified according to the quality of attachment to their mother. An attempt was then made to find relationships between the attachment classification and specific maternal behaviors observed earlier. The results of this study indicated that mothers of securely attached infants were *sensitive* to their children's signals, noticing their cues and interpreting them correctly. These mothers were *accepting* of their role as caregiver. They displayed *cooperation*; mothers of securely attached infants would wait until the child finished her activity or was in a good mood before imposing a request. They used gentle persuasion rather than assertive control. Mothers in this group were also *accessible*, providing quick responses to the child's signals, particularly crying. They were not distracted by their own thoughts and activities. In contrast, mothers of the insecurely attached group were often rigid, unresponsive, and demanding in their parenting style and did not feel positively about their role as caregiver.

A meta-analysis of sixty-six studies showed that maternal sensitivity is indeed strongly related to attachment (De Wolff & van IJzendoorn, 1997). However, research shows that the emotional tone of early mother-child interactions may be just as important to consider. Mothers of securely attached children have been found to be more affectionate, more positive, and less intrusive in their vocalizations than mothers of insecurely attached infants, toddlers, and young school-age children (Bates, Maslin, & Frankel, 1985; Isabella, 1993; Izard et al., 1991; Stevenson-Hinde & Shouldice, 1995). In a study of children who were about to enter school, those who were insecurely attached and who showed the most behavior problems two years later had mothers who displayed the highest levels of negativity and tension of all the participants (Moss et al., 1998).

Interactive synchrony also influences the emergence of attachments. One group of researchers observed the interactions of mothers and their infants at one, three, and nine months of age, recording each instance in which the infants' and mothers' behaviors co-occurred and produced a mutually satisfying outcome. For example, if the infant gazed at the mother, the mother verbalized, or if the infant fussed and cried, the mother soothed him. The infants' attachments were then assessed at one year of age. According to the results, securely attached infants had experienced a greater number of synchronous interactions in the prior months, a finding that other researchers have replicated (Isabella, Belsky, & von Eye, 1989; Scholmerich et al., 1995). Therefore, in accounting for the emergence of secure attachment, it is important to consider maternal behavior *as it is related to the child's behavior*.

It is worth noting that siblings reared in the same family are at least moderately similar to one another in their attachment classifications and that identical twins are no more similar than fraternal twins in their attachment styles (O'Connor & Croft, 2001; van IJzendoorn et al., 2000). This pattern of results is consistent with the notion that the events that transpire within the family are a key ingredient in shaping attachments.

Attachments to Fathers Because mothers traditionally have fulfilled the role of primary caregiver, most of the emphasis in research has been on the emotional bond that develops between child and mother. With large numbers of women participating in the labor force, however, and challenges to the assumption that females have the exclusive role in child care, many caregiving responsibilities have been assumed by others either within or outside the family. Moreover, researchers in developmental psychology have recognized the glaring absence of information on how another important family member, the father, interacts with his children. The result has been a growing literature on father-child interaction.

In this chapter, we have underscored maternal sensitivity and responsiveness as key factors in fostering optimal child development. Studies have shown that fathers are just as responsive as mothers to the signals of their infants, and when given the opportunity, they interact with their babies in ways similar to mothers. One team of researchers measured the physiological responsiveness of mothers and fathers as they observed quiet, smiling, or crying babies on a video monitor (Frodi et al., 1978). Mothers and fathers showed similar changes in heart rate, blood pressure, and skin conductance when the babies smiled or cried. In another study of maternal and paternal behaviors toward infants in the newborn nursery, Ross Parke and Sandra O'Leary (1976) found that fathers were just as likely as mothers to hold, touch, and vocalize to their babies.

After the newborn period, fathers and mothers begin to manifest somewhat different styles of interacting with their infants. When they play face to face with their babies, fathers tend to provide physical and social stimulation in staccato bursts, whereas mothers tend to be more rhythmic, positive in emotional tone, and soothing (Forbes et al., 2004; Yogman et al., 1977). Fathers typically engage in physical and unpredictable "idiosyncratic" play with their infants—throwing them up in the air, moving their limbs, and tickling them—whereas mothers spend more time in caregiving activities or calm games like "pat-a-cake" (Lamb, 1997; Yogman, 1982). As a consequence, infants prefer fathers when they wish to play and seek out mothers when they desire care and comfort. At the same time, fathers from diverse backgrounds have also been observed to engage in at least moderate amounts of responsive, positively toned interaction with their young infants (Shannon, Tamis-LeMonda, & Margolin, 2005). Physical play is not the exclusive style that fathers display.

Infants show clear signs of attachment to fathers, especially when fathers spend time in rewarding, mutually engaging interactions with them. Research shows that children who have healthy attachments to mothers *and* fathers show higher self-esteem and greater social competence than children who are securely attached to only one or neither parent.

In general, fathers spend less time interacting with and caring for their children than mothers do. Nevertheless, infants clearly do form attachments to their fathers. In the Strange Situation, infants show signs of separation anxiety when the father leaves the room and greet him on his return. They also use him as a secure base for exploration (Kotelchuk, 1976). In most cases, when infants are attached to their mother, they are also attached to their father (Rosen & Burke, 1999). As is the case with mothers, when fathers spend time in face-to-face interactions with their infants, but particularly when they show sensitivity in their play, their infants show clear signs of attachment to them (Cox et al., 1992; Grossmann et al., 2002). Securely attached infants also tend to have fathers who are sociable, are agreeable, and express positive emotions (Belsky, 1996). Given the opportunity to be nurturant and responsive, fathers, like mothers, can become partners in strong, secure attachments.

Key Theme
Risk/Resilience

The opportunity for infants to develop attachments to fathers matters. Children who have secure attachments to *both* mothers and fathers show higher self-esteem and greater social competence than children who have secure attachments to only one or to neither parent (Verschueren & Marcoen, 1999). Moreover, healthy relationships with fathers can buffer children who are at risk due to impaired interactions with their mother. Recall how infants with a depressed mother often have poor-quality interactions with them. One group of researchers found that infants with a depressed mother often developed more positive interactions with their father (Hossain et al., 1994). Studies like these suggest that fathers fulfill a very important role in the family—one that simply cannot be ignored.

Temperament and Attachment Caregivers are not solely responsible for the emergence of attachment. Because attachments form in the context of interactions between caregiver and infant, it seems reasonable to postulate that the infant's own style as a communication partner contributes significantly to the growth of an affectional bond.

Several researchers have reported a link between infant characteristics, such as irritability and proneness to distress, and subsequent attachment behaviors in the Strange Situation (Bates et al., 1985; Goldsmith & Alansky, 1987; Miyake, Chen, & Campos, 1985). For example, two-day-old infants' proneness to distress when a pacifier is removed from their mouth is related to insecure attachment at fourteen months of age (Calkins & Fox, 1992). Similarly, in a study of Dutch infants who were identified as very irritable newborns, 74 percent were classified as insecurely attached at eighteen months of age (van den Boom, 1994, 1995). Yet early irritability does not necessarily predispose children to become insecurely attached. In the same study of Dutch infants, a second group of irritable newborns and their mothers participated in an intervention program that resulted in only 28 percent being scored as insecurely attached later in infancy.

RESEARCH APPLIED TO PARENTING

Promoting Secure Attachment in Irritable Infants

The phone call turned out to be from Gwen, Cindy's close friend. The two of them had shared many life experiences since their childhood days, but Cindy still found it remarkable that they had had their babies within three months of each other. Cindy knew, though, that motherhood was a challenge for Gwen. Gwen's son, unlike Michael, was hard to figure out and to keep happy. He didn't seem to like being held very much and was often cranky both before and after feeding. Gwen was a loving mother, but at times she was at her wits' end trying to think of ways to soothe her baby. When Cindy picked up the phone, she could tell from Gwen's strained voice that she was looking for help on how to handle her difficult child.

What can parents do if their infant is born with a "difficult" temperamental style, showing more negative than positive emotions, fussing and crying, and smiling infrequently? Research carried out in the Netherlands, in which mother-child interaction was observed in the home monthly until the infants were six months of age, shows that mothers of irritable infants displayed distinct patterns of reactions. They exhibited less visual and physical contact with their babies, were less involved with them, and responded less when their babies smiled or showed other positive social behaviors (van den Boom & Hoeksma, 1994). Although many of the differences between mothers of irritable and nonirritable infants disappeared by the time their children were six months old, such negative parent-child interactions may predispose children to develop insecure attachments.

In a second study (van den Boom, 1994, 1995), mothers of irritable newborns were randomly assigned to either an intervention group or a control group when their infants were six months of age. During three in-home training sessions conducted every three weeks, mothers in the intervention group were taught to be more responsive to the cues their infants provided. The infants and mothers were observed again when the children were twelve, eighteen, twenty-four, and forty-two months of age. The benefits of the intervention were clear: children in the experimental group were far more likely to be securely attached than children in the control group, even into toddlerhood. These children were also more cooperative, displayed fewer behavior problems, and engaged in more activities and verbal interactions with their mothers than the control group children. Even though mothers had received training up to several years earlier, they continued to show responsive, sensitive parenting.

What exactly were mothers in the intervention group taught? Following are the essential ingredients of the training package:

1. ***Attend to the infant's signals, especially by imitating the baby's behaviors and repeating one's own verbalizations.*** If the infant coos, respond by making a similar sound. When speaking to the infant, say words slowly and repeat them. If the infant averts his gaze, remain silent, because gaze aversion often means the caregiver has not interpreted the child's signals correctly. These techniques aim to slow down the tempo of mother-infant interactions and to simplify them. The overall goal of these procedures is to help the mothers perceive and interpret infant signals accurately.

2. *Try to soothe the fussing or crying infant.* Because some infants seem to respond negatively to being cuddled or held in close physical contact, try to find a technique suitable for the particular child and her preferences, for example, feeding or vocalizing to her. Once an effective technique is identified, stick with it. Again, the idea is to avoid rapid changes in maternal behavior that might create further frustration and distress in the infant.

3. *Pay attention to the infant's positive signals instead of focusing on his negative behaviors.* Mothers of irritable infants are often so focused on their negative behaviors that they ignore the infant's positive signals. Create opportunities for positive interactions. Play with the infant using games and toys, paying attention to how he she responds, especially if the response is a smile or a laugh.

In general, the goal of the program was to help mothers correctly read and respond to their own infants' signals, characteristics of mothering that Ainsworth's early studies identified as precursors of secure attachment. As the results described earlier indicate, infants who participated in this intervention showed many desirable outcomes even years after the intervention itself was terminated.

KEY THEME
SOCIOCULTURAL INFLUENCE

Cross-Cultural Variations in Patterns of Attachment Overall, children in most countries around the world show behaviors indicating secure attachment even if they have been reared in very different circumstances (Posada et al., 1995; Van IJzendoorn, 1995). Studies of children in Israel are good examples. Many Israeli infants are raised in the group setting of the kibbutz. While parents go to work, children are cared for by the *metapelet*, or caregiver, beginning sometime between six and twelve weeks of age and continuing after the first year. Children go to the group caregiving center (called the "children's house") in the morning and return home in the late afternoon, but most of their time is spent with the nonparental caregiver and peers. Do such arrangements interfere with the formation of attachments to mothers? One study showed that 80 percent of infants were securely attached to their mother; interestingly, however, this finding held true only for infants who came home to sleep for the evening. Some infants sleep overnight at the "children's house," in keeping with more traditional practices of the kibbutz; among this group, only 48 percent were securely attached to their mother (Sagi et al., 1994). Children raised on the kibbutz also showed notable attachments to their metapelet; 53 percent of infants were classified as securely attached to the nonmaternal caregiver (Sagi et al., 1985).

Observations of infants in Germany show a different pattern of results. In one study, about 49 percent of infants were scored as avoidantly attached (Grossmann et al., 1985). As in the Ainsworth studies, these researchers noted a relationship between maternal sensitivity and infant attachment: securely attached infants had mothers who interacted with them in a warm, responsive manner. However, although mothers varied in the sensitivity of responding when infants were two months of age, they did not vary by the time the infants were ten months old; most mothers had *low* sensitivity ratings by this time. Grossmann and her colleagues interpreted their findings in the context of the different attitudes toward child rearing held by parents in Germany and the United States. The emphasis in German culture is on fostering independence in one's offspring, encouraging the development of an obedient child who does not make demands on the parents. Responding to the infant's every cry is considered inappropriate. Thus German mothers' tendency to pick up their children less frequently and for shorter periods of time, and to display less affection, reflects the goals of socialization in that culture.

Finally, a study of Dogon mothers and infants in northwestern Africa found that, although infants assessed in the Strange Situation fell into the secure category at the same rate as Western samples, no infants were classified as avoidant. Recall that in North America about 20 percent of infants are avoidant. The researchers attribute the results to the fact that Dogon mothers feed their infants on demand, responding immediately to their infants' cries of hunger and distress. The high degree of responsiveness of mothers, say the researchers, makes avoidant behavior highly unlikely (True, Pisani, & Oumar, 2001).

Taken together, these studies suggest that the central ideas of attachment theory hold up under a wide variety of cultural circumstances. They show, in particular, that the mother's sensitivity and responsiveness is indeed related to the type of attachment style the infant displays. Yet some researchers caution that the Strange Situation may not take into account specific cultural practices as they relate to separation of the mother and infant. In Japan, for example, mothers and infants are rarely apart from each other, and infants respond with distress when the mother departs but also when she returns as part of the Strange Situation. Because of their persistent anxiety, infants may be classified as insecure when they are really just responding to a breech of cultural practice (Takahashi, 1990). More broadly, say the critics, theorists need to consider the goals of socialization in a particular culture; not all cultures may value the emergence of independence and exploration, as we do in our culture. Nor do all cultures define maternal sensitivity and responsiveness in the same way. Thus attachment should be studied within the context of a particular culture's belief systems and practices (Rothbaum et al., 2000).

Child Care and Attachment One of the most difficult decisions many parents face concerns alternative child care arrangements when they work. As Table 7.2 shows, almost 70 percent of mothers with preschool-age children work, and almost 60 percent of women with infants under two years of age are employed (U.S. Bureau of the Census, 2005). In fact, this latter group represents the fastest-growing category of women in the labor force. A substantial number of children are therefore receiving nonparental care, many beginning very early in life. Does this form of early experience influence the formation of attachments?

One problem in answering this question is that many variables operate when the child receives nonparental care. Is it the mother's absence or the quality of substitute care that produces observable effects on child behavior? These two factors are difficult to separate. Does it matter whether the child receives full-time or

Table 7.2 Labor Force Participation Rates for Women with Children Under Age 18

This table shows the percentage of women with children under age eighteen who are employed outside the home (the table shows only the data for married women whose husbands are present in the home). The labor force participation rates for mothers have grown substantially since 1975, including women with children two years of age and under.

	Percentage of Women in the Labor Force		
Age of Child	*1975*	*1990*	*2003*
Under 18	44.9	66.3	69.2
Under 6, total	36.7	58.9	59.8
Under 3	32.7	55.5	56.5
1 year or under	30.8	53.9	54.7
2 years	37.1	60.9	61.3
3–5 years	42.2	64.1	64.8
6–13 years	51.8	73.0	75.1
14–17 years	53.5	75.1	81.6

Source: Data from U.S. Bureau of the Census (2005).

part-time care? Perhaps, but the tremendous variation in caregiving schedules has made this factor difficult to control in research studies. In addition, the kinds of alternative care that children receive vary a great deal, ranging from a single caregiver's coming to the home, to out-of-home family daycare in which another parent provides care for several children, to center-based care.

Studies conducted in the 1980s suggested that children in daycare behaved differently than home-reared children on some components of the Strange Situation. Although daycare children showed similar patterns of separation anxiety when the mother departed, a sizable minority showed avoidant responses when reunited with their mother (Clarke-Stewart & Fein, 1983). This pattern was especially true for infants who received more than twenty hours per week of nonmaternal care, although even among this group over 50 percent of infants formed secure attachments (Belsky & Rovine, 1988). The most recent information, though, shows that early daycare experiences do not put children at risk for insecure attachments. In a major study of more than 1,000 infants attending ten centers, researchers found that children who attended daycare did not differ from home-reared children in their behaviors during reunions with their mother and in overall attachment security. In addition, age at which daycare began, the amount of weekly time spent in daycare, the quality of care, and the type of care (for instance, home with a relative, home with a nonrelative, center-based care) did not influence children's attachments in infancy or during the preschool years. There were some conditions under which insecure attachments were more likely, however: when maternal insensitivity co-occurred with extensive or poor-quality child care. In these cases, children were particularly at risk for ambivalent attachments (NICHD Early Child Care Research Network, 1997; 2001b).

A study conducted in Australia reiterates that what is important is the attitude and behaviors of the mother. The researchers found that mothers who returned to work by the time an infant was five months of age and who were committed to combining their roles as mothers with their work roles were more likely to have secure infants. These mothers, as it turned out, were also less anxious about child care and more sensitive in their parenting style (Harrison & Ungerer, 2002). Taken together, the studies on child care and attachment indicate that what matters most is the context in which child care is taking place—the emotional climate that parents create in the home and the quality of the interactions infants have with their parents.

DISRUPTIONS IN ATTACHMENT

KEY THEME
RISK/RESILIENCE

In some contexts, the ideal pattern of caregiver-child interaction may be disrupted, for example, when mother and infant are physically separated during the early days of their partnership due to the infant's premature birth or when the child is placed for adoption and nonbiological parents assume the caregiving role. Other children are the victims of physical abuse or neglect. Is there any evidence that attachments suffer in such cases? A consideration of these issues will further illuminate the ways in which early caregiver-child relationships influence subsequent child development.

Prematurity The preterm infant looks and behaves differently than the infant with the benefit of a full thirty-eight weeks in utero. In all likelihood, the premature infant will be very small and fragile looking, less alert and responsive to stimulation, and more difficult to comfort. Cries, but not smiles, are very frequent (Goldberg, 1979). In addition, mothers and their premature infants usually are separated physically, sometimes for several weeks, while the baby receives the medical care necessary to ensure well-being and even survival. If attachments were based largely on mutually rewarding infant-caregiver interactions, we might expect premature infants to develop insecure attachments with their mothers.

In the hospital nursery, mothers of premature infants indeed behave in a markedly different manner than do mothers of full-term infants. Mothers of premature babies touch, hold, and smile at their babies less often than do mothers of full-term

FIGURE 7.3

Maternal Interactions with Premature Babies

After an initial period of inactivity following the births of their children, mothers of premature infants become more active in their exchanges with their infants than mothers of full- and postterm infants. At the same time, premature babies display more gaze aversion, as though they are seeking to terminate their mothers' overstimulation.

Source: Adapted from Field (1982).

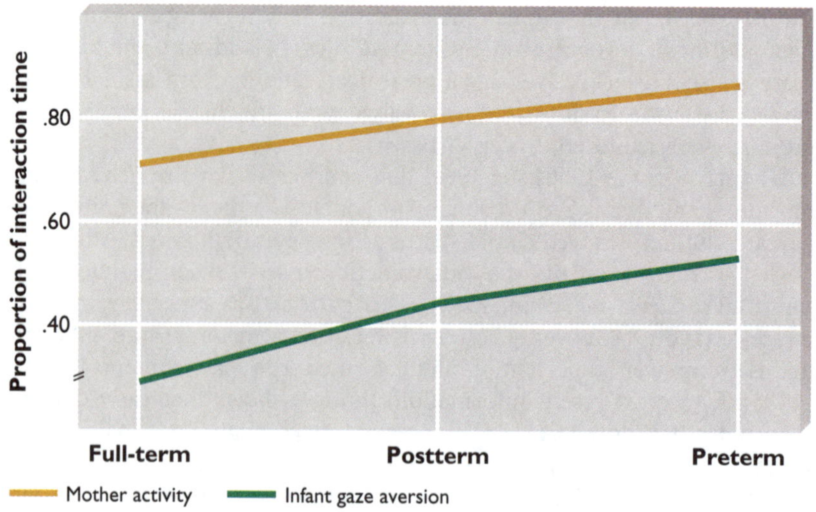

infants (DiVitto & Goldberg, 1979). As their babies get older, however, mothers of premature infants actually become more active than mothers of full-term babies in stimulating them: they initiate and maintain more interactions, even to the point of being excessive. These behaviors may stem from the mother's desire to alter the premature's unresponsive pattern or to stimulate the child in an effort to spur slowed development. As Figure 7.3 shows, infants often react to these maternal behaviors by averting their gaze, as though to shut out the added stimulation (Field, 1977, 1982).

Given the differences in maternal styles with premature babies, is there a corresponding impact on the attachments of these infants? In a comparison of twenty full-term and twenty premature infants at eleven months of age, Ann Frodi and Ross Thompson (1985) observed no significant differences in the patterns of attachments. Most of the children in both groups were observed to be securely attached. By one year of age, many premature infants "rebound" from the negative effects of early birth, especially if they encounter a responsive, supportive environment. Mothers may also adapt their styles in later months to conform more closely to the rhythms and needs of the child. Thus the early developmental risk posed by prematurity does not automatically lead to persistent problems in mother-child relations or other developmental patterns. On the other hand, very-low-birth-weight infants—those under 1,250 grams—have been found to be at risk for insecure attachments at nineteen months of age (Mangelsdorf et al., 1996). These infants in particular may present greater stresses and challenges for their caregivers.

Adoption and Foster Care By the time they reach middle childhood and adolescence, adopted children show a noticeably higher incidence of psychological and academic problems compared with nonadopted children (Brodzinsky et al., 1984; Fergusson, Lynskey, & Horwood, 1995; Sharma, McGue, & Benson, 1998). They are at greater risk for substance abuse, physical and mental health problems, emotional distress, and fighting (Juffer & van IJzendoorn, 2005; B. C. Miller et al., 2000). Because most adoptions involve the separation of the child from the biological parent during infancy, disruption of the attachment process may be a factor.

KEY THEME
CONTINUITY/DISCONTINUITY

Investigations of this issue show that separation of the infant from the biological parents at six to seven months of age can produce socioemotional difficulties even ten years later, particularly in the child's ability to form relationships with others (Yarrow et al., 1973). Separation at an earlier age, however, may have a lesser impact. When Leslie Singer and her colleagues assessed the attachments of adopted and nonadopted infants between thirteen and eighteen months of age, they found no difference in the classifications of attachments between these two groups (Singer et al., 1985). Most of the infants fell in the securely attached category. In this group, most of the adoptive placements had occurred at fairly early ages, the majority by three months of age. At this age children have not yet developed the early manifestations of attachment, such as stranger and separation anxiety. It is also important to keep in mind that maternal sensitivity is important for adopted children, just as it is for biological caregivers and their infants. In a Dutch study of 146 children adopted before six months of age, maternal sensitive responsiveness—more than such factors as the child's temperament or gender—predicted better cognitive and social functioning when these children were seven years old (Stams, Juffer, & van IJzendoorn, 2002).

If the studies of adoption generally suggest that early placement is better for children than later placement, what are the implications for another group of children who experience disrupted relationships with their biological parents—foster children? Mary Dozier and her colleagues (Dozier et al., 2001) found that infants placed in foster homes at age eighteen months can still develop secure attachments provided that their caregivers both value relationships and had strong attachments to their own parents. This pattern occurred even if the infants had experienced neglect, physical abuse, and frequent turnover in caregivers. These data speak to the remarkable resilience of young children when they are provided with loving, nurturant homes. They also reemphasize the important role played by the sensitivity of the child's caregiver.

Abuse Physically or psychologically abused children are at risk for an assortment of cognitive and socioemotional difficulties. Because the trauma that accompanies within-family violence can be enduring, especially with repeated episodes of abuse, it is not surprising that attachments between abused children and their parents take on an aberrant character.

Infants and toddlers who have been maltreated by their caregivers are likely to fall into the category of insecure attachment called *disorganized/disoriented attachment.* Approximately 80 percent of maltreated infants fit this attachment profile (Carlson et al., 1989; Cicchetti, Toth, & Lynch, 1995). Like other attachment categories, the disorganized/disoriented pattern may predict later developmental outcomes. In one study, 71 percent of preschoolers who showed high levels of hostile behavior toward peers had been categorized as having disorganized attachments during infancy (Lyons-Ruth, Alpern, & Repacholi, 1993). In another, researchers found that, when children with disorganized/disoriented attachments were six years old, they tended to be depressed, disorganized in behavior, and even self-destructive in response to questions about their parents or family life (Main, Kaplan, & Cassidy, 1985). Disorganized children also tend to express more anger over time (Kochanska, 2001).

Why do these maladaptive attachments form? Abusive parents tend to react negatively to many of their children's social signals, even positive ones. When Ann Frodi and Michael Lamb (1980) observed the reactions of abusive and nonabusive mothers to videotapes of smiling and crying infants, abusive mothers were more aroused physiologically by both cries and smiles than were nonabusive mothers and were less willing to interact with an infant, even a smiling one. These findings suggest, at the very least, that the abused infant has an unwilling and psychologically distant interaction partner. In addition, mothers of disorganized/disoriented children tend to be intrusive and insensitive in their parenting styles, independent of the temperamental characteristics of their children (Carlson, 1998).

Studies of premature and adopted children reveal that secure attachment relationships can develop in circumstances that are less than optimal during the early part of infancy. At the same time, however, when interactions between caregivers and infants deviate too widely from the ideal, especially in terms of the emotional tone of interactions, the consequences for the child can be serious and enduring.

ATYPICAL DEVELOPMENT

Failure-to-Thrive Syndrome

Some infants just don't seem to grow at the same pace as their agemates. If they remain in the third percentile for weight for at least one month, or if they show a notable deceleration in their rate of gaining weight from the time of birth, infants may be diagnosed as **failure to thrive**. Their small physical size is often accompanied by delays in acquiring developmental milestones—the ages at which they crawl, walk, or say their first words. Later in childhood, they may show lower intelligence test scores or other signs of problematic cognitive or social development.

The causes of failure-to-thrive syndrome are not entirely understood. For some infants, the origins may lie in a preceding medical condition which may have required lengthy hospitalization. But, for others, there is no clear organic basis. At one time, a great deal of attention was focused on the nature of the attachment relationship between these infants and their caregivers. According to this line of thinking, infants and parents never developed the positive, close emotional bonds that characterize secure attachment. More recently, however, researchers have come to realize that failure to thrive is often accompanied by a constellation of factors that may put the infant at risk: less responsive or more intrusive parenting, negative emotional experiences, but also greater familial exposure to poverty, violence, and other sources of stress. Attributing the infant's condition simply to poor parenting, say the researchers, is too simplistic (Benoit, 2000; Drotar & Robinson, 2000).

Infants diagnosed with failure to thrive often respond well to medical or psychological interventions that aim to improve their nutritional intake. Infants may be given medications, be fitted with a feeding tube, or participate in a program of behavior therapy to increase food intake and help them gain weight. However, social and cognitive deficits may persist, perhaps because of the initial effects of undernutrition. Researchers generally agree that we need to know more about the developmental processes at work in failure-to-thrive syndrome (Drotar & Robinson, 2000).

Early Emotional Experiences and the Brain One of the most valuable outcomes of the studies that have been conducted on disrupted infant-caregiver attachments has been an accumulating appreciation for the role of early experiences in children's emotional lives. Recent physiological evidence suggests that changes in the functioning of the nervous system may accompany early social-emotional interactions and, furthermore, that the first two to three years of life may represent a critical period in laying down the "hard-wiring" of emotional responding.

One physiological system that has been examined is the action of the stress hormone *cortisol*. Researchers have observed that infants with a tendency to be fearful, inhibited, or angry sometimes show elevation of the amount of cortisol in their saliva, reflecting their experience of stress (Stansbury & Gunnar, 1994). In one study, though, inhibited infants with secure attachments did not show these typical elevations when confronted with fear-provoking stimuli, as indicated in Figure 7.4 (Nachmias et al., 1996). In contrast, inhibited infants who were insecurely attached did show a rise in levels of cortisol. Because these data are correlational, the usual precautions about interpreting the results apply. Nonetheless, there are some interesting potential implications of studies like this one. Cortisol is released by the adrenal glands and can influence the hippocampus (which is involved in learning and memory), the frontal areas of the brain, and portions of the limbic system (connected with emotional responding). In animals, excessive exposure to cortisol results in the death of neurons and the atrophy of dendrites. Although the impact of too much exposure to cortisol on the human brain has not yet been studied directly, one implication is that early and prolonged exposure to stress can have negative consequences on the structure of important brain systems. Healthy attachments, however, might buffer those effects (Gunnar, 1998; Gunnar & White, 2001).

KEY THEME
RISK/RESILIENCE

failure to thrive Label applied to any child whose growth in height or weight is below the third percentile for children of the same age.

Another biochemical substance, the neurotransmitter norepinephrine, has also been implicated in early emotional development. Infant monkeys deprived of

FIGURE 7.4

Physiological Stress Responses in Young Infants

In a study in which inhibited and uninhibited eighteen-month-olds were exposed to stressful situations (such as a noisy mechanical robot), inhibited children showed elevated levels of the stress hormone cortisol, but only if they were insecurely attached. The lightly shaded bars represent baseline levels of cortisol in the saliva prior to the fearful situation, and the darkly shaded bars represent levels of cortisol after the fearful event. These findings suggest that secure attachments might buffer the physiological stress responses of inhibited children.

Source: Adapted from Nachmias et al. (1996).

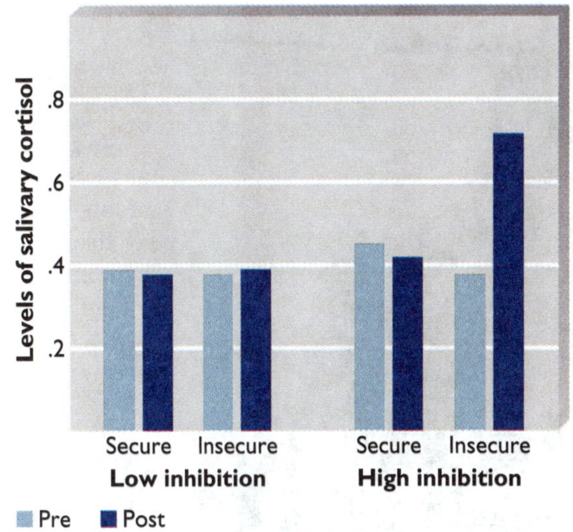

contact with their mother show depressed levels of norepinephrine. Similarly, emotionally disturbed children who have suffered neglect show lower levels of norepinephrine than children who were not neglected (Rogeness & McClure, 1996). Researchers are beginning to explore the relationship of attachment with this biochemical system as well (Nelson & Panksepp, 1998).

We now know that many of the brain systems involved in emotional responding—the hippocampus, the amygdala, and the prefrontal cortex—are malleable and plastic in early infancy. Because of their malleability, they may be especially vulnerable to the differing types of emotional experiences, positive and negative, to which children are exposed (Post & Weiss, 1997). Given these findings, it is vital that researchers continue to explore the role that early emotional experiences play in brain development.

FOR • YOUR • REVIEW

- What theoretical perspectives have influenced our understanding of attachment?
- What changes in attachment behaviors are typically seen over the course of development? Which behaviors are special hallmarks of attachment?
- How is attachment assessed in young children? What categories are used to classify children?
- What factors have been shown to promote secure attachments?
- What are the consequences of attachment styles for later development?
- How are attachment behaviors similar or different across cultures? What is the significance of these findings?
- What is the impact of child care on attachment?
- What do the cases of prematurity, adoption, and abuse tell us about the concept of attachment?
- What is the relationship between early emotional experiences and the development of the brain?

In touching her nose while looking in the mirror, this eighteen-month-old illustrates one way a toddler tells us something about the knowledge she has about herself. After having a small spot of rouge surreptitiously placed on the tip of her nose, she seems to be indicating by touching her nose that the reflection is of "me." Before about fifteen to eighteen months of age, children typically do not respond to their reflection in the mirror because they still have a very limited understanding of self.

SELF AND OTHERS

For most infants in our culture, social interactions center largely on exchanges with caregivers. Although we have focused mostly on the emotional elements in these interactions, there are probably some other important lessons that are learned in these shared psychological contexts. For one thing, infants become aware of themselves as entities distinct from others. This is not to say that they have a full-blown "self-concept" in the sense of understanding one's own unique traits and characteristics. But they do begin to recognize their physical self, an important first step in the emergence of selfhood. They also begin to show signs of recognizing at least some of the psychological dimensions of others—caregivers and even other infants.

THE CONCEPT OF SELF

Self-awareness is usually said to begin when children declare or indicate in a fairly specific way, "That's me!" They may recognize themselves in a family photo or a vacation video, or stake a claim to a particular toy with a boisterous self-reference of "That's mine!" But do infants, even before they begin to talk, show any signs of this "idea of me"?

The seeds of such awareness already may be sown in the infant's recognition of how his own body movements take place. For example, the attentional preferences of babies as young as three months suggest that they recognize when the left and right position and movements of their legs, viewed on videotape, are inverted (Rochat & Morgan, 1995, 1998). Other research reveals that infants recognize their own voice, face, and body movements as different from those of others, suggesting the origins of a rudimentary understanding of self as separate and distinct from other people and objects well before the end of the first year (Legerstee, Anderson, & Schaffer, 1998; Rochat & Striano, 2002; Tomasello, 1995). These capacities very likely serve as precursors to the fuller representation of self.

The household mirror has become an especially helpful research tool in answering the question of when self-recognition emerges. A toddler younger than fifteen to eighteen months shows little evidence of recognizing herself in a mirror. How do we know? If a spot of rouge is placed surreptitiously on her nose, it is not until she is older than this age that she will touch or rub her nose while looking in the mirror. Such behavior suggests that she has formed a concept of the details that ordinarily make up her appearance. In just a few more months she will also say, "That's me" when asked, "Who's that?" as she stares at a picture or a reflection of herself. Moreover, this self-recognition emerges about the same time in children from widely varying backgrounds (Cicchetti et al., 1997).

The implications of becoming aware of one's physical appearance can be enormous. For one thing, it may signal the appearance of self-conscious emotions, such as embarrassment, shame, and pride, which emerge in toddlers (Lewis et al., 1989). For another, self-recognition seems to develop hand in hand with a growing awareness of others as distinct individuals. For example, a child who displays self-recognition on the mirror task is also likely to attend to a partner of a similar age and to encourage him or her to play with matching toys, an indication of increased interest in sharing and enjoyment of the other child's activities (Asendorpf & Baudonnière, 1993). Thus, at a very young age, children have begun to unwrap a major piece of the total package of their self-concept, the first of many steps in the development of their identity.

SENSE OF AGENCY

Just as we can ask a child what she knows about her physical features or personal characteristics, so, too, can we ask whether she realizes that she influences and controls her surroundings, remains the same person over time, or is a unique individual.

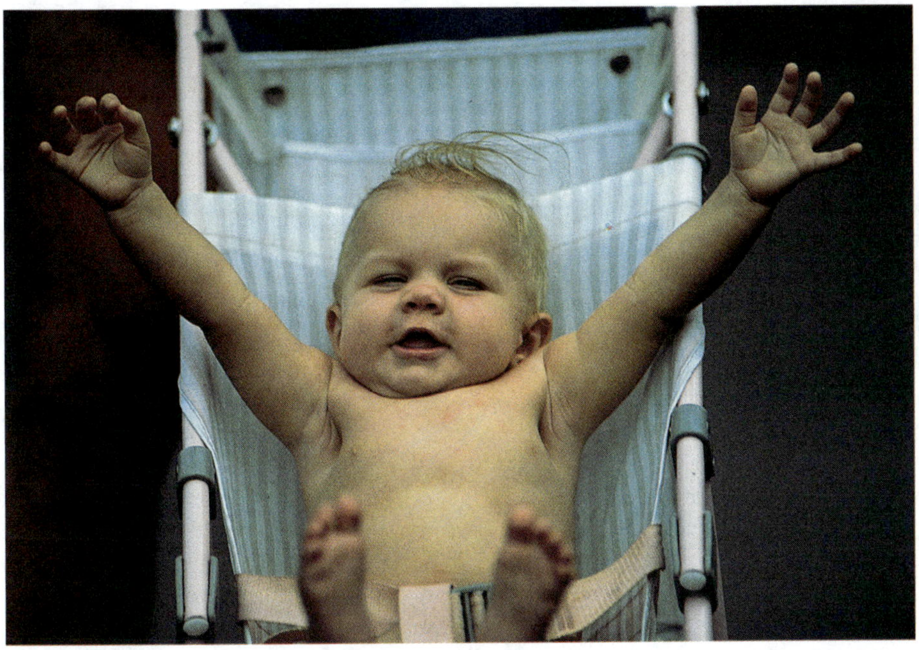

This infant may have already gained a rudimentary sense of agency. His outstretched arms seem to shout "Pick me up!" His behavior illustrates one of the many ways even babies actively influence the things that happen to them.

Such questions inquire about a child's understanding of her sense of agency or autonomy. What do children know about such matters?

The belief that a person can determine and influence his or her surroundings probably has its roots in infancy. Robert White (1959) suggested that babies are born with a desire to master their environment, an ambition he termed **effectance motivation**. The active infant repeatedly stacks blocks, bangs pots, smiles at caregivers, and plays peekaboo, activities that often lead to consequences that he anticipates. If he cries, he typically is picked up, rocked, and comforted. The one-year-old who says, "Mama" or another new word often becomes the center of attention. From the feedback associated with these actions, infants may learn to expect outcomes and how to make them happen again. Eventually, they see themselves as being in control, capable of reaching desired goals, and having the means to do so as they interact with both their physical and social environments (Wachs & Combs, 1995). For example, when babies can make a mobile rotate rapidly by moving their head on a pressure-sensitive pillow, they quickly learn to do so. But if their head movements on the pillow initially fail to have any consequences, they are far less likely to learn a contingency-related outcome when it is established (Watson, 1971; Watson & Ramey, 1972).

Many of the early accomplishments exhibited by infants are accompanied by positive emotional responses, such as delight and laughter (Case, 1991; Harter, 1998). For example, when four-month-olds learn that moving their arms will activate a picture of an infant and voices of children singing, they display positive emotions (Lewis, Hitchcock, & Sullivan, 2004). Toward the end of the first year and continuing into the second, children start to initiate efforts to share interesting sights and activities with caregivers and playmates, an important step in becoming aware of their ability to influence what others see and do.

UNDERSTANDING OTHERS

An important element in social relationships and interactions is the ability to understand the psychological states of other people—their intentions and feelings, for example. A number of research studies are beginning to reveal the remarkable

effectance motivation Inborn desire theorized by Robert White to be the basis for the infant's and child's efforts to master and gain control of the environment.

sensitivities that infants show to the social cues displayed by the individuals who surround them. We have already alluded to this idea in our discussion of language development. Infants who display *intersubjectivity* with their caregivers seem to be particularly attuned to learning the meanings of new words, for example. Even earlier in this chapter, we highlighted infants' tendencies to exhibit *social referencing*, modulating their own reactions to strange or new events depending on how they interpret the emotional expressions of others. Some would argue that, in the world of the infant, this "social intelligence" is at least as important as knowledge about physical objects and events (Trevarthen & Aitken, 2001).

The first signs of the infant's readiness to enter a social world appear at about two months of age, when she begins to have lengthier periods of alertness, displays a social smile, shows a distinct preference for scanning the human face, and exhibits a peak in crying (Rochat & Striano, 1999). The convergence of so many factors that just so happen to prepare the infant for social interactions has been dubbed the "two-month revolution" by Philippe Rochat (2001). The consequence of this newfound orientation is that caregivers and infants begin to participate in mutually rewarding playful exchanges, whether they are a game of peekaboo or a melodic exchange of smiles and vocalizations.

At nine months of age, the infant's social sophistication is even more obvious. Imagine a scene in which an adult shows an infant an interesting toy, and just as the infant is about to reach for it, the adult playfully pulls it away. Contrast this scenario with another one: the adult seems to accidentally drop the toy and is unable to reach for it. The infant is unable to touch the toy in both cases, but in the first, the adult apparently intends to tease the child. In the second case, the adult does not aim to frustrate the child. Nine-month-olds show signs of being able to tell the difference in adults' intentions; they reach for the toy more often in the "teasing" situation and also express more frustration (Behne et al., 2005). The infant's understanding of the motives of others can be thought of as a breakthrough acquisition. It signals the infant's more deliberate and *intentional* participation in the social world (Rochat, 2001).

EARLY REACTIONS TO PEERS

There is one more way in which infants show their growing awareness of self and others—in the distinct reactions they show to peers even in the first few months of life. The sight of another baby often prompts a three-month-old to become generally aroused and active, a reaction that is very different from the ritualized greeting she usually reserves for her mother (Fogel, 1979) or the rapt and quiet attention she displays to her reflected image (Field, 1979). At six months, diffuse responses to peers give way to more specific signals, such as smiles, squeals, touching, and leaning in their direction (Hay, Nash, & Pedersen, 1983; Vandell, Wilson, & Buchanan, 1980). Older babies crawl toward one another and explore one another's facial features (Vandell & Mueller, 1980). Thus, from early on, infants recognize something special and interesting about strangers who resemble them in size and features. At the same time, most peer interactions during infancy are brief, lasting only a few seconds, and usually do not involve mutual exchanges of behaviors (Eckerman, Whatley, & Kutz, 1975; Vandell & Wilson, 1982). Truly interactive play and friendship, hallmarks of young children's peer relationships, are usually not seen until at least the preschool years and beyond.

FOR • YOUR • REVIEW

- What are the early indications of the concept of self during infancy? How do researchers measure self-recognition?
- How does effectance motivation begin and develop?
- What are the infant's major accomplishments in the understanding of others?
- How do infants typically react to other children of similar ages?

CHAPTER RECAP

Summary of Developmental Themes

NATURE & NURTURE

How do nature and nurture interact in social and emotional development in infancy?

Both nature and nurture contribute to the child's socioemotional development. Biology assumes a role in the infant's ability to express and detect basic emotions, such as joy and sadness. However, socialization becomes a more prominent force as children learn to manage and regulate their emotions. Ethologists and child temperament researchers also maintain that nature guides the formation of attachments between children and caregivers, although it is also apparent that parenting style plays a role on the emergence of attachments.

SOCIOCULTURAL INFLUENCE

How does the sociocultural context influence social and emotional development in infancy?

Different cultures place varying emphases on emotionality itself and on the specific emotions considered appropriate to display. For example, a culture's beliefs and values can influence the child's responses in the Strange Situation. Japanese children are more frequently classified as insecurely attached, but their behavior may simply reflect a response to changes in normative cultural practices.

CONTINUITY/DISCONTINUITY

Are social and emotional development in infancy continuous or discontinuous?

Attachment patterns established during the first year of life endure for relatively long periods of time and forecast many desirable developmental outcomes. Thus many researchers believe that infancy is a sensitive period for the formation of attachments. Studies of adopted children in particular suggest that better socioemotional outcomes result when infants are placed with their adoptive parents prior to six months of age.

INTERACTION AMONG DOMAINS

How do social and emotional development during infancy interact with other domains of development?

Emotions are intimately connected with the rhythm and flow of social interactions, as in the case of interactive synchrony. Emotions are also related to advances in cognition. For example, young children's interpretations of feeling states, as well as the phenomenon of social referencing, likely depend on their growing cognitive skills.

RISK/RESILIENCE

What factors promote risk or resilience in social and emotional development during infancy?

Individual differences are especially evident in the enduring emotional moods that infants display. For example, children may be "easy," "difficult," or "slow to warm up" in temperament, or may display inhibited or uninhibited styles. These relatively stable individual differences may affect how parents and others react to the child and, in turn, influence other developmental outcomes, such as attachment.

Chapter Review

EMOTIONS IN INFANCY

What are the three components of emotions?

Emotions are a complex set of behaviors produced in response to some event. Emotions have physiological, expressive, and experiential components.

What are the different ways in which researchers measure emotions?

Because of their varied dimensions, emotions can be measured in an assortment of ways. Physiological measures (such as heart rate, EEGs, and fMRI), analyses of facial expressions, and self-report measures have all been used to study emotions.

What are the main ways in which biological, cognitive-socialization, and social-contextual theories of emotion differ from one another?

Biological theories state that infants are born with the ability to express certain basic emotions. Making the facial expressions for these emotions leads to the experience of the emotion. Cognitive-socialization theories emphasize the child's knowledge about the appropriate times and ways of expressing emotions, knowledge that is gleaned from socialization experiences. Social-contextual theories state that emotions must be understood as processes embedded in social interactions. The positive or negative tone and their intensity are especially important.

What are some of the basic emotions that researchers have observed in young infants?

Researchers have observed the *basic (primary) emotions* of interest, distress, disgust, joy, sadness, anger, and surprise in young infants.

What are some of the changes in crying and smiling that occur during infancy?

Smiling shifts from a reflexlike behavior to a controlled, voluntary response important to social interactions with the caregiver. Crying changes from a way of expressing physical needs to including demands for objects and actions.

Why is the emergence of social referencing so significant in the course of emotional development?

Social referencing, looking to another individual for emotional cues on how to act, indicates that an infant interprets emotional expressions as having meaning.

What are the dynamics of interactive synchrony between infant and caregiver? What is the significance of these types of interactions for the infant's development?

During *interactive synchrony*, infants' emotional expressions occur in a contingent exchange with the caregiver. The reactions of one individual follow the expressions of the other. Infants may learn important lessons about the rules of interaction and the ability to regulate interactions in the context of these, as well as asynchronous interactions, as studies of depressed mothers and their infants show.

What strategies do infants typically use to regulate their emotional states?

Infants may distract themselves, look away, or look at the caregiver in order to regulate their emotional states.

What are the different ways in which child temperament has been characterized?

Different *temperament* categories include the easy, difficult, and slow-to-warm-up styles identified by Chess and Thomas, the inhibited versus uninhibited styles researched by Kagan and his colleagues, and the dimensions of reactivity and self-regulation focused on by Rothbart and her colleagues.

What is the evidence for a biological basis for temperament?

Children with different temperament styles show differences in such physiological responses as heart rate, EEG patterns, and cardiac vagal tone. Thus there is reason to believe that biology plays some part in temperament.

How is temperament in infancy related to later development?

Early temperament styles predict social behaviors, peer relations, and cognitive functioning later in development.

ATTACHMENT

What theoretical perspectives have influenced our understanding of attachment?

Learning theory has emphasized the mother's association with feeding *(a primary reinforcer)* and other activities that the infant finds pleasurable. As a result of this association, she is said to acquire *secondary reinforcing* attributes. Harlow's classic experiments with surrogate monkeys showed that contact comfort played a more important role in *attachment* than feeding did. Ethological theorists view attachment as an innate, adaptive phenomenon that promotes proximity between infant and caregiver and thus ensures the infant's survival.

What changes in attachment behaviors are typically seen over the course of development? Which behaviors are special hallmarks of attachment?

Several behaviors mark the child's emerging attachment to the caregiver at about six months of age. These include using the caregiver as a *secure base, separation anxiety, reunion behavior,* and *stranger anxiety*.

How is attachment assessed in young children? What categories are used to classify children?

Attachment is measured by observing the infant's responses to the *Strange Situation,* a standardized laboratory task that assesses the infant's use of the mother as a secure base for exploration; stranger anxiety; separation anxiety; and reunion behavior. The different attachment categories include *secure attachment* and three categories of insecure attachment—*avoidant, ambivalent* (or *resistant*), and *disorganized/disoriented attachment*.

What factors have been shown to promote secure attachments?

Several variables predict the formation of secure attachments, including the sensitivity and responsiveness of the caregiver, the synchrony of child-caregiver interactions, and the temperament of the child. Fathers who are high on sensitivity and responsiveness are fully capable of being objects of attachment.

What are the consequences of attachment styles for later development?

Security of attachment predicts a number of important developmental outcomes, including cognitive performance, social competence, and high self-esteem.

How are attachment behaviors similar or different across cultures? What is the significance of these findings?

The proportion of infants placed in the various attachment categories can vary cross-culturally, but these studies still confirm that maternal sensitivity is an important factor in the emergence of secure attachment. However, it is important to consider the goals of socialization in a particular culture as attachment concepts are applied in different cultural contexts.

What is the impact of child care on attachment?

The most recent data show that, in general, early experiences in child care do not lead to disruptions in attachment. Rather, it is important to consider the emotional climate of the home and the quality of interactions that parents and infants have when both parents work.

What do the cases of prematurity, adoption, and abuse tell us about the concept of attachment?

Studies of premature infants, adoptees, foster children, and abused children indicate that attachments can form under less-than-optimal circumstances but that extreme deviations in caregiver-child interaction patterns can have serious negative consequences for the child, including *failure to thrive*.

What is the relationship between early emotional experiences and the development of the brain?

There is growing evidence to suggest that early emotional experiences are linked to changes in the underlying physiology of the central nervous system. Changes in the action of cortisol and neurotransmitters have been observed in young organisms that experience prolonged early stress.

SELF AND OTHERS

What are the early indications of the concept of self during infancy? How do researchers measure self-recognition?

Infants recognize the movement of their own legs at three months and their own voice and face especially between fifteen and eighteen months of age. In order to get a measure of self-recognition, researchers often observe infants' reactions to a spot of rouge placed on the nose as infants look in the mirror.

How does effectance motivation begin and develop?

Infants seem to be born with an intrinsic desire (*effectance motivation*) to gain control of their world. To the extent that an environment provides consistent feedback, children acquire an increasing sense of agency.

What are the infant's major accomplishments in the understanding of others?

At two months of age, infants show a distinct orientation to social stimuli. At about nine months of age, infants exhibit more intentional participation in social interactions.

How do infants typically react to other children of similar ages?

At about three months, infants react with arousal and activity to the presence of other infants. By six months, they smile at and touch other infants, and by the time they are mobile, they crawl toward and explore the faces of infant strangers.

KEY TERMS AND CONCEPTS

ambivalent (resistant) attachment (p. 250)
attachment (p. 247)
avoidant attachment (p. 250)
basic (primary) emotion (p. 240)
disorganized/disoriented attachment (p. 250)
effectance motivation (p. 263)
emotion (p. 237)
failure to thrive (p. 260)
interactive synchrony (p. 242)
primary reinforcer (p. 248)
reunion behavior (p. 249)
secondary reinforcer (p. 248)
secure attachment (p. 250)
secure base (p. 250)
separation anxiety (p. 249)
social referencing (p. 242)
stranger anxiety (p. 249)
Strange Situation (p. 250)
temperament (p. 245)

Pathways: Connecting the Story of Development

Infancy (0–2 years)		Early Childhood	Middle Childhood	Adolescence
Physical Development	• Evidences rapid gains in height and weight, with faster rates of growth in the head region and regions nearer the center of the body • Shows period of rapid brain development, including formation and pruning of synapses • Shows basic learning capabilities in the form of habituation, operant and classical conditioning, and imitation • Shows improvements in visual accommodation, saccadic movements, acuity, and vergence • Attracted first to external features of objects and to movement, and later to internal features of objects • Localizes sounds • Recognizes melodic rhythms and other features of music • Shows sensitivity to smells, tastes, and tactile stimuli	See p. 376	See p. 493	See pp. 576–577
Cognitive/ Language Development	• Attends to increasingly complex patterns including those with facelike organization • Responsive to biological motion • Shows signs of depth perception • Shows intermodal perception • Develops *means-ends behavior* • Attains the *object concept* • Shows sensitivity to changes in number • Relies on egocentric and landmark cues to locate objects • Classifies objects according to physical similarities, as well as thematic and simple taxonomic relations • Distinguishes between animate and inanimate objects • Shows recognition memory for simple stimuli • Shows long-term recall in elicited imitation tasks • Shows simple problem-solving behaviors, including transfer • Discriminates among phonemes • Discriminates own language from others • Detects words in speech stream • Produces gestures to communicate • Comprehends many words • Speaks in single-word utterances			
Social/ Emotional Development	• Displays basic emotions • Imitates emotional expressions of others • Recognizes others' emotions • Begins to regulate own emotions through withdrawal or distraction • Forms attachments • Recognizes self • Begins to be able to delay gratification • Shows early signs of agency • Shows intersubjectivity • Shows early signs of empathy			

8 PHYSICAL, COGNITIVE, AND LANGUAGE DEVELOPMENT

Jeremy! Let's play hide-and-seek!" shouted Tommy to his three-year-old brother. "See. You hide. I'll count to ten. Then I'll find you. It's fun, Jeremy. Let's try it." Tommy took pride in being a big brother; with seven years between them, he often baby-sat while his parents did chores around the house, and he especially enjoyed teaching Jeremy new things like this favorite game of his.

"Okay," smiled Jeremy. "I hide." The toddler stepped carefully over the family's Labrador retriever and plunked himself squarely behind the couch, or so he thought since he could not see his older brother. In the distance, he heard Tommy say, "Ten! Ready or not, here I come!" and held his breath. In barely a few seconds, though, Tommy was right in front of him, grinning widely. "Silly Jeremy," chuckled Tommy, "You can't let your legs stick out like that from behind the couch. I can see you!"

KEY THEMES in Physical, Cognitive, and Language Development

NATURE & NURTURE How do nature and nurture interact in physical, cognitive, and language development in early childhood?

SOCIOCULTURAL INFLUENCE How does the sociocultural context influence physical, cognitive, and language development in early childhood?

CONTINUITY/DISCONTINUITY Are physical, cognitive, and language development in early childhood continuous or discontinuous?

INTERACTION AMONG DOMAINS How do physical, cognitive, and language development in early childhood interact with other domains of development?

RISK/RESILIENCE What factors promote risk or resilience in physical, cognitive, and language development during early childhood?

There is no doubt about it. Young children act, think, and speak differently than older children, as the preceding scene suggests. They do not understand, for example, that other individuals may have different information about objects and events in the world than they themselves do. They may not have mastered the complexities of counting, especially when the numbers go past ten, nor do they verbalize quite like sophisticated orators. Yet at the same time, it is obvious that preschoolers are functioning in more advanced ways on many fronts when compared with infants. Sometimes when you watch three- or four-year-olds, you can almost "feel the wheels turning" in their heads, so obvious are their deliberate efforts to gain information, remember the past, or solve problems. Armed with the ability to communicate and notorious for their "why" questions, most preschoolers are literally bursting to learn about the world around them, and they are developing the requisite skills to do precisely that.

The early childhood years are marked by noticeable changes in physical size and motor capabilities. Running, trying out various tricks on the backyard climbing gym, or coloring a picture become a normal part of many young children's daily routines. Preschoolers also show tremendous advances in the breadth and detail of their general knowledge, in large part because of enhancement in cognitive skills. Another extremely important dimension of the preschool years is children's nearly complete acquisition of the complexities of language. Astonishingly, most preschoolers have mastered the bewildering variety of sounds in their native language to produce thousands of recognizable words, and they understand the meanings of those words reasonably well. They also become more proficient in using the rules of grammar of their language and become aware of the interactive and sociocultural rules of communication. The end result of the child's progress in these three areas of development is an active, delightful, and sometimes challenging being that is getting ready to take its place in human society.

PHYSICAL DEVELOPMENT IN EARLY CHILDHOOD

In contrast to the dramatic gains in height and weight that we see during infancy, physical growth rate generally follows a slow and steady pace throughout much of early childhood. The average preschooler grows from a little under three feet tall at age two to a little under four feet tall at age six. Weight gains are smallest during childhood between ages two and three and gradually increase so that by age six, most children weigh between thirty-five and sixty pounds.

The brain, too, has passed its period of most rapid growth in size. By age four years, the size of the brain is about 80 percent of its adult weight (Spreen et al., 1984). The total volume of the brain does not change very much after about the age of five. Such a statement is a bit misleading, though, because the volume of the white matter increases throughout childhood and into adulthood largely because of continuing myelination of neurons. In contrast, the volume of gray matter, usually associated with the neurons, decreases largely as a result of pruning and perhaps cell death (Durston et al., 2001).

DETERMINANTS OF BODY GROWTH AND DEVELOPMENT

KEY THEME
NATURE & NURTURE

What are the roles of nature and nurture in human physical growth? On the one hand, the contributions of nature, or heredity, are suggested by research indicating significant biological influences on physical development, as well as correlations among related family and cultural members in mature size and in the onset and pattern of physical changes. On the other hand, nurture, or environment—including diet and disease—has a bearing on physical growth as well. We take the time here to examine the determinants of physical growth because the foundation that it lays at this early time in development may have implications for cognitive and social functioning now as well as later in life.

Genetic Factors A person's height is likely to be closely related to that of his or her mother and father. What is true for the family in miniature is also true for larger human populations that are genetically related. The Lese of Zaire, for example, are much taller as a group than their nearby neighbors the Efe, the pygmies of the Ituri rain forest. Even body proportions differ among groups. For example, although many individual differences and much overlap occur among people of different ethnic backgrounds, leg and arm lengths tend to be relatively greater in individuals of African descent, and even more so in Australian aborigines, than in other ethnic groups when length of the torso is equated (Eveleth & Tanner, 1990). Such similarities and differences implicate genetic factors in physical development. But genes do not control growth *directly*. Genes regulate physical development by means of neural and hormonal activity in different organs and body systems.

Neural Control Many researchers believe that the brain includes a growth center, a genetically established program or template that monitors and compares expected and actual rates and levels of growth for the individual. The claim has been supported by observations of **catch-up growth**, an increase in growth rate that often occurs if some environmental factor interferes with normal increases in height during infancy or childhood. Illness or malnutrition, for example, may disrupt physical growth. However, if the duration and severity are limited and do not occur at some critical time, the child's rate of growth often accelerates once she or he recovers. The acceleration continues until height "catches up" to the level expected had no disruption occurred.

The presence of a growth center is also suggested by the converse finding: **lagging-down growth** (Prader, 1978). Some rare congenital and hormonal disorders produce unusually rapid growth. If the disorder is corrected, growth halts or slows until actual and projected height match the trajectory established before the disruption. Where might this neural control center be located? Researchers theorize that the *hypothalamus*, a small region near the base of the brain, orchestrates the genetic instructions for growth.

Hormonal Influences **Hormones**, chemicals produced by various glands that are secreted directly into the bloodstream and can therefore circulate to influence cells in other locations of the body, furnish another key mechanism for converting genetic instructions into physical development. For example, hormones produced by cells in the hypothalamus, the suspected site of the growth center, trigger or inhibit production of still other hormones in the nearby *pituitary gland*, including one known as *human growth hormone (HGH)*. Infants with insufficient HGH may be nearly normal in size at birth, but their growth slows dramatically over the ensuing months and years; they typically reach an adult height of only about four to four-and-a-half feet. HGH, however, only indirectly promotes growth. It spurs the

catch-up growth Increase in growth rate after some factor, such as illness or poor nutrition, has disrupted the expected, normal growth rate.

lagging-down growth Decrease in growth rate after some factor, such as a congenital or hormonal disorder, has accelerated the expected normal growth rate.

hormones Chemicals produced by various glands which are secreted directly into the bloodstream and can therefore circulate to influence cells in other locations of the body.

production of *somatomedins*, specialized hormones manufactured by many other cells in the body that directly regulate cell division for growth (Underwood, 1991).

However, variations in amounts of hormones, as long as they fall within a reasonable range, do not account for individual differences in height. Individual differences seem to depend on the sensitivity of cells to the hormones (Tanner, 1978). For example, the pygmy Efe produce normal quantities of HGH but seem unable to use it to produce one kind of somatomedin important for growth to heights typical of other groups (Merimee, Zapf, & Froesch, 1981).

Nutrition and Health For a large proportion of the world's children, adequate nutrition and exposure to diseases may be the primary determinants of whether physical growth proceeds normally or even at all. We pointed out some consequences of malnutrition for fetal development in the chapter titled "The Prenatal Period and Birth." Illness and nutritional deprivation can affect postnatal growth as well. During much of the first half of the twentieth century in Western Europe, for example, the average height gain of children at various ages increased gradually over the years, except during World Wars I and II and periods of agricultural and economic crisis, when food was far more limited. In 1984 a severe, three-month-long drought struck Kenya while researchers were engaged in a study of malnutrition in that region (McDonald et al., 1994). Food intake was cut sharply. The normal rate of weight gain among children was halved.

KEY THEME
SOCIOCULTURAL INFLUENCE

KEY THEME
RISK/RESILIENCE

Severe protein-energy malnutrition can have a particularly devastating effect on growth. Children with *marasmus* fail to grow because they lack sufficient calories. Consequences include eventual loss in weight; wrinkly, aged-looking skin; an often-shrunken abdomen; and a hollow body appearance, suggesting emaciation. Another prevalent form of protein-energy malnutrition is *kwashiorkor*, or failure to develop because the diet either contains an inadequate balance of protein or includes potentially harmful toxins. Kwashiorkor typically appears in one- to three-year-old children who have been weaned, usually because of the arrival of a newborn sibling, and whose subsequent sources of protein are inadequate or contaminated.

The symptoms of kwashiorkor include lethargic behavior and apathy, wrinkled skin, and thin, wispy, slightly reddish-orange hair, but most defining is edema or swelling, especially of the stomach, giving the child a bloated appearance (Balint, 1998). Kwashiorkor leads not only to disruption in growth of the body but also to deterioration of the brain. Although some of the damage can be quickly reversed when adequate nutrition is reinstated early (Gunston et al., 1992), long-term cognitive deficits and poorer school-related performance may persist due to impaired attention and memory (Galler et al., 1990). Studies of the effects of supplementary feeding during the first few years of life, provided for nutritionally deprived families in Colombia, Guatemala, Jamaica, Taiwan, and Indonesia, indicate that both motor and mental development are enhanced (Pollitt, 1994).

KEY THEME
INTERACTION AMONG DOMAINS

As Figure 8.1 suggests, malnutrition operates at many levels to produce negative consequences for development. For example, cognitive deficits may stem from lessened motivation or curiosity and an inability to respond to or engage the environment (Brown & Pollitt, 1996). To illustrate, during the relatively brief drought in Kenya, schoolchildren became less attentive in class and less active on the playground (McDonald et al., 1994). To counter the disruption in motivation, attention, and activity level that can accompany malnutrition, some projects have been designed to encourage mothers to become more competent and effective teachers and caregivers for their young children. When nutritionally deprived children in Jamaica have been given extra play opportunities and mothers have been taught how to positively influence their children's development, children have shown substantially higher performance on developmental and intelligence tests over a fourteen-year time period compared to children not receiving the intervention (Grantham-McGregor et al., 1994). However, the scores of malnourished children, even those given this kind of intervention, continue to fall below those of children

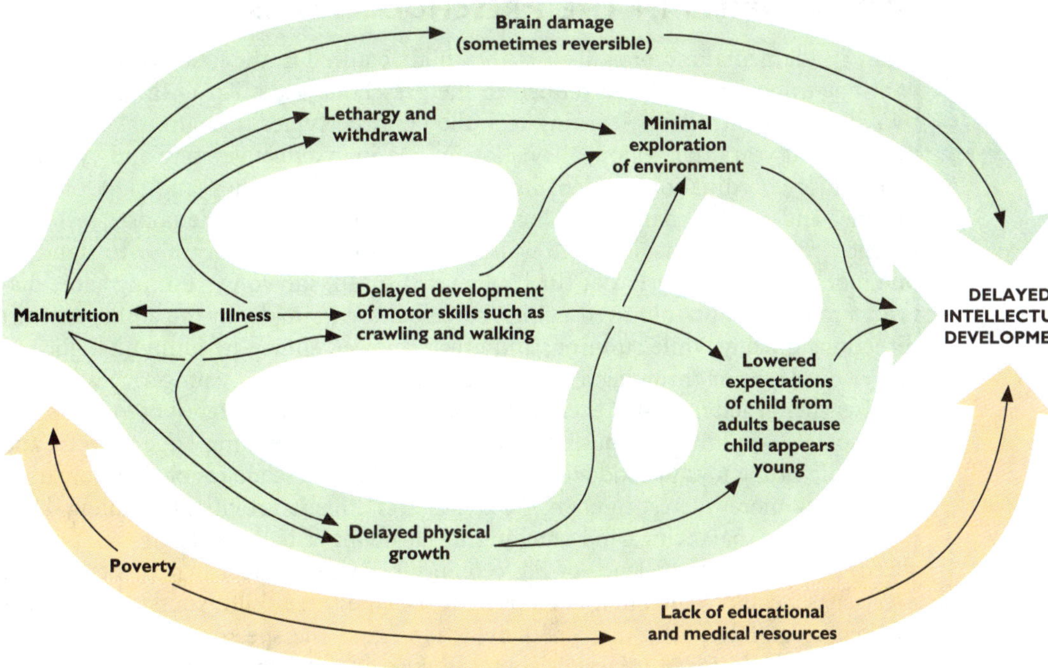

FIGURE 8.1

The Many Routes by Which Malnutrition Affects Development

Nutritional deprivation can influence development at many different levels. More frequent and severe illness, delayed growth, and slower motor skill development are among the more visible consequences. Lower intellectual development is often an outcome as well. Malnutrition can damage the brain directly. However, limited capacity to engage the environment and other repercussions from the kinds of experiences a malnourished child receives may take a further toll on intellectual development. The context in which it often persists, such as poverty and the lack of essential resources, must also be factored into a consideration of how nutritional deprivation affects development.

Source: From *Malnutrition, Poverty and Intellectual Development* by J. Larry Brown and Ernesto Pollitt.

who have been adequately nourished, a finding consistently reported in studies on the long-term consequences of malnutrition (Drewett et al., 2001). Even in the United States, lower academic performance and less positive interpersonal relationships are reported among large numbers of children living in families in which inadequate amounts of nutritional food are available (Alaimo, Olson, & Frongillo, 2001).

KEY THEME
RISK/RESILIENCE

Deficiencies in specific nutritional elements—for example, vitamins A, B complex, D, and K, as well as iron and calcium—are also linked to growth disorders affecting hundreds of thousands of children throughout the world (Balint, 1998; Hansen, 1990). Some of these disorders, especially iron-deficiency anemia, spawn lower performance on intelligence and other kinds of psychological tests. Although the problem is often assumed to be limited to low-income countries, iron-deficiency anemia is a major nutritional concern in the United States, affecting perhaps as much as 20 percent of some ethnic groups (Pollitt, 1994). More alarming is the claim that, for more than three-quarters of the children in the United States, the quality of their diet is poor or in need of improvement (Federal Interagency Forum on Child and Family Statistics, 2005).

Motor Skills in the Preschool Years

Many fundamental motor skills that the child acquired in the first two years of life continue to be modified and refined in the preschool years. For example, between two and six months after learning to walk, children typically begin to run. In the months and years that follow, they show increasingly effective body and eye-hand or eye-foot coordination, evident in their greater ability to hop and skip, or kick, dribble, and catch a ball. With increasing age, children also demonstrate better balance, reflected in the ability to walk greater distances on a beam or to stand on one foot for a longer period of time; increased speed, shown by running short distances more rapidly; improved agility, revealed, for example, in the ability to shift directions quickly while running; and greater power, shown by jumping higher or longer distances or throwing a ball farther and faster than at younger ages.

In general, activities that exercise large muscles attract the interest of toddlers and preschoolers—pulling and pushing things, stacking and nesting large objects, and eventually riding toys like kiddy cars and tricycles. As preschoolers begin to organize and display more interest in energetic games and athletic activities—jumping, hopping, running, balancing, and catching or throwing a ball—feats that emphasize speed, strength, and efficiency of performance become frequent ingredients of their everyday schedule. When first attempting to execute these skills, young children fail to prepare or follow through on their actions, and the speed or force needed to complete them in a mature way is absent. Before finally demonstrating mastery of a skill, children may also have difficulty synchronizing all of the complex movements. But, as any childhood observer can attest, gross motor skills undergo substantial improvements in the time between two and six years of age.

Fine motor skills advance, too. Older preschoolers supplement their large-muscle and athletic exercises with coloring and drawing, cutting and sculpting, and other activities that demand greater neural control and small-muscle coordination, a longer attention span, and more sophisticated planning and organization.

Implicit Learning

Whether it is figuring out how to pedal a tricycle or getting one's first lessons in gymnastics, many motor abilities, especially those requiring some level of skill, involve learning and practice. Implicit learning has become of increasing interest to researchers because it may help to explain the acquisition of some fundamental aspects of knowledge, not just procedural routines that accompany many motor behaviors in children, but also language and concepts. **Implicit learning** refers to knowledge that is not available to conscious reflection. It is knowledge incidentally acquired from processing structured information; the learning is unintentional. Because much of the stimulation to which we are exposed—for example, the visual-spatial environment and language—is organized by patterns and rules, learning these systematic relationships is important for adaptation to both the physical and social worlds. Essentially, as a result of the frequent covariation of specific features and attributes in experience, we implicitly become sensitive to these patterns or rules.

Research by Annie Vinter and Pierre Perruchet (2000) illustrates how the concept of implicit learning applies to a motor skills task. When we draw a figure, such as a circle, we tend to do so either clockwise or counterclockwise, depending on the position of the starting point. For example, if the starting point is above an imaginary line drawn to connect the positions of approximately eleven o'clock and five o'clock on the circle, we tend to draw it counterclockwise; if below the line, clockwise. Of course, the requirement of drawing the entire circle is the same no matter which direction is employed. In Vinter and Perruchet's study, children practiced drawing the circle but were instructed at what point to start and in which direction to draw it. Some children received far more experience drawing the circle in the direction opposite to the one they would spontaneously employ. When no longer instructed to draw the circle in a particular direction, they were much more likely to draw it in

implicit learning Abstract knowledge not available to conscious reflection; acquired accidentally from processing structured information.

the direction with which they had more experience. The children (as is true of adults as well) did not realize that they had drawn the circle in one direction more frequently than the other during the practice session. Nevertheless, they continued to display this behavior, a kind of implicit learning, as much as an hour after the practice session. These findings suggest that learning takes place in many contexts and situations of which we are totally unaware and by different mechanisms than those involved in, for example, classical and operant conditioning. In other words, even young children's behavior could be dramatically influenced and driven by the various kinds of regularities that they experience in their world.

FOR • YOUR • REVIEW

- How do genetic factors, neural control, and hormonal variations affect growth?
- What are catch-up and lagging-down growth?
- What are the consequences of poor nutrition for growth?
- What are the child's major achievements in motor skills in the years from two to six?
- What is implicit learning?

PERCEPTION IN EARLY CHILDHOOD

Richard Aslin and Linda Smith (1988) have noted a predicament facing anyone interested in learning about perceptual development after infancy. As research has increasingly documented sophisticated abilities in newborns and infants, interest in studying perceptual development at older ages appears to have faded. Nonetheless, researchers do find evidence of improved sensory processing during childhood (Ellemberg et al., 1999; Tschopp et al., 1999).

Perception also becomes more difficult to investigate without considering at the same time the child's developing attentional, linguistic, and cognitive skills. All of these factors may contribute to the observation that perceptual skills become more focused, organized, and confined to the meaningful and important features of the environment; in other words, perception becomes increasingly efficient with development. Eleanor Gibson (1969, 1982, 1988) has outlined an influential view of perceptual learning to account for these kinds of findings.

PERCEPTUAL LEARNING

Eleanor Gibson's theory of perceptual learning emphasizes three changes with age: increasing specificity in perception, improved attention, and more economical and efficient acquisition of perceptual information. As we have seen earlier in this text, much of the child's first year is spent learning the sensory properties of objects, the spatial layout of her world, and the perceptual repercussions of her actions. But perceptual learning continues. For example, children acquire new kinds of visual discriminations when they learn to read. They must begin to pay attention to consistencies and variations in letters and text.

To study perceptual learning, Eleanor Gibson and her colleagues (Gibson et al., 1962) created sets of letterlike figures, such as those shown in Figure 8.2. One member of each set was designated a standard, but each set included variations of that standard. A straight line, for example, might be redrawn as a curved line, the standard rotated or reversed, a break introduced in a continuous line, or the line's perspective changed by tipping or elongating some aspect of the figure. Children four through eight years of age were shown a stack of each set of figures and asked to pick out only those identical to the standard.

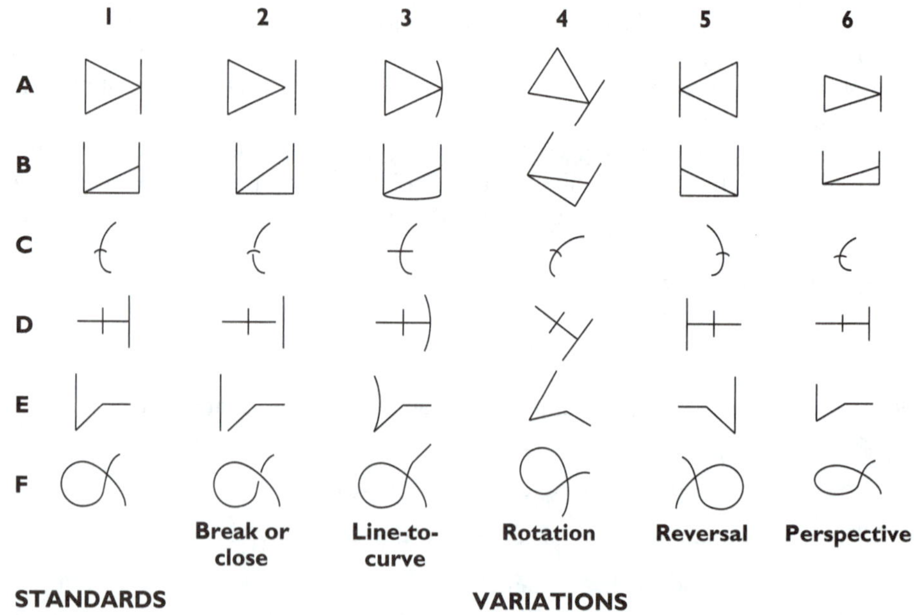

FIGURE 8.2
Sensitivity to Perceptual Differences

Column 1 gives different letterlike forms used as standards in a sorting task. Columns 2 through 6 display various transformations of each standard. Four- to eight-year-olds, when shown a stack of the figures and asked to select only those identical to the standard, commit relatively few errors on variations that involve a break in the figure, presumably because the distinction is important for identifying many objects, as well as alphabetic symbols. With increasing age, errors involving rotation, reversal, and line/curve variations decrease substantially because, according to Eleanor Gibson, children who are beginning to learn to read must pay attention to these features of the stimuli. Errors involving perspective remain high at all ages, perhaps because the transformation is not important for identifying either objects or letters of the alphabet.

Source: Adapted from Pick (1965).

Children made many more errors for some kinds of variations than for others. Children of all ages seldom confused the standard with versions that contained breaks, perhaps because these features are important for identifying objects in the environment, as well as letters of the alphabet. However, older children did substantially better than younger children in discriminating rotations, reversals, and line-curve transformations, presumably because children who are learning to read must begin to distinguish such variations. Finally, children of all ages found it difficult to discriminate changes in perspective from the standard, a variation that can and normally should be ignored for identifying both physical objects and letters of the alphabet.

Eleanor Gibson believed the age-related improvements in performance on this activity do not come about by reinforcing children to make the discriminations. In fact, when asked to classify the letterlike forms over a series of trials, children showed steady improvement in sorting, without any feedback about their accuracy. Gibson argued that, through repeated exposure to and inspection of letters of the alphabet, children are afforded the opportunity to recognize certain critical features distinguishing such figures, an example of the powerful influence of implicit learning discussed earlier.

Still other changes are evident in perceptual development. Young children, for example, have difficulty making precise and systematic judgments about the similarity of objects based on a single dimension or attribute (Smith, 1989). Preschoolers

FIGURE 8.3

Perceiving Ambiguous Figures

What do you see in these ambiguous figures? If you look at each figure long enough, you will most likely see (in one or the other order) a vase and two people looking at each other, a duck and a rabbit, and a rat and an old man with glasses. In fact, your perception of the figures may often shift back and forth between the two interpretations. If you did not see both initially, you will readily detect them when told about the two possible representations. However, children less than five years of age seem unable to see more than one representation even when told about the alternative interpretation. Cognitive limitations associated with attributing multiple representations to a stimulus may be a factor in seeing both aspects of the ambiguous figures.

Source: Gopnick & Rosati (2001), p. 176.

might put a red rubber ball with a slightly smaller ball of pink yarn because the overall appearance of the two is similar, whereas older children are likely to lump the red rubber ball with a white foam ball on the basis of their being exactly the same size. Preschoolers also do not perceive the two distinctive interpretations that typically can be given to ambiguous figures (see Figure 8.3). Even after looking at an ambiguous figure for a long period of time, children younger than about five years of age fail to see the figures reverse, as do older children and adults (Gopnik & Rosati, 2001). Perhaps cognitive limitations in organizing perceptual information and in understanding that arrays can have multiple meanings are factors contributing to the difficulty that young children have with these kinds of perceptual tasks.

EXPERIENCE AND PERCEPTUAL DEVELOPMENT

KEY THEME
NATURE & NURTURE

How do experience and inborn sensory capacities interact to determine perception? Throughout the history of psychology this has been an important question, and it continues to be so as medical and technical advances provide opportunities to compensate for some kinds of sensory disabilities. For example, blind children can perceive the existence of distant objects, presumably from changes in auditory cues they receive while moving about (Ashmead, Hill, & Talor, 1989). As a consequence, blind children are now being fitted with sonic devices to help them hear echoes to signal the direction, distance, and other qualities of objects.

The effects of these efforts with blind children are still to be demonstrated, but we can be sure of one thing from research we discussed earlier that showed evidence for sensitive periods in the development of vision: experience is extremely important for maintaining many perceptual capacities. Experience also helps to explain cross-cultural differences in perception. Environments around the world differ in their degree of "carpenteredness" (Segall, Campbell, & Herskovits, 1966). In most urban, technically advanced societies, houses are constructed according to rectilinear principles, which involve perpendicular and right-angle dimensions. Even the layouts of roads and other artifacts of the environment often follow these principles. In other environments, such as in Oceanic and many African cultures, walls and roofs may be curved, and straight lines and angular intersections may be few.

KEY THEME
Sociocultural Influence

In one study, field workers administered several optical illusions, such as the Müller-Lyer and horizontal-vertical illusions, whose effects depend on straight lines that intersect, to samples of children and adults in Africa, the Philippines, and the United States (Segall et al., 1966). The researchers theorized that individuals living in a carpentered environment, who often see intersecting rectangular contours, would be more susceptible to these illusions than people living in noncarpentered environments. In fact, their results conformed to their prediction. In a related set of findings, children and adults in cultures with minimal formal education, little experience with pictures, or artworks that incorporate few depth cues were unlikely to perceive pictures or photos in three dimensions (Pick, 1987). Thus the ways in which children and adults interpret their sensory environment can be greatly affected by cultural opportunities, a finding that fits well with the conclusion that perception is influenced by experience.

FOR • YOUR • REVIEW

- What are the basic elements of Gibson's perceptual learning theory?
- What aspects of objects do children have difficulty perceiving?
- How might cross-cultural factors influence perceptual development?

Cognition in Early Childhood

Much of our exploration of cognitive development in early childhood continues to be grounded in the foundational ideas of Jean Piaget, who outlined major advances in the thinking of children who have grown past infancy. However, contemporary research has added an abundance of fascinating details to the initial portrait Piaget painted of the emerging thinker that we find in the preschool-age child. In this section, we describe several types of conceptual knowledge, memory, and problem-solving skills that we observe in the period from two to six years of age. Because the end of early childhood signals the entrance of most children into a formal educational system, it is especially important to consider how the child's skills match the demands that will be placed on her or him as that landmark first day of school approaches.

Piaget's Theory and Early Childhood

In Piaget's theory, the period of early childhood is characterized by thought that is *preoperational*. Piaget employed a classic series of problem-solving tasks to reveal the major features of children's thinking during this developmental stage.

The Preoperational Stage (About Two to Seven Years) The key feature of the young child's thought in the **preoperational stage** is the *semiotic function*, the child's ability to use a symbol, an object, or a word to stand for something. The child can play with a cardboard tube as though it were a car or draw a picture to represent the balloons from her third birthday party. The semiotic function is a powerful cognitive ability because it permits the child to think about past and future events and to employ language. In fact, Piaget asserted that language would not be possible without this significant characteristic of thought; the child must possess the general cognitive ability to let one thing stand for another before she can use words to represent objects, events, and relationships. The semiotic function is also a prerequisite for imitation, imagery, fantasy play, and drawing, all of which the preschool child begins to manifest.

Despite this tremendous advance in thinking, preoperational thought has distinct limitations. One is that children in this stage are said to be **egocentric**, a term that describes the child's inability to separate his own perspective from others'. Put into words, his guiding principle might be "You see what I see, you think what I

preoperational stage In Piagetian theory, the second stage of development, from approximately two to seven years of age, in which thought becomes symbolic in form.

egocentric Term applied to the preoperational child's inability to separate his or her own perspective from those of others.

think," much like Jeremy in this chapter's opening scene, who thinks he is hiding from his older brother by crouching behind a couch. Even though his legs and feet might be sticking out for all present to see, the youngster believes he is well concealed because he himself is unable to see anyone. According to Piaget, the preschooler's egocentrism has ramifications for both his social communicative behavior and his perceptual skills. Piagetian theory predicts that children under age seven years may neither be fully attentive to the needs of a listener in a conversation nor able to appreciate the perspectives of others in perceptual tasks.

The second limitation of preoperational thought lies in the child's inability to solve problems flexibly and logically. The major tasks Piaget used to assess the status of the child's cognitive development are called the **conservation tasks**. These "thinking problems" generally require the child to observe some transformation in physical quantities that are initially equivalent and to reason about the impact of the transformation. Figure 8.4 shows several conservation tasks.

We can use the conservation of liquid quantity task to illustrate how the preoperational child thinks. The four- or five-year-old will usually quickly agree that two equal-size glasses of water contain the same amount of liquid. If the liquid from one glass is poured into a tall cylinder, however, the child will state that the cylinder now contains more than the glass does. According to Piaget, this error is the result of several limitations in preoperational thinking. One is **centration**; that is, focusing on one aspect of the problem—in this case, the height of the cylinder—to the exclusion of all other information, such as its narrower width, that could help to produce a correct solution.

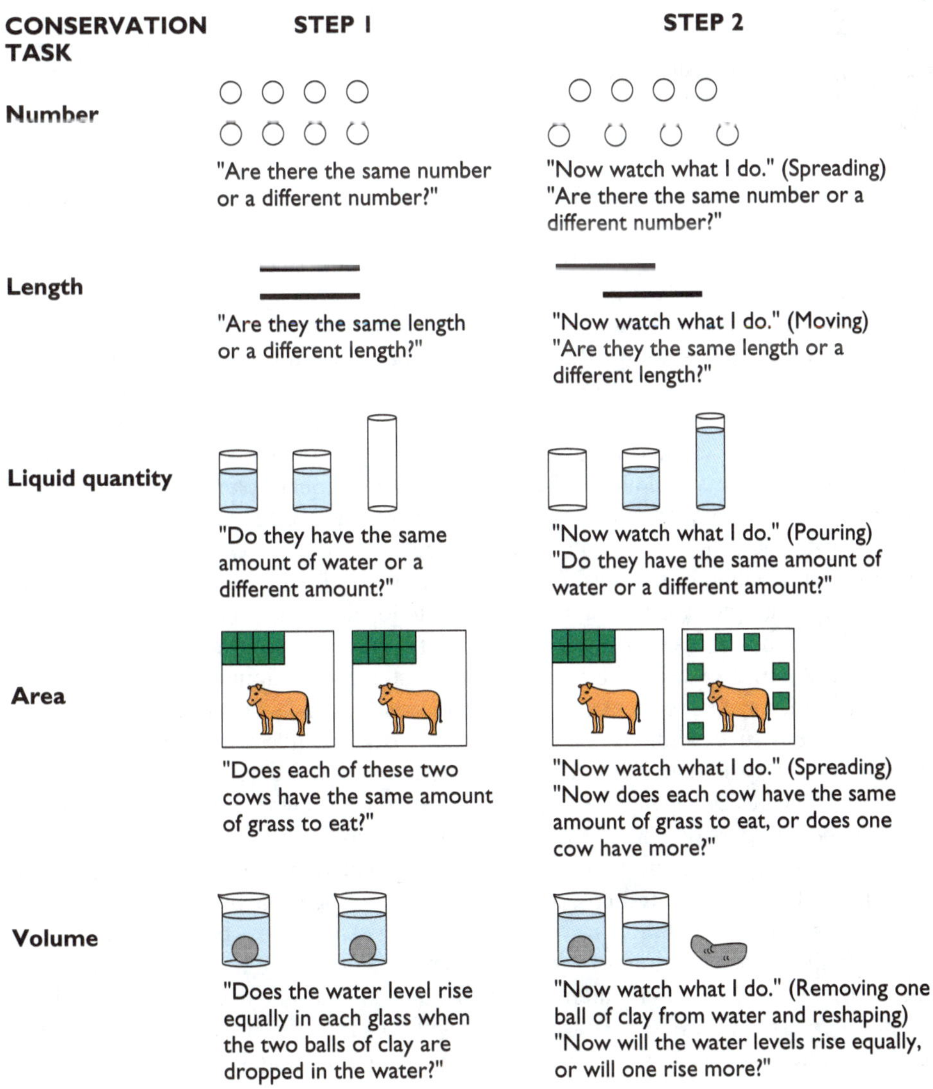

FIGURE 8.4

Examples of Conservation Tasks

Depicted here are several Piagetian conservation tasks that children can solve once they reach the stage of concrete operations. Preoperational children usually say the quantities change after the transformation. Piaget believed they lack the logical thought structures necessary to reason correctly.

conservation task Problem that requires the child to make judgments about the equivalence of two displays; used to assess stage of cognitive development.

centration In Piagetian theory, tendency of the child to focus on only one aspect of a problem.

An important question concerning cognitive development is whether changes in thinking are domain-general, as Piaget claimed, or domain-specific. For example, proponents of a domain-specific view believe that children's understanding of numerical concepts advances more quickly than knowledge in other domains.

A second cognitive trait at work here is lack of **reversibility**. The preoperational child cannot mentally reverse the action of pouring from the tall cylinder to the shorter glass; if she could, she would realize that the two containers still hold the same amount of liquid that they did at the start of the problem. Third, the preoperational child tends to **focus on states** rather than on the events that occur between states. It is as though he has stored two static photographs of the two equal-size glasses, followed by static photographs of the shorter glass and the tall cylinder, rather than a video of the sequence of events. He fails to realize the connection between the two components of the conservation problem and, as a result, fails the conservation task.

How Accurate Was Piaget About Thinking in Early Childhood? Piaget is widely acknowledged as one of the most influential of all thinkers in the history of psychology and a founder of the study of cognitive development as we know it (Brainerd, 1996; Flavell, 1996). By introducing questions about what develops as well as how development occurs, Piaget went well beyond the descriptions of norms of behavior that had been the staple of the early years of research in developmental psychology. Moreover, once American psychologists learned of his ideas in the 1960s and early 1970s, they could no longer conceptualize development solely in terms of learning theory, which was a dominant psychological view at that time. Piaget's method of closely watching the nuances of children's behaviors and listening as they explained their reasoning provided an important and inspiring lesson for developmental psychologists: that "grand questions can actually be answered by paying attention to the small details of the daily lives of our children" (Gopnik, 1996, p. 225). At the same time, though, like all good theories, Piaget's ideas have spawned a host of debates about the fundamental nature of cognitive change. Two important issues concern the generality of cognitive growth and the precise nature of the processes that underlie advances in thinking.

Piaget maintained that, for the most part, changes in mental structures—like the shift from sensorimotor to preoperational thought—are broad, sweeping reorganizations that influence thinking in multiple domains. Development, in this view, is said to be *domain-general*. However, some theorists maintain that advances in thinking occur more rapidly in some domains than in others; that is, development is seen as *domain-specific* (Hirschfeld & Gelman, 1994). One example of domain-specific processes is children's rapid acquisition of certain concepts, such as the properties of biological entities. Children seem to acquire a vast amount of information about animals, plants, and other living things at very young ages and at a particularly rapid pace (Gelman & Williams, 1998). Moreover, this knowledge does not seem to "spill over" into other kinds of conceptual understanding. Children's acquisition of basic numerical concepts—which we already noted starts during infancy—is another candidate for domain-specific knowledge.

Many studies have confirmed Piaget's general claims about the patterns of behavior that children display at different ages. Without special training, for example, most children under age six or seven years fail conservation tasks, whereas older children perform them successfully. Yet many psychologists disagree with Piaget about the precise mechanisms that account for such patterns in the development of thinking processes. The basic challenge to Piaget's theory centers on whether cognitive development is best understood in terms of emerging symbolic, logical, and (later) hypothetical thought structures or whether some other explanation is more tenable. A case in point is the successful training of conservation by Rochel Gelman (1969). Gelman suggests that young children normally fail conservation tasks because they fail to attend to the correct portions of the problem, not because they lack mental operations like reversibility. If children's attention is directed to the salient cues, such as length or number, Gelman and others argue, they will be successful in conserving. Younger children may also be less skilled at remembering than older children, forgetting

reversibility In Piagetian theory, the ability to mentally reverse or negate an action or a transformation.

focus on states Preoperational child's tendency to treat two or more connected events as unrelated.

elements of problems that are essential to reaching the correct solutions. Thus cognitive development may result from a change in how information is gathered, manipulated, and stored, rather than from the alteration of cognitive structures themselves.

CLASSIFICATION

We have already seen in Chapter 6 that infants learn about relationships that can exist among sets of objects. They use shared *perceptual* features to group items together, and by age two, can also use *thematic* and occasionally *taxonomic* relations. They will put a banana and an apple together, presumably because they belong to the higher-order conceptual group "fruit." Piaget believed that, before age seven years, children's ability to classify objects, particularly in the hierarchical manner of the latter example, is limited. Ask a young child who sees six brown beads and three white beads, all of which are wooden, "Do I have more brown beads or more wooden beads?" Chances are the four- or five-year-old will respond, "More brown beads." According to Piaget, preoperational children lack the logical thought structures to permit understanding that some classes can be subsets of others (Piaget, 1952a). Piaget was right in claiming that classification skills undergo changes with development, but the research that followed his work has revealed a far more complex portrait of this cognitive skill. Rather than showing a single kind of progression in classification skills, children evidence a range of types of conceptual skills depending on the kind of information with which they are confronted (Gelman & Kalish, 2006).

Basic-Level Categories Some groupings of objects can be described as *basic level*; that is, objects go together when they look alike and can be used in similar ways, and when we can think of "average" members of the class. "Chair" is an example of a basic-level concept because virtually all chairs have seats, legs, and backs; all are used for sitting; and we can think of such a thing as a "typical" chair. In contrast, other concepts are *superordinate level*. Members of superordinate-level groups, such as "furniture," do not necessarily share many perceptual attributes, and they are broader and more general than basic-level concepts. Figure 8.5 illustrates this example of a basic-level and a superordinate-level grouping.

Eleanor Rosch and her colleagues believe that, because basic-level groups carry more information, especially perceptual information, than superordinate-level groups, they are easier for children to process. Children under age five years readily put together four pictures of different shoes or four pictures of different cars; that is, they can sort according to basic-level groupings (Rosch et al., 1976). Children in Rosch's study could not, however, proficiently sort on the basis of superordinate category by putting a shoe, shirt, sock, and pants together until they reached age eight or nine years. In fact, other research shows that the ability to sort basic-level stimuli does indeed appear early in development; it is evident as early as eighteen months of age (Gopnik & Meltzoff, 1992).

Even though Rosch's theory of basic-level categories has had widespread appeal, there are two important points of contention. First, do children really evidence knowledge and use of superordinate categories later (as opposed to early) in development? Not according to findings by Behl-Chadha (1996), which indicate that children as young as three to four months can categorize superordinate items when the habituation procedure is used. Second, do children's early categories really rely primarily on perceptual information, as the notion of basic-level concepts suggests? Jean Mandler thinks the answer is no (Mandler, 2004). Consider the items shown in Figure 8.6, which are perceptually similar but belong to two different conceptual categories. A group of seven- to eleven-month-olds was allowed to examine several items from one category, say birds, until they were familiar with them. Then two more objects, a new bird and a new plane, were presented. Infants spent more time looking at and manipulating the item from the new category—in this particular instance, planes—than the item from the familiar category, despite the striking perceptual similarities between the two groups (Mandler & McDonough, 1993). Mandler argues that, during the latter portion of the first year, infants form categories based on *meanings* rather than perceptual similarities.

FIGURE 8.5

Basic- and Superordinate-Level Categories

The left panel gives an example of objects that are considered a basic-level grouping. These stimuli share perceptual features, and an "average" member of the class can be conceptualized. The right panel gives an example of superordinate-level grouping. Members of such classes do not necessarily share many perceptual features, and it is more difficult to think of an "average" class member. Basic-level categories are easier for young children to employ than superordinate-level groupings.

FIGURE 8.6

How Do Infants Group Birds and Airplanes?

According to research by Mandler and McDonough (1993), seven- to eleven-month-old infants treated these stimuli as belonging to two separate categories, birds and planes, despite the strong perceptual similarities between them. Thus, Mandler argues, young children's categories are based on meanings rather than shared perceptual features.

Source: Mandler (1997).

Moreover, rather than starting with basic-level categories and progressing to superordinate categories as Rosch has postulated, Mandler and her colleagues maintain that infants begin with broad, general categories. They understand, for example, that different animals (both a dog and a bird) can drink water from a cup but that an airplane cannot. These broad categories of "animalness" become increasingly more fine-tuned and refined with experience (Mandler & McDonough, 1998, 2000), processes that presumably continue through the preschool years and perhaps beyond.

Natural Domains Several developmental psychologists have asserted that some concepts or categories of objects are easier to acquire than others. Children seem to be biologically "programmed" to learn about certain conceptual domains quickly and effortlessly. In other words, some objects and events in the environment offer "privileged relationships" for the child to learn about (Gallistel et al., 1991). Among these so-called **natural domains** is knowledge about biological entities.

KEY THEME
NATURE & NURTURE

Children show a dramatically early ability to classify animate versus inanimate objects. For example, a twenty-four-month-old will show obvious surprise when a chair seems to move forward on its own (Golinkoff et al., 1984), and a twelve-month-old will fuss and cry more when a robot starts to move, as opposed to a human stranger (Poulin-Dubois, Lepage, & Ferland, 1996). Three-year-olds know that living things can feel emotions but inanimate objects cannot; they say that a person can feel sad, but a doll or a rock cannot (Gelman, Spelke, & Meck, 1983). Preschoolers also begin to recognize that other processes, such as growth, illness, healing, and death, are unique to biological organisms (Backscheider, Shatz, & Gelman, 1993; Rosengren et al., 1991; Siegal, 1988).

Part of the usefulness of concepts, of course, is that they permit us to make assumptions about other category members. In other words, we go beyond the information given, perhaps even beyond the similarities of perceptual features of objects, to make conceptually based judgments or inductions about them. According to Susan Carey (1985) and Frank Keil (1989), children's inductions are largely guided by "theories" they construct about the nature of specific concepts. For the domain of biological entities, Carey found that children's theories undergo revision with development to allow more and more accurate judgments. For example, a four-year-old who is told that humans have "omenta" will say that only other animals that are very similar to humans also have "omenta." The child's theory about biology centers on what he knows about humans. In contrast, an older child would state that even animals physically dissimilar from humans have "omenta." Her theory of biology extends beyond resemblances to human beings to the broader properties that characterize living things. Theories do seem to play a role in children's categorization. When provided with theories about fictitious animals and their features, for example ("Wugs are animals that like to fight" and "Gillies are animals that like to hide in trees"), children were more successful in categorizing pictures of "wugs" and "gillies" than when they were trained to focus solely on their features ("Wugs are animals that have claws") (Krascum & Andrews, 1998).

Individual and Cultural Variations in Classification Implicit in Piagetian ideas about classification is the notion that there should be many similarities in concept development among children, even those from different cultures. However, research suggests that this is not the case. For example, some three-year-olds show a clear propensity to use thematic classification, whereas others prefer taxonomic classification. Interestingly, these individual differences in classification preferences are linked to earlier unique profiles in play and language use. As one-year-olds, "thematic" children have been noted to play with objects in spatial, functional ways and, at age two, use words such as *in* and *down* more than "taxonomic" children do; that is, they have seemingly stable preferences to focus on how objects work in relation to one another (Dunham & Dunham, 1995).

natural domain Concept or category that children acquire especially rapidly and effortlessly.

Like this four-year-old, many preschoolers are able to count and understand at least some principles of numerical relationships, such as *cardinality*. By claiming that preoperational children do not have a conceptual understanding of number, Piaget probably underestimated children's numerical competence.

Cultural variations in classification occur, too. One group of researchers found that residents of rural Mexico with little formal schooling tended to group objects on the basis of their functional relations. "Chicken" and "egg" were frequently classified together because "the chicken lays eggs." On the other hand, individuals with more education relied on taxonomic classification, grouping "chicken" with "horse" because "they are animals" (Sharp, Cole, & Lave, 1979). It may be that taxonomic classification strategies are taught explicitly in schools or that education fosters the development of more abstract thought, a basic requirement for taxonomic grouping. Any full explanation of the development of classification skills will have to take into account the experiences of children within their specific sociocultural contexts.

NUMERICAL CONCEPTS

Children as young as two years of age frequently use number terms, either to count toys, snacks, or other items or in playful ways, such as shouting, "One, two, three, jump!" as they bounce off their bed (Saxe, Guberman, & Gearhart, 1987). But do young children really understand the full significance of numbers as a tool for establishing quantitative relationships? Or are they merely repeating a series of words they have heard someone else say, without fully appreciating the conceptual underpinnings of those words?

Piaget's (1952a) position was that children under age seven years or so, before they enter the concrete operational stage, lack a full grasp of the meaning of numbers. One indication is the failure of preoperational children to succeed in the conservation of number task. In this problem, you will recall, children see two equal rows of objects—say, red and white poker chips—as was shown in Figure 8.4. Initially the rows are aligned identically, and most children will agree that they have equal numbers of chips. But when the chips in one row are spread out, the majority of children state that this row now has more chips, even though no chips have been added or taken away.

Preoperational children, Piaget maintained, fail to comprehend the **one-to-one correspondence** that still exists among items in the two rows; that is, each element in a row can be mapped onto an element in the second row, with none left over. Moreover, he believed young children have not yet attained an understanding of two important aspects of number. The first is **cardinality**, or the total number of elements in a class, as in six red poker chips. The second is **ordinality**, the order in which an item appears in the set, as in the second poker chip. According to Piaget, the child must grasp both these concepts to judge two sets of items as being equivalent.

Many contemporary researchers believe that Piaget underestimated preschool children's understanding of number concepts. For example, two-year-olds will correctly point to a picture with three items, and not a picture with one item, when asked, "Can you show me the three fish?" (Wynn, 1992b). By age four years, many children count—they say number words in sequence and, in so doing, appreciate at least some basic principles of numerical relationships. Rochel Gelman and her associates have argued that young children have knowledge of certain important fundamental principles of counting (Gelman & Gallistel, 1978; Gelman & Meck, 1983). Among these principles are (1) using the same sequence of counting words when counting different sets, (2) employing only one counting word per object, (3) using the last counting word in the set to represent the total number, (4) understanding that any set of objects can be counted, and (5) appreciating that objects can be counted in any order.

one-to-one correspondence Understanding that two sets are equivalent in number if each element in one set can be mapped onto a unique element in the second set with none left over.

cardinality Principle that the last number in a set of counted numbers refers to the number in that set.

ordinality Principle that a number refers to an item's order within a set.

When young children count, their words are not devoid of numerical meaning. In one experiment, three- and four-year-olds saw six dolls and five rings and were asked, "There are six dolls. Is there a ring for every doll?" Most of the four-year-olds used number words to answer questions about one-to-one correspondence. For example, many said, "No, because there are six dolls and five rings" (Becker, 1989). In addition, four-year-olds are able to compare quantities, answering correctly such questions as "Which is bigger, five or two?" (Siegler & Robinson, 1982). Thus their understanding of number terms includes relations such as "larger" and "smaller." One interesting pattern, though, is that young children have more difficulty in making such comparisons when the numbers themselves are large (ten versus fourteen) or when the difference between two numbers is small (eight versus nine). The same is true when children have to add, subtract, and perform other calculations with numbers (Levine, Jordan, & Huttenlocher, 1992).

In fact, children seem to have a good basic grasp of even more complex numerical concepts, such as fractions, by age four. Suppose a preschooler sees three-fourths of a circle hidden by a screen and then one-half of a circle come out from behind the screen. How much is left behind the screen? A surprising number of four-year-olds can select a picture of one-fourth of a circle from a set of alternatives (Mix, Levine, & Huttenlocher, 1999). In addition, even a brief training session can help young children understand the basic concepts of fractions. When five-year-olds in one study had the opportunity to observe a whole pizza divided among different numbers of recipients, they began to understand that the size of each share of pizza depended on the number of individuals who were going to eat it (Sophian, Garyantes, & Chang, 1997).

SPATIAL CONCEPTS

Earlier in this text, we saw that infants already showed some remarkably good spatial abilities, including the capacity to use landmarks to locate objects in large spatial environments. Linda Acredolo and her colleagues demonstrated that this skill is clearly present among older children. Three- through eight-year-olds were taken on a walk through an unfamiliar building in one of two conditions (Acredolo, Pick, & Olsen, 1975). In the first condition, the hallway through which the experimenter led each child contained two chairs; in the second, there were no chairs. The children saw the experimenter drop a set of keys during the walk, and in the "landmark" condition this event occurred near one of the chairs. Later, when children were asked to retrieve the keys, performance was best in the "landmark" condition for the preschoolers; older children did well regardless of the experimental condition.

Young children can also use geometric cues—the shape of a room, for example—to orient themselves in space. In one study, an experimenter showed three- and four-year-old children a green square in the corner of a rectangular room. The experimenter then flipped the square over so that it was blue, like the squares in all of the other corners. She also spun each child around approximately four times to disorient him or her. How did children locate the green square? Because there were no landmarks or distinguishing features in this particular condition of the experiment, successful performance depended on noticing the relationship of the short and long sections of the room in the corner in which the square was located. Children directed about 40 percent of their searches to the corners that provided the correct spatial information, for example, "the short wall is on the left" (Learmonth, Nadel, & Newcombe, 2002).

One of the practical ways in which spatial skills are exercised is in reading maps. From participating in a treasure hunt at a birthday party to traveling or learning geography in school, reading maps is part of many children's experiences, at least occasionally. Making use of a map involves several types of skills, including understanding that the symbols on the page refer to real objects or places, appreciating the scale and alignment of the map in relation to the actual physical space, and, if one is actually navigating, planning an efficient route in order to get from one place to another.

Four-year-olds begin to show an ability to use simple maps to navigate a U-shaped route through a series of rooms (Uttal & Wellman, 1989). However, their skills are limited to maps for which there is a clear one-to-one correspondence between representations on the map (in this case, photographs of stuffed animals) and real objects in each of the rooms (actual stuffed animals). Also, the map must be aligned to match the actual physical space; rotating it to a different orientation presents problems. Map-reading skills improve in the next two years, though, so that by the time they are six, many children can use a map to plan an efficient route through a large-scale space (Sandberg & Huttenlocher, 2001). However, understanding maps that are not oriented in the same direction as the physical space remains challenging for children through the early school years (Liben & Downs, 1993).

Why do children improve in map reading? One way to answer this question is to see which kinds of experiences improve children's ability to use maps. When experimenters highlight the connection between objects on the map and objects in the physical space by making explicit comparisons, young children's performance improves (Loewenstein & Gentner, 2001). Organizing the spatial relations among objects in the map—by making them into a drawing, for example—helps, too (Uttal et al., 2001). Thus improvements in children's ability to reason about relations among objects are one likely source of better performance. Creating an efficient map route to follow also depends on the emergence of good planning skills. In fact, many of the problem-solving skills we will discuss later in this chapter are relevant to children's facility with maps.

FOR • YOUR • REVIEW

- What are the major characteristics of preoperational thought according to Piaget?
- What are the some criticisms of Piaget's theory about thought in early childhood?
- What developmental changes have researchers observed in children's classification, numerical reasoning, and spatial concepts in the preschool years?

Understanding Psychological States

Our knowledge extends beyond understanding of physical objects, classes, number, and space. It also includes an awareness of our minds and how they and the minds of others work. How do children understand and judge the motives, feelings, needs, interests, capacities, and thoughts of playmates, siblings, parents, and others? And how and when do children come to understand and reflect on the psychological states of the self? This type of cognition, thinking about the self and its relationship to the social world, is called *social cognition* and is a vital aspect of successful communication and social interaction. In comparison to the world of physical objects and events, thinking about the social world presents unique challenges to the developing child. People may act unpredictably; their feelings and moods, even their appearance, may shift unexpectedly. Just how children piece together their understanding of social experiences has been the focus of several lines of research. Here, too, contemporary researchers owe Piaget recognition for his initial efforts in studying how children think about thinking.

Perspective Taking: Taking the Views of Others **Perspective taking** is the ability to put oneself in another person's place, to consider that person's thoughts, feelings, or knowledge. One basic element of perspective taking is understanding what others see. For example, does the child realize that his sister, who is standing across the room, cannot see the brightly colored pictures in the book he is eagerly examining?

perspective taking Ability to take the role of another person and understand what that person is thinking, is feeling, or knows.

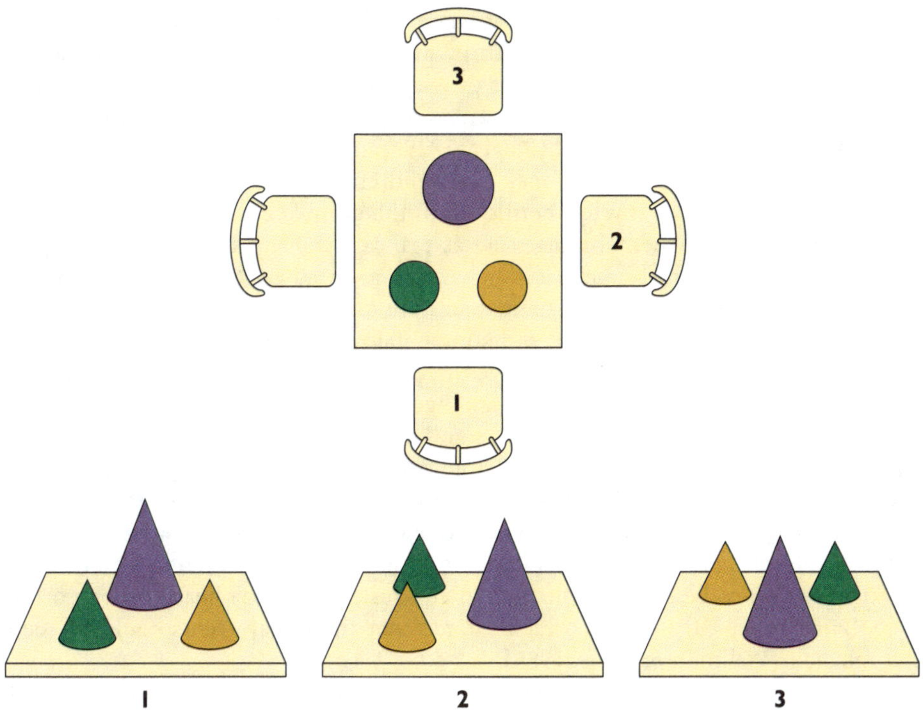

FIGURE 8.7
Visual Perspective Taking
How well can children adopt another person's perspective? Piaget asked this question by seating a child at a table (location 1) containing three "mountains" of different size and color, then asking the child how the scene would look to a doll (or another person) seated at other locations (locations 2 and 3) around the table. Piaget found that preschoolers often chose a view similar to their own. More recent research indicates that preschoolers can more successfully accomplish this task when familiar and easily distinguishable scenes are used.

In 1956, Jean Piaget and Barbel Inhelder published a classic experiment illustrating children's limited knowledge of the visual perspective of others. Children seated in front of three different papier-mâché mountains (see Figure 8.7) were asked to indicate what a doll would see in viewing the array from various locations. Four- to six-year-olds showed considerable *egocentrism* in their responses; they typically indicated that the doll's view would be identical to their own. By six to nine years of age, children began to realize that the doll's perspective would differ, although they still had difficulty figuring out what the doll would actually see. Nine- and ten-year-olds were able to determine the doll's perspective accurately. More recent research has shown that the difficulty of the doll and mountain task may have led Piaget and Inhelder to underestimate children's role-taking competence. When simpler visual arrays or familiar everyday scenes are used, or when the method of interviewing children is simplified, three- and four-year-olds can answer some of these kinds of questions reasonably well (Borke, 1975; Newcombe & Huttenlocher, 1992).

Visual perspective taking develops in two phases. At first, from late infancy until about age three years, children come to realize that their own and another's view are not identical. This is called *Level 1 perspective taking.* More advanced *Level 2 perspective taking* appears in three- and four-year-olds and continues to be refined for several years thereafter. Now children can determine the specific limitations of another's view—for example, whether an object or picture another person sees will look right side up or not (Flavell, 1978). These advances reflect cognitive gains in differentiating oneself from another and in knowledge of spatial relationships (Shantz, 1983).

The Child's Theory of Mind Children's understanding of their social world extends beyond visual perspective-taking skills. Emerging among their competencies is an expanding and increasingly coherent appreciation of the kinds of mental qualities that contribute to the behavior of self and others. Did the playmate who broke a favorite toy *intend* to do the damage? Would a close friend *believe* that Mom will not let them go to the park alone? Many of our social behaviors are guided by the judgments and inferences we make about the desires, feeling states, beliefs, and thoughts of other people (Astington, Harris, & Olson, 1988; Slomkowski & Dunn, 1996; Wellman, 1990). In fact, it would be rare *not* to be concerned with the mental states of others in the normal course of interactions with them.

When and how do children become aware of the concept of mental states, their own and those of others? In other words, when and how do children develop a **theory of mind**? Once again, Piaget has provided much of the impetus for research on this topic. His position was quite clear. As Piaget put it, "The child knows nothing about the nature of thought" (Piaget, 1929, p. 37). Dubbing this characteristic of children **realism**, Piaget maintained that children are not capable of distinguishing between mental and physical entities until the school years. To the child under age eight, dreams and mental images are as real as any event in waking, conscious life. To the same child, thinking is a behavior produced by the body, usually the mouth or the head; physical and mental acts are one and the same.

Despite Piaget's strong claims, developmental researchers have uncovered considerable evidence to the contrary. By age three, children readily distinguish between mental and physical entities and, after that age, show further developments in their understanding of their own mental states and those of others (Flavell, 1993). In one classic experiment, three-year-olds were told stories like the following: "Judy doesn't have a kitty, but right now she is thinking about a kitty." Could they see or touch the kitty? Could the kitty be seen by someone else or touched at some time in the future? Children had no problem identifying this as a mental event, one in which the kitty could not be seen or touched. In contrast, when they heard other stories, as in "Judy had a kitty," they correctly stated that these real events could be seen and touched (Wellman & Estes, 1986).

Some of the earliest signs of awareness of mental states are actually evident at eighteen months, when infants follow the gaze of an adult in episodes of joint attention. Infants react to these actions as if the adult "intends" to communicate something (Butler, Caron, & Brooks, 2000). From there, preschoolers display an increasing repertoire of knowledge of mental states that starts with understanding the meaning of "desire," then "belief," and finally the concept of "false belief" (Wellman & Liu, 2004). The typical "false belief" task involves testing children's knowledge about what a naïve observer does or does not know about a visual scene that has been transformed. In one version, children are shown a doll named Maxi who puts some chocolate in a cupboard and leaves the scene. Maxi's mother moves the chocolate to a new location. When Maxi returns, children are asked, "Where will he look for the chocolate?" Most three-year-olds say that he will look in the new location. Four-year-olds, though, recognize that Maxi holds a "false belief" and will look for the chocolate in the cupboard (Wimmer & Perner, 1983).

KEY THEME
NATURE & NURTURE

What factors account for the child's growing success on the false belief task and presumably their theory of mind? There is an ongoing debate. Some researchers argue that the theory of mind is an innate, prepackaged, modular form of knowledge that becomes more elaborate as the child's cognitive skills develop (Baron-Cohen, 1995; Fodor, 1992; Leslie, 1994). In support of this view, it is interesting to note that children from several cultures, including China, Japan, and the preliterate Baka society of Cameroon, show similar developmental improvements in their understanding of mental state terms, such as *desire* and *belief* (Avis & Harris, 1991; Flavell et al., 1983; Gardner et al., 1988; Tardif & Wellman, 2000). Likewise, performance on the false belief task shows consistent developmental trends across many studies and across cultures as diverse as Canada, India, Peru, Samoa, and Thailand (Callaghan et al., 2005; Wellman, Cross, & Watson, 2001).

KEY THEME
INTERACTION AMONG DOMAINS

Other researchers believe that a theory of mind arises from the child's socialization experiences, especially those that encourage an appreciation of others' mental states. Mothers who use more language to describe mental states to their preschoolers, for example, have children who are more successful on the false belief task several months later (Ruffman, Slade, & Crowe, 2002). Theory of mind may also depend on the extent to which a culture emphasizes this type of understanding. For example, among the Illongot people of the Philippines, there is not a great deal of concern with the concept of mind, so we might not expect to see the emergence of a strong theory of mind (Lillard, 1997, 1998). The child's theory of mind, in particular, is a key cognitive attainment bridging the self and the social world. Researchers have

theory of mind Awareness of the concept of mental states, both one's own and those of others.

realism Inability to distinguish between mental and physical abilities.

noted, for example, that performance on the false belief task is related to the child's social skills with peers (Watson et al., 1999). You will encounter several other examples of the link between theory of mind and the child's social and emotional functioning in other chapters.

Atypical Development

Childhood Autism

Childhood autism is a puzzling disorder affecting about 1 or 2 of every 1,000 children born. The disorder, more common among boys than girls, is characterized by the child's preference to be alone, poor eye contact and general lack of social skills, often the absence of meaningful language, and a preference for sameness and elaborate routines. Some autistic children show unusual skills, such as being able to recite lengthy passages from memory, put together complex jigsaw puzzles, or create intricate drawings. Often these children show a fascination with spinning objects or repeating the speech patterns of someone else. The hallmark trait, though, is the lack of contact these children have with the social world, starting at an early age. Kanner's (1943) description of one autistic boy captures the syndrome well: "He seems almost to draw into his shell and live within himself" (p. 218).

Since Leo Kanner first identified this psychopathology, numerous causes of autism have been proposed, ranging from deprived early emotional relationships with parents to defective neurological wiring in the brain (Waterhouse, Fein, & Modahl, 1996). An intriguing more recent suggestion is that autistic children, for biological reasons, lack the ability to think about mental states; that is, they lack a "theory of mind" that most children begin to develop during the preschool years. Consider how autistic children behave in the "false belief" task described earlier. Whereas most normal four-year-olds are successful, most nine-year-old autistic children fail this problem (Baron-Cohen, Tager-Flusberg, & Cohen, 1993; Peterson, Wellman, & Liu, 2005). These results suggest that autistic children cannot conceptualize the mental state of another individual. Autistic children, the argument proceeds, have severe deficits in communication and social interaction precisely because they cannot appreciate what the contents of another person's mind might be (Frith & Happé, 1999).

Not all researchers believe that the absence of a "theory of mind" explains childhood autism. Some maintain that autistic children cannot disengage their attention from a stimulus on which they are focusing, such as the hiding location in the "false belief" task (Hughes & Russell, 1993). Others suggest that problems with memory or executive control processes are responsible (Bennetto, Pennington, & Rogers, 1996; Carlson, Moses, & Hix, 1998). Moreover, even if autistic children lack a theory of mind, it may not be because of a neurological deficit. Deaf children who are not exposed to sign language for several years, for example, perform similarly to autistic children on the false belief task. Thus, as discussed earlier, the opportunity to engage in conversations from which one might glean information about the mental states of others may be a crucial factor in the development of a theory of mind (Peterson & Siegal, 1999; Woolfe, Want, & Siegal, 2002). Whatever the ultimate basis for autism, however, it seems likely that understanding basic cognitive processes will be helpful in deciphering the mechanisms underlying this perplexing childhood disorder. One outcome of this active area of research, for example, is awareness that autistic children show deficits in joint attention in the preschool years and as early as age one (Dawson et al., 2002; Leekam, Lopez, & Moore, 2000; Osterling & Dawson, 1994), a finding that can be useful in early diagnosis and treatment of this disorder.

FOR • YOUR • REVIEW

- What developmental changes in visual perspective taking have been identified by researchers?
- What is meant by the child's "theory of mind"? What contrasting positions have been suggested as explanations for the development of a theory of mind?
- What is childhood autism? What are some hypotheses about its causes?

Memory

Given the excellent memory skills of infants, especially in recognition and elicited imitation tasks, it should be no surprise that preschoolers, too, show superb memory in similar situations. Yet the advent of language permits something new: preschoolers can now *talk* about past events. They can talk about specific events in their lives, a form of memory called **episodic memory** (as in "What did you do at your birthday party?"). In addition, they can talk about the general knowledge they have acquired and stored, a phenomenon called **semantic memory** (as in "How many legs does a dog have?"). Interestingly, this general knowledge in turn has an impact on the ability to remember new events. For example, when preschoolers witness a logically ordered event, such as making "fun dough," they remember more details about the sequence than when the event consists of arbitrary segments, such as different activities in sand play (Fivush, Kuebli, & Clubb, 1992). In other words, knowledge about logical and causal relations among events helps memory.

Scripts One way to describe the effect of a growing knowledge base on memory is in terms of scripts. **Scripts** are the organized schemes of knowledge that individuals possess about commonly encountered events. For example, by the time they are three or four years old, most children have a general schematic representation for the events that occur at dinnertime—cooking the food, setting the table, sitting down to eat—as well as for other routine events, such as going to school or attending a birthday party (Fivush, 1984; Nelson & Gruendel, 1981). When asked to remember stories based on such familiar scripts, children typically recall script-based activities, such as "eating dinner," better than other details less closely related to scripts (McCartney & Nelson, 1981). Thus scripts serve as general frameworks within which specific memories can be stored and may be one of the earliest building blocks for memory.

Conversations with parents and others probably foster the formation of scripts. When parents reminisce using rich and detailed language about past events with their children, children have better recall about the past (Reese & Fivush, 1993; Reese, Haden, & Fivush, 1993). Thus scripts are likely to be influenced by the types of social experiences the child has. Within this framework, memory is better conceptualized as something children *use* than as something they *have* (Fivush, 1997).

Autobiographical Memory Think back to your childhood and try to identify your earliest memory. How old were you? It is unlikely that you will report that you were an infant or perhaps even a toddler. Most people are not able to recount memories for experiences prior to age three years (Pillemer & White, 1989; West & Bauer, 1999), a phenomenon called **infantile amnesia**. The question of why infantile amnesia occurs has intrigued psychologists for decades, especially in light of the ample evidence that infants and young children can display impressive memory capabilities.

episodic memory Memory for events that took place at a specific time and place.

semantic memory Memory for general concepts or facts.

script Organized scheme or framework for commonly experienced events.

infantile amnesia Failure to remember events from the first two to three years of one's life.

Many find that understanding the general nature of **autobiographical memories**, memories of events that have occurred in one's own life, can provide some important clues to this mystery. Between ages three and four, children begin to give fairly lengthy and cohesive descriptions of events in their past, often marking them with explicit references to time ("last Halloween" or "on my birthday") (Fivush, Haden, & Adam, 1995; Nelson & Fivush, 2004). What factors are responsible for this developmental turning point?

One explanation goes back to an idea raised by Piaget, namely, that children under age two years represent events in a qualitatively different form than older children. According to this line of thought, the verbal abilities that blossom in the two-year-old allow events to be coded in a form radically different from the action-based codes of the infant. The child's emerging verbal skills are, in fact, related to memory for personal experiences. Preverbal children who see unique events at age two do not describe them in verbal terms six months later when they are able to talk. Thus early memories seem to be encoded in a format that cannot be translated into verbal terms later on (Simcock & Hayne, 2002).

Another suggestion is that, before children can talk about past events in their life, they need to have a reasonable understanding of the self as a psychological entity (Howe & Courage, 1993, 1997). As we saw in Chapter 7, the development of the self becomes evident between the first and second years of life and shows rapid elaboration in subsequent years. The realization that the physical self has continuity in time, according to this hypothesis, lays the foundation for the emergence of autobiographical memory. Research has confirmed that the ability to recognize the self at nineteen months of age predicts the frequency with which children talk about past events when they are a few months older (Harley & Reese, 1999).

A third possibility is that children will not be able to tell their own "life story" until they understand something about the general form stories take; that is, the structure of narratives (Nelson, 1993a). Knowledge about narratives arises from social interactions, particularly the storytelling children experience with parents and the attempts parents make to talk with children about past events in their life (Reese et al., 1993). When parents talk with children about "what we did today" or "last week" or "last year," they guide the children's formation of a framework for talking about the past. They also provide children with reminders about the memory and relay the message that memories are valued as part of the cultural experience (Nelson, 1993b). It is interesting to note that Caucasian children have earlier childhood memories than Korean children do (Mullen, 1994). American children also provide more extensive, detailed descriptions of events in their past than do Korean and Chinese children (Han, Leichtman, & Wang, 1998; Wang, 2004). By the same token, Caucasian mother-child pairs talk about past events three times more often than do Korean mother-child pairs (Mullen & Yi, 1995). Moreover, Caucasian mothers who ask their children many questions about past events, elaborating on their children's comments or asking for more details ("And what did Daddy do on the boat?"), tend to have children who talk more about the past (Harley & Reese, 1999). Thus the types of social experiences children have factor into the development of autobiographical memories.

KEY THEME
INTERACTION AMONG DOMAINS

KEY THEME
SOCIOCULTURAL INFLUENCE

A final suggestion is that children must begin to develop a "theory of mind" before they can talk about their own past memories. Once children begin to accurately answer questions like "What does it mean to *remember*?" and "What does it mean to *know* something?" improvements in memory also seem to occur (Perner & Ruffman, 1995).

It may be that the developments just described are intertwined with and influence one another, that the ability to talk about one's past arises from the interplay of several factors, not just one (Pillemer, 1998). Talking with parents about the past may enhance the development of the self-concept, for example, as well as help the child understand what it means to "remember" (Welch-Ross, 1995).

autobiographical memory
Memory for specific events in one's own life.

CONTROVERSY: THINKING IT OVER

How Reliable Is Children's Eyewitness Testimony?

The research on children's memory, particularly recognition memory, suggests that their ability to remember events from the past is very impressive. But when children are called on to testify in court after they have witnessed or been victims of abuse, neglect, or other crimes, their capability to render an accurate account of past events has been called into question.

What Is the Controversy?

Just how reliable is children's memory when they are called on to give eyewitness testimony? Children's memory for events, even those that occurred months or years in the past, is remarkably good. On the other hand, children's memory is also susceptible to suggestive or leading questions by attorneys, clinicians, and other interrogators (Bruck & Ceci, 1999, 2004). The stakes are high regarding these issues. If children have been the victims of crime, the perpetrators should be punished; but if children's memories are inaccurate in these contexts, a criminal suspect might be falsely accused.

What Are the Opposing Arguments?

Some research indicates that children's recall of distinctive events, such as a trip to Disney World or a medical emergency, is surprisingly complete and accurate even four or five years after the event (Fivush & Schwarzmueller, 1998; Peterson & Whalen, 2001). For example, in one study of two- to thirteen-year-old children who had been treated in a hospital emergency room, even two-year-olds remembered a substantial amount about their injuries when they were interviewed five years later (Peterson & Whalen, 2001). Data like these suggest that children's memories are reliable.

On the other hand, other studies have shown that children, especially preschoolers, are likely to misreport a past event if they are asked misleading questions. In some of the original studies of "false memory" in children, Stephen Ceci and his colleagues tested children ages three through twelve years on their ability to remember the details of a story (Ceci, Ross, & Toglia, 1987). A day later, children in one of the experimental conditions were asked leading questions that distorted the original information, such as "Do you remember the story about Loren, who had a headache because she ate her cereal too fast?" In the original story, Loren had a stomachache from eating her eggs too fast. Compared with children who did not hear misleading questions, children who heard biased questions made more errors on a subsequent test that required them to select pictures depicting the original story: they chose the pictures showing a girl eating cereal and having a headache. This tendency to err was especially pronounced in children ages four and under.

What Answers Exist? What Questions Remain?

Many factors may influence just how suggestible children are. One is exactly who is doing the questioning. For example, in Ceci's study just described, misinformation provided by an adult tended to distort memory more than misinformation provided by another child; the perceived power of the questioner may make a difference. Second, when children are asked questions repeatedly, particularly yes-no questions, they are likely to change their answers or speculate inappropriately (Poole & White, 1991, 1993). Preschoolers in particular may perceive the repeated question as a signal that their first answer was incorrect. Repeated questions, even when they are neutral, can lead to false memories because the information contained in them can be incorporated into the "gist" of the real memory (Brainerd & Mojardin, 1998). Third, supplying dolls and props for children to reenact the event can lead to elevated false reports, especially among younger children (age three) and when this form of interview occurs after a delay of several weeks (Greenhoot et al., 1999). Finally, suggestibility may be reduced when children first are reminded to consider the basis of their information, a phenomenon called *source monitoring* (Poole & Lindsay, 2002; Thierry & Spence, 2002). In one laboratory study, for example, preschoolers were first asked to answer "Did you see it on the tape?" or "Did I tell you?" before they were asked leading questions about the story. This group was less likely to be influenced by leading questions compared with a group of children who were asked the leading questions first (Giles, Gopnik, & Heyman, 2002).

An important, and perhaps obvious, consideration in this discussion is that memories—those of both children and adults—generally decline with the passage of time. The results of a recent experiment showed that the amount and accuracy of information that children spontaneously recalled about past events went down after two years, especially if they did not have an opportunity to be reminded of the original event. Under the latter conditions, up to 50 percent of the new information that children added to their memories after being prompted by an experimenter was found to be inaccurate (Pipe et al., 1999). Because extended periods of time often elapse between a criminal event and the trial, these findings are especially relevant.

Given this information, what is the best way for professionals in the criminal justice system to encourage children to give reliable eyewitness accounts based on what we know from research?

PROBLEM-SOLVING SKILLS

Problem-solving skills become more elaborate and complex as children pass through early childhood. Although these children are not yet in school, an environment that explicitly demands more focused problem solving, many are enrolled in child care centers or preschools, which often present children with educational tasks that include elements of problem solving. Furthermore, during their play, children may encounter their own "problem situations" which require some form of resolution. Whether it is completing a simple puzzle or figuring out how to arrange blocks to make a bridge over a road, preschoolers often find themselves in circumstances in which they have to think through some options in order to achieve specific goals.

Representation One of the most basic capacities required for problem solving is the ability to use symbols—images, words, numbers, pictures, maps, or other configurations that represent real objects in the world. Piaget argued that children are unable to think with symbols—that is, use representations—until near the end of the sensorimotor stage of development at about eighteen months of age. Others, however, have challenged this position and argue that representational capacities are evident much earlier in infancy. Jean Mandler (1988, 1998) has pointed out that a number of early abilities that infants display support this thesis. For example, infants begin to use gestures to stand for objects or events prior to age one year. Similarly, young infants' apparent knowledge about the physical properties of objects, described in Chapter 6, suggests that they must hold some internal representation of them.

Although infants may have basic representational capacities, toddlers and older children far more readily recognize that external symbols of real objects in the world can be used to further their problem-solving efforts. For example, Judy DeLoache (1987) asked two- and three-year olds to search for a small toy hidden in a scale model of a room. Next, the children were brought into a life-size room that corresponded to the scale model they had just seen. Could they find the real-life toy that corresponded to the smaller replica in the previous segment of the experiment? If they saw a small Snoopy toy under a miniature couch, would they look for a large

An important cognitive skill that emerges at about age three is the understanding that a model may *represent* a real-life event. Representation is a fundamental skill necessary for problem solving.

Snoopy under the couch in the life-size room? The three-year-olds could find the hidden object on more than 70 percent of the trials. But the two-year-olds could do so on only 20 percent of the trials. Later, when both age groups were asked to locate the toy back in the scale model, they did so with few errors. Thus the search failures of two-year-olds in the life-size room were not due to memory problems. DeLoache believes that two-year-olds have difficulty with *dual representation*; that is, with understanding that a scale model can be both an object in its own right and a representation of a life-size room. By age three, however, children have the cognitive capacity, flexibility, and conceptual knowledge to appreciate that a symbol, such as a model, can "stand for" a real-life event. In other words, children gain **representational insight** (DeLoache, 2000; DeLoache & Smith, 1999).

Some factors can accelerate young children's tendency to develop representational insight. Repeated exposure to scale models, drawings, and live video photography helps children younger than three years to understand that these are symbols of real-world events (Callaghan & Rankin, 2002; DeLoache, 2004; Troseth, 2003). So do explicit explanations that scale models have been created for the purpose of standing for corresponding large-scale objects and spaces. As young children generally become more aware of the intentions of others, they are better able to grasp that people create representations for this purpose (Sharon, 2005). The great interest that contemporary researchers have in illuminating the development of representational skills is understandable given the growing presence of images and graphic symbols in contemporary culture.

Transferring Skills One essential element in higher-order thinking is the ability to use what you have learned in one situation and apply it to other, similar problems. How well do children extend their existing problem-solving skills to new circumstances? This has been a long-standing question in psychology, particularly among researchers who have studied the role of generalization in learning. It has also been a question of paramount importance to educators, who assume that children will find some application in their everyday life for what they have learned in the classroom. The ability to transfer knowledge requires that children learn the original

representational insight The child's ability to understand that a symbol or model can stand for a real-life event.

problem well, note the resemblance between the old and the new problem, and apply the appropriate activities to the new problem. This process is called **analogical transfer**, in that the child must notice the one-to-one correspondence that exists between the elements of one problem and those of another, and then apply the familiar skills to the novel context.

An experiment by Ann Brown and her coresearchers illustrates how this process can occur (Brown, Kane, & Echols, 1986). Three- to five-year-olds were read a story in which a magical genie had to move his jewels from one bottle across a high wall to another bottle. Several items were available to help the genie: glue, paper clips, sheets of paper, and so on. The experimenter and each child enacted the solution, rolling up the paper into a tube and using it to transport the jewels from one bottle to the other. The children were then presented with a different problem having the same general solution (a rabbit that needs to get its Easter eggs across a river can roll paper into a tube to transport them). Whether the children were able to transfer the solution to a new problem depended on whether they recalled the goal structure of the previous problem. If they remembered the major actor, his goal, and the solution to his problem, even three-year-olds could solve the new problem. Other research by Zhe Chen has shown that four- and five-year-olds can profit from viewing a series of drawings depicting a rabbit using sticks to obtain an apple from the bottom of a container. When faced with a similar problem, these children were more likely to enact the solution than children who had seen irrelevant drawings (Chen, 2003). Based on studies like these, as well as the research on infants' problem-solving capabilities that we have already encountered in Chapter 6, it seems clear that young children are capable of a very important cognitive skill—analogical transfer.

FOR • YOUR • REVIEW

- What forms of memory are evident in preschool children?
- What role do scripts play in the memory processes of preschool-age children?
- What explanations have been offered for the emergence of autobiographical memory?
- What has research told us about the reliability of eyewitness testimony among young children?
- What kinds of changes have researchers observed in young children's ability to demonstrate representational insight?
- What factors encourage children to transfer skills from one situation to another?

LANGUAGE IN EARLY CHILDHOOD

Around the child's second birthday, a significant achievement in language production appears: the child becomes able to produce more than one word at a time to express ideas, needs, and desires. At first, two-word utterances, such as "Doggie go" and "More juice," prevail, but the child soon combines greater numbers of words in forms that loosely resemble the grammatical structure of his or her native language. When children combine words, they are stating more than just labels for familiar items; they are expressing relationships among objects and events in the world. Most impressive is that most of this process is conducted with relatively little deliberate instruction about grammar from adults. All of this represents no small feat for a two-year-old who is now mastering some of the more complex aspects of language.

analogical transfer Ability to employ the solution to one problem in other, similar problems.

The effective use of language includes a host of nonverbal behaviors, rules of etiquette, and even changing the content of speech according to the identity of the listener and the situation surrounding the communication. How do you ask someone for a favor? Not, the child soon learns, by saying, "Hey, you, get me that ball!" The child also learns that, if someone did not hear what she said, she can sometimes add a gesture to complete the communication. And the proper way to speak to an adult who has some authority will probably include more polite forms and fewer terms of familiarity than when speaking to a peer.

Clearly, language is a multifaceted skill with many overlapping dimensions, from understanding and uttering sounds to appreciating the sometimes subtle rules of social communication. Despite the complexities, by the time they are four or five years old, most children speak much as adults do. Their progress in mastering vocabulary, syntax, and pragmatics continues during the school years and thereafter, but they acquire the essential elements of the language system in an impressively brief period.

SEMANTICS

The number of new words that the child learns grows rapidly from age eighteen months through the preschool years. By the time they enter school, children know more than 14,000 words (Carey, 1978). How do children learn the meanings of so many new words in such a short period of time?

Many researchers believe that certain biases operate in the child's literal "search for meaning." Consider the toddler who hears a new word, such as *eggbeater*. What does that word mean? Logically, it could refer to a host of objects or perhaps an action instead of an object. Testing the numerous hypotheses could take an inordinate amount of time. Several researchers argue that children are biased to form more restricted hypotheses about the meanings of words; if they were not, they would not learn language so rapidly and with so few errors. *Constraints* on word learning give young children an edge in figuring out the meanings of words from the vast array of possibilities.

One way that the child acquires word meanings is by a process called **fast-mapping**, in which the context in which the child hears words spoken provides the key to their meanings. Often the child's initial comprehension of a word is an incomplete guess, but a fuller understanding of its meaning follows from successive encounters with it in other contexts (Carey, 1978). Upon hearing the word *eggbeater* while watching someone unload various implements from the dishwasher, the child may think it is some kind of cooking tool; hearing the word again, as someone uses a specific object to mix a bowl of eggs, refines the meaning of the word in the child's mind. Children are often able to derive the meanings of words quickly, even when the exposure is brief, if the context in which they hear those words is meaningful (Rice & Woodsmall, 1988).

Young children also tend to assume that new words label unfamiliar objects, a phenomenon called the **mutual exclusivity bias** (Littschwager & Markman, 1994; Markman, 1987, 1990). Researchers have been able to demonstrate that children tend to treat new words as labels for new objects rather than as synonyms for words they already know. For example, Ellen Markman and Gwyn Wachtel (1988) showed three-year-olds pairs of objects; in each set, one object was familiar and the other was unfamiliar (for example, a banana and a pair of tongs). When children were told, "Show me the X" where X was a nonsense syllable, they tended to select unfamiliar objects. The mutual exclusivity bias emerges at about age three and is evident even in deaf children who use American Sign Language (Lederberg, Prezbindowski, & Spencer, 2000).

Another bias in word learning, the **shape bias**, refers to the child's assumption that a new word labels an entire object, specifically its form. Young children learning that a new object is called a *zup*, for example, apply that word to other objects

fast-mapping Process through which the context in which the child hears words spoken provides the key to their meanings.

mutual exclusivity bias Tendency for children to assume that unfamiliar words label new objects.

shape bias The child's assumption that a new word labels an entire object, specifically its form.

similar in shape, but not in color, rigidity, or other characteristics (Graham & Poulin-Dubois, 1999; Samuelson & Smith, 2000). Children extend new words to objects that come from a similar conceptual category, too. Consider a study conducted by Ellen Markman and Jean Hutchinson (1984). Four- and five-year-olds looked at a picture as the experimenter labeled it with a nonsense syllable. For example, a cow was called a *dax*. Then two other pictures were presented: in this case, a pig and milk. When asked, "Can you find another *dax?*" most children pointed to the pig, not the milk. In contrast, when children heard no label for the cow and were simply instructed to "find another one," they tended to associate the cow with milk.

Where do constraints on word learning come from? Some researchers believe they are innate and unique to word learning (Waxman & Booth, 2000). Others suggest that they arise from growth in general knowledge about objects and their relationships to one another (Smith, 1995; Smith, 1999). It may also be that some word-learning biases, such as the "whole object bias," are more important in the early stages of semantic development, whereas others, such as the "category bias," play a larger role in later stages (Golinkoff, Mervis, & Hirsh-Pasek, 1994).

KEY THEME
NATURE & NURTURE

GRAMMAR

As the child begins to combine words, she learns the principles of **grammar**, the rules pertaining to the structure of language. Grammar includes two components, *syntax* and *morphology*. **Syntax** refers to the rules that dictate how words can be combined. The order in which words are spoken conveys meaning; for example, "Eat kitty" and "Kitty eat" do not mean the same thing, even in the simplified language of the young child. A word's position in a sentence can signify whether the word is an agent or the object of an action, for example. The rules of syntax vary widely from one language to another, but within a given language they operate with consistency and regularity.

Morphology refers to the rules for combining the smallest meaningful units of language to form words. For example, the word *girl* has one morpheme. Adding *-s* to form *girls* makes the number of morphemes two and changes the meaning from singular to plural. Similarly, morphemes like *-ed* and *-ing* create a change in the tense of words. One of the most remarkable features of language acquisition is the child's ability to detect the rules of syntax and morphology and to use them to create meaningful utterances of his own with little direct instruction.

Early Grammars: The Two-Word Stage At first, children's two-word utterances consist of combinations of nouns, verbs, and adjectives, and omit the conjunctions, prepositions, and other modifiers that give speech its familiar flow. In addition, young talkers use very few morphemes to mark tense or plurals. Because speech at this stage usually contains only the elements essential to getting the message across, it has sometimes been described as **telegraphic speech**.

In his systematic observations of the language of three children, Martin Braine (1976) noted that speech at this stage contained a unique structure which he dubbed *pivot grammar*. The speech of the children he observed contained noticeable regularities: one word often functioned in a fixed position, and other words filled in the empty slot. For example, one child said, "More car, more cookie, more juice, more read." Table 8.1 contains several other examples of a two-year-old's early word combinations.

More recent research has confirmed that children use nouns in particular in these pivot-type constructions, even when the noun is a nonsense word, such as *wug*. Thus, if a caregiver says, "Look! A wug!" children would say "More wug" or "Wug gone" (Tomasello et al., 1997). Children do not yet produce utterances according to a well-developed grammar, though; their constructions are probably based on the phrasings they hear as the adults around them speak (Tomasello & Brooks, 1999).

grammar Rules pertaining to the structure of language.

syntax Grammatical rules that dictate how words can be combined.

morphology Rules of how to combine the smallest meaningful units of language to form words.

telegraphic speech Early two-word speech that contains few modifiers, prepositions, or other connective words.

Table 8.1 One Child's Early Grammar

This table shows several examples of one two-year-old's two-word speech. Frequently, one word—the pivot word—is repeated, while several other words fill the other slot. The pivot word can occupy either the first or second position in the child's utterances.

no bed	boot off	more car	airplane all gone
no down	light off	more cereal	Calico all gone
no fix	pants off	more cookie	Calico all done
no home	shirt off	more fish	all done milk
no mama	shoe off	more high	all done now
no more	water off	more hot	all gone juice
no pee	off bib	more juice	all gone outside
no plug		more read	all gone pacifier
no water		more sing	salt all shut
no wet		more toast	
		more walk	
		outside more	

Source: Adapted from Braine (1976).

Roger Brown (1973) also studied the regularities of child speech in the two-word stage in ten different cultures. Table 8.2 summarizes some of the results. In children's verbalizations, agents consistently precede actions, as in "Mommy come" or "Daddy sit." At the same time, inanimate objects are usually not named as agents. The child rarely says, "Wall go." To avoid making this utterance, the child must know the meaning of wall and that walls do not move. Thus the child's semantic knowledge is related to the production of highly ordered two-word utterances.

Table 8.2 Examples of Semantic Relations in Child Syntax

Children's word orders often reflect knowledge of semantic relationships, such as the idea that agents precede actions or that actions are followed by locations. Roger Brown believes the semantic relations shown in this table are incorporated into the syntactic constructions of children in many different cultures.

Semantic Relation	Examples
agent + action	Mommy come; Adam write
action + object	eat cookie; wash hand
agent + object	Mommy sock; Eve lunch
action + location	sit chair; go park
entity + location	lady home; baby highchair
possessor + possession	my teddy; Daddy chair
entity + attribute	block yellow; box shiny
demonstrative + entity	dat book; dis doggie

Source: Adapted from Brown (1973).

Many experts believe that no one syntactic system defines the structure of early language for all children (Maratsos, 1983; Tager-Flusberg, 1985). Some children speak with nouns, verbs, adjectives, and sometimes adverbs, whereas others pepper their speech with pronouns and other words such as *I*, *it*, and *here* (Bloom, Lightbown, & Hood, 1975). Most researchers agree, however, that individual children frequently use consistent word orders and that their understanding of at least a small set of semantic relationships is related to that word order. Moreover, numerous detailed observations of children's language indicate that they never construct "wild grammars"; some utterances, such as "Big he" or "Hot it," are simply never heard (Bloom, 1990). Such observations have distinct implications for explanations of syntactic development.

As we saw with semantics, children just starting to use more complex speech are able to comprehend more information conveyed by different grammatical structures than they are able to produce. Two-year-olds, for example, demonstrate an understanding of the difference between past, present, and future tenses, even though these distinctions do not typically appear in their own speech (Wagner, 2001). They also show that they understand the different meanings conveyed by transitive versus intransitive verbs (those with and without objects, respectively). In one study, twenty-five-month-old children saw a video of a duck bending a bunny over as both animals made arm circles. The experimenter said either, "The duck is blicking the bunny" or "The duck and the bunny are blicking," constructions that are more complex syntactically than the child's own spontaneous utterances. Then children saw two screens, one that portrayed bending and one that portrayed arm circling. When asked to "Find blicking," children who had heard the term as a transitive verb looked at bending, and those who had heard the term as an intransitive verb looked at arm circling (Naigles, 1990). What cues are children using to make this correct distinction? Two-year-olds can detect the difference between transitive and intransitive verbs when subject and object are represented by nouns and also when they are made more ambiguous in the form of pronouns, as in "She pilks her back and forth" versus "She pilks back and forth." These results suggest that information denoted by the number of arguments or relationships expressed in the sentence helps children decipher its meaning (Fisher, 2002).

Later Syntactic Development At age two and a half, children's speech often exceeds two words in length and includes many more of the modifiers and connective words that enrich the quality of speech. Adjectives, pronouns, and prepositions are added to the child's repertoire (Valian, 1986). Between ages two and five, the child's speech also includes increasingly sophisticated grammatical structures. *Morphemes*, such as *-s*, *-ed*, and *-ing*, are added to words to signal plurals or verb tense, and more articles and conjunctions are incorporated into routine utterances. The child also comes to use negatives, questions, and passives correctly.

Several other sophisticated forms of speaking emerge after age two, one of which is the use of negatives. In her examination of language acquisition in four children, Lois Bloom (1991) found a predictable sequence in the use of negatives. Initially, children use the negative to express the *nonexistence* of objects, as in "No pocket," said as the child searches for a pocket in her mother's skirt. In the second stage, children use the negative as they *reject* objects or events. For example, one of Bloom's participants said, "No sock" as she pulled her sock off her foot. Finally, negatives are used to express *denial*, such as when the child states, "No dirty" in response to his mother's comment about his dirty sock. This sequence has also been observed cross-culturally, among Chinese children learning to speak Cantonese (Tam & Stokes, 2001). Young children form negatives not just by putting the negative marker at the beginning of an utterance but also by embedding it deep within a statement, as in "My sweetie's no gone" (de Villiers & de Villiers, 1979).

Questions, too, are formed in a fairly consistent developmental sequence, although not all children display the pattern we are about to describe (Maratsos, 1983). Children's earliest questions do not contain inverted word order but consist instead of an affirmative sentence or a declarative preceded by a *wh*- word (*who, what, why, when, where*), with a rising intonation at the end of the statement ("Mommy is tired?"). Subsequently, children form questions by inverting word order for affirmative questions ("Where will you go?") but not negative ones ("Why you can't do it?"). Finally, by age four, children form questions for both positive and negative instances as adults do (Klima & Bellugi, 1966).

One of the more difficult linguistic constructions for children to understand is the passive voice, as in "The car was hit by the truck." Children typically begin to comprehend the meaning of a passive construction by the later preschool years, but they may not use this grammatical form spontaneously and correctly until several years later. Prior to age four, children are also limited in their ability to generate sentences using subject-verb-object (the transitive) with novel verbs they have just learned, as in "He's meeking the ball" (Tomasello & Brooks, 1998). Michael Tomasello maintains that, when two- and three-year-olds do use more complex syntactic constructions, such as the passive and transitive voices, they are initially imitating what adults say. Only later in the preschool and early school years do they have a deeper appreciation for the forms that grammatical constructions can take (Brooks & Tomasello, 1999; Tomasello, 2000).

One particularly interesting phenomenon of the preschool and early school years is the child's tendency to use **overregularizations,** the application of grammatical rules to words that require exceptions to those rules. From time to time, for example, young children use words like *goed* or *runned* to express past tense, even if they previously used the correct forms, *went* and *ran*. Perhaps children make these mistakes because they forget the exception to the general rule for forming a tense (Marcus, 1996). Whatever the reason, these constructions suggest that the child is learning the general rules for forming past tense, plurals, and other grammatical forms (Marcus et al., 1992).

KEY THEME
Interaction Among Domains

How exactly do children master the rules of syntax? Some clues may come from the phonology or sounds of language. Is the word *record* a noun or a verb, for example? The answer depends on which syllable is stressed; if the first, the word is a noun; if the second, it is a verb. Children may pick up cues from stress, the number of syllables in a word, or other tips from the sounds of language to help them classify words as nouns, verbs, or other grammatical categories (Kelly, 1992). Other cues about syntax may come from the meanings of words. According to the **semantic bootstrapping hypothesis,** for example, when children learn that a certain animal is called a "dog," they also notice that it is a thing (noun) and, later in development, that it is an agent (subject) or a recipient (object) of action (Pinker, 1984, 1987). Noticing that adults use certain patterns of speech and understanding their contents may help, too. For example, when young children hear adults say, "Look! The dog's hurling the chair. See? He's hurling it," the pronouns in the pattern "He's [verb]ing it!" may help children understand the unfamiliar verb *hurling* and its use with a subject and object in a transitive sentence. In other words, children's knowledge of semantics influences their mastery of grammar (Childers & Tomasello, 2001).

Pragmatics

Just as important as semantic and syntactic rules are cultural requirements or customs pertaining to the proper use of speech in a social context. Is the child speaking with an elder or a peer? Is the context formal or informal? How does the speaker express politeness? Each situation suggests some unique characteristics of speech, a tone of voice, a formal or more casual syntactic structure, and the choice of specific words. In the context of playing with a best friend, saying, "Gimme that" might be perfectly appropriate; when speaking with the first-grade teacher, saying, "Could I please have that toy?" will probably produce a more favorable reaction. These examples demonstrate the child's grasp of **pragmatics,** the rules for using language effectively and appropriately according to the social context.

overregularization Inappropriate application of grammatical rules to words that require exceptions to those rules.

semantic bootstrapping hypothesis Idea that children derive information about syntax from the meaning of words.

pragmatics Rules for using language effectively within a social context.

Acquiring Social Conventions in Speech When do children first understand that different situations call for different forms of speech? When Jean Gleason and Rivka Perlmann (1985) asked two- to five-year-olds and their parents to play "store," they observed that, at age three, some children modified their speech depending on the role they were playing. For example, one three-and-a-half-year-old boy who was the "customer" pointed to a fake milk bottle and said, "I want ... I would like milk." His revision showed an understanding that an element of politeness is required of a customer. Preschoolers also have some limited understanding that different listeners are typically spoken to in different ways. In a study in which four- and five-year-olds were asked to speak to dolls portraying adults, peers, or younger children, the participants used more imperatives with dolls representing children and fewer with dolls representing adults and peers (James, 1978).

The child's facility with social forms of politeness increases with age. Researchers in one study instructed two- to six-year-olds to *ask* or *tell* another person to give them a puzzle piece. Older children were rated by adults as being more polite than the younger children, particularly when they were asking for the puzzle piece. Usually, older children included such words as *please* in their requests of another person (Bock & Hornsby, 1981).

Parents undoubtedly play a significant role in at least some aspects of the acquisition of pragmatics, especially because they deliberately train their children to speak politely. Esther Greif and Jean Gleason (1980) observed the reactions of parents and children after children had received a gift from a laboratory assistant. If the child did not say, "Thank you" spontaneously (and most of the preschoolers in the sample did not), the parent typically prompted the child with "What do you say?" or "Say thank you." Parents also serve as models for politeness routines; most parents in the study greeted the laboratory assistant upon entry and said good-bye when the assistant departed. In cultures such as Japan, in which politeness is a highly valued social behavior, children begin to show elements of polite language as early as age one year (Nakamura, 2001), probably because parents model and reinforce these verbal forms.

Key Theme
Sociocultural Influence

Incorporating social conventions into language often involves learning subtle nuances in behaviors, the correct words, vocal intonations, gestures, or facial expressions that accompany speech in different contexts. Children may get direct instruction on the use of verbal forms of politeness, but it is not yet clear exactly how they acquire the other behaviors that accompany socially skilled communication.

Referential Communication A group of experiments that has been especially useful in providing information on children's awareness of themselves and others as effective communicators centers on **referential communication,** situations that require the child to either talk about a topic specified by the experimenter or evaluate the effectiveness of a message describing some sequence of events. Researchers note whether the child's message is sufficient to communicate his or her intent or, alternatively, whether the child is able to detect ambiguous or uninformative components in the messages heard.

In a classic study of referential communication, Robert Krauss and Sam Glucksberg (1969) asked four- and five-year-olds to describe a series of unfamiliar geometric forms to another child who could not see them (see Figure 8.8). The speaker had to provide the listener with enough information to duplicate an array the speaker was constructing. The results showed that children at this age often rely on personal descriptions of the stimuli (for instance, "It looks like Daddy's shirt"), messages that are not at all helpful to the listener. Thus young children's ability to understand the requirements of the listener and to adjust their speech accordingly is limited when they are describing unfamiliar items and when the interaction is not face to face.

On the other hand, observations of children in more natural interactions with one another suggest that, well before they enter school, children appreciate at least some of the requirements of the listener and can modify their speech to make their communication effective. In a study of the communication skills of preschool-age

referential communication Communication in situations that require the child to describe an object to a listener or to evaluate the effectiveness of a message.

FIGURE 8.8

An Experiment in Referential Communication

In Krauss and Gluckberg's (1969) study of referential communication, four- and five-year-olds had to describe a series of unfamiliar geometric forms (pasted on blocks) to other children who could not see them. In this illustration, for example, the speaker on the left must explain to the listener on the right which forms to place on the stacking peg. The results showed that children this age are generally ineffective in transmitting this type of information. Research in more naturalistic settings, however, demonstrates that preschoolers can engage in effective referential communication.

Source: Adapted from Krauss & Glucksberg (1969).

children, Marilyn Shatz and Rochel Gelman (1973) asked four-year-olds to describe a toy to either an adult or a two-year-old listener. When the children spoke to the younger child, they shortened their utterances, used simple constructions, repeated utterances, and employed more attention-getting devices than when they spoke to the adult. Other researchers have also observed that even two-year-olds use techniques to make sure their messages get across during the normal interactions that occur in a nursery school. Children point, seek eye contact with listeners, and use verbal attention getters, such as "Hey," to ensure that listeners hear what they have to say (Wellman & Lempers, 1977). In addition, when a listener somehow indicates that he has misunderstood or says, "What?" two- and three-year-olds attempt to make their communication more effective. They may repeat their statement or restate the utterance with a better choice of words, a change in verb form, or some other linguistic correction (Ferrier, Dunham, & Dunham, 2000; Levy, 1999; Shwe & Markman, 1997).

The mature use of language involves the ability to understand the demands of the situation, be sensitive to the needs of the listener, and employ subtle nuances in speech that are compatible with the situation. The child's failure to acquire the social skills that are part of effective communication can have broad consequences for the qualities of relationships that she or he establishes with parents, teachers, and peers, among others.

The Linguistic Perspective on Language Development

When you consider the sequence of language acquisition, three points are especially noteworthy. First, language development proceeds in an orderly fashion. Although individuals may vary in the age at which they attain language milestones or in the precise form of those achievements, children do not acquire language in a haphazard fashion. Second, children learn language rapidly and with seemingly little effort. With the exception of those with some serious physical or psychological problem, all children learn to speak within only a few years, despite the diverse range of skills required. Third, children produce *generative* language; that is, they do not merely duplicate what others say, but create novel and unique expressions of their own. How do children accomplish all of this? An important theoretical perspective—the linguistic perspective—attempts to account for these remarkable achievements.

Noam Chomsky (1980, 1986) and other linguists emphasize the structures that all languages share, those syntactic regularities that the young language learner quickly identifies in the course of everyday exposure to speech, such as when the child learning English notices that nouns representing agents precede verbs and nouns representing the objects of actions follow verbs. According to Chomsky, children possess an innate system of language categories and principles, called *universal grammar*, which predisposes them to notice the general linguistic properties of any language. As children are exposed to a specific language, a process called *parameter setting* takes place; that is, "switches" for the grammatical rules that distinguish English from Japanese or Arabic from French are set. After abstracting the general rules of language, children apply them to form their own novel and creative utterances. Language learning, say most linguists, is different from other forms of learning; there are constraints on what the child will be predisposed to learn, and language learning is governed by its own set of principles. In other words, language learning is *modular*, separate and distinct from other kinds of processing. Furthermore, many linguists believe language is a uniquely human enterprise, one that is not part of the behavioral repertoire of other species.

Research evidence generally supports the idea that learning and applying rules is part of the process of learning language. Children rapidly learn syntactic rules for forming plurals, past tense, and other grammatical forms in their first five years, and can even apply them to words they have never heard before. In a famous experiment, Jean Berko (1958) demonstrated this phenomenon by presenting children with several nonsense words, such as *wug*. Children were able to state correctly that the plural form of *wug* is *wugs*, although they had never heard made-up words like these. Even seven-month-old infants show evidence of being able to learn rules that can help them to learn language. In one study, infants heard several three-word sentences from an artificial language until they showed a decline in interest in them. For example, they heard constructions that had an ABA form such as "ga ti ga" and "li na li." During the test phase, though, they showed a distinct preference for sentences with an ABB construction, such as "wo fe fe." Likewise, infants who were habituated to the ABB structure preferred sentences with the ABA structure during the test phase (Marcus et al., 1998). Moreover, linguistic theories provide a plausible explanation of the occurrence of *overregularizations*; these can be seen as the product of a language learner who has done too good a job, implementing rules even in cases in which exceptions exist. The drive to find structure in language is evident in another interesting way—in the development of *creole* languages, in which children in a particular cohort permanently embellish or expand the organization of the language they hear. Researchers have discovered a deaf community in Nicaragua in which individuals created their own version of sign language. With each new generation of children, the complexity of that language's structure has increased (Senghas & Coppola, 2001). The implication is that children do not simply pattern their speech after what they hear; rather, they use language in creative and highly organized ways.

Linguistic approaches help to explain just how children can master the complex, abstract rules that characterize all languages, given what some have called the "impoverished input"—the incomplete or ungrammatical utterances—that they typically hear (Lightfoot, 1982). They also help us understand how children learn language without explicit teaching of the rules of grammar or lists of vocabulary words. However, critics point out that linguistic approaches may reflect more closely the biases of adult theoreticians who attempt to describe the logical necessities of language achievements than the actual processes children use. Michael Tomasello (2000), for example, maintains that young children's use of language does not always reflect an appreciation of abstract principles of syntax. When children first learn how to use verbs, they use some in very restricted ways ("cut paper," "cut it") and others in varied types of constructions ("I draw on man," "Draw it by Santa Claus"). This lack of consistency suggests that children are not using general rules about how verbs work to produce their utterances.

What about the linguists' claim that language is uniquely human? In the past several decades, numerous attempts have been made to train members of the ape family to use language, all with some apparent success (Gardner & Gardner, 1971;

Premack, 1971; Rumbaugh, Gill, & von Glasersfeld, 1973), although many early studies were criticized on methodological grounds (Terrace et al., 1979). Nevertheless, in one well-controlled study, an ape named Kanzi was raised from infancy with exposure to human speech similar to that provided to a young girl named Alia. When Kanzi was eight years old and Alia was two, they were tested on their ability to comprehend an assortment of novel sentences, such as "Take the potato outdoors." On many of the sentences, ape and child performed equally well (Savage-Rumbaugh et al., 1993). Scientists have also identified areas in the left hemisphere of the chimpanzee brain that seem to correspond to Broca's area and Wernicke's area in humans (Cantalupo & Hopkins, 2001; Gannon et al., 1998). However, compare the ages of Kanzi and Alia; it took many more years to bring the ape to the two-year-old child's level of mastery. Furthermore, although apes may be able to use visual props or sign language to form two-word communications, they rarely generate more complex grammatical structures. Perhaps most important, when observed in their natural habitat, apes do not point to or show objects to other apes. In other words, although they do use highly patterned signals to communicate with one another, they do not use signs or gestures in referential or symbolic ways (Tomasello, 1998). Perhaps their limitation is a cognitive rather than a linguistic one, so questions about the modularity of language skills in humans cannot be answered from these observations. Even so, apes are evidently limited in their ability to use language, despite intensive efforts to teach them.

FOR • YOUR • REVIEW

- What are the processes by which young children acquire the meanings of words?
- What are the major grammatical accomplishments of children in the two-word stage of language acquisition?
- What syntactic accomplishments follow the two-word stage?
- What aspects of pragmatics do children acquire in the preschool years?
- How does the linguistic perspective account for language acquisition? What research findings are consistent with a linguistic perspective?

CHAPTER RECAP

Summary of Developmental Themes

NATURE & NURTURE

How do nature and nurture interact in physical, cognitive, and language development in early childhood?

Genetic factors, brain centers that regulate growth, and hormones such as HGH are biological factors that contribute to physical growth. Nutrition is an example of an environmental factor that influences physical growth. According to Gibson, perceptual development involves perceptual *learning*—in particular, noticing consistencies and variations among stimuli in the environment. In Piaget's theory, maturation, in conjunction with experience, is responsible for the child's cognitive growth. Linguistic theories emphasize the child's innate tendencies to process language information in particular ways. However, the child must be exposed to linguistic input to manifest these tendencies.

SOCIOCULTURAL INFLUENCE

How does the sociocultural context influence physical, cognitive, and language development in early childhood?

Knowledge of and access to nutrition can have important consequences for children's physical growth. Perceptual development may be influenced by cultural factors, such as the degree of "carpenteredness" in the environment.

Elements of language acquisition, such as learning pragmatics, are also influenced by the unique cultural context in which the child is developing.

Continuity/Discontinuity

Are physical, cognitive, and language development in early childhood continuous or discontinuous?

Piaget stressed stagelike attainments as the child progresses from sensorimotor to preoperational thought. However, changes in cognitive skills, such as memory, appear to arise from successive increments, not qualitative stagelike changes.

Interaction Among Domains

How do physical, cognitive, and language development in early childhood interact with other domains of development?

The child's emergent cognitive skills interact with social capabilities. For example, children's decreasing cognitive egocentrism will affect their ability to make judgments in perspective-taking tasks, which have important social ramifications. At the same time, social experiences influence cognitive skills. For example, autobiographical memory emerges in the context of learning how to tell a narrative.

Risk/Resilience

What factors promote risk or resilience in physical, cognitive, and language development during early childhood?

Exposure to malnutrition poses a serious risk to children's physical and intellectual development. Deficiencies in certain vitamins, iron, and calcium are also linked to physical and cognitive risks.

Chapter Review

Physical Development in Early Childhood

How do genetic factors, neural control, and hormonal variations affect growth?

Genetic factors predict a person's height and body proportions. Genetic factors work primarily through neural and *hormonal* activity. The hypothalamus contains cells that may determine whether growth is proceeding according to genetic instructions. These cells trigger human growth hormone, a substance that interacts in complex ways with other hormones to influence growth.

What are catch-up and lagging-down growth?

Catch-up growth refers to the tendency for the rate of growth to increase for a period of time after disease or illness. *Lagging-down growth* is the tendency for it to decrease for a period of time after rapid gains.

What are the consequences of poor nutrition for growth?

Poor nutrition can result in decreased height and weight, deterioration of the brain, long-term cognitive deficits, and, ultimately, death.

What are the child's major achievements in motor skills in the years from two to six?

During early childhood, children show advances in gross motor skills such as running, jumping, and skipping. They also show major improvements in fine motor skills which enable children to use scissors, hold crayons, and perform other actions requiring small muscle movements.

What is implicit learning?

Implicit learning refers to knowledge acquisition that is not always within conscious awareness. Motor skills are often acquired in this fashion.

Perception in Early Childhood

What are the basic elements of Gibson's perceptual learning theory?

Gibson's theory helps us to understand how, with experience, children show steady improvements in the ability to classify different stimuli that share similar features, such as certain letters of the alphabet. Reinforcement is not necessary for this form of learning to take place.

What aspects of objects do children have difficulty perceiving?

Children have difficulty making similarity judgments among stimuli based on just one feature. They also have difficulty seeing both interpretations in ambiguous figures.

How might cross-cultural factors influence perceptual development?

Environments that are highly "carpentered" may be responsible for children's being more susceptible to visual illusions like the Müller-Lyer and horizontal-vertical illusions. Also, children who live in cultures that do not emphasize formal education have difficulty perceiving depth cues in pictures and photographs.

Cognition in Early Childhood

What are the major characteristics of preoperational thought according to Piaget?

Children in the *preoperational stage* can think using symbols, but their thought is limited in that it is *egocentric*. Children fail *conservation tasks* because they do not yet have the logical thought structures that allow them to think about *reversibility*. They also focus on only one aspect of a problem (*centration*), and they tend to *focus on states*.

What are some criticisms of Piaget's theory? What research evidence supports these criticisms?

Some critics maintain that cognitive development is not as general as Piaget maintained, but rather shows more rapid advances in some domains than in others. One example is children's early sensitivity to biological entities. Researchers have also proposed explanations for the behaviors Piaget observed. Some data suggest that changes in information processing—such as the ability to pay attention to the correct cues in a problem—lie behind advances in cognition.

What developmental changes have researchers observed in children's classification, numerical reasoning, and spatial concepts in the preschool years?

Some researchers believe that children begin to classify with basic-level categories and progress to superordinate relations. Others maintain that children's early concepts are global and based on meanings, and that they become more refined with age. The learning of concepts in *natural domains* occurs at an accelerated pace. Children also seem to form theories about the meanings of concepts, ideas that become more elaborated with age.

Piaget maintained that preoperational children fail to comprehend *one-to-one correspondence, cardinality,* and *ordinality*. However, by age four, children are able to count, and they display some knowledge of important numerical principles. Preschoolers understand relations such as "bigger" and "smaller," and have basic intuitions about fractions, but have more difficulty with large number sets and numbers that are close together.

Preschoolers are able to use landmark and geometric cues to orient themselves in space. They can use simple maps to navigate a route, but map-reading skills improve over the next few years. Children learn to understand that symbols on a map refer to corresponding real-world objects, understand the scale and alignment of a map, and become able to plan an efficient route using a map.

What developmental changes in visual *perspective taking* have been identified by researchers?

Children first recognize that their own view is not identical to that of another person (Level 1). Later in development, about age three or four years, they can determine the specifics of the other's view (Level 2).

What is meant by the child's "theory of mind"? What contrasting positions have been suggested as explanations for the development of theory of mind?

Theory of mind refers to the child's awareness of his or her own mental states, as well as the mental states of others. In contrast to Piaget's claims for early childhood *realism*, children can distinguish between mental and physical phenomena in the preschool years. Some researchers feel that theory of mind is an innate, modular form of knowledge, whereas others claim it arises from the child's experiences with language.

What is childhood autism? What are some hypotheses about its causes?

Childhood autism is a disorder in which children display a lack of contact with the social world which is manifested by communication deficits. Some researchers believe autism arises from the lack of a theory of mind. Others suggest that information-processing deficits, such as attention, memory, or executive control processes, are responsible.

What forms of memory become evident in preschool-aged children?

Preschoolers evidence both *episodic* and *semantic memory*. In the first case, they begin to talk about specific events that took place in their life. In the second case, they evidence general knowledge about things and events in the world.

What role do scripts play in the memory processes of preschool-aged children?

Preschoolers have clearly formed *scripts* for common events; these are organized schemes that include the repeated general elements of those events. Preschoolers show evidence of using scripts to recall the details of stories they have heard.

What explanations have been offered for the emergence of autobiographical memory?

Few people can remember events that occurred prior to age three, a phenomenon called *infantile amnesia*. Improvements in memory for specific events in one's life, or *autobiographical memory*, are tied to the child's emerging verbal skills, a growing awareness of the self, and increasing understanding of the form of a narrative.

What has research told us about the reliability of eyewitness testimony among young children?

Young children's memories, like adults', are vulnerable to the influence of misleading questions. In fact, children under age four years may be especially susceptible. Factors such as a powerful questioner, the use of repeated questions, and the use of props can exacerbate the distortion of memory. Encouraging source monitoring can reduce the influence of leading questions.

What kinds of changes have researchers observed in young children's ability to demonstrate representational insight?

By age three, children attain *representational insight*, the ability to use a symbol for a real-world event.

What factors encourage children to transfer skills from one situation to another?

Analogical transfer, the ability to employ the solution to one problem in other similar problems, can be encouraged by helping children to see the goal structure of the problem.

Language in Early Childhood

What are the processes by which young children acquire the meanings of words?

Children seem to learn the meanings of words by relying on constraints such as *fast-mapping*, the *mutual exclusivity bias*, and the *shape bias*.

What are the major grammatical accomplishments of children in the two-word stage of language acquisition?

Two-year-olds begin to use two-word utterances, sometimes called *telegraphic speech* because it contains few modifiers, prepositions, and connective words. They also use few morphemes to mark tense or plurals. Although no single syntactic system defines the structure of language at this stage, acquisition for individual children is orderly and may rely on semantic knowledge.

What syntactic accomplishments follow the two-word stage?

As children begin to speak more words, they learn and apply the rules of *grammar.* These rules include both *syntax* and *morphology.* Children add morphemes, modifiers, prepositions, pronouns, and connective words to their speech. They begin to use negatives, questions, and eventually the passive voice. One interesting type of error they sometimes make is called *overregularization*, the application of grammatical rules to words that are exceptions. Children also evidence *semantic bootstrapping*, using the meanings of words to help them apply the rules of syntax.

What aspects of *pragmatics* do children acquire in the preschool years?

Children begin to show that different situations call for different forms of speech around age three. They adjust their speech, depending on the listener, and begin to use polite forms, probably because parents instruct them to. Some research indicates that preschoolers have problems with *referential communication*, but when observed in natural settings, young children evidence sensitivity to the needs of their communication partners.

How does the linguistic perspective account for language acquisition? What research findings are consistent with a linguistic perspective?

Linguistic theorists emphasize the child's abstraction of general grammatical principles from the stream of speech. They tend to take a nativist stance and believe that language skills are modular. Data showing that children are able to learn rules, that they creolize language, and that animals are limited in their ability to learn language are consistent with linguistic theory.

Key Terms and Concepts

analogical transfer (p. 295)
autobiographical memory (p. 291)
cardinality (p. 284)
catch-up growth (p. 271)
centration (p. 279)
conservation task (p. 279)
egocentric (p. 278)
episodic memory (p. 290)
fast-mapping (p. 296)
focus on states (p. 280)
grammar (p. 297)
hormones (p. 271)
implicit learning (p. 274)
infantile amnesia (p. 290)
lagging-down growth (p. 271)
morphology (p. 297)
mutual exclusivity bias (p. 296)
natural domain (p. 283)
one-to-one correspondence (p. 284)
ordinality (p. 284)
overregularization (p. 300)
perspective taking (p. 286)
pragmatics (p. 300)
preoperational stage (p. 278)
realism (p. 288)
referential communication (p. 301)
representational insight (p. 294)
reversibility (p. 280)
script (p. 290)
semantic bootstrapping hypothesis (p. 300)
semantic memory (p. 290)
shape bias (p. 296)
syntax (p. 297)
telegraphic speech (p. 297)
theory of mind (p. 288)

9 SOCIAL AND EMOTIONAL DEVELOPMENT

"Nicky," the author said to her then-five-year-old son. "What do you think should be on the cover of this book? It's about children, you know."

"Well … ," he thought for a moment.

"How about a picture of a child?"

"A boy or a girl?" asked the mother.

"How about one of each?" he suggested. The mother was pleased that her son chose a girl as well as a boy. She had tried hard to teach him to think about gender in nonstereotypical ways, and his willingness to include girls seemed to indicate that her efforts were successful.

"What should they be doing?" the mother continued.

"Well, how about having the boy play with a computer?" he quickly responded.

"And the girl?" she asked.

"I think she should have a tea party or something."

KEY THEMES in Social and Emotional Development

NATURE & NURTURE How do nature and nurture interact in social and emotional development in early childhood?

SOCIOCULTURAL INFLUENCE How does the sociocultural context influence social and emotional development in early childhood?

CONTINUITY/DISCONTINUITY Are social and emotional development during early childhood continuous or discontinuous?

INTERACTION AMONG DOMAINS How do social and emotional development in early childhood interact with other domains of development?

RISK/RESILIENCE What factors promote risk or resilience in social and emotional development during early childhood?

As this brief scene suggests, preschoolers are becoming very much aware of the intricacies of their social world. Not only do they know the obvious and sometimes subtle elements of *gender stereotypes*—beliefs and expectations about the characteristics of males and females—but they are also learning about other important dimensions of human interactions. They make important strides in mastering the world of emotions, develop a more complex sense of self, and evidence the beginnings of moral awareness. Growing cognitive and language skills permit the child's self-expression—her wants, needs, and desires—in the full-blown sense of the word. Perhaps for the first time, as they experience the full force of the preschooler's growth as a social being, parents feel the need to start to guide or limit their child's behaviors. Social and emotional development occurs at a remarkably swift pace during the preschool years. In this chapter, we focus on the most significant elements of that growth.

EMOTIONAL DEVELOPMENT IN EARLY CHILDHOOD

Anyone who has spent time with preschoolers is probably aware of the intensity and range of the emotions they express. From their infectious bursts of unbridled laughter to their sometimes distressing temper tantrums, preschoolers are for the most part the epitome of emotionally expressive beings. One of the major developmental tasks for this age group is to learn to regulate and control their emotional displays in keeping with the social norms and values of their background culture.

EXPRESSING EMOTIONS

We have already learned that infants express such basic emotions as joy, sadness, and fear. Preschoolers build on this initial repertoire, expanding in both the number of specific emotions they communicate and the ways in which they convey them. In addition, basic emotions, such as fear, undergo developmental changes, particularly in the types of stimuli that elicit them. Whereas early expressions of fear result from physical events, such as loud noises or strange people, now fear occurs as a response to more complex psychological events, such as the possibility of failing an academic task or being rejected by peers (Morris & Kratchowill, 1983; Rutter & Garmezy, 1983). As you can see, the child's cognitive skills and social awareness are very much intertwined with emotional development.

The Emergence of Self-Conscious Emotions By their second year, many children begin to show emotions that reflect a more complex understanding of the self and social relationships: shame, guilt, and envy, for example. Each of these emotions requires the child to understand the perspective of another person—that the person may be disappointed with the child, may be hurt, or may feel affection for a third party. Such emotions also require a consciousness about the self and about one's

By the time they are two years old, children start to show more complex emotions such as jealousy. As they get older, children become better able to manage their emotions when they are in front of other people.

relations to others (Campos et al., 1983; Lewis, 1989). Accordingly, emotions like envy and guilt are known as **self-conscious emotions**.

The visible signs of self-conscious emotions can be multifaceted: a child displaying shame lowers her head and eyes, collapses her body, and often has an odd smile on her face (Lewis, Alessandri, & Sullivan, 1992). Asked to dance in front of people or told that he or she has failed a task, a preschooler might show embarrassment with a smiling face, a look away, and nervous body movements (Lewis & Ramsay, 2002). The expression of self-conscious emotions changes with age. At age two years, children show discernible signs of jealousy through physical actions. The child may wedge himself between his mother and father as they are hugging or hit a sibling whom his parent just kissed (Cummings, Zahn-Waxler, & Radke-Yarrow, 1981). But as children get older, they are better able to manage their jealousy, especially in front of their parents (Miller, Volling, & McElwain, 2000).

KEY THEME
INTERACTION AMONG DOMAINS

Talking About and Understanding Emotions With the advent of language, children can communicate feelings by verbalizing instead of just furrowing their brow and crying or making some other facial display. Children begin to use language to describe feeling states between eighteen and thirty-six months of age, shortly after they begin to talk. Inge Bretherton and Marjorie Beeghly (1982) asked mothers of twenty-eight-month-olds to keep a diary of their children's verbalizations that referred to psychological states. Besides being able to apply a wide range of terms to express both positive and negative feelings, these children were able to discuss the conditions that led to a specific emotion and the actions that followed as a consequence. Several children, for example, made statements similar to "Grandma mad. I wrote on wall," suggesting an understanding of the reasons for another's emotion. Another type of utterance made by several children—"I cry. Lady pick me up and hold me"—signifies an understanding that emotions may be related to subsequent actions.

From age three to four years and older, children use more varied and complex emotion words (Fabes, Eisenberg, et al., 2001). At this age, children also become more proficient in verbally describing the causes and consequences of emotions (Barden et al., 1980). They tend to agree that certain events, such as receiving a compliment, lead to happy emotions, whereas others, such as being shoved, lead to negative feelings. Furthermore, they are able to suggest ways to ameliorate another's negative emotions, such as hugging a crying sibling or sharing toys to placate an angered playmate (Fabes et al., 1988).

self-conscious emotion Emotion, such as guilt and envy, that appears later in childhood and requires more knowledge about the self as related to others.

By age three or four, children's understanding of emotions includes knowledge about how to soothe others' negative emotions. Preschoolers might suggest hugging or sharing a toy with a distressed child, for example.

Sex Differences in Emotions According to the familiar stereotype, females are more emotionally expressive and more sensitive to the emotional states of others than are males. Do boys and girls actually differ in any facet of emotional development? It seems that for the most part the answer is yes—girls are more emotionally expressive and more attuned to emotions than are boys.

During the preschool years, there do not appear to be strong, clear-cut sex differences. Some studies find that girls tend to show more positive emotions than boys (e.g., Matias & Cohn, 1993), but other researchers report that boys are more expressive in general (Weinberg et al., 1999). Eventually, though, sex differences in emotion show up. By elementary school, girls show a greater range of emotions than do boys (Casey, 1993). Boys, in contrast, tend to express one particular emotion—anger—more often than do girls (Hubbard, 2001). Finally, to some degree, girls show a heightened sensitivity to emotions compared with boys. For example, female children and adults from widely varying cultures are better than males at identifying the positive and negative emotions displayed on faces (Brown & Dunn, 1996; Hall, 1984).

Key Theme
Nature & Nurture

Observations of parents' behaviors suggest that many of these sex differences that appear later in childhood may be taught or modeled directly in interactions that begin in infancy but are especially apparent in the preschool years. Mothers of preschoolers mention feeling states more often and discuss a wider variety of emotions when they talk with their daughters than when conversing with their sons (Dunn, Bretherton, & Munn, 1987; Kuebli, Butler, & Fivush, 1995). Mothers are also more facially expressive when they play with their two-year-old girls than with boys, thus exposing girls to a greater range of emotions and displaying more social smiles to them (Malatesta et al., 1989). In general, parents encourage girls to maintain close emotional relationships and to show affection, whereas they instruct boys to control their emotions (Block, 1973). Thus, although biological explanations of sex differences cannot be ruled out completely, many of the emotional behaviors we see in males and females appear to be influenced by their learning histories.

Caregivers start to expect preschoolers to regulate their emotions. Once children become more facile with language, they start to express their feelings by speaking rather than with tantrums or by crying.

Regulating Emotions

By the preschool years, most caregivers begin to expect children to control their emotional displays. Two-year-olds continue to use the emotion regulation strategies we saw in infants, such as distraction; when they are presented with a snack or a gift but must wait to obtain it, they typically shift their attention to other objects. Normally, this strategy alleviates their distress (Grolnick, Bridges, & Connell, 1996). But when young children focus on the source of their frustration, their anger tends to increase (Gilliom et al., 2002). By age three, many children show fewer tantrums and intense negative outbursts as they increasingly rely on language to communicate their intents and desires (Kopp, 1992). Physiological maturation probably contributes, too. Researchers believe that early childhood is a time when the frontal portions of the brain, which control excitation and inhibition of emotion-linked behavior, are maturing (Fox, 1994; Schore, 1996).

Key Theme
Interaction Among Domains

Key Theme
Risk/Resilience

One of the most important aspects of emotion regulation is what it predicts later in development. Preschoolers and elementary-age children who express a great deal of anger, hostility, and other negative emotions show poorer social competence in school and are isolated from or rejected by peers (Eisenberg et al., 1997; Fabes et al., 2002; Hubbard, 2001). Perhaps of most concern, researchers have found that the inability to regulate negative emotions is part of the behavioral profile of children with conduct problems. In one study, preschool-age children, some of whom were identified as being at risk for behavior problems, were invited to a laboratory to participate in several cognitive tasks. After each child finished the session, he or she was offered a prize that was undesirable and disappointing. The children's emotional expressions were observed in both the presence and absence of the experimenter. As Figure 9.1 indicates, boys who were at risk for conduct problems expressed more anger, speaking rudely and with obvious negative emotion, compared with low-risk boys. High-risk boys also maintained that anger for longer periods of time while in the presence of the experimenter. Low-risk boys showed anger, too, but only when they were alone. The pattern for girls differed: girls from almost all risk categories expressed fewer negative emotions. These results suggest that boys who are reported by parents and teachers to have fewer behavior problems are better able to manage their emotions when in a social setting. Boys with conduct problems, on the other hand, seem to have difficulty regulating their anger, a fact that could be a source of their generally disruptive behavior (Cole, Zahn-Waxler, & Smith, 1994). The evidence linking emotion regulation and later social development continues to mount, not only for children in the United States but also for those in other cultures, such as Indonesia and China (Eisenberg, Pidada, & Liew, 2001; Zhou et al., 2004).

Is there anything that parents can do to encourage healthy emotion regulation in their preschoolers? Researchers have reported that mothers who at least *attempt*

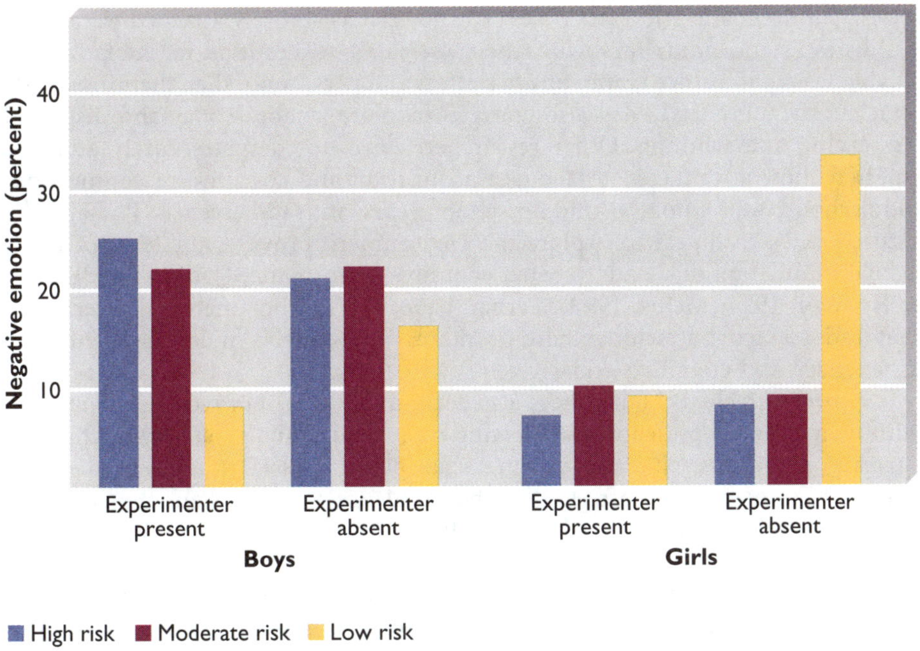

FIGURE 9.1

Emotion Regulation in Children at Risk for Conduct Problems

What happens when children who are at risk for behavior problems experience disappointment? In a study assessing this question, children who had been identified as being at high, medium, or low risk for conduct problems were given a prize that was disappointing to them. The graph shows that boys who were at risk showed a higher percentage of negative emotions whether or not the experimenter was in the room with them. Low-risk boys were better able to regulate their negative feelings when someone was present in the room with them. Girls, in general, expressed fewer negative emotions regardless of whether or not they were with someone. The exception was low-risk girls, who expressed more negative emotions when alone.

Source: Cole, Zahn-Waxler, & Smith (1994).

to manage their thirty-month-old children's emotions have children who display appropriate emotional responses at age five. However, mothers who give in to children's emotional displays, by saying "OK, you can have that toy!" for example, or who question children's emotions ("Why are you crying?") have children who express more negative affect in later years (Spinrad, Stifter, et al., 2004).

It should be apparent that emotion regulation is a very significant developmental accomplishment, especially because of its implications for relationships with parents, teachers, peers, and other significant individuals in the child's life. Emotion regulation can be viewed as part of the more general process of self-regulation, a topic to which we turn later in this chapter.

Attachment and Development in Early Childhood

Key Theme
Interaction Among Domains

We have already seen that the concept of attachment has been a key facet of our thinking about emotional development in infancy. The importance of attachment has been underscored by research findings showing that secure attachments in infancy are related to positive developmental outcomes in both social and cognitive spheres when children reach early childhood. Leah Matas and her associates assessed the quality of attachments of forty-eight infants when they were eighteen months of age (Matas, Arend, & Sroufe, 1978). Six months later, these same children were observed for the quality of their play and their problem-solving styles. Children who had earlier been categorized as securely attached were more enthusiastic and compliant with their mother's suggestions in the problem-solving tasks and showed more positive affect and persistence than their insecurely attached counterparts. They also engaged in more symbolic play and displayed less crying and whining. Other researchers have noted that securely attached children show advantages in language acquisition and cognitive reasoning from toddlerhood well into the middle school years and adolescence. Perhaps the secure child's readiness to explore the environment provides the kind of intellectual stimulation that leads to better cognitive performance (Jacobsen, Edelstein, & Hofman, 1994; Meins, 1998). Perhaps, too, the style of maternal interaction that leads to secure attachment also promotes other aspects of development, such as language and cognitive skills.

Key Theme
Interaction Among Domains

Securely attached children have also been found to be more socially competent with their peers as preschoolers, showing more leadership, greater sympathy, less aggression, and less withdrawal from social interactions (DeMulder et al., 2000; Waters, Wippman, & Sroufe, 1979). They evidence stronger signs of "ego resiliency" at age five years, meaning that they respond to problems in a flexible, persistent, and resourceful manner (Arend, Gove, & Sroufe, 1979). In contrast, insecurely attached infants, particularly those who show avoidant patterns, do not fare so well in the preschool years, according to other research. Children with this attachment classification are found to display many maladaptive and undesirable behaviors, such as high dependency, noncompliance, and poor social skills in peer interactions. They are described by teachers as hostile, impulsive, and withdrawn (Erickson, Sroufe, & Egeland, 1985; Laible & Thompson, 2000). Moreover, avoidant children tend to have negative representations of peers, interpret peers' behaviors as hostile, and become more fearful with age (Cassidy et al., 1996; Kochanska, 2001).

For • Your • Review

- What are self-conscious emotions? Give some examples.
- What types of knowledge about emotions emerge in early childhood?
- How do boys and girls differ in the expression of emotions? What factors might be responsible for these differences?
- What strategies do young children typically use to regulate their emotions? What is the significance of the ability to do so?
- How can parents and caregivers promote emotion regulation among children?
- What are the consequences of attachment styles for development in early childhood?

Self and Self-Regulation in Early Childhood

The early childhood years herald several important changes in concepts of self. Especially important is the child's emerging ability to manage his or her own behaviors. Most societies uphold the importance of shifting responsibilities from parent to child for all sorts of conduct, from self-care activities, such as dressing and grooming, to speaking and acting in socially appropriate ways. That is, after all, a main goal of socialization. In this process, parents serve as the main guides, offering advice and supervision, and expecting compliance from the child in return.

The Concept of Self

How does a preschooler think of himself or herself? If asked to answer the question "Who are you?" a preschooler might say, "I'm a boy. I'm strong. I know the letters of the alphabet. I like pizza. I live with my mother and father. I go to nursery school." During the preschool years, knowledge of self includes one's own physical features but also extends to include activities the child likes and is good at, his possessions, and his relationships with others. In defining themselves, children at this age commonly establish a **categorical self**; that is, they classify themselves in terms of membership in certain groups based on their sex, age, skills, what they own, where they live, and who their friends are.

Are very young children also aware of having psychological and social attributes? As we pointed out in Chapter 8, preschoolers know quite a bit about their own mental activities. They possess knowledge of themselves that goes beyond physical appearance and actions. Thus responses like "I have a friend" or "I'm a happy person" are among their self-descriptions, as are other comments about moods, feelings, achievements, and other psychological and social orientations. Self as object, as *me*, even for a young child, includes a sense of a psychological and social being (Damon & Hart, 1988; Harter, 1999).

Does the preschool-age child know that she cannot become someone else? In other words, what do children understand about *individuality* and uniqueness? In one study participants were asked, "What makes you different from everybody else in the world?" Preschoolers usually answered with their name ("Cause there is only one person with my name"), their possessions, or specific features of their body (Damon & Hart, 1988). What about the child's sense of *stability*? Is an individual essentially the same person today that she was a year ago or will be a year from now? As with the sense of individuality, a child's understanding of continuity begins quite early, but the explanation for this stability changes with development. Preschoolers have more difficulty than older children recognizing that changes in mood, weight, and even age or height are possible while still retaining one's identity (Bales & Sera, 1995). When asked, "If you change from year to year, how do you know it's still always you?" preschoolers cite their name ("My name, and then I would know if it was me if someone called me"), physical features, possessions, or other categorical qualities as proof. By age four or five, though, many children are able to link the "I" that existed some time ago with the "I" that exists right now (Povinelli, 2001).

Sense of Agency

There are several indicators of a growing sense of agency in early childhood. After about two years of age, many children will protest the attempts of caregivers to help them in an activity like dressing or eating. Some researchers believe that such protests reveal the desire to be an agent or to master an activity (Kagan, 1981; Lutkenhaus, Bullock, & Geppert, 1987).

At about this same time, children also look to adults after completing a task as if to share their success or turn away and hunch their shoulders after failure (Stipek, Recchia, & McClintic, 1992). The feedback that mothers provide to two-year-olds following their efforts to solve a problem plays an important role in the way children subsequently respond to a challenging task. When mothers are more negative and critical, their children are increasingly likely to display shame in confronting a difficult problem as three-year-olds. When mothers are more supportive and provide a scaffold to assist in solving a problem, their children display greater persistence when confronted with an achievement-oriented task when they are older (Kelley, Brownell, & Campbell, 2000).

categorical self Self-classification in terms of membership in certain groups based on sex, age, skills, what one owns, where one lives, and who one's friends are.

Self-Regulation and Self-Control

Impulsive and easily upset, young children typically have difficulty behaving in a patient or deliberate manner. Eventually, however, parents and others demand that children acquire **effortful control**, the ability to suppress undesirable responses for less dominant ones that are considered socially or morally more acceptable. A three-year-old needs to stay away from an attractive fireplace, use the toilet, say thank you, and share and put away toys. But becoming responsible and self-reliant can be a long and difficult transition.

Self-regulation refers to the capacity to monitor and direct one's behaviors and activities to achieve certain goals or meet the demands imposed by others. **Self-control**, a related concept, is the ability to comply with expectations of caregivers or other adults concerning moral or ethical behavior, especially in their absence. The degree to which preschool children achieve the ability to regulate their own behaviors has been linked to important outcomes even many years later. For example, adolescents who had greater self-regulatory capacities as preschoolers are described by their parents as more academically and socially competent and better able to handle frustration and temptation. They are also reported to be more attentive, deliberate, and intelligent, and seem better able to tolerate stress and cope with social and personal problems, even when their intellectual performance is similar to that of peers less able to self-regulate (Mischel, Shoda, & Rodriguez, 1989; Shoda, Mischel, & Peake, 1990).

Key Theme
Risk/Resilience

Developmental Changes in Self-Regulation and Self-Control For young children, regulation of behavior might best be labeled *co-regulation* (Kopp, 1987), because children and their caregivers jointly manage behavior. In many families, efforts to limit activities begin when babies are about eight or nine months old. At this time, newly acquired motor skills increase risk of injury, heralding the need for restraining devices, such as playpens and gates. Infants about one year of age may be warned to avoid dangerous or health-threatening objects and situations ("Don't touch the knife," "Don't play with the cat litter," "Hold onto my hand"). Efforts to preserve possessions ("Stay away from the VCR") and avoid harm to others ("Don't pinch") are also common concerns at about this time (Gralinski & Kopp, 1993).

As toddlers move beyond eighteen months of age, adults often supplement these *caregiving demands* with additional *demands for appropriate behavior*, such as keeping quiet and sitting up straight, and *demands for competent action*, such as helping to set the table or participating in social and family activities (Kuczynski & Kochanska, 1995). These efforts focus on encouraging acceptable social interactions, taking part in family routines and chores, and cultivating self-care and greater independence, such as walking rather than being carried (Gralinski & Kopp, 1993). By the time children reach twenty-four to thirty months of age, parental demands may decline in frequency as children become familiar with and respond to requests more routinely (Kopp, 1987). In general, girls tend to be more compliant than boys (Kochanska, Murray, & Harlan, 2000).

Children's self-initiated attempts to obey appear during the second year. A thirteen-month-old, for example, may look at, and perhaps even approach and touch, an electrical outlet while saying, "No, no!" But over the next few years, self-restraint improves rapidly. For example, in a **delay-of-gratification** task, in which the child is asked to wait some period of time before performing an activity or attaining some highly desired outcome (such as playing with an attractive toy or eating a piece of candy), eighteen-month-olds have great difficulty complying. Between two and three years of age, children become increasingly more effective in delaying their behavior (Vaughn, Kopp, & Krakow, 1984). Thus, although self-control begins with attempts by others to govern the young child's actions, their efforts are transferred and gradually relinquished as warnings and guidance become less direct and as the child takes on more responsibility for regulating his behavior.

effortful control Ability to suppress undesirable responses for less dominant ones that are considered socially or morally more acceptable.

self-regulation Process by which children come to control their own behaviors in accordance with the standards of their caregivers and community, especially in the absence of other adults.

self-control Ability to comply with sociocultural prescriptions concerning ethical or moral behavior.

delay of gratification Capacity to wait before performing a tempting activity or attaining some highly desired outcome; a measure of ability to regulate one's own behavior.

Research Applied to Parenting

Encouraging Children's Compliance

Even though preschoolers are beginning to exert signs of self-control, most parents still provide their young children with a hefty dose of supervision. And with their rising independence, children are not always ready to accept it. The frequency with which conflict occurs between parents and children in American families—for example, asking the child to delay a response, slow down an activity, stop an unacceptable behavior, pay attention, or help out with an uninteresting task—is typically high, perhaps on the order of fifteen to twenty times per hour (Laible & Thompson, 2002). The commitment to complying with a "don't" uttered by caregivers appears to be acquired somewhat earlier and more rapidly by children in American families than consistency in responding to a "do." This difference may be due to parents' enforcement of the former more often than the latter or to their greater persistence in prohibiting negative behaviors, thus promoting more fear in children about initiating (or continuing to produce) these behaviors (Kochanska, 2002; Kochanska, Coy, & Murray, 2001). Can caregivers do anything to encourage the emergence of socially acceptable and compliant behaviors during early childhood? Research findings suggest that there is a link between child compliance and several characteristics of caregivers.

1. ***Be supportive, responsive, accepting, sensitive, and emotionally available to children.*** In one study of the predictors of children's compliance, researchers noticed that, when mothers showed eager responsiveness to their toddlers and were generally positive in the emotions they expressed, their children often responded in kind, with cooperation and enthusiasm. When mother-child pairs displayed this *mutually responsive orientation,* as the researchers called it, the children were likely to comply with mothers' requests even when they were observed several years later (Kochanska & Murray, 2000).
2. ***Justify the need for children to act in certain ways.*** Researchers have noted that, when mothers used a high level of justification when their children were thirty months old, children were more compliant with adult requests six months later. When caregivers make statements like "You need to eat your dinner, so that you will not be hungry later," they are helping their children to understand multiple perspectives on social conflicts, offering an opportunity for growth (Laible & Thompson, 2002).
3. ***Offer a compromise or provide a benefit for alternative responses.*** When caregivers show an interest in putting an end to a conflict ("I'll let you have a piece of candy if you eat your dinner"), children are learning an important lesson: that relationships are important and that conflict resolution skills are useful in preserving those relationships (Laible & Thompson, 2002).
4. ***Emphasize behaving competently over inhibiting activities.*** When mothers emphasize "do" over "don't" in their toddlers and preschoolers, fewer compliance and behavior problems arise at age five. Perhaps by encouraging children to perform various activities, such as household tasks ("Clean up") or self-care behaviors ("Tie your shoe"), parents are fostering feelings of competence that have repercussions for the child's future willingness to comply with parental requests (Kuczynski & Kochanska, 1995).

Key Theme
Interaction Among Domains

The Influence of Language and Attention Attention and language also appear to be critical elements in the child's ability to regulate his or her own behavior without the assistance of an adult. Lev Vygotsky (1962) and his students, particularly Alexander

Luria (1961, 1969), theorized that language plays a pivotal role in behavioral regulation. A preschool child, for example, may engage in the expression of *private speech*, speech intended for no one else but that helps to direct attention to key dimensions and features of a task. Private speech also assists in establishing and organizing ways to carry out an activity, and in preserving important task-related information in memory (Meichenbaum, 1977). Yet children's observable private speech is not always correlated with effective problem solving. Perhaps this finding should be expected, as the production of private speech is more likely in especially challenging circumstances where successes are harder to come by (Frauenglass & Diaz, 1985). Preschoolers at risk for behavior problems, however, tend to produce more spontaneous private speech than those who are not at risk. This finding raises an interesting possibility—that the failure to progress from overt speech-for-self to internalized speech-for-self may contribute to greater risk for behavioral problems in some children (Winsler et al., 2000).

Attentional factors also seem important. For example, the child directed not to eat a marshmallow who says, "The marshmallow is yummy"—words that focus attention on the forbidden treat—or who talks about sad things, such as falling and hurting himself—ideas that provide little diversion—shows less ability to inhibit his behavior than a child who sings a pleasant but distracting nursery rhyme, such as "Three Blind Mice" (Mischel, Ebbesen, & Zeiss, 1972). For very young children, caregivers are more likely to initiate attempts to focus or distract the child. To illustrate this point, George Holden (1983) observed mothers and their two-and-a-half-year-olds as they completed grocery shopping, an activity that can test the limits of most caregivers because grocery displays are enticing. In this setting, mothers were frequently forced to respond to their children's requests and used a variety of tactics to do so: reasoning, not responding, physically or verbally intervening, acknowledging children's desires, and attempting to distract children. Mothers who tried to anticipate conflicts, either by diverting children's attention in advance or by engaging them in an interesting conversation, were most effective in preventing conflict while grocery shopping. Sensitive and consistent mothers who learned to use strategies to direct, maintain, and redirect their children's attention appeared to be most successful in regulating their behavior (Holden & West, 1989; Kopp, 1987).

During the later preschool and early school years, children display their own attentional strategies to keep on track and support their goals. For example, in a delay-of-gratification task, preschoolers often place a tempting reward in front of themselves rather than a picture of it or some other, irrelevant item. In doing so, they increase their exposure to the forbidden object, look at it more, and have greater difficulty delaying their response to it. By age five, children are less likely to create such self-defeating arrangements. They prefer to wait with the tempting reward covered rather than uncovered (Mischel & Mischel, 1983). Some will even shield their eyes, play games with their hands and feet, or try to go to sleep to help manage the delay (Cournoyer & Trudel, 1991; Mischel, Shoda, & Rodriguez, 1989).

FOR • YOUR • REVIEW

- What are the features of the self-concept during early childhood?
- What are some signs of the preschool child's growing sense of agency?
- What is the difference between self-regulation and self-control?
- How does self-regulation change during early childhood?
- What factors seem to promote children's compliance?

MORAL DEVELOPMENT IN EARLY CHILDHOOD

As children gain increasing knowledge of the self and greater skill in regulating their own behavior, they are expected to increasingly conform to the socially acceptable rules and regulations of their community. We are talking here about *moral development*, the process by which an individual comes to understand what society accepts as right and wrong. Researchers have focused on two key components of moral development: *moral thinking*, or what some would call conscience, and *moral behavior*, the performance of actions consistent with principles of right and wrong.

THE DEVELOPMENT OF CONSCIENCE

Conscience seems to arise in the child's third year of life. Conscience has two components: the ability to feel moral emotions, such as guilt and empathy, and the tendency to follow rules set forth by adults, even when children are not being watched (Aksan & Kochanska, 2005). We see evidence of both of these elements in early childhood. By age three years, some children willingly comply with the requests of their parents to complete certain activities (such as putting away toys) and to avoid others (such as touching prohibited objects), even when the parents are no longer present (Kochanska, Aksan, & Koenig, 1995). Three-year-olds also notice flawed objects (such as a teddy bear with stuffing coming out or a broken cup), and if led to believe the flaws are the consequence of their own behavior, may voice apologies ("Sorry," "Didn't mean to"), offer reparations ("Put back in," "Clean up"), and exhibit distress ("Take this away," "I wanna go"), expressions of guilt and shame that are frequently manifestations of conscience (Kochanska, Casey, & Fukumoto, 1995). Girls tend to display more guilt than boys (Kochanska et al., 2002). This combination of moral feelings and moral actions tends to meld into a more cohesive form of conscience by the time the child approaches age four years (Aksan & Kochanska, 2005).

This young girl shows the beginnings of conscience development, which includes feelings of guilt and a desire to comply with the requests of adults. Conscience arises from children's observations of the anger and displeasure of their caregivers. Children's growing ability to regulate and inhibit their behaviors also plays a part.

What forces are responsible for the emergence of conscience? One factor may be the child's ability to recognize positive emotional reactions as well as anger or displeasure in the communications of caregivers. These emotions give children clear messages about what adults deem to be appropriate behavior. Another factor is that the ability to regulate and inhibit behavior increases (Kochanska, 2002; Kochanska, Murray, & Coy, 1997; Kochanska, Tjebkes, & Forman, 1998). Parental behaviors are related, too. Positive emotional relationships and mutual responsiveness between mother and child are closely aligned with a healthy conscience for both boys and girls (Kochanska, Aksan, & Koenig, 1995; Kochanska & Murray, 2000). But the relationship between parenting style and the child's conscience is especially strong when children show a secure attachment to their parents (Kochanska et al., 2004). At the same time, some young children seem to be more willing and eager than others to learn what parents teach, including behaviors in the moral domain. For example, the degree to which fourteen-month-olds imitated their mothers in a teaching task like "Clean the Table" predicted their levels of conscience and guilt at three and four years of age (Forman, Aksan, & Kochanska, 2004). The sources of these individual differences in readiness to learn are still not well understood.

SOCIAL LEARNING THEORY AND MORAL BEHAVIOR

KEY THEME
NATURE & NURTURE

KEY THEME
CONTINUITY/DISCONTINUITY

Social learning theories emphasize the child's acquisition of *moral behaviors*, such as behaving acceptably and resisting temptation. According to social learning theory, the rewards and punishments dispensed by parents and others shape the child's conduct, as do the actions and verbalizations that a child sees parents and that others use. In this sense, moral values are learned just like any other behavior. Social learning theorists see morality as a process of incremental growth in appropriate actions and increasing conformity with the rules of society.

How convincingly does the social learning model explain moral development? Studies investigating the child's ability to resist temptation have often used the "forbidden toy" situation; the child must learn not to play with an attractive and enticing toy placed in the room with them. The results suggest that reinforcement history is indeed a factor in moral behavior. Children quickly learn not to touch an attractive toy if an adult mildly reprimands them for initiating activities with it. In other words, they respond to the punishments the adult doles out.

Several factors influence children's tendency to transgress when left alone in a room with a forbidden toy after they have been punished. First, as social learning theory predicts, the timing of the punishment plays a role. Punishments are most effective if they closely follow the undesired behavior—for example, when the child first reaches for a forbidden toy rather than after he has picked it up. Second, providing a verbal explanation of why the toy is prohibited also has an effect. When children are told, for example, that the attractive toy might break if it is handled, they are much less likely to violate the adult's prohibition. According to social learning theorists, verbalizations facilitate the internalization of morally acceptable and unacceptable behaviors (Aronfreed, 1976).

Parents and others also serve as models for moral behavior. Children who observe a model commit a prohibited act, such as touching a forbidden toy, are more likely to perform the act themselves, whereas children observing a model who resists temptation will commit fewer transgressions (Rosenkoetter, 1973). However, models appear to be more powerful in *disinhibiting* than in inhibiting behavior that violates a rule or an expectation. Children are more likely to follow someone's deviant behaviors than his or her compliant ones (Hoffman, 1970).

Newer versions of social learning theory assign a larger role to cognitive processes in the emergence of moral values. In Albert Bandura's social cognitive theory (1986), children develop internalized standards of conduct, cognitive representations derived from observing others and processing their explanations for moral behavior. Children, especially to the extent to which they accept and accurately perceive

Even preschoolers display care and concern about others. Here a boy brushes sand from the face of his younger sister in an effort to keep her from becoming upset. These kinds of actions suggest that prosocial behavior is an early aspect of human development. Moreover, its expression very likely is greatly influenced by the socialization practices of parents and other caregivers.

communications, attempt to behave in ways consistent with those representations (Grusec & Goodnow, 1994). Nevertheless, describing changes in the child's ability to reason about moral questions has been left largely to other theorists, such as Jean Piaget and Lawrence Kohlberg, whose ideas on moral development we will encounter in later chapters.

Prosocial Behavior and Altruism

A young child consoles a friend in distress, helps her pick up the pieces of a broken toy, or shares a snack. These **prosocial behaviors**, social actions performed to benefit others and perhaps the self, have come under increasing investigation in recent years as another way to understand the development of values and moral behavior in children. Among prosocial behaviors is **altruism**, behavior carried out to help others without expectation of rewards for oneself. Acts of kindness or assistance are often discretionary but highly valued in many communities.

Several contemporary theorists believe an essential element underlying prosocial or altruistic behavior is **empathy**, a vicarious, shared emotional response involving an understanding and appreciation of the feelings of others, which includes sympathetic concern for the person in need of assistance (Eisenberg, Fabes, & Spinrad, 2006). Perhaps humans are biologically predisposed to exhibit such a trait. Even infants show signs of sensitivity to the distress of others. Two-and three-day-olds may cry when other infants cry, but not in response to other, equally loud noises (Simner, 1971). In addition to crying, ten-to fourteen-month-olds may whimper or silently attend to expressions of distress from another person. Often they respond by soothing themselves, sucking their thumb, or seeking a parent for comfort (Radke-Yarrow & Zahn-Waxler, 1984). Perhaps because the boundary between self and another individual is not yet clear at this age, consoling the self is a form of coping with another's distress, a self-focused emotional reaction more than a genuine prosocial behavior.

Between one and two years of age, empathy promotes new behaviors, typically called *sympathy*: touching or patting the distressed person as though to provide solace, seeking assistance for the person, or even giving the person something to provide comfort, such as a cookie, blanket, or teddy bear. The person's emotional

prosocial behavior Positive social action performed to benefit others.

altruism Behavior carried out to help another without expectation of reward.

empathy Understanding and sharing of the feelings of others.

state may also be labeled with such expressions as "Cry," "Oh-oh!" or "Hurting." Slightly older children display more varied and complex responses, including comforting and helping the troubled child, asking questions of her, punishing the agent of the child's distress, protecting the child, and asking an adult for help (Radke-Yarrow & Zahn-Waxler, 1984; Zahn-Waxler et al., 1992). Such expressions are not uncommon. In one study of toddlers playing at home with familiar peers, almost half of the children who observed distress in their peers responded with an attempt to comfort or assist them. They were especially likely to do so if they themselves had caused the distress (Demetriou & Hay, 2004)

FOR • YOUR • REVIEW

- What are the signs of the development of conscience in the early childhood years?
- What factors are related to the development of conscience?
- How does social learning theory account for the development of moral behaviors?
- What is the evidence that children are capable of prosocial behaviors in early childhood?

Gender Roles in Early Childhood

Many **gender stereotypes** exist in our society; that is, most of us have beliefs and expectations about the characteristics of females and males. Boys, according to these stereotypes, are active, aggressive, independent, and interested in science. Girls, on the other hand, are passive, not aggressive, and socially oriented. At what ages and to what extent do children have knowledge of these stereotypes? Furthermore, are such common beliefs actually manifested in the everyday behaviors of children? Are any differences we might observe due to the biological makeup of males and females? What part do socialization and cognitive development play in this process? We will address these central questions as we discuss **gender-role development**, the process by which children acquire the characteristics and behaviors prescribed for males and females in their culture. Before the mid-1960s, most psychologists regarded the socialization of children into traditional masculine and feminine roles as both a natural and a desirable outcome of development. Behavioral sex differences were viewed as inevitable and were linked to comparable sex differences among nonhumans (Kohlberg, 1966; Mischel, 1966; Shaw & Darling, 1985). But changes in social values in the mid-1960s, especially those accompanying the women's movement, shifted the ways in which psychologists approached sex differences and gender-role socialization. Many of the questions that interest developmental psychologists today represent both a challenge to traditional assumptions about the nature and origins of gender roles and sex differences and a concerted effort to determine the developmental processes that underlie children's acquisition and enactment of gender roles.

gender stereotype Expectation or belief that individuals within a given culture hold about the behaviors characteristic of males and females.

gender-role development Process by which individuals acquire the characteristics and behaviors prescribed by their culture for their sex. Also called *sex typing.*

instrumental characteristics Characteristics associated with acting on the world; usually considered masculine.

Gender Stereotypes

Suppose a group of college students is asked to rate the "typical" boy or girl on a number of psychological attributes. Will they rate certain traits as more typical of males than of females, and vice versa? College students respond that characteristics like independence, aggression, and self-confidence are associated with masculinity. In general, attributes like these, which are associated with acting on the world, are classified as **instrumental**. In contrast, emotional expressiveness, kindness, and gentleness are linked with femininity. These perceived feminine characteristics are often classified as

expressive, or associated with emotions and interactions with other people. Table 9.1 shows other traits often associated with masculinity and femininity (Martin, 1995).

These gender stereotypes are not limited to our own society. Researchers asked children and adults from thirty nations in North and South America, Europe, Africa, and Asia to indicate whether certain traits are more frequently associated with men or women in their culture. The results showed many cross-cultural similarities in the stereotypes that adults attributed to males and females (Williams & Best, 1982).

Table 9.1 Stereotypic Characteristics Attributed to Males and Females

When college students were asked to rate a typical boy or girl on a number of personality traits, strong patterns emerged among traits that were seen as being associated with each sex. Male traits generally fall into a cluster called *instrumentality* and female traits into a cluster labeled *expressiveness*.

	Mean Typicality Ratings by Sex of Child Target[a]	
Item Type	*Boys*	*Girls*
Sex-typed Masculine[b]		
Self-reliant	5.05	3.69
Does dangerous things	4.96	2.57
Enjoys mechanical objects	5.57	2.68
Dominant	5.36	3.54
Enjoys rough play	6.09	3.07
Independent	4.95	3.59
Competitive	5.70	4.16
Noisy	5.78	3.93
Physically active	6.23	4.80
Aggressive	5.60	3.41
Conceited	4.38	3.46
Sex-typed Feminine[c]		
Gentle	3.21	5.36
Neat and clean	3.05	5.42
Sympathetic	3.42	5.33
Eager to soothe hurt feelings	3.35	5.33
Well-mannered	4.01	5.44
Cries and gets upset easily	3.20	4.95
Easily frightened	3.27	4.89
Soft-spoken	3.00	4.64
Helpful around the house	3.27	5.31
Gullible	3.74	4.33
Reliable	4.33	4.74
Truthful	4.31	4.91
Likeable	4.99	5.68
Nonsex-typed		
Adaptable	4.90	4.72

[a]Maximum scores = 7.0
[b]Indicates the ratings for boys were significantly higher than for girls.
[c]Indicates that ratings for girls were significantly higher than for boys.

Source: Martin (1995).

expressive characteristics
Characteristics associated with emotions or relationships with people; usually considered feminine.

Children show an awareness of gender stereotypes remarkably early in development. Like this boy, many two-year-olds play with toys in a manner that is consistent with gender stereotypes.

KEY THEME
SOCIOCULTURAL INFLUENCE

Despite the many similarities in gender stereotypes across cultures, some differences occurred among nations in the specific characteristics attributed to males and females. For example, Italian adults stereotypically associated "endurance" with women, although most adults in other countries believed this is a masculine trait. Nigerian adults believed "affiliation" is neutral, whereas adults in other countries said it is a feminine characteristic. Thus we cannot say that specific characteristics are always attributed to males or to females. We can say, however, that the tendency to stereotype on the basis of sex is found in a variety of cultural settings.

Children begin to acquire gender-role stereotypes and employ them as guides for their behavior at a surprisingly early age—from about two years onward. At eighteen months of age, infants prefer to look at toys stereotypically associated with their own sex (Serbin et al., 2001). By age two, boys prefer to play with cars, balls, and trains, whereas girls prefer dolls, cooking utensils, and brush and comb sets (Campbell, Shirley, & Caygill, 2002). Preschoolers' knowledge about gender stereotypes includes personality traits, occupations, appearance qualities, and household activities that are associated with males and females (Bauer, Liebl, & Stennes, 1998; Poulin-Dubois et al., 2002). Their thinking about gender stereotypes even extends beyond these qualities to items that may serve as metaphors for masculinity and femininity; they believe, for example, that fir trees and bears are "for boys," and that maple trees and butterflies are "for girls" (Leinbach, Hort, & Fagot, 1997).

GENDER DIFFERENCES IN BEHAVIORS

In light of such durable and pervasive stereotypes about "femaleness" and "maleness," it is logical to ask whether researchers have documented actual differences in the characteristics or behaviors of females and males. For many human traits, the data show that average differences between the sexes are smaller than the variability in performance within each sex. Nonetheless, in some domains the characteristics of females and males have been found to differ, and often these differences start to show up in the early childhood years.

Physical Development Females and males physically differ in a number of ways, including the makeup of their chromosomes, their genitalia, and levels of certain hormones. Females are physically more mature at birth, whereas males show a special physical vulnerability during infancy. Compared with females, males are more likely to be miscarried, die in infancy, or develop hereditary diseases (Jacklin, 1989). Later in infancy and childhood, females walk, talk, and reach other developmental milestones, especially those that are tied to neurological development, earlier than males. Males, on the other hand, are more physically active and are more likely to engage in vigorous rough-and-tumble play (Pellegrini & Smith, 1998; Ruble, Martin, & Berenbaum, 2006).

Cognition One aspect of cognition for which males and females have been thought to differ is verbal abilities. The popular belief has been that girls are more skilled than boys at verbal tasks, a belief that was modestly substantiated by an early review of the relevant research (Maccoby & Jacklin, 1974). Meta-analyses of cognitive sex differences, however, indicate only small sex differences in verbal skills favoring females (Feingold, 1988; Hyde & Linn, 1988). Females have a slight advantage on tests that measure reading comprehension, spelling, word meaning, or grammar (Feingold, 1993; Halpern, 1997), but most researchers agree that the differences are not large enough to warrant much notice.

In another meta-analysis of more than one hundred studies of sex differences in mathematics skills, the investigators concluded that boys and girls showed no overall differences in performance (Hyde, Fennema, & Lamon, 1990). When the scores of participants of different ages and from specific groups were examined more closely, however, sex differences in certain aspects of mathematics performance did emerge. During elementary school, for example, girls showed a slight superiority over boys in the area of computation; in the high school and college years, on the other hand, males did moderately better than females on tests of mathematical problem solving. Among groups selected for exceptional performance (such as students in gifted and talented programs), males performed better than females in tests of mathematics. The scores of males on mathematics tests are more variable than the scores of females, at least for children in the United States (Feingold, 1992). When differences across all the studies are averaged, males show only a very slight advantage. Figure 9.2 illustrates the overall magnitude of this sex difference.

In fact, the only notable sex difference in cognitive skills currently supported by empirical evidence involves visual-spatial abilities. Visual-spatial skills include a number of processes, all of which require the ability to visualize and transform figures or objects in the mind. Figure 9.3 illustrates three tests of visual-spatial skills: spatial perception, mental rotation, and spatial visualization. As you can see, spatial perception tasks require participants to ignore distracting information to locate horizontal and vertical orientation. Mental rotation tasks demand that participants transform two-and three-dimensional figures "in their heads." Spatial visualization tasks require them to analyze relationships among different spatial representations.

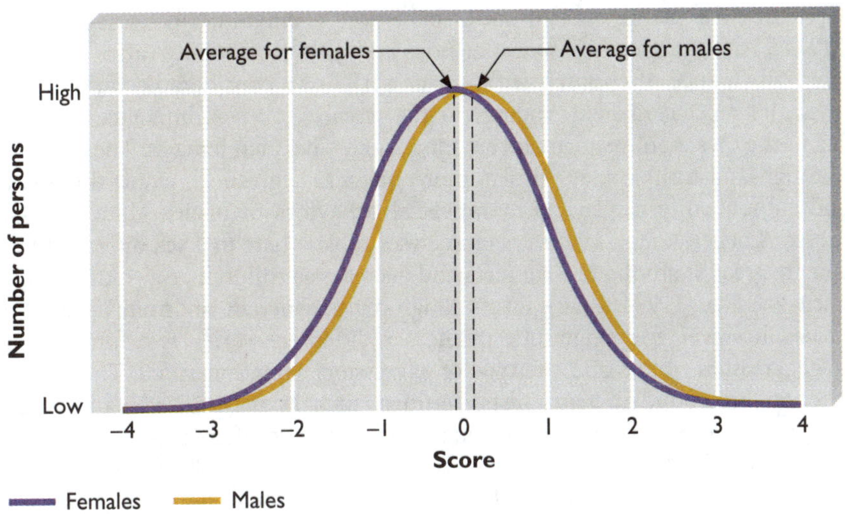

FIGURE 9.2

Sex Differences in Mathematics Skills

Although sex differences in mathematics skill do exist, the differences are quite small. This graph illustrates the size of the average sex differences. The horizontal axis represents scores converted to a standardized form.

Source: Adapted from Hyde, Fennema, & Lamon (1990).

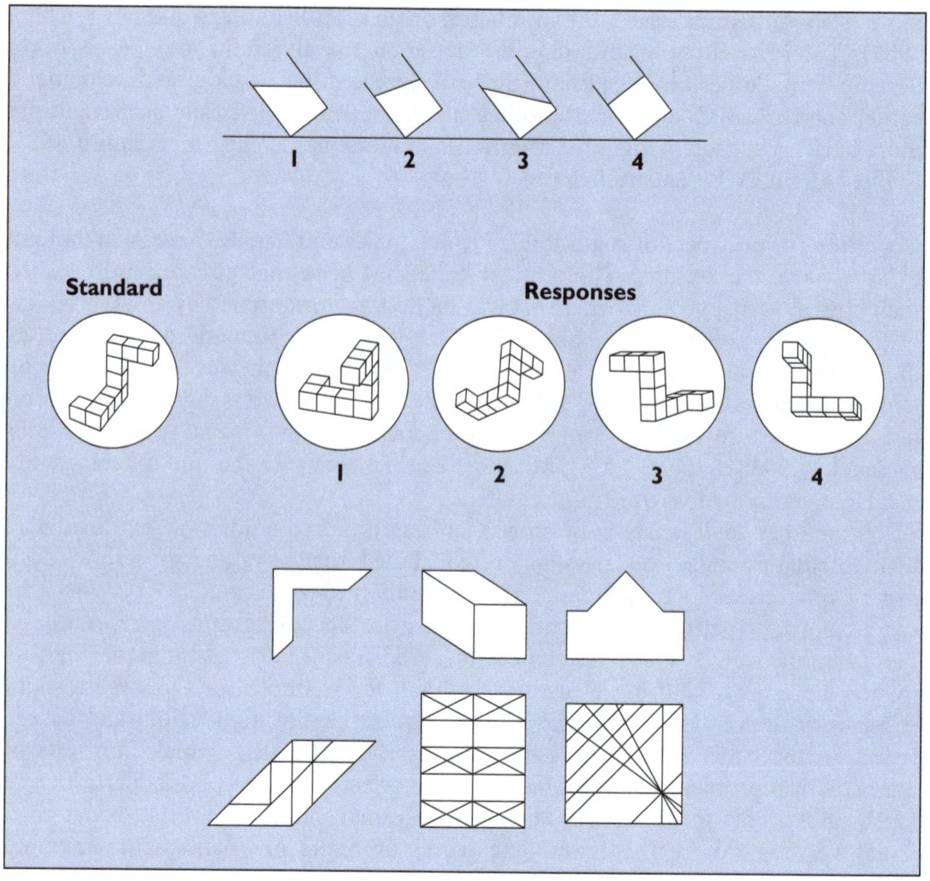

FIGURE 9.3

Sex Differences in Visual-Spatial Skills

Tests of visual-spatial skills typically assess spatial perception (top), mental rotation (middle), or spatial visualization (bottom). In the top panel, participants are asked to indicate which bottle has a horizontal water line. In the middle panel, participants must identify the two responses that depict rotated versions of the standard. In the bottom panel, participants are asked to identify the simple geometric figure on the top within the more complex figure underneath. Generally, males perform better than females on spatial perception and mental rotation tasks.

Source: Adapted from Linn & Peterson (1985).

In general, results indicate no sex differences on spatial visualization tasks. Males do, however, show superior performance on mental rotation and, to a lesser extent, spatial perception (the tasks depicted in the middle and top portions of Figure 9.3, respectively) (Linn & Peterson, 1985, 1986; Voyer, Voyer, & Bryden, 1995). As with mathematical skills, boys show greater variability in their visual-spatial scores than do girls in our society (Feingold, 1992). Sex differences in visual-spatial skills are evident in children by age four and a half years (Levine et al., 1999), but the magnitude of sex differences in this domain increases with age (Voyer et al., 1995).

Social Behaviors Researchers who have examined the results of hundreds of studies of social behaviors and personality characteristics have concluded that few actual sex differences exist in the area of social behaviors (Feingold, 1994; Maccoby & Jacklin, 1974). Although average scores of boys and girls consistently differ in some areas, the performance of children within each sex shows considerable variability.

One of the most consistent findings in the research on sex differences is that, beginning in the preschool years, males are more aggressive than females. They engage in more rough-and-tumble play, display more physical aggression, try to dominate peers, and subsequently display more antisocial behaviors than girls (Block, 1983; Huston, 1985; Loeber & Hay, 1997). Meta-analyses substantiate that sex differences in aggression are greatest among preschoolers and decrease as children grow older (Eagly & Steffen, 1986; Hyde, 1984, 1986). Even though males generally are more aggressive than females, however, the magnitude of the sex difference varies as a function of where the aggression occurs and the type of aggression being measured. The largest sex differences are found in naturalistic settings, such as playgrounds, and when physical aggression is being measured. Conclusions about sex differences in aggression must be tempered by how this construct is defined, however. When aggression is described as an attempt to harm another person through manipulation, gossip, or excluding peers from a social group (called *indirect* or *relational aggression*), girls are found to be more aggressive than boys, starting in the preschool years (Bjorkqvist, 1994; Crick, Casas, & Mosher, 1997; Crick & Grotpeter, 1995).

Other sex differences occur in the verbal and nonverbal behaviors that boys and girls use as they participate in social communication. Boys generally issue more directive statements ("Put that block over here!"), attempt to gain the floor, and engage in one-upmanship as they speak. Girls, on the other hand, tend to verbally reinforce their conversation partners and follow the ongoing themes of conversations (Carli & Bukatko, 2000). Girls are especially likely to display these affiliative behaviors when they are interacting with other girls (Strough & Berg, 2000). Girls also display more social smiles and gazing than boys do (Eisenberg & Lennon, 1983; Hall & Halberstadt, 1986).

Theories of Gender-Role Development

What are the origins of sex differences in behavior? Even though contemporary research shows that actual sex differences in behavior are relatively few, boys and girls still show different profiles in some domains of behavior, as we just saw with social behaviors in early childhood. Three major theoretical perspectives—biological, social learning, and cognitive-developmental theories—each make unique and important contributions to our understanding of these differences.

Key Theme
Nature & Nurture

Biological Theories Biologically based explanations for sex differences focus largely on the influence of chromosomes, hormones, and the structure of the brain on behavior. These factors often work in ways that illustrate the complex interactions of biological systems to produce sex-differentiated behaviors.

As we saw in the chapter titled "Genetics and Heredity," the presence of an X or a Y sex chromosome begins a complex process that leads to sexual differentiation. Between six and twelve weeks after conception, the XY chromosomal configuration leads to the development of testes and the secretion of a class of male hormones called **androgens**, a process that results in further sexual differentiation. The penis and scrotum develop in response to the metabolism of testosterone, an androgen that is actually present in both sexes but in greater amounts in males (Whalen, 1984). In the absence of an XY configuration and the associated greater amounts of androgens, the female structures develop (Breedlove, 1994; Hood et al., 1987). These differences in biological structures form the bases by which a child is labeled "boy" or "girl," the social categorization of biological sex.

Prenatal exposure to hormones, particularly androgens, influences the developing fetus in ways that may have an impact on biology and, perhaps, postnatal behavior. Most important for our discussion, androgens influence the developing organization of the central nervous system and the brain (Gorski, 1980; MacLusky & Naftolin, 1981; Overman et al., 1997). Hormone-related sex differences in the central nervous system may, in turn, have important influences on behavior and abilities.

Take the example of aggression. Explanations of sex differences in aggression from a biological perspective have relied largely on experiments in which androgens were administered systematically to female animals during prenatal development. The animal studies show that these hormonally treated females subsequently display increased aggressive behaviors, such as threats and rough-and-tumble play, compared with normally developing females. These findings have been replicated in rats, monkeys, and a number of other species (Goy, 1970; Parsons, 1980).

Although this type of evidence implies a causal link between male hormones and aggression, some controversy concerning the relationship exists (Tieger, 1980). First, although hormones have been shown to precede and presumably influence certain behaviors, such as aggression, those behaviors may themselves have an impact on hormone levels. That is, levels of hormones, including testosterone, can also change *in response to* changes in the environment (Hood et al., 1987). Among nonhuman males, for example, increases in androgen levels frequently follow, rather

androgen Class of male or masculinizing hormones.

than precede, an aggressive encounter (Hood et al., 1987). Thus the link between aggression and levels of androgens is not unidirectional, and it is difficult to make causal statements. Second, because human beings have a nervous system that differs in important ways from those of other species—particularly in the size of the cortex, which directs voluntary behavior—it is not clear that the findings from animal studies can be generalized to humans (Fausto-Sterling, 1992). Nevertheless (and still keeping the aforementioned cautions in mind), the data from a recent study with humans show that the more testosterone women had in their bloodstream during pregnancy, the more likely their daughters were to show preferences for masculine activities when they were preschoolers. In contrast, social factors such as parental sex-role beliefs did not predict these girls' behaviors (Hines et al., 2002).

ATYPICAL DEVELOPMENT

Hormonal Disorders in Children

Among humans, there are several conditions in which genetic males or females may be exposed to a hormonal environment that is not typical for their sex. One such disorder is *congenital adrenal hyperplasia* (CAH), a condition that occurs in about 1 in 5,000 to 1 in 15,000 births (Miller & Levine, 1987). This genetic disorder causes a deficiency in the production of adrenal steroids, with the result that high levels of androgens begin to be produced during the prenatal period. If the child is a genetic female, for example, she will be born with masculinized genitalia. Usually her physical appearance is surgically corrected, hormone therapy is begun to regulate the levels of androgens circulating in her body, and the child is raised as a girl. Even following treatment, however, CAH girls have been found to show many behavioral patterns that are "typical" of boys. They prefer toys geared for boys, like rough-and-tumble play, and show enhanced visual-spatial skills, a domain in which males sometimes excel (Collaer & Hines, 1995; Hampson, Rovet, & Altmann, 1998).

Among boys, a failure of androgen to bind with its receptors can result in *androgen insensitivity syndrome (AI)*. Because the boy is born with female-looking genitalia, he is usually raised as a girl; the disorder is typically discovered at puberty, when menstruation fails to begin (Breedlove, 1994). These children commonly show "female" play interests and visual-spatial skills that are poorer than those of normal females who served as controls (Collaer & Hines, 1995).

It is tempting to conclude from these unusual hormonal disorders that biological factors are responsible for sex differences in patterns of social behaviors and cognitive skills. CAH girls do, in fact, have masculine-typed behaviors and were exposed to unusually high levels of androgens even though they were later socialized as girls. AI boys have lower levels of androgens and, even though they are socialized as girls, their performance on some cognitive tasks is actually lower than that of the average female.

Thus it is difficult to argue simply for the effect of socialization on their behavior. On the other hand, studies of androgenized girls are difficult to interpret because parents were aware of their daughters' masculinized appearance at birth and may have tolerated or even encouraged more "boylike" behaviors. Moreover, their enhanced visual-spatial skills may be the result of their masculine play styles rather than hormone levels per se (Liben et al., 2002). Thus, although these studies suggest a role for biology in the emergence of some sex-linked behaviors, it is still premature to rule out the effects of socialization.

KEY THEME
NATURE & NURTURE

Social Learning Theory One of the primary mechanisms accounting for sex differences in behavior, social learning theorists maintain, is sex-differentiated treatment of boys and girls. According to this position, boys and girls are reinforced and punished differentially for specific behaviors, which leads them to behave in sex-typed ways. Girls, for example, may be rewarded for playing with dolls and punished for climbing trees, whereas boys may receive the opposite treatment. Thus, because children are motivated to seek reinforcement and avoid punishment, they will behave in a sex-typed fashion.

Children attend both to the consequences of their own behavior and to the consequences others face for their behavior. In fact, imitation, or modeling, may be an even more powerful means by which children learn gender roles. By observing the experiences of other people, children develop expectations for reinforcement and punishment of their own behavior. These expectations may influence their behavior as strongly as the actual experiences of reward or punishment do (Bandura, 1969, 1977a). Children have numerous opportunities to observe models behaving in stereotypic ways in the home, in the outside world, and in the media. Recent studies show that gender stereotypes are frequently evident in television, video games, and children's literature (Dietz, 1998; Furnham & Mak, 1999; Turner-Bowker, 1996). They also show that, within families, women still do the bulk of such household tasks as cooking and cleaning (Coltrane, 2000). Each time a child sees that Dad fixes things around the house and Mom does the cleaning, or that most little boys play baseball and most little girls play house, she is adding to her growing storehouse of sex-typed behaviors.

Several factors influence whether children will imitate the sex-typed behaviors of others. Albert Bandura and other researchers have proposed that children's *attention* to models in the first place is influenced by both the sex of the model and the **sex typicality** of the model's behavior, that is, how characteristic it is of the model's own sex (Bandura, 1977a; Perry & Bussey, 1979). According to this hypothesis, boys would, in general, be more likely than girls to attend to the behavior of male models, although they would be less likely to attend a male model who was exhibiting "feminine" behavior. The prediction that individuals will pay greater attention to same-sex models is based on the notion that observation of same sex models should provide children with greater information about potential consequences for their own behavior. In addition, Bandura suggests, children *recognize* that certain behaviors are sex-typed, especially as they observe the frequency with which males and females, as a group, perform certain behaviors. Finally, Bandura (1977a) proposes that *motivational* factors, such as reward seeking and attempts to retain a sense of mastery, will influence behavior in a variety of realms. As children grow older, they rely less on others to regulate their behavior and more on self-regulation, based on personal standards of gender-appropriate behavior (Bandura, 1986).

Research has supported several of the predictions of social learning theory. Children are indeed more likely to imitate same-sex than other-sex models (Bussey & Bandura, 1984; Bussey & Perry, 1982). Thus same-sex parents, peers, and characters in the media can be powerful influences on the child. In addition, children are more likely to imitate models who behave in sex-typical ways than models who behave in sex-atypical ways (Perry & Bussey, 1979). Finally, self-regulation of sex-typed behavior does seem to increase with development, as a study by Kay Bussey and Albert Bandura (1992) shows. Two- to four-year-olds privately rated how they would feel if they played with a series of toys, some of which were masculine (a dump truck), some feminine (a baby doll), and some neutral (a xylophone). As Figure 9.4 shows, younger children expressed relatively neutral self-evaluations regarding playing with masculine and feminine toys. Older children, in contrast, indicated more positive self-evaluations when visualizing themselves playing with toys geared for their own sex.

Social learning theory makes an important contribution to our understanding of gender-role development in that it provides a way for us to understand how broader societal beliefs and values are transmitted to individual children. As Bussey and Bandura (1999) state, labeling boys as boys and girls as girls would have very little consequence if there were no social repercussions to acting in masculine and feminine ways.

Key Theme
Interaction Among Domains

Cognitive-Developmental Theories Cognitive-developmental theories focus on the ways children understand gender roles in general and themselves as males or females in particular. In cognitive-developmental theories, gender is emphasized as a conceptual category, a way of classifying people on the basis of their overt appearance or behaviors.

sex typicality Extent to which a behavior is usually associated with one sex as opposed to the other.

FIGURE 9.4

Self-Evaluation During Same-Sex Activities

Two- and four-year-olds rated how they would feel while playing with masculine, feminine, or neutral toys. The higher the score, the more favorable the self-evaluation. As the graph indicates, the younger children, especially girls, gave relatively neutral self-evaluations for playing with masculine and feminine toys. In contrast, older children said they would feel better about themselves when they played with same-sex toys.

Source: Bussey & Bandura (1992).

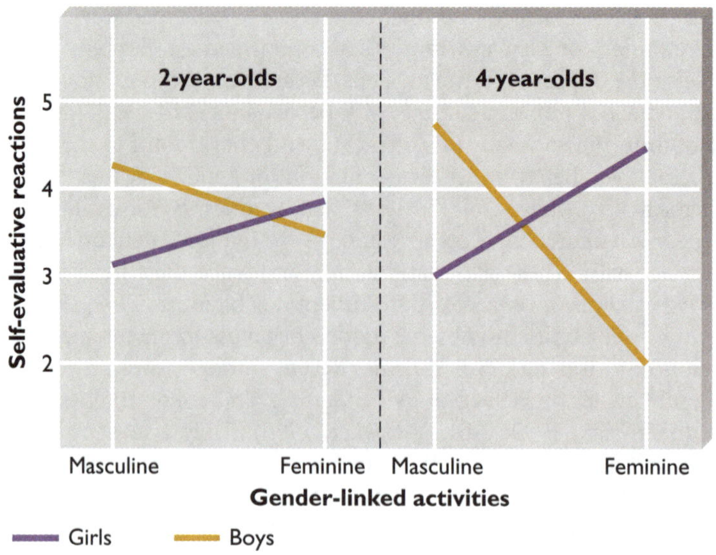

KEY THEME
CONTINUITY/DISCONTINUITY

Lawrence Kohlberg (1966) proposed that gender roles emerge as a consequence of stagelike developments in cognition. The most basic of these cognitive milestones is acquisition of **gender identity,** the knowledge that self and others are female or male. This concept, which is acquired between ages two and three years, is crucial to later gender-role development because it provides a basic categorizing principle with which children begin to divide the world. After acquiring gender identity, around their fourth birthday children develop **gender stability,** a sense that gender does not change over time. Children who have acquired gender stability recognize that they were born one sex and will grow up to be a member of that same sex. Despite this knowledge, however, they may not yet be aware of the fact that genitalia determine biological sex. Rather, children assume that external factors (such as clothing or hair length) are the determinants of sex. Thus a young boy may believe he was a baby boy and will grow up to be a "daddy" (gender stability), but only if his behavior and physical characteristics (such as hair length) remain masculine. By age six, most children acquire **gender constancy,** the awareness that changes in external characteristics, behaviors, or desires do not lead to a change in biological sex. Thus a boy may wear a dress and a girl may play with toy soldiers without altering their respective biological sexes. For Kohlberg, the acquisition of gender constancy marks the child's mature awareness of the concept of gender differentiation.

Research has confirmed that children progress from attaining gender identity to gender stability and, finally, gender constancy from about two to nine years of age (Fagot, 1985; Slaby & Frey, 1975; Szkrybalo & Ruble, 1999). This trend appears among children from several cultures, including Argentina, Belize, Kenya, Nepal, and American Samoa (DeLisi & Gallagher, 1991; Munroe, Shimmin, & Munroe, 1984). At about eighteen months of age, children show some knowledge of gender categories by matching up the faces and voices of adult males and females (Poulin-Dubois, Serbin, & Derbyshire, 1998). Between ages two and three, most children are able to label themselves as male or female (Huston, 1985). Precisely when children develop this distinction can forecast subsequent patterns of behavior. Beverly Fagot and Mary Leinbach (1989) found that some children developed gender identity early (before age twenty-eight months) and others not until later. Boys and girls who were early identifiers engaged in significantly more gender-typical play, such as play with building toys for boys and doll play for girls, than did late identifiers. At two to three years of age, children who are able to apply gender labels correctly to others also have greater knowledge of gender stereotypes (Fagot, Leinbach, & O'Boyle, 1992).

Another important cognitive-developmental theory is **gender schema theory** (Bem, 1981; Martin & Halverson, 1981, 1987). Like Kohlberg's theory, gender schema

gender identity Knowledge, usually gained by age three years, that one is male or female.

gender stability Knowledge, usually gained by age four years, that one's gender does not change over time.

gender constancy Knowledge, usually gained around age six or seven years, that one's gender does not change as a result of alterations in appearance, behaviors, or desires.

gender schema theory Cognitive-developmental theory that stresses the importance of the acquisition of gender identity and children's intrinsic motivations to behave in a gender-typical manner.

theory stresses the importance of the acquisition of gender identity and children's intrinsic motivations to behave in a gender-typical manner. Unlike Kohlberg's theory, however, gender schema theory does not stress the attainment of gender constancy; rather, it focuses on the influence of children's active construction of gender knowledge on their behavior (Bem, 1981; Martin & Halverson, 1987; Signorella, 1987).

Carol Martin and Charles Halverson (1981) have proposed that children first acquire gender identity and then, in their attempts to create order in their social worlds, begin to construct two **gender schemas,** or cognitive organizing structures for information relevant to gender. The first one, the *same-sex/opposite-sex schema,* refers to the child's knowledge of one sex or the other. This is a fairly primitive cognitive structure composed largely of gender stereotypes, such as "Boys fix cars" and "Girls sew." Children also develop a second, more elaborate gender schema about behaviors relevant to their own sex. This *own-sex schema* provides a basis for guiding children's behavior. Thus, even though both boys and girls know that girls sew, girls are more likely to be motivated to learn to sew, whereas they may not want to learn how to fix a car. Researchers have confirmed that children explore and prefer neutral objects labeled as intended for their own sex more than they do for objects labeled for the other sex. Moreover, up to one week later, children remember more details about the "same-sex" objects than they do about the "other-sex" objects, even when they are offered a reward for remembering details (Bradbard et al., 1986; Martin, Eisenbud, & Rose, 1995).

According to Martin and Halverson (1981), children's gender schemas serve as a potent means of organizing information about their social world. Some children tend to be *gender schematic*; that is, they possess a strong gender schema, exhibit more consistent sex typing in their behavior, and process information along gender lines. In contrast, children who are *gender aschematic* possess a weaker gender schema, are less sex typed behaviorally, and focus their attention on aspects of information that are not related to gender. Gender-schematic children often distort information according to their beliefs about gender and are unlikely to remember events that are inconsistent with those beliefs. For example, gender-schematic children find it difficult to remember information about pictures of people engaged in sex-atypical activities, such as a boy playing with a doll, whereas they can easily remember information about people engaged in sex-typical activities, such as a girl playing with a tea set (Signorella, 1987; Welch-Ross & Schmidt, 1996). These effects are apparent as early as age twenty-five months, at least among boys (Bauer, 1993). Even more dramatic is the finding that children distort stereotype-inconsistent information by actually changing the sex of the person engaged in the sex-atypical behavior. Gender-schematic children who see a picture of a boy playing with a doll are more likely to remember seeing a picture of a girl playing with a doll than a picture of a boy playing with a gender-typical toy (Carter & Levy, 1988).

Why do many children become gender schematic? According to Bem (1983), children become gender schematic to the extent that they experience gender as a relevant social category. Thus, for example, when differences between males and females are frequently highlighted by parents, teachers, or peers, children themselves will use gender as a way to classify social information. Furthermore, both peers and adults in our society stress children's conformity to gender-typical roles, a fact that makes it difficult for them to become truly gender aschematic.

To sum up, each of the preceding theories has some value for explaining the different aspects of sex differences. The biological theories provide a basis for understanding the physiological underpinnings of male and female behavior. Social learning theory provides a mechanism for explaining how children learn discrete elements of sex-typical behavior. Cognitive-developmental approaches explain how children's concepts of gender become integrated in their mind. Although researchers have obtained data to support each theoretical position, none of the theories taken alone is adequate to explain the multifaceted nature of this aspect of development. An important task for researchers is to identify how biology, experience, and thought combine to produce masculine and feminine behavior patterns.

gender schema Cognitive organizing structure for information relevant to sex typing.

The Socialization of Gender Roles

Key Theme
Nature & Nurture

Whatever biological tendencies are associated with being a male and a female, it is worth exploring further the influences of the social environment on gender-role development and how they intersect with the child's developing cognitions about gender. We need to understand, in particular, how social experiences can promote optimal development for both sexes.

The earliest messages about the social world, of course, come from the child's parents. From the moment of birth, when parents in our culture ask, "Is it a boy or a girl?" the sex of their child is a very prominent characteristic, one that elicits specific behaviors and reactions from mother and father. As children branch out to social relationships with peers, gender-role socialization continues in very powerful ways—in the games children play, the relationships they form, and how they react to one another's behaviors.

The Influence of Parents Traditionally, developmental psychologists have believed that one of the most important sources of information about gender for children is the behavior of their parents and the environment parents create (Katz, 1987). Sometimes the messages are subtle. Parents commonly provide their children with sex-differentiated toys and room furnishings (Rheingold & Cook, 1975). They buy sports equipment, tools, and vehicles for their sons, and dolls and doll furniture for their daughters. Boys' rooms typically are decorated in blue, girls' in yellow (Pomerleau et al., 1990). When parents supply boys and girls with different physical environments, they send messages that boys are different from girls and set sex-related limits on the types of behavior that are acceptable and appropriate.

Another way in which parents influence their children's gender-role development is through their own general viewpoints about masculine and feminine roles. Many parents believe that children as young as two years differ along gender-stereotypic lines (McGuire, 1988). They report, for example, that their sons like sports, enjoy tools, and are energetic. On the other hand, parents of girls say that their daughters like to be admired, enjoy playing with dolls, and like clothes. Parents' gender beliefs are related to their children's gender beliefs (Tenenbaum & Leaper, 2002). And those beliefs are frequently translated into sex-differentiated patterns in the types of chores boys and girls are assigned to do around the house: boys take out the garbage and mow the lawn; girls do more chores within the house, such as cleaning and cooking (Goodnow, 1988; Lackey, 1989).

Sometimes parents' messages about gender are more direct. Some research shows that parents treat children differently on the basis of sex in early infancy, beginning at ages younger than those at which actual behavioral sex differences emerge (Fagot & Leinbach, 1987). Right in the first week following the birth of their child, parents of daughters describe their infants as more delicate and less strong and as having finer features than do parents of boys (Karraker, Vogel, & Lake, 1995). Adults play more roughly with a male infant, tossing him in the air and tickling him vigorously, than they do with a female infant (Huston, 1983). During infancy and early childhood, girls are more likely than boys to be protected and sheltered by adults, whereas boys are given greater opportunities than girls to explore their environment (Block, 1983; Burns, Mitchell, & Obradovich, 1989). When their children are preschoolers, parents react more negatively when their daughters assert themselves than when their sons do. Fathers in particular tend to react positively when their daughters display compliant behavior and to reward their sons for assertiveness (Kerig, Cowan, & Cowan, 1993). In addition, parents give boys more positive evaluations and girls more negative evaluations when children are working on solving problems (Alessandri & Lewis, 1993). Both mothers and fathers use more emotion words when speaking with their preschool-age daughters than with their sons (Adams et al., 1995; Kuebli, Butler, & Fivush, 1995). Parents also respond positively to boys who play with blocks, manipulate objects, and engage in physical play. With girls they encourage play that involves dolls, domestic themes, and "pretending" (Fagot & Leinbach, 1987; Farver & Wimbarti, 1995; Lindsay, Mize, & Pettit, 1997). Fathers appear to be especially concerned about what they perceive as masculinity in their sons, at least during the preschool years (Jacklin, DiPietro, & Maccoby, 1984). Such concern is often expressed in parental interviews, as well as in the consistently negative manner in which fathers respond to sex-atypical behavior in their sons.

However, a meta-analysis of 172 studies of parents' differential socialization of girls and boys suggests that we must be cautious about how much weight we give to the role of direct parental reinforcement in accounting for the various facets of gender-role development. In general, the overall impact of parental behaviors was judged to be small in most areas of socialization, including achievement expectations, dependency, and aggression. The only socialization area that showed a significant effect was parental encouragement of sex-typed activities, such as doll play for girls and tool play for boys (Lytton & Romney, 1991).

There are several ways to interpret these somewhat surprising findings. First, it may be that children's participation in sex-typed play is a particularly important context for acquiring behaviors typical of masculinity and femininity. Recent studies show that children's activity interests and how they spend their leisure time are gender-stereotyped—even more so than their beliefs about gender or their personality characteristics. Boys tend to prefer and engage in such activities as competitive sports and building, whereas girls prefer and participate in such activities as dancing, reading, and writing (McHale, Crouter, & Tucker, 1999, 2001). Even at age three, girls spend more of their weekend time in socializing, personal care activities, and educational activities, whereas boys engage in more video game playing (Huston et al., 1999). Some of these contexts are more conducive to fostering collaboration, whereas others tend to promote competition and assertiveness (Leaper, 2000). Second, children's gender-role socialization may be more heavily influenced by broader social forces than by parental behaviors (Harris, 1995; Martin & Ruble, 1997). For example, peer experiences and exposure to gender-typed media messages may be far more important in gender socialization than the behaviors encouraged by mothers and fathers. Finally, parents' roles in gender-role socialization may generally be more indirect, but still powerful. For example, mothers in one recent study were observed as they spoke to their preschoolers about a picture book they were reading together. A substantial proportion of mothers were observed to make implicit references to gender by making statements like "That's a lady sewing a dress, right?" and "Can girls play football?" By highlighting gender as a social category and by contrasting male versus female roles, parents may be inadvertently sending signals about gender stereotypes to children whose minds are actively processing social information (Gelman, Taylor, & Nguyen, 2004).

Gender Roles in Nontraditional Families A series of profound changes in the traditional American family over the last several decades has had an impact on gender-role development. Mothers increasingly are employed outside the home while their children are still young. These women may be providing their children with alternative models for feminine behavior.

In general, maternal employment facilitates the development of flexibility in children's conceptions of gender roles. Children with employed mothers are more likely to believe that both males and females can exhibit a wide variety of behaviors and personality characteristics than are children whose mothers are not employed outside the home. The effects on daughters of employed mothers are particularly dramatic. Daughters of mothers who work outside the home show higher levels of achievement motivation and are more likely to have personality styles that blend male-typed and female-typed traits than are the daughters of nonworking mothers (Hoffman, 1979; Huston, 1983).

Psychologists are also interested in the effects of nontraditional mothers and fathers—those who take on approximately equal responsibility for child care—on children's gender-role development. Children whose mothers and fathers make a deliberate effort to share parenting are slower to adopt gender labels and show less knowledge of gender stereotypes during the preschool years (Fagot & Leinbach, 1995).

The Influence of Peers An extremely powerful influence on children's gender-role development is the peer group. Peer groups not only provide children with opportunities for particular kinds of play but also offer a forum in which children can learn about social behavior and social interactions by watching models and obtaining feedback about their own behaviors. Although peers influence children in a variety of social dimensions, nowhere is their impact more marked than in the area of gender-role socialization (Carter, 1987).

The role of peers in gender-role development can be observed even among very young children. Carol Jacklin and Eleanor Maccoby (1978) observed same-sex and mixed-sex pairs of unacquainted two-year-olds to determine the influence of peers on toddlers' behavior. Children were dressed in a sex-neutral fashion (in yellow jumpsuits) and allowed to play in a room with their mothers present but nondirective. As Figure 9.5 shows, the toddlers' behavior varied as a function of the sex of their play partner even though the children were unaware of the true sex of the other child. In general, children displayed more social behaviors, both positive overtures and negative acts, when they played with a peer of the same sex. Girls were more likely to be passive when they played with a boy than when they played with a girl. In addition, girls in girl-girl pairs exhibited greater sharing of toys and were less likely to become upset and cry than when they were in mixed-sex pairs. Finally, boys were less likely to obey a verbal prohibition from a girl than from a boy. Already at this young age, the dynamics of peer interactions were markedly affected by the sex of the partners.

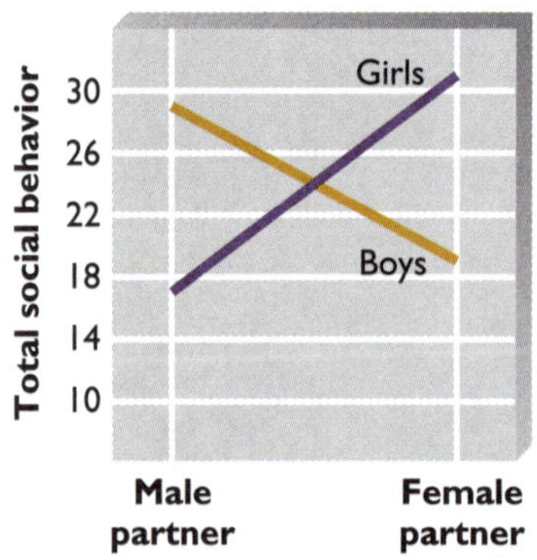

FIGURE 9.5

Social Behavior as a Function of the Child's Play Partner

In a study by Jacklin and Maccoby, unacquainted two-year-olds were observed as they interacted with either a same-sex or opposite-sex partner. The amount of social behavior (both positive overtures and negative acts such as aggression) was greater when children played with a peer of the same sex.

Source: Adapted from Jacklin & Maccoby (1978).

Peers continue to exert a strong influence on children's adoption of sex-typical behaviors as they begin preschool. A number of studies have shown, for example, that children respond differentially to sex-typical and sex-atypical behavior in their peers. Children may reward behavior they like by complimenting a child or by engaging in mutual play, and they may punish a behavior they do not approve of by name calling. Preschoolers and kindergartners reliably punish boys who engage in sex-atypical behavior, such as playing with dolls, while rewarding them for engaging in sex-typical behavior, such as playing with trucks (Fagot, 1977; Lamb, Easterbrooks, & Holden, 1980; Lamb & Roopnarine, 1979). In contrast, girls are rewarded for engaging in sex-typical behavior, such as playing house, but apparently they experience no consequences when they engage in sex-atypical behavior (Fagot, 1977).

The pressures the peer group exerts apparently work. Children are responsive to the positive and negative feedback they receive from their peers. They are likely to continue to engage in a sex-typical behavior in response to reinforcement and to terminate behaviors that their peers punish (Lamb et al., 1980). Furthermore, feedback from same-sex peers is especially important. Beverly Fagot (1978) found that both girls and boys two years of age were more likely to continue a behavior if a same-sex peer responded positively and to discontinue a behavior if a same-sex peer reacted negatively. If the peer was of the other sex, however, the peer's feedback was largely ineffective.

Cross-Gender Behaviors Some children (between 20 and 40 percent), more often girls than boys, fail to respond to their peers' disapproval of sex-atypical behaviors (Sandberg et al., 1993). These children exhibit cross-gender behavior; that is, they adopt, in whole or in part, a variety of characteristics typical of the other sex (Fagot, 1977). Cross-gender boys, for example, exhibit a strong interest in feminine games and activities, and play "dress-up" in girls' clothes. Cross-gender boys are likely to become social isolates over time because their male peers refuse to interact with them even when they play in a masculine fashion, and their female peers seem to merely tolerate their presence. Cross-gender girls, in contrast, appear to suffer very little for their sex-atypical behavior, at least in the preschool years.

Key Theme
Sociocultural Influence

The tendency of children to disapprove of cross-gender behavior is more pronounced in cultures that emphasize the importance of traditions and adherence to social norms (for example, Taiwan) as opposed to freedom to break from traditions and individualism, as in Israel (Lobel et al., 2001). This tendency also increases with age. When researchers interviewed kindergartners through sixth-graders to determine how these children would respond to hypothetical cases of cross-gender behavior in their peers, older children reported that they would respond more negatively to cross-gender behavior than did younger children. Moreover, children stated that they would respond more negatively to cross-gender behavior in their male peers than in their female peers. The degree of negativity that children exhibited was particularly surprising. Children were virtually unanimous in their assertion that they would not want to play with a cross-gender child. Children's reports of how they would respond ranged from fairly innocuous comments (such as "I'd stay away") to statements indicating that they would physically abuse cross-gender children (Carter & McCloskey, 1984).

For • Your • Review

- What are the characteristics associated with masculine and feminine stereotypes?
- What do cross-cultural studies reveal about the nature of gender stereotypes?
- What is the nature of children's knowledge about gender stereotypes during the early childhood years?
- What actual sex differences exist in the physical, cognitive, and social domains?
- What are the major ways in which biology is thought to influence gender-role development? What specific research findings support a biological perspective? What research findings challenge the idea that biology alone is responsible for role development?
- How does social learning theory account for gender-role development? What research findings support the social learning perspective?
- What are the essential features of Kohlberg's cognitive-developmental theory of role development? What specific research findings support Kohlberg's theory?
- What are the elements of gender schema theory? What specific research findings support gender schema theory?
- What are some of the ways in which parents influence children's gender-role development?
- What effects do nontraditional parents have on gender-role development?
- What do early play patterns reveal about the role of peers in gender-role development?
- What role do peers play in the enforcement of sex-typed behaviors?
- What are the consequences of cross-gender behaviors for boys and for girls?

Chapter Recap

Summary of Developmental Themes

Nature & Nurture

How do nature and nurture interact in social and emotional development in early childhood?

Socialization becomes a more prominent force in explaining emotional development during early childhood, particularly in the emergence of self-conscious emotions, such as guilt and envy, and in emotion regulation. Socialization also plays a major role in shaping other aspects of the child's behaviors, including self-regulation and moral orientation. The development of gender roles is a good example of the interaction of biological and social forces.

Sociocultural Influence

How does the sociocultural context influence social and emotional development in early childhood?

Although there appear to be many commonalities in social and emotional development in early childhood, cultural variations are apparent in concepts of gender roles and in tolerance for cross-gender behaviors.

Continuity/Discontinuity

Are social and emotional development during early childhood continuous or discontinuous?

Most of the research on the child's social and emotional development implies that development is continuous. However, Lawrence Kohlberg's theory of gender role development describes a stagelike process. Children are hypothesized to progress through a sequence of attaining gender identity, gender stability, and gender constancy.

Interaction Among Domains

How do social and emotional development in early childhood interact with other domains of development?

Emotional development is closely intertwined with language and cognitive development. For example, the self-conscious emotions require the child to understand the perspectives of other people, a significant cognitive achievement. Similarly, gender-role development relies on cognitive processes. In Bandura's work, attention influences which models, male or female, children will imitate.

Risk/Resilience

What factors promote risk or resilience in social and emotional development during early childhood?

The child's ability to regulate his or her emotions is an important predictor of successful social development later in childhood. The child's attachment status also continues to have repercussions for social and cognitive development in early childhood.

Chapter Review

Emotional Development in Early Childhood

What are self-conscious emotions? Give some examples.

Self-conscious emotions are those that require knowledge of the self as related to others. Some examples include guilt, envy, and shame.

What types of knowledge about emotions emerge in early childhood?

Preschoolers begin to understand many of the situations that give rise to specific emotions and the consequences of displaying them. They also begin to understand how to ameliorate negative emotions.

How do boys and girls differ in the expression of emotions? What factors might be responsible for these differences?

Sex differences in emotions are more likely to show up later in childhood than in the preschool years. Girls tend to express a wider range of emotions and are better at identifying emotional expressions in others than boys. However, these sex differences may arise from socialization experiences that take place in early childhood. Mothers are more expressive with and tend to engage in more "emotion talk" with their daughters than with their sons. Parents also encourage girls to maintain emotional closeness and boys to control their emotions.

What strategies do young children typically use to regulate their emotions? What is the significance of the ability to do so?

Young children typically use distraction to regulate their emotions. The ability to regulate emotions is important because it predicts behavioral conduct and the quality of social relationships later in childhood.

How can parents and caregivers promote emotion regulation among children?

Parents who provide supportive guidance and who at least attempt to help children manage their emotions have children who are better at emotion regulation.

What are the consequences of attachment styles for development in early childhood?

Secure attachment in infancy is related to successful problem-solving, more symbolic play, advanced language development, social competence, more positive emotions, and the development of conscience in the early childhood years.

SELF AND SELF-REGULATION IN EARLY CHILDHOOD

What are the features of the self-concept during early childhood?

Preschool-aged children typically define themselves in terms of a *categorical self*; that is, by referring to various categories that provide membership in one group or another.

What are some signs of the preschool child's growing sense of agency?

Preschoolers show signs of protest when caregivers attempt to help them with an activity such as dressing or feeding. They also show signs of emotion after either success or failure in a problem-solving situation.

What is the difference between self-regulation and self-control?

Parents expect preschoolers to begin to display *effortful control*, the ability to suppress undesirable responses. *Self-regulation* refers to the child's ability to control his or her own behaviors in accordance with the expectations of caregivers and other adults. *Self-control* refers to the ability to comply with moral and ethical expectations, especially when adults are not present.

How does self-regulation change during early childhood?

Regulation of the child's behaviors typically shifts from parents to children in the second year. On *delay-of-gratification tasks*, in which children are asked to wait for some period of time before attaining a highly desirable object, children become increasingly able to delay their behavior. Progress in language development and attentional capacities seems to be related to this ability.

What factors seem to promote children's compliance?

Children's compliance is facilitated when parents are responsive and supportive, justify their demands, offer compromises, and focus on "do" rather than "don't."

MORAL DEVELOPMENT IN EARLY CHILDHOOD

What are the signs of the development of conscience in the early childhood years?

Some signs of conscience development include the display of moral emotions, such as guilt or shame, as well as increasing willingness to comply with adult rules, even when adults are not present.

What factors are related to the development of conscience?

Children are increasingly able to recognize the adult emotions that give them feedback about appropriateness of their own actions. They are also better able to regulate their own behaviors. Positive and mutually responsive interactions with caregivers are also important in conscience development.

How does social learning theory account for the development of moral behaviors?

Social learning theory emphasizes the reinforcements that children receive from parents and other agents of socialization, as well as their observations of the behaviors of others, in explaining moral development.

What is the evidence that children are capable of prosocial behaviors in early childhood?

Prosocial behaviors, social actions performed to benefit others, include *altruism*, behavior carried out to help others without expecting a reward for one's self. Some signs of this capacity in early childhood include the following: displays of *empathy* (a vicarious, shared emotional response) for the distress of others, soothing a person in distress, and seeking assistance for that person.

GENDER ROLES IN EARLY CHILDHOOD

What are the characteristics associated with masculine and feminine stereotypes? What do cross-cultural studies reveal about the nature of gender stereotypes?

Gender stereotypes are the expectations or beliefs that individuals within a given culture hold about the characteristics of women and men. Children learn these stereotypes as part of the process of *gender-role development*. Stereotypes of masculinity center on *instrumentality*, qualities associated with acting on the world. Stereotypes of femininity center on *expressiveness*, qualities associated with emotions and relationships. There are many cross-cultural similarities in the content of gender stereotypes but also a few notable variations.

What is the nature of children's knowledge about gender stereotypes during the early childhood years?

Children demonstrate knowledge of gender stereotypes as early as age two. They are familiar with the personality traits, occupations, appearance qualities, and household activities associated with males and females. They are also familiar with many metaphors for masculinity and femininity.

What actual sex differences exist in the physical, cognitive, and social domains?

Males and females differ in several physical qualities, including activity level, rate of maturity, and physical size. The most notable sex differences in cognition are in visual-spatial tasks, such that males tend to perform better than females on mental rotation and spatial perception tasks. In the social domain, males tend to be more physically aggressive than females.

What are the major ways in which biology is thought to influence gender-role development? What specific research findings support a biological perspective? What research findings challenge the idea that biology alone is responsible for role development?

Biological theories emphasize the role of hormones, such as *androgens*, and differences in the structures of the male and female brains in explaining sex differences. Animal and human studies show that prenatal exposure to androgens is related to aggressive, rough-and-tumble behavior and more male-type play. However, hormone levels can change in response to environmental experiences, indicating that caution is in order when interpreting findings about biology and gender.

How does social learning theory account for gender-role development? What research findings support the social learning perspective?

Social learning theory emphasizes the roles of reinforcement, imitation, and eventually self-regulation in producing sex-typed behaviors. An important factor in influencing the likelihood of imitation is the *sex typicality* of the model's behavior. Research shows that children are more likely to imitate same-sex than other-sex models and that self-regulation of sex-typed behavior increases with development.

What are the essential features of Kohlberg's cognitive-developmental theory of role development? What specific research findings support Kohlberg's theory?

Kohlberg's theory hypothesizes that children's awareness of gender grows through successive mastery of *gender identity*, *gender stability*, and *gender constancy*. Cross-cultural research has confirmed this developmental progression. For example, by age two or three, most children can label themselves as male or female.

What are the elements of gender schema theory? What specific research findings support gender schema theory?

Gender schema theory states that children first form cognitive representations of the same-sex/opposite-sex schema and then form more elaborate *gender schemas* for their own sex. Research has shown that children prefer neutral objects labeled for their own sex and that gender schemas can have an impact on social information processing. For example, gender-schematic children distort information about sex-atypical behaviors.

What are some of the ways in which parents influence children's gender-role development?

Many parents express stereotypical attitudes and beliefs about their male and female children. They also treat children differently based on their biological sex, from the way they furnish their rooms to the kinds of activities and play they encourage.

What effects do nontraditional parents have on gender-role development?

Children who have nontraditional parents show less knowledge of gender stereotypes, and girls show more independence and achievement.

What do early play patterns reveal about the role of peers in gender-role development?

Children display more positive and negative social behaviors when they play with a peer of the same sex. Girls in mixed-sex pairs are more likely to be passive and to become upset. Thus gender-role dynamics are already apparent at age two years.

What role do peers play in the enforcement of sex-typed behaviors?

Peers reward sex-typical play and reliably punish sex-atypical behaviors in children, especially boys.

What are the consequences of cross-gender behaviors for boys and for girls?

Children who consistently display cross-gender behaviors are likely to be isolated from their peer groups.

Key Terms and Concepts

altruism (p. 321)
androgen (p. 327)
categorical self (p. 315)
delay of gratification (p. 316)
effortful control (p. 316)
empathy (p. 321)
expressive characteristics (p. 323)
gender constancy (p. 330)
gender identity (p. 330)
gender schema (p. 331)
gender schema theory (p. 330)
gender stability (p. 330)
gender stereotype (p. 322)
gender-role development (p. 322)
instrumental characteristics (p. 322)
prosocial behavior (p. 321)
self-conscious emotion (p. 310)
self-control (p. 316)
self-regulation (p. 316)
sex typicality (p. 329)

10 Contexts of Development

Four-year-old Joey looked at his loaded dinner plate and announced, "I'm not hungry. Can I just have dessert?" "No, you may not!" his embarrassed mother replied as she turned toward her house guest. "I can't think why he gets like this. He's stubborn as a mule." The guest wondered why no one mentioned that Joey, in full view of his mother, had eaten most of a gift box of cookies before dinner.

"I don't want this! It stinks! You stink!" Joey shouted. He pushed away his plate, got up from the table, and ran to the television, which he turned up to full volume.

"Turn that down this minute or go to your room!" his mother ordered. Joey ignored her. Spying Joey reaching for the cookie box, she warned, "Don't take that cookie!" Joey removed his hand from the box and gave his mother a mournful, pleading look. "All right, but just one!" she conceded. Joey took two and returned to the TV.

KEY THEMES in Contexts of Development

SOCIOCULTURAL INFLUENCE How do sociocultural factors influence the contexts of development in early childhood?

RISK/RESILIENCE What contextual factors promote risk or resilience in early childhood?

By the time children are two or three years old, caregivers begin to be concerned with **socialization**, the process by which children acquire the social knowledge, behaviors, and attitudes valued by the larger society. Among many other things, we start to expect children to eat their dinner before dessert, to be polite to visitors to their home, and to listen to the requests made by parents. These behaviors do not always come easily, as the above scene with Joey suggests. And guiding children to maturity on the social and cognitive fronts takes more than a mere couple of years and one or two parents. As children grow beyond infancy, the wider world—peers, teachers, neighbors, and the media—also begins to exert its influence. For the great majority of children ages two through six, though, the family is the primary context for the process of development. Parents, siblings, and others within the family unit are the people with whom the child usually spends the most time and forms the strongest emotional bonds, and they thus play an undeniable role in the child's life. Therefore, in this chapter, we examine more closely the ways in which the family has an impact on children's social and cognitive development. Because children also have increasing opportunities to spend time with peers, and because, for a significant proportion of children, a considerable amount of time is spent in some form of child care, we also take a look at the influence of these two other important contexts in the life of the young child. Finally, we provide a beginning glimpse of how the powerful force of the media impinges on the life of the preschool-aged child.

THE FAMILY IN EARLY CHILDHOOD

In a sense, virtually every domain of development is deeply influenced by the family environment. Cognition, moral awareness, gender identity, and emotional growth are all nurtured largely within the family. However, the study of the impact of the family is no simple matter, primarily because the direction of influence within families runs along several paths. Just as parents and siblings affect the child's behavior, the child affects the reactions of other family members. Because the family experience includes fluid, constantly changing effects and outcomes for its various members, studying the influence of the family presents a special research challenge to developmental psychologists.

STUDYING THE FAMILY

We begin by considering the question of just what we mean by "family." Is there a typical structure in contemporary families? Has the composition of the family undergone any significant shifts in recent years? Then we elaborate on the idea that families are contexts for development in which the effects are reciprocal and multifaceted. This discussion will allow you to understand the family's role in socialization in a richer and more meaningful way.

The Demographics of the American Family Historians, sociologists, and anthropologists who study the family as a social unit point to the changes in its structure and functions over the last two centuries. With the industrialization of nineteenth-century America, for example, the extended family, in which secondary relatives, such as grandparents, aunts and uncles, or cousins, lived in the same household as the primary family, gave way to the nuclear family, consisting solely of parents and their offspring living in a single household. Similarly, as we saw in the chapter titled "Themes and Theories," the modern notion that families are havens for nurturing the child's growth and development was not always prevalent. As we look back in

socialization Process by which children acquire the social knowledge, skills, and attitudes valued by the larger society.

FIGURE 10.1

Demographic Changes in Family Structure

The percentage of children living with two parents has declined since 1970, and the percentage living with a single parent (most frequently the mother) has increased dramatically. About one-fourth of American children live with a single parent. The higher rates of divorce and single-parent births have contributed to this trend.

Source: U.S. Bureau of the Census (2005).

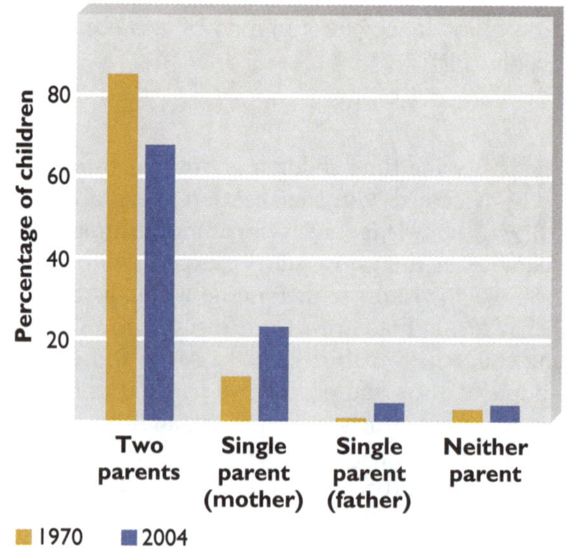

history, we see that the family has been a changing social structure, and all signs indicate that it will continue to take different shapes in the future to reflect larger social, economic, and historical trends.

No one family structure typifies contemporary American society. The 1950s' model of a two-parent family with two children and a nonworking mother no longer applies. For example, as Figure 10.1 shows, only 68 percent of children younger than eighteen years lived with two parents in 2004, compared with 85 percent in 1970. Today, 28 percent of American children live with only one parent (U.S. Bureau of the Census, 2005). High rates of divorce and single-parent births have contributed to this trend. Current data show that a little over 40 percent of current marriages end in divorce (compared with about 15 percent in 1960), and about 35 percent of all births are to single women (Bramlett & Mosher, 2001; Federal Interagency Forum on Child and Family Statistics, 2005). Moreover, about 2 percent of children live with their grandparents (Federal Interagency Forum on Child and Family Statistics, 2005), and a growing number live with gay or lesbian parents. Finally, more than 70 percent of married women with children younger than eighteen years work outside the home, compared with about 45 percent in 1975 (U. S. Bureau of the Census, 2005). All of these changes in family structure have distinct implications for the child's experiences within the family.

Family structures vary greatly in contemporary society. For example, today, about 28 percent of American children live with a single parent.

A Systems Approach Many child development researchers have found it fruitful to focus on family dynamics, the interactions among all members of the group, rather than on the structure of the family per se as they study the impact of the family. An important influence on contemporary thinking about the family is **systems theory**. Its premise is that all members influence one another simultaneously and that the interactions flow in a circular, reciprocal manner. In systems theory (see Figure 10.2), the individual child's development is understood as being embedded in the complex network of multidirectional interactions among all family members (Bronfenbrenner, 1986; Cox & Paley, 2003).

Systems theory assumes that families undergo periods of stability and change. The family tends to adapt in order to maintain a state of *homeostasis*, or equilibrium. Thus, as children attain significant milestones like going to preschool, the family system must readjust to absorb the child's new routines or demands for independence. At other times, families may experience crises, such as financial hardship, moving, or divorce. In these instances, changing external circumstances require the

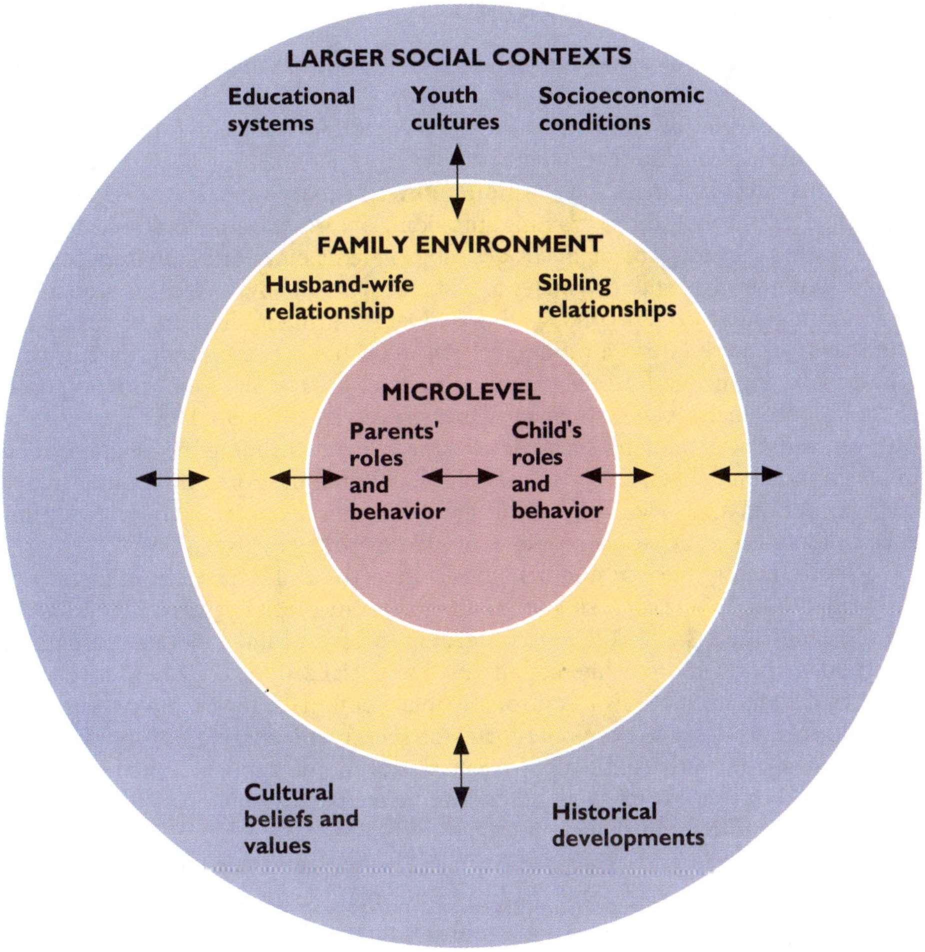

FIGURE 10.2

The Systems Model of the Family

According to systems theorists, reciprocal influences among family members occur at three levels: the individual or micro-level, the family environment, and the larger social context. At the microlevel, parent and child influence each other directly. Within the family, relationships between particular individuals, such as husband and wife, can affect interactions with children. Finally, larger social factors, such as the presence of economic stress, can affect parent-child relations. The individual child's development is thus embedded in this network of multidirectional interactions.

Source: Adapted from Peterson & Rollins (1987).

child and all other family members to adapt to the new situation. Systems theory, then, regards families as dynamic, self-regulating social groups (Minuchin, 1988).

Families usually contain several subsystems, such as the relations maintained between spouses, among siblings, and between parent and child. A single family member is usually a member of more than one subsystem at the same time. The child has a relationship with each parent, as well as with one or more siblings; mothers and fathers are spouses as well as parents. The quality of each of these separate relationships can have an impact on other relationships. Thus, for example, when parents have high-quality marital relationships, their relationships with their children are warmer, and their children show more favorable psychological adjustment (Davies & Scummings, 1998; Harold et al., 1997; Miller et al., 1993). Siblings have more positive interactions with one another, too (MacKinnon, 1988). Within the systems model, family members have reciprocal influences on one another, and there are several layers of such interactions.

KEY THEME
SOCIOCULTURAL INFLUENCE

The family system itself is embedded in larger social networks, including the economic, political, legal, and educational forces that are part of the larger culture. Events in the workplace, school, and other extrafamilial settings can affect individual family members and hence the interactions that occur within the family unit. When one or both parents becomes unemployed, for example, the family experiences stress that often is expressed in increased conflict between parents and children (Flanagan, 1990). In other instances, both parents may be employed outside the home, and their experiences of stress at work can have an impact on the quality of interactions with their children (Crouter & Bumpus, 2001). The social ecology of child development—that is, the direct or indirect impact of broad sociocultural factors on the child's social, cognitive, and emotional growth—is critical to understand, according to psychologists.

systems theory Model for understanding the family that emphasizes the reciprocal interactions among various members.

PARENTS AND SOCIALIZATION

In most cultures, the primary agents of the child's socialization are parents. Teachers, peers, and broader social factors also play a significant role; but perhaps no other individuals in the child's life have the powerful influence on future behaviors, attitudes, and personality that parents do.

Parents affect children's socialization in three primary ways. First, they socialize their children through direct training, providing information or reinforcement for the behaviors they find acceptable or desirable. Parents may, for example, encourage their children to share with playmates or instruct them on how to become acquainted with an unfamiliar peer. Second, as they interact with their children, parents serve as models for the children's attitudes, beliefs, and actions. For example, parents who are warm, engaging, and verbally stimulating tend to have children who are popular in school. Finally, parents manage other aspects of their children's lives that in turn can influence children's social development. Parents choose the neighborhood in which the family lives; they also may enroll children in sports programs, arrange birthday parties, and invite children's friends to spend the night, all of which influence children's peer networks (Parke et al., 1988; Parke & O'Neil, 1999).

Parents' major concerns and activities shift as the child moves from infancy to early childhood. Whereas parents of infants focus on caregiving activities and helping the child learn such skills as self-feeding, dressing, and toileting, parents of preschoolers begin more deliberate attempts at socialization. They help their children regulate their emotions—controlling angry outbursts, for example—and start to instill social skills, such as polite forms of speech and sharing during play with peers. Throughout early childhood, parents closely monitor much of their children's activity and begin to expect their children to be cooperative members of the family by avoiding conflicts and sharing in household tasks. (Maccoby, 1984; Maccoby & Martin, 1983). The child's own development often precipitates shifts in parental roles. As the child's language and cognitive skills mature, for example, parents place greater expectations on her social communication behaviors. As systems theory suggests, the individual child's development within the family represents an ongoing give-and-take between child and parent, necessitating continual readjustment by all members to reinstate family equilibrium.

Styles of Parenting Even the casual observer of parents interacting with their children in public places, such as parks, shopping malls, and supermarkets, will notice markedly different styles of parental behavior. Some parents are extremely controlling, using crisp, firm commands devoid of explanations to restrict their children's behavior. Others seem not to notice as their charges create chaos and pandemonium. Researchers have established that the pattern of interactions that a parent adopts is an important variable in influencing the child's later development.

In a landmark series of observational studies, Diana Baumrind (1971, 1972) recorded the interpersonal and behavioral styles of nursery school children as they engaged in normal school activities. She also watched as they worked on a series of standardized problem-solving tasks, such as completing a set of puzzles. In addition, Baumrind gathered information on parenting styles by observing how mothers interacted with their children in both play and structured teaching settings, watching parents and their children in the home, and interviewing parents about their child-rearing practices. The children and parents were observed again when the children were eight or nine years old. Based on these extensive observations, Baumrind identified several distinct patterns of parenting.

authoritarian parent Parent who relies on coercive techniques to discipline the child and displays a low level of nurturance.

Some parents, Baumrind found, were extremely restrictive and controlling. They valued respect for authority and strict obedience to their commands, and relied on coercive techniques, such as threats or physical punishment, rather than on reasoning or explanation, to regulate their children's actions. They were also less nurturant toward their children than other parents in the study. Baumrind identified this group as **authoritarian parents**. The second parenting style belonged to

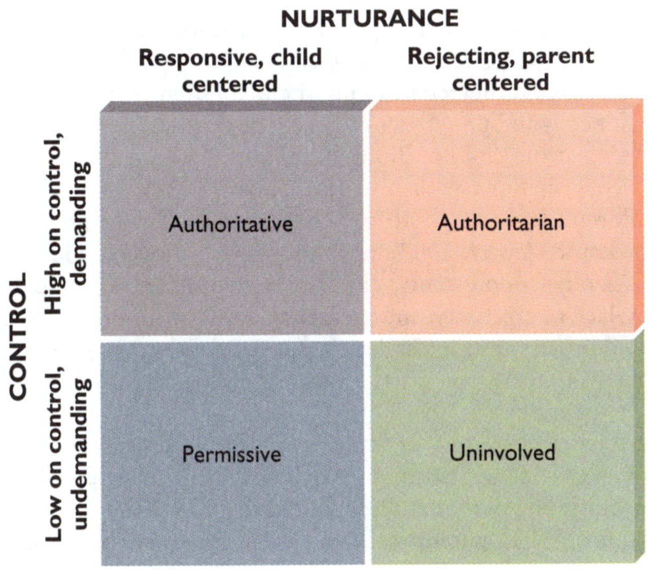

FIGURE 10.3

Patterns of Parenting as a Function of Control and Nurturance

Four parenting styles can be identified in terms of the extent to which parents set limits on the child's behavior (control) and the level of nurturance and responsiveness they provide.

Source: Adapted from Maccoby & Martin (1983).

the group she called **permissive parents**. These parents set few limits and made few demands for mature behavior from their children. Children were permitted to make their own decisions about many routine activities, such as TV viewing, bedtime, and mealtimes, for example. Permissive parents tended to be either moderately nurturant or cool and uninvolved. The third group of parents was high on both control and nurturance. These **authoritative parents** expected their children to behave in a mature fashion but tended to use rewards more than punishments to achieve their ends. They communicated their expectations clearly and provided explanations to help their children understand the reasons for their requests. They also listened to what their children had to say and encouraged a dialogue with them. Authoritative parents were distinctly supportive and warm in their interactions with their children. Figure 10.3 summarizes the characteristics of these three parental styles, as well as a fourth style, *uninvolved parents*, which has been described in later research and will be discussed shortly.

Baumrind found a cluster of behavioral characteristics in children linked with each parental style. The offspring of authoritative parents were friendly with peers, cooperative with adults, independent, energetic, and achievement oriented. They also displayed a high degree of self-control. This set of characteristics often is termed **instrumental competence**. In marked contrast, children of authoritarian and permissive parents did not exhibit the social responsibility and independence associated with instrumental competence. Children who had authoritarian parents appeared unhappy; also, boys tended to be aggressive, whereas girls were likely to be dependent. Children of permissive parents, on the other hand, were low on self-control and self-reliance.

The effects of parenting style extend to other dimensions of child development and reach into the adolescent years. Authoritarian parenting, especially with its use of coercive techniques for controlling behavior, is associated with less advanced moral reasoning and less prosocial behavior (Boyes & Allen, 1993; Krevans & Gibbs, 1996), lower self-esteem (Loeb, Horst, & Horton, 1980), and poorer adjustment when starting school (Barth, 1989). Extremely controlling parenting and the use of coercive techniques are also associated with higher levels of aggression in children (Dodge, Coy, & Lynam, 2006), poor peer relations (Pettit et al., 1996; Putallaz, 1987), and lower school achievement in adolescence (Dornbusch et al., 1987). In contrast, by the time children reach adolescence, those with authoritative parents show more prosocial behaviors; fewer problem behaviors, such as substance abuse; greater academic achievement; and higher self-confidence than adolescents whose parents use other parenting styles (Baumrind, 1991; Lamborn et al., 1991; Radziszewska et al., 1996).

permissive parent Parent who sets few limits on the child's behavior.

authoritative parent Parent who sets limits on a child's behavior using reasoning and explanation and displays a high degree of nurturance.

instrumental competence Child's display of independence, self-control, achievement orientation, and cooperation.

Researchers have identified a fourth parenting style: the **uninvolved**, or *neglectful*, **parent** (Maccoby & Martin, 1983). These parents seem to be uncommitted to their parental role and emotionally detached from their children, often giving greater priority to their own needs and preferences than to the child's. These parents may be uninterested in events at the child's school, unfamiliar with his playmates, and have only infrequent conversations with him (Pulkkinen, 1982). Uninvolved parenting is related to children's lower self-esteem (Loeb et al., 1980), heightened aggression (Hatfield, Ferguson, & Alpert, 1967), and lower control over impulsive behaviors (Block, 1971). As older adolescents, children with uninvolved parents show more maladjustment, lack of creativity, and greater alcohol consumption than adolescents who experienced other parenting styles (Weiss & Schwarz, 1996). Some believe that uninvolved parenting may present the greatest risks of all for healthy long-term development (Steinberg et al., 1994).

KEY THEME
RISK/RESILIENCE

Why does authoritative parenting work so well? Several explanations are possible. First, when parents make demands for mature behavior from their children, they make explicit the responsibilities that individuals have toward one another when they live in social groups. When parents set forth clear, consistent guidelines for behavior, they make the child's job of sorting out the social world much easier. Second, when parental demands are accompanied by reasonable explanations, the child is more likely to accept the limitations on her actions. Third, when parents take into account the child's responses and show affection, he is likely to acquire a sense of control over his actions and derive the sense that he has worth (Glasgow et al., 1997; Steinberg, Elmen, & Mounts, 1989). Thus the net outcome of authoritative parenting is a competent child who shows successful psychological adjustment.

Parental Warmth A series of recent studies has singled out parental warmth, the tendency of parents to express positive emotions and approval toward their children, as an important feature of effective parenting. Children whose parents express warmth and support tend to have higher self-esteem, greater empathy, and fewer behavioral problems (Cox & Harter, 2003; Zhou et al., 2002). On the other hand, parental hostility and negativity is related to less compliance on the part of the child, poor peer relationships, and persistent and ongoing patterns of aggressive behavior (Deater-Deckard et al., 2001; Isley et al., 1999; Rubin et al., 2003; Simons et al., 2001). Parental warmth may even serve as a protection of sorts for children who are highly aggressive as youngsters and who are at risk for later developmental problems. When these children experience warm and affectionate parenting, they are less likely to show the declines in empathy and school problems that many other children in this category display (Hastings et al., 2000).

Parental warmth is a key dimension of effective parenting. Parental expression of positive emotions is associated with higher self-esteem, fewer behavior problems, and a range of other positive developmental outcomes in children.

Parental warmth probably works in a number of ways. One outcome of parental warmth and supportiveness is the child's perception of his or her own competence. Parental support is an important contributor to the growth of children's self-esteem, which in turn has consequences for many other aspects of the child's social and cognitive development. Moreover, warm parents, in their expression of positive emotions, may encourage a process of "emotion matching" in their children. Positive parental emotions are associated with positive emotions in children (Kochanska, 1997). A recent survey shows that many fathers and mothers report showing warmth and affection to their children every day (see Figure 10.4) (Child Trends Databank, 2002b). Given the importance of parental warmth in child rearing, these statistics are encouraging to see.

Punishment One of the most common problems parents face is the oppositional behavior their children show, often beginning at age two or three. A parent makes a request ("Time to go to bed"), and the child simply refuses to comply, adding a loud "No!" for emphasis. The child's response may reflect a healthy, growing desire for independence and self-assertion. But this pattern, if repeated for a length of time, can quickly

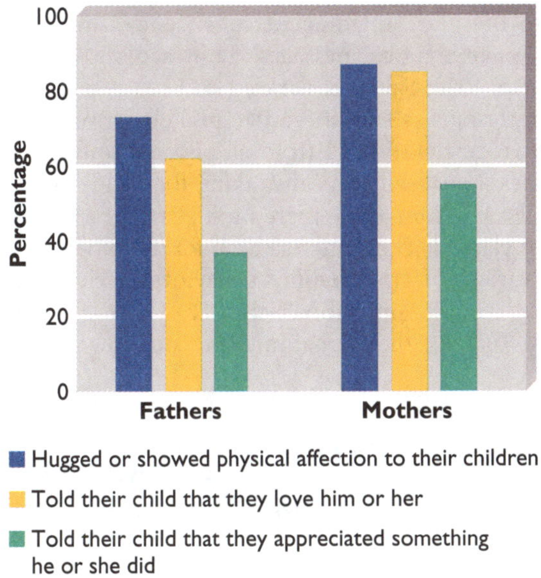

FIGURE 10.4

Expressing Parental Warmth

To what degree do mothers and fathers express warmth to their children? This graph shows the percentage of fathers and mothers who say that they provide various visible signs of warmth to their children (under age thirteen) on a daily basis. Numerous studies confirm that parental warmth is a key feature in effective parenting.

Source: Child Trends Databank (2002b).

lead to conflicts with parents. How should parents respond to these situations? In recent decades, the most widely discussed parental control technique has been *punishment*, the administration of an aversive stimulus or withdrawal of rewards to decrease the frequency of undesirable behaviors. Punishment can include sharp verbal rebukes or the loss of such privileges as TV-viewing time or playtime with friends.

Laboratory studies carried out in the tradition of learning theory show that certain ways of administering punishment are more effective than others. One important factor is making sure the punishment closely follows the child's transgression so that the child makes the connection between her behavior and the consequences. Another powerful factor is providing an explanation for why the behavior is not desirable (Parke, 1969). The effectiveness of punishment also depends on the consistency with which it is applied. As we saw in the case of Joey and the cookies at the beginning of this chapter, children become particularly disobedient and aggressive when parents prohibit a behavior on one occasion and permit it on another. Consistency among caregivers (**interagent consistency**) and consistency of

One effective technique for managing a child's behavior is the use of "time-out," sending the child to a neutral area for a specific amount of time after he or she misbehaves. Time-out has been found to reduce or eliminate a variety of behavior problems among children.

uninvolved parent Parent who is emotionally detached from the child and focuses on his or her own needs as opposed to the child's.

interagent consistency Consistency in application of disciplinary strategies among different caregivers.

one caregiver from one occasion to the next (**intra-agent consistency**) are both important in giving children clear, unambiguous messages about acceptable and unacceptable behaviors (Deur & Parke, 1970; Sawin & Parke, 1979).

Many experts favor the use of a technique called **time-out**, especially for younger children. To use time-out, caregivers remove the child from all possible sources of reward, even subtle or accidental ones. Usually this means taking the child immediately to a quiet, neutral place and leaving him alone there until a short period of time, usually two to five minutes, has elapsed. Time-out has been found to be effective in reducing or eliminating a variety of troublesome behaviors in children, including temper tantrums, fighting, and self-injurious behaviors (Varni, 1983). Time-out also gives both children and parents the opportunity to "cool down" after all parties have become aroused.

CONTROVERSY: THINKING IT OVER

Should Parents Spank Their Children?

Most often, when parents think of punishment, they think of spanking the child. In a survey of almost 1,000 parents, Murray Straus and Julie Stewart found that 94 percent of parents of three- and four-year-olds reported striking their children in the previous year. Infants and adolescents were spanked less often (Straus & Stewart, 1999). However, even half of adolescents report being hit by their parents, with an average of six to eight times in a year (Straus & Donnelly, 1993). Thus, in the United States, many parents resort to physical punishment, at least on occasion, to control their child's behavior.

What Is the Controversy?

Many psychologists believe that physical tactics, such as hitting and spanking, should not be used at all. Some groups of lay individuals feel so strongly about the negative effects that they are working to make physical punishment of children illegal. Others maintain that moderate spanking in the context of a warm, supportive family life has no long-lasting negative effects and in fact can be an effective way to manage children's misbehavior.

What Are the Opposing Arguments?

Many researchers argue that, by using physical punishment, parents are serving as models for aggression. Following the tenets of social learning theory, we should not be surprised if the chief lesson children learn from parents who spank is that physical aggression is a way to resolve conflicts (Parke & Slaby, 1983). Also, an overreliance on physical punishment may, in some cases, set the stage for child abuse (Parke & Collmer, 1975). Caught up in the escalating emotions of a confrontation with their children, parents who are already willing to spank, hit, or pinch do not have far to go before they cause more serious physical injury.

A contrasting position is that occasional spanking has no long-lasting negative effects. In fact, spanking, judiciously used, may be a necessary tactic when children are unrelentingly noncompliant. In this line of thinking, parents should consider spanking only when other nonphysical disciplinary tactics have failed. When parents are warm and supportive, an occasional spanking is not harmful; rather, it may be necessary to help children learn to be compliant and to regulate their own behavior (Baumrind, 1996).

What Answers Exist? What Questions Remain?

Some research suggests that the children of parents who use occasional spanking do not have different profiles than children whose parents never spank. In one study of twenty-one-month-olds, for example, children whose mothers used frequent physical punishment scored lower on their ability to regulate their behaviors. However, children whose mothers used occasional physical punishment

intra-agent consistency Consistency in a single caregiver's application of discipline from one situation to the next.

time-out Disciplinary technique that involves immediately removing a child from all possible sources of reward and leaving the child alone in a quiet, neutral place for a short time.

did not differ from children whose mothers never spanked them—both fared better than the high-physical-punishment group (Power & Chapieski, 1986). Additional evidence suggests that the links between spanking and aggression in children, and between spanking and child abuse, are not necessarily clear. For example, since 1995, when Sweden passed a law to ban physical punishment, aggression among children has increased (and not decreased), as has the number of cases of child abuse (Baumrind, 1996).

Supporting the other side of the debate are the results of a recent meta-analysis of eighty-eight studies evaluating the impact of physical punishment on children. The findings indicated that physical punishment has a strong relationship to the child's immediate compliance. Children who are spanked do listen in the short run. However, there was also a strong association between the use of physical punishment and incidence of child abuse. Lesser, but still significant associations were found between increased use of physical punishment and heightened aggression, risk of mental health problems, and lower moral internalization in children (Gershoff, 2002).

The meta-analysis has been criticized for including studies in which physical punishment was more extreme than an occasional spanking (Baumrind, Larzelere, & Cowan, 2002). Would the same relationships have been found if only cases of mild physical punishment were evaluated? What kinds of studies might provide more compelling evidence about the appropriateness of spanking? For example, Alan Kazdin (Kazdin & Benjet, 2003) states that many of the goals of discipline can be accomplished without the use of corporal punishment. Yet research has not directly compared the effectiveness of spanking versus techniques such as time-out, positive reinforcement, or other behavior management techniques.

Parental Cognitions As is the case with most human interactions, the dynamics of parent-child relations are complex. As they engage in exchanges with each other, parents and children interpret each other's behaviors; these mental judgments, in turn, influence the specific behaviors parents and children subsequently display toward each other. In addition, parents hold beliefs about their own competence and effectiveness as parents; these beliefs are also related to the quality of parenting (Coleman & Karraker, 1998). Finally, children's behaviors, specifically the extent to which they escalate the intensity of interactions, can influence parental styles. In short, parenting strategies arise from a complex interplay of cognitions and behaviors in the context of dynamic interchanges with the child.

One way to understand parents' cognitions is in terms of their *attributions* about children's behaviors: why are their children acting the way they do? Theodore Dix and Joan Grusec (1985; Dix, 1993) hypothesize that the kinds of attributions parents make about the causes of their children's behaviors will influence the parenting strategies they adopt. If, for example, a parent believes his three-year-old is throwing a tantrum at the dinner table because she wants her dessert immediately, he will probably insist that she first eat all her vegetables. If, on the other hand, the parent suspects the child is ill, he will probably remove the child from the dinner table and nurture and console her.

Figure 10.5 presents a schematic diagram of Dix and Grusec's (1985) attribution model of socialization. The flow of events proceeds as follows. First, the parent observes the child's behavior and judges whether it is typical for the child or normative for her age group. The parent assesses whether the child has the skills, knowledge, and motive to behave intentionally in a certain way. Do most three-year-olds throw tantrums to get dessert? Is throwing a tantrum a typical behavior for that child? Parents make a causal attribution about the child's intentions. Next, parents' attributions affect their emotional and behavioral responses to the child. Parents become more upset and act more forcefully if they believe the child intends to misbehave—in this case, screaming for the explicit purpose of getting dessert.

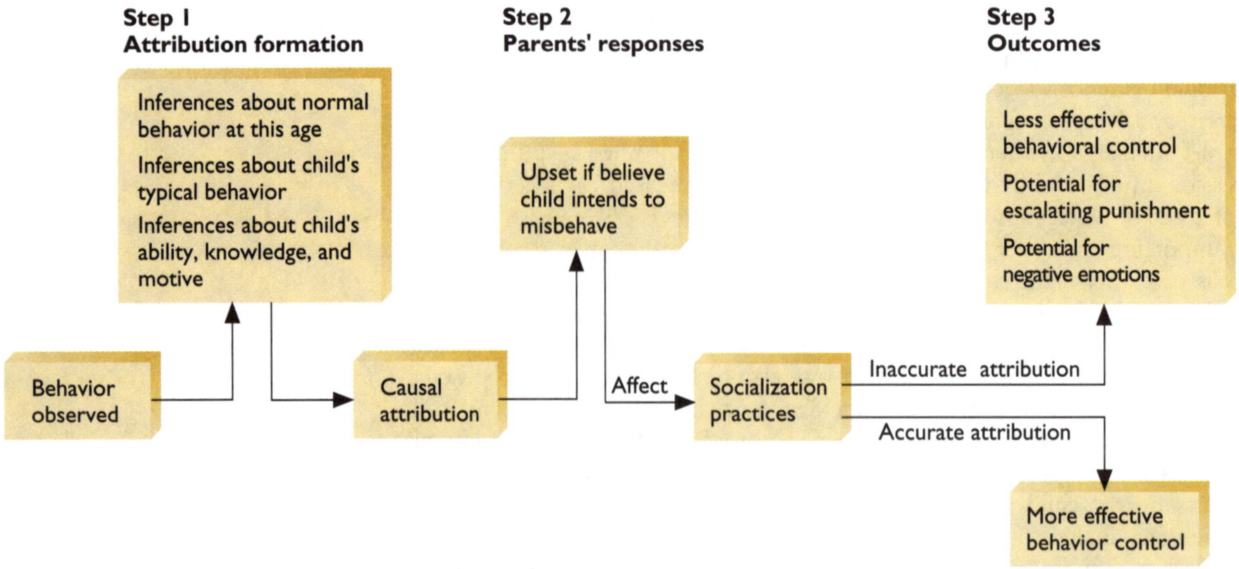

FIGURE 10.5

The Attribution Model of Socialization

Dix and Grusec (1985) hypothesized that parents' judgments about the child's intentionality in misbehaving are critical in determining their response. Parents become more upset if they believe the child intended to transgress and select more forceful control strategies than they do if they believe the transgression was intentional. If their attributions are correct, they will effectively control behavior. If they make an incorrect attribution, however, they will be less effective, may escalate the level of punishment, and may produce negative emotions in themselves and the child.

Source: Adapted from Dix & Grusec (1985).

Finally, if parents have made the correct attribution, they will be effective in controlling the child. But if they are wrong, the child may continue to misbehave, and both parents and child may feel negative emotions rising.

Research confirms that parents make more attributions about children's intentions as the children get older. Furthermore, when parents believe that a child intends to misbehave, they feel more upset and think it is important to respond forcefully (Dix et al., 1986; Dix, Ruble, & Zambarano, 1989). Mothers who tend to attribute hostile intentions to children's actions are likely, in fact, to use harsh discipline practices; their children, in turn, tend to have problems with aggression (Nix et al., 1999).

Another dimension of parental cognitions is their beliefs about their own *efficacy:* do parents see themselves as competent and able to control their children's behaviors? For example, some parents see themselves as powerless relative to their children. Often, in an attempt to regain their power and control, these parents engage in conflict and harsh discipline with their children (Bugental & Lewis, 1998; Bugental et al., 1997). However, their inconsistent style may send mixed messages to the child. For example, a harsh command might be followed by "Just kidding" or some other form of appeasement (Bugental, Blue, & Cruzcosa, 1989). Children tend to become inattentive when they experience this type of ambiguous communication style from adults and may thus become unresponsive to their requests (Bugental et al., 1999). Parental beliefs about their own efficacy can be influenced by diverse factors, including financial stress (Brody, Flor, & Gibson, 1999), the degree to which the child's temperament challenges the parent (Teti & Gelfand, 1991), and the parent's "working models" of interpersonal relationships (Grusec, Hastings, & Mammone, 1994).

Finally, it is important to consider the different goals that parents have as they raise their children. These goals typically extend beyond simply controlling their children's behavior—parents want their children to be happy, have strong values, and have a trusting and loving relationship with them. Parents rely on different strategies depending on the goals they have in mind. When parents want to quickly resolve a disagreement with the child, for example, they most often use power assertion. When they wish to teach a child specific values, on the other hand, they tend to use explanation and open communication (Hastings & Grusec, 1998).

The Child's Characteristics and Behaviors In his pioneering **control theory**, Richard Bell (1968; Bell & Harper, 1977) suggested that children play a distinct role in the types of behaviors that parents display toward them. Parents and children have upper and lower limits of tolerance for the types of behavior each shows the other. When the behavior of one person approaches the other's upper limit, the recipient tries to reduce the excessive behavior with increasing levels of intensity. Thus, for example, a parent whose son is having a temper tantrum might first try to talk to him, then remove him to his room, and finally resort to physical punishment. Likewise, if the child's behavior approaches the parent's lower limits—in the child's shyness or withdrawal at the doctor's office, for example—the parent may try to stimulate the child by coaching her to speak and then promising her a reward if she vocalizes.

Control theory implies that, when children's behavior pushes parents to their limits, parents will respond with more forceful and firmer control techniques. Some children may transgress to this extent more frequently than others. Support for this idea comes from research that shows that aggressive, difficult children elicit more negative reactions from adults than more compliant, nonaggressive children (Anderson, Lytton, & Romney, 1986). In addition, in a study of identical and fraternal twins, and biologically related and unrelated siblings, genetic factors accounted for the relationship between parents' negativity and problem behaviors (Neiderhiser et al., 1999). The idea that the child's temperament influences parental reactions is consistent with these data.

The research of Grazyna Kochanska and her colleagues is adding to the growing body of evidence that some children are easier to socialize than others. Some children, she finds, display *committed compliance*. Even as fourteen-month-old infants, these children seem eager to respond to their mothers, imitating them readily as they teach or complying quickly and enthusiastically with their requests. Other children may comply with parental requests only as particular situations demand, and still others seem to be generally unresponsive to their parents (Forman & Kochanska, 2001). These qualities of the child are, in turn, related to parenting styles. When children display committed compliance, for example, parents are less likely to use power-assertive techniques (Kochanska, 1997). Another study involving school-age children shows similar findings: mothers who scolded, yelled, and used other ineffective discipline techniques reported that their children were very difficult to manage during their first five years of life. These children had frequent temper tantrums, were strong-willed, did not obey, and were very active (Stoolmiller, 2001).

Children's cognitions about their parents' demands probably also make a difference in how they react. Do children see their parents' requests as fair and appropriate? Are children motivated to comply? Do they feel internally motivated rather than pressured by others to respond? These are some of the factors that likely play a part in the tone and outcomes of parent-child interactions (Grusec & Goodnow, 1994). Researchers are just beginning to explore the role of children's cognitions in parent-child interactions.

Child Abuse In 2003 more than 900,000 children in the United States were the victims of abuse or neglect. Children under age three years are most likely to be victims (U. S. Department of Health and Human Services, 2005). Table 10.1 shows some of the characteristics of children who are the victims of maltreatment. Aside from the immediate physical and psychological consequences of abuse, children who are the victims of family violence are predisposed to a number of developmental problems. Maltreated infants and toddlers are more likely to be anxiously attached to their mothers than are children who are not maltreated (Egeland & Sroufe, 1981; Schneider-Rosen et al., 1985). These children are thus vulnerable to the social, emotional, and cognitive impairments associated with insecure attachment. Preschool and school-age children with a history of abuse score lower on tests of cognitive maturity and academic engagement, show delayed language development, and manifest low self-esteem and school learning problems (Eckenrode, Laird, & Doris, 1993;

control theory Hypothesis about parent-child interactions suggesting that the intensity of one partner's behavior affects the intensity of the other's response.

Table 10.1 Characteristics of Victims of Child Maltreatment

The table shows some of the characteristics of American children who experienced child abuse or neglect, as well as the specific type of maltreatment they experienced (expressed in terms of percentages), for the year 1999. The percentages for type of maltreatment reflect the fact that some children experience multiple forms of abuse and neglect.

Number of Victims		826,162
Rate per 1,000		11.8
Gender	Male	48
	Female	52
Age of Victim	1 year and younger	14
	2–5 years old	24
	6–9 years old	25
	10–13 years old	20
	14–17 years old	15
	18 and older	1
Type of Maltreatment	Neglect	56
	Physical Abuse	21
	Sexual Abuse	11
	Psychological or Emotional Abuse	8
	Medical Neglect	2
	Other and Unknown	28

Source: Child Trends Databank (2002a).

Eigsti & Cicchetti, 2004; Hoffman-Plotkin & Twentyman, 1984; Shonk & Cicchetti, 2001). Emotionally, they may display withdrawal and passivity or, on the other hand, aggressive, oppositional patterns of behavior, patterns that are linked to their generally poor relationships with peers (Salzinger et al., 1993; Shonk & Cicchetti, 2001). They also frequently display symptoms of clinical depression (Sternberg et al., 1993). Finally, abused and neglected children are at risk for delinquency and violent criminal behavior in adulthood (Widom, 1989) and may be prone to become abusive parents themselves (Egeland, Jacobvitz, & Papatola, 1987).

KEY THEME
RISK/RESILIENCE

The causes of abuse are neither simple nor easily ameliorated. Research on the interaction patterns in abusive families suggests that they differ in several respects from those in nonabusive families. Perhaps most significantly, parents in abusive families tend to rely on coercive or negative strategies to modify their children's behavior, even for routine or mild discipline problems. In one study, abusive and nonabusive mothers were observed as they engaged in a sequence of preparing a meal, playing, and cleaning up with their preschool-age children. Abusive mothers relied heavily on power-assertive techniques, such as threats, humiliation, or physical contact, to alter their children's behavior, whereas nonabusive mothers used predominantly positive strategies, including reasoning, bargaining, or modeling. Abusive mothers issued more than twice as many commands to their children as nonabusive mothers and also were inconsistent in reinforcing their children's compliance (Oldershaw, Walters, & Hall, 1986). As we saw earlier, inconsistent punishment usually leads to the persistence of undesirable behaviors in children.

Certain characteristics of children are also more commonly observed in abusive families. Parents often describe the abused child as irritable, difficult to put to sleep, and prone to excessive crying (Ounsted, Oppenheimer, & Lindsay, 1974). A group at special risk for abuse is premature infants, who tend to have high-pitched, aversive cries and a less attractive appearance (Parke & Collmer, 1975). Abusive parents become especially sensitized to some of the child's objectionable behaviors and show heightened emotional reactivity to the child's cries or noncompliance (Frodi & Lamb, 1980; Wolfe et al., 1983). Abuse is especially likely to occur when mothers of premature and at-risk children feel unable to control their children's behavior and experience depression (Bugental & Happaney, 2004).

Finally, abusive families tend to be isolated from the outside world and have fewer sources of social support than nonabusive families. In one study, abusive parents reported that they were less involved with the community than were nonabusive parents; they tended not to join sports teams, go to the library, or take classes (Trickett & Susman, 1988). In another study, some mothers who were at risk for becoming abusive because of their own family history had normal, positive relationships with their children. These mothers also had extensive emotional support from other adults, a therapist, or a mate. In contrast, high-risk mothers who subsequently became abusive experienced greater life stress and had fewer sources of psychological support (Egeland, Jacobvitz, & Sroufe, 1988).

How can the spiral of abuse be broken? Researchers suggest that interventions should teach basic parenting skills, provide parents with mechanisms to cope with their emotional tension, and offer social support, such as child care or counseling services (Belsky, 1993; Wolfe, 1985). Especially promising are programs in which home visitors provide parent education and support (MacMillan et al., 1994). Moreover, observers have noted our society's general acceptance of violence as a means of solving problems. This tendency is evident in the widespread endorsement of physical punishment as a technique for disciplining children, as well as in the pervasive displays of violence in the media (Belsky, 1980, 1993; Hart & Brassard, 1987). Altering broader societal attitudes about violence may thus be an additional and necessary step in breaking the cycle of child abuse. Finally, a national study of more than 6,000 households showed that violence toward children was more prevalent in families experiencing unemployment, substance abuse, and financial difficulties (Wolfner & Gelles, 1993). As daunting as the task may seem, a broad attack on more general social problems may help to ameliorate the problem of child abuse.

ATYPICAL DEVELOPMENT

Posttraumatic Stress Disorder

Approximately one-fourth to one-half of children who are the victims of physical or sexual abuse experience the symptoms of posttraumatic stress disorder, or PTSD (Dubner & Motta, 1999; Famularo et al., 1994; Wolfe, Sas, & Wekerle, 1994). This diagnosis was originally formulated in studies of adults' responses to extremely stressful events, such as wars and natural disasters, but many of the symptoms have also been observed in children who have experienced psychological traumas. Chief among those symptoms is the reexperiencing of the traumatic event; children may show repetitive, intrusive thoughts or have vivid flashbacks of the episode. They may also show sleep disturbances and nightmares, have angry outbursts, suffer from stomachaches and headaches, display signs of depression, and have difficulties in school (Milgram, 1998; Yule, 1998).

Physiological changes in the central nervous system may accompany PTSD. Studies with animals and adult humans have shown that extreme stress is associated with decreases in the size of the hippocampus and declines in short-term memory performance (Bremner, 1999; Bremner & Narayan, 1998). More volatile functioning of the neurochemical system that responds to stress has also been observed in adults and adolescents who have experienced trauma (Golier & Yehuda, 1998; Southwick, Yehuda, & Charney, 1997). The possibility that stress can cause permanent changes to the structure of the brain and affect children's learning abilities is particularly disturbing.

The most successful treatments of PTSD in children and adults have used a cognitive-behavioral approach (Foa & Meadows, 1997). Typically, the child is given relaxation training along with suggestions for how to control thoughts about the traumatic event. For example, in one study of four sexually abused children who were given this type of intervention, all four reported a decline in the symptoms of PTSD (Farrell, Hains, & Davies, 1998). Because of the seriousness of the problems associated with PTSD in children, many researchers are eager to devise more precise ways to diagnose and treat this disorder.

Fathers

Do fathers have a different influence than mothers on the process of child development? During the 1960s and 1970s psychologists believed that they do, based on studies of the effects of father absence, especially on boys. Boys growing up without a father were more likely to have problems in academic achievement, gender-role development, and control of aggression (Biller, 1974; Lamb, 1981). An important theoretical construct driving much of the research was *identification*: the idea that boys assimilate the characteristics, attitudes, and behaviors of their father as they form an intense emotional bond with him. Presumably, boys without a father did not have an identity figure or model for appropriate masculine, instrumentally competent behavior and thus suffered deficits in cognitive, social, and emotional domains.

Identification with the father may be less important than other variables, however. Michael Lamb (1987) points out that the effects of father absence may result not from the loss of a masculine identity figure for the son, but from the loss of a source of emotional and financial support for the entire family. The tension and stress that result may produce maladaptive patterns of parenting, which in turn generate undesirable developmental outcomes for boys. Boys may be particularly vulnerable because they seem to be more generally susceptible than girls to the effects of deviant environments (Rutter, 1986).

A more contemporary view is that fathers make recognizable contributions to family life in general and child development in particular but that those contributions simply reflect aspects of good parenting. In other words, good fathering resembles good mothering, and the child will thrive by having two parents who fill those roles instead of just one. For example, studies are beginning to show that the mere presence of a father is not associated with benefits to children's development. Instead, it is only when fathers are nurturant, are involved with their children, and display low levels of antisocial behavior that children show higher cognitive and social functioning (Black, Dubowitz, & Starr, Jr., 1999; Jaffee et al., 2003). Several other studies also show that a father's warmth and involvement are associated with children's competence and academic achievement, and with less rigid gender-role stereotypes (Radin, 1981, 1994; Wagner & Phillips, 1992). This influence holds true even when children live in single-parent families with their mother but have contact with their biological father (Coley, 1998).

Despite their responsiveness and competence as parents, most fathers spend less time with their children than do mothers. In general, fathers spend about one-half to two-thirds the time mothers do in direct contact with their children, even when the mother works outside the home (National Research Council and Institute of Medicine, 2003). This pattern has been found in diverse ethnic groups and cultures, including African American, Chinese, and Japanese families (Hossain & Roopnarine, 1994; Ishii-Kuntz, 1994; Sun & Roopnarine, 1996). Why are fathers less involved? Some fathers (and mothers) may hold traditional beliefs about which family member should be responsible for child care. Another reason may be that fathers are not confident in their caregiving skills. Because males typically are not exposed to child care through such experiences as baby-sitting and home economics courses, they may feel insecure about feeding, bathing, or diapering a child (Lamb et al., 1987). On the other hand, certain circumstances predict greater father involvement in child care: fewer hours at work, the fact that the mother works, and the father's memories of his own relationship with his father (Gottfried, Bathurst, & Gottfried, 1994; NICHD Early Child Care Research Network, 2000a; Radin, 1994). In some cases, the father may have learned to extend his caregiving role from observing the participation of his father; in other cases, he may be trying to have a better relationship with his own children than he had with his uninvolved father.

Demographers project that more and more children will be cared for by fathers for longer periods of time (Casper & O'Connell, 1998). It seems, then, that the concept of the father as an equal partner in parenthood is starting to emerge (Pleck & Pleck, 1997).

SIBLINGS

Like parents, siblings serve as important sources of the child's social attitudes, beliefs, and behaviors. Although they may not wield as much power as parents, siblings certainly do attempt to control one another's behaviors (ask anyone who is not an only child!) and may be models for both desirable and undesirable actions. An emerging body of research on sibling relationships has provided yet another perspective on how families influence development.

The Only Child One way to assess the impact of siblings on development is to examine children who have none. Are there notable differences between only children and children with one or more sisters or brothers? Popular opinion depicts the only child as spoiled, demanding, self-centered, and dependent (Thompson, 1974). But research evidence suggests the contrary, that only children may enjoy the benefits of having their parents' exclusive attention. Toni Falbo and Denise Polit (1986) summarized the results of 115 studies of only children and concluded that, overall, only children showed higher achievement and intelligence scores than children with siblings. In addition, only-borns ranked higher on measures of character—that is, tendencies toward leadership, personal control, and maturity—than children with siblings. No overall differences emerged between only children and children with siblings on assessments of sociability and personal adjustment.

In explaining these findings, Falbo and Polit (1986) found support for the hypothesis that features of the parent-child relationship account for the advantages only children enjoy in certain domains. Only children were found to have more positive relationships with their parents than children with siblings. This effect probably occurs because parents of one child have more time to spend with their son or daughter and generally have high-quality interactions with their child (Falbo & Cooper, 1980). Parents and children in one study, for example, exchanged more in mealtime conversations in one-child families than in families having two or three children (Lewis & Feiring, 1982). First-time parents are also more anxious about their child-rearing techniques and may thus be more vigilant and responsive to their child's behaviors (Falbo & Polit, 1986).

Falbo and Polit's (1986) meta-analysis showed that parent-child relations in one- and two-child families are actually more similar than different. Only when a third child is born does the quality of parent-child relations diminish significantly. Parents of more than two children probably become more relaxed about their child-rearing strategies and also have significantly more demands placed on their time. The result is less responsiveness and fewer deliberate attempts to instruct their children, aspects of parenting found to be related to cognitive achievements.

Family Size and Birth Order Children growing up in contemporary American society have fewer siblings than children in earlier eras. In 2004 the typical American family with children had one or two children (U.S. Bureau of the Census, 2005). Many children thus grow up with only one other sibling. Does the size of the family make any difference in child development?

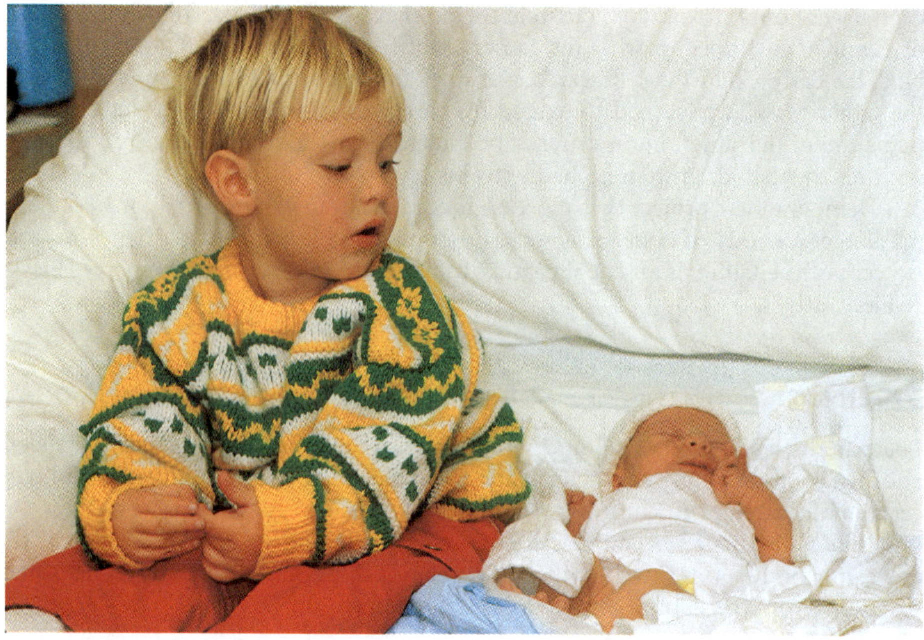

This young boy's reaction to a new sibling is typical. Although many children become clingy, withdrawn, and are demanding when a new sibling first arrives, these reactions can be diminished if parents prepare the older child for the infant's arrival and involve him in the infant's care. Adjustment is also more difficult if the older child perceives that he must compete for the parents' affection and attention.

In general, children from smaller families have higher intelligence test scores, achieve higher levels of education, and display greater self-esteem (Blake, 1989; Wagner, Schubert, & Schubert, 1985). As we have just seen, one reason for these effects may be that parents in larger families have less time to spend with their children and may not provide the kind of cognitive stimulation that children in smaller families receive. Another important factor is financial circumstances: parents with a larger number of children often experience greater economic stress, which in turn may affect the quality of their parenting (Rutter & Madge, 1976).

Regardless of family size, the child's birth order, whether first born or later born, can also be a factor in development. Like only children, first-borns tend to score higher on IQ tests and have higher achievement motivation than other children (Glass, Neulinger, & Brim, 1974; Zajonc, Markus, & Markus, 1979). They also tend to be more obedient and socially responsible (Sutton-Smith & Rosenberg, 1970). All these effects probably stem from the greater attention parents give to their first children. Later-borns seem to have an advantage in the social sphere, however. Youngest siblings tend to have better peer relationships than first-borns and are more confident in social situations (Lahey et al., 1980; Miller & Maruyama, 1976).

The Impact of a Sibling's Arrival The birth of a sibling can have a dramatic on the life of a first-born child, and often this momentous event occurs during the early childhood years. Research on the consequences of a second child's arrival generally confirms that "sibling rivalry" is no myth. Judy Dunn and Carol Kendrick (1982) followed the progress of family relationships among forty first-born children who experienced the arrival of a sibling sometime between their first and fourth birthdays. Dunn and Kendrick observed normal home routines during the mother's last month of pregnancy and again when the baby sibling was one, eight, and fourteen months old. They also interviewed the mother at each stage about the older child's eating and sleeping habits, moods, and other routine behaviors.

For the majority of first-born children, the arrival of a sister or brother led to marked changes in behavior: they became more demanding, clingy, unhappy, or withdrawn. Accompanying these changes in behavior were significant decreases in maternal attention toward them: mothers engaged in less joint play, cuddling, and verbalization with their first-borns and in general initiated fewer interactions with them. At the same time, restrictive and punitive maternal behaviors increased. Over time, Dunn and Kendrick (1982) noted, two distinct patterns of sibling relationships emerged. Among some sibling pairs, almost all interactions eventually became friendly and positive; for others, a persistent pattern of hostility and aggression became the norm. The first pattern was more likely if mothers had previously prepared the older child for the newborn's arrival by referring to the infant as a person with needs and desires. Engaging the older child in caring for the infant also seemed to have positive consequences. In contrast, negative relationships between siblings resulted if the older child experienced a sharp drop in maternal contact. The discrepancy in pre- and postsibling maternal contact made the most difference: children who had less contact with their mother before the sibling's birth were less profoundly affected by her attention to the new infant.

The timing of a sibling's arrival may also be important. Researchers have noted a drop in the security of a child's attachment to the mother following the birth of a second child. However, the decrease in attachment security was less noticeable if the older child was twenty-four months of age or younger (Teti et al., 1996). Younger children may not yet have the social cognitive capacities to see the new arrival as a threat or cause of change in family routines.

The arrival of a sibling demands a big adjustment for the older child, especially because another individual begins to compete for the parents' attention and affection. Siblings are aware of the differential treatment parents may knowingly or unwittingly bestow on them (Kowal & Kramer, 1997; McHale et al., 1995). The greater the perceived discrepancy is, the greater the sibling conflict will be (Dunn, 1988). But certainly not all aspects of sibling relationships are negative. Dunn and Kendrick (1982) noted that, in certain circumstances, siblings fill a void in parent-child relationships. When the mother and her older child have difficulties in their interactions, siblings may provide the attention and affection missing from the maternal relationship, thus helping to keep the family system in equilibrium. When parents display a high degree of marital conflict or even undergo divorce, siblings show an increase in emotional closeness and positive, friendly behavior toward one another (Dunn, 1996).

FOR • YOUR • REVIEW

- What is socialization? At what age do parents begin serious efforts to socialize their children?
- What major changes have occurred in the structure of American families in the past thirty years?
- What does it mean to take a systems approach to understanding the family? Give examples of how influences on one subsystem within the family can have consequences for another subsystem.
- What are the characteristics of the four major styles of parenting? What child behaviors are associated with each parenting style?
- What are some of the specific effects of parental warmth on the developing child?
- What are principles of the effective use of punishment?
- In what ways do cognitions play a role in parenting strategies?
- What are some of the ways in which characteristics of the child can influence parenting strategies?
- What are some of the factors associated with the incidence of child abuse?
- In what ways do fathers make important contributions to child development?
- How do family size and birth order have an impact on child development?
- In what ways can parents facilitate the child's transition to having a new sibling?

Peer Relationships in Early Childhood

A significant development in early childhood is that the child's social world typically expands to include peers. In the second year, social exchanges with peers may start out as very brief, transitory episodes, but they quickly become longer and more coordinated. Two children will jointly manipulate toys and other objects, each child taking a turn playing and then offering the object to the playmate. Children also begin to play simple games together, such as hide-and-seek or tag, activities that require taking turns and switching roles (Howes, 1987a, 1987b). Later in toddlerhood, between ages two and three years, children engage in peer interactions more frequently. Instead of revolving around objects such as toys, these interactions contain many positive social and affiliative behaviors, such as giving attention, smiling, sharing, and cooperating (Bronson, 1981). Before age four, most peer interactions tend to occur in dyads, or groups of two; after age four, children's play starts to take place in larger groups (Benenson, Apostoleris, & Parnass, 1997).

Play in Early Childhood

In her classic studies of children's play, Mildred Parten (1932) found that the peer relations of young children are characterized by three forms. In **solitary play**, children play alone with toys, apart from other children and without regard for what they are doing. One child might be stacking rings while another does a puzzle; neither notices or cares about the other's activities. In **parallel play**, children play independently while alongside or close to other children. Several children might be gathered at a sandbox, one digging with a shovel, another making "pies," and still another dragging a truck through the sand. Even though they are in close proximity, one child's activities do not influence the play of the others. In **cooperative play**, children interact. They share toys, follow one another, and make mutual suggestions about what to do next. Although Parten believed that a stagelike developmental progression takes place from solitary to parallel and then cooperative play, other research suggests that all three types of play occur among preschoolers (Barnes, 1971; Rubin, Maioni, & Hornung, 1976).

Key Theme
Sociocultural Influence

The type of play exhibited by preschoolers may depend on the socialization goals of parents and teachers. For example, in Korean American preschools, teachers encourage individual academic achievement and task persistence rather than social interaction with other children. Korean American preschoolers engage in significantly less cooperative play and more parallel play than Anglo American preschoolers do (Farver, Kim, & Lee, 1995). A child's preferred form of play might also be an early indicator of possible problems in peer relationships. In one recent study, the findings suggested that preschoolers who engaged in higher levels of solitary play had, in earlier months, exhibited less ability to regulate their behaviors. They were also more likely to be excluded by peers than children with lower levels of solitary play (Spinrad, Eisenberg, et al., 2004). In other words, solitary play may be linked less with an immature developmental stage than with the nature of budding relationships with peers.

One of the most interesting forms of play seen in preschoolers is **social pretend play** (also called *sociodramatic play*), in which they invoke "make-believe" to change the functions of objects, create imaginary situations, and enact pretend roles, often with the cooperation of one or two peers (Goncu, Patt, & Kouba, 2002; Rubin, Fein, & Vandenberg, 1983). Children use sticks and pots as band instruments, ride "magic carpets" together, and play "Mommy and Daddy." Growth in the child's cognitive, perspective-taking, and communication skills helps to explain these changes (Hartup, 1983; Howes, 1987a). To conceive of a stick as representing a flute, for example, the child must develop symbolic capabilities that allow him to let one object represent another. To play "Mommy," a young girl must relinquish her own perspective and appreciate another person's social role: what "mommies" do and how they speak to children. Finally, for complex and coordinated exchanges of pretend play to occur,

solitary play Individual play, performed without regard for what others are doing.

parallel play Side-by-side, independent play that is not interactive.

cooperative play Interactive play in which children's actions are reciprocal.

social pretend play Play that makes use of imaginary and symbolic objects and social roles, often enacted among several children. Also called *sociodramatic play*.

such as when one child sets the table and prepares the food while the other cries like a baby, children must understand the rules of social dialogue and communication. When we watch three-year-olds engage in pretend play with one another, we are witnessing an intersection of their growing competence in several arenas: social, language, and cognitive skills (Howes, Unger, & Seidner, 1989).

The tendency for three- and four-year-olds to engage in social pretend play has been observed among children from diverse cultural backgrounds, including Chinese, Korean American, and Irish American groups, suggesting that this form of play may be a universal developmental acquisition. It is interesting to note that this is the age at which children from different cultures acquire a "theory of mind" and that children who engage in pretend play are advanced in theory-of-mind tasks (Dunn & Hughes, 2001). At the same time, the child's background culture influences the specific content of pretend play. Korean American children, for example, typically enact family and everyday themes (such as eating, sleeping, and going places) in their play, whereas American children display themes of danger (crashes, injuries) and fantasy characters (Farver & Shin, 1997). Irish American children spend substantial time pretending with toys purchased by their family, whereas Chinese children rely more on social routines than on props (Haight et al., 1999). Thus cultural values and resources are often vividly reflected in children's play.

Key Theme
Sociocultural Influence

Friendship

Certain peer relations are special. They are marked by shared thoughts and experiences, trust, intimacy, and joy in the other's company. Children's relationships with friends differ from those with other peers. Friends express more emotion and loyalty toward each other, see each other more frequently, and both cooperate and disagree more than do mere acquaintances (Bigelow, Tesson, & Lewko, 1992; Hartup & Sancilio, 1986; Newcomb & Bagwell, 1995). Even though childhood friendships may not endure, their impact on social and emotional development can rival that of the family and may provide a needed buffer when children feel psychological strains. Friendships are also an important source of cognitive and social support (Hartup, 1996).

About 80 percent of three- to four-year-olds spend a substantial amount of time with at least one peer who is a "strong associate" or friend. Most preschoolers observed in their nursery school classrooms spend at least 30 percent of their time with one other peer, usually someone of the same sex (Hinde et al., 1985). For the three-year-old, however, the concept of "friend" does not encompass the full range of psychological complexities that it does for the older child. At this age, the term is virtually synonymous with playmate.

Preschoolers' activities with friends usually consist of games, object sharing, and pretend sequences (such as "You be the baby and I'll be the mommy"). Conversations between friends often contain a good deal of social comparison, a search for differences as well as similarities. Preschool children are fascinated not so much by the specific things they have in common as by the fact that they have things in common. Hence the following typical conversation recorded by Jeffrey Parker and John Gottman (1989):

Child A: *We both have chalk in our hands.*

Child B: *Right!*

Preschoolers try to avoid disagreements and negative affect in their interactions with friends more than older children do (Gottman & Parkhurst, 1980). Preschoolers especially value friends who give them positive feedback, prefer to play with them over other children, and engage in low levels of conflict with them (Ladd, Kochenderfer, & Coleman, 1996). The qualities of preschoolers' friendships are associated with other dimensions of their social functioning. When children offer support to their friends, they tend to be more prosocial in general. When they have a high degree of conflict in their friendships, they tend to be more aggressive in general. Perhaps most interesting is the finding that preschoolers who tend to have close, intimate friendships with only a few peers tend to show greater relational aggression. These children may already be learning how to manipulate their peers through gossip, threats, or exclusion in order to achieve their personal and social goals (Sebanc, 2003).

FOR • YOUR • REVIEW

- What are the different forms of play usually exhibited in early childhood? What factors are related to the emergence of these different types of play?
- What are the qualities of children's friendships during the preschool years?

CHILD CARE

As we noted at the start of this chapter, in the past three decades the percentage of married women with children in the labor force has increased dramatically. The working mother is now the norm. So is the child care experience for the majority of children in the United States. Today, more than 60 percent of children under age six receive care from someone other than a parent, with an average of forty hours per week in that care (National Center for Education Statistics, 2001; National Research Council and Institute of Medicine, 2003). What are the effects of maternal employment and child care, two experiences that usually go together, on development? It turns out that neither variable is simple or "neat." Take maternal employment, for example. Some mothers work out of sheer economic necessity, whereas others are more concerned with realizing personal or career goals. As researchers point out, the impact of maternal employment is best understood through its effects on family dynamics, parental attitudes, and the quality of the alternative child care arrangements the family chooses (Beyer, 1995; Hoffman, 1989; Marshall, 2004). In this section, we examine all of these factors, with special attention to the daycare center as an increasingly important context for early childhood development.

MATERNAL EMPLOYMENT

Mothers who work full time outside the home spend less time caring for their children, no matter what their age, than mothers who stay at home (Hill & Stafford, 1980). In terms of direct, one-to-one mother-child interaction, however, no significant differences have been found between employed and nonemployed mothers (Richards & Duckett, 1994). Employed mothers often compensate for the time they miss with their children during the work week by allocating more time for them during mornings and evenings (Ahnert, Rickert, & Lamb, 2000). In many instances, fathers assume more responsibilities for child care when the mother works, especially when parents have nonstandard work schedules and when they hold nontraditional beliefs about child care (Han, 2004; NICHD Early Child Care Research Network, 2000b).

Overall, what matters more than whether or not the mother works is her attitude toward mothering and work, and why she is working or staying at home. In one study, mothers who remained at home contrary to their preference had higher scores on tests of depression and stress compared with mothers who preferred to be at home and were not in the labor force and with employed mothers who valued their positions in the work world (Hock & DeMeis, 1990). We saw earlier in this chapter that parental stress has been implicated as a factor in less consistent and less nurturant parenting. Likewise, when maternal employment produces tension, parenting practices may also suffer. Researchers have found that mothers who worked more than forty hours per week, for example, were more anxious and unhappy, and had less sensitive and less animated interactions with their children than mothers who worked less than forty hours per week (Owen & Cox, 1988).

When psychologists compare children of employed mothers with children of women who remain at home, few differences emerge on measures of cognitive achievement and socioemotional development, at least among middle-class participants. If anything, daughters of employed mothers derive some benefit: they are likely to show greater independence, greater achievement, and higher self-esteem than daughters of nonworking mothers (Gottfried et al., 1994; Hoffman, 1989). Apparently these girls profit from having a successful, competent role model, at least as the larger society recognizes these qualities. (Women who remain at home "work," too, but traditionally have not been afforded recognition or status for that role.) In general, the clearest effect of maternal employment involves the gender-role attitudes of both sons and daughters. When mothers work outside the home, their children are less likely than children of at-home mothers to hold stereotypical beliefs about males and females, and are more likely to see both sexes as competent (Hoffman, 1989). When both mothers and fathers work, sons and daughters have the opportunity to see both parents in multiple roles—as powerful, competent wage earners and as nurturant, warm caregivers—a factor that probably contributes to more egalitarian beliefs.

When mothers work outside the home, their children are less likely to hold stereotyped beliefs about gender, probably because they see both parents in multiple roles.

When a mother returns to work might be important to consider. In one analysis of data collected from several thousand participants in the National Longitudinal Survey of Youth, Elizabeth Harvey (1999) found that the timing of the mother's entry or return to the work force was not associated with children's development. Another study found, though, that when mothers returned to work when their children were nine months of age, the children tended to have lower scores on measures of cognitive development (Brooks-Gunn, Han, & Waldfogel, 2002). The number of hours mothers work can make a difference, too. Two studies of mostly Caucasian middle-class women found that the more hours mothers worked, the lower was the academic achievement of their preschool and early school-age children (Brooks-Gunn, Han, & Waldfogel, 2002; Goldberg, Greenberger, & Nagel, 1996). On the other hand, comprehensive longitudinal studies of children from infancy through age twelve have found that, although academic achievement was negatively related to the number of hours the mothers worked when children were ages five and six, this relationship was modest and was not apparent as children grew older (Gottfried et al., 1994; Harvey, 1999).

For low-income families, maternal employment is related to benefits for children. One longitudinal study examined 189 second-graders; most were born to adolescent mothers, and 41 percent lived in households with incomes below the poverty level. For this sample, maternal employment during the child's first three years was associated with greater household income, a higher-quality home environment, and higher mathematics achievement in school for the child compared with the effects when mothers did not work (Vandell & Ramanan, 1992).

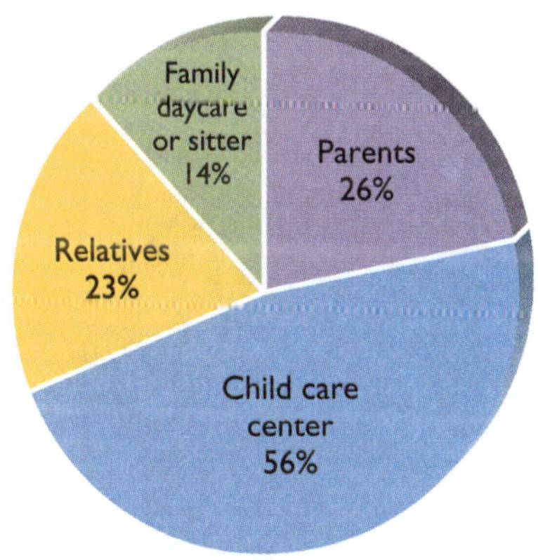

Note: The percents do not add up to 100 percent because some children receive more than one form of care.

FIGURE 10.6
Child Care Arrangements for Children Age 6 and Under, 2001
This chart shows the percentage of American children who receive different forms of child care. About forty percent of infants, toddlers, and preschoolers are cared for by parents. Of the remainder, most attend a formal child care center.

Source: National Center for Educational Statistics (2006).

THE EFFECTS OF DAYCARE

About one-fourth of children enter child care during the first five months after birth, according to one national survey. About half begin regular child care before they turn three (Singer et al., 1998). Child care arrangements take various forms, from in-home care provided by a relative or paid caregiver to group care in a formal, organized center. Often, parents use multiple forms of care. As Figure 10.6 shows, about 70 percent of children under age six are cared for by someone other than their parents. Of those who receive full-time nonparental care, the largest percentage attend organized child care centers. There has been a steady increase in the last thirty years in the proportion of children attending child care centers as opposed to family daycare or being cared for by a relative or a sitter (Hofferth, 1996).

One area in which some researchers have noted an effect of daycare is in intellectual performance. Daycare children tend to outperform children reared at home by parents on standardized tests of IQ, as well as measures of problem-solving ability, creativity, language development, and arithmetic skills when the quality of child care is high (Lamb & Ahnert, 2006). Daycare programs that stress cognitive activities and provide rich language stimulation tend to have children who score higher on IQ tests and measures of cognitive skills than those that simply provide caregiving or allow children to watch long hours of television (McCartney et al., 1985; NICHD Early Child Care Research Network, 2003b). Moreover, the effect of daycare on intellectual achievements shows up years later, when children are in elementary school. In one study that examined the academic achievements of sixth-graders, the amount of time children had spent in high-quality daycare centers during infancy was positively related to their mathematics grades and their tendency to be enrolled in programs for gifted children (Field, 1991). In two other studies, conducted in Sweden, children who had daycare experience performed better on measures of verbal and mathematics abilities and obtained better grades in school seven years later and beyond when compared with children who had no experience with out-of-home care (Andersson, 1992; Broberg et al., 1997).

Daycare is also associated with effects in the realm of social development. Specifically, children with experience in daycare are more socially competent with peers. They show more frequent nonnegative interactions, more complex and reciprocal play, and more positive engagement with peers compared with children not in child care. Important to note is the finding that responsiveness of caregivers in daycare centers was associated with these positive peer interactions (NICHD Early Child Care Research Network, 2001a). In addition to children's showing more positive behaviors, some studies suggest that daycare children may display more aggression with peers and noncompliance with adults (Bates et al., 1994; Baydar & Brooks-Gunn, 1991). A national study of more than 1,000 children in daycare centers across the United States found that the amount of time spent in child care predicted children's problem social behaviors at age four and a half (NICHD Early Child Care Research Network, 2003a). However, if there are negative effects, some caution, they may arise from experiences in low-quality centers (Lamb, 1998; Love et al., 2003).

It is important to remember that many studies of daycare have been conducted in high-quality centers, often associated with universities and populated by children from middle- to upper-class families. But not all parents have the opportunity or resources to send their children to such high-caliber programs. In a disturbing report on the quality of child care centers in the United States, only 14 percent of centers were judged to offer care that promotes children's development; most provided only custodial-level care, and 12 percent were found to jeopardize children's development

Research shows that daycare has few negative effects on young children and may even facilitate cognitive and social development. High-quality centers generally have small group size, favorable staff-to-child ratios, and responsive, warm caregivers.

(Children's Defense Fund, 1996). Another national report characterizes the average level of child care in the United States as "mediocre" (National Research Council and Institute of Medicine, 2003). What are the effects of less-than-excellent programs on children? Research suggests that, when children are enrolled in low-quality centers before age one, they have more difficulty with peers and are distractible and less task oriented in kindergarten than children who are enrolled at later ages and those who attend high-quality centers (Howes, 1990). Children in low-quality child care also tend to score lower on tests of cognitive and language skills than children in high-quality care (Burchinal et al., 2000; NICHD Early Child Care Research Network, 2000b; Peisner-Feinberg et al., 2001). Evidence is accumulating that quality of child care makes a big difference. Thus it is essential that parents be aware of the elements of high-quality daycare.

There is one final, important point to make about the child care experience: even when mothers work and their children are enrolled in full-time child care, family factors still continue to predict child outcomes. Variables such as parental child-rearing style, psychological well-being, and sensitivity are all associated with children's cognitive and social development regardless of the child's caregiving context (NICHD Early Child Care Research Group, 1998b). First and foremost, it is the parents who play the primary role.

RESEARCH APPLIED TO PARENTING

Choosing a Daycare Center

After her dinner guest left and Joey was put to bed (with yet another struggle), his mother sat exhausted on the couch and thought about the difficulties she was having in controlling her child's behavior. Because of her recent divorce, she was now a single parent, and she knew she would have to spend a lot of more time at work in order to provide for her son. She was worried that all of these changes had taken a toll on both Joey and her, and that some of the problems they were having were because she was more stressed and a little less attentive to her parenting than usual. Now the thought of sending him to a child care center made her even more anxious. Would this experience add to those problems? Fortunately, her new employer had a child care center right in the building where she worked. She had heard great things about it, and it looked bright, clean, and inviting. But how could she tell if it would provide for Joey all those things she had heard good daycare could provide?

What factors should parents consider as they select a daycare center for their children? Both the federal government and many states have set minimum requirements for daycare services, which regulate the qualifications of teachers, staff-child ratios, the size and safety of the physical facility, and the provision of nourishing meals. Although the guidelines and laws provide for minimum standards, most parents are concerned with providing their children with the best possible care during the hours they are at work. Alison Clarke-Stewart (1993) has drawn on the body of research findings on daycare to compile the following suggestions for parents:

1. ***Center-based care is more likely to include educational opportunities for children than home-based care, like that provided by baby-sitters and family daycare.*** Many teachers in center-based daycare develop daily plans that expose children to stories and introduce them to numbers, the letters of the alphabet, shapes, colors, and other concepts that help to prepare children for school. On the other hand, children are more likely to receive one-to-one supervision and authoritative discipline in home-based care. Because of the mere fact that teachers in center-based care typically have half a dozen or more children in the classroom, it is difficult to respond to each child's needs from one moment to the next.

2. ***Children are most likely to thrive intellectually and emotionally in programs that offer a balance between structured educational activities and an open, free environment.*** The advantage of center-based care is that there is often a curriculum that guides children in developing school readiness skills. Yet it is important to remember that part of what we hope to encourage in early childhood is creativity and having fun in "school."
3. ***The caregiving environment should provide ample physical space (at least twenty-five square feet per child) and a variety of materials and activities to foster sensorimotor, social, and cognitive development.*** High-quality centers provide children with room to move around and explore, as well as the toys, crayons, books, and other resources that stimulate learning and foster social exchanges with peers.
4. ***Class size should be small and should include children within a two-year age range. Small centers usually have better staff-child ratios than centers with more children.*** Small class size, of course, means that teachers are better able to respond to children in a manner that is sensitive to each child's needs.
5. ***The interaction style of the caregiver is a key aspect of quality care.*** The caregiver should be actively involved but not restrictive with the children. The caregiver should also be responsive and offer positive encouragement.
6. ***Caregivers who have training in child development and continuing opportunities for education are most likely to provide high-quality care.*** Well-educated caregivers understand the cognitive, social, and emotional capabilities and needs of their charges, and are aware of the best ways to respond to children's behavior (and misbehavior).
7. ***The individual characteristics of the child should be taken into account.*** Some children will probably do well in a program that balances structure and openness; others may profit from either more structure or a more flexible and relaxed program.

Other important factors include a high staff-child ratio and low staff turnover. Research shows, for example, that, when the staff-child ratio is at least one to three for infants, one to four for toddlers, and one to nine for preschoolers, the quality of caregiving and of children's activities within the center are both good. Likewise, when the overall class size is six or fewer for infants, twelve or fewer for toddlers, and eighteen or fewer for preschoolers, children have better-quality experiences than those in larger groups (Howes, Phillips, & Whitebook, 1992).

In essence, the qualities of good daycare mirror the qualities of good parenting. In fact, the reason why such factors as good staff-child ratios and education of caregivers are important is that they are related to the quality of caregiving (NICHD Early Child Care Research Network, 2002). In choosing a daycare center, parents should seek a warm, responsive environment that provides the child, at least some of the time, with opportunities for structured play and prosocial learning.

EARLY INTERVENTION PROGRAMS

KEY THEME
RISK/RESILIENCE

As we noted above, some research has shown that daycare experiences are associated with gains in intellectual performance. If there are, indeed, benefits of early childcare experiences for children's cognitive development, can they be extended to children who are at risk for not performing well once they get to school? During the 1960s, the idea of compensatory education became popular in the United States. Researchers wanted to see whether the poor performance of children from lower socioeconomic classes on IQ and achievement tests could improve if the children received the kinds of cognitive stimulation presumably available to middle-class children.

Early experiences might be especially important if we believe that experiences during the first three or four years of life are important for optimal brain development. Because we now understand that neurotransmitter functioning, synaptic formation, and gene activation are influenced by environmental conditions, some researchers argue that there is more urgency for providing optimal learning environments for young children (Shore, 1997). Are there certain things that parents and teachers do that are linked to the child's intellectual development? Some of the answers come from studies of how parents and children interact in their home.

The HOME Inventory In 1970 an ambitious project got under way in Little Rock, Arkansas. Initiated by Bettye Caldwell and her associates (Caldwell & Bradley, 1978), the project had as its goal identifying characteristics of the young child's environment that might be related to later competence, including intellectual achievement. A sample of infants and their parents was recruited for a longitudinal study that would last eleven years.

The *Home Observation for Measurement of the Environment (HOME)* inventory was designed to measure a number of characteristics of the child's home surroundings, including the quality of caregiver-child interactions, the availability of objects and activities to stimulate the child, and the types of experiences family members provide to nurture the child's development (see Table 10.2 for the subscales and some sample items). Researchers collected data for the inventory through interviews and direct observations in the children's homes and gave children in the sample standard intelligence and school achievement tests.

The results identified several key features of the home environment as being related to subsequent IQ (Bradley, 1989). Significant correlations were found among measures of the home environment taken at age twelve months and children's IQ scores at ages three and four and a half years. Particularly important were scales that measured parental emotional and verbal responsivity to the child, the availability of appropriate play materials, and parental involvement with the child (Bradley & Caldwell, 1976; Elardo, Bradley, & Caldwell, 1975). In addition, HOME scores at age two years were significantly related to language competencies at age three years (Elardo, Bradley, & Caldwell, 1977). The same three scales on the HOME inventory were especially

Table 10.2 Subscales of the Home Observation for Measurement of the Environment (HOME)

The HOME inventory assesses several features of the home environment. Subscales 1, 4, and 5 were found to be significantly correlated with the child's later IQ and language competence.

1. Emotional and verbal responsivity of mother

Sample item: Mother caresses or kisses child at least once during visit.

2. Avoidance of restriction and punishment

Sample item: Mother does not interfere with child's actions or restrict child's movements more than three times during visit.

3. Organization of physical and temporal environment

Sample item: Child's play environment appears safe and free of hazards.

4. Provision of appropriate play materials

Sample item: Mother provides toys or interesting activities for child during interview.

5. Maternal involvement with child

Sample item: Mother tends to keep child within visual range and to look at the child often.

6. Opportunities for variety in daily stimulation

Sample item: Child eats at least one meal per day with mother and father.

Source: Adapted from Elardo & Bradley (1981).

related to the children's linguistic competence. A follow-up of these children showed that parental involvement and availability of toys at age two years were significantly related to school achievement at age eleven years (Bradley, 1989).

This series of studies shows that important processes occur between children and their parents early in life that can have long-lasting implications for future intellectual achievement. For one thing, children who have responsive parents may develop a sense of control over their environments, and their resulting general socioemotional health may facilitate intellectual growth. In addition, the opportunity to play with toys may provide contexts for children to learn problem-solving skills from their parents, as well as the chance to develop knowledge from direct manipulation of the play materials. Language development is also enhanced because verbal interactions with parents during play and at other times teach children the properties of spoken speech (Bradley & Caldwell, 1984). One project demonstrated that, when mothers provided an environment rich in learning experiences like those described in the HOME studies, the difference in IQ scores between African American and Caucasian children—usually found to be in the range of 15 points—dropped by 28 percent (Brooks-Gunn, Klebanov, & Duncan, 1996).

Project Head Start The first federally funded program for compensatory education was Project Head Start, begun in the 1960s as a preschool enrichment program for "underprivileged children." Currently enrolling more than 900,000 children, the program includes nutritional and medical assistance, as well as a structured educational program designed to provide cognitive stimulation. The first evaluations of Head Start were disappointing. In 1969 the Westinghouse Learning Corporation/Ohio University report compared the intellectual development of about 4,000 children from similar backgrounds, half of whom had participated in the first Head Start programs around the country and half of whom did not participate. Essentially no differences were found in the intellectual performance of the two groups; both remained below the norm for their age group (Westinghouse Learning Corporation, 1969). This evaluation, however, was criticized on a number of grounds, including the fact that the evaluation was done prematurely, just barely after the program got off the ground.

Subsequent evaluations of Head Start have yielded more optimistic results. The Head Start Evaluation, Synthesis, and Utilization Project was an attempt to summarize all research on the impact of Head Start (McKey et al., 1985). This review concluded that Head Start produced significant effects on the intellectual performance of program participants, at least for the short term. Head Start children performed well in the first year or two after they started elementary school, showing average gains of 10 points in IQ score, but the effects of the program faded in subsequent years.

The Carolina Abecedarian Project Another important early intervention project, the Carolina Abecedarian Project, begun in 1972, aimed to prevent the lower intellectual functioning of children at risk (Ramey & Campbell, 1981; Ramey, Lee, & Burchinal, 1989). A sample of 121 low-income, pregnant women with low educational achievement and low IQ scores (an average of 84) was selected. Once the infants were born, roughly half were assigned to the experimental group and half to the control group. Infants in the experimental group received medical care, nutritional supplements, and a structured program of day care that emphasized the development of cognitive, language, social, and motor skills. In addition, the researchers provided a toy-lending library and a home visiting program, as well as parent support groups. During the first year, few differences on IQ scores were found between infants in the experimental and control groups. From age eighteen months onward, however, the IQs of the experimental group consistently exceeded those of the control group, even when the children reached young adulthood (see Figure 10.7) (Campbell & Ramey, 1994; Campbell et al., 2001). Yet some researchers remain pessimistic about the significance of these findings. For example, Herman

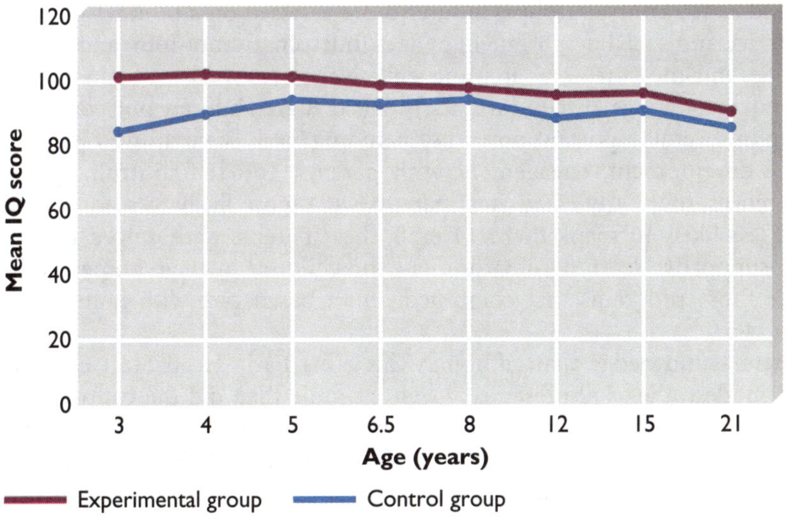

FIGURE 10.7

Early Intervention and IQ

Children who participated in the Abecedarian Project from infancy have been followed longitudinally through early adulthood. As the graph shows, compared with a control group, participants in this program had higher IQ scores at each test time, suggesting a modest but long-term impact of intensive early intervention.

Source: Campbell et al. (2001).

Spitz (1986) pointed out that, by age five years, the differences between the experimental and control groups diminished to an average of only 7 points. Also, scores for the experimental group never really increased (Spitz, 1999). In the end, say the critics, the effects of this intensive intervention were not substantial.

An important issue concerns why the initial gains of Head Start and Abecedarian children "washed out" in successive years. Perhaps early intervention is not enough to overcome the pervasive and continuing effects of poverty and understimulating environments on children as they advance into the school years. Perhaps, too, IQ scores are not the best indicators of the impact of Head Start and other early intervention programs. One collaborative study of the effects of eleven early intervention programs showed that children who had participated were less likely than nonparticipants to be assigned to special education classes, less likely to be "held back" in grade, and more likely to cite their school achievements as a source of pride (Lazar & Darlington, 1982). Data from the Chicago Longitudinal Study, assessing the impact of intensive center-based preschool programs for children living in poverty, show that, by the time children were teenagers, they finished more years of school and had lower rates of juvenile delinquency than nonparticipants (Reynolds et al., 2001). Statistical analyses suggest that these effects are connected to growth in children's scholastic skills, good-quality educational experiences following the preschool program, and a high level of parental involvement (Reynolds, Ou, & Topitzes, 2004). Many believe that these multifaceted outcomes are just as important as gains in IQ scores.

Craig and Sharon Ramey (1998), pioneers in the Abecedarian Project, suggest that, in order to be effective, early intervention programs need to target children early in development, include substantial contact with children and families who participate, and provide direct learning experiences for children. Programs should also provide a broad array of services, including health and social services, as well as transportation. Finally, in order to have long-lasting impact, continuous intervention and support should take place beyond the preschool years. Assessments of early intervention programs are providing strong support for these ideas.

Early Head Start In 1994 the federal government launched Early Head Start, a comprehensive national early intervention program targeted toward low-income children from birth to three years of age. Providing center-based services, home-based services, or both, the program focuses on health care, nutrition, early education of children, and parent education and support. Currently, slightly over 60,000 children participate in Early Head Start. In order to evaluate the impact of the program, 3,000 families from seventeen programs in diverse regions of the country were recruited; half were randomly assigned to receive Early Head Start services, and half served as the control group. Children were assessed on a number of measures of cognitive and social development at ages fourteen, twenty-four, and thirty-six months. Several measures of parenting effectiveness were also obtained. The results showed that by age three years, Early Head Start children outscored the control group in several important domains, including levels of cognitive functioning, language development, engagement with parents, and self-control. Parents showed differences, too; Early Head Start parents were more likely to read to their children and less likely to spank them. Overall, these parents were judged to provide a more supportive learning environment for children in their homes. Most effective were those programs that combined center-based care with home visits (Love et al., 2005).

Researchers acknowledge that, although the gains Early Head Start children showed were modest, they still presented a better profile than did the control children (Love et al., 2005), no small accomplishment considering that their annual family income was at the federal poverty level (for example, $19,350 for a family of four in 2005). The data indicate that intensive intervention, started early and involving parents, can indeed have an impact on children who are at risk.

FOR • YOUR • REVIEW

- What are some of the effects of maternal employment on child development? How are mother-child interactions affected?
- What has research shown about the effects of daycare on the cognitive and social development of children?
- What are some important factors to consider in selecting a daycare center?
- What features of the home environment have been linked to positive intellectual development?
- What has research revealed about the effects of early intervention programs for children? What factors are most important in promoting successful outcomes?

MEDIA

KEY THEME
SOCIOCULTURAL INFLUENCE

The second half of the twentieth century has brought what some have called a "media revolution" into the lives of children (Comstock & Scharrer, 2006; Roberts & Foehr, 2004). Television, DVDs, video games, computers, and other electronic devices have become a staple in the everyday lives of many young children. Some wonder if the influence of media has encroached on the ability of parents to control the events and experiences to which their children are exposed. Does the violence in much of contemporary media have a detrimental impact on young children? Is there any consequence of media on children's cognitive development? In this chapter, we begin to explore some of these issues by focusing on television, probably the most prevalent form of media with which many young children have contact.

American children watch a great deal of television. Babies as young as six months of age attend to television and on average are exposed to more than one hour per day (Hollenbeck & Slaby, 1979). The amount of time children spend attending to television increases dramatically during the preschool years, especially after age two-and-a-half. Children regularly watch between two and three hours of television per day between the ages of three and six (Comstock & Sharrer, 2006). Individual patterns of TV viewing tend to remain stable over the years; the television-viewing habits that children acquire in early childhood can be relatively long lasting (Huston & Wright, 1998).

What do children watch on television? Preschoolers tend to view educational programs specifically designed for children, such as *Sesame Street*, children's entertainment programs, and cartoons. Interest in child-centered educational programs is relatively greater among younger preschoolers than older children (Wright et al., 2001). By the age of five or so, children begin to watch comedies and entertainment shows aimed at general audiences, shows that make increasing demands on their ability to comprehend plots and themes (Huston et al., 1990). Boys tend to watch more television than girls (Huston & Wright, 1998) and African American children more than European American children (Comstock, 1991). Children from lower socioeconomic levels are more frequent viewers than children from higher-income backgrounds (Greenberg, 1986).

Children's Comprehension of Television Programs

Contrary to popular belief, television viewing is usually not a passive process in which a mesmerized child sits gazing at the screen. The fact that preferences for shows change with age is just one example of the ways children actively control their TV viewing. Daniel Anderson and his colleagues have conducted numerous studies demonstrating that children's selection of television programs is influenced by their ability to comprehend content (Anderson & Burns, 1991). Certain formal, or structural, features of television serve to draw the viewer in, particularly such sound effects as laughter, music, and children's and women's voices. Other features, such as visual cuts, motion, and special sound effects, hold the child's attention (Alwitt et al., 1980; Schmitt, Anderson, & Collins, 1999). But the formal features of television programs are not the sole determinants of what children watch.

When preschoolers view segments of *Sesame Street* in which the comprehensibility of the program has been altered, that is, presented in a foreign language or played backward, attention declines even though the formal features remain constant (Anderson et al., 1981). In other words, children actively direct their attention to those portions of the show that they most readily understand; they are not influenced by sound effects or visual cuts alone. Many television shows have complex plots and use subtle cues that require inferences about characters' motives, intentions, and feelings. In addition, most programs contain changes of scene that require viewers to integrate information across several scenes. Research indicates that clear developmental differences exist in children's ability to understand information from television shows, differences that accompany changes in cognitive processing. Preschoolers can understand short story segments and remember the most central elements of each story (Lorch, Bellack, & Augsbach, 1987). When the plots and themes of television shows thicken, however, young children have difficulties. More specifically, when they watch programs designed for general audiences, younger children are less likely than older children to remember the explicit content, that is, the discrete scenes that are essential to understanding the plot. As children's general knowledge about the world grows, their comprehension of more detailed, specific information in television programs expands as well.

One other important developmental change is in children's ability to recognize that most television programming is fictional. Children under four years of age often have difficulty distinguishing the boundaries between events that occur on television and those that take place in the real world (Flavell et al., 1990; Jaglom & Gardner, 1981). For example, young preschoolers may think that Sesame Street is a place where others live, that individuals portrayed on television can see and hear their viewers, and that the things seen on TV exist inside it (Nikken & Peeters, 1988). Moreover, many five- and six-year-olds do not fully understand that television characters are actually actors playing roles; not until age eight and older do the majority of children grasp this concept. However, even kindergartners realize that cartoons are fantasy. They are also quite accurate about deciding whether their favorite programs occur as part of real life or just on television. In fact, they tend to be biased in assuming that most television programming does not occur in real life (Wright et al., 1994). Thus the developmental course seems to progress from failing to make a distinction between events on television and events in the real world, to a belief that few events depicted on television occur in the real world to, finally, a more complete understanding of which events occurring on television are fictional and which are not (Wright et al., 1994).

TELEVISION AND DEVELOPMENT IN EARLY CHILDHOOD

Today many preschoolers in the United States and most Western countries have ready access to programs specifically designed to teach cognitive skills. Evaluations of the effects of such shows as *Sesame Street* demonstrate that television can teach children a range of problem-solving, mathematical, reading, and language skills (Huston & Wright, 1998). But children also learn a lot more, according to research on television. Concerns have been raised about the effects of other types of programming to which many young children are exposed, especially on their social development.

Cognition *Sesame Street* was specifically designed to provide entertaining ways to teach children, especially those who might be underprepared for school, the letters of the alphabet, counting, vocabulary, and similar school-readiness skills. The programs also deliberately include both male and female characters from many racial and ethnic backgrounds. Early research showed that preschoolers who watched the show most frequently demonstrated the greatest gains on several skills, including writing their names and knowing letters, numbers, and forms. Frequent viewers also obtained higher scores on a standardized vocabulary test, adapted better to school, and had more positive attitudes toward school and people of other races than nonwatchers (Bogatz & Ball, 1972; Rice et al., 1990). Thus the show had effects not only on children's cognitive skills but also on their prosocial attitudes.

Not only does educational programming have immediate effects on children's cognitive abilities, but evidence is also accumulating to indicate that these effects can be long lasting. For example, children in low-income families who spent relatively greater amounts of time watching *Sesame Street* and other television shows geared to educational goals at two and three years of age did well on measures of reading, math, language abilities, and other indicators of school readiness three years later (Wright et al., 2001). This effect may, in part, stem from their increased interest in continuing to watch informative television as they become older. Moreover, a longitudinal study carried out on high schoolers in working- and middle-class families for whom television viewing habits had been recorded as preschoolers suggests a positive impact of having watched informative educational programming more than a decade earlier. Compared with those who watched more violent or entertainment-oriented shows as preschoolers, those who watched more educational programming had higher grades in English, math, and science, read more books, and were more achievement oriented as teenagers (D. R. Anderson et al., 2001). This relationship was somewhat greater for males than females, although a similar pattern was found for both sexes. Because the data on long-term effects of television viewing are correlational in nature, it is not possible to completely rule out other factors that could account for the positive relationships that were observed in the longitudinal study. For example, either individual differences or parental encouragement of educational and achievement goals throughout childhood may help to explain these findings. Nevertheless, the results considerably blunt many of the strong objections that have been raised about television's negative influence on development, especially if children are observing programming designed to be educationally informative.

Language Language skills may also be influenced by television. Mabel Rice and her colleagues (1990) suggest that television promotes children's language development.

Many programs targeted for children include simplified speech, repetitions, recasts, and elaboration on the meanings of words. As we saw earlier in this text, these devices can enhance the child's acquisition of vocabulary and syntax (Rice, 1983). Parents also sometimes use television as a "video picture book" in which events portrayed on the show stimulate verbal exchanges and language learning. For example, when mothers watch television with their preschoolers, they frequently identify objects, repeat new words, ask questions, or relate the content of the show to the child's own experiences (Lemish & Rice, 1986).

Is there direct evidence that television can function as a vehicle for vocabulary acquisition? Investigators exposed three- and five-year-olds to twenty new words in a fifteen-minute animated television story and found that both age groups showed gains in comprehension after only two viewings. Three-year-olds learned an average of one to two new words, and five-year-olds learned four to five words (Rice & Woodsmall, 1988). These findings are all the more impressive considering the brevity of the children's exposure to new vocabulary items and the limited efforts of the experimenters to highlight or exaggerate the new words.

Social Development Whipping a towel over his shoulders, a six-year-old jumps off the couch after watching the movie Superman on television. A brother and sister brandish toy swords, the brother mimicking in great detail the actions of a favorite cartoon character. These common scenes in American households illustrate the power of television to influence children's behavior by providing models for direct imitation. Psychologists and social policymakers have been particularly concerned about how television affects the child's social behavior and understanding, for better or worse.

Any child who turns on the television in the United States has an extraordinarily good chance of encountering a portrayal of violence. Approximately 60 percent of the programming shown between 6:00 a.m. and 11:00 p.m. contains violent scenes (and sometimes many of them). Moreover, that rate is even higher in children's programming, especially cartoons (Center for Communication and Social Policy, 1998). As a consequence, children will see an average of 10,000 acts of violence every year (Federman, 1998). Does this heavy dose of televised violence viewing produce aggression in children? Hundreds of research studies have examined this issue, and the consensus is clearly yes. Meta-analyses of the large number of studies investigating the relationship arrive at the same conclusion: a small but consistent causal relationship exists between viewing aggression on TV and aggressive behavior in children (Comstock & Scharrer, 2006; Anderson et al., 2003).

In keeping with the principles of social learning theory, a regular diet of viewing aggressive models may suggest to the child that physical attacks are acceptable in a person's repertoire of behaviors. Two processes could be operating. First, children can learn new acts of aggression from the models they observe. Second, aggressive behaviors already in the child's repertoire may be disinhibited (Bandura, 1969). Albert Bandura and his colleagues (Bandura, Ross, & Ross, 1963a, 1963b) designed a number of classic laboratory studies to explore the effects of viewing aggression. Nursery school children in one experiment were randomly assigned to one of five experimental conditions. The first group watched from behind a one-way mirror as a model in the next room performed a series of unusual acts of physical and verbal aggression on a plastic, inflated Bobo doll. For example, the model hit the doll with a hammer, kicked it, and said, "Hit the Bobo doll!" and "Kick the Bobo doll!" A second group of children watched a model perform the same actions, but the presentation was on film. A third group watched an adult disguised as a cartoon figure behave like the models in the previous two conditions. A fourth group observed an adult model behaving in a nonaggressive manner, sitting quietly and ignoring the Bobo doll and the toys associated with aggressive behavior. The last group of children saw no model at all. Children who had seen an aggressive model performed a large number of imitative aggressive acts, copying even the subtle details of the model's behaviors. In addition, they frequently added their own forms of physical and verbal aggression. Moreover, the performance of children in the film-model group was no different from that of children who saw the real-life model. Models on film were just as powerful as "live" models in eliciting aggression.

One study of almost 1,000 children showed that aggression and televised violence are actually linked in a reciprocal way (Huesmann, Lagerspetz, & Eron, 1984). The investigators asked each child's peers to rate how aggressive the child was, and they also noted how much television violence each child watched. The number of violent TV shows children watched at the start of the study predicted how aggressive they were three years later. In turn, aggression also influenced TV viewing. Children who were aggressive at the start of the study watched more violent shows three years later than they did initially. The findings are consistent with a bidirectional model of influence: children become more aggressive after a diet of violent television, and their aggression seems to stimulate even more viewing of violent shows. The tendency to view high amounts of violence as preschoolers correlates with more aggression as far down the road as adolescence, and also correlates with poorer academic success (D. R. Anderson et al., 2001).

Key Theme
Risk/Resilience

Can parents do anything to mitigate the potentially harmful consequences of television shows on their children's behavior? One obvious tactic is to limit the amount of time children are permitted to watch violent programs. Another is to encourage critical viewing skills in children, a topic that we will amplify in upcoming chapters.

For • Your • Review

- How much time do preschoolers spend watching television, and what kinds of television programs do they prefer?
- What do young children comprehend about television programming?
- How are cognitive and language development influenced by viewing television?
- What is the relationship between watching television and aggression in young children?

Chapter Recap

Summary of Developmental Themes

Sociocultural Influence

How do sociocultural factors influence the contexts of development in early childhood?

Cultural variations have been noted in the nature of young children's experiences with peers, particularly in the types of pretend play in which they engage. In addition, the emergence of multiple forms of media in the last several decades has provided a new and powerful context in which child development takes place.

Risk/Resilience

What contextual factors promote risk or resilience in early childhood?

Certain styles of parenting or parenting behaviors may put children at risk. In general, authoritative parents who display warmth and responsiveness are most effective. In addition, associations have been reported between the quality of children's home and child care environments and their cognitive and social development. Early intervention programs have been shown to improve children's scores on measures of cognitive, language, and social development. Exposure to a heavy diet of media violence early in childhood may put the child at risk for aggression later in childhood.

Chapter Review

THE FAMILY IN EARLY CHILDHOOD

What is socialization? At what age do parents begin serious efforts to socialize their children?

Socialization refers to the child's acquisition of the social knowledge, skills, and attitudes valued by the larger society. Most parents begin serious efforts to socialize their children by age two or three years.

What major changes have occurred in the structure of American families in the past thirty years?

In today's society, more children live with single parents, grandparents, gay or lesbian parents, or in families in which both parents work outside the home, compared with thirty years ago.

What does it mean to take a systems approach to understanding the family? Give examples of how influences on one subsystem within the family can have consequences for another subsystem.

Systems theory recognizes that reciprocal relations occur among various members of the family. For example, problems in marital relationships can have an impact on parent-child interactions.

What are the characteristics of the four major styles of parenting? What child behaviors are associated with each parenting style?

Authoritarian parents display a low degree of warmth and tend to use coercive techniques. Their children tend to be unhappy; boys are more aggressive and girls are more dependent. *Permissive parents* set few limits on children's behaviors. Their children tend to be low on self-control and self-reliance. *Uninvolved parents* are emotionally detached from their children and uncommitted to the parental role. Their children tend to be more aggressive, display low self-esteem, and engage in risky behaviors. *Authoritative parents* are high on warmth and use reasoning and explanation to control their children. Their children tend to display a high degree of *instrumental competence*, showing independence, self-control, achievement orientation, and cooperation.

What are some of the specific effects of parental warmth on the developing child?

Parental warmth is associated with higher self-esteem, greater empathy, and fewer behavioral problems, such as aggression, in children.

What are principles of the effective use of punishment?

To be effective, punishment should closely follow the child's transgression, and should be consistently applied. Both *inter-agent* and *intra-agent consistency* are important. Punishment should also be accompanied by an explanation for why the behavior is undesirable. An effective alternative to physical punishment is a technique called *time-out*.

In what ways do cognitions play a role in parenting strategies?

Parents' attributions about their children's behaviors, their beliefs in their own efficacy, and their socialization goals all affect parenting strategies.

What are some of the ways in which characteristics of the child can influence parenting strategies?

Control theory holds that children's behavior can influence the intensity of a parent's response. The child's temperament and the degree to which he or she exhibits committed compliance are often related to parenting strategies.

What are some of the factors associated with the incidence of child abuse?

Child abuse is more likely to occur when parents rely on harsh, coercive control techniques, are isolated from the outside world, and have few sources of social support. Certain children, such as those born prematurely, are at risk for abuse.

In what ways do fathers make important contributions to child development?

Sensitive, responsive fathering is associated with children's higher academic achievement, better social functioning, and less rigid gender-role stereotypes.

How do family size and birth order have an impact on child development?

In general, children raised in smaller families tend to display higher levels of achievement, probably because they experience higher- quality interactions with their parents. First-borns tend to excel in academic and intellectual achievements, whereas later-borns tend to be more socially oriented.

In what ways can parents facilitate the child's transition to having a new sibling?

The child's adjustment to the arrival of a new sibling is smoother when parents prepare him or her for the arrival of the new child and when the older child is involved in the new sibling's care.

Peer Relationships in Early Childhood

What are the different forms of play usually exhibited in early childhood? What factors are related to the emergence of these different types of play?

Preschoolers typically engage in three forms of play: *solitary play, parallel play,* and *cooperative play.* They also engage in *social pretend play,* a form of play that is linked to advances in cognition, language, and social understanding. Cultural values can influence the types of play in which preschoolers engage.

What are the qualities of children's friendships during the preschool years?

Preschoolers view friends as peers to play with, rather than as individuals valued for their psychological qualities.

Child Care

What are some of the effects of maternal employment on child development? How are mother-child interactions affected?

Maternal employment is associated with higher levels of achievement, independence, and self-esteem in girls, and with less stereotyped gender-role attitudes in both boys and girls. More important than the fact of maternal employment is the mother's interaction style and the quality of substitute care that the child receives. Mothers who are satisfied with their life circumstances and who display adaptive parenting techniques tend to have well-adjusted children regardless of their employment status.

What has research shown about the effects of daycare on the cognitive and social development of children?

Studies generally show that children who attend high-quality daycare are more cognitively and socially competent than children reared solely at home with their parents.

What are some important factors to consider in selecting a daycare center?

High-quality child care provides the same sensitive, responsive caregiving that good parenting provides. Parents should consider the following in selecting a daycare center: the types of educational opportunities provided for children, a balance between structured and more open environments, ample physical space and play materials, the interaction style of caregivers, training of caregivers in child development, the match between the characteristics of the child and the nature of the daycare program, child-staff ratios, staff turnover rate, and overall class size.

What features of the home environment have been linked to positive intellectual development?

Studies using the HOME inventory show that several factors in the child's home environment are related to higher IQ scores. Particularly important are parental responsiveness to the child, provision of appropriate play materials, and parental involvement with the child.

What has research revealed about the effects of early intervention programs for children? What factors are most important in promoting successful outcomes?

Evaluations of the effectiveness of early intervention programs, such as Head Start and the Abecedarian Project, show intellectual gains by children who have participated. However, the increases shown by Head Start children often fade after a few years. Critics of the Abecedarian Project say that increases in IQ scores are modest at best. Some researchers argue that more intensive and continuous intervention is necessary to produce more dramatic outcomes. Research on Early Head Start confirms the importance of these factors.

Media

How much time do preschoolers spend watching television, and what kinds of television programs do they prefer?

On average, young children watch between two and three hours of television each day. They prefer children's educational programming, children's entertainment programming, and cartoons, but by age five, they also begin to watch comedies and general entertainment shows.

What do young children comprehend about television programming?

Although the formal features of television often guide their attention, children actively attend to the portions of programs they comprehend. Young children progress from failing to make a distinction between events on television and events in the real world, to a belief that events depicted on television do not occur in the real world, to a more complete understanding of which events occurring on television are fictional and which are not.

How are cognitive and language development influenced by viewing television?

Television can promote certain pre-reading skills, such as knowledge of the alphabet and numbers. Television can also promote language development and increase children's vocabulary.

What is the relationship between watching television and aggression in young children?

Children who observe aggressive events on television learn such behaviors and can demonstrate them in similar situations. Viewing high levels of violence on television is associated with greater aggression in children and youth.

KEY TERMS AND CONCEPTS

authoritarian parent (p. 344)
authoritative parent (p. 345)
control theory (p. 351)
cooperative play (p. 358)
instrumental competence (p. 345)
interagent consistency (p. 347)
intra-agent consistency (p. 348)
parallel play (p. 358)
permissive parent (p. 345)
social pretend play (p. 358)
socialization (p. 341)
solitary play (p. 358)
systems theory (p. 343)
time-out (p. 348)
uninvolved parent (p. 347)

Pathways: Connecting the Story of Development

Infancy	Early Childhood (2–6 years)		Middle Childhood	Adolescence
See p. 268	**Physical Development**	• Shows advances in gross motor skills such as running, jumping, and skipping • Evidences slower but regular increases in size • Shows evidence of implicit learning	See p. 493	See pp. 576–577
	Cognitive/ Language Development	• Shows gains in ability to make perceptual discriminations • Can classify according to basic-level concepts • Understands the meaning of simple number terms, and eventually the basic principles of counting • Displays good intuitions about mathematical operations such as addition and forming fractions • Uses landmark cues to negotiate spatial environments • Uses geometric cues to aid spatial location • Begins to be able to read maps • Realizes that others can have different visual perspectives • Develops a *theory of mind* • Shows elementary planning activities • Displays knowledge of scripts • Displays autobiographical memory • By age three, attains *representational insight* • Uses two- and then multiword utterances • Uses morphemes, negatives, questions, and passive voice • Shows rapid growth in vocabulary and use of syntax • Displays overregularizations • Shows growth in referential communication and other aspects of pragmatics		
	Social/ Emotional Development	• Displays self-conscious emotions • Uses language to express emotions • Understands causes and consequences of emotions • Shows more effective emotion regulation strategies and, eventually, a decline in tantrums • Displays more complex aspects of attachment by considering motives, feelings of caregiver • Shows decline in separation distress and other attachment behaviors typical of infants • Has notion of categorical self • Displays overt behaviors signaling independence • Shows first signs of self-control • Shows early signs of conscience and altruism • Thinks in terms of preconventional ideas • Shows awareness of own gender and gender stereotypes		

PHYSICAL, COGNITIVE, AND LANGUAGE DEVELOPMENT 11

"Tomorrow's geography test is going to be really tough," Nate lamented to his friend on the way home from school. "I should have paid more attention in class and kept up with my assignments. Now I have to study so much!" Normally a good student, Nate had been preoccupied with the success of his baseball team. As pitcher, he was proud to be a contributor to that success. Now there was a price to be paid as he prepared for the next day's test, and he was decidedly anxious about it. Nate had made up one "trick" for remembering the states in the Southeast: he strung their first letters to make the phrase "True aces for-get no states" for Tennessee, Alabama, Florida, Georgia, North Carolina, and South Carolina, respectively. And it helped him to identify some of the states by tying their shapes to things he knew; for example, Florida really did look as though it had a "panhandle." But there was so much more to remember! Maybe he could just repeat the capitals of the states over and over to himself. One thing he knew for sure: next time he would not save all of his studying for the night before the test.

KEY THEMES in Physical, Cognitive, and Language Development

NATURE & NURTURE How do nature and nurture interact in physical, cognitive, and language development in middle childhood?

SOCIOCULTURAL INFLUENCE How does the sociocultural context influence physical, cognitive, and language development in middle childhood?

CONTINUITY/DISCONTINUITY Are cognition and language development during middle childhood continuous or discontinuous?

INTERACTION AMONG DOMAINS How do physical, cognitive, and language development interact with other domains in middle childhood?

Nate, as it turns out, had a pretty good understanding of his mental capabilities. He knew that paying attention in class was helpful and that certain techniques, such as rehearsal, mental imagery, and other "tricks," could help him remember information. He also knew there were limits to what he could accomplish in the few hours he had to prepare for his exam. In fact, many aspects of Nate's own thinking—attention, memory, and even the fact that he could evaluate his thought capabilities—have been topics of great interest to developmental psychologists. Middle childhood is a time, of course, when the child's cognitive skills have significant import; children must apply their thinking skills as they go to school and learn to read, do mathematics, and master an assortment of other academic subjects. Nate's involvement in baseball also reflects children's growing physical stature and mastery of complex motor skills. In this chapter, we start with a summary of physical development during the middle school years. Next, we focus on the main accomplishments in children's thinking during those all-important early school years. We will begin by revisiting Piaget's theory. Then we will survey several topics that have been studied extensively from the stance of information-processing theory, including attention, memory, and problem solving. Finally, we discuss the main features of the child's accomplishments in language use.

PHYSICAL DEVELOPMENT IN MIDDLE CHILDHOOD

One of the most obvious differences you would notice between a six-year-old standing next to an eleven-year-old is the disparity in their physical size—about a foot on average and more than thirty pounds. Accompanying the steady pace of growth in height and weight in middle childhood are noticeable changes in motor skills, as anyone who has coached a softball team or watched children draw can testify. As we document changes in these arenas, it is important to be thinking about the implications of these skills and characteristics for the psychological functioning of the child, especially as he or she enters school, with all of the new expectations and opportunities it affords.

MOTOR SKILLS

Motor skills during middle childhood become more efficient and better controlled, involve complex and coordinated movements, and are exhibited quickly and in a wider variety of contexts and circumstances (Keogh & Sugden, 1985). With the exception of balance, boys tend to slightly outperform girls on many gross-motor tasks by the time they enter elementary school (Gallahue, 1989). However, differences between boys and girls may become especially large for some activities as children approach the end of middle childhood and enter the adolescent years, as Figure 11.1 indicates for running speed and the distance a youngster can throw a ball.

Fine-motor coordination improves dramatically during the school years. For example, writing as a motor activity independent of drawing emerges around six years of age (Adi-Japha & Freeman, 2001). In addition, children may begin to construct models or do needlework, master the complex finger sequencing needed to play musical instruments, and produce more detailed drawings. All of these activities confirm that motor skills are undergoing significant developmental advances.

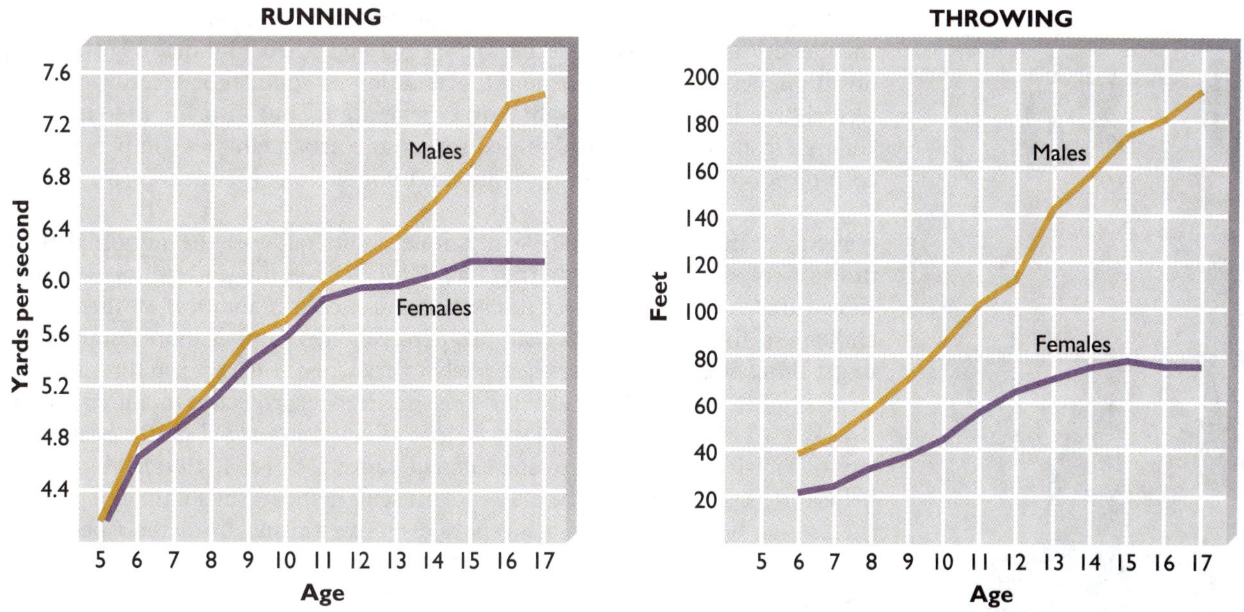

FIGURE 11.1

Running Speed and Throwing Distance for Boys and Girls at Different Ages

Boys tend to outperform girls on many motor skill tasks during the elementary school years, as indicated by these data on speed of running and distance throwing a ball, summarized from a number of studies carried out since 1960. The differences between girls and boys often increase substantially as children enter adolescence.

Source: Gallahue (1989), adapted from Haubenstricker & Seefeldt (1986).

As children grow older, differences in individual abilities often increase. Of course, to some degree, this may stem from practice—some children focus on acquiring particular competence relevant to their social and cultural milieus. The acquisition of expertise or specialized motor skills in sports, dance, crafts, hobbies, playing of musical instruments, and, in some cultures, trade- or work-related endeavors permits older children to become more effective members of their society and gain greater social status among peers and adults.

Body Growth

Children also undergo dramatic changes in physical size, a highly visible indicator of development. For parent and child alike, the ever-higher marks penciled on the bathroom wall give eloquent testimony to increasing maturity. A long-absent aunt who cries, "My, how you've grown!" may summon a grin or a blush from the wary seven-year-old, but she is confirming the social importance of this sign of change. Throughout childhood, boys and girls grow at similar rates, although individual children, of course, may differ enormously. Is physical size important to development and the way others interact with a child? If so, perhaps it is because the adult world appears to have strong preferences concerning height and weight.

Secular Trends Increased knowledge of nutrition and the ability to treat disease have yielded dramatic changes in patterns of growth in many societies in recent generations. These generational changes are termed **secular trends.** Children today grow faster and become taller as adults than did previous generations in most regions of the world.

Between 1880 and 1950, the average height of Western European and American children increased by nearly four inches. A slower increase or even stability in size has been found since the 1960s. Similar findings have been reported for other

secular trend Consistent pattern of change over generations.

Many children become sensitive to physical appearance, and weight, in particular, in the middle school years. Overweight individuals are viewed negatively in many contemporary Western cultures.

cultures, although at different times. For example, in Japan the most substantial changes in height took place between 1950 and 1970 (Tanner, 1978). Improved nutrition, better medical care, and the abolition of child labor account not only for secular trends in greater height across generations but also for the larger size of children from professional, highly educated, and urban families compared with children of poorer families and those in rural populations (Tanner, 1978).

Height Many societies share a mystique about tallness, the notion that height directly correlates with such traits as competence and leadership. Research has shown that height does affect impressions of a child's abilities. Mothers of young children of the same age, for example, perceive taller boys as more competent (able to get along better with others, less likely to cry when frustrated, and so forth). They treat smaller boys as younger and in a more overprotective manner (Sandberg, Brook, & Campos, 1994). The same is true of children judged on the basis of maturity of facial features (Zebrowitz, Kendall-Tackett, & Fafel, 1991). Moreover, boys believe it is important to be tall and muscular; those substantially shorter than the average height for their age report extensive teasing from their peers; greater dissatisfaction with their skill in athletic endeavors; and increasing unhappiness as they approach adolescence (Finch, 1978).

Despite these observations, lower self-esteem and other behavioral problems among children of short stature have not been consistently reported. And short adults typically function well within the norm socially and intellectually (Kranzler et al., 2000; Sandberg et al., 1994; Zimet et al., 1997). Until 1985, little could be done to alter the course of growth or eventual height for most children. Today, human growth hormone (HGH) can be produced synthetically. For children whose lack of growth stems from insufficient HGH, the breakthrough represented an enormously positive step toward more typical growth. However, increasing numbers of children who are genetically short or whose delay in growth is a normal part of their pattern of maturation are also being given HGH to speed up growth or increase their height, even though this practice is not officially recommended in many countries, including the United States (Cuttler et al., 1996).

Should such treatments, which tend to be motivated by perceptions and expectations about the benefits of being tall rather than by a medical condition, be encouraged? It is an expensive course of treatment and many children who are not HGH deficient gain few long-term benefits from its administration (Brook, 2000). Nor is the potential for negative side effects fully understood (Betts, 2000; Drug and Therapeutics Committee, 1995), although some pediatric endocrinologists believe it is very safe. In some countries (for instance, France, Japan, and Sweden) HGH is officially approved for use with individuals born with Turner syndrome and with children of short stature or who are simply failing to grow at normal rates (Bercu, 1996). However, attempting to alter normal physical development to conform to a cultural stereotype is a drastic action that raises many ethical issues.

Obesity Most estimates of obesity today make use of a measure called the *body mass index (BMI)*. The BMI is determined by dividing the weight of a child or adult (in kilograms) by the square of his or her height (in meters). Children and adults above the 95th percentile for their age on this measure compared with a reference population (which for the United States usually has been a large sample of children and adults who were tested in this country in the 1970s) or whose BMI is above 30 are considered obese. Children between the eighty-fifth and ninety-fifth percentile or who show rapid changes in weight relative to other children their age also are considered at risk for becoming obese (Strauss, 1999; Styne, 2001). Estimates are that, today, approximately 16 percent of children are either obese or at risk for being obese (Federal Interagency Forum on Child and Family Statistics, 2005).

KEY THEME
SOCIOCULTURAL INFLUENCE

Being overweight has strong social-emotional consequences in most cultures. At earlier times it carried positive connotations of substance and prosperity in industrialized societies and still does in many developing countries today (Sobal & Stunkard,

1989). For example, females in some regions of the world are encouraged to increase their body fat in preparation for marriage (Brown & Konner, 1987). However, in contemporary Western cultures obesity is often viewed negatively. For example, children as young as six, when describing drawings or photographs of people who are chubby or thin, are likely to label obese figures as "lazy," "cheater," or "liar" and are unlikely to select a chubby child as a "best friend" (Kirkpatrick & Sanders, 1978; Lawson, 1980; Musher-Eizenman et al., 2004). In addition, overweight children as young as seven years old experience more negative interactions with parents and peers than do other children (Davison & Birch, 2002). Although research has revealed a mixed pattern of findings, self-esteem may suffer as well (Klesges et al., 1992; Pierce & Wardle, 1997), especially for children who feel (or are made to feel) that they are responsible for being overweight (say, because of overeating or insufficient exercise) even as early as five years of age among girls (Davison & Birch, 1999).

Key Theme
Nature & Nurture

Genetic factors predispose some children to obesity. At least five single gene disorders are known to be related to its early onset (Farooqi & O'Rahilly, 2000). Behavioral genetics studies further suggest a relationship as a function of multiple genes, perhaps because of inherited differences in metabolic processes (Strauss, 1999). Not surprisingly, either because of a genetic component or because parents serve as models for their children's eating and exercise habits, overweight parents are more likely to have obese children (Birch & Davison, 2001). Early obesity, as well as the length of time a child continues to be overweight, increase the likelihood he or she will be obese as an adult (Strauss, 1999; Whitaker et al., 1997).

Controlling weight is complicated by heavy children's tendency to be more sensitive to external food-related cues and less responsive to internal hunger cues compared with their normal-weight peers (Ballard et al., 1980; Costanzo & Woody, 1979). Infants and children are responsive to the amount of energy provided by the foods they consume (Birch & Davison, 2001; Fomon, 1993). However, eleven-year-old obese children tend to eat faster than other children. They also fail to slow down their rate of food intake as they near the end of their meal, a pattern of responding that is at odds with what is typically observed in children of normal weight (Barkeling, Ekman, & Rössner, 1992). Obese children are also somewhat less accurate in reporting how much they eat (Maffeis et al., 1994).

Leann Birch and her colleagues (cf. Birch & Davison, 2001) believe that children can learn to become unresponsive to internal satiation cues through child-feeding practices imposed by parents. For example, some parents express concerns about

Parents can play an influential role in the development of childhood eating habits. When parents encourage children to finish everything on their plate or reward good behavior with sweets, children begin to rely more on external than internal cues for satiation, placing them at risk for obesity.

FIGURE 11.2

Trends in Overweight (BMI ≥ 95th Percentile): United States

These data, collected from a series of studies carried out in the United States between 1963 and 1999, reveal the marked increase that has taken place in the number of children who are considered obese. Some believe obesity has become a health epidemic in this and other countries because of the dramatic change and accompanying health risks that are associated with being overweight.

Source: Centers for Disease Control and Prevention (2002).

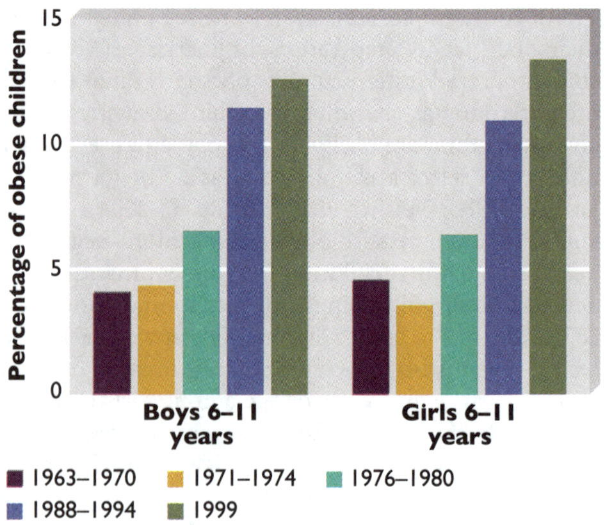

their infants' gaining sufficient weight. As a consequence, they may initiate meal-related practices designed to encourage food consumption ("clean their plates") and use certain foods, such as sweets, to reward good behavior and to calm and quiet the child. These efforts, however, could have the unintended effect of shifting the child's reliance on internal signals for hunger to external signals based on how much has been eaten and of increasing preferences for some foods that may not be so healthy. In addition, if concerns begin to emerge about weight, parents may attempt to restrict ingestion of high-calorie foods, an action that seems to have the unintended consequence of making the forbidden foods even more attractive to children.

KEY THEME
SOCIOCULTURAL INFLUENCE

Recent health surveys reveal a worrisome increase in obesity among children and adolescents in the United States (see Figure 11.2). Increases have been greatest among African American, Hispanic American, and Native American children (Crawford et al., 2001). Although less information is available from other countries, increases in obesity in children also have been reported in England (Reilly & Dorosty, 1999) and are taking place in many other regions of the world if the reports of the rise of obesity for adults are any indication (Taubes, 1998).

What are the reasons for this secular trend? Researchers have advanced various hypotheses. For example, compared with a generation ago, children today spend more time in sedentary activities, such as watching television. In general, children who watch more television per day have a higher BMI (Andersen et al., 1998; Robinson, 2001); the likelihood of becoming overweight is correlated with the number of hours spent watching television, as can be seen in Figure 11.3. Perhaps an even greater influ-

FIGURE 11.3

The Relationship Between Becoming Overweight and Hours of Television Viewing per Day

The more time children spend watching television each day, the more likely they are to be overweight. Ten- to fifteen-year-olds who were reported to watch more than five hours of television each day in 1990 were greater than eight times (8× in the figure) more likely to have become overweight (BMI greater than 85th percentile) between 1986 and 1990 than children who watched less than two hours each day. These findings provide powerful arguments for the view that obesity is increasing among children because they do not spend enough time engaging in physical activity or because the advertising messages on television encourage excessive food consumption.

Source: Adapted from Strauss (1999). Data from Gortmaker et al. (1996).

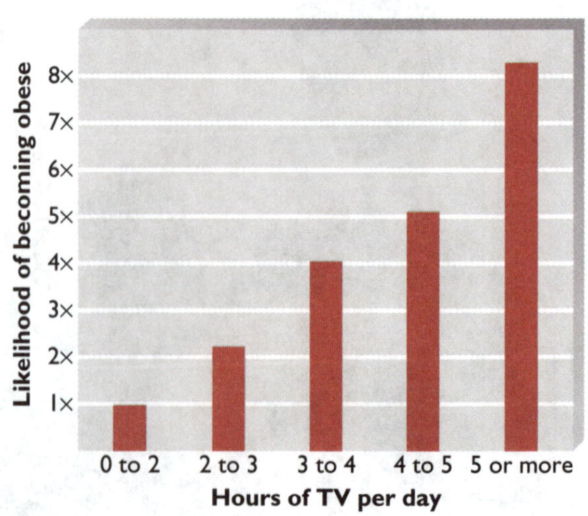

ence stems from television advertising, which rarely promotes consumption of fresh fruits and vegetables over calorie-laden snack and convenience foods; consumption of these latter foods has gone up substantially over the last twenty-five years (Jahns, Siega-Riz, & Popkin, 2001). Although culture may attach a negative label to being overweight on the one hand, television actively serves to promote it on the other.

FOR • YOUR • REVIEW

- What kinds of improvements in motor skills are observed during the middle school years?
- What is a secular trend?
- What are the concerns about short stature and obesity in many cultures?
- What factors may be contributing to the increase in obesity observed in many Western nations?

COGNITION IN MIDDLE CHILDHOOD: PIAGET'S THEORY

Recall Piaget's description of the preschooler who views much of the world from his own perspective and who lacks the thought structures to solve problems like the conservation of number or liquid tasks. As children begin the early school years, the change in their thought capabilities is dramatic, according to Piaget. Shedding his or her earlier egocentrism and beginning to reason logically, the child is well on the way to becoming a mature thinker and skilled problem solver.

THE CONCRETE OPERATIONAL STAGE

KEY THEME
CONTINUITY/DISCONTINUITY

In Piaget's theory, children are said to be in the **concrete operational stage** from approximately seven to eleven years of age. Children enter this stage when they begin to be able to solve the conservation tasks correctly. At first, the six- or seven-year-old may solve only a few of the simpler problems, such as conservation of length, number, or liquid quantity. Later, she will succeed on tasks that involve area or volume. Piaget called this extension of the same cognitive structures to solve increasingly difficult problems within a given stage *horizontal décalage.*

The reason for this shift is that the child is now capable of performing **operations**, mental actions such as *reversibility,* that allow him to reason about the events that have transpired. He can pour the liquid back from the cylinder to the glass "in his head" or think about the narrow width of the tall cylinder as compensating for its height. In other words, the child now thinks logically, although the physical components of the problem must still be present (if not externally in the world, then as images in the mind). The child's growing logical capabilities are also manifested in his ability to *seriate* objects, putting sticks of varied lengths into a systematic series arranged from shortest to longest, for example. Unlike the preoperational child who performs this task in a haphazard way, the concrete operational child starts with the shortest (or tallest) and compares each successive stick with those that are shorter and longer so that an orderly array results. The child's thought in this stage is also less egocentric, allowing him to understand that other individuals' perceptions, beliefs, and feelings may differ from his own. The concrete operational child is becoming a true "thinker," as long as there are specific objects or events to which he can apply his logic.

concrete operational stage In Piagetian theory, the third stage of development, from approximately seven to eleven years of age, in which thought is logical when stimuli are physically present.

operation In Piagetian theory, a mental action that allows a child to reason about events that have transpired.

CONCEPTS OF CAUSALITY

Piaget (1930, 1974) believed that, up until the early school years, ages seven or eight years, children lack a mature awareness of physical causality. Once they are verbal and can discuss causality, they make some interesting errors. One type of error is **animism**, attributing lifelike properties to inanimate objects. In one of Piaget's examples of animism, a six-year-old boy named Vern was asked why a boat floats on water but a little stone sinks. Vern answered, "The boat is more intelligent than the stone" (Piaget, 1929, p. 223). Another child, age seven, is asked if the sun can do whatever it likes. The child responds affirmatively; asked why the sun doesn't stop giving light, the child says, "It wants it to be fine weather" (Piaget, 1929, p. 227). Animism is often accompanied by **artificialism**, the belief that people cause naturally occurring events. Piaget provides the example of a six-year-old named Hub.

PIAGET: *Has the sun always been there?*

HUB: *No, it began.*

PIAGET: *How?*

HUB: *With fire ...*

PIAGET: *How did that start?*

HUB: *With a match ...*

PIAGET: *Who struck it?*

HUB: *A man. (Piaget, 1929, p. 266)*

In Piaget's view, children are slow to shed their animistic and artificial beliefs; the latter may persist until age ten years or so (Piaget, 1929).

Susan Gelman and Kathleen Kremer (1991) attempted to replicate some of Piaget's studies by asking preschoolers, "Do you think people made (or make) _____?" in which the blank was filled in by an object, such as the sun, the moon, dogs, flowers, dolls, and shoes. Few of the children showed evidence of artificialism; most recognized that objects like dolls are made by humans but that the sun and moon are not. Moreover, these young children often cited natural causes for the behaviors of living things (birds fly because they have wings) and human causes for the things artificial objects do (cars go uphill because people make them do so). Why the discrepancy from Piaget's observations? Gelman and Kremer (1991) postulate that direct questions, like the ones they used, were more likely to tap children's underlying knowledge of causality than the free-ranging interview questions Piaget employed. Their findings add to the body of research we have already discussed, suggesting that Piaget may have underestimated the cognitive capabilities of young children.

IMPLICATIONS FOR EDUCATION

Many educators have found inspiration in Piaget's distinctive ideas about child development. His theory carries some clear implications for teaching children. The first is that the individual child's current stage of development must be carefully taken into account as teachers plan lessons. For example, a seven-year-old who is in the stage of concrete operations should be given problems involving actual physical objects to observe or manipulate, rather than abstract word problems or diagrams (Flavell, 1963).

A second, related implication is that what the child already knows will determine what new information she is able to absorb. Because her current cognitive structures limit what she will be able to assimilate, it is important that the teacher be aware of the child's current state of knowledge. In addition, cognitive advances are made most optimally when new material is only slightly different from what the child already knows (Ginsburg & Opper, 1988). Thus the teacher's task is to plan lessons that are tailored to the needs of the individual child rather than to the class as a whole and to be flexible in devising instructional materials that stretch the child one step beyond what she already knows.

One of Piaget's most important statements about cognitive development is that it is the result of the *active engagement of the child*. Early sensorimotor schemes and

animism Attribution of lifelike qualities to inanimate objects.

artificialism Belief that naturally occurring events are caused by people.

later mental operations are all founded first on the child's physical activity and later on mental actions. Thus education, too, must be structured in such a way that it will promote the child's active participation. Instead of emphasizing rote learning, teachers following a Piagetian model provide children, for example, with experiments that allow them to discover scientific principles on their own. Children do not memorize numerical relationships, such as the multiplication tables, but discern them by manipulating sets of objects under the close guidance of the teacher. According to Piagetian thinking, active learning of this sort promotes deeper and more enduring understanding.

FOR • YOUR • REVIEW

- What are the major features of thinking in the concrete operational stage?
- What are Piaget's ideas about concepts of causality during the middle childhood years?
- What are the implications of Piaget's theory for education?

COGNITION IN MIDDLE CHILDHOOD: THE INFORMATION-PROCESSING APPROACH

Most of the child's cognitive attainments during the school years have been understood through the information-processing perspective. As we saw in the chapter titled "Themes and Theories," information-processing theorists believe that human cognition is best understood as the management of information through a system with limited space or resources. In the information processing approach, mental processing is usually broken down into several components or levels of activity. For example, memory processes are often partitioned into *encoding, storage,* and *retrieval* phases. Information is assumed to move forward through the system, and each stage of processing takes some time (Massaro & Cowan, 1993; Palmer & Kimchi, 1986).

Many traditional information-processing models are called **multistore models**, because they posit several mental structures through which information flows, much as data pass through a computer. One example of this type of model is shown in Figure 11.4. Most multistore models distinguish between psychological structures and control processes. *Psychological structures* are analogous to the hardware of a computer. The *control processes* are mental activities that move information from one structure to another, much as software functions for the computer.

Suppose someone asks you to repeat a list of words, such as *shoe, car, truck, hat, coat, bus.* If you have paid attention to all of the words and, like an efficient computer, have "input" them into your cognitive system, processing will begin in the **sensory register**. Information is held here for a fraction of a second in a form very close to the original stimuli—in this case, the audible sounds you experienced. Next, the words may move to the memory stores. **Working memory** (sometimes called *short-term memory*) holds information for no more than a couple of minutes. Many researchers consider working memory to be a kind of work space in which various kinds of cognitive tasks can be conducted. If you were to repeat the words over and over to yourself—that is, rehearse them—you would be employing a control process to retain information in working memory. You might also use the second memory store, **long-term memory**, the repository of more enduring information, and notice that the items belong to two categories, clothing and vehicles. The *executive control* oversees this communication among the structures of the information-processing system. Finally, when you are asked to say the words aloud, your *response system* functions to help you reproduce the sounds you heard moments earlier.

Other theorists in this field have advanced a **limited-resource model** of the cognitive system that emphasizes a finite amount of available cognitive energy that

multistore model Name for many traditional information-processing models which posit several mental structures through which information flows.

sensory register Memory store that holds information for very brief periods of time in a form that closely resembles the initial input.

working memory Short-term memory store in which mental operations such as rehearsal and categorization take place.

long-term memory Memory that holds information for extended periods of time.

limited-resource model Information-processing model that emphasizes the allocation of finite energy within the cognitive system.

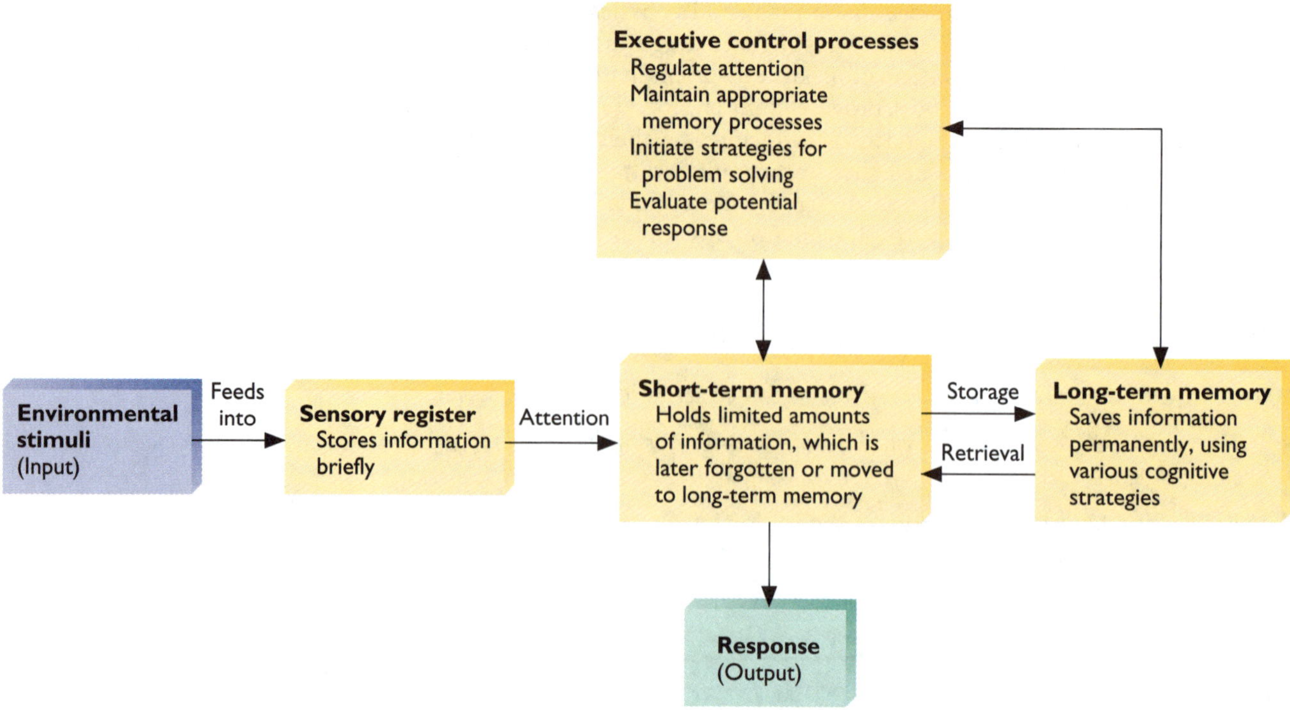

FIGURE 11.4

A Schematic Model of Human Information Processing

This highly simplified model includes several cognitive structures and processes that many information-processing theorists believe to be important in cognitive development. As the arrows indicate, information often flows in several directions between various structures. The goal of information-processing models is to identify those structures and processes that are at work when a child responds to his or her environment.

Source: Adapted from Atkinson & Shiffrin (1968).

can be deployed in numerous ways, but only with certain tradeoffs. Limited-resource models emphasize the allocation of energy for various cognitive activities rather than the mental structures themselves. The basic assumption is that the pool of resources available for processing, retaining, and reporting information is finite (Bjorklund & Harnishfeger, 1990). In one such model, Robbie Case proposes an inverse relationship between the amount of space available for operating on information and that available for storage (Case, 1985; Case, Kurland, & Goldberg, 1982). *Operations,* as we have seen, include processes such as identifying the stimuli and recognizing relationships among them; *storage* refers to the retention of information for use at a later time. If a substantial amount of mental effort is expended on operations, less space is available for storage or retention.

In the simple memory experiment we just examined, the effort used to identify the words and notice the categorical relationships among them will determine the space left over for storing those words. If we are proficient at recognizing words and their relationships, storage space will be available. If these tasks cost us substantial effort, however, our resources will be taxed and little will be left for the task of remembering. Robert Kail's research (1986, 1991a, 1991b) supports the idea that a central component of cognitive development is an increase in processing speed with age. As children grow older, they can mentally rotate images, name objects, or add numbers more rapidly. More resources then become available for other cognitive tasks.

How do these two general information-processing frameworks, the multistore model and the limited-resource model, account for cognitive development? Multistore models allow for two possibilities. Changes in cognition can stem from either an increase in the size of the structures—the "hardware"—or increasing proficiency in employing the "software," or control processes. For example, the capacity of the mental structure working memory may increase with age, or, as children grow older, they may increase their tendency to rehearse items to keep information in working memory or even push it into long-term memory. Limited-resource models suggest that what changes during development is processing efficiency. As children become more proficient in manipulating information, more internal space is freed up for storage.

ATTENTION

Attention changes in the middle childhood years. By this age, children are better able to control where their eyes look (Kramer, Gonzalez de Sather, & Cassavaugh, 2005) and improve in the ability to be *selective*. In other words, older children are much more likely than younger children to ignore information that is irrelevant or distracts from some central activity or problem. For example, in one study, children ages six, nine, and twelve years participated in a *speeded classification task*. They were given decks of cards that varied on one or more stimulus dimensions: form (circle or square), orientation of a line (horizontal or vertical), and location of a star (above or below the center). The objective was to sort the cards on the basis of one predetermined dimension as quickly as they could. But what happened when an irrelevant dimension was added to the cards in the deck? This change interfered with six-year-olds' ability to sort the cards but had little effect on the performance of older children (Strutt, Anderson, & Well, 1975). Other research confirms that the ability to filter out distracting information continues to mature at least until early adolescence (Goldberg, Maurer, & Lewis, 2001).

The ability to attend to some parts of an event or activity to the exclusion of others signals the child's increasing skill at controlling his own cognitive processing. This ability likely depends to some extent on the maturation of the prefrontal cortex, which we know is involved in selective attention in adults (Husain & Kennard, 1997). Also contributing to this change is the child's growing understanding that his attentional capacity is limited and that cognitive tasks are best accomplished with attention. Growth in this knowledge occurs during the preschool and early school years. Six-year-olds state that a person who is concentrating on one task will not pay much attention to other things, whereas four-year-olds do not exhibit this understanding (Flavell, Green, & Flavell, 1995).

KEY THEME
SOCIOCULTURAL INFLUENCE

To some degree, the child's knowledge about attention may be gleaned from the kinds of behaviors that are emphasized in his or her culture. In our society, focusing on one thing at a time is probably considered by most parents and teachers to be a desirable goal (Ruff & Rothbart, 1996). However, this pattern is not universal. Children of Mexican heritage, when observed as they learned to make origami figures in a group context, engaged in much more simultaneous attention to multiple events than did European American children (Correa-Chávez, Rogoff, & Mejía Arauz, 2005). Cultural preferences or demands may thus guide the particular attentional style a child develops.

ATYPICAL DEVELOPMENT
Attention Deficit Hyperactivity Disorder

Between 3 and 5 percent of school-age children in the United States, usually boys, show a pattern of impulsivity, high levels of motor activity, and attention problems called *attention deficit hyperactivity disorder,* or *ADHD* (American Psychiatric Association, 2002). The disorder is puzzling because its cause is not completely understood, and an unambiguous diagnosis can be difficult to obtain. At the same time, for parents, teachers, and the children themselves, the consequences of the disorder—poor school achievement, behavior management problems, poor peer relationships, negative moods, and low self-esteem among them—can be serious (Erhardt & Hinshaw, 1994; Rapport, 1995; Whalen et al., 2002). Whereas hyperactivity and impulsivity may decline in adolescence, problems with attention often persist for years (Hart et al., 1995).

As the diagnostic label implies, a major assumption about the nature of ADHD is that these children have some type of deficit in attention. But what precisely is the nature of that deficit? A prominent current hypothesis is that children with ADHD have problems with higher-order executive control processes, especially those that help children to inhibit their tendencies to respond (Barkley, 1997; Pennington, 1998). In one type of experiment, children sitting in front of a computer screen are instructed to hit one key if they see the letter *X* appear and to hit another key if the letter *O* pops up. However, if they first hear a tone, they must not hit a key at all. Children with ADHD have difficulty stopping themselves unless the tone is played much earlier than the letter appears (Schachar et al., 2000).

Children with ADHD also have difficulty being selective when confronted with numerous stimuli that compete for their attention. An experiment comparing six- to twelve-year-old ADHD boys with non-ADHD boys as they watched television demonstrates this effect (Landau, Lorch, & Milich, 1992). Each boy watched four segments of a show for fourteen minutes, half the time with several distracting toys in the room and half the time without toys. All participants were told they would have to answer some questions about the televised segments at the end of the viewing period. When distracting toys were present, ADHD boys paid about half as much attention to the shows as the non-ADHD boys. However, the two groups did not differ in their attention in the absence of distracting toys. These results suggest that ADHD children do not have a pervasive problem in sustaining attention; rather, they have difficulty in the presence of extraneous stimulation.

Some researchers now hypothesize that the specific cognitive problem that children with ADHD have is with working memory, the memory store in which "cognitive work" occurs (Tannock & Martinussen, 2001). In this line of thinking, the process of selective attention takes place in working memory. A recent study showed that normal adults, too, are distracted by stimuli when they are overloaded with another demanding cognitive task, such as remembering a set of digits. When less stress is placed on the cognitive system, problems in attention diminish (de Fockert et al., 2001).

Why do children with ADHD have these difficulties? Several studies implicate biological factors. Individuals with ADHD show abnormal brain wave activity, slower blood flow, and lower glucose metabolism in the prefrontal regions of the brain that are associated with regulating attention and motor activity (Rapport, 1995). Also, several brain regions, including the prefrontal cortex, are smaller in children with ADHD than in children without the diagnosis (Giedd et al., 2001). Accumulating evidence points to a strong genetic component to ADHD (Stevenson et al., 2005). In one investigation, 65 percent of the ADHD children in the sample had at least one relative with the disorder (Biederman et al., 1990). Other risk factors for attention problems include prenatal exposure to alcohol (Streissguth et al., 1995) and possibly nicotine, cocaine, or other drugs that may affect the developing brain of the fetus (National Institute of Mental Health, 1996).

ADHD children are frequently treated with medications, such as Ritalin or Concerta, which are classified as stimulants but that actually serve to "slow them down." This treatment helps many children, as does a combination of medication and behavior therapy, according to a major national study conducted by the National Institute of Mental Health (MTA Cooperative Group, 1999). But some experts worry that too many children are placed on this medication simply because they exhibit behavior problems, rather than because they have genuine ADHD. Clearly, a better understanding of ADHD is needed to sharpen its clinical diagnosis and develop effective treatment strategies for these children.

memory span Number of stimulus items that can be recalled after a brief interval of time.

FOR • YOUR • REVIEW

- What are the major differences between multistore and limited-resource models of information processing? How do they differ in accounting for developmental changes in cognition?
- What is selective attention? How does it change by the time a child gets to the early school years?
- What is ADHD? What factors may be responsible for its occurrence?

MEMORY

Nate, the underprepared student described at the beginning of the chapter, is getting ready for a geography test that requires him to use a specific form of memory, *recall memory*, in order to perform well. By its very nature, recall memory seems harder than recognition memory. Instead of indicating which states named in a list are from the southeastern part of the United States, Nate will have to look at a blank map and fill in the names on his own. Researchers have used different types of tasks to assess the development of recall memory. Some of these tasks have been focused on short-term memory, whereas others have tapped memories over longer durations. Regardless of the delay period involved, the child's use of memory strategies seems to be an important factor in preserving past events. However, alternative conceptualizations of memory development emphasizing different aspects of processing have also offered explanations of memory improvement.

Memory Span Suppose someone asks you to repeat a string of digits, such as a phone number. Like most adults, you should be able to repeat between seven and nine digits with relatively little difficulty as long as no more than approximately thirty seconds elapse after you first hear the digits. Tasks such as these measure **memory span**, the number of stimulus items that can be recalled after a brief interval. Children under age ten years remember fewer items than do adults. As Figure 11.5 shows, two-year-olds typically remember only about two items, but seven-year-olds remember about five (Dempster, 1981).

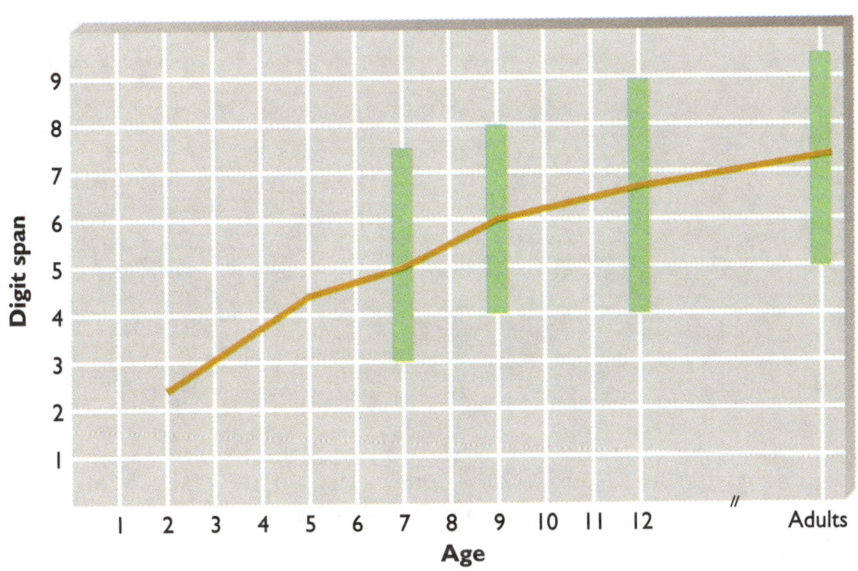

FIGURE 11.5

Developmental Changes in Memory Span

In the memory span task, participants are asked to repeat a string of digits after an interval of a few seconds. The points on the curve represent the average number of digits participants are able to recall. The bars represent the ranges of typical performance at each age. Memory span increases throughout childhood and approaches the adult level between the ages of ten and twelve years.

Source: Adapted from Dempster (1981).

Do these changes in memory span occur because the storage capacity of memory increases? Numerous memory experiments suggest that this is not necessarily the case. Instead, children's ability to employ **memory strategies**, activities to enhance the encoding and retrieval of information, increases with age. Children seven years and older are more likely than younger children to rehearse items or reorganize them into more meaningful, and hence more memorable, units. For instance, noting that the numbers 1, 3, 5, and 7 form the sequence of odd numbers makes the list easier to recall. So does simply repeating them over and over. Alternatively, as we saw at the start of this chapter, Robbie Case and his colleagues have proposed that increases in memory span can be understood as a result of the increasing operational efficiency children display as they mature (Case, Kurland, & Goldberg, 1982). As operational efficiency increases, more cognitive resources are available for storage.

Changes in **processing speed**, the rapidity with which cognitive activities are carried out, might indeed contribute to developmental gains in memory span. Researchers have suggested that two types of processing speed are important. Among children ages seven to eight, the ability to speak digits or words rapidly—presumably indexing the *rate of verbal rehearsal*—is related to their memory span. Among children ages eleven and twelve, memory span is more closely linked to shorter silent pauses between the items as they are being recalled. This second measure is presumed to index the rate at which items are actually *retrieved* from short-term memory. The data suggest that these different aspects of processing speed mature at different ages (Cowan, 1999; Cowan et al., 1998).

The memory span task is usually believed to tap short-term memory because the interval between presentation of the stimuli and the memory test is relatively brief. Other techniques have been used to study the ability of children to remember lists of words, sentences, or other items for longer than a few seconds.

Recall Many studies of memory with school-aged children have used *free-recall* tasks in which they are given a list of words or objects that they are to repeat, after a specified delay period, in any order they wish. As Figure 11.6 shows, few developmental differences in recall are usually noted for items later in the list (Ornstein & Naus, 1978; Ornstein, Naus, & Liberty, 1975). Children of all ages recall these items well, at least by the time they are of elementary school age. This elevated recall for later items, called the **recency effect**, is viewed as the extraction of information from more immediate memory, a task that is usually not too demanding for children age four years and older. Older children, however, show a clear advantage for recalling items that appeared in the early or middle positions in the list. The fact that older children show good memory for early items is called the **primacy effect**. Developmental

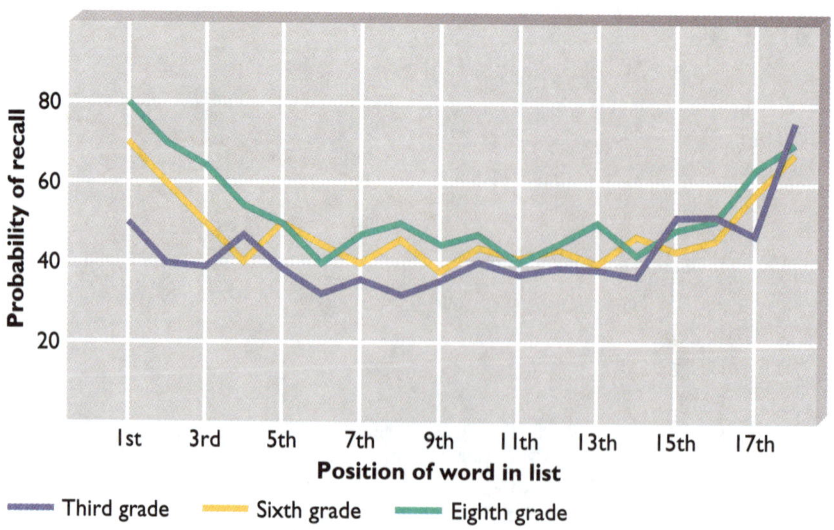

FIGURE 11.6

Developmental Differences in Free Recall

This graph shows the probability that a word will be recalled by third-, sixth-, and eighth-graders in a free-recall task. Few developmental differences appear in memory for the last few items in the list, but older children show elevated levels of recall for the first few items. This pattern suggests that older children are more likely than younger children to employ memory strategies, such as rehearsal, to remember the early items.

Source: Adapted from Ornstein, Naus, & Liberty (1975).

differences in the primacy effect can be explained as the result of the tendency of older children, those age seven years or older, to engage in deliberate strategies to improve recall. They repeat items aloud, make up sentences connecting the items, or think of mental images that connect the items. Research on memory development has told us quite a bit about the types of strategies children of different ages display.

Memory Strategies How do you make sure you remember your grocery list or where you hung your coat in a restaurant coatroom? Or, as in the case of Nate, how do you make sure you remember important facts and concepts for a test in school? Ordinarily, you must perform some activity to ensure that the stimuli are correctly and enduringly encoded in the first place. As a mature rememberer, you often capitalize on cues that may later "trigger" retrieval. Thus you might say the words in your grocery list over and over to yourself ("milk, eggs, bread; milk, eggs, bread") or note the characteristics of the location of an object ("next to the bright red coat"). In general, as children grow older, they become more likely to employ self-generated strategies for both encoding and retrieval and to take advantage of external information that can potentially aid recall.

We already identified one useful memory tactic, **rehearsal**—simply repeating, either aloud or silently, items to be remembered. The fact that young children are unlikely to engage spontaneously in rehearsal is well documented. In a classic study of children's memory, investigators asked kindergartners, second-graders, and fifth-graders to observe as an experimenter pointed to three specific pictures in an array of seven (Flavell, Beach, & Chinsky, 1966). When asked to point to the same sequence after a fifteen-second delay, fifth-graders showed significantly greater accuracy than the other two age groups. More important, during the delay period the researchers recorded any signs that the children may have been rehearsing the items to be remembered, such as moving their lips or vocalizing to themselves. They found that 85 percent of the fifth-graders engaged in spontaneous rehearsal, whereas only 10 percent of the kindergartners did. Moreover, children who rehearsed showed the best recall. In other words, there was a direct link between the children's production of this strategy and memory performance.

Older children also exhibit another important memory strategy called **organization**, the tendency to reorder items to fit some category or higher-order scheme. If the items to be recalled can be grouped conceptually, older children do so, and the amount they recall increases accordingly. For example, if the stimulus list contains words from the categories *animals, furniture, vehicles,* and *clothing* (such as *sofa, dog, chair,* and so forth.), ten- and eleven-year-olds spontaneously cluster conceptually related items together as they recall them, whereas five- and six-year-olds do not (Moely et al., 1969). Furthermore, instructing children to group the words or objects they are to remember into categories significantly enhances recall (Bjorklund, Ornstein, & Haig, 1977; Black & Rollins, 1982).

Still another helpful memory technique is the use of **elaboration**, thinking of a sentence or an image that links together items to be remembered. If you have to remember the list *cat, shoe, piano,* you might construct the sentence "The cat wearing shoes played the piano" or think of a visual image portraying this scene. Elaboration is one of the latest memory strategies to appear; usually children do not spontaneously use images or elaborative verbalizations until adolescence or later (Pressley & Levin, 1977).

The strategies just discussed pertain mostly to *encoding,* or getting information into the memory stores; but older children are also better at retrieval, or getting it out. Figure 11.7 shows the sketches made by a first-grader and a seventh-grader who were asked in one recent study to "write or draw anything you want to help you win the game" as they played the memory game "Concentration." Notice how the first-grader's drawing has little to do with the game; it is simply a picture depicting an unrelated event. In contrast, the seventh-grader's notations contain important details about what the items are and their specific locations on the game board. Not surprisingly, the results of the study showed that the better the quality of children's notations, the fewer turns it took for them to win the memory game (Eskritt & Lee, 2002).

memory strategy Mental activity, such as rehearsal, that enhances memory performance.

processing speed Rapidity with which cognitive activities are carried out.

recency effect Tendency for individuals to show good recall for the last few items in a list.

primacy effect Tendency for individuals to display good recall for early items in a list.

rehearsal Memory strategy that involves repetition of items to be remembered.

organization Tendency to reorder items to fit some category or higher-order scheme.

elaboration Memory strategy in which individuals link items to be remembered in the form of an image or a sentence.

FIGURE 11.7

Generating Retrieval Cues for Memory

Older children are more skilled than younger children at producing notes to help them remember information. The drawing on the left was made by a first-grader playing a memory game. The items in this child's drawing have little to do with the stimulus items to be remembered. In contrast, the seventh-grader's notations on the right include the stimulus items themselves, as well as their specific locations. Children who produce good external notes are more successful in memory tasks.

Source: Eskritt & Lee (2002).

Throughout this discussion, the recurring theme has been the tendency of children over seven years of age to initiate some activity that will improve their recall. Research has also revealed that children sometimes use multiple strategies—not just one—while engaged in a memory task, employing a mix of rehearsal and organization, for example (Coyle & Bjorklund, 1997). Thus development is not characterized by the replacement of simple strategies, such as rehearsal, with more sophisticated ones, such as organization. Instead, the array of study techniques available to children seems to expand with development.

Controlling Cognitive Processing Until recently, most explanations of developmental changes in memory have focused on children's increasing use of deliberate strategies to enhance their recall. However, theorists now recognize that this focus does not capture the full complexities of cognitive processing in children. Developmental changes in memory are now understood in terms of the child's increasing efficiency and control over cognitive processes.

Metamemory, the child's understanding of memory, is one aspect of this process. It includes the ability to assess one's own memory characteristics and limitations, the demands made by different memory tasks, and the strategies likely to benefit memory (Flavell & Wellman, 1977; Guttentag, 1987). It also includes the ability to monitor the contents of one's own memory and to make decisions about how to allocate cognitive resources ("Have I memorized everything thoroughly? Do I still need to study some items?"; Kail, 1990). Advances in each of these aspects of metamemory are, to some degree, related to improvements in memory as children get older. For example, older children have a better understanding than younger children that longer lists are harder to remember than shorter ones and that events from the distant past are more difficult to remember than more recent events (Kreutzer, Leonard, & Flavell, 1975; Lyon & Flavell, 1993; Wellman, 1977). One consequence of this awareness is that children begin to see the need to use strategies (Schneider, 2000).

The child also displays a growing ability to engage in *cognitive inhibition*, to regulate how much irrelevant information gets processed. Older children are better able than younger children to filter out information that is not pertinent to the task at hand, so that the space allocated to cognitive processing is greater. For example, older children can selectively forget irrelevant information; they can intentionally keep it "out of mind" (Harnishfeger & Pope, 1996; Pope & Kipp, 1998). Accomplishments like these are good examples of the child's increasing control over the management of his own thinking.

metamemory The child's understanding of his or her own memory.

Charles Brainerd and Valerie Reyna's *fuzzy trace theory* (Brainerd & Gordon, 1994; Reyna & Brainerd, 1995) provides still another example of growing cognitive efficiency. According to this theory, a continuum exists for how literally memories are stored. On one end, memories are very true to the original event, containing verbatim information. On the other end, they may be stored as "fuzzy traces" or "gists," containing the essence or core of the event without the literal details. Both types of memory representations coexist, but they are used for different purposes. Gists, according to this theory, are extracted by children of all ages, but younger children are more predisposed toward verbatim memories. Difficulties can arise, though, because verbatim memories are more vulnerable to disruption; they also make more demands on the cognitive system, in that they take more time to process. Young children's performance is affected by these demands.

To illustrate this theory, consider a study in which preschoolers and second-graders were given the following problem: "Farmer Brown owns many animals. He owns three dogs, five sheep, seven chickens, nine horses, and eleven cows." Children were then asked verbatim questions, such as "How many chickens does Farmer Brown own—seven or five?" or gist questions, such as "Does Farmer Brown have more cows or horses?" Among preschoolers, performance was better on the verbatim questions than on the gist questions, whereas the reverse was true for the second-graders. In addition, preschoolers and second-graders performed at equal levels on the verbatim questions, but second-graders had better recall for the gist questions (Brainerd & Gordon, 1994). Children who can focus on the gist of information do not get distracted by irrelevant details and retain the core of essential information for longer periods of time.

Memory and the Growth of General Knowledge Do younger children ever remember more than older children or adults? In a unique experiment, Michelene Chi (1978) found that in certain situations they do. Adults and children averaging ten years of age were asked to remember lists of ten digits presented by the experimenter. Typically, the adults' performance surpassed the children's. However, when the memory task consisted of reproducing chess positions previously seen for only ten seconds on a chessboard, children significantly outperformed adults. How did they accomplish this remarkable feat? Chi explains that the children who participated were experts in the game of chess, whereas the adults (who were college educated) had only casual knowledge of the game. By having greater knowledge, these children probably could encode the familiar patterns of chess pieces more efficiently, whereas adults were probably seeing random arrangements of rooks, knights, and pawns. Thus *domain-specific knowledge*, information about a specific content area, can influence the individual's ability to remember.

FOR • YOUR • REVIEW

- What have memory span and free recall studies told us about age changes in memory performance?
- What factors are primarily responsible for developmental improvements in recall memory?

PROBLEM SOLVING

Just think about the typical day of the average school-age child and you will undoubtedly come up with many problem-solving situations that the child encounters: a set of arithmetic problems to complete on a worksheet at school or a computer maze or jigsaw puzzle to solve for fun. More mature and efficient problem solvers deploy several "executive" cognitive skills, much as the central processor directs the various functions of a computer. For instance, can I add these numbers in my head or should I get a calculator? What is the best strategy to use—should the puzzle be started with the edge pieces or the entire top left corner? Will learning how to do a simple computer maze provide any clues about how to do a more complex one?

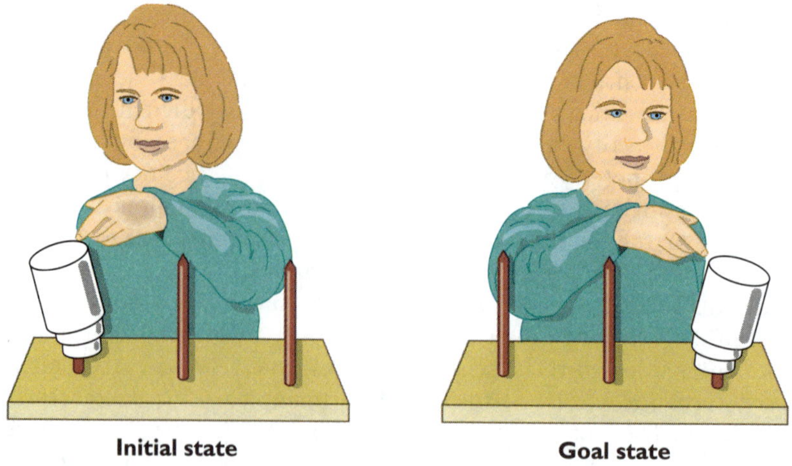

FIGURE 11.8

The Tower of Hanoi

In the Tower of Hanoi problem, the child must move three cans stacked on the first peg to the third peg so that they end up in the same order. Only one can may be moved at a time, and a smaller can may not be placed on a larger one. This problem gives researchers the opportunity to study developmental changes in children's planning activities as they solve problems.

Planning One of the hallmarks of a mature problem solver is the ability to plan an approach to obtaining a goal. Planning, of course, depends on representational capacities, because symbols may be employed or manipulated as part of the plan. It also depends on having general knowledge about the events being planned for—what is involved in going grocery shopping versus taking a trip to the beach, for example (Hudson, Shapiro, & Sosa, 1995). Moreover, planning has at least two aspects: (1) deciding on the steps one needs to take ahead of time and (2) knowing when to be flexible and perhaps modify or discard advance plans if the situation calls for it (Baker-Sennett, Matusov, & Rogoff, 1993).

David Klahr's classic research using the Tower of Hanoi problem, illustrated in Figure 11.8, shows that there are clear developmental improvements in planning (Klahr, 1978; Klahr & Robinson, 1981). In this problem, one of three pegs has three cans of different sizes stacked on it. The goal is to move the cans to the third peg so that they end up in the same order they were on the first peg. Two rules apply: only one can may be moved at a time, and a smaller can cannot be placed on a larger one.

Klahr found that six-year-olds were better planners than three-year-olds in two respects: they were more likely to pursue long-term goals, and they could keep more subgoals in mind as they attempted to solve the problem. For example, three-year-olds single-mindedly moved the cans to the third peg without thinking of the intermediate steps that might be necessary; their plan encompassed only the short-term goal to get the cans to the final peg. They could think of only one or two steps to attain the goal and broke the rules of the game. In contrast, six-year-olds used five or six steps to solve the problem, looking ahead a step or more as they planned their moves and anticipating potential traps in or obstacles to their placement of the cans.

With development, children also show changes in the flexibility of their planning. This phenomenon is illustrated by another study in which children were asked to plan a route through a maze (Gardner & Rogoff, 1990). When the task involved no time pressure, seven- to ten-year-olds planned the entire route through the maze before they drew in the path. However, when the experimenter told children to work as fast as they could, these older children used a more efficient approach under the circumstances: they planned less. Younger children, ages four to seven years, were less likely to adapt their planning strategies to the particular demands of the task.

KEY THEME
NATURE & NURTURE

Planning is likely to develop as children gain experiences with everyday routines in which specific events occur in a temporal order. Parental verbalizations about plans and the child's own emerging ability to verbalize probably also contribute (Benson, 1997). Another ingredient, according to Marshall Haith, is the child's "future orientation," his or her ability to think about events that are yet to come. Although early signs of future orientation are evident in infants—as they show anticipation about events in familiar routines, for example—a sense about the future probably undergoes more complex elaboration as the child matures (Haith, 1997).

Strategy Choice When a child encounters a problem—say, an addition problem—he will most likely choose from among several strategies. Robert Siegler has closely examined children's strategies as they solve simple addition problems and has found that children often rely on more than one approach (Siegler & Crowley, 1991; Siegler & Jenkins, 1989; Siegler & Shrager, 1984). Most children, he noted, first turned to one strategy but also usually had a backup strategy or two. Having multiple strategies affords the child useful flexibility as she encounters new situations and gains new knowledge (Siegler, 1989).

Suppose the child's assignment is to add the numbers 3 and 1. Several strategies are possible. The child can represent each number on his fingers and then count all of them to find the total. Alternatively, he can represent the larger number on his fingers and then count off the smaller number. Or he can simply retrieve the information from memory. Siegler found that, if the problem was simple, children drew on memory for the answer because that approach is the fastest (Siegler & Shrager, 1984). If the problem was more difficult, however, children used other strategies that ensured greater accuracy, such as counting on their fingers.

With development, as children have more successes with solving problems and become more confident about their approach, they are more likely to use memory as opposed to finger counting to solve addition problems. They also learn new strategies, often when they fail to solve a problem and need to search for alternative solutions. But children can learn from their successes, too. Siegler and Jenkins (1989) noticed that children often came up with new strategies for problems they had solved correctly earlier in the experiment. Children may also discover strategies simply by interacting with the materials for a problem (Thornton, 1999) or by hearing an expert explain a successful strategy (Crowley & Siegler, 1998).

Siegler's research shows that children do not merely substitute one strategy for another as they become more mature problem solvers. Rather, they incorporate new blends of strategies as they learn new ones and discard older ones. Children are constantly selecting from a pool of multiple strategies, depending on whether the task demands that they be fast or accurate and on what they remember about the success of the particular strategy in the past (Siegler, 1989). In their use of strategies, children frequently show variability from one problem-solving session to another, from one child to the next, and from one context to another, such as playing a board game versus doing math (Bjorklund & Rosenblum, 2002; Kuhn et al., 1995; Siegler, 1994). Variability, in fact, may enhance learning because it provides experiences with different problem-solving approaches and opportunities to discover those that work (Siegler, 1996).

Transfer You read earlier in this book that three-year-olds in Ann Brown's study of the magical genie moving jewels could transfer the solution of one problem to another similar problem. Brown hypothesized that, for transfer of problem solving to take place, the child must represent the problem in general mental terms; that is, abstract out the goal, problem, and solution dissociated from the specific fact that it was a genie that had to transfer jewels. Children can be encouraged to discern such common goal structures in a series of consecutive problems. Zhe Chen and Marvin Daehler (1989) found that, when six-year-olds were explicitly prompted to formulate an answer to the question of how problems were alike, they then performed significantly better on a transfer problem than control participants who did not receive this training. Thus parents and teachers may play a crucial role in facilitating the transfer of learning by pointing out commonalities across several problems.

RESEARCH APPLIED TO EDUCATION

Facilitating Transfer in the Classroom

As the teacher collected each student's paper, Nate was thinking how glad he was to have the geography test over with. Science was next, and science was without doubt his favorite subject in school. The class was studying electricity and had learned about how to make a circuit, the properties of conductors and insulators, and the role of a battery. Now the teacher was asking pairs of students to make a series of three light bulbs work by putting together wires and batteries in the correct order. Nate and his partner, Eliza, looked at the equipment before them and were stumped. How would they even begin? As they experimented, though, the principles they had discussed in the previous day's lesson began to creep into their thinking. By the end of only a few minutes, their bulbs were assembled and shining as brightly as their proud faces.

If you stop and think about it, probably the greatest overarching goal of education is to ensure that students transfer what they learn in one lesson, problem, or assignment to new situations both in and outside of the classroom. We expect students to go beyond the specific content of one particular mathematics problem, scientific experiment, or writing assignment and apply what they have learned in new situations. Is there anything teachers can do to promote this important process?

One technique that teachers can use to facilitate transfer of knowledge from one situation to another is to present information using obvious organizational structure. Explaining to students why the material they are learning is important can also be helpful.

Robert Sternberg and Peter Frensch (1993) offer the following suggestions based on their review of numerous studies of both memory and transfer:

1. ***"Teach for transfer" by providing multiple settings in which information is encoded.*** This tactic, according to numerous studies of memory, should make retrieval of information more likely because there are more cues associated with it. Teachers should demonstrate to students how information they learn can be applied in different contexts and even ask students to think of applications themselves. In other words, knowledge should not be "encapsulated" or taught as a "stand alone" topic. As an example, principles of algebra could be taught in the context of a science class as well as a math class. The results should be that those principles are remembered well and their usefulness in different subject areas is apparent to students.
2. ***Organize information so that transfer is more likely to occur.*** Classroom presentations should have an obvious organizational structure and should be connected to information that students already have. Such an approach would provide students with a framework, much like a script, that would enhance understanding and learning. Sternberg and Frensch (1993) add that teachers rarely begin lessons with a discussion of why the information is important in students' lives (where it fits in their personal scheme of things), but to enhance learning, they should.
3. ***Help students see the general features that are common across different content areas to be learned and that are specific to a given lesson.*** Sternberg and Frensch (1993) describe a personal experience in learning Spanish in which the general features of the language were explicitly pointed out. At the same time, pronunciations and vocabulary that were unique to a given region or country were also highlighted for students. Learning should proceed more efficiently under circumstances in which common themes and exceptions to those themes are deliberately highlighted.
4. ***Test students on their ability to apply what they have learned to new situations rather than on their ability to recall specific pieces of information.*** This approach would establish in students a "mental set" for the idea that they will have to engage in transfer—that this is an important expectation of them.

All of these pointers have a common aim: to make students aware of transfer as an explicit goal of learning. In a sense, the preceding suggestions ask teachers and students to be more "metacognitive" about the learning process, to overtly and frequently discuss and reflect on how transfer might be promoted. The more teachers incorporate this goal into their daily classroom instruction, according to these researchers, the more likely students will learn in the truest sense of the word.

Learning Mathematics Once children enter school, of course, they are expected to master the formal properties of numbers through mathematics. Lauren Resnick (1986) believes that, before children learn the systematic rules for addition, subtraction, algebra, and other mathematical systems, they develop intuitive concepts about how numbers can be manipulated. How would Pitt, one of her seven-year-old participants, add 152 and 149?

> I would have the two 100's, which equals 200. Then I would have 50 and the 40, which equals 90. So I have 290. Then plus the 9 from 49, and the 2 from the 52 equals 11. And then I add the 90 plus the 11 ... equals 102. 102? 101. So I put the 200 and the 101, which equals 301. (p. 164)

All of this came from a young boy who had mastered only first-grade arithmetic!

In fact, children seem to have a good basic grasp of even more complex numerical concepts, such as fractions, by age four. Suppose a preschooler sees three-fourths of a circle hidden by a screen and then one-half of a circle come out from the screen. How much is left behind the screen? A surprising number of four-year-olds can select a picture of one-fourth of a circle from a set of alternatives (Mix, Levine, & Huttenlocher, 1999). In addition, even a brief training session can help young children understand the basic concepts of fractions. When five-year-olds in one study had the opportunity to observe a whole pizza divided among different numbers of recipients, they began to understand that the size of each share of pizza depended on the number of individuals who were going to eat it (Sophian, Garyantes, & Chang, 1997). Given such findings, it is puzzling that many children experience difficulties with mathematics in school. Perhaps, as Resnick suggests, teachers should frame more complex mathematical operations, such as ratios and algebraic expressions, in terms of simple additive properties or other intuitions that children have about numbers, at least when they are first being learned (Resnick, 1995; Resnick & Singer, 1993).

Key Theme
Sociocultural Influence

Because Asian students score significantly higher than students from the United States on tests of mathematics (Fuligni & Stevenson, 1995; Geary et al., 1993; Stevenson, Chen, & Lee, 1993), examining the source of their mathematical proficiency can be especially instructive. Asian children use different strategies to solve mathematics problems than American children usually do. Korean and Japanese children, for example, add the numbers 8 + 6 by first trying to reach 10; that is, they add 8 + 2 to make 10 and then add the difference between 6 and 2 to reach the answer, 14. It is interesting to note that, in these Asian languages, names for numbers in the teens are "ten one" (eleven), "ten two" (twelve), and so on. Thus children may be used to thinking in terms of tens. Addition and subtraction strategies based on a system of tens are also taught explicitly in Korea and Japan (Fuson & Kwon, 1992; Naito & Miura, 2001); as amount of schooling increases, so does children's use of the base ten approach (Naito & Miura, 2001). Findings like these offer interesting potential ways of enhancing children's already-sound mathematical understanding.

For • Your • Review

- What are the major ways in which children show changes in problem-solving skills as they develop?
- What factors encourage children to transfer skills from one situation to another?
- What basic forms of mathematical reasoning do children display in the early school years?

Cognition in Middle Childhood: Vygotsky and the Sociocultural Context of Learning

No account of cognition during the school years would be complete without a return to some of Vygotsky's seminal concepts about how learning and development progress. In addition to providing an explanation for how children move forward in their thinking, Vygotsky's theory, like Piaget's, has important implications for the kinds of educational experiences we should be providing to children.

The Role of Scaffolding

Key Theme
Sociocultural Influence

Recall our earlier discussion of Vygotsky's theory in which we defined the concept of *scaffolding*. Scaffolding involves a teaching/learning relationship that uses the expert or tutor who intervenes as required and gradually withdraws as assistance becomes unnecessary. Patricia Greenfield (1984) observed this phenomenon among girls learning to weave in Zinacantan, Mexico. Beginners, in the presence of at least one expert weaver (usually the mother), started by weaving small items and performed only the simpler parts of the task. The more experienced the learner, the less likely the teacher was to intervene to complete the more technically difficult steps. Novices were more likely to receive direct commands from the teacher, whereas experienced weavers were more likely to receive statements or comments. Both verbal and nonverbal assistance declined as the girls became increasingly proficient weavers, although the expert continued to be a role model for both specific techniques and more general principles of weaving. Remarkably, the scaffolding that the tutor provided yielded a woven product from beginners indistinguishable from those completed by expert weavers. These examples illustrate what Vygotsky (1978) called the **zone of proximal development**, the span or disparity between what children are able to do without the assistance of others and what they are often able to accomplish by having someone more expert assist them at key points. Vygotsky claimed that the most effective assistance from the expert is that just slightly beyond or ahead of the child's current capacities.

THE ROLE OF SKILLED COLLABORATORS

As the phenomena of scaffolding and the zone of proximal development suggest, a role model who is sensitive to the learner's level of knowledge contributes greatly to the effective transmission of skills. The effect can be demonstrated in tasks as diverse as learning to distinguish the colors and shapes of pictures (Diaz, Neal, & Vachio, 1991) to finding out how to carry out long division in mathematics assignments (Pratt et al., 1992). Of course, some tutors may be better at these activities than others. Barbara Radziszewska and Barbara Rogoff (1988) examined how nine- and ten-year-olds learned to plan errands. One group of children worked with their parents to organize a shopping trip through an imaginary town, while a second group of children worked with a peer to plan the expedition. Children who worked with adults were exposed to more sophisticated planning strategies; they explored a map of the town more frequently, planned longer sequences of activities, and verbalized more of their plans. Instead of using a step-by-step strategy ("Let's go from this store to the next-closest store"), as the peer pairs did, children working with adults formulated an integrated sequence of actions ("Let's mark all the stores we have to go to in blue and see what is the best way between them"). In the second part of the experiment, all of the children were observed as they planned a new errand in the same town, this time by themselves. Children who had initially worked with their parents employed more efficient planning strategies than children who had worked with peers.

Why does collaboration with adults work so well? In a follow-up study, Radziszewska and Rogoff (1991) observed that, when children worked with adults, they participated in more discussion of the best planning strategy—more "thinking out loud"—than when they worked with peers who had expertise in planning. When working with adults, children were generally more actively involved in the cognitive task, whereas they tended to be more passive observers when their tutor was another child.

Barbara Rogoff and her colleagues (1993) have suggested that the extent to which children and adults take an active role in learning the skills, values, and knowledge of their community differs across cultures. In general, in all communities adults provide scaffolding for children to begin engaging in mature activities, a process the researchers label *guided participation*. However, children take on a greater burden of responsibility for managing their attention, desire, and interest in mature activities in communities in which they are routinely in the company of adults. The guidance that caregivers provide in this context is likely to be in the form of supporting children's observations and efforts rather than in the form of instruction. In contrast, when much of a child's day is spent separate from adults, the child will need more directed lessons and training to acquire mature skills. In this context,

zone of proximal development Range of various kinds of support and assistance provided by an expert (usually an adult) who helps children to carry out activities they currently cannot complete but will later be able to accomplish independently.

When children work with skilled collaborators, such as parents or teachers, they are often encouraged to think aloud and participate actively. The result is greater transmission of problem-solving skills than when working on a project with another child.

the caregivers assume comparatively greater responsibility in helping children to observe and understand the world.

Key Theme
Sociocultural Influence

Rogoff and her colleagues (1993) found that, in communities in India and Guatemala, where young children could watch and enter into adult social and work activities, caregivers were likely to assist and support children in carrying out more mature responsibilities, such as learning to dress themselves or play with a new toy. On the other hand, in middle-income communities in Turkey and the United States, where children were more likely to be segregated (and parents could not be as consistently attentive and supportive), caregivers were likely to promote play and conversation or provide lessons or learning opportunities in interacting with children to teach them new skills. These interactions, in other words, looked more like the kind typically found with older children in formal school settings. Thus, although all caregivers provided guidance for more mature behavior in each community, its specific form differed, a confirmation of the diverse ways learning may be encouraged in various cultural contexts.

Developmental psychologists have shown widespread interest in Vygotsky's theory. Many have accepted his claims for the social basis of cognitive development and the importance of understanding the sociocultural context in which the child grows up.

For • Your • Review

- How do the processes of scaffolding and guided participation contribute to cognitive development according to Vygotsky?
- What do research findings tell us about the role of skilled collaborators in promoting children's cognitive advances?

Language in Middle Childhood

By about age five, the speech of most children sounds like that of adults. They have figured out the sounds of their native language, and by the time they enter school, children know more than 14,000 words (Carey, 1978). By age ten, they comprehend almost 40,000 words. These numbers translate into an astonishing rate of learning—between 6 and 12 new words per day among school-age children (Anglin, 1993)! Children have also mastered the basic rules of grammar and many of the nuances of pragmatics that characterize their language. What is unique about middle childhood is that children can now think about their use of language from a more mature vantage point, reflecting on their own skill with language and even using it in a playful manner.

METALINGUISTIC AWARENESS

Prior to age five, children may lack a full understanding of what it means for a sentence to be grammatical or how to gauge their linguistic competencies, even when their speech is syntactically correct and effective in delivering a communication. The ability to reflect abstractly on the properties of language and to conceptualize the self as a more or less proficient user of this communication tool is called **metalinguistic awareness**. By most accounts, children show thinking about language in this way during the early school years.

Reflecting on Properties of Language One of the first studies to explore children's thinking about language was conducted by Lila Gleitman and her colleagues (Gleitman, Gleitman, & Shipley, 1972); these researchers were interested in children's ideas about the function of grammar. The investigators had mothers read grammatically correct and incorrect passages to their two-, five-, and eight-year-old children. After each sentence, an experimenter said, "Good" at the end of an acceptable passage, such as "Bring me the ball," or "Silly" at the end of an unacceptable one, such as "Box the open." When the children were given the opportunity to judge sentences themselves, even the youngest children were generally able to discriminate between correct and incorrect versions. They were not able, however, to correct improper constructions or to explain the nature of a syntactic problem until age five.

In addition, it is not until age six or seven that most children appreciate that words are different from the concepts to which they are linked. For example, four-year-olds frequently believe *train* is a long word because its referent is long, in contrast to older children who understand the distinction (Berthoud-Papandropoulou, 1978). Such changes in metalinguistic understanding are undoubtedly linked to advances in cognition, particularly the development of more flexible and abstract thought.

Humor and Metaphor One visible way in which children demonstrate their metalinguistic awareness is through language play: intentionally mislabeling objects, creating funny words, telling jokes or riddles, or using words in a figurative sense. The earliest signs of humor have been documented shortly after the child begins speaking. Researcher Carolyn Mervis noted that her son Ari, at age fifteen months, called a hummingbird a "duck" (a word he had previously used correctly) and then looked at his mother and laughed (Johnson & Mervis, 1997). However, the ways in which children comprehend and produce humorous verbalizations undergo clear developmental changes from the preschool to later school years. Three- to five-year-olds experiment with the sounds of words, altering phonemes to create humorous facsimiles (for example, *watermelon* becomes *fatermelon*) (McGhee, 1979). By the early school years, the basis of children's humor expands to include riddles or jokes based on semantic ambiguities, as in the following:

QUESTION: *How can hunters in the woods find their lost dogs?*

ANSWER: *By putting their ears to a tree and listening to the bark.*

Still later—as every parent who has ever had to listen to a seemingly endless string of riddles and jokes from a school-age child can testify—children begin to understand and be fascinated by jokes and riddles that require them to discern syntactic ambiguities (Hirsch-Pasek, Gleitman, & Gleitman, 1978), as in the following:

QUESTION: *Where would you go to see a man-eating shark?*

ANSWER: *A seafood restaurant.*

metalinguistic awareness Ability to reflect on language as a communication tool and on the self as a user of language.

One way in which children manifest a more sophisticated mastery of language is through their use of humor, which often contains instances of language play.

Thus children's appreciation of humor mirrors their increasingly sophisticated knowledge of the various features of language, beginning with its fundamental sounds and culminating with the complexities of syntactic and semantic rules.

Similarly, children's understanding of **metaphor**, figurative language in which a term that typically describes one object or event is applied to another context (for example, calling a shadow a "piece of the night" or skywriting a "scar in the sky"), undergoes developmental change. Preschoolers show a rudimentary ability to understand and produce figurative language, especially when it refers to perceptual similarities between two objects (Gottfried, 1997). A four-year-old understands expressions like "A string is like a snake," for example (Winner, 1979). But by middle childhood, children understand and even prefer metaphors grounded in conceptual relationships, like "The volcano is a very angry man" (Silberstein et al., 1982).

Atypical Development

Language-Impaired Children

About 7 percent of children fail to develop normal speech and language despite having normal hearing and general intellectual skills (Leonard, 1998). They may have trouble pronouncing words, have a limited spoken vocabulary, and show poor language comprehension. For many of these children, delayed language skills can mean severe reading difficulties, called *dyslexia*, once they enter school. Many researchers now believe that this wide array of problems is due to phonological processing deficits (Olson, 1994; Siegel, 1993; Stanovich, 1993; Whitehurst & Fischel, 2000). These children have particular difficulty in discriminating phonemes. Compared with normal children, these children are slower and less accurate when asked to read nonsense words like *calch* and *tegwop*; they also have difficulty when asked to make words into a familiar children's language called pig Latin (for instance, making the word *pig* into *igpay*) (Connors & Olson, 1990). These processing deficits can persist well into adulthood (Bruck, 1993). They also occur among poor readers from a wide variety of language backgrounds, including Arabic, Chinese, Punjabi, and Norwegian (Chiappe & Siegel, 1999; Høien et al., 1995; Siegel, 1998).

metaphor Figurative language in which a term is transferred from the object it customarily designates to describe a comparable object or event.

Paula Tallal and her colleagues (1996) have found that many of these children can be helped by being trained with taped exercises in which speech has been modified to help them identify auditory sounds that change quickly. In these exercises, the speech signal was slowed down by 50 percent, but its natural quality was preserved. In addition, the elements of speech that typically change rapidly were amplified in volume. The children had to act out commands they heard in the exercises or repeat syllables, words, and phrases. The program was intensive; children worked on the exercises three hours each weekday and were also given homework every night. At the end of only one month, the children's scores on several measures of language development improved by two years on average.

Just why language-impaired children lag behind in phonological processing skills is still not completely understood. Tallal and her colleagues believe that the problem lies in a general deficit in processing auditory stimuli of any sort, be they speech sounds or not (Tallal et al., 1997). Another ingredient may be poor executive processing skills, such as the ability to maintain two pieces of information in memory at once or to select the best strategy from a number of competing options in a task (Swanson, Mink, & Bocian, 1999). Other experts argue that the problem is not cognitive but rather is specific to processing linguistic stimuli, because children from a wide range of intellectual levels—even those with high IQ—can show dyslexia (Siegel, 1998). Whatever the explanation, this body of research makes very clear the importance of mastering phonology in the acquisition of language and reading for all children, not just those who have dyslexia. The ability to decipher the basic sound units of language is now a widely recognized predictor of children's eventual skill in reading (Comeau et al., 1999; Ehri, 1998; Ho & Bryant, 1997).

BIOLOGY AND LANGUAGE ACQUISITION

The discussion of language in middle childhood provides a good opportunity to reflect on the role that brain development plays in this process. To what extent has biology played a role in the child's acquisitions to this point, and to what degree is language development constrained by what happens to the brain up until the period of adolescence? The human brain contains several areas associated with the understanding and production of language. The right and left hemispheres of the brain have specialized functions, a phenomenon called *lateralization*. The primary regions that control language processing in most people are found in the left hemisphere. A major question arising from knowledge of the brain's involvement in language is the extent to which the milestones of language acquisition are controlled by physiological maturation of brain structures and, more specifically, by lateralization.

KEY THEME
NATURE & NURTURE

The Brain and Language Neuropsychological studies reveal that several portions of the temporal, prefrontal, and visual areas of the brain are involved in language processing (Neville et al., 2001). However, studies of individuals who have suffered brain damage due to stroke, traumatic injury, or illness have pinpointed two specific regions in the left hemisphere that play a special role in the ability to use language. The first is **Broca's area**, located in the left frontal region near the motor cortex (see Figure 11.9). Patients who have damage in this region evidence **expressive aphasia**, or the inability to speak fluently, although their comprehension abilities remain intact. The second region, **Wernicke's area**, is in the temporal region of the left hemisphere, close to the areas of the brain responsible for auditory processing. Damage to Wernicke's area results in **receptive aphasia**, in which speech seems fluent—at least on the surface—but contains nonsense or incomprehensible words; the ability to understand the speech of others is also impaired. An important finding is that children are more likely than adults to recover language functions following injury to the left hemisphere (Annett, 1973; Basser, 1962), an illustration of the brain's greater *plasticity* during childhood.

Broca's area Portion of the cerebral cortex that controls expressive language.

expressive aphasia Loss of the ability to speak fluently.

Wernicke's area Portion of the cerebral cortex that controls language comprehension.

receptive aphasia Loss of the ability to comprehend speech.

FIGURE 11.9

The Two Portions of the Left Cortex of the Brain Responsible for Language Processing

Broca's area governs the production of speech, and Wernicke's area is responsible for the comprehension of speech. Damage to the former produces expressive aphasia, whereas damage to the latter leads to receptive aphasia.

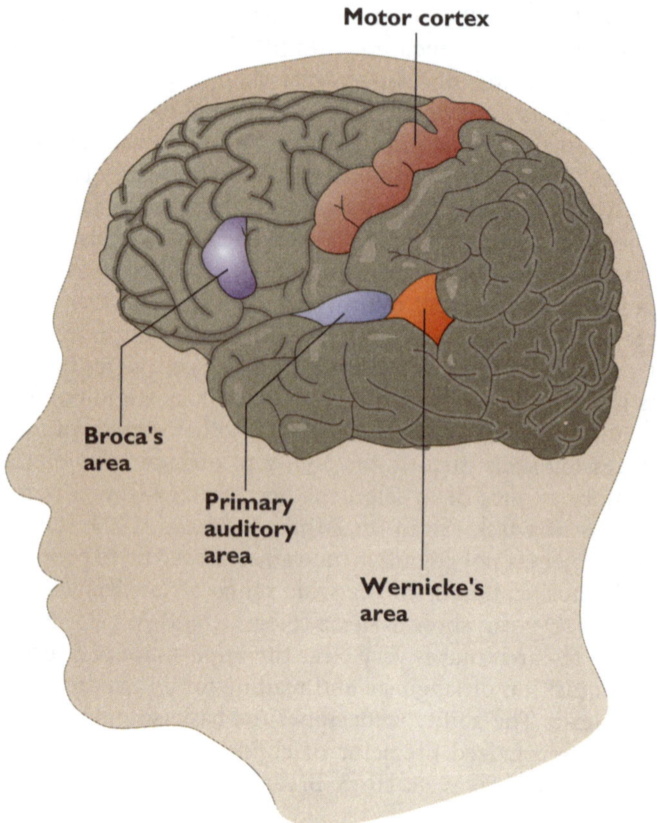

Recent advances in the ability to record electrical activity and blood flow in the brain have yielded further information on the brain's involvement in language. Before young children begin speaking, brain wave activity as they listen to words they comprehend is distributed across many regions of the brain. Once they start speaking, brain waves become more focused in the left hemisphere (Mills, Coffey-Corina, & Neville, 1993, 1994, 1997). In addition, children for whom fMRI data indicate left hemisphere damage at sixteen to twenty-four months of age show delayed language acquisition at age four years (Chilosi et al., 2001). Studies like these suggest that some (but not all) language processing is localized in the left hemisphere shortly after the first year. By the time children reach age seven years, patterns of brain activation indicate adultlike lateralization of language in the left hemisphere (Lee et al., 1999). Even deaf individuals learning sign language show brain activity in the left hemisphere similar to that of hearing individuals (Corina et al., 1999; McGuire et al., 1997).

Several other features of language acquisition suggest a strong biological component. Like motor milestones, language milestones are attained in a predictable sequence, regardless of the environment in which the child grows up (except for a few rare cases of extreme environmental deprivation). In addition, all languages share such features as phonology, semantics, and grammar, elements that Erik Lenneberg (1967) and others believed derive from the biologically determined capabilities of human beings. Indeed, children do seem to be driven to learn language, even in the absence of linguistic stimulation. One group of researchers studied a group of congenitally deaf preschool-age children who had not been taught sign language because parents were led to believe it would impede their ability to learn oral communication. None of them had learned to speak yet. Even so, the children had developed a unique gestural system of communication that followed the same sequence used by hearing children; that is, a one-symbol stage, followed by a two-symbol stage, and so forth (Feldman, Goldin-Meadow, & Gleitman, 1978). For these children, language literally "dripped" out of their fingers.

Critical Periods and Language Learning Lenneberg (1967) claimed that, to speak and comprehend normally, children must acquire all language basics by adolescence, when physiological changes in the brain make language learning more difficult. He thus proposed a *critical period* for the acquisition of language. A few rare case studies of children who have been isolated from social contact or linguistic experience for protracted periods support his position. One girl, Genie, had minimal human contact from age twenty months until thirteen years, due to isolation imposed by her parents. She did not speak at all. After she was found and received extensive therapy, Genie made some progress in learning words but never learned to speak normally, showing special difficulty in completely mastering the rules of syntax (Curtiss, 1977). Another nineteen-year-old boy from rural Mexico, deaf since birth but given hearing aids at age fifteen years, spoke only in one- or two-word utterances and had difficulties with verb tenses, negation, and other elements of syntax, despite three years of exposure to language (Grimshaw et al., 1998). Studies of deaf people who learned American Sign Language (ASL) at different times in life provide additional support for the critical-period hypothesis. Elissa Newport (1990) found that individuals who learned ASL after age twelve showed consistent errors in the use of grammar, whereas those who were exposed to ASL from birth displayed a normal course in the development of the language.

Lenneberg's hypothesis also implies that children will find it difficult to learn a second language if they begin during or after adolescence. Here, too, there is evidence to support his ideas. Jacqueline Johnson and Elissa Newport (1989) assessed the ability of Chinese and Korean immigrants who learned English as a second language to judge the grammatical correctness of more than 200 English sentences. Some participants started to learn English as early as age three, others not until age seventeen or later. The older they were before learning English, the poorer were their scores on the grammar test. Moreover, factors such as length of experience with English, amount of formal instruction in English, or identification with American culture could not account for the findings. Early exposure to a second language can also affect one's ability to pronounce it. One study found that, when individuals merely overheard Spanish before age six, they sounded more like native speakers when they went on to study Spanish as adults, as compared with individuals without that early experience (Au et al., 2002). Newport (1990) aptly summarizes findings like these by stating that "in language … the child, and not the adult, appears to be especially privileged as a learner" (p. 12).

Neuropsychological findings with bilingual speakers complement these findings. Participants in one study were Chinese adults who had acquired English as a second language at different points in their lifetime. While participants read sentences that were either correct or violated semantic or syntactic rules, the researchers monitored their brain wave activity. Brain wave patterns suggested that the age of second-language acquisition made a special difference for syntactic tasks; if English had been acquired after age four, electrical activity in the left hemisphere showed a different pattern than if English had been acquired earlier in childhood (Weber-Fox & Neville, 1996). In another study, magnetic resonance imaging was used to study patterns of brain activation as bilingual individuals performed linguistic tasks in their native and second languages. When the second language was learned in adulthood, images of brain functioning showed that two adjoining but separate regions in Broca's area were activated (see the left panel of Figure 11.10). In contrast, when the second language was learned during infancy, overlapping regions in Broca's area showed activity (see the right panel of Figure 11.10) (Kim et al., 1997). Thus the brain seems to respond, and perhaps become organized, differently depending on when the second language was learned.

Critics point to problems in interpreting some of the research cited in support of the critical-period hypothesis. Genie, for example, may have suffered serious cognitive, physiological, and emotional deficits because of her prolonged isolation from other humans, deficits that could well account for her lack of mature language. Furthermore, most studies of second-language learning, although controlling for many relevant variables, have not taken into account how much the later-learned second language is actually used (Bruer, 2001). One study showed that, even though they were learning English at age seventeen or later, the amount of English used by native Spanish speakers in speaking to others predicted their facility with English (Birdsong & Molis, 2001). Finally, some individuals who learn a second language in

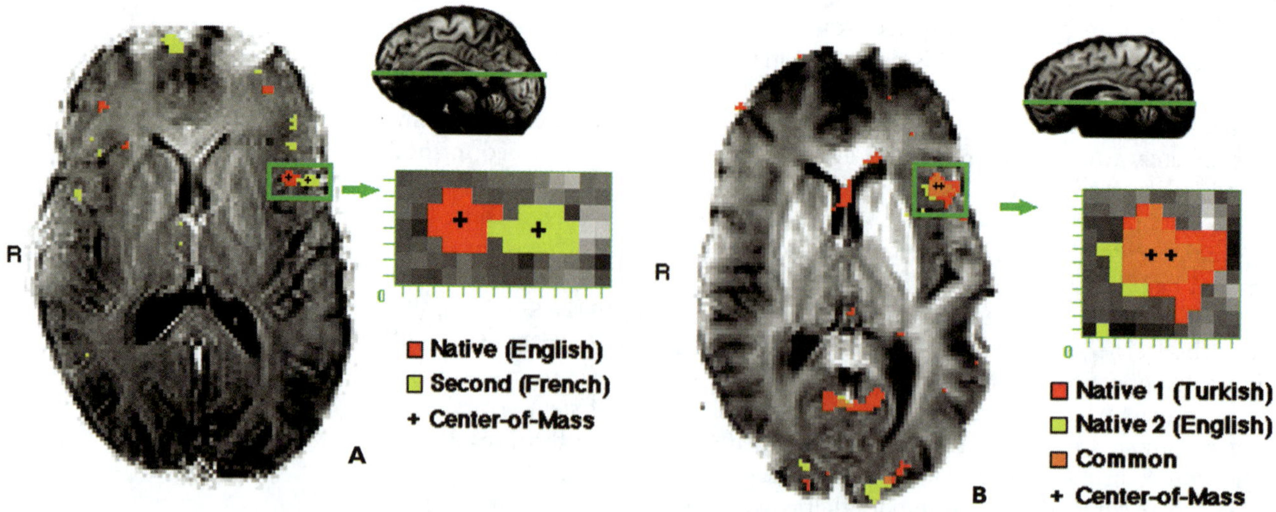

FIGURE 11.10

Brain Functioning in Bilingual Individuals

These two panels show activity patterns in the brains of two bilingual individuals as they engage in linguistic tasks in their native and second languages. The panel on the left shows brain activity for a native speaker of English who learned French in adulthood. Notice that two adjacent areas show activation. The panel on the right shows brain activity for a native speaker of Turkish who learned English in infancy. Here the areas activated for each language overlap. Neuropsychological findings like these provide support for the critical-period hypothesis of language acquisition.

Source: Kim et al. (1997).

adulthood acquire the phonology, vocabulary, and syntax of that language with nativelike proficiency (Birdsong & Molis, 2001; Bongaerts, 1999; Snow, 1987). Thus the window of opportunity for learning language may not be as restricted by biology as initially thought. Nonetheless, most experts would probably agree that children have a distinct advantage over adults in language learning, which makes early childhood an ideal time to acquire a second language.

Ample and convincing evidence exists for the role of biology in language acquisition—few would debate that claim. Yet a biological account, although necessary for a comprehensive understanding of language development, is not sufficient. The world's languages often differ, for example, in how they express ideas, some using patterns of intonation instead of words for a given concept (Maratsos, 1989). How would brain structures account for such cultural variations? In addition, knowing that biology is involved still does not reveal the details of many other aspects of language development that we reviewed in earlier chapters—children's early facility with nouns in one culture versus verbs in others, for example. In other words, we need to be able to explain how the language environment to which the child is exposed feeds into whatever biological language structures exist.

The Functions of Language

Key Theme
Interaction Among Domains

Aside from its obvious usefulness as a social communication tool, what other functions does language serve? Does the human propensity to learn and employ language affect other aspects of functioning, specifically, mental processes, the regulation of behavior, and socialization? At the very least, language enriches the human experience by providing a useful vehicle for enhancing cognition and behavior; it also exerts powerful influences on other areas of human activity. In this section, we will examine briefly some broad effects of language on the domains of cognition, behavior, and socialization.

Language and Cognition The relationship between language and cognition has been a controversial subject for many years, especially with respect to which activity precedes the other. Some psychologists and anthropologists have argued that language shapes thinking, whereas others contend that cognition paves the way for language. Most now acknowledge that the link between language and cognition is bidirectional and that each domain influences the other. How exactly might language have a powerful influence on the child's cognitive attainments?

If you ask a child to perform a cognitive task, such as remembering a list of words or grouping a set of similar objects, you will notice that he will often spontaneously use language to aid his performance. The best examples of this behavior come from research findings on developmental changes in children's memory. We have seen earlier in this chapter that there are distinct differences in the way preschool and school-age children approach the task of remembering. Older children are far more likely than younger children to employ deliberate strategies for remembering, strategies that typically involve the use of verbal skills (Flavell, Beach, & Chinsky, 1966). The use of verbal labels seemed to bridge the gap between the time the items were first seen and the time they were to be recalled.

Language can also influence how children categorize related groups of objects. Stan Kuczaj and his colleagues showed children twelve unfamiliar objects that could be grouped into three sets (Kuczaj, Borys, & Jones, 1989). Children who were taught the names of one category member from each group were more successful in sorting the objects than children who were not given labels. Language provides children with cues that classes of stimuli differ from one another, and these cues can influence how children form conceptual groups. If some four-legged animals are called dogs and others are called cats, the different linguistic labels will highlight for the child that the features of these two groups differ.

Bilingualism and Cognition One of the more interesting ways in which the influence of language on thought has been studied has been to compare, on a variety of tasks, the performances of bilingual children equally fluent in two languages with monolinguals fluent in only one. Bilingual children have been characterized as more analytic and flexible in their approach to different types of thought problems. For example, bilingual children perform better than monolinguals on certain nonverbal problems, such as the Raven Progressive Matrices (see Figure 11.11) (Hakuta & Diaz, 1985). Bilingual children have also been found to display greater metalinguistic awareness than monolingual children, even those who are chronologically older. When given sentences like "Why is the cat barking so loudly?" bilingual children were more likely than monolingual children to ignore conflicting semantic information and state that the sentences were grammatically correct (Bialystok, 1986). Finally, bilingual children perform better than monolingual children on tasks that require selective attention. If instructed to sort a deck of cards based on one dimension—say, color—and then re-sort the deck on the basis of a different dimension, shape, bilingual children are better able to inhibit responses from the first task (Bialystok, 2001; Bialystok & Martin, 2004).

One hypothesis to explain their superior performance is that bilingual children are forced to think more abstractly and analytically because they have had experience with analyzing the structure and detail of not just one language but two. A second possibility is that they are generally more verbally oriented in their thinking and have a greater tendency to produce verbalizations that enhance their performance even in

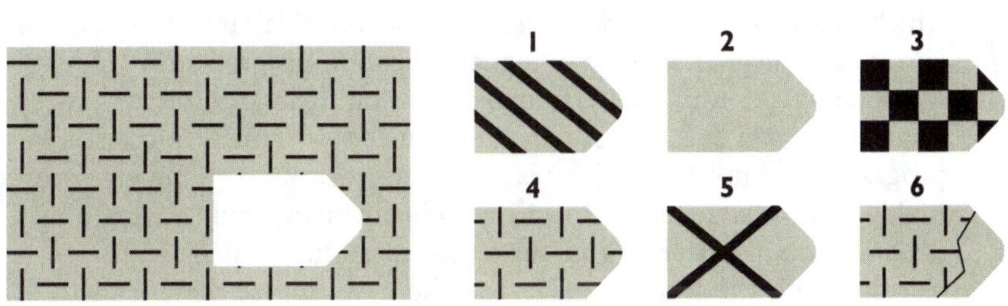

FIGURE 11.11

Cognitive Achievements of Bilingual and Monolingual Children

Bilingual children outperform monolingual children on nonverbal tasks, such as the Raven Progressive Matrices, which requires participants to select the segment that correctly fits into the larger pattern. Bilingual children generally seem to be more analytical than monolingual children in their approach to various problem-solving tasks.

Source: Raven (1962).

KEY THEME
INTERACTION AMONG DOMAINS

nonverbal tasks. Finally, they may have more control over cognitive processing because they are constantly having to inhibit one language when they speak (Bialystok, 1999, 2001; Diaz & Klingler, 1991). Whatever the mechanism, these studies demonstrate that speaking a second language affects cognitive processes, often in a favorable way.

CONTROVERSY: THINKING IT OVER

How Should Bilingual Education Programs Be Structured?

Estimates are that almost 10 percent of school-age children in the United States have limited English proficiency (National Clearinghouse for English Language Acquisition, 2002), a characteristic that could understandably hinder success in school. Given the ease with which young children learn language and the apparent connection between bilingualism and certain cognitive processes, are there any implications for how children learning English as a second language should be taught?

What Is the Controversy?

Philosophies of teaching language-minority children have varied. Some believe that children should receive most of their education in their primary language, whether it is Spanish, Cambodian, or French, and make the transition to English only when they are ready. At the other extreme are the advocates of immersion, the idea that children should be totally surrounded by the second language, learning it in the same way the young child learns the first language. Immersion has been in the public spotlight as states such as California and Massachusetts have mandated this approach to teaching children with limited English proficiency. Many bilingual programs, in reality, fall between these two extremes, such that English is taught as an extra subject by a bilingual teacher while children take their core academic subjects in their native language.

What Are the Opposing Arguments?

Proponents of easing children into English by starting them in classes in their native language say that this approach promotes basic language development, which in turn creates the foundation for acquiring the second language. In addition, children will develop a sense of belonging in the school, and their self-esteem will be high (Fillmore & Meyer, 1992). Advocates of immersion generally say that children will have to learn English eventually and that it is better not to delay. This view is also consistent with a belief that language learning is generally easier for younger than for older children.

What Answers Exist? What Questions Remain?

Some research findings suggest that allowing students to build their competence in their own native language assists in learning both core academic subjects and English (Bialystok, 2001; Meyer & Fienberg, 1992). On the other hand, immersion programs have been successful in Canada, Spain, and other countries (Artigal, 1991; Tucker & d'Anglejan, 1972). Unfortunately, evaluations of the effectiveness of bilingual education programs have been fraught with methodological difficulties (Willig & Ramirez, 1993). One issue is that many language-minority children come from a background of poverty, the effects of which may contribute to difficulties with school (Hakuta, 1999). Another problem is that the goal of most bilingual education programs for language-minority children is not, in reality, to make them bilingual but to emphasize speaking English (Hakuta & Mostafapour, 1996). In contrast, many successful immersion programs in Europe involve teaching both the native language and another highly valued language (Brisk, 1998). Finally, many children learning a second language are also learning about a second culture. Their degree of success in learning both the new language and the new culture may depend, at least in part, on how their culture of origin is viewed: is it valued or is there discrimination against it? In other words, learning a second language often takes place against a backdrop of complex social factors that are just as important to consider as the elements of linguistic development (Snow & Kang, 2006).

What does the research on the process of language development suggest about the best way to structure bilingual education programs? Aside from economic status, what other variables should future research evaluating bilingual education take into account?

Language and Self-Regulation Language takes on an increasingly important role in regulating behavior as the child develops, according to prominent Russian psychologist Lev Vygotsky. Vygotsky (1962) believed the child's initial utterances during infancy serve an interpersonal function, signaling others about the child's affective state. In the preschool years, however, speech takes on a different function. Specifically, the child's **private speech**, or overt, audible "speech-for-self," comes to guide his or her observable activities. If you have ever observed a toddler coloring and simultaneously saying something like "Now, I'll use the blue crayon. I'll make the sky blue," you have seen an example of private speech. Eventually, speech-for-self becomes interiorized; **inner speech** dictates the direction of the child's thoughts. Research has confirmed that audible private speech declines during middle childhood, but talking to one's self covertly increases (Winsler & Naglieri, 2003).

How important is private speech in directing behavior? You may have noticed that you tend to talk to yourself when you are under stress or when you have a lot to do. Research has confirmed that children, like adults, use private speech when they find tasks difficult or when they make errors. In one study, researchers found that about 13 percent of three and four-year-olds used private speech in some way during their spontaneous activities in preschool, but as Figure 11.12 shows, the older children were more likely to use private speech in the context of focused, goal-directed activities, such as doing a puzzle, rather than for nongoal-directed activities, such as wandering around the classroom (Winsler, Carlton, & Barry, 2000).

Similarly, Laura Berk (1986) noted that, when first-graders were solving math problems in school, they engaged in high levels of externalized private speech to guide their problem solving. Third-graders also showed evidence of private speech, but a more internalized form—through mutterings and lip movements—as they attempted to solve math problems. When children use task-relevant private speech, their performance on a variety of tasks improves (Berk, 1992). One longitudinal

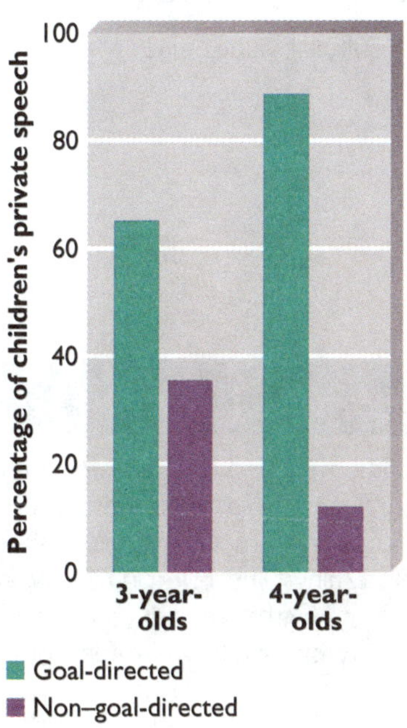

FIGURE 11.12

Private Speech in Young Children

Both three- and four-year-olds use private speech in the natural context of preschool, but older children are more likely to use private speech when they are engaged in focused, goal-directed activities. Private speech is one way in which language can regulate children's behaviors.

Source: Winsler, Carlton, & Barry (2000).

private speech Children's vocalized speech to themselves that directs behavior.

inner speech Interiorized form of private speech.

study demonstrated that, as children progress from overt to more internal private speech, they also show fewer distracting body movements and greater sustained attention in school (Bivens & Berk, 1990). Such studies suggest that language becomes an increasingly powerful regulator of children's behavior as they develop.

KEY THEME
SOCIOCULTURAL INFLUENCE

Language and Cultural Socialization Still another way in which language can have a broad influence on development is by helping children discern the social roles, relationships, and values of their culture. Many languages have specific grammatical forms that are used to convey gender, age, or social power. In acquiring language, children are sensitized to the specific ways their own culture creates social order. For example, in Japanese, the word particle *zo* signifies affective intensity and a male speaker, and the particle *wa* conveys hesitancy and a female speaker. Children learning Japanese are therefore likely to associate hesitancy with females and forcefulness with males (Ochs, 1990). In many other languages, specific words have formal and informal versions, with the formal used when speaking with individuals who have more authority or power and the informal with individuals who share equal status or are related. Again, such linguistic distinctions highlight important social relationships within the cultural group.

A good example of how language can influence socialization comes from traditional Samoan culture, which emphasizes community and group accomplishments over the attainments of individuals. In Samoan speech, few verbalizations include praise or blame for individuals. Most statements concern the success or failure of the group and emphasize the life of the community. When Samoan children are exposed to verbalizations of this type, they are being socialized into the collective orientation of their culture (Ochs, 1990).

Researchers are just beginning to explore the ways in which the words and social conventions within a specific language are related to cultural values and beliefs. However, it is apparent that, through language, children learn far more than simply how to communicate; they also learn about the broader belief systems of their society.

FOR • YOUR • REVIEW

- What are some examples of children's metalinguistic awareness?
- What have neuropsychological studies revealed about the involvement of the brain in language acquisition?
- In what ways does language influence cognitive processing? What are the particular effects of bilingualism on cognition?
- What are the functions of private speech for the developing child?
- In what ways does language provide cues about cultural values and socialization goals?

CHAPTER RECAP

Summary of Developmental Themes

NATURE & NURTURE

How do nature and nurture interact in physical, cognitive, and language development in middle childhood?

As we have seen before, in Piaget's theory, maturation, in conjunction with experience, is responsible for the child's cognitive growth. Sociocultural theories and the research they have generated point to the influence of parents and teachers as important guides in how children learn such cognitive skills as planning and transfer of learning. The role of biology in language development is illustrated by the fact that certain portions of the brain are devoted to specific language functions.

SOCIOCULTURAL INFLUENCE

How does the sociocultural context influence physical, cognitive, and language development in middle childhood?

According to Vygotsky, cultural beliefs and values are transmitted to children through the scaffolding provided by experts. In the domain of language development, the content and structure of language often provide cues about the culture's social order and values.

CONTINUITY/DISCONTINUITY

Are cognition and language development during middle childhood continuous or discontinuous?

Piaget stressed stagelike attainments as the child progresses from preoperational to concrete operational thought. However, information-processing theorists suggest that changes in such cognitive skills as attention and memory arise from successive increments, not qualitative, stagelike changes.

INTERACTION AMONG DOMAINS

How do physical, cognitive, and language development interact with other domains in middle childhood?

Social interactions with parents, teachers, and others form the basis for cognitive development within a given cultural context. For language development, we have seen that bilingualism may have an impact on such cognitive functions as analytic thinking and mental flexibility.

Chapter Review

PHYSICAL DEVELOPMENT IN MIDDLE CHILDHOOD

What kinds of improvements in motor skills are observed during the middle school years?

Children become more adept at fine-motor coordination and show more controlled, coordinated, and complex motor movements.

What is a secular trend?

A *secular trend* refers to a change in some aspect of development that occurs across generations. Height is an example of a secular trend, in that today's children grow faster and taller than in previous generations.

What are the concerns about short stature and obesity in many cultures?

Children, especially boys, prefer being tall, but little evidence exists to indicate that those who develop normally but are constitutionally small are seriously disadvantaged. Nevertheless, parents of children with short stature may request synthetic growth hormone despite lack of evidence that it provides long-term gains in height. Being overweight typically has negative connotations in today's society. Overweight children have more negative interactions with parents and peers, and may display low self-esteem.

What factors may be contributing to the increase in obesity observed in many Western nations?

The numbers of children who are obese have increased dramatically over the past several decades, in part because of a more sedentary lifestyle as well as increasing availability of calorie-laden convenience foods and drinks.

COGNITION AND MIDDLE CHILDHOOD: PIAGET'S THEORY

What are the major features of thinking in the concrete operational stage?

The *concrete operational stage* is characterized by logical thought but only in the presence of real objects or images. Because children are capable of performing *operations*, they are successful in increasingly difficult conservation tasks, as well as seriation tasks.

What are Piaget's ideas about concepts of causality during the middle childhood years?

Piaget claims that children may show *animism* and *artificialism* up until even ten years of age. However, when children are asked direct questions about the causes of things, they show a more mature understanding of causality than Piaget acknowledged.

What are the implications of Piaget's theory for education?

Piaget's theory implied that teachers must take into account the child's current stage of development and supply activities consistent with his or her capabilities. Teachers should also be aware of the individual child's current state of knowledge, so that new material can be readily assimilated. Piagetian theory supports the active role of the child in the educational process.

Cognition and Middle Childhood: The Information-Processing Approach

What are the major differences between multistore and limited-resource models of information processing? How do they differ in accounting for developmental changes in cognition?

Multistore models include such structures as the *sensory register*, *working memory*, and *long-term memory*, as well as control processes, such as rehearsal. Developmental changes are due largely to increased use of control processes to move information from one part of the system to another. *Limited-resource models* describe tradeoffs between energy used to operate on stimuli and the capacity left over for storage. Developmental change is characterized in terms of increased cognitive efficiency.

What is selective attention? How does it change by the time a child gets to the early school years?

As children grow older, they are better able to select certain aspects of the environment to attend to. Physiological maturation and the child's increasing control over cognitive processing are responsible for these changes.

What is ADHD? What factors may be responsible for its occurrence?

ADHD is a developmental disorder linked to problems of attention. Problems with executive control and allocating resources in working memory are thought to underlie this disorder.

What have memory span and free recall studies told us about age changes in memory performance?

From preschool to preadolescence, children show an increase in *memory span*, the number of items that can be recalled after a brief period of time. Changes in *processing speed*, the rapidity with which cognitive activities can be carried out, contribute to this increase. Children participating in free-recall tasks typically show *primacy* and *recency effects*. The former refers to elevated recall at the beginning of the list and reflects rehearsal. The latter refers to good recall for the last few items in a list.

What factors are primarily responsible for developmental improvements in recall memory?

As children progress through the school years, they show an increase in the deliberate production of *memory strategies* for both encoding and retrieval. Among these are *rehearsal* (repeating items), *organization* (reordering items on the basis of higher-order relationships), and *elaboration* (linking items in an image or sentence). Improvements in memory are tied to the child's increasing control over his or her cognitive processing. One aspect of cognitive control is *metamemory*, the child's understanding of memory as a process. Improvements in cognitive inhibition and reliance on the gist of an event are also part of memory development.

What are the major ways in which children show changes in problem-solving skills as they develop?

With development, children are better able to plan the steps in problem solving. They also become more flexible in their strategy use.

What factors encourage children to transfer skills from one situation to another?

An important factor that can influence the likelihood of transfer is making the parallels between problems more obvious to children. Similar skills should be taught in a variety of contexts, information should be presented to children in an organized fashion, and tests should assess the ability to apply already-learned information in new situations.

What basic forms of mathematical reasoning do children display in the early school years?

Young children display good intuitions about mathematical operations such as addition and forming fractions. These understandings can form the basis for mathematical instruction.

Cognition and Middle Childhood: Vygotsky and the Sociocultural Context of Learning

How do the processes of scaffolding and guided participation contribute to cognitive development according to Vygotsky?

Novice learners often get more scaffolding from experts, but as their skills improve, that support is gradually withdrawn. This process is called guided participation. Tutors often work within the child's *zone of proximal development*, the distance between what the child can do alone and what she can do with guidance.

What do research findings tell us about the role of skilled collaborators in promoting children's cognitive advances?

Research shows that adults play a critical role in the transmission of skills, probably because they encourage children to be active and think out loud. Some communities afford children more opportunities for guided participation than others, especially when the children are routinely in the company of adults.

Language in Middle Childhood

What are some examples of children's metalinguistic awareness?

Examples of *metalinguistic awareness* include the ability to create humor and showing an understanding of *metaphor*.

What have neuropsychological studies revealed about the involvement of the brain in language acquisition?

Specific brain structures are associated with *expressive aphasia* (*Broca's area*) and *receptive aphasia* (*Wernicke's area*). Children sustaining damage to these areas show a greater ability to recover language functions than adults do. Neuropsychological studies suggest that language functions begin to become lateralized shortly after the first year and look adult-like by age seven. The predictability of language milestones and the universality of certain language structures also support the role of biology. Research on later language learners and neuropsychological evidence support a critical period for language learning, although not a strong version of it.

In what ways does language influence cognitive processing? What are the particular effects of bilingualism on cognition?

Language has been shown to influence specific cognitive processes, such as memory and classification. Bilingual children are more flexible and analytic in certain cognitive tasks. They also perform better than monolingual children on tasks that require response inhibition.

What are the functions of private speech for the developing child?

Children often use *private speech* and, later, *inner speech*, to direct their behavior. They tend to use private speech when tasks are difficult or goal directed.

In what ways does language provide cues about cultural values and socialization goals?

Language can be a vehicle to transmit to children the specific values and expectations of their native culture through formal and informal versions of words, gender categories of words, and even the specific words that are included (or not included) in the language.

Key Terms and Concepts

animism (p. 384)
artificialism (p. 384)
Broca's area (p. 403)
concrete operational stage (p. 383)
elaboration (p. 391)
expressive aphasia (p. 403)
inner speech (p. 409)
limited-resource model (p. 385)
long-term memory (p. 385)
memory span (p. 388)
memory strategy (p. 391)
metalinguistic awareness (p. 401)
metamemory (p. 392)
metaphor (p. 402)
multistore model (p. 385)
operation (p. 383)
organization (p. 391)
primacy effect (p. 391)
private speech (p. 409)
processing speed (p. 391)
recency effect (p. 391)
receptive aphasia (p. 403)
rehearsal (p. 391)
secular trend (p. 379)
sensory register (p. 385)
Wernicke's area (p. 403)
working memory (p. 385)
zone of proximal development (p. 399)

12 Social and Emotional Development

Michael had just finished his math assignment when he heard the door slam. Then he heard the loud, angry voice. "Kids today!" his grandfather fumed to no one in particular. "A couple of 'em almost ran me down on the sidewalk. Didn't bother to apologize. One even yelled, 'Get out of my way!' as she chased after her friends. Kids don't respect anybody, not even themselves—wearing those weird clothes, dying their hair every color you can think of, poking holes in their ears, even their noses! I suppose if I had stopped 'em, they'd have taken a swing at me or even worse. ..." His voice trailed off to a mutter.

Michael had heard such tirades before: how the world has changed, how children today don't know right from wrong. Michael also worried about reports on the news: the first-grader who punched his teacher, the large number of sixth-graders who felt cheating was okay. Did his grandfather have a valid point? But he also thought about the fund raiser he and his friends had held to help hurricane victims whose homes and neighborhoods had been destroyed in the

KEY THEMES in Social and Emotional Development

NATURE & NURTURE How do nature and nurture interact in social and emotional development in middle childhood?

SOCIOCULTURAL INFLUENCE How does the sociocultural context influence social and emotional development in middle childhood?

CONTINUITY/DISCONTINUITY Are social and emotional development in middle childhood continuous or discontinuous?

INTERACTION AMONG DOMAINS How do social and emotional development in middle childhood interact with other domains?

RISK/RESILIENCE What factors promote risk or resilience in social and emotional development during middle childhood?

southern part of the country. Collecting bottles and cans from the school cafeteria, as well as those brought by community members to a drop-off spot at school, they had managed to raise over $500 to send to a relief agency. It made him feel good to be able to do even such a small thing to help people in that devastated region. "Grandpa," he now said, hoping to placate his grandfather, "Don't worry. Next time you go out for a walk, I'll go with you. Now would you like me to make you a cup of hot tea?"

To instill in children a sense of satisfaction with who they are and recognition of the standards of conduct considered acceptable and ethical within their community are among the most important goals of society. We expect children and adults to take pride in their accomplishments, learn to judge right from wrong, and refrain from actions that harm family, friends, or neighbors. Broadly speaking, survival in a social community depends on helping, cooperation, and sharing, behaviors that benefit others. Children display an awareness of self and the consequences of their conduct, both good and bad, early on, but these understandings undergo noticeable changes in the middle school years.

Michael's grandfather believes his generation has witnessed a decline in a positive sense of self and in courtesy and concern for others. Although one might debate whether such a change has actually taken place, the concerns voiced by Michael's grandfather are not new. Philosophers, theologians, and scientists have argued for decades about whether human nature is good or evil and whether experience serves to channel children's inborn tendencies in either direction. In this sense, the interaction of nature and nurture remains embedded in contemporary discussions of the roots of self, moral behavior, and values. In this chapter, we look first at the continuing course of emotional development in middle childhood. We next examine self-identity, self-esteem, and self-regulation. We spend a good portion of this chapter examining several theories of moral development and how society promotes the development of prosocial values. Finally, we revisit the topic of gender-role development to highlight its main features in middle childhood.

EMOTIONAL DEVELOPMENT IN MIDDLE CHILDHOOD

There are two main aspects to emotional development in middle childhood: continuing growth of children's knowledge about the emotions themselves and progress in the management of their own emotional states. Researchers increasingly recognize the integral role that emotions play in communication and the social interactions that children have with adults and with their peers. At the core of successful social development is the ability to make judgments about the emotions displayed by others as well as the emotions one decides to display oneself.

During middle childhood, children learn the rules that their culture prescribes for the display of emotions. In many cultures, for example, children learn that they should exhibit happiness when they receive a gift.

Knowledge About Emotions

Much of what we know about emotional development in middle childhood has to do with how children think and reason about emotions. Between about ages eight and ten, for example, many children understand the emotional behaviors prescribed by cultural rules (you are supposed to look happy when you receive a gift even if you don't like it) and the behaviors necessary to obtain certain goals (you should smile even if you don't feel well if you want your mother to allow you to go to a friend's party). In such cases, the individual masks or "fakes" an emotional state. Paul Harris and his associates (Harris et al., 1986) examined this skill in using emotional **display rules**, the cultural guidelines governing when and how to express emotions, by asking six- and ten-year-olds to listen to stories in which the central character felt either a positive or a negative emotion but had to hide it. After hearing the story, children were asked to describe verbally the facial expression of the protagonist, along with how this person really felt. Even six-year-olds could state that the emotion displayed would not match the emotion felt, although ten-year-olds provided a fuller explanation. These results suggest that, by the middle school years, children have developed a broad understanding of the social norms and expectations that surround the display of feelings.

Knowledge about emotions can have significant ramifications for the child's social development. For example, five-year-old children who are able to correctly label facial expressions of emotions are more likely to display positive social behaviors at age nine (Izard et al., 2001). Moreover, children who have substantial knowledge about the emotions have higher scores on tests of moral development, are less likely to evidence behavior problems, and are better liked by their peers (Cook, Greenberg, & Kusche, 1994; Denham et al., 1990; Dunn, Brown, & Maguire, 1995). The reason may be that children who have greater knowledge about emotions are more likely to respond appropriately to the emotional expressions of their agemates—they have greater social skills (Mostow et al., 2002).

Key Theme
Nature & Nurture

Knowledge about emotions is probably gleaned, at least in part, from parents. Children who have greater knowledge about emotions—who can label emotional expressions on faces, describe the feelings of another person in an emotion-related situation, and talk about the causes of emotions—typically have mothers who discuss and explain emotions, often in the context of the child's expressing a negative emotion himself. In other words, these mothers are good "emotion coaches." On the other hand, when parents display more negative affect themselves or dismiss children's experiences of emotions ("You're overreacting!"), children's understanding of emotions is poorer and they are less socially competent (Denham et al., 1997; Dunn & Brown, 1994; Laible & Thompson, 2002). Parents who engage in such behaviors are probably missing opportunities to explain to their children the important elements of emotional responding. The extreme case is represented by children who are physically abused or neglected by their parents. These children have noticeable deficits in their ability to identify the emotional expressions that correspond to particular situations, such as going to the zoo and getting a balloon or losing a pet dog to disease. Physically abused children, perhaps not surprisingly, have a bias toward selecting angry expressions no matter what the context (Pollak et al., 2000).

Key Theme
Risk/Resilience

Key Theme
Interaction Among Domains

display rule Cultural guideline concerning when, how, and to what degree to display emotions.

Emotional development is closely affiliated with advances in cognition that allow children to think in more complex, abstract terms. By the time they enter school, children begin to understand that changes in thoughts may lead to changes in feelings—that thinking happier thoughts, for example, might make a sad mood go away (Weiner & Handel, 1985). In addition, they comprehend the possibility of experiencing two contrasting emotions at the same time, such as feeling happy at receiving a gift but disappointed that it cannot yet be opened (Brown & Dunn, 1996). As children approach adolescence, their concepts of emotions center increasingly on internal psychological states. In other words, whereas younger children identify their own emotional states based on the situations they are in ("I'm happy when it's my birthday"), older children refer more frequently to their mental state ("I'm happy when I feel good inside") (Harris, Olthof, & Meerum Terwogt, 1981).

REGULATING EMOTIONS

In addition to becoming more adept at understanding various emotions, during the middle childhood years children generally become better able to regulate their own emotional states. Part of the process of enacting display rules—to smile even when a gift is not exactly what one wanted—depends on the capacity to control one's actions (Kieras et al., 2005). These behaviors, as well as others, such as calming down after getting angry, have important repercussions for the child's social relationships and perhaps even mental health in the United States, China, and probably many other cultures (Cicchetti, Ackerman, & Izard, 1995; Zhou et al., 2004). In fact, much of the development of emotion that we have described in this book—expressing, recognizing, and understanding emotions, as well as socialization experiences regarding emotions—culminates in the ability to regulate one's affective state (Denham, 1998).

KEY THEME
RISK/RESILIENCE

The way children learn to manage their emotions depends, at least in part, on the kinds of experiences their parents provide (for example, do parents provide opportunities for children to become aroused or to calm down?), as well as what children learn are the consequences of their own emotional displays (what happened when I had an angry tantrum versus when I "used my words"?). When parents become distressed at their children's displays of negative emotions and punish them, children later tend to express more anger and hostility, and have more behavior problems and poorer social functioning in school (Eisenberg, Fabes, et al., 1999; Fabes, Leonard, et al., 2001). On the other hand, when parents provide supportive coaching and guidance for children's expression of emotion—by helping children talk about how they feel and suggesting ways of dealing with their emotions—children are better able to soothe themselves and moderate their negative emotions (Gottman, Katz, & Hooven, 1997). The general emotional tone of interactions with parents may play a role, too. Nancy Eisenberg and her colleagues have found that mothers who were more positive in their emotional expressivity, in contrast to mothers who generally expressed negative emotions, had children who were better able to regulate their own emotions. The children of more negative mothers, in turn, behaved more aggressively and were rated as less socially competent by parents and teachers (Eisenberg, Gershoff, et al., 2001; Eisenberg, Valiente, et al., 2003).

It is important to remember that all of these findings need to be considered within the context of the child's temperament style. Some children tend to be more impulsive and quick to react than others, qualities that are related to their greater emotional expressiveness. Other children are cautious and deliberate, and more likely to hide their feelings. Parental behaviors can both shape and be a reaction to their children's tendencies (Eisenberg, Zhou, et al., 2003), yet another manifestation of the complex ways in which developmental outcomes are influenced by dynamic, mutually influential interactions. Recent longitudinal evidence suggests, though, that the sequence of events that seems to make the most sense given the data is parental warmth, followed by children's emotion regulation, and then fewer behavior problems as rated by parents and teachers (Eisenberg et al., 2005). In terms of emotion regulation, with development, too, children probably become more aware of their own emotional styles and seek out experiences that are compatible with their needs; some children may learn that sitting alone and playing is soothing, whereas others may seek the emotional release of a fast-paced basketball game (Thompson, 1994).

New research indicates that children's increasing ability to regulate behaviors, and emotions in particular, is accompanied by distinct changes in how the brain functions. In one study, children played a computer game in which they were required

FIGURE 12.1

Brain Areas Associated with Inhibition

Recent fMRI studies have shown that children display elevated activation in the prefrontal cortex and the parietal lobes when they are involved in tasks that require them to inhibit a response. Adults show less dramatic levels of activation in these brain areas.

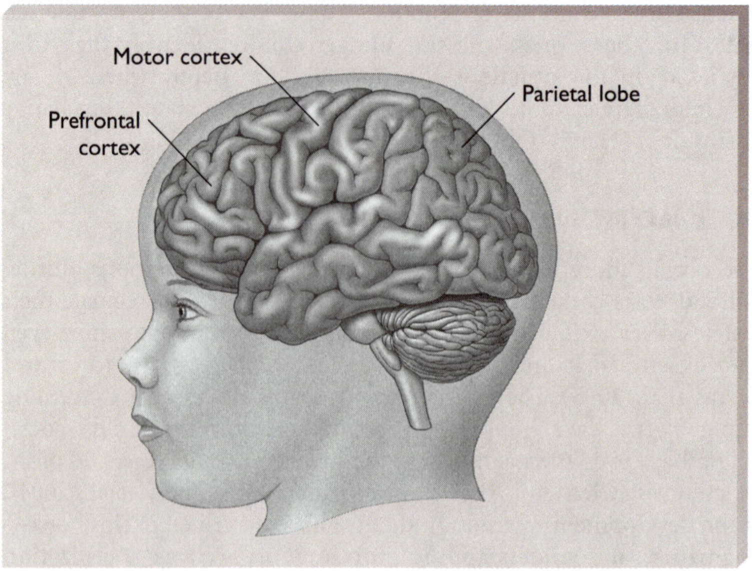

to press a button when certain target stimuli appeared on the screen, but not to press when a nontarget showed up. In this case, children were told, "Catch all the Pokemon except for Meowth." Brain scans (fMRI) obtained while children played this game revealed that there was pronounced activation of the prefrontal and parietal regions of the brain when responses had to be inhibited (see Figure 12.1), much more so than was observed when adults played the same game (Durston et al., 2002). Other researchers have focused on changes in electrophysiological responding of regions of the brain involved in the inhibition and control of behaviors. When children played a computer game in which they suddenly and briefly lost all of the "points" they had earned (and thus experienced a negative emotion), areas of the prefrontal cortex showed particular patterns of electrophysiological activity. For older children, those physiological responses were quicker, less dramatic, and more localized in the prefrontal regions, a pattern suggesting that development of emotion regulation corresponds to greater neural efficiency in specific regions of the brain (Lewis et al., 2006).

CULTURAL DIFFERENCES IN EMOTIONS

KEY THEME
SOCIOCULTURAL INFLUENCE

The tendency of children to express and detect emotions varies as a function of the culture in which they are raised. American children, for example, tend to smile more than Chinese children as early as infancy (Camras et al., 1998). On the other end of the emotional spectrum, Chinese children are better able to identify fearful and sad situations than are American children, and they cry less (Borke, 1973; Camras et al., 1998). These differences may reflect the child's incorporation of particular cultural beliefs about emotions.

A study of two different cultural groups in rural Nepal further illustrates this concept. Pamela Cole and her colleagues (Cole, Bruschi, & Tamang, 2002) studied children in two small villages, each comprising a different ethnic group—one Brahmin and the other Tamang. The Brahmins subscribe to a caste system in which strict rules dictate which social groups may interact. They are very oriented to status differences and the power of authority, and they have a great deal of pride in their own ethic group. The Tamang, on the other hand, place great value on community rather than on the individuals within the group. Resources are shared, and important decisions are made by consulting all group members, in accordance with their Buddhist values of selflessness. How do school-age children in these two very different cultures express emotions? All children were asked to react to scenarios likely to lead to an emotional reaction, such as having a friend snatch away a piece of candy or watching as a parent spills tea all over homework papers. Brahmin children, although they expected to feel anger in such situations, clearly stated that anger should not be expressed, primarily because authority needed to be respected and group orderliness preserved. Tamang children, in contrast, did not express anger; rather, they reported a feeling of *thiken*, or making the mind calm, in accordance with their Buddhist beliefs. American children, also participants in this study, endorsed anger as an appropriate response. This belief is consistent with the value we place on self-assertion and independence in our culture (Cole et al., 2002).

Cultural belief systems extend even to the kinds of temperamental styles that are valued within a particular society. A good example is the dimension of shyness and inhibition. In European-heritage families, shyness is often seen as a liability; instead, children are expected to be outgoing, sociable, and eager to interact with the environment. In Chinese society, however, shyness has traditionally been a valued trait. Parents and teachers believe that shy children are well behaved, and as testimony to that belief, shy children in China assessed up until just a few years ago expressed positive views of themselves (Chen, Rubin, & Li, 1997; Chen et al., 1999). In an interesting example of how historical forces interact with culture, though, a more contemporary sample of urban Chinese children showed links between shyness and academic, social, and behavioral problems (Chen et al., 2005). Even long-standing cultural values are not immune to the influences of an increasingly global and interconnected world.

Why is it important to recognize cultural differences in the values placed on various emotions? Simply put, cultural beliefs are likely to be expressed in the socialization practices that parents and others employ as they respond to the child's emotional displays.

FOR • YOUR • REVIEW

- What kinds of knowledge do children acquire about emotions during middle childhood?
- What factors influence children's acquisition of knowledge about emotions?
- What factors are involved in children's increasing ability to regulate emotions?
- How does culture play a role in emotional development?

THE DEVELOPMENT OF SELF IN MIDDLE CHILDHOOD

"I know how."
"Look! See what I did!"
"I'm smart."
"I'm stronger than you!"
"I'm really good at this!"

These declarations express in no uncertain terms what children believe they can do, what they think they are like, and how they feel about their abilities. The statements reveal the school-age child's awareness of self. How does this understanding of self—as someone who is an independent, unique person, able to reflect on his or her own beliefs and characteristics—develop?

To answer this question, it will be useful to adopt a distinction first offered by William James (1892) more than a century ago. The distinction continues to be every bit as useful today (Harter, 1999). For James, there were two components of self: the "me," or *objective self*, and the "I," or *subjective self*. James's objective, or the "me" aspect of self, is often called *self-concept*. An individual's self-concept includes an understanding of his or her physical qualities, possessions and status, skills, and psychological characteristics, including personality, beliefs, and value systems. To a large extent, many of the developments we have described up to middle childhood reflect acquisitions in this objective self.

The "I," or the subjective component, is made up of several key realizations about the self: (1) I can be an agent of change and can control events in my life (sense of autonomy); (2) my experiences are unique and accessible to no one else in exactly the same way (sense of individuality); (3) my past, present, and future are continuous (sense of stability); and (4) I can reflect on—that is, think about—my self (sense of reflection, or self-consciousness). We see progress in all of these aspects of self during the period of middle childhood.

THE CONCEPT OF SELF

When children reach about seven years of age, a new element enters their self-descriptions. Whereas younger children describe themselves in terms of typical physical characteristics and activities ("I run fast"), older children begin to make relational statements. For example, in response to the question "Who are you?" a fifth-grader might say, "I can run faster than anyone else in my class," "I'm not as pretty as my older sister," or "Other kids in my class are better than I am at math." In other words, instead of itemizing their skills, actions, or social and psychological qualities, they compare their qualities with those of others (Harter, 1999; Ruble, 1983).

As children become older, they also view self in terms of increasingly differentiated qualities (Harter & Monsour, 1992). During the elementary school years, children effectively distinguish self in terms of separate skills: academic abilities, physical appearance, behavioral conduct, social skills, and athletic competence (Cole et al., 2001; Hymel et al., 1999). As children acquire a better understanding of their strengths and limitations, their evaluation of self may be somewhat less positive than during the preschool years. Their self-concept shows some positive increases in most domains in the later elementary school years but then tends to dip again as they begin to enter the adolescent years. Moreover, gender differences exist in how favorable these different domains of self are perceived, as can be seen in Figure 12.2.

An important factor to consider in the development of the concept of self is the culture in which the child is growing up. Children in Western societies tend to use many personal references in responding to questions about things that "tell about you." They might say, "I am a very smart person" or "I like hockey." Children from China, however, tend to comment on their social networks or social interactions, saying, for example, "I like to help my mom wash dishes" or "I am in second grade," responses that are consistent with their culture's emphasis on the connections among individuals in the social group (Wang, 2004).

Social Comparison During the early and middle school years, as we already indicated, children begin to reference others in describing themselves. Whether Jim

FIGURE 12.2

Evaluations of Self as a Function of Gender

The different domains of self are not always evaluated equally. Females consistently give less favorable ratings (on a 4-point scale) to their appearance and to their athletic ability than do males. These data have been averaged over thirteen different studies carried out by Susan Harter with children from elementary school through high school (Harter, 1999). In addition, research cited by Harter (1999) and carried out by others in England, Ireland, Australia, and many non–English-speaking countries, including Switzerland, Italy, Holland, China, Japan, and Korea, reveals a similar pattern of findings.

Source: Harter (1999), p. 131.

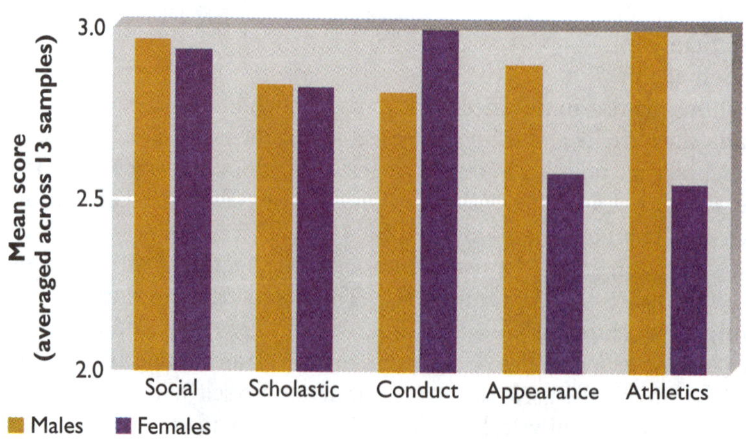

feels he is nice or can run fast, or Ellen believes she is smart or throws a ball well, depends on how Jim or Ellen thinks he or she stacks up against agemates and friends. How important is this process, called **social comparison**, the tendency of people to use others as mirrors to evaluate their own abilities, interests, and values? The answer appears to be that it becomes increasingly important as children move through the elementary school years. For example, nine-year-olds who could not actually determine their success but were told that they did better than, or not as well as, peers in a ball-throwing contest predicted future performance based on the feedback they received. If told they were successful, they expected to show continued superior ability; if told they were less successful, they expected to continue to perform more poorly than children who received no feedback. Five- and seven-year-olds, however, were unaffected by the information; they predicted that they would do equally well, regardless of how they compared with others (Ruble et al., 1980).

This fifth-grade boy exhibits pride in the certificate of achievement he received as he describes his work on a project designed to save energy. Such positive feedback can play an important role in promoting continued academic effort. As he enters into and proceeds through the adolescent years, he will increasingly rely on his own standards for determining whether he has done a good job in the various activities he undertakes.

In fact, young children frequently are unrealistic about their skills; they claim they will do far better than they actually can (Butler, 1990; Harter, 1999). Kindergartners rate themselves more positively than older children do and tend to ignore feedback to adjust their evaluations, particularly when information about failure is given to them (Ruble, Eisenberg, & Higgins, 1994). However, by attending to the attributes and qualities of others, children may gain a more realistic means of predicting how well they can do. For example, Diane Ruble (1987) found that children in kindergarten and first grade who more frequently made social comparisons involving achievement tended to have greater knowledge of their relative standing in the classroom. Comments from classmates make a difference, too. When other children say things like "You're good at math," children acquire a sense of academic areas they are good at and those they are not (Altermatt et al., 2002).

Older school-age children engage in increasingly subtle, indirect social comparisons to determine how well they are doing, perhaps because more conspicuous forms of information gathering are perceived as inappropriate behaviors. For example, nine- or ten-year-olds are more likely than younger children to ask classmates, "What question are you on?" to assess their progress among peers (Pomerantz et al., 1995). On the other hand, the kind of educational environment in which children participate also influences this behavior. In Israel, for example, children in kibbutz schools, which place greater emphasis on cooperative activity than more traditional urban schools in that country, continue to be more likely to interpret glances among one another as efforts to increase mastery rather than as social comparisons (Butler & Ruzany, 1993).

Self-Determination Children become increasingly sophisticated about how the world responds to their actions. For example, if asked, "How did you get to be the way you are?" a preschooler is likely to refer to uncontrollable factors ("I just grew. ... My body just got bigger"), whereas a ten-year-old mentions her own efforts ("From getting good grades in school from studying"). Most children believe individual effort is an important aspect of achieving success and avoiding failure, even in societies that have emphasized a more collective orientation, such as Russia (Stetsenko al., 1995). For example, elementary school children in Los Angeles, Tokyo, Berlin, Moscow, and Prague are in close agreement in their views that effort in particular, rather than other factors, such as the teacher or luck or even ability, is the most important determinant of school performance (Little & Lopez, 1997). Yet, within every community, individuals can differ substantially in their sense of self-determination and control. Some children are convinced that what happens to them depends on their actions; that their choices, decisions, and abilities govern whether outcomes are good or bad, successful or unsuccessful. When asked how to find a friend, such a child might say, "Go up to someone you like and ask them to play with you." When asked how to do well on a test, the child might answer, "Study for it and you'll get smarter!" Such children have a strong **mastery orientation**, a belief that success stems from trying hard; failures,

social comparison Process in which individuals define themselves in relation to the skills, attributes, and qualities of others; an important contributor to self-concept during middle childhood.

mastery orientation Belief that achievements are based on one's own efforts rather than on luck or other factors beyond one's control.

these children presume, are conditions to be overcome by working more or by investing greater effort (Dweck & Elliott, 1983).

Other children, in contrast, believe luck, fate, or other people have an inordinate influence on what happens to them. When asked why he cannot catch a ball, such a child might say, "The others throw it too fast." When asked why he got a poor grade, he might say, "The teacher doesn't like me." His explanation for a good grade might be "I was lucky." Such children often express little confidence in their ability and feel powerless to influence the future. They perceive themselves as being unable to achieve, perhaps because their efforts have not led to regular success. In place of a sense of mastery, they have a sense of **learned helplessness** (Dweck & Elliott, 1983).

These differing interpretations about success and failure are linked to another property of the belief system. To the extent that children think the characteristics they and others display are stable *entities*—that is, fixed or unchangeable qualities or traits, such as being smart, friendly, or popular—the more vulnerable they are to a helpless orientation. As a consequence, when faced with a challenging situation, the focus tends to be on evaluating how well they perform or "measure up" rather than on what steps might be taken to improve their performance or activity. In contrast, when children hold beliefs that characteristics or traits of individuals are *incremental* or malleable and can therefore be changed, their focus in challenging situations is more likely to be directed toward learning procedures and strategies reflecting resilience and increased effort (Erdley et al., 1997; Heyman & Dweck, 1998). Why might this be so? If traits are seen as enduring characteristics, little can be done to change them; thus the child places greater emphasis on determining the degree to which he or she (and others) possesses them as indicated by *performance* on the problem or task. On the other hand, if traits are seen as temporary characteristics, then the child can focus on the processes required to improve on or modify them, that is, on better ways of *learning* the task or how to solve the problem (Dweck, 1999).

KEY THEME
RISK/RESILIENCE

Differing beliefs about the degree to which traits are fixed or modifiable and the causes of success or failure have a powerful bearing on academic achievement, participation in athletics and other physical activities, efforts to establish social relationships, self-esteem, and career aspirations (Bandura et al., 2001; Chapman, Skinner, & Baltes, 1990; Heyman & Dweck, 1998). Children who display evidence of learned helplessness in school, for example, may be caught in a vicious cycle involving self-fulfilling anticipation of failure accompanied by excuses that they have little control over what happens to them (Bandura et al., 1996). They are especially likely to expect failure on tasks found difficult in the past and may avoid them when given further opportunity to work on them (Dweck, 1991; Erdley et al., 1997). Note that high ability is not the factor that determines a mastery orientation (Dweck, 1999). Deborah Phillips (1984) reported that nearly 20 percent of fifth-graders with high ability limit their goals and persistence in school activities. In the academic realm, this pattern occurs more frequently among girls than boys, perhaps because girls are more likely than boys to view their failures in terms of such uncontrollable factors as lack of ability (Crandall, 1969; Dweck, Goetz, & Strauss, 1980; Stipek & Hoffman, 1980).

A mastery-versus-helplessness orientation can be observed in kindergartners and remains stable for up to five years (Ziegert et al., 2001). However, teachers can have an important influence on children's beliefs about their academic competence. When teachers provide a supportive, responsive learning environment, children come to believe that they have greater control over their understanding of academic materials and, as a consequence, become more actively engaged, as well as more successful in their efforts. Where learning environments are unsupportive, children are more likely to conclude that external factors are responsible for what happens, which, in turn, leads to less satisfaction and lower achievement in the classroom. Longitudinal data reveal that these differences in perceived control form a cyclic pattern of confidence and success that feeds into and magnifies individual differences in children's views of beliefs about their achievements and failures in the classroom (Skinner, Zimmer-Gembeck, & Connell, 1998).

learned helplessness Belief that one has little control over situations, perhaps because of lack of ability or inconsistent outcomes.

RESEARCH APPLIED TO PARENTING

Preventing Learned Helplessness

The rule in Michael's house was that, once homework was finished, the remaining time before bedtime was his to do with as he wished. He often played chess with his grandfather. This evening, however, his grandfather had become busy on another project. "Perhaps just as well," thought Michael as he reflected on the earlier exchange that had so angered his grandfather. Michael dialed his friend Jonathon. "Can you play some catch?" he queried when Jonathon answered the phone. "You must have finished your math already," Jonathon retorted. "I hate math, still have a lot more problems to do," he continued. But Michael quickly interjected, "You did really well on that last test." But before he could finish, Michael knew what Jonathon's reply would be: "I was lucky. The teacher asked the right questions. I wish I were good at math."

Children who gain little mastery over their environment or who face conflicting and inconsistent reactions, such as those they might receive from abusive parents, are among the most likely to display learned helplessness. But even well-intentioned parents and teachers may unwittingly help to foster a sense of helplessness. The seeds of a sense of helplessness, Carol Dweck (1999) believes, are sown in preschoolers who tend to judge their performance on tasks as "good" or "bad." When the value of self becomes contingent on feeling worthy or unworthy, young children become especially vulnerable to learned helplessness.

A study conducted by Melissa Kamins and Carol Dweck (1999) provides some experimental evidence to indicate that certain types of feedback with respect to either criticism or praise can lead to a more helpless orientation when children are subsequently confronted with similar situations involving a setback. In this study, five- and six-year-olds engaged in role-playing a series of four different stories that involved various tasks. In each of these tasks, children acted in the role of a doll, either making an error or completing the task successfully. At the end of each story the experimenter (who was engaged in role-playing as the teacher) provided one of three different types of feedback. When the task involved an error, the feedback from the "teacher" was directed either at the person ("I'm very disappointed in you"), at the outcome of the task ("That's not the right way to do it"), or at the process that contributed to the error in the task ("Maybe you can think of another way to do it"). (Special effort was made to ensure that the children understood they were role-playing and that the scenarios were "pretend" situations.) When praise for success was administered, the child heard something like "I'm very proud of you" or "That's the right way to do it" or "You must have tried really hard" for the person, outcome, and process feedback conditions, respectively.

How would children respond after role-playing in a similar but new task when a setback occurred? To answer this question the researchers asked children to evaluate how well the new problem had been completed (product rating); how performance in the task reflected such abilities as being good, bad, smart, not so smart, and so forth (self-assessment); whether they felt happy or sad (affect); and their willingness to continue in the role-playing activity or to attempt to correct the error (persistence). The results are shown in Figure 12.3. Higher scores indicate a more positive rating.

The results revealed a consistent pattern of reactions typical of helplessness when the emphasis in the feedback had been on the person (and, to a lesser extent, on the outcome) than when the feedback focused on the process of completing the task effectively. Somewhat surprisingly, this relationship held up whether the children had been exposed earlier to criticism or to praise in the role-playing activity, a finding reported by other researchers as well (Henderlong

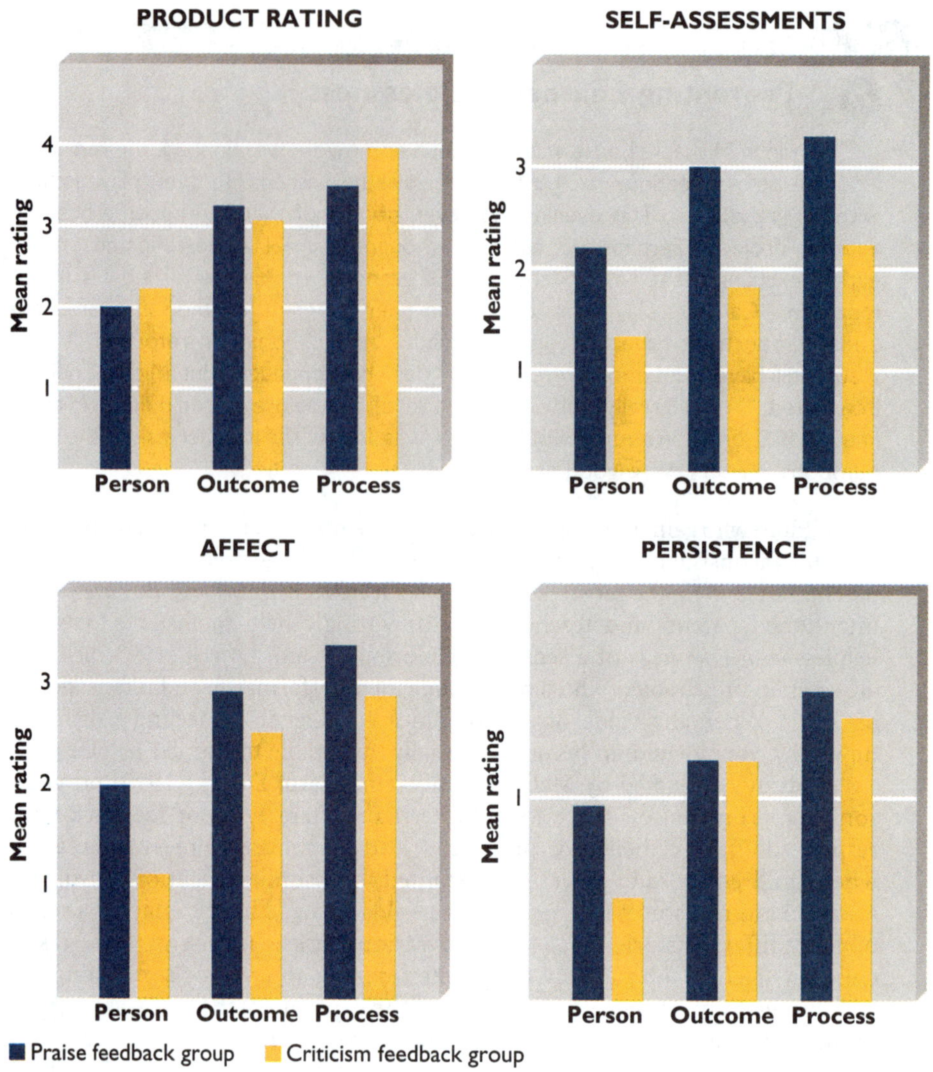

FIGURE 12.3

The Consequences of Different Types of Feedback for Learned Helplessness

When given praise or criticism for their work on a task, children may hear comments that are directed at them as a person ("good," "bad"), at the outcome ("right way to do it," "wrong way to do it"), or at the process ("really tried hard," "think of another way"). Hearing these different types of feedback influences how children subsequently respond to a setback on a similar task. Children who have heard person-oriented feedback evaluate the outcome of the new work less positively (product rating), view themselves as having fewer positive abilities (self-assessment), feel less happy with themselves (affect), and are less willing to continue the activity (persistence) than children who experience process-oriented feedback and, to a lesser extent, outcome-oriented feedback. Moreover, these kinds of responses are produced even though errors have not occurred in the previous tasks and children heard praise. The results suggest that the extent to which children express a sense of helplessness after experiencing a setback is affected by the specific form of praise or criticism they have heard in previous similar situations.

Source: Adapted from Kamins & Dweck (1999).

& Lepper, 2002). These findings and the research of many others suggest that parents can take several steps to reduce the likelihood that children will acquire a sense of learned helplessness.

1. *Avoid frequent criticism and punishment, especially of younger children.* The younger child who is often criticized or punished for, say, being messy or failing to finish a task may be particularly susceptible to the belief that he is "bad." In arriving at this stable view of his personality, he may have little reason to try to do better or may shun similar challenges to avoid receiving further negative evaluations. Thus it is important that parents help the younger child to avoid feelings of shame or limited self-worth when evaluating behavior (Kelley, Brownell, & Campbell, 2000).
2. *Motivate effort by identifying positive process approaches to problem solving.* As children become older and more knowledgeable, parents and teachers can promote a mastery orientation by emphasizing the various skills and procedures important to success; that is, what children can do to more effectively achieve a goal. Such feedback should help children to appreciate the malleability of traits and capacities.
3. *Attribute poor performance to factors other than ability.* When a child does perform poorly, a parent's or teacher's evaluation should focus on nonintellectual and temporary factors that may have reduced the child's performance

rather than on her intrinsic ability, thereby inspiring effort when the next opportunity arises.

4. *View activities as opportunities to learn rather than as tests of ability.* Parents and teachers can encourage children to approach academic tasks as opportunities to learn rather than as situations in which their performance will be evaluated in terms of competence (or lack of competence) (Dweck, 1999; Erdley et al., 1997).

Younger children must be convinced that their failures and successes are not the outcome of being "bad" or "good." Older children should be assured that shortcomings in performance on, say, academic tasks stem less from lack of ability than from insufficient effort or some other factor that can be modified. Children who have already acquired an orientation to learned helplessness can benefit from *attribution retraining*, a procedure designed to change their beliefs about the cause of their failures. This procedure emphasizes tying lack of success more directly to poor or ineffective effort than to inability. Attribution retraining has become an effective method of replacing self-limiting styles with positive approaches to success, a means of converting learned helplessness into a greater sense of mastery and agency (Dweck, 1986).

SELF-ESTEEM

A child's description of self often includes an evaluation component. **Self-esteem** or self-worth is specifically concerned with the positive feelings of merit and the extent to which the child believes his attributes and actions are good, desired, and valued (Davis-Kean & Sandler, 2001). This aspect of self appears to be related to social affiliations, success in school, and overall mental health (Dusek, 2000; Harter, 1999; Kling et al., 1999). For example, later life satisfaction and happiness have been linked to high self-esteem (Bachman, 1970; Crandall, 1973); depression, anxiety, and poor adjustment in school and social relationships have been associated with low self-esteem (Damon, 1983; Zimmerman et al., 1997).

Defining Self-Esteem How should we describe a child's self-esteem if the child takes pride in how smart she is, concludes that she is not very good at sports (but sports are unimportant anyway), and is unsure whether she is pretty enough to become a movie star? Work by Susan Harter and others (Eccles, Wigfield, et al., 1993; Harter, 1999; Marsh, Craven, & Debus, 1998) has revealed that children often give different evaluations of self when asked about academic competence, athletic skill, social acceptance, or physical appearance. Still, by about eight years of age, children can give answers to such global questions as "Do you like yourself?" and "Are you happy the way you are?" The responses to these broad inquiries, however, are not simply the sum of all the different evaluations made of one's attributes and abilities, and they can vary across situations and time (Harter, Waters, & Whitesell, 1998). What, then, are some of the factors that influence how a child arrives at a global sense of worth?

Origins of Self-Esteem William James (1892) theorized that self-esteem depends on the success a person feels in areas in which she wants to succeed. Other theories emphasize that self-esteem originates in how a person thinks others see him; the *generalized other*—the combined perceived evaluations of parents, peers, and teachers influential in a person's life—helps to determine sense of worth (Cooley, 1902; Felson, 1993; Mead, 1934).

Both success in a highly regarded domain and the perceived evaluations of others do appear to affect self-esteem. Susan Harter (1987) obtained ratings of how children viewed themselves in scholastic competence, athletic competence, social acceptance, physical appearance, and behavioral conduct, as well as in terms of

self-esteem One's feelings of worth; extent to which one senses that one's attributes and actions are good, desired, and valued.

global success. Children were also asked how critical it was for them to do well in each of these domains. Harter reasoned that greater discrepancies between perceived competence and the importance of a domain, especially one highly valued, would be linked to lower self-esteem. Children also rated how others (parents, peers) viewed them, felt they were important, liked them, and so on.

For children in the third to eighth grades, the more an area rated as important outstripped a child's perception of her competence, the lower was the child's sense of her overall worth. In fact, children with low self-esteem seemed to have trouble disregarding the significance of domains in which they were not skilled (Harter, 1985). In contrast, children with high self-esteem minimized the value of those fields in which they were not especially competent and gained considerable satisfaction from areas in which they were relatively successful. Are some domains more important than others for a child's overall sense of worth? The answer appears to be yes. Boys and girls of elementary and middle school age who are dissatisfied with and keenly concerned about their physical appearance tend to have lower self-esteem. Although discrepancies are also important in other domains, they correlate less highly with judgments of overall self-worth. Harter (1987, 1998) speculates that, in American culture, the relationship stems from the enormous emphasis in movies, television, and magazines on physical appearance as the key to success and acceptance. As children become older, discrepancy scores on social acceptance take on increasingly greater significance, whereas discrepancy scores on athletic competence show a decline in importance (Harter, 1987). Nevertheless, positive assessments of physical appearance continue to be an important predictor of higher self-esteem for boys and girls as they enter the adolescent years (DuBois et al., 2000; Lord, Eccles, & McCarthy, 1994).

Harter also found that the perceived social support of others was correlated with the child's sense of self-worth. As Figure 12.4 shows, elementary school children with low discrepancy *and* high social support scores showed superior levels of self-worth. Children with high discrepancy and low social support displayed the lowest levels of self-esteem. The opinions of others do matter in children's feelings of self-worth, but the need for approval from others diminishes as children grow older. Moreover, some children seem to respond more to the degree of approval they get from others, some to how much disapproval they receive, and still others to both (Rudolph, Caldwell, & Conley, 2005). Thus efforts to improve self-esteem in children may require the formation and acceptance of realistic personal goals, as well as an understanding of how the need for approval works for each individual child.

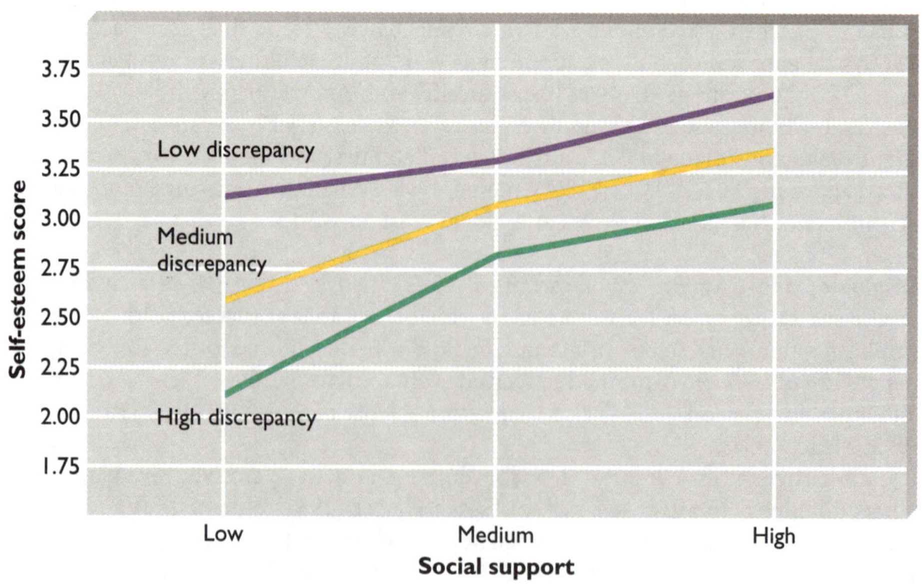

FIGURE 12.4

How Self-Esteem Develops

Self-esteem reflects the combined influence of social support and the discrepancy between the child's perceived and desired competence in some ability or attribute. Harter divided elementary school children into three groups based on these two measures. Those with the highest self-esteem reported high social support and a low discrepancy between perceived and desired competence. Those with the lowest self-esteem reported low social support and a high discrepancy between perceived and desired competence. The findings suggest that parents, teachers, and others concerned with increasing self-esteem need to consider both the kind of social encouragement and positive regard they provide and the children's own beliefs about what is important.

Source: Adapted from Harter (1987).

CONTROVERSY: THINKING IT OVER

Is Praise Always a Good Thing?

In the discussion of ways to prevent learned helplessness, one finding by Kamins and Dweck (1999) may come as a surprise to many. These researchers noted that praise directed toward children for success did not necessarily inoculate the children from reporting a greater sense of helplessness when faced with a setback in a new task. Are we to conclude that praise (such as "I am really proud of you," "You are really smart," "You are a star") is not a particularly good means of promoting effective behavior?

What Is the Controversy?

If there is one prescription that many parents and professionals in Western societies, particularly in the United States, would offer for encouraging the development of a competent child, it would very likely be to praise generously for his or her accomplishments. As Carol Dweck (1999) points out, it is one of our most treasured assumptions. Enlightened parents attempt to (and often do) follow such a practice, and many teachers and others working with children are advised to unstintingly administer praise to promote learning. Yet in their recent examination of the effects of praise on children, Jennifer Henderlong and Mark Lepper (2002) have concluded that the research literature often paints a far different picture of its motivational consequences for children.

What Are the Opposing Arguments?

Learning theory has long recognized the importance of reinforcement for enhancing behavior. Telling a child that he or she is good, excellent, or really smart after completing a task should be reinforcing and promote continuing efforts to engage in that behavior. Moreover, a common belief is that such praise helps to bring about and strengthen intrinsic motivation for accomplishing various goals. To top it off, praise is routinely viewed as an effective way of enhancing a child's self-esteem, another desirable goal, as our discussion of this concept has suggested.

Yet others have raised serious questions about the effectiveness of frequent praise. The concern is that praise, although a presumably positive source of feedback for a child, is nevertheless a *judgment*. As a consequence, it can lead a child to become concerned about performing well and to avoid risks (Henderlong & Lepper, 2002). In other words, the child may place greater value on receiving the praise at the expense of working autonomously or of learning from one's own mistakes. Moreover, when given indiscriminately, such as for an easy task, praise may be interpreted by the child as indicating low ability. Thus frequent praise can have the paradoxical effect of lowering motivation and of promoting a kind of *contingent self-worth*; that is, of feeling worthy only when successful (Dweck, 1999).

What Answers Exist? What Questions Remain?

When is praise beneficial to a child? In their summary of the research literature, Henderlong and Lepper (2002) suggest a number of conditions under which some types of praise may have positive consequences for a child. These conditions include praise that is sincere and appropriate; that focuses on the type of effort, strategies, and self-corrections the child initiates in an activity rather than on his or her stable attributes (being good, smart, and so on); that encourages the child to be autonomous in his or her activity rather than serving as a way of controlling behavior; that emphasizes effectiveness in the task rather than social comparison; and that is informative in providing feedback about realistic expectations for the task.

Still, many questions remain about praise as a motivational tool. How could professionals and the public be so convinced of its unbridled value, whereas still others have now come to question its general effects on children's development? Thus controversy continues over what kind of and how frequently praise should be administered. Moreover, virtually all of the research on the consequences of praise has been completed on children in the United States (Henderlong & Lepper, 2002). However, cultures differ dramatically in the extent to which children are praised. For example, could its effects on children be very different in a collectivist society in which the emphasis is on improving oneself for the good of the group rather than on self-enhancement? Methodological limitations in the research that has been carried out on this topic present further challenges to some of the conclusions about the effects of praise. Broad acceptance of the value of praise for self-esteem and of its motivational consequences for effort remain controversial and in need of further examination. What kinds of evidence must researchers obtain to decide whether this long-cherished assumption needs to be amended?

FOR • YOUR • REVIEW

- What are the primary distinctions between self as object and self as subject? What are the typical behaviors that illustrate these two characterizations of self?
- How does social comparison contribute to concept of self in middle childhood?
- What factors contribute to mastery orientation and learned helplessness? What steps can parents and teachers take to reduce learned helplessness?
- What factors contribute to high self-esteem?
- What role does praise play in self-esteem and in promoting achievement motivation?

Moral Development in Middle Childhood

Like Michael, the child in this chapter's opening vignette, school-aged children typically have daily opportunities to make decisions that have a moral dimension to them. From choosing how to respond to a sibling who absconds with a favorite toy ("Should I hit him, or should I share?") to deciding whether to tell parents about a misbehavior at school (Should I confess, or should I hide the truth for as long as I can?"), to selecting a way to handle an irritated grandfather ("Should I talk back, or should I find a way to make him feel better?"), children's behaviors often reflect the value system that their parents, teachers, and others have tried to pass on to them. But when parents and teachers engage in "moral education," what can they expect the child to understand about these all-important lessons? And even if children understand what is right and what is wrong, how can they be encouraged to behave in ways that reflect those judgments? Some of the answers arise from a long line of theory and research on children's moral development.

Cognitive-Developmental Theories

Cognitive-developmental explanations of moral development highlight the ways children *reason* about moral problems. Should a person ever steal, even if the transgression would help another person? Are there circumstances under which lying is acceptable? The child's capacity to think through the answers to such questions depends on his ability to consider the perspectives, needs, and feelings of others. In other words, moral development is intimately connected with advances in general thinking abilities. The two most prominent cognitive-developmental theorists concerned with moral development, Jean Piaget and Lawrence Kohlberg, have suggested stage theories in which children's reasoning about moral issues is qualitatively different depending on their level of development.

Key Theme
Interaction Among Domains

Key Theme
Continuity/Discontinuity

Piaget's Theory Piaget (1932/1965) derived many of his ideas about moral development from two contexts: as children played a formal game with a shared set of rules and as they encountered moral dilemmas created to assess thinking about ethical problems. For example, Piaget observed and interviewed children playing marbles, a popular children's game. Children were asked questions about this game: What are the rules? Can new rules be invented? Where do rules come from? Have they always been the same?

Preschoolers, Piaget stated, are not guided by rules. They engage in the activity for the pure pleasure it provides, and their play is largely solitary. Thus young children may hide marbles or throw them randomly, ignoring the formal rules of the game. By about age six, however, children come to regard rules as sacred and inviolable. Rules, handed down by adults, must be respected and have always existed in the same form; people played marbles in exactly the same way over the years. By about ten years of age, children understand rules to be the result of cooperation and mutual consent among all the participants in the game. Thus rules may be modified to suit the needs of the situation if all the players agree.

The second method Piaget used to study moral development consisted of noting children's responses to moral dilemmas, stories in which a central character committed a transgression. The intentions of that character and the consequences of his or her act varied, as the following stories illustrate:

A. A little boy who is called John is in his room. He is called to dinner. He goes into the dining room. But behind the door there was a chair, and on the chair there was a tray with fifteen cups on it. John couldn't have known that there was all this behind the door. He goes in, the door knocks against the tray, bang go the fifteen cups, and they all get broken!

B. Once there was a little boy whose name was Henry. One day when his mother was out he tried to get some jam out of the cupboard. He climbed up onto a chair and stretched out his arm. But the jam was too high up and he couldn't reach it and have any. But while he was trying to get it he knocked over a cup. The cup fell down and broke. (Piaget, 1932/1965, p. 122)

Which boy is naughtier? Younger children typically choose John, the child who broke more cups. According to Piaget, children younger than about ten are in the stage of moral development called **moral realism**, or *heteronomy*. They judge the rightness or wrongness of an act by the objective visible consequences—in this case, how many cups were broken. They do not consider the boys' intentions to behave well or improperly.

In the stage of moral realism, rules are viewed as unbreakable; if the rules are violated, the child sees punishment as the inevitable consequence. The belief in **immanent justice** is reflected in such statements as "That's God punishing me," made when the child accidentally falls off a bike after lying to her mother, for example. Although the fall is unrelated to the child's transgression, she believes the causal link exists. Children in this stage also believe that a punishment need not be related to the wrongful act if it is severe enough to teach a lesson. Thus stealing a friend's toy can be punished by any means, not necessarily by returning the toy or making reparations.

From a limited ability to reason about moral issues, children progress to **moral relativism**, or *autonomy*. Now the transgressor's motives are taken into account. Thus Henry is named as the naughtier boy. In addition, the child no longer believes

moral realism In Piaget's theory of moral development, the first stage of moral reasoning, in which moral judgments are made on the basis of the consequences of an act. Also called *heteronomy*.

immanent justice Young child's belief that punishment will inevitably follow a transgression.

moral relativism In Piaget's theory of moral development, the second stage of moral reasoning, in which moral judgments are made on the basis of the actor's intentions. Also called *autonomy*.

every violation will be punished. Punishments, however, should relate to the misdemeanor so that the individual appreciates the consequences of his act.

What precipitates the shift from moral realism to moral relativism? Piaget points to changes in the child's cognitive capabilities, especially decreasing egocentrism, as one important element. To understand another's intentions, for example, the child must be able to appreciate the point of view of that person as distinct from her own. Another important factor is the opportunity to interact with peers. Peer interactions force the child to consider the thoughts and feelings of others and eventually lead to an understanding of their intentions and motives. Parents can further promote the shift from realism to relativism, notes Piaget, by encouraging mutual respect and understanding, pointing out the consequences of the child's actions for others, and articulating their needs and feelings as parents.

Evaluating Piaget How well does Piaget's theory stand up? Research confirms that reasoning about moral problems shifts as children grow older. With development, children from diverse cultures, from different social classes, and of varying intellectual abilities more fully consider intentions in judging the actions of another person. But in contrast to Piaget's claims, children younger than age ten can be sensitive to the motives behind a given act—that intentional hitting is worse than accidental hitting, for example (Zelazo, Helwig, & Lau, 1996). In addition, as early as the preschool years, children recognize that actions that produce harmful psychological consequences (such as causing embarrassment or frightening another person) are as unacceptable as behaviors that produce physical harm (Helwig, Zelazo, & Wilson, 2001).

As Piaget described, beliefs in immanent justice and arbitrary punishment decline with age (Hoffman, 1970; Lickona, 1976). Moreover, as children reach the stage of concrete operations, become less egocentric, and demonstrate improved ability to take the perspective of another person, they are more likely to recommend punishment appropriate to the moral transgression (Lee, 1971). However, the manner in which *both* parents and peers reason with younger children influences the level of reasoning the children display concerning moral conflicts later in their development (Walker, Hennig, & Krettenauer, 2000). In other words, parents and not just peers (as Piaget claimed) have a significant impact on moral reasoning.

It is clear from Piaget's work that the child's conceptualization of what is moral becomes more elaborate and complex with age, and that any attempt to understand moral development must include an explanation of the child's thought as well as behavior. Subsequent theorists, Lawrence Kohlberg in particular, have found Piaget's writings a useful springboard for their own theoretical formulations.

Kohlberg's Theory Like Piaget, Kohlberg (1969, 1976) proposed a stage theory of moral development in which progress through each stage proceeds in a universal order and regression to earlier modes of thinking is rare. Kohlberg based his theory on children's responses to a set of dilemmas that put obedience to authority or the law in direct conflict with helping a person in need ("Should a man steal an overpriced drug that he cannot obtain legally in order to save his wife?").

Using an analysis of the reasoning of boys ranging in age from ten to sixteen, Kohlberg identified three general levels of moral orientation, each with two substages, to explain the varying responses of his participants (see Table 12.1). At the **preconventional level**, the child's behavior is motivated by external pressures: avoidance of punishment, attainment of rewards, and preservation of self-interests. Norms of behavior are not yet derived from internalized principles, and the child's needs and desires are primary. At the **conventional level**, conforming to the norms of the majority and maintaining the social order have become central to the child's reasoning. The child now considers the points of view of others, along with their intentions and motives. The child also feels a sense of responsibility to contribute to society and to uphold the laws and institutions that serve its members. Finally, at the **postconventional level**, the individual has developed a fuller understanding

preconventional level In Kohlberg's theory, the first level of moral reasoning, in which morality is motivated by the avoidance of punishments and attainment of rewards.

conventional level In Kohlberg's theory, the second level of moral reasoning, in which the child conforms to the norms of the majority and wishes to preserve the social order.

postconventional level In Kohlberg's theory, the third level of moral reasoning, in which laws are seen as the result of a social contract and individual principles of conscience may emerge.

Table 12.1 Kohlberg's Six Stages of Moral Development

Stage	Motivation	Typical Moral Reasoning
Preconventional Level		
1 Punishment and obedience orientation	The primary motive for action is the avoidance of punishment:	*Pro:* If you let your wife die, you will get in trouble. You'll be blamed for not spending the money to save her and there'll be an investigation of you and the druggist for your wife's death. *Con:* You shouldn't steal the drug because you'll be caught and sent to jail if you do. If you do get away, your conscience would bother you thinking how the police would catch up to you any minute. (Kohlberg, 1984, p. 52)
2 Naive instrumental hedonism	Actions are motivated by the desire for rewards:	*Pro:* If you do happen to get caught you could give the drug back and you wouldn't get much of a sentence. It wouldn't bother you much to serve a little jail term, if you have your wife when you get out. *Con:* He may not get much of a jail term if he steals the drug, but his wife will probably die before he gets out, so it wouldn't do him much good. If his wife dies, he shouldn't blame himself; it isn't his fault she has cancer. (Kohlberg, 1984, p. 52)
Conventional Level		
3 Good-boy morality	The child strives to avoid the disapproval of others (as distinct from avoidance of punishment):	*Pro:* No one will think you're bad if you steal the drug but your family will think you're an inhuman husband if you don't. If you let your wife die, you'll never be able to look anyone in the face again. *Con:* It isn't just the druggist who will think you're a criminal, everyone else will, too. After you steal it, you'll feel bad thinking how you've brought dishonor on your family and yourself; you won't be able to face anyone again. (Kohlberg, 1984, p. 52)
4 Authority-maintaining morality	An act is always wrong if it violates a rule or does harm to others:	*Pro:* You should steal it. If you did nothing you'd be letting your wife die, it's your responsibility if she dies. You have to take it with the idea of paying the druggist. *Con:* It is a natural thing. . . to want to save his wife but it's always wrong to steal. He still knows he's stealing and taking a valuable drug from the man who made it. (Kohlberg, 1984, p. 50)
Postconventional Level		
5 Morality of contract and democracy	The individual is concerned with self-respect and maintaining the respect of others. Laws must be obeyed, because they represent a social contract, but they may sometimes conflict with moral values:	*Pro:* The law wasn't set up for these circumstances. Taking the drug in this situation isn't really right, but it's justified to do it. *Con:* You can't completely blame someone for stealing, but extreme circumstances don't really justify taking the law in your own hands. You can't have everyone stealing when they get desperate. The end may be good, but the ends don't justify the means. (Kohlberg, 1984, p. 50)
6 Morality of individual principles of conscience	Individuals are concerned with upholding their personal principles and may sometimes feel it necessary to deviate from rules when the rules conflict with moral principles:	*Pro:* This is a situation that forces him to choose between stealing and letting his wife die. In a situation in which the choice must be made, it is morally right to steal. He has to act in terms of the principle of preserving and respecting life. *Con:* [The man] is faced with the decision of whether to consider other people who need the drug just as badly as his wife. [He] ought to act not according to his particular feelings toward his wife but considering the value of all the lives involved. (Kohlberg, 1984, p. 51)

of the basis for laws and rules. They are now seen as a social contract that all individuals must uphold because of shared responsibilities and duties. The individual recognizes the relative and sometimes arbitrary nature of rules, which may vary from group to group. Certain principles and values—in particular, justice and human dignity—must be preserved at all costs. Kohlberg emphasized that changes in the child's perspective-taking ability are the basis for shifts in moral reasoning. According to Kohlberg, changes in perspective-taking ability are promoted by opportunities for children to discuss others' points of view, a position for which research provides some support (Walker et al., 2000).

Evaluating Kohlberg Numerous investigations of Kohlberg's theory have confirmed stagelike transitions in moral reasoning. For example, Anne Colby and her colleagues (1983) followed Kohlberg's original sample during a twenty-year period and noted that their responses to moral dilemmas fit within the developmental stages delineated by Kohlberg (see Figure 12.5). With few exceptions, participants progressed upward. In another study, six- through fifteen-year-olds tested during a two-year period gained in moral reasoning, and few children skipped stages or regressed to earlier forms of reasoning (Walker, 1989). Children also judge the sophistication of alternative responses to moral dilemmas in accordance with stage theory, as long as the alternatives are below their current level of reasoning about moral development (Boom, Brugman, & van der Heijden, 2001).

Cross-cultural studies in countries as diverse as India, Turkey, Japan, Nigeria, and Finland have also found that children show development of moral reasoning, from preconventional to conventional levels, without skipping stages and without regressing to previous stages. However, most individuals as adults still reason at the conventional level (see Figure 12.5). The highest level of moral maturity, which might be termed *moral excellence* (the kind, for example, displayed by Mahatma Gandhi, Martin Luther King, or Abraham Lincoln), probably requires more than postconventional reasoning about moral dilemmas. Such reasoning very likely must combine with high standards, a responsive conscience, a strong sense of personal agency and understanding of one's place in society, a sensitive and compassionate concern about others, and a willingness to act on one's convictions (Colby & Damon, 1992; Hart & Fegley, 1995; Walker & Pitts, 1998).

Moral development has been found to correlate positively with IQ and educational level, consistent with Kohlberg's emphasis on the cognitive basis of moral judgment. As with Piaget's theory, however, researchers have been unable to confirm some specific propositions in Kohlberg's outline of moral development. For example, do individuals within a stage respond consistently to different moral dilemmas, as Kohlberg maintains they should? In one study of seventy-five college students

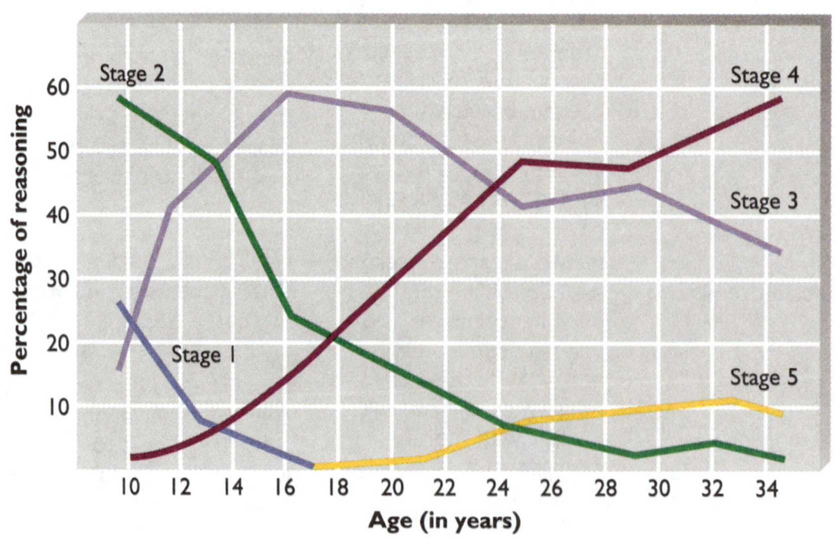

FIGURE 12.5

The Development of Moral Reasoning

In a longitudinal follow-up study of Kohlberg's original sample, Anne Colby and her colleagues confirmed that participants showed consistent upward advances in moral reasoning with age. The graph shows the extent to which participants gave responses characteristic of each of Kohlberg's six stages from age ten through adulthood. With development, responses associated with the preconventional level (stages 1 and 2) declined, and responses associated with the conventional level (stages 3 and 4) increased. Few young adults moved to the postconventional level of moral reasoning.

Source: Adapted from Colby et al. (1983).

Kohlberg's theory of moral development has been criticized for failing to measure the values found in other cultures. Until researchers have a greater understanding of cultural values, such as those conveyed by this mother in Somalia as she assists her children in studying the Koran, our understanding of the development of moral reasoning will remain incomplete.

who responded to five moral dilemmas, not one person received the same stage score for all stories (Fishkin, Keniston, & MacKinnon, 1973). Thus, although individuals may exhibit a particular stage, they also display considerable variation in their reasoning about moral issues.

A major criticism of Kohlberg's theory is that it fails to capture the many modes of moral reasoning evident in individuals and different cultural groups. In responding to moral dilemmas, people growing up on the Israeli kibbutz often address the importance of the principle of happiness for everyone (Snarey, 1985). Asian cultures are more likely to emphasize the idea of the collective good and a harmonious social order than are Western cultures. From this perspective, the desirable way to resolve disputes is to reconcile people who are in conflict rather than rely on laws to control their behavior. Thus families often preserve harmony by holding conferences to settle disputes. Kohlberg's moral dilemmas, which require a choice between rules and the needs of individuals to bring about justice, do not permit the expression of this cultural principle (Dien, 1982; Ma & Cheung, 1996). Evaluations of the appropriateness of telling the truth or lying also differ between Chinese and Canadian children, as might be predicted from the differing emphasis on modesty and humility reported for these two cultures (Lee et al., 1997). Likewise, Indian cultures emphasize the value of all life, not just human life; thus a most serious transgression, as expressed by Hindu children and adults, is eating beef, chicken, or fish (Shweder, Mahapatra, & Miller, 1987). Such a concept does not appear in Kohlberg's outline of moral development. Buddhist beliefs about limits to self and to the value of intervention in preventing suffering are also difficult to reconcile within Kohlberg's framework (Huebner & Garrod, 1991). Thus the movement of the individual toward the fullest understanding of the principle of justice, at least as conceptualized by Kohlberg, may be a singularly Western phenomenon.

Gilligan's Theory The failure to consider alternative modes of moral reasoning has been an especially sensitive issue with respect to possible sex differences in moral development. In one early study, Kohlberg reported that most males function at the higher stage, whereas most females reason at the lower stage, within the conventional level of moral reasoning (Kohlberg & Kramer, 1969). The report provoked a strong reaction from some members of the psychological community and led Carol Gilligan to propose that moral development takes a different, not an inferior, course in females (Gilligan, 1982, 1988; Gilligan & Attanucci, 1988). Gilligan states that, because females tend to be concerned with relationships, caregiving, and intimacy, they typically develop a **morality of care and responsibility** in contrast to the **morality of justice** described by Kohlberg. The morality of care and responsibility concerns self-sacrifice and relationships with others, rather than the tension between rules and the needs and rights of the individual.

An eleven-year-old girl's response to the story about whether or not to steal a drug illustrates the ethic of care that Gilligan holds to be typical of females:

> If he stole the drug, he might save his wife then, but if he did, he might have to go to jail, and then his wife might get sicker again, and he couldn't get more of the drug, and it might not be good. So, they should really just talk it out and find some other way to make the money. (Gilligan, 1982, p. 28)

Although this girl's response might receive a low score in Kohlberg's system because of its seemingly wavering and noncommittal nature, Gilligan believes it reflects a mature understanding of the crisis a relationship might undergo when a law is broken.

Are there sex differences in moral development? Of the large number of investigations based on Kohlberg's tasks, very few report substantial differences between males and females (Walker, 1984, 1991; Wark & Krebs, 1996). Both males and females tend to interpret moral decisions about impersonal situations (such as whether a man should steal a drug for his wife) in terms of justice and rights; decisions about dilemmas that they have personally confronted are more frequently made in terms of the ethic of care (Walker, 1996). Regardless of whether sex differences in moral development exist, Gilligan's work has shown that researchers need to expand their understanding of what constitutes moral values.

Morality as Domain-Specific Knowledge As we have just seen, definitions of morality can vary enormously and are often embedded within the broad fabric of social knowledge and values represented in culture (Turiel & Wainryb, 1994; Turiel, 1998). But perhaps a distinction needs to be made between moral and societal beliefs. The moral domain consists of rules that regulate a person's own or another's rights or welfare; examples are the concepts of justice and responsibility toward others. The societal domain pertains to knowledge of **social conventions**, the rules that regulate such social interactions as how to dress appropriately for a given occasion and what degree of formality to use in speaking to someone, factors that can vary dramatically from one culture to another.

Elliot Turiel (2006) hypothesizes that the moral and societal domains develop along separate paths and that most theories of moral development have confused the two. Children begin distinguishing moral and social-conventional rules by age three (Smetana & Braeges, 1990). To illustrate, young children will respond differently to their playmates' transgressions depending on whether the actions violate a social or a moral rule. When a child violates a moral rule, for example, by intentionally inflicting harm or taking another's possessions, other children typically react by physically intervening or making statements about the pain the victim experienced. On the other hand, when children observe another person violating a social convention, such as eating while standing instead of sitting, they either do not react or simply comment on the rules that surround proper social behavior (Nucci & Turiel, 1978). When questioned about social-conventional transgressions, most children say such an act would be acceptable if no rule existed about it in school, whereas moral transgressions are wrong, are more serious, and should receive greater punishment, even if the school has no rule pertaining to them (Smetana, Schlagman, & Adams, 1993). Children are likely to be relatively intolerant about others' holding moral beliefs with which they disagree, but they also readily recognize that others need not share beliefs about social conventions (Wainryb et al., 2001).

How do children come to appreciate the distinction between moral and social conventions? Perhaps through the greater emotional affect associated with moral transgressions than with social infractions. When a child observes a peer hitting

morality of care and responsibility Tendency to make moral judgments on the basis of concern for others.

morality of justice Tendency to make moral judgments on the basis of reason and abstract principles of equity.

social convention Behavioral rules that regulate social interactions, such as dress codes and degrees of formality in speech.

someone or is a victim of retaliation himself, the abuse may arouse a high degree of emotion in him. For example, when first- and third-graders are asked to rate how they would feel if they were hit without provocation or if another child stole their toys, they are more likely to indicate a negative emotion than if the scenario described lining up outside the wrong classroom. Furthermore, children frequently justify intervening in a moral transgression by referring to their own or the victim's emotional state (Arsenio & Ford, 1985). Finally, adults may react differently to transgressions associated with moral issues compared with social conventions; as a result, the child learns to discriminate between these two domains (Glassman & Zan, 1995).

Moral Reasoning versus Moral Behavior Cognitive-developmental approaches fill a void left by social learning theories by acknowledging that how the child thinks about moral situations and social conflict is every bit as important as how she behaves. However, a major concern is whether moral reasoning is related to moral behavior. As one researcher put it, "Knowing the good is not always sufficient to motivate someone to do the good" (Nucci, 2001, p. 196). Scores on moral reasoning tests do not always correlate with tendencies to avoid cheating, to help others, or to abide by rules (Richards et al., 1992). The closest relationships are found between moral reasoning and specific negative social behaviors, such as aggression and delinquency (Blasi, 1980; Gregg, Gibbs, & Basinger, 1994). These issues aside, it remains important to understand how children make judgments about what is right and wrong and, in addition, to know more about how the motivations to act on those judgments arise (Arsenio & Lemerise, 2004).

PROSOCIAL BEHAVIOR AND ALTRUISM

In contrast to research that focuses on justice and rights, prosocial and altruistic responses have a less obligatory, legalistic quality about them (Kahn, 1992). Acts of kindness or assistance are often discretionary but highly valued in many communities. Many researchers report that helping and sharing increase with age, but others note that older children may actually help or share less (Radke-Yarrow, Zahn-Waxler, & Chapman, 1983). Beyond age six, increasing concerns about self-interest, the expectations of others, and greater consideration of the consequences of their actions can enter into children's decisions about assisting a person in need or performing another prosocial activity (Eisenberg et al., 1995; Krebs & Van Hesteren, 1994). Nevertheless, a meta-analysis of research on this issue has revealed that prosocial behavior does generally increase with age (Fabes et al., 1999).

Are girls, often believed to be more nurturing, caring, and empathic than boys, also more altruistic? On the whole, children display few sex differences in the amount of helping and sharing they exhibit (Radke-Yarrow et al., 1983). For example, when in the presence of a crying baby, girls are no more likely to assist than boys (Zahn-Waxler, Friedman, & Cummings, 1983). But some sex differences are observed favoring girls, and the differences tend to increase with age (Fabes et al., 1999). These differences are more evident when measures of prosocial behavior involve being kind or considerate, rather than when the activity demands helping, comforting, or sharing. In addition, they are more likely to be found when self-reports rather than observational methods are used to measure prosocial activity (Eisenberg & Fabes, 1998).

The Relationship Between Empathy and Helping Behaving prosocially, such as attempting to alleviate distress in others, may be a way to relieve a child's own empathic distress (Hoffman, 1976, 1982). Thus, if a boy sees that a friend who has just fallen down on the playground is crying, he feels uncomfortable. He knows how painful a skinned knee feels and shares his friend's anguish. To feel better himself, the boy rushes to help his playmate to the school nurse's office.

How strong is the connection between empathy and prosocial behavior? When children are asked to report their feelings, a consistent link between empathy and assisting others has not always been shown. When empathy is assessed by using nonverbal measures, such as facial expressions (such as sadness) or behavioral gestures that connote empathy or lack of it (looking away from the distressed person), there is a relationship with helping and sharing. As children grow older, that relationship grows distinctly stronger (Eisenberg, 1986; Eisenberg & Miller, 1987; Roberts & Strayer, 1996).

A younger child may show signs of empathic distress but not know exactly how to help (Hoffman, 1976). If a playmate is crying as the result of a fall, should she be helped to stand up or be left alone? Should the child say something comforting or reassuring, or simply keep silent? As children mature, they are learning about the social and emotional worlds on a number of fronts. They are better able to interpret the emotions they are feeling (including empathy), may experience them more strongly, and learn about the range of prosocial behaviors they can express. Unfortunately, if the emotional arousal is either too limited or becomes too great, children may either ignore the other person or focus on their own uncomfortable feelings at the expense of helping (Fabes et al., 1994; Miller et al., 1996; Young, Fox, & Zahn-Waxler, 1999). The distinction between self and other also matures and, with it, the realization that the other person's distress can be relieved by taking some action. In this regard, individual differences in helpfulness do exist (Hay et al., 1999). Children who show more prosocial behaviors are better able to take the perspective of another and therefore to feel sympathy for that individual.

Prosocial Reasoning Just as moral reasoning associated with justice changes with development, so does reasoning associated with prosocial behavior. Nancy Eisenberg (1986) formulated prosocial dilemmas in which the interests of one person are in conflict with those of another individual or group. For example, a child on the way to a birthday party sees another child who has hurt her leg. Should she go find that child's parent in order to get her to a doctor? Or should she continue on to the birthday party so as not to miss the fun? In justifying their answers to such a dilemma, many preschool and some young school-age children in the United States use a *hedonistic orientation* in their reasoning, saying they would help in order to gain affection or material rewards, such as candy or cake. A *needs-of-others orientation* prevails in the reasoning of early elementary school children, who typically express a concern for the physical or psychological needs of others ("He needs help"; "She's hurt"). An *approval and interpersonal orientation* is more prevalent in the middle childhood years as the child's responses increasingly take into consideration the reactions of others ("The child should help because the other person would like her"). During the later elementary years and into high school, a more *self-reflective, empathic orientation* emerges ("I'm trying to put myself in that person's shoes"). Older adolescents develop an *internalized orientation,* focusing on the importance of such emotions as happiness and pride to match internalized abstract principles of behavior concerned with fulfilling societal obligations, avoiding guilt, and maintaining self-respect.

Table 12.2 outlines the stages of prosocial reasoning. As with other views of moral development, reasoning progresses from concern for external consequences to a more internalized, principled foundation. However, hedonistic responses do show some increase during the adolescent years, especially in boys (Eisenberg et al., 1995). As expected, level of orientation relates to behavior and how children are perceived by others. For example, children who reason hedonistically tend to donate toys, stickers, or other valued objects to other children less frequently and are evaluated less positively by peers than children of a similar age who reason at higher levels (Carlo et al., 1996; Eisenberg & Shell, 1986).

KEY THEME
SOCIOCULTURAL INFLUENCE

Culture and Altruism When asked to reason about prosocial dilemmas, children in other Western industrialized societies display similar patterns of development. German, Italian, and Polish children, for example, show the same progression from

Table 12.2 Levels of Prosocial Reasoning

Nancy Eisenberg has outlined the accompanying progression in prosocial reasoning. Children move from a concern with the self to a concern for others and show more internal, abstract bases for helping as they grow older.

Level	Age	Characteristics
Hedonistic orientation	Preschoolers and young elementary school children	Preoccupation with gain for the self as a result of being or not being altruistic
Needs-of-others orientation	Early and middle elementary school children	Concern for the physical and psychological needs of others although they may conflict with own
Approval and interpersonal orientation	Middle elementary and high school students	Reliance on stereotypes of good and bad and seeking approval from others for helping or not helping
Self-reflective, empathetic orientation	Late elementary and high school students	Concern for feelings of others and use of norms for prosocial behavior
Internalized orientation	High school students	Maintenance of self-respect for living up to internalized values and beliefs; belief in rights of all individuals and importance of fulfilling societal obligations

Source: Adapted from Eisenberg (1986).

a hedonistic to a needs-of-others orientation that children in the United States do (Boehnke et al., 1989; Eisenberg et al., 1985). In other cultures, however, variations have been found. For example, elementary school children reared on the Israeli kibbutz reflect a more mature level of prosocial reasoning, voicing concern about the humaneness of the central character and the importance of internalized norms ("She has a duty to help others") (Eisenberg, Hertz-Lazarowitz, & Fuchs, 1990). A somewhat different picture emerges for children from the Maisin tribe, a coastal village society of Papua New Guinea. Here children maintain a needs-of-others orientation well into adolescence and even adulthood (Tietjen, 1986). These developmental patterns mirror the values emphasized by each culture. On the Israeli kibbutz, the goal of contributing to the good of the entire community is stressed, whereas, among the Maisin, children are taught explicitly to be aware of and respond to the needs of specific others rather than to those of the larger social group.

Might children also show cross-cultural differences in their tendency to behave prosocially related to their prosocial reasoning? Nancy Graves and Theodore Graves (1983) studied the inhabitants of Aitutaki Island, one of the Cook Islands in the South Pacific. A tremendous economic shift, from a subsistence to an industrialized market economy, took place on parts of this island and produced corresponding changes in family structure and the roles of family members. Children living in the unaffected rural villages grow up in extended families in which they make substantial contributions to family and community goals. They participate in most community affairs, are sent by elders to share food and goods with other village members, and bring the family contribution to church each week. In contrast, children growing up in urban, more modernized settings are reared in nuclear families and participate less in both family and community functions.

Graves and Graves (1983) observed that children five and six years of age in the urban communities were less likely to assist others in their home and surrounding environs than were children in rural settings. The researchers conclude that prosocial behavior is more likely in societies in which the predominant ethic is one of interdependence and group orientation, and in which the child participates in cooperative work experiences, than it is in cultures that emphasize individualism and self-reliance. In general, children from traditional rural communities tend to

Some children grow up in cultures in which they contribute to the needs of the entire community. Here children in India assist by carrying firewood to their local rural village. Children reared in group-oriented societies tend to engage in more prosocial behavior than children reared in settings that emphasize individualism.

be more cooperative than children from urban cultures (Eisenberg & Mussen, 1989). Also, children from more communal cultures (typical of Asian countries) tend to share more than children from cultures emphasizing individualism (typical of Western countries) (Rao & Stewart, 1999).

KEY THEME
NATURE & NURTURE

The Role of Socialization What role do child-rearing techniques play in the emergence of prosocial behavior? As social learning theory would predict, reinforcement can be influential. Both material rewards (money, candy, tokens) and social rewards ("You're a good boy!") increase the likelihood that children will share with or help others, although social rewards and acknowledgments seem to motivate greater care and concern for others (Grusec, 1991). Opportunities for observational learning are another potent factor. When a child sees someone make a donation to a needy person or group, he is likely to be charitable as well (Grusec & Skubiski, 1970).

What models do appears to be more important than what they say (Rushton, 1975); yet the nature of caregivers' verbal communications also has a bearing on prosocial behavior. When parents use **induction**—that is, explain why transgressions are wrong, provide a rationale for rules and regulations, present a reason for prosocial activity, and express disappointment at specific behaviors when exhibited inappropriately—their children are more likely to practice prosocial behaviors (Hastings et al., 2000; Hoffman, 1975; Krevans & Gibbs, 1996). For example, a parent might say, "Don't pull Sam's hair! That hurts him. You don't like to have your hair pulled, do you?" Such messages emphasize clear communication about standards for behavior, arouse empathic feelings, and stimulate perspective taking (Eisenberg & Mussen, 1989). In contrast, a far less effective means of fostering prosocial behavior involves **power assertion**, using forceful commands, physical punishment, or removal of material objects or privileges to influence behavior. For example, the parent might yell, "Stop that! You're not watching TV tonight!" as her son pulls his brother's hair.

induction Parental control technique that relies on the extensive use of reasoning and explanation as well as the arousal of empathic feelings.

power assertion Parental control technique that relies on the use of forceful commands, physical punishment, and removal of material objects or privileges.

Assigning responsibility to children, particularly for tasks that benefit others rather than oneself, also has an impact. For example, having children contribute to household chores, such as gardening, helping to prepare meals, keeping the family room clean, or other activities beneficial to the family as a whole, is related to more prosocial activities than is taking responsibility for tasks that directly profit only oneself, such as taking care of one's own room or cleaning up one's own space

(Grusec, Goodnow, & Cohen, 1996). Moreover, prosocial actions are increased when children are "expected" to initiate and routinely complete these helping activities—that is, when children must self-regulate their actions in these realms rather than when they are requested to carry out the chores only on particular occasions.

Another socialization technique that may be as effective as induction is to emphasize the child's prosocial characteristics. When a child is told, "I guess you're the kind of person who helps others whenever you can," her tendency to behave prosocially increases greatly (Mills & Grusec, 1989). Perhaps attributing to the child a sense of concern for others changes her self-concept, and she strives to behave in a manner consistent with that image (Grusec, 1982). Parents do not make prosocial attributions about their children often, but it is precisely the rarity of these comments that may make them so powerful in the eyes of the child (Grusec, 1991).

Additional Influences on Prosocial Behavior Surprisingly, developmental researchers have seldom investigated the many potential influences that exposure to religious education and other social organizations, such as scouting, boys' and girls' clubs, and other community programs, may have on the development of prosocial responses and values. Yet many parents would claim that such activities also play a vital role in the development of socially acceptable behaviors. In one study of children given training in their Jewish or Christian faith, participants as young as ten years were found to distinguish between moral issues that they considered to be unalterable (stealing, hitting, damaging another's property) and conventional religious practices that might change in certain circumstances or not apply to other individuals (dress customs, dietary laws, worship activities). Thus they could distinguish moral issues involving justice and human welfare from social conventions that arise from exposure to their particular faith (Nucci & Turiel, 1993). In other words, recognizing what is moral and what is socially determined very likely is influenced not only by parental teachings and school practices but also by the myriad other activities and examples to which children are exposed in their particular social contexts. Issues of fairness and rights, caring and cooperation, and duties and personal responsibility are among those that individuals in most cultures believe are too important to be left to just one component of the child's experiences.

Prosocial Behavior and Other Aspects of Development Grade school children who tend to help others have better social skills (Eisenberg & Mussen, 1989), are more popular with peers (Gottman, Gonso, & Rasmussen, 1975; McGuire & Weisz, 1982), and are more self-confident, self-assured, and better adjusted than those who do not. Children who think prosocially—who tend to think in terms of helping others in distress—have more friends and higher-quality relationships with their friends (Rose & Asher, 2004). Perhaps it is not surprising that prosocial behaviors are associated with many desirable outcomes, particularly in children's social relationships.

However, recent research has revealed other intriguing links, as well. For example, relationships have been reported between prosocial behavior and academic achievement. In one study carried out by Gian Caprara and colleagues (Caprara et al., 2000), eight- to nine-year-olds in a community near Rome, Italy, were revisited five years later as adolescents. In contrast to the more traditional focus, in which negative factors, such as aggression in young children, are studied as a condition predicting poor academic achievement, this study examined the consequences of prosocial behavior on success in the later school years. Teachers, peers, and the children themselves rated their willingness to help, share, be cooperative, and be kind. Even after controlling for level of early academic achievement as third-graders, the researchers found that higher levels of prosocial behavior displayed at this younger age subsequently predicted greater achievement in school as adolescents (Caprara et al., 2000). In another study carried out in Shanghai, China, a greater prosocial orientation among sixth-graders also was correlated with greater academic achievement two years later (Chen et al., 2000). These results suggest that educational environments might benefit from emphasizing prosocial behaviors as much as, if not more than, from the fairly widespread practice of focusing on reducing negative behaviors.

FOR • YOUR • REVIEW

- What are the basic elements of Piaget's theory of moral development? What elements of his theory are supported or refuted by research evidence?
- What are the primary stages of moral development according to Kohlberg? What kinds of data support his theory? What are some of the major criticisms of his perspective?
- What is the distinction between a morality of justice and a morality of care and responsibility?
- What evidence suggests that the development of knowledge in the moral domain should be distinguished from the development of knowledge about social conventions?
- What is the relationship between empathy and prosocial behavior?
- What are the stages of prosocial reasoning according to recent theory and research?
- How do cross-cultural differences in child rearing influence displays of prosocial behavior?
- What roles do socialization practices play in displays of prosocial behavior?
- What factors outside of the family can influence prosocial behavior?
- What is the relationship between prosocial behavior and other aspects of development?

GENDER ROLES IN MIDDLE CHILDHOOD

Despite shifting cultural beliefs about gender over the last several decades, the world of the middle child is still decidedly "gendered." In their knowledge and in their behaviors, school-age children demonstrate very clearly that they know full well what society expects of them as boys and girls, and that, for better or for worse, fulfilling those social roles plays an important part in their self-identity.

GENDER STEREOTYPES

By age six or seven, children's knowledge of gender stereotypes is well elaborated. Lisa Serbin and her colleagues (Serbin, Powlishta, & Gulko, 1993) asked five- through twelve-year-olds to state whether twenty stereotyped objects (for example, *hammer*, *rifle*, *stove*, *broom*) belonged to a male or female category. As Figure 12.6 indicates, all children, regardless of age, showed extensive knowledge of the stereotypes. The figure also shows that children's knowledge of stereotyped personality traits (*gentle*, *emotional*, *adventurous*, *messy*) expands through the middle school years. As children grow older, however, their knowledge of stereotypes also becomes more flexible, in that they are more likely to say that both males and females can possess certain traits (Katz & Ksansnak, 1994; Levy, Taylor, & Gelman, 1995; Serbin et al., 1993).

Given their far-reaching knowledge, to what degree do children actually enact gender stereotypes? Quite a bit, according to studies that have asked children to report how they spend their leisure time. Eight-year-old girls in one recent study said that they spent much more time in feminine activities, such as dance, crafts,

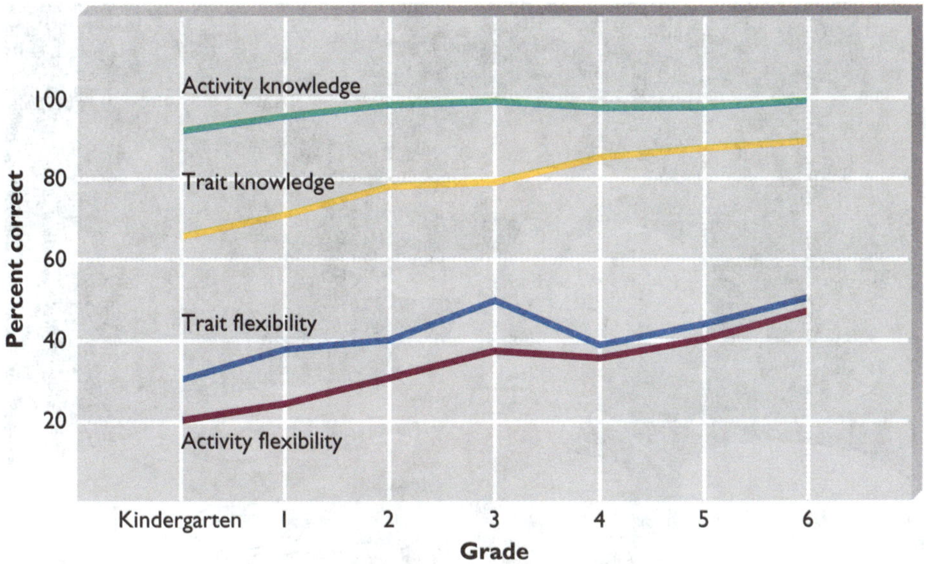

FIGURE 12.6

Development Trends in Gender-Role Knowledge

When kindergartners through sixth-graders were asked to identify which of twenty stereotyped objects were masculine and which were feminine, all children gave at least 90 percent correct answers (see the line for "Activity knowledge"). If they were asked to indicate whether objects could be used by both sexes, a developmental increase in flexibility was also observed (see the line for "Activity flexibility"). In addition, knowledge of stereotyped traits and flexibility with regard to those traits both increased over the age span studied.

Source: Serbin, Powlishta, & Gulko (1993).

gymnastics, and art, than in masculine activities, such as competitive sports, building, and fishing. As they grew older, however, the difference between time spent in feminine and masculine activities diminished (McHale, Shanahan, et al., 2004). Boys tend to be even more stereotyped in their activities, especially when they are with other boys. In this context, they spend seven times the amount of time in masculine activities as compared with feminine ones (McHale, Kim, et al., 2004).

KEY THEME
SOCIOCULTURAL INFLUENCE

The strong pattern of preferring sex-typed activities breaks down under certain circumstances. Playing with a sibling of the opposite sex makes a difference (McHale, Kim, et al., 2004). Culture matters, too. Perhaps the most comprehensive cross-cultural comparison of children and the factors that influence their development was conducted by Beatrice Whiting and Carolyn Pope Edwards. In their Six-Culture study, these researchers examined aggression, nurturance, help seeking, sociability, and other social behaviors in children ages three to eleven living in Kenya, Okinawa, India, the Philippines, Mexico, and the United States (Whiting & Edwards, 1988;

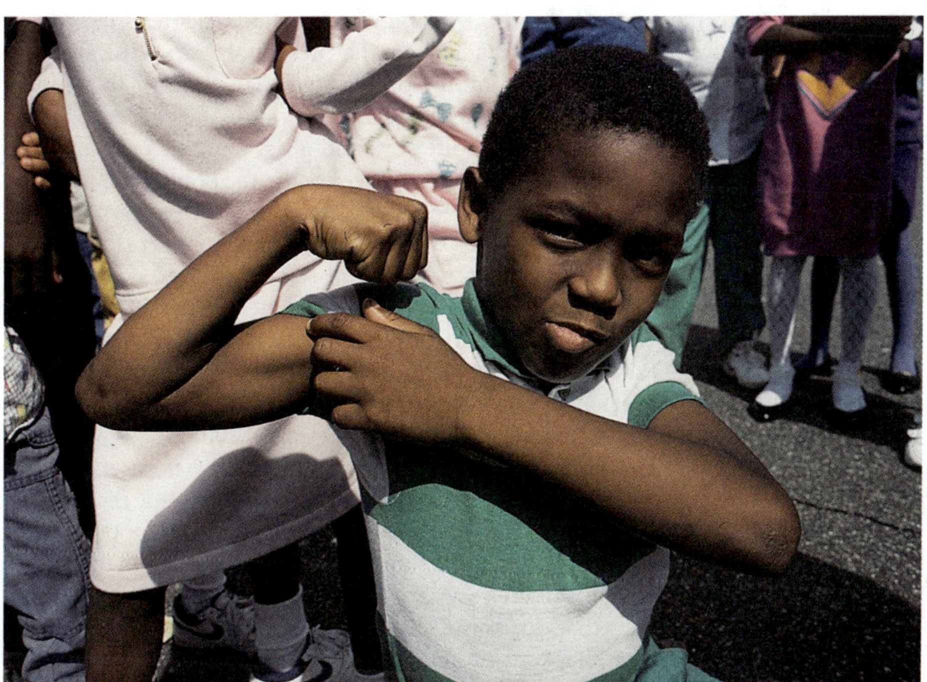

By two or three years of age, children show a fairly extensive understanding of gender stereotypes, beliefs about the characteristics of males and females. Through the early and middle school years, this knowledge becomes even more fully elaborated.

Similar gender-typed behaviors have been observed in several different cultures, including Mexico, this girl's home. Women and girls are expected to participate in household tasks and the care of children. Variations in gender roles across cultures have also been observed, however, suggesting that biology alone cannot account for their occurrence.

Whiting & Whiting, 1975). The results showed that differences between boys and girls were more exaggerated in some cultures than in others; in fact, they were least pronounced for the American children in the sample. Furthermore, sex differences between males and females diminished when both boys and girls were involved in household tasks, particularly the care of younger siblings. For example, Nyansango boys in East Africa scored higher than girls on their tendency to offer help and support to others; they were also as likely as girls to retreat from aggression. Interestingly, many boys in this culture tend to babies and perform other domestic chores, tasks that encourage nurturance and collaboration.

Gender Identity

Gender identity, in the sense of the child's being able to state whether she or he is a boy or a girl, is well established as far back as the preschool years. However, the concept of gender identity is actually more complicated than that. In the middle childhood years, children begin to think about *gender typicality*, the degree to which they conform to society's expectations about boys and girls. They also make evaluative judgments about the extent to which they feel content about their assigned gender. Research has shown that the degree to which children view themselves as compatible with their gender is related to psychological adjustment. Preadolescents who express contentment with their own gender and see themselves as typical for their sex have higher self-esteem, for example (Egan & Perry, 2001). When preteens score low on measures of gender typicality, however, they are at risk for low self-esteem in later years. These children are also more likely to experience internalizing problems, such as depression and anxiety, if they feel pressured to conform to gender expectations for boys and girls (Yunger, Carver, & Perry, 2004).

Some preadolescents also begin to question their identities as heterosexual individuals. They may be unsure of whether they will get married, have a family, take on traditional parental roles, or fall in love with a member of the opposite sex. Children who express these ideas tend to feel subsequent distress about their relationships with peers, although these effects are not necessarily very large. Perhaps the most important point is that, for some children, ideas about the nature of the "sexual self" begin to take shape prior to adolescence, contrary to what many researchers had previously thought (Carver, Egan, & Perry, 2004).

ATYPICAL DEVELOPMENT

Gender Identity Disorder

According to the *Diagnostic and Statistical Manual of Mental Disorders (DSM-IV)* of the American Psychiatric Association, some children may qualify for a diagnosis of *gender identity disorder* if they express a strong desire to be a member of the opposite sex or claim to be unhappy as a boy or a girl (American Psychiatric Association, 2000). Children may insist on wearing clothing or hairstyles of the opposite sex or may display significant problems at home or school, sometimes to the extent that parents seek out professional help (Zucker & Bradley, 2000). The criteria for mental disorder in the DSM-IV include an individual's experience of severe distress or increased risk of harm.

There is controversy about whether gender identity disorder is truly a psychiatric condition. Some mental health professionals note that children with gender identity disorder are prone to depression and behavior problems similar to those of children with other clinical diagnoses (Zucker & Bradley, 2000). Therefore, they say that gender identity disorder is a legitimate psychiatric problem. Critics point out that gender identity disorder does not necessarily lead to adjustment problems later in adolescence and adulthood. Many of these children, for example, eventually identify themselves as homosexual, which is not a psychiatric condition in the DSM-IV. Moreover, the distress that children experience is not due to cross-gender behaviors—these children are perfectly happy when they perform such behaviors. It is the reactions of peers and others that cause them such great difficulty. The critics believe that gender identity disorder should be removed from the DSM-IV (Bartlett, Vasey, & Bukowski, 2000).

The main point of contention is whether gender identity disorder is a genuine problem residing within an individual or whether the problem lies in our broader society's intolerance for behaviors that violate gender boundaries. When these children experience distress, for example, is it because of some inner turmoil associated with personal adjustment issues, or is it due to the highly negative reactions of peers and parents to cross-gender behaviors? When children with gender identity disorder report distress, the cause is usually problems with peers or unhappiness at having to stop their cross-gender behaviors, not a disturbance of gender. Also important to consider is the fact that definitions of masculinity and femininity can vary across cultures and historical times. Nancy Bartlett and her colleagues point out that, in other eras, for example, men who stayed at home with their children might have been seen as mentally ill for violating a gender norm (Bartlett et al., 2000). It would be helpful to conduct more longitudinal studies of cross-gender children to observe developmental changes in their adjustment, as well as the specific antecedents and consequences of their cross-gender behaviors.

SEX SEGREGATION

One of the things even a casual observer would notice on the typical school playground is that boys and girls tend to interact in separate groups: boys play with boys and girls play with girls (Maccoby, 1988, 1990). This phenomenon is called **sex segregation.** In one observation of one hundred children on their preschool playgrounds, four-year-olds spent three times as much time with same-sex partners as with opposite-sex partners. By age six, they spent eleven times more time with peers of the same sex (Maccoby & Jacklin, 1987). In fact, only about 10 percent of young children's peer interactions are with members of the opposite sex (Martin & Fabes, 2001). This tendency to prefer same-sex peers persists at least until early adolescence (Maccoby, 1990). Interestingly enough, when young children are asked if a

sex segregation Clustering of individuals into same-sex groups.

boy can join a group of girls playing with dolls (or if a girl can join a group of boys playing with trucks), almost 90 percent say, "Yes" and justify their responses on moral grounds. It wouldn't be right or fair, they say, to exclude the member of the opposite sex (Killen et al., 2001). Yet, when confronted with social interactions with an opposite-sex peer, elementary school–age children express more negative emotion toward and less liking of that child (Underwood, Schockner, & Hurley, 2001). Sex segregation is a potent phenomenon in the social lives of young children.

Eleanor Maccoby (1990, 2002) believes that children's experiences in same-sex groups constitute an extremely powerful socialization environment. As boys play in their characteristic rough-and-tumble fashion or in team sports and games, they develop assertive, dominance-seeking styles of interaction. In contrast, girls' groups, which are oriented toward relationships and shared intimacy, promote cooperation and mutual support, as well as a tendency to preserve the cohesiveness of the group. A study of preschool and kindergarten children over a six-month period confirmed that, as children spent more time in same-sex groups, their conformity with gender-stereotyped behaviors increased. Boys who spent more time with boys became more active and rough in their play. Similarly, girls who spent more time with girls played more calmly over time and engaged in more gender-stereotyped play, such as dressing up and interacting with dolls (Martin & Fabes, 2001).

FOR • YOUR • REVIEW

- How do children's concepts of gender stereotypes change during middle childhood?
- What changes in gender identity occur during middle childhood?
- How does sex segregation contribute to the development of gender roles?

CHAPTER RECAP

Summary of Developmental Themes

NATURE & NURTURE

How do nature and nurture interact in social and emotional development in middle childhood?

Many changes in emotions during middle childhood occur through the process of socialization. Parents and others transmit their culture's messages about emotional display rules and about the need to regulate one's emotions. The role of biology in emotional development is illustrated by the fact that certain portions of the brain are active during attempts to regulate emotions.

Many aspects of the development of self-concept occur in a social context. By engaging in the process of social comparison, for example, children develop a sense of their strengths and weaknesses compared with those of other children their age. Social support from parents and peers plays a role in the development of self-esteem. Feedback from parents and others can also influence the child's mastery orientation or learned helplessness.

Piaget and Kohlberg suggest that maturation contributes in part to changes in moral reasoning, but so do children's experiences with peers and socializing agents. Research on the development of prosocial behaviors shows that certain parental socialization techniques are associated with children's altruism.

Many of the child's beliefs and attitudes about gender are formed in a social context, particularly in the same-sex groups in which children tend to participate.

SOCIOCULTURAL INFLUENCE

How does the sociocultural context influence social and emotional development in middle childhood?

Different cultures place varying emphasis on emotionality itself and on the specific emotions considered appropriate to display. Cultural values can impinge on growing concepts of self, especially the terms that are used to describe the self. Cultures also vary in the degree to which they stress an orientation to the community, an emphasis that is associated with greater prosocial behavior.

Continuity/Discontinuity

Are social and emotional development in middle childhood continuous or discontinuous?

Piaget's and Kohlberg's theories of moral development are stage theories. However, much of the research on social and emotional development portrays the child's acquisitions as continuous.

Interaction Among Domains

How do social and emotional development in middle childhood interact with other domains?

Emotions are closely intertwined with both cognition and social behavior. As children begin to think in more complex ways, they begin to understand the complexities of emotional communication. Children who are skilled at understanding, expressing, and regulating emotions have better relations with their peers. Similarly, advances in the child's cognition pave the way for development of self-concept and moral reasoning.

Risk/Resilience

What factors promote risk or resilience in social and emotional development in middle childhood?

Children who show poor knowledge about emotions and lack the ability to regulate emotions are at risk for poor social relations and behavior problems. Likewise, learned helplessness, low self-esteem, and a lower prosocial orientation are linked to poorer outcomes later in development.

Chapter Review

Emotional Development in Middle Childhood

What kinds of knowledge do children acquire about emotions during middle childhood?

School-age children begin to appreciate cultural *display rules* that dictate when and how emotions should be displayed. They also understand that they can control emotions with their own thoughts and that sometimes two emotions can be experienced simultaneously.

What factors influence children's acquisition of knowledge about emotions?

Knowledge about emotions is learned, at least in part, from interactions with parents. Parents who discuss and explain emotions and who display less negative affect themselves have children with greater understanding of emotions.

What factors are involved in children's increasing ability to regulate emotions?

Parents who provide supportive guidance and positively toned interactions have children who are better able to regulate their own emotions. Changes in the functioning of certain regions of the brain also seem to be associated with better self-regulation.

How does culture play a role in emotional development?

Different cultures encourage the expression of some emotions over others, depending on the broader values and belief systems they hold. They may also value some temperament styles over others.

The Development of Self in Middle Childhood

What are the primary distinctions between self as object and self as subject? What are the typical behaviors that illustrate these two characterizations of self?

Self as object consists of the perceptions, ideas, and beliefs that a person holds to be true of himself or herself, including physical qualities, possessions, skills, and personality. Self as subject includes the child's sense of agency, individuality, stability, and identity.

How does social comparison contribute to the concept of self in middle childhood?

By engaging in *social comparison*, children gain knowledge of their relative standing among their peers, an important component in their understanding of self. Most five- to seven-year-olds do not respond to this form of feedback about their successes or failures in assessing themselves, but older school-age children do.

What factors contribute to mastery orientation and learned helplessness? What steps can parents and teachers take to reduce learned helplessness?

Children with a *mastery orientation* believe they have considerable influence over what happens to them. Those who experience *learned helplessness* believe they have little influence over what happens to them. Mastery orientation and learned helplessness are determined in part by the extent to which children perceive their abilities as entity-based or as a result of their own effort. Learned helplessness can be reduced by a focus on effort and by avoiding praise or criticism of stable traits.

What factors contribute to high self-esteem?

Self-esteem arises from the evaluations of others, as well as the extent to which the child feels successful in those areas thought be to important.

What role does praise play in self-esteem and in promoting achievement motivation?

Unlimited and unqualified praise does not always contribute to positive self-esteem and achievement motivation. To be effective, praise should be sincere and focused on the child's efforts, encourage the child to be autonomous, avoid social comparison, and provide realistic feedback.

Moral Development in Middle Childhood

What are the basic elements of Piaget's theory of moral development? What elements of his theory are supported or refuted by research evidence?

In Piaget's theory, children progress from *moral realism* to *moral relativism* as their cognitive capabilities mature. In moral realism, children focus on the visible consequences of an act, believe in *immanent justice*, and do not see a need for punishments to fit the transgression. In moral relativism, children focus on the intentions behind an act, shed their belief in immanent justice, and believe that punishments should relate to misdemeanors. The child's increasing perspective-taking skills, as well as opportunities to interact with peers, are major factors in promoting this shift.

Research confirms that children more fully consider intentions and show fewer beliefs in immanent justice and arbitrary punishment as they grow older. But even preschoolers have been shown to recognize actors' intentions, and the contributions of parents (not just peers) have also been demonstrated in children's moral reasoning.

What are the primary stages of moral development according to Kohlberg? What kinds of data support his theory? What are some of the major criticisms of his perspective?

In Kohlberg's view, most children advance through *preconventional*, *conventional*, and *postconventional* levels of moral reasoning. Kohlberg maintains that the child's increasing perspective-taking skills, amplified by opportunities to discuss the points of view of others, are responsible for progress through the stages.

Research supports the idea that there are stagelike progressions in moral thinking and that moral reasoning is related to advances in cognition. But critics point out that most people do not reason above the conventional level and that values drawn from various cultures are not well-represented in the theory.

What is the distinction between a morality of justice and a morality of care and responsibility?

Kohlberg's theory focuses on a *morality of justice*, the tendency to make moral judgments based on considerations of rules versus the rights of the individual. A *morality of care and responsibility* refers to moral judgments based on concerns of self-sacrifice and relationships with others.

What evidence suggests that the development of knowledge in the moral domain should be distinguished from the development of knowledge about social conventions?

Children tend to take action when moral rules, as opposed to *social conventions*, are violated. They also believe that moral transgressions are wrong, even if there are no explicit rules about them. Social conventions, they say, are dependent on rules.

What is the relationship between empathy and prosocial behavior?

When empathy is assessed via facial expressions or other observable behaviors, it has been shown to be related to prosocial behavior. This relationship grows stronger with development.

What are the stages of prosocial reasoning according to recent theory and research?

Children typically progress through the following steps in prosocial reasoning: believing that prosocial behaviors should be displayed because they are rewarded, a concern for the needs of others, a concern for the approval of others, an empathy orientation, and finally, a focus on self-respect and fulfillment of societal obligations.

How do cross-cultural differences in child rearing influence displays of prosocial behavior?

Children are more likely to engage in mature prosocial reasoning and display a greater number of prosocial behaviors in cultures that promote a community orientation and group values.

What roles do socialization practices play in displays of prosocial behavior?

Children who are rewarded for prosocial behaviors and who observe parents and others acting prosocially tend to be more helpful than other children. Children whose parents use *induction* rather than *power assertion* as a disciplinary technique are also more likely to demonstrate care and concern for others.

What factors outside of the family can influence prosocial behavior?

Religious education and participation in other social organizations is likely to encourage children to engage in more prosocial behavior.

What is the relationship between prosocial behavior and other aspects of development?

Children who display prosocial behaviors are more popular with peers and have stronger friendships. They are also more likely to have higher academic achievement.

Gender Roles in Middle Childhood

How do children's concepts of gender stereotypes change during middle childhood?

During middle childhood, knowledge about gender stereotypes becomes more extensive but also more flexible. Stereotypes are often enacted by children in the types of activities in which they choose to participate.

What changes in gender identity occur during middle childhood?

Gender identity begins to include assessments of gender typicality during middle childhood. Children who see themselves as typical for their sex have higher self-esteem and lower incidence of internalizing disorders.

How does sex segregation contribute to the development of gender roles?

Sex segregation is a robust phenomenon that provides different socialization experiences for boys and girls. Boys' groups promote dominance and assertiveness, whereas girls' groups promote a relationship orientation and shared intimacy.

Key Terms and Concepts

conventional level (p. 430)
display rule (p. 416)
immanent justice (p. 429)
induction (p. 438)
learned helplessness (p. 422)
mastery orientation (p. 421)
moral realism (p. 429)
moral relativism (p. 429)
morality of care and responsibility (p. 434)
morality of justice (p. 434)
postconventional level (p. 430)
power assertion (p. 438)
preconventional level (p. 430)
self-esteem (p. 425)
sex segregation (p. 443)
social comparison (p. 421)
social convention (p. 434)

13 Contexts of Development

It was the start of the first day of school. Ms. Klein, the third-grade teacher, surveyed her new charges as they played in the schoolyard before the bell rang. It was a familiar scene: the boys played a raucous game of kickball, cheering their teammates and urging victory. The girls gathered in small groups, talking with great animation about their summer experiences and their excitement to see each other again. As always, certain children in both groups were the center of activity; they seemed to attract their peers as a pot of honey draws bees. Other children stayed on the fringes of the playground; few of their peers approached or spoke to them. Already, Ms. Klein has a sense that third grade, with all of its academic and social challenges, will be easier on some of these fresh new faces than on others.

Key Themes in Contexts of Development

Sociocultural Influence How do sociocultural factors influence the contexts of development in middle childhood?

Risk/Resilience What contextual factors promote risk or resilience in middle childhood?

Middle childhood brings a host of new experiences for children and, consequently, new contexts for their development. The most significant is the start of formal schooling. The child's typical day is now more highly structured, involves serious work, and requires greater independence than ever before. And with the start of school come other new opportunities for children—to make new friends, participate in athletics, or perhaps begin music or art instruction. The family still plays a pivotal role to be sure, but the sphere of influences on children's development—peers, teachers, media—is now greatly expanded. In this chapter, we take the opportunity to focus on these important new circumstances in which growth takes place.

The Family in Middle Childhood

As we have already pointed out in this text, in today's society we see the concept of family undergoing somewhat of a transition. There are now many variations from the traditional two-parent nuclear family. Single-parent families, families in which parents have divorced, and same-sex parents are more prevalent. What are the effects of these emerging family structures on child development? Research shows that development is influenced not so much by changes in family arrangement as by the ways in which interpersonal relations take place within the family.

During middle childhood, relationships between parents and children are no longer so one-sided. Instead of playing such a large supervisory role, parents now begin to nurture greater independence, especially as children enter school. Parents and children begin to negotiate as they make decisions and solve family problems.

In this portion of the chapter, we examine variations in families, across cultures and across the different forms and structures they may take. It should become apparent that the principles of effective parenting that we described in the chapter on early childhood continue to apply during the middle childhood years. Parents who are warm and nurturant but also set clear, consistent limits for their children provide a healthy, positive context for the child's continuing growth. These principles apply regardless of who the parents are and how many of them live in the child's immediate environment.

Cross-Cultural Differences in Parenting

Key Theme
Sociocultural Influence

Beatrice Whiting and Carolyn Pope Edwards (1988) have provided an extended analysis of variations in parenting by comparing societies as diverse as rural Kenya, Liberia, and the Philippines with urban America. Despite vast differences in economic, social, and political conditions, many similar, overarching patterns were apparent in the ways parents socialized their children. Whereas parents of infants and toddlers emphasized nurturance and, slightly later, corrections of misbehavior, when children reached school age parents became concerned with training them in the skills and social behavior valued by their cultural group.

At the same time, though, Whiting and Edwards (1988) observed notable differences. For example, mothers from rural villages in Kenya and Liberia emphasized training children to do chores responsibly and placed a high premium on obedience. From an early age, children were taught how to care for the family's fields and animals, and they assumed a major role in caring for younger siblings. Children were punished for performing tasks irresponsibly and were rarely praised. Consistent

Children's socialization experiences are influenced by cultural values and beliefs. For example, in rural Kenya, children care for the family's fields and animals, and have responsibility for younger siblings. Children growing up in such communities were found to display a high degree of compliance with mothers' requests.

with this orientation to child rearing was the family's dependence on women and children for producing food. Because women in these cultures typically had an enormous workload, they delegated some tasks to children as soon as children were physically capable of managing them; because accidents and injury to infants and the family's resources must be prevented, deviant behaviors were not tolerated in children. Children growing up in these communities were highly compliant with mothers' commands and suggestions.

An even more controlling style characterized the Tarong community in the Philippines, in which subsistence farming is the mainstay but responsibilities for producing food are more evenly distributed among the group's members. When the mother did not rely so heavily on her children to work for the family's survival and when the goals of training were thus less clear, arbitrary commands and even punishment became more common. Children were scolded frequently for being in the way of adults or for playing in inappropriate places. By middle childhood, Tarong children showed a marked decline in their tendency to seek attention from or be close to their parents.

These patterns provided a striking contrast to the "sociability" that characterized the middle-income American mothers in the sample. Interactions between mothers and children consisted of significant information exchange and warm, friendly dialogues. Mothers emphasized verbalization, educational tasks, and play, and they were liberal in their use of praise and encouragement. Because children in American society normally do not work to ensure the economic survival of the family unit, firm training and punishing were not part of these parents' styles. The emphasis on verbalization and educational activities was consistent with the high value Americans place on social interactions and schooling.

Other researchers examining parent-child relationships in Asian cultures have reaffirmed the idea that culture affects parenting styles. Japanese mothers use less physical punishment and more verbal reasoning to control their children than American mothers (Kobayashi-Winata & Power, 1989). Japanese culture emphasizes responsibilities and commitments to others, a socialization goal that is achieved more effectively through reasoning than through power-assertive techniques. Japanese children, in fact, comply with rules at home and in school more than their American counterparts do. Similarly, when Chinese parents are asked to describe their child-rearing practices, they report a greater emphasis on control and achievement in children than American parents (Chao, 1994; Lin & Fu, 1990). In Chinese society, character development and educational attainment are highly valued, and parental practices follow directly from these larger societal goals.

As Whiting and Edwards (1988) point out, parents around the world resemble one another in numerous ways because of the universal needs children have as they grow and develop. But it is also true that the specific ecology of each culture, its socialization goals, and the demands it places on the family unit can dramatically shape parenting practices and the course of the individual child's socialization.

Divorce

Key Theme
Risk/Resilience

The statistics are dramatic: the divorce rate among couples in the United States is a little under 50 percent, and estimates suggest that 40 percent of children in contemporary society will live through the divorce of their parents (Bramlett & Mosher, 2001; Cherlin, 1992; Furstenberg, 1994). Far from being an atypical event, divorce affects a significant proportion of American children. Unfortunately, the effects of divorce on children are rarely positive; the absence of one parent, the emotional and financial tension, and sometimes the continuing conflicts between parents that accompany divorce can lead to a range of psychological problems for

Parents around the world look similar on some dimensions because of the universal needs of children. For example, like this father, many parents across a variety of cultures express nurturance but also expect children to conform to specific cultural-linked values.

both boys and girls, at least in the period immediately following the breakup of the family. Children's ability to cope with the stresses of divorce, particularly in the long run, depends on a number of variables. Most important is the way parents manage the transition in family structure.

Consequences of Divorce A major longitudinal study of the effects of divorce on parents and children, conducted by E. Mavis Hetherington and her associates, illuminated how parental separation affects children and how the nature of parent-child interactions changes (Hetherington, Cox, & Cox, 1982). The researchers compared two groups over a period of two years, a sample of forty-eight preschool-age, middle-class children whose parents divorced and another group of forty-eight middle-class children matched on several variables, such as age and sex, whose families were intact. In all the divorced families, mothers had custody of their children. During the course of the study, the researchers made several assessments of both parents and children, including parental interviews, observations of parent-child interactions in the laboratory and at home, observations and ratings of children's behavior in the home and at school, and personality tests.

The results of the study indicated that the worst period for most children was the first year after the divorce, when they exhibited many negative characteristics such as aggression, distractibility, and noncompliance. The extent of their undesirable behaviors surpassed those of children from intact families with a high level of conflict; it was particularly noticeable in boys. Two years after the divorce, many of the effects on children had diminished, especially for girls. In a six-year follow-up, however, many boys continued to show patterns of aggression and noncompliance, academic difficulties, poor relations with peers, and extremely low self-esteem (Hetherington, 1989).

A look at family interaction styles after divorce helps to account for the poor initial adjustment of children. Hetherington and her colleagues noted that, soon after they separated from their husbands, mothers tended to adopt a more authoritarian style of parenting (Hetherington et al., 1982; Hetherington & Kelly, 2002). They gave out numerous commands and prohibitions, and displayed little affection or responsiveness to their children. These mothers were undoubtedly having problems coping, in both emotional and practical terms, with their new status as single parents. At the same time, the fathers withdrew, participating little in the management of their children's behavior. Children, particularly boys, became less compliant, and mothers in turn responded with increased restrictiveness and punitiveness. Caught up in a spiral of frustration, helplessness, and feelings of incompetence, these mothers responded negatively to many of their children's behaviors, even those that were neutral or positive, and, despite their harsh threats, followed up on few of the directives they gave. The result was a negative cycle of parent-child interactions.

Other researchers have confirmed that many children show more heightened aggression, lower academic achievement, more disruptions in peer relationships, and more depression after their parents' divorce than previously (Amato, 2001; Emery, 1999b; Stolberg & Anker, 1984; Wallerstein, Corbin, & Lewis, 1988). Research on how children respond to parental conflict suggests that children either blame themselves or perceive a personal threat when their parents fight, judgments that are linked to their own psychological adjustment (Grych, Harold, & Miles, 2003). Sibling interactions also suffer. Carol MacKinnon (1989) observed elementary school–age children as they played games with their siblings in the laboratory. Siblings whose parents had been divorced for one year or longer showed more teasing, quarreling, physical attacks, and other negative behaviors toward one another than children from intact families. Children ages six to eight years seem to have the most difficulty adjusting to divorce; they are old enough to recognize the seriousness of the family's situation but do not yet have the coping skills to deal with the feelings of sadness and guilt that often accompany the change in family structure (Wallerstein & Kelly, 1980). Older children often have a better understanding of divorce and the notion that conflicts between parents must somehow be resolved (Kurdek, 1989). However, even adolescents often suffer negative psychological consequences after their parents divorce. Adolescent boys in particular were found to be more likely to use alcohol or illicit drugs after their parents separated than boys in a control group whose parents remained married (Doherty & Needle, 1991).

For some individuals, the aftermath of divorce may last well into young adulthood. According to data collected as part of a major longitudinal study in Great Britain, young adults whose parents had previously divorced reported more depression, anxiety, and other emotional problems than adults from intact families (Chase-Lansdale, Cherlin, & Kiernan, 1995). In addition, in a twenty-year follow-up of her original sample, Hetherington (1999) found that young adults whose parents had divorced were less likely to finish high school, had smaller social networks, experienced more conflicts with siblings and friends, and had more conflicts in their own marriages. The results of another longitudinal study showed that adults whose parents had divorced were more likely to experience a breakup of their own marriages (Amato, 1999).

Key Theme
Risk/Resilience

Adjusting to Divorce The consequences of divorce are not always so grim for all children. In fact, most children whose parents have divorced do not look different from children in intact families when they are followed over time (Emery, 1999a). We need to remember that the psychological distress experienced by children at the time of the divorce is different from a long-term psychological disorder (Emery, Otto, & O'Donohue, 2005). E. Mavis Hetherington (1989) observed that, after six years, some of the children in her original study recovered from the family crisis and showed a healthy adaptation to their new family lifestyle, whether or not their mother remarried. These children displayed few behavior problems, high self-esteem, successful academic performance, and positive relations with peers.

What factors were associated with this favorable pattern of adjustment? For one thing, mothers of children in this group had become less authoritarian and more authoritative in their parental style, encouraging independence but also providing a warm, supportive climate for their sons and daughters. If the mother was not available, many of these children had contact with some other caring adult, such as a relative, teacher, or neighbor. In addition, several children in this category had responsibility for the care of another individual: a younger sibling, an aging grandparent, or someone with a physical or emotional problem. These relationships may have offered children an opportunity to feel needed and provided an alternative source of emotional gratification and support. In contrast, mothers of children with long-lasting adjustment problems continued to manifest coercive negative styles of interaction. Mothers and sons were especially likely to fall into this pattern. Children are also more likely to show successful adjustment to divorce when conflict between divorced parents is low, when the child does not feel "caught" between the two parents, and when the child does not feel that he or she will be abandoned (Amato & Rezac, 1994; Buchanan, Maccoby, & Dornbusch, 1991; Wolchik et al., 2002). Maintaining a close relationship with grandparents can also help (Lussier et al., 2002).

Divorce represents a difficult transition for all members of the family. Some of the effects of divorce on children may actually be due to personal attributes in parents that are passed on genetically to children. Parents and children may share biological predispositions to poor social and academic skills, and these may be the very characteristics that lead to marital problems for parents, as well as problematic postdivorce behaviors in children (O'Connor et al., 2000). However, research also suggests that a key variable in understanding the effects of divorce is the quality of relationships among all family members: the more conflict and negative emotion associated with the process and the more prolonged the maladaptive patterns of interaction, the worse the outcomes for the child. In addition, the child's overall adjustment needs to be considered in the broader context of such factors as socioeconomic status, neighborhood, and parental emotional state. These risk factors operate in a similar fashion whether the parents are divorced or not (Deater-Deckard & Dunn, 1999).

Custody Arrangements After divorce, most children reside with their mother, in large part because of long-standing societal beliefs about the privileged nature of mother-child relationships. Yet when children live with their mother after a divorce, they are more likely to experience economic hardship than if they live with their father. Studies have found that income for divorced women with children declines an average of 30 percent, whereas income for fathers declines much less or even increases (Burkhauser et al., 1991; Weitzman, 1985). Children living with their mother also typically show a dramatic impairment in their relationship with their father. For example, according to one national study, more than one-third of the children in the sample did not see their father *at all* or saw him only a few times a year (Selzer, 1991).

Many states now have laws that favor joint custody of children following divorce. In most cases, this means that both parents have equal responsibility for making decisions about the child's medical care and education; that is, they have *joint legal custody*. In other cases, children reside for substantial periods of time with each parent; this arrangement refers to *joint physical custody*. A meta-analysis of studies comparing the effects of joint custody versus sole custody shows that joint custody—whether it is legal or physical—is generally associated with greater benefits for children. Children in joint custody display higher self-esteem and fewer behavioral and emotional problems than children in sole custody. An important factor related to these benefits is children's ability to spend time with each parent; also, parents of children in joint custody tend to have fewer conflicts than parents in a sole-custody situation (Bauserman, 2002). However, it may not be the custody situation per se that influences children's well-being. Rather, it may be that parents who select this custody arrangement tend to have a low conflict style to begin with (Emery, Otto, & O' Donohue, 2005). Researchers have also reported that parental participation in a wide range of activities, even such everyday ones as shopping and watching TV together, predicted children's successful adjustment better than the frequency of special trips or activities (Clarke-Stewart & Hayward, 1996).

SINGLE-PARENT FAMILIES

KEY THEME
RISK/RESILIENCE

Slightly over one-third of American children are born to single mothers (Hamilton et al., 2005). Children growing up in single-parent families are at greater risk for a broad array of developmental problems, including poor academic achievement, behavior problems, and high-risk behaviors, such as substance abuse (Barber & Eccles,

1992; Demo & Acock, 1996; Turner, Irwin, & Millstein, 1991). It is also important to note that the poverty rate for families headed by single mothers is almost 30 percent, higher than for any other family type (DeNavas-Walt, Proctor, & Lee, 2005).

In light of these risks, it is important for research to identify the factors associated with more successful child outcomes in single-parent families. One of these is more involved parenting (Avenevoli, Sess, & Steinberg, 1999). In a study of almost 200 inner-city African American and Hispanic families, most of whom earned less than $20,000 per year, adolescent boys from mother-only families showed fewer problem behaviors when mothers used effective discipline strategies (firm but warm), allowed for the child's growing autonomy, provided a structured family environment, and facilitated the growth of relationships with other male family members (Florsheim, Tolan, & Gorman-Smith, 1998). In contrast, when parents are too punitive, children may not fare so well. In a study of 290 single-parent, poor families, most of whom were African American, children with fewer behavior problems and better school readiness had parents who were less likely to use harsh discipline (Zaslow et al., 1999).

Another factor is the involvement of mothers in religion. Among single-parent, poor African American families in the rural South, maternal religiosity was related to use of "no-nonsense" parenting (firm but warm), higher quality of mother-child relationships, and more maternal involvement in school. These latter variables, in turn, were linked to the child's overall successful development in cognitive, social, and behavioral domains (Brody & Flor, 1998).

Studies of single-parent families, as well as families that are undergoing other types of transitions, emphasize that it is important to find ways to promote healthy, positive interactions between parents and children. Effective parents are involved and nurturant, and provide firm, steady guidance to their children. When parents are stressed or distracted, or when they are unaware of the importance of parenting style, they are less likely to engage in successful interactions with their children. Assistance with child care, parent training programs, and counseling support for families experiencing stress are some of the societal programs that can be helpful.

Gay and Lesbian Parents

Because of the legal and social controversies surrounding gay and lesbian parenting, it is difficult to obtain accurate estimates of how many children grow up in families with same-sex parents. But most experts agree that the numbers are rising and might be in the millions. Research on the impact of growing up in families in which parents are gay or lesbian is clearer, however. When children whose parents are homosexual are compared with children whose parents are heterosexual, there are virtually no identifiable differences in their academic performance, social development, peer relationships, mental health, or sexual orientation (Patterson, 2000; Wainright, Russell, & Patterson, 2004). As with most studies of the impact of the family on child development, what matters most, say the results, is the quality of the day-to-day interactions that family members have with one another.

A study by Susan Golombok and her colleagues (Golombok et al., 2003) is representative of this body of research. Samples of seven-year-old children with two lesbian parents, two heterosexual parents, or single heterosexual mothers were compared on a number of measures of social and emotional well-being, including self-esteem, peer relations, gender-role activities, and mental health. Parental warmth, emotional involvement, and conflict resolution styles were also assessed. The findings showed that, in general, lesbian mothers were not significantly different from heterosexual mothers on most dimensions of parenting. In fact, lesbian mothers spanked their children less and engaged in more imaginative play. No differences were found in the adjustment scores of children from the various groups. Most revealing was the finding that the strongest predictor of children's adjustment was not mothers' sexual orientation or the structure of the family, but rather the amount of stress parents reported. For children in all families, the greater the difficulty mothers reported in their parental roles, the more likely were children to experience adjustment problems.

SIBLINGS

Siblings play an important but often unacknowledged role within the family. Older siblings act as teachers and role models, and can be important sources of emotional support for younger siblings. For better or worse, they instruct younger brothers and sisters on how to think and act, and in times of conflict or trouble within the family, they can buffer younger siblings from emotional distress (Jenkins, 1992). Aside from their direct impact on other children in the family, however, siblings can have effects that are more indirect (Brody, 2004). Consider what happens when an older sibling is rebellious or cooperative, successful in school or not. Parents' positive or negative experiences with an older sibling can color their expectations of the younger sibling (Whiteman & Buchanan, 2002). Moreover, older siblings who do well academically and who have good relationships with their peers give their parents confidence in their parenting skills, which in turn has an impact on their interactions with younger children in the family. Positive parenting results in better self-control and fewer behavioral problems in younger siblings (Brody et al., 2003). These kinds of findings provide vivid examples of how families function as systems with multiple layers of reciprocal influences.

How do older children interact as siblings? For one thing, children tend to fight more with their siblings than with their friends. When fifth- through eighth-graders were asked to describe conflicts with their siblings, they reported that they allowed quarrels with siblings to escalate, whereas they tried to resolve conflicts with friends. Most of the time, siblings fight about privacy and interpersonal boundaries (Raffaelli, 1989). Typically, parents do not intervene in sibling conflicts, and when they do not, those conflicts continue (Perozynski & Kramer, 1999). On the other hand, when parents discuss each child's needs (as opposed to using controlling tactics), subsequent conflicts between siblings are less likely (Kramer, Perozynski, & Chung, 1999). Siblings also express more positive behaviors with one another when their fathers, in particular, are nurturant and try to be fair to each child (Brody, Stoneman, & McCoy, 1992). Researchers have noted that the degree of conflict in sibling relationships is related to the amount of aggression a child shows in school, whereas the amount of warmth in sibling relationships is linked to emotional control and social competence in school (Garcia et al., 2000; Stormshak et al., 1996).

Whether positive or negative in character, the quality of sibling relationships initiated in early childhood tends to remain stable through middle childhood (Dunn, Slombowski, & Beardsall, 1994) and then typically changes from middle childhood through adolescence. Duane Buhrmester and Wyndol Furman (1990) administered the Sibling Relationship Questionnaire to third-, sixth-, ninth-, and twelfth-graders to assess several dimensions of sibling interactions. Older siblings reported being more dominant and nurturant toward their younger siblings, and younger siblings confirmed that they received more often than dispensed dominance and nurturance. These differences between older and younger siblings disappeared over time, however. The older children in the sample reported having more egalitarian relationships with their siblings, as well as less intense feelings of both warmth and conflict. Initial differences in power and nurturance usually disappeared when the younger sibling was twelve years old, by which time she or he had become more competent and needed less guidance and emotional support.

Although the presence of siblings may mean that the child has fewer opportunities to interact with parents, it also provides the context for developing other unique skills. Older siblings have opportunities to become nurturant and assertive, and younger siblings have more models for a range of behaviors than do only children.

FOR • YOUR • REVIEW

- In what ways do parenting strategies vary across different cultural groups?
- What are the effects of divorce on child development?
- What factors can help children adjust to the divorce of their parents?
- What kinds of custody arrangements are best for children?
- What factors are associated with successful outcomes in single-parent families?
- What does the research indicate about the impact of having gay or lesbian parents?
- What role do siblings play in the development of younger children in the family?

PEER RELATIONSHIPS IN MIDDLE CHILDHOOD

Research evidence suggests that the ability to have successful and rewarding interactions with peers during childhood can be the harbinger of successful later adjustment and that poor peer relations are often associated with a range of developmental problems. Boys and girls who have good peer relationships enjoy school more and are less likely to experience academic difficulties, drop out of school, or commit delinquent acts in later years than agemates who relate poorly with their peers (Bagwell, Newcomb, & Bukowski, 1998; Morison & Masten, 1991; Parker & Asher, 1987). Children who are accepted by their peers are also less likely to report feeling lonely, depressed, and socially anxious than children who are rejected (Boivin & Hymel, 1997; Cassidy & Asher, 1992; Crick & Ladd, 1993). Of course, the quality of peer relations is not the only factor that predicts later developmental outcomes. But it is hard to deny that experiences with peers play a substantial role in the lives of most children. Thus, peer relationships have become an important focus of developmental research.

What do child development theorists say about the role of peers? Social learning theorists believe that peers exert a powerful influence on the child's socialization by means of modeling and reinforcement. Piaget (1932/1965) and Vygotsky (1978) have discussed the ways in which peer contacts alter the child's cognitions, which can in turn direct social behavior. Piaget contends that peer interactions prompt or even coerce the child to consider the viewpoints of others, thus broadening her social perspective-taking ability and diminishing her egocentrism. The result is a greater capacity for social exchange. Vygotsky maintains that contact with peers, especially those who are more skilled in a given domain, stretches the child's intellectual and social capacities. As a result of experiences with peers, the child internalizes new modes of thinking and social interaction and then produces them independently.

PEER GROUP FORMATION

How do peer groups form in the first place? Undoubtedly, they coalesce on the basis of children's shared interests, backgrounds, or activities. Children associate with other members of their classroom, soccer team, or school band, for example. Other variables, such as socioeconomic status or ethnic and racial group membership, can also contribute. Youngsters often join with others of similar social class or ethnic/racial background (Clasen & Brown, 1985; Larkin, 1979). Gender is another powerful variable; groups for the most part tend to be of the same sex throughout childhood and early adolescence.

A particularly enlightening description of how peer groups form and operate can be found in a classic experiment called the Robbers Cave study, named after the state park in Oklahoma where it took place. Muzafer Sherif and his colleagues invited twenty-two fifth-grade boys who did not know one another to participate in a summer camp program (Sherif et al., 1961). The boys were divided into two groups housed in separate parts of the state park. Initially, each group participated in its own program of typical camp activities—hiking, crafts, structured games—and was unaware of the existence of the other group. In this initial period of the experiment, each group began to develop a unique identity, and individual members performed distinct roles in relation to this group identity. One group became "tough"; the boys swore, acted rough, and ridiculed those who were "sissies." Members of the other group were polite and considerate. As group solidarity grew, members decided to name themselves, the former calling themselves the Rattlers and the latter the Eagles.

The experimenters found that, when they deliberately structured certain situations to encourage cooperation, group identities could be further strengthened. One day, for example, each group returned to the campsite only to find that the staff had not prepared dinner; only the uncooked ingredients were available. The boys quickly took over, dividing up the tasks so that some cooked, others prepared drinks, and so forth. Some boys assumed a leadership role, directing the suppertime activities, and others followed their directives. It was quite apparent that the boys had a strong sense of identity with the group and that the group had a clear structure. In other words, for both the Rattlers and the Eagles, there was strong intragroup cooperation and identity.

Another change in circumstances made the group identities even more pronounced. The camp counselors arranged for the Rattlers and Eagles to meet and organized a series of competitions for them, including games, such as baseball and tug-of-war. The effects of losing in these competitions were dramatic. The losing group became very disharmonious and conflict ridden. Members accused one another of causing the loss, and some boys who had previously enjoyed status and prestige were demoted in standing if they had contributed to the group's humiliation. After these initial conflicts, however, group identity became stronger than ever. The effects of competition on behavior *between* the groups were even more pronounced. The Rattlers and Eagles verbally antagonized each other and retaliated for a loss in the day's competition by raiding each other's campsites and stealing possessions, such as comic books and clothing. Each episode forged intragroup identity but also increased intergroup hostility.

In the last phase of this social experiment, the counselors attempted to lessen the bad feelings between the Rattlers and the Eagles by having them share meals or watch movies together. Instead of promoting harmony between the groups, however, this tactic produced continuing hostilities, punctuated with fights and verbal assaults. In contrast, when the experimenters created situations in which the two groups had to work together to achieve some common goal, antagonisms between them began to crumble. One hot day, for example, when the counselors "discovered" that the water pipeline for the campsites was broken, boys from both Rattlers and Eagles began to search together for the broken pipes. On another occasion, the food delivery truck broke down; again, the boys all worked together to restart the engine. The acrimonious behavior between the two groups diminished, and boys from the two groups actually began to form friendships with one another.

Few studies of the formation and function of peer groups match the scope of the Robbers Cave study. However, a more recent series of studies sheds further light on the factors that promote peer group identity. Rebecca Bigler and her colleagues (Bigler, Jones, & Lobliner, 1997) divided children in each of several summer school classrooms into a "blue" group and a "yellow" group. For some children, their assignment to a group was based on a biological characteristic: whether their hair color was light or dark. For others, assignment to a group was random. Teachers in both groups were instructed to emphasize group membership with verbal comments and by other overt actions, such as seating children and having them line up for recess according to their group. Children in all the groups wore T-shirts bearing the color of their group. The researchers also included a control group, in which children wore either yellow or blue T-shirts but did not experience emphasis on the groups from their teachers. At the end of four weeks, children were asked a series of questions evaluating their attitudes toward their own group (the in-group) and the other group (the out-group). Children in the experimental conditions showed a strong tendency to ascribe positive traits to *all* members of the in-group and *none* of the members of the out-group. The control group, in contrast, did not show this pattern. Thus, when adults actively use obvious perceptual categories to describe children's groups, children exhibit strong favoritism toward their own group and bias against the out-group. In-group favoritism does not operate in all circumstances, however. In a subsequent study, Bigler and her colleagues manipulated the status of the yellow and blue groups by displaying photographs of past winners of athletic and academic competitions on posters placed around the classrooms. They purposely showed more "winners" from the yellow group. Under these conditions, children in the low-status group, the blue group, did not show a bias toward their own group, whereas children in the high-status group did (Bigler, Brown, & Markell, 2001). These studies, together with the Robbers Cave study, reveal important information about the factors that influence peer group dynamics. In particular, they provide clues about the strategies that either promote or break down animosities among children's groups, findings that have implications for interventions aimed at reducing gender or racial and ethnic biases.

Peer Popularity

Key Theme
Risk/Resilience

Parents, teachers, and others who have the opportunity to observe children over time usually notice the two extreme ends of the sociability spectrum: some children seem to be at the center of many activities, from school projects to playground games, whereas others are ridiculed or ignored. Frequently the patterns of peer acceptance that become established in the early school years persist for years afterward, along with the psychological rewards or disappointments that accompany them. Research shows that, once children are rejected by peers, they are on a trajectory that often leads to lower school achievement and emotional problems. In

Children who lack social skills may be rejected or neglected by their peers. In contrast, popular children display prosocial behaviors and a wide range of social knowledge.

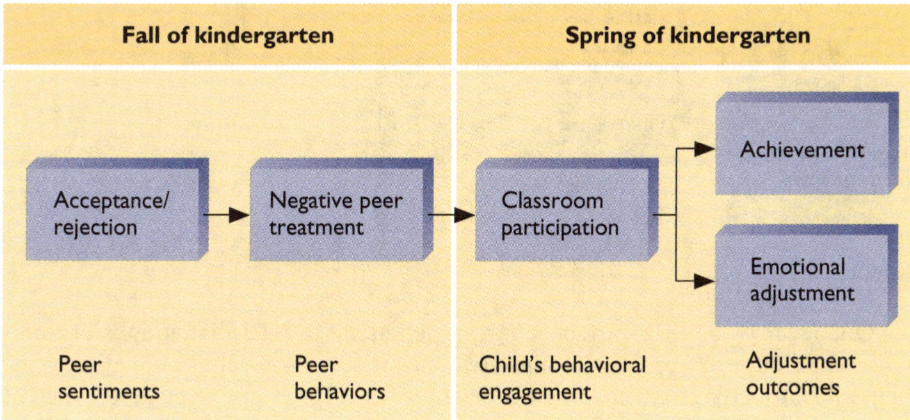

FIGURE 13.1
The Impact of Peer Rejection
Peer rejection is associated with negative consequences among children, including emotional and academic problems. To study more closely the dynamics of this process, Eric Buhs and Gary Ladd (2001) monitored kindergarten children's peer status, peer interactions, classroom participation, and eventual adjustment over the school year. They found that the results of the study generally supported a model like that depicted here.

Source: Buhs & Ladd (2001).

one study, Gary Ladd observed children in both the fall and the spring of their kindergarten year, noting their peer status, peer interactions, classroom participation, and emotional adjustment over the school year. The data fit the model depicted in Figure 13.1. Unpopular children were subjected to more negative treatment from peers (such as exclusion from peer activities and victimization) and participated less in classroom activities, which in turn predicted lower achievement and emotional difficulties (Buhs & Ladd, 2001). Given the developmental pathway that many rejected children follow, finding ways to help them negotiate their social world, especially as they begin school, seems all the more important. Psychologists have uncovered several factors related to peer acceptance and popularity.

Assessing Popularity Psychologists usually assess the quality of peer relations by administering questionnaires to children, asking about the social standing of their agemates. Peer assessments frequently consist of a **sociometric nomination** measure in which children are asked to name a specified number of peers (usually between three and five) who fit a certain criterion. For example, children might be asked to "Name three classmates you especially like (or dislike)" or "List three peers you would like to walk home from school with." The number of positive or negative nominations the child receives from other children serves as a measure of his popularity. Alternatively, children are sometimes asked to rate each peer in the class or group on a **sociometric rating scale,** a series of items like "How much do you like to be with this person at school?" The target child's average rating by the other children is the index of peer acceptance.

Peer nomination measures, in turn, are used to classify children's *peer status*. *Popular* children receive many more positive ("like") than negative ("dislike") nominations. *Rejected* children, in contrast, receive few positive but many negative nominations. *Neglected* children receive low numbers of nominations in either category; although they lack friends, they are not actively disliked (Asher & Dodge, 1986). *Controversial* children receive high numbers of both positive and negative nominations. They have a high degree of "social impact" because they are active and visible, but they are generally not preferred as social partners (Coie, Dodge, & Coppotelli, 1982). Finally, *average* children do not receive extreme scores on peer nomination measures. Figure 13.2 summarizes these categories of peer status.

Characteristics of Popular and Unpopular Children What exactly is it about unpopular children that makes them so unappealing to their agemates and places them so consistently in an undesirable status? This is a particularly important question for those attempting to intervene in these children's "at-risk" circumstances. Peer popularity, as defined by sociometric measures, is related to a number of variables, some of which lie within the child's control and some of which, unfortunately, do not.

sociometric nomination Peer assessment measure in which children are asked to name a specified number of peers who fit a certain criterion, such as "peers you would like to walk home with."

sociometric rating scale Peer assessment measure in which children rate peers on a number of social dimensions.

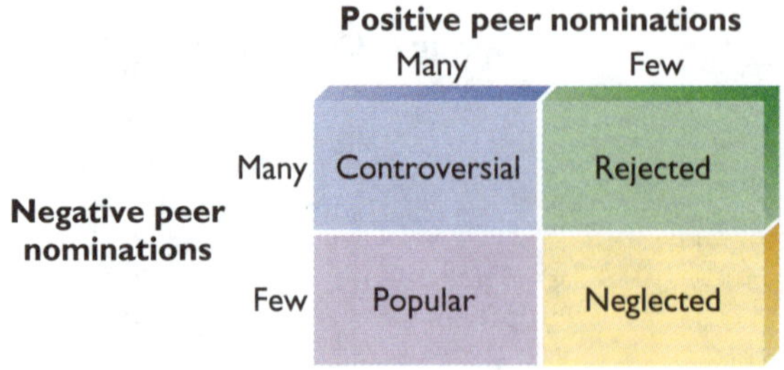

FIGURE 13.2
Classification of Peer Status
The number of positive and negative peer nominations received determines whether a child's peer status is classified as controversial, rejected, neglected, or popular. Average children receive less extreme scores on peer nomination measures.

One factor is physical attractiveness. When asked to rate photographs of unfamiliar children, both preschool- and elementary school–age children believe children with attractive faces to be more friendly, intelligent, and socially competent than unattractive children (Dion & Berscheid, 1974; Langlois & Stephan, 1981). Correlations between children's ratings of peers' attractiveness and sociometric measures of peer acceptance typically range between +0.35 and +0.50, indicating a moderately strong relationship between these two variables (Cavior & Dokecki, 1973; Lerner & Lerner, 1977). Body type makes a difference, too. For example, boys with broad shoulders and large muscles are the most popular, and short, chubby boys are the least popular (Staffieri, 1967). The reasons for these stereotypic beliefs are unknown, but they can lead to self-fulfilling behaviors in children who have been labeled (Hartup, 1983). For example, a child who receives peer attention because of attractiveness may have numerous opportunities to develop the social skills that lead to even greater peer acceptance.

Another factor related to peer acceptance is the child's proficiency in motor activities. Both boys and girls who are coordinated, strong, and skilled in such activities as throwing a ball are rated as more popular by peers and as more socially competent by their teachers and parents (Hops & Finch, 1985). It may be that the value our society places on athletic prowess is reflected in children's preferences in playmates. Alternatively, motor skill may facilitate the manipulation of objects and game playing that constitute the majority of children's shared activities. Those who are talented in this arena will naturally have more peer contacts and eventually be better liked.

One of the most important factors in peer acceptance is the constellation of social behaviors displayed by popular and unpopular children. Researchers who have observed the overt activities of accepted and unaccepted peers have learned that each presents a distinct behavioral profile. In general, popular children engage in prosocial, cooperative, and normative behaviors and show a high degree of social skill. In contrast, about 50 percent of rejected children are aggressive (Bierman, Smoot, & Aumiller, 1993), and about 20 percent are highly socially withdrawn (Volling et al., 1993). Both of these types of rejected children, as well as neglected children, display socially inappropriate behaviors for which they receive little social reinforcement (Parkhurst & Asher, 1992; Pettit et al., 1996).

For example, when Gary Ladd (1983) observed third- and fourth-grade students during recess, he noted several differences in the behavioral styles of popular and rejected children. Popular children spent more time in cooperative play, social conversation, and other positive social interactions with peers than did their rejected counterparts. Rejected children, on the other hand, spent more time engaging in antagonistic behaviors, such as arguing and playing in a rough-and-tumble fashion, or playing or standing alone, at a distance from peers. According to the results of another study that examined the peer-directed behaviors of first- and third-grade boys, neglected and controversial children display still other clusters of behaviors (Coie & Dodge, 1988). Neglected boys were the least aggressive of any group observed. They tended to engage in isolated activities and had low visibility with peers. Controversial boys were intellectually, athletically, or socially talented and very active, but they were sometimes prone to anger and rule violations. The mixture of their positive and negative social behaviors thus elicited a similarly mixed reaction from their classmates. Thus children may be unpopular with their peers for a number of reasons, ranging from social withdrawal to outright aggression.

Finally, research is increasingly pointing to a link between children's ability to regulate their own emotions and the reactions they receive from peers. For example, in one study, peers reported that children they had categorized as rejected were irritable and inattentive in their behaviors. Peers saw them as complaining and getting upset when things went wrong and as being easily distracted (Pope & Bierman, 1999). In fact, rejected children do tend to express more anger, in both their facial expressions and their verbalizations, in contexts such as losing a game (Hubbard, 2001). Or they may show inappropriate happiness as they behave aggressively with their peers (Arsenio, Cooperman, & Lover, 2000). Observations of young children also show that there is a relationship between the ability to inhibit undesirable behaviors and social competence with peers. Children who are able to control their behaviors (that is, those who are attentive and follow directions) tend to express fewer negative emotions and generally have more positive interactions with their classmates (Fabes et al., 1999). This pattern of findings has been observed in varying cultures, such as Indonesia, for example (Eisenberg, Pidada, & Liew, 2001).

Atypical Development

Social Withdrawal

Some children are "loners." They have few or no friends, and they end up playing or doing their schoolwork on their own, even if surrounded by other children. Along with aggression, social withdrawal is considered by many child development experts to be one of the two most important indicators of a behavior problem (Rubin & Asendorpf, 1993). Withdrawn children are prone to express anxiety, loneliness, negative conceptions of themselves, and depression (Boivin & Hymel, 1997; Rubin, Hymel, & Mills, 1989). Moreover, lack of social contact is a feature of several clinical categories of psychopathology (Rubin & Asendorpf, 1993).

Children may have limited interactions with their peers for a number of reasons. Some children may simply prefer to play by themselves, curling up with a book or becoming involved with an interesting toy. This pattern is usually noted in the preschool and early school years, and is not necessarily an indication that the child is at risk for abnormal development. A second pattern is that of the shy child, who is nervous about being in new environments or with strangers but generally desires social interactions. This characteristic may stem from a biologically based temperament that results in the child's wariness and inhibition (Kagan, Snidman, & Arcus, 1993). If either of these patterns persists, peers may react negatively and reject the child outright (Gazelle & Ladd, 2003; Rubin, 1993). Early negative experiences like these can escalate into more severe social withdrawal, and even depression, as the childhood years progress (Gazelle & Rudolph, 2004). A third category is children who desire social interactions but, because of their inept social skills, are avoided by their peers. These children may react with aggression, which further contributes to their isolation (Rubin & Asendorpf, 1993).

Researchers are just beginning to understand some of the factors, aside from biological temperament, that may contribute to social withdrawal in children. For example, Rosemary Mills and Kenneth Rubin (1993) found that mothers of withdrawn children were highly controlling and directive when attempting to teach their children how to interact with peers. They also expressed more anger, disappointment, and guilt about their children's behaviors than mothers of aggressive and "average" children. The reactions of peers may make a difference, too. First-grade children do not seem to think about social withdrawal as a liability when asked to rate the likeability of children described in vignettes. By age ten, though, social withdrawal was viewed as an abnormal behavior

(Younger, Gentile, & Burgess, 1993). Interestingly, even in China, where adults value shyness as a personality trait, children shift from positive to negative evaluations of shy children at around age twelve (Chen, Rubin, & Li, 1995). These studies, along with the different patterns of social withdrawal described here, suggest the complex nature of this style of social functioning.

Despite these complexities, it is important that researchers continue to examine the nature of social withdrawal in childhood because of its potential lingering impact even well into adulthood. Kenneth Rubin gives one example in a letter he received from a fifty-one-year-old individual who had read about his research.

> I recall one instance in my third year of grade school and my teacher approached me after recess with the enquiry "have you no one to play with—I have noticed you standing by yourself at recess for several days now." I recalled replying and LYING—"yes I've friends." The teacher was observant and I give her credit for this, however, I wish, oh how I wish, something had been done about my isolation at the tender age of 7 or 8. It has been a long, lonely road. (Rubin & Asendorpf, 1993, p. 4)

THE ORIGINS OF SOCIAL COMPETENCE

What factors are responsible for the skilled social behaviors of some children but not others? Researchers draw their answers from a number of perspectives, from the early attachment relationships children form with their caregivers to capabilities in processing the subtle cues that form such an integral part of social interactions.

Attachment Relationships Attachment teaches children about emotional ties: how to recognize affection and how to show it. This knowledge about the central ingredients of relationships and the "internal working models" that children construct regarding relationships may assist them as they expand their social world (Hay, 1985; Sroufe, 1983). In their early relationships with caregivers, children have the opportunity to learn and practice a variety of social skills, such as turn taking, compromise, and effective communication. Once honed and refined, these abilities can later be employed with peers and other individuals in the child's life. Longitudinal studies confirm that children who have more positive relationships with peers tended to have secure attachments with their parents during infancy and toddlerhood (Booth et al., 1995; Sroufe, Egeland, & Carlson, 1999; Youngblade & Belsky, 1992). Other researchers have noted that seven- to twelve-year-olds who reported positive relationships with their mother also had positive cognitions about relationships with peers. For example, those who characterized their mother as being indifferent made similar judgments about interactions with peers (Rudolph, Hammen, & Burge, 1995).

Parental Influences Parents play an influential role in the relationships their children form with peers. Broadly speaking, parents who exhibit an authoritative style—that is, are responsive, are nurturant, and provide verbal explanations—tend to have children who are popular and who display prosocial behaviors with peers. In contrast, children of authoritarian, power-assertive parents are more likely to be classified as rejected (Dekovic & Janssens, 1992; Hart et al., 1992; Pettit et al., 1996).

Parents serve as important models of social competence for their children; they may also provide explicit instruction on appropriate ways to behave in social situations. In one study, mothers of popular and unpopular preschoolers were observed as they introduced their children to a pair of peers busily playing with blocks. Mothers of unpopular children tended to disrupt the ongoing play and use their authority to incorporate their own child into the group. In contrast, mothers of popular children encouraged them to become involved in play without intervening in the activity of the host peers. Moreover, in a subsequent interview, these mothers displayed greater knowledge of how to encourage their children to make friends, resolve conflicts, and display other positive social behaviors (Finnie & Russell, 1988). Others have noted that, compared with parents of less popular children, parents of popular and socially competent children are generally less disagreeable and demanding, and express less negative affect when they play with their children (Isley et al., 1999; Putallaz, 1987). In addition, both mothers and fathers of unpopular children have been found to shift conversations to irrelevant topics, speak while someone else is talking, and ignore their children's requests. Perhaps not surprisingly, their children showed similar ineffective communication styles (Black & Logan, 1995).

Finally, parents can influence children's social competence on another level: by managing their children's social activities. Parents vary in the extent to which they create opportunities for their children to interact with peers, experiences that provide the context for the emergence of social skills. Some parents seek out play groups for their children or periodically get together with friends who have children. When parents deliberately arrange peer contacts for their children, children have a greater variety of playmates and a larger number of consistent play partners, display more prosocial behaviors at school, and have higher sociometric status (at least among boys) than when parents do not make such efforts (Ladd & Golter, 1988; Ladd & Hart, 1992).

Social-Cognitive Development Children's social competence includes an array of intertwined cognitive and behavioral skills. An information-processing model of social competence formulated by Nicki Crick and Kenneth Dodge (see Figure 13.3) suggests more precisely how cognitions and behaviors are related and where problems in social functioning might occur (Crick & Dodge, 1994).

According to the model, the first step in processing social information is to focus on the correct cues. For example, suppose a boy initiates a conversation with a peer. It is more important for the child to encode the peer's facial expression ("Is that a smile or a sneer?") than to encode the color of her clothing. Second, the child must meaningfully interpret the social cues based on his past experiences. Most

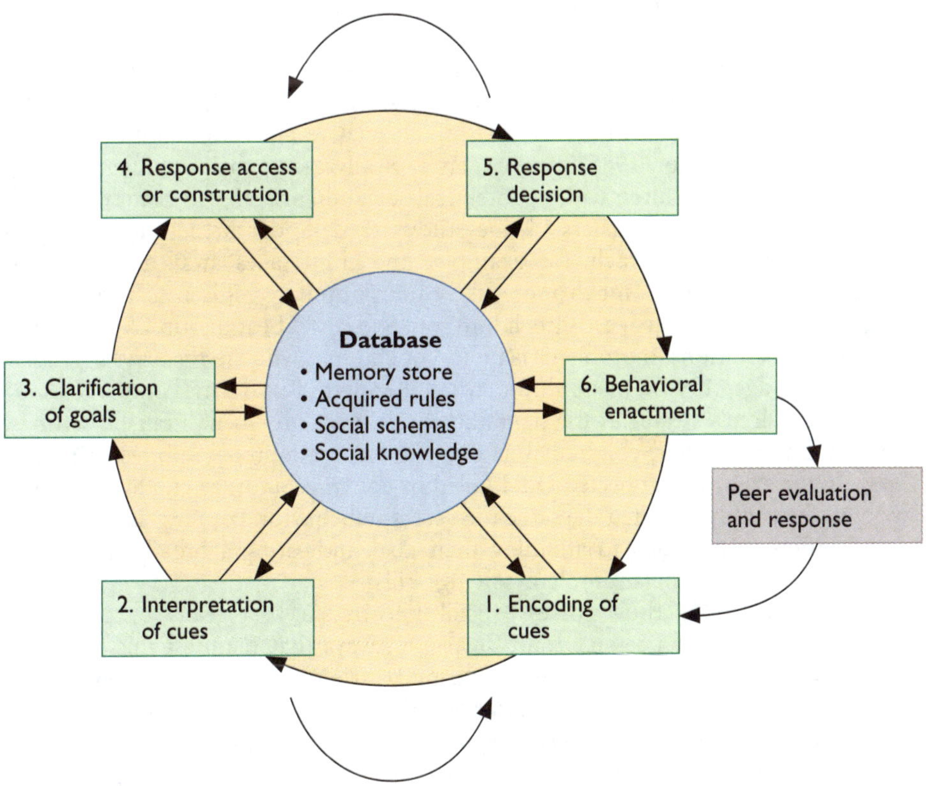

FIGURE 13.3

Social Competence: An Information-Processing Model

Crick and Dodge (1994) have proposed a six-step model of social competence based on the child's growing social information-processing skills. The process begins when the child is able to correctly encode and then interpret a social cue. Next, the child generates a set of social goals and possible responses to achieve them. Finally, the child evaluates those responses and enacts the behavior that he or she internally selected. Children low in social competence may have difficulty in any step in this model.

Source: Adapted from Linn et al. (1985).

children would interpret a scowl on a peer's face as a sign of hostility and a smile as a mark of friendliness. In the third step of processing, the child selects a goal for the situation, such as retaliating against an aggressor or making a friend. Fourth, the child generates one or more potential behavioral responses. If he perceives the peer as hostile, he may contemplate avoiding her or matching her hostility. If he reads her signals as friendly, he may consider smiling back or beginning to talk. Fifth, the child evaluates the potential consequences of each possible behavior. Hostility and aggression could lead to physical harm whereas avoidance might not; hence, avoidance might be preferable. Finally, the child enacts the chosen response verbally or physically, monitors the outcome of his behavior, and, if necessary, modifies it, engaging in the six-step cycle over again. This model thus includes a number of steps where things can go wrong and disrupt a smooth, mutually rewarding social interaction.

Studies of peer relations suggest that popular children are more skillful than unpopular (and, in particular, rejected) children at several steps in the model. First, they are better able to encode and decipher social information correctly. In one study, elementary school children were asked to label the emotions depicted in sets of pictures. For example, one was a series of faces depicting anger, happiness, sadness, disgust, surprise, and fear. Rejected children were less able than popular children to correctly identify the emotions represented in these stimuli (Monfries & Kafer, 1987).

Second, some rejected children tend to make incorrect attributions about the behaviors of peers. In one experiment, researchers asked children to view videotaped episodes of an actor destroying a second actor's toy with hostile, prosocial, accidental, or ambiguous intent. Both rejected and neglected children tended to attribute hostile intentions to the actor's actions, even when the acts were accidental or prosocial. Popular children were more often correct in their judgments (Dodge, Murphy, & Buchsbaum, 1984). Numerous studies have confirmed that aggressive children in particular tend to make more hostile attributions about the intentions of others than nonaggressive children (Orobio de Castro et al., 2002). The tendency to hold negative beliefs about peers is linked to two factors: prior negative experiences with parents and past low social acceptance from peers (MacKinnon-Lewis, Rabiner, & Starnes, 1999). As a result of these mistaken attributions, aggressive children often retaliate with further negative behavior. Children who exhibit this style of overattributing hostile intent are called *reactive aggressive* (Crick & Dodge, 1996).

Third, some rejected children tend to suggest inappropriate strategies to resolve social problems and have difficulty devising alternative paths to attain their social goals (Rubin & Krasnor, 1986). Researchers typically assess social problem-solving skills by presenting children with hypothetical social dilemmas and examining their proposed solutions. Researchers in one study asked kindergartners to react to a series of dilemmas in which, for example, one child takes away another's toy. Unpopular children were much more likely than popular children to recommend an aggressive solution, such as "Punch him" or "She could beat her up." A preference for aggressive solutions to problems is typical of children who are *proactive aggressive* (Crick & Dodge, 1996). In addition, when Kenneth Rubin and Linda Krasnor observed children's strategies for handling social problems in naturalistic settings, they noted that rejected children were rigid in their attempts (Rubin & Krasnor, 1986). If, for example, a rejected child failed to convince another child to give him an object, he simply repeated the same unsuccessful behavior. Popular children often tried a different approach to attaining their goal, indicating a broader and more flexible repertoire of social problem-solving skills.

Popular children thus possess social knowledge that leads to successful interactions with their peers and also behave in ways that manifest this expertise. They know what strategies are needed to make friends (ask others their names, invite them to do things) and can describe prosocial behaviors that tend to foster peer relationships (be generous, keep promises) (Wentzel & Erdley, 1993). They also recognize that the achievement of their social goals may require time and work, and adjust their behaviors according to the sometimes-subtle demands of the situation (Asher, 1983). Rejected children, on the other hand, have a more limited awareness of how to solve social problems, believing particularly in the effectiveness of aggression. Unfortunately, their antagonistic actions frequently lead to a spiral of continuing rejection. As they become disassociated from more socially skilled, popular peers, they have fewer opportunities to learn the basics of successful social interaction from them. Moreover, the child who receives consistently negative feedback from peers would probably be hard pressed to be positive, cooperative, and friendly. In this context, it is perhaps not surprising that aggression tends to remain a fairly stable trait, or may even accelerate, among rejected children during the school years (Dodge et al., 2003; Ladd & Burgess, 1999). Neglected children have their own special problems. Rubin and Krasnor (1986) believe that children in this special category do not display social cognitive deficits, but insecurities and anxieties about the consequences of their social actions. What they need is more self-confidence in their abilities to interact with and be accepted by their peers.

Research Applied to Education

Preventing Bullying

Ms. Klein's attention was drawn to the loud shouts of a circle of boys at the back of the playground. As she approached, she saw two boys in the middle of the circle, one waving clenched fists and yelling at the other. Quickly she stepped in and broke up the fight, fortunately before anyone got hurt. She recognized the older of the two boys; he was a fourth-grader who had a reputation for being a "bully." The other child was a small, frightened-looking second-grader who was on the verge of tears. Ms. Klein knew she would have to do some talking to both of them and probably to their parents as well.

Researchers have documented many of the characteristics of children who are rejected, particularly those who are aggressive with their peers. But what about children who are the victims of aggression? About 9 percent of children are chronic targets of peer aggression, a pattern that can begin as early as kindergarten age. Being a victim is associated with poorer school adjustment, anxiety, low self-esteem, loneliness, and depression (Boulton & Underwood, 1992; Egan & Perry, 1998; Kochenderfer & Ladd, 1996; Olweus, 1993a). Given these characteristics of victims, is there anything parents and teachers can do to stop this negative cycle?

Dan Olweus has studied the problem of bullies and victims among children in grades one through nine in Norway and Sweden. He found that victims are often anxious, sensitive, and quiet children who react to bullying by crying and giving in. Often they are physically weaker than most children their age and generally have few friends. Olweus believes this pattern of passive characteristics signals to other children that they are unlikely to retaliate against aggression (Olweus, 1993a). Other researchers, including those who have studied children from varying cultures, such as China, have confirmed that chronic victims tend to be unassertive and submissive when they are with their peers (Schwartz, Chang, & Farver, 2001; Schwartz, Dodge, & Coie, 1993). A major intervention program to deal with the problems of bullying was launched in Norway over a three-year period. The program involved about 2,500 students from forty-two elementary and junior high schools, as well as their parents and teachers. Advice to the parents of chronic victims included the following:

1. ***Help the child to develop self-confidence by encouraging special talents or abilities he displays.*** Children who gain confidence are more likely to be assertive and refuse to tolerate the behaviors of bullies.

One way to help children who are the victims of bullies is to encourage their physical development so that they do not send cues suggesting "weakness" to potential aggressors. Building the victim's confidence by encouraging abilities and talents can also be beneficial.

2. *Encourage the child to undertake some form of physical training or to participate in sports.* By doing so, he will feel less anxiety about his body and send out signals of strength rather than weakness to potential aggressors.
3. *Help the child get to know a friendly student in the class who has similar interests or is also looking for a friend.* A relationship with another peer can help with feelings of loneliness and depression.
4. *Encourage the child's attempts to become involved with people or activities outside the family.* This suggestion is especially helpful if the family tends to attempt to protect the child every time he is attacked.

This advice was combined with several other programmatic changes involving the school, including teachers' institution of class rules against bullying, better supervision of lunch and recess, talks with the parents of bullies, and promotion of more positive classroom experiences and cooperative learning (Olweus, 1993b). The results showed a 50 percent reduction in the number of children being bullied (and in those acting as bullies as well). In addition, the incidence of other antisocial behavior, such as thefts and vandalism, was reduced, and the social climate of the classroom became more positive. A key to the program's success was the involvement of all children in the program (not just bullies and victims), greater supervision of children during the school day, and good communication between teachers and parents (Olweus, 1994, 1997). Other researchers support the idea that, to be most effective, antibullying interventions in schools should take a broad-based approach. When all of the children in a classroom are exposed to prosocial beliefs and learn skills in conflict resolution and establishing positive relationships with peers, not only does bullying decline, but so does the participation of children as bystanders who reward and perhaps even assist the bullies (Frey et al., 2005).

Friendship

In the middle childhood years, children are very concerned with being accepted by their peers and with avoiding the insecurity that peer rejection brings; both factors motivate friendship formation. Most friends are of the same age and sex, although

Boys and girls differ in the patterns of their friendships and the types of activities they engage in with friends. Boys tend to have larger networks of friends, with whom they tend to participate in shared activities. Girls' networks, on the other hand, are smaller and center on affective communication and self-disclosure.

relationships with younger and older children occasionally occur as well. Cross-sex friendships are rare, however, constituting only about 5 percent of the mutual friendships reported in one study of more than 700 third- and fourth-graders (Kovacs, Parker, & Hoffman, 1996). In fact, researchers in another study found their fifth-grade participants to be openly resistant to the idea that they might have a friend of the opposite sex (Buhrmester & Furman, 1987). By the time children approach preadolescence, the time they spend with same-sex friends surpasses the time they spend with either parent.

Friendship partners may change, though, sometimes rather frequently, over the childhood years. As part of a comprehensive longitudinal study of the social development of children beginning in fourth grade, Robert and Beverly Cairns (1994) asked children to name their best friend each year through eleventh grade. Figure 13.4 shows that the friend named in fourth grade was unlikely to be named again in successive years. Friendships can shift even within a time span of a few weeks. When this same research group observed the nature of fourth- and seventh-graders' friendships, they found that children who mutually nominated each other as friends the first time they were interviewed usually did not name each other as close friends

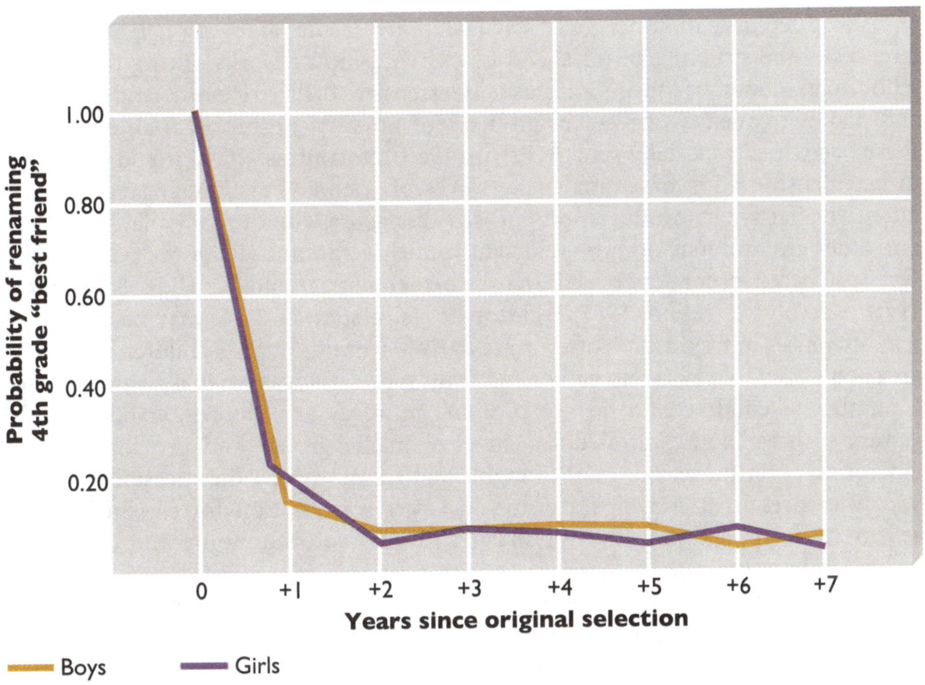

FIGURE 13.4

Changes in Best Friends

In a longitudinal study of best friends, Cairns and Cairns (1994) found that children named as best friends in fourth grade were seldom renamed as best friends in successive years. Friendships may therefore be less stable than generally thought. On the other hand, other research suggests that the stability of friendships over time may depend on the specific personality characteristics of individual children.

Source: Cairns & Cairns (1994).

three weeks later (Cairns et al., 1995). However, the tendency for children to have new mutual friends at different points in time may depend on the characteristics of the child. In another project, children who switched friends more frequently over the four weeks of a summer camp session tended to be perceived by other children as playful, humorous, and "gossipy," but also as aggressive, unreliable, and untrustworthy; that is, they had qualities that probably both attracted and disappointed friends (Parker & Seal, 1996).

In middle childhood, friendship interactions typically include conflicts as well as cooperation (Hartup et al., 1993), and gossip becomes a predominant format for communication, as the following episode between two girls illustrates:

> E: *Oh, see, um, you know that tub she gave us for the spider?*
>
> M: *Yeah.*
>
> E: *She acts like she owns the whole thing.*
>
> M: *The whole spider.*
>
> E: *I know. (Parker & Gottman, 1989, p. 114)*

Parker and Gottman (1989) believe that gossip allows children to sample the attitudes and beliefs of their agemates without taking the risk of revealing their own views. Because gossip involves the sharing of "privileged" information, it also solidifies the child's membership in the friendship circle.

During this age period, the internal psychological aspects of friendship grow in importance. When sixth-graders are asked, "How do you know that someone is your best friend?" they respond with statements such as "I can talk to her about problems" or "He'll keep a secret if you tell him." In other words, intimacy and trust, as well as loyalty, generosity, and helpfulness, become integrated into the child's understanding of friendship (Berndt, 1981). Girls in particular speak about the value they place on intimacy in friendship relations. Girls cite the importance of sharing confidences and private feelings with friends far more frequently than boys do and find that their same-sex friendships provide more support than boys' same-sex friendships do (Buhrmester & Furman, 1987; Furman & Buhrmester, 1992; Jones & Dembo, 1989). This tendency, however, may stem in part from their stereotyped knowledge that female relationships are supposed to be close (Bukowski & Kramer, 1986).

Sex differences in concepts of friendship are accompanied by heightened differences in the structure of boys' and girls' friendship networks during the middle school years. Boys' friendships are usually extensive; their circle of friends is larger, and play is frequently enacted in groups. For boys, friendship is oriented around shared activities, especially sports (Erwin, 1985). In contrast, girls' friendships tend to be intensive. Girls have smaller networks of friends, but they engage in more intensive affective communication and self-disclosure. Girls usually play with only one other girl and may even be reluctant to include a third girl in the relationship. Girls also become more distressed over the breakup of a friendship (Eder & Hallinan, 1978; Maccoby & Jacklin, 1987; Waldrop & Halverson, 1975). It may be that these sex differences in friendship patterns are derived from the games children play. Boys are encouraged to play group games and team sports, such as baseball, which involve a number of children and do not promote intimacy and close interaction. Girls' games, such as "house" and "dolls," involve smaller groups and provide an ideal environment for the exchange of thoughts and emotions. Another possibility is that sex differences in friendships are due to larger socialization forces which foster sensitivity to others and affective sharing in girls and autonomy and emotional reserve in boys (Winstead, 1986).

Some children tend to have more friends and better-quality friendships than other children. Their relationships with friends are marked by shared intimacy, caring, support, companionship, and the ability to resolve conflicts. In responding to vignettes about potential situations involving good friends (for example, watching a friend being laughed at for botching a class presentation), these children did not propose to avoid or blame the friend ("I'd stay away from my friend"; "It was his own fault") (Rose & Asher, 2004). In other vignettes in which there was a conflict with a friend (for example, the friend changes the television channel), these children refrained from using revenge as a motive for their actions (Rose & Asher, 1999). Information about the specific goals and behaviors used by children who are good friendship partners can be useful in interventions for children with fewer friends.

Becoming Friends How do two previously unacquainted children form a friendship? What behaviors must occur to produce an affiliative bond between these two peers? A time-intensive investigation by John Gottman (1983) provides a fascinating glimpse into the process of friendship formation among children who initially met as strangers. Gottman's method involved tape-recording the conversations of eighteen unfamiliar dyads ages three to nine years as they played in their homes for three sessions. Even in this short time, friendships among some of the pairs began to emerge. In all cases, each member of the pair was within one year of the age of the other. Some were same-sex pairs, others opposite-sex. The behaviors of the child whose home it was (the host child) and the visiting child (the guest) were coded separately; the sequences of behaviors these children displayed—that is, how one child's behavior influenced the other's—were also analyzed.

Children who "hit it off" in the first play session showed several distinct patterns of interaction. First, they were successful in exchanging information, as in the following conversation one pair had:

A: *Hey, you know what?*

B: *No, what?*

A: *Sometime you can come to my house.*

Children who became friends made efforts to establish a common ground by finding activities they could share or by identifying similarities and differences between them.

In addition, any conflicts that occurred as they played were successfully resolved, either by one member of the dyad's explaining the reason for the disagreement or by one child's complying with the other child's demands, as long as they were not excessive or unreasonable. Alternatively, as activities escalated from simply coloring side by side ("I'm coloring mine green.") to one child's issuing a command ("Use blue. That'd be nice."), children who became friends tempered potential conflict by de-escalating the intensity of play (in this case, going back to side-by-side coloring) or using another element of play that was "safe"—namely, information exchange ("I don't have a blue crayon. Do you?"). In contrast, children who did not become friends often persisted in escalating their play until the situation was no longer amicable. Children who became friends thus modulated their interactions to preserve a positive atmosphere. Over time, other social processes also came into play; clear communication and self-disclosure (the revelation of one's feelings) were among these.

Generally speaking, children become friends with agemates who resemble themselves on a number of dimensions. Young children and their friends often share similar play styles and language skills (Dunn & Cutting, 1999; Rubin et al., 1994). Among older children, friends are similar in temperament, popularity, and the tendency to behave prosocially or aggressively (Haselager et al., 1998). By becoming friends with like-minded agemates, children select contexts in which some of their own initial tendencies—their aggression or prosocial behavior, for example—may become even more accentuated. In fact, friends become more similar to one another as their relationship continues (Newcomb, Bukowski, & Bagwell, 1999).

FIGURE 13.5

Friendship as a Buffer Against Loneliness

Having even one best friend can significantly lower children's reports of loneliness. In this study, third- through sixth-graders filled out a questionnaire assessing their feelings of loneliness and social dissatisfaction partway through the school year. A high score indicated greater feelings of loneliness. Children who had a reciprocal relationship with at least one friend had significantly lower loneliness scores than children who had no such relationship.

Source: Renshaw & Brown (1993).

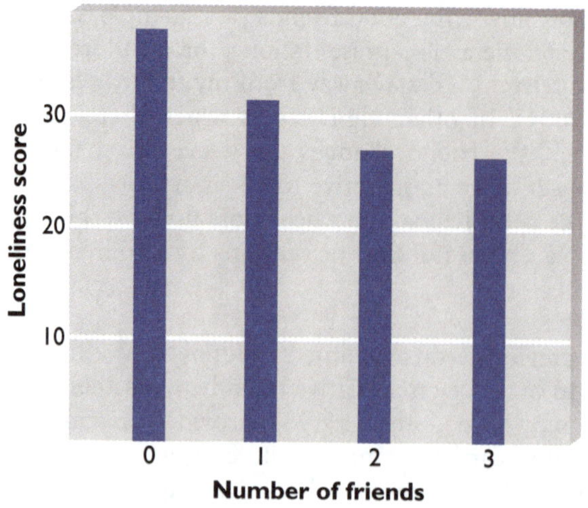

KEY THEME
RISK/RESILIENCE

The Functions of Friendship By virtue of their special qualities, friendships contribute to the child's development in ways that differ from other, more transient peer interactions. Friendships involve a distinct sense of mutual reciprocity between peers and a significant affective investment from each child (Hartup & Stevens, 1999). Thus they provide a fertile ground for the child's social and emotional development.

Because friendships include the sharing of affection and emotional support, especially among older children, they may play a vital role in protecting children from anxiety and stress, particularly when there are problems in the family. For example, boys seem to adjust better to the practical and psychological consequences of divorce when they have friends (Wallerstein & Kelly, 1980). Likewise, when children come from harsh, punitive home environments, they are at risk for becoming the victims of peer aggression and for behaving aggressively and defiantly; however, this risk is diminished for children who have friends (Criss et al., 2002; Schwartz et al., 2000). Children who have close and intimate friendships have higher levels of self-esteem, experience less anxiety and depression, and are more sociable in general than those with few close friends (Buhrmester, 1990; Mannarino, 1978). Because many studies of friendship are correlational, the direction of influence is not always clear. In other words, less anxious children may be more capable of forming intimate friendships, or the reverse may be true: friendships may make them less anxious. Nonetheless, it is reasonable to hypothesize that friends provide an important source of social support for and feedback about one's competence and self-worth. In fact, as Figure 13.5 shows, having even just one "best friend" can mean less loneliness for the child (Parker & Asher, 1993; Renshaw & Brown, 1993).

FOR • YOUR • REVIEW

- What factors promote the formation of peer group identities? What factors can lessen hostilities among groups of peers?
- How do researchers assess children's peer status?
- What are some of the characteristics displayed by popular children?
- What are some of the influences on the development of children's social competence?
- What are the qualities of children's friendships during middle childhood?
- What factors influence the formation of children's friendships?
- How do friendships contribute to the child's social and emotional development?

SCHOOL

The main aim of education is to provide children with the skills necessary to function as independent, responsible, and contributing members of society. Schools reinforce cultural practices for how to get things done (Matusov, Bell, & Rogoff, 2002). Academic accomplishment and the development of cognitive skills are the chief points of emphasis. For example, school experience cultivates rote memory, classification, and logical reasoning (Morrison, Smith, & Dow-Ehrensberger, 1995; Rogoff, 1981). One especially important goal of schooling is the development of literacy, the ability to read and write using the symbol system of the culture's language. Literacy is virtually a prerequisite for survival in most societies; more and more jobs in the professional and technical sectors require not only reading and writing skills but also the ability to communicate, reason, and apply mathematical and scientific concepts (Jackson & Hornbeck, 1989). Yet societies vary in the extent to which they stress the experience of formal schooling; rural and agrarian subcultures in some countries, for example, do not have compulsory schooling.

How well are children learning in schools? Major national surveys often conclude that academic achievement among American students is not high and compares unfavorably with that of students from other industrialized countries. The United States ranks below many countries in student performance on tests in science and mathematics, as indicated by the results of the Trends in International Mathematics and Science Study (TIMSS). This research project has included evaluations of academic performance by fourth-graders and twelfth-graders, as well as for eighth-graders whose relative level of performance is shown in Figure 13.6. Because children in many East Asian and European nations perform better than those in the United States, the findings are among those that have created concern about the adequacy of our educational system.

STARTING SCHOOL

Few occasions in a child's life are as momentous as the first day of school. Parents typically find this a time of mixed emotions, of eager anticipation about the child's future accomplishments coupled with anxieties about whether school will provide positive and rewarding experiences for their child. Children have many major adjustments to handle, including accommodating to a teacher and a new physical environment, making new friends, and mastering new academic challenges. Success in making the initial transition to school can set the tone for later academic and socioemotional development.

School policies that prepare young children and their parents for the start of school make a difference. Providing parents with information about the kindergarten program, inviting preschoolers and their parents to visit the kindergarten classroom, or sponsoring an orientation program are all tactics associated with better academic performance and greater parental involvement by the end of the kindergarten year. These policies were especially predictive of success for children from middle- or lower-income backgrounds (Schulting, Malone, & Dodge, 2005).

In addition, children who bring to school certain entry-level skills, such as a battery of positive social behaviors (for instance, cooperativeness in their preschool play or friendliness in their interactions with peers), and who exhibit cognitive and linguistic maturity (such as ability to engage in or be ready for school-related activities as a result of preschool and family experiences) do better in kindergarten (Entwisle, 1995; Ladd, Birch, & Buhs, 1999; Ladd & Price, 1987). Gary Ladd and his colleagues (Ladd et al., 1999), testing several hundred kindergartners throughout the school year, found that positive behavioral orientations exhibited by children in the first weeks of kindergarten fostered the formation of friendships and peer acceptance, whereas antisocial behaviors resulted in children's being less liked by peers over the year and having greater conflict with teachers. Cognitive and linguistic

FIGURE 13.6

International Data on Mathematics and Science Achievement

This table presents the average scores of eighth-graders for the countries included in the Trends in International Mathematics and Science Study (TIMMS). These findings typically receive considerable interest from educators and politicians, and may have policy implications for education.

Source: Gonzalez et al. (2004).

MATHEMATICS

Nation	Average
Singapore	605
Korea, Republic of	589
Hong Kong SAR	586
Chinese Taipei	585
Japan	570
Belgium-Flemish	537
Netherlands	536
Estonia	531
Hungary	529
Malaysia	508
Latvia	508
Russian Federation	508
Slovak Republic	508
Australia	505
United States	**504**
Lithuania	502
Sweden	499
Scotland	498
Israel	496
New Zealand	494
Slovenia	493
Italy	484
Armenia	478
Serbia	477
Bulgaria	476
Romania	475
Norway	461
Moldovia, Republic of	460
Cyprus	459
Macedonia, Republic of	435
Lebanon	433
Jordan	424
Iran, Islamic Republic of	411
Indonesia	411
Tunisia	410
Egypt	406
Bahrain	401
Palestinian National Authority	390
Chile	387
Morocco	387
Philippines	378
Botswana	366
Saudi Arabia	332
Ghana	276
South Africa	264
Average international score	466

SCIENCE

Nation	Average
Singapore	578
Chinese Taipei	571
Korea, Republic of	558
Hong Kong	556
Estonia	552
Japan	552
Hungary	543
Netherlands	536
United States	**527**
Australia	527
Sweden	524
Slovenia	520
New Zealand	520
Lithuania	519
Slovak Republic	517
Belgium-Flemish	516
Russian Federation	514
Latvia	512
Scotland	512
Malaysia	510
Norway	494
Italy	491
Israel	488
Bulgaria	479
Jordan	475
Moldova, Republic of	472
Romania	470
Serbia	468
Armenia	461
Iran, Islamic Republic of	453
Macedonia, Republic of	449
Cyprus	441
Bahrain	438
Palestinian National Authority	435
Egypt	421
Indonesia	420
Chile	413
Tunisia	404
Saudi Arabia	398
Morocco	396
Lebanon	393
Philippines	377
Botswana	365
Ghana	255
South Africa	244
Average international score	473

Average is higher than the U.S. average
Average is not measurably different from the U.S. average
Average is lower than the U.S. average

maturity directly facilitated classroom participation and higher achievement. In addition, classroom participation, which ultimately plays an important part in contributing to achievement in kindergarten, was influenced by the relationships children established with their peers and their teachers. The negative qualities displayed by some children (lack of friends, peer rejection, poor teacher-child relationship) seemed to be increasingly detrimental for adjustment to this new environment (Ladd et al., 1999). These findings confirm that many factors working within the school, as well as the qualities that children bring to the school environment, affect their early academic success.

The presence of familiar peers in the kindergarten classroom also facilitates peer acceptance (Ladd & Price, 1987) and is related to more positive attitudes toward school and fewer anxieties at the start of the school year. In general, factors promoting continuity between the preschool and kindergarten experiences seem beneficial to the child's adjustment, suggesting that parents should consider ways to foster their children's friendships with peers who will be future classmates. These results underscore the fact that the transition to school can be a particularly crucial time and that successes in one domain, peer relations, are related to successes in another, competence in school.

One major controversy that surrounds this first school transition is the age of the child upon school entry. Most children begin kindergarten at age five or six. Some researchers claim that younger members of the classroom do not perform as well academically as older members and continue to have difficulty in the later school years (Breznitz & Teltsch, 1989; May, Kundert, & Brent, 1995). Others, however, have pointed out methodological and other problems in this research and have failed to find evidence that younger and older children in the classroom differ in any meaningful way (Alexander & Entwisle, 1988; Shepard & Smith, 1986). Frederick Morrison and his colleagues have carried out further work on this issue with Canadian schoolchildren (Morrison, Griffith, & Alberts, 1997). They found that younger children do tend to score below older children on reading and mathematics achievement tests at the end of the school year. However, the same is true even at the beginning of the school year. In fact, when measures of progress in reading and mathematics were used as the criteria, younger first-graders gained just as much as older first-graders did. Furthermore, the first-graders, whether younger or older, gained more than children who remained in kindergarten but could have been enrolled in first grade. Although additional research needs to be carried out, these findings suggest that entrance age by itself may not be an important factor in academic progress and that children should not be delayed in entering school on that basis alone.

SCHOOL ACHIEVEMENT

Schools can vary substantially in their organization and structure. Although the one-room classroom is rarely found today, schools and classes can be large or small depending on the community, and both are likely to increase in size in the upper grades. Of course, the people involved in the child's schooling probably play the biggest role. Parents, peers, and teachers all contribute to the mix of how children experience school. What are some of the effects of these factors on children's achievement?

Parents, Peers, and School Achievement Several factors aside from aspects of the school curriculum itself are associated with academic success. Not surprisingly, parents are of paramount importance. Consider, for example, a model proposed by Wendy Grolnick and her colleagues (Grolnick, Ryan, & Deci, 1991) and illustrated in Figure 13.7. According to these researchers, parental support for their children's autonomy (such as encouraging independent decision making) and involvement with their children (such as spending time talking with them about the children's problems) are related to the strength of children's "inner resources." In other words, children develop

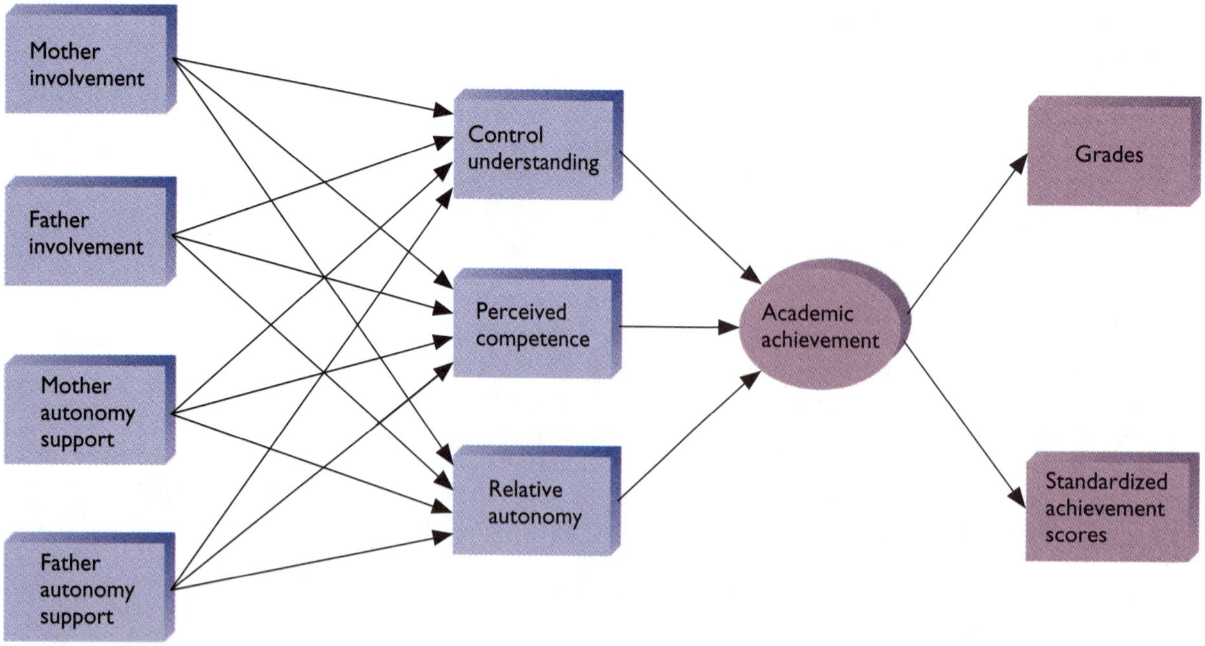

FIGURE 13.7

A Model of Parental Influence on Children's Academic Achievement

One model of children's academic achievement suggests that parental involvement and support of children's autonomy predict children's "inner resources." These resources include children's feelings of control, competence, and autonomy. These characteristics in turn predict academic achievement. Research has found support for major elements of this model.

Source: Grolnick, Ryan, & Deci (1991).

feelings of competence, autonomy, and control, which in turn influence academic performance. To test these ideas, the researchers measured both parental and child qualities that were components of the model, as well as children's academic success. Using sophisticated statistical techniques, they were able to show the relationships they had predicted. Other researchers add that authoritative parenting (characterized by warmth and extensive verbal explanation) and the social support that parents provide predict, at least indirectly, exactly how well children will do in school during middle childhood (DeBaryshe, Patterson, & Capaldi, 1993; Dubow et al., 1991; Steinberg et al., 1992). Frequent transitions in parenting (such as divorce and remarriage followed by another divorce) and a more discordant family climate, on the other hand, are related to less positive outcomes in school (Kurdek, Fine, & Sinclair, 1995).

An especially important way that parents can bolster their children's school-related motivations is to be involved in schooling. When parents attend open houses, parent-teacher conferences, and other school functions, and keep track of how their children are doing in school, children show higher academic motivation and, ultimately, better performance in school (Grolnick & Slowiaczek, 1994). By being involved, parents learn about how to handle the challenges their children face in school, and children receive an important message—that parents and teachers agree on objectives and standards for behavior (Hill & Taylor, 2004).

Peers make a difference, too. As early as fourth grade, children tend to sort themselves into groups that have different levels of school motivation, and children who are members of a particular group at the start of the school year become even more aligned with the group's motivation level by the end of this period (Kindermann, 1993). For example, when a student at the beginning of the school year has friends who consider themselves disruptive in school, that student will begin to demonstrate more disruptive behavior as the school year progresses (Berndt & Keefe, 1995).

Class Size Many countries around the world, as well as numerous states within the United States, have invested huge amounts of money to reduce class size (Ehrenberg et al., 2001b). For example, the number of students per teacher in elementary school classrooms in the United States has fallen from 25.1 to 18.3 over the past three decades; a similar decrease, from 19.7 to 14.0, has occurred in secondary schools (Ehrenberg et al., 2001b). Although research has not always revealed a consistent benefit from such efforts, the general consensus is that children in small classes, especially in the earlier grades, show academic advances over children in large classes (Ehrenberg et al., 2001a). Perhaps the most influential of these studies was carried out in Tennessee and involved seventy-six schools. Kindergarten children and teachers were randomly assigned to classes of different sizes (thirteen to seventeen versus twenty-two to twenty-five pupils per class). By the end of first grade, children in the small classes showed marked improvement performance on standardized tests of reading and mathematics compared with children from regular-size classes. The benefits of small classes were especially pronounced for minority children (Finn & Achilles, 1990).

The long-term consequences of smaller class size have also been investigated. Children in small classes in kindergarten through third grade in the Tennessee study continued to do better than their classmates assigned to larger classes, even after entering regular-size classrooms beginning in fourth grade (Mosteller, 1995). The benefits of the smaller-class experience were exhibited by children in later grades as well. Moreover, when small class sizes were introduced to the poorest districts in the state, children in these districts moved from displaying reading and mathematics scores that were well below average to scores above average for the state.

Why do smaller classes work? For one thing, teachers probably have greater enthusiasm and higher morale when they are not burdened with large numbers of students. Teachers also have more time to spend with individual children, and students are more likely to be attentive and engaged in classroom activities, and show fewer behavioral problems in small classes (Finn & Achilles, 1990; Mosteller, 1995). But it is likely that benefits of reduced class size emerge only when teachers are trained to take advantage of the opportunities of working with smaller numbers of students (Bennett, 1998; Ehrenberg et al., 2001a, 2001b).

Teacher Expectations No single factor in the school experience plays a more critical role in student achievement and self-esteem than teachers. One way that they have an influence is through the expectations they have of their students. A highly publicized study by Robert Rosenthal and Lenore Jacobson (1968) documented just how readily teachers' expectations of students' performance can affect students' actual attainments. The researchers told teachers that certain elementary school children could be expected to show sudden gains in intellectual skills during the course of the school year based on their scores on an IQ test administered at the beginning of the term. In reality, the students they designated as "rapid bloomers" were chosen randomly. An IQ test administered at the end of the school year revealed that the targeted children indeed showed significantly greater improvement than other students in the class, an outcome called the *Pygmalion effect.* The investigators explained the findings by suggesting that teachers somehow treated the targeted children differently based on their beliefs about the children's intellectual potential, thereby creating a self-fulfilling prophecy.

Differing expectations, especially when they are clearly evident to students, have consequences for achievement. Margaret Kuklinski and Rhona Weinstein (2001) looked at children in grades one through five to determine whether teacher expectations affected performance on reading achievement. As Figure 13.8 suggests, the researchers anticipated that teacher expectations about reading ability would influence not only achievement in reading at the end of the school year but also the children's own self-perceptions of their reading ability. These self-perceptions would, in turn, also influence their reading achievement. The results of the study generally supported these hypotheses, especially in classrooms in which teacher expectations

FIGURE 13.8

Teacher Expectancy Effects on Children's Reading Achievement

Teacher expectancies not only may have a direct effect on reading achievement but also can influence behavior by modifying children's own expectations for themselves, as this model suggests. Margaret Kuklinsky and Rhona Weinstein (2001) obtained support for this model, especially in classrooms in which teacher expectancies could be recognized easily by children. The impact of the children's own self-perceptions pertaining to reading, as influenced by teacher expectations, was especially evident when children were in the fifth grade but far less evident in earlier grades.

Source: Kuklinsky & Weinstein (2001), p. 1557.

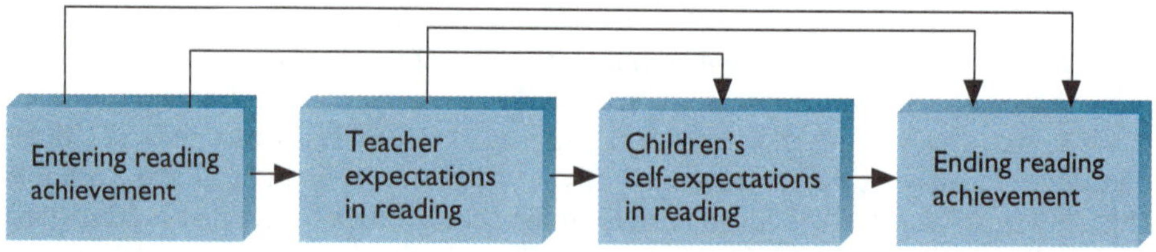

were more readily apparent to children, although children's self-perceptions tended not to become a factor until they reached the fifth grade.

Other studies have confirmed that high achievers *are* treated differently in the classroom by many teachers; they are given more opportunities to participate, given more time to answer questions, receive more praise for being correct, and receive less criticism than lower achievers (Minuchin & Shapiro, 1983). In other words, the classroom climate is most supportive for those who have already demonstrated success, whereas those who most need the teacher's attention and encouragement may actually get it least.

Classroom Management Strategies Students achieve most in school when their teachers maximize the time spent in actual learning. This statement may seem obvious, but not all school time is spent in direct instruction. Effective teachers plan their lessons well, monitor the entire classroom continuously, minimize the time spent in disciplining children who misbehave, and keep transitions between activities brief and smooth (Brophy, 1986). They make sure there is little "dead time" in the classroom when students are unoccupied, and they keep the focus on instruction.

Another key ingredient in a teacher's success is active involvement in the learning process. This means that teachers remain personally involved in every phase of instruction, from the initial presentation of a new lesson to supervising the individual work of students. Involvement also refers to the teacher's enjoyment and knowledge of students. Even when students are working in groups, teachers who guide the discussion or progress of the group will foster higher levels of mastery and greater feelings of competence than those who leave students completely on their own (Brophy, 1986; Skinner & Belmont, 1993). Effective teachers also provide students with clear feedback on the quality of their performance and on what is expected of them (Rutter, 1983).

One of the most important factors in a child's school experience is teacher encouragement. This boy is receiving the kind of assistance with writing that will promote learning. Effective teachers are involved in all phases of instruction, provide clear feedback, and create a positive emotional climate in the classroom.

Creating peer-centered learning experiences can be an effective means of involving students in the educational enterprise of the school. In studies of **cooperative learning**, students work in groups rather than individually to solve academic problems. These groups may consist of, for example, four or five students, some boys and some girls, with a range of abilities and from diverse backgrounds. The teacher is usually instrumental in introducing a topic or set of materials, but then the team members work and study together on the problems, quizzing one another until they decide collectively that they understand the unit. Cooperative learning has been found to increase affiliations among students from diverse backgrounds (for instance, cross-racial friendships), improve self-esteem, and produce more favorable attitudes toward academic achievement (Slavin, 1990).

As an illustration of the effectiveness of cooperative learning, Hanna Shachar and Shlomo Sharan (1994) compared the communication and achievement skills of 197 eighth-graders assigned to cooperative learning classrooms in history and geography with those of 154 students in classrooms taught by traditional teacher-led methods. The study, carried out in Israel, included Jewish students from Western and Middle Eastern backgrounds. The classes were taught for six months. The cooperative learning groups were reconstituted several times throughout the year to give students the opportunity to work with a number of different peers. At the end of the year, a videotaped discussion of a topic in history and geography involving six-person groups revealed that those who participated in cooperative learning expressed themselves more frequently, were more likely to take a personal position and expand on the ideas brought up by another student, and were less likely to interrupt their peers than students who participated in traditional classrooms. The gains in communication skills were especially great for Middle Eastern students; those with this background who came from the traditional classroom were far less likely to express themselves than their peers from Western backgrounds. Gains in scores on achievement tests in history were also much higher among students who participated in the cooperative groups than among students in the traditional classroom.

Another form of peer-centered education is called **collaborative learning**. Here students work jointly on the same problems, often without competing with other groups but with the goal of arriving at solutions jointly, solutions that would be unlikely to arise from students working by themselves (Littleton & Häkkinen, 1999). For example, in one study, fourth-graders worked in pairs on mathematics and spatial reasoning problems, some that required rote learning and copying and some that required formal reasoning (Phelps & Damon, 1989). After six sessions of collaboration, children showed significant gains in performance on math and spatial problems compared with a control group of children who did not participate in collaborative efforts. This effect occurred for tasks that required formal reasoning but not for those that required rote learning or copying. Another interesting outcome was that the superiority of boys over girls on spatial problems at the start of the study significantly diminished. In fact, other research indicates that cooperative and collaborative learning may be especially beneficial in certain areas for students, such as, for example, girls learning math or science. These gains could come about because girls now have a chance to take on leadership roles or because cooperative or collaborative learning more closely fits their preferred style of learning and helps to maintain interest in these subjects (Eccles & Roeser, 1999; Peterson, Johnson, & Johnson, 1991).

The Classroom Climate When students participate in cooperative and collaborative learning efforts, they may get the idea that the teacher and the school are promoting *autonomy*, or increased student initiative within the classroom, a perception that appears to be beneficial to student progress (Boggiano et al., 1992; Valeski & Stipek, 2001). Children who view their teachers as giving them greater responsibility within the classroom have higher self-esteem scores than those who perceive teachers as controlling and directive (Ryan & Grolnick, 1986). Moreover, teachers who

cooperative learning Peer-centered learning experience in which students work together in small groups to promote the learning of each group member.

collaborative learning Peer-centered learning in which students work together on academic problems with the goal of arriving at solutions that are more effective than solutions that could have been derived from individual effort alone.

display the kinds of qualities associated with good parenting—that is, who have high expectations for their students and who show caring, supportive, and nurturant qualities in contrast to an emphasis on negative feedback in their educational approach—are more effective in promoting student adjustment to the classroom and high academic performance (Linney & Seidman, 1989; Rutter, 1983; Wentzel, 2002).

Children as early as first grade are able to recognize the strength of their interpersonal relationship with a teacher. When they perceive that teachers care about them, children have more favorable attitudes toward school (Valeski & Stipek, 2001). Moreover, teacher-child relationships that begin early in the schooling process have long-term outcomes. Bridget Hamre and Robert Pianta (2001) asked kindergarten teachers in a small community to assess their personal relationships with each of their students. Nearly 200 of these students were followed through eighth grade. Those reported to have had a negative relationship with the teacher as kindergartners (for example, conflict and overdependency) continued to have difficulties with school over the next eight years. However, if children who displayed behavior problems in kindergarten were able to develop positive relationships with their kindergarten teachers, it helped to counter behavioral difficulties in the later school years, a finding that has considerable implications for the importance of a young student's relationship with his or her teacher and academic success.

KEY THEME
SOCIOCULTURAL INFLUENCE

CULTURAL DIFFERENCES IN SCHOOL ACHIEVEMENT

The school experience is not the same for children of different racial and ethnic backgrounds. Children who attend school bring with them attitudes about school that are first nurtured within their families, as well as cultural beliefs that may be in synchrony or in conflict with the predominant belief system of the school (Gibson & Ogbu, 1991). For example, are schools a vehicle for economic and personal advancement? Cultural and ethnic groups may vary in their responses to this question. Is verbal, rational expression (which schools emphasize) the optimal means of human communication, as opposed to emotional or spiritual sharing? Again, cultures differ in the extent to which they value these skills. One of the major challenges facing educators is how to ensure the academic success of children who come from a range of cultural and ethnic backgrounds.

School Achievement Among African American Children A persistent finding in past research on school achievement in the United States is that children from some minority groups—for example, African American children—score significantly lower than Caucasian children on many measures of academic performance. In the 1960s, the prevailing explanation for the school difficulties of minority children centered on the *cultural deficit hypothesis,* the notion that some deficiency in the backgrounds of minority children hindered their preparation for the academic demands of school. However, Herbert Ginsberg (1972) pointed out that, rather than being culturally deficient, minority children are *culturally different*; that is, the behaviors that minority children display help them to adapt to their specific life circumstances. For example, rather than having poor language skills, African American children display rich images and poetic forms when speaking to one another in Black English. According to the **cultural compatibility hypothesis**, school instruction produces greater improvements in learning if it is consistent with the practices of the child's own culture (Tharp, 1989).

In a study of children in the first two years of school, Karl Alexander and Doris Entwisle (1988) found that African American and Caucasian first-graders did not differ significantly on a standardized test of verbal and quantitative achievement when they were assessed at the beginning of the school year. But by the end of the year and during the second year, the scores of African American and Caucasian students began to diverge noticeably. In keeping with the cultural compatibility hypothesis, some have argued that, for many African American students, a conflict

cultural compatibility hypothesis Theory that school instruction is most effective if it is consistent with the practices of the child's background culture.

exists between their background culture and the social and cognitive structure of traditional schools. For example, the spiritualism, expressiveness, and rich oral tradition characteristic of the African American heritage frequently clash with the materialism, emotional control, and emphasis on printed materials characteristic of European Americans and their schools (Boykin, 1986; Heath, 1989; Slaughter-Defoe et al., 1990). Some African American children may also perceive that academic success does not necessarily lead to occupational or economic success and therefore do not take academic performance seriously (Ogbu, 1974). Furthermore, many African American children believe they will do well in school even though past performance indicates they are likely to do otherwise. These children may need not only to overcome the hurdles imposed by racism and economic hardship but also to more fully understand what behaviors will be necessary to achieve their expectations, that is, to become motivated to master the academic materials and skills necessary to achieve their goals (Alexander, Entwisle, & Bedinger, 1994; Steinberg, 1996).

In focusing on cultural differences, however, researchers need to recognize that they may be unwittingly contributing to stereotypes. After all, many children in all cultural and ethnic groups in the United States are doing well in school. In fact, children of immigrant families in the United States, who are often poor and members of minority groups, generally do better in mathematics and English courses in high school than children of native families (Fuligni, 1997). What factors contribute to their success? Tom Luster and Harriette McAdoo (1994, 1996) have provided some answers for African American children, and the answers should not be too surprising. African American children who are high achieving, just like other children who are high achieving, experience relatively supportive home environments in which mothers display self-esteem and are members of smaller families whose incomes are above the poverty line. Luster and McAdoo (1996) followed African American children from preschool age until young adulthood. All the children lived in families with low socioeconomic status during the preschool period. Consistent with our earlier discussion emphasizing the importance of parents in promoting school success, the cognitive competence and academic motivation that these children brought to the public school setting, as well as their degree of social adjustment, predicted performance on achievement tests during the elementary school years. Children of mothers who were more involved with their children's schooling also tended to do better in the lower grades, although this relationship did not hold up during adolescence. However, parents' expectations for success in the classroom were correlated with achievement throughout the school years. These findings further confirm the important role families play in the education of African American children, just as in the education of all children (Fuligni, 1997; Steinberg, 1996).

Achievement Among Asian Children Beginning in the mid-1980s, Harold Stevenson and his associates have conducted comparative research on the academic abilities of Taiwanese Chinese, Japanese, and American students. This research has been guided by an effort to understand why Asian students seem to do particularly well in the areas of mathematics and science. First- and fifth-grade students from middle- to upper-class backgrounds in all three countries were tested on a battery of specially designed cognitive tasks that assessed, among other things, spatial relations, perceptual speed, auditory and verbal memory, and vocabulary, along with reading and mathematics achievement (Stevenson, Lee, & Stigler, 1986).

Most noteworthy about the findings was that American children scored far lower in mathematics than the other two groups (see Figure 13.9). The distinctive patterns of achievement could not be explained by superior cognitive skills in any one group. The researchers found no predictive relationships between scores on the various cognitive assessments and scores on achievement tests. In fact, the children's cognitive profiles were quite similar across cultural groups by the time

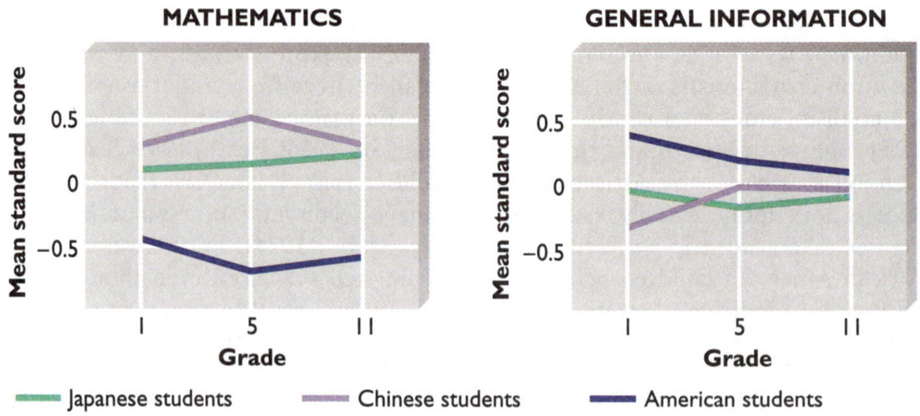

FIGURE 13.9

Mathematics Achievement and General Information Scores as a Function of Sociocultural Context

Chinese and Japanese students score higher than American students on tests of mathematics achievement beginning in first grade, and their superiority in this area continues throughout high school. However, on tests of general information, children from all three cultures perform at similar levels, especially in the higher grades. The better performance on mathematics tests by East Asian children may reflect both school- and family-related cultural influences.

Source: Stevenson, Chen, & Lee (1993).

they reached fifth grade (Stevenson et al., 1985). When again tested in eleventh grade, American children continued to lag well behind the Chinese and Japanese in mathematics achievement, although, as Figure 13.9 shows, on age-appropriate tests of general information ("What are two things a plant needs in order to grow?" or "Why has it been possible to make smaller computers in recent years?"), the Asian children were not superior to the American children (Stevenson, Chen, & Lee, 1993).

What accounts for this pattern of findings? Stevenson's research group reported significant differences in children's school routines and parents' attitudes and beliefs among the Taiwanese Chinese, Japanese, and American groups, as well as differences between Asian American and Caucasian American families. For example, during the year, Taiwanese Chinese and Japanese children attended school about fifty more days than American children (Fuligni & Stevenson, 1995). The percentage of classroom time actually spent in academic activities also differed. For fifth-grade students, the figures were 64.5 percent of the time for American children, 91.5 percent for Taiwanese Chinese children, and 87.4 percent for Japanese children. Furthermore, American children studied language arts more than twice as long as they did mathematics, whereas the Asian children spent equal amounts of time on each subject. Thus the American children received far less instruction in mathematics than did their Taiwanese Chinese and Japanese counterparts (Stevenson, Lee, & Stigler, 1986). Moreover, the Asian teachers were far more likely to use their time in mathematics classes directly teaching the entire class, whereas American children spent more than half their time in mathematics classes working alone (Stigler, Lee, & Stevenson, 1987).

Stevenson's research group also examined attitudes and behaviors related to homework. American children devoted substantially less time to doing homework—an average of 46 minutes per day among fifth-graders, according to mothers' estimates—compared with 114 and 57 minutes for Taiwanese Chinese and Japanese children, respectively. American mothers were not dissatisfied with the small amount of homework their children received, nor were Taiwanese Chinese and Japanese mothers dissatisfied with the large amounts their children were assigned (Stevenson, Lee, & Stigler, 1986). In addition, compared with Americans, students, their peers, and their parents in the two Asian cultures seemed to expect higher standards and voiced greater concern about education, with Asian Americans surpassing their Caucasian American counterparts on these measures (Chen & Stevenson, 1995). Finally, Asian students (including Asian Americans) were more likely than American students to believe that their own effort was the best route to accomplishment (Chen & Stevenson, 1995). Indeed, effort is a central component of the socialization process in many Asian cultures; that is, the procedures by which one achieves a goal are considered extremely important (Bempechat & Drago-Severson, 1999).

These data confirm that a number of factors other than pure cognitive ability determine the child's level of achievement in school. As we have seen throughout this section, the events that transpire in the classroom, parental attitudes, and larger cultural influences are all related to patterns of academic success or failure. If we are concerned about the educational attainments of students and their overall psychological development, research on the influence of schools reveals that there are many ways to more fully engage children of all ability levels and diverse sociocultural backgrounds (Steinberg, 1996).

Gender Issues in School

Teachers, like peers and parents, treat children differentially according to sex, reinforce and punish sex-typed behaviors, and model sex-typical behavior for their students. Moreover, schools may foster sex typing through the teaching materials and curriculum to which children are exposed. For example, one survey of children's readers found that, although boys and girls were portrayed with almost equal frequency, girls were more often the characters in stories in need of rescue, and boys were rarely shown doing housework or displaying emotions (Purcell & Stewart, 1990).

Teacher Attitudes and Behaviors Teachers, like other adults, may express stereotypical, gender-based views about the capacities of their students. They believe that female students are feminine and male students are masculine, although more experienced teachers are less likely to hold stereotyped beliefs and more likely to treat in an egalitarian fashion than are less experienced teachers (Fagot, 1978; Huston, 1983). When teachers are asked to nominate their best students or those with the most potential, they are more likely to nominate boys than girls. They are especially likely to name boys as most skilled in mathematics. When asked to think of students who excel in language or social skills, teachers are more likely to name girls (BenTsvi-Mayer, Hertz-Lazarowitz, & Safir, 1989). These patterns in teacher responses occur despite the fact that actual sex differences in many of these domains are minimal.

In addition, teachers respond differently to students on the basis of sex as opposed to behavior. Boys, for example, receive more disapproval from teachers than girls, even when boys and girls engage in similar amounts of disruptive behavior (Huston, 1983; Serbin et al., 1973). Teachers' responses may reflect a belief that boys are more likely than girls to cause trouble in the classroom unless rules are strictly enforced (Huston, 1983). On the other hand, teachers pay more attention to a girl when she sits quietly in the front of the classroom, whereas the amount of attention paid to a boy is high regardless of where he sits (Serbin et al., 1973). Within elementary school classrooms, teachers tend to call on boys more often than girls and give them more explicit feedback regarding their answers. When girls answer, they are more likely to receive a simple acceptance from the teacher ("Okay"), whereas boys tend to receive more praise, constructive criticism, or encouragement to discover the correct answer (Sadker & Sadker, 1994). Thus boys receive more explicit academic instruction and tend to dominate classroom interactions.

Teachers can influence the degree to which children pay attention to stereotypes when they highlight gender as a relevant social grouping. In one study, teachers in one set of classrooms were told to behave in ways that emphasized gender groups. For example, they used separate bulletin boards to display girls' and boys' artwork, and made frequent comments like "All the boys should be sitting down" or "Amber, you can come up for the girls." Teachers in this group made an average of 7.2 references to gender per twenty-minute time period. Compared with a control group in which teachers were instructed to refer to children as individuals rather than according to gender, children in the "gendered" classrooms showed significant increases in stereotyping over the course of four weeks (Bigler, 1995).

Research Applied to Education

Promoting Gender Equity in the Classroom

Nicky is sitting in a circle with the other third-graders in his class, listening to Brittany read the story she wrote during Writing Workshop. The children seem captivated by her story; even the most restless among them sits quietly, eyes glued on the storyteller. When Brittany is done, Ms. Klein says, "Okay, does anyone have any questions or comments about Brittany's story? Go ahead, Brittany. You can call on someone." Hands fly up eagerly.

"Stephen," says Brittany.

"Why did you make the character live by a pond?" asks Stephen.

"Because he has a lot of animal friends that live there," she responds.

More hands churn in the air. "Nicky," she calls out next. "Wait a minute," says Ms. Klein. "Remember our rule. You have to call on a girl next."

"Reesha," Brittany calls out.

"I like how the words you picked make me think of beautiful pictures in my head," comments Reesha.

"Thank you," responds Brittany, a little shyly.

Nicky's mother, observing all of this, thinks that maybe her son feels slighted for being passed over. Later, when she asks him about this, he firmly proclaims, "All Ms. Klein is trying to do is to be fair to the boys and girls in the class. I didn't feel bad at all. I think it's the right thing to do."

Just as teacher behavior can perpetuate stereotypes, it can also change sex-typing patterns among children in classroom settings. A collection of studies suggests some specific techniques that teachers can use to reduce sex segregation, modify children's attitudes about gender, and promote girls' participation in the classroom.

1. *Use reinforcement to facilitate cooperative cross-sex play.* In one study involving preschoolers and kindergartners, teachers praised children who played in mixed-sex groups by pointing out their cooperative play to the class and complimenting the children. Cross-sex play subsequently increased (Serbin, Connor, & Iler, 1979; Serbin, Tonick, & Sternglanz, 1977).
2. *Prepare lessons that explicitly allow children to question gender stereotypes about personal qualities, occupations, and activities.* Researchers in Dublin, Ireland, had student teachers present a series of lessons to children in the first through sixth grades. The lessons encouraged children to think of counterexamples to common stereotypes—for example, instances in which women show an interest in football or in which men have been observed to be warm and gentle. Discussions were supplemented by opportunities to meet people who worked in nontraditional roles, such as a male nurse and a female veterinary surgeon. In addition, children read poetry and fairy tales, as well as worksheets, that brought up themes counter to traditional stereotypes. At the end of four months, children who had experienced the lessons had significantly lower stereotype scores than those in a control group (Gash & Morgan, 1993).
3. *Be conscious of the need to give girls a chance to participate.* One way to do this is to wait three to five seconds before calling on a student to answer a question. Girls, especially those who are shy or less confident, may need time to formulate their answers and decide that they are willing to share them with the class. Also, don't call only on students who volunteer, because these are more likely to be boys. Teachers can even have an observer record the number of times they call on boys versus girls. Myra and David Sadker (1994) found that, when teachers saw the results of such observations, and,

further, when they received training on how to be more gender equitable, girls in their elementary and secondary school classrooms became more equal partners with boys in class participation.

Student Attitudes Toward Coursework For several decades, research has indicated that students, teachers, and parents alike view some academic subjects as masculine and others as feminine (Huston, 1983). As we noted earlier, mathematics has generally been seen as a masculine activity and reading as feminine (Eccles, 1983; Eccles, Wigfield, et al., 1993; Huston, 1983; Yee & Eccles, 1988). Such sex typing has not been limited to American schoolchildren. In a study of first- through fifth-grade Chinese, Japanese, and American boys and girls, the investigators found that most children believed boys are better in mathematics and girls are better at reading (Lummis & Stevenson, 1990). Moreover, boys in these three societies predicted that they would do better in mathematics in high school than girls predicted they would do, although no sex differences were found in children's predictions of their future reading skills.

Society's messages about girls' mathematical abilities may be changing, however. In a recent study including data from children in first through twelfth grades, researchers asked children to report how competent they felt in math. Although in the early grades boys clearly felt more capable in math than girls, the gender gap in beliefs declined with age, such that by twelfth grade there was virtually no difference between boys and girls. The researchers suggest that one reason for this shift may be a general societal push for girls to participate in math courses and activities (Fredricks & Eccles, 2002).

Sex Differences in Academic Self-Evaluations Girls generally show greater self-criticism of their academic work than boys do. Karin Frey and Diane Ruble (1987) have studied instances of self- and peer criticism for academic work in classroom settings. Children between ages five and ten years were observed at work in academic tasks in their classrooms, and their spontaneous critical and complimentary comments about themselves and their peers were tallied. Several sex differences emerged in the nature of comments children made. Overall, both girls and boys made more self-compliments than self-criticisms, but boys made a greater number of self-congratulatory statements relative to self-criticisms than girls did. Boys complimented themselves and criticized their peers more than girls did, whereas girls criticized themselves and complimented their peers more than boys did. Girls also were more likely to attribute their failures to a lack of ability ("I'm so stupid") than boys were. If girls tend to take greater responsibility for their own failures than boys do, it is possible that there may be emotional consequences for them—for example, greater anxiety and depression.

The link between emotions and academic self-evaluations was demonstrated in a longitudinal study in which third- and sixth-graders were asked to evaluate their scholastic competence each year for a period of three years. Teachers also evaluated children's academic abilities. Boys and girls were similar in their estimates of their academic ability in grade three, but in successive years, their profiles diverged. As Figure 13.10 illustrates, starting at about fourth grade and continuing through eighth grade, boys tended to overestimate their academic abilities, and girls tended underestimate theirs. In addition, symptoms of anxiety and depression were correlated with the tendency to overestimate one's abilities (Cole et al., 1999). Thus gender differences in self-evaluations can have important connections to children's emotional well-being.

KEY THEME
SOCIOCULTURAL INFLUENCE

The preceding findings should be a concern in light of the findings of a cross-cultural study that found that, in settings as diverse as Japan, Germany, and Russia, girls who outperformed boys on academic measures did not see themselves as more talented than boys (Stetsenko et al., 2000). Just why talented girls tend to underplay their abilities and the repercussions of this tendency are key questions for developmental researchers.

FIGURE 13.10

Gender Differences in Academic Self-Evaluations

In a study by Cole et al. (1999), third- and sixth-graders were asked to evaluate their scholastic competence each year for a period of three years. Teachers also evaluated children's academic abilities. The graph shows that there are sex differences in children's tendency to overestimate their academic abilities, starting at about fourth grade and continuing through eighth grade. (The *y*-axis shows a statistical estimate of the tendency to overestimate, such that a higher positive number indicates greater overestimation.)

Source: Cole et al. (1999).

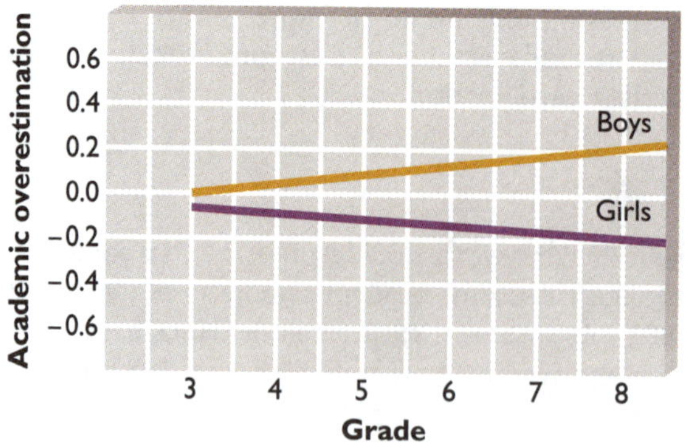

For • Your • Review

- What factors help to promote a smooth transition to the start of school?
- How do parents and peers influence school achievement?
- What is the role of class size in children's school achievement?
- How do teacher behaviors influence school achievement?
- What factors seem to facilitate learning among minority-group children? What factors seem to be responsible for the unique achievement patterns of Asian children?
- In what ways do teachers sometimes contribute to gender-typed behaviors and attitudes among children?
- How do children's own attitudes contribute to gender bias in school achievement?

Media

Media in all its forms—television, movies, radio, and magazines—has an undoubtedly enormous influence on school-age children. Perhaps there is no more visible symbol of the technological and "digital" age than the computer. Just as most adults in many countries are now likely to encounter computers in their daily experiences, so, too, are children. For example, within the United States, *100 percent* of children now have access to computers and the Internet in school (National Center for Education Statistics, 2005). Furthermore, the availability of computers in the homes of school-age children in the United States has increased dramatically within the last few years. About 65 percent of all children under age eighteen in the United States currently operate a home computer for educational and entertainment purposes, as well as for communicating with others. However, the level of home computer use drops substantially for African American, Hispanic, and poor children. Some refer to this disparity as the "digital divide." Children spend the largest proportion of time on the computer playing games, using the Internet, and working on school assignments (DeBell & Chapman, 2003). Figure 13.11 shows just how prevalent computer and Internet use are for school-age children. In this section we examine the question "What is the effect of computers on children's development?" In addition, we consider some of the research on the impact of television viewing on children, especially on their attitudes about gender and ethnicity, and on their consumer behavior.

Computers and Child Development

Does experience with computers influence the ways children tackle problem solving and other cognitive tasks? Are young "keyboard junkies" who spend long hours glued

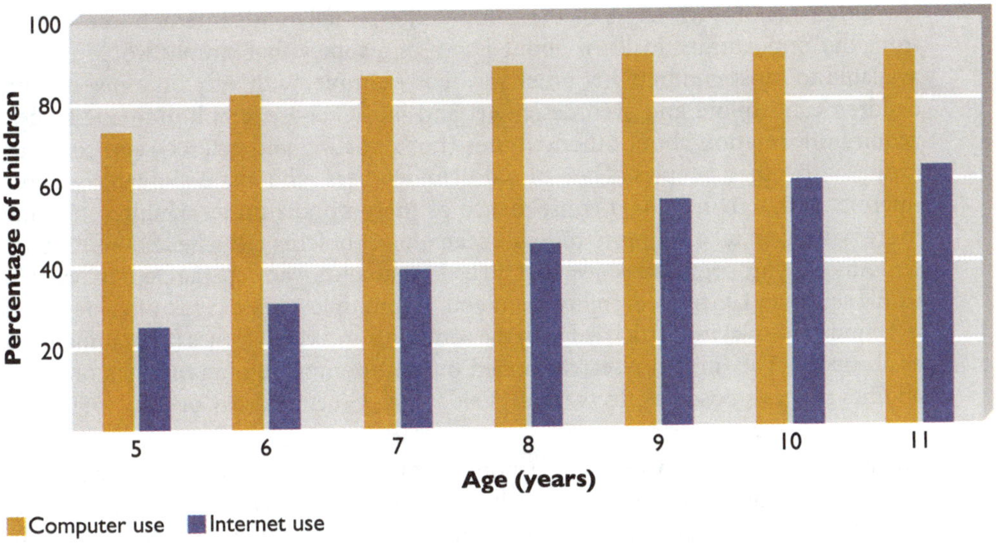

FIGURE 13.11

Percentage of School-Age Children Using Computers and the Internet

As the graph shows, a high percentage of school-age children use computers, either at home or at school, even at age five years. Most young children do not use the Internet, but usage rises dramatically over the next several years.

Source: DeBell & Chapman (2003).

to the video screen missing other critical experiences, particularly the social interactions crucial to their socioemotional development? The pervasive presence of computers in today's world makes these questions well worth exploring. The emerging answer is clear: there is no such thing as an "effect of computers" per se on child development. What matters, rather, is the way children use them (Behrman, 2000).

Academic Mastery and Cognition The first relatively widespread use of computers in education began in the 1960s, when computer-assisted instruction (CAI) was touted as a valuable, efficient educational tool. CAI programs serve primarily to supplement classroom instruction, providing highly structured tutorial information along with drill-and-practice exercises in content areas such as mathematics and reading.

Newer educational software places less emphasis on rote memorization and more on providing children with opportunities to use higher-order thinking skills as they master academic subjects. To date, the effects of these efforts have been mixed (Roschelle et al., 2000). For example, math education programs designed to encourage children to think more fully seem to have positive effects, whereas those that are oriented toward making repetitive math learning more fun seem to have no, and perhaps even detrimental, effects on learning (Wenglinsky, 1998). In general, however, the areas in which computer learning seems to have the greatest benefits are in science and mathematics (Roschelle et al., 2000). Being able to visualize and observe simulations of scientific concepts appears to encourage children to engage in levels of thinking generally more advanced than had been thought possible (Gordin & Pea, 1995; White & Fredriksen, 1998). Another factor associated with computers, which may have powerful benefits, is the opportunity to work on real-world problems that are available through the Internet. More specifically, with increased access to recently collected data from scientific research, children can engage in the very same types of activities of experimentation, design, and reflection that scientists and researchers carry out in their efforts to make contributions to understanding the environment, society, and the physical and biological world.

Other major advantages of the computer, especially with Internet access, stem from the opportunity to learn about issues and topics that simply would not be available to most children any other way. For example, with very little investment, children can explore and even design art and music, choreograph dramatic scenes, acquire information about other cultures (both existing and extinct), and communicate with other peoples. They can also find others who share similar academic interests and activities. As a consequence of these opportunities, children become more willing to take on more difficult academic problems (Roschelle et al., 2000).

Among the cognitive skills that may be enhanced are spatial representation, iconic skills, and increased ability to attend to multiple events, as is often required in action game playing associated with the computer and video games (Subrahmanyam et al., 2001). The limited research carried out on the impact of computers on these abilities suggests positive effects (Greenfield, 1998; Greenfield & Cocking, 1996).

Social Development Contrary to popular opinion, the interactions a child has with the computer do not necessarily displace other activities of a more social nature, nor is computer use itself necessarily a solitary activity (Crook, 1992). In one survey of more than 500 children, those with computers at home resembled nonowners in the frequency with which they visited friends, participated in club meetings, and engaged in sports (Lieberman, 1985). Furthermore, children who work on computer projects in school tend to collaborate and share ideas more in these settings than they do in other school activities (Hawkins et al., 1982). Thus, rather than inhibiting social interactions, computer activities may actually promote them, especially when teachers encourage group problem solving as opposed to individual projects (Bergin, Ford, & Hess, 1993).

Older children do spend much of their time at the computer alone. Nevertheless, a substantial portion of children's involvement with the computer, especially after it is no longer a novelty in the home, is devoted to communicating and maintaining social relationships with others via e-mail, with instant messaging, by playing games, or in chat rooms (Subrahmanyam et al., 2000; Subrahmanyam et al., 2001). Of course, one major concern is what kinds of social interactions may be occurring during some of these on-line activities, especially with individuals with whom the young person is not acquainted.

Gender Differences Ask children ranging from kindergarten age to twelfth grade to rate the word *computer* on a scale labeled M (for "male") at one end and F (for "female") at the other. Ask them also to rate how much they like the item. Researchers who have followed these and other procedures have found that children place computers toward the "male" side of the rating scale. In general, boys like computers more than girls do (Culley, 1993), and children sometimes perceive school computers as "belonging more" to boys (Cassell & Jenkins, 1998). Yet these gender differences are apparent primarily at the elementary and high school levels and are not present at younger ages; preschoolers and kindergartners are much less likely to display these stereotypes, at least with respect to interest in the computer (Bergin et al., 1993; Collis & Ollila, 1990; Krendl & Broihier, 1992). Moreover, the gender gap appears to be narrowing; girls now indicate that they use their home computer as much as boys do (DeBell & Chapman, 2003; Subrahmanyam et al., 2000). And boys and girls use the Internet about equally often, although the sites they access may differ (Clark, 2001). New computer games designed for girls have helped to reduce the disparity (Subrahmanyam & Greenfield, 1998), as has the increasing availability of websites responsive to girls' interests (Subrahmanyam et al., 2000).

TELEVISION AND DEVELOPMENT IN MIDDLE CHILDHOOD

Children, at least in the United States, spend more time watching television than at any other activity except sleep (Roberts et al., 1999). In fact, by high school graduation, three years will, on average, have been given to watching television, usually general entertainment shows (Roberts & Foehr, 2004; Strasburger, 1993). Moreover, with the advent of cable television, DVDs, and digital games, children have more opportunities than ever to spend time in front of a television screen. We have already discussed how television can influence cognitive and language development, as well as the incidence of aggressive behaviors, in early childhood. Here, we look more closely at the relationship between TV viewing and a number of other dimensions of social development.

Gender Stereotypes Television occasionally portrays males and females in nontraditional roles: fathers cook and care for their children, and women are employed in customarily masculine jobs. These programs, however, are not standard fare on commercial television. The portrayal of working women has increased over recent decades, but women are still more likely to be found in situation comedies and dramas than in action-adventure shows (Signorielli & Bacue, 1999). Consistent with stereotypes of female behavior, girls and women on television act nurturantly, passively, or emotionally. In contrast, males are more frequently the central characters of television shows, and they act forcefully, have more power and authority than women, and display reason rather than emotion (Lovdal, 1989; Signorielli & Bacue, 1999).

These stereotypical portrayals are likely to have some impact on children. When asked to write about their favorite shows, both boys and girls focus more on male than female characters and write about more masculine than feminine behaviors (Calvert et al., 2003). Children's attention to gender stereotypes very likely depends on other developmental changes children undergo. For example, boys who demonstrate gender constancy are more likely to watch male characters on television and prefer programs that contain a greater proportion of males than boys who do not display gender constancy (Luecke-Aleksa et al., 1995). In addition, gender-constant boys are more likely to watch shows created for adult entertainment, particularly sports and action shows, than their counterparts who still do not exhibit gender constancy. This difference in viewing preferences does not seem to be linked to earlier maturity in other cognitive abilities. In contrast, gender constancy in girls has relatively little effect on their television preferences or viewing habits. Perhaps this sex difference reflects the greater attractiveness of male roles on much of television and, therefore, accounts for such programs' increased interest value for gender-constant boys. Alternatively, perhaps this sex difference reflects a lessened need on the part of girls to exploit television as a basis for gender-role differentiation.

Ethnic Attitudes The characters on American television are predominantly white. African Americans are occasionally shown, but Hispanic, Asian, and Native American individuals are not commonly seen (Greenberg & Brand, 1994). This portrait applies even more strongly to commercial entertainment programs for children, although in both commercial and public educational programming for children about one-fourth to more than one-third of the characters are minorities, and minorities are becoming represented in increasing numbers on American television (Calvert, 1999). Relatively little research has been carried out to determine how important the representation of ethnic minorities may be to children. However, evidence shows that African American young people tend to prefer to watch and identify with African American characters (Greenberg & Brand, 1994). The extent to which they do so has been found to be positively related to self-esteem (McDermott & Greenberg, 1984) and, in some cases, although not consistently, to positive attitudes about their own race (Graves, 1993). Findings like these point to the potential for television to influence attitudes toward the self and toward other ethnic groups.

Consumer Behavior Because of their tremendous spending power, either directly or through their parents, children are the targets of a significant number of television commercials. According to some estimates, the average child sees almost 40,000 television commercials each year (Comstock & Scharrar, 2006). Of concern to many child advocates is the proliferation of television shows linked to specific toys and product endorsements for expensive items, such as athletic shoes, by popular sports figures and other celebrities, all of which put pressure on children to spend money.

Children certainly respond to the messages of commercials. For one thing, they frequently request the cereals and other foods they see advertised (Taras et al., 1989). By age five, children distinguish commercials from other programming, but they do not always recognize commercials as messages specifically intended to influence their behavior; four- and five-year-olds, for example, believe "commercials are to help and entertain you" (Kunkel, 2001; Ward, Reale, & Levinson, 1972). Young children are especially likely to confuse programs with commercials if toys or cartoon characters appear in both (Wilson & Weiss, 1992). It is usually not until children are eight years of age or older that they understand that commercials are intended to influence viewers' buying habits (Blosser & Roberts, 1985). Because young children are not able to critically evaluate the information presented to them in commercials, they may pressure their parents to purchase expensive toys and clothes, heavily sugared foods, and other products (Kunkel & Roberts, 1991).

In more recent years, controversy has swirled around the introduction of Channel One in public schools. This program consists of ten minutes of news and two minutes of commercials for products of interest to young people. If a school agrees to air these broadcasts to students, free televisions are provided. It has become a popular idea in American school systems; approximately 12,000 schools and an estimated 7 million young people have access to the program. In general, students seem to learn about current events from such programming, and it is liked by teachers and principals (Johnston, Brzezinski, & Anderman, 1994). But the commercials also are reported to be effective as well; students more positively evaluate and express greater interest in buying the products that are advertised (Brand & Greenberg, 1994). Other companies are providing school computer labs with free equipment in which the advertising is available on a small part of the screen continuously. In addition, based on information provided when the student logs on, these companies are collecting information about the age and gender of children working with the computer, as well as the kinds of Web sites they visit. Although schools are being provided with state-of-the-art computer facilities, critics worry about the potential invasion of privacy and the consequences of what could be interpreted as school-sanctioned commercialism from these kinds of arrangements.

RESEARCH APPLIED TO PARENTING

Encouraging Critical Skills in Television Viewing

Nicky finished his homework just before his mother came home. Fortunately, there still was enough daylight for his best friend, Aaron, to come over for a visit. As soon as he arrived, the conversation turned to the afternoon's television fare and some of the toys that were advertised on their favorite shows. "Hey, did you see that car that spins off the race track? That is really awesome!" "Yeah," Aaron replied. "I really want to get one." "Me, too. And I want that robot they showed after that," Nicky proclaimed. Nicky's mother worried when she overheard this conversation. Was this generation of kids being steered to buy more consumer goods than children in prior years? These fears were added to her growing concerns about the effects of watching all of that violence on television. Was there anything she could do to control the large impact of television on the thinking and behavior of her young son?

As we have seen, television holds enormous promise to enhance children's intellectual and social functioning. However, there is also clear evidence of potential dangers, especially when television viewing takes up much of a child's time or is directed at programs that are age inappropriate. Apart from the option not to have a television set available in the home (an alternative that relatively few parents defend), what steps might parents take to promote positive benefits from this medium? Any recommendations will, of course, depend on the maturity of the child, as well as the values caregivers wish to promote. However, developmental psychologists and others concerned about the influence of television on children generally agree with the following guidelines:

1. ***Be aware of how much time is being spent watching television and what is being watched.*** Parents may not always realize how much of the day their children spend in front of the television set, what they are watching, or how the program is affecting them. Continuous supervision may not be possible when parents are busy with other household duties or away at work. However, knowing what children are watching, and for how long, is the first step in understanding what they might be learning from television.

2. ***Decide what is acceptable to watch.*** Even young children may be attracted to programming that is frightening or inappropriate, not because they necessarily enjoy it but because the rapid pace of events or some other convention of the programming is attracting their attention. Parents have the responsibility to determine which programs are permissible and ensure that children limit their television viewing those programs. Recognize, however, that as children become older and more independent, parental monitoring will be more difficult. Older children must learn to take increasing responsibility for their own television viewing.

3. ***Establish acceptable times for watching television.*** Family members need to know when they can watch television. For example, can the television be on during the dinner hour? Is watching television permitted if homework, chores, or other obligations are not yet finished? How late in the evening is television viewing allowed?

4. ***Watch television with children whenever possible.*** When jointly watching programs with their children, parents have the opportunity to discuss such things as what is real and what is fantasy, how conflict might be resolved other than through violence, the stereotypes being portrayed, the goals of advertising, and many other issues presented through this medium that are valued or not approved within the household. In addition, by commenting on the material, parents can stimulate vocabulary development and provide different perspectives that may promote cognitive and social skills. Unfortunately, coviewing involving active discussion of television content appears to be infrequent in most families (Huston & Wright, 1998).

FOR • YOUR • REVIEW

- What benefits do computers provide in the mastery of academic material?
- What has been the impact of computers on children's social development?
- How do boys and girls differ in their use of computers?
- What influence does television viewing have on children's gender role beliefs?
- How is television viewing related to children's ethnic group attitudes?
- How is television viewing related to children's consumer behavior?

Chapter Recap

Summary of Developmental Themes

Sociocultural Influence

How do sociocultural factors influence the contexts of development in middle childhood?

Culture has been shown to influence parenting demands, especially in the degree to which children are expected to be compliant and helpful in order to help the family survive.

Risk/Resilience

What contextual factors promote risk or resilience in middle childhood?

Divorce and single parenthood can put children at risk, but the practice of effective parenting overrides the effects that these variations in family structure might have. Children can be at risk for negative developmental outcomes if they experience poor peer relationships. However, research has identified several ways in which success with peers can be promoted. For example, fostering prosocial behaviors, good social skills, and effective social-information processing can help children in their interactions with peers. Certain characteristics of schools can promote or discourage academic achievement. Children thrive when they experience smooth transitions to school, have small classes, and interact with teachers who encourage autonomy and initiative.

Chapter Review

The Family in Middle Childhood

In what ways do parenting strategies vary across different cultural groups?

Cultures vary in the degree to which children must contribute to the family's subsistence, do chores, and obey their parents. In some cultures, parents demand a very high degree of compliance, whereas in others, the emphasis in parent-child interactions is sociability.

What are the effects of divorce on child development?

Children whose parents divorce evidence socioemotional and academic difficulties, especially boys. Many effects disappear after the first year following divorce, however.

What factors can help children adjust to the divorce of their parents?

More positive adjustment to divorce is associated with a shift from power-assertive to authoritative parenting, low parental conflict after separation, and the presence of sources of social support for children outside of the immediate family.

What kinds of custody arrangements are best for children?

Research suggests that joint custody, whether legal or physical, has the greatest benefits for children.

What factors are associated with successful outcomes in single-parent families?

Children do best when single parents are involved, use effective discipline strategies, and display warmth. Assistance with sources of stress, such as help with child care and counseling, can be helpful in alleviating some of the stresses that single parents face.

What does the research indicate about the impact of having gay or lesbian parents?

Research shows that children growing up with same-sex parents do not differ from children with heterosexual parents on academic, social, or emotional traits. What matters most for all children is the quality of caregiver interactions that they experience.

What role do siblings play in the development of younger children in the family?

Older siblings act as teachers, models, and sources of social support for young children in the family. Older siblings are usually more dominant and nurturant than younger siblings, but these differences diminish as children get older.

Peer Relationships in Middle Childhood

What factors promote the formation of peer group identities? What factors can lessen hostilities among groups of peers?

Children show especially strong identity with peer groups when their groups compete against others. Peer groups show in-group favoritism when their groups are highly defined and have high status. Intergroup hostilities can be reduced by having groups work together on some common goal.

How do researchers assess children's peer status?

Peer status is usually measured through *sociometric nominations* or *sociometric rating scales*. Based on the outcomes, children are classified as popular, rejected, neglected, or controversial.

What are some of the characteristics displayed by popular children?

Popular children tend to engage in prosocial behaviors. The child's peer status is also related to physical attractiveness, motor skills, and emotion regulation.

What are some of the influences on the development of children's social competence?

Social competence has its roots in the child's earliest attachment relationships but is also influenced by parental styles of social interaction, as well as social-cognitive skills, such as the ability to perceive social cues accurately.

What are the qualities of children's friendships during middle childhood?

During middle childhood, children begin to value friends for their psychological qualities, rather than the fact that friends share activities with them.

What factors influence the formation of children's friendships?

Children become friends with peers who share interests, personality qualities, or other behaviors and characteristics with them. Children form friendships by keeping social interactions positive in tone and de-escalating conflicts.

How do friendships contribute to the child's social and emotional development?

Friendships seem to protect children from anxiety and stress, and are associated with higher levels of self-esteem.

SCHOOL

What factors help to promote a smooth transition to the start of school?

Children who initially demonstrate competence with respect to social behaviors and cognitive/linguistic skills tend to make smoother transitions to the start of school. Entering school with familiar peers has advantages as well.

How do parents and peers influence school achievement?

Parents who are involved with their children and who encourage their children's autonomy tend to have children with higher academic achievement. The peers with whom a child aligns himself or herself can affect school motivation.

What is the role of class size in children's school achievement?

Smaller classes, especially during the early grades, appear to have positive consequences for children. The research shows that, for early grades, class sizes of thirteen to seventeen students are associated with greater achievement on standardized tests of reading and mathematics.

How do teacher behaviors influence school achievement?

Teacher expectations about students' abilities can have important consequences for their school achievement. Certain classroom management styles can be influential; studies of *cooperative learning* and *collaborative learning* reveal more favorable outcomes for students. In addition, teachers have a positive impact on students when they encourage autonomy and initiative, and when they form close interpersonal relationships with their students.

What factors seem to facilitate learning among minority-group children?

According to the *cultural compatibility hypothesis*, children's academic performance rises when educational practices incorporate elements of the child's background culture.

What factors seem to be responsible for the unique achievement patterns of Asian children?

Children in Asian societies display higher levels of achievement in mathematics and science perhaps because of the amount of time spent learning these subjects, demands for homework, concerns of parents for successful school performance, and the central role that effort plays in many Asian cultures.

In what ways do teachers sometimes contribute to gender-typed behaviors and attitudes among children?

Teachers may contribute to gender-role socialization through their attitudes and behaviors. For example, they may have different expectations about the academic skills of boys and girls, and often focus more attention on boys than on girls.

How do children's own attitudes contribute to gender bias in school achievement?

Girls and boys often believe that girls are better at reading and boys are better at mathematics. In the domain of mathematics, however, girls' beliefs in their competence seem to be increasing. Girls often underestimate their academic abilities and attribute failures to lack of ability.

MEDIA

What benefits do computers provide in the mastery of academic material?

Computers appear to enhance the learning of science and mathematics, especially by providing opportunities to visualize concepts. Children can access real-world data on-line and learn about a wide array of topics and issues that might not normally be available to them.

What has been the impact of computers on children's social development?

Computers can promote social involvement, especially when they are used for group projects. Even when children are on the computer alone, they are often engaged in social networking through e-mail and instant messaging.

How do boys and girls differ in their use of computers?

Younger children do not show gender differences in their used of computers. Although the stereotype is that computers are for boys, gender differences in computer use are diminishing in contemporary society.

What influence does television viewing have on children's gender role beliefs?

Gender stereotypes are commonly exhibited in television programming. Children show evidence of learning these stereotypes, although their attention to them appears to be dependent on an understanding of their own gender.

How is television viewing related to children's ethnic group attitudes?

Children watch and identify with television characters that belong to their own ethnic group, and the extent to which they do so is linked to positive self-esteem.

How is television viewing related to children's consumer behavior?

Children do not understand that commercials are intended to influence consumer behavior until about age eight. Children tend to request the products they have seen on television commercials.

KEY TERMS AND CONCEPTS

collaborative learning (p. 477)
cooperative learning (p. 477)
cultural compatibility hypothesis (p. 478)
sociometric nomination (p. 459)
sociometric rating scale (p. 459)

Pathways: Connecting the Story of Development

Infancy	Early Childhood	Middle Childhood (6–11 years)		Adolescence
See p. 268	See p. 376	**Physical Development**	• Shows more efficient and better-controlled motor skills • Becomes more adept at fine-motor coordination • Shows steady growth in physical size	See pp. 576–577
		Cognitive/ Language Development	• Shows systematic and efficient attention strategies • Shows logical thought on conservation tasks but only in the presence of real objects or images • Develops increasing memory span • Produces various kinds of memory strategies to enhance recall • Shows greater control of cognitive processing • Shows gains in ability to plan the steps in problem solving • Becomes more flexible in strategy use • Shows growth in metacognition • Shows metalinguistic awareness including appreciation of humor and metaphor	
		Social/ Emotional Development	• Shows understanding of display rules • Engages in social-comparison • Displays global self-esteem • Shows mastery orientation • Exercises self-regulation through internalized language • Thinks in terms of moral realism or conventional ideas • Shows greater knowledge of and greater flexibility toward gender stereotypes	

PHYSICAL AND COGNITIVE DEVELOPMENT 14

She stared intently at the thirteen-year-old who had just finished her routine. Danielle couldn't believe what she had just seen. How could any girl her own age do that? Danielle's words expressed admiration and awe, but her voice was tinged with envy as she confided to her best friend, "We've been in gymnastics ever since we were five. If we tried that, we'd probably break our necks!"

Even as a toddler, Danielle had seemed captivated by leaping and tumbling. Her parents took great pride in their daughter's graceful athleticism and precocious motor skills. Danielle enrolled in ballet and gymnastics at an early age. Both activities had been fun. As Danielle became older and more skilled, she especially seemed to thrive on the competition that permeated gymnastics meets. She liked being good at what she did; she preferred being the best. Through the applause, her friend had no difficulty hearing Danielle mutter, "I'll bet I can do that. Watch me next time we're at practice." But she also knew that her body had changed. All of a sudden her legs seemed too long for the pommel horse, and her own program took more effort to carry out. She wondered silently if she really could complete a routine as challenging and remarkable as the one she was now observing.

Key Themes in Physical and Cognitive Development

Nature & Nurture How do nature and nurture interact in physical and cognitive development in adolescence?

Sociocultural Influence How does the sociocultural context influence physical and cognitive development in adolescence?

Continuity/Discontinuity Are physical and cognitive development during adolescence continuous or discontinuous?

Interaction Among Domains How do physical and cognitive development in adolescence interact with other domains of development?

Danielle, who is physically poised and skilled, displays a fair amount of confidence in the demands of learning a new and difficult gymnastic routine. Toward the end of childhood, many skills become highly specialized talents: youngsters like Danielle are already accomplished athletes; others her age are concert musicians. On the verge of adulthood, adolescents undergo sweeping changes on all fronts—the physical, cognitive, emotional, and social. Interpreting and orchestrating all these changes is the increasingly sophisticated and complex brain. And part and parcel of the myriad transformations that the brain directs during this developmental phase are notable advances in the way adolescents think and solve problems.

Physical Development in Adolescence

Probably the most obvious changes that signal the transition to adolescence occur in the domain of physical development. Although parents may long ago have dropped the typical childhood practice of penciling ever-higher marks on the bathroom wall, a long-absent aunt might still cry out, "My, how you've grown!" upon seeing her thirteen-year-old niece. And by this she might be referring

Variations in height and weight are just two of the many ways that children of similar ages differ in their physical development. These middle school children joining together to socialize after school illustrate a wide variation in height. Some may not have begun their adolescent growth spurt, others may be in the middle of this developmental phase, and still others may have completed it.

not just to a conspicuous change in height, but also to numerous changes in physical characteristics that signify the emergence of adulthood. Her proclamation might just mean "You look grown up."

Physical Growth

In the United States, the onset of rapid adolescent growth typically occurs between ages ten and fourteen for girls and between ages twelve and sixteen for boys (Sinclair, 1985). During this period, height increments occur at nearly double the rate in childhood. Because the growth spurt usually does not start in boys until about two years later, girls may be head and shoulders over their male peers for a brief period in early adolescence. During the approximately three years over which the growth spurt occurs, girls add about twenty-eight centimeters (eleven inches) and boys about thirty centimeters (twelve inches), or about 17 percent of their total height (Abbassi, 1998). Figure 14.1 illustrates the growth typically observed in many populations of children during their first eighteen years.

Individual differences in growth are especially evident during the adolescent years, when children are likely to show enormous variation in the timing, speed, and duration of the adolescent growth spurt. A girl who once towered over her childhood girlfriends may suddenly find at age thirteen that she is looking up to them, at least temporarily. A boy whose athletic skills were unremarkable may find himself the starting center for the middle school basketball team if he undergoes an early adolescent growth spurt.

In earlier chapters, we pointed to the fact that much physical growth during childhood follows the *cephalocaudal* and *proximodistal* principles. However, physical growth

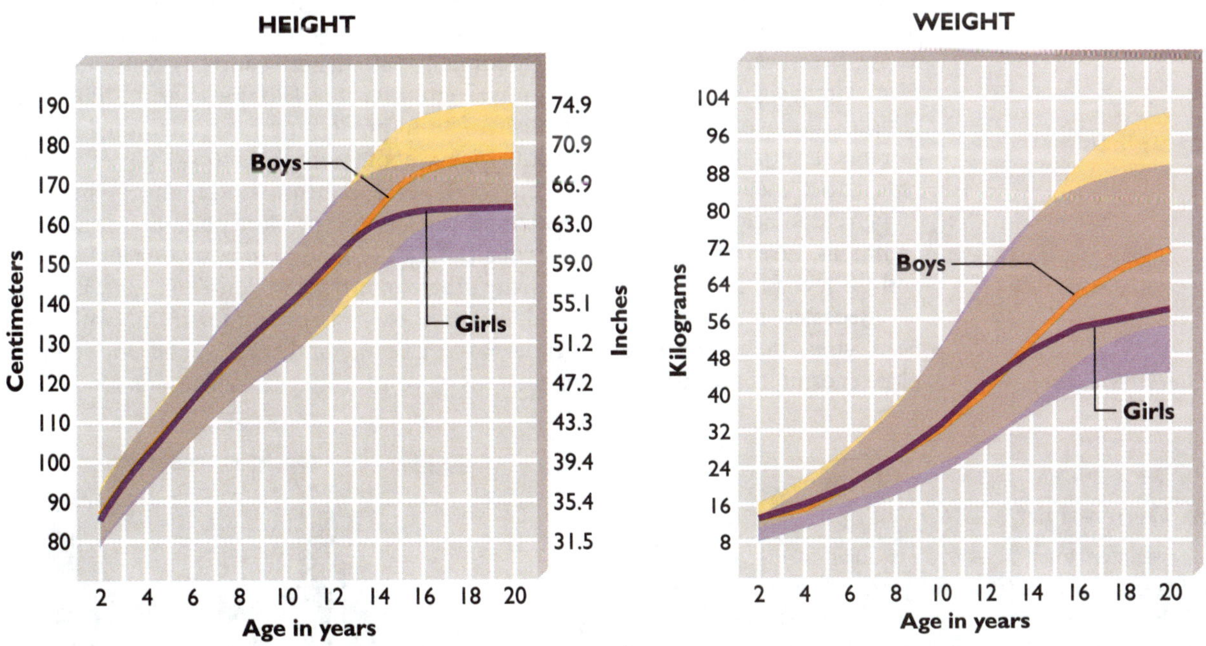

FIGURE 14.1

Growth in Height and Weight over the First Twenty Years

Height and, to a lesser extent, weight rapidly increase in the first two years following birth. Changes in height and weight continue at a fairly modest rate throughout childhood, followed by a brief, more rapid upturn sometime during the preadolescent or adolescent years. However, there is a wide range in height and weight among children, especially during the adolescent years. This figure (based on children in the United States) shows height and weight growth charts for boys and girls between the third and ninety-seventh percentiles.

Source: Centers for Disease Control and Prevention, National Center for Health Statistics (2000).

does not necessarily conform to these principles during adolescence. During the adolescent growth spurt, for example, some parts of the body undergo rapid growth in a pattern almost the reverse of the proximodistal principle. We are all familiar with the teenager who seems to be all hands and feet. Hands and feet are in fact among the first body parts to show a dramatic change during this period; they are followed by arms and legs and, last of all, the trunk (Tanner, 1978). An adolescent, in other words, is likely to outgrow his shoes first, then his trousers, and finally his jacket.

The organ systems, which have been growing at a stable rate throughout the childhood years, show a rapid increase during adolescence. However, the reproductive system follows a strikingly different pattern: only during adolescence do organs associated with reproduction begin to mature and rapidly approach their adult size. These different patterns mirror the functional importance of various systems of the body at specific points in development.

Weight

Just as we pointed to concerns about the climbing rate of obesity in younger children, so, too, do health experts express similar concerns about adolescents. As Figure 14.2 indicates, the prevalence of being overweight in this age group has climbed substantially over the last 40 years. This increase has been especially pronounced among adolescents who grow up in poor families (Miech et al., 2006). At the same time, one-third of high school students report that they do not engage in regular physical activity (National Center for Health Statistics, 2005). This factor, along with poor dietary habits, no doubt contributes to adolescent overweight.

Key Theme
Sociocultural Influence

In many cultures, a concern with being overweight seems to have contributed to another problem: efforts to initiate dieting, even by children who are within a normal weight range. In the United States, many young people, especially women, are dissatisfied with their weight. Concerns about becoming obese are expressed as early as age five (Feldman, Feldman, & Goodman, 1988). These concerns continue to be seen among eight-year-olds from nearly all ethnic groups (Robinson et al., 2001), and various studies report that up to half of third-grade girls have attempted to diet (Strauss, 1999). By the time they get to high school, more than 40 percent of women report that they are dieting (Centers for Disease Control, 1991), and as many as 75 percent indicate that they have attempted to lose five or more pounds at some time (Emmons, 1996). Similar percentages of girls have been found to be dieting in Australia, and the levels may be the same in many other countries (Paxton et al., 1991).

Repeated messages from fashion magazines, and sometimes from family and peers, stress the importance of slenderness for beauty and success, and undoubtedly place enormous pressure even on preteens to control weight. When girls report that

FIGURE 14.2
Trends in Overweight

These data, collected from a series of studies carried out in the United States between 1963 and 1999, reveal the marked increase that has taken place in the number of children and adolescents who are considered obese. Some believe that obesity has become a health epidemic in this and other countries because of the dramatic changes and accompanying health risks that are associated with being overweight.

Source: Centers for Disease Control and Prevention (2002).

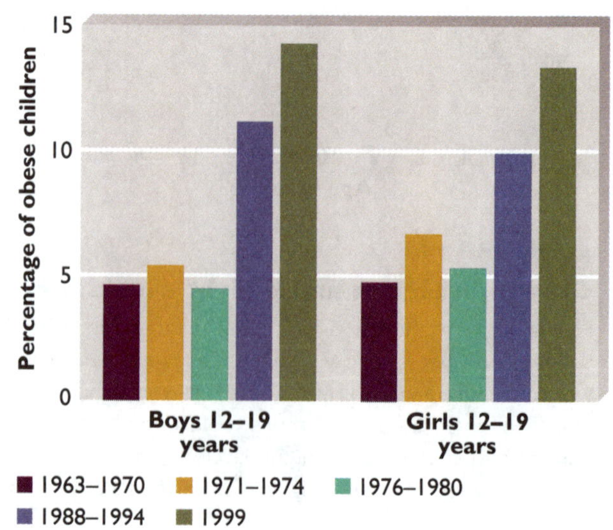

they feel pressure from family and friends to be thin, they are also likely to express dissatisfaction with their body (Stice & Whitenton, 2002).

During the adolescent years, many girls believe it is important to have a boyfriend and to be physically attractive. Having dates, at least among Caucasian girls and African American girls whose mothers are more highly educated, is correlated with lower body fat, an indication that concern about weight has some basis in real experience (Halpern et al., 1999). Many teenage girls also tend to talk a lot with their friends about appearance—about how to look good and how to improve physical appearance. The extent to which they do so, as well as the extent to which they compare themselves with celebrities or other girls in school, predicts the degree of body dissatisfaction that they report (Jones, 2004).

ATYPICAL DEVELOPMENT

Dieting and Eating Disorders

The large number of girls who attempt to diet has become an almost normative, although troubling, aspect of growing up in many cultures. Sometimes, however, young people initiate more drastic steps to encourage weight loss. For example, in one study, nearly 10 percent of girls and 4 percent of boys in the sixth through eighth grades indicated that they have resorted to vomiting or use of laxatives in their efforts to remain thin (Krowchuck et al., 1998). A substantial number of teenagers, especially girls, including many who are not obese, go to great and even life-threatening lengths to reduce their weight. Anorexia nervosa and bulimia nervosa are two self-initiated forms of extreme weight control efforts, disorders that affect perhaps as many as 3 percent of women in industrialized countries at some time during their lifetime (Walsh & Devlin, 1998). *Anorexia nervosa* is a kind of self imposed starvation. Individuals with anorexia appear to be obsessed with the fear of appearing too heavy and as a consequence become dangerously thin. As weight loss becomes severe, muscle tissue degenerates, bone marrow changes, menstrual periods are disrupted in girls, and cardiac stress and arrhythmias can occur. *Bulimia nervosa* is an eating disorder in which the individual often engages in recurrent bouts of binge eating, sometimes consuming enormous quantities of high-calorie, easily digested food. For many, binge eating alternates with self-induced vomiting, actions sometimes accompanied by use of laxatives or diuretics. Although they share with anorexics an intense concern about their body, individuals suffering from bulimia often fall within a normal weight range for their age and height.

A substantial increase in these disorders, particularly the more frequent of the two, bulimia, has been reported since the 1970s (Bryant-Waugh & Lask, 1995). Its incidence is greatest among Caucasian, middle- to upper-income young women (Harris, 1991), but both disorders appear to be increasing in males and in some cultural groups that have begun to adopt Western values. Their frequency may also be greater in certain groups, such as athletes and dancers, who are especially concerned about weight gain. Eating disorders may begin as part of the larger spectrum of anxieties that children, adolescents, and young adults experience about physical changes, especially as they approach and continue through puberty (Keel, Fulkerson, & Leon, 1997). For some individuals, an inherited, biological susceptibility, particularly in cases of anorexia nervosa, may exist (Katzman et al., 2000). Because sociocultural, psychological, and biological factors appear to interact, it should not be surprising that the treatments most effective for dealing with such disorders have been difficult to identify. However, about two-thirds of individuals who display anorexia nervosa show good recovery if treatment is begun early (Herpetz-Dahlmann et al., 2001). Because eating disorders can have serious long-term consequences, individuals experiencing one of them should be strongly encouraged to seek professional help.

Physical Maturity

The growth spurt of early adolescence is only one of numerous indicators of approaching physical maturity. Accompanying the growth spurt are important progressions indicating sexual maturity. We briefly consider these and the psychological issues a young person may confront during the passage from late childhood to early adulthood.

Defining Maturity Because rate and final level of growth vary so greatly among individuals and for different parts of the body, researchers have turned to other criteria to define physical maturity. One reliable indicator is **skeletal maturity**, the extent to which *ossification,* the chemical transformation of cartilage into bony tissue, has been completed. The change begins prenatally about the eighth week after conception, when cartilage in the ribs and in the center of the long bones of the arms and legs is transformed. The process continues into late adolescence or early adulthood, when bones in the wrist and ankle are finally completely formed. Although skeletal maturity has become the standard for defining the end of physical growth, other, visible markers of approaching maturity appear just before and during the adolescent years. These important markers comprise a series of events associated with **puberty**, the developmental milestone reached when a young person gains the ability to reproduce.

During puberty, the *primary sexual organs*—testes and penis in males; vagina, uterus, and ovaries in females—enlarge and become capable of functioning. *Secondary sexual characteristics* that distinguish men from women, such as facial hair or breasts, also mature. Boys take on a more muscular and angular look as shoulders widen and the fat tissue of childhood is replaced with muscle. Girls' hips broaden, a change especially adaptive to bearing children. Girls also tend to retain a higher proportion of fat to muscle tissue and assume a more rounded appearance overall than boys. Like the growth spurt, the timing of each of the many events associated with puberty differs enormously from one young person to another. As a rule, however, this cluster of characteristics tends to appear somewhat earlier in girls than in boys.

Although there are numerous indicators of increasing sexual maturity, perhaps none are more significant than **menarche**, the first menstrual period in females, and **spermarche**, the occurrence of the first ejaculation of sperm in males. Menarche typically takes place between about twelve and thirteen years of age for females and spermarche between thirteen and fourteen years of age for males. However, as with other indicators of puberty, their initial appearance varies considerably from one individual to the next. For example, in the United States, the events accompanying sexual maturity begin somewhat earlier in African American girls than in Caucasian American girls (Biro et al., 2001).

Key Theme

Nature & Nurture

What triggers these remarkable changes? The brain, including the hypothalamus and pituitary gland, and various hormones are centrally involved. *Adrenarche* initiates many of the changes taking place during early adolescence (McClintock & Herdt, 1996). Adrenarche refers to the maturation of the adrenal glands, small glands located above the kidneys. These glands release hormones important for the growth spurt and the emergence of underarm and pubic hair in girls. In addition, adrenarche may play an important role in the emergence of sexual attraction, which Martha McClintock and Gilbert Herdt (1996) argue typically occurs as early as ten years of age. In girls the hypothalamus may monitor metabolic cues associated with body size or the ratio of fat to muscle, because body mass index appears to be a good, although not the only, predictor of onset of menarche (Kaplowitz et al., 2001).

Still other *gonadotropic* (gonad-seeking) hormones released by the pituitary gland stimulate, in the case of females, the production of estrogen and progesterone by the ovaries and regulate the menstrual cycle. Estrogen promotes the development of the breasts, uterus, and vagina, as well as the broadening of the pelvis. Even family relationships, such as greater stress in the family, which can affect hormonal balances,

skeletal maturity Extent to which cartilage has ossified to form bone; provides the most accurate estimate of how much additional growth will take place in the individual.

puberty Developmental period during which a sequence of physical changes takes place that transforms the person from an immature individual to one capable of reproduction.

menarche First occurrence of menstruation.

spermarche The first ejaculation of sperm by males entering puberty.

may accelerate female development (Ellis & Garber, 2000). In the case of males, hormones contribute to the production of sperm and elevate the production of testosterone by the testes. Testosterone, in turn, promotes further growth in height, an increase in size of the penis and testes, and the appearance of secondary sexual characteristics, such as pubic and facial hair.

Early Versus Late Maturity Today adult height in most industrialized societies is typically reached by about age seventeen; a century ago, it often was not achieved until about age twenty-three (Rallison, 1986). Changes in the age of menarche reveal a similar trend toward increasingly early occurrences over recent generations (see Figure 14.3).

The secular changes stem from improved socioeconomic conditions, including more adequate nutrition. Do the individual differences that are a part of this transition affect socioemotional development? The answer appears to be yes. For example, girls who are unprepared for menarche, either due to lack of information or because of its early onset, perceive the event more negatively than other girls, whose reactions are often a mixture of positive and negative feelings (Koff & Rierdan, 1995; Ruble & Brooks-Gunn, 1982). Thanks to greater communication within the family, including emotional support and assurance that menstruation is normal and healthy, girls' reactions to menarche today seem more positive (Brooks-Gunn & Ruble, 1980; Koff & Rierdan, 1995).

KEY THEME
SOCIOCULTURAL INFLUENCE

The limited research conducted with boys suggests that they are often uninformed, surprised, and confused about spermarche (Stein & Reiser, 1994). For many boys, sex education classes may either fail to explain what they need to know or are provided too late to prepare them. Their feelings about the event are mixed, and they seldom talk about it with others (Gaddis & Brooks-Gunn, 1985; Stein & Reiser, 1994). Nevertheless, early maturity seems to have positive aspects for boys (Alsaker, 1992; Petersen, 1988). Compared with early maturers, late-maturing boys report more negative feelings about themselves, feel more rejected, express stronger dependency and affiliative needs, and are more rebellious toward their parents (Mussen & Jones, 1957). Although late maturers want to be well liked and accepted, their efforts to obtain social approval often translate into attention-getting, compensatory, and childish behaviors disruptive to success with peers and adults (Mussen & Jones, 1958). The differences continue to be observed even into adulthood (Jones, 1965).

KEY THEME
INTERACTION AMONG DOMAINS

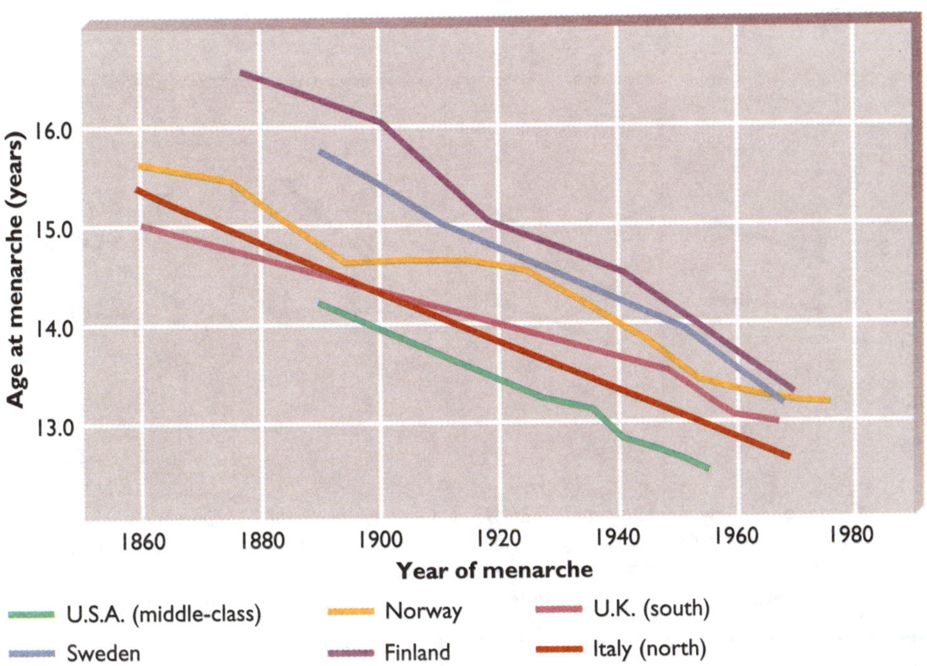

FIGURE 14.3
Secular Trends in the Age of Menarche
Evidence exists for a secular trend in the decrease in age of the onset of menarche from 1845 through 1960. Although most of the data were obtained by questioning adolescents and young adults, some, especially those from earlier generations, depended on the memories of older individuals.
Source: Adapted from Tanner (1990).

What are girls' reactions to early and late maturity? Here the picture differs (Alsaker, 1992; Greif & Ulman, 1982; Simmons, Blyth, & McKinney, 1983). Early maturity may enhance status and prestige for girls just as for boys, but it can also be embarrassing; decrease their popularity, at least among agemates; and lead to greater social pressure and expectations from older friends, parents, and other adults to conform to more mature behavior patterns (Brooks-Gunn, 1989). In research in Sweden, girls who reached menarche early were more likely than late-maturing girls to engage in a variety of norm-breaking activities, such as staying out late, cheating on exams, pilfering, or using alcohol (Magnusson, Stattin, & Allen, 1986). Early-maturing girls preferred older and more mature friends, who may have inspired their greater independence from socially approved conventions of behavior. Indeed, among those maturing early but reporting no older friends, the frequency of norm-breaking activities was about the same as for girls who matured later.

As they grew older, early maturers with and without older friends began to look more alike in their frequency of many norm-breaking activities, and late maturers began to engage in such activities as use of alcohol as often as early maturers. Still, a few unacceptable behaviors, such as the use of drugs, remained higher throughout adolescence among early-maturing than among late-maturing girls.

As illustrated in Figure 14.4, another important component of girls' responses to early maturity appears to be whether their group of friends includes only other girls or also boys (Ge, Conger, & Elder, 1996). Early-maturing girls growing up in a rural area of the United States reported that they felt somewhat more stress than their on-time or late-maturing counterparts. They continued to report this greater stress over several years but particularly if their friends included boys. Although peer influences may be a factor in norm breaking, other changes taking place within the family, including less careful monitoring by parents, may contribute as well (Dick et al., 2000).

KEY THEME
SOCIOCULTURAL INFLUENCE

Some of the negative consequences of early maturity for females may also spring from the cultural ideals of beauty and maturity that exist in most Western societies. Slenderness and long legs are considered desirable traits in women. Although initially taller than their peers during the growth spurt, early-maturing girls have less opportunity to grow tall and often end up somewhat shorter, heavier, and more robust than their later-maturing peers (Biro et al., 2001). Not surprisingly, early-maturing girls are therefore initially less satisfied with their weight and appearance than are late-maturing girls (Williams & Currie, 2000). Personality disturbances, such as depression, are also more frequent among girls who mature

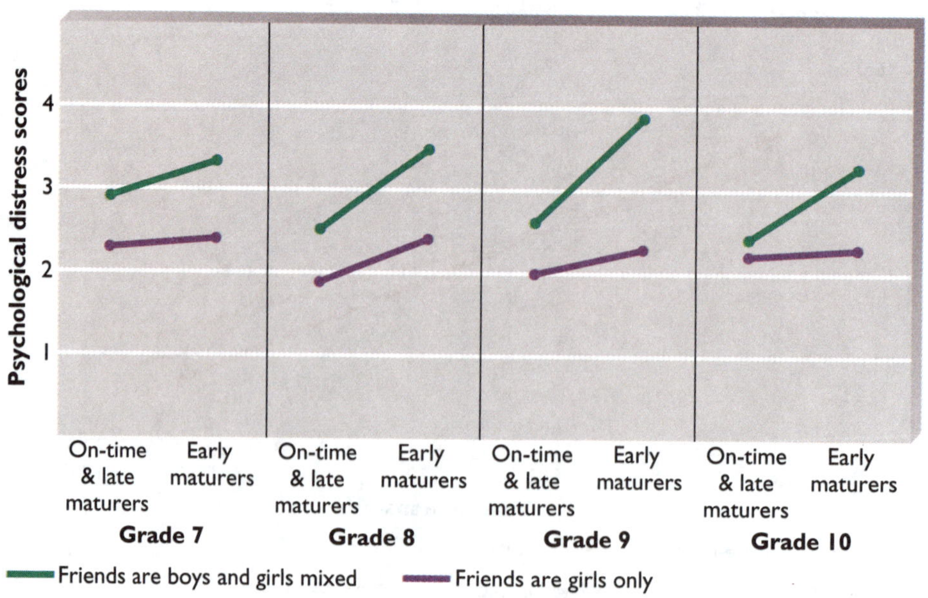

FIGURE 14.4

Psychological Distress Reported by Early-, On-Time, and Late-Maturing Girls as a Function of Sex Composition of Their Friends

In general, early-maturing girls report somewhat greater stress than girls who mature later or on time. However, this increased stress in early maturers is especially evident when their group of friends includes boys as well as girls. Early-maturing girls undergoing greater stress may initiate friendships that include boys, which continue to heighten their concerns throughout the adolescent years.

Source: Ge, Conger, & Elder (1996).

early (Ge et al., 2003; Stice, Presnell, & Bearman, 2001). In contrast, early-maturing boys more quickly assume the rugged, muscular physique stereotypically portrayed in American society as ideal for men and are more pleased by their weight and appearance than late-maturing boys (Petersen, 1988). Even if they show depressive symptoms early in puberty, boys seem to bounce back two years later, a pattern that is not found for early-maturing girls (Ge et al., 2003).

Girls who mature early and boys who mature late are also out of step with most of their classmates. Young people usually prefer friends who share interests, and interests change with increasing maturity. Late-maturing boys may find that their peers move on to other pursuits, making it more difficult to maintain positive relationships with their friends. Early-maturing girls may redirect friendships to older peers and boys. But this desire can be a problem, because it can contribute to increased behavioral and school problems, as well as greater personal unhappiness caused by pressures to conform to the interests of these older peers or boys. In other words, biological, immediate social, and broader cultural factors combine to help define the consequences of early and late maturity.

SEXUAL BEHAVIOR

KEY THEME
SOCIOCULTURAL INFLUENCE

Few changes accompanying puberty are as contentious in many families as the sexuality that attends physical maturity. Anthropological research indicates that the majority of cultures are likely to permit or at least tolerate some sexual activity during the teen years. But Western societies have generally been more restrictive in its expression (Schlegel & Barry, 1991). Many mothers in the United States tend to underestimate the extent of sexual activity among their offspring; their children, in turn, tend to underestimate the degree to which their mothers disapprove of this activity (Jaccard, Dittus, & Gordon, 1998). Nevertheless, large numbers of teenagers are sexually active, and at young ages. In one study, for example, 30 percent of students entering sixth grade (averaging 11.7 years of age) in impoverished areas of one major city in the United States reported that they have engaged in sexual intercourse (Kinsman et al., 1998). Although teen sexual activity has declined from 1993 to 2003, 47 percent of ninth- through twelfth-graders still state that they have engaged in sexual intercourse (Kaiser Family Foundation, 2005).

What factors play a role in whether a teenager will engage in sexual activity? Several different family variables seem to be instrumental, according to a review by Brent Miller, Brad Benson, and Kevin Galbraith (2001). One especially important parameter is how the members of the family "connect" with one another. More specifically, when parents are warm and supportive of their children—that is, seem to be close and responsive to them—teenagers are more likely to remain sexually abstinent until they are somewhat older. Additionally, a similar outcome occurs when parents maintain relatively closer supervision and monitoring of their children's behavior, although evidence exists that there is a limit to this factor; when parents become intrusive and overcontrolling, sexual activity may be started somewhat earlier by their offspring. Not surprisingly, another important factor is the values parents hold concerning the appropriateness of sexual activity among teenagers. On the other hand, research on the extent to which parents communicate with their sons and daughters about sexual issues does not appear to be related to the timing with which sexual activity initiated. However, few studies have examined when such communications begin; information about this subject may often be initiated by parents only after they are aware that their children are sexually active.

Other contextual variables associated with the family are also related to sexual activity. In general, children in families living in neighborhoods where there is greater poverty, higher crime rates, and less stability—factors that are generally correlated with lower education and income—tend to engage in earlier onset of sexual activity. Children of single parents are more likely to initiate sexual behavior earlier, and so are children who are growing up in abusive family environments or who have older teenage siblings who are already parents (East & Jacobson, 2001).

Aside from the moral and ethical issues that adolescent sexual behavior raises, there are important health and social consequences. Among the most frequent concerns are sexually transmitted diseases (STDs), teenage pregnancy, and the tendency of teenage parents to drop out of school. Adolescents appear to be more susceptible than adults to STDs; an estimated 3 million are infected each year by one of these diseases—a number that has spread considerable alarm among members of the medical profession (Eng & Butler, 1997; McIlhaney, 2000). In the 1980s approximately 20 percent of unmarried American women of European heritage eighteen years or younger and 40 percent of African heritage became pregnant during their adolescent years (Furstenberg, Brooks-Gunn, & Chase-Lansdale, 1989). The rate of teen pregnancy has shown some decline throughout the 1990s and early 2000s but still remains far higher in the United States than in other technologically advanced countries (Hamilton et al., 2005). Moreover, approximately 300,000 of the nearly half a million teenage women delivering their first child and 75 percent of all adolescents giving birth to a child each year will remain unmarried, a substantial increase from forty years ago, when only 15 percent who gave birth were unmarried (Allen et al., 1997; Coley & Chase-Lansdale, 1998). Only about half of these women will finish high school (Hotz, McElroy, & Sanders, 1997). Moreover, their children will often have difficulty when they begin school (Brooks-Gunn & Chase-Lansdale, 1995).

Controversy: Thinking It Over

What Should Sex Education Programs Emphasize?

Because of the risks associated with sexual activity, such as pregnancy and contracting AIDS or other STDs, many individuals working with elementary, middle school, and high school students in the United States and other countries around the world have argued that young people need to be better educated about their sexuality.

What Is the Controversy?

Nearly everyone agrees that sex education should begin in the home at a young age, taught by parents. Moreover, parents generally wish to see instruction about sexuality provided in the schools. Most adults in the United States believe that sex education is appropriate, and when given the opportunity, only a small proportion of parents ask to have their children excused from sex education classes (Kaiser Family Foundation, 2004). In fact, sex education is either required or recommended in all states today and in most other countries in which formal education is offered. But beyond that, much less accord exists about sex education and, in particular, on what the focus of the instructional content should be, especially in the United States. Should the emphasis be on encouraging young people to abstain from sexual relationships until they are married? Or should sex education in the schools attempt to promote the acquisition of skills to handle maturely the complexities and consequences of relationships and provide clear information and access to resources that will help young people to think clearly about and be comfortable with their emerging sexuality?

What Are the Opposing Arguments?

From the perspective of some, the only effective way for teenagers to avoid the negative outcomes associated with sexual relationships is to abstain from them. Harmful consequences, both psychological and physical, are the inevitable result of such premature activity. Moreover, to promote anything other than abstinence in sex education classes sends a mixed message that communicates a double

Sex education is part of the school curriculum in most states and in many countries. There is considerable controversy about what the content of sex education programs should be, but some recent programs show promise in lowering the rate of teen sexual activity and exposure to sexually transmitted diseases.

standard: "Avoid sexual relationships, but in case you can't, here is what you should know."

To others, however, a message that focuses only on abstinence ignores the fact that many teenagers are already engaging in sexual relationships. In fact, somewhere between 800,000 and 900,000 adolescent girls less than nineteen years of age will become pregnant each year in the United States alone, and about half of them can be expected to deliver babies (Centers for Disease Control, 2000). The number who are sexually active is substantially higher. Youths need information on the best ways to avoid pressure to initiate sexual activity and to prevent becoming infected with sexually transmitted diseases and becoming pregnant. Thus a more balanced perspective is to encourage postponing sexual involvement but, for those already involved or likely to initiate it, to emphasize engaging in it responsibly and safely.

What Answers Exist? What Questions Remain?

Tests of the effectiveness of various sex education curricula have yielded mixed results, although some success has been reported. Knowledge of sexuality typically increases, but young people do not consistently report that they are involved in fewer sexual relationships or practice sex more responsibly or safely after exposure to many of these programs. Moreover, little evidence exists to indicate that abstinence-only programs are any more effective than other programs in reducing initiation into sexual activity or risky behaviors associated with it. Rarely have sex education programs been found to lead to an increase in sexual activity, another fear that is occasionally expressed (Grunseit et al., 1997). Nevertheless, some types of programs seem to hold considerable promise for delaying the onset of sexual activity or reducing the number of partners, unplanned pregnancies, or rate of sexually transmitted diseases (Franklin al., 1997; Grunseit et al., 1997; Kirby, 1997). One example is Teen Outreach. This program is designed to involve high schoolers in voluntary community service and encourages them to reflect on the normative tasks of adolescence, such as career goals and appropriate social relationships; only a small component of the curriculum is geared to sex education. Students participating in it, however, displayed a significant decline in pregnancy and other school-related problems compared with other students who did not participate (Allen et al., 1997). What makes this or other sex education programs more effective? At the present time, the essential ingredients are unknown. In that many young people are already sexually active before they participate in sex education classes, do programs need to be offered at earlier ages? Should the curricula include emphasis on more than the biology of reproduction? For example, could young people benefit from learning the social skills needed to respond to the many pressures they face to engage in sexual relationships? Have programs stressing abstinence, which for the most part have only recently gained widespread adoption, not been in schools long enough to prove themselves? Or are these programs too biased and narrow in their focus, often emphasizing fear instead of knowledge, extolling a simplistic solution to a complex problem that can have life-and-death consequences?

Brain Development

For many years, scientists believed that, by adolescence, the growth of the brain is essentially complete. However, growing evidence indicates that remodeling of the brain continues well into adulthood (Spear, 2000; Tanapat, Hastings, & Gould, 2001). For adolescents, most of the changes appear to occur in the frontal regions of the cortex. One important development is that axons in this region continue to grow and become myelinated, speeding the transmission of signals among neurons within this area of the brain as well as to other portions of the brain (Paus, 2004; Yakovlev & Lecours, 1967). Thus, not only is communication among brain cells faster, it is also more integrated among brain regions. A second change is in the number of synapses in the frontal cortex. At the start of puberty, there is an abundance of synapses in this region of the brain, but over time, synaptic density declines, probably because of synaptic pruning, the elimination of weaker synaptic connections (Huttenlocher, 1979). In some ways, this pattern of overabundance of synapses followed by a decline resembles the pattern of brain development that we saw in prenatal development and early infancy. However, it is not yet clear that the physiological processes underlying these major two waves of brain development are the same (Spear, 2003).

Key Theme
Interaction Among Domains

Studies using fMRI scans show that, in general, activity in the prefrontal cortex increases in adolescents as they perform a variety of cognitive tasks, in particular those that involve inhibition of responses. For example, if individuals are required to suppress the movement of their eyes to a visual stimulus, adolescents show greater activation of the prefrontal region than children or adults (Luna et al., 2001). In another experiment, adolescents were instructed to press a button in response to one visual target, but avoid pressing when they saw a different target. While they were performing, fMRI scans were obtained. Of special interest was how the brain responded when participants had to inhibit their responses. When scans of children at age nine were compared to their scans at age eleven, they showed an age-related decrease in activity in the prefrontal cortex. In addition, the areas that were activated were more localized rather than diffuse (Durston et al., 2006). All of this suggests that, with development, brain functioning seems to become more efficient and more specialized. As brain researcher Linda Spear (2003) puts it, "The adolescent brain is a brain in the process of becoming leaner, more efficient, and less energy consuming" (p. 66).

Researchers are intrigued by all of these changes in the brain because they seem to correspond to such behaviors as planning, higher-level reasoning, and impulse control in adolescents. If we see notable changes in thinking, social behavior, and even risk taking in the teen years, the reason may be, say some researchers, that underlying brain physiology is at least partly responsible.

SLEEP

Ask any parent of a teenager—adolescents tend to be night owls. They go to bed later, often after 11:30 P.M. At the same time, because most high schools have earlier start times than elementary schools, adolescents must wake up early, typically at 6 A.M. or even earlier, in order to make it to school on time. About 26 percent of adolescents get less than 6.5 hours of sleep per night (Wolfson & Carskadon, 1998). But teens may actually need more sleep, as much as 9 hours daily compared to the typical 7 or 8 hours that we think of for adults (Carskadon, Harvey, & Duke, 1980). This means that many teenagers are not getting enough rest to be alert during the day; by some estimates, as many as 85 percent can be categorized as sleep deprived (Dahl & Lewin, 2002; Wolfson & Carskadon, 1998).

Besides needing more sleep, adolescents also experience a phase shift in sleep cycle—a biological tendency to go to bed later and wake up later in the morning—which appears to be triggered by the onset of puberty (Carskadon, Acebo, & Jenni, 2004). Several other factors add to the tendency for teens to stay up later. In contrast to the regulation of bedtimes that most parents practice with younger children, very few parents of teenagers tell them when to go to sleep. Homework, computers and the Internet, and work schedules also contribute to this pattern (Wolfson & Carskadon, 1998). Sometimes teens try to catch up by sleeping more on weekends and holidays, but this further upsets the sleep-wake rhythm when they have to awaken early on the next school day (Dahl & Lewin, 2002).

What are the consequences of insufficient sleep for adolescents? Lack of sleep is associated with lower grades in school, moodiness and depression, and lower self-esteem (Fredriksen et al., 2004; Wolfson & Carskadon, 1998). Excessive sleepiness is a special concern when teenagers drive; it is associated with the tendency to be involved in serious automobile accidents. The consequences of adolescent sleepiness are serious enough that several school districts across the United States have made changes toward later school start times for high school students. According to early reports from one of these districts, school attendance is up, and daytime sleepiness among students has declined (Wahlstrom, 2002).

FOR • YOUR • REVIEW

- What patterns of physical growth are observed during adolescence?
- Why are dieting and eating disorders of concern? What factors lead to efforts to control weight?
- How is physical maturity defined?
- What are the developmental changes that accompany puberty?
- What are the social and behavioral consequences of early and late maturity for males and females?
- What factors are related to sexual behavior in adolescents? What are the health implications of such behavior?
- What are the controversies associated with sex education programs in the public schools?
- What major changes occur in the brain during adolescence?
- How do patterns of sleep change in adolescence?

COGNITIVE DEVELOPMENT IN ADOLESCENCE

Earlier in this text, we documented the growth in children's cognitive processes from infancy through middle childhood. The range and scope of these changes might lead you to surmise that, by adolescence, cognitive development is complete. However, research shows that this supposition would be incorrect. For example, by looking at how participants perform when they are asked to locate a target in a string of letterlike stimuli or to judge how a spatial figure would look if it were rotated a few degrees, researchers have concluded that there are increases in the speed of processing information from middle childhood to adolescence (Kail & Miller, 2006). The ability to perform accurately in tasks in which memory must be used to locate a visual target improves up until age nineteen years, and the ability to suppress a behavioral response (such as looking at an intruding visual stimulus when instructed not to) improves until age fourteen years (Luna et al., 2004). Generally speaking, cognition in adolescence becomes more controlled, better coordinated, and in many instances, more subject to self-reflection.

PIAGET'S THEORY AND ADOLESCENCE

KEY THEME
CONTINUITY/DISCONTINUITY

By the time the child reaches adolescence, she will most likely have moved to the final stage in Piaget's theory, the **formal operational stage**. Thinking in this stage is both logical and abstract. Problems like "Bill is shorter than Sam but taller than Jim. Who is tallest?" can now be solved without seeing the individuals or conjuring up concrete images of them. The adolescent can also engage in **hypothetical reasoning**; that is, she can generate potential solutions to problems in a thoroughly systematic fashion, much as a scientist approaches an experiment. According to Piaget, the development of formal operational thought represents the culmination of the reorganizations in thought that have taken place throughout each preceding stage in childhood. By adolescence, thought has become logical, flexible, and abstract, and its internal guiding structures are now highly organized.

Piaget's pendulum problem allows us to examine the thinking of the formal operational adolescent. In this task, the person is shown an object hanging from a string and asked to determine the factor that influences the frequency of oscillation, or the rate at which the pendulum swings. The length of the string, the weight of the object, the force of the push on the object, and the height from which the object is released can all be varied. How do children in earlier Piagetian stages approach this problem? Children in the preoperational and concrete operational stages typically try various manipulations in a haphazard fashion. They might compare the effect of a long string attached to a heavy weight and a short string tied to a light weight. Or they might vary the weight of the object and the force of the push, but leave out the length of the string. In contrast, formal operational children are both systematic and complete in testing the potential influences on oscillation. For example, while keeping weight constant, they observe the effects of varying length, push, and height; while keeping length the same, they investigate the effects of varying weight, push, and height; and so forth. Most adolescents, Piaget observed, could correctly determine that the length of the string was the critical factor in how fast the pendulum swings (Inhelder & Piaget, 1958).

In the social realm, achieving abstract thought means that the adolescent can think about the nature of society and his own future role in it. Idealism is common at this developmental stage because he understands more fully such concepts as justice, love, and liberty, and thinks about possibilities rather than just realities. In some ways, the adolescent may be more of a "dreamer" or a utopian than the adult because he has not yet had to confront the practical facts of living and working in the world (Inhelder & Piaget, 1958).

The contemplative nature of adolescent thought may manifest itself in two other ways, according to David Elkind (1976, 1981). First, adolescents may believe that others scrutinize and evaluate them as much as they think about themselves. This belief, called the **imaginary audience**, may cause a young girl to avoid going out because she just got braces on her teeth ("Everybody will see me!") or make a teenage boy avoid answering a question in class because he is certain all his classmates will think he is "dumb." Second, adolescents may show signs of holding a **personal fable**, the belief that they are unique, that no one can fully understand them, and

formal operational stage In Piagetian theory, the last stage of development, from approximately eleven to fifteen years of age, in which thought is abstract and hypothetical.

hypothetical reasoning Ability to systematically generate and evaluate potential solutions to a problem.

imaginary audience Individual's belief that others are examining and evaluating him or her.

personal fable Belief that one is unique and perhaps even invulnerable.

Many adolescents have the false belief that others inspect them in the same detail as they evaluate themselves, a phenomenon called the "imaginary audience."

even that they are invulnerable. A teenage boy prohibited from going to a late-night rock concert by his parents might say, "You just don't understand how important this is to me!"

You will recall that Piaget made strong claims that the sequence of development is universal. Yet not all children reach the stage of formal operations, and some do not even attain the highest levels of concrete operations. Many American adults, in fact, fail to display formal operational thought (Neimark, 1979). Members of many non-Western cultures do not display formal operational thinking, especially when they have little experience with formal schooling (Dasen, 1972; Rogoff, 1981). Other research shows that adolescents today receive higher scores on tests of formal operations than adolescents did twenty and thirty years ago (Flieller, 1999). Studies like these imply that the child's experiences in the sociocultural context may shape the nature of thought to a greater degree than Piaget acknowledged.

KEY THEME
SOCIOCULTURAL INFLUENCE

THE DEVELOPMENT OF SCIENTIFIC THINKING

Most of us have received at least some formal training in the complex type of reasoning called *scientific thinking*. Scientific reasoning involves formulating a hypothesis, designing experiments in which one factor varies while others are held constant, and deciding on the validity of the hypothesis based on the observable evidence. We have just seen that, according to Piaget, this form of logical thought is not observed prior to the start of the formal operational stage. Contemporary research confirms that there are indeed observable developmental accomplishments in scientific reasoning; however, the foundations of this type of thinking are evident early in childhood. Even children who are just starting school show impressive knowledge about some of the basic tenets of scientific thinking.

One element of scientific thinking is the ability to distinguish between theory and evidence. Preschoolers often behave as if there is no distinction between the two. Shown a series of pictures depicting two runners in a race, younger children typically answer the questions "Who won?" and "How do you know?" with theory ("He has fast sneakers") rather than evidence ("He's holding the trophy"). By age six, though, children are likely to cite objective evidence (Kuhn & Pearsall, 2000).

A related skill is the capacity to see which conclusions are warranted by the evidence. Let us consider one example in which the child is presented with a series

Research shows that when children have the opportunity to engage in repeated scientific problem solving, they become more proficient in designing controlled experiments.

of pictures depicting the phases of the moon, along with two theories about why they occur: (1) clouds cover different portions of the moon at different times, or (2) the moon has a dark and a light side. Then the child hears the evidence: an astronaut reports that the moon is dry and has no water, that he landed on some white rock, and that he later walked on black gravel. Which theory about the moon could possibly be correct? Most first-, third-, and fifth-graders in this study chose the second theory, the one that was consistent with the evidence (Samarapungavan, 1992). Other researchers have confirmed that first-graders can go even further and correctly identify whether a specific piece of empirical evidence provides conclusive or inconclusive support for a hypothesis (Sodian, Zaitchik, & Carey, 1991).

Yet scientific thinking involves greater complexities. For example, hypotheses must be formed in the first place, and usually several hypotheses are concurrently in the mind of the scientist. Often, several variables operate at the same time. Experiments must be designed and conducted, and their outcomes coordinated with the hypotheses, to determine which variable causes the observed outcomes (Klahr & Dunbar, 1988). It is here that developmental changes are most apparent. When third-graders are asked to generate and evaluate hypotheses by running a series of experiments, they usually are not systematic in designing experiments that isolate the key variable and do not write down the outcomes of their experiments. Sixth-graders show improvements but still design a limited number of experiments, and their experiments are often difficult to interpret. In one study in which sixth-graders were asked to use a software package to test which variables played a role in the risk of earthquakes, 83 percent of the students investigated three or more variables at once (Kuhn & Dean, 2005). Adults do the best, but not because their reasoning about the relationship between theory and evidence is stronger. Rather, adults can coordinate the generation of hypotheses with the design of the set of experiments necessary to test them (Klahr, Fay, & Dunbar, 1993).

When children are encouraged to engage repeatedly in scientific problem solving, their skills improve noticeably. Deanna Kuhn and her colleagues (Kuhn, Schauble, & Garcia-Mila, 1992) asked preadolescents to identify which variables affected the speed of a model boat being towed in a tank of water: the water depth, boat size, boat weight, sail color, or sail size. The instructor gave minimal feedback to the students, but they were encouraged to make a plan about what they wished to find out, state what they found out after each experiment, and record their findings in a notebook.

The results showed that, over only a few weeks of repeated exposure to these problems, students became markedly more proficient at designing valid and focused experiments, and at drawing valid inferences from the data they collected. Follow-up studies show that this knowledge is subsequently applied to new problems (Kuhn et al., 1995; Schauble, 1996). Even hinting to students that they should limit their investigations to a single variable helps. Sixth-graders who received this tip during science instruction were more likely than those in a control group to conduct valid experiments and to draw appropriate conclusions (Kuhn & Dean, 2005).

Direct instruction helps children master principles of scientific reasoning, too. In one study, seven- to ten-year-olds received explicit training on the concept "controlling variables in an experiment." They were provided with examples of confounded and unconfounded experiments, and were then asked to apply their knowledge to a sample experiment. Children who had received this training were able to apply the principle of "controlling variables" to several different experiments and were more likely to do so than children who had not received instruction. Thus the ability to reason like a scientist is clearly within the grasp of elementary school students and preadolescents (Chen & Klahr, 1999; Klahr, Chen, & Toth, 2001).

A good way to capture the development of scientific thinking is provided by Deanna Kuhn and her colleagues, who say that children acquire increasing control over their own thought processes. By becoming aware of the differences between theory and evidence, fact and opinion, and by coordinating theories with evidence, children begin to be able to "know how they know" (Kuhn & Pearsall, 2000). In that sense, the steps in the development of scientific reasoning may reflect broader accomplishments in the cognitive domain.

The Executive Function

In earlier chapters, we mentioned that, with development, children are better able to control their cognitive processing—their attention and memory, for example. As children mature, they become better able to analyze the tasks they face, size up their own capabilities, deploy and modify strategies, inhibit certain behaviors if they have to, and monitor the effectiveness of their approaches. The control of cognitive processing is also very important in problem solving, which, as we saw earlier, can involve complex tasks, such as planning and transfer. Researchers have recently begun to turn their attention to understanding the role and development of this **executive function**. A key aspect of the executive function is *coordination* of the various components of cognitive processing in order to achieve some goal (Welsh, 2002). A growing body of research indicates that the development of the executive function is a central feature of cognition in adolescence.

On the behavioral level, one manifestation of the child's executive function skills is the growth of **metacognition**, the child's awareness and knowledge of thinking and cognitive processes. The beginnings of this process are evident in the preschooler's emerging theory of mind, discussed earlier in this text. Children become aware of the difference between *thinking* about something and *seeing* it, and they understand the meanings of other psychological states, such as *belief* and *desire.* Young children, though, often perform cognitive tasks without being fully reflective about their actions. Metacognitive awareness grows through the school years and into adolescence, as does the ability to act on that awareness. By adolescence, for example, children are able to judge whether they have studied enough to remember and know the strategies they must use, as well as how much effort they need to allocate in order to improve recall (Schneider & Lockl, 2002). More broadly speaking, adolescents decide what to think about in the first place and when (Kuhn, 2006). In essence, they become masters of their mental life.

One of the laboratory tasks that researchers have used to examine executive function is a spatial working memory task in which an array of colored squares appears on a computer screen. The goal is to touch the squares one at a time in

executive function Portion of the information-processing system that coordinates various component processes in order to achieve some goal.

metacognition Awareness and knowledge of cognitive processes.

order to locate tokens hidden within and then "place" them in a special bin. How organized is the search process? And do individuals touch squares that have already been searched? Optimal performance requires participants to be systematic in their search—maybe by proceeding left to right or top to bottom—and once a token has been found and placed in the bin, to resume search where it was left off. Touching squares in which tokens have already been found is considered an "error." This task is presumed to assess executive control because it has several components that have to be regulated; it requires participants to be organized, to remember, to monitor their performance, and to update information as progress is made. When nine- through twenty-year-olds were assessed on this task, individuals who were thirteen years of age and older did significantly better than younger children (Luciana et al., 2005).

Another situation that has been used to examine executive control is the Iowa Gambling Task. Here, four decks of cards are presented to individuals. Two decks have cards with high monetary rewards but also a few cards with high losses; the other two decks offer cards with smaller rewards but also many cards with small losses. The goal is to select cards from the decks to obtain the most money; in the long run, the decks with smaller rewards and losses are the best to choose. How do adolescents respond to this task, in which the lure of big gains must be suppressed in order to "win" the most money? Monica Luciana and her colleagues (Hooper et al., 2004) found that preteens aged nine to ten years seemed to understand the task but were still tempted by the promise of big wins. Their choices tended to center on the decks with big wins and losses. In contrast, fourteen- to seventeen-year-olds were more likely to shift from the risky "big money" decks to the "safer" decks over the course of several trials. But even the older teenagers tended to make a greater number of riskier choices than did older adults. In other words, executive control shows signs of development throughout adolescence.

Neuropsychological studies of children who have experienced brain damage indicate that executive function skills seem to stand apart from other cognitive abilities; affected children may show normal language and sensory abilities but have difficulties with planning and inhibition (Espy & Kaufmann, 2002). We have already seen that the prefrontal cortex of the brain has been implicated as one area responsible for the executive function, although there may be others. Thus, as this region of the brain matures, we would expect children to show gains in their executive function capabilities.

Like many adults, adolescents are prone to exhibit judgment biases, overlooking relevant facts in favor of strong personal beliefs. Some experts tie this tendency to the occurrence of risky behaviors.

JUDGMENT AND DECISION MAKING

Adolescents (or even adults) do not necessarily reach the most mature levels of metacognition (Kuhn, 2000a, 2000b). For example, adolescents and adults engaged in decision making are often influenced by their current belief systems, especially when confronted with real-life as opposed to laboratory problems. People of all ages, adolescents included, display **judgment biases**, tendencies to be influenced by inappropriate information at the expense of important and perhaps more relevant facts. They also often operate according to their personal beliefs about social groups or how things look.

Most adolescents, for example, are vulnerable to the *gambler's fallacy*, saying that if a person has just won 75 percent of the time in video poker, she is destined to lose on the next turn. Rather than using information about statistics and probability, concepts that are within the grasp of children and adolescents, individuals make judgments on the basis of a small sample of events in which certain dramatic outcomes stand out (Klaczynski, 2001). Children and adolescents are also influenced by biases toward their own group, such as the social categories or religion to which they belong (Klaczynski, 2000). In the following scenario, for example, individuals can respond on the basis of statistical probability or a social stereotype:

> In Juanita's class, ten girls are trying out to be cheerleaders, and twenty are trying out for the band. Juanita is very popular and very pretty. She is always telling jokes and loves to be around people. Do you think Juanita is trying out to be a cheerleader or for the band?

Children and preadolescents tend to say, "cheerleader," responding to these types of questions on the basis of stereotypes (Jacobs & Potenza, 1991).

Even though the story of cognitive development suggests that the eventual outcome is more efficient and rational, the research on decision making suggests that thought does not always stem purely from well-developed logic. Especially when situations involve self-interest or uncertainty, judgments are likely be swayed by more informal, and sometimes emotional, beliefs (Jacobs & Klaczynski, 2002). What may develop, then, is the ability to inhibit quick, belief-based responding in favor of more reasoned, well-thought-out choices (Klaczynski, 2004).

FOR • YOUR • REVIEW

- According to Piaget, what are the major features of thinking in the formal operational stage?
- What changes are observed in children's scientific reasoning skills as they progress to adolescence?
- What role does the executive function play in cognitive processing? In what ways does the executive function change with development?
- What are the main features of adolescents' decision-making behaviors?

INTELLIGENCE

Children and adults sometimes show noticeable differences in individual performance on tests of word meanings, general knowledge, and visual-spatial performance, a phenomenon that is described by some psychologists in terms of the concept of intelligence. To the layperson, the term *intelligence* usually includes the abilities to reason logically, speak fluently, solve problems, learn efficiently, and display an interest in the world at large (Siegler & Richards, 1982; Sternberg et al., 1981). Most of us probably have a sense that the abilities to profit from experience and adapt to the environment are also part of intelligent human functioning. Yet, despite the average person's ability to give what sounds like a

judgment bias Tendency to be influenced by inappropriate information at the expense of important and perhaps more relevant facts.

reasonable description of intelligent behavior, in the field of psychology the formal definition of intelligence has proven surprisingly elusive. Although the concept has been the subject of research and theorizing for more than a century, no single definition has been commonly agreed on, and no one measurement tool assesses intelligence to everyone's satisfaction.

Despite the lack of consensus on how to define and measure intelligence, we now have many tests designed to measure it in children as well as adults. Most of the commonly used tests assess the kinds of thinking people do in academic settings, as opposed to common sense or "practical intelligence" (Sternberg, 1995). These tests are routinely used in schools, as well as in other settings, to make decisions about educational strategies or therapeutic interventions. We mention this topic here because it is often when preadolescents and adolescents are in middle school and high school that decisions are made about the educational track (general academic, college prep, or honors, for example) in which they will participate. In other words, judgments are made about children's abilities. Thus in this chapter we examine more closely the concept of intelligence and how it is measured.

Psychometric Approaches

The notion that human beings may differ from one another in certain skills originated in the late nineteenth century with the work of Sir Francis Galton. Galton (1883) believed that people differ in their ability to discriminate among varying physical stimuli, such as auditory tones of different pitch, and in their speed of reaction to sensory stimuli. Such differences, according to Galton, are largely innate. Expanding on these ideas, James McKeen Cattell (1890) devised a series of psychophysical tests that assessed a person's ability to sense physical stimuli or perform different motor actions. It was Cattell who coined the term *mental test.* The first formal intelligence test was created in 1905 by Alfred Binet and Theodore Simon. Commissioned by the minister of public instruction in Paris to devise an instrument that would identify children who could not profit from the regular curriculum in the public schools due to lower mental abilities, Binet and Simon (1905) designed a test that assessed children's ability to reason verbally, solve simple problems, and think logically. With the Binet-Simon test, the mental testing movement was born, and psychometrics became firmly entrenched as a model for understanding intelligence.

Psychometric models of intelligence are based on the testing of large groups of individuals to quantify differences in abilities. The basic assumption is that some people will perform better than others and that those who perform below some average or normative level are less intelligent, whereas those who perform above that level are more intelligent. Within the general psychometric framework, however, theorists have taken contrasting positions on the exact nature of intelligence. Charles Spearman (1904) believed that intelligence consists of two parts: *g*, a general intelligence factor that he equated with "mental energy," and *s*'s, specific knowledge and abilities, such as verbal reasoning or spatial problem solving, which are evident only in certain tasks. According to Spearman, *g* is a central aspect of any task requiring cognitive activity and accounts for commonalities in levels of performance that people typically demonstrate in various kinds of intellectual tasks. Thus the influence of *g* might enable a person to obtain a high score on a verbal test, as well as on a test of visual-spatial skill. In contrast, Louis Thurstone (1938) believed that intelligence is composed of several distinct fundamental capabilities that are completely independent of one another. He proposed that the following seven *primary mental abilities* are components of intelligence: *visual comprehension*, as measured by vocabulary and reading comprehension tests; *word fluency*, the ability to generate a number of words (for example, those beginning with *b*) in a short period of time; *number facility*, the ability to solve arithmetic problems; *spatial visualization*, the mental manipulation of geometric forms or symbols; *memory*, the ability to recall lists of words, sentences, or pictures; *reasoning*, the ability to solve analogies or other problems involving formal relations; and *perceptual speed*, the ability to recognize symbols rapidly.

psychometric model Model of intelligence based on the testing of large groups of individuals to quantify differences in abilities.

There is one other way that intelligence has been conceptualized within the psychometric tradition. According to Raymond Cattell and John Horn, a distinction can be made between two types of intelligence, each with a unique developmental course (Cattell, 1971; Horn, 1968; Horn & Cattell, 1967). **Fluid intelligence** consists of biologically based mental abilities that are relatively free of cultural influence, such as the ability to remember a list of words or to group abstract figures together. **Crystallized intelligence** consists of skills that one acquires as a result of living in a specific culture, such as knowledge of vocabulary, reading comprehension, or general information about the world. Cattell and Horn believed that fluid intelligence is tied to physiological maturation and that it increases until adolescence, when it levels off, and then declines in later adulthood. On the other hand, they hypothesized that crystallized intelligence increases over much of the life span because individuals continually acquire knowledge from the cultural groups in which they live.

Researchers have found that fluid intelligence does eventually decline with age, especially after ages seventy to eighty. Crystallized intelligence increases from childhood through the middle adult years but also declines with aging, although on a somewhat slower trajectory than fluid intelligence (Kaufman, 2001; McArdle et al., 2002). These decreases are probably linked to physiological changes in the ability of the brain and other portions of the nervous system to process information. It is important to note, however, that wide individual differences occur in age-related changes in intelligence (Brody, 1992).

INFORMATION-PROCESSING APPROACHES

Alternative theoretical ideas about intelligence are directly derived from the information-processing model of cognition. Rather than identifying the structures of mental ability, as the psychometricians do, information-processing theorists have focused on describing the mental processes necessary to accomplish different types of tasks. Thus each step involved in the chain of cognitive processes from encoding to retrieval, such as speed of processing, a growing knowledge base, or metacognitive skill, provides important insights about defining intelligence.

Intelligence as Speed of Processing Individuals vary in the speed with which they conduct certain cognitive activities. For example, consider a typical *choice reaction-time* task. A participant sits in front of an apparatus that contains eight lights, her finger resting on a "home" button. As soon as one of the eight lights comes on, the participant must move her finger to a button below that light to turn it off. People show notable differences in the speed with which they carry out this task. Several researchers have proposed that such individual differences in speed of processing information may be related to intelligence, particularly *g*, the general intelligence originally described by Spearman (Jensen, 1982; Jensen & Munroe, 1979; Vernon, 1983).

Is there evidence that speed of information processing is a component of intelligence? Researchers have observed at least moderate relationships between reaction-time measures and scores on standardized tests of intelligence among adults (Jensen, 1982; Vernon, 1983); these relationships are weaker among young children (Miller & Vernon, 1996).

It is important to keep in mind that individuals may differ in their processing speed because of variations in motivation and attention to the task rather than differences in intellectual ability. Some participants in the choice reaction-time task may be distracted by the equipment in the experimental room or may become anxious, and hence slower, in their attempts to do their best. Because reaction times are measured in fractions of a second, they are particularly vulnerable to these types of disruptions. In addition, different cultures and ethnic groups place varying emphases on the value of speed in mental processes. In our own Western culture, we place high priority on getting things done quickly, but the same may not be true for cultures in which time is not a major factor in daily routines. A person who does not have a heightened consciousness of time and speed may not choose to perform mental tasks rapidly, even

fluid intelligence Biologically based mental abilities that are relatively uninfluenced by cultural experiences.

crystallized intelligence Mental skills derived from cultural experience.

when he or she has the capability to do so (Marr & Sternberg, 1987). Finally, not all intelligent problem solving is done in a speedy way. Consider the problem of deciding on a career or whom to marry. Rushing to a solution can hardly be considered "smart" in these situations (Sternberg, 1982). Thus we must be cautious about interpreting the results of tasks that assess speed of processing as an element of intelligence.

Intelligence and Working Memory A promising new approach to understanding intelligence involves examining individual differences in working memory. Recall that working memory involves a short-term psychological "work space" in which complex (and sometimes multiple) tasks are performed on incoming information. Individuals might be asked to read and confirm the truth value of a sentence and also to remember the last word in the sentence, for example. Researchers have reported that successful performance on working memory tasks is related to intelligence test scores and is also linked to specific patterns of brain activity in the parietal and occipital lobes (Van Rooy et al., 2001). Other research suggests that the capacity of working memory is an even better predictor of intelligence test scores than processing speed (Conway et al., 2002). Working memory probably involves some form attentional control, the ability to regulate the amount of cognitive resources necessary to perform the components of a complex task (Engle, 2002; Miyake et al., 2001). Some researchers postulate that individual differences in this ability represent an element of g, the concept of general intelligence identified by Spearman (Engle, Kane, & Tuholski, 1999).

Sternberg's Triarchic Theory of Intelligence Robert Sternberg (1985) has proposed a broad contemporary theory of intelligence based on the principles of information processing. The **triarchic theory** of intelligence (see Figure 14.5) consists of three major subtheories that describe mental functioning in terms of what cognitive psychologists have learned in the past three decades about how people think.

The first of these subtheories, called the *contextual subtheory*, asserts that intelligence must be considered as an adaptation to the unique environment in which the individual lives. This means, for example, that we would not administer an intelligence test designed for children in the United States to children from a completely different culture, such as that of the Australian aborigines. In Sternberg's words, intelligence consists of "purposive adaptation to, and selection and shaping of, real-world environments relevant to one's life" (1985, p. 45). Intelligent people are thus able to meet the specific demands that their environment places on them—by learning to hunt if their culture requires that skill or by perfecting reading or mathematical skills in societies that stress formal education. By the same token, intelligent people will change their

FIGURE 14.5
The Triarchic Theory of Intelligence
According to Robert Sternberg, intelligence has three major facets, or "subtheories," all based on the individual's ability to process information.

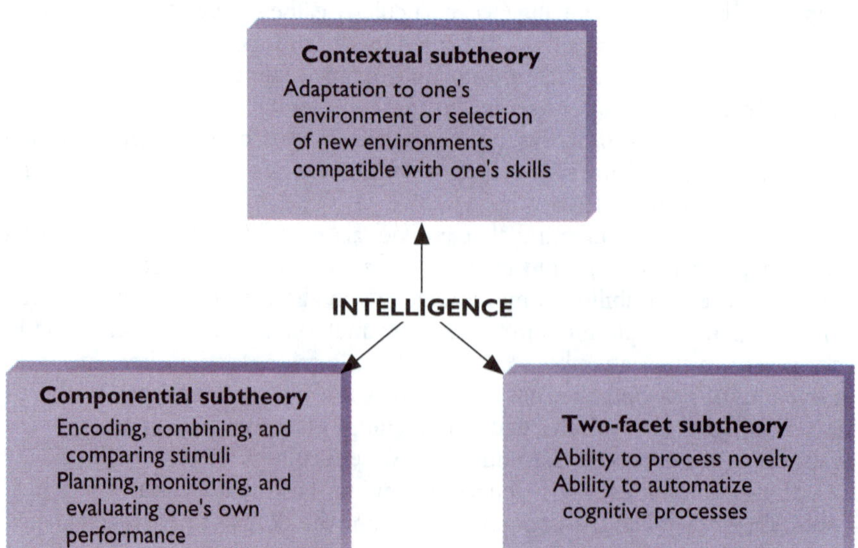

environment to utilize their unique skills and abilities most effectively. For instance, changing jobs or moving to a different locale may demonstrate what Sternberg calls "successful intelligence," which may be equally as important as or more important than "academic intelligence" (Sternberg, 2001).

The *componential subtheory* focuses on the internal mental processes involved in intelligent functioning, including the ability to encode, combine, and compare stimuli—the basic aspects of the information-processing system. Other components of intelligence are higher-order mental processes, such as relating new information to what one already knows. Finally, the ability to plan, monitor, and evaluate one's performance—the metacognitive activities we described earlier in this chapter—is also part of intelligent functioning. Thus Sternberg stresses how individuals acquire knowledge rather than what they know as indicators of intelligence.

The *two-facet subtheory* describes intelligent individuals in terms of (1) their ability to deal with novelty and (2) their tendency to automatize cognitive processes. Devising a creative solution to an unfamiliar problem or figuring out how to get around in a foreign country are examples of coping successfully with novelty. Automatization takes place when the individual has learned initially unfamiliar routines so well that executing them requires little conscious effort. Learning to read is a good example of this process. The beginning reader concentrates on the sounds symbolized by groups of letters and is very aware of the process of decoding a string of letters. The advanced reader scans groups of words effortlessly and may not even be aware of his mental activities while in the act of reading.

By including practical abilities, analytical abilities, and creative abilities, the triarchic theory captures the enormous breadth and complexity of what it means to be intelligent (Sternberg, 1998; Sternberg & Kaufman, 1998). Sternberg believes it is difficult to assess this human quality with one measure or test score, because such a number would mask the extremely different patterns of abilities that individuals show. One child may have exceptional componential skills but behave maladaptively in her environment. Another may be highly creative in tackling novel problems but show poor componential skills.

Gardner's Theory of Multiple Intelligences Howard Gardner defines intelligence as "an ability (or skill) to solve problems or to fashion products which are valued within one or more cultural settings" (1986, p. 74). Like Sternberg, Gardner believes that information-processing abilities are at the core of intelligence. Gardner's (1983, 1998) emphasis, though, is on the idea that people often show marked individual differences in their ability to process specific kinds of information. Accordingly, he identified the following eight distinct intelligences:

Linguistic. A sensitivity to the meanings and order of words, as well as the functions of language

Musical. A sensitivity to pitch, tone, and timbre, as well as musical patterns

Logico-mathematical. The ability to handle chains of reasoning, numerical relations, and hierarchical relations

Spatial. The capacity to perceive the world accurately and to transform and re-create perceptions

Bodily-kinesthetic. The ability to use one's body or to work with objects in highly differentiated and skillful ways

Intrapersonal. The capacity to understand one's own feelings and use them to guide behavior

Interpersonal. The ability to notice and make distinctions among the moods, temperaments, motivations, and intentions of others

Naturalistic. The ability to distinguish among, classify, and see patterns in aspects of the natural environment

triarchic theory Theory developed by Robert Sternberg that intelligence consists of three major components: (1) the ability to adapt to the environment, (2) the ability to employ fundamental information-processing skills, and (3) the ability to deal with novelty and automatize processing.

Gardner claims support for the existence of these discrete areas of intelligence on several fronts. For each skill, he says, it is possible to find people who excel or show genius, such as Mozart, T. S. Eliot, and Einstein. It is also possible, in many instances, to show a loss of or a deficit in a specific ability due to damage to particular areas of the brain. Lesions to the parts of the left cortex specifically dedicated to language function, for example, produce a loss of linguistic intelligence. Yet the other intelligences usually remain intact. Finally, it is possible to identify a core of information-processing operations uniquely relevant to each area. For musical intelligence, one core process is sensitivity to pitch. For bodily-kinesthetic intelligence, it is the ability to imitate the movement made by another person.

How does each of the intelligences develop? Gardner believes propensities or talents in certain areas may be inborn, but the child's experiences are also of paramount importance. Some children, for example, may show a unique ability to remember melodies, but all children would profit from exposure to musical sequences. Moreover, Gardner reminds us that it is important to remember the cultural values to which the child is exposed. In our culture, linguistic and logico-mathematical skills are highly valued and emphasized as measures of school success. Among the Puluwat Islanders of the South Pacific, the navigational skills required for successful sailing are critical, and hence spatial intelligence receives great recognition in that culture.

Gardner's theory has appealed to many educators and parents in its positive emphasis on each child's unique talents, but some researchers caution that more independent empirical evidence is necessary to fully evaluate it (Klein, 1997).

Measuring Intelligence

Over the years, we have come to use the term *IQ* as a synonym for intelligence. In fact, the abbreviation IQ stands for "intelligence quotient" and refers only to the score a person obtains on the standardized intelligence tests now widely used in Western societies. The results of these tests have become so closely associated with intelligence as an attribute of human functioning that we have virtually ceased to make a distinction between them. Yet the IQ score may or may not be a good indicator of intelligent functioning.

The Distribution of IQ Scores Standardized tests of intelligence are based on many shared assumptions about how this characteristic is distributed among individuals. As Figure 14.6 shows, IQ scores are assumed to be normally distributed in the population, with the majority falling in the middle of the distribution and

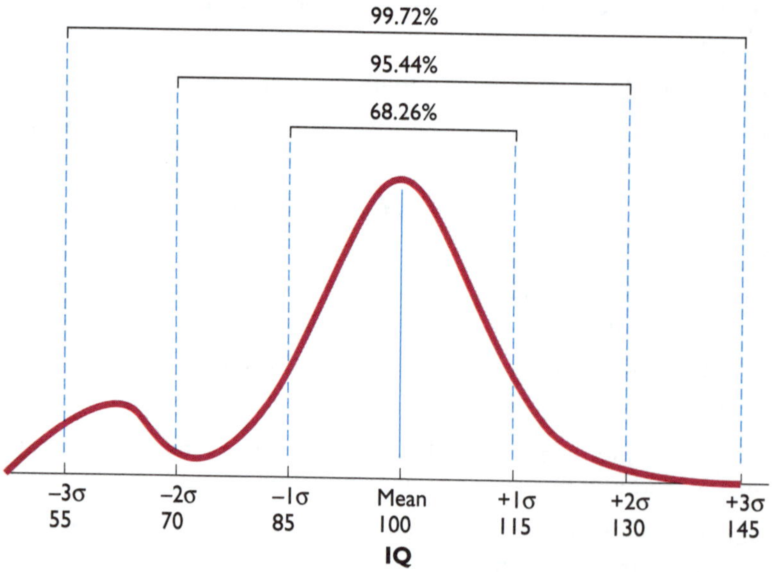

FIGURE 14.6
How Intelligence Is Distributed in the General Population of Intelligence

Intelligence scores are assumed to be normally distributed in the population, with a mean score of 100. Most people's scores fall within 15 points (or one standard deviation) above or below the mean, and almost the entire population falls within three standard deviation units of the mean. In reality, a slightly greater number of individuals than we would theoretically expect fall at the lower end of the distribution, probably due to genetic, prenatal, or early postnatal risks that can affect intelligence.

fewer at the upper and lower extremes. The average, or *mean*, IQ score on most tests is 100. Usually a statistical measure of the average variability of scores around the mean, or the *standard deviation*, is also calculated. The standard deviation gives a picture of how clustered or spread out the scores are around the mean. On many tests, the standard deviation has a value of 15.

The normal distribution of scores can also be partitioned into "standard deviation units." As Figure 14.6 shows, the majority of IQ scores (about 68 percent) fall within one standard deviation on either side of the mean, and almost all scores in the population (about 99 percent) fall within three standard deviations above or below the mean. In reality, the percentage of scores below the mean is slightly greater than the theoretical normal distribution would predict. This fact is probably the result of genetic, prenatal, or early postnatal factors that can put young infants at risk for lower intellectual development (Vandenberg & Vogler, 1985; Zigler, 1967).

KEY THEME
SOCIOCULTURAL INFLUENCE

There is one interesting point to mention about the distribution of IQ scores. Across twenty countries in North America, Europe, and Asia, as well as in rural Kenya, IQ scores have risen 15 points or more every thirty years on culture-fair tests, such as the Raven Progressive Matrices (Daley et al., 2003; Flynn, 1998, 1999). Perhaps better nutrition, increased access to schooling, or greater availability of technology (which may foster certain cognitive skills) are responsible (Neisser, 1998).

ATYPICAL DEVELOPMENT

Giftedness

Less than 3 percent of the population falls outside the typical range of intelligence; that is, beyond two standard deviation units of the mean for IQ scores. A child who obtains an IQ score greater than 130 is generally regarded as gifted. According to the U.S. Department of Education (1993), gifted children show "high performance capability in intellectual, creative, and/or artistic areas, possess an unusual leadership capacity, or excel in specific academic fields." Gifted children may already display remarkably high levels of performance compared with other children of similar age or background experiences, or they may show the potential to perform at those high levels. Although unusual talent has traditionally been measured by IQ scores, more contemporary views provide alternative ways of understanding giftedness.

For example, drawing on his triarchic theory of intelligence, Robert Sternberg (1981, 1986) has demonstrated that gifted children show several unique information-processing skills. First, when solving problems, they tend to spend much of their time in planning—selecting and organizing strategies and information, for example—and less time in encoding the details stated in the problem. In other words, their approach tends to be more "global" than "local," reflecting greater metacognitive skills, an idea that has received support in several studies of gifted children (Alexander, Carr, & Schwanenflugel, 1995). Second, Sternberg hypothesizes that gifted children are better able to deal with novelty and to automatize their information processing. Given novel, unusual insight problems, for example, gifted children are better able than children of average ability to recognize useful strategies for solutions (Sternberg, 1986).

Gifted children are also apparently more efficient and speedier in processing stimuli that match their particular talents. Veronica Dark and Camilla Benbow (1993) asked extremely gifted seventh- and eighth-graders to judge, as quickly as they could, whether two stimuli were the same or different. When the stimuli were digits, the response patterns of students most gifted in mathematics showed faster access to numerical representations than those of other children. The response patterns of students most gifted in verbal skills showed faster access to verbal representations when the stimuli were words. Based on their analyses of many studies of giftedness, Dark and Benbow concluded that the difference between gifted and other children is not qualitative; rather, it is simply a matter of degree—in this case, the degree to which basic cognitive skills are used quickly and efficiently.

What else do we know about the characteristics of gifted children? One of the most extensive studies was conducted by Lewis Terman beginning in 1921 (Terman, 1954; Terman & Oden, 1959). More than 1,000 children with IQ scores of 140 or greater were studied longitudinally from early adolescence into their adult years. Contrary to popular stereotypes, they were not frail, sickly, antisocial, "bookish" types. They tended to be taller than average, were physically healthy, and often assumed positions of leadership among their peers. By the time they were young adults, about 70 percent of those in the sample had completed college (a very high proportion for that generation), and many had obtained advanced degrees. The majority entered professional occupations in which they became very productive as adults—authoring books, plays, and scientific articles, for example. Unfortunately, however, because the children in Terman's sample were nominated by their teachers, gifted children who were quieter or did not fit a teacher's conception of a "good student" were probably overlooked. Thus Terman's results must be viewed with caution. Other, more recent research has found that gifted children take advantage of accelerated educational opportunities and are far more likely to pursue postgraduate degrees than is the norm (Lubinski et al., 2001). They generally show healthy peer relationships, good self-concepts, and are well adjusted. Those at the extreme end of the continuum, though, are more likely to be socially isolated and feel unhappy, probably because they are so different from their peers and have trouble "fitting in" (Robinson & Clinkenbeard, 1998; Winner, 1996, 1997).

Does giftedness simply reveal itself naturally during the childhood years? Not according to other researchers examining the underpinnings of exceptional talent. In one study, two children who were expert chess players and one who was an accomplished musician were found to spend many hours practicing their skills under the tutelage of special teachers (Feldman, 1979). In another study, world-class musicians, mathematicians, and athletes reported that their childhood years were marked by strong encouragement of their early natural abilities. Parents, coaches, and teachers were important sources of motivation, and typically these talented individuals spent years in intensive training of their skills (Bloom, 1982). Because of the exceptional drive and hard work involved in achieving high levels of success, most gifted children do not become unusually accomplished or eminent adults (Winner, 1997). A special concern for many researchers and educators is that the talents of gifted children be nurtured so that their potential can be realized (Winner, 2000).

IQ Tests Educators, clinicians, and others who must assess and diagnose children have a number of standardized tests to choose from. Usually intelligence tests are administered in special situations, such as when parents or teachers suspect that a child is unusually gifted. Alternatively, there may be a need to assess a child whose schoolwork falls below the level of other children in the class. Does the child have a learning disability (which is usually accompanied by normal intellectual functioning), or is the child's general ability to learn impaired? Are there other reasons (for example, emotional factors) the child is not performing well? A special educational plan designed to meet the needs of the student is then implemented. Intelligence tests may also be employed to assess the developmental progress of children who are at risk for any one of a number of reasons; perhaps they were premature at birth or suffered some trauma that could affect the ability to learn. Although many children will not have the experience of taking an IQ test, a variety of special circumstances may dictate administering such a test.

How are IQ tests designed? Psychometricians, psychologists who specialize in the construction and interpretation of tests, typically administer a new test to a large sample of individuals during the test construction phase, both to assess the test's reliability and validity (see the chapter titled "Studying Child Development") and to establish the norms of performance against which to compare other individuals. A central concern is to ensure that each item included in the test is related to the overall concept being measured—in this case, intelligence. Moreover, if the test is valid, the scores obtained should be related to scores on other, similar tests. Needless to say, the business of designing intelligence tests requires careful thought and skill. Some intelligence tests are designed to be administered to individual children; others can be given to large groups. Ethical standards dictate that psychologists be carefully trained in both the administration and the scoring of IQ tests before being permitted to administer them.

The two most widely used individually administered intelligence tests for school-age children are the Stanford-Binet Intelligence Scales and the Wechsler Intelligence Scales for Children–III (or WISC-III). Both are based on the psychometric model and measure similar mental skills.

The *Stanford-Binet Intelligence Scales*, adapted from the original Binet scales by Lewis Terman of Stanford University, were most recently revised in 2003 (Roid, 2003; Terman, 1916). When Binet originally designed the test, he chose mental tasks that the average child could perform at each age. He also assumed that children of a specific age—say, twelve years—who performed as their older counterparts—say, fourteen years—did had a higher mental age. By the same token, a twelve-year-old who passed only the items that the average ten-year-old could answer had a lower mental age. Thus intelligence was thought to be the extent to which children resemble their agemates in performance.

Terman translated, modified, and standardized the Binet scales for use in the United States. He also borrowed from William Stern, a German psychologist, an equation for expressing the results of the test. The child's **intelligence quotient**, or **IQ**, was computed as follows:

$$\text{IQ} \times \text{Mental age/Chronological age} = 100$$

Thus a twelve-year-old who obtained a mental age score of 14 would have an IQ of 117. The Stanford-Binet Intelligence Scales rapidly came into use among educators and clinicians eager to find a useful diagnostic tool for children.

The Stanford-Binet test assesses five broad areas of mental functioning: verbal reasoning, knowledge, visual reasoning, quantitative reasoning, and working memory. The test is scaled for use with individuals from two years of age through adulthood. In the Stanford-Binet, the concept of mental age has been replaced by a **deviation IQ**. The child's score in each of the test areas is compared with those of similar-age children in the standardization sample, and verbal and nonverbal IQ scores are obtained. An overall IQ score can also be computed. Thus this test permits psychologists not only to assess the child's overall abilities but also to isolate specific areas of strength and weakness.

The *Wechsler Intelligence Scale for Children*, the major alternative to the Stanford-Binet, is scaled for use with children ages six through sixteen years. The original version was constructed in 1949 by David Wechsler and most recently revised in 1991 (Wechsler, 1991). The revised version, called the WISC-III, contains three scales: (1) the Verbal Scale, which includes items assessing vocabulary, arithmetic skills, digit span performance, and knowledge of general information; (2) the Performance Scale, which includes tests of visual-spatial skill, puzzle assembly, and arranging pictures to form a story; and (3) a Full Scale IQ, which represents a composite of the two scales. Thus, like the Stanford-Binet, this test allows the examiner to assess patterns of strength and weakness in the child's mental abilities. In addition, like the Stanford-Binet, the child's score on the WISC-III is computed on the basis of the deviation IQ. Figure 14.7 shows some items resembling those from the verbal and performance scales of the WISC-III.

intelligence quotient (IQ) Numerical score received on an intelligence test.

deviation IQ IQ score computed by comparing the child's performance with that of a standardization sample.

FIGURE 14.7

Sample Items from the Wechsler Intelligence Scale for Children–III

The WISC-III contains two scales, the Verbal Scale and the Performance Scale. Shown here are examples that resemble items from the several subsets that contribute to each scale.

Source: Simulated items similar to those in the Wechsler Intelligence Scale for Children: Third Edition. Copyright © 1991 by the Psychological Corporation, a Harcourt Assessment Company. Reproduced by permission. All rights reserved. "Wechsler Intelligence Scale for Children" and "WISC-III" are registered trademarks of The Psychological Corporation.

VERBAL SCALE

General Information

1. How many nickels make a dime?
2. Who wrote *Tom Sawyer?*

General Comprehension

1. What is the advantage of keeping money in a bank?
2. Why is copper often used in electrical wires?

Arithmetic

1. Sam had three pieces of candy and Joe gave him four more. How many pieces of candy did Sam have all together?
2. If two buttons cost fifteen cents, what will be the cost of a dozen buttons?

Similarities

1. In what way are a saw and a hammer alike?
2. In what way are an hour and a week alike?

Vocabulary

This test consists simply of asking, "What is a ________?" or "What does ________mean?" The words cover a wide range of difficulty.

PERFORMANCE SCALE

Picture Arrangement

I want you to arrange these pictures in the right order so they tell a story that makes sense. Work as quickly as you can. Tell me when you have finished.

Object Assembly

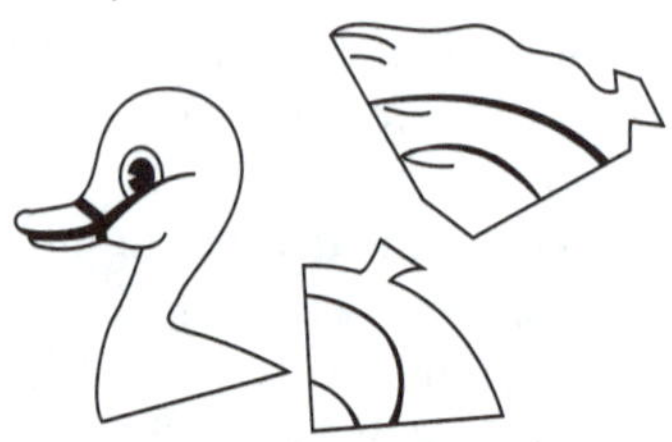

Put this one together as quickly as you can.

THE PREDICTIVE UTILITY OF IQ TESTS

What do IQ tests predict? IQ tests do a good job of telling us which children will be successful in school and which will have difficulties. Most studies have found that the correlations between intelligence tests and measures of educational achievement average about .50, with the correlations slightly higher for elementary school children than for high school or college students (Brody & Brody, 1976; Jensen, 1980). In addition, the correlations are strongest with academic subjects that emphasize verbal skills, such as reading (Horn & Packard, 1985). One reason IQ scores predict school achievement so successfully is that many of the skills assessed in intelligence tests overlap with the skills essential to educational success. Verbal fluency, the ability to solve arithmetic problems, and rote memory, some of the abilities IQ tests measure, are part of most children's school routines. Thus IQ tests predict best exactly what Binet originally designed them to foretell.

Do IQ tests predict any developmental outcomes other than school success? IQ scores are related to job status during adulthood, according to one research program.

In his longitudinal study of children with IQs of 140 or higher, Lewis Terman (Terman, 1925; Terman & Oden, 1959) found that many of these exceptionally bright individuals eventually became scientists, executives, and college faculty members. As usual, however, we must be cautious about how we interpret correlational data. As we saw earlier, IQ scores are strongly related to educational achievement. They are also related to how many years an individual will actually spend in school (Neisser et al., 1996). It may be that occupational success is the result of education and not a direct outcome of IQ (Ceci & Williams, 1997; Fulker & Eysenck, 1979; Jencks, 1972).

Aside from these relationships, do IQ scores predict other measures of success in life? Social scientists disagree. According to some, IQ scores predict economic status in adulthood (Herrnstein & Murray, 1994); others claim that IQ scores do not necessarily forecast the amount of money an individual earns, physical or mental health, job satisfaction, or general life satisfaction (Lewis, 1983; McClelland, 1973; Sternberg, 1995). The debate abounds with disagreements about the proper use of statistical techniques, as well as whether various measures of IQ are valid (Fraser, 1995). Suffice it to say that this topic has strong roots in the nature-nurture controversy; generally, advocates of a strong nature position believe that intelligence is a stable trait that affects later developmental outcomes, whereas those who favor a nurture position believe that intelligence is malleable depending on the quality of a child's experiences.

KEY THEME
NATURE & NURTURE

GROUP DIFFERENCES IN IQ SCORES

Children from different socioeconomic and ethnic backgrounds do not perform equally well on traditional IQ tests. One well-established finding is that African American children in the United States typically score 15 points lower than Caucasian children on tests such as the Stanford-Binet and the WISC (Jensen, 1980; Loehlin, Lindzey, & Spuhler, 1975). Another finding is that children from lower socioeconomic classes obtain lower IQ scores than those from middle and upper classes (Deutsch, Katz, & Jensen, 1968; Lesser, Fifer, & Clark, 1965). Of the many hypotheses put forward about the sources of these differences, some have rekindled the nature-nurture debate, and others focus on the validity of IQ tests for children who are members of minority and lower socioeconomic groups.

KEY THEME
NATURE & NURTURE

Race, IQ, and Nature Versus Nurture In 1969, Arthur Jensen published a paper suggesting that racial differences in IQ scores could, in large part, be accounted for by heredity. According to Jensen, there is a high degree of *heritability* in IQ; that is, about 80 percent of the variation in IQ scores in the population could be explained by genetic variation. He argued that, because racial and ethnic subgroups within the population tend not to marry outside their groups, African American–Caucasian differences in IQ scores have a strong genetic component.

Jensen's propositions created a storm of controversy, one that has reemerged as a result of similar claims made more recently by Richard Herrnstein and Charles Murray (1994). One of the most immediate criticisms of Jensen's argument (which has also been applied to its modern-day counterpart) was that within-group estimates of heritability cannot be used to explain between-group differences in performance. Even if the heritability of IQ were .80 for both Caucasian and African American populations (actually the heritability estimates for IQ were derived solely from samples of Caucasian children and their families), other factors, such as differences in the environmental experiences of each group, could not be ruled out in explaining racial differences in IQ scores (Loehlin et al., 1975). For example, a 15-point difference in IQ could still arise if most Caucasian children grew up in enriched environments and most African American children experienced environments that did not promote optimal intellectual development.

A *cross-fostering study* by Sandra Scarr and Richard Weinberg (1976, 1978, 1983), which examined children who were raised in environments markedly different from those of their biological families, demonstrated just how this effect might take place. In their transracial adoption study, Scarr and Weinberg selected 101 Caucasian middle-class families that had adopted African American children, most of whom were under one year of age at the time of adoption. Many of these families also had biological children of their own. The adoptive families were highly educated, were above average in occupational status and income, and had high IQ scores. The biological families of the adopted children had lower educational levels and lower-status occupations. Scarr and Weinberg found that the average IQ among the African American adopted children was 106, higher than the average score of both African American children and those in the general population. The researchers argued that, because the adopted children were raised in environments that exposed them to Caucasian culture and to the verbal and cognitive skills customarily assessed in IQ tests, they performed better than African American children with similar genetic backgrounds who did not have that experience. At the same time, however, the IQs of the adopted children were more strongly correlated with the educational levels of their biological parents ($r = 0.36$) than with the IQs of their adoptive parents ($r = 0.19$). Thus the role of heredity cannot be ruled out either.

Many researchers reject a genetic explanation of racial differences in IQ as too simplistic. We saw in the chapter titled "Genetics and Heredity" that heredity and environment interact in complex ways to produce varied developmental outcomes; neither by itself is sufficient to explain most human behaviors. In fact, because an individual's genotype influences the type of environment he or she will experience, heritability estimates may actually include environmental effects (Dickens & Flynn, 2001). Furthermore, in the United States race is a variable confounded by the other variables of social class, educational achievement, educational opportunities, and income. All of these factors can contribute to the types of learning experiences to which young children are exposed. Parents with greater financial resources can provide the books, toys, and other materials that stimulate intellectual growth. Moreover, families with economic stability are likely to experience less stress than economically unstable families, a factor that can be related to intellectual performance. Finally, research shows that heritability estimates can vary depending on family background variables. For families in which parents were well educated, heritability of verbal IQ for children was estimated to be .74, whereas the heritability estimate was .26 when parents were poorly educated (Rowe, Jacobson, & Van den Oord, 1999). Rather than settling the nature-nurture question, then, racial differences in IQ have served to highlight the complexity of interactions among variables associated with intelligence.

KEY THEME
SOCIOCULTURAL INFLUENCE

Test Bias A major hypothesis put forth to account for group differences in IQ scores is based on the notion of **test bias**. According to this view, the content of traditional tests is unfamiliar to children from some social or cultural backgrounds. In other words, traditional psychometric tests are not culturally fair. For example, suppose a question on an IQ test asks, "Who discovered America?" Individuals who have not encountered such specific information in their own cultural experiences will fail those items and score lower on many intelligence tests (Fagan & Holland, 2002).

What happens when tests that are more culturally fair are administered to children from varied sociocultural backgrounds? The research findings are mixed. Earlier in this textbook, you were introduced to the Raven Progressive Matrices, a nonverbal test of reasoning ability that is assumed to contain minimal cultural bias. Caucasian children still score significantly higher on this test than African American children do (Jensen, 1980). Yet when another culturally fair test, the Kaufman Assessment Battery, was administered to children of different cultural backgrounds, the difference in test scores between Caucasian and African American children was smaller than when more traditional IQ tests were given (Kaufman, Kamphaus, & Kaufman, 1985).

Finally, there are questions about whether minority children have the same experiences with and attitudes toward taking tests that majority children do. Some of the skills required to perform well on standardized tests include understanding directions, considering all response alternatives before selecting one, and attending

test bias Idea that the content of traditional standardized tests does not adequately measure the competencies of children from diverse cultural backgrounds.

stereotype threat The psychological impact of negative social stereotypes in an individual.

to one item at a time (Oakland, 1982). Minority children may lack this basic "savvy" regarding how to take tests. Because most tests do not permit examiners to be flexible in administering them, they may underestimate minority children's skills (Miller-Jones, 1989). Moreover, minority children may score lower simply because they do not see the point of performing well or have not acquired the same drive to achieve in academic settings that is part of the majority culture (Gruen, Ottinger, & Zigler, 1970; Zigler & Butterfield, 1968). For some, IQ tests may even represent a part of the majority culture that is to be rejected outright (Ogbu, 1994). Still another factor to consider is the extent to which children are accustomed to having questions asked of them by adults. Greenfield (1997) points out that, in Asian, African, and Hispanic cultures, children are expected not to speak to adults but to listen to them and respect their authority. By answering questions posed by an adult, the child may be violating cultural norms.

Not all researchers are convinced that test bias and motivational factors play a large part in explaining the lower IQ scores of certain groups of children (Jensen, 1980). Even for the skeptics, however, these ideas have highlighted the importance of structuring test situations so that all children are given the opportunity to display their best performance.

Stereotype Threat How an individual thinks about his or her abilities in relation to negative stereotypes about gender or race can affect performance on different tasks, a concept called **stereotype threat**. This phenomenon has been demonstrated among adults: African American individuals initially primed to think that an upcoming test would assess their abilities scored lower on a challenging verbal test than did Caucasian individuals. However, there was no difference in performance when the groups were given instructions that did not emphasize ability testing (Steele & Aronson, 1995). Similar findings have been reported with upper and lower elementary and middle school Asian American girls given a standardized math test. Right before taking the test, each girl colored a picture that activated stereotypes about either "girls" or "Asians." A third group colored a neutral landscape scene. Figure 14.8 shows the performance of each of the groups on the math component of the Iowa Test of Basic Skills. For the youngest and oldest age groups, activating stereotypes about girls resulted in lower math test scores, whereas activating stereotypes about ethnicity resulted in higher scores (Ambady et al., 2001). (It is unclear why upper elementary students did not fit this pattern of performance.) Results like these suggest that stereotype threat may be an important factor in interpreting racial and ethnic group differences in IQ scores.

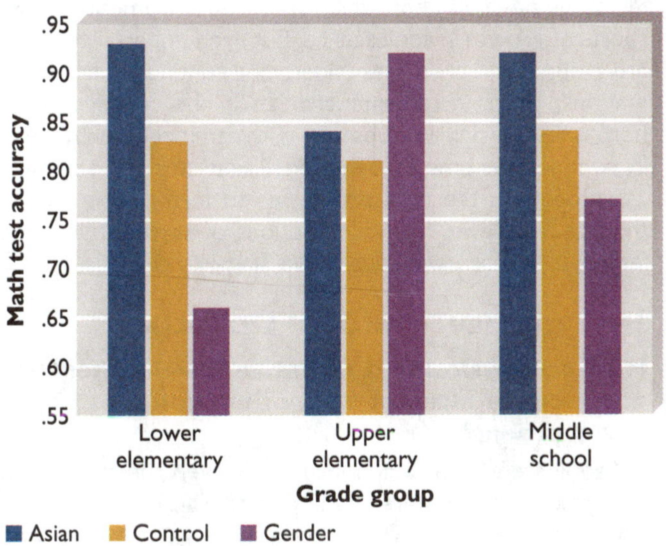

FIGURE 14.8

Stereotype Threat and Test Performance

In a study of lower and upper elementary and middle school Asian American girls, Nalini Ambady and her colleagues found that activation of gender stereotypes resulted in lower math test scores but that activation of ethnic stereotypes resulted in higher scores at least for the youngest and oldest groups. These findings suggest that it is important to consider the phenomenon of stereotype threat in evaluating ethnic differences in intelligence test scores.

Source: Ambady et al. (2001).

FOR • YOUR • REVIEW

- What are the main features of psychometric approaches to intelligence?
- What are the main features of information-processing approaches to intelligence?
- What are the principal ideas in Sternberg's and Gardner's theories of intelligence?
- What assumptions do psychologists make about the distribution of IQ scores in the population?
- How is giftedness defined? What are the unique ways in which gifted children process information? What are the behavioral characteristics of gifted children?
- What are the major features of the tests that have been used to assess intelligence in children?
- What kinds of developmental outcomes do IQ scores predict?
- What are the complexities in trying to assess the contributions of heredity to group differences in IQ?
- How might concepts like test bias and stereotype threat play a part in explaining group differences in IQ?

Chapter Recap

Summary of Developmental Themes

Nature & Nurture

How do nature and nurture interact in physical and cognitive development in adolescence?

The processes of physical growth and physical maturity are set in motion by biological forces, but social variables like body image can lead to behaviors such as dieting and eating disorders that influence health and physical well-being among adolescents. In Piaget's theory, maturation, in conjunction with experience, is responsible for the child's entry into the stage of formal operations. Some changes in cognition, such as executive control, are linked to development of the brain in adolescence, especially in the prefrontal region. However, the child's exposure to experiences that nurture the emergence of cognitive skills—for example, the elements of scientific reasoning—is also important.

Sociocultural Influence

How does the sociocultural context influence physical and cognitive development in adolescence?

Secular trends in the age of menarche are linked to sociohistorical shifts in economic conditions, especially access to good nutrition. The influence of culture is also seen in the fact that not all children in all cultures attain formal operational thought. Finally, culture broadly influences the kinds of skills that its members value and nurture, which are believed to constitute "intelligence."

Continuity/Discontinuity

Are physical and cognitive development during adolescence continuous or discontinuous?

Physical development and brain development show spurts of growth in adolescence. But even pubertal changes are grounded in processes undergoing continuous transformations. Small, incremental changes in the production of hormones may initiate substantive, dynamic reorganizations in complex systems of behavior. Piaget stressed stagelike attainments as the child progresses to formal operational thought. However, many descriptions of cognition in adolescence do not reveal qualitative stagelike changes.

Interaction Among Domains

How do physical and cognitive development in adolescence interact with other domains of development?

An adolescent's physical appearance, even the degree to which he or she matures early or late, can have dramatic influences on the responses of caregivers and peers, and can influence the child's evaluation of self. Brain development in adolescence is linked to cognitive attainments, such as speeded processing of information and greater ability to control behaviors and cognition.

Chapter Review

Physical Development in Adolescence

What patterns of physical growth are observed during adolescence?

Most adolescents show a final growth spurt before or during early adolescence. Unlike the pattern observed earlier in childhood, physical growth at this time does not conform to the principles of cephaolcaudal and proximodistal development.

Why are dieting and eating disorders of concern? What factors lead to efforts to control weight?

Of concern is the trend for an increasing number of individuals, especially girls, to engage in dieting and to display such eating disorders as anorexia and bulimia. Cultural pressures to be thin, as well as the influence of parents and peers, may contribute to these trends.

How is physical maturity defined?

Maturity is defined not by size but by ossification of bone material, or *skeletal maturity*. This process ends in late adolescence when bones in the wrists and ankles complete their formation.

What are the developmental changes that accompany puberty?

Puberty is defined as the period during which the individual gains the ability to reproduce. *Menarche*, or the first occurrence of menstruation, and *spermarche*, the initial occurrence of ejaculation of sperm, signal the ability to reproduce in females and males, respectively. The primary sexual organs enlarge, and secondary sexual characteristics, such as facial hair and breasts, emerge.

What are the social and behavioral consequences of early and late maturity for males and females?

Boys seem to benefit from early maturity. They have more positive feelings about themselves and have better relationships with their parent and peers. For girls, early maturity is associated with a decline in body satisfaction, depression, and association with norm-breaking peers.

What factors are related to sexual behavior in adolescents? What are the health implications of such behavior?

Among the factors that are related to whether youth engage in sexual behavior are the connectedness they feel with their families, the extent to which they are supervised, and the attitudes their parents hold with respect to sexual activity. Fewer resources in the family and the presence of a teenage sibling who is already a parent are also factors. Health concerns include increase in the incidence of sexually transmitted diseases and pregnancy.

What are the controversies associated with sex education programs in the public schools?

Some programs focus on encouraging abstinence; others acknowledge that teens are sexually active and seek to promote responsible and safe sexual practices. The effectiveness of various kinds of sex education programs to reduce sexual activity among young people remains uncertain.

What major changes occur in the brain during adolescence?

Most brain changes during adolescence occur in the frontal regions. Neurons continue to become myelinated, and after a period of overabundance of synapses, the number of synapses declines. The prefrontal cortex is more active in adolescents than in other age groups when certain kinds of cognitive tasks are performed, leading some to conclude that the brain areas that control inhibition and other regulatory behaviors are immature.

How do patterns of sleep change in adolescence?

Adolescents tend to need more sleep than younger children and show a shift toward a later sleep-wake cycle. Because these tendencies conflict with many of the daily demands placed on adolescents by school, work, and other forces, many adolescents are sleep-deprived.

Cognitive Development in Adolescence

According to Piaget, what are the major features of thinking in the formal operational stage?

By the time children reach the *formal operational stage*, they can think abstractly and *hypothetically*, generating multiple solutions to a problem. Thought is also systematic. Adolescents in this stage may display beliefs in the *imaginary audience* and the *personal fable*.

What changes are observed in children's scientific reasoning skills as they progress to adolescence?

Before adolescence, children display the ability to distinguish between theory and evidence and can identify which evidence supports a given hypothesis. Developmental changes are most apparent in the ability to design systematic experiments to test hypotheses. This ability can be enhanced with increased experiences in scientific problem solving, as well as with direct instruction on how to design an experiment without confounds.

What role does the executive function play in cognitive processing? In what ways does the executive function change with development?

An important element in cognitive development is the ability to control and coordinate one's own cognitive processes, a concept called *executive function*. One element of executive function is *metacognition*, the child's awareness and knowledge of cognitive processes. This awareness, as well as the ability to regulate and monitor one's thinking, grow throughout the adolescent years. Still, adolescents may opt for risky choices in the face of promising large rewards.

What are the main features of adolescents' decision-making behaviors?

Decisions may not always be made on the basis of rational, logical thinking but may be influenced by *judgment biases*, opinions based on vivid evidence or personal/social beliefs.

Intelligence

What are the main features of psychometric approaches to intelligence?

Psychometric approaches to intelligence emphasize individual differences in test scores. Several historically important ideas in this tradition include those of Spearman, who conceptualized a general intelligence factor called *g*, and Thurstone, who believed in seven primary mental abilities. In Cattell and Horn's view, intelligence could be seen as having two components: *fluid intelligence*, which was free of cultural influence, and *crystallized intelligence*, which referred to culturally derived skills. Fluid intelligence shows an earlier developmental decline than crystallized intelligence.

What are the main features of information-processing approaches to intelligence?

Information-processing models focus on the mental activities of individuals as they engage in problem solving. Speed of processing and working memory capacity are two information-processing activities thought to be involved in intelligence.

What are the principal ideas in Sternberg's and Gardner's theories of intelligence?

Sternberg's *triarchic theory* points to (1) the ability to adapt to the environment; (2) the ability to encode, combine, and compare stimuli; and (3) the ability to deal with novelty and to automatize as components of intelligence. Gardner's theory of multiple intelligences states that individuals can differ in discrete skill areas, such as language, music, mathematics, spatial perception, physical activities, personal awareness, social interaction, and nature.

What assumptions do psychologists make about the distribution of IQ scores in the population?

IQ scores are normally distributed in the population. The mean IQ is 100 and the standard deviation is 15. Individuals who fall beyond two standard deviations from the mean are considered to be exceptional.

How is giftedness defined? What are the unique ways in which gifted children process information? What are the behavioral characteristics of gifted children?

A child who obtains an IQ score greater than 130 is generally regarded as gifted. Gifted children are good planners and show skill in dealing with novelty. They are also efficient and fast in processing information. Gifted children tend to take advantage of educational opportunities, have good relationships with peers, and are generally well adjusted.

What are the major features of the tests that have been used to assess intelligence in children?

IQ tests are designed by being administered to large groups of individuals to assess norms of performance and to establish the validity and reliability of the test. School-age children are most frequently tested with the Stanford-Binet Intelligence Scales or the Wechsler Intelligence Scale for Children–III (WISC-III). These tests are based on the psychometric model and assess a range of verbal, visual-spatial, quantitative, and problem-solving skills.

What kinds of developmental outcomes do IQ scores predict?

IQ scores generally predict academic success but are not necessarily related to other measures of life satisfaction.

What are the complexities in trying to assess the contributions of heredity to group differences in IQ?

Social class and racial differences in IQ scores illustrate the difficulty of drawing simple conclusions about the sources of intelligence. One problem is that estimates of heritability do not necessarily explain between-group differences in scores. Cross-fostering studies of children who were raised in environments that differed from those of their biological parents indicate that IQ scores rise in enriched environments but that scores are still more strongly related to educational levels of biological parents than to IQ levels of adoptive parents.

How might concepts like test bias and stereotype threat play a part in explaining group differences in IQ?

Test bias, the idea that the content of IQ tests may not be fair to children from different cultural backgrounds, can help to explain group differences in IQ scores. Other factors in the testing situation may also interfere with children's optimal performance. *Stereotype threat*, the negative psychological impact of being sensitized to a stereotype about gender or ethnicity, has been linked to diminished performance on standardized tests.

KEY TERMS AND CONCEPTS

crystallized intelligence (p. 515)
deviation IQ (p. 521)
executive function (p. 511)
fluid intelligence (p. 515)
formal operational stage (p. 508)
hypothetical reasoning (p. 508)
imaginary audience (p. 508)
intelligence quotient (IQ) (p. 521)
judgment bias (p. 513)
menarche (p. 500)
metacognition (p. 511)
personal fable (p. 508)
psychometric model (p. 514)
puberty (p. 500)
skeletal maturity (p. 500)
spermarche (p. 500)
stereotype threat (p. 524)
test bias (p. 524)
triarchic theory (p. 517)

15 Social and Emotional Development

Kelsey burst in the door of her house, dropped her backpack on the floor, and shrieked, "Mom! You'll never guess what happened in school today. I got the lead in the school musical! I am soooo excited! Can you believe it? It's me! Star of the show! Tah dah!" Kelsey was literally skipping around the kitchen, singing a verse from one of the songs she had been so earnestly rehearsing for the past two weeks.

"Honey, that's wonderful," her mother responded, at the same time giving her fourteen-year-old daughter a big bear hug. "I know you worked so hard for this, especially with all of the practicing you've been doing. What great news!"

"Yeah, it is great." But almost in a flash, Kelsey's exuberance waned. Her mother had turned away to finish unpacking groceries, but she wondered about Kelsey's long, silent pause.

"Mom, I forgot to tell you. I actually need to get back to school in half an hour. First rehearsal for everyone who was picked for the cast is actually today. We have to hurry." Kelsey knew that her mother didn't like to have last-minute plans sprung upon her.

Key Themes in Social and Emotional Development

Nature & Nurture How do nature and nurture interact in social and emotional development in adolescence?

Sociocultural Influence How do sociocultural factors influence social and emotional development in adolescence?

Continuity/Discontinuity Are social and emotional development during adolescence continuous or discontinuous?

Interaction Among Domains How do social and emotional development in adolescence interact with other domains of development?

Risk/Resilience What factors promote risk or resilience during adolescence?

"Oh, sweetheart," Kelsey's mother replied, "We need to go pick up your brother at soccer practice in half an hour. It's completely on the other side of town. Let's see, can we call a friend to get you a ride?"

"Mom, you can't do this to me. I have to be at school, and I have to be there on time. I don't have time for phone calls. I have the lead—I can't just not show up! Charlie can wait. Or *he* can get a ride. Please, you have to get me there on time!"

Kelsey's sudden shift in tone caught her mother off guard. How could someone who was dancing and singing with such joy just a few moments ago become so angry and forceful in the blink of an eye? But this was not the first time Kelsey's mother had seen such a dramatic shift in her daughter's disposition; it seemed to have become a pattern lately. She knew she needed to draw on all of the patience she could muster right now. She was simply not in the mood to argue with her newly anointed star.

Adolescence is a time when most children begin to form a solid sense of identity, a fuller sense of self-awareness, and greater feelings of confidence. For many adolescents, this can mean that they feel freer to express themselves, giving voice to any of the range of emotions that they are feeling at a given time. Sometimes this comes as a surprise to parents, who may not be used to hearing such frank and sometimes intense reactions, or who are bewildered, as was Kelsey's mother, by just how quickly their child's emotional states can change. However, this newfound need to express one's self can be understood as part of a larger process of constructing a "true self," a sense of who one really is at the core, one of the dimensions of identity that seems to be forged at this time in development (Harter, 1999). We begin this chapter by documenting some of the major aspects of emotional functioning in adolescence. We also continue to examine the development of self, in particular the forming of an identity that is seen by many theorists as one of the central developmental tasks of adolescence. Intermingled with these advances are changes in moral reasoning and concepts of gender. The socioemotional development of adolescents is, in fact, not neatly and readily partitioned into separate topics. In this chapter, you should be able to detect how emotions, a moral sense, gender concepts, and notions of self and identity are very much related to one another, a fact that researchers are increasingly acknowledging.

Emotional Development in Adolescence

By adolescence, the brain and cognitive processes that are presumed to support the regulation of emotions are maturing (Spear, 2000). In addition, cognitive advances make it possible for adolescents to consider the complexities of many situations, including the possibility that events and experiences

Key Theme
Interaction Among Domains

can lead to feelings that are equally complex, even sometimes in opposition to one another. Children are now more likely to express conflicting emotions, making statements such as "I love my dad even though I am mad at him right now" or "Watching the end of that movie makes me feel both sad and happy at the same time" (Harter & Whitesell, 1989; Larsen, To, & Fireman, 2006). The abilities to consider multiple sides of a problem and to think abstractly no doubt play a part in the emergence of such many-sided feelings.

For many children, the various facets of emotional development that we have discussed throughout this text now culminate in a more mature state of *emotional self-efficacy*, the ability to accept and feel in control of one's emotions. By the time they pass through adolescence, well-adjusted individuals are able to handle challenging emotional encounters with an appropriate emotional tone. They accept their emotional experiences, both good and bad, and feel they are able to manage them. Emotional challenges are met with a sense of wanting to move forward in a positive way. All of these qualities are part and parcel of an evolving general sense of positive self-regard (Saarni et al., 2006). You can probably see, too, that developing emotional self-efficacy has enormous implications for the success of the adolescent's social interactions, not only with casual acquaintances, but also with those who form his or her network of close relationships.

EMOTIONAL STATES IN ADOLESCENCE

By many popular accounts, adolescence is a unique phase in emotional development. Many laypeople, as well as professionals, believe that adolescence is a time of "storm and stress," of emotional turmoil and extreme moodiness. Does research substantiate this belief? Although the evidence is somewhat mixed, several studies suggest that adolescents do experience more negative emotions than children of other ages and, in some cases, may be at risk for psychological problems, such as depression (Larson & Lampman-Petraitis, 1989; Petersen & Hamburg, 1986; Rutter, 1991).

In one study, for example, fifth- through ninth-graders wore electronic pagers for one week as they went through their normal daily routines. At random times over the week, the researchers "beeped" the participants to indicate that they should rate their mood just before the signal. In addition, the children and their parents filled out questionnaires assessing the number of positive and negative life events they experienced in the past six months. Figure 15.1 shows the results. Ninth-graders reported more negative affect than fifth-graders; moreover, for these young

FIGURE 15.1

Frequency of Negative Affect Among Adolescents

To assess the types of emotions experienced by older children and adolescents, researchers "beeped" participants during their daily routines and asked them to report how they felt. The mean percentage of negative affect is shown along the vertical axis. The percentages indicated within the graph show the proportion of students in each grade reporting low, medium, or high stress associated with negative life events. Ninth-graders reported more negative affect than did fifth-graders, and those who reported more stress in their life were especially likely to experience negative emotions.

Source: Larson & Ham (1993).

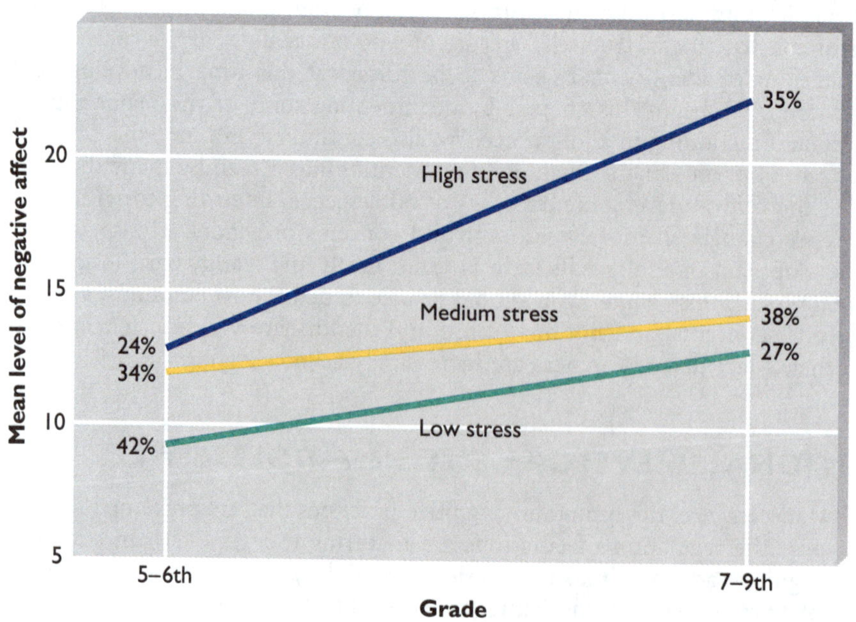

adolescents, negative emotions were associated with a greater number of negative life events, such as changing schools, breaking up with a boyfriend or girlfriend, or getting along poorly with parents (Larson & Ham, 1993). By grade ten, though, adolescents' emotional states become more stable and stop moving in a negative direction (Larson et al., 2002).

In addition, adolescents and their parents express increased negative emotions to each other from age twelve to about age fifteen, after which negativity declines. These parent-child interactions involve mutual reciprocal influences. Parents who receive a large amount of expressed negative affect from their adolescent children escalate in their own negative emotions over time; likewise, adolescents whose parents express negative emotions toward them increase in their negative affect (Kim et al., 2001). These results illustrate an important principle that we have stressed throughout this book: that parents and their children are often involved in a mutually influencing spiral of interactions, sometimes affecting each other in important and enduring ways.

Emotion Regulation in Adolescence

A new school, perhaps a new circle of friends, budding romantic relationships, greater challenges and pressures in academics, shifting relationships with parents—adolescents have reasons to experience more numerous and powerful bouts of emotion. Just how adolescents manage these emotions, as it turns out, can be a significant predictor of their mental health. Psychologists typically describe two broad categories of adjustment problems that sometimes face older children and adults. **Internalizing problems** refer to disturbances of mood, such as experiences of guilt and sadness, and, in more severe cases, anxiety and depression. As the name implies, this emotional style of the individual is inner-directed but exacts a psychological cost. **Externalizing problems** pertain to outward-directed behavioral manifestations, usually aggression or temper tantrums, which are typically driven by anger. Research is beginning to suggest that adolescents who develop and use ineffective emotion regulation strategies are more prone to both types of problematic styles.

Key Theme
Risk/Resilience

In one study, seventh- and tenth-graders were cued at various times of the day to report on their feelings over the past hour. Then, thinking about their most negative emotions, participants were asked to indicate which strategies they used in order to cope with their stress. Adolescents reported feeling a wide range of emotions, some connected to embarrassing situations, others to romantic relationships, sexual activity, or substance use. The most frequent ways adolescents dealt with their negative emotions included expressing their feelings, trying to solve the problem, acceptance of the problem, distraction, or thinking more positively. These strategies did not always work to make participants feel better, but they did signal active attempts to try to resolve their feelings. A smaller proportion of participants reported using less effective strategies, such as denial or rumination (persistent worrying). These adolescents were more likely to continue to feel anger or sadness. Most importantly, frequent use of strategies like denial or rumination was correlated with a greater incidence of internalizing and externalizing problems (Silk, Steinberg, & Morris, 2003).

In studying how adolescents cope with stress in their lives, Bruce Compas has proposed that it is first important to establish the context within which negative pressures are occurring. Is the factor causing stress perceived as controllable or not? For example, adolescents are less likely to perceive control when their distress is associated with parental divorce or economic strain within the family. Under such conditions, coping strategies like distraction seem to be most helpful. On the other hand, adolescents may perceive more control over other sources of stress, such as getting a poor grade on an exam or having an argument with a friend. In this latter case, the use of active problem-solving strategies is most beneficial. In most cases, though, denial and avoidance are ineffective coping strategies regardless of the degree of perceived control (Compas, 2004). The links between emotion regulation and

internalizing problem Disturbance of mood, such as guilt and sadness, and, in more severe cases, anxiety and depression.

externalizing problem Outward-directed behavioral manifestation, usually aggression or a temper tantrum, which is typically driven by anger.

psychopathology suggest that this is a very important area for future research and intervention. Promoting healthy coping skills may be one of the best ways to promote resilience among adolescents, not only those who experience normal developmental challenges, but also those who are exposed to aversive conditions, such as parental depression, poverty, abuse, and violence (Compas, 2004; Compas et al., 2002).

Atypical Development

Adolescent Depression and Suicide

For some adolescents, negative emotional states become more extreme and manifest themselves as depression, a psychological disorder characterized by dejected mood for lengthy periods of time, eating and sleeping problems, low self-esteem, loss of energy, and other symptoms. According to recent estimates, roughly 35 percent of adolescents experience depressed mood, and about 7 percent meet the criteria for clinical depression, with girls experiencing higher rates of depression than boys (Ge et al., 1994; Petersen et al., 1993; Wichstrøm, 1999).

Key Theme
Nature & Nurture
Risk/Resilience

The causes of depression in adolescents are complex and not completely understood by psychologists, but researchers have noticed that depressed children often have depressed parents. Studies of family relationships suggest that there is a genetic component to depression (Pike et al., 1996) but also that certain family climates are typical among children who are depressed. Parents who express less warmth and supportiveness and who participate in more conflicts with their children are more likely to have adolescents who are depressed (Ge, Best, et al., 1996; Greenberger & Chen, 1996; Messer & Gross, 1995). Children who witness or are victims of domestic violence are also at risk for depression (Downey et al., 1994; Sternberg et al., 1993). Perhaps these parents, whose poor parenting skills may be due to their own depression, weaken their children's ability to regulate their own emotions or influence their children to form negative ideas about social relationships (Cummings, 1995). The result is that the child, too, becomes depressed.

Key Theme
Interaction Among Domains

Why are adolescents especially vulnerable to depression? Several explanations are possible. Cognitive growth may mean that the adolescent thinks more about the self and the future, and perhaps the worries that are part of that reflection contribute. A switch from elementary to secondary school may mean adjustments in peer group relationships. Family relationships may be changing; parents may have reached a stage in their relationship at which they are considering divorce, for example (Petersen et al., 1993; Rutter, 1991). Changes in self-image may accompany the many biological changes in the body that are associated with puberty. For girls, depression is linked to issues of self-concept and interpersonal stress (Donnelly & Wilson, 1994; Rudolph & Hammen, 1999). In fact, girls show a sharp rise in the rates of depression they experience compared with boys; by late adolescence, they are twice as likely as boys to be depressed. According to Susan Nolen-Hoeksma (2001), these findings can be understood as the result of several factors that girls experience to a greater degree than boys: greater exposure to stressful life events (such as sexual abuse), greater biological responses to stress, and coping styles that involve focusing inward on feelings of distress (Nolen-Hoeksma, 2001). Finally, some researchers believe that changes in hormone levels that occur during puberty may activate genes that put individuals at risk for psychological problems (Walker, 2002). Clearly, understanding and preventing depression in adolescents requires a consideration of several domains of development.

The most serious concern about adolescents who are depressed is their risk for committing suicide. Surveys suggest that 6 to 13 percent of adolescents have attempted suicide (Garland & Zigler, 1993). Between 1960 and 1990, the rate of adolescent suicide tripled (Bennett, 1994). Suicide is now the third leading cause of death among fifteen- to twenty-four-year-olds and the fourth leading cause of death among children ages ten to fourteen (National Institute of Mental Health, 2002). Although the number of attempted suicides is greater in females than in males, completed suicides are more frequent among males than females. This difference is the consequence of the fact that males typically choose more lethal means of attempting suicide than females do. Homosexual male adolescents are at particular risk for suicide (Remafedi et al., 1998).

Some of the warning signs that a young person may be thinking about suicide include falling grades in school, drug or alcohol use, withdrawal from family or friends, or avoidance of social and sporting events. When these behaviors are combined with becoming especially quiet, changes in eating or sleeping patterns, giving away valued possessions, or talking or writing about suicide, the adolescent may be signaling a need for help. The Centers for Disease Control (1992) suggest that strategies to address the problem must include helping teachers and community leaders identify those most at risk; educating young people to become more knowledgeable about risk factors and intervention; developing screening, referral, and peer-support programs; supporting crisis centers and hotlines; and reducing access to lethal means of suicide.

ATTACHMENT AND ADOLESCENCE

Throughout this book, we have made reference to attachment theory and the role that early emotional relationships play in healthy development. The effects of early attachments seem to carry over well into adolescence and the adult years. Longitudinal data suggest that children who showed the ambivalent attachment pattern as infants are more prone than secure infants to develop anxiety disorders and have poorer social competence many years later during adolescence (Warren et al., 1997; Weinfield, Ogawa, & Sroufe, 1997). Adolescents who evidence secure attachments to their parents, in the sense of expressing affection for and trust in them, generally have high self esteem, a strong sense of personal identity, fewer depressive symptoms, and social competence (Cooper, Shaver, & Collins, 1998; Rice, 1990). They also engage in more constructive problem solving when discussing controversial topics, such as dating and household rules, with their parents (Kobak et al., 1993).

In a sense, parents of securely attached adolescents provide the same kind of "secure base" for exploration that they do for much younger children, only now the sphere of exploration reaches beyond the physical environment. As teens press to attain independence, develop a personal identity, and consider possible paths for their future, caregivers of those who are securely attached provide support and feedback that is nuanced to meet the child's emotional and social needs. Even when conflicts and disagreements between these parents and adolescents arise, they are resolved in an amicable manner within the safety net provided by warm, responsive parenting (Allen et al., 2003).

One of the most provocative and interesting findings emerging in attachment research is that the quality of an individual's attachment during childhood may influence his or her interpersonal relationships as an adolescent or adult. In Bowlby's (1973) theory, as children experience ongoing interactions with parents, they develop mental frameworks of those relationships called **internal working models of relationships**. These internal working models can, in turn, influence representations of other close relationships that emerge later in life, such as those with friends and romantic partners. Secure attachments, according to the theory, help foster healthy close relationships later in life; insecure attachments, however, can forecast problems in subsequent close relationships. Consistent with this theory are the results of a meta-analysis of sixty-three studies of attachment which found that secure attachment was more strongly associated with friendship quality than with peer relations in general (Schneider, Atkinson, & Tardif, 2001). In a more direct

internal working model of relationships Mental framework of the quality of relationships with others, developed as a result of early ongoing interactions with caregivers.

exploration of how early representations of relationships are related to later representations, Wyndol Furman and his colleagues (Furman et al., 2002) administered the Adult Attachment Interview to a group of high school seniors. This attachment measure requires participants to describe and evaluate their own childhood attachment relations; participants were then placed in the appropriate attachment category based on their responses. Working models of friendships and romantic partners were also assessed, using questions about support, caregiving, and cooperation in these relationships. The results showed a strong relationship between working models of relationships with parents and those with friends, but those with romantic relationships were less strong.

Internal working models of relationships may even extend to how a parent conceptualizes his or her relationship and interacts with the child (Bowlby, 1973; Main, Kaplan, & Cassidy, 1985). Researchers have noted significant relationships between the attachment classifications given to parents through the Adult Attachment Interview and the attachment styles of their infants (Benoit & Parker, 1994; Steele, Steele, & Fonagy, 1996; Van IJzendoorn, 1995). Mothers who have positive concepts of their own attachments express more joy and pleasure in the relationship with their own child; they also display more emotional availability and use more positive and sensitive parenting behaviors (Aviezer et al., 1999; Pederson et al., 1998; Slade et al., 1999). In contrast, as the results of one recent study showed, adolescent mothers who indicated disorganized concepts of attachment displayed disrupted styles of interaction with their infants, who in turn evidenced disorganized attachments themselves (Madigan, Moran, & Pederson, 2006).

FOR • YOUR • REVIEW

- What are the distinctive features of emotional development in adolescence?
- What is the relationship between emotion regulation and healthy adaptation in adolescence?
- What factors are related to depression in adolescence?
- How do secure attachments play a role in adolescent development?

THE DEVELOPMENT OF SELF IN ADOLESCENCE

Although the spotlight has traditionally been on identity formation in adolescence, there are several other dimensions to concepts of self that are at least as important to recognize. When you read the descriptions of changes in self that are discussed below, you should keep in mind the changes in cognitive skills that we have already mentioned. Multifaceted, abstract thinking is applied not only to academic situations, but also to the social world, especially to how one thinks about one's self.

THE CONCEPT OF SELF

As we have done in earlier chapters, we consider the concept of self from the historical perspective of "me" versus "I" formulated by William James (1892). With regard to the former, we focus here on changes in self-definition. With regard to the latter, we continue to examine concepts of agency, individuality, stability, and reflection.

Self-Definition During adolescence, "self" as a concept begins to be viewed from multiple or even opposing perspectives. Susan Harter (1986a) asked children whether someone can have both positive and negative qualities. Can a person be both "smart" and "dumb" or "nice" and "nasty"? She found a substantial increase in the belief in this possibility between the seventh and ninth grades. The number of opposite perspectives, as well as concerns about feeling confused or bothered by qualities of

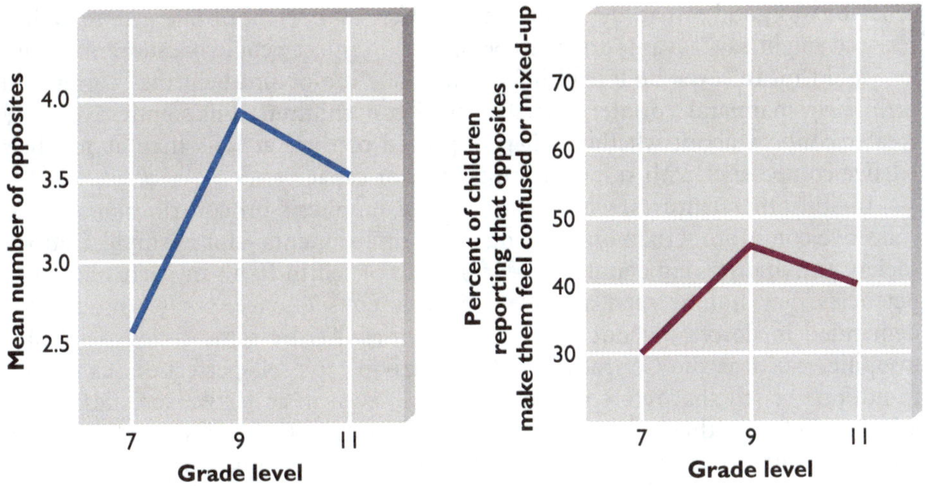

FIGURE 15.2

Concerns About Opposing Attributes

From early to middle adolescence, students increasingly report conflicting descriptions of self that depend on whether their evaluations are framed within the perspective of classroom, friends, close relationships, or parents. Concerns about these conflicting views increase at the same time. However, both the number of opposite attributes assigned to self and concerns about their effects on defining self begin to decline in later adolescence, as young people establish a more integrated identity and recognize that contradictions may be normal and even of some value.

Source: Harter & Monsour (1992).

self that conflict when, for example, interacting with parents, with friends, in a romantic relationship, or as a member of the classroom, become greatest during middle adolescence, as Figure 15.2 indicates (Harter & Monsour, 1992).

The impetus for conflicting selves may arise from a desire to impress or gain increased acceptance or simply as part of experimentation during the teenage years. Teens are certainly sensitive to the social implications of their self-portrayals. This awareness is evident in such responses from young adolescents as "I play sports … because all the kids like athletes" and "I'm an honest person … people trust me because of it" (Damon & Hart, 1988). Under these circumstances, "false" selves appear to be a normal and even healthy aspect of development. However, if inconsistencies arise from a belief that approval is contingent on "showing different faces" at the expense of one's "true self," these conflicts may lead to more serious consequences, such as feeling depressed and confused about self (Harter et al., 1996). Fortunately, concerns about conflicting selves typically lessen for most adolescents as they become older. With increasing maturity, they come to establish a higher-order, coherent picture of self based on principled ideas and comprehensive plans, which include a more extended future and greater understanding of their strengths and limitations (Harter, 2006).

Unlike younger children, as children approach the adolescent years and become more competent, they are less likely to look to others to evaluate themselves. In some domains, such as academic achievement, they use their own measures of performance on a task to judge success (Ruble & Flett, 1988). This indicates a shift from social comparison to a more self-reliant and principled standard for evaluating self. This basis for a self-concept, rooted in internalized values and norms of mastery and competence, fits the criteria that mature individuals use to evaluate their identity and that often is observed in later adolescence and early adulthood. But throughout the early and middle adolescent years, concern with the views and expectations of others, especially peers, and in many cases parents and teachers, is still far reaching (Harter, 1999).

KEY THEME
SOCIOCULTURAL INFLUENCE

Can cultural, religious, and social class differences, which are highly laden with values in their own right, influence the development of self-concepts? William Damon and Daniel Hart (1988) believe that such influence is likely. In some societies, for example, possessions or membership in the family or a social group may be far more important in determining perceptions of self than individual qualities, abilities, and achievements (LeVine & White, 1986). To illustrate their point, Damon and Hart (1988) studied children living in a fishing village in Puerto Rico. The residents were relatively poor and had few educational and social services available to them. Children typically attended school for no more than three or four years, and obtaining a job often depended on a network of family and social relationships. Compared with middle-income youngsters from mainland regions of the United States, Puerto Rican children voiced far more apprehension about whether their behavior was good or bad than whether they were competent or talented. A twelve-year-old might say it is important to be nice and respect people because misbehavior would mean "everybody will hit me and hate me or not help me." Compared with their mainland counterparts, Puerto Rican children consistently expressed greater concern about whether others approved of their actions than about their relative competence with respect to some skill or capacity.

In still other cultures, which place greater emphasis on contributions to the collective community than on individual accomplishments—for example, Samoan society and many Asian countries—evaluations of self in terms of particular competencies may not be seen as desirable. As a consequence, greater modesty is demanded in describing one's personal qualities. At the same time, social philosophies, such as the Confucian belief in striving for self-perfection, can result in notions of self that reference the individual, even in collective societies. When asked to describe themselves as learners, for example, Chinese adolescents often talk about enhancing their own skills, personal achievements, and self-fulfillment (Li, 2006). Because children's views of themselves are heavily influenced by social structure and the expectations of the community, as well as styles of parenting and formal education, the picture of an emerging self in many societies is remarkably complex and may differ substantially from that typically observed in many Western nations.

Self as Subject The subjective component of self—the "I"—undergoes changes in adolescence, too. For example, by age thirteen, children acknowledge the contributions of others to their sense of agency ("I learned from my parents, I even learned from friends, just listening to them and talking to them"). This point of view stands in contrast to younger children, who focus almost exclusively on their own efforts in their notions of agency. In addition, older adolescents incorporate into their reasoning principled personal and moral qualities ("Well, I decided to be kind to people because I've seen lots of kids hurt other kids' feelings for no reason, and it's not right or fair"; Damon & Hart, 1988). Perhaps this is a reflection of their growing sense of identity as well as the integration of different elements of their thinking about self; the moral is not distinct from the self after all.

Young adolescents typically have a strong sense of individuality. Asked to describe what makes them different from others, they are more likely than younger children to list unique psychological and other traits ("Yeah, I worry too much and about a lot of things that a lot of kids don't care about"). Older adolescents adopt even stronger views involving unique personal feelings and orientations ("Nobody else sees things or feels the same way about things as I do"; Damon & Hart, 1988).

The sense of the self as stable likewise draws on expanded ways of thinking. Asked how they know they are still the same person despite changes from year to year, young adolescents display a sense of continuity to others ("I'll still have my family. They always know I'm me and not someone else"). Older adolescents are likely to state their certainty more abstractly ("Well, nothing about me always stays the same, but I am always kind of like I was awhile ago"; Damon & Hart, 1988). As in the case of individuality, children's sense of a stable self gradually expands from physical, highly observable attributes to include both inner psychological and broader contextual elements. Moreover, as children mature, they judge inner psychological qualities as increasingly important in decisions about their stability of self (Aboud & Skerry, 1983). Children and adolescents are also more likely to anticipate greater similarity between their present and future selves than between past and present selves (Hart, Fegley, & Brengelman, 1993). Still, anticipated changes in future selves are positive ones; children and adolescents expect to lose their undesirable characteristics as they mature.

Finally, early adolescence is the time when the ability to reflect on or contemplate the self emerges. Its advent, along with new ways of thinking abstractly, helps to explain the preoccupations of young teenagers with appearance and worth; that is, a growing self-consciousness about who they are (Elkind, 1981; Selman, 1980).

Another consequence of the capacity to reflect on the self is a greater appreciation of how the mind contributes to experience. A fourteen-year-old may say, "I can fool myself into thinking I don't miss my lost puppy." Yet an older adolescent often realizes that completely controlling her feelings, even if she is unaware of them, may not be possible. Thus the sense of reflection forms the basis for eventually distinguishing between the influence of conscious and unconscious psychological processes on behavior (Damon & Hart, 1988).

SELF-ESTEEM

In general, the self-esteem of children in early elementary school is high. Yet, according to some research, as they approach adolescence, self-esteem for a substantial portion, especially girls, declines (Block & Robins, 1993; Simmons & Blyth, 1987; Wigfield & Eccles, 1994). Surveys of middle-class girls indicate that, when they reach adolescence, girls report a drop in their feelings about their self-worth (American Association of University Women, 1992). The change accompanies major transitions, such as the onset of puberty, entry into junior high school, and substantial realignments in friendship patterns. Often the decline accompanies a lowering of perceived competence in academic subjects, such as math. More recent research, however, indicates that the size of the difference in self-esteem between boys and girls is generally small (Kling et al., 1999) and that there is actually more variability in self-esteem within groups of boys and girls than there is between them (Eccles et al., 1999).

During the change to junior high, daily hassles tend to increase, whereas teacher support and extracurricular activities decline, all factors correlated with a decrease in self-esteem, especially among disadvantaged children regardless of ethnic or racial background (Seidman et al., 1994). However, when adolescents retain a warm, strong orientation toward others and perceive their parents as being attuned to and supportive of their efforts in decision making, they are more likely to maintain high self-esteem throughout these transitions (Lord et al., 1994). Coping strategies that lead young people to attribute success to their competence and mastery are another critical element in maintaining high self-esteem (Brooks, 1992).

High self-esteem continues to be associated with positive developmental outcomes for adolescents, just as it is for younger children. High self-esteem is a key factor in predicting low levels of emotional and behavioral problems in the teenage years; externalizing problems are especially less likely when parents (as opposed to peers) are the source of children's self-esteem (DuBois et al., 2002). A major longitudinal study conducted in New Zealand adds further weight to the importance of self-esteem. The data indicate that low self-esteem in adolescence is correlated with several negative outcomes in adulthood (age twenty-six years), among them poorer physical and mental health, money and work problems, and more criminal convictions (Trzesniewski et al., 2006).

KEY THEME
SOCIOCULTURAL INFLUENCE

Relatively little cross-cultural research on self-esteem has been reported, although several studies comparing children from the United States and Taiwan have revealed a consistent pattern: Taiwanese children report lower self-esteem than their counterparts in the United States (Chiu, 1992–1993; Stigler, Smith, & Mao, 1985; Turner & Mo, 1984). The reasons may stem from cultural practices in Taiwan that emphasize humility rather than pride in one's accomplishments or qualities and provide less opportunity to receive social or public displays of success in academic and other settings. Also, Taiwanese family-rearing patterns emphasize obedience rather than individual achievement, and although children in Taiwan often do excel academically, other ways of gaining high self-esteem may be less available to them.

IDENTITY

The burgeoning sense of self, along with the capacity to reflect on individual qualities, serves as the nucleus for the construction of an identity, a broad,

Parents are not always enthusiastic about some of the things their children do. During the adolescent years, decisions about dress and appearance are especially common sources of tension within families. However, efforts to distinguish themselves are typically part of an ordinary developmental process accompanying the transition to mature adulthood. They probably reflect the increasing independence that young people desire, and may need, in their efforts to construct their own identity.

coherent, internalized view of who a person is and what a person wants to be, believes, and values. A sense of identity solidifies and gives meaning to such fundamental questions about self as: Who am I? Why do I exist? What am I to become? The development of a healthy identity, as Erik Erikson pointed out (see the chapter titled "Themes and Theories"), is a lifelong process that builds on earlier gains in accepting and trusting others, in being encouraged to explore interests and desires, and in acquiring feelings of competence and skill. However, it undergoes further important changes during adolescence and early adulthood. By formulating a unified sense of self as an agent separate from others and as someone capable of reflecting on one's own agency, the adolescent creates a more fully integrated identity and sets the stage for developing a healthy personality to accompany the transition to mature adulthood (Blasi & Glodis, 1995). Nevertheless, the popular idea that the emergence of identity at this time follows a stagelike progression has been challenged (e.g., Bosma & Kunnen, 2001). For example, alternative conceptualizations place greater emphasis on the view that one's identity is constantly being modified and adjusted as part of an individual's efforts to make sense out of the story of his or her life (Dien, 2000). Despite these differing perspectives, the adolescent period in identity development typically has generated the most interest from researchers.

The Adolescent Identity Crisis The period of adolescence has sometimes been viewed as filled with stress and uncertainty about self, riddled with sudden and frequent mood shifts, a time dubbed the **identity crisis**. Increased conflict with parents and the initiation of more risky and socially disruptive behavior are said to be a part of this developmental period as well (Arnett, 1999).

As they approach the teen years, children frequently engage in new ways of behaving and thinking that involve greater autonomy, independence, and expressions of intimacy with others. For example, teenagers increasingly view their actions and conduct as personal—their own business, so to speak (Smetana, 1988)—and believe that such matters as family chores, eating habits, curfews, and personal appearance are up to them, not their parents. Needless to say, this view can introduce conflict within the family, especially for parents who wish to maintain control. Meta-analyses of the findings of numerous studies reveal that the frequency of conflict within the family is greatest early in adolescence and declines over the teenage years (Laursen, Coy, & Collins, 1998). For many adolescents, however, conflict is far less frequent than the idea of a crisis would suggest (Hill, 1987; Powers, Hauser, & Kilner, 1989).

Mood disruptions are greater during the adolescent years than during other major periods of development (Arnett, 1999). Still, substantial differences among individuals are found here as well. Youth who experience negative life events—that is, who are less popular, are not doing well in school, and are experiencing stress within the family—are especially susceptible to mood shifts (Brooks-Gunn & Warren, 1989; Petersen et al., 1993). In addition, risk-taking behaviors that involve the potential for harm to self and others peak during the late adolescent years, although again substantial individual differences exist in these activities (Arnett, 1999).

KEY THEME
RISK/RESILIENCE

One key to successfully negotiating this period appears to be a family, an educational environment, and a social milieu that support the needs and interests of adolescents (Eccles, Midgley, et al., 1993). For example, as children progress from elementary to junior high school, they find greater emphasis on control and discipline, less positive personal support from teachers, and more competitiveness and public evaluation of their work (Lord et al., 1994). Such changes may conflict with adolescents' need for fewer intellectual pressures and more opportunity to take charge in exploring and resolving uncertainties about their identity (Eccles, Midgley, et al., 1993). From bargaining over their choices of friends and activities to use of the telephone or the family car, adolescents also test new ways of communicating with and relating to parents and others in authority (Powers et al., 1989). Being able to establish a point of view seems to promote a strong sense of personal identity (Grotevant & Cooper, 1986; Hauser et al., 1987). Parents, teachers, and others play an important role in providing reassurance and support while permitting teenagers to weigh their ideas.

KEY THEME
SOCIOCULTURAL INFLUENCE

Cultural differences exist in the extent to which storm and stress during adolescence are reported as well (Arnett, 1999). Problems associated with the adolescent years seem to be most severe in Western and other cultures in which greater independence is encouraged and in which the transition from childhood to the adult world is relatively greater. Within the United States, less conflict is reported between adolescents and adults in Mexican American families than in Caucasian American middle-class families (Suarez-Orozco & Suarez-Orozco, 1996). Nevertheless, as families assimilate Western culture over generations, the conflict seems to increase. For example, adolescents in those generations of Asian American families that have been in the United States longer are more likely to display greater evidence of characteristics suggestive of an identity crisis (Steinberg, 1996).

KEY THEME
SOCIOCULTURAL INFLUENCE

Ethnic Identity Among the factors affecting a young person's identity is ethnic and racial background. **Ethnic identity** refers to the sense of belonging to a specific cultural group as opposed to simply adopting its social practices, known more generally as *acculturation* (Phinney, 1990). Thinking about one's ethnic roots is not particularly common among European American adolescents who generally describe themselves as "White" or "American," rather than referring to their ancestors' countries of origin. On the other hand, Mexican and Chinese youth in the United States, particularly those who are immigrants, frequently identify themselves solely in terms of their country of origin. Second- and third-generation youth add hyphenated terms, saying that they are "Mexican-American" or "Asian-American" (Fuligni, Witkow, & Garcia, 2005).

Because the majority culture often views minority groups in a stereotypical and negative light, identifying with a minority ethnic or racial group was once thought to set the stage for personal conflict and confusion. Early studies with preschool and younger children reported a bias for choosing dolls or pictures that depict the majority group—in this case, Caucasian children—even by members of a minority group. But this measure may be methodologically biased, or other factors may be influencing children's choices; the preference has been observed even in the West Indies, where Caucasians are the minority. Other measures used to assess the value given to one's own racial group have not shown any disadvantage to children with a strong ethnic identity (Gray-Little & Hafdahl, 2000). In fact, two large-scale meta-analyses of self-esteem in majority and minority groups in the United States have revealed that self-esteem among African American children and adolescents, especially for girls, is higher than among Caucasians. It does, however, tend to be lower for Hispanic, Asian, and Native Americans than for Caucasians among both boys and girls (Gray-Little & Hafdahl, 2000; Twenge & Crocker, 2002).

Ethnic identity formation is thought to involve at least two components: *group-esteem*, or feeling pride in belonging to an ethnic group, and *exploration*, attempting to learn more about the meaning of being part of an ethnic group. Longitudinal research including African American, Latino American, and European American youth shows that each component takes a slightly different developmental course. As Figure 15.3 shows, group-esteem rises in early and middle adolescence, and growth is especially pronounced for non-European children. Exploration of ethnic identity seems to be a later-occurring process and may be facilitated when adolescents find themselves in more diverse environments, such as racially mixed schools (French et al., 2000; 2006).

identity crisis Period, usually during adolescence, characterized by considerable uncertainty about the self and the role the individual is to fulfill in society.

ethnic identity The sense of belonging to a particular cultural group.

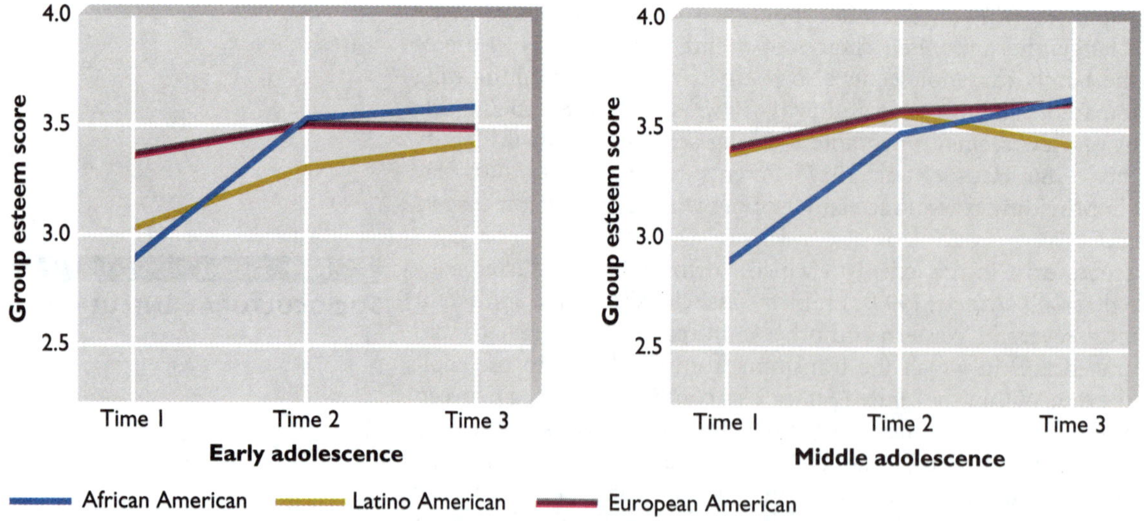

FIGURE 15.3
Ethnic Identity in Adolescence
Group-esteem, one component of ethnic identity, was assessed over a three-year period in two groups of adolescents, one whose average age was eleven years at the start of the study and another whose average age was fourteen years. Non-European children showed growth in group-esteem over this time period.

Source: Adapted from French et al. (2006).

KEY THEME
RISK/RESILIENCE

Becoming comfortable with one's own ethnic identity is associated with several positive outcomes. For one thing, it can lead to greater acceptance of and a more favorable attitude toward other ethnic groups (Phinney, Ferguson, & Tate, 1997; Valk, 2000). A strong ethnic identity, especially in the sense of feeling pride and emotional attachment to one's ethnic group, can also serve as a buffer against the negative consequences of perceived discrimination from peers (Greene, Way, & Pahl, 2006). Valuing one's ethnicity seems to be fostered by responsive parents who are sensitive to ethnic issues (Phinney & Rosenthal, 1992). However, ethnic socialization for minority parents is usually carried out within, not at the expense of, broader child-rearing goals emphasized in most families: getting a good education, being a good human being, feeling satisfied about oneself, and working hard (Marshall, 1995).

FOR • YOUR • REVIEW

- What are the main features of self-definitions in adolescence?
- In what ways does self as subject change during adolescence?
- What changes in self-esteem have been reported in adolescence?
- What is an identity crisis? Is there evidence that this is a significant part of adolescent development?
- How important is ethnic group identity for young people?

MORAL DEVELOPMENT IN ADOLESCENCE

Our discussions of moral development earlier in childhood focused primarily on moral reasoning, the kinds of judgments children make when they are faced with ethical dilemmas. As we have seen, most of these theories of moral development emphasize the relationship between growing cognitive skills and children's responses to the dilemmas. Here, in our chapter on adolescence, we highlight some of the key behavioral manifestations of moral development—the outcomes, in a sense, of years of moral socialization.

In the past, psychological research on moral behaviors in adolescence has centered predominantly on aggression, violence, and crime—the negative side of moral actions. Indeed, crime statistics show that, among all age groups, teenagers are overrepresented when it comes to violent crime. For example, youth from fifteen to seventeen years of age have the highest homicide rate in the United States (U.S. Department of Justice, 2005). Violent crimes among juveniles have declined substantially in the last twenty years. Nonetheless, if an individual is going to be involved in serious violence, adolescence is the time when it begins (Dodge, Coie, & Lynam, 2006). Clearly, the reason for this stark fact needs to be understood.

More recently, many members of the research community have called for a shift to what is called *positive youth development*. Rather than stressing the problems and deficits of adolescents, the emphasis is on promoting well-being and locating the *assets* that adolescents possess (Roth & Brooks-Gunn, 2000). Thus qualities like caring, honesty, responsibility, and integrity need to be nurtured by the larger community so that adolescents can make the most of their education and work lives, and offer contributions to their communities. Social policies, say the advocates of positive youth development, need to promote adolescent health and well-being (Benson et al., 2004). As just one example of the many ways in which youth contribute in prosocial ways to their family, school, and neighborhood, we discuss community service involvement among adolescents.

Antisocial Behavior

Conduct disorders range from highly aggressive and violent behaviors directed toward people or animals to the destruction of property, deceitfulness, theft, and truancy. These behaviors share the common denominator of violating or seriously disregarding the social norms and rules of the family, school, or society. The factors hypothesized to contribute to the development of conduct disorders in children and adolescents are as varied as the types of problem behaviors that are identified as antisocial. For example, genetic and temperamental predispositions, along with inconsistent and coercive parenting practices—especially when discipline is based on physical punishment or includes abuse and maltreatment, frequent parental discord and conflict, or limited cognitive skills associated with perspective taking—may play some part in contributing to conduct disorders (Gabel, 1997; Horne, Glaser, & Calhoun, 1999).

Key Theme
Nature & Nurture

Is it possible that a child or adolescent who is aggressive and actually injures another person, who displays cruelty to pets, who intentionally and maliciously destroys another's property, or who often lies or engages in other threatening and harmful activities that violate the basic rights of others might be deficient in empathy? In other words, are some children unable to emotionally share others' feelings and to understand the negative impact of their actions on others? To examine this question, Douglas Cohen and Janet Strayer (1996) asked young people (ages fourteen to seventeen) who had been diagnosed as conduct disordered and were residing in a residential treatment center, and a comparison group of normal young people from the same community, to observe and respond to a videotaped set of vignettes depicting individuals in emotionally laden situations. They also completed a set of questionnaires about how certain types of situations made them feel ("Seeing [a child] who is crying makes me feel like crying" or "I am often very touched by the things that I see happen"). These various measures revealed that young people who display conduct disorders exhibit substantially less empathy than a comparison group; they are less likely to identify the emotions of others and to show responses concordant with and responsive to the emotional states of others.

Cohen and Strayer's research did not reveal why the differences in empathy between conduct-disordered and normal adolescents might exist. Perhaps family socialization practices that differ in the extent to which the youths' emotional needs are met or experienced are part of the answer. For example, concern for others is found more frequently in families in which warmth is high, in which parents point out the consequences of harmful behavior, and in which altruistic activities are modeled (Robinson, Zahn-Waxler, & Emde, 1994). Perhaps, too, children who begin to engage in antisocial conduct become less sensitive to and less willing to interpret empathic cues in others, growing increasingly callous to such information. Children who, as preschoolers, show signs of behavioral problems display levels of concern for others that are similar to those of children who display normative behavior. But by six to seven years of age, they no longer exhibit as much concern for others (Hastings et al., 2000). These results raise the question of how important empathic training might be for effective treatment of children who display conduct disorders. Many therapeutic efforts, especially when begun later in development, have not always benefited children with conduct disorders (Gabel, 1997; Horne et al., 1999); perhaps increased efforts to foster empathy need further consideration.

KEY THEME
NATURE & NURTURE

KEY THEME
RISK/RESILIENCE

Rather than focusing on any one cause of antisocial behavior, some contemporary researchers have found it useful to understand aggression in terms of how multiple forces, some positive and some negative, interact with each other (Dodge & Pettit, 2003; Pettit, 2004; Rutter, 2003). Which factors put children at risk, which are protective, and how do they interrelate? One good example of this approach comes from research showing that, when males are victims of maltreatment, they tend to become aggressive, but only when they have a particular genotype, the one that depresses levels of MAO-A. MAO-A is an enzyme that metabolizes certain neurotransmitters and is found on the X chromosome (Caspi et al., 2002). Thus genetic risk alone is not sufficient to predict aggressive behavior, nor is maltreatment alone. Rather, it is the co-occurrence of the two circumstances that produces elevated aggression. Another example comes from a study of twelve- and thirteen-year-olds whose risk for aggressive behaviors was related to poverty within the family and neighborhood. The likelihood of aggression for this vulnerable group was reduced when parents monitored their child's location and peer contacts (Pettit et al., 1999). Studies like these underscore that understanding adolescent antisocial behavior requires casting a wide net—considering characteristics of the person, his

Many adolescents participate in some form of community service, an activity that is related to the growth of identity and civic awareness. Experts recognize such activities as a way of promoting positive youth development, focusing on the ways that youth contribute to society rather than on problem behaviors.

social environment, and the larger community—rather than targeting one or two causal variables.

VOLUNTEERING AND COMMUNITY SERVICE

A substantial number of high school students participate in community service of one form or another. National data show that 83 percent of public high schools organize or recognize student service activities and that almost 60 percent of students do some sort of volunteer work, either sponsored by their school or on their own (National Center for Education Statistics, 1999, 2001). Religious organizations also provide many opportunities for youth to do community service (Youniss, McLellan, & Yates, 1999). Students volunteer to clean up neighborhoods, help the elderly, raise money for educational projects, staff soup kitchens—all sorts of activities that suggest prosocial motives.

What are the characteristics of adolescents who volunteer? Usually, these individuals are extraverted in personality, idealistic, and high in self-understanding. They often express moral feelings in explaining why they volunteer (Yates & Youniss, 1996b). Frequently, their parents and peer group are also involved in community service, providing models and support for service activities. When teenagers are members of the "school crowd"—those students who tend to be oriented to achievement and participation in school activities—they are especially likely to be engaged in community service, express interest in being politically active, and say they will continue to be involved in service in the future (Youniss, McLellan, & Mazur, 2004).

Volunteer activities provide adolescents with a powerful context in which to grow in their identity, feelings of connectedness to society, and political awareness, (Yates & Youniss, 1996a, 1996b). Teenagers who participate in volunteer activities tend to show high educational achievement and low levels of risky behavior (Eccles & Barber, 1999). Youth who volunteer also show greater knowledge of civics and awareness of principles of government, the political system, and the nature of citizenship (National Center for Education Statistics, 2001). Consider the following passage, written by a high school student who volunteered in a soup kitchen for the homeless:

> As I left, I realize that this epidemic in America is not a black, white, Indian, Chinese, man, woman, or child problem; it's a human problem. It is our responsibility to see that every individual crippled by the lack of opportunities, and that one chance, is nourished, loved, and cared for. (Yates, & Youniss, 1996a, p. 283)

These words provide vivid testimony to a way of thinking that might be fostered by encouraging community service and enhancing the assets that youth bring to society.

FOR • YOUR • REVIEW

- What are the main contributors to antisocial behaviors in adolescence?
- How do volunteering and community service promote positive youth development?

GENDER ROLES IN ADOLESCENCE

The physical changes associated with puberty offer clear signals to adolescents (and their parents and teachers) that they are sexual beings, becoming ready to participate in adult roles as males and females. That fact suggests that perhaps gender stereotypes and the behaviors that accompany them become amplified in the lives of teens. At the same time, more sophisticated cognitive skills and a striving for individuality might position adolescents to challenge

According to the gender intensification hypothesis, adolescents may revert to more traditional beliefs about gender when they begin dating and feel they have to assume more stereotypical masculine or feminine roles. Research evidence regarding the gender intensification hypothesis is mixed, however.

societal gender norms. Compared to what we see for earlier periods in childhood, there is less research on gender roles in adolescence than you might expect. The evidence we do have offers a fairly complex, and sometimes conflicting, portrait of the role of gender in adolescents' lives.

GENDER CONCEPTS AND BEHAVIORS

How children *think* about gender apparently changes to some degree in adolescence. Some researchers have found that flexibility concerning gender stereotypes increases during adolescence. Many teens say that "independence" can be a male or a female trait, or that both boys and girls can be "gentle" (Liben & Bigler, 2002). Flexibility about gender roles is especially high right when young adolescents experience a life transition that may involve reevaluation of past beliefs: entering junior high school (Alfieri, Ruble, & Higgins, 1996).

How children *behave* changes in some ways, too. Sex segregation breaks down as children enter adolescence and begin to think about dating (Richards et al., 1998). In addition, the presence of cross-sex personality characteristics does not lead to isolation from peers in the same way that it does for younger children (Huston & Alvarez, 1990; Katz & Ksansnak, 1994). Adolescents' greater tolerance for sex-atypical personality characteristics in their peers probably reflects their increasing cognitive abilities, specifically their ability to consider multiple dimensions as they make judgments about individuals, including such abstract qualities as trustworthiness and loyalty. However, for some, the pressures of heterosexual interactions may enhance rather than diminish the push toward conformity with gender-role norms (Eccles, 1987; Petersen, 1980). This pattern is particularly obvious among teenage girls, many of whom abandon "tomboyish" behaviors that were acceptable earlier in development (Huston & Alvares, 1990).

THE GENDER INTENSIFICATION HYPOTHESIS

Some evidence suggests that, later in adolescence, when individuals are more likely to be thinking about their future roles and responsibilities, flexibility regarding gender stereotypes declines (Alfieri, Ruble, & Higgins, 1996). Researchers have described this return to traditional beliefs about gender during adolescence as **gender intensification** (Hill & Lynch, 1983). Societal expectations that teens will begin dating may create pressures to conform to more rigid masculine and feminine roles. Those who socialize them—their parents, teachers, and others—may feel they have to encourage that conformity as well. Do adolescent boys, then, become increasingly masculine and girls more feminine?

To some extent, yes, particularly in the context of conventional parental influences. When parents assume traditional roles in household tasks, or when they openly encourage stereotyped chores, girls and boys do indeed assume more gender-typed roles around the house over time. Teenage girls do more of the cleaning, food preparation, and laundry, whereas boys take out the garbage, do yard work, and repair household items (Antill et al., 1996; Crouter, Manke, & McHale, 1995). Furthermore, when high school students were asked in one study to consider their "possible selves"—that is, the future roles they envisioned for themselves—girls favored the arts and communication, whereas boys favored math and science (Lips, 2004). However, other longitudinal research indicates that gender differences in some areas might actually decrease over adolescence. For example, boys and girls express differences in their feelings of math competence in elementary school, but those differences practically vanish by the senior year of high school. Similarly, sex differences in ratings of language competence diminish over the middle and high school years (Jacobs et al., 2002). Given the ambiguities in the data, perhaps the safest conclusion is that gender intensification is not a robust phenomenon (Galambos, 2004; Ruble, Martin, & Berenbaum, 2006).

gender intensification Return to traditional beliefs about gender during adolescence.

SEXUAL HARASSMENT

A recent national survey of more than 2,000 middle and high school students reveals that a surprising number, 83 percent of girls and 79 percent of boys, report that they have experienced sexual harassment from either a peer or an adult (American Association of University Women Educational Foundation, 2001). Sexual harassment in one form or another is part of the routine, everyday experiences of many teens. Forms of harassment can vary from spreading rumors about sexual activity, to telling sexual jokes, to forcing participation in kissing or a sexual act. Of most concern, of course, is the impact on the victims; the consequences can range from feeling embarrassed to extreme upset. For girls, who are more likely than boys to experience physical forms of harassment, fear of the perpetrator is often the outcome (Hand & Sanchez, 2000).

Sexual harassment is in violation of Title IX, the federal law protecting the civil rights of students. Most schools have formal policies against sexual harassment, in part to protect against litigation. Then why is sexual harassment so common? First, even though schools may have policies, it is not always clear how students are made aware of them. Researcher Nan Stein (1995) also notes that there tends to be tacit approval by teachers and parents when they witness sexual harassment. Adults are not always prepared to challenge this behavior when they witness adolescents displaying it in school hallways, classrooms, and sports playing fields. Finally, students themselves may not be fully aware of the behaviors that fall within the scope of sexual harassment. High schoolers are usually able to identify physical acts as harassment but often do not label sexist jokes or sexual remarks in the same way. Perhaps these latter behaviors have simply become normative in the high school environment (Terrance, Logan, & Peters, 2004).

Adolescents are less likely to assume gender-typed roles when their parents are less traditional in how they assume household tasks and when they refrain from encouraging stereotyped chores in their children.

RESEARCH APPLIED TO EDUCATION

Educating Students About Sexual Harassment

As Kelsey sat at the edge of the stage and looked over her script, one of her friends came over to her and tapped her on the shoulder. "Kelsey," she said with a distinct look of concern on her face. "Did you see what happened to Alison at her locker today? Did you see how the pictures and names that were tacked up on the outside of it? It was awful!" Kelsey felt bad when she heard this. She knew Alison was trying to start a support group at school for gay and lesbian students, but she also knew that many of her peers were mocking Alison behind her back for these activities. Was there something she could do to support her longtime friend, Alison? Should she tell a teacher? Retaliate against the suspected perpetrators? Or should she just keep quiet? That was probably the easiest thing to do.

Despite the fact that most schools have formal sexual harassment policies, and may even have formal education programs about sexual harassment, students are often at a loss for what they should do if they confront an incident. They may want to take action, but may not know exactly what to do or who to tell about it. Research suggests that there are concrete steps that schools can take in order to tackle more effectively the problem of sexual harassment.

1. ***Use opportunities provided in the regular curriculum to discuss issues of harassment and relationship violence.*** Many sexual harassment programs are "stand alone" programs taught by individuals who are not the students' regular teachers. Program teachers may come into the classroom only one time in a school year or may talk to an auditorium full of students only once in a student's high school career. However, talking about violence or harm in relationships in any meaningful way takes more than a one-shot approach. Nan Stein (Stein & Cappello, 1999) suggests that there are many high school classes in literature, social studies, health, and other academic subjects in

which it is appropriate and natural to bring up issues of sexual harassment and relationship violence. One recommendation is that at least four or five class sessions be devoted to discussions such as these.

2. *Identify a staff member in the school to whom questions or complaints about harassment can be directed.* Students may know that sexual harassment is not permitted but may not know the individuals responsible for handling these issues in their school. Although all school staff should receive training in how to respond to episodes of harassment and should be encouraged to respond immediately when they see it, it is very helpful to designate one person in the school who is specially trained to deal with these reports (Smith, 2001).
3. *Start programs at least by ninth grade.* Many students report that they have been victims of gender violence by age 14 or 15. Thus, middle school is an appropriate time to educate children about this topic (Stein & Cappello, 1999).
4. *Involve parents and the community in prevention programs.* Invite parents to form discussion groups with their children so that information about how to deal with harassment and gender violence can be shared. Children often do not realize that their parents have likely been through similar experiences; parents are in a good position to model or suggest appropriate ways to respond (Smith, 2001).

FOR • YOUR • REVIEW

- What is the nature of gender concepts and behaviors during adolescence?
- What is the gender intensification hypothesis? Does research provide support for this hypothesis?
- What kinds of problems do adolescents experience with sexual harassment?

CHAPTER RECAP

Summary of Developmental Themes

NATURE & NURTURE

How do nature and nurture interact in social and emotional development in adolescence?

Many aspects of social and emotional development in adolescence highlight the interaction between heredity and environment. Depression and antisocial behavior, for example, can best be understood as emerging from biological risks that meet with socialization or contextual risks.

SOCIOCULTURAL INFLUENCE

How do sociocultural factors influence social and emotional development in adolescence?

Cultural, religious, and social class differences can influence identity formation. For example, cultures that encourage a group orientation may lead to heightened modesty in self-concepts.

CONTINUITY/DISCONTINUITY

Are social and emotional development during adolescence continuous or discontinuous?

Many have characterized the identity crisis, often considered a hallmark of adolescence, to be an example of a unique stage in development. However, alternate accounts see identity formation as the culmination of many earlier, gradual changes.

INTERACTION AMONG DOMAINS

How do social and emotional development in adolescence interact with other domains of development?

Emotional development is a key factor in the successful social development of adolescents. The ability to respond with appropriate emotional tone, for example, can facilitate social interactions. Emotional, moral, and gender-role development, as well as the development of self and identity, are linked to advances in cognition.

Risk/Resilience

What factors promote risk or resilience during adolescence?

Many factors can put adolescents at risk in their social and emotional development. For example, the failure to regulate emotions, genetic propensities for depression and antisocial behaviors, and environments that are unsupportive of positive development are among them. Research has also identified several factors that are protective. Ethnic identity and community service are two examples of positive forces in the lives of adolescents.

Chapter Review

Emotional Development in Adolescence

What are the distinctive features of emotional development in adolescence?

Adolescents experience more negative emotions and have more negative interactions with their parents than children of other ages.

What is the relationship between emotion regulation and healthy adaptation in adolescence?

Adolescents who use active emotion regulation strategies, such as problem solving rather than denial or rumination, are less likely to develop adjustment problems, such as *internalizing* or *externalizing*.

What factors are related to depression in adolescence?

Depression may have a genetic component but is also linked to family conflict, lack of parental warmth, and family violence. Adolescents may be especially prone to depression because of the large number of cognitive, physical, emotional, and social changes that take place at this time.

How do secure attachments play a role in adolescent development?

Adolescents who have secure attachments display many positive qualities, including high self-esteem, a strong sense of personal identity, fewer depressive symptoms, and social competence. Secure attachments also help adolescents to develop *internal working models of relationships,* which can serve as the basis for the quality of their own relationships with friends, romantic partners, and eventually their own children.

The Development of Self in Adolescence

What are the main features of self-definitions in adolescence?

Definitions of self may include conflicting dimensions, probably in response to demands from different social groups (for instance, friends versus parents). A reliance on social comparison diminishes in concepts of self as adolescents develop a firm sense of personal identity.

In what ways does self as subject change during adolescence?

Adolescents widen the scope of their concepts of agency, individuality, stability, and reflection. They are more likely than younger children to acknowledge the influence of others and to draw on psychological, internal qualities as opposed to physical traits.

What changes in self-esteem have been reported in adolescence?

Some researchers have reported a drop in self-esteem as children enter adolescence, especially for girls, but others claim that the changes are small and that within-group differences are larger than differences between boys and girls. The most important aspect of self-esteem is that it is associated with a number of positive developmental outcomes, including those that are long term.

What is an identity crisis? Is there evidence that this is a significant part of adolescent development?

The *identity crisis* refers to the idea that adolescents, in particular, experience a period of uncertainty about who they are and what roles they will fill in society. Although research indicates that this is a time of heightened conflicts with parents as they explore new ways of behaving, most teenagers negotiate this time without undergoing a "crisis."

How important is ethnic group identity for young people?

Ethnic identity, a sense of belonging to one's own cultural group, seems to benefit children and improve their understanding of others. It can also serve as a buffer against perceived discrimination.

Moral Development in Adolescence

What are the main contributors to antisocial behaviors in adolescence?

Researchers have identified genetic, socialization, and contextual factors that contribute to the emergence of antisocial behaviors in youth. A decline in feelings of empathy may play a special role in the development of highly aggressive youth. Contemporary viewpoints emphasize the convergence of multiple risk and protective factors that result in antisocial behaviors.

How do volunteering and community service promote positive youth development?

A substantial number of young people participate in some form of community service. Volunteering provides opportunities to develop identity, social connectedness, and civic knowledge.

Gender Roles in Adolescence

What is the nature of gender concepts and behaviors during adolescence?

Adolescents show greater flexibility in their gender-role concepts. They show less sex segregation in their interactions with peers and are more tolerant of cross-sex behavior.

What is the gender intensification hypothesis? Does research provide support for this hypothesis?

Gender intensification refers to a period of heightened adherence to traditional gender-role beliefs during the period of adolescence. Although some studies provide support for this concept, other research indicates that gender differences in beliefs diminish over adolescence.

What kinds of problems do adolescents experience with sexual harassment?

Sexual harassment is a common occurrence in the lives of adolescents. Victims of harassment evidence a variety of reactions to these episodes, ranging from embarrassment to fear.

Key Terms and Concepts

ethnic identity (p. 541)
externalizing problem (p. 533)
gender intensification (p. 546)
identity crisis (p. 541)
internalizing problem (p. 533)
internal working model of relationships (p. 535)

CONTEXTS OF DEVELOPMENT

16

Kevin's mother had come home from work early so that she could get ready for his soccer team's pasta party, scheduled at their house that night. As busy as she was with work, she wanted to participate in this tradition of having a pregame event to build team spirit. She knew that Kevin was incredibly busy, too, with homework, sports, band practice, and a peer tutoring project for which he had just volunteered. As she was thinking about the impossibly rapid pace of their lives, she heard Kevin's car pull into the driveway, and then his steps on the front porch.

"Hi, honey!" she sang out. "How was school today?"

"Fine," Kevin replied. And with that brief statement and a quick smile, he vanished into his room.

"Probably instant-messaging his friends," she thought. She recalled how the very same question about the school day would lead to a full-blown conversation only a few short years ago. She had learned from other parents that this was the way things went in many households with teenagers, both boys and

SOCIOCULTURAL INFLUENCE How do sociocultural factors influence the contexts of development in adolescence?

RISK/RESILIENCE What factors promote risk or resilience during adolescence?

girls. It was taking her some time to understand the world of adolescence—the need for privacy and independence, spending so much time with friends, and being on that computer! She knew, though, that she and her husband had to make some adjustments in their relationship with their son. He was, after all, about to enter the world as a full-fledged adult in only two years.

Throughout this text, as we have discussed the various contexts that impinge on child development, we have emphasized the primary role of the family in shaping cognitive, social, and emotional development. For adolescents, who are at the life stage at which forging autonomy and independence are pivotal developmental tasks, might it be that the family diminishes in importance as peers, media, and other outside influences assume a more prominent role? Kevin's behaviors, for example, suggest that friends and technology are certainly significant factors in his daily life. And even if the family does not assume a secondary role, how might roles in the family shift in response to adolescents' sometimes dramatic demands that they be treated as mature, responsible individuals, a lesson that Kevin's parents are in the process of learning?

As we discuss the different contexts in which adolescent development occurs, we need to emphasize an important point: the contexts for development are interrelated. This idea was highlighted in a major longitudinal study of the well-being of over 12,000 adolescents in the suburbs of Washington, DC. Children who had warm, supportive parents also tended to have stable friendships with peers who engaged in less deviant behavior. Children who grew up in "good neighborhoods" also had opportunities to attend high-quality schools. Most importantly, while there were statistical effects of families, peers, schools, and neighborhoods on successful academic performance, positive behaviors, and mental health among adolescents, the *combined* effect of these four contexts explained the most variation in positive development (Cook et al., 2002).

THE FAMILY IN ADOLESCENCE

Perhaps because of the popular idea that adolescence involves rebellion against the adults in their lives, most of the research on family processes during this developmental time has centered on parents, as opposed to siblings or other family members. Do parent-child interactions indeed change during the teen years and, if so, how? Furthermore, what are the most effective parenting strategies for caregivers to use in order to promote healthy social and emotional adjustment and reduce the risky behaviors that some youth begin to manifest?

RELATIONSHIPS WITH PARENTS

It is precisely adolescents' needs to express autonomy that typically precipitate a change in parent-child relations. As children press for independence, many parents find that they must adjust to form more egalitarian relationships with their children (Adams & Laursen, 2001; Collins, 1995). Perhaps contributing to the shifting nature of power relations within the family are changes in the way adolescents even think about their parents. Rather than seeing their parents as perfect and idealized individuals, they begin to consider them as people with both strengths and weaknesses

(Allen & Land, 1999). Gains in cognitive skills and, in particular, the ability to think in more complex and abstract ways likely contribute to these changing perceptions of parents.

Communication with parents changes, too. Adolescents admit that they keep secrets from their parents, and for some topics they feel that is perfectly appropriate. For example, adolescents feel it is proper to disclose information about their own health and safety, but they do not feel obligated to discuss personal issues, such as how they spend their money or who their latest "crush" is. In general, adolescents disclose more information to their mother than to their father (Smetana et al., 2006).

Beginning in early adolescence, conflicts with parents increase, especially for girls. Young teens generally perceive their relationship with parents to be less positive (McGue et al., 2005). However, clashes with parents are usually over day-to-day issues and do not threaten the basic strength of relationships with parents. In fact, parents seem to experience more emotional distress as a result of these conflicts than do their children (Steinberg, 2001). Although there are wide individual differences, for the most part conflicts with parents decline over the course of mid- to late adolescence (Collins & Laursen, 2004a).

Even though the nature of parent-child interactions changes, it is important to note that parents still remain a key source of social and emotional support for their adolescents and that they still have significant influence on the decisions their children make (Steinberg, 2001). The biggest factor in predicting the nature of parent-child relations in adolescence is the history of their interactions. If they had warm, close relationships with their parents in earlier years, children are more likely to remain close and connected in adolescence, too (Collins & Laursen, 2004b).

Effective parenting of adolescents is not much different than effective parenting with younger children—parental warmth and moderate behavioral control are still key dimensions. Especially important with adolescents is open parent-child communication.

EFFECTIVE PARENTING

Our discussions of effective parenting earlier in this text pointed to authoritative parenting as a generally constructive and desirable style. The benefits of authoritative parenting extend to adolescence as well. Adolescents who have authoritative parents demonstrate all sorts of positive developmental outcomes. They show higher school achievement, have higher self-esteem, display lower depression and anxiety, and perform fewer risky and antisocial behaviors (Collins & Steinberg, 2006; Steinberg, 2001).

Parents who express warmth and support, who are good communicators with their adolescents, and who continue to retain some control over them seem to buffer their children against risks such as the propensity to engage in violence and to use alcohol, tobacco, and marijuana (Brookmeyer, Henrich, & Schwab-Stone, 2005; Cleveland et al., 2005; Fletcher, Steinberg, & Williams-Wheeler, 2004). The two basic elements of authoritative parenting, as you probably recall, are warmth and moderate control. In general, research shows that the role of parental firmness is to protect against antisocial behavior, while parental warmth contributes in important ways to mental health (Gray & Steinberg, 1999).

Parental Warmth Several messages are communicated to adolescents when parents express warmth and affection: "You are secure, you are valued, and you are worthwhile." These messages may be especially critical for children to hear at a time when they are at risk for experiencing a drop in self-esteem or feelings of anxiety or depression. In contrast to parents who express hostility to their adolescent children, parents who are high on warmth tend to have children with fewer internalizing and externalizing problems overall. Furthermore, warm parenting seems to slow many teens' tendency to increase in acting-out behaviors, depression, and anxiety over time (Scaramella, Conger, & Simons, 1999).

Some researchers believe that the real underlying value of parental warmth is that it sets a positive emotional tone in parent-child interactions, one that fosters harmony and connection among family members (Collins & Steinberg, 2006). In addition, in keeping with the tenets of social learning theory, studies have shown that, when parents express a high level of negative affect, adolescents increase in their own expressions of negative emotions, and vice versa (Kim et al., 2001). Considering that negative emotions are generally associated with unsuccessful social interactions, not just with parents but also with peers and others, learning how to maintain a positive emotional tone may be an important social skill for children to learn.

Parental Control Effective parenting also includes parents' ability to control their children's behavior, setting limits when appropriate. However, researchers are finding that a distinction needs to be made between *behavioral control*, monitoring and regulating the child's actions, and *psychological control*, intrusive and domineering parenting that can interfere with the child's growing autonomy. Gregory Pettit and his colleagues found that adolescents whose parents were high on monitoring (that is, they were aware of their activities, friends, and how they spent their time) were less likely to become involved in delinquent behaviors. In contrast, parents who exerted a high degree of psychological control were more likely to have children who displayed delinquent behaviors and also expressed higher levels of anxiety and depression (Pettit et al., 2001).

Other studies support the importance of parental monitoring and supervision, at least in terms of knowing about what children are doing (Herman et al., 1997; Li, Stanton, & Feigelman, 2000). Effective parents do not engage in close surveillance or spying. Rather, they create an atmosphere in which adolescents feel comfortable talking with parents and disclosing information about how things are going in school or where they are spending their free time. According to some experts, it is parental knowledge, rather than monitoring per se, that predicts less risky and delinquent behavior in teens (Soenens et al., 2006; Stätten & Kerr, 2000). Moreover, fewer risky behaviors occur when parents have developed a close relationship with their children, which allows for disclosure, than when parents gain knowledge about their children from other sources, such as teachers, neighbors, and the child's friends (Crouter et al., 2005).

KEY THEME
RISK/RESILIENCE

As you can see, parenting of adolescents can require a delicate balancing act between controlling children's behavior and respecting children's need to develop a sense of identity and independent decision making. When parents allow autonomy in decisions about how to spend allowance or free time, self-esteem rises and depression declines (Hasebe, Nucci, & Nucci, 2004; Smetana, Campione-Barr, & Daddis, 2004). But when they are overbearing and controlling, parents are simply exerting their power in a style reminiscent of authoritarian parenting. It should not be surprising, then, that the consequences of this approach to parental control are often negative (Barber & Harmon, 2002). Research shows that, if teens experienced a high level of parental intrusiveness in seventh grade, they had more unsupervised peer contact in eighth grade and more problem behaviors in eleventh grade. By the same token, a similar pattern unfolded if seventh-graders had high levels of freedom in deciding how late to stay out or whether they could date (Goldstein, Davis-Kean, & Eccles, 2005). Balance is indeed the key, and as Kevin's mother in the opening vignette portrays, finding the right balancing point between control and autonomy promotion often offers a distinct challenge to parents.

KEY THEME
SOCIOCULTURAL INFLUENCE

Social Class and Ethnic Group Differences in Parenting Reliable social class differences exist in parenting practices. Middle-class mothers more frequently use induction, or reasoning, as they discipline their children than do lower-class mothers, who tend to use power-assertive techniques. Middle-class mothers also praise their children liberally and generally verbalize more than lower-class mothers, who in turn more frequently utter such commands as "Do it because I say so!" and dispense less positive reinforcement (Hoffman, 1984).

Social class (typically defined by the father's occupation) by itself, however, is not a variable that provides neat or meaningful explanations, because it is usually associated with other variables, such as access to health care, nutrition, physical environment, and educational experiences. Moreover, even within low-income families, significant variations in parenting styles can occur; a single characteristic style may not exist. For example, among low-income families, older mothers and mothers who are more religious tend to rely less on power-assertive parenting styles than younger mothers or those who are less religious (Kelley, Power, & Wimbush, 1992). Another factor to consider is how parenting practices might be related to the type of peer influence to which children are exposed. In one study, African American adolescents from lower- and working-class families were divided into two groups: those who were above and those who were below average in their exposure to peer problem behaviors. As Figure 16.1 shows, for adolescents exposed to negative peer influences, fewer behavior problems occurred when parents exerted more control over their children. When exposure to negative peer influences was lower, the type of parental control made less of a difference (Mason et al., 1996). Although we have seen in this chapter that high parental control is often associated with negative child outcomes, under some circumstances this type of parenting may actually be advantageous.

KEY THEME
RISK/RESILIENCE

Vonnie McLoyd (McLoyd, 1990; McLoyd et al., 1994) has provided an extended analysis of the growing literature on families under economic stress which illuminates the effects of social class. Because African American children experience a disproportionate share of the problems of poverty (a rate of 41 percent for African American children at the time of her analysis, compared with 13 percent for Caucasian children), McLoyd focused on the social and family dynamics that can affect this racial minority. In McLoyd's analysis, economic hardship has a serious negative impact on children's socioemotional development because of the psychological distress it causes parents. Parents under stress have a diminished ability to provide nurturant, consistent, involved care for their children. Children growing up with poverty are thus at risk for depression, poor peer relations, lower self-esteem, and conduct disorders. In one study of African American mothers, mothers' job loss was related to the tendency to report symptoms of depression. This fact was, in turn, related to their use of punishment and less parental nurturance (McLoyd et al., 1994). Similar findings have been reported for Caucasian

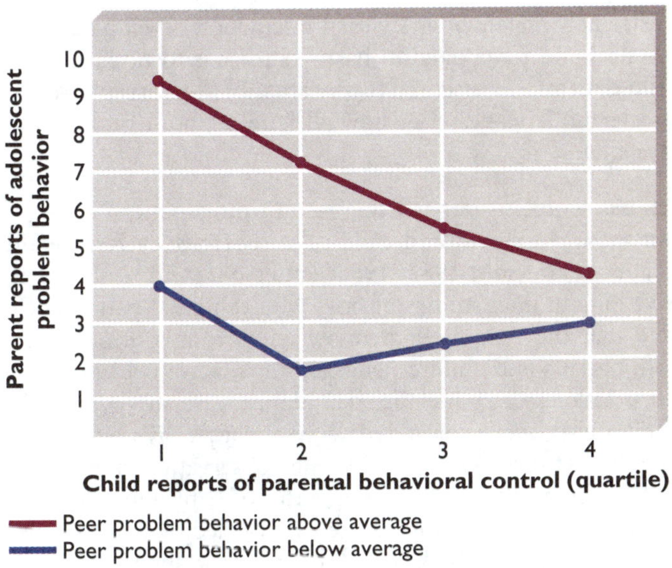

FIGURE 16.1

Effective Parenting and Peer Influences

The style of parenting that best predicts successful developmental outcomes may depend on other influences in the child's life. For example, researchers have found that, for lower- and working-class adolescents, a more controlling style of parenting may lead to fewer problem behaviors if peers exert a negative influence. In this study, adolescents were divided into two groups: those who were above and those who were below average in their exposure to negative peer influences. The amount of control that parents exhibited was divided into four categories, from least to most control (where 1 was equal to least control). As the graph shows, for adolescents exposed to higher-than-average negative peer influences, greater parental control was associated with fewer behavioral problems. Levels of parental control mattered less for adolescents exposed to lower-than-average negative peer influences.

Source: Adapted from Mason et al. (1996).

middle-class families from the midwestern United States during a time of economic downturn. Rand Conger and his colleagues (Conger et al., 1992) found that parents who experienced economic hardship reported greater emotional distress; this factor, in turn, was related to less skillful parenting. The disruptions in parenting were associated with adjustment problems among the adolescent boys in the sample. These seventh-graders reported more feelings of hostility and depression than those whose families were not experiencing economic hardship. The effects of financial stress have been observed in many types of families. Both one- and two-parent families of African American and European American backgrounds show more negative parent-child relationships in the context of financial strain (Conger et al., 2002; Gutman & Eccles, 1999; Jackson et al., 2000).

The demands that poverty makes on many African American families may be related to unique family structures that are adaptive for their situation and help them to cope. For example, a significant number of African American children grow up in an extended family. About 10 percent of African American children younger than eighteen years—three times as many as Caucasian children—grow up with a live-in grandparent (Beck & Beck, 1989). Extended family members often bring additional income, child care assistance, and emotional support and counseling to families under stress, especially when the parent is single (Wilson, 1986). Extensive networks of social support have, in turn, been associated with responsive and involved parenting styles among low-income African American mothers (Burchinal, Follmer, & Bryant, 1996). Among African American adolescents, those who perceived their family as having extensive social support from relatives also perceived their home as being organized and their parents as being involved in their schooling; these beliefs were linked to fewer problem behaviors, greater self-reliance, and higher grades in school than for adolescents whose perceptions differed (Taylor, 1996). The higher levels of involvement of African American families in religion also have a positive impact on children. Children of religious parents show less aggression and depression than those whose parents are less involved in religion (Brody, Stoneman, & Flor, 1996). Thus, although economic stress can have a negative effect on family dynamics, it can also foster alternative family structures and socialization goals that help to meet the needs of children.

Challenges in Parenting

In some instances, such extremely maladaptive styles of interaction develop between parent and child that physical and psychological harm can occur to both. Understanding these parent-child dynamics is essential to any attempt at intervention and also provides an even greater understanding of how all families, both healthy and dysfunctional, work as systems.

Coercive Cycles Sometimes problems in parenting result from a pattern of negative reciprocal interactions between parent and child called **coercive cycles**. Gerald Patterson and his colleagues (Patterson, 1982, 1986; Patterson, Reid, & Dishion, 1992) conducted extensive longitudinal studies of boys who exhibited pathological aggression and concluded that they acquired their behavior from routine family interactions in which both parents and children engaged in coercive behavior.

In Patterson's studies, preadolescent boys labeled as highly aggressive by schools, courts, or the families themselves were compared with nonaggressive boys from "normal" families over a period of several months. Detailed observations were made of family interactions in the home, including the sequences of behaviors displayed by parents, the target children, and their siblings. Patterson learned that the families of antisocial boys were characterized by high levels of aggressive interaction that rewarded coercive behaviors. When younger, the antisocial boys exhibited minor negative behaviors, such as whining, teasing, or yelling, in response to the aggression of another family member. About 70 percent of these behaviors were reinforced by the acquiescence of the child's interaction partner; in other words, the parent or

coercive cycle Pattern of escalating negative reciprocal interactions.

sibling backed down, and the submission negatively reinforced the child's aggression. In addition, although parents were observed to nag, scold, or threaten their children, they seldom followed through on their threats. Such sequences between the target child and other family members occurred as often as hundreds of times each day in the aggressive families. Over time, the target boys' aggression escalated in frequency and progressed to physical assaults.

KEY THEME
RISK/RESILIENCE

At this point, many parents attempted to control their sons' aggressive behaviors, but in doing so they, too, became highly aggressive. The chains of coercion increased in duration to form long bursts of negative interactions and often resulted in hitting between parent and child. After extended experience in these maladaptive familial exchanges, boys became out of control and acted violently in settings outside the home, such as the school. Aggression in school was related, in turn, to poor peer relations and academic failure, adding to the chain of negative events in the boys' lives.

Can such extreme patterns of aggression be controlled? Patterson and his colleagues have intervened in the maladaptive interactions of aggressive families by training parents in basic child management skills (Patterson et al., 1975; Snyder, Reid, & Patterson, 2003). They focused on teaching parents to use discipline more effectively by dispensing more positive reinforcements for prosocial behaviors, using reasoning, disciplining consistently, and setting clear limits on even minor acts of aggression. Children significantly decreased their rates of deviant behavior after only a few weeks, and the results were maintained for as long as twelve months after the initial training period (Patterson & Fleischman, 1979). As an added benefit, parents' perceptions of their children became more positive (Patterson & Reid, 1973).

Relationships with Stepparents Approximately 75 to 80 percent of divorced individuals remarry, the majority within five years after their divorce (Cherlin, 1992). As a consequence, a significant number of children, often teenagers by virtue of the timing of these events, live with a stepparent. For children who have experienced the separation of their own parents, the introduction of a new "parent" can represent yet another difficult transition, even though parental remarriage holds the promise of greater financial security and emotional support for both parents and children (Zill, Morrison, & Coiro, 1993).

KEY THEME
RISK/RESILIENCE

Like divorce, a parent's remarriage often leads to aggression, noncompliance, poor peer relations, and academic difficulties among children (Bray, 1988; Zill, 1988). In fact, children with stepparents often resemble children with single parents on measures of problem behavior, academic success, and psychological adjustment (Hetherington & Henderson, 1997). As Figure 16.2 shows, a survey of more than

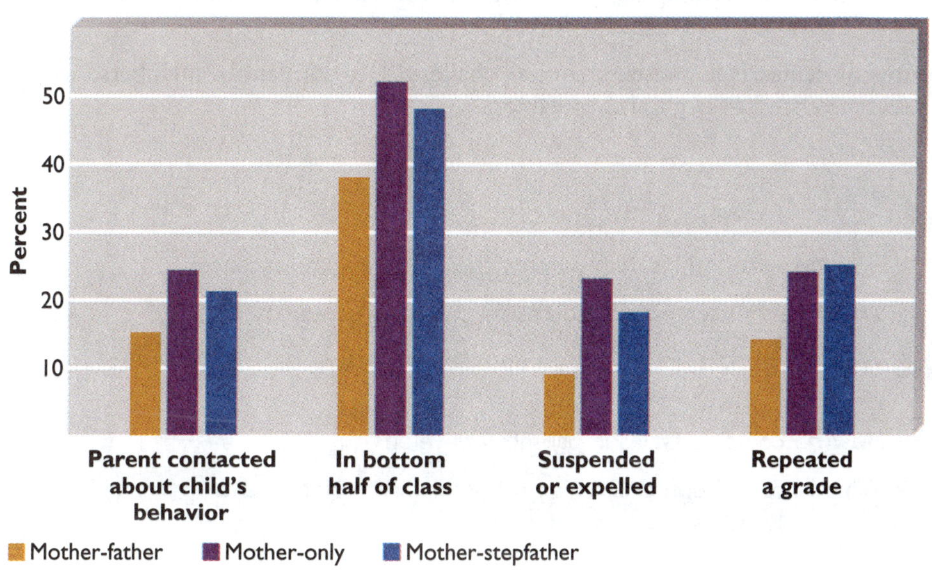

FIGURE 16.2

Family Type and Percentage of Children Experiencing Problems in School

According to a national study involving more than 10,000 children in grades six though twelve, children living in stepfamilies resemble those living in single-parent homes (with their mother) in the patterns of difficulties they show in school. Both groups have more problems than children living in two-parent families, probably due to differences in parenting style among the groups.

Source: Adapted from Zill (1994).

10,000 children in grades six through twelve showed that children in stepfamilies look similar to children from single-parent families in the number of school-related problems experienced; both groups have more problems than children from two-parent families (Zill, 1994). The child usually has more difficulty adjusting when stepparents have larger numbers of their own children, when children from two previous marriages are assimilated into one family, and when the custodial parent and stepparent have a new biological child of their own (Hetherington, 1999; Hetherington, Henderson, & Reiss, 1999; Santrock & Sitterle, 1987; Zill, 1988). Adolescents have more problems adjusting to their new family than younger children, perhaps because their growing autonomy leads them to be more confrontational with parents (Brand, Clingempeel, & Bowen-Woodward, 1988; Hetherington & Jodl, 1994). Even if children had shown previous adjustment to the remarriage of their parents, problems can resurface in adolescence (Bray, 1999). In addition, girls in the middle school and adolescent years do not adjust as well as boys to parental remarriage; girls especially withdraw from their stepfather (Brand et al., 1988; Vuchinich et al., 1991).

Drawing from data collected in a national survey of parent-adolescent relations, Frank Furstenberg (1987) found that stepparents had reservations about their ability to discipline and provide affection to stepchildren. At the same time, stepchildren corroborated that stepparents were less involved than their biological parents in care and supervision. Other researchers examining stepparent-stepchild relationships over time confirm that stepparents typically do not fit the profile of authoritative parenting described earlier in this chapter (Hetherington & Jodl, 1994), and thus the benefits of that parenting style for children are not realized. If anything, stepparents often look like the disengaged parents described earlier in this book; they provide less support for and control over the behavior of their stepchildren compared with their biological children (Mekos, Hetherington, & Reiss, 1996). Moreover, when stepparents do exert control, adolescents tend to show greater aggression, noncompliance, and other problem behaviors (Kim, Hetherington, & Reiss, 1999).

Some difficulties in stepfamilies may stem from the uncertain social roles of stepparents. Stepparents believe that they should play an active role in parenting but are also reluctant to become too involved with their stepchildren (Fine, Coleman, & Ganong, 1999). The advice given by one sixteen-year-old stepson reveals just how precise a balance stepparents must strike.

> The stepparent first would be to give room to the children, but still on the same spectrum, keep control basically, keep disciplining but I wouldn't say that you should make them, kinda let them ease into it. You shouldn't jump into something right away which is completely new. (Fine et al., 1999, p. 283)

Parental remarriage presents special challenges to all family members, which researchers are just beginning to explore.

FOR ◆ YOUR ◆ REVIEW

- How do relationships with parents change during adolescence?
- What are the elements of successful parenting of adolescents?
- What social class and ethnic group differences have been observed in parenting?
- How do coercive cycles in parenting develop?
- What issues arise in children's relationships with stepparents?

Table 16.1 How Do Adolescents Spend Their Free Time?

Reed Larson compiled the results of forty-five studies of how adolescents in various cultures spend their work and free-time hours per day. A portion of the results is shown here. You should note that several of the activities in the "free time" category include opportunities to interact with peers. What do the data suggest about cross-cultural differences in how adolescents spend their time?

Activity	United States	Europe	East Asia
Household labor	20–40 min	20–40 min	10–20 min
Paid labor	40–60 min	10–20 min	1–10 min
Schoolwork	3.0–4.5 hr	4.0–5.5 hr	5.5–7.5 hr
Total work time	**4–6 hr**	**4.5–6.5 hr**	**6–8 hr**
TV viewing	1.5–2.5 hr	1.5–2.5 hr	1.5–2.5 hr
Talking	2–3 hr	Insufficient data	45–60 min
Sports	30–60 min	20–80 min	1–20 min
Structured voluntary activities	10–20 min	1.0–20 min	0–10 min
Total free time	**6.5–8.0 hr**	**5.5–7.5 hr**	**4.0–5.5 hr**

Source: Larson (2001).

PEER RELATIONSHIPS IN ADOLESCENCE

By the time they reach adolescence, children spend considerable free time with their peers, at least in the United States. In a review of forty-five studies of how adolescents in different countries spend their daily time (see Table 16.1), Reed Larson found that American youth have more unrestricted time than children in Europe or Asia and that much of this time is spent with friends (Larson, 2001). Although time spent with peers might provide important opportunities to develop social skills and supportive relationships, some research is beginning to indicate that the amount of unstructured time spent with peers without adult supervision is related to depression, conduct problems, and lower grades in school. On the other hand, free time spent with parents and other adults or participating in such structured activities as hobbies, sports, and extracurricular activities at school predicts better school success and fewer conduct problems (Mahoney, 2000; McHale, Crouter, & Tucker, 2001).

Peer relations during adolescence become more intense on one level and involve larger networks on another level. Adolescents form close, intimate friendships with a subset of their peers, often those who resemble themselves in certain traits, such as an orientation to academics (Iervolino et al., 2002). Many children also form **cliques**, groups of five to ten children, usually in the same class at school, who frequently interact together (Brown, 1989). Clique membership is frequently supplemented by identification with a **crowd**, a larger group of peers with a specific reputation, such as "jocks" or "brains" Members of crowds do not necessarily spend time together but share a label based on a stereotype. Interestingly, even though youngsters may see themselves as members of particular cliques, their membership in crowds is often identified or labeled by others (Brown, 1989). In other words, a girl may not see herself as a "brain" but receive that label from peers who observe her academic achievements and studious behaviors. Membership in cliques and crowds in the middle and later school years reflects the child's growing need for group belonging at a time when he is orienting away from parents and other adults. At the same time, the values that parents encourage can influence the crowds with which their adolescent children affiliate themselves. If a parent encourages achievement, for example, the child's academic success may place her in the group of "brains" (Brown et al., 1993). The norms of cliques and crowds can be powerful shapers of behavior; they often provide the adolescent with prescriptions on how

clique Peer group of five to ten children who frequently interact together.

crowds Large group of peers characterized by specific traits or reputation.

Adolescents who spend time with their peers in structured activities such as extracurricular clubs at school (as opposed to unstructured time with peers) are at less risk for academic and behavioral problems.

to dress, act, and even what ambitions to have for the future. However, the degree to which the group has influence depends on how strongly the adolescent identifies with that group (Kiesner et al., 2002).

As adolescents approach young adulthood and feel more secure about their self-identity, they are less interested in cliques and crowds, and become oriented once again toward relationships with individuals. In one study, third- through twelfth-graders were asked to list their closest friends in the entire school, as well as the people they spent time with (Shrum & Cheek, 1987). Analysis of the patterns of relationships among children showed a sharp decline toward later adolescence in the percentage of students who were members of cliques.

One other significant change in adolescence is that some peer relations begin to reflect interest in the opposite sex. The time spent with same-sex peers does not decline in adolescence, but time spent with an opposite-sex peer increases substantially during high school (Richards et al., 1998). As they grow older, and as they begin to spend increasing time with their romantic partners, adolescents spend less time with family members. Nonetheless, they still maintain close emotional ties with the family, rating parents and romantic partners as their most influential relationships (Laursen & Williams, 1997).

Peer Pressure and Conformity

One of the most widely accepted beliefs about peer groups is that they control the behavior of children, sometimes more than parents and other adults would like. In fact, peer pressure *is* a very real phenomenon. When seventh- through twelfth-graders were asked to rate how much pressure they felt from agemates in several domains, they did report pressure, and the greatest pressure was simply to be involved with peers: spend time with them, go to parties, and otherwise associate with them (Brown, Clasen, & Eicher, 1986; Clasen & Brown, 1985). They also felt pressure to excel and to complete their education. Contrary to popular opinion, however, they reported the least peer pressure to engage in misconduct, such as smoking, drinking, or having sexual relations. Older adolescents, however, felt more pressure to engage in misconduct than younger adolescents did.

How willing are children to conform to these peer pressures? Again, when researchers ask them, children give different answers depending on their age (Berndt, 1979; Brown, Clasen, & Eicher, 1986; Gavin & Furman, 1989). Relative to

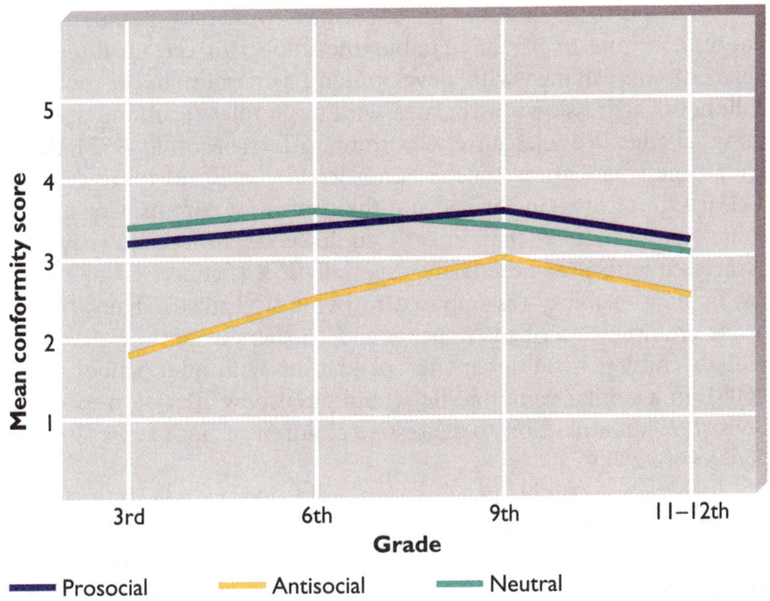

FIGURE 16.3

Developmental Changes in Conformity to Peer Pressure

Conformity to peer pressure, whether it involves prosocial, antisocial, or neutral behavior, peaks in early adolescence, then declines. The higher numbers in this graph represent greater willingness to conform.

Source: Adapted from Berndt (1979).

other ages, vulnerability to peer pressure peaks in early adolescence, usually between the sixth and ninth grades (see Figure 16.3). However, note in Figure 16.3 that, in terms of actual conformity scores, most children would not succumb to peer pressure; their average ratings are in the middle of the rating scale and correspond to a neutral response (Berndt, 1999). By late adolescence the influence of peers on conformity declines even further.

For some children, though, the peer group plays an important part in influencing behaviors and choices. By virtue of their style of parenting, parents may be responsible for adolescents' tendencies to seek out the peer group. When parents of adolescents are unresponsive to their children and maintain their power and restrictiveness, their children tend to be more noticeably oriented to their peer group (Bogenschneider et al., 1998; Fuligni & Eccles, 1993). Adolescents who develop an extreme orientation to their peer group, to the extent that they will ignore parents and schoolwork in order to remain popular, are more likely to become involved with alcohol and drug use, to skip classes, and to demonstrate other problem behaviors (Fuligni et al., 2001).

Researchers now believe that studying "peer pressure" as a general phenomenon is not as revealing as examining the roles that *specific* peers play in the child's development. For example, some friends may be more influential than others, and their influence may be greater in some domains than in others, such as aggression as opposed to school achievement. In addition, a child's vulnerability to peer influences probably depends to some degree on his level of emotional and cognitive development (Berndt, 1999; Hartup, 1999). Thus a full understanding of peer influences will have to take these complexities into account.

PEER POPULARITY

Peer popularity has both positive and negative consequences associated with it. In one study, popular teens tended to show good self-control, sensitivity to the views of others, and healthy emotional relationships with parents and friends. At the same time, those who were popular at age thirteen were more likely to show increases in alcohol and marijuana use and minor delinquent behavior a year later. According to the *popularity-socialization hypothesis*, popular teens experience more opportunities to be socialized by their agemates than those who are less popular, subjecting them to both the positive and the negative influences of peers (Allen et al., 2005).

What personal qualities are associated with peer popularity? Social skills, no doubt, continue to play a role, but the impact of certain dimensions of personal behavior may change with development. For example, we noted that, in middle childhood, aggression is associated with unpopularity among peers. To some degree, things change in adolescence. According to Terrie Moffit (1993), the adolescent years are a time when some teens see antisocial behavior as more desirable because it is a clear sign of breaking away from the control of parents. Consistent with this idea, some studies indicate that, in early adolescence, antisocial behavior may actually be associated with peer popularity, especially if it is conceived of as *perceived popularity*, or high visibility (as opposed to being well liked). Thus, for example, eighth-grade children described by peers and teachers as antisocial were named as individuals children would want to spend time with after school (Kiesner & Pastore, 2005). In a similar vein, middle school girls show attraction to aggressive boys, and boys show an attraction to aggressive children of both sexes (Bukowski, Sippola, & Newcomb, 2000).

Two recent studies provide some additional clues about the social dynamics of aggression and popularity. Thomas Farmer and his colleagues (Farmer et al., 2003) surveyed seventh- and eighth-graders, as well as their peers and teachers, and found two types of aggressive children: "tough" boys who were aggressive but also popular and socially skilled, and "troubled boys" who were aggressive, unpopular, and unskilled socially. The first group, more than the second, tended to be leaders who were involved in extracurricular activities and were very influential in peer groups. Other researchers have also shown that overt, but especially *relational,* aggression is associated with perceived popularity (Cillessen & Mayeux, 2004; Rose et al., 2004). Recall that relational aggression refers to tactics such as ignoring others or leaving them out of social activities. Together, these research findings seem to tell a more complicated story: that, in the transition from elementary school to middle school, when many peer groups become shifted or realigned, some children find forceful ways to exert social power. They manipulate others, assert themselves, and generally "call the shots" with their peers. In many cases, their efforts at using aggression to attain social status are successful, at least in the short run. However, the long-term outcomes of behaving in this way are still not known (Cillessen & Rose, 2005).

FRIENDSHIPS

By adolescence, the importance of close friendship is firmly solidified. Adolescents from such diverse cultures as China and Iceland claim strong loyalty to their close friends (Keller et al., 1998). Why are friends important? In our culture, adolescents say they value the ability to share thoughts and feelings with friends and expect mutual understanding and self-disclosure in friendships (Bigelow & LaGaipa, 1975; Furman & Bierman, 1984). They share problems, solutions to those problems, and private feelings with friends. These qualities fit the needs of individuals who are struggling to define who they are and who they will become. A sample exchange between two adolescent friends drawn from Parker and Gottman's (1989) research illustrates these themes:

A: *I don't know. Gosh, I have no idea what I want to do. And it really doesn't bother me that much that I don't have my future planned.* [laughs]

B: [laughs]

A: [laughs] *Like it bothers my Dad a lot, but it doesn't bother me.*

B: *Just tell your dad what I always tell my Dad: "Dad, I* am."

A: [laughs] *Exactly!*

B: *And whatever happens tomorrow, I still will be!*

Adolescents continue to prefer same-sex friends, although the frequency of boy-girl interactions increases. At this age, similarities in attitudes about academics, dating, drinking, smoking, and drug use influence whether children become friends (Dishion, Andrews, & Crosby, 1995; Epstein, 1983; Tolson & Urberg, 1993). Adolescent friendships become more selective with age; teenagers have fewer mutual friends than younger children do, but mutual friends comprise a greater proportion of their total network of friends. The tendency for girls to have smaller friendship networks than boys, observed earlier in childhood, disappears to some degree, but girls' friendships remain marked by emotional intensity and, perhaps because of this, even fragility (Benenson & Christakos, 2003; Urberg et al., 1995). Adolescents also say that the time they spend with their friends is the most enjoyable part of their day (Csikszentmihalyi & Larson, 1984). Friendship is thus a key element in the social and emotional life of the older child.

The relationship styles cultivated in friendships may extend to relations with others later in life. Harry Stack Sullivan (1953) believed that the capacity for intimacy nurtured by same-sex friendships in childhood provides the foundation for intimacy in more mature adult relationships. The failure to acquire this capacity in the formative years of childhood may impair a person's later functioning as a romantic partner, spouse, or parent. More recent studies confirm that there is a correlation between relational styles used with friends and romantic partners (Furman, 1999). For example, adolescents who perceive their friendships as supportive also tend to see their romantic relationships as supportive (Connolly, Furman, & Konarski, 2000).

Friends can encourage many positive qualities, such as the tendency to engage in prosocial behavior. When their friends are prosocial, adolescents express altruistic goals (for instance, they say that they try to share or cheer someone up if something has gone wrong), and are described by peers as behaving prosocially a year later (Barry & Wentzel, 2006). But research has also revealed that friendships may not always be positive and emotionally supportive. Among rejected children, for example, interactions with their friends tend to be more negative than among other children (Rubin, Bukowski, & Parker, 1998). Friends can also be a factor in deviant behavior, especially among children who are predisposed to have conduct problems themselves. Thomas Dishion and his colleagues (Dishion, Patterson, & Griesler, 1994) observed that ten-year-old aggressive boys who had been rejected by most of their peers often became friends with other aggressive boys. Over time, they conversed more about deviant behavior, such as substance abuse and delinquency, a form of talk for which deviant peers typically reward one another (Dishion et al., 1996). By age fourteen, association with antisocial friends was found to contribute statistically to the tendency to engage in deviant behaviors. These findings suggest that breaking the cycle of antisocial behavior may require more than intervening in an individual child's pattern of behaviors; monitoring his or her friendship networks may be just as important. Adolescence is an especially vulnerable time for the negative influences of antisocial friends (Berndt, Hawkins, & Jiao, 1999). In addition, association with deviant friends is especially likely when parents fail to be nurturant and involved and to monitor their adolescents' behaviors (Ary et al., 1999; Scaramella et al., 2002).

KEY THEME
RISK/RESILIENCE

ROMANTIC RELATIONSHIPS

Romantic relationships seem to grow in a specific sequence for many adolescents. They usually begin with mixed-sex interactions that involve casual and informal boy-girl groups in early adolescence. This type of interaction is often followed by group dating, and finally romantic relationships with a single partner (Connolly et al., 2004). Most teens report that they have "fallen in love" and that they have been involved in a serious romantic relationship in high school, according to the results of one study (Regan et al., 2004). However, although teenagers are deeply interested in romantic relationships, their relationships are generally not long-enduring, especially early in adolescence (Davies & Windle, 2000). Only about 33 percent report having a current girlfriend or boyfriend by age 15 or 16 (Connolly & Johnson, 1996).

Unlike more mature romantic relationships, which offer mutual support and caregiving, romantic relationships at this time take on significance merely because adolescents feel it is important to be involved with someone romantically (Furman, 2002). Early romantic relationships function as opportunities to explore sexuality and are a source of companionship. Later in adolescence, however, romantic relationships take on a greater caregiving and mutual support function, qualities associated with mature relationships in adulthood (Furman & Wehner, 1994).

FOR • YOUR • REVIEW

- What are the characteristics of peer relationships during adolescence?
- When does peer pressure reach its peak? What factors are related to vulnerability to peer pressure?
- What factors are related to peer popularity in adolescence?
- What are the qualities of children's friendships during adolescence?
- What are the qualities of romantic relationships in adolescence?

School

Clearly, a significant part of most adolescents' daily life continues to be the school experience. Academic demands increase, as do opportunities to explore personal interests, such as sports, drama, music, and other domains, through formal study or extracurricular activities. There is much more that can be said about teenagers' experiences in the educational system than can be discussed in this book. In this section, we take the opportunity to describe two school-related topics that seem to be especially relevant to development in adolescence.

School Transitions

Aside from the transition to kindergarten, a second important shift occurs when children move from elementary school to a middle or junior high school. In the United States, this transition is usually the visible signal of childhood's end and the beginning of adolescence. Children must adapt to a new physical environment, new teachers, and, often, new peers; and now, rather than staying with the same classmates in the same room for most of the school day, they move from class to class, each usually with its own set of students. Frequently the difference in student body size is dramatic. In one study, the mean school size from grade six to grade seven increased from 466 to 1,307, and the mean number of children in each grade went from 59 to 403 (Simmons et al., 1987). It is no wonder that many researchers report a decline in school satisfaction and academic motivation in pre- and early adolescence, as well as a drop in grades and participation in extracurricular activities (Eccles, Midgley, et al., 1993; Hirsch & Rapkin, 1987; Schulenberg, Asp, & Petersen, 1984; Simmons & Blyth, 1987).

We have already noted that some researchers have observed a decline in self-esteem at this time, particularly among preadolescent girls (Hirsch & Rapkin, 1987; Simmons et al., 1979). Early-maturing sixth-grade girls display better images of themselves when they attend schools with kindergarten through eighth-grade classes, presumably because they feel less pressured to adopt dating and other activities that become prevalent among seventh- and eighth-graders. On the other hand, those girls entering puberty at more typical ages and at about the same time that they enter a new school program or undergo other significant transitions tend to have lower self-image and more difficulties in school, possibly because multiple changes in life are difficult to handle (Simmons et al., 1987). Boys and girls who feel they have little control over their academic progress and are less personally invested in succeeding in school also benefit by not having to undergo a school transition between fifth and sixth grades (Rudolph et al., 2001).

For some adolescents, the difficulties encountered during school transitions continue to be reflected in lower self-esteem, high levels of depression, and greater drug and alcohol use through the later school years (Rudolph et al., 2001). These difficulties may even set in motion a pattern of academic decline that leads them to drop out of school (Eccles et al., 1997; Eccles & Midgley, 1989). Perhaps school transitions do not fit the specific developmental needs of many preadolescents. At a time during which youngsters seek stronger peer associations and a supportive climate for resolving identity issues, they confront an educational environment that is more impersonal than elementary school and fragments peer relationships. Compared with elementary school, junior high school classrooms also tend to emphasize greater teacher control and discipline, offer fewer personal and positive teacher-student interactions, use a higher standard of evaluating student competence while focusing on more public evaluation of the quality of work, and can often be less cognitively challenging, as classrooms become more teacher directed and provide fewer opportunities for student-initiated learning (Eccles, Midgley, et al., 1993; Eccles & Roeser, 1999).

KEY THEME
RISK/RESILIENCE

What happens when alternatives to the traditional middle school and high school structures are instituted? When teachers offer greater academic and personal counseling, contact parents when students are absent, and encourage communication with parents, and when students are assigned to classes with many of the same classmates, students show higher levels of academic success, less psychological dysfunction, and a substantially lower school dropout rate than students who experience more traditional school changes (Felner & Adan, 1988; Felner, Ginter, & Primavera, 1982).

SCHOOL VIOLENCE

In recent years violence in the schools has become a growing concern. Violent behavior may range from attacks on children or teachers that result in physical and psychological damage, even death. Youth violence resulting in deaths in U.S. schools increased substantially in the late 1980s in disadvantaged urban schools among African American and Hispanic youths. However, in the latter half of the 1990s, violence was reported more and more frequently in suburban and rural communities, and at the hands of middle-class Caucasian American youths (National Research Council and Institute of Medicine, 2002b). Shootings in schools have resulted in deaths not only in the United States but also in Western Europe and other nations. Fortunately, such incidents remain quite rare. Nevertheless, they have received enormous attention in the media and have contributed to considerable public alarm (M. Anderson et al., 2001).

KEY THEME
SOCIOCULTURAL INFLUENCE

The violence associated with inner-city schools often appears to be an extension of the violence found in urban neighborhoods (National Research Council and Institute of Medicine, 2002b). Problems involving poverty, racial segregation, and illegal drug activity very likely spill over from the neighborhood and into the school in urban communities, and typically involve specific grievances held by the perpetrators against particular individuals. However, in suburban and rural schools the violence seems more like the kind of "rampage" shootings by adults that occur in workplaces or other public locations (National Research Council and Institute of Medicine, 2002b). Although the youths who commit violence in suburban and rural communities also hold grievances, their dissatisfactions tend to be more abstract and less concerned with specific issues or threats. Case studies of a number of these rampage-type events reported by researchers reveal few similarities among the students committing these acts of violence other than that the perpetrators are virtually always male. But among other factors shared by some of the perpetrators are a recent drop in grades, the tendency to be associated with or engage in delinquent behavior, serious mental health problems (not typically recognized by either parents or the school), and easy access to guns. The stereotyped picture of a child who is a member of a dysfunctional family, who is a loner, and whom adults believe to be at high risk for committing violence is not usually supported in the cases that have been studied. Although the youths who committed lethal violence were often members of some student groups and informal cliques—that is, they were not completely outside the configuration of social participation with other peers—they were more likely to be only marginally associated with the group. At least some adults had hints that these boys might commit violent acts; however, the gap between the young persons who displayed such clues and their parents or others who might have been able to obtain help was never bridged. Some of the youths' friends had an even greater sense of the potential danger of violence. However, they, too, failed to communicate this information to appropriate authorities who might have been able to intervene.

Key Theme
Risk/Resilience

Perhaps many steps can be taken to reduce or eliminate such rampages in the future and to make schools safer. For example, more extensive mental health services should be provided in the schools for children in need of them. Additionally, greater efforts may be required to limit young people's access to weapons such as guns, because their use has been the primary means by which violent acts resulting in death have occurred. However, the most important step in reducing violent lethal behavior may be to establish a climate, not just in the schools but also in other locations within the community, in which adults and young people can communicate with one another and work together to provide a supportive network committed to the safety and well-being of all youth (National Research Council and Institute of Medicine, 2002b).

For • Your • Review

- What are the effects of the transition from elementary school to middle school or junior high school?
- What explanations exist for violent behavior in schools?

Media

There is no question that technology and media are an integral part of the lives of most adolescents in the United States. It seems hard to locate a teenager who does not regularly download music onto his or her computer, engage in on-line social networking, or use a feature-loaded cell phone to communicate with friends and family. A recent national survey indicates just how involved adolescents are with media: on average, teenagers spend over eight hours per day in contact with some form of media, and for about one-quarter of teens, this figure includes contact with multiple forms of media at the same time (Roberts, Foehr, & Rideout, 2005). What are the effects of this large amount of time with computers, video games, television, and other electronic tools? They are both negative and positive.

In one study, twelve- to fourteen-year-old children were interviewed about the television shows, music, movies, and magazines they used. The researchers were able to compute an index of these teens' "sexual media diet" by noting the extent of sexual content in the shows, music, movies, and magazines. When the participants were interviewed again two years later, those who had experienced heavy exposure to sexual content in the media were more than twice as likely to report engaging in sexual intercourse (Brown et al., 2006). Among African American teenagers, heavy exposure to music videos and sports programming on television was found to be linked to lower self-esteem. However, adolescents who expressed strong identification with popular Black (and not white) television characters had high self-esteem (Ward, 2004). Thus, the way in which media influences children—either positively or negatively—depends not only on the content of what they watch but also on the characteristics of the viewer.

Approximately nine out of ten teenagers between ages twelve and seventeen now have access to the Internet (Pew Internet & Family Life Project, 2005). Older children and adolescents spend much of their time at the computer alone. Adolescents who put in relatively large amounts of time on the computer—for example, more than two hours a day—report fewer and poorer social interactions with parents and friends (Sanders et al., 2000). Nevertheless, a substantial portion of children's involvement with the computer is devoted to communicating and maintaining social relationships with others via e-mail, instant messaging, game playing, or chat rooms (Subrahmanyam et al., 2000; Subrahmanyam et al., 2001). Researchers know very little about the impact of these new forms of social communication on adolescent development. Of course, one major concern is what kinds of social interactions may be occurring during some of these on-line activities, especially with individuals with whom the young person is not acquainted.

CONTROVERSY: THINKING IT OVER

What Regulations Should Exist for Children's Access to the Internet?

With the emergence of new technologies often come new challenges and dilemmas for parents and society. Because computers and the Internet have become such a prevalent part of the environment for many children, this relatively new resource has generated its own set of controversies.

What Is the Controversy?

Many positive advantages can exist for children using the Internet. These benefits may come from being able to move from one site to another in exploring or addressing a question and in obtaining in-depth information about a topic. But readily accessible sites may provide access to some material not considered appropriate for children, including ways to engage in violent activity, information from groups that promote hatred and bigotry, and sexually explicit imagery. Children also may be constantly bombarded with advertising and other images that can promote certain points of view that children have difficulty understanding and that parents may find objectionable.

What Are the Opposing Arguments?

The issues related to this matter bear closely on questions of free speech and rights to information. Few would argue in support of the unfettered availability to children of some types of material. Parents can take steps in limiting their children's exposure to unacceptable information in the home. However, applying the same restrictions to the schools and, particularly, to children's access to the Internet in public libraries or other public places may be far more difficult. Should filters and blocking devices be installed on computers in these publicly accessible locations as well? Would such restrictions be inappropriate in public facilities, given that they interfere with the rights of adults? Still others are concerned that efforts to regulate public sites, and even efforts by parents in the home, may promote a false sense of security among caregivers that overlooks the myriad ways in which inappropriate material can become available to their children via the computer.

Other debates arise over how to determine when it becomes reasonable for children and adolescents to have access to various kinds of information—for example, in cases in which a young person (and his or her parents) may feel uncomfortable or unwilling to discuss sexuality with their children. The timetable for such access may differ considerably depending on a child's age, the parents' beliefs about such matters, and community standards (National Research Council and Institute of Medicine, 2001). Additionally, young people must ultimately learn to engage in responsible use of the Internet, an educational goal that could receive little attention when parents and others rely on filters or blocking devices to monitor website activity.

What Answers Exist? What Questions Remain?

Parents may need to become more fully aware of how their children are using the computer. For example, whereas only 30 percent of parents think their adolescent children have ever corresponded with a stranger via e-mail, more than 50 percent of teenagers report having done so. Moreover, whereas only 17 percent of parents believe that their teenage children have provided personal information over the computer, 45 percent of young people report having done so (Penn, Schoen, & Berland Associates, 2000). In addition, little research exists on what children are actually viewing or saying on the Internet. One recent study of the chat room conversations of over 500 teenagers found that almost thirty percent of participants talked about sexual themes, and that within communications, there was one sexual comment per minute (Subrahmanyam, Smahel, & Greenfield, 2006). Another analysis found that over 400 message boards on the Internet were devoted to the topic of self-injurious behaviors in teens. Although many of these provided a way for adolescents with this problem to engage in mutual support for each other, a fair number were judged to encourage even more of these damaging and harmful behaviors (Whitlock, Powers, & Eckenrode, 2006).

Experts have called for the creation of websites that offer balanced and healthy information on topics that young people search for. There is also a growing need for psychologists and educators to develop programs to teach children and adolescents about appropriate on-line computer usage. Indeed, in order to address the question about what regulations are needed for children's access to the Internet, perhaps it is important to first ask to what extent *mentoring* or *monitoring* is needed to effectively deal with the problem (National Research Council and Institute of Medicine, 2001).

FOR • YOUR • REVIEW

- What has research revealed about media effects during adolescence?
- What controversies exist concerning children's access to computers?

NEIGHBORHOODS

In many cultures and societies, rearing children is considered a communal effort. Even in the United States, with its emphasis on the family as the bedrock for the transmission of cultural values and beliefs, neighbors and other community members often provide resources to families in their efforts to create a supportive rearing environment (National Research Council and Institute of Medicine, 2002a). Of course, at one time, neighbors might often have included distant family members. But today, increased family mobility, less visibility in the community because of long absences for work, more heterogeneous interests among the residents, and the deterioration of some areas as a result of crime, drugs, and poverty have made questions about the neighborhood's role in development—that is, the broader ecological context in which children live—even more important.

NEIGHBORHOOD EFFECTS

KEY THEME
SOCIOCULTURAL INFLUENCE
RISK/RESILIENCE

A review by Tama Leventhal and Jeanne Brooks-Gunn (2000) of the literature on their effects on developmental outcomes indicates that neighborhoods do matter. They matter, for example, with respect to school readiness and achievement; children who grow up in neighborhoods in which the residents have higher socioeconomic status do better in school and are more likely to graduate from high school and to attend college. Neighborhoods matter, too, with respect to behavioral and emotional problems; both are more likely to be present among children residing in neighborhoods with lower socioeconomic status. And youths living in neighborhoods with higher socioeconomic status tend to delay engaging in sexual activity and are less likely to bear children as teenagers.

These findings are probably not too surprising. However, a more important question is how neighborhoods might influence these kinds of outcomes (Jencks & Mayer, 1990). Leventhal and Brooks-Gunn (2000) propose three different pathways by which neighborhoods can have an impact. One pathway is via the availability of institutional resources, such as libraries, educational programs, and museums designed to promote achievement. Such resources also extend to the availability of quality child care; the presence of good schools and medical services; and in the case of adolescents, employment opportunities that encompass visible opportunities for "getting ahead" through the acquisition of job-relevant skills. The benefits of high-quality child care and good schools are well documented, although evidence that other institutional resources make a difference needs more thorough research.

A second pathway by which neighborhoods may have an effect on development is through the parenting styles of caregivers and the interpersonal support networks that are available to parents. Indeed, parenting is affected by a mother's perception of the neighborhood, such as how safe it is. As an illustration, mothers who have a negative view of their neighborhood are more likely to show greater supervision of their children's activities than mothers who view their neighbors as a source of help (O'Neil, Parke, & McDowell, 2001). As it turns out, more restrictive parental practices in poorer, high-crime neighborhoods may be beneficial to children, as the findings of a recent study carried out by Rosario Ceballo and Vonnie McLoyd (2002) indicate. Perhaps such parental practices reduce opportunities for children to be influenced by peers who may encourage them to engage in less desirable activities (Jarrett, 1997). Even so, an important beneficial component to children of concerned and involved parents in poor neighborhoods continues to be nurturance, rather than harsh and inconsistent

One way in which neighborhoods have an impact on children's development is through the institutional resources they provide. For example, "good neighborhoods" typically have good schools that promote academic and personal success.

Adolescents thrive in communities where residents provide opportunities to act on shared values and goals.

socialization practices (Brody et al., 2001). When parents have greater social support from family and friends within the community, the negative effects that often accompany increased parental stress in poor neighborhoods may also be reduced.

Yet a third pathway for influences on development occurs through the individual and community-level offerings provided within neighborhoods to supervise young people and to reduce the risks that they may experience. This pathway is sometimes referred to in terms of the norms or collective efforts of neighbors (Leventhal & Brooks-Gunn, 2000). The social cohesion—that is, the willingness of residents to intervene or establish such alternatives as athletic activities, after-school programs, and social clubs designed to promote the values and goals of the community—may differ substantially from one neighborhood to another. Yet, when residents are willing to take the initiative in monitoring or overseeing the doings of children and youths, neighborhoods tend to experience less violence and fewer deviant behaviors among the young (Brody et al., 2001; Elliott et al., 1996; Sampson, Raudenbush, & Earls, 1997).

These various neighborhood effects on development are not large (Caspi et al., 2000; Leventhal & Brooks-Gunn, 2000). For example, research involving identical twins growing up in a range of communities suggests that neighborhood differences account for about 5 percent of the variability associated with their mental health. Although this impact may seem small, when the interventions designed to improve institutional resources, interpersonal support, and the norms and collective efforts of a community are extended to a large number of children within a neighborhood, the costs are small and the benefits quite high. Thus social policies designed to enhance the institutional resources within the community, parental perceptions of support and other features that uphold desirable parenting practices, and the individual and collective efforts of community members to monitor and assist in the supervision of children and adults may be important avenues for promoting child and youth development.

Exposure to Violence

KEY THEME
Risk/Resilience

Among youth living in urban neighborhoods, about 76 percent have witnessed or been victimized by violence in their community (Ozer & Weinstein, 2004). This experience puts them at risk for posttraumatic stress disorder, depression, anxiety, and substance use (Gorman-Smith & Tolan, 1998; Sullivan, Kung, & Farrell, 2004). Moreover, children who witness violence are also more likely to enact violent behaviors themselves (Farrell & Bruce, 1997).

A recent study showed that parents play an influential role in how adolescents cope with exposure to violence. Young adolescents and their female caregivers living in a violent section of an urban area were interviewed about how they coped with this problem. Caregivers were also asked to describe the types of discussions they had with children about violence in their neighborhood. Children whose parents encouraged them to take an active, problem-focused, or preventive approach showed gains in self-esteem, grades in school, and mental health. These gains were not observed when children were encouraged to ignore the problem or to respond with aggression. Talking to children about violence, as opposed to ignoring it, and serving as a good role model for how to cope can provide children with a means to achieve successful outcomes (Kliewer et al., 2006). In addition, adolescents who report that they are religious, in the sense of being spiritual and engaging in personal religious experiences, seem to be protected to some degree from the negative impact of exposure to violence (Pearce et al., 2003).

AFFLUENT COMMUNITIES

KEY THEME
RISK/RESILIENCE

We often think that children growing up in affluent communities are protected from risks in development, but this is not necessarily the case. Suniya Luther and her colleagues have conducted several studies that show that, for some children from wealthy families, the pressures placed on them by families with hard-driving schedules and high expectations may be associated with psychological costs. In one study, one in five tenth-grade girls reported that they were depressed, a rate that was three times higher than average among girls this age. In addition, 72 percent of adolescents reported that they had used alcohol at least once in the past, compared with 61 percent for teens of this age on average (Luther & D'Avanzo, 1999). In another study, a sample of 300 sixth- and seventh-graders from a high-income neighborhood (the median income was about $100,000 per year) showed high rates of depression among girls and high levels of substance use among boys and girls, a phenomenon that was linked to their anxiety and depression. Related to these behaviors was the feeling of being pressured toward academic achievement, a sentiment that caused them to set very high standards for themselves.

Researchers do not yet fully understand why children from privileged backgrounds might experience such serious social and emotional problems, but they have some suspicions. For one thing, apparently many of the parents of these children focused more on their children's accomplishments than on their personal qualities and character. Many of these children also experienced a lack of emotional connection to their parents. Involved in a pattern of extensive after-school activities, or spending significant time alone while their professional parents worked, these children did not feel much emotional closeness to their parents (Luther & Becker, 2002; Luther & Latendresse, 2005). Students and parents were both apparently caught up in highly overscheduled days, with little "down time" in which emotional support could be provided.

WAR AND CHILDREN

KEY THEME
SOCIOCULTURAL INFLUENCE

Perhaps no other tragedy aside from such natural calamities as earthquakes, floods, or famine is more disruptive to neighborhoods than war. But wars often have an impact on large numbers of communities and are the result of human motivation; they are therefore subject to a form of intervention that is not available for many other kinds of disasters. The consequences of war for young people can be devastating. As a result of conflicts between 1990 and 2000, perhaps as many as 2 million children around the world have lost their lives, 6 million have been injured or disabled, 12 million have been left homeless, and 1 million have been orphaned (UNICEF, 2002).

Of children who experience and survive war in their neighborhood, a high percentage, typically on the order of 40 to 50 percent, display posttraumatic stress disorder (PTSD), a disorder that was described earlier in this text. In the case of war, multiple factors may contribute to the appearance of PTSD. Children may witness violent acts, such as killing, rape, and torture (or even experience some of these), or see the physical manifestations of war, including dead bodies and destroyed buildings. They may also be subjected to homelessness, starvation, relocation to refugee camps, and separation from family and friends. All of these factors can contribute to the occurrence of PTSD (Allwood, Bell-Dolan, & Husain, 2002), and the extent of stress reported by children is influenced by the degree to which they report experiencing the more traumatizing aspects of war (Smith et al., 2001).

Key Theme
Risk/Resilience

In general, the symptoms of PTSD are most evident within the first year of exposure to war events; after one year, they decline. However, some stressors, such as relocation and separation from family, may continue for years, and as a consequence, children may remain vulnerable to PTSD for long periods of time (Thabet & Vostanis, 2000). Nevertheless, some children show exceptional resilience in the face of such tragedy. At the present time, researchers know little about the factors that might promote this resilience; however, the availability of some kind of social support is often theorized to be one important element (Cairns & Dawes, 1996). That support usually comes from a mother. Her reactions to the war experience, research shows, do have an impact on the child's level of distress (Smith et al., 2001).

Effective ways to treat children experiencing the stresses of war remain uncertain (Yule, 2000). Perhaps a first step is to establish a secure environment for children, often an extremely difficult task given the possibilities of continued conflict, the uncertainties associated with living under refugee conditions, and the suspicions that can pervade attitudes toward others who may not be well known by the children. Psychosocial intervention efforts designed to assist the mothers of children exposed to war so that they, in turn, can be more helpful to their children show promise of positive benefits (Dybdahl, 2001).

Vast amounts of support may be needed for children who have experienced this degree of disruption in their lives. Well-designed research to evaluate the procedures that can help the most should be a priority until such time as neighborhoods are safe, no matter where children reside.

FOR • YOUR • REVIEW

- What aspects of development are known to be influenced by neighborhoods?
- What is the impact on adolescents of exposure to violence? What factors promote successful adaptation to this exposure?
- What adverse developmental outcomes do some children from affluent families manifest?
- What are the most serious consequences for children experiencing war, and what procedures may be most effective in dealing with those consequences?

CHAPTER RECAP

Summary of Developmental Themes

SOCIOCULTURAL INFLUENCE

How do sociocultural factors influence the contexts of development in adolescence?

Social class has been shown to influence parenting styles with adolescents, such that parents from lower-income groups tend to use more power-assertive techniques than middle-income groups. Neighborhoods, in the resources they provide as well as the degree of violence they include, also play a significant role in development. One other important sociocultural factor is exposure of children to war.

RISK/RESILIENCE

What factors promote risk or resilience during adolescence?

Many contextual factors can put adolescents at risk. Among them are coercive or controlling parenting styles, peers who engage in deviant or antisocial behaviors, the transition to a new school, certain forms of media content, and neighborhoods with poor resources or violence. In each case, however, research shows that certain strategies or interventions can be protective or help children to recover from the negative impact of being exposed to risk.

Chapter Review

THE FAMILY IN ADOLESCENCE

How do relationships with parents change during adolescence?

Adolescents communicate less with parents, especially about personal matters. At least at the start of adolescence, conflicts with parents typically become more frequent. Still, parents remain an important source of support and advice for children in the teenage years.

What are the elements of successful parenting of adolescents?

Authoritative parenting, with its emphasis on warmth and moderate control, remains an effective parenting style for adolescents, just as it was for younger children. However, parents also need to be attuned to adolescents' growing need for autonomy. Thus effective parenting involves creating an atmosphere in which children disclose information to parents and in which cooperative decision making can take place.

What social class and ethnic group differences have been observed in parenting?

Lower-class mothers tend to use more power-assertive parenting techniques than do middle-class mothers. Economic stress is associated with a diminished ability of parents to offer warm, supportive care. African American families experience a disproportionate share of poverty, but the support of extended families and involvement in religion seem to have a positive influence on children.

How do coercive cycles in parenting develop?

Coercive cycles develop when parents do not deliver consequences to the aggressive behaviors of their children, thus tacitly reinforcing them. Children's aggression increases, and a cycle of escalating negative interactions ensues.

What issues arise in children's relationships with stepparents?

Adolescents often have difficulty adjusting to life with stepparents. Part of the problem may be the reluctance of stepparents to exhibit the qualities of authoritative parenting that are associated with positive child outcomes—in particular, support for and control over their stepchildren's behaviors.

PEER RELATIONSHIPS IN ADOLESCENCE

What are the characteristics of peer relationships during adolescence?

Adolescents form larger peer groups called *cliques* and *crowds*. They also form more intense relationships with friends and start to spend more time with peers of the opposite sex.

When does peer pressure reach its peak? What factors are related to vulnerability to peer pressure?

Susceptibility to peer pressure heightens during early adolescence but declines as young adulthood approaches. Children may be more vulnerable to peer pressure when parents are unresponsive and uninvolved.

What factors are related to peer popularity in adolescence?

In a shift from earlier periods in childhood, for some children popularity with peers during adolescence seems to be related to aggression. Because many of these adolescents are socially skilled and involved in school activities, they may use aggression as a means of establishing social status and power.

What are the qualities of children's friendships during adolescence?

Adolescents see friends as providing trust and intimacy. Opposite-sex as well as same-sex friendships are observed. Friends can influence prosocial as well as antisocial behaviors.

What are the qualities of romantic relationships in adolescence?

Adolescents' romantic relationships do not show the same mutually supportive, caregiving qualities as more mature adult relationships. Romantic relationships among teens evolve from more casual mixed-sex groups and provide opportunities for companionship and exploration of sexuality.

School

What are the effects of the transition from elementary school to middle school or junior high school?

The move from elementary to middle or junior high school can be difficult for many children, especially if they experience other developmental transitions at the same time. Children may exhibit a drop in self-esteem, depression, anxiety, and greater participation in risky behaviors. The kinds of interactions that occur in the more advanced grades may be difficult for children if they feel they have little control over their academic progress or if they are not personally invested in succeeding in the classroom.

What explanations exist for violent behavior in schools?

In urban communities, school violence tends to reflect an extension of violence found in the neighborhood. In suburban and rural communities, violence is more likely the result of youth engaging in a "rampage." Few commonalities are shared by perpetrators, and although both adults and peers may detect signals that anticipate these actions, they are often not sufficiently visible to lead to intervention.

Media

What has research revealed about media effects during adolescence?

Adolescents who consume a heavy diet of sexual content via various forms of media tend to have sexual relations earlier. Exposure to certain forms of television programming can boost or lower self-esteem, depending on the characteristics of the viewer.

What controversies exist concerning children's access to computers?

Controversies exist over how to regulate access to the Internet, as some material on it may not be suitable for children. A major unresolved issue is the extent to which children should be educated about versus monitored in their use of the Internet.

NEIGHBORHOODS

What aspects of development are known to be influenced by neighborhoods?

The neighborhoods in which children grow up have an effect on academic success, mental health, and sexual behavior. Neighborhoods influence development through the institutional resources they provide, the parenting styles practiced in response to safety, the support network perceived to exist in the neighborhood, and the individual and collective efforts of community residents to supervise and monitor the development of youth.

What is the impact on adolescents of exposure to violence? What factors promote successful adaptation to this exposure?

Exposure to violence is linked to PTSD, depression, anxiety, substance use, and the tendency to commit aggressive acts. Modeling and coaching youth in active, problem-focused coping strategies can help to mitigate these effects, as does the practice of religious and spiritual behaviors.

What adverse developmental outcomes do some children from affluent families manifest?

For some children from affluent families, high pressures to achieve, combined with lack of emotional connection to parents, are associated with depression, anxiety, and substance use.

What are the most serious consequences for children experiencing war, and what procedures may be most effective in dealing with those consequences?

Children who witness war evidence the symptoms of PTSD, especially within the first year of their exposure. Successful interventions have involved placing children in a secure environment, as well as providing support to caregivers, who have the potential to, in turn, be helpful to their children.

KEY TERMS AND CONCEPTS

clique (p. 559)
coercive cycle (p. 556)
crowds (p. 559)

Pathways: Connecting the Story of Development

	Infancy (0–2 years)	Early Childhood (2–6 years)
Physical Development	• Evidences rapid gains in height and weight, with faster rates of growth in the head region and regions nearer the center of the body • Shows period of rapid brain development, including formation and pruning of synapses • Shows basic learning capabilities in the form of habituation, operant and classical conditioning, and imitation • Shows improvements in visual accommodation, saccadic movements, acuity, and vergence • Attracted first to external features of objects and to movement, and later to internal features of objects • Localizes sounds • Recognizes melodic rhythms and other features of music • Shows sensitivity to smells, tastes, and tactile stimuli	• Shows advances in gross motor skills such as running, jumping, and skipping • Evidences slower but regular increases in size • Shows evidence of implicit learning
Cognitive/ Language Development	• Attends to increasingly complex patterns including those with facelike organization • Responsive to biological motion • Shows signs of depth perception • Shows intermodal perception • Develops *means-ends behavior* • Attains the *object concept* • Shows sensitivity to changes in number • Relies on egocentric and landmark cues to locate objects • Classifies objects according to physical similarities, as well as thematic and simple taxonomic relations • Distinguishes between animate and inanimate objects • Shows recognition memory for simple stimuli • Shows long-term recall in elicited imitation tasks • Shows simple problem-solving behaviors, including transfer • Discriminates among phonemes • Discriminates own language from others • Detects words in speech stream • Produces gestures to communicate • Comprehends many words • Speaks in single-word utterances	• Shows gains in ability to make perceptual discriminations • Can classify according to basic-level concepts • Understands the meaning of simple number terms, and eventually the basic principles of counting • Displays good intuitions about mathematical operations such as addition and forming fractions • Uses landmark cues to negotiate spatial environments • Uses geometric cues to aid spatial location • Begins to be able to read maps • Realizes that others can have different visual perspectives • Develops a *theory of mind* • Shows elementary planning activities • Displays knowledge of scripts • Displays autobiographical memory • By age three, attains *representational insight* • Uses two- and then multiword utterances • Uses morphemes, negatives, questions, and passive voice • Shows rapid growth in vocabulary and use of syntax • Displays overregularizations • Shows growth in referential communication and other aspects of pragmatics
Social/ Emotional Development	• Displays basic emotions • Imitates emotional expressions of others • Recognizes others' emotions • Begins to regulate own emotions through withdrawal or distraction • Forms attachments • Recognizes self • Begins to be able to delay gratification • Shows early signs of agency • Shows intersubjectivity • Shows early signs of empathy	• Displays self-conscious emotions • Uses language to express emotions • Understands causes and consequences of emotions • Shows more effective emotion regulation strategies and, eventually, a decline in tantrums • Displays more complex aspects of attachment by considering motives, feelings of caregiver • Shows decline in separation distress and other attachment behaviors typical of infants • Has notion of categorical self • Displays overt behaviors signaling independence • Shows first signs of self-control • Shows early signs of conscience and altruism • Thinks in terms of preconventional ideas • Shows awareness of own gender and gender stereotypes

	Middle Childhood (6–11 years)	Adolescence (11–18 years)
Physical Development	• Shows more efficient and better-controlled motor skills • Becomes more adept at fine-motor coordination • Shows steady growth in physical size	• Shows a physical growth spurt that does not conform to the principles of cephalocaudal and proximodistal development • Shows signs of sexual maturity and gains the ability to reproduce • Evidences maturation of frontal regions of the brain
Cognitive/ Language Development	• Shows systematic and efficient attention strategies • Shows logical thought on conservation tasks but only in the presence of real objects or images • Develops increasing memory span • Produces various kinds of memory strategies to enhance recall • Shows greater control of cognitive processing • Shows gains in ability to plan the steps in problem solving • Becomes more flexible in strategy use • Shows growth in metacognition • Shows metalinguistic awareness including appreciation of humor and metaphor	• Can think abstractly and *hypothetically,* generating multiple solutions to a problem • May display beliefs in the *imaginary audience* and the *personal fable* • Shows growth in scientific reasoning skills • Shows growth in *executive function* • Shows evidence of *judgment biases*
Social/ Emotional Development	• Shows understanding of display rules • Engages in social-comparison • Displays global self-esteem • Shows mastery orientation • Exercises self-regulation through internalized language • Thinks in terms of moral realism or conventional ideas • Shows greater knowledge of and greater flexibility toward gender stereotypes	• Shows more negative emotions than before • Uses early attachments as basis for more mature relationships • Defines self in terms of social roles • Views self from multiple and conflicting perspectives • Period of identity formation • Thinks in terms of moral relativism or postconventional ideas • Shows signs of gender intensification

Glossary

Accommodation In Piagetian theory, a component of adaptation; process of modification in thinking (schemes) that takes place when old ways of understanding something no longer fit.

Adaptation In Piagetian theory, the inborn tendency to adjust or become more attuned to conditions imposed by the environment; takes place through assimilation and accommodation.

Age-history confound In longitudinal studies, the co-occurrence of historical factors with changes in age; affects the ability to interpret results.

Allele Alternate form of a specific gene; provides a genetic basis for many individual differences.

Altruism Behavior carried out to help another without expectation of reward.

Ambivalent (resistant) attachment Insecure attachment in which the infant shows separation protest but also distress upon the caregiver's return.

Amniocentesis Method of sampling the fluid surrounding the developing fetus through insertion of a needle; used to diagnose fetal genetic and developmental disorders.

Amniotic sac Fluid-filled, transparent protective membrane surrounding the fetus.

Analogical transfer Ability to employ the solution to one problem in other, similar problems.

Androgen Class of male or masculinizing hormones.

Animism Attribution of lifelike qualities to inanimate objects.

A-not-B error Error that an infant makes when an object is hidden in location A, found by the infant, and then, in full view of the infant, moved to location B. Piaget observed that the child will mistakenly but persistently search for the object in location A.

Artificialism Belief that naturally occurring events are caused by people.

Assimilation In Piagetian theory, a component of adaptation; process of interpreting an experience in terms of current ways (schemes) of understanding things.

Attachment Strong emotional bond that emerges between infant and caregiver.

Attention State of alertness or arousal that allows the individual to focus on a selected aspect of the environment.

Authoritarian parent Parent who relies on coercive techniques to discipline the child and displays a low level of nurturance.

Authoritative parent Parent who sets limits on a child's behavior using reasoning and explanation and displays a high degree of nurturance.

Autobiographical memory Memory for specific events in one's own life.

Autosome One of twenty-two pairs of homologous chromosomes. The two members of each pair are similar in size, shape, and genetic function. The two sex chromosomes are excluded from this class.

Babbling Consonant-vowel utterances that characterize the infant's first attempts to vocalize.

Basic (primary) emotion Emotion, such as joy, sadness, or surprise, that appears early in infancy and seems to have a biological foundation.

Behavior analysis Learning theory perspective that explains the development of behavior according to the principles of classical and operant conditioning.

Behavior genetics Study of how characteristics and behaviors of individuals, such as intelligence and personality, are influenced by the interaction between genotype and experience.

Broca's area Portion of the cerebral cortex that controls expressive language.

Canalization Concept that the development of some attributes is governed primarily by the genotype and that only extreme environmental conditions will alter the phenotypic pattern for these attributes.

Canonical babbling Repetition of simple consonant-vowel combinations in well-formed syllables.

Cardinality Principle that the last number in a set of counted numbers refers to the number in that set.

Case study In-depth description of psychological characteristics and behaviors of an individual, often in the form of a narrative.

Catch-up growth Increase in growth rate after some factor, such as illness or poor nutrition, has disrupted the expected, normal growth rate.

Categorical perception Inability to distinguish among sounds that vary on some basic physical dimension except when those sounds lie at opposite sides of a critical juncture point on that dimension.

Categorical self Self-classification in terms of membership in certain groups based on sex, age, skills, what one owns, where one lives, and who one's friends are.

Centration In Piagetian theory, tendency of the child to focus on only one aspect of a problem.

Cephalocaudal development Pattern in which organs, systems, and motor movements near the head tend to develop earlier than those near the feet.

Chorionic villus sampling Method of sampling fetal chorionic cells; used to diagnose embryonic genetic and developmental disorders.

Chromosome Threadlike structure of DNA, located in the nucleus of cells, which forms a collection of genes. A human body cell normally contains forty-six chromosomes.

Chronosystem In Bronfenbrenner's ecological systems theory, the constantly changing temporal component of the environment that can influence development.

Clinical method Flexible, open-ended interview method in which questions are modified in reaction to the child's responses.

Clique Peer group of five to ten children who frequently interact together.

Codominance Condition in which individual, unblended characteristics of two alleles are reflected in the phenotype.

Coercive cycle Pattern of escalating negative reciprocal interactions.

Cognition Processes involved in thinking and mental activity, such as attention, memory, and problem solving.

Cognitive-developmental theory Theoretical orientation, most frequently associated with Piaget, emphasizing the active construction of psychological structures to interpret experience.

Cohort effect All the characteristics shared by individuals growing up in a specific social and historical context.

Collaborative learning Peer-centered learning in which students work together on academic problems with the goal of arriving at solutions that are more effective than solutions that could have been derived from individual effort alone.

Concepts Definition of a set of information on the basis of some general or abstract principle.

Concordance rate Percentage of pairs of twins in which both members have a specific trait identified in one twin.

Concrete operational stage In Piagetian theory, the third stage of development, from approximately seven to eleven years of age, in which thought is logical when stimuli are physically present.

Conditioned response (CR) Learned response that is exhibited to a previously neutral stimulus (CS) as a result of pairing the CS with an unconditioned stimulus (UCS).

Conditioned stimulus (CS) Neutral stimulus that begins to elicit a response similar to the unconditioned stimulus (UCS) with which it has been paired.

Conservation task Problem that requires the child to make judgments about the equivalence of two displays; used to assess stage of cognitive development.

Contextual models theories of development that are concerned with the effects of a broad range of biological, physical, and sociocultural settings on the process of development.

Control theory Hypothesis about parent-child interactions suggesting that the intensity of one partner's behavior affects the intensity of the other's response.

Conventional level In Kohlberg's theory, the second level of moral reasoning, in which the child conforms to the norms of the majority and wishes to preserve the social order.

Cooing Vowel-like utterances that characterize the infant's first attempts to vocalize.

Cooperative learning Peer-centered learning experience in which students work together in small groups to solve academic problems.

Cooperative play Interactive play in which children's actions are reciprocal.

Core knowledge hypothesis The idea that infants possess innate knowledge of certain properties of objects.

Correlation coefficient (*r*) Statistical measure, ranging from +1.00 to −1.00, that summarizes the strength and direction of the relationship between two variables; does not provide information about causation.

Correlational study Study that assesses whether changes in one variable are accompanied by systematic changes in another variable.

Cross-cultural study Study that compares individuals in different cultural contexts.

Crossing over Process during the first stage of meiosis when genetic material is exchanged between autosomes.

Cross-sectional study Study in which individuals of different ages are examined at the same point in time.

Crowds Large group of peers characterized by specific traits or reputation.

Crystallized intelligence Mental skills derived from cultural experience.

Cultural compatibility hypothesis Theory that school instruction is most effective if it is consistent with the practices of the child's background culture.

Debriefing Providing research participants with a statement of the true goals of a study after initially deceiving them or omitting information about its purposes.

Deferred imitation Ability to imitate a model's behavior hours, days, and even weeks after observation.

Delay of gratification Capacity to wait before performing a tempting activity or attaining some highly desired outcome; a measure of ability to regulate one's own behavior.

Deoxyribonucleic acid (DNA) Long, spiral staircaselike sequence of molecules created by nucleotides identified with the blueprint for genetic inheritance.

Dependent variable Behavior that is measured; suspected effect of an experimental manipulation.

Development Physical and psychological changes in the individual over a lifetime.

Developmental delay The condition children are said to have when they deviate noticeably from motor, cognitive, or language milestones in one or more areas.

Developmental psychology Systematic and scientific study of changes in human behaviors and mental activities over time.

Deviation IQ IQ score computed by comparing the child's performance with that of a standardization sample

Disorganized/disoriented attachment Infant-caregiver relations categorized by the infant's fear of the caregiver, confused facial expressions, and a combination of avoidant and ambivalent attachment behaviors.

Display rule Cultural guideline concerning when, how, and to what degree to display emotions.

Dominant allele Allele whose characteristics are reflected in the phenotype even when part of a heterozygous genotype. Its genetic characteristics tend to mask the characteristics of other alleles.

Down syndrome Disorder resulting from an extra chromosomal material on pair number twenty-one; associated with mental retardation and distinct physical features.

Dynamic systems theory Theoretical orientation that explains development as the emerging organization arising from the interaction of many different processes.

Ecological systems theory Bronfenbrenner's theory that development is influenced by experiences arising from broader social and cultural systems as well as a child's immediate surroundings.

Effectance motivation Inborn desire theorized by Robert White to be the basis for the infant's and child's efforts to master and gain control of the environment.

Effortful control Ability to suppress undesirable responses for less dominant ones that are considered socially or morally more acceptable.

Egocentric Term applied to the preoperational child's inability to separate his or her own perspective from those of others.

Elaboration Memory strategy in which individuals link items to be remembered in the form of an image or a sentence.

Elicited imitation Method in which older infants and preschoolers must repeat a sequence of actions demonstrated by the experimenter.

Embryonic period Period of prenatal development during which major biological organs and systems form; begins about the tenth to fourteenth day after conception and ends about the eighth week after conception.

Emotion Complex behavior involving physiological, expressive, and experiential components produced in response to some internal or external event.

Empathy Understanding and sharing of the feelings of others.

Empiricism Theory that environmental experiences shape the individual; more specifically, that all knowledge is derived from sensory experiences.

Episodic memory Memory for events that took place at a specific time and place.

Equilibration In Piagetian theory, an innate self-regulatory process that, through accommodation and assimilation, results in more organized and powerful schemes for adapting to the environment.

Ethnic identity The sense of belonging to a particular cultural group.

Ethnography Set of methods, including observations and interviews, used by researchers to describe the behaviors and underlying meaning systems within a given culture.

Ethology Theoretical orientation and discipline concerned with the evolutionary origins of behavior and its adaptive and survival value in animals, including humans.

Executive function Portion of the information-processing system that coordinates various component processes in order to achieve some goal.

Exosystem In Bronfenbrenner's ecological systems theory, environmental settings that indirectly affect the child by influencing the various microsystems forming the child's immediate environment.

Expansion Repetition of a child's utterance along with more complex forms.

Experimental design Research method in which one or more independent variables are manipulated to determine the effect on other, dependent variables.

Explicit memory Conscious recollection of a past event or experience.

Expressive aphasia Loss of the ability to speak fluently.

Expressive characteristics Characteristics associated with emotions or relationships with people; usually considered feminine.

Expressive style Type of early language production in which the child uses many social words.

Externality effect Tendency for infants younger than two months to focus on the external features of a complex stimulus and explore the internal features less systematically.

Externalizing problem Outward-directed behavioral manifestation, usually aggression or a temper tantrum, which is typically driven by anger.

Failure to thrive Label applied to any child whose growth in height or weight is below the third percentile for children of the same age.

Fast-mapping Process through which the context in which the child hears words spoken provides the key to their meanings.

Fetal alcohol syndrome (FAS) Cluster of fetal abnormalities stemming from mother's consumption of alcohol; includes growth retardation, defects in facial features, and intellectual retardation.

Fetal blood sampling Method of withdrawing blood from the umbilical cord of the fetus; used to diagnose genetic disorders, especially those that affect the blood.

Fetal monitoring device Medical device used to monitor fetal heartbeat during delivery.

Fetal period Period of prenatal development, from about the eighth week after conception to birth, marked by rapid growth and preparation of body systems for functioning in the postnatal environment.

Field experiment Study in which the experimental manipulations are carried out in a natural setting.

Fluid intelligence Biologically based mental abilities that are relatively uninfluenced by cultural experiences.

Focus on states Preoperational child's tendency to treat two or more connected events as unrelated.

Formal operational stage In Piagetian theory, the last stage of development, from approximately eleven to fifteen years of age, in which thought is abstract and hypothetical.

Fragile X syndrome Disorder associated with a pinched region of the X chromosome; a leading genetic cause of mental retardation in males.

Fraternal twins Siblings who share the same womb at the same time but originate from two different eggs fertilized by two different sperm cells. Also called *dizygotic twins*.

Gamete Sperm cell in males, egg cell in females, normally containing only twenty-three chromosomes.

Gender constancy Knowledge, usually gained around age six or seven years, that one's gender does not change as a result of alterations in appearance, behaviors, or desires.

Gender identity Knowledge, usually gained by age three years, that one is male or female.

Gender intensification Return to traditional beliefs about gender during adolescence.

Gender-role development Process by which individuals acquire the characteristics and behaviors prescribed by their culture for their sex. Also called *sex typing*.

Gender schema Cognitive organizing structure for information relevant to sex typing.

Gender schema theory Cognitive-developmental theory that stresses the importance of the acquisition of gender identity and children's intrinsic motivations to behave in a gender-typical manner.

Gender stability Knowledge, usually gained by age four years, that one's gender does not change over time.

Gender stereotype Expectation or belief that individuals within a given culture hold about the behaviors characteristic of males and females.

Gene Large segment of nucleotides within a chromosome that codes for the production of proteins and enzymes. These proteins and enzymes underlie traits and characteristics inherited from one generation to the next.

Genetic counseling Medical and counseling specialty concerned with determining and communicating the likelihood that prospective parents will give birth to a baby with a genetic disorder.

Genetic screening Systematic search using a variety of tests to detect developmental risk due to genetic anomalies.

Genomic imprinting Instances of genetic transmission in which the expression of a gene is determined by whether the particular allelic form has been inherited from the mother or the father.

Genotype Total genetic endowment inherited by an individual.

Germinal period Period lasting about ten to fourteen days following conception before the fertilized egg becomes implanted in the uterine wall. Also called *period of the zygote*.

Gestational age Age of fetus derived from onset of mother's last menstrual period.

Glial cell Brain cell that provides the material from which myelin is created, nourishes neurons, and provides a scaffolding for neuron migration.

Grammar Rules pertaining to the structure of language.

Habituation Gradual decline in the intensity, frequency, or duration of a response over repeated or lengthy occurrences of the same stimulus.

Heritability Proportion of variability in the phenotype that is estimated to be accounted for by genetic influences within a known environmental range.

Heterozygous Genotype in which two alleles of a gene are different. The effects on a trait will depend on how the two alleles interact.

Homozygous Genotype in which two alleles of a gene are identical, thus having the same effects on a trait.

Hormones Chemicals produced by various glands which are secreted directly into the bloodstream and can therefore circulate to influence cells in other locations of the body.

Human genome Entire inventory of nucleotide base pairs that compose the genes and chromosomes of humans.

Hypothetical reasoning Ability to systematically generate and evaluate potential solutions to a problem.

Identical twins Two individuals who originate from a single zygote (one egg fertilized by one sperm), which early in cell division separates to form two separate cell masses. Also called *monozygotic twins.*

Identity In Eriksonian psychosocial theory, the acceptance of both self and society, a concept that must be achieved at every stage but is especially important during adolescence.

Identity crisis Period, usually during adolescence, characterized by considerable uncertainty about the self and the role the individual is to fulfill in society.

Imaginary audience Individual's belief that others are examining and evaluating him or her.

Immanent justice Young child's belief that punishment will inevitably follow a transgression.

Implicit learning Abstract knowledge not available to conscious reflection; acquired accidentally from processing structured information.

Implicit memory Nonconscious recollections of how to do something behaviorally.

Imprinting Form of learning, difficult to reverse, during a sensitive period in development in which an organism tends to stay near a particular stimulus.

Independent variable Variable manipulated by the experimenter; the suspected cause.

Individual differences Unique characteristics that distinguish a person from other members of a larger group.

Induction Parental control technique that relies on the extensive use of reasoning and explanation as well as the arousal of empathic feelings.

Infantile amnesia Failure to remember events from the first two to three years of one's life.

Information processing Theoretical approach that views humans as having a limited ability to process information, much like computers.

Informed consent Participant's formal acknowledgment that he or she understands the purposes, procedures, and risks of a study, and agrees to participate in it.

Inner speech Interiorized form of private speech.

Instrumental characteristics Characteristics associated with acting on the world; usually considered masculine.

Instrumental competence Child's display of independence, self-control, achievement orientation, and cooperation.

Intelligence quotient (IQ) Numerical score received on an intelligence test.

Interactive synchrony Reciprocal, mutually engaging cycles of caregiver-child behaviors.

Interagent consistency Consistency in application of disciplinary strategies among different caregivers.

Intermodal perception Coordination of sensory information to perceive or make inferences about the characteristics of an object.

Internal working model of relationships Mental framework of the quality of relationships with others, developed as a result of early ongoing interactions with caregivers.

Internalizing problem Disturbance of mood, such as guilt and sadness, and, in more severe cases, anxiety and depression.

Intersubjectivity Mutual attention and shared communication that take place between two individuals.

Intra-agent consistency Consistency in a single caregiver's application of discipline from one situation to the next.

Joint attention Episodes in which the child and another individual share the same "psychological space" as they encounter experiences in the world.

Judgment bias Tendency to be influenced by inappropriate information at the expense of important and perhaps more relevant facts.

Karyotype Pictorial representation of an individual's chromosomes.

Lagging-down growth Decrease in growth rate after some factor, such as a congenital or hormonal disorder, has accelerated the expected normal growth rate.

Lateralization Process by which one hemisphere of the brain comes to dominate the other; for example, processing of language in the left hemisphere or of spatial information in the right hemisphere.

Learned helplessness Belief that one has little control over situations, perhaps because of lack of ability or inconsistent outcomes.

Learning Relatively permanent change in behavior as a result of such experiences as exploration, observation, and practice.

Limited-resource model Information-processing model that emphasizes the allocation of finite energy within the cognitive system.

Longitudinal study Research in which the same participants are repeatedly tested over a period of time, usually years.

Long-term memory Memory that holds information for extended periods of time.

Macrosystem In Bronfenbrenner's ecological systems theory, major historical events and the broad values, practices, and customs shared by a culture.

Mastery orientation Belief that achievements are based on one's own efforts rather than on luck or other factors beyond one's control.

Maternal blood screening Tests performed on a woman's blood to determine whether the fetus she is carrying has an increased risk for some types of chromosomal and metabolic disorders.

Means-ends behavior Deliberate behavior employed to attain a goal.

Meiosis Process of cell division that forms the gametes; normally results in twenty-three chromosomes in each human egg and sperm cell rather than the full complement of forty-six.

Memory span Number of stimulus items that can be recalled after a brief interval of time.

Memory strategy Mental activity, such as rehearsal, that enhances memory performance.

Menarche First occurrence of menstruation.

Mesosystem In Bronfenbrenner's ecological systems theory, the environment provided by the interrelationships among the various settings of the microsystem.

Meta-analysis Statistical examination of a body of research studies to assess the effect of the common central variable.

Metacognition Awareness and knowledge of cognitive processes.

Metalinguistic awareness Ability to reflect on language as a communication tool and on the self as a user of language.

Metamemory The child's understanding of his or her own memory.

Metaphor Figurative language in which a term is transferred from the object it customarily designates to describe a comparable object or event.

Microgenetic study A research approach in which close observations are made of the individual child's behavior from one trial to the next.

Microsystem In Bronfenbrenner's ecological systems theory, the immediate environment provided in such settings as the home, school, workplace, and neighborhood.

Mitosis Process of cell division that takes place in most cells of the human body and results in a full complement of identical material in the forty-six chromosomes in each cell.

Moral realism In Piaget's theory of moral development, the first stage of moral reasoning, in which moral judgments are made on the basis of the consequences of an act. Also called *heteronomy*.

Moral relativism In Piaget's theory of moral development, the second stage of moral reasoning, in which moral judgments are made on the basis of the actor's intentions. Also called *autonomy*.

Morality of care and responsibility Tendency to make moral judgments on the basis of concern for others.

Morality of justice Tendency to make moral judgments on the basis of reason and abstract principles of equity.

Morphology Rules of how to combine the smallest meaningful units of language to form words.

Motherese (parentese) Simple, repetitive, high-pitched speech of caregivers to young children; includes many questions.

Multistore model Name for many traditional information-processing models which posit several mental structures through which information flows.

Mutation Sudden change in molecular structure of a gene; may occur spontaneously or be caused by an environmental event such as radiation.

Mutual exclusivity bias Tendency for children to assume that unfamiliar words label new objects.

Myelin Sheath of fatty cells that insulates and speeds neural impulses by about tenfold.

Natural domain Concept or category that children acquire especially rapidly and effortlessly.

Naturalistic observation Study in which observations of naturally occurring behavior are made in real-life settings.

Nature-nurture debate Ongoing theoretical controversy over whether development is the result of the child's genetic endowment or environmental influences.

Negative correlation Relationship in which changes in one variable are accompanied by systematic changes in another variable in the opposite direction.

Negative punishment Removal or loss of a desired stimulus or reward, which weakens or decreases the frequency of a preceding response.

Negative reinforcement Removal of an aversive stimulus, which strengthens a preceding response.

Neuron Nerve cell within the central nervous system that is electrochemically designed to transmit messages between cells.

Niche picking Tendency to actively select an environment compatible with a genotype.

Nominal Word that labels objects, people, or events; the first type of word most children produce.

Norm Quantitative measure that provides typical values and variations in such characteristics as height and weight for children.

Nucleotide Repeating basic building block of DNA consisting of nitrogen-based molecules of adenine, thymine, cytosine, and guanine.

Object concept Realization that objects exist even when they are not within view. Also called *object permanence*.

Observational learning Learning that takes place by simply observing another person's behavior.

Observer bias Tendency of researchers to interpret ongoing events as being consistent with their research hypotheses.

One-to-one correspondence Understanding that two sets are equivalent in number if each element in one set can be mapped onto a unique element in the second set with none left over.

Operation In Piagetian theory, a mental action that allows a child to reason about events that have transpired.

Operational definition Specification of variables in terms of measurable properties.

Ordinality Principle that a number refers to an item's order within a set.

Organization In Piagetian theory, the inborn tendency for structures and processes to become more systematic and coherent; tendency to reorder items to fit some category or higher-order scheme.

Overextension Tendency to apply a label to a broader category than the term actually signifies.

Overregularization Inappropriate application of grammatical rules to words that require exceptions to those rules.

Parallel play Side-by-side, independent play that is not interactive.

Participant reactivity Tendency of individuals who know they are under observation to alter natural behavior.

Perception Process of organizing and interpreting sensory information.

Perceptual differentiation Process postulated by Eleanor and James Gibson in which experience contributes to the ability to make increasingly finer perceptual discriminations and to distinguish stimulation arising from each sensory modality.

Perinatal period Period beginning about the seventh month of pregnancy and continuing until about four weeks after birth.

Permissive parent Parent who sets few limits on the child's behavior.

Personal fable Belief that one is unique and perhaps even invulnerable.

Perspective taking Ability to take the role of another person and understand what that person is thinking, is feeling, or knows.

Phenotype Observable and measurable characteristics and traits of an individual; a product of the interaction of the genotype with the environment.

Phenylketonuria (PKU) Recessive genetic disorder in which phenylalanine, an amino acid, fails to be metabolized. Unless dietary changes are made to reduce intake of phenylalanine, severe mental retardation occurs.

Phoneme Smallest unit of sound that changes the meanings of words.

Phonology Fundamental sound units and combinations of units in a given language.

Placenta Support organ formed by cells from both blastocyst and uterine lining; serves as exchange site for oxygen, nutrients, and waste products.

Plasticity Capacity of immature systems, including regions of the brain and the individual neurons within those regions, to take on different functions as a result of experience.

Polygenic Phenotypic characteristic influenced by two or more genes.

Positive correlation Relationship in which changes in one variable are accompanied by systematic changes in another variable in the same direction.

Positive punishment Occurrence of an aversive stimulus that serves to weaken or decrease the frequency of a preceding response.

Positive reinforcement Occurrence of a stimulus that strengthens a preceding response. Also known as a *reward.*

Postconventional level In Kohlberg's theory, the third level of moral reasoning, in which laws are seen as the result of a social contract and individual principles of conscience may emerge.

Postnatal period Period in development following birth.

Power assertion Parental control technique that relies on the use of forceful commands, physical punishment, and removal of material objects or privileges.

Pragmatics Rules for using language effectively within a social context.

Preconventional level In Kohlberg's theory, the first level of moral reasoning, in which morality is motivated by the avoidance of punishments and attainment of rewards.

Prenatal development Period in development from conception to the onset of labor.

Preoperational stage In Piagetian theory, the second stage of development, from approximately two to seven years of age, in which thought becomes symbolic in form.

Prepared (natural) childbirth Type of childbirth that involves practicing procedures during pregnancy and childbirth that are designed to minimize pain and reduce the need for medication during delivery.

Primacy effect Tendency for individuals to display good recall for early items in a list.

Primary reinforcer Reward that gratifies biological need or drives.

Private speech Children's vocalized speech to themselves that directs behavior.

Processing speed Rapidity with which cognitive activities are carried out.

Productive language Meaningful language spoken or otherwise produced by an individual.

Prosocial behavior Positive social action performed to benefit others.

Prosody Patterns of intonation, stress, and rhythm that communicate meaning in speech.

Protodeclarative communication Use of a gesture to call attention to an object or event.

Protoimperative communication Use of a gesture to issue a command or request.

Proximodistal development Pattern in which organs and systems of the body near the middle tend to develop earlier than those near the periphery.

Psychometric model Model of intelligence based on the testing of large groups of individuals to quantify differences in abilities.

Psychosocial theory of development Erikson's theory that personality develops through eight stages of adaptive functioning to meet the demands framed by society.

Puberty Developmental period during which a sequence of physical changes takes place that transforms the person from an immature individual to one capable of reproduction.

Quasi-experiment Study in which researchers investigate the effects of independent variables that they do not manipulate themselves but that occur as a result of participants' natural experiences.

Questionnaire Set of standardized questions administered to participants in written form.

Random assignment Use of principles of chance to assign participants to treatment and control groups; avoids systematic bias.

Range of reaction Range of phenotypic differences possible as a result of different environments' interacting with a specific genotype.

Realism Inability to distinguish between mental and physical abilities.

Recall memory Ability to reproduce stimuli that one has previously encountered.

Recast Repetition of a child's utterance along with grammatical corrections.

Recency effect Tendency for individuals to show good recall for the last few items in a list.

Receptive aphasia Loss of the ability to comprehend speech.

Receptive language Ability to comprehend spoken speech.

Recessive allele Allele whose characteristics do not tend to be expressed when part of a heterozygous genotype. Its genetic characteristics tend to be masked by other alleles.

Recognition memory Ability to identify whether a stimulus has previously been encountered.

Recovery from habituation (dishabituation) Renewed response to a change in a stimulus, which indicates that the infant has detected that change.

Referential communication Communication in situations that require the child to describe an object to a listener or to evaluate the effectiveness of a message.

Referential style Type of early language production in which the child uses mostly nominals.

Reflex Involuntary reaction to touch, light, sound, and other kinds of stimulation.

Rehearsal Memory strategy that involves repetition of items to be remembered.

Reliability Degree to which a measure will yield the same results if administered repeatedly.

Representational insight The child's ability to understand that a symbol or model can stand for a real-life event.

Reunion behavior The child's style of greeting a caregiver after a separation.

Reversibility In Piagetian theory, the ability to mentally reverse or negate an action or a transformation.

Rhythmical stereotypy Repeated sequence of movements, such as leg kicking, hand waving, or head banging, that has no apparent goal.

Saccades Rapid eye movement to inspect an object or view a stimulus in the periphery of the visual field.

Scaffolding Temporary aid provided by one person to encourage, support, and assist a lesser-skilled person in carrying out a task or completing a problem. The model provides knowledge and skills that are learned and gradually transferred to the learner.

Scheme In Piagetian theory, the mental structure underlying a coordinated and systematic pattern of behaviors or thinking applied across similar objects or situations.

Scientific method Use of objective, measurable, and repeatable techniques to gather information.

Script Organized scheme or framework for commonly experienced events.

Secondary reinforcer Object or person that attains rewarding value because of its association with a primary reinforcer.

Secular trend Consistent pattern of change over generations.

Secure attachment Attachment category defined by the infant's distress at separation from the caregiver and enthusiastic greeting upon his or her return. The infant also displays stranger anxiety and uses the caregiver as a secure base for exploration.

Secure base An attachment behavior in which the infant explores the environment but periodically checks back with the caregiver.

Self-conscious emotion Emotion, such as guilt and envy, that appears later in childhood and requires more knowledge about the self as related to others.

Self-control Ability to comply with sociocultural prescriptions concerning ethical or moral behavior.

Self-esteem One's feelings of worth; extent to which one senses that one's attributes and actions are good, desired, and valued.

Self-regulation Process by which children come to control their own behaviors in accordance with the standards of their caregivers and community, especially in the absence of other adults.

Semantic bootstrapping hypothesis Idea that children derive information about syntax from the meaning of words.

Semantic memory Memory for general concepts or facts.

Semantics Meanings of words or combinations of words.

Sensation Basic information in the external world that is processed by the sensory receptors.

Sensitive period Brief period during which specific kinds of experiences have significant positive or negative consequences for development and behavior; also called *critical period.*

Sensorimotor stage In Piagetian theory, the first stage of cognitive development, from birth to approximately two years of age, in which thought is based primarily on action.

Sensory register Memory store that holds information for very brief periods of time in a form that closely resembles the initial input.

Separation anxiety Distress that the infant shows when the primary caregiver leaves the immediate environment.

Sequential study Study that examines groups of individuals of different ages over a period of time; usually shorter than a longitudinal study.

Sex segregation Clustering of individuals into same-sex groups.

Sex typicality Extent to which a behavior is usually associated with one sex as opposed to the other.

Shape bias The child's assumption that a new word labels an entire object, specifically its form.

Sickle cell disease Genetic blood disorder common in regions of Africa and other areas where malaria is found and among descendants of the people of these regions. Abnormal blood cells carry insufficient oxygen.

Sickle cell trait Symptoms shown by those possessing a heterozygous genotype for sickle cell anemia.

Single-case design Study that follows only one or a few participants over a period of time, with an emphasis on systematic collection of data.

Skeletal maturity Extent to which cartilage has ossified to form bone; provides the most accurate estimate of how much additional growth will take place in the individual.

Smooth visual pursuit Consistent, unbroken tracking by the eyes that serves to maintain focus on a moving visual target.

Social comparison Process in which individuals define themselves in relation to the skills, attributes, and qualities of others; an important contributor to self-concept during middle childhood.

Social convention Behavioral rules that regulate social interactions, such as dress codes and degrees of formality in speech.

Social learning theory Theoretical approach emphasizing the importance of learning through observation and imitation of behaviors modeled by others.

Social policy Programs and plans established by local, regional, or national public and private organizations and agencies designed to achieve a particular social purpose or goal.

Social pretend play Play that makes use of imaginary and symbolic objects and social roles, often enacted among several children. Also called *sociodramatic play.*

Social referencing Looking to another individual for emotional cues in interpreting a strange or ambiguous event.

Socialization Process by which children acquire the social knowledge, skills, and attitudes valued by the larger society.

Sociohistorical theory Vygotsky's developmental theory emphasizing the importance of cultural tools, symbols, and ways of thinking that the child acquires from more knowledgeable members of the community.

Sociometric nomination Peer assessment measure in which children are asked to name a specified number of peers who fit a certain criterion, such as "peers you would like to walk home with."

Sociometric rating scale Peer assessment measure in which children rate peers on a number of social dimensions.

Solitary play Individual play, performed without regard for what others are doing.

Sound localization Ability to determine a sound's point of origin.

Spermarche The first ejaculation of sperm by males entering puberty.

Stage Developmental period during which the organization of thought and behavior is qualitatively different from that of an earlier or later period.

Stereopsis The ability to fuse the two distinct images from the eyes to perceive a single object.

Stereotype threat The psychological impact of negative social stereotypes in an individual.

Strange Situation Standardized test that assesses the quality of infant-caregiver attachment.

Stranger anxiety Fear or distress that an infant shows at the approach of an unfamiliar person.

Structured interview Standardized set of questions administered orally to participants.

Structured observation Study in which behaviors are recorded as they occur within a situation constructed by the experimenter, usually in the laboratory.

Sudden infant death syndrome (SIDS) Sudden, unexplained death of an infant or a toddler as a result of cessation of breathing during sleep.

Syntax Grammatical rules that dictate how words can be combined.

Systems theory Model for understanding the family that emphasizes the reciprocal interactions among various members.

Telegraphic speech Early two-word speech that contains few modifiers, prepositions, or other connective words.

Temperament Stable, early-appearing constellation of individual personality attributes believed to have a hereditary basis; includes sociability, emotionality, and activity level.

Teratogen Any environmental agent that can cause deviations in prenatal development. Consequences may range from behavioral problems to death.

Test bias Idea that the content of traditional standardized tests does not adequately measure the competencies of children from diverse cultural backgrounds.

Theory Set of ideas or propositions that helps to organize or explain observable phenomena.

Theory of mind Awareness of the concept of mental states, both one's own and those of others.

Time-out Disciplinary technique that involves immediately removing a child from all possible sources of reward and leaving the child alone in a quiet, neutral place for a short time.

Triarchic theory Theory developed by Robert Sternberg that intelligence consists of three major components: (1) the ability to adapt to the environment, (2) the ability to employ fundamental information-processing skills, and (3) the ability to deal with novelty and automatize processing.

Trisomy Inheritance of an extra chromosome.

Turn taking Alternating vocalization by parent and child.

Turnabout Element of conversation that requests a response from the child.

Ultrasonography Method of using sound wave reflections to obtain a representation of the developing fetus; used to estimate gestational age and detect fetal physical abnormalities.

Umbilical cord Conduit of blood vessels through which oxygen, nutrients, and waste products are transported between placenta and embryo.

Unconditioned response (UCR) Response that is automatically elicited by the conditioned stimulus (CS).

Unconditioned stimulus (UCS) Stimulus that, without prior training, elicits a reflexlike response (unconditioned response).

Underextension Application of a label to a narrower class of objects than the term signifies.

Uninvolved parent Parent who is emotionally detached from the child and focuses on his or her own needs as opposed to the child's.

Validity Degree to which an assessment procedure actually measures the variable under consideration.

Variable Factor having no fixed or constant value in a given situation.

Vergence Ability of the eyes to rotate in opposite directions to fixate on objects at different distances; improves rapidly during first few months after birth.

Viability Ability of the baby to survive outside the mother's womb.

Visual accommodation Visuomotor process by which small involuntary muscles change the shape of the lens of the eye so that images of objects seen at different distances are brought into focus on the retina.

Visual acuity Ability to make fine discriminations among elements in a visual array by detecting contours, transitions in light patterns that signal borders and edges.

Visual cliff Experimental apparatus used to test depth perception, in which the surface on one side of a glass-covered table is made to appear far below the surface on the other side.

Vocabulary spurt Period of rapid word acquisition that typically occurs early in language development.

Wernicke's area Portion of the cerebral cortex that controls language comprehension.

Williams syndrome Dominant genetic disorder involving the deletion of a set of genes, which results in affected individuals' typically having a strong social orientation, good musical ability, and some unusual linguistic capabilities; accompanied by mental retardation and severe deficits in numerical and spatial ability.

Working memory Short-term memory store in which mental operations such as rehearsal and categorization take place.

X chromosome Larger of the two sex chromosomes associated with genetic determination of sex. Normally females have two X chromosomes and males, only one.

Y chromosome Smaller of the two sex chromosomes associated with genetic determination of sex. Normally males have one Y chromosome and females, none.

Zone of proximal development Range of various kinds of support and assistance provided by an expert (usually an adult) who helps children to carry out activities they currently cannot complete but will later be able to accomplish independently.

Zygote Fertilized egg cell.

References

Abbassi, V. (1998). Growth and normal puberty. *Pediatrics, 102, 507–511.*

Abel, E. L. (1989). *Behavioral teratogenesis and behavioral mutagenesis: A primer in abnormal development.* New York: Plenum Press.

Aboud, F. E., & Skerry, S. (1983). Self and ethnic concepts in relation to ethnic constancy. *Canadian Journal of Behavioral Science, 15,* 14–26.

Achenbach, T. M., Howell, C. T., Aoki, M. F., & Rauh, V. A. (1993). Nine-year outcome of the Vermont Intervention Program for Low Birth Weight Infants. *Pediatrics, 91,* 45–55.

Ackerman, B. P., Abe, J. A., & Izard, C. E. (1998). Differential emotions theory and emotional development. In M. F. Mascolo & S. Griffin (Eds.), *What develops in emotional development?* (pp. 85–106). New York: Plenum.

Acredolo, L. P., & Goodwyn, S. W. (1988). Symbolic gesturing in normal infants. *Child Development, 59,* 450–466.

Acredolo, L. P., & Goodwyn, S. W. (1990a). Sign language among hearing infants: The spontaneous development of symbolic gestures. In V. Volterra & C. J. Erting (Eds.), *From gesture to language in hearing and deaf children.* New York: Springer-Verlag.

Acredolo, L. P., & Goodwyn, S. W. (1990b). Sign language in babies: The significance of symbolic gesturing for understanding language development. In R. Vasta (Ed.), *Annals of child development* (Vol. 7, pp. 1–42). Greenwich, CT: JAI Press.

Acredolo, L. P., Pick, H. L., Jr., & Olsen, M. G. (1975). Environmental differentiation and familiarity as determinants of children's memory for spatial location. *Developmental Psychology, 11,* 495–501.

Adams, R. J., & Courage, M. L. (1998). Human newborn color vision: Measurement with chromatic stimuli varying in excitation purity. *Journal of Experimental Child Psychology, 68,* 22–34.

Adams, R., & Laursen, B. (2001). The organization and dynamics of adolescent conflict with parents and friends. *Journal of Marriage and the Family, 63,* 97–110.

Adams, S., Kuebli, J., Boyle, P. A., & Fivush, R. (1995). Gender differences in parent-child conversations about past emotions: A longitudinal investigation. *Sex Roles, 33,* 309–323.

Adi-Japha, E., & Freeman, N. H. (2001). Development of differentiation between writing and drawing systems. *Developmental Psychology, 37,* 101–114.

Adler, S. P. (1992). Cytomegalovirus and pregnancy. *Current Opinions in Obstetrics and Gynecology, 4,* 670–675.

Adoh, T. O., & Woodhouse, J. M. (1994). The Cardiff Acuity Test used for measuring visual acuity development in toddlers. *Vision Research, 34,* 555–560.

Adolph, K. E. (1997). Learning in the development of infant locomotion. *Monographs of the Society for Research in Child Development, 62*(3, Serial No. 251).

Adolph, K. E. (2000). Specificity of learning: Why infants fall over a veritable cliff. *Psychological Science, 11,* 290–295.

Adolph, K. E., Vereijken, B., & Denny, M. A. (1998). Learning to crawl. *Child Development, 69,* 1299–1312.

Adolph, K. E., Vereijken, B., & Shrout, P. E. (2003). What changes in infant walking and why. *Child Development, 74,* 475–497.

Agustines, L. A., Lin, Y. G., Rumney, P. J., Lu, M. C., Bonebrake, R., Asrat, T., & Nageotte, M. (2000). Outcomes of extremely low-birth-weight infants between 500 and 750 g. *American Journal of Obstetrics and Gynecology, 182,* 1114–1116.

Ahmed, A., & Ruffman, T. (1998). Why do infants make A not B errors in a search task, yet show memory for location of hidden objects in a nonsearch task? *Developmental Psychology, 34,* 441–453.

Ahnert, L., Rickert, H., & Lamb, M. E. (2000). Shared caregiving: Comparisons between home and child-care settings. *Developmental Psychology, 36,* 339–351.

Ainsworth, M. D. S., Bell, S. M., & Stayton, D. J. (1971). Individual differences in Strange Situation behavior of one-year-olds. In H. R. Schaffer (Ed.), *The Origins of human social relations.* London: Academic Press.

Ainsworth, M. D. S., Bell, S. M., & Stayton, D. J. (1972). Individual differences in the development of some attachment behaviors. *Merrill-Palmer Quarterly, 18,* 123–143.

Ainsworth, M. D. S., Bell, S. M., & Stayton, D. J. (1974). Infant-mother attachment and social development: "Socialization" as a product of reciprocal responsiveness to signals. In M. R. Richards (Ed.), *The integration of the child into a social world.* London: Cambridge University Press.

Ainsworth, M. D. S., Blehar, M. C., Waters, E., & Wall, S. (1978). *Patterns of attachment: A psychological study of the strange situation.* Hillsdale, NJ: Erlbaum.

Akhtar, N., Carpenter, M., & Tomasello, M. (1996). The role of discourse novelty in early word learning. *Child Development, 67,* 635–645.

Akhtar, N., Jipson, J., & Callanan, M. A. (2001). Learning words through overhearing. *Child Development, 72,* 416–430.

Aksan, N., & Kochanska, G. (2005). Conscience in childhood: Old questions, new answers. *Developmental Psychology, 41,* 506–516.

Alaimo, K., Olson, C. M., & Frongillo, E. A., Jr. (2001). Food insufficiency and American school-aged children's cognitive, academic, and psychosocial development. *Pediatrics, 108,* 44–53.

Alan Guttmacher Institute. (1993). *Facts in Brief, March* (pp. 1–2). Chicago: Alan Guttmacher Innstitute.

Alessandri, S. M., & Lewis, M. (1993). Parental evaluation and its relation to shame and pride in young children. *Sex Roles, 29,* 335–343.

Alexander, J. M., Carr, M., & Schwanenflugel, P. J. (1995). Development of metacognition in gifted children: Directions for future research. *Developmental Review, 15,* 1–37.

Alexander, K. L., & Entwisle, D. R. (1988). Achievement in the first 2 years of school: Patterns and processes. *Monographs of the Society for Research in Child Development, 53*(2, Serial No. 218).

Alexander, K. L., Entwisle, D. R., & Bedinger, S. D. (1994). When expectations work: Race and socioeconomic differences in school performance. *Social Psychology Quarterly, 57,* 283–299.

Alfieri, T., Ruble, D. N., & Higgins, E. T. (1996). Gender stereotypes during adolescence: Developmental changes and the transition to junior high school. *Developmental Psychology, 32,* 1129–1137.

Allaire, A. D. (2001). Complementary and alternative medicine in the labor and delivery suite. *Clinical Obstetrics and Gynecology, 44,* 681–691.

Allanson, J., & Graham, G. (2002). Sex chromosome abnormalities. In D. L. Rimoin, J. M. Connor, R. E. Pyeritz, & B. R. Korf (Eds.), *Emery and Rimoin's principles and practice of medical genetics* (4th ed., Vol. 1, pp. 1184–1201). London: Churchill Livingston.

Allen, J. P., & Land, D. (1999). Attachment in adolescence. In J. Cassidy & P. R. Shaver (Eds.), *Handbook of attachment: Theory, research, and clinical applications* (pp. 319–335). New York: Guilford.

Allen, J. P., McElhaney, K. B., Land, D. J., Kuperminc, G. P., Moore, C. W., O'Beirne-Kelly, H., & Kilmer, S. L. (2003). A secure base in adolescence: Markers of attachment security in the mother-adolescent relationship. *Child Development, 74,* 292–307.

Allen, J. P., Philliber, S., Herrling, S., & Kuperminc, G. P. (1997). Preventing teen pregnancy and academic failure: Experimental evaluation of a developmentally based approach. *Child Development, 64,* 729–742.

Allen, J. P., Porter, M. R., McFarland, F. C., Marsh, P., & McElhaney, K. B. (2005). The two faces of adolescents' success with peers: Adolescent popularity, social adaptation, and deviant behavior. *Child Development, 76,* 747–760.

Allwood, M. A., Bell-Dolan, D., & Husain, S. A. (2002). Children's trauma and adjustment reactions to violent and nonviolent war experiences.

Journal of the American Academy of Child and Adolescent Psychiatry, 41, 450–457.

Als, H., Lawhon, G., Duffy, F. H., McAnulty, G. B., Gibes-Grossman, R., Blickman, J. G. (1994). Individualized developmental care for the very low-birth-weight preterm infants: Medical and neurofunctional effects. *Journal of the American Medical Association, 272,* 853–858.

Alsaker, F. D. (1992). Pubertal timing, overweight, and psychological adjustment. *Journal of Early Adolescence, 12,* 396–419.

Altermatt, E. R., Pomerantz, E. M., Ruble, D. N., Frey, K., & Greulich, F. K. (2002). Predicting changes in children's self-perceptions of academic competence: A naturalistic examination of evaluative discourse among class mates. *Developmental Psychology, 38,* 903–917.

Alwitt, L. F., Anderson, D. R., Lorch, E. P., & Levin, S. R. (1980). Preschool children's visual attention to attributes of television. *Human Communication Research, 7,* 52–67.

Amato, P. R. (1999). Children of divorced parents as young adults. In E. M. Hetherington (Ed.), *Coping with divorce, single parenting, and remarriage* (pp. 147–163). Mahwah, NJ: Erlbaum.

Amato, P. R. (2001). Children of divorce in the 1990s: An update of the Amato and Keith (1990) meta-analysis. *Journal of Family Psychology, 15,* 355–370.

Amato, P. R., & Rezac, S. J. (1994). Contact with nonresident parents, in-terparental conflict, and children's behavior. *Journal of Family Issues, 15,* 191–207.

Ambady, N., Shih, M., Kim, A., & Pittinsky, T. L. (2001). Stereotype susceptibility in children: Effects of identity activation on quantitative performance. *Psychological Science, 12,* 385–390.

American Academy of Pediatrics Committee on Drugs. (2001). The transfer of drugs and other chemicals into human milk. *Pediatrics, 108,* 776–789.

American Academy of Pediatrics Committee on Environmental Health. (1997). Environmental tobacco smoke: A hazard to children. *Pediatrics, 99,* 639–642.

American Academy of Pediatrics Task Force on Infant Sleep Position and Sudden Infant Death Syndrome. (2000). Changing concept of sudden infant death syndrome: Implications for infant sleeping environment and sleep position. *Pediatrics, 105,* 650–656.

American Academy of Pediatrics, Committee on Substance Abuse and Committee on Children with Disabilities. (2000). Fetal alcohol syndrome and alcohol-related neurodevelopmental disorders. *Pediatrics, 106,* 358–361.

American Academy of Pediatrics. (2001). Developmental surveillance and screening of infants and young children. *Pediatrics, 108,* 192–196.

American Academy of Pediatrics. (2005). *AAP revises recommendations on reducing the risk of SIDS.* Retrieved May 12, 2006, from www.aap.org/ncepr/sids.htm.

American Association of University Women. (1992). *How schools shortchange girls.* Washington, DC: AAUW Educational Foundation.

American College of Obstetricians and Gynecologists Committee on Ethics. (2002). Sex selection. *Ethics in Obstetrics and Gynecology* (pp. 85–88). Washington, DC: The American College of Obstetricians and Gynecologists.

American College of Obstetricians and Gynecologists. (1994). Substance abuse in pregnancy. *ACOG Technical Bulletin No. 195.*

American Psychiatric Association. (1994). *Diagnostic and statistical manual of mental disorders* (4th ed.). Washington, DC.

American Psychiatric Association. (2000). *Diagnostic and statistical manual of mental disorders–TR* (4th ed.). Arlington, VA: Author.

American Psychiatric Association. (2002). *Fact sheet: Attention deficit/hyperactivity disorder.* Retrieved December 9, 2002, from www.psych.org/publicinfo/adhdfactsheet42401.pdf

Anand, K. J. S., and the International Evidence-Based Group for Neonatal Pain. (2001). Consensus statement for the prevention and management of pain in the newborn. *Archives of Pediatric and Adolescent Medicine, 155,* 173–180.

Andersen, R. E., Crespo, C. J., Bartlett, S. J., Cheskin, L. J., & Pratt, M. (1998). Relationship of physical activity and television watching with body weight and level of fatness among children: Results from the Third National Health and Nutrition Examination Survey. *Journal of the American Medical Association, 279,* 938–942.

Anderson, C. A., Berkowitz, L., Donnerstein, E., Huesmann, L. R., Johnson, J. D., Linz, D., et al. (2003). The influence of media violence on youth. *Psychological Science in the Public Interest, 4,* 81–110.

Anderson, D. R., & Burns, J. (1991). Paying attention to television. In J. Bryant & D. Zillmann (Eds.), *Responding to the screen: Reception and reaction processes* (pp. 3–25). Hillsdale, NJ: Erlbaum.

Anderson, D. R., Huston, A. C., Schmitt, K. L., Lineberger, D. L., & Wright, J. C. (2001). Early childhood television viewing and adolescent behavior: The recontact study. *Monographs of the Society for Research in Child Development, 66*(Serial No. 264).

Anderson, D. R., Lorch, E. P., Field, D. E., & Sanders, J. (1981). The effects of TV program comprehensibility on preschool children's television viewing behavior. *Child Development, 52,* 151–157.

Anderson, M., Kaufman, J., Simon, T. R., Barrios, L., Paulozzi, L., Ryan, G., et al. (2001). School-associated violent deaths in the United States, 1994–1999. *Journal of the American Medical Association, 286,* 2695–2702.

Andersson, B. (1992). Effects of day-care on cognitive and socioemotional competence of thirteen-year-old Swedish schoolchildren. *Child Development, 63,* 20–36.

Anglin, J. M. (1993). Vocabulary development: A morphological analysis. *Monographs of the Society for Research in Child Development, 59* (5, Serial No. 242).

Angoff, W. H. (1988). The nature-nurture debate: Aptitudes and group differences. *American Psychologist, 43,* 713–720.

Anisfeld, M. (1996). Only tongue protrusion modeling is matched by neonates. *Developmental Review, 16,* 149–161.

Annett, M. (1973). Laterality of childhood hemiplegia and the growth of speech and intelligence. *Cortex, 9,* 4–33.

Antell, S. E., & Keating, D. P. (1983). Perception of numerical invariance in neonates. *Child Development, 54,* 695–701.

Antill, J. K., Goodnow, J. J., Russell, G., & Cotton, S. (1996). The influence of parents and family context on children's involvement in household tasks. *Sex Roles, 34,* 215–236.

Antonov, A. N. (1947). Children born during the siege of Leningrad in 1942. *Journal of Pediatrics, 30,* 250–259.

Apgar, V. (1953). A proposal for a new method of evaluation of the newborn infant. *Anesthesia and Analgesia: Current Researches, 32,* 260–267.

Arend, R., Gove, F. L., & Sroufe, L. A. (1979). Continuity of individual adaptation from infancy to kindergarten: A predictive study of egoresiliency and curiosity in preschoolers. *Child Development, 50,* 950–959.

Ariès, P. (1962). *Centuries of childhood: A social history of family life* (R. Baldick, Trans.). New York: Vintage.

Arnett, J. J. (1999). Adolescent storm and stress, reconsidered. *American Psychologist, 54,* 317–326.

Arnold, D. S., & Whitehurst, G. J. (1994). Accelerating language development through picture book reading: A summary of dialogic reading and its effects. In D. K. Dickinson (Ed.), *Bridges to literacy: Children, families, and schools* (pp. 103–128). Cambridge, MA: Blackwell.

Aronfreed, J. (1976). Moral development from the standpoint of a general psychological theory. In T. Lickona (Ed.), *Moral development and moral behavior.* New York: Holt, Rinehart & Winston.

Arsenio, W. F., Cooperman, S., & Lover, A. (2000). Affective predictors of preschoolers' aggression and peer acceptance: Direct and indirect effects. *Developmental Psychology, 36,* 438–448.

Arsenio, W. F., & Ford, M. E. (1985). The role of affective information in social-cognitive development: Children's differentiation of moral and conventional events. *Merrill-Palmer Quarterly, 31,* 1–17.

Arsenio, W. F., & Lemerise, E. A. (2004). Aggression and moral development: Integrating social information processing and moral domain models. *Child Development, 75,* 987–1002.

Artigal, J. M. (1991). *The Catalan immersion program: A European point of view.* Norwood, NJ: Ablex.

Ary, D. V., Duncan, T. E., Biglan, A., Metzler, C. W., Noell, J. W., & Smolkowski, K. (1999). Development of adolescent problem behavior. *Journal of Abnormal Child Psychology, 27,* 141–150.

Asendorpf, J. B., & Baudonnière, P-M. (1993). Self-awareness and other-awareness: Mirror self-recognition and synchronic imitation among unfamiliar peers. *Developmental Psychology, 29,* 88–95.

Asher, S. R. (1983). Social competence and peer status: Recent advances and future directions. *Child Development, 54,* 1427–1434.

Asher, S. R., & Dodge, K. A. (1986). The identification of socially rejected children. *Developmental Psychology, 22,* 444–449.

Ashima-Takane, Y., Goodz, E., & Derevensky, J. L. (1996). Birth order effects on early language development: Do secondborn children learn from overheard speech? *Child Development, 67,* 621–634.

Ashley-Koch, A., Yang, Q., & Olney, R. S. (2000). Sickle hemoglobin (HbS) allele and sickle cell disease: A HuGE review. *American Journal of Epidemiology, 151,* 839–845.

Ashmead, D. H., Clifton, R. K., & Perris, E. E. (1987). Precision of auditory localization in human infants. *Developmental Psychology, 23,* 641–647.

Ashmead, D. H., Hill, E. W., & Talor, C. R. (1989). Obstacle perception by congenitally blind children. *Perception & Psychophysics, 46,* 425–433.

Aslin, R. N. (1987a). Motor aspects of visual development in infancy. In P. Salapatek & L. Cohen (Eds.), *Handbook of infant perception: From sensation to perception* (Vol. 1). Orlando, FL: Academic Press.

Aslin, R. N. (1987b). Visual and auditory development in infancy. In J. D. Osofsky (Ed.), *Handbook of infant development* (2nd ed., pp. 5–97). New York: Wiley.

Aslin, R. N. (1993). Perception of visual direction in human infants. In C. Granrud (Ed.), *Visual perception and cognition in infancy* (pp. 91–119). Hillsdale, NJ: Erlbaum.

Aslin, R. N. (2000). Why take the cog out of infant cognition? *Infancy, 1,* 463–470.

Aslin, R. N., & Smith, L. B. (1988). Perceptual development. *Annual Review of Psychology, 39,* 435–473.

Astington, J. W., Harris, P. L., & Olson, D. R. (1988). *Developing theories of mind.* New York: Cambridge University Press.

Atkinson, R. C., & Shiffrin, R. M. (1968). Human memory: A proposed system and its control processes. In K. W. Spence & J. T. Spence (Eds.), *The psychology of learning and motivation: Advances in research and theory* (Vol. 2, pp. 90–95). New York: Academic Press.

Au, T. K.-F., Knightly, L. M., Jun, S.-A., & Oh, J. S. (2002). Overhearing a language during childhood. *Psychological Science, 13,* 238–243.

Avenevoli, S., Sess, F. M., & Steinberg, L. (1999). Family structure, parenting practices, and adolescent adjustment: An ecological examination. In E. M. Hetherington (Ed.), *Coping with divorce, single parenting, and remarriage* (pp. 65–90). Mahwah, NJ: Erlbaum.

Aviezer, O., Sagi, A., Joels, T., & Ziv, Y. (1999). Emotional availability and attachment representations in kibbutz infants and their mothers. *Developmental Psychology, 35,* 811–821.

Avis, J., & Harris, P. L. (1991). Belief-desire reasoning among Baka children: Evidence for a universal conception of mind. *Child Development, 62,* 460–467.

Aylward, G. P., Pfeiffer, S. I., Wright, A., & Verhulst, S. J. (1989). Outcome studies of low birth weight infants published in the last decade: A metaanalysis. *Journal of Pediatrics, 115,* 515–520.

Bachevalier, J., Brickson, M., & Hagger, C. (1993). Limbic-dependent recognition memory in monkeys develops early in infancy. *Neuro Report, 4,* 77–80.

Bachevalier, J., Hagger, C., & Mishkin, M. (1991). Functional maturation of the occipitotemporal pathway in infant rhesus monkeys. In N. A. Lassen, D. H. Ingvar, M. E. Raichle, & L. Friberg (Eds.), *Brain work and mental activity* (pp. 231–240). Copenhagen: Munksgaard.

Backscheider, A. G., Shatz, M., & Gelman, S. A. (1993). Preschoolers' ability to distinguish living kinds as a function of regrowth. *Child Development, 64,* 1242–1257.

Bader, A. P., & Phillips, R. D. (1999). Father's proficiency at recognizing their newborns by tactile cues. *Infant Behavior and Development, 22,* 405–409.

Bagwell, C. L., Newcomb, A. F., & Bukowski, W. M. (1998). Preadolescent friendship and peer rejection as predictors of adult adjustment. *Child Development, 69,* 140–153.

Bahrick, L. E. (2002). Generalization of learning in three-and-a-half-month-old infants on the basis of amodal relations. *Child Development, 73,* 667–681.

Bahrick, L. E., & Lickliter, R. (2000). Intersensory redundancy guides attentional selectivity and perceptual learning in infancy. *Developmental Psychology, 36,* 190–201.

Bahrick, L. E., Netto, D., & Hernandez-Reif, M. (1998). Intermodal perception of adult and child faces and voices by infants. *Child Development, 69,* 1263–1275.

Baillargeon, R. (1987a). Object permanence in 31/2- and 41/2-month-old infants. *Developmental Psychology, 23,* 655–664.

Baillargeon, R. (1987b). Young children's reasoning about the physical and spatial characteristics of a hidden object. *Cognitive Development, 2,* 179–200.

Baillargeon, R. (1995). Physical reasoning in infancy. In M. S. Gazzaniga (Ed.), *The cognitive neurosciences* (pp. 181–204). Cambridge, MA: MIT Press.

Baillargeon, R. (2001). Infants' physical knowledge: Of acquired expectations and core principles. In E. Dupoux (Ed.), *Language, brain, and cognitive development: Essays in honor of Jacques Mehler* (pp. 341–361). Cambridge, MA: MIT Press.

Baillargeon, R., & DeVos, J. (1991). Object permanence in young infants: Further evidence. *Child Development, 62,* 1227–1246.

Baille, M.-F., Arnaud, C., Cans, C., Grandjean, H., du Mazaubrun, C., & Rumeau-Rouquette, C. (1996). Prevalence, aetiology, and care of severe and profound hearing loss. *Archives of Disease in Childhood, 75,* 129–132.

Baker-Sennett, J., Matusov, E., & Rogoff, B. (1993). Planning as a developmental process. In H. W. Reese (Ed.), *Advances in child development and behavior* (Vol. 24). San Diego, CA: Academic Press.

Balaban, M. T., Anderson, L. M., & Wisniewski, A. B. (1998). Lateral asymmetries in infant melody perception. *Developmental Psychology, 34,* 39–48.

Baldwin, J. M. (1930). [Autobiography]. In C. Murchison (Ed.), *A history of psychology in autobiography* (Vol. 1). Worcester, MA: Clark University Press.

Bales, D. W., & Sera, M. D. (1995). Preschoolers' understanding of stable and changeable characteristics. *Cognitive Development, 10,* 69–107.

Balint, J. P. (1998). Physical findings in nutritional deficiences. *Pediatric Clinics of North America, 45,* 245–260.

Ballard, B. D., Gipson, M. T., Guttenberg, W., & Ramsey, K. (1980). Palatability of food as a factor influencing obese and normal-weight children's eating habits. *Behavior Research and Therapy, 18,* 598–600.

Bandura, A. (1965). Vicarious processes: A case of no-trial learning. In L. Berkowitz (Ed.), *Advances in experimental social psychology* (Vol. 2, pp. 1–55). New York: Academic Press.

Bandura, A. (1969). *Principles of behavior modification.* New York: Holt, Rinehart & Winston.

Bandura, A. (1977a). Self-efficacy: Toward a unifying theory of behavioral change. *Psychological Review, 84,* 191–215.

Bandura, A. (1977b). *Social learning theory.* Englewood Cliffs, NJ: Prentice-Hall.

Bandura, A. (1986). *Social foundations of thought and action: A social cognitive theory.* Englewood Cliffs, NJ: Prentice-Hall.

Bandura, A. (1989). Social cognitive theory. In R. Vasta (Ed.), *Annals of child development: Vol. 6. Six theories of child development: Revised formulations and current issues* (pp. 1–60). Greenwich, CT: JAI Press.

Bandura, A., Barbaranelli, C., Caprara, G. V., & Pastorelli, C. (1996). Multifaceted impact of self-efficacy beliefs on academic functioning. *Child Development, 67,* 1206–1222.

Bandura, A., Barbaranelli, C., Caprara, G. V., & Pastorelli, C. (2001). Self-efficacy beliefs as shapers of children's aspirations and career trajectories. *Child Development, 72,* 187–206.

Bandura, A., Ross, D., & Ross, S. A. (1963a). Imitation of film-mediated aggressive models. *Journal of Abnormal and Social Psychology, 66,* 3–11.

Bandura, A., Ross, D., & Ross, S. A. (1963b). Vicarious reinforcement and imitative learning. *Journal of Abnormal and Social Psychology, 67,* 601–607.

Bandura, A., & Walters, R. H. (1959). *Adolescent aggression.* New York: Ronald Press.

Bandura, A., & Walters, R. H. (1963). *Social learning and personality development.* New York: Holt, Rinehart & Winston.

Banks, M. S., Aslin, R. N., & Letson, R. D. (1975). Sensitive period for the development of human binocular vision. *Science, 190,* 675–677.

Barber, B. K., & Harmon, E. L. (2002). Violating the self: Parental psychological control of children and adolescents. In B. K. Barber (Ed.), *Parental psychological control of children and adolescents* (pp. 15–52). Washington, DC: American Psychological Association.

Barber, B. L., & Eccles, J. S. (1992). Long-term influence of divorce and single-parenting on adolescent family- and work-related values, behaviors, and aspirations. *Psychological Bulletin, 111,* 108–126.

Barden, R. C., Zelko, F., Duncan, S. W., & Masters, J. C. (1980). Children's consensual knowledge about the experiential components of emotion. *Journal of Personality and Social Psychology, 39,* 968–976.

Barela, J. A., Jeka, J. J., & Clark, J. E. (1999). The use of somatosensory information during the acquisition of independent upright stance. *Infant Behavior and Development, 22,* 87–102.

Barkeling, B., Ekman, S., & Rössner, S. (1992). Eating behaviour in obese and normal weight 11-year-old children. *International Journal of Obesity, 16,* 355–360.

Barkley, R. A. (1997). *ADHD and the nature of self-control.* New York: Guilford Press.

Barnes, K. (1971). Preschool play norms: A replication. *Developmental Psychology, 5,* 99–103.

Barnhart, H. X., Caldwell, M. B., Thomas, P., Mascola, L., Ortiz, I., Hus, H. W., et al. (1996). Natural history of human immunodeficiency virus disease in perinatally infected children: An analysis from the Pediatric Spectrum of Disease Project. *Pediatrics, 97,* 710–716.

Baron-Cohen, S. (1995). *Mindblindness: An essay on autism and theory of mind.* Cambridge, MA: MIT Press.

Baron-Cohen, S., Tager-Flusberg, H., & Cohen, D. J. (1993). *Understanding other minds: Perspectives from autism.* New York: Oxford University Press.

Barr, R., Dowden, A., & Hayne, H. (1996). Developmental change in deferred imitation by 6- to 24-month-old infants. *Infant Behavior and Development, 19,* 159–170.

Barrett, K. C. (1998). A functionalist perspective to the development of emotions. In M. F. Mascolo & S. Griffin (Eds.), *What develops in emotional development?* (pp. 109–133). New York: Plenum.

Barrett, M. D. (1985). Issues in the study of children's single-word speech. In M. D. Barrett (Ed.), *Children's single-word speech.* Chichester, UK: Wiley.

Barrett, M. D. (1986). Early semantic representations and early word usage. In S. A. Kuczaj & M. D. Barrett (Eds.), *The development of word meaning.* New York: Springer-Verlag.

Barrett, M. D. (1989). Early language development. In A. Slater & G. Bremner (Eds.), *Infant development.* London: Erlbaum.

Barry, C. M., & Wentzel, K. R. (2006). Friend influence on prosocial behavior: The role of motivational factors and friendship characteristics. *Developmental Psychology, 42,* 153–163.

Barth, J. M. (1989, April). *Parent-child relationships and children's transition to school.* Paper presented at the biennial meeting of the Society for Research in Child Development, Kansas City, MO.

Bartlett, N. H., Vasey, P. L., & Bukowski, W. M. (2000). Is gender identity disorder in children a mental disorder? *Sex Roles, 43,* 753–785.

Baruch, C., & Drake, C. (1997). Tempo discrimination in infants. *Infant Behavior and Development, 20,* 573–577.

Basser, L. S. (1962). Hemiplegia of early onset and the faculty of speech with special reference to the effects of hemispherectomy. *Brain, 85,* 427–460.

Bates, E. (1979). *The emergence of symbols: Cognition and communication in infancy.* New York: Academic Press.

Bates, E., Bretherton, I., & Snyder, L. (1988). *From first words to grammar.* Cambridge, UK: Cambridge University Press.

Bates, E., Camaioni, L., & Volterra, V. (1975). The acquisition of performatives prior to speech. *Merrill-Palmer Quarterly, 21,* 205–224.

Bates, J., Marvinney, D., Kelly, T., Dodge, K., Bennett, T., & Pettit, G. (1994). Child-care history and kindergarten adjustment. *Developmental Psychology, 30,* 690–700.

Bates, J. E., Maslin, C. A., & Frankel, K. A. (1985). Attachment security, mother-child interaction, and temperament as predictors of behavior-problem ratings at age three years. In I. Bretherton & E. Waters (Eds.), *Growing points of attachment theory and research. Monographs of the Society for Research in Child Development, 50*(1–2, Serial No. 209).

Bauer, P. J. (1993). Memory for gender-consistent and gender-inconsistent event sequences by twenty-five-month-old children. *Child Development, 64,* 285–297.

Bauer, P. J. (2002). Long-term recall memory: Behavioral and neuro-developmental changes in the first 2 years of life. *Current Directions in Psychological Science, 11,* 137–141.

Bauer, P. J. (2004). Getting explicit memory off the ground: Steps toward construction of a neuro-developmental account of changes in the first two years of life. *Developmental Review, 24,* 347–373.

Bauer, P. J., Liebl, M., & Stennes, L. (1998). PRETTY is to DRESS as BRAVE is to SUITCOAT: Gender-based property-to-property inferences by 4-1/2-year-old children. *Merrill-Palmer Quarterly, 44,* 355–377.

Bauer, P. J., Wenner, J. A., Dropik, P. L., & Wewerka, S. S. (2000). Parameters of remembering and forgetting in the transition from infancy to early childhood. *Monographs of the Society for Research in Child Development, 65*(4, Serial No. 263).

Baumrind, D. (1971). Current patterns of parental authority. *Developmental Psychology Monographs, 4*(1, Pt. 2).

Baumrind, D. (1972). From each according to her ability. *School Review, 80,* 161–197.

Baumrind, D. (1991). The influence of parenting style on adolescent competence and substance abuse. *Journal of Early Adolescence, 11,* 56–94.

Baumrind, D. (1993). The average expectable environment is not good enough: A response to Scarr. *Child Development, 64,* 1299–1317.

Baumrind, D. (1996). Parenting: The discipline controversy revisited. *Family Relations, 45,* 405–414.

Baumrind, D., Larzelere, R. E., & Cowan, P. A. (2002). Ordinary physical punishment: Is it harmful? Comment on Gershoff (2002). *Psychological Bulletin, 128,* 580–589.

Bauserman, R. (2002). Child adjustment in joint-custody versus sole-custody arrangements: A meta-analytic review. *Journal of Family Psychology, 16,* 91–102.

Baydar, N., & Brooks-Gunn, J. (1991). Effects of maternal employment and child care arrangements on preschoolers' cognitive and behavioral outcomes: Evidence from the children of the National Longitudinal Survey of Youth. *Developmental Psychology, 27,* 932–945.

Bayley, N. (1993). *Bayley Scales of Infant Development* (2nd ed.). San Antonio: The Psychological Corporation.

Beauchamp, G. K., & Cowart, B. J. (1990). Preference for high salt concentrations among children. *Developmental Psychology, 26,* 539–545.

Beauchamp, G. K., & Moran, M. (1982). Dietary experience and sweet taste preferences in human infants. *Appetite, 3,* 139–152.

Beauchamp, T. L., Faden, R. R., Wallace, R. J., Jr., & Walters, L. (1982). *Ethical issues in social science research.* Baltimore, MD: Johns Hopkins University Press.

Beaudet, A. L., Scriver, C. R., Sly, W. S., & Valle, D. (2001). Genetics, biochemistry, and molecular bases of variant human phenoypes. In C. R. Scriver, A. L. Beaudet, W. S. Sly, & D. Valle (Eds.), *The metabolic and molecular bases of inherited disease* (8th ed., Vol. 1, pp. 3–45). New York: McGraw-Hill.

Beck, R. W., & Beck, S. H. (1989). The incidence of extended households among middle-aged black and white women. *Journal of Family Issues, 10,* 147–168.

Becker, A. B., Manfreda, J., Ferguson, A. C., Dimich-Ward, H., Watson, W. T. A., Chan-Yeung, M. (1999). Breast-feeding and environmental tobacco smoke exposure. *Archives of Pediatric and Adolescent Medicine, 153,* 689–691.

Becker, J. (1989). Preschoolers' use of number words to denote one-to-one correspondence. *Child Development, 60,* 1147–1157.

Beckett, K. (1995). Fetal rights and "crack moms": Pregnant women in the war on drugs. *Contemporary Drug Problems, 22,* 587–612.

Behl-Chadha, G. (1996). Basic-level and superordinate-like categorical representations in early infancy. *Cognition, 60,* 105–141.

Behne, T., Carpenter, M., Call, J., & Tomasello, M. (2005). Unwilling versus unable: Infants' understanding of intentional action. *Developmental Psychology, 41,* 328–337.

Behrman, R. E. (Ed.). (2000). Children and computer technology [Special issue]. *The Future of Children, 10*(2).

Beilin, H. (1989). Piagetian theory. In R. Vasta (Ed.), *Annals of child development: Vol. 6. Six theories of child development: Revised formulations and current issues.* Greenwich, CT: JAI Press.

Beilin, H., & Fireman, G. (1999). The foundation of Piaget's theories: Mental and physical action. *Advances in child development and behavior* (Vol. 27, pp. 221–246). San Diego: Academic Press.

Bell, M. A., & Fox, N. A. (1992). The relations between frontal brain electrical activity and cognitive development during infancy. *Child Development, 63,* 1142–1163.

Bell, R. Q. (1968). A reinterpretation of the direction of effects in studies of socialization. *Psychological Review, 75,* 81–95.

Bell, R. Q., & Harper, L. V. (1977). *Child effects on adults.* Hillsdale, NJ: Erlbaum.

Bell, S. M., & Ainsworth, M. D. S. (1972). Infant crying and maternal responsiveness. *Child Development, 43,* 1171–1190.

Belsky, J. (1980). Child maltreatment: An ecological integration. *American Psychologist, 35,* 320–335.

Belsky, J. (1981). Early human experience: A family perspective. *Developmental Psychology, 17,* 3–23.

Belsky, J. (1993). Etiology of child maltreatment: A developmental-ecological analysis. *Psychological Bulletin, 114,* 413–434.

Belsky, J. (1996). Parent, infant, and social-contextual antecedents of father-son attachment security. *Developmental Psychology, 32* 905–913.

Belsky, J., & Rovine, M. J. (1988). Nonmaternal care in the first year of life and the security of infant-parent attachment. *Child Development, 59,* 157–167.

Bem, S. L. (1981). Gender schema theory: A cognitive account of sex-typing. *Psychological Review, 88,* 354–364.

Bem, S. L. (1983). Gender schema theory and its implications for child development: Raising gender aschematic children in a gender schematic society. *Signs, 8,* 598–616.

Bempechat, J., & Drago-Severson, E. (1999). Cross-national differences in academic achievement: Beyond etic conceptions of children's understanding. *Review of Educational Research, 69,* 287–314.

Bender, B. G., Harmon, R. J., Linden, M. G., & Robinson, A. (1995). Psychosocial adaptation of 39 adolescents with sex chromosome abnormalities. *Pediatrics, 96,* 302–308.

Bendersky, M., & Lewis, M. (1999). Prenatal cocaine exposure and neonatal condition. *Infant Behavior and Development, 22,* 353–366.

Benenson, J., Apostoleris, N., & Parnass, J. (1997). Age and sex differences in dyadic and group interaction. *Developmental Psychology, 33,* 538–543.

Benenson, J. F., & Christakos, A. (2003). The greater fragility of females' versus males' closest same-sex friendships. *Child Development, 74,* 1123–1129.

Bennett, N. (1998). Annotation: Class size and the quality of educational outcomes. *Journal of Child Psychology and Psychiatry, 39,* 797–804.

Bennett, W. J. (1994). *The index of leading cultural indicators: Facts and figures on the state of American society.* New York: Simon & Schuster.

Bennetto, L., Pennington, B. F., & Rogers, S. J. (1996). Intact and impaired memory functions in autism. *Child Development, 67,* 1816–1835.

Benoit, D. (2000). Feeding disorders, failure to thrive, and obesity. In C. H. Zeanah, Jr. (Ed.), *Handbook of infant mental health* (2nd ed., pp. 339–352). New York: Guilford.

Benoit, D., & Parker, K. (1994). Stability and transmission of attachment across three generations. *Child Development, 65,* 1444–1456.

Benson, J. B. (1997). The development of planning: It's about time. In S. L. Friedman & E. K. Scholnick (Eds.), *The developmental psychology of planning: Why, how, and when do we plan?* (pp. 43–75). Mahwah, NJ: Erlbaum.

Benson, P. L., Mannes, M., Pittman, K., & Ferber, T. (2004). Youth development, developmental assets, and public policy. In R. M. Lerner & L. Steinberg (Eds.), *Handbook of adolescent psychology* (2nd ed., pp. 747–780). Hoboken, NJ: Wiley.

BenTsvi-Mayer, S., Hertz-Lazarowitz, R., & Safir, M. P. (1989). Teachers' selections of boys and girls as prominent pupils. *Sex Roles, 21,* 231–245.

Bercu, B. B. (1996). Growing conundrum: Growth hormone treatment of the non-growth hormone deficient child. *Journal of the American Medical Association, 276,* 567–568.

Bergin, D. A., Ford, M. E., & Hess, R. D. (1993). Patterns of motivation and social behavior associated with microcomputer use of young children. *Journal of Educational Psychology, 85,* 437–445.

Berk, L. E. (1986). Relationship of elementary school children's private speech to behavioral accompaniment to task, attention, and task performance. *Developmental Psychology, 22,* 671–680.

Berk, L. E. (1992). Children's private speech: An overview of theory and the status of research. In R. M. Diaz & L. E. Berk (Eds.), *Private speech: From social interaction to self-regulations.* Hillsdale, NJ: Erlbaum.

Berko, J. (1958). The child's learning of English morphology. *Word, 14,* 150–177.

Berndt, T. J. (1979). Developmental changes in conformity to peers and parents. *Developmental Psychology, 15,* 608–616.

Berndt, T. J. (1981). Relations between social cognition, nonsocial cognition, and social behavior: The case of friendship. In J. H. Flavell & L. D. Ross (Eds.), *Social cognitive development: Frontiers and possible futures.* Cambridge, UK: Cambridge University Press.

Berndt, T. J. (1999). Friends' influence on school adjustment. In W. A. Collins & B. Laursen (Eds.), *Minnesota Symposia on Child Psychology: Vol. 30. Relationships as developmental contexts* (pp. 85–107). Mahwah, NJ: Erlbaum.

Berndt, T. J., Hawkins, J. A., & Jiao, Z. (1999). Influences of friends and friendships on adjustment to junior high school. *Merrill-Palmer Quarterly, 45,* 13–41.

Berndt, T. J., & Keefe, K. (1995). Friends' influence on adolescents' adjustment to school. *Child Development, 66,* 1312–1329.

Bernstein, I. M., Mongeon, J. A., Badger, G. J., Solomon, L., Heil, S. H., & Higgins, S. T. (2005). Maternal smoking and its association with birth weight. *Obstetrics & Gynecology, 106,* 986–991.

Bertenthal, B. I. (1993). Infants' perception of biomechanical motions: Intrinsic image and knowledge-based constraints. In C. Granrud (Ed.), *Visual perception and cognition in infancy* (pp. 175–214). Hillsdale, NJ: Erlbaum.

Berthier, N. E. (1996). Learning to reach: A mathematical model. *Developmental Psychology, 32,* 811–823.

Berthier, N. E., DeBlois, S., Poirier, C. R., Novak, M. A., & Clifton, R. K. (2000). Where's the ball? Two- and three-year-olds reason about unseen events. *Developmental Psychology, 36,* 394–401.

Berthier, N. E., & Robin, D. J. (1998). Midreach correction in 7-month-olds. *Journal of Motor Behavior, 30,* 290–300.

Berthoud-Papandropoulou, I. (1978). An experimental study of children's ideas about language. In A. Sinclair, R. J. Jarvella, & W. J. M. Levelt (Eds.), *The child's conception of language.* Heidelberg: Springer-Verlag.

Betts, P. (2000) Which children should receive growth hormone treatment: Long term side effects possible with high doses. *Archives of Disease in Childhood, 83,*177–178.

Beyer, S. (1995). Maternal employment and children's academic achievement: Parenting styles as mediating variable. *Developmental Review, 15,* 212–253.

Bialystok, E. (1986). Factors in the growth of linguistic awareness. *Child Development, 57,* 498–510.

Bialystok, E. (1999). Cognitive complexity and attentional control in the bilingual mind. *Child Development, 70,* 636–644.

Bialystok, E. (2001). *Bilingualism in development: Language, literacy, and cognition.* Cambridge, UK: Cambridge University Press.

Bialystok, E., & Martin, M. M. (2004). Attention and inhibition in bilingual children: Evidence from the dimensional change card sort task. *Developmental Science, 7,* 325–339.

Biederman, J., Faraone, S. V., Keenan, K., Knee, D., & Tsuang, M. T. (1990). Family-genetic and psychosocial risk factors in DSM-III attention deficit disorder. *Journal of the American Academy of Child and Adolescent Psychiatry, 29,* 526–533.

Bierman, K. L., Smoot, D. L., & Aumiller, K. (1993). Characteristics of aggressive-rejected, aggressive (nonrejected), and rejected (nonaggressive) boys. *Child Development, 64,* 139–151.

Bigelow, A. E., & DeCoste, C. (2003). Sensitivity to social contingency from mothers and strangers in 2-, 4-, and 6-month-old infants. *Infancy, 4,* 111–140.

Bigelow, B. J., & LaGaipa, J. J. (1975). Children's written descriptions of friendship: A multidimensional analysis. *Developmental Psychology, 11,* 857–858.

Bigelow, B. J., Tesson, G., & Lewko, J. H. (1992). The social rules that children use: Close friends, other friends, and "other kids" compared to parents, teachers, and siblings. *International Journal of Behavioral Development, 15,* 315–335.

Bigler, R. S. (1995). The role of classification skill in moderating environmental effects on children's gender stereotyping: A study of the functional use of gender in the classroom. *Child Development, 66,* 1072–1087.

Bigler, R. S., Brown, C. S., & Markell, M. (2001). When groups are not created equal: Effects of group status on the formation of intergroup attitudes in children. *Child Development, 72,* 1151–1162.

Bigler, R. S., Jones, L. C., & Lobliner, D. B. (1997). Social categorization and the formation of intergroup attitudes in children. *Child Development, 68,* 530–543.

Bijou, S. W. (1989). Behavior analysis. In R. Vasta (Ed.), *Annals of child development: Vol 6. Six theories of child development: Revised formulations and current issues.* Greenwich, CT: JAI Press.

Biller, H. B. (1974). *Paternal deprivation: Family, school, sexuality and society.* Lexington, MA: Heath.

Billing, L., Eriksson, M., Jonsson, B., Steneroth, G., & Zetterström, R. (1994). The influence of environmental factors on behavioral problems in 8-year-old children exposed to amphetamine during fetal life. *Child Abuse & Neglect, 18,* 3–9.

Binet, A., & Simon, T. (1905). Méthodes nouvelles pour le diagnostic du niveau intellectuel des anormaux. *L'Anée Psychologique, 11,* 191–244.

Birch, L. L., & Davison, K. K. (2001). Family environmental factors influencing the developing behavioral controls of food intake and childhood overweight. *Pediatric Clinics of North America, 48,* 893–907.

Birdsong, D., & Molis, M. (2001). On evidence for maturational constraints in second-language acquisition. *Journal of Memory and Language, 44,* 235–249.

Biro, F. M., McMahon, R. P., Striegel-Moore, R., Crawford, P. B., Obarzanek, E., Morrison, J. A., et al. (2001). Impact of timing of pubertal maturation on growth in black and white female adolescents: The National Heart, Lung, and Blood Institute Growth and Health Study. *Journal of Pediatrics, 138,* 636–643.

Bivens, J. A., & Berk, L. E. (1990). A longitudinal study of the development of elementary school children's private speech. *Merrill-Palmer Quarterly, 36,* 443–463.

Bjorklund, D. F., & Harnishfeger, K. K. (1990). The resources construct in cognitive development: Diverse sources of evidence and a theory of inefficient inhibition. *Developmental Review, 10,* 48–71.

Bjorklund, D. F., Ornstein, P. A., & Haig, J. R. (1977). Development of organization and recall: Training in the use of organizational techniques. *Developmental Psychology, 13,* 175–183.

Bjorklund, D. F., & Rosenblum, K. E. (2002). Context effects in children's selection and use of simple arithmetic strategies. *Journal of Cognition and Development, 3,* 225–242.

Bjorkqvist, K. (1994). Sex differences in physical, verbal, and indirect aggression: A review of recent research. *Sex Roles, 30,* 177–188.

Black, B., & Logan, A. (1995). Links between communication patterns in mother-child, father-child, and child-peer interactions and children's social status. *Child Development, 66,* 255–271.

Black, M. M., Dubowitz, H., & Starr, R. H., Jr. (1999). African American fathers in low income, urban families: Development, behavior, and home environment of their three-year-old children. *Child Development, 70,* 967–978.

Black, M. M., & Rollins, H. A., Jr. (1982). The effects of instructional variables on young children's organization and recall. *Journal of Experimental Child Psychology, 33,* 1–19.

Blake, J. (1989). Number of siblings and educational attainment. *Science, 245,* 32–36.

Blasco, P. A. (1994). Primitive reflexes: Their contribution to the early detection of cerebral palsy. *Clinical Pediatrics, 33,* 388–397.

Blasi, A. (1980). Bridging moral cognition and moral action: A critical review of the literature. *Psychological Bulletin, 88,* 1–45.

Blasi, A., & Glodis, K. (1995). The development of identity: A critical analysis from the perspective of the self as subject. *Developmental Review, 15,* 404–433.

Blass, E. M., Ganchrow, J. R., & Steiner, J. E. (1984). Classical conditioning in newborn humans 2–48 hours of age. *Infant Behavior and Development, 7,* 223–235.

Block, J. H. (1971). *Lives through time.* Berkeley, CA: Bancroft Books.

Block, J. H. (1973). Conceptions of sex role: Some cross-cultural and longitudinal perspectives. *American Psychologist, 28,* 512–526.

Block, J. H. (1983). Differential premises arising from differential socialization of the sexes: Some conjectures. *Child Development, 54,* 1335–1354.

Block, J. H., & Robins, R. W. (1993). A longitudinal study of consistency and change in self-esteem from early adolescence to early adulthood. *Child Development, 64,* 909–923.

Bloom, B. S. (1982). The role of gifts and markers in the development of talent. *Exceptional Children, 48,* 510–522.

Bloom, L. (1973). *One word at a time.* The Hague: Mouton.

Bloom, L. (1991). *Language development from two to three.* Cambridge, UK: Cambridge University Press.

Bloom, L. (1998). Language acquisition in its developmental context. In W. Damon (Series Ed.) & D. Kuhn & R. S. Siegler (Vol. Eds.), *Handbook of child psychology: Vol. 2: Cognition, perception, and language.* (5th ed., pp. 309–370). New York: Wiley.

Bloom, L., Lightbown, P., & Hood, L. (1975). Structure and variation in child language and the acquisition of grammatical morphemes. *Monographs of the Society for Research in Child Development, 40* (2, Serial No. 160).

Bloom, P. (1990). Syntactic distinctions in child language. *Journal of Child Language, 17,* 343–355.

Bloom, P. (2000). *How children learn the meanings of words.* Cambridge, MA: MIT Press.

Blosser, B. J., & Roberts, D. F. (1985). Age differences in children's perceptions of message intent: Responses to TV news, commercials, educational spots, and public service announcements. *Communication Research, 4,* 455–484.

Bock, J. K., & Hornsby, M. E. (1981). The development of directives: How children ask and tell. *Journal of Child Language, 8,* 151–163.

Boehnke, K., Silbereisen, R. K., Eisenberg, N., Reykowski, J., & Palmonari, A. (1989). Developmental pattern of prosocial motivation: A cross-national study. *Journal of Cross-Cultural Psychology, 20,* 219–243.

Bogartz, R. S., Shinskey, J. L., & Schilling, T., H. (2000). Object permanence in five-and-a-half-month-olds? *Infancy, 1,* 403–428.

Bogatz, G., & Ball, S. (1972). *The second year of Sesame Street: A continuing evaluation.* Princeton, NJ: Educational Testing Service.

Bogenschneider, K., Wu, M., Raffaeilli, M., & Tsay, J. C. (1998). Parent influences on adolescent peer orientation and substance abuse: The interface of parenting practices and values. *Child Development, 69,* 1672–1688.

Boggiano, A. K., Shields, A., Barrett, M., Kellam, T., Thompson, E., Simons, J., & Katz, P. (1992). Helplessness deficits in students: The role of motivation orientation. *Motivation and Emotion, 16,* 271–296.

Boivin, M., & Hymel, S. (1997). Peer experiences and social self-perceptions: A sequential model. *Developmental Psychology, 33,* 135–145.

Bongaerts, T. (1999). Ultimate attainment in foreign language pronunciation: The case of very advanced foreign language learners. In D. Birdsong (Ed.), *Second language acquisition and the critical period hypothesis* (pp. 133–159). Mahwah, NJ: Erlbaum.

Bookstein, F. L., Sampson, P. D., Streissguth, A. P., & Barr, H. M. (1996). Exploiting redundant measure of dose and developmental outcome: New methods from the behavioral teratology of alcohol. *Developmental Psychology, 32,* 404–415.

Boom, J., Brugman, D., & van der Heijden, P. G. M. (2001). Hierarchical structure of moral stages assessed by a sorting task. *Child Development, 72,* 535–548.

Booth, C. L., Rose-Krasnor, L., McKinnon, J., & Rubin, K. H. (1995). Predicting social adjustment in middle childhood: The role of preschool attachment security and maternal style. *Social Development, 3,* 189–204.

Borke, H. (1973). The development of empathy in Chinese and American children between three and six years of age: A cross-culture study. *Developmental Psychology, 9,* 102–108.

Borke, H. (1975). Piaget's mountains revisited: Changes in the egocentric landscape. *Developmental Psychology, 11,* 240–243.

Bornstein, M. H., Haynes, O. M., Pascual, L., Painter, K. M., & Galperín, C. (1999). Play in two societies: Pervasiveness of process, specificity of structure. *Child Development, 70,* 317–331.

Bornstein, M. H., Tal, J., Rahn, C., Galperín, G. Z., Pêcheux, M., Lamour, M., et al. (1992). Functional analysis of the contents of maternal speech to infants of 5 and 13 months in four cultures: Argentina, France, Japan, and the United States. *Developmental Psychology, 28,* 593–603.

Borstelmann, L. J. (1983). Children before psychology: Ideas about children from antiquity to the late 1800s. In W. Kessen (Ed.), *Handbook of child psychology: Vol. I. History, theory, and methods* (4th ed., pp. 1–40). New York: Wiley.

Bortfeld, H., Morgan, J. L., Golinkoff, R. M., & Rathbun, K. (2005). Mommy and me: Familiar names help launch babies into speech-stream segmentation. *Psychological Science, 16,* 298–304.

Bosma, H. A., & Kunnen, E. S. (2001). Determinants and mechanisms in ego identity development: A review and synthesis. *Developmental Review, 21,* 39–66.

Bouchard, T. J., Jr. (1984). Twins reared together and apart: What they tell us about human diversity. In S. W. Fox (Ed.), *Individuality and determinism: Chemical and biological bases.* New York: Plenum Press.

Bouchard, T. J., Jr. (1997). IQ similarity in twins reared apart: Findings and responses to critics. In R. J. Sternberg & E. Grigorenko (Eds.), *Intelligence, heredity and environment* (pp. 126–160). New York: Cambridge University Press.

Bouchard, T. J., Jr., Lykken, D. T., McGue, M., Segal, N. L., & Tellegen, A. (1990). Sources of human psychological differences: The Minnesota Study of Twins Reared Apart. *Science, 250,* 223–228.

Boulton, M. J., & Underwood, K. (1992). Bully/victim problems among middle school children. *British Journal of Educational Psychology, 62,* 73–87.

Bowerman, M. (1978). The acquisition of word meaning: An investigation of some current conflicts. In N. Waterson & C. Snow (Eds.), *The development of communication.* New York: Wiley.

Bowlby, J. (1958). The nature of the child's tie to his mother. *International Journal of Psychoanalysis, 39,* 350–373.

Bowlby, J. (1969). *Attachment and loss: Vol. 1. Attachment.* New York: Basic Books.

Bowlby, J. (1973). *Attachment and loss. Vol. 2. Separation: Anxiety and anger.* New York: Basic Books.

Boyes, M. C., & Allen, S. G. (1993). Styles of parent-child interaction and moral reasoning in adolescence. *Merrill-Palmer Quarterly, 39,* 551–570.

Boykin, A. W. (1986). The triple quandary and the schooling of Afro-American children. In U. Neisser (Ed.), *The school achievement of minority children: New perspectives.* Hillsdale, NJ: Erlbaum.

Boysson-Bardies, B. de, Halle, P., Sagart, L., & Durand, C. (1989). A cross-linguistic investigation of vowel formants in babbling. *Journal of Child Language, 16,* 1–17.

Brackbill, Y. (1975). Continuous stimulation and arousal level in infancy: Effects of stimulus intensity and stress. *Child Development, 46,* 364–369.

Brackbill, Y., McManus, K., & Woodward, L. (1985). *Medication in maternity: Infant exposure and maternal information.* Ann Arbor: University of Michigan Press.

Bradbard, M. R., Martin, C. L., Endsley, R. C., & Halverson, C. F. (1986). Influence of sex stereotypes on children's exploration and memory: A competence versus performance distinction. *Developmental Psychology, 22,* 481–486.

Bradley, R. H. (1989). The use of the HOME inventory in longitudinal studies of child development. In M. H. Bornstein & N. A. Krasnegor (Eds.), *Stability and continuity in mental development: Behavioral and biological perspectives.* Hillsdale, NJ: Erlbaum.

Bradley, R. H., & Caldwell, B. M. (1976). The relation of infants' home environments to mental test performance at fifty-four months: A follow-up study. *Child Development, 47,* 1172–1174.

Bradley, R. H., & Caldwell, B. M. (1984). The relation of infants' home environments to achievement test performance in first grade: A follow-up study. *Child Development, 55,* 803–809.

Braine, M. D. S. (1976). Children's first word combinations. *Monographs of the Society for Research in Child Development, 41*(1, Serial No. 164).

Brainerd, C. J. (1996). Piaget: A centennial celebration. *Psychological Science, 7,* 191–195.

Brainerd, C. J., & Gordon, L. L. (1994). Development of verbatim and gist memory for numbers. *Developmental Psychology, 30,* 163–177.

Brainerd, C. J., & Mojardin, A. H. (1998). Children's and adults' spontaneous false memories: Long-term persistence and mere-testing effects. *Child Development, 69,* 1361–1377.

Bramlett, M. D., & Mosher, W. D. (2001). *First marriage dissolution, divorce, and remarriage: United States* (Advance Data from Vital and Health Statistics No. 323). Hyattsville, MD: National Center for Health Statistics.

Brand, E., Clingempeel, W. E., & Bowen-Woodward, K. (1988). Family relationships and children's psychological adjustment in stepmother and stepfather families: Findings and conclusions from the Philadelphia Stepfamily Research Project. In E. M. Hetherington & J. D. Arasteh (Eds.), *Impact of divorce, single-parenting, and stepparenting on children* (pp. 299–324). Hillsdale, NJ: Erlbaum.

Brand, J. E., & Greenberg, B. S. (1994). Commercials in the classroom: The impact of Channel One advertising. *Journal of Advertising Research, 34,* 18–27.

Bray, J. H. (1988). Children's development during early remarriage. In E. M. Hetherington & J. D. Arasteh (Eds.), *Impact of divorce, single parenting, and stepparenting on children* (pp. 279–298). Hillsdale, NJ: Erlbaum.

Bray, J. H. (1999). From marriage to remarriage and beyond: Findings from the Developmental Issues in Stepfamilies Research Project. In E. M. Hetherington (Ed.), *Coping with divorce, single parenting, and remarriage* (pp. 253–271). Mahwah, NJ: Erlbaum.

Brazelton, T. B. (1973). *Neonatal Behavioral Assessment Scale.* Philadelphia: J. B. Lippincott.

Brazelton, T. B., Nugent, K. J., & Lester, B. M. (1987). Neonatal Behavioral Assessment Scale. In J. D. Osofsky (Ed.), *Handbook of infant development* (2nd ed., pp. 780–817). New York: Wiley.

Breedlove, S. M. (1994). Sexual differentiation of the human nervous system. *Annual Review of Psychology, 45,* 389–418.

Bregman, J. (1998). Developmental outcome in very low birthweight infants: Current status and future trends. *Pediatric Clinics of North America, 45,* 673–690.

Bremner, A., & Bryant, P. (2001). The effect of spatial cues on infants' responses in the AB task, with and without a hidden object. *Developmental Science, 4,* 408–415.

Bremner, J. D. (1999). Does stress damage the brain? *Biological Psychiatry, 45,* 797–805.

Bremner, J. D., & Narayan, M. (1998). The effects of stress on memory and the hippocampus throughout the life cycle: Implications for childhood development and aging. *Development and Psychopathology, 10,* 871–885.

Bremner, J. G. (1978). Egocentric versus allocentric spatial coding in nine-month-old infants: Factors influencing the choice of code. *Developmental Psychology, 14,* 346–355.

Bremner, J. G. (1998). From perception to action: The early development of knowledge. In F. Simion & G. Butterworth (Eds.), *The development of sensory, motor and cognitive capacities in early infancy* (pp. 239–255). East Sussex, England: Psychology Press.

Bremner, J. G., & Bryant, P. E. (1977). Place versus response as the basis for spatial errors made by young infants. *Journal of Experimental Child Psychology, 23,* 162–171.

Brendgen, M., Dionne, G., Girard, A., Boivin, M., Vitaro, F., & Pérusse, D. (2005). Examining genetic and environmental effects on social aggression: A study of 6-year-old twins. *Child Development, 76,* 930–946.

Brenner, R. A., Simons-Morton, B. G., Bhaskar, B., Mehta, N., Melnick, V., Revenis, M., et al. (1998). Prevalence and predictors of the prone sleep position among inner-city infants. *Journal of the American Medical Association, 280,* 341–346.

Bretherton, I., & Beeghly, M. (1982). Talking about internal states: The acquisition of an explicit theory of mind. *Developmental Psychology, 18,* 906–921.

Breznitz, Z., & Teltsch, T. (1989). The effect of school entrance age on academic achievement and social-emotional adjustment of children: Follow-up study of fourth graders. *Psychology in the Schools, 26,* 62–68.

Brisk, M. (1998). *Bilingual education: From compensatory to quality schooling.* Mahwah, NJ: Erlbaum.

Broberg, A. G., Wessels, H., Lamb, M. E., & Hwang, C. P. (1997). Effects of day care on the development of cognitive abilities in 8-year-olds: A longitudinal study. *Developmental Psychology, 33,* 62–69.

Brody, E. B., & Brody, N. (1976). *Intelligence: Nature, determinants, and consequences.* New York: Academic Press.

Brody, G. H. (2004). Siblings' direct and indirect contributions to child development. *Current Directions in Psychological Science, 13,* 124–126.

Brody, G. H., & Flor, D. L. (1998). Maternal resources, parenting practices, and child competence in rural, single-parent African American families. *Child Development, 69,* 803–816.

Brody, G. H., Flor, D. L., & Gibson, N. M. (1999). Linking maternal efficacy beliefs, developmental goals, parenting practices, and child competence in rural single-parent African American families. *Child Development, 70,* 1197–1208.

Brody, G. H., Ge, X., Conger, R., Gibbons, F. X., Murry, V. M., Gerrard, M., & Simons, R. L. (2001). The influence of neighborhood disadvantage, collective socialization, and parenting on African American children's affiliation with deviant peers. *Child Development, 72,* 1231–1246.

Brody, G. H., Kim, S., Murry, V. M., & Brown, A. C. (2003). Longitudinal direct and indirect pathways linking older sibling competence to the development of younger sibling competence. *Developmental Psychology, 39,* 618–628.

Brody, G. H., & Stoneman, Z. (1994). Sibling relationships and their association with parental differential treatment. In E. M. Hetherington, D. Reiss, & R. Plomin (Eds.), *Separate social worlds of siblings* (pp. 129–142). Hillsdale, NJ: Erlbaum.

Brody, G. H., Stoneman, Z., & Flor, D. (1996). Parental religiosity, family processes, and youth competence in rural, two-parent African American families. *Developmental Psychology, 32,* 696–706.

Brody, G. H., Stoneman, Z., & McCoy, J. K. (1992). Associations of maternal and paternal direct and differential behavior with sibling relationships: Contemporaneous and longitudinal analyses. *Child Development, 63,* 82–92.

Brody, N. (1992). *Intelligence* (2nd ed.). San Diego: Academic Press.

Brodzinsky, D. M., Schecter, D. E., Braff, A. M., & Singer, L. M. (1984). Psychological and academic adjustment in adopted children. *Journal of Consulting and Clinical Psychology, 52,* 582–590.

Bronfenbrenner, U. (1977). Toward an experimental ecology of human development. *American Psychologist, 32,* 513–531.

Bronfenbrenner, U. (1986). Ecology of the family as a context for human development: Research perspectives. *Developmental Psychology, 22,* 723–742.

Bronfenbrenner, U. (1989). Ecological systems theory. In R. Vasta (Ed.), *Annals of child development: Vol 6. Six theories of child development: Revised formulations and current issues* (pp. 187–251). Greenwich, CT: JAI Press.

Bronfenbrenner, U. (1995). Developmental ecology through space and time: A future perspective. In P. Moen, G. H. Elder, & K. Luescher (Eds.), *Examining lives in context: Perspectives on the ecology of human development* (pp. 619–647). Washington, DC: American Psychological Association.

Bronson, G. W. (1994). Infants' transitions toward adult-like scanning. *Child Development, 65,* 1243–1261.

Bronson, W. (1981). Toddlers' behavior with age-mates: Issues of interaction, cognition, and affect. In L. Lipsitt (Ed.), *Monographs on infancy* (Vol. 1). Norwood, NJ: Ablex.

Brook, C. G. D. (2000). Which children should receive growth hormone treatment: Reserve it for the GH deficient. *Archives of Disease in Childhood, 83,* 176.

Brookmeyer, K. A., Henrich, C. C., & Schwab-Stone, M. (2005). Adolescents who witness community violence: Can parent support and prosocial cognitions protect them from committing violence? *Child Development, 76,* 917–929.

Brooks, P. J., & Tomasello, M. (1999). Young children learn to produce passives with nonce verbs. *Developmental Psychology, 35,* 29–44.

Brooks, R. B. (1992). Self-esteem during the school years: Its normal development and hazardous decline. *Pediatric Clinics of North America, 39,* 537–550.

Brooks, R., & Meltzoff, A. N. (2000). The importance of eyes: How infants interpret adult looking behavior. *Developmental Psychology, 38,* 958–966.

Brooks-Gunn, J. (1989). Pubertal processes and the early adolescent transition. In W. Damon (Ed.), *Child development today and tomorrow.* San Francisco: Jossey-Bass.

Brooks-Gunn, J., & Chase-Lansdale, P. L. (1995). Adolescent parenthood. In M. H. Bornstein (Ed.), *Handbook of parenting: Vol. 3. Status and social conditions of parenting* (pp. 113–149). Mahwah, NJ: Erlbaum.

Brooks-Gunn, J., Han, W. J., & Waldfogel, J. (2002). Maternal employment and child cognitive outcomes in the first three years of life: The NICHD study of early child care. *Child Development, 73,* 1052–1072.

Brooks-Gunn, J., Klebanov, P. K., & Duncan, G. J. (1996). Ethnic differences in children's intelligence test scores: Role of economic deprivation, home environment, and maternal characteristics. *Child Development, 67,* 396–408.

Brooks-Gunn, J., Klebanov, P. K., Liaw, F., & Spiker, D. (1993). Enhancing the development of low-birthweight, premature infants: Changes in cognition and behavior over the first three years. *Child Development, 64,* 736–754.

Brooks-Gunn, J., & Ruble, D. (1980). Menarche: The interaction of physiology, cultural, and social factors. In A. J. Dan, E. A. Graham, & C. P. Beecher (Eds.), *The menstrual cycle: A synthesis of interdisciplinary research* (pp. 141–159). New York: Springer-Verlag.

Brooks-Gunn, J., & Warren, M. P. (1989). Biological and social contributions to negative affect in young adolescent girls. *Child Development, 60,* 40–55.

Brophy, J. (1986). Teacher influences on student achievement. *American Psychologist, 41,* 1069–1077.

Brown, A. L., Kane, M. J., & Echols, C. H. (1986). Young children's mental models determine analogical transfer across problems with a common goal structure. *Cognitive Development, 1,* 103–121.

Brown, B. B. (1989). The role of peer groups in adolescents' adjustment to secondary school. In T. J. Berndt & G. W. Ladd (Eds.), *Peer relationships in child development.* New York: Wiley.

Brown, B. B., Clasen, D. R., & Eicher, S. A. (1986). Perceptions of peer pressure, peer conformity dispositions, and self-reported behavior among adolescents. *Developmental Psychology, 22,* 521–530.

Brown, B. B., Mounts, N., Lamborn, S. D., & Steinberg, L. (1993). Parenting practices and peer group affiliation in adolescence. *Child Development, 64,* 467–482.

Brown, J. D., L'Engle, K. L., Pardun, C. J., Guo, G., Kenneavy, K., & Jackson, C. (2006). Sexy media matter: Exposure to sexual content in music, movies, television, and magazines predicts Black and White adolescents' sexual behavior. *Pediatrics, 117,* 1018–1027.

Brown, J. L., & Pollitt, E. (1996, February). Malnutrition, poverty and intellectual development. *Scientific American, 274,* 38–43.

Brown, J. R., & Dunn, J. (1996). Continuities in emotion understanding from three to six years. *Child Development, 67,* 789–802.

Brown, L. K., Lourie, K. J., & Pao, M. (2000). Children and adolescents living with HIV and AIDS: A review. *Journal of Child Psychology and Psychiatry, 41,* 81–96.

Brown, M. L. (2001). The effects of environmental tobacco smoke on children: Information and implications for PNPs. *Journal of Pediatric Health Care, 15,* 280–286.

Brown, P. J., & Konner, M. (1987). An anthropological perspective on obesity. *Annals of the New York Academy of Sciences, 499,* 29–46.

Brown, R. (1973). *A first language: The early stages.* Cambridge, MA: Harvard University Press.

Bruck, K. (1962). Temperature regulation in the newborn infant. *Biological Neonatorum, 3,* 65–119.

Bruck, M., & Ceci, S. J. (1999). The suggestibility of children's memory. *Annual Review of Psychology, 50,* 419–439.

Bruck, M., & Ceci, S. (2004). Forensic developmental psychology. *Current Directions in Psychological Science, 13,* 229–232.

Bruer, J. T. (1999). *The myth of the first three years.* New York: Free Press.

Bruer, J. T. (2001). A critical and sensitive period primer. In D. B. Bailey, J. T. Bruer, F. J. Symons, & J. W. Lichtman (Eds.), *Critical thinking about critical periods* (pp. 3–26). Baltimore, MD: Brookes.

Bruner, J. S. (1981). Intention in the structure of action and interaction. In L. P. Lipsitt (Ed.), *Advances in infancy research* (Vol. 1, pp. 41–56). Norwood, NJ: Ablex.

Bruner, J. S. (1983). *Child's talk: Learning to use language.* New York: W. W. Norton.

Bryant-Waugh, R., & Lask, B. (1995). Annotation: Eating disorders in children. *Journal of Child Psychology and Psychiatry, 36,* 191–202.

Buchanan, C. M., Maccoby, E. E., & Dornbusch, S. M. (1991). Caught between parents: Adolescents' experience in divorced homes. *Child Development, 62,* 1008–1029.

Bugental, D. B., Blue, J. B., & Cruzcosa, M. (1989). Perceived control over caregiving outcomes: Implications for child abuse. *Developmental Psychology, 25,* 532–539.

Bugental, D., & Happaney, K. (2004). Predicting infant maltreatment in low-income families: The interactive effects of maternal attributions and child status at birth. *Developmental Psychology, 40,* 234–243.

Bugental, D. B., & Lewis, J. (1998). Interpersonal power repair in response to threats to control from dependent others. In M. Kofta, G. Weary, & G. Sedek (Eds.), *Personal control in action: Cognitive and motivational mechanisms* (pp. 341–362). New York: Plenum.

Bugental, D. B., Lyon, J. E., Krantz, J., & Cortez, V. (1997). Who's the boss? Accessibility of dominance ideation among individuals with low perceptions of interpersonal power. *Journal of Personality and Social Psychology, 72,* 1297–1309.

Bugental, D. B., Lyon, J. E., Lin, E. K., McGrath, E. P., & Bimbela, A. (1999). Children "tune out" in response to the ambiguous communication styles of powerless adults. *Child Development, 70,* 214–230.

Buhrmester, D. (1990). Intimacy of friendship, interpersonal competence, and adjustment during preadolescence and adolescence. *Child Development, 61,* 1101–1111.

Buhrmester, D., & Furman, W. (1987). The development of companionship and intimacy. *Child Development, 58,* 1101–1113.

Buhrmester, D., & Furman, W. (1990). Perceptions of sibling relationships during middle childhood and adolescence. *Child Development, 61,* 1387–1398.

Buhs, E. S., & Ladd, G. W. (2001). Peer rejection as an antecedent of young children's school adjustment: An examination of mediating processes. *Developmental Psychology, 37,* 550–560.

Buitendijk, S., & Bracken, M. B. (1991). Medication in early pregnancy: Prevalence of use and relationship to maternal characteristics. *American Journal of Obstetrics and Gynecology, 165,* 33–40.

Bukowski, W. M., & Kramer, T. L. (1986). Judgments of the features of friendship among early adolescent boys and girls. *Journal of Early Adolescence, 6,* 331–338.

Bukowski, W. M., Sippola, L. K., & Newcomb, A. F. (2000). Variations in patterns of attraction to same- and other-sex peers during early adolescence. *Developmental Psychology, 36,* 147–154.

Burchinal, M. R., Follmer, A., & Bryant, D. M. (1996). The relations of maternal social support and family structure with maternal responsiveness and child outcomes among African American families. *Developmental Psychology, 32,* 1073–1083.

Burchinal, M. R., Roberts, J. E., Riggins, R., Jr., Zeisel, S. A., Neebe, E., & Bryant, D. (2000). Relating quality of center-based child care to early cognitive and language development longitudinally. *Child Development, 71,* 338–357.

Burgess, T. (2001). Determinants of transmission of HIV from mother to child. *Clinical Obstetrics and Gynecology, 44,* 198–209.

Burkhauser, R. V., Duncan, G. J., Hauser, R., & Bernsten, R. (1991). Wife or frau, women do worse: A comparison of men and women in the United States and Germany after marital dissolution. *Demography, 28,* 353–360.

Burns, A. L., Mitchell, G., & Obradovich, S. (1989). Of sex role and strollers: Female and male attention to toddlers at the zoo. *Sex Roles, 20,* 309–315.

Bushnell, E. W. (1981). The ontogeny of intermodal relations: Vision and touch in infancy. In R. D. Walk & H. L. Pick, Jr. (Eds.), *Intersensory perception and sensory integration.* New York: Plenum Press.

Bushnell, I. W. R., Sai, F., & Mullin, J. T. (1989). Neonatal recognition of the mother's face. *British Journal of Developmental Psychology, 7,* 3–15.

Buss, K. A., & Goldsmith, H. H. (1998). Fear and anger regulation in infancy: Effects on the temporal dynamics of affective expression. *Child Development, 69,* 359–374.

Bussey, K., & Bandura, A. (1984). Influence of gender constancy and social power on sex-linked modeling. *Journal of Personality and Social Psychology, 47,* 1292–1302.

Bussey, K., & Bandura, A. (1992). Self-regulatory mechanisms governing gender development. *Child Development, 63,* 1236–1250.

Bussey, K., & Bandura, A. (1999). Social cognitive theory of gender development and differentiation. *Psychological Bulletin, 106,* 676–713.

Bussey, K., & Perry, D. G. (1982). Same-sex imitation: The avoidance of cross-sex models or the acceptance of same-sex models. *Sex Roles, 8,* 773–784.

Butler, J., Abrams, B., Parker, J., Roberts, J. M., & Laros, R. K., Jr. (1993). Supportive nurse-midwife care is associated with a reduced incidence of cesarean section. *American Journal of Obstetrics and Gynecology, 168,* 1407–1413.

Butler, R. (1990). The effects of mastery and competitive conditions on self-assessment at different ages. *Child Development, 61,* 201–210.

Butler, R., & Ruzany, N. (1993). Age and socialization effects on the development of social comparison motives and normative ability assessment in kibbutz and urban children. *Child Development, 64,* 532–543.

Butler, S. C., Berthier, N. E., & Clifton, R. K. (2002). Two-year-olds' search strategies and visual tracking in a hidden displacement task. *Developmental Psychology, 38,* 581–590.

Butler, S. C., Caron, A. J., & Brooks, R. (2000). Infant undestanding of the referential nature of looking. *Journal of Cognition and Development, 1,* 359–377.

Butz, A. M., Pulsifer, M., Marano, N., Belcher, H., Lears, M. K., & Royall, R. (2001). Effectiveness of a home intervention for perceived child behavioral problems and parenting stress in children with in utero drug exposure. *Archives of Pediatric and Adolescent Medicine, 155,* 1029–1037.

Caccia, N., Johnson, J. M., Robinson, G. E., & Barna, T. (1991). Impact of prenatal testing on maternal-fetal bonding: Chorionic villus sampling versus amniocentesis. *American Journal of Obstetrics and Gynecology, 165,* 1122–1125.

Cacioppo, J. T., & Gardner, W. L. (1999). Emotion. *Annual Review of Psychology, 50,* 191–214.

Cairns, E., & Dawes, A. (1996). Children: Ethnic and political violence: A commentary. *Child Development, 67,* 129–139.

Cairns, R. B. (1992). The making of developmental science: The contributions and intellectual heritage of James Mark Baldwin. *Developmental Psychology, 28*, 17–24.

Cairns, R. B., & Cairns, B. D. (1994). *Lifelines and risks: Pathways of youth in our time.* Cambridge, UK: Cambridge University Press.

Cairns, R. B., & Cairns, B. D. (2006). The making of developmental psychology. In W. Damon & R. M. Lerner (Editors-in-Chief) & R. M. Lerner (Vol. Ed.), *Handbook of child psychology: Vol. 1. Theoretical models of human development* (6th ed., pp. 89–165). Hoboken, NJ: Wiley.

Cairns, R. B., Leung, M., Buchanan, L., & Cairns, B. D. (1995). Friendships and social networks in childhood and adolescence: Fluidity, reliability, and interrelations. *Child Development, 66*, 1330–1345.

Cairns, R. B., & Ornstein, P. A. (1979). Developmental psychology. In E. Hearst (Ed.), *The first century of experimental psychology.* Hillsdale, NJ: Erlbaum.

Caldwell, B. M., & Bradley, R. H. (1978). *Home Observation for Measurement of the Environment.* Little Rock: University of Arkansas.

Calkins, S. D., & Fox, N. A. (1992). The relations among infant temperament, security of attachment, and behavioral inhibition at twenty-four months. *Child Development, 63*, 1456–1472.

Calkins, S. D., Fox, N. A., & Marshall, T. R. (1995). Behavioral and physiological antecedents of inhibition in infancy. *Child Development, 67*, 523–540.

Callaghan, T. C., & Rankin, M. P. (2002). Early understanding and production of graphic symbols. *Child Development, 70*, 1314–1324.

Callaghan, T., Rochat, P., Lillard, A., Claux, M. L., Oden, H., Itakura, S., et al. (2005). Synchrony in the onset of mental-state reasoning: Evidence from five cultures. *Psychological Science, 16*, 378–384.

Calvert, S. (1999). *Children's journeys through the information age.* New York: McGraw-Hill.

Calvert, S. L., Kotler, J. A., Zehnder, S. M., & Schockey, E. M. (2003). *Gender* stereotyping in *children's* reports about educational and informational *television* programs. *Media Psychology, 5*, 139–162.

Campbell, A., Shirley, L., & Caygill, L. (2002). Sex-typed preferences in three domains: Do two-year-olds need cognitive variables? *British Journal of Psychology, 93*, 203–317.

Campbell, F. A., Pungello, E., Miller-Johnson, S., Burchinal, M., & Ramey, C. T. (2001). The development of cognitive and academic abilities: Growth curves from an early childhood educational experiment. *Developmental Psychology, 37*, 231–242.

Campbell, F. A., & Ramey, C. T. (1994). Effects of early intervention on intellectual and academic achievement: A follow-up study of children from low-income families. *Child Development, 65*, 684–698.

Campbell, S. B., Cohn, J. F., & Meyers, T. (1995). Depression in first-time mothers: Mother-infant interaction and depression chronicity. *Developmental Psychology, 31*, 349–357.

Campos, J. J., Barrett, K. C., Lamb, M. E., Goldsmith, H. H., & Stenberg, C. (1983). Socioemotional development. In M. M. Haith & J. J. Campos (Eds.), *Handbook of child psychology: Vol. II. Infancy and developmental psychobiology* (pp. 783–915). New York: Wiley.

Campos, J. J., Langer, A., & Krowitz, A. (1970). Cardiac responses on the visual cliff in prelocomotor human infants. *Science, 170*, 196–197.

Campos, J., Mumme, D., Kermoian, R. , & Campos, R. G. (1994). A functionalist perspective on the nature of emotion. In N. Fox (Ed.), The development of emotion regulation: Behavioral and biological considerations. *Monographs of the Society for Research in Child Development, 59*(2–3, Serial No. 240).

Camras, L. A., Oster, H., Campos, J., Campos, R., Ujie, T., Miyake, K., et al. (1998). Production of emotional facial expressions in European, American, Japanese, and Chinese infants. *Developmental Psychology, 34*, 616–628.

Canfield, R. L., & Smith, E. G. (1996). Number-based expectations and sequential enumeration by 5-month-olds. *Developmental Psychology, 32*, 269–279.

Cantalupo, C., & Hopkins, W. D. (2001). Asymmetric Broca's area in great apes: A region of the ape brain is uncannily similar to one linked with speech in humans. *Nature, 414*, 505.

Caplan, D. N., & Gould, J. L. (2003). Language and communication. In. L. Squire, F. Bloom, S. McConnell, J. Roberts, N. Spitzer, & M. Zigmond (Eds.), *Fundamental neuroscience* (2nd ed., pp. 1329–1352). San Diego, CA: Academic Press.

Caprara, G. V., Barbaranelli, C., Pastorelli, C., Bandura, A., & Zimbardo, P. G. (2000). Prosocial foundations of children's academic achievement. *Psychological Science, 11*, 302–306.

Capron, A. M. (1998). Punishing mothers. *Hastings Center Report, 28*, 31–33.

Carey, S. (1978). The child as word learner. In M. Halle, J. Bresnan, & G. A. Miller (Eds.), *Linguistic theory and psychological reality.* Cambridge, MA: MIT Press.

Carey, S. (1985). *Conceptual changes in childhood.* Cambridge, MA: MIT Press.

Carli, L. L., & Bukatko, D. (2000). Gender, communication, and social influence: A developmental perspective. In T. Eckes & H. M. Trautner (Eds.), *The developmental social psychology of gender.* Mahwah, NJ: Erlbaum.

Carlo, G., Koller, S. H., Eisenberg, N., Da Silva, M. S., & Frohlich, C. B. (1996). A cross-national study on the relations among prosocial moral reasoning, gender role orientations, and prosocial behaviors. *Developmental Psychology, 32*, 231–240.

Carlson, E. A. (1998). A prospective longitudinal study of attachment disorganization/disorientation. *Child Development, 69*, 1107–1128.

Carlson, S. M., Moses, L. J., & Hix, H. R. (1998). The role of inhibitory processes in young children's difficulties with deception and false belief. *Child Development, 69*, 672–691.

Carlson, V., Cicchetti, D., Barnett, D., & Braunwald, K. (1989). Contributions of the study of maltreated infants to the development of the disorganized ("D") type of attachment relationship. In D. Cicchetti & V. Carlson (Eds.), *Child maltreatment: Theory and research on the causes and consequences of child abuse and neglect.* Cambridge, UK: Cambridge University Press.

Carmichael, C. A., & Hayes, B. K. (2001). Prior knowledge and exemplar encoding in children's concept acquisition. *Child Development, 72*, 1071–1090.

Carpenter, M., Akhtar, N., & Tomasello, M. (1998). Fourteen- through 18-month-old infants differentially imitate intentional and accidental actions. *Infant Behavior and Development, 21*, 315–330.

Carpenter, M., Nagell, K., & Tomasello, M. (1998). Social cognition, joint attention, and communicative competence from 9 to 15 months of age. *Monographs of the Society for Research in Child Development, 63*(4, Serial No. 176).

Carskadon, M. A., Acebo, C., & Jenni, O. G. (2004). Regulation of adolescent sleep: Implications for behavior. *Annals of the New York Academy of Sciences, 1021*, 276–291.

Carskadon, M. A., Harvey, K., & Duke, P. (1980). Pubertal changes in daytime sleepiness. *Sleep, 2*, 453–460.

Carter, D. B. (1987). The roles of peers in sex role socialization. In D. B. Carter (Ed.), *Current conceptions of sex roles and sex-typing: Theory and research.* New York: Praeger.

Carter, D. B., & Levy, G. D. (1988). Cognitive aspects of early sex-role development: The influence of gender schemas on preschoolers' memories and preferences for sex-typed toys and activities. *Child Development, 59*, 782–792.

Carter, D. B., & McCloskey, L. A. (1984). Peers and the maintenance of sex-typed behavior: The development of children's understanding of cross-gender behavior in their peers. *Social Cognition, 2*, 294–314.

Carver, P. R., Egan, S. K., & Perry, D. G. (2004). Children who question their heterosexuality. *Developmental Psychology, 40*, 43–53.

Casasola, M., & Cohen, L. B. (2000). Infants' association of linguistic labels with causal actions. *Developmental Psychology, 36*, 155–168.

Case, R. (1985). *Intellectual development: A systematic reinterpretation.* New York: Academic Press.

Case, R. (1991). Stages in the development of the young child's first sense of self. *Developmental Review, 11*, 210–230.

Case, R., Kurland, D. M., & Goldberg, J. (1982). Operational efficiency and the growth of short term memory span. *Journal of Experimental Child Psychology, 33,* 386–404.

Casey, B. J., Thomas, K. M., & McCandless, B. (2001). Applications of magnetic resonance imaging to the study of development. In C. A. Nelson & M. Luciana (Eds.), *Handbook of developmental cognitive neuroscience* (pp. 137–148). Cambridge, MA: MIT Press.

Casey, R. J. (1993). Children's emotional experience: Relations among expression, self-report, and understanding. *Developmental Psychology, 29,* 119–129.

Casper, L. M., & O'Connell, M. (1998). Work, income, the economy, and married fathers as child care providers. *Demography, 35,* 243–250.

Caspi, A., McClay, J., Moffitt, T., Mill, J., Martin, J., Craig, I., Taylor, A., & Poulton, R. (2002). Evidence that the cycle of violence in maltreated children depends on genotype. *Science, 297,* 851–854.

Caspi, A., Taylor, A., Moffitt, T. E., & Plomin, R. (2000). Neighborhood deprivation affects children's mental health: Environmental risks identified in a genetic design. *Psychological Science, 11,* 338–342.

Cassel, W. S., Roebers, C. E. M., & Bjorklund, D. F. (1996). Developmental patterns of eyewitness responses to repeated and increasingly suggestive questions. *Journal of Experimental Child Psychology, 61,* 116–133.

Cassell, J., & Jenkins, H. (1998). Chess for girls? Feminism and computer games. In J. Cassell & H. Jenkins (Eds.), *From Barbie to Mortal Kombat: Gender and computer games* (pp. 2–45). Cambridge, MA: MIT Press.

Cassia, V. M., Turati, C., & Simion, F. (2004). Can a nonspecific bias toward top-heavy patterns explain newborns' face preference? *Psychological Science, 15,* 379–383.

Cassidy, J., & Asher, S. R. (1992). Loneliness and peer relations in young children. *Child Development, 63,* 350–365.

Cassidy, J., Kirsh, S. J., Scolton, K. L., & Parke, R. D. (1996). Attachment and representations of peer relationships. *Developmental Psychology, 32,* 892–904.

Castles, A., Datta, H., Gayan, J., & Olson, R. K. (1999). Varieties of developmental reading disorder: Genetic and environmental influences. *Journal of Experimental Child Psychology, 72,* 73–94.

Cattell, J. M. (1890). Mental tests and measurements. *Mind, 15,* 373–381.

Cattell, R. B. (1971). *Abilities: Their structure, growth, and action.* Boston: Houghton Mifflin.

Cavior, N., & Dokecki, P. R. (1973). Physical attractiveness, perceived attitude similarity, and academic achievement as contributors to interpersonal attraction among adolescents. *Developmental Psychology, 9,* 44–54.

Ceballo, R., & McLoyd, V. C. (2002). Social support and parenting in poor, dangerous neighborhoods. *Child Development, 73,* 1310–1321.

Ceci, S. J., & Bruck, M. (1993). Suggestibility of the child witness: A historical review and synthesis. *Psychological Bulletin, 113,* 403–439.

Ceci, S. J., Ross, D. F., & Toglia, M. P. (1987). Suggestibility of children's memory: Psychological implications. *Journal of Experimental Psychology: General, 116,* 38–49.

Ceci, S. J., & Williams, W. M. (1997). Schooling, intelligence, and income. *American Psychologist, 52,* 1051–1058.

Center for Communication and Social Policy. (1998). *National Television Violence Study* (Vol. 3). Newbury Park, CA: Sage.

Centers for Disease Control. (1991). Premarital sexual experience among adolescent women-United States, 1970–1988. *Morbidity and Mortality Weekly Report, 39,* 929–932.

Centers for Disease Control. (1992). Youth suicide prevention programs: A resource guide. Atlanta: U.S. Department of Health and Human Services, Public Health Service.

Centers for Disease Control and Prevention. (2000). State-specific pregnancy rates among adolescents—United States, 1992–1995. *Morbidity and Mortality Weekly Report, 49,* 605–611.

Centers for Disease Control and Prevention. (2004a). *Alcohol consumption among women who are pregnant or who might become pregnant—United States, 2002.* Retrieved May 10, 2006, from www.cdc.gov/mmwr/preview/mmwrhtml/mm5350a4.htm

Centers for Disease Control and Prevention. (2004b). *Toxoplasmosis.* Retrieved May 7, 2006, from www.dpd.cdc.gov/dpdx/HTML/Toxoplasmosis.asp?body=Frames/S-Z/Toxoplasmosis/body_Toxoplasmosis_pagel.htm.

Centers for Disease Control and Prevention. (2005a). *2003 assisted reproductive technology success rates: National summary and fertility clinic reports.* Retrieved May 7, 2006, from www.cdc.gov/ART/ART2003/PDF/ART03part1.pdf.

Centers for Disease Control and Prevention. (2005b). *CDC announces rubella, once a major cause of birth defects, is no longer a health threat in the U.S.* Retrieved May 3, 2006, from www.cdc.gov/od/oc/media/transcripts/t050321.htm.

Centers for Disease Control and Prevention. (2005c). Trends in Cesarean rates for first births and repeat Cesarean rates for low-risk women: United States, 1990–2003. *National Vital Statistics Reports, 54,* No. 4.

Centers for Disease Control and Prevention, National Health and Nutrition Examination Survey, National Center for Health Statistics. (2002). *Overweight among U.S. children and adolescents.* Retrieved January 13, 2003, from www.cdc.gov/nchs/nhanes.htm

Chan, K., Ohlsson, A., Synnes, A., Lee, D. S. C., Chien, L.-Y., Lee, S. K., and the Canadian Neonatal Network. (2000). Survival, morbidity, and resource use of infants of 25 weeks' gestational age or less. *American Journal of Obstetrics and Gynecology, 185,* 220–226.

Chao, R. K. (1994). Beyond parental control and authoritarian parenting style: Understanding Chinese parenting through the cultural notion of training. *Child Development, 65,* 1111–1119.

Chapman, M., Skinner, E. A., & Baltes, P. B. (1990). Interpreting correlations between children's perceived control and cognitive performance: Control, agency, or means-ends beliefs? *Developmental Psychology, 26,* 246–253.

Charpak, N., Ruiz, J. G., de Calume, Z. F., & Charpak, Y. (1997). Kangaroo mother versus "traditional" care for newborn infants < 2000 grams: A randomized, controlled trial. *Pediatrics, 100,* 682–688.

Chase-Lansdale, P. L., Cherlin, A. J., & Kiernan, K. E. (1995). The long-term effects of parental divorce on the mental health of young adults: A developmental perspective. *Child Development, 66,* 1614–1634.

Chasnoff, I. J. (1986). Perinatal addiction: Consequences of intrauterine exposure to opiate and nonopiate drugs. In I. J. Chasnoff (Ed.), *Drug use in pregnancy: Mother and child.* Lancaster, UK: MTP Press.

Chasnoff, I. J. (1992). Cocaine, pregnancy, and the growing child. *Current Problems in Pediatrics, 22,* 302–321.

Chavkin, W. (2001). Cocaine and pregnancy: Time to look at the evidence. *Journal of the American Medical Association, 285,* 1626–1627.

Chen, C., & Stevenson, H. W. (1995). Motivation and mathematics achievement: A comparative study of Asian-American, Caucasian-American, and East Asian high school students. *Child Development, 66,* 1215–1234.

Chen, X., Cen, G., Li, D., & He, Y. (2005). Social functioning and adjustment in Chinese children: The imprint of historical time. *Child Development, 76,* 182–195.

Chen, X., Li, D., Li, Z., Li, B., & Liu, M. (2000). Sociable and prosocial dimensions of social competence in Chinese children: Common and unique contributions to social, academic, and psychological adjustment. *Developmental Psychology, 36,* 302–314.

Chen, X., Rubin, K. H., Li, B., & Li, D. (1999). Adolescent outcomes of social functioning in Chinese children. *International Journal of Behavioral Development, 23,* 199–223.

Chen, X., Rubin, K. H., & Li, D. (1997). Maternal acceptance and social and school adjustment: A four-year longitudinal study. *Merrill-Palmer Quarterly, 43,* 663–681.

Chen, X., Rubin, K. H., & Li, Z. (1995). Social functioning and adjustment in Chinese children: A longitudinal study. *Developmental Psychology, 31,* 531–539.

Chen, Z. (2003). Worth one thousand words: Children's use of pictures in analogical problem-solving. *Journal of Cognition and Development, 4,* 415–434.

Chen, Z., & Daehler, M. W. (1989). Positive and negative transfer in analogical problem-solving by 6-year-olds. *Cognitive Development, 4,* 327–344.

Chen, Z., & Klahr, D. (1999). All other things being equal: Acquisition and transfer of the control of variables strategy. *Child Development, 70,* 1098–1120.

Chen, Z., Sanchez, R. P., & Campbell, T. (1997). From beyond to within their grasp: The rudiments of analogical problem solving in 10- and 13-month-olds. *Developmental Psychology, 33,* 790–801.

Cherlin, A. J. (1992). *Marriage, divorce, remarriage* (Rev. ed.). Cambridge, MA: Harvard University Press.

Chess, S., & Thomas, A. (1982). Infant bonding: Mystique and reality. *American Journal of Orthopsychiatry, 52,* 213–222.

Chess, S., & Thomas, A. (1990). Continuities and discontinuities in temperament. In L. N. Robins & M. Rutter (Eds.). *Straight and devious pathways from childhood to adolescence.* Cambridge, UK: Cambridge University Press.

Chess, S., & Thomas, A. (1991). Temperament and the concept of goodness of fit. In J. Strelau & A. Angleitner (Eds.), *Explorations in temperament: International perspectives on theory and measurement.* New York: Plenum.

Chi, M. T. H. (1978). Knowledge structure and memory development. In R. Siegler (Ed.), *Children's thinking: What develops?* (pp. 73–96). Hillsdale, NJ: Erlbaum.

Chiappe, P., & Siegel, L. S. (1999). Phonological awareness and reading acquisition in English- and Punjabi-speaking Canadian children. *Journal of Educational Psychology, 91,* 20–28.

Child Trends Databank. (2002a). *Child maltreatment.* Retrieved December 23, 2002, from www.childtrendsdatabank.org/family/thefamily/40ChildMaltreatment.htm

Child Trends Databank. (2002b). *Parental warmth and affection.* Retrieved December 23, 2002, from www.childtrendsdatabank.org/family/thefamily/52ParentalWarmthAffection.htm

Childers, J. B., & Tomasello, M. (2001). The role of pronouns in young children's acquisition of the English transitive construction. *Developmental Psychology, 37,* 739–748.

Children's Defense Fund. (1996). *The state of America's children: Yearbook.* Washington, DC: Author.

Children's Defense Fund. (2002). *Facts on Black youths, violence, and crimes.* Retrieved on May 21, 2006, from www.childrendefense.org/education/prevention/factsheets/blackyouth.as

Chilosi, A. M., Cipriani, P., Bertuccelli, B., Pfanner, L., & Cioni, G. (2001). Early cognitive and communication development in children with focal brain lesions. *Journal of Child Neurology, 16,* 309–316.

Chiu, L. H. (1992–93). Self-esteem in American and Chinese (Taiwanese) children. *Current Psychology: Research & Reviews, 11,* 309–313.

Choi, S. (1998). Verbs in early lexical and syntactic development in Korean. *Linguistics, 36,* 755–780.

Choi, S., & Gopnik, A. (1995). Early acquisition of verbs in Korean: A cross-linguistic study. *Journal of Child Language, 22,* 497–529.

Chomsky, N. (1980). *Rules and representations.* New York: Columbia University Press.

Chomsky, N. (1986). *Knowledge of language: Its nature, origin, and use.* New York: Praeger.

Christianson, A., Howson, C. P., & Modell, B. (2006). *March of Dimes global report on birth defects: The hidden toll of dying and disabled children.* White Plains, NY: March of Dimes Defects Foundation.

Chugani, H. T. (1994). Development of regional brain glucose metabolism in relation to behavior and plasticity. In G. Dawson & K. Fischer (Eds.), *Human behavior and the developing brain* (pp. 153–175). New York: Guilford.

Cicchetti, D., Ackerman, B., & Izard, C. (1995). Emotions and emotion regulation in developmental psychopathology. *Development and Psychopathology, 7,* 1–10.

Cicchetti, D., Rogosch, F. A., Toth, S. L., & Spagnola, M. (1997). Affect, cognition, and the emergence of self-knowledge in the toddler offspring of depressed mothers. *Journal of Experimental Child Psychology, 67,* 338–362.

Cicchetti, D., Toth, S. L., & Lynch, M. (1995). Bowlby's dream comes full circle: The application of attachment theory to risk and psychopathology. *Advances in Clinical Child Psychology, 17,* 1–75.

Cillessen, A. H. N., & Mayeux, L. (2004). From censure to reinforcement: Developmental changes in the association between aggression and social status. *Child Development, 75,* 147–163.

Cillessen, A. H. N., & Rose, A. J. (2005). Understanding popularity in the peer system. *Current Directions in Psychological Science, 14,* 102–105.

Clark, E. V. (1973). What's in a word? On the child's acquisition of semantics in his first language. In T. E. Moore (Ed.), *Cognitive development and the acquisition of language.* New York: Academic Press.

Clark, W. (2001, Autumn). Kids and teens on the net. *Canadian Social Trends,* No. 62 (Catalogue Number 11-008-XPE). Retrieved on November 27, 2002, from www.statcan.ca/english/IPS/Data/11-008-XPE20010025821.htm

Clarke-Stewart, K. A. (1993). *Daycare* (Rev. ed.). Cambridge, MA: Harvard University Press.

Clarke-Stewart, K. A., & Fein, G. G. (1983). Early childhood programs. In M. M. Haith & J. J. Campos (Eds.), *Handbook of child psychology: Vol. II. Infancy and developmental psychobiology* (4th ed., pp. 917–999). New York: Wiley.

Clarke-Stewart, K. A., & Hayward, C. (1996). Advantages of father custody and contact for the psychological well-being of school-age children. *Journal of Applied Developmental Psychology, 17,* 239–270.

Clarkson, M. G. (1996). Infants' intensity discrimination: Spectral profiles. *Infant Behavior and Development, 19,* 181–190.

Clarren, S. K., Alvord, E. C., Suni, S. M., & Streissguth, A. P. (1978). Brain malformations related to prenatal exposure to ethanol. *Journal of Pediatrics, 92,* 64–67.

Clasen, D. R., & Brown, B. B. (1985). The multidimensionality of peer pressure in adolescence. *Journal of Youth and Adolescence, 14,* 451–468.

Claxton, L. J., Keen, R., & McCarty, M. E. (2003). Evidence of motor planning in infant reaching behavior. *Psychological Science, 14,* 354–356.

Clearfield, M. W., & Mix, K. S. (1999). Number versus contour length in infants' discrimination of small visual sets. *Psychological Science, 10,* 408–411.

Clearfield, M. W., & Mix, K. S. (2001). Amount versus number: Infants' use of area and contour length to discriminate small sets. *Journal of Cognition and Development, 2,* 243–260.

Cleveland, M. J., Gibbons, F. X., Gerrard, M., Pomery, E. A., & Brody, G. H. (2005). The impact of parenting on risk cognitions and risk behavior: A study of mediation and moderation in a panel of African American adolescents. *Child Development, 76,* 900–916.

Clifton, R., Muir, D. W., Ashmead, D. H., & Clarkson, M. G. (1993). Is visually guided reaching in early infancy a myth? *Child Development, 64,* 1099–1110.

Clifton, R., Perris, E., & Bullinger, A. (1991). Infants' perception of auditory space. *Developmental Psychology, 27,* 187–197.

Cohen, D., & Strayer, J. (1996). Empathy in conduct-disordered and comparison youth. *Developmental Psychology, 32,* 988–998.

Cohen, L. B., & Cashon, C. H. (2006). Infant cognition. In W. Damon & R. M. Lerner (Editors-in-Chief) & D. M. Kuhn & R. S. Siegler (Vol. Eds.), *Handbook of child psychology: Vol. 2. Cognition, perception, and language* (6th ed., pp. 214–251). Hoboken, NJ: Wiley.

Cohen, R. L. (1966). Experimental and clinical chemateratogenesis. *Advances in Pharmacology, 4,* 263–349.

Cohn, J. F., Matias, R., Tronick, E. Z., Connell, D., & Lyons-Ruth, D. (1986). Face-to-face interactions of depressed mothers and their infants. In E. Z. Tronick & T. M. Field (Eds.), *New directions for child development: No. 34. Maternal depression and infant disturbance.* San Francisco: Jossey-Bass.

Cohn, J. F., & Tronick, E. Z. (1983). Three-month-old infants' reaction to simulated maternal depression. *Child Development, 54,* 185–193.

Cohn, J. F., & Tronick, E. Z. (1987). Mother-infant face-to-face interaction: The sequence of dyadic states at 3, 6, and 9 months. *Developmental Psychology, 23,* 68–77.

Coie, J. D., & Dodge, K. A. (1988). Multiple sources of data on social behavior and social status in the school: A cross-age comparison. *Child Development, 59,* 815–829.

Coie, J. D., Dodge, K. A., & Coppotelli, H. (1982). Dimensions and types of social status: A cross-age perspective. *Developmental Psychology, 18,* 557–570.

Colby, A., & Damon, W. (1992). *Some do care: Contemporary lives of moral commitment.* New York: Free Press.

Colby, A., Kohlberg, L., Gibbs, J., & Lieberman, M. (1983). A longitudinal study of moral judgment. *Monographs of the Society for Research in Child Development, 48*(1–2, Serial No. 200).

Cole, D. A., Martin, J. M., Peeke, L. A., Seroczynski, A. D., & Fier, J. (1999). Children's over- and underestimation of academic competence: A longitudinal study of gender differences, depression, and anxiety. *Child Development, 70,* 459–473.

Cole, D. A., Maxwell, S. E., Martin, J. M., Peeke, L. G., Seroczynski, A. D., Tram, J. M., et al. (2001). The development of multiple domains of child and adolescent self-concept: A cohort sequential longitudinal design. *Child Development, 72,* 1723–1746.

Cole, P. M., Bruschi, C. J., & Tamang, B. L. (2002). Cultural differences in children's emotional reactions to difficult situations. *Child Development, 73,* 983–996.

Cole, P. M., Zahn-Waxler, C., & Smith, K. D. (1994). Expressive control during a disappointment: Variations related to preschoolers' behavior problems. *Developmental Psychology, 30,* 835–846.

Coleman, P. K., & Karraker, K. H. (1998). Self-efficacy and parenting quality: Findings and future applications. *Developmental Review, 18,* 47–85.

Coley, R. L. (1998). Children's socialization experiences and functioning in single-mother households: The importance of fathers and other men. *Child Development, 69,* 219–230.

Coley, R. L., & Chase-Lansdale, P. L. (1998). Adolescent pregnancy and parenthood: Recent evidence and future directions. *American Psychologist, 53,* 152–166.

Collaer, M. L., & Hines, M. (1995). Human behavioral sex differences: A role for gonadal hormones during early development? *Psychological Bulletin, 118,* 55–107.

Collins, J. A. (1995). A couple with infertility. *Journal of the American Medical Association, 274,* 1159–1164.

Collins, W. A., (1995). Relationships and development: Family adaptation to individual change. In S. Shulman (Ed.), *Close relationships and socioemotional development* (pp. 128–154). New York: Ablex.

Collins, W. A., & Laursen, B. (2004a). Parent-adolescent relationships and influences. In R. M. Lerner & L. Steinberg (Eds.), *Handbook of adolescent psychology* (2nd ed., pp. 331–361). Hoboken, NJ: Wiley.

Collins, W. A., & Laursen, B. (2004b). Changing relationships, changing youth: Interpersonal contexts of adolescent development. *Journal of Early Adolescence, 24,* 55–62.

Collins, W. A., Maccoby, E. E., Steinberg, L., Hetherington, E. M., & Bornstein, M. H. (2000). Contemporary research on parenting: The case for nature and nurture. *American Psychologist, 55,* 218–232.

Collins, W. A., & Steinberg, L. (2006). Adolescent development in interpersonal context. In W. Damon & R. M. Lerner (Editors-in-Chief) & N. Eisenberg (Vol. Ed.), *Handbook of child psychology: Vol. 3. Social, emotional, and personality development* (6th ed., pp. 1003–1067). Hoboken, NJ: Wiley.

Collis, B., & Ollila, L. (1990). The effects of computer use on grade 1 children's gender stereotypes about reading, writing, and computer use. *Journal of Research and Development in Education, 24,* 14–20.

Coltrane, S. (2000). Research on household labor: Modeling and measuring the social embeddedness of routine family work. *Journal of Marriage and the Family, 62,* 1208–1233.

Comeau, L., Cormier, P., Grandmaison, È., & Lacroix, D. (1999). A longitudinal study of phonological processing skills in children learning to read in a second language. *Journal of Educational Psychology, 91,* 29–43.

Committee on Genetics. (1996). Newborn screening fact sheet. *Pediatrics, 98,* 473–501.

Compas, B. E. (2004). Processes of risk and resilience during adolescence: Linking contexts and individuals. In R. M. Lerner & L. Steinberg (Eds.), *Handbook of adolescent psychology* (2nd ed., pp. 263–296). Hoboken, NJ: Wiley.

Compas, B. E., Langrock, A. M., Keller, G., Merchant, M. J., & Copeland, M. E. (2002). Coping with parental depression: Processes of adaptation to chronic stress. In S. H. Goodman & I. H. Gotlib (Eds.), *Children of depressed parents: Mechanisms of risk and implications for treatment* (pp. 227–252). Washington, DC: American Psychological Association.

Comstock, G. (1991). *Television and the American child.* Orlando, FL: Academic Press.

Comstock, G., & Scharrer, E. A. (2006). Media and popular culture. In W. Damon & R. M. Lerner (Editors-in-Chief) & K. A. Renninger & I. E. Sigel (Vol. Eds.), *Handbook of child psychology: Vol. 4. Child psychology in practice* (6th ed., pp. 817–863). Hoboken, NJ: Wiley.

Conger, R. D., Conger, K. J., Elder, G. H., Jr., Lorenz, F. O., Simons, R. L., & Whitbeck, L. B. (1992). A family process model of economic hardship and adjustment of early adolescent boys. *Child Development, 63,* 526–541.

Conger, R. D., Wallace, L. E., Sun, Y., Simons, R. L., McLoyd, V. C., & Brody, G. H. (2002). Economic pressure in African American families: A replication and extension of the family stress model. *Developmental Psychology, 38,* 179–193.

Connolly, J. A., Craig, W., Goldberg, A., & Pepler, D. (2004). Mixed gender groups, dating, and romantic relationships in early adolescence. *Journal of Research on Adolescence, 14,* 185–207.

Connolly, J., Furman, W., & Konarski, R. (2000). The role of peers in the emergence of heterosexual romantic relationships in adolescence. *Child Development, 71,* 1395–1408.

Connolly, J. A., & Johnson, A. (1996). Adolescents' romantic relationships and the structure and quality of their close interpersonal ties. *Personal Relationships, 3,* 185–195.

Connors, F., & Olson, R. K. (1990). Reading comprehension in dyslexic and normal readers: A component-skills analysis. In D. A. Balota, G. B. Flores d'Arcais, & K. Rayner (Eds.), *Comprehension processes in reading.* Hillsdale, NJ: Erlbaum.

Conway, A. R. A., Cowan, N., Bunting, M. F., Therriault, D. J., & Minkoff, S. R. B. (2002). A latent variable analysis of working memory capacity, short-term memory capacity, processing speed, and general fluid intelligence. *Intelligence, 30,* 163–184.

Cook, E. T., Greenberg, M. T., & Kusche, C. (1994). The relations between emotional understanding, intellectual functioning, and disruptive behavior problems in elementary-school-aged children. *Journal of Abnormal Child Psychology, 22,* 205–219.

Cook, T. D., Herman, M. R., Phillips, M., & Settersten, Jr., R. A. (2002). Some ways in which neighborhoods, nuclear families, friendship groups, and schools jointly affect changes in early adolescent development. *Child Development, 73,* 1283–1309.

Cooley, C. H. (1902). *Human nature and the social order.* New York: Scribner's.

Cooper, M. L., Shaver, P. R., & Collins, N. L. (1998). Attachment styles, emotion regulation, and adjustment in adolescence. *Journal of Personality and Social Psychology, 74,* 1380–1397.

Copper, R. L., Goldenberg, R. L., Cliver, S. P., DuBard, M. B., Hoffman, H. J., & Davis, R. O. (1993). Anthropometric assessment of body size differences of full-term male and female infants. *Obstetrics and Gynecology, 81,* 161–164.

Corina, D. P., McBurney, S. L., Dodrill, C., Hinshaw, K., Brinkley, J., & Ojemann, G. (1999). Functional roles of Broca's area and supramarginal gyrus: Evidence from cortical stimulation mapping of a deaf signer. *NeuroImage, 10,* 570–581.

Correa-Chávez, M., Rogoff, B., & Mejía Arauz, R. (2005). Cultural patterns in attending to two events at once. *Child Development, 76,* 664–678.

Costanzo, P. R., & Woody, E. Z. (1979). Externality as a function of obesity in children: Pervasive style or eating-specific attribute? *Journal of Personality and Social Psychology, 37,* 2286–2296.

Courage, M. L., & Howe, M. L. (2004). Advances in early memory development research: Insights about the dark side of the moon. *Developmental Review, 24,* 6–32.

Cournoyer, M., & Trudel, M. (1991). Behavioral correlates of self-control at 33 months. *Infant Behavior and Development, 14,* 497–503.

Coustan, D. R., & Felig, P. (1988). Diabetes mellitus. In G. N. Burrow & T. F. Ferris (Eds.), *Medical complications during pregnancy* (3rd ed.). Philadelphia: W.B. Saunders.

Cowan, N. (1999). The differential maturation of two processing rates related to digit span. *Journal of Experimental Child Psychology, 72,* 193–209.

Cowan, N., Wood, N. L., Wood, P. K., Keller, T. A., Nugent, L. D., & Keller, C. V. (1998). Two separate verbal processing rates contribute to short-term memory span. *Journal of Experimental Psychology: General, 127,* 141–160.

Cowan, W. M. (1979, September). The development of the brain. *Scientific American, 241,* 113–133.

Cox, M., & Harter, K. S. M. (2003). Parent-child relationships. In M. H. Bornstein & L. Davidson, C. Keyes, & K. Moore (Eds.), *Well-being: Positive development across the lifespan.* Mahwah, NJ: Erlbaum.

Cox, M. J., Owen, T. J., Henderson, V. K., & Margand, N. A. (1992). Prediction of infant-father and infant-mother interaction. *Developmental Psychology, 28,* 474–483.

Cox, M. J., & Paley, B. (2003). Understanding families as systems. *Current Directions in Psychological Science, 5,* 193–196.

Coyle, T. R., & Bjorklund, D. F. (1997). Age differences in, and consequences of, multiple- and variable-strategy use on a multitrial sort-recall task. *Developmental Psychology, 33,* 372–380.

Crain-Thoreson, C., & Dale, P. S. (1992). Do early talkers become early readers? Linguistic precocity, preschool language, and emergent literacy. *Developmental Psychology, 28,* 421–429.

Crandall, V. C. (1969). Sex differences in expectancy of intellectual and academic reinforcement. In C. P. Smith (Ed.), *Achievement-related motives in children.* New York: Russell Sage.

Crawford, P. B., Story, M., Wang, M. C., Ritchie, L. D., & Sabry, Z. I. (2001). Ethnic issues in the epidemiology of childhood obesity. *Pediatric Clinics of North America, 48,* 855–875.

Crick, N. R., Casas, J. F., & Mosher, M. (1997). Relational and overt aggression in preschool. *Developmental Psychology, 33,* 579–588.

Crick, N. R., & Dodge, K. A. (1994). A review and reformulation of social information-processing mechanisms in children's social adjustment. *Psychological Bulletin, 115,* 74–101.

Crick, N. R., & Dodge, K. A. (1996). Social information-processing mechanisms in reactive and proactive aggression. *Child Development, 67,* 993–1002.

Crick, N. R., & Grotpeter, J. K. (1995). Relational aggression, gender, and social-psychological adjustment. *Child Development, 66,* 710–722.

Crick, N. R., & Ladd, G. W. (1993). Children's perceptions of their peer experiences: Attributions, loneliness, social anxiety, and social avoidance. *Developmental Psychology, 29,* 244–254.

Criss, M. M., Pettit, G. S., Bates, J. E., Dodge, K. A., & Lapp, A. L. (2002). Family adversity, positive peer relationships, and children's externalizing behavior: A longitudinal perspective on risk and resilience. *Child Development, 73,* 1220–1237.

Crook, C. (1992). Cultural artifacts in social development: The case of computers. In H. McGurk (Ed.), *Childhood social development: Contemporary perspectives* (pp. 207–231). Hove, UK: Erlbaum.

Crouter, A. C., & Bumpus, M. F. (2001). Linking parents' work stress to children's and adolescents' psychological adjustment. *Current Directions in Psychological Science, 10,* 156–159.

Crouter, A. C., Bumpus, M. F., Davis, K. D., & McHale, S. M. (2005). How do parents learn about adolescents' experiences? Implications for parental knowledge and adolescent risky behavior. *Child Development, 76,* 869–882.

Crouter, A. C., Manke, B. A., & McHale, S. M. (1995). The family context of gender intensification in early adolescence. *Child Development, 66,* 317–329.

Crouter, A. C., McHale, S. M., & Tucker, C. J. (1999). Does stress exacerbate parental differential treatment of siblings? A pattern-analytic approach. *Journal of Family Psychology, 13,* 286–299.

Crowley, K., & Siegler, R. S. (1998). Explanation and generalization in young children's strategy learning. *Child Development, 70,* 304–316.

Csikszentmihalyi, M., & Larson, R. (1984). *Being adolescent.* New York: Basic Books.

Culley, L. (1993). Gender equity and computing in secondary schools. In J. Benyon & H. McKay (Eds.), *Computers into classrooms* (pp. 73–95). London: Falmer Press.

Cummings, E. M. (1995). Security, emotionality, and parental depression: A commentary. *Developmental Psychology, 31,* 425–427.

Cummings, E. M., Zahn-Waxler, C., & Radke-Yarrow, C. (1981). Young children's responses to expressions of anger and affection by others in the family. *Child Development, 52,* 1274–1282.

Cuniff, C., & Committee on Genetics. (2004). Prenatal screening and diagnosis for pediatricians. *Pediatrics, 114,* 889–894.

Cunningham, J. D. (1993). Experiences of Australian mothers who gave birth either at home, at a birth centre, or in hospital labour wards. *Social Science and Medicine, 36,* 475–483.

Curtiss, S. (1977). *Genie: A psycholinguistic study of a modern-day "wild child."* New York: Academic Press.

Cuttler, L., Silvers, J. B., Singh, J., Marrero, U., Finkelstein, B., Tannin, G., & Neuhauser, D. (1996, August 21). Short stature and growth hormone therapy: A national study of physician recommendation patterns. *Journal of the American Medical Association, 276,* 531–537.

Dahl, R. E., & Lewin, D. S. (2002). Pathways to adolescent health: Sleep regulation and behavior. *Journal of Adolescent Health, 31,* 175–184.

Dahl, R. E., Scher, M. S., Williamson, D. E., Robles, N., & Day, N. (1995). A longitudinal study of prenatal marijuana use: Effects on sleep and arousal at age 3 years. *Archives of Pediatric and Adolescent Medicine, 149,* 145–150.

Daley, T. C., Whaley, S. E., Sigman, M. D., Espinosa, M. P., & Neumann, C. (2003). IQ on the rise: The Flynn effect in rural Kenyan children. *Psychological Science, 14,* 215–219.

Dalterio, S., & Bartke, A. (1979). Perinatal exposure to cannabinoids alters male reproductive function in mice. *Science, 205,* 1420–1422.

Damon, W. (1983). *Social and personality development: Infancy through adolescence.* New York: W. W. Norton.

Damon, W., & Hart, D. (1988). *Self-understanding in childhood and adolescence.* New York: Cambridge University Press.

Daniels, K. (1989). Waterbirth: The newest form of safe, gentle and joyous birth. *Journal of Nurse-Midwifery, 34,* 198–205.

Daniels, K., & Taylor, K. (1993). Formulating selection policies for assisted reproduction. *Social Science & Medicine, 37,* 1473–1480.

Dapretto, M., & Bjork, E. L. (2000). The development of word retrieval abilities in the second year and its relation to early vocabulary growth. *Child Development, 71,* 635–648.

Dark, V. J., & Benbow, C. P. (1993). Cognitive differences among the gifted: A review and new data. In D. K. Detterman (Ed.), *Current topics in human intelligence. Vol. 3. Individual differences and cognition* (pp. 85–120). Norwood, NJ: Ablex.

Darnovsky, M. (2004). Revisiting sex selection: The growing popularity of new sex selection methods revives an old debate. *Gene Watch, 17,* 3–6.

Darwin, C. (1877). A biographical sketch of an infant. *Mind, 2,* 285–294.

Dasen, P. R. (1972). Cross-cultural Piagetian research: A summary. *Journal of Cross-Cultural Psychology, 3,* 23–39.

Davidoff, M. J., Dias, T., Damus, K., Russell, R., Bettegowda, V. R., et al. (2006). Changes in gestational age distribution among U. S. singleton births: Impact on rates of late preterm birth, 1992–2002. *Seminars in Perinatology, 30,* 8–15.

Davies, P. T., & Scummings, E. M. (1998). Exploring children's emotional security as a mediator of the link between marital relations and child adjustment. *Child Development, 69,* 124–139.

Davies, P. T., & Windle, M. (2000). Middle adolescents' dating pathways and psychosocial adjustment. *Merrill-Palmer Quarterly, 44,* 231–337.

Davis, B. L., MacNeilage, P. F., Matyear, C. L., & Powell, J. K. (2000). Prosodic correlates of stress in babbling: An acoustical study. *Child Development, 71,* 1258–1270.

Davis, S. C., & Roberts, I. A. G. (1996). Bone marrow transplant for sickle cell disease: An update. *Archives of Disease in Childhood, 75,* 448–450.

Davis-Kean, P. E., & Sandler, H. M. (2001). A meta-analysis of measures of self-esteem for young children: A framework for future measures. *Child Development, 72,* 887–906.

Davison, K. K., & Birch, L. L. (1999). Weight status, parent reaction, and self-concept in five-year-old girls. *Pediatrics, 107,* 46–53.

Davison, K. K., & Birch, L. L. (2002). Processes linking weight status and self-concept among girls from ages 5 to 7 years. *Developmental Psychology, 38,* 735–748.

Dawson, G. (1994). Development of emotion expression and emotion regulation in infancy. In G. Dawson & K. W. Fischer (Eds.), *Human behavior and the developing brain* (pp. 346–379). New York: Guilford.

Dawson, G., Munson, J., Estes, A., Osterling, J., McPartland, J., Toth, K., et al. (2002). Neurocognitive function and joint attention ability in young children with autism spectrum disorder versus developmental delay. *Child Development, 73,* 345–358.

Day, N. L., & Richardson, G. A. (1994). Comparative teratogenicity of alcohol and other drugs. *Alcohol Health and Research World, 18,* 42–48.

de Fockert, J. W., Rees, G., Frith, C. D., & Lavie, N. (2001). The role of working memory in visual selective attention. *Science, 291,* 1803–1806.

de Haan, M., & Nelson, C. A. (1997). Brain activity differentiates face and object processing in 6-month-olds. *Developmental Psychology, 35,* 1113–1121.

de Villiers, P. A., & de Villiers, J. G. (1979). Form and function in the development of sentence negation. *Papers and Reports in Child Language, 17,* 57–64.

De Wolff, M. S., & van IJzendoorn, M. H. (1997). Sensitivity and attachment: A meta-analysis on parental antecedents of attachment. *Child Development, 68,* 571–591.

Deák, G. O., & Bauer, P. J. (1996). The dynamics of preschoolers' categorization choices. *Child Development, 67,* 740–767.

Deater-Deckard, K., & Dunn, J. (1999). Multiple risks and adjustment in young children growing up in different family settings: A British community study of stepparent, single mother, and nondivorced families. In E. M. Hetherington (Ed.), *Coping with divorce, single parenting, and remarriage* (pp. 65–90). Mahwah, NJ: Erlbaum.

Deater-Deckard, K., Pike, A., Petrill, S. A., Cutting, A. L., Hughes, C., & O'Connor, T. G. (2001). Nonshared environmental processes in social-emotional development: An observational study of identical twin differences in the preschool period. *Developmental Science, 4,* F1 F6.

DeBaryshe, B. D. (1993). Joint picture-book reading correlates of early oral language skill. *Journal of Child Language, 20,* 455–461.

DeBaryshe, B. D., Patterson, G. R., & Capaldi, D. M. (1993). A performance model for academic achievement in early adolescent boys. *Developmental Psychology, 29, 795–804.*

DeBell, M., & Chapman, C. (2003). U.S. Department of Education, National Center for Education Statistics. *Computer and Internet use by children and adolescents in 2001* (NCES 2001–014). Washington, DC: U.S. Government Printing Office.

DeCasper, A. J., & Fifer, W. P. (1980). Of human bonding: Newborns prefer their mothers' voices. *Science, 208,* 1174–1176.

DeCasper, A. J., Lecanuet, J.-P., Busnel, M.-C., Granier-Deferre, C., & Maugeais, R. (1994). Fetal reactions to recurrent maternal speech. *Infant Behavior and Development, 17,* 159–164.

DeCasper, A. J., & Spence, M. J. (1986). Prenatal maternal speech influences newborns' perception of speech sounds. *Infant Behavior and Development, 9,* 133–150.

Declercq, E. R. (1993). Where babies are born and who attends their births: Findings from the revised 1989 United States Standard Certificate of Live Birth. *Obstetrics and Gynecology, 81,* 997–1004.

DeFries, J. C., Gervais, M. C., & Thomas, E. A. (1978). Response to 30 generations of selection for open-field activity in laboratory mice. *Behavior Genetics, 8,* 3–13.

Dekovic, M., & Janssens, J. (1992). Parents' child-rearing style and child's sociometric status. *Developmental Psychology, 28,* 925–932.

DeLisi, R., & Gallagher, A. M. (1991). Understanding of gender stability and constancy in Argentinian children. *Merrill-Palmer Quarterly, 37,* 483–502.

DeLoache, J. (1987). Rapid change in the symbolic functioning of young children. *Science, 238,* 1556–1557.

DeLoache, J. S. (2000). Dual representation and young children's use of scale models. *Child Development, 71,* 329–338.

DeLoache, J. S. (2004). Becoming symbol-minded. *Trends in Cognitive Sciences, 8,* 66–70.

DeLoache, J. S., & Smith, C. M. (1999). Early symbolic representation. In I. E. Sigel (Ed.), *Development of mental representation: Theories and applications* (pp. 61–86). Mahwah, NJ: Erlbaum.

Demany, L., McKenzie, B., & Vurpillot, E. (1977). Rhythm perception in early infancy. *Nature, 266,* 718–719.

Demetriou, H., & Hay, D. F. (2004). Toddlers' reactions to the distress of familiar peers: The importance of context. *Infancy, 6,* 299–318.

Demo, D. H., & Acock, A. C. (1996). Family structure, family process, and adolescent well-being. *Journal of Research on Adolescence, 6,* 457–488.

Dempster, F. N. (1981). Memory span: Sources of individual and developmental differences. *Psychological Bulletin, 89,* 63–100.

DeMulder, E. K., Denham, S., Schmidt, M., & Mitchell, J. (2000). Q-sort assessment of attachment security during the preschool years: Links from home to school. *Developmental Psychology, 36,* 274–282.

DeNavas-Walt, C., Proctor, B. D., & Lee, C. H. (2005). Income, poverty, and health insurance coverage in the United States: 2004. *Current Population Reports* (P60-229). Washington, DC: U.S. Government Printing Office.

Denham, S. A. (1998). *Emotional development in young children.* New York: Guilford.

Denham, S. A., McKinley, M., Couchoud, E. A., & Holt, R. (1990). Emotional and behavioral predictors of preschool ratings. *Child Development, 61,* 1145–1152.

Denham, S. A., Mitchell-Copeland, J., Strandberg, K., Auerbach, S., & Blair, K. (1997). Parental contributions to preschoolers' emotional competence: Direct and indirect effects. *Motivation and Emotion, 21,* 65–86.

Dennis, W. (1960). Causes of retardation among institutional children: Iran. *Journal of Genetic Psychology, 96,* 47–59.

Dennis, W., & Dennis, M. G. (1940). The effect of cradling practices upon the onset of walking in Hopi children. *Journal of Genetic Psychology, 56,* 77–86.

Desrochers, S., Ricard, M., Decarie, T. G., & Allard, L. (1994). Developmental synchrony between social referencing and Piagetian sensorimotor causality. *Infant Behavior and Development, 17,* 303–309.

Deur, J. L., & Parke, R. D. (1970). Effects of inconsistent punishment on aggression in children. *Developmental Psychology, 2,* 403–411.

Deutsch, M., Katz, I., & Jensen, A. R. (1968). *Social class, race, and psychological development.* New York: Holt, Rinehart & Winston.

Devoe, L. D., Murray, C., Youssif, A., & Arnaud, M. (1993). Maternal caffeine consumption and fetal behavior in normal third-trimester pregnancy. *American Journal of Obstetrics and Gynecology, 168,* 1105–1112.

Dhont, M., De Sutter, P., Ruyssinck, G., Martens, G., & Bekaert, A. (1999). Perinatal outcome of pregnancies after assisted reproduction: A case-control study. *American Journal of Obstetrics and Gynecology, 181,* 688–695.

Diamond, A. (1985). The development of the ability to use recall to guide action as indicated by infants' performance on A–B. *Child Development, 56,* 868–883.

Diamond, A. (1991). Neuropsychological insights into the meaning of object concept development. In S. Carey & R. Gelman (Eds.), *The epigenesis of mind: Essays on biology and cognition* (pp. 67–110). Hillsdale, NJ: Erlbaum.

Diamond, A., & Goldman-Rakic, P. S. (1989). Comparison of human infants and rhesus monkeys on Piaget's A–B task: Evidence for dependence on dorsolateral prefrontal cortex. *Experimental Brain Research, 74,* 24–40.

Diamond, A., Prevor, M. B., Callender, G., & Druin, D. P. (1997). Prefrontal cortex cognitive deficits in children treated early and continuously for PKU. *Monographs of the Society for Research in Child Development, 62*(4, Serial No. 252).

Diaz, R. M., & Klingler, C. (1991). Towards an explanatory model of the interaction between bilingualism and cognitive development. In E. Bialystok (Ed.), *Language processing in bilingual children.* Cambridge, UK: Cambridge University Press.

Diaz, R. M., Neal, C. J., & Vachio, A. (1991). Maternal teaching in the zone of the proximal development: A comparison of low- and high-risk dyads. *Merrill-Palmer Quarterly, 37,* 83–108.

Dick, D. M., Rose, R. J., Viken, R. J., & Kaprio, J. (2000). Pubertal timing and substance use: Associations between and within families across late adolescence. *Developmental Psychology, 36,* 180–189.

Dickens, W. T., & Flynn, J. R. (2001). Heritability estimates versus large environmental effects: The IQ paradox resolved. *Psychological Review, 108,* 346–369.

Dick-Read, G. (1959). *Childbirth without fear.* New York: Harper & Row.

Dien, D. S. (1982). A Chinese perspective on Kohlberg's theory of moral development. *Developmental Review, 2,* 331–341.

Dien, D. S.-F. (2000). The evolving nature of self-identity across four levels of history. *Human Development, 43,* 1–18.

Dietz, T. L. (1998). An examination of violence and gender role portrayals in video games: Implications for gender socialization and aggressive behavior. *Sex Roles, 38,* 425–442.

DiMatteo, M. R., Lepper, H. S., Damush, T. M., Morton, S. C., Carney, M. F., Pearson, M., & Kahn, K. L. (1996). Cesarean childbirth and psychosocial outcomes: A meta-analysis. *Health Psychology, 15,* 303–314.

Dion, K. K., & Berscheid, E. (1974). Physical attractiveness and peer perception among children. *Sociometry, 37,* 1–12.

Dishion, T. J., Andrews, D. W., & Crosby, L. (1995). Anti-social boys and their friends in early adolescence: Relationship characteristics, quality, and interactional process. *Child Development, 66,* 139–151.

Dishion, T. J., Patterson, G. R., & Griesler, P. C. (1994). Peer adaptations in the development of antisocial behavior: A confluence model. In L. R. Huesmann (Ed.), *Aggressive behavior: Current perspectives* (pp. 61–95). New York: Plenum.

Dishion, T.J., Spracklen, K. M., Andrews, D. W., & Patterson, G. R. (1996). Deviancy training in male adolescent friendships. *Behavior Therapy, 27,* 373–390.

DiVitto, B., & Goldberg, S. (1979). The effect of newborn medical status on early parent-infant interactions. In T. M. Field, A. M. Sostek, S. Goldberg, & H. H. Shuman (Eds.), *Infants born at risk.* New York: S. P. Medical & Scientific Books.

Dix, T. (1993). Attributing dispositions to children: An interactional analysis of attribution in socialization. *Personality and Social Psychology Bulletin, 19,* 633–643.

Dix, T. H., & Grusec, J. E. (1985). Parent attribution processes in the socialization of children. In I. E. Sigel (Ed.), *Parental belief systems: The psychological consequences for children.* Hillsdale, NJ: Erlbaum.

Dix, T. H., Ruble, D. N., Grusec, J. E., & Nixon, S. (1986). Social cognition in parents: Inferential and affective reactions to children of three age levels. *Child Development, 57,* 879–894.

Dix, T. H., Ruble, D. N., & Zambarano, R. J. (1989). Mothers' implicit theories of discipline: Child effects, parent effects, and the attribution process. *Child Development, 60,* 1373–1391.

Dixon, S., Tronick, E., Keeler, C., & Brazelton, T. B. (1981). Mother-infant interaction among the Gusii of Kenya. In T. M. Field, A. M. Sosteck, P. Vietze, & P. H. Leiderman (Eds.), *Culture and early interactions.* Hillsdale, NJ: Erlbaum.

Dixon, W. E., Jr., & Shore, C. (1997). Temperamental predictors of linguistic style during multiword acquisition. *Infant Behavior and Development, 20,* 99–103.

Dixon, W. E., Jr., & Smith, P. H. (2000). Links between early temperament and language acquisition. *Merrill-Palmer Quarterly, 46,* 417–440.

Dodge, K. A., Coie, J. D., & Lynam, D. (2006). Aggression and antisocial behavior in youth. In W. Damon & R. M. Lerner (Editors-in-Chief) & N. Eisenberg (Vol. Ed.), *Handbook of child psychology: Vol. 3. Social, emotional, and personality development* (6th ed., pp. 719–788). Hoboken, NJ: Wiley.

Dodge, K. A., Lansford, J. E., Burks, V. S., Bates, J. E., Pettit, G. S., et al. (2003). Peer rejection and social information-processing factors in development of aggressive behavior problems in children. *Child Development, 74,* 374–393.

Dodge, K. A., Murphy, R. R., & Buchsbaum, K. (1984). The assessment of intention-cue detection skills in children: Implications for developmental psychopathology. *Child Development, 55,* 163–173.

Dodge, K. A., & Pettit, G. S. (2003). A biopsychosocial model of the development of chronic conduct problems in adolescence. *Developmental Psychology, 39,* 349–371.

Dodge, K. A., Pettit, G. S., & Bates, J. E. (1994). Socialization mediators of the relation between socioeconomic status and child conduct problems. *Child Development, 65,* 649–665.

Doherty, W. J., & Needle, R. H. (1991). Psychological adjustment and substance use among adolescents before and after parental divorce. *Child Development, 62,* 328–337.

Donnelly, M., & Wilson, R. (1994). The dimensions of depression in early adolescence. *Personality and Individual Differences, 17,* 425–430.

Dooley, S. L. (1999). Routine ultrasound in pregnancy. *Clinical Obstetrics and Gynecology,* 737–748.

Dornbusch, S. M., Ritter, P. L., Leiderman, P. H., Roberts, D. F., & Fraleigh, M. J. (1987). The relation of parenting style to adolescent school performance. *Child Development, 58,* 1244–1257.

Dowling, J. E. (1998). *Creating mind: How the brain works.* New York: Norton.

Downey, G., Feldman, S., Khuri, J., & Friedman, S. (1994). Maltreatment and childhood depression. In W. M. Reynolds & H. F. Johnston (Eds.), *Handbook of depression in children and adolescents: Issues in clinical child psychology* (pp. 481–508). New York: Plenum.

Dozier, M., Stovall, K. C., Albus, K. E., & Bates, B. (2001). Attachment for infants in foster care: The role of caregiver state of mind. *Child Development, 72,* 1467–1477.

Dreher, M. C., Nugent, K., & Hudgins, R. (1994). Prenatal marijuana exposure and neonatal outcomes in Jamaica: An ethnographic study. *Pediatrics, 93,* 254–260.

Drewett, R., Wolke, D., Asefa, M., Kaba, M., & Tessema, F. (2001). Malnutrition and mental development: Is there a sensitive period? A nested case-control study. *Journal of Child Psychology and Psychiatry, 42,* 181–187.

Dromi, E. (1999). Early lexical development. In M. Barrett (Ed.), *The development of language* (pp. 99–131). East Sussex, UK: Psychology Press.

Drotar, D., & Robinson, J. (2000). Developmental psychopathology of failure to thrive. In A. J. Sameroff & M. L. Lewis (Eds.), *Handbook of developmental psychopathology* (2nd ed., pp. 351–364). Dordrecht, Netherlands: Kluwer.

Drug and Therapeutics Committee of the Lawson Wilkins Pediatric Endocrine Society. (1995). Guidelines for the use of growth hormone in children with short stature. *Journal of Pediatrics, 127,* 857–867.

Dubner, A. E., & Motta, R. W. (1999). Sexually and physically abused foster care children and posttraumatic stress disorder. *Journal of Consulting and Clinical Psychology, 67,* 367–373.

DuBois, D. L., Burk-Braxton, C., Swenson, L. P., Tevendale, H. D., Lockerd, E. M., & Moran, B. L. (2002). Getting by with a little help from self and others: Self-esteem and social support as resources in early adolescence. *Developmental Psychology, 38,* 822–839.

DuBois, D. L., Tevendale, H. D., Burk-Braxton, C., Swenson, L. P., & Hardesty, J. L. (2000). Self-system influences during early adolescence: Investigation of an integrative model. *Journal of Early Adolescence, 20,* 12–43.

Dubow, E. F., Tisak, J., Causey, D., Hryshko, A., & Reid, G. (1991). A two-year longitudinal study of stressful life events, social support, and social problem-solving skills: Contributions to children's behavioral and academic adjustment. *Child Development, 62,* 583–599.

Dunham, P., & Dunham, F. (1995). Developmental antecedents of taxonomic and thematic strategies at 3 years of age. *Developmental Psychology, 31,* 483–493.

Dunn, J. (1988). Connections between relationships: Implications of research on mothers and siblings. In R. A. Hinde & J. Stevenson-Hinde (Eds.), *Relationships within families: Mutual influences.* Oxford: Clarendon Press.

Dunn, J. (1996). Brothers and sisters in middle childhood and early adolescence: Continuity and change in individual differences. In G. H. Brody (Ed.), *Sibling relationships: Their causes and consequences.* Norwood, NJ: Ablex.

Dunn, J., Bretherton, I., & Munn, P. (1987). Conversations about feeling states between mothers and their young children. *Developmental Psychology, 23,* 132–139.

Dunn, J., & Brown, J. R. (1994). Affect expression in the family, children's understanding of emotions, and their interactions with others. *Merrill Palmer Quarterly, 40,* 120–137.

Dunn, J., Brown, J. R., & Maguire, M. (1995). The development of children's moral sensibility: Individual differences and emotion understanding. *Developmental Psychology, 31,* 649–659.

Dunn, J., & Cutting, A. L. (1999). Understanding others, and individual differences in friendship interactions in young children. *Social Development, 8,* 201–219.

Dunn, J., & Hughes, C. (2001). "I got some swords and you're dead!": Violent fantasy, antisocial behavior, and moral sensibility in young children. *Child Development, 72,* 491–505.

Dunn, J., & Kendrick, C. (1982). *Siblings: Love, envy, and understanding.* Cambridge, MA: Harvard University Press.

Dunn, J., & McGuire, S. (1994). Young children's nonshared experiences: A summary of studies in Cambridge and Colorado. In E. M. Hetherington, D. Reiss, & R. Plomin (Eds.), *Separate social worlds of siblings: The impact of nonshared environment on development* (pp. 111–128). Hillsdale, NJ: Erlbaum.

Dunn, J., Slombowski, C., & Beardsall, L. (1994). Sibling relationships from the preschool period through middle childhood and early adolescence. *Developmental Psychology, 30,* 315–324.

Durik, A. M., Hyde, J. S., & Clark, R. (2000). Sequelae of Cesarean and vaginal deliveries: Psychosocial outcomes for mothers and infants. *Developmental Psychology, 36,* 251–260.

Durston, S., Davidson, M. C., Tottenham, N., Galvan, A., Spicer, J., et al. (2006). A shift from diffuse to focal cortical activity with development. *Developmental Science, 9,* 1–8.

Durston, S., Hulshoff, H. E., Casey, B. J., Giedd, J. N., Buitelaar, J. K., & van Engeland, H. (2001). Anatomical MRI of the developing human brain: What have we learned? *Journal of the American Academy of Adolescent Psychiatry, 40* 1012–1020.

Durston, S., Thomas, K. M., Yang, Y., Ulug, A. M., Zimmerman, R. D., & Casey, B. J. (2002). A neural basis for the development of inhibitory control. *Developmental Science, 5,* F9–F16.

Dusek, J. B. (2000). Commentary on the special issue: The maturing of self-esteem research with early adolescents. *Journal of Early Adolescence, 20,* 231–240.

Dweck, C. S. (1986). Motivational processes affecting learning. *American Psychologist, 41,* 1040–1048.

Dweck, C. S. (1991). Self-theories and goals: Their role in motivation, personality, and development. In R. Diestbier (Ed.), *Nebraska Symposium on Motivation, 1990* (Vol. 36, pp. 199–235). Lincoln: University of Nebraska Press.

Dweck, C. S. (1999). *Self-theories: Their role in motivation, personality, and development.* Philadelphia, PA: Psychology Press.

Dweck, C. S., & Elliott, E. S. (1983). Achievement motivation. In E. M. Hetherington (Ed.), *Handbook of child psychology: Vol. IV. Socialization, personality, and social development* (4th ed., pp. 643–691). New York: Wiley.

Dweck, C. S., Goetz, T. E., & Strauss, N. L. (1980). Sex differences in learned helplessness: IV. An experimental and naturalistic study of failure generalization and its mediators. *Journal of Personality and Social Psychology, 38,* 441–452.

Dybdahl, R. (2001). Children and mothers in war: An outcome study of a psychosocial intervention program. *Child Development, 72,* 1214–1230.

Dye, N. S. (1986). The medicalization of birth. In P. S. Eakins (Ed.), *The American way of birth.* Philadelphia: Temple University Press.

Eagly, A. H., & Steffen, V. J. (1986). Gender and aggressive behavior: A meta-analytic review of the social psychological literature. *Psychological Bulletin, 100,* 309–330.

East, P. L., & Jacobson, L. J. (2001). The younger siblings of teenage mothers: A follow-up of their pregnancy risk. *Developmental Psychology, 37,* 254–264.

Ebrahim, S. H., Luman, E. T., Floyd, R. L.,Murphy, C. C., Bennett, D. M., & Boyle, C. A. (1998). Alcohol consumption by pregnant women in the United States during 1988–1995. *Obstetrics and Gynecology, 92,* 187–192.

Eccles, J. (1983). Expectancies, values, and academic behaviors. In J. T. Spence (Ed.), *Achievement and achievement motives: Psychological and sociological approaches.* San Francisco: W.H. Freeman.

Eccles, J. S. (1987). Adolescence: Gateway to androgyny? In D. B. Carter (Ed.), *Current conceptions of sex roles and sex typing: Theory and research* (pp. 225–241). New York: Praeger.

Eccles, J. S., & Barber, B. L. (1999). Student council, volunteering, basketball, or marching band: What kind of extracurricular involvement matters? *Journal of Adolescent Research, 14,* 10–43.

Eccles, J., Barber, B., Jozefowicz, D., Malenchuk, O., & Vida, M. (1999). Self-evaluations of competence, task values, and self-esteem. In N. G. Johnson, M. C. Roberts, & J. Worell (Eds.), *Beyond appearance: A new look at adolescent girls* (pp. 53–83). Washington, DC: American Psychological Association.

Eccles, J. S., Lord, S. E., Roeser, R. W., Barber, B. L., & Jozefowicz, D. M. H. (1997). The association of school transitions in early adolescence with developmental trajectories through high school. In J. Schulenberg, J. Maggs, & K. Hurrelmann (Eds.), *Health risks and developmental transitions during adolescence* (pp. 283–320). New York: Cambridge University Press.

Eccles, J. S., & Midgley, C. (1989). Stage/environment fit: Developmentally appropriate classrooms for early adolescents. In R. E. Ames & C. Ames (Eds.), *Research on motivation in education* (Vol. 3, pp. 139–186). San Diego, CA: Academic Press.

Eccles, J. S., Midgley, C., Wigfield, A., Buchanan, C. M., Reuman, D., Flanagan, C., & Mac Iver, D. (1993). Development during adolescence: The impact of stage-environment fit on young adolescents' experiences in schools and families. *American Psychologist, 48,* 90–101.

Eccles, J. S., & Roeser, R. W. (1999). School and community influences on human development. In M. H. Bornstein & M. E. Lamb (Eds.), *Developmental psychology: An advanced textbook* (4th ed., pp. 503–554). Mahwah, NJ: Erlbaum.

Eccles, J., Wigfield, A., Harold, R. D., & Blumenfeld, P. (1993). Age and gender differences in children's self- and task perceptions during elementary school. *Child Development, 64,* 830–847.

Eckenrode, J., Laird, M., & Doris, J. (1993). School performance and disciplinary problems among abused and neglected children. *Developmental Psychology, 29,* 53–62.

Eckerman, C. O., Whatley, J. L., & Kutz, S. L. (1975). Growth of social play with peers during the second year of life. *Developmental Psychology, 11,* 42–49.

Eder, D., & Hallinan, M. T. (1978). Sex differences in children's friendships. *American Sociological Review, 43,* 237–250.

Egan, S. K., & Perry, D. G. (1998). Does low self-regard invite victimization? *Developmental Psychology, 34,* 299–309.

Egan, S. K., & Perry, D. G. (2001). Gender identity: A multidimensional analysis with implications for psychosocial adjustment. *Developmental Psychology, 37,* 451–463.

Egeland, B., & Sroufe, L. A. (1981). Attachment and early maltreatment. *Child Development, 52,* 44–52.

Egeland, B., Jacobvitz, D., & Papatola, K. (1987). Intergenerational continuity of abuse. In R. J. Gelles & J. B. Lancaster (Eds.), *Child abuse and neglect: Biosocial dimensions.* Hawthorne, NY: Aldine de Gruyter.

Ehrenberg, R. G., Brewer, D. J., Gamoran, A., & Willms, J. D. (2001a). Class size and student achievement. *Psychological Science in the Public Interest, 2,* 1–30.

Ehrenberg, R. G., Brewer, D. J., Gamoran, A., & Willms, J. D. (2001b, November). Does class size matter? *Scientific American, 285,* 79–85.

Ehri, L. C. (1998). Grapheme-phoneme knowledge is essential for learning to read words in English. In J. L. Metsala & L. C. Ehri (Eds.), *Word recognition in beginning literacy* (pp. 3–40). Mahwah, NJ: Erlbaum.

Eigsti, I., & Cicchetti, D. (2004). The impact of child maltreatment on expressive syntax at 60 months. *Developmental Science, 7,* 88–102.

Eilers, R. E., & Berlin, C. (1995). Advances in early detection of hearing loss in infants. *Current Problems in Pediatrics, 25,* 60–66.

Eimas, P. D., Siqueland, E. R., Jusczyk, P., & Vigorito, J. (1971). Speech perception in infants. *Science, 171,* 303–306.

Eisenberg, N. (1986). *Altruistic emotion, cognition, and behavior.* Hillsdale, NJ: Erlbaum.

Eisenberg, N., Boehnke, K., Schuhler, P., & Silbereisen, R. K. (1985). The development of prosocial behavior and cognition in German children. *Journal of Cross-Cultural Psychology, 16,* 69–82.

Eisenberg, N., Carol, G., Murphy, B., & Van Court, P. (1995). Prosocial development in late adolescence: A longitudinal study. *Child Development, 66,* 1179–1197.

Eisenberg, N., & Fabes, R. A. (1998). Prosocial development. In W. Damon (Series Ed.) & N. Eisenberg (Vol. Ed.), *Handbook of child psychology: Vol. 3. Social, emotional, and personality development* (5th ed., pp. 701–778). New York: Wiley.

Eisenberg, N., Fabes, R. A., Shepard, S. A., Guthrie, I. K., Murphy, B. C., & Reiser, M. (1999). Parental reactions to children's negative emotions: Longitudinal reactions to the quality of children's social functioning. *Child Development, 70,* 513–534.

Eisenberg, N., Fabes, R. A., Shepard, S. A., Murphy, B. C., Guthrie, I. K., Jones, S., et al. (1997). Contemporaneous and longitudinal prediction of children's social functioning from regulation and emotionality. *Child Development, 68,* 642–664.

Eisenberg, N., Fabes, R. A., & Spinrad, T. L. (2006). Prosocial development. In W. Damon & R. M. Lerner (Editors-in-Chief) & N. Eisenberg (Vol. Ed.), *Handbook of child psychology: Vol. 3. Social, emotional, and personality development* (6th ed., pp. 646–718). Hoboken, NJ: Wiley.

Eisenberg, N., Gershoff, E. T., Fabes, R. A., Shepard, S. A., Cumberland, A. J., Losoya, S. H., et al. (2001). Mother's emotional expressivity and children's behavior problems and social competence: Mediation through children's regulation. *Developmental Psychology, 37,* 475–490.

Eisenberg, N., Hertz-Lazarowitz, R., & Fuchs, I. (1990). Prosocial moral judgment in Israeli kibbutz and city children: A longitudinal study. *Merrill-Palmer Quarterly, 36,* 273–285.

Eisenberg, N., & Lennon, R. (1983). Sex differences in empathy and related capacities. *Psychological Bulletin, 94,* 100–131.

Eisenberg, N., & Miller, P. A. (1987). The relation of empathy to prosocial and related behaviors. *Psychological Bulletin, 101,* 91–119.

Eisenberg, N., & Mussen, P. H. (1989). *The roots of prosocial behavior in children.* Cambridge, UK: Cambridge University Press.

Eisenberg, N., Pidada, S., & Liew, J. (2001). The relations of regulation and negative emotionality to Indonesian children's social functioning. *Child Development, 72,* 1747–1763.

Eisenberg, N., & Shell, R. (1986). Prosocial moral judgment and behavior in children: The mediating role of cost. *Personality and Social Psychology Bulletin, 12,* 426–433.

Eisenberg, N., Valiente, C., Morris, A. S., Fabes, R. A., Cumberland, A., et al. (2003). Longitudinal relations among parental emotional expressivity, children's regulation, and quality of socioemotional functioning. *Developmental Psychology, 39,* 3–19.

Eisenberg, N., Zhou, Q., Losoya, S. H., Fabes, R. A., Shepard, S. A., et al. (2003). The relations of parenting, effortful control, and ego control to children's emotional expressivity. *Child Development, 74,* 875–895.

Eisenberg, N., Zhou, Q., Spinrad, T., Valiente, C., Fabes, R. A., & Liew, J. (2005). Relations among positive parenting, children's effortful control, and externalizing problems: A three-wave longitudinal study. *Child Development, 76,* 1055–1071.

Eizenman, D. R., & Bertenthal, B. I. (1998). Infants' perception of object unity in translating and rotating displays. *Developmental Psychology, 34,* 426–434.

Ekman, P. (1972). Universals and cultural differences in facial expressions of emotion. In J. K. Cole (Ed.), *Nebraska symposium on motivation, 1971.* Lincoln: University of Nebraska Press.

Ekman, P. (1973). Cross-cultural studies of facial expression. In P. Ekman (Ed.), *Darwin and facial expression.* New York: Academic Press.

Elardo, R., & Bradley, R. H. (1981). The Home Observation for Measurement of the Environment (HOME) scale: A review of research. *Developmental Review, 1,* 113–145.

Elardo, R., Bradley, R. H., & Caldwell, B. M. (1975). The relation of infants' home environments to mental test performance from six to thirty-six months: A longitudinal analysis. *Child Development, 46,* 71–76.

Elardo, R., Bradley, R., & Caldwell, B. M. (1977). A longitudinal study of the relation of infants' home environments to language development at age three. *Child Development, 48,* 595–603.

Eley, T. C. (1997). General genes: A new theme in developmental psychopathology. *Current Directions in Psychological Science, 6,* 90–95.

Elfenbein, H. A., & Ambady, N. (2002). On the universality and cultural specificity of emotion recognition: A meta-analysis. *Psychological Bulletin, 128,* 203–235.

Elias, S., Simpson, J. L., & Shulman, L. P. (2002). Techniques for prenatal diagnosis. In D. L. Rimoin, J. M. Connor, R. E. Pyeritz, & B. R. Korf (Eds.), *Emery and Rimoin's principles and practice of medical genetics* (4th ed., Vol. 1, pp. 802–825). London: Churchill Livingston.

Eliez, S., & Reiss, A. L. (2000). Genetics of childhood disorders: 77 Fragile X syndrome. *Journal of the American Academy of Child and Adolescent Psychiatry, 39,* 264–266.

Elkind, D. (1976). *Child development and education.* New York: Oxford.

Elkind, D. (1981). *Children and adolescents: Interpretive essays on Jean Piaget* (3rd ed.). New York: Oxford University Press.

Ellemberg, D., Lewis, T. L., Liu, C. H., & Maurer, D. (1999). Development of spatial and temporal vision during childhood. *Vision Research, 39,* 2325–2333.

Elliott, D. S., Wilson, W. J., Huizinga, D., Sampson, R. J., Elliott, A., & Rankin, B. (1996). The effects of neighborhood disadvantage on adolescent development. *Journal of Crime and Delinquency, 33,* 389–426.

Ellis, B. J., & Garber, J. (2000). Psychosocial antecedents of variation in girls' pubertal timing: Maternal depression, stepfather presence, and marital and family stress. *Child Development, 71,* 273–287.

Emde, R. N., & Koenig, K. L. (1969). Neonatal smiling, frowning and rapid eye movement states. *Journal of the American Academy of Child Psychiatry, 8,* 57–67.

Emde, R. N., Plomin, R., Robinson, J., Corley, R., DeFries, J., Walker, D. W., et al. (1992). Temperament, emotion, and cognition at fourteen months: The MacArthur longitudinal twin study. *Child Development, 63,* 1427–1455.

Emery, R. E. (1999a). Changing the rules for determining child custody in divorce cases. *Clinical Psychology: Science and Practice, 6,* 323–327.

Emery, R. E. (1999b). *Marriage, divorce, and children's adjustment* (2nd ed.). Thousand Oaks, CA: Sage.

Emery, R. E., Otto, R. K., & O'Donohue (2005). A critical assessment of child custody evaluations. *Psychological Science in the Public Interest, 6,* 1–29.

Emmons, L. (1996). The relationship of dieting to weight in adolescents. *Adolescence, 31,* 167–178.

Emory, E. K., Schlackman, L. J., & Fiano, K. (1996). Drug-hormone interactions on neurobehavioral responses in human neonates. *Infant Behavior and Development, 19,* 213–220.

Eng, T. R., & Butler, W. T. (Eds.). (1997). *The hidden epidemic: Confronting sexually transmitted disease.* Washington, DC: Institute of Medicine, National Academy Press.

Engle, R. W. (2002). Working memory capacity as executive attention. *Current Directions in Psychological Science, 11,* 19–23.

Engle, R. W., Kane, M. J., & Tuholski, S. W. (1999). Individual differences in working memory capacity and what they tell us about controlled attention, general fluid intelligence, and functions of the prefrontal cortex. In A. Miyake & P. Shah (Eds.), *Models of working memory: Mechanisms of active maintenance and executive control* (pp. 102–134). New York: Cambridge University Press.

Enright, M. K., Rovee-Collier, C. K., Fagen, J. W., & Caniglia, K. (1983). The effects of distributed training on retention of operant conditioning in human infants. *Journal of Experimental Child Psychology, 36,* 512–524.

Ensembl Human. (2006). *Explore the* Homo sapiens *genome.* Retrieved May 5, 2006, from www.ensembl.org/Homo_sapiens/index.html.

Entwisle, D. (1995). The role of schools in sustaining early childhood program benefits. *The Future of Children: Long-term Outcomes of Early Childhood Programs, 5,* 133–143.

Epstein, C. J. (2001). Down syndrome (Trisomy 21). In C. R. Scriver, A. L. Beaudet, W. S. Sly, & D. Valle (Eds.), *The metabolic and molecular bases of inherited disease* (8th ed., Vol. 1, pp.1223–1256). New York: McGraw-Hill.

Epstein, J. L. (1983). Examining theories of adolescent friendship. In J. L. Epstein & N. L. Karweit (Eds.), Friends in school. San Diego: Academic Press.

Erbe, R. W., & Levy, H. L. (2002). Neonatal screening. In D. L. Rimoin, J. M. Connor, R. E. Pyeritz, & B. R. Korf (Eds.), *Emery and Rimoin's principles and practice of medical genetics* (4th ed., Vol. 1, pp. 826–841). London: Churchill Livingston.

Erdley, C. A., Cain, K. M., Loomis, C. C., Dumas-Hines, F., & Dweck, C. S. (1997). Relations among children's social goals, implicit personality theories, and responses to social failure. *Developmental Psychology, 33,* 263–272.

Erhardt, D., & Hinshaw, S. P. (1994). Initial sociometric impressions of attention-deficit hyperactivity disorder and comparison boys: Predictions from social behaviors and from nonbehavioral variables. *Journal of Consulting and Clinical Psychology, 62,* 833–842.

Erickson, M. F., Sroufe, L. A., & Egeland, B. (1985). The relationship between quality of attachment and behavior problems in preschool in a high-risk sample. In I. Bretherton & E. Waters (Eds.), *Growing points of attachment theory and research. Monographs of the Society for Research in Child Development, 50*(1–2, Serial No. 209).

Erikson, E. H. (1950). *Childhood and society.* New York: W. W. Norton

Ernst, M., Moolchan, E. T., & Robinson, M. L. (2001). Behavioral and neural consequences of prenatal exposure to nicotine. *Journal of the Academy of Adolescent Psychiatry, 40,* 630–641.

Eron, L. D., Huesmann, L. R., & Zelli, A. (1991). The role of parental variables in the learning of aggression. In D. J. Pepler & K. H. Rubin (Eds.), *The development and treatment of childhood aggression* (pp. 169–188). Hillsdale, NJ: Erlbaum.

Erwin, P. (1985). Similarity of attitudes and constructs in children's friendships. *Journal of Experimental Child Psychology, 40,* 470–485.

Eskenazi, B., Stapleton, A. L., Kharrazi, M., & Chee, W. Y. (1999). Associations between maternal decaffeinated and caffeinated coffee consumption and fetal growth and gestational duration. *Epidemiology, 10,* 242–249.

Eskritt, M., & Lee, K. (2002). "Remember where you last saw that card": Children's production of external symbols as a memory aid. *Developmental Psychology, 38,* 254–266.

Espy, K. A., & Kaufmann, P. M. (2002). Individual differences in the development of executive function in children: Lessons from the delayed response and A-not-B tasks. In D. L. Molfese & V. J. Molfese (Eds.), *Developmental variations in learning: Applications to social, executive function, language, and reading skills* (pp. 113–137). Mahwah, NJ: Erlbaum.

European Collaborative Study. (2001). Fluctuations in symptoms in human immunodeficiency virus-infected children: The first 10 years of life. *Pediatrics, 108,* 116–122.

Eveleth, P. B., & Tanner, J. M. (1990). *Worldwide variation in human growth* (2nd ed.). Cambridge, UK: Cambridge University Press.

Everman, D. B., & Cassidy, S. B. (2000). Genetics of childhood disorders: 12 Genomic imprinting: Breaking the rules. *Journal of the American Academy of Child and Adolescent Psychiatry, 39,* 386–389.

Eyler, F. D., Behnke, M., Conlon, M., Woods, N. W., & Wobie, K. (1998). Birth outcomes from a prospective matched study of prenatal crack cocaine use: II. Interactive and dose effects on neurobehavioral assessment. *Pediatrics, 101,* 237–241.

Ezzell, C. (2000, July). Beyond the human genome. *Scientific American, 283,* 64–69.

Fabes, R. A., Eisenberg, N., Hanish, L. D., & Spinrad, T. L. (2001). Preschoolers' spontaneous emotion vocabulary: Relations to likability. *Early Education and Development, 12,* 11–27.

Fabes, R. A., Eisenberg, N., Jones, S., Smith, M., Guthries, I, Poulin, R., et al. (1999). Regulation, emotionality, and preschoolers' socially competent peer interactions. *Child Development, 70,* 432–442.

Fabes, R. A., Eisenberg, N., Karbon, M., Troyer, D., & Switzer, G. (1994). The relations of children's emotion regulation to their vicarious emotional responses and comforting behaviors. *Child Development, 65,* 1678–1693.

Fabes, R. A., Eisenberg, N., McCormick, S. E., & Wilson, M. S. (1988). Preschoolers' attributions of the situational determinants of others' naturally occurring emotions. *Developmental Psychology, 24,* 376–385.

Fabes, R. A., Hanish, L. D., Martin, C. L., & Eisenberg, N. (2002). Young children's negative emotionality and social isolation: A latent growth curve analysis. *Merrill Palmer Quarterly, 48,* 284–307.

Fabes, R. A., Leonard, S. A., Kupanoff, K., & Martin, C. L. (2001). Parental coping with children's negative emotions: Relations with children's emotional and social responding. *Child Development, 72,* 907–920.

Fackelmann, K. (1998). It's a girl! Is sex selection the first step to designer children? *Science News, 154,* 350–351.

Fagan, J. F., III. (1974). Infant recognition memory: The effects of length of familiarization and type of discrimination task. *Child Development, 45,* 351–356.

Fagan, J. F., & Holland, C. R. (2002). Equal opportunity and racial differences in IQ. *Intelligence, 30,* 361–387.

Fagot, B. I. (1977). Consequences of moderate cross-gender behavior in preschool children. *Child Development, 48,* 902–907.

Fagot, B. I. (1978). The influence of sex of child on parental reactions to toddler children. *Child Development, 49,* 459–465.

Fagot, B. I. (1985). Changes in thinking about early sex role development. *Developmental Review, 5,* 83–98.

Fagot, B. I., & Leinbach, M. D. (1987). Socialization of sex roles within the family. In D. B. Carter (Ed.), *Current conceptions of sex roles and sex typing: Theory and research.* New York: Praeger.

Fagot, B. I., & Leinbach, M. D. (1989). The young child's gender schema: Environmental input, internal organization. *Child Development, 60,* 663–672.

Fagot, B. I., & Leinbach, M. D. (1995). Gender knowledge in egalitarian and traditional families. *Sex Roles, 32,* 513–526.

Fagot, B. I., Leinbach, M. D., & O'Boyle, C. (1992). Gender labeling, gender stereotyping, and parenting behaviors. *Developmental Psychology, 28,* 225–230.

Falbo, T., & Cooper, C. R. (1980). Young children's time and intellectual ability. *Journal of Genetic Psychology, 173,* 299–300.

Falbo, T., & Polit, D. F. (1986). Quantitative review of the only child literature: Research evidence and theory development. *Psychological Bulletin, 100,* 176–189.

Famularo, R., Fenton, T., Kinscherff, R., Ayoub, C., & Barnum, R. (1994). Maternal and child posttraumatic disorder in cases of child maltreatment. *Child Abuse and Neglect, 18,* 27–36.

Fancher, R. E. (1998). Alfred Binet, general psychologist. In G. A. Kimble & M. Wertheimer (Eds.), *Portraits of pioneers in psychology* (Vol. 3, pp. 67–83). Washington, DC: American Psychological Association.

Fangman, J. J., Mark, P. M., Pratt, L., Conway, K. K., Healey, M. L., Oswald, J. W., & Uden, D. L. (1994). Prematurity prevention programs: An analysis of successes and failures. *American Journal of Obstetrics and Gynecology, 170,* 744–750.

Fantz, R. L. (1961, May). The origin of form perception. *Scientific American, 204,* pp. 66–72.

Farmer, T. W., Estell, D. B., Bishop, J. L., O'Neal, K. K., & Cairns, B. D. (2003). Rejected bullies or popular leaders? The social relations of aggressive subtypes of rural African American early adolescents. *Developmental Psychology, 39,* 992–1004.

Farooqi, I. S., & O'Rahilly, S. (2000). Recent advances in the genetics of severe childhood obesity. *Archives of Disease in Childhood, 83,* 31–34.

Farr, K. A. (1995). Fetal abuse and the criminalization of behavior during pregnancy. *Crime and Delinquency, 41,* 235–245.

Farrar, M. J. (1992). Negative evidence and grammatical morpheme acquisition. *Developmental Psychology, 28,* 90–98.

Farrell, A. D., & Bruce, S. E. (1997). Impact of exposure to community violence on violent behavior and emotional distress among urban adolescents. *Journal of Clinical Child Psychology, 26,* 2–17.

Farrell, S. P., Hains, A. A., & Davies, W. H. (1998). Cognitive behavioral interventions for sexually abused children exhibiting PTSD symptomology. *Behavior Therapy, 29,* 241–255.

Farrington, D. P. (1991). Childhood aggression and adult violence: Early precursors and later-life outcomes. In D. J. Pepler & K. H. Rubin (Eds.), *The development and treatment of childhood aggression* (pp. 5–29). Hillsdale, NJ: Erlbaum.

Farver, J. M., Kim, Y. K., & Lee, Y. (1995). Cultural differences in Korean- and Anglo-American preschoolers' social interaction and play behaviors. *Child Development, 66,* 1088–1099.

Farver, J. M., & Shin, Y. L. (1997). Social pretend play in Korean- and Anglo-American preschoolers. *Child Development, 68,* 544–556.

Farver, J. M., & Wimbarti, S. (1995). Paternal participation in toddlers' pretend play. *Social Development, 4,* 17–31.

Fausto-Sterling, A. (1992). *Myths of gender: Biological theories about women and men* (2nd ed.). New York: Basic Books.

Federman, J. (1998). *National Television Violence Study III.* Thousand Oaks, CA: Sage.

Federal Interagency Forum on Child and Family Statistics. (2005). *Backgrounder: Healthy eating index shows most children and adolescents have a diet that is poor or needs improvement.* Retrieved January 13, 2003, from childstats.gov/ac1999/heirel.asp

Federal Interagency Forum on Child and Family Statistics. (2005). *America's children: Key national indicators of well-being 2005.* Washington, DC: U.S. Government Printing Office.

Feinberg, M. E., & Hetherington, E. M. (2000). Sibling differentiation in adolescence: Implications for behavioral genetic theory. *Child Development, 71,* 1512–1524.

Feingold, A. (1988). Cognitive gender differences are disappearing. *American Psychologist, 43,* 95–103.

Feingold, A. (1992). Sex differences in variability in intellectual abilities: A new look at an old controversy. *Review of Educational Research, 62,* 61–84.

Feingold, A. (1993). Cognitive gender differences: A developmental perspective. *Sex Roles, 29,* 91–112.

Feingold, A. (1994). Gender differences in personality: A meta-analysis. *Psychological Bulletin, 116,* 429–456.

Feldman, D. (1979). The mysterious case of extreme giftedness. In H. Passow (Ed.), *The gifted and talented.* Chicago: University of Chicago Press.

Feldman, H., Goldin-Meadow, S., & Gleitman, L. (1978). Beyond Herodotus: The creation of language by linguistically deprived children. In A. Locke (Ed.), *Action, gesture, and symbol: The emergence of language.* New York: Academic Press.

Feldman, P. J., Dunkel-Schetter, C., Sandman, C. A., & Wadhwa, P. D. (2000). Maternal social support predicts birth weight and fetal growth in human pregnancy. *Psychosomatic Medicine, 62,* 715–725.

Feldman, R., Weller, A., Sirota, L., & Eidelman, A. I. (2002). Skin-to-skin contact (kangaroo care) promotes self-regulation in premature infants: Sleep-wake cyclicity, arousal modulation, and sustained exploration. *Developmental Psychology, 38,* 194–207.

Feldman, W., Feldman, E., & Goodman, J. T. (1988). Culture versus biology: Children's attitudes toward fatness and thinness. *Pediatrics, 81,* 190–194.

Felner, R. D., & Adan, A. M. (1988). The School Transitional Environment Project: An ecological intervention and evaluation. In R. H. Price, E. L. Cowan, R. P. Lorion, I. Serrano-Garcia, & J. Ramos-McKay (Eds.), *14 ounces of prevention: A casebook for practitioners.* Washington, DC: American Psychological Association.

Felner, R. D., Ginter, M., & Primavera, J. (1982). Primary prevention during school transitions: Social support and environmental structure. *American Journal of Community Psychology, 10,* 277–290.

Felson, R. B. (1993). The (somewhat) social self: How others affect self-appraisals. In J. Suls (Ed.), *Psychological perspectives on the self* (Vol. 4, pp. 1–26). Hillsdale, NJ: Erlbaum.

Fenson, L., Dale, P. S., Reznick, J. S., Bates, E., Thal, D. J., & Pethick, S. J. (1994). Variability in early communicative development. *Monographs of the Society for Research in Child Development, 59* (5, Serial No. 242).

Fergusson, D. M., Lynskey, M., & Horwood, L. J. (1995). The adolescent outcomes of adoption: A 16-year longitudinal study. *Journal of Child Psychology and Psychiatry and Allied Disciplines, 36,* 597–615.

Fergusson, D. M., Woodward, L. J., & Horwood, L. J. (1998). Maternal smoking during pregnancy and psychiatric adjustment in late adolescence. *Archives of General Psychiatry, 55,* 721–727.

Fernald, A. (1985). Four-month-olds prefer to listen to motherese. *Infant Behavior and Development, 8,* 181–195.

Fernald, A. (1991). Prosody in speech to children: Prelinguistic and linguistic features. In R. Vasta (Ed.), *Annals of child development: Vol. 8.* London: Jessica Kingsley.

Fernald, A., & Mazzie, C. (1991). Prosody and focus in speech to infants and adults. *Developmental Psychology, 27,* 209–221.

Fernald, A., & Morikawa, H. (1993). Common themes and cultural variations in Japanese and American mothers' speech to infants. *Child Development, 64,* 637–656.

Fernald, A., Perfors, A., & Marchman, V. A. (2006). Picking up speed in understanding: Speech processing efficiency and vocabulary growth across the 2nd year. *Developmental Psychology, 42,* 98–116.

Fernald, A., Swingley, D., & Pinto, J. P. (2001). When half a word is enough: Infants can recognize spoken words using partial phonetic information. *Child Development, 72,* 1003–1015.

Ferrier, S., Dunham, P., & Dunham, F. (2000). The confused robot: Two-year-olds' responses to breakdowns in conversation. *Social Development, 9,* 337–347.

Feuerstein, R., Rand, Y., & Rynders, J. (1988). *Don't accept me as I am: Helping "retarded" people to excel.* New York: Plenum.

Field, J., Muir, D., Pilon, R., Sinclair, M., & Dodwell, P. (1980). Infants' orientation to lateral sounds from birth to three months. *Child Development, 51,* 295–298.

Field, T. (1979). Differential behavior and cardiac responses of 3-month-olds to a mirror and a peer. *Infant Behavior and Development, 2,* 179–184.

Field, T. (1995). Infants of depressed mothers. *Infant Behavior and Development, 18,* 1–13.

Field, T. (2001). Massage therapy facilitates weight gain in preterm infants. *Current Directions in Psychological Science, 10,* 51–54.

Field, T. M. (1977). Effects of early separation, interactive deficits, and experimental manipulations on infant-mother face-to-face interactions. *Child Development, 48,* 763–771.

Field, T. M. (1982). Affective displays of high-risk infants during early interactions. In T. Field & A. Fogel (Eds.), *Emotion and early interaction.* Hillsdale, NJ: Erlbaum.

Field, T. M., Cohen, D., Garcia, R., & Greenberg, R. (1984). Mother-stranger face discrimination by the newborn. *Infant Behavior and Development, 7,* 19–25.

Field, T., Fox, N. A., Pickens, J., & Nawrocki, T. (1995). Relative right frontal EEG activation in 3- to 6-month-old infants of "depressed" mothers. *Developmental Psychology, 31,* 358–363.

Field, T., Healy, B., Goldstein, S., Perry, S., Bendell, D., Schanberg, S., et al. (1988). Infants of depressed mothers show "depressed" behavior even with nondepressed adults. *Child Development, 59,* 1569–1579.

Field, T., Scafidi, F., Pickens, J., Prodromidis, M., Pelaez-Nogueras, M., Torquati, J., et al. (1998). Polydrug-using adolescent mothers and their infants receiving early intervention. *Adolescence, 33,* 117–143.

Field, T. M., Woodson, R., Cohen, D., Greenberg, R., Garcia, R., & Collins, K. (1983). Discrimination and imitation of facial expressions by term and preterm neonates. *Infant Behavior and Development, 6,* 485–489.

Field, T. M., Woodson, R., Greenberg, R., & Cohen, D. (1982). Discrimination and imitation of facial expressions by neonates. *Science, 218,* 179–181.

Fillmore, L. W., & Meyer, L. (1992). The curriculum and linguistic minorities. In P. Jackson (Ed.), *Handbook of research on curriculum.* New York: Macmillan.

Finch, E. (1978). *Clinical assessment of short stature.* Unpublished medical school thesis, Yale University.

Fine, M. A., Coleman, M., & Ganong, L. H. (1999). A social constructionist multi-method approach to understanding the stepparent role. In E. M. Hetherington (Ed.), *Coping with divorce, single parenting, and remarriage* (pp. 273–294). Mahwah, NJ: Erlbaum.

Finn, J. D., & Achilles, C. M. (1990). Answers and questions about class size: A statewide experiment. *American Educational Research Journal, 27,* 557–577.

Finnie, V., & Russell, A. (1988). Preschool children's social status and their mothers' behavior and knowledge in the supervisory role. *Developmental Psychology, 24,* 789–801.

Fioravanti, F., Inchingolo, P., Pensiero, S., & Spanio, M. (1995). Saccadic eye movement conjugation in children. *Vision Research, 35,* 3217–3228.

Fischbein, S. (1981). Heredity-environment influences on growth and development during adolescence. In L. Gedda, P. Parisi, & W. E. Nance (Eds.), *Twin research 3: Pt. B. Program in clinical and biological research.* New York: Liss.

Fischer, K. W., & Bidell, T. R. (2006). Dynamic development of action and thought. In W. Damon & R. M. Lerner (Editors-in-Chief) & R. M. Lerner (Vol. Ed.), *Handbook of child psychology: Vol. 1. Theoretical models of human development* (6th ed., pp. 313–399). Hoboken, NJ: Wiley.

Fisher, C. (2002). Structural limits on verb mapping: The role of abstract structure in 2.5-year-olds' interpretations of novel verbs. *Developmental Science, 5,* 55–64.

Fisher, C. B. (1994). Reporting and referring research participants: Ethical challenges for investigators studying children and youth. *Ethics & Behavior, 4,* 87–95.

Fisher, C. B., Higgins D'Alessandro, A., Rau, J. M. B., Kuther, T. L., & Belanger, S. (1996). Referring and reporting research participants at risk: Views from urban adolescents. *Child Development, 67,* 2086–2100.

Fishkin, J., Keniston, K., & MacKinnon, C. (1973). Moral reasoning and political ideology. *Journal of Personality and Social Psychology, 27,* 109–119.

Fivush, R. (1984). Learning about school: The development of kindergartners' school scripts. *Child Development, 55,* 1697–1709.

Fivush, R. (1997). Event memory in early childhood. In N. Cowan (Ed.), *The development of memory in childhood* (pp. 139–161). East Sussex, UK: Psychology Press.

Fivush, R., & Schwarzmueller, A. (1998). Children remember childhood: Implications for childhood amnesia. *Applied Cognitive Psychology, 12,* 455–473.

Fivush, R., Haden, C., & Adam, S. (1995). Structure and coherence of preschoolers' personal narratives over time: Implications for childhood amnesia. *Journal of Experimental Child Psychology, 60,* 32–56.

Fivush, R., Kuebli, J., & Clubb, P. A. (1992). The structure of events and event representations: A developmental analysis. *Child Development, 63,* 188–201.

Flanagan, C. A. (1990). Change in family work status: Effects on parent-adolescent decision making. *Child Development, 61,* 163–177.

Flannagan, D., & Hardee, S. D. (1994). Talk about preschoolers' interpersonal relationships: Patterns related to culture, SES, and gender of child. *Merrill-Palmer Quarterly, 40,* 523–537.

Flavell, J. H. (1963). *The developmental psychology of Jean Piaget.* New York: Van Nostrand Reinhold.

Flavell, J. H. (1970). Developmental studies of mediated memory. In H. W. Reese & L. P. Lipsitt (Eds.), *Advances in child development and behavior* (Vol. 5). New York: Academic Press.

Flavell, J. H. (1978). The development of knowledge about visual perception. In C. B. Keasey (Ed.), *Nebraska symposium on motivation* (Vol. 25). Lincoln: University of Nebraska Press.

Flavell, J. H. (1993). Young children's understanding of thinking and consciousness. *Current Directions in Psychological Science, 2,* 40–43.

Flavell, J. H. (1996). Piaget's legacy. *Psychological Science, 7,* 200–203.

Flavell, J. H., Beach, D. H., & Chinsky, J. M. (1966). Spontaneous verbal rehearsal in a memory task as a function of age. *Child Development, 37,* 283–299.

Flavell, J. H., Flavell, E. R., Green, F. L., & Korfmacher, J. E. (1990). Do young children think of television images as pictures or real objects? *Journal of Broadcasting & Electronic Media, 34,* 399–419.

Flavell, J. H., & Wellman, H. M. (1977). Metamemory. In R. V. Kail & J. W. Hagen (Eds.), *Perspectives on the development of memory and cognition* (pp. 3–33). Hillsdale, NJ: Erlbaum.

Flavell, J. H., Green, F. L., & Flavell, E. R. (1995). The development of children's knowledge about attentional focus. *Developmental Psychology, 31,* 706–712.

Flavell, J. H., Zhang, X-D, Zou, H., Dong, Q., & Qi, S. (1983). A comparison of the appearance-reality distinction in the People's Republic of China and the United States. *Cognitive Psychology, 15,* 459–466.

Fletcher, A. C., Steinberg, L., & Williams-Wheeler, M. (2004). Parental influences on adolescent problem behavior: Revisiting Stattin and Kerr. *Child Development, 75,* 781–796.

Fletcher-Flinn, C. M., & Thompson, G. B. (2000). Learning to read with underdeveloped phonemic awareness but lexicalized phonological recoding: A case study of a 3-year-old. *Cognition, 74,* 177–208.

Flick, L., Vemulapalli, C., Stulac, B. B., & Kemp, J. S. (2001). The influence of grandmothers and other senior caregivers on sleep position used by African American infants. *Archives of Pediatrics and Adolescent Medicine, 155,* 1231–1237.

Flieller, A. (1999). Comparison of the development of formal thought in adolescent cohorts aged 10 to 15 years (1967–1996 and 1972–1993). *Developmental Psychology, 35,* 1048–1058.

Florsheim, P., Tolan, P., & Gorman-Smith, D. (1998). Family relationship, parenting practices, the availability of male family members, and the behavior of inner-city boys in single-mother and two parent families. *Child Development, 69,* 1437–1447.

Flynn, J. R. (1998). IQ gains over time: Toward finding the causes. In U. Neisser (Ed.), *The rising curve: Long-term gains in IQ and related measures* (pp. 25–66). Washington, DC: American Psychological Association.

Flynn, J. R. (1999). Searching for justice: The discovery of IQ gains over time. *American Psychologist, 54,* 5–20.

Foa, E. B., & Meadows, E. A. (1997). Psychosocial treatments for post-traumatic stress disorder: A critical review. *Annual Review of Psychology, 48,* 449–480.

Fodor, J. A . (1992). A theory of the child's theory of mind. *Cognition, 44,* 283–296.

Fodor, J. A. (1983). *The modularity of mind.* Cambridge, MA: MIT Press.

Fogel, A. (1979). Peer- vs. mother-directed behavior in 1- to 3-month-old infants. *Infant Behavior and Development, 2,* 215–226.

Fogel, A. (1982). Early adult-infant face-to-face interaction: Expectable sequences of behavior. *Journal of Pediatric Psychology, 7,* 1–22.

Fomon, S. J. (1993). *Nutrition of normal infants.* St. Louis, MO: Mosby-Yearbook.

Food and Drug Aministration. (2005). *Public Health Advisory: Strengthened risk management program for isotretinoin.* Retrieved May 3, 2006, from www.fda.gov/cder/drug/advisory/isotretinoin2005.htm.

Forbes, E. E., Cohn, J. F., Allen, N. B., & Lewinsohn, P. M. (2004). Infant affect during parent-infant interaction at 3 and 6 months: Differences between mothers and fathers and influence of parent history of depression. *Infancy, 5,* 61–84.

Forman, D. R., & Kochanska, G. (2001). Viewing imitation as child responsiveness: A link between teaching and discipline domains of socialization. *Developmental Psychology, 37,* 198–206.

Forman, D. R., Aksan, N., & Kochanska, G. (2004). Toddlers' responsive imitation predicts preschool-age conscience. *Psychological Science, 15,* 699–704.

Foulon, W., Villena, I., Stray-Pedersen, B., Decoster, A., Lappalainen, M., Pinon, J.-M., et al. (1999). Treatment of toxoplasmosis during pregnancy: A multicenter study of impact on fetal transmission and children's sequelae at age 1 year. *American Journal of Obstetrics and Gynecology, 180,* 410–415.

Fox, N. A. (1991). If it's not left, it's right: Electroencephalograph asymmetry and the development of emotion. *American Psychologist, 46,* 863–872.

Fox, N. A. (1994). Dynamic cerebral processes underlying emotion regulation. In N. A. Fox (Ed.), *The development of emotion regulation: Biological and behavioral considerations. Monographs of the Society for Research in Child Development, 59* (Nos. 2–3, Serial No. 240).

Fox, N. A., & Davidson, R. J. (1986). Psychophysiological measures of emotion: New directions in developmental research. In C. E. Izard & P. B. Read (Eds.), *Measuring emotions in infants and children* (Vol. 2). Cambridge, UK: Cambridge University Press.

Fox, R., Aslin, R. N., Shea, S. L., & Dumais, S. T. (1980). Stereopsis in human infants. *Science, 207,* 323–324.

Fraiberg, S. (1977). *Insights from the blind.* New York: Basic Books.

Franco, P., Groswasser, J., Hassid, S., Lanquart, J. P., Scaillet, S., & Kahn, A. (1999). Prenatal exposure to cigarette smoking is associated with a decrease in arousal in infants. *Journal of Pediatrics, 135,* 34–38.

Frank, D. A., Augustyn, M., Knight, W. G., Pell, T., & Zuckerman, B. (2001). Growth, development, and behavior in early childhood following prenatal cocaine exposure: A systematic review. *Journal of the American Medical Association, 285,* 1613–1625.

Franklin, C., Grant, D., Corcoran, J., O'Dell-Miller, P., & Bultman, L. (1997). Effectiveness of prevention programs for adolescent pregnancy: A meta-analysis. *Journal of Marriage and the Family, 59,* 551–567.

Fraser, S. (1995). *The bell curve wars: Race, intelligence, and the future of America.* New York: Basic Books.

Frauenglass, M. H., & Diaz, R. M. (1985). Self-regulatory functions of children's private speech: A critical analysis of recent challenges to Vygotsky's theory. *Developmental Psychology, 21,* 357–364.

Frazier, J. A., & Morrison, F. J. (1998). The influence of extended-year schooling on growth of achievement and perceived competence in early elementary school. *Child Development, 69,* 495–517.

Fredricks, J. A., & Eccles, J. S. (2002). Children's competence and value beliefs from childhood through adolescence: Growth trajectories in two male-sex-typed domains. *Developmental Psychology, 38,* 519–533.

Fredriks, A. M., Van Buren, S., Burgmeijer, R. J. F., Meulmeester, J. F., Beuker, R J., Brugman, E., et al. (2000). Continuing positive secular growth change in the Netherlands 1955–1997. *Pediatric Research, 47,* 316–323.

Fredriksen, K., Rhodes, J., Reddy, R., & Way, N. (2004). Sleepless in Chicago: Tracking the effects of adolescent sleep loss during the middle school years. *Child Development, 75,* 84–95.

Freedland, R. L., & Bertenthal, B. I. (1994). Developmental changes in interlimb coordination: Transition to hands-and-knees crawling. *Psychological Science, 5,* 26–32.

French, S. E., Seidman, E., Allen, L., & Aber, J. L. (2000). Racial/ethnic identity, congruence with the social context, and the transition to high school. *Journal of Adolescent Research, 15,* 587–602.

French, S. E., Seidman, E., Allen, L., & Aber, J. L. (2006). The development of ethnic identity during adolescence. *Developmental Psychology, 42,* 1–10.

Frey, K. S., Hirschstein, M. K., Snell, J. L., Edstrom, L. V. S., MacKenzie, E. P., & Broderick, C. J. (2005). Reducing playground bullying and supporting beliefs: An experimental trial of the *Steps to Respect* program. *Developmental Psychology, 41,* 479–491.

Frey, K. S., & Ruble, D. N. (1987). What children say about classroom performance: Sex and grade differences in perceived competence. *Child Development, 58,* 1066–1078.

Fried, P. A., Watkinson, B., & Gray, R. (1998). Differential effects on cognitive functioning in 9- to 12-year-olds prenatally exposed to cigarettes and marijuana. *Neurotoxicology and Teratology, 20,* 293–306.

Friedman, J. M., & Hanson, J. W. (2002). Clinical teratology. In D. L. Rimoin, J. M. Connor, R. E. Pyeritz, & B. R. Korf (Eds.), *Emery and Rimoin's principles and practice of medical genetics* (4th ed., Vol. 1, pp. 1011–1045). London: Churchill Livingston.

Friedman, J. M., & Polifka, J. E. (1996). *The effects of drugs on the fetus and nursing infant: A handbook for health care professionals.* Baltimore: Johns Hopkins University Press.

Frith, U., & Happé, F. (1999). Theory of mind and self-consciousness: What is it like to be autistic? *Mind & Language, 14,* 1–22.

Frodi, A. M., & Lamb, M. E. (1980). Child abusers' responses to infant smiles and cries. *Child Development, 51,* 238–241.

Frodi, A. M., Lamb, M. E., Leavitt, L. A., & Donovan, W. L. (1978). Fathers' and mothers' responses to infant smiles and cries. *Infant Behavior and Development, 1,* 187–198.

Frodi, A. M., & Thompson, R. (1985). Infants' affective responses in the strange situation: Effects of prematurity and of quality of attachment. *Child Development, 56,* 1280–1290.

Fuligni, A. J. (1997). The academic achievement of adolescents from immigrant families: The roles of family background, attitudes, and behavior. *Child Development, 68,* 351–363.

Fuligni, A. J., & Eccles, J. S. (1993). Perceived parent-child relationships and early adolescents' orientation toward peers. *Developmental Psychology, 29,* 622–632.

Fuligni, A. J., & Stevenson, H. W. (1995). Time use and mathematics achievement among American, Chinese, and Japanese high school students. *Child Development, 66,* 830–842.

Fuligni, A. J., Eccles, J. S., Barber, B. L., & Clements, P. (2001). Early adolescent peer orientation and adjustment during high school. *Developmental Psychology, 37,* 28–36.

Fuligni, A. J., Witkow, M., & Garcia, C. (2005). Ethnic identity and the academic adjustment of adolescents from Mexican, Chinese, and European backgrounds. *Developmental Psychology, 41,* 799–811.

Fulker, O. W., & Eysenck, H. J. (1979). Nature, nurture and socioeconomic status. In H. J. Eysenck (Ed.), *The structure and measurement of intelligence.* Berlin: Springer-Verlag.

Furman, W. (1999). Friends and lovers: The role of peer relationships in adolescent romantic relationships. In W. A. Collins & B. Laursen (Eds.), *Minnesota symposia on child psychology: Vol. 30. Relationships as developmental contexts* (pp. 133–154). Mahwah, NJ: Erlbaum.

Furman, W. (2002). The emerging field of adolescent romantic relationships. *Current Directions in Psychological Science, 11,* 177–180.

Furman, W., & Bierman, K. L. (1984). Children's conceptions of friendship: A multimethod study of developmental changes. *Developmental Psychology, 20,* 925–931.

Furman, W., & Buhrmester, D. (1992). Age and sex differences in perceptions of networks of personal relationships. *Child Development, 63,* 103–115.

Furman, W., Somin, V. A., Shaffer, L., & Bouchey, H. A. (2002). Adolescents' working models and styles for relationships with parents, friends, and romantic partners. *Child Development, 73,* 241–255.

Furman, W., & Wehner, E. A. (1994). Romantic views: Toward a theory of adolescent romantic relationships. In R. Montemayor, G. R. Adams, & G. P. Gullota (Eds.), *Advances in adolescent development: Vol. 6. Relationships during adolescence* (pp. 168–175). Thousand Oaks, CA: Sage.

Furnham, A., & Mak, T. (1999). Sex-role stereotyping in television commercials: A review and comparison of fourteen studies done on five continents over 25 years. *Sex Roles, 41,* 413–437.

Furstenberg, F. F. (1994). History and current status of divorce in the United States. *The Future of Children, 4,* 29–43.

Furstenberg, F. F., Jr. (1987). The new extended family: The experience of parents and children after remarriage. In K. Paley & M. Ihinger-Tallman (Eds.), *Remarriage and stepparenting.* New York: Guilford Press.

Furstenberg, F. F., Jr., Brooks-Gunn, J., & Chase-Lansdale, L. (1989). Teenaged pregnancy and childbearing. *American Psychologist, 44,* 313–320.

Fuson, K. C., & Kwon, Y. (1992). Korean children's understanding of multidigit addition and subtraction. *Child Development, 63,* 491–506.

Gabbe, S. G., & Turner, L. P. (1997). Reproductive hazards of the American lifestyle: Work during pregnancy. *American Journal of Obstetrics and Gynecology, 176,* 826–832.

Gabel, S. (1997). Conduct disorder in grade-school children. In J. D. Noshpitz (Series Ed.) & P. F. Kernberg & J. R. Bemporad (Vol. Eds.), *Handbook of child and adolescent psychiatry* (Vol. 2, pp. 309–401). New York: Wiley.

Gaddis, A., & Brooks-Gunn, J. (1985). The male experience of pubertal change. *Journal of Youth and Adolescence, 14,* 61–69.

Gagnon, M., & Ladouceur, R. (1992). Behavioral treatment of child stutterers: Replication and extension. *Behavior Therapy, 23,* 113–129.

Galambos, N. L. (2004). Gender and gender role development in adolescence. In R. M. Lerner & L. Steinberg (Eds.), *Handbook of adolescent psychology* (2nd ed., pp. 233–262). Hoboken, NJ: Wiley.

Gallahue, D. L. (1989). *Understanding motor development: Infants, children, adolescents.* Indianapolis, IN: Benchmark Press.

Galler, J. R., Ramsey, F. C., Morley, D. S., Archer, E., & Salt, P. (1990). The long-term effects of early kwashiorkor compared with marasmus. IV. Performance on the National High School Entrance Exam. *Pediatric Research, 28,* 235–239.

Gallistel, C. R., Brown, A. L., Carey, S., Gelman, R., & Keil, F. C. (1991). Lessons from animal learning for the study of cognitive development. In S. Carey & R. Gelman (Eds.), *The epigenesis of mind: Essays on biology and cognition* (pp. 3–36). Hillsdale, NJ: Erlbaum.

Galton, F. (1883). *Inquiries into human faculty and its development.* London: Macmillan.

Gannon, P. J., Holloway, R. L., Broadfield, D. C., & Braun, A. R. (1998). Asymmetry of chimpanzee planum temporale: Humanlike pattern of Wernicke's brain language area homolog. *Science, 279,* 220–222.

Garabino, J. (1982). Sociocultural risk: Dangers to competence. In C. Kopp & J. Krakow (Eds.), *Child development in a social context.* Reading, MA: Addison-Wesley.

Garcia, M. M., Shaw, D. S., Winslow, E. B., & Yaggi, K. E. (2000). Destructive sibling conflict and the development of conduct problems in young boys. *Developmental Psychology, 36,* 44–53.

Gardner, B. T., & Gardner, R. A. (1971). Two-way communication with an infant chimpanzee. In A. M. Schrier & F. Stollnitz (Eds.), *Behavior of nonhuman primates.* New York: Academic Press.

Gardner, D., Harris, P. L., Ohmoto, M., & Hamasaki, T. (1988). Japanese children's understanding of the distinction between real and apparent emotion. *International Journal of Behavioral Development, 11,* 203–218.

Gardner, H. (1983). *Frames of mind: The theory of multiple intelligences.* New York: Basic Books.

Gardner, H. (1986). The waning of intelligence tests. In R. J. Sternberg & D. K. Detterman (Eds.), *What is intelligence?* (pp. 73–76). Norwood, NJ: Ablex.

Gardner, H. (1998). Are there additional intelligences? The case for naturalistic, spiritual, and existential intelligences. In J. Kane (Ed.), *Education, information, and transformation: Essays on learning and thinking* (pp. 111–131). Upper Saddle River, NJ: Prentice Hall.

Gardner, M., & Steinberg, L. (2005). Peer influence on risk taking, risk preference, and risky decision making in adolescence and adulthood: An experimental study. *Developmental Psychology, 41,* 625–635.

Gardner, W., & Rogoff, B. (1990). Children's deliberateness of planning according to task circumstances. *Developmental Psychology, 26,* 480–487.

Garland, A. F., & Zigler, E. (1993). Adolescent suicide prevention: Current research and social policy implications. *American Psychologist, 48,* 169–182.

Gash, H., & Morgan, M. (1993). School-based modifications of children's gender-related beliefs. *Journal of Applied Developmental Psychology, 14,* 277–287.

Gavin, L. A., & Furman, W. (1989). Age differences in adolescent's perceptions of their peer groups. *Developmental Psychology, 25,* 827–834.

Gazelle, H., & Ladd, G. W. (2003). Anxious solitude and peer exclusion: A diathesis-stress model of internalizing trajectories in childhood. *Child Development, 74,* 257–278.

Gazelle, H., & Rudolph, K. D. (2004). Moving toward and away from the world: Approach and avoidance trajectories in anxious solitary youth. *Child Development, 75,* 829–849.

Ge, X., Best, K. M., Conger, R. D., & Simons, R. L. (1996). Parenting behaviors and the occurrence and co-occurrence of adolescent depressive symptoms and conduct problems. *Developmental Psychology, 32,* 717–731.

Ge, X., Conger, R. D., & Elder, G. H., Jr. (1996). Coming of age too early: Pubertal influences on girls' vulnerability to psychological distress. *Child Development, 67,* 3386–3400.

Ge, X., Kim, I. J., Brody, G. H., Conger, R. D., Simons, R. L., et al. (2003). It's about timing and change: Pubertal transition effects on symptoms of major depression among African American youths. *Developmental Psychology, 39,* 430–439.

Ge, X., Lorenz, F. O., Conger, R. D., Elder, G. H., Jr., & Simons, R. L. (1994). Trajectories of stressful life events and depressive symptoms during adolescence. *Developmental Psychology, 30,* 467–483.

Geary, D. C., Bow-Thomas, C. C., Fan, L., & Siegler, R. S. (1993). Even before formal instruction, Chinese children outperform American children in mental addition. *Cognitive Development, 8,* 517–529.

Geldart, S., Maurer, D., & Carney, K. (1999). Effects of the height of the internal features of faces on adult's aesthetic ratings and 5-month-old's looking times. *Perception, 28,* 839–850.

Gelman, R. (1969). Conservation acquisition: A problem of learning to attend to relevant attributes. *Journal of Experimental Child Psychology, 7,* 167–187.

Gelman, R., & Gallistel, C. R. (1978). *The child's understanding of number.* Cambridge, MA: Harvard University Press.

Gelman, R., & Meck, E. (1983). Preschoolers' counting: Principles before skill. *Cognition, 13,* 343–359.

Gelman, R., Spelke, E. S., & Meck, E. (1983). What preschoolers know about animate and inanimate objects. In D. Rogers & J. A. Sloboda (Eds.), *The acquisition of symbolic skills.* New York: Plenum.

Gelman, R., & Williams, E. M. (1998). Enabling constraints for cognitive development: Domain specificity and epigenesis. In W. Damon (Series Ed.) & D. Kuhn & R. S. Siegler (Vol. Eds.), *Handbook of child psychology: Vol. 2. Cognition, perception, and language* (5th ed., pp. 575–630). New York: Wiley.

Gelman, S. A., Coley, J. D., Rosengren, K. S., Hartman, E., & Pappas, A. (1998). Beyond labeling: The role of maternal input in the acquisition of richly structured categories. *Monographs of the Society for Research in Child Development, 63*(1, Serial No. 253).

Gelman, S. A., & Kalish, C. W. (2006). Conceptual development. In W. Damon & R. M. Lerner (Editors-in-Chief) & D. M. Kuhn & R. S. Siegler (Vol. Eds.), *Handbook of child psychology: Vol. 2. Cognition, perception, and language* (6th ed., pp. 687–733). Hoboken, NJ: Wiley.

Gelman, S. A., & Kremer, K. E. (1991). Understanding natural cause: Children's explanations of how objects and their properties originate. *Child Development, 62,* 396–414.

Gelman, S. A., Taylor, M. G., & Nguyen, S. P. (2004). Mother-child conversations about gender. *Monographs of the Society for Research in Child Development, 69*(1, Serial No. 275).

Gershkoff-Stowe, L. (2001). The course of children's naming errors in early word learning. *Journal of Cognition and Development, 2,* 131–155.

Gershkoff-Stowe, L., & Smith, L. B. (1997). A curvilinear trend in naming errors as a function of early vocabulary growth. *Cognitive Psychology, 34,* 37–71.

Gershoff, E. T. (2002). Corporal punishment by parents and associated child behaviors and experiences: A meta-analytic and theoretical review. *Psychological Bulletin, 128,* 539–579.

Geschwind, M., & Galaburda, A. M. (1987). *Cerebral lateralization.* Cambridge, MA: MIT Press.

Gesell, A., & Thompson, H. (1934). *Infant behavior: Its genesis and growth.* New York: McGraw-Hill.

Gesell, A., & Thompson, H. (1938). *The psychology of early growth.* New York: Macmillan.

Gewirtz, J. L., & Peláez-Nogueras, M. (1992). B. F. Skinner's legacy to human infant behavior and development. *American Psychologist, 47,* 1411–1422.

Ghim, H-R. (1990). Evidence for perceptual organization in infants: Perception of subjective contours by young infants. *Infant Behavior and Development, 13,* 221–248.

Gibson, E. J. (1969). *Principles of perceptual learning and development.* New York: Appleton.

Gibson, E. J. (1982). The concept of affordances in development: The renascence of functionalism. In W. A. Collins (Ed.), *The Minnesota symposia on child psychology: Vol. 15. The concept of development.* Hillsdale, NJ: Erlbaum.

Gibson, E. J. (1988). Exploratory behavior in the development of perceiving, acting, and the acquiring of knowledge. *Annual Review of Psychology, 39,* 1–41.

Gibson, E. J., Gibson, J. J., Pick, A. D., & Osser, H. (1962). A developmental study of the discrimination of letter-like forms. *Journal of Comparative and Physiological Psychology, 55,* 897–906.

Gibson, E. J., & Walker, A. (1984). Development of knowledge of visual-tactual affordances of substance. *Child Development, 55,* 453–460.

Gibson, J. J. (1966). *The senses considered as perceptual systems.* Boston: Houghton Mifflin.

Gibson, J. J. (1979). *The ecological approach to visual perception.* Boston: Houghton Mifflin.

Gibson, M., & Ogbu, J. (Eds.). (1991). *Minority status and schooling: A comparative study of immigrant and involuntary minorities.* New York: Garland.

Giedd, J. N., Blumenthal, J., Molloy, E., & Castellanos, F. X. (2001). Brain imaging of attention deficit/hyperactivity disorder. *Annals of the New York Academy of Sciences, 931,* 33–49.

Gilbert, S. F. (2003). *Developmental biology* (7th ed.). Sunderland, MA: Sinauer Associates.

Gilbert, W. M., Nesbitt, T. S., & Danielsen, B. (1999). Childbearing beyond age 40: Pregnancy outcome in 24,032 cases. *Obstetrics and Gynecology, 93,* 9–14.

Giles, J. W., Gopnik, A., & Heyman, G. D. (2002). Source monitoring reduces the suggestibility of preschool children. *Psychological Science, 13,* 288–291.

Gilligan, C. (1982). *In a different voice: Psychological theory and women's development.* Cambridge, MA: Harvard University Press.

Gilligan, C. (1988). Remapping the moral domain: New images of self in relationship. In C. Gilligan, J. V. Ward, J. M. Taylor, & B. Bardige (Eds.), *Mapping the moral domain.* Cambridge, MA: Harvard University Press.

Gilligan, C., & Attanucci, J. (1988). Two moral orientations: Gender differences and similarities. *Merrill-Palmer Quarterly, 34,* 223–237.

Gilliom, M., Shaw, D. S., Beck, J. E., Schonberg, M. A., & Lukon, J. L. (2002). Anger regulation in disadvantaged preschool boys: Strategies, antecedents, and the development of self-control. *Developmental Psychology, 38,* 222–235.

Ginsberg, H. P. (1972). *The myth of the deprived child: Poor children's intellect and education.* Englewood Cliffs, NJ: Prentice-Hall.

Ginsburg, H. P. & Opper, S. (1988). *Piaget's theory of intellectual development* (3rd ed.). Englewood Cliffs, NJ: Prentice-Hall.

Ginsburg, H. P., Pappas, S., & Seo, K. H. (2001). Everyday mathematical knowledge: Asking young children what is developmentally appropriate. In S. L. Golbeck (Ed.), *The Rutgers invitational symposium on education series: Psychological perspectives on early childhood education: Reframing dilemmas in research and practice* (pp. 181–219). Mahwah, NJ: Erlbaum.

Glasgow, K. L., Dornbusch., S. N., Troyer, L., Steinberg, L., & Ritter, P. (1997). Parenting styles, adolescents' attributions, and educational outcomes in nine heterogeneous high schools. *Child Development, 68,* 507–529.

Glass, D. C., Neulinger, J., & Brim, O. G. (1974). Birth order, verbal intelligence, and educational aspiration. *Child Development, 45,* 807–811.

Glassman, M., & Zan, B. (1995). Moral activity and domain theory: An alternative interpretation of research on young children. *Developmental Review, 15,* 434–457.

Gleason, J. B., & Perlmann, R. Y. (1985). Acquiring social variation in speech. In H. Giles & R. N. St. Clair (Eds.), *Recent advances in language, communication, and social psychology.* London: Erlbaum.

Gleason, J. B., & Weintraub, S. (1978). Input language and the acquisition of communicative competence. In K. Nelson (Ed.), *Children's language* (Vol. 1). New York: Gardner Press.

Gleitman, L. R., Gleitman, H., & Shipley, E. F. (1972). The emergence of the child as grammarian. *Cognition, 1,* 137–164.

Gleitman, L. R., Newport, E. L., & Gleitman, H. (1984). The current status of the motherese hypothesis. *Journal of Child Language, 11,* 43–79.

Glynn, L. M., Wadhwa, P. O., Dunkel-Schetter, C., Chicz-DeMet, A., & Sandman, C. A. (2001). When stress happens matters: Effects of earthquake timing on stress responsivity in pregnancy. *American Journal of Obstetrics & Gynecology, 184,* 637–642.

Gogate, L. J., Bahrick, L. E., & Watson, J. D. (2000). A study of multimodal motherese: The role of temporal synchrony between verbal labels and gestures. *Child Development, 71,* 878–894.

Goldberg, M. C., Maurer, D., & Lewis, T. L. (2001). Developmental changes in attention: The effects of endogenous cueing and of distractors. *Developmental Science, 4,* 209–219.

Goldberg, S. (1979). Premature birth: Consequences for the parent-infant relationship. *American Scientist, 67,* 582–590.

Goldberg, W. A., Greenberger, E., & Nagel, S. K. (1996). Employment and achievement: Mothers' work involvement in relation to children's achievement behaviors and mothers' parenting behaviors. *Child Development, 67,* 1512–1527.

Golden, F. (1998, September 21). Boy? Girl? Up to you. *Time,* pp. 82–83.

Goldenberg, R. L., Clivar, S. P., Cutter, G. R., Hoffman, H. J., Cassady, G., Davis, R. O., & Nelson, K. G. (1991). Black-white differences in newborn anthropometric measurements. *Obstetrics and Gynecology, 78,* 782–788.

Goldfield, B. A., & Reznick, J. S. (1990). Early lexical acquisition: Rate, content, and the vocabulary spurt. *Journal of Child Language, 17,* 171–183.

Goldin-Meadow, S. (2006). Nonverbal communication: The hand's role in talking and thinking. In W. Damon & R. M. Lerner (Editors-in-Chief) & D. M. Kuhn & R. S. Siegler (Vol. Eds.), *Handbook of child psychology: Vol. 2. Cognition, perception, and language* (6th ed., pp. 336–369). Hoboken, NJ: Wiley.

Goldsmith, H. H., & Alansky, J. A. (1987). Maternal and infant temperamental predictors of attachment: A meta-analytic review. *Journal of Consulting and Clinical Psychology, 55,* 805–816.

Goldsmith, H. H., Buss, K. A., & Lemery, K. S. (1997). Toddler and childhood temperament: Expanded content, stronger genetic evidence, new evidence for the importance of environment. *Developmental Psychology, 33,* 891–905.

Goldstein, S. E., Davis-Kean, P. E., & Eccles, J. S. (2005). Parents, peers, and problem behavior: A longitudinal investigation of the impact of relationship perceptions and characteristics on the development of adolescent problem behavior. *Developmental Psychology, 41,* 401–413.

Golier, J., & Yehuda, R. (1998). Neuroendocrine activity and memory-related impairments in posttraumatic stress disorder. *Development and Psychopathology, 10,* 857–869.

Golinkoff, R. M., Harding, C. G., Carlson, V., & Sexton, M. E. (1984). The infant's perception of causal events: The distinction between animate and inanimate objects. In L. L. Lipsitt & C. Rovee-Collier (Eds.), *Advances in infancy research. Vol. 3.* Norwood, NJ: Ablex.

Golinkoff, R. M., Mervis, C. B., & Hirsh-Pasek, K. (1994). Early object labels: The case for a developmental lexical principles framework. *Journal of Child Language, 21,* 125–155.

Golombok, S., Cook, R., Bish, A., & Murray, C. (1995). Families created by the new reproductive technologies: Quality of parenting and social and emotional development of the children. *Child Development, 66,* 285–298.

Golombok, S., MacCallum, F., & Goodman, E. (2001). The "test-tube" generation: Parent-child relationships and the psychological well-being of in vitro fertilization in children at adolescence. *Child Development, 72,* 599–608.

Golombok, S., MacCallum, F., Goodman, E., & Rutter, M. (2002). Families with children conceived by donor insemination: A follow-up at stage twelve. *Child Development, 73,* 952–968.

Golombok, S., Perry, B., Burston, A., Murray, C., Mooney-Somers, J., Stevens, M., & Golding, J. (2003). Children with lesbian parents: A community study. *Developmental Psychology, 39,* 20–33.

Goncu, A., Patt, M. B., & Kouba, E. (2002). Understanding young children's pretend play in context. In P. K. Smith & C. H. Hart (Eds.), *Blackwell handbook of childhood social development* (pp. 418–437). Malden, MA: Blackwell.

Gonzalez, P., Guzman, J. C., Partelow, L., Pahlke, E., Jocelyn, L., Kastberg, D., & Williams, T. (2004). *Highlights from the Trends in International Mathematics and Science Study (TIMMS) 2003* (NCES 2005–05). U.S. Department of Education, National Center for Education Statistics. Washington, DC: U.S. Government Printing Office.

Goodnow, J. (1988). Children's household work: Its nature and functions. *Psychological Bulletin, 103,* 5–26.

Goodwin, S. W., & Acredolo, L. P. (1993). Symbolic gesture versus word: Is there a modality advantage for onset of symbol use? *Child Development, 64,* 688–701.

Gopnik, A. (1996). The post-Piaget era. *Psychological Science, 7,* 221–225.

Gopnik, A., & Meltzoff, A. N. (1986). Relations between semantic and cognitive development in the one-word stage: The specificity hypothesis. *Child Development, 57,* 1040–1053.

Gopnik, A., & Meltzoff, A. N. (1987). The development of categorization in the second year and its relation to other cognitive and linguistic attainments. *Child Development, 58,* 1523–1531.

Gopnik, A., & Rosati, A. (2001). Duck or rabbit? Reversing ambiguous figures and understanding ambiguous representations. *Developmental Science, 4,* 175–183.

Gordin, D., & Pea, R. D. (1995). Prospects for scientific visualization as an educational technology. *The Journal of Learning Science, 4,* 249–279.

Gordon, I., & Slater, A. (1998). Nativism and empiricism: The history of two ideas. In A. Slater (Ed.), *Perceptual development: Visual, auditory, and speech perception in infancy* (pp. 73–103). East Sussex, UK: Psychology Press.

Gorman-Smith, D., & Tolan, P. (1998). The prevalence and consequences of exposure to violence among African-American youth. *Development and Psychopathology, 10,* 101–116.

Gorski, P. A. (1991). Developmental intervention during neonatal hospitalization: Critiquing the state of the science. *Pediatric Clinics of North America, 38,* 1469–1479.

Gorski, R. A. (1980). Sexual differentiation of the brain. In D. T. Krieger & J. C. Hughes (Eds.), *Neuroendocrinology.* New York: Rockefeller University Press.

Gortmaker, S. L., Must, A., Sobol, A. M., Peterson, K., Colditz, G. A., & Dietz, W. H. (1996). Television viewing as a cause of increasing obesity among children in the United States, 1886–1990. *Archives of Pediatrics and Adolescent Medicine, 150,* 356–362.

Gottesman, I. I., & Shields, J. (1982). *Schizophrenia: The epigenetic puzzle.* Cambridge, UK: Cambridge University Press.

Gottfried, A. E., Bathurst, K., & Gottfried, A. W. (1994). Role of maternal and dual-earner employment status in children's development. In A. E. Gottfried, & A. W. Gottfried (Eds.), *Redefining families: Implications for children's development.* New York: Plenum.

Gottfried, G. M. (1997). Using metaphors as modifiers: Children's production of metaphoric compounds. *Journal of Child Language, 24,* 567–601.

Gottlieb, G. (1991). Experimental canalization of behavioral development: Theory. *Developmental Psychology, 27,* 4–13.

Gottlieb, G. (2000). Environmental and behavioral influences on gene activity. *Current Directions in Psychological Science, 9,* 93–97.

Gottlieb, G., Wahlsten, D., & Lickliter, R. (2006). The significance of biology for human development: A developmental psychobiological systems view. In W. Damon & R. M. Lerner (Editors-in-Chief) & R. M. Lerner (Vol. Ed.), *Handbook of child psychology: Vol. 1. Theoretical models of human development* (6th ed., pp. 210–257). Hoboken, NJ: Wiley.

Gottman, J. M. (1983). How children become friends. Monographs of the Society for Research in Child Development, 48(2, Serial No. 201).

Gottman, J. M., Gonso, J., & Rasmussen, B. (1975). Social interaction, social competence, and friendship in children. *Child Development, 46,* 709–718.

Gottman, J. M., Katz, L. F., & Hooven, C. (1997). *Metaemotion: How families communicate emotionally.* Mahwah, NJ: Erlbaum.

Gottman, J. M., & Parkhurst, J. T. (1980). A developmental theory of friendship and acquaintanceship processes. In W. A. Collins (Ed.), *The Minnesota symposia on child development: Vol. 13. Development of cognition, affect, and social relations.* Hillsdale, NJ: Erlbaum.

Goubet, N., & Clifton, R. K. (1998). Object and event representation in 6 1/2-month-old infants. *Developmental Psychology, 34,* 63–76.

Goy, R. (1970). Early hormonal influences on the development of sexual and sex-related behavior. In F. Schmitt, G. Quarton, T. Melnechuck, & G. Adelman (Eds.), *The neurosciences: Second study program.* New York: Rockefeller University Press.

Graham, S. A., & Poulin-Dubois, D. (1999). Infants' reliance on shape to generalize novel labels to animate and inanimate objects. *Journal of Child Language, 26,* 295–320.

Gralinski, J. H., & Kopp, C. B. (1993). Everyday rules for behavior: Mothers' requests to young children. *Developmental Psychology, 29,* 573–584.

Grandjean, H., Larroque, D., Levi, S., and the Eurofetus Study Group. (1999). The performance of routine ultrasonographic screening of pregnancies in the Eurofetus Study. *American Journal of Obstetrics and Gynecology, 181,* 446–454.

Grantham-McGregor, S., Powell, C., Walker, S., Change, S., & Fletcher, P. (1994). The long-term follow-up of severely malnourished children who participated in an intervention program. *Child Development, 65,* 428–439.

Graves, S. B. (1993). Television, the portrayal of African Americans, and the development of children's attitudes. In G. L. Berry & J. K. Asamen (Eds.), *Children and television: Images in a changing sociocultural world* (pp. 179–190). Newbury Park, CA: Sage.

Graves, N. B., & Graves, T. D. (1983). The cultural context of prosocial development: An ecological model. In D. L. Bridgeman (Ed.), *The nature of prosocial development: Interdisciplinary theories and strategies.* New York: Academic Press.

Gray, M., & Steinberg, L. (1999). Unpacking authoritative parenting: Reassessing a multidimensional construct. *Journal of Marriage and the Family, 61,* 574–587.

Gray-Little, B., & Hafdahl, A. R. (2000). Factors influencing racial comparisons of self-esteem: A quantitative review. *Psychological Bulletin, 126,* 26–54.

Greenberg, B. S. (1986). Minorities and the mass media. In J. Bryant & D. Zillman (Eds.), *Perspectives on mass media effects.* Hillsdale, NJ: Erlbaum.

Greenberg, B. S., & Brand, J. E. (1994). Minorities and the mass media: 1970s to 1990s. In J. Bryant & D. Zillmann (Eds.), *Media effects: Advances in theory and research* (pp. 273–314). Hillsdale, NJ: Erlbaum.

Greenberger, E., & Chen, C. (1996). Perceived family relationships and depressed mood in early and late adolescence: A comparison of European and Asian Americans. *Developmental Psychology, 32,* 707–716.

Greene, M. L., Way, N., & Pahl, K. (2006). Trajectories of perceived adult and peer discrimination among Black, Latino, and Asian American adolescents: Patterns and psychological correlates. *Developmental Psychology, 42,* 218–236.

Greenfield, P. M. (1984). A theory of the teacher in the learning activities of everyday life. In B. Rogoff & J. Lave (Eds.), *Everyday cognition: Its development in social context.* Cambridge, MA: Harvard University Press.

Greenfield, P. M. (1997). You can't take it with you: Why ability assessments don't cross cultures. *American Psychologist, 52,* 1115–1124.

Greenfield, P. M. (1998). The cultural evolution of IQ. In U. Neisser (Ed.), *The rising curve: Long-term gains in IQ and related measures* (pp. 85–94). Washington, DC: American Psychological Association.

Greenfield, P. M., & Cocking, R. R. (Eds.). (1996). *Interacting with video.* Norwood, NJ: Ablex.

Greenhoot, A. F., Ornstein, P. A., Gordon, B. N., & Baker-Ward, L. (1999). Acting out the details of a pediatric check-up: The impact of interview condition and behavioral style on children's memory reports. *Child Development, 70,* 363–380.

Greenhouse, L. (2000, October 5). Justices consider limits of the legal response to risky behavior by pregnant women. *New York Times,* p. A6.

Greenough, W. T., Black, J. E., & Wallace, C. S. (1987). Experience and brain development. *Child Development, 58,* 539–559.

Gregg, V., Gibbs, J. C., & Basinger, K. S. (1994). Patterns of developmental delay in moral judgment by male and female delinquents. *Merrill-Palmer Quarterly, 40,* 538–553.

Greif, E. B., & Gleason, J. B. (1980). Hi, thanks, and goodbye: More routine information. *Language in Society, 9,* 159–166.

Greif, E. B., & Ulman, K. J. (1982). The psychological impact of menarche on early adolescent females: A review of the literature. *Child Development, 53,* 1413–1430.

Gressens, P. (2000). Mechanisms and disturbances of neuronal migration. *Pediatric Research, 48,* 725–730.

Grimshaw, G. M., Adelstein, A., Bryden, M. P., & MacKinnon, G. E. (1998). First-language acquisition in adolescence: Evidence for a critical period for language development. *Brain and Language, 63,* 237–255.

Grolnick, W. S., Bridges, L. J., & Connell, J. P. (1996). Emotion regulation in two-year-olds: Strategies and emotional expression in four contexts. *Child Development, 67,* 928–941.

Grolnick, W. S., Ryan, R. M., & Deci, E. L. (1991). Inner resources for school achievement: Motivational mediators of children's perceptions of their parents. *Journal of Educational Psychology, 83,* 508–517.

Grolnick, W. S., & Slowiaczek, M. L. (1994). Parents' involvement in children's schooling: A multidimensional conceptualization and motivation model. *Child Development, 65,* 237–252.

Groome, L. J., Swiber, M. J., Atterbury, J. L., Bentz, L. S., & Holland, S. B. (1997). Similarities and differences in behavioral state organization during sleep periods in the perinatal infant before and after birth. *Child Development, 68,* 1–11.

Grossmann, K., Grossmann, K. E., Fremmer-Bombik, E., Kindler, H., Scheurer-Englisch, H., & Zimmermann, P. (2002). The uniqueness of the child-father attachment relationship: Fathers' sensitive and challenging play as a pivotal variable in a 16-year longitudinal study. *Social Development, 11,* 307–331.

Grossmann, K., Grossmann, K. E., Spangler, G., Suess, G., & Unzner, L. (1985). Maternal sensitivity and newborns' orientation responses as related to quality of attachment in northern Germany. In I. Bretherton & E. Waters (Eds.), *Growing points of attachment theory and research. Monographs of the Society for Research in Child Development, 50* (1–2, Serial No. 209).

Grotevant, H. D., & Cooper, C. R. (1986). Individuation in family relationships. *Human Development, 29,* 82–100.

Gruen, G., Ottinger, D., & Zigler, E. (1970). Level of aspiration and the probability learning of middle- and lower-class children. *Developmental Psychology, 3,* 133–142.

Grunseit, A., Kippax, S., Aggleton, P., & Baldo, M.,& Slutkin, G. (1997). Sexuality education and young people's sexual behavior: A review of studies. *Journal of Adolescent Research, 12,* 421–453.

Grusec, J. E. (1982). The socialization of altruism. In N. Eisenberg (Ed.), *The development of prosocial behavior.* New York: Academic Press.

Grusec, J. E. (1991). Socializing concern for others in the home. *Developmental Psychology, 27,* 338–342.

Grusec, J. E. (1992). Social learning theory and developmental psychology: The legacies of Robert Sears and Albert Bandura. *Developmental Psychology, 28,* 776–786.

Grusec, J. E., & Goodnow, J. J. (1994). Impact of parental discipline methods on the child's internalization of values: A reconceptualization of current points of view. *Developmental Psychology, 30,* 4–19.

Grusec, J. E., Goodnow, J. J., & Cohen, L. (1996). Household work and the development of concern for others. *Developmental Psychology, 32,* 999–1007.

Grusec, J. E., Hastings, P., & Mammone, N. (1994). Parenting cognitions and relationship schemas. In J. G. Smetana (Ed.), *Beliefs about parenting: Origins and developmental implications* (pp. 5–19). San Francisco: Jossey-Bass.

Grusec, J. E., & Skubiski, L. (1970). Model nurturance, demand characteristics of the modeling experiment, and altruism. *Journal of Personality and Social Psychology, 14,* 352–359.

Grych, J. H., Harold, G. T., & Miles, C. J. (2003). A prospective investigation of appraisals as mediators of the link between interparental conflict and child adjustment. *Child Development, 74,* 1176–1193.

Guerra, B., Lazzarotto, T., Quarta, S., Lanari, M., Bovicelli, L., Nicolosi, A., & Landini, M. P. (2000). Prenatal diagnosis of symptomatic congenital cytomegalovirus infection. *American Journal of Obstetrics and Gynecology, 183,* 476–482.

Guinan, M. E. (1995). Artificial insemination by donor: Safety and secrecy. *Journal of the American Medical Association, 273,* 890–891.

Gunnar, M. R. (1998). Quality of early care and buffering of neuroendocrine stress reactions: Potential effects on the developing brain. *Preventive Medicine, 27,* 208–211.

Gunnar, M. R., Porter, F., Wolf, C., Rigatuso, J., & Larson, M. (1995). Neonatal stress reactivity: Predictions to later emotional development. *Child Development, 66,* 1–13.

Gunnar, M. R., & White, B. P. (2001). Salivary cortisol measures in infant and child assessment. In L. T. Singer & P. S. Zeskind (Eds.), *Biobehavioral assessment of the infant* (pp. 167–189). New York: Guilford Press.

Gunston, G. D., Burkimsher, D., Malan, H, & Sive, A. A. (1992). Reversible cerebral shrinkage in kwashiorkor: An MRI study. *Archives of Disease in Childhood, 67,* 1030–1032.

Guntheroth, W. G., & Spiers, P. S. (2001). Thermal stress in sudden infant death: Is there an ambiguity with the rebreathing hypothesis? *Pediatrics, 107,* 693–698.

Gutman, L. M. , & Eccles, J. S. (1999). Financial strain, parenting behaviors, and adolescents' achievement: Testing model equivalence between African American and European American single- and two-parent families. *Child Development, 70,* 1464–1476.

Guttentag, R. E. (1987). Memory and aging: Implications for theories of memory development during childhood. *Developmental Review, 5,* 56–82.

Hafner-Eaton, C., & Pearce, L. K. (1994). Birth choices, the law, and medicine: Balancing individual freedoms and protection of the public's health. *Journal of Health Politics, Policy and Law, 19,* 813–835.

Hagay, Z. J., Biran, G., Ornoy, A., & Reece, E. A. (1996). Congenital cytomegalovirus infection: A long-standing problem still seeking a solution. *American Journal of Obstetrics and Gynecology, 174,* 241–245.

Hahn, C.-S., & DiPietro, J. A. (2001). In vitro fertilization and the family: Quality of parenting, family functioning, and child psychosocial adjustment. *Developmental Psychology, 37,* 37–48.

Haight, W. L., Wang, X., Fung, H., Williams, K., & Mintz, J. (1999). Universal, developmental, and variable aspects of young children's play: A cross-cultural comparison of pretending at home. *Child Development, 70,* 1477–1488.

Hainline, L. (1998). The development of basic visual abilities. In A. Slater (Ed.), *Perceptual development: Visual, auditory, and speech perception in infancy* (pp. 5–50). East Sussex, UK: Psychology Press.

Hainline, L., & Riddell, P. M. (1995). Binocular alignment and vergence in early infancy. *Vision Research, 35,* 3229–3236.

Haith, M. M. (1997). The development of future thinking as essential for the emergence of skill in planning. In S. L. Friedman & E. K. Scholnick (Eds.), *The developmental psychology of planning: Why, how, and when do we plan?* (pp. 25–42). Mahwah, NJ: Erlbaum.

Haith, M. M. (1998). Who put the cog in cognition? Is rich interpretation too costly? *Infant Behavior and Development, 21,* 167–179.

Hakuta, K. (1999). The debate on bilingual education. *Journal of Developmental & Behavioral Pediatrics, 20,* 36–37.

Hakuta, K., & Diaz, R. M. (1985). The relationship between degree of bilingualism and cognitive ability: A critical discussion and some new longitudinal data. In K. E. Nelson (Ed.), *Children's language* (Vol. 5). Hillsdale, NJ: Erlbaum.

Hakuta, K., & Mostafapour, E. F. (1996). Perspectives from the history and politics of bilingualism amd bilingual education in the United States. In I. Parasnis (Ed.), *Cultural and language diversity and the deaf experience* (pp. 38–50). Cambridge, UK: Cambridge University Press.

Haley, D. W., & Stansbury, K. (2003). Infant stress and parent responsiveness: Regulation of physiology and behavior during still-face and reunion. *Child Development, 74,* 1534–1546.

Hall, G. S. (1891). The contents of children's minds on entering school. *Pedagogical Seminary, 1,* 139–173.

Hall, J. A. (1984). *Nonverbal sex differences: Communication accuracy and expressive style.* Baltimore: Johns Hopkins University Press.

Hall, J. A., & Halberstadt, A. G. (1986). Smiling and gazing. In J. S. Hyde & M. C. Linn (Eds.), *The psychology of gender: Advances through meta-analysis.* Baltimore: Johns Hopkins University Press.

Halpern, C. T., Udry, J. R., Campbell, B., & Suchindran, C. (1999). Effects of body fat on weight concerns, dating, and sexual activity: A longitudinal analysis of black and white adolescent girls. *Developmental Psychology, 35,* 721–736.

Halpern, D. F. (1986). *Sex differences in cognitive abilities.* Hillsdale, NJ: Erlbaum.

Halpern, L. F., MacLean, W. E., Jr., & Baumeister, A. A. (1995). Infant sleep-wake characteristics: Relation to neurological status and the prediction of developmental outcome. *Developmental Review, 15,* 255–291.

Hamilton, B. E., Martin, J. A., Ventura, S. J., Sutton, P. D., & Menacker, F. (2005). *Births. Preliminary data for 2004* (National Vital Statistics Reports, Vol. 54, No. 8). Hyattsville, MD: National Center for Health Statistics.

Hampson, E., Rovet, J. F., & Altmann, D. (1998). Spatial reasoning in children with congential adrenal hyperplasia due to 21-hydroxylase deficiency. *Developmental Neuropsychology, 14,* 299–320.

Hamre, B. K., & Pianta, R. C. (2001). Early teacher-child relationships and the trajectory of children's outcomes through eighth grade. *Child Development, 72,* 625–638.

Han, J. J., Leichtman, M. D., & Wang, Q. (1998). Autobiographical memory in Korean, Chinese, and American children. *Developmental Psychology, 34,* 701–713.

Han, W. J. (2004). Nonstandard work schedules and child care decisions: Evidence from the NICHD Study of Early Child Care. *Early Childhood Research Quarterly, 19,* 231–256.

Hand, J. Z., & Sanchez, L. (2000). Badgering or bantering? Gender differences in experience of, and reaction to, sexual harassment among U.S. high school students. *Gender & Society, 14,* 718–746.

Hansen, J. D. L. (1990). Malnutrition review. *Pediatric Reviews and Communication, 4,* 201–212.

Hansen, M., Bower, C., Milne, E., de Klerk, N., & Kurinczuk, J. J. (2005). Assisted reproductive technologies and the risk of birth defects—a systematic review. *Human Reproduction, 20,* 328–338.

Hanson, J. W. (1986). Teratogen update: Fetal hydantoin effects. *Teratology, 33,* 349–353.

Hanson, J. W. (1997). Human teratology. In D. L. Rimoin, J. M. Connor, & R. E. Pyeritz (Eds.), *Emory and Rimoin's principles and practices of medical genetics* (3rd Ed., Vol. 1, pp. 697–724). New York: Churchill Livingstone.

Harbison, R. D., & Mantilla-Plata, B. (1972). Prenatal toxicity, maternal distribution and placental transfer of tetrahydrocannabinol. *Journal of Pharmacology and Experimental Therapeutics, 180,* 446–453.

Hareven, T. (1985). Historical changes in the family and the life course: Implications for child development. In A. B. Smuts & J. W. Hagen (Eds.), *History and research in child development. Monographs of the Society for Research in Child Development, 50*(4–5, Serial No. 211).

Harley, K., & Reese, E. (1999). Origins of autobiographical memory. *Developmental Psychology, 35,* 1338–1348.

Harlow, H. F., & Zimmerman, R. R. (1959). Affectional responses in the infant monkey. *Science, 130,* 421–432.

Harman, C., Rothbart, M. K., & Posner, M. I. (1997). Distress and attention interactions in early infancy. *Motivation and Emotion, 21,* 27–43.

Harnishfeger, K. K., & Pope, S. (1996). Intending to forget: The development of cognitive inhibition in directed forgetting. *Journal of Experimental Child Psychology, 62,* 292–315.

Harold, G. T., Fincham, F. D., Osborne, L. N., & Conger, R. D. (1997). Mom and Dad are at it again: Adolescent perceptions of marital conflict and adolescent psychological distress. *Developmental Psychology, 33,* 333–350.

Harpin, V., Chellappah, G., & Rutter, N. (1983). Responses of the newborn infant to overheating. *Biology of the Neonate, 44,* 65–75.

Harriman, A. E., & Lukosius, P. A. (1982). On why Wayne Dennis found Hopi children retarded in age at onset of walking. *Perceptual and Motor Skills, 55,* 79–86.

Harris, J. R. (1995). Where is the child's environment? A group socialization theory of development. *Psychological Review, 102,* 458–489.

Harris, J. R. (1998). *The nurture assumption: Why children turn out the way they do.* New York: Free Press.

Harris, J. R. (2000). Socialization, personality development, and the child's environments: Comment on Vandell (2000). *Developmental Psychology, 36,* 711–723.

Harris, P. L., Donnelly, K., Guz, G. R., & Pitt-Watson, R. (1986). Children's understanding of the distinction between real and apparent emotion. *Child Development, 57,* 895–909.

Harris, P. L., Olthof, T., & Meerum Terwogt, M. (1981). Children's knowledge of emotion. *Journal of Child Psychology and Psychiatry, 22,* 247–261.

Harris, R. T. (1991, March). Anorexia nervosa and bulimia nervosa in female adolescents. *Nutrition Today* pp. 30–34.

Harrison, L. J., & Ungerer, J. A. (2002). Maternal employment and infant-mother attachment security at 12 months postpartum. *Developmental Psychology, 38,* 758–773.

Harrison, M. R. (1996). Fetal surgery. *American Journal of Obstetrics and Gynecology, 174,* 1255–1264.

Hart, C. H., De Wolf, D. M., Wozniak, P., & Burts, D. C. (1992). Maternal and paternal disciplinary styles: Relations with preschoolers' playground behavioral orientations and peer status. *Child Development, 63,* 879–892.

Hart, D., & Fegley, S. (1995). Prosocial behavior and caring in adolescence: Relations to self-understanding and social judgment. *Child Development, 66,* 1346–1359.

Hart, D., Fegley, S., & Brengelman, D. (1993). Perceptions of past, present and future selves among children and adolescents. *British Journal of Developmental Psychology, 11,* 265–282.

Hart, E. L., Lahey, B. B., Loeber, R., Applegate, B., & Frick, P. J. (1995). Developmental change in attention-deficit hyperactivity disorder in boys: A four-year longitudinal study. *Journal of Abnormal Child Psychology, 23,* 729–749.

Hart, S. N., & Brassard, M. R. (1987). A major threat to children's mental health. *American Psychologist, 42,* 160–165.

Harter, S. (1986a). Cognitive-developmental processes in the integration of concepts about emotions and the self. *Social Cognition, 4,* 119–151.

Harter, S. (1986b). Processes underlying the construct, maintenance and enhancement of the self-concept in children. In J. Suls & A. Greenwald (Eds.), *Psychological perspectives on the self* (Vol. 3, pp. 136–182). Hillsdale, NJ: Erlbaum.

Harter, S. (1987). The determinants and mediational role of global self-worth in children. In N. Eisenberg (Ed.), *Contemporary topics in developmental psychology.* New York: Wiley.

Harter, S. (1998). The development of self-representations. In W. Damon (Series Ed.) & N. Eisenberg (Vol. Ed.), *Handbook of child psychology: Vol. 3. Social, emotional, and personality development* (5th ed., pp. 553–617). New York: Wiley.

Harter, S. (1999). *The construction of the self: A developmental perspective.* New York: Guilford Press.

Harter, S. (2006). The self. In W. Damon & R. M. Lerner (Editors-in-Chief) & N. Eisenberg (Vol. Ed.), *Handbook of child psychology: Vol. 3. Social, emotional, and personality development* (6th ed., pp. 505–570). Hoboken, NJ: Wiley.

Harter, S., Marold, D. B., Whitesell, N. R., & Cobbs, G. (1996). A model of the effects of perceived parent and peer support on adolescent false self behavior. *Child Development, 67,* 360–374.

Harter, S., & Monsour, A. (1992). Developmental analysis of conflict caused by opposing attributes in the adolescent self-portrait. *Developmental Psychology, 28,* 251–260.

Harter, S., Waters, P., & Whitesell, N. R. (1998). Relational self-worth: Differences in perceived worth as a person across interpersonal contexts among adolescents. *Child Development, 69,* 756–766.

Harter, S., & Whitesell, N. R. (1989). Developmental changes in children's understanding of single, multiple, and blended emotion concepts. In C. Saarni & P. Harris (Eds.), *Children's understanding of emotion* (pp. 81–116). Cambridge, UK: Cambridge University Press.

Hartshorn, K., Rovee-Collier, C., Gerhardstein, P., Bhatt, R. S., Klein, P. J., Aaron, F., et al. (1998). Developmental changes in the specificity of memory over the first year of life. *Developmental Psychobiology, 33,* 61–78.

Hartup, W. W. (1983). Peer relations. In E. M. Hetherington (Ed.), *Handbook of child psychology: Vol. IV. Socialization, personality, and social development* (4th ed., pp. 103–196). New York: Wiley.

Hartup, W. W. (1996). The company they keep: Friendships and their developmental significance. *Child Development, 67,* 1–13.

Hartup, W. W. (1999). Constraints on peer socialization: Let me count the ways. *Merrill-Palmer Quarterly, 45,* 172–183.

Hartup, W. W., French, D. C., Laursen, B., Johnston, M. K., & Ogawa, J. R. (1993). Conflict and friendship relations in middle childhood: Behavior in a closed field situation. *Child Development, 64,* 445–454.

Hartup, W. W., & Sancilio, M. F. (1986). Children's friendships. In E. Shopler & G. B. Mesibov (Eds.), *Social behavior in autism.* New York: Plenum Press.

Hartup, W. W., & Stevens, N. (1999). Friendships and adaptation across the life span. *Current Directions in Psychological Science, 3,* 76–79.

Harvey, E. (1999). Short-term and long-term effects of early parental employment on children of the National Longitudinal Survey of Youth. *Developmental Psychology, 35,* 445–459.

Hasebe, Y., Nucci, L., & Nucci, M. S. (2004). Parental control of the personal domain and adolescent symptoms of psychopathology: A cross-national study in the United States and Japan. *Child Development, 75,* 815–828.

Haselager, G. J. T., Hartup, W. W., van Lieshout, C. F. M., & Riksen-Walraven, J. M. A. (1998). Similarities between friends and nonfriends in middle childhood. *Child Development, 69,* 1198–1208.

Hastings, P. D., & Grusec, J. E. (1998). Parenting goals as organizers of responses to parent-child disagreement. *Developmental Psychology, 34,* 465–479.

Hastings, P. D., Zahn-Waxler, C., Robinson, J., Usher, B., & Bridges, D. (2000). The development of concern for others in children with behavior problems. *Developmental Psychology, 36,* 531–546.

Hatfield, J. S., Ferguson, L. R., & Alpert, R. (1967). Mother-child interaction and the socialization process. *Child Development, 38,* 365–414.

Haubenstricker, J., & Seefeldt, V. (1986). Acquisition of motor skills during childhood. In V. Seefeldt (Ed.), *Physical activity and well-being.* Reston, VA: American Alliance for Health, Education, Recreation, and Dance.

Hauck, F. R., & Hunt, C. E. (2000). Sudden infant death syndrome in 2000. *Current Problems in Pediatrics, 30,* 241–261.

Hauk, F. R. (2001). Changing epidemiology. In R. W. Byard & H. F. Kraus (Eds.), *Sudden infant death syndrome: Problems, progress, & possibilities* (pp. 31–57). London: Arnold.

Hauk, F. R., Omojokun, O. O., & Siadaty, M. S. (2005). Do pacifiers reduce the risk of Sudden Infant Death Syndrome? A meta-analysis. *Pediatrics, 116,* 716–723.

Hauser, S. T., Powers, S. I., Noam, G. G., & Bowlds, M. K. (1987). Family interiors of adolescent ego development trajectories. *Family Perspectives, 21,* 263–282.

Hawkins, J., Sheingold, K., Gearhart, M., & Berger, C. (1982). Microcomputers in classrooms: Impact on the social life of elementary classrooms. *Journal of Applied Developmental Psychology, 3,* 361–373.

Hawn, P. R., & Harris, L. J. (1983). Hand differences in grasp duration and reaching in two- and five-month old infants. In G. Young, S. Segalowitz, C. M. Carter, & S. E. Trehub (Eds.), *Manual specialization and the developing brain.* New York: Academic Press.

Hay, D. F. (1985). Learning to form relationships in infancy: Parallel attainments with parents and peers. *Developmental Review, 5,* 122–161.

Hay, D. F., Castle, J., Davies, L., Demetriou, H., & Stimson, C. A. (1999). Prosocial action in very early childhood. *Journal of Child Psychology and Psychiatry, 40,* 905–916.

Hay, D. F., Nash, A., & Pedersen, J. (1983). Interaction between 6-month-old peers. *Child Development, 54,* 557–562.

Hayne, H. (2004). Infant memory development: Implications for childhood amnesia. *Developmental Review, 24,* 33–73.

Hayne, H., & Rovee-Collier, C. (1995). The organization of reactivated memory. *Child Development, 66,* 893–906.

Heath, S. B. (1989). Oral and literate traditions among black Americans living in poverty. *American Psychologist, 44,* 367–373.

Hebb, D. O. (1980). *Essay on mind.* Hillsdale, NJ: Erlbaum.

Held, R., Birch, E., & Gwiazda, J. (1980). Stereoacuity in human infants. *Proceedings of the National Academy of Sciences of the U.S.A., 77,* 5572–5574.

Helwig, C. C., Zelazo, P. D., & Wilson, M. (2001). Children's judgments of psychological harm in normal and noncanonical situations. *Child Development, 72,* 66–81.

Henderlong, J., & Lepper, M. R. (2002). The effects of praise on children's intrinsic motivation: A review and synthesis. *Psychological Bulletin, 128,* 774–795.

Henifin, M. S. (1993). New reproductive technologies: Equity and access to reproductive health care. *Journal of Social Issues, 49,* 61–74.

Hepper, P. G., & Shahidullah, B. S. (1994). Development of fetal hearing. *Archives of Disease in Childhood, 71,* F81–F87.

Hepper, P. G., Wells, D. L., & Lynch, C. (2005). Prenatal thumbsucking is related to postnatal handedness. *Neuropsychologia, 43,* 313–315.

Herman, M. R., Dornbusch, S. M., Herron, M. C., & Herting, J. R. (1997). The influence of family regulation, connection, and psychological autonomy on six measures of adolescent functioning. *Journal of Adolescent Research, 12,* 34–67.

Hernandez-Reif, M., Field, T., Diego, M., & Largie, S. (2003). Haptic habituation to temperature is slower in newborns of depressed mothers. *Infancy, 4,* 47–63.

Herpetz-Dahlmann, B., Müller, B., Herpetz, S., Heussen, N., Hebebrand, J., & Remschmidt, H. (2001). Prospective 10-year follow-up in adolescent anorexia nervosa: Course, outcome, psychiatric comorbidity, and psychosocial adaptation. *Journal of Child Psychology and Psychiatry, 42,* 603–612.

Herrnstein, R. J., & Murray, C. (1994). *The bell curve: Intelligence and class structure in American life.* New York: Free Press.

Hertsgaard, L., Gunnar, M., Erickson, M. F., & Nachmias, M. (1996). Adrenocortical responses to the Strange Situation in infants with disorganized/disoriented attachment relationships. *Child Development, 66,* 1100–1106.

Hetherington, E. M. (1989). Coping with family transitions: Winners, losers, and survivors. *Child Development, 60,* 1–14.

Hetherington, E. M., Cox, M., & Cox, R. (1982). Effects of divorce on parents and children. In M. Lamb (Ed.), *Nontraditional families.* Hillsdale, NJ: Erlbaum.

Hetherington, E. M., & Henderson, S. H. (1997). The effects of divorce on fathers and their children. In M. E. Lamb (Ed.), *The role of the father in child development* (pp. 191–211). New York: Wiley.

Hetherington, E. M., Henderson, S. H., & Reiss, D. (1999). Adolescent siblings in stepfamilies: Family functioning and adolescent adjustment. *Monographs of the Society for Research in Child Development, 64*(4, Serial No. 259).

Hetherington, E. M., & Jodl, K. M. (1994). Stepfamilies as settings for child development. In A. Booth & J. Dunn (Eds.), *Stepfamilies: Who benefits? Who does not?* (pp. 55–79). Hillsdale, NJ: Erlbaum.

Hetherington, E. M., & Kelly, J. (2002). *For better or for worse: Divorce reconsidered.* New York: Norton.

Heyman, G. D., & Dweck, C. S. (1998). Children's thinking about traits? Implications for judgments of the self and others. *Child Development, 69,* 391–403.

Heynen, A. J., Yoon, B-J., Liu, C-H., Chung, H. J., Huganir, R. L., & Bear, M. F. (2003). Molecular mechanism for loss of visual cortical responsiveness following brief monocular deprivation. *Nature Neuroscience, 8,* 854–862.

Hilgard, J. R. (1932). Learning and maturation in preschool children. *Journal of Genetic Psychology, 41,* 36–56.

Hill, C. R., & Stafford, F. P. (1980). Parental care of children: Time diary estimates of quantity, predictability, and variety. *Journal of Human Resources, 15,* 219–289.

Hill, J. P. (1987). Research on adolescents and their families: Past and prospect. In C. E. Irwin (Ed.), *Adolescent social behavior and health.* San Francisco: Jossey-Bass.

Hill, J. P., & Lynch, M. E. (1983). The intensification of gender-related role expectations during early adolescence. In J. Brooks-Gunn & A. C. Petersen (Eds.), *Girls at puberty: Biological and psychosocial perspectives* (pp. 201–228). New York: Academic Press.

Hill, N. E., & Taylor, L. C. (2004). Parental school involvement and children's academic achievement: Pragmatics and issues. *Current Directions in Psychological Science, 13,* 161–164.

Hinde, R. A. (1989). Ethological and relationships approaches. In R. Vasta (Ed.), *Annals of child development: Six theories of child development: Revised formulations and current issues* (Vol. 6, pp. 251–285). Greenwich, CT: JAI Press.

Hinde, R. A., Titmus, G., Easton, D., & Tamplin, A. (1985). Incidence of "friendship" and behavior to strong associates versus non-associates in preschoolers. *Child Development, 56,* 234–245.

Hines, M., Golombok, S., Rust, J., Johnston, K. J., Golding, J., & ALSPAC Study Team. (2002). Testosterone during pregnancy and gender role behavior of preschool children: A longitudinal population study. *Developmental Psychology, 73,* 1678–1687.

Hirsch, B. J., & Rapkin, B. D. (1987). The transition to junior high school: A longitudinal study of self-esteem, psychological symptomatology, school life, and social support. *Child Development, 58,* 1235–1243.

Hirschfeld, L. A., & Gelman, S. A. (1994). Toward a topography of mind: An introduction to domain specificity. In L. A. Hirschfeld & S. A. Gelman (Eds.), *Mapping the mind: Domain specificity in cognition and culture* (pp. 3–35). Oxford, UK: Oxford University Press.

Hirsch-Pasek, K., Gleitman, L. R., & Gleitman, H. (1978). What does the brain say to the mind? A study of the detection and report of ambiguity by young children. In A. Sinclair, R. J. Jarvella, & W. J. M. Levelt (Eds.), *The child's conception of language.* Berlin: Springer-Verlag.

Ho, C. S., & Bryant, P. (1997). Phonological skills are important in learning to read Chinese. *Developmental Psychology, 33,* 946–951.

Hock, E., & DeMeis, D. K. (1990). Depression in mothers of infants: The role of maternal employment. *Developmental Psychology, 26,* 285–291.

Hoff, E., & Naigles, L. (2002). How children use input to acquire a lexicon. *Child Development, 73,* 418–433.

Hoff, T. L. (1992). Psychology in Canada one hundred years ago: James Mark Baldwin at the University of Toronto. *Canadian Psychology, 33,* 683–694.

Hofferth, S. (1996). Child care in the United States today. *The Future of Children, 6*(2), 41–61.

Hoff-Ginsberg, E. (1986). Function and structure in maternal speech: Their relation to the child's development of syntax. *Developmental Psychology, 22,* 155–163.

Hoff-Ginsberg, E. (1991). Mother-child conversation in different social classes and communicative settings. *Child Development, 62,* 782–796.

Hoffman, L. W. (1979). Maternal employment: 1979. *American Psychologist, 34,* 859–865.

Hoffman, L. W. (1984). Maternal employment and the young child. In M. Perlmutter (Ed.), *The Minnesota symposia on child psychology: Vol. 17. Parent-child interaction and parent-child relations in child development.* Hillsdale, NJ: Erlbaum.

Hoffman, L. W. (1989). Effects of maternal employment in the two-parent family. *American Psychologist, 44,* 283–292.

Hoffman, L. W., & Kloska, D. D. (1995). Parents' gender-based attitudes toward marital roles and child rearing: Development and validation of new measures. *Sex Roles, 32,* 273–295.

Hoffman, M. L. (1970). Moral development. In P. H. Mussen (Ed.), *Carmichael's manual of child psychology* (Vol. 2, pp. 261–359). New York: Wiley.

Hoffman, M. L. (1975). Altruistic behavior and the parent-child relationship. *Journal of Personality and Social Psychology, 31,* 937–943.

Hoffman, M. L. (1976). Empathy, role-taking, guilt, and the development of altruistic motives. In T. Lickona (Ed.), *Moral development and moral behavior: Theory, research, and social issues.* New York: Holt, Rinehart & Winston.

Hoffman, M. L. (1982). Development of prosocial motivation: Empathy and guilt. In N. Eisenberg (Ed.), *The development of prosocial behavior.* New York: Academic Press.

Hoffman-Plotkin, D., & Twentyman, C. (1984). A multimodal assessment of behavioral and cognitive deficits in abused and neglected preschoolers. Child Development, 52, 13–30.

Høien, T., Lundberg, I., Stanovich, K. E., & Bjaalid, I. K. (1995). Components of phonological awareness. *Reading and Writing: An Interdisciplinary Journal, 7,* 171–188.

Holden, G. W. (1983). Avoiding conflict: Mothers as tacticians in the supermarket. *Child Development, 54,* 233–240.

Holden, G. W., & West, M. J. (1989). Proximate regulation by mothers: A demonstration of how differing styles affect young children's behavior. *Child Development, 60,* 64–69.

Hollenbeck, A. R., & Slaby, R. G. (1979). Infant visual and vocal responses to television. *Child Development, 50,* 41–45.

Holowka, S., & Petitto, L. A. (2002). Left hemisphere cerebral specialization for babies while babbling. *Science*, 297, 1515.

Hood, K. E., Draper, P., Crockett, L. J., & Petersen, A. C. (1987). The ontogeny and phylogeny of sex differences in development: A biopsychosocial synthesis. In D. B. Carter (Ed.), *Current conceptions of sex roles and sex typing: Theory and research.* New York: Praeger.

Hooper, C. J., Luciana, M., Conklin, H. M., & Yarger, R. S. (2004). Adolescents' performance on the Iowa Gambling Task: Implications for the development of decision making and ventromedial prefrontal cortex. *Developmental Psychology, 40,* 1148–1158.

Hopkins, B., & Westra, T. (1990). Motor development, maternal expectations, and the role of handling. *Infant Behavior and Development, 13,* 117–122.

Hops, H., & Finch, M. (1985). Social competence and skill: A reassessment. In B. H. Schneider, K. H. Rubin, & J. E. Ledingham (Eds.), *Children's peer relations: Issues in assessment and intervention.* New York: Springer-Verlag.

Horn, J. L. (1968). Organization of abilities and the development of intelligence. *Psychological Review, 75,* 242–259.

Horn, J. L., & Cattell, R. B. (1967). Refinement and test of the theory of fluid and crystallized ability intelligences. *Journal of Educational Psychology, 57,* 253–270.

Horn, J. M., & Packard, T. (1985). Early identification of learning problems: A meta-analysis. *Journal of Educational Psychology, 77,* 349–360.

Horne, A. M., Glaser, B. A., & Calhoun, G. B. (1999). Conduct disorders. In R. T. Ammerman, M. Hersen, & C. G. Last (Eds.), *Handbook of prescriptive treatments for children and adolescents* (2nd ed., pp. 84–101). Boston: Allyn & Bacon.

Horowitz, F. D. (2000). Child development and the PITS: Simple questions, complex answers, and developmental theory. *Child Development, 71,* 1–10.

Hosmer, L. (2001). Home birth. *Clinical Obstetrics and Gynecology, 44,* 671–680.

Hossain, Z., & Roopnarine, J. L. (1994). African-American fathers' involvement with infants: Relationship to their functioning style, support, education, and income. *Infant Behavior and Development, 17,* 175–184.

Hossain, Z., Field, T., Gonzalez, J., Malphurs, J., Del Valle, C., & Pickens, J. (1994). Infants of "depressed" mothers interact better with their non-depressed fathers. *Infant Mental Health Journal, 15,* 348–357.

Hotz, V. J., McElroy, S. W., & Sanders, S. G. (1997). The costs and consequences of teenage childbearing for mothers. In R. A. Maynard (Ed.), *Kids having kids* (pp. 55–94). Washington, DC: Urban Institute.

Howe, M. L. & Courage, M. L. (1993). On resolving the enigma of infantile amnesia. *Psychological Bulletin, 113,* 305–326.

Howe, M. L., & Courage, M. L. (1997). The emergence and early development of autobiographical memory. *Psychological Review, 104,* 499–523.

Howes, C. (1987a). Peer interaction of young children. *Monographs of the Society for Research in Child Development, 53* (1, Serial No. 217).

Howes, C. (1987b). Social competence with peers in young children. *Developmental Review, 7,* 252–272.

Howes, C. (1990). Can age of entry and the quality of childcare predict adjustment in kindergarten? *Developmental Psychology, 26,* 292–303.

Howes, C., Phillips, D. A., & Whitebook, M. (1992). Thresholds of quality: Implications for the social development of children in center-based child care. *Child Development, 63,* 449–460.

Howes, C., Unger, O., & Seidner, L. B. (1989). Social pretend play in toddlers: Parallels with social play and with solitary pretend. *Child Development, 60,* 77–84.

Hoyert, D. L., Freedman, M. A., Strobino, D. M., & Guyer, B. (2001). Annual summary of vital statistics: 2000. *Pediatrics, 108,* 1241–1255.

Hoyert, D. L., Kung, H., & Smith, B. L. (2005). Deaths: Preliminary data for 2003. *National Vital Statistics Reports, Vol. 53, No. 15.* Bethesda, MD: National Center for Health Statistics.

Hsieh, F.-J., Shyu, M.-K., Sheu, B.-C., Lin, S.-P., Chen, C.-P., & Huang, F.-Y. (1995). Limb defects after chorionic villus sampling. *Obstetrics and Gynecology, 85,* 84–88.

Hsu, H.-C., & Fogel, A. (2001). Infant vocal development in a dynamic mother-infant communication system. *Infancy, 2,* 87–109.

Hsu, H-C., & Fogel, A. (2003). Stability and transitions in mother-infant face-to-face communication during the first 6 months: A microhistorical approach. *Developmental Psychology, 39,* 1061–1082.

Hubbard, J. A. (2001). Emotion expression processes in children's peer interaction: The role of peer rejection, aggression, and gender. *Child Development, 72,* 1426–1438.

Hubbs-Tait, L., Nation, J. R., Krebs, N. F., & Bellinger, D. C. (2005). Neurotoxicants, micronutrients, and social environments: Individual effects on children's development. *Psychological Science in the Public Interest, 6,* 57–121.

Hubel, D. H., & Wiesel, T. N. (1979, September). Brain mechanisms of vision. *Scientific American, 241,* pp. 150–162.

Hudson, J. A., Shapiro, L. R., & Sosa, B. B. (1995). Planning in the real world: Preschool children's scripts and plans for familiar events. *Child Development, 66,* 984–998.

Huebner, A., & Garrod, A. (1991). Moral reasoning in a karmic world. *Human Development, 34,* 341–352.

Huesmann, L. R., Lagerspetz, K., & Eron, L. D. (1984). Intervening variables and the TV violence-aggression relation: Evidence from two countries. *Developmental Psychology, 20,* 746–775.

Huffman, L. C., Bryan, Y. E., del Carmen, R., Pedersen, F. A., Doussrad-Roosevelt, J. A., & Porges, S. W. (1998). Infant temperament and cardiac vagal tone: Assessments at twelve weeks of age. *Child Development, 69,* 624–635.

Hughes, C., & Russell, J. (1993). Autistic children's difficulty with mental disengagement from an object: Its implications for theories of autism. *Developmental Psychology, 29,* 498–510.

Human Genome Project Information. (2006). *Gene therapy.* Retrieved May 5. 2006, from www.ornl.gov/sci/techresources/Human_Genome/medicine/genetherapy.shtml.

Hur, Y.-M., & Bouchard, T. J., Jr. (1995). Genetic influences on perceptions of childhood family environment: A reared apart twin study. *Child Development, 1995,* 330–345.

Hurley, J. C., & Underwood, M. K. (2002). Children's understanding of their research rights before and after debriefing: Informed assent, confidentiality, and stopping participation. *Child Development, 73,* 132–143.

Husain, M., & Kennard, C. (1997). Distractor-dependent frontal neglect. *Neuropsychologia, 35,* 829–841.

Huston, A. C. (1983). Sex typing. In E. M. Hetherington (Ed.), *Handbook of child psychology: Vol. IV. Socialization, personality, and social development* (4th ed., pp. 387–467). New York: Wiley.

Huston, A. C. (1985). The development of sex typing: Themes from recent research. *Developmental Review, 5,* 1–17.

Huston, A. C., & Alvarez, M. M. (1990). The socialization context of gender role development in early adolescence. In R. Montemayor, G. R. Adams, & T. P. Gullota (Eds.), *From childhood to adolescence: A transitional period?* (pp. 156–179). Newbury Park, CA: Sage.

Huston, A. C., & Wright, J. C. (1998). Mass media and children's development. In W. Damon (Series Ed.) & R. Lerner (Vol. Ed.), *Handbook of child psychology: Vol. 4. Child psychology in practice* (5th ed., pp. 999–1058). New York: Wiley.

Huston, A. C., Wright, J. C., Marquis, J., & Green, S. B. (1999). How young children spend their time: Television and other activities. *Developmental Psychology, 35,* 912–925.

Huston, A. C., Wright, J. C., Rice, M. L., Kerkman, D., & St. Peters, M. (1990). Development of television viewing patterns in early childhood: A longitudinal investigation. *Developmental Psychology, 26,* 409–420.

Huttenlocher, J., Haight, W., Bryk, A., Seltzer, M., & Lyons, T. (1991). Early vocabulary growth: Relation to language input and gender. *Developmental Psychology, 27,* 236–248.

Huttenlocher, P. R. (1979). Synaptic density in human frontal cortex—developmental changes and effects of aging. *Brain Research, 163,* 195–205.

Huttenlocher, P. R. (1994). Synaptogenesis in human cerebral cortex. In G. Dawson & K. W. Fischer (Eds.), *Human behavior and the developing brain* (pp. 137–152). New York: Guilford.

Hyde, J. S. (1984). How large are gender differences in aggression? A developmental meta-analysis. *Developmental Psychology, 20,* 722–736.

Hyde, J. S. (1986). Gender differences in aggression. In J. S. Hyde & M. C. Linn (Eds.), *The psychology of gender: Advances through meta-analysis.* Baltimore: Johns Hopkins University Press.

Hyde, J. S., Fennema, E., & Lamon, S. J. (1990). Gender differences in mathematics performance: A meta-analysis. *Psychological Bulletin, 107,* 139–155.

Hyde, J. S., & Linn, M. C. (1988). Gender differences in verbal ability: A meta-analysis. *Psychological Bulletin, 104,* 53–69.

Hymel, S., LeMare, L., Ditner, E., & Woody, E. Z. (1999). Assessing self-concept in children: Variations across self-concept domains. *Merrill-Palmer Quarterly, 45,* 602–623.

Iervolino, A. C., Pike, A., Manke, B., Reiss, D., Hetherington, E. M., & Plomin, R. (2002). Genetic and environmental influences in adolescent peer socialization: Evidence from two genetically sensitive designs. *Child Development, 73,* 162–174.

Ingram, D. (1999). Phonological acquisition. In M. Barrett (Ed.), *The development of language.* Hove, UK: Psychology Press.

Inhelder, B., & Piaget, J. (1958). *The growth of logical thinking from childhood to adolescence.* New York: Basic Books.

International Human Genome Sequencing Consortium. (2004). Finishing the euchromatic sequence of the human genome. *Nature, 431,* 931–945.

Isabella, R. A. (1993). Origins of attachment: Maternal interactive behavior across the first year. *Child Development, 64,* 605–621.

Isabella, R. A., Belsky, J., & von Eye, A. (1989). Origins of infant-mother attachment: An examination of interactional synchrony during the infant's first year. *Developmental Psychology, 25,* 12–21.

Isensee, W. (1986, September 3). *The Chronicle of Higher Education,* 33.

Ishii-Kuntz, M. (1994). Paternal involvement and perception toward fathers' roles: A comparison between Japan and the United States. *Journal of Family Issues, 15,* 30–48.

Isley, S. L., O'Neil, R., Clatfelter, D., & Parke, R. D. (1999). Parent and child expressed affect and children's social competence: Modeling direct and indirect pathways *Developmental Psychology, 35,* 547–560.

Iverson, J. M., & Goldin-Meadow, S. (2001). The resilience of gesture in talk: Gesture in blind speakers and listeners. *Developmental Science, 4,* 416–422.

Iverson, J. M., & Goldin-Meadow, S. (2005). Gesture paves the way for language development. *Psychological Science, 16,* 367–371.

Izard, C. E. (1978). On the ontogenesis of emotions and emotion-cognition relationships in infancy. In M. Lewis & L. A. Rosenblum (Eds.), *The development of affect.* New York: Plenum Press.

Izard, C., & Ackerman, B. P. (2000). Motivational, organizational, and regulatory functions of discrete emotions. In M. Lewis & J. M. Haviland-Jones (Eds.), *Handbook of emotions* (2nd ed., pp. 253–280). New York: Guilford Press.

Izard, C. E., & Dougherty, L. M. (1982). Two complementary systems for measuring facial expressions in infants and children. In C. E. Izard (Ed.), *Measuring emotions in infants and children* (Vol. 1). Cambridge, UK: Cambridge University Press.

Izard, C. E., Fantauzzo, C. A., Castle, J. M., Haynes, O. M., Rayias, M. F., & Putnam, P. H. (1995). The ontogeny and significance of infants' facial expressions in the first 9 months of life. *Developmental Psychology, 31,* 997–1013.

Izard, C., Fine, S., Schultz, D., Mostow, A., Ackerman, B., & Youngstrom, E. (2001). Emotion knowledge as a predictor of social behavior and academic competence in children at risk. *Psychological Science, 12,* 18–23.

Izard, C. E., Haynes, O. M., Chisolm, G., & Baak, K. (1991). Emotional determinants of infant-mother attachment. *Child Development, 62,* 906–917.

Izard, C. E., Huebner, R. R., Risser, D., McGinnes, G., & Dougherty, L. (1980). The young infant's ability to produce discrete emotion expressions. *Developmental Psychology, 16,* 132–140.

Izard, C. E., Kagan, J., & Zajonc, R. B. (1984). Introduction. In C. E. Izard, J. Kagan, & R. B. Zajonc (Eds.), *Emotions, cognition, and behavior.* Cambridge, UK: Cambridge University Press.

Izard, C. E., & Malatesta, C. Z. (1987). Perspectives on emotional development: I. Differential emotions theory of early emotional development. In J. D. Osofsky (Ed.), *Handbook of infant development* (2nd ed., pp. 494–554). New York: Wiley.

Jaccard, J., Dittus, P. J., & Gordon, V. V. (1998). Parent-adolescent congruency in reports of adolescent sexual behavior and in communications about sexual behavior. *Child Development, 69,* 247–261.

Jacklin, C. N. (1989). Female and male: Issues of gender. *American Psychologist, 44,* 127–133.

Jacklin, C. N., DiPietro, J. A., & Maccoby, E. E. (1984). Sex-typing behavior and sex-typing pressure in child/parent interaction. *Archives of Sexual Behavior, 13,* 413–425.

Jacklin, C. N., & Maccoby, E. E. (1978). Social behavior at thirty-three months in same-sex and mixed-sex dyads. *Child Development, 49,* 557–569.

Jackson, A. P., Brooks Gunn, J., Huang, C. C., & Glassman, M. (2000). Single mothers in low-wage jobs: Financial strain, parenting, and preschoolers' outcomes. *Child Development, 71,* 1409–1423.

Jackson, A. W., & Hornbeck, D. W. (1989). Educating young adolescents: Why we must restructure middle grade schools. *American Psychologist, 44,* 831–836.

Jackson, J. F. (1993). Human behavioral genetics, Scarr's theory, and her views on interventions: A critical review and commentary on their implications for African American children. *Child Development, 64,* 1318–1332.

Jacobs, J. E., & Klaczynski, P. A. (2002). The development of judgment and decision making during childhood and adolescence. *Current Directions in Psychological Science, 11,* 145–149.

Jacobs, J. E., & Potenza, M. (1991). The use of judgment heuristics to make social and object decisions: A developmental perspective. *Child Development, 62,* 166–178.

Jacobs, J. E., Lanza, S., Osgood, D. W., Eccles, J. S., & Wigfield, A. (2002). Changes in children's self-competence and values: Gender and domain differences across grades one through twelve. *Child Development, 73,* 509–527.

Jacobs, P. A., & Hassold, T. J. (1995). The origin of numerical chromosome abnormalities. *Advances in Genetics, 33,* 101–133.

Jacobsen, T., Edelstein, W., & Hofman, V. (1994). A longitudinal study of the relation between representations of attachment in childhood and cognitive functioning in childhood and adolescence. *Developmental Psychology, 30,* 112–124.

Jacobson, J. L., & Jacobson, S. W. (1996). Methodological considerations in behavioral toxicology in infants and children. *Developmental Psychology, 32,* 390–403.

Jaffee, S. R., Moffitt, T. E., Caspi, A., & Taylor, A. Life with (or without) father: The benefits of living with two biological parents depend on the father's antisocial behavior. *Child Development, 74,* 109–126.

Jaglom, L. M., & Gardner, H. (1981). The preschool television viewer as anthropologist. In H. Kelly & H. Gardner (Eds.), *New directions in child development: Viewing children through television* (pp. 9–30). San Francisco: Jossey-Bass.

Jahns, L., Siega-Riz, A. M., & Popkin, B. M. (2001). The increasing prevalence of snacking among U.S. children from 1977 to 1996. *Journal of Pediatrics, 138,* 493–498.

Jahromi, L. B., Putnam, S. P., & Stifter, C. A. (2004). Maternal regulation of infant reactivity from 2 to 6 months. *Developmental Psychology, 40,* 477–487.

James, S. (1978). Effect of listener age and situation on the politeness of children's directives. *Journal of Psycholinguistic Research, 7,* 307–317.

James, W. (1890). *The principles of psychology.* New York: Henry Holt.

James, W. (1892). *Psychology: The briefer course.* New York: Henry Holt.

Janicki, M. P., & Dalton, A. J. (2000). Prevalence of dementia and impact on intellectual disability services. *Mental Retardation, 38,* 276–288.

Jarrett, R. L. (1997). Bringing families back in: Neighborhoods' effects on child development. In J. Brooks-Gunn, G. J. Duncan, & J. L. Aber (Eds.), *Neighborhood poverty: Vol. 2. Policy implications in studying neighborhoods* (pp. 48–64). New York: Russell Sage Foundation.

Jegalian, K., & Lahn, B. T. (2001, February). Why the Y is so weird. *Scientific American, 284,* pp. 56–61.

Jencks, C. (1972). *Inequality: A reassessment of the effect of family and schooling in America.* New York: Basic Books.

Jencks, C., & Mayer, S. (1990). The social consequences of growing up in a poor neighborhood. In L. E. Lynn & M. F. H. McGeary (Eds.), *Inner-city poverty in the United States* (pp. 111–186). Washington, DC: National Academy Press.

Jenkins, J. (1992). Sibling relationships in disharmonious homes: Potential difficulties and protective effects. In R. A. Hinde & J. Stevenson-Hinde (Eds.), *Children's sibling relationships: Developmental and clinical issues* (pp. 125–138). Hillsdale, NJ: Erlbaum.

Jensen, A. R. (1969). How much can we boost IQ and scholastic achievement? *Harvard Educational Review, 39,* 1–123.

Jensen, A. R. (1980). *Bias in mental testing.* New York: Free Press.

Jensen, A. R. (1982). The chronometry of intelligence. In R. J. Sternberg (Ed.), *Advances in the psychology of human intelligence* (Vol. 1). Hillsdale, NJ: Erlbaum.

Jensen, A. R., & Munroe, E. (1979). Reaction time, movement time, and intelligence. *Intelligence, 3,* 121–126.

Johnson, J., & Newport, E. (1989). Critical period effects in second language learning: The influence of maturational state on the acquisition of English as a second language. *Cognitive Psychology, 21,* 60–99.

Johnson, K. E., & Mervis, C. M. (1997). First steps in the emergence of verbal humor: A case study. *Infant Behavior & Development, 20,* 187–196.

Johnson, M. H. (1992). Imprinting and the development of face recognition: From chick to man. *Current Directions in Psychological Science, 1,* 52–55.

Johnson, M. H. (2000). Functional brain development in infants: Elements of an interactive specialization framework. *Child Development, 71,* 75–81.

Johnson, M. H., Dziurawiec, S., Ellis, H. D., & Morton, J. (1991). Newborns' preferential tracking of face-like stimuli and its subsequent decline. *Cognition, 40,* 1–21.

Johnson, M. H., Farroni, T., Brockbank, M., & Simion, F. (2000). Preferential orienting to faces in 4-month-olds: Analysis of temporal-nasal visual field differences. *Developmental Science, 3,* 41–45.

Johnson, S. P. (2004). Development of perceptual completion in infancy. *Psychological Science, 15,* 769–775.

Johnson, S. P., Bremner, J. G., Slater, A. M., & Mason, U. C. (2000). The role of good form in young infant's perception of partly occluded objects. *Journal of Experimental Child Psychology, 76,* 1–25.

Johnson, S. P., & Mason, U. (2002). Perception of kinetic illusory contours by two-month-old infants. *Child Development, 73,* 22–34.

Johnston, J., Brzezinski, E. J., & Anderman, E. M. (1994). *Taking the measure of Channel One: A three year perspective.* Ann Arbor, MI: University of Michigan, Institute for Social Research.

Joint Committee on Infant Hearing. (2000). Year 2000 Position Statement: Principles and Guidelines for Early Hearing Detection and Intervention Program. *Pediatrics, 106,* 798–817.

Jones, D. C. (2004). Image among adolescent girls and boys: A longitudinal study. *Developmental Psychology, 40,* 823–835.

Jones, G. P., & Dembo, M. H. (1989). Age and sex role differences in intimate friendships during childhood and adolescence. *Merrill-Palmer Quarterly, 35,* 445–462.

Jones, K. L., & Smith, D. W. (1973). Recognition of the fetal alcohol syndrome in early infancy. *Lancet, 2,* 999–1001.

Jones, M. C. (1965). Psychological correlates of somatic development. *Child Development, 36,* 899–911.

Jones, S. S. (1996). Imitation or exploration? Young infants' matching of adults' oral gestures. *Child Development, 67,* 1952–1969.

Joseph, R. (2000). Fetal brain behavior and cognitive development. *Developmental Review, 20,* 81–98.

Joyce, B. A., Keck, J. F., & Gerkensmeyer, J. (2001). Evaluation of pain management interventions for neonatal circumcision pain. *Journal of Pediatric Health Care, 15,* 105–114.

Juffer, F., & van IJzendoorn, M. A. (2005). Behavior problems and mental health referrals of international adoptees. *Journal of the American Medical Association, 293,* 2501–2515.

Jusczyk, P. W., Cutler, A., & Redanz, L. (1993). Infants' sensitivity to predominant stress patterns in English. *Child Development, 64,* 675–687.

Jusczyk, P. W., Friederici, A. D., Wessels, J. M. I., Svenkerud, V. Y., & Jusczyk, A. M. (1993). Infants' sensitivity to the sound patterns of native language words. *Journal of Memory and Language, 32,* 402–420.

Jusczyk, P. W., Hirsh-Pasek, K., Kemler Nelson, D. G., Kennedy, L. J., Woodward, A. & Piwoz, J. (1992). Perception of acoustic correlates of major phrasal units by young infants. *Cognitive Psychology, 24,* 252–293.

Kagan, J. (1981). *The second year: The emergence of self-awareness.* Cambridge, MA: Harvard University Press.

Kagan, J. (1994). *Galen's prophecy: Temperament in human nature.* New York: Basic Books.

Kagan, J., Arcus, D., Snidman, N., Feng, W. Y., Hendler, J., & Greene, S. (1994). Reactivity in infants: A cross-national comparison. *Developmental Psychology, 30,* 342–345.

Kagan, J., & Fox, N. A. (2006). Biology, culture, and temperamental biases. In W. Damon & R. M. Lerner (Editors-in-Chief) & N. Eisenberg (Vol. Ed.), *Handbook of child psychology: Vol. 3. Social, emotional, and personality development* (6th ed., pp. 167–225). Hoboken, NJ: Wiley.

Kagan, J., Reznick, J. S., & Snidman, N. (1988). Biological basis of childhood shyness. *Science, 240,* 167–171.

Kagan, J., Snidman, N., & Arcus, D. M. (1992). Initial reactions to unfamiliarity. *Current Directions in Psychological Science, 1,* 171–174.

Kagan, J., Snidman, N., & Arcus, D. (1993). On the temperamental categories of inhibited and uninhibited children. In K. H. Rubin & J. B. Asendorpf (Eds.), *Social withdrawal, inhibition, and shyness in children* (pp. 19–28). Hillsdale, NJ: Erlbaum.

Kahn, P. H., Jr. (1992). Children's obligatory and discretionary moral judgments. *Child Development, 63,* 416–430.

Kail, R. (1986). Sources of age differences in speed of processing. *Child Development, 57,* 969–987.

Kail, R. (1990). *The development of memory in children* (3rd ed.). New York: W.H. Freeman.

Kail, R. (1991a). Development of processing speed in childhood and adolescence. In H. W. Reese (Ed.), *Advances in child development and behavior* (Vol. 23). San Diego, CA: Academic Press.

Kail, R. (1991b). Processing time declines exponentially during childhood and adolescence. *Developmental Psychology, 27,* 259–266.

Kail, R. V., & Miller, C. A. (2006). Developmental change in processing speed: Domain specificity and stability during childhood and adolescence. *Journal of Cognition and Development, 7,* 119–137.

Kaiser, J. (2005). An early look at baby's genes. *Science, 309,* 1476–1478.

Kaiser Family Foundation. (2004). *Sex education in America: General public/Parents survey.* Washington, DC: Kaiser Family Foundation.

Kaiser Family Foundation. (2005). *U. S. teen sexual activity.* Washington, DC: Henry J. Kaiser Family Foundation.

Kaitz, M., Lapidot, P., Bronner, R., & Eidelman, A. I. (1992). Parturient women can recognize their infants by touch. *Developmental Psychology, 28,* 35–39.

Kaitz, M., Shiri, S., Danziger, S., Hershko, Z., & Eidelman, A. I. (1994). Fathers can also recognize their newborns by touch. *Infant Behavior and Development, 17,* 205–207.

Kajii, T., Kida, M., & Takahashi, K. (1973). The effect of thalidomide intake during 113 human pregnancies. *Teratology, 8,* 163–166.

Kamins, M. L., & Dweck, C. S. (1999). Person versus process praise and criticism: Implications for contingent self-worth and coping. *Developmental Psychology, 35,* 835–847.

Kanner, L. (1943). Autistic disturbances of affective contact. *Nervous Children, 2,* 217–250.

Kaplan, H., & Dove, H. (1987). Infant development among the Ache of Eastern Paraguay. *Developmental Psychology, 23,* 190–196.

Kaplowitz, P. B., Slora, E. J., Wasserman, R. C., Pedlow, S. E., & Herman-Giddens, M. E. (2001). Earlier onset of puberty in girls: Relation to increased body mass index and race. *Pediatrics, 108,* 347–353.

Karmiloff-Smith, A. (1995). Annotation: The extraordinary cognitive journey from foetus through infancy. *Journal of Child Psychology and Psychiatry, 36,* 1293–1313.

Karraker, K. H., Vogel, D. A., & Lake, M. A. (1995). Parents' gender-stereotyped perceptions of newborns: The eye of the beholder revisited. *Sex Roles, 33,* 687–701.

Karrass, J., & Braungart-Rieker, J. M. (2005). Effects of shared parent-infant book reading on early language acquisition. *Applied Developmental Psychology, 26,* 133–148.

Katz, P. A. (1987). Variations in family constellation: Effects on gender schemata. In L. S. Liben & M. L. Signorella (Eds.), *New directions for child development: No. 38. Children's gender schemata.* San Francisco: Jossey-Bass.

Katz, P. A., & Ksansnak, K. R. (1994). Developmental aspects of gender role flexibility and traditionality in middle childhood and adolescence. *Developmental Psychology, 30,* 272–282.

Katz, P., Natchtigall, R., & Showstack, J. (2002). The economic impact of the assisted reproductive technologies. *Nature Cell Biology, 4,* s29–32.

Katzman, D. K., Golden, N. H., Neumark-Sztainer, D., Yager, J., & Strober, M. (2000). From prevention to prognosis: Clinical research update on adolescent eating disorders. *Pediatric Research, 47,* 709–712.

Kaufman, A. S. (2001). WAIS-III IQs, Horn's theory, and generational changes from young adulthood to old age. *Intelligence, 29,* 131–167.

Kaufman, A. S., Kamphaus, R. W., & Kaufman, N. L. (1985). New directions in intelligence testing: The Kaufman Assessment Battery for Children (K-ABC). In B. B. Wolman (Ed.), *Handbook of intelligence* (pp. 663–698). New York: Wiley.

Kaye, K., & Marcus, J. (1981). Infant imitation: The sensorimotor agenda. *Developmental Psychology, 17,* 258–265.

Kayne, M. A., Greulich, M. B., & Albers, L. L. (2001). Doulas: An alternative yet complementary addition to care during childbirth. *Clinical Obstetrics and Gynecology, 44,* 692–703.

Kazdin, A., & Benjet, C. (2003). Spanking children: Evidence and issues. *Current Directions in Psychological Science, 12,* 99–103.

Keel, P. K., Fulkerson, J. A., & Leon, G. R. (1997). Disordered eating precursors in pre- and early adolescent girls and boys. *Journal of Youth and Adolescence, 26,* 203–216.

Keen, R. E., & Berthier, N. E. (2004). Continuities and discontinuities in infants' representation of objects and events. In R. V. Kail (Ed.), *Advances in child development and behavior* (Vol. 32, pp. 243–279). San Diego: Elsevier.

Keil, F. C. (1989). *Concepts, kinds, and cognitive development.* Cambridge, MA: MIT Press.

Keller, M., Edelstein, W., Schmid, C., Fang, F., & Fang, G. (1998). Reasoning about responsibilities and obligations in close relationships: A comparison across two cultures. *Developmental Psychology, 34,* 731–741.

Kelley, M. L., Power, T. G., & Wimbush, D. D. (1992). Determinants of disciplinary practices in low-income black mothers. *Child Development, 63,* 573–582.

Kelley, S. A., Brownell, C. A., & Campbell, S. B. (2000). Mastery motivation and self-evaluative affect in toddlers: Longitudinal relations with maternal behavior. *Child Development, 71,* 1061–1071.

Kellman, P. J. (1996). The origins of object perception. In R. Gelman & T. Au (Eds.), *Perceptual and cognitive development* (pp. 3–48). New York: Academic Press.

Kellman, P. J., & Arterberry, M. E. (1998). *The cradle of knowledge: Development of perception in infancy.* Cambridge, MA: MIT Press.

Kellman, P. J., & Arterberry, M. E. (2006). Infant visual perception. In W. Damon & R. M. Lerner (Editors-in-Chief) & D. M. Kuhn & R. S. Siegler (Vol. Eds.), *Handbook of child psychology: Vol. 2. Cognition, perception, and language* (6th ed., pp. 109–160). Hoboken, NJ: Wiley.

Kellman, P. J., & Banks, M. S. (1998). Infant visual perception. In W. Damon (Series Ed.) & R. Siegler & D. Kuhn (Vol. Eds.), *Handbook of child psychology: Vol. 2. Cognition, perception, and language* (5th ed., pp. 103–146). New York: Wiley.

Kellman, P. J., & Spelke, E. S. (1983). Perception of partly occluded objects in infancy. *Cognitive Psychology, 15,* 483–524.

Kelly, M. H. (1992). Using sound to solve syntactic problems: The role of phonology in grammatical category assignments. *Psychological Review, 99,* 349–364.

Kemler Nelson, D. G., Hirsh-Pasek, K., Jusczyk, P. W., & Cassidy, K. W. (1989). How the prosodic cues in motherese might assist language learning. *Journal of Child Language, 16,* 55–68.

Kemp, J. S., Livne, M., White, D. K., & Arfken, C. L. (1998). Softness and potential to cause rebreathing: Differences in bedding used by infants at high and low risk for sudden infant death syndrome. *Journal of Pediatrics, 132,* 234–239.

Kendler, K. S., Prescott, C. A., Neale, M. C., & Pedersen, N. L. (1997). Temperance Board registration for alcohol abuse in a national sample of Swedish male twins, born 1902–1949. *Archives of General Psychiatry, 54,* 178–184.

Kennedy, C. R. (2000). Neonatal screening for hearing impairment. *Archives of Disease in Childhood, 83,* 377–383.

Keogh, J., & Sugden, D. (1985). *Movement skill development.* New York: Macmillan.

Kerig, P. K., Cowan, P. A., & Cowan, C. P. (1993). Marital quality and gender differences in parent-child interaction. *Developmental Psychology, 29,* 931–939.

Kersten, A. W., & Smith, L. B. (2002). Attention to novel objects during verb learning. *Child Development, 73,* 93–109.

Kieras, J. E., Tobin, R. T., Graziano, W. G., & Rothbart, M. K. (2005). You can't always get what you want: Effortful control and children's responses to undesirable gifts. *Psychological Science, 16,* 391–396.

Kiesner, J., Cadinu, M., Poulin, F., & Bucci, M. (2002). Group identification in early adolescence: Its relation with peer adjustment and its moderator effect on peer influence. *Child Development, 73,* 196–208.

Kiesner, J., & Pastore, M. (2005). Differences in the relations between antisocial behavior and peer acceptance across contexts and across adolescence. *Child Development, 76,* 1278–1293.

Kilbride, H., Castor, C., Hoffman, E., & Fuger, K. L. (2000). Thirty-six-month outcome of prenatal cocaine exposure for term or near-term infants: Impact of early case management. *Journal of Developmental and Behavioral Pediatrics, 21,* 19–26.

Killen, M., Pisacane, K., Lee Kim, J., & Ardila Rey, A. (2001). Fairness or stereotypes? Young children's priorities when evaluating group exclusion and inclusion. *Developmental Psychology, 37,* 587–596.

Kim, J. E., Hetherington, E. M., & Reiss, D. (1999). Associations among family relationships., antisocial peers, and adolescents' externalizing behaviors: Gender and family type differences. *Child Development, 70,* 1209–1230.

Kim, K. H. S., Relkin, N. R., Lee, K., & Hirsch, J. (1997). Distinct cortical areas associated with native and second languages. *Nature, 388,* 171–174.

Kim, K. J., Conger, R. D., Lorenz, F. O., & Elder, G. H., Jr. (2001). Parent-adolescent reciprocity in negative affect and its relation to early adult social development. *Developmental Psychology, 37,* 775–790.

Kinsman, S. B., Romer, D., Furstenberg, F. F., & Schwartz, D. F. (1998). Early sexual initiation: The role of peer norms. *Pediatrics, 102,* 1185–1192.

Kirby, D. (1997). *No easy answers: Research findings on programs to reduce teen pregnancy.* Washington, DC: National Campaign to Prevent Teen Pregnancy.

Kirkpatrick, S. W., & Sanders, D. M. (1978). Body image stereotypes: A developmental comparison. *Journal of Genetic Psychology, 132,* 87–95.

Kisilevsky, B. S., Hains, S. M. J., & Low, J. A. (1999). Differential maturation of fetal responses to vibroacoustic stimulation in a high risk population. *Developmental Science, 2,* 234–245.

Kisilevsky, B. S., & Low, J. A. (1998). Human fetal behavior: 100 years of study. *Developmental Review, 18,* 1–29.

Kisilevsky, B. S., & Muir, D. W. (1991). Human fetal and subsequent newborn responses to sound and vibration. *Infant Behavior and Development, 14,* 1–26.

Klaczynski, P. A. (2000). Motivated scientific reasoning biases, epistemological beliefs, and theory polarization: A two-process approach to adolescent cognition. *Child Development, 71,* 1347–1366.

Klaczynski, P. A. (2001). Analytic and heuristic processing influences on adolescent reasoning and decision-making. *Child Development, 72,* 844–861.

Klaczynski, P. A. (2004). A dual-process model of adolescent development: Implications for decision making, reasoning, and identity. In R. V. Kail (Ed.), *Advances in child development and behavior* (Vol. 32, pp. 73–123). San Diego, CA: Elsevier.

Klahr, D. (1978). Goal formation, planning, and learning by preschool problem solvers or: "My socks are in the dryer." In R. S. Siegler (Ed.), *Children's thinking: What develops?* (pp. 181–212). Hillsdale, NJ: Erlbaum.

Klahr, D. (1989). Information-processing approaches. In R. Vasta (Ed.), *Annals of child development: Vol 6. Six theories of child development: Revised formulations and current issues.* Greenwich, CT: JAI Press.

Klahr, D., Chen, Z., & Toth, E. E. (2001). Cognitive development and science education: Ships that pass in the night or beacons of mutual illumination? In S. M. Carver & D. Klahr (Eds.), *Cognition and instruction: Twenty-five years of progress* (pp. 75–119). Mahwah, NJ: Erlbaum.

Klahr, D., & Dunbar, K. (1988). Dual space search during scientific reasoning. *Cognitive Science, 12,* 1–55.

Klahr, D., Fay, A. L., & Dunbar, K. (1993). Heuristics for scientific experimentation: A developmental study. *Cognitive Psychology, 25,* 111–146.

Klahr, D., & MacWhinney, B. (1998). Information processing. In W. Damon (Series Ed.) & D. Kuhn & R. S. Siegler (Vol. Eds.), *Handbook of child psychology: Vol. 2. Cognition, perception, and language* (5th ed., pp. 631–678). New York: Wiley.

Klahr, D., & Robinson, M. (1981). Formal assessment of problem solving and planning processes in preschool children. *Cognitive Psychology, 13,* 113–148.

Klaus, M., & Kennell, J. (1982). *Parent-infant bonding.* St. Louis: C. V. Mosby.

Klebanov, P. K., Brooks-Gunn, J., & McCormick, M. C. (1994). Classroom behavior of very low birth weight elementary school children. *Pediatrics, 94,* 700–708.

Klein, P. D. (1997). Multiplying the problems of intelligence by eight: A critique of Gardner's theory. *Canadian Journal of Education, 22,* 377–394.

Klesges, R. C., Haddock, C. K., Stein, R. J., Klesges, L. M., Eck, L. H., & Hanson, C. L. (1992). Relationship between psychosocial functioning and body fat in preschool children: A longitudinal investigation. *Journal of Consulting and Clinical Psychology, 60,* 793–796.

Kliewer, W., Adams Parrish, K., Taylor, K. W., Jackson, K., Walker, J. M., & Shivy, V. A. (2006). Socialization of coping with community violence: Influences of caregiver coaching, modeling, and family context. *Child Development, 77,* 605–623.

Klima, E. S., & Bellugi, U. (1966). Syntactic regularities in the speech of children. In J. Lyons & R. J. Wales (Eds.), *Psycholinguistic papers: The proceedings of the 1966 Edinburgh conference.* Edinburgh: Edinburgh University Press.

Kling, K. C., Hyde, J. S., Showers, C. J., & Buswell, B. N. (1999). Gender differences in self-esteem: A meta-analysis. *Psychological Bulletin, 125,* 470–500.

Knowles, R. V. (1985). *Genetics, society and decisions.* Columbus, OH: Merrill.

Kobak, R. R., Cole, H. E., Ferenz-Gillies, R., & Fleming, W. S. (1993). Attachment and emotion regulation during mother-teen problem-solving: A control theory analysis. *Child Development, 64,* 231–245.

Kobayashi-Winata, H., & Power, T. G. (1989). Child rearing and compliance: Japanese and American families in Houston. *Journal of Cross-Cultural Psychology, 20,* 333–356.

Kochanek, K. D., Murphy, S. L., Anderson, R. N., & Scott, C. (2004). *Deaths: Final data for 2002. National Vital Statistics Report, 53*(5), 1–116.

Kochanska, G. (1994). Beyond cognition: Expanding the search for the early roots of internalization and conscience. *Developmental Psychology, 30,* 20–22.

Kochanska, G. (1997). Mutually responsive orientation between mothers and their young children: Implications for early socialization. *Child Development, 68,* 94–112.

Kochanska, G. (2001). Emotional development in children with different attachment histories: The first three years. *Child Development, 72,* 474–490.

Kochanska, G. (2002). Committed compliance, moral self, and internalization: A mediational model. *Developmental Psychology, 38,* 339–351.

Kochanska, G., Aksan, N., Knaack, A., & Rhines, H. M. (2004). Maternal parenting and children's conscience: Early security as a moderator. *Child Development, 75,* 1229–1242.

Kochanska, G., Aksan, N., & Koenig, A. L. (1995). A longitudinal study of the roots of preschoolers' conscience: Committed compliance and emerging internalizations. *Child Development, 66,* 1752–1769.

Kochanska, G., Casey, R. J., & Fukumoto, A. (1995). Toddlers' sensitivity to standard violation. *Child Development, 66,* 643–656.

Kochanska, G., Coy, K. C., & Murray, K. T. (2001). The development of self-regulation in the first four years of life. *Child Development, 72,* 1091–1111.

Kochanska, G., Gross, J. N., Lin, M.-H., & Nichols, K. E. (2002). Guilt in young children: Development, determinants, and relations with a broader system of standards. *Child Development, 73,* 461–482.

Kochanska, G., & Murray, K. T. (2000). Mother-child responsive orientation and conscience development: From toddler to early school age. *Child Development, 71,* 417–431.

Kochanska, G., Murray, K., & Coy, K. C. (1997). Inhibitory control as a contributor to conscience in childhood: From toddler to early school age. *Child Development, 68,* 263–277.

Kochanska, G., Murray, K. T., & Harlan, E. T. (2000). Effortful control in early childhood: Continuity and change, antecedents, and implications for social development. *Developmental Psychology, 36,* 220–232.

Kochanska, G., Tjebkes, T. L., & Forman, D. R. (1998). Children's emerging regulation of conduct: Restraint, compliance, and internalization from infancy to the second year. *Child Development, 69,* 1378–1389.

Kochenderfer, B. J., & Ladd, G. W. (1996). Peer victimization: Cause or consequence of school maladjustment? *Child Development, 67,* 1305–1317.

Koff, E., & Rierdan, J. (1995). Preparing girls for menstruation: Recommendations from adolescent girls. *Adolescence, 30,* 795–811.

Kohlberg, L. (1966). A cognitive-developmental analysis of children's sex-role concepts and attitudes. In E. E. Maccoby (Ed.), *The development of sex differences* (pp. 82–173). Stanford, CA: Stanford University Press.

Kohlberg, L. (1969). Stage and sequence: The cognitive-developmental approach to socialization. In D. A. Goslin (Ed.), *The handbook of socialization theory and research* (pp. 347–380). Chicago: Rand McNally.

Kohlberg, L. (1976). Moral stages and moralization: The cognitive developmental approach. In T. Lickona (Ed.), *Moral development and moral behavior: Theory, research, and social issues* (pp. 31–53). New York: Holt, Rinehart & Winston.

Kohlberg, L. (1984). *Essays on moral development: Vol. 2. The psychology of moral development.* San Francisco: Harper & Row.

Kohlberg, L., & Kramer, R. (1969). Continuities and discontinuities in childhood moral development. *Human Development, 12,* 93–120.

Kolata, G. (2001, September 28). Fertility ethics authority approves sex selection. *New York Times,* p. A16.

Kopp, C. (1989). Regulation of distress and negative emotions: A developmental view. *Developmental Psychology, 25,* 343–354.

Kopp, C. B. (1987). The growth of self-regulation: Caregivers and children. In N. Eisenberg (Ed.), *Contemporary topics in developmental psychology* (pp. 34–55). New York: Wiley.

Kopp, C. B. (1992). Emotional distress and control in young children. In N. Eisenberg & R. A. Fabes (Eds.), *Emotion and its regulation in early development (New Directions in Child Development,* No. 55). San Francisco: Jossey-Bass.

Korner, A. F. (1972). State as a variable, as obstacle, and mediator of stimulation in infant research. *Merrill-Palmer Quarterly, 18,* 77–94.

Korner, A. F. (1987). Preventive intervention with high-risk newborns: Theoretical, conceptual, and methodological perspectives. In J. D. Osofsky (Ed.), *Handbook of infant development* (2nd ed.). New York: Wiley.

Kotelchuk, M. (1976). The infant's relationship to the father: Experimental evidence. In M. E. Lamb (Ed.), *The role of the father in child development.* New York: Wiley.

Kovacs, D. M., Parker, J. G., & Hoffman, L. W. (1996). Behavioral, affective, and social correlates of involvement in cross-sex friendship in elementary school. *Child Development, 67,* 2269–2286.

Kowal, A., & Kramer, L. (1997). Children's understanding of potential differential treatment. *Child Development, 68,* 113–126.

Kraemer, H. C., Korner, A., Anders, T., Jacklin, C. N., & Dimiceli, S. (1985). Obstetric drugs and infant behavior: A re-evaluation. *Journal of Pediatric Psychology, 10,* 345–353.

Krafchuk, E. E., Tronick, E. Z., & Clifton, R. K. (1983). Behavioral and cardiac responses to sound in preterm infants varying in risk status: A hypothesis of their paradoxical reactivity. In T. Field & A. Sostek (Eds.), *Infants born at risk: Physiological, perceptual, and cognitive processes.* New York: Grune & Stratton.

Kramer, A. F., Gonzalez de Sather, J. C. M., & Cassavaugh, N. D. (2005). Development of attentional and oculomotor control. *Developmental Psychology, 41,* 760–772.

Kramer, L., Perozynski, L. A., & Chung, T. (1999). Parental responses to sibling conflict: The effects of development and parent gender. *Child Development, 70,* 1401–1414.

Kranzler, J. H., Rosenbloom, A. L., Proctor, B., Diamond, F. B., Jr., & Watson, M. (2000). Is short stature a handicap? A comparison of the psychosocial functioning of referred and nonreferred children with normal short stature and children with normal stature. *Journal of Pediatrics, 136,* 96–102.

Krascum, R. M., & Andrews, S. (1998). The effects of theories on children's acquisition of family-resemblance structures. *Child Development, 69,* 333–346.

Krauss, R. H., & Glucksberg, S. (1969). The development of communication. *Child Development, 40,* 255–266.

Krebs, D. L., & Van Hesteren, F. (1994). The development of altruism: Toward an integrative model. *Developmental Review, 14,* 103–158.

Krendl, K. A., & Broihier, M. (1992). Student responses to computers: A longitudinal study. *Journal of Educational Computing Research, 8,* 215–227.

Kreutzer, M. A., Leonard, S. C., & Flavell, J. H. (1975). An interview study of children's knowledge about memory. *Monographs of the Society for Research in Child Development, 40*(1, Serial No. 159).

Krevans, J., & Gibbs, J. C. (1996). Parents' use of inductive discipline: Relations to children's empathy and prosocial behavior. *Child Development, 67,* 3263–3277.

Kroll, J. (1977). The concept of childhood in the Middle Ages. *Journal of the History of the Behavioral Sciences, 13,* 384–393.

Krowchuck, D. P., Kreiter, S. R., Woods, C. R., Sinal, S. H., & DuRant, R. H. (1998). Problem dieting behavior among young adolescents. *Archives of Pediatric and Adolescent Medicine, 152,* 884–888.

Krumhansl, C. L., & Jusczyk, P. W. (1990). Infants' perception of phrase structure in music. *Psychological Science, 1,* 70–73.

Kuczaj, S. A., Borys, R. H., & Jones, M. (1989). On the interaction of language and thought: Some thoughts and developmental data. In A. Gellatly, D. Rogers, & J. A. Sloboda (Eds.), *Cognition and social worlds.* Oxford: Clarendon Press.

Kuczynski, L., & Kochanska, G. (1995). Function and content of maternal demands: Developmental significance of early demands for competent action. *Child Development, 66,* 616–628.

Kuebli, J., Butler, S., & Fivush, R. (1995). Mother-child talk about past emotions: Relations of maternal language and child gender over time. *Cognition and Emotion, 9,* 265–283.

Kuhl, P. K. (1987). Perception of speech and sound in early infancy. In P. Salapatek & L. Cohen (Eds.), *Handbook of infant perception: From perception to cognition* (Vol. 2). Orlando, FL: Academic Press.

Kuhl, P. K., & Miller, J. D. (1978). Speech perception by the chinchilla: Identification functions for synthetic VOT stimuli. *Journal of the Acoustical Society of America, 63,* 905–917.

Kuhl, P. K., & Padden, D. M. (1983). Enhanced discriminability at the phonetic boundary for the place feature in macaques. *Journal of the Acoustical Society of America, 73,* 1003–1010.

Kuhl, P. K., Stevens, E., Hayashi, A., Deguchi, T., Kiritani, S., & Iverson, P. (2006). Infants show a facilitation effect for native language phonetic perception between 6 and 12 months. *Developmental Science, 9,* F13–F22.

Kuhl, P. K., Williams, K. A., Lacerda, F., Stevens, K. N., & Lindblom, B. (1992). Linguistic experience alters phonetic perception in infants by 6 months of age. *Science, 255,* 606–608.

Kuhn, D. (2000a). Metacognitive development. *Current Directions in Psychological Science, 9,* 178–181.

Kuhn, D. (2000b). Theory of mind, metacognition, and reasoning: A lifespan perspective. In P. Mitchell & K. J. Riggs (Eds.), *Children's reasoning and the mind* (pp. 301–326). Hove, UK: Psychology Press.

Kuhn, D. (2006). Do cognitive changes accompany developments in the adolescent brain? *Perspectives on Psychological Science, 1,* 59–67.

Kuhn, D., & Dean, D., Jr. (2005). Is developing scientific thinking all about learning to control variables? *Psychological Science, 16,* 866–870.

Kuhn, D., Garcia-Mila, M., Zohar, A., & Andersen, C. (1995). Strategies of knowledge acquisition. *Monographs of the Society for Research in Child Development, 60* (No. 4, Serial No. 245).

Kuhn, D., & Pearsall, S. (2000). Developmental origins of scientific thinking. *Journal of Cognition and Development, 1,* 113–129.

Kuhn, D., Schauble, L., & Garcia-Mila, M. (1992). Cross-domain development of scientific reasoning. *Cognition and Instruction, 9,* 285–327.

Kuklinski, M. R., & Weinstein, R. S. (2001). Classroom and developmental differences in a path model of teacher expectancy effects. *Child Development, 72,* 1554–1578.

Kunkel, D. (2001). Children and television advertising. In D. Singer & J. Singer (Eds.), *Handbook of children and the media* (pp. 375–393). Thousand Oaks, CA: Sage.

Kunkel, D., & Roberts, D. (1991). Young minds and marketplace values: Issues in children's television advertising. *Journal of Social Issues, 47,* 57–72.

Kunzig, R. (1998, August). Climbing through the brain. *Discover, 19,* 61–69.

Kuppermann, M., Gates, E., & Washington, A. E. (1996). Racial ethnic differences in prenatal diagnostic test use and outcomes: Preferences, socioeconomics, or patient knowledge? *Obstetrics and Gynecology, 87,* 675–682.

Kurdek, L. A. (1989). Siblings' reactions to parental divorce. *Journal of Divorce, 12,* 203–219.

Kurdek, L. A., Fine, M. A., & Sinclair, R. J. (1995). School adjustment in sixth graders: Parenting transitions, family climate, and peer norm effects. *Child Development, 66,* 430–445.

LaBarbera, J. D., Izard, C. E., Vietze, P., & Parisi, S. A. (1976). Four- and six-month-old infants' visual responses to joy, anger, and neutral expressions. *Child Development, 47,* 535–538.

Lackey, P. N. (1989). Adults' attitudes about assignments of household chores to male and female children. *Sex Roles, 20,* 271–281.

Ladd, G. W. (1983). Social networks of popular, average, and rejected children in school settings. *Merrill-Palmer Quartlerly, 29,* 283–307.

Ladd, G. W., Birch, S. H., & Buhs, E. S. (1999). Children's social and scholastic lives in kindergarten: Related spheres of influence? *Child Development, 70,* 1373–1400.

Ladd, G. W., & Burgess, K. B. (1999). Charting the relationship trajectories of aggressive, withdrawn, and aggressive/withdrawn children during early grade school. *Child Development, 70,* 910–929.

Ladd, G. W., & Golter, B. S. (1988). Parents' management of preschooler's peer relations: Is it related to children's social competencies? *Developmental Psychology, 24,* 109–117.

Ladd, G. W., & Hart, C. H. (1992). Creating informal play opportunities: Are parents' and preschoolers' initiations related to children's competence with peers? *Developmental Psychology, 28,* 1179–1187.

Ladd, G. W., Kochenderfer, B. J., & Coleman, C. C. (1996). Friendship quality as a predictor of young children's early school adjustment. *Child Development, 67,* 1103–1118.

Ladd, G. W., & Price, J. M. (1987). Predicting children's social and school adjustment following the transition from preschool to kindergarten. *Child Development, 58,* 1168–1189.

Lahey, B. B., Hammer, D., Crumrine, P. L., & Forehand, R. L. (1980). Birth order sex interactions in child behavior problems. *Developmental Psychology, 16,* 608–615.

Laible, D. J., & Thompson, R. A. (2000). Mother-child discourse, attachment security, shared positive affect, and early conscience development. *Child Development, 71,* 1424–1440.

Laible, D. J., & Thompson, R. A. (2002). Mother-child conflict in the toddler years: Lessons in emotion, morality, and relationships. *Child Development, 73,* 1187–1203.

Lamaze, F. (1970). *Painless childbirth: Psychoprophylactic method.* Chicago: Henry Regnery.

Lamb, M. E. (1981). *The role of the father in child development* (rev. ed.). New York: Wiley.

Lamb, M. E. (1987). Introduction: The emergent American father. In M. E. Lamb (Ed.), *The father's role: Cross-cultural perspectives.* Hillsdale, NJ: Erlbaum.

Lamb, M. E. (1997). The development of father–infant relationships. In M. E. Lamb (Ed.), *The role of the father in child development* (3rd ed., pp. 104–120). New York: Wiley.

Lamb, M. E. (1998). Nonparental child care: Context, quality, correlates, and consequences. In W. Damon (Series Ed.) & I. E. Sigel & K. A. Renninger (Vol. Eds.), *Handbook of child psychology: Vol. 4. Child psychology in practice* (5th ed., pp. 73–133). New York: Wiley.

Lamb, M. E., & Ahnert, L. (2006). Nonparental child care: Context, concepts, correlates, and consequences. In W. Damon & R. M. Lerner (Editors-in-Chief) & K. A. Renninger & I. E. Sigel (Vol. Eds.), *Handbook of child psychology: Vol. 4. Child psychology in practice* (6th ed., pp. 950–1016). Hoboken, NJ: Wiley.

Lamb, M. E., Easterbrooks, M. A., & Holden, G. (1980). Reinforcement and punishment among preschoolers: Characteristics and correlates. *Child Development, 51,* 1230–1236.

Lamb, M. E., Pleck, J. H., Charnov, E. L., & Levine, J. A. (1987). A biosocial perspective on paternal behavior and involvement. In J. B. Lancaster, J. Altmann, A. S. Rossi, & L. R. Sherrod (Eds.), *Parenting across the life span: Biosocial dimensions.* New York: Aldine de Gruyter.

Lamb, M. E., & Roopnarine, J. L. (1979). Peer influences on sex-role development in preschoolers. *Child Development, 50,* 1219–1222.

Lamborn, S. D., Mounts, N. S., Steinberg, L., & Dornbusch, S. M. (1991). Patterns of competence and adjustment among adolescents from authoritative, authoritarian, indulgent, and neglectful families. *Child Development, 62,* 1049–1065.

Lammer, E. J., Chen, D. T., Hoar, R. M., Agnish, N. D., et al. (1985). Retinoic acid embryopathy. *New England Journal of Medicine, 313,* 837–841.

Lampl, M., Veldhuis, J. D., & Johnson, M. L. (1992). Saltation and stasis: A model of human growth. *Science, 258,* 801–803.

Landau, S., Lorch, E. P., & Milich, R. (1992). Visual attention to and comprehension of television in attention-deficit hyperactivity disordered and normal boys. *Child Development, 63,* 928–937.

Landry, M. L. (2004). Viral infections. In G. N. Burrow, T. P. Duffy, & J. Copel (Eds.), *Medical complications during pregnancy* (6th ed., pp. 347–374). Philadelphia: Saunders.

Langlois, J. H., & Stephan, C. (1981). Beauty and the beast: The role of physical attractiveness in the development of peer relations and social behavior. In S. S. Brehm, S. H. Kassin, & F. X. Gibbons (Eds.), *Developmental social psychology* (pp. 152–168). New York: Oxford University Press.

Larkin, R. W. (1979). *Suburban youth in cultural crisis.* New York: Oxford University Press.

Larsen, J. T., To, Y. M., & Fireman, G. (2006). Children's understanding and experience of mixed emotions. *Psychological Science.*

Larson, R. W. (2001). How U.S. children and adolescents spend time: What it does (and doesn't) tell us about development. *Current Directions in Psychological Science, 10,* 160–164.

Larson, R. W., & Ham, M. (1993). Stress and "storm and stress" in early adolescence: The relationship of negative events with dysphoric affect. *Developmental Psychology, 29,* 130–140.

Larson, R. W., & Lampman-Petraitis, C. (1989). Daily emotional stress as reported by children and adolescents. *Child Development, 60,* 1250–1260.

Larson, R. W., Moneta, G., Richards, M. H., & Wilson, S. (2002). Continuity, stability, and change in daily emotional experience across adolescence. *Developmental Psychology, 73,* 1151–1165.

Laskari, A., Smith, A. K., & Graham, J. M., Jr. (1999). Williams-Beuren syndrome: An update and review for the primary physician. *Clinical Pediatrics, 38,* 189–208.

Latz, S., Wolf, A. W., & Lozoff, B. (1999). Cosleeping in context: Sleep practices and problems in young children in Japan and the United States. *Archives of Pediatrics and Adolescent Medicine, 153,* 339–346.

Laursen, B., Coy, K. C., & Collins, W. A. (1998). Reconsidering changes in parent-child conflict across adolescence: A meta-analysis. *Child Development, 69,* 817–832.

Laursen, B., & Williams, V. A. (1997). Perceptions of interdependence and closeness in family and peer relationships among adolescents with and without romantic partners. In S. Shulman & W. Andrew Collins (Eds.), *New Directions for Child Development: No. 78. Romantic relationships in adolescence: Developmental perspectives* (pp. 3–20). San Francisco: Jossey-Bass.

Lawson, M. (1980). Development of body build stereotypes, peer ratings, and self-esteem in Australian children. *Journal of Psychology, 104,* 111–118.

Lazar, I., & Darlington, R. (1982). Lasting effects of early education: A report from the Consortium for Longitudinal Studies. *Monographs of the Society for Research in Child Development, 47* (2–3, Serial No. 195).

Leaper, C. (2000). Gender, affiliation, assertion, and the interactive context of parent-child play. *Developmental Psychology, 36,* 381–393.

Learmonth, A. E., Nadel, L., & Newcombe, N. S. (2002). Children's use of landmarks: Implications for modularity theory. *Psychological Science, 13,* 337–341.

LeBoyer, F. (1975). *Birth without violoence.* New York: Knopf.

Lecanuet, J.-P. (1998). Foetal responses to auditory and speech stimuli. In A. Slater (Ed.), *Perceptual development: Visual, auditory, and speech perception in infancy* (pp. 317–355). East Sussex, UK: Psychology Press.

Lederberg, A. R., Prezbindowski, A. K., & Spencer, P. E. (2000). Word-learning skills of deaf preschoolers: The development of novel mapping and rapid word-learning strategies. *Child Development, 71,* 1571–1585.

Lee, B. C. P., Kuppusamy, K. G. R., El-Ghazzawy, O., Gordon, R. E., Lin, W., & Haacke, M. (1999). Hemispheric language dominance in children demonstrated by functional magnetic resonance imaging. *Journal of Child Neurology, 14,* 78–82.

Lee, K., Cameron, C. A., Xu, F., Fu, G., & Board, J. (1997). Chinese and Canadian children's evaluations of lying and truth telling: Similarities and differences in the context of pro- and antisocial behavior. *Child Development, 68,* 924–934.

Lee, L. C. (1971). The concommitant development of cognitive and moral modes of thought: A test of selected deductions from Piaget's theory. *Genetic Psychology Monographs, 83,* 93–146.

Lee, R. V. (1988). Sexually transmitted infections. In G. N. Burrow & T. F. Ferris (Eds.), *Medical complications during pregnancy.* Philadelphia: W.B. Saunders.

Leekam, S. R., Lopez, B., & Moore, C. (2000). Attention and joint attention in preschool children with autism. *Developmental Psychology, 36,* 261–273.

Legerstee, M., Anderson, D., & Schaffer, A. (1998). Five- and eight-month-old infants recognize their faces and voices as familiar and social stimuli. *Child Development, 69,* 37–50.

Leinbach, M. D., Hort, B. E., & Fagot, B. I. (1997). Bears are for boys: Metaphorical associations in young children's gender stereotypes. *Cognitive Development, 12,* 107–130.

Lemish, D., & Rice, M. (1986). Television as a talking picture book: A prop for language acquisition. *Journal of Child Language, 13,* 251–274.

Lenneberg, E. (1967). *Biological foundations of language.* New York: Wiley.

Leonard, L. B. (1998). *Children with specific language impairment.* Cambridge, MA: MIT Press.

Leonard, L. B., Newhoff, M., & Meselam, L. (1980). Individual differences in early child phonology. *Applied Psycholinguistics, 1,* 7–30.

Lerner, R. M., & Lerner, J. V. (1977). Effects of age, sex, and physical attractiveness on child-peer relations, academic performance, and elementary school adjustment. *Developmental Psychology, 13,* 585–590.

Lesser, G. S., Fifer, F., & Clark, D. H. (1965). Mental abilities of children of different social-class and cultural groups. *Monographs of the Society for Research in Child Development, 30*(4, Serial No. 102).

Lester, B. M., & Brazelton, T. B. (1982). Cross-cultural assessment of neonatal behavior. In D. Wagner & H. W. Stevenson (Eds.), *Cultural perspectives on child development.* San Francisco: W.H. Freeman.

Lester, B. M., & Dreher, M. (1989). Effects of marijuana use during pregnancy on newborn cry. *Child Development, 60,* 765–771.

LeVay, S., & Hamer, D. H. (1994, May). Evidence for a biological influence in male homosexuality. *Scientific American, 270,* 43–57.

Leventhal, T., & Brooks-Gunn, J. (2000). The neighborhoods they live in: The effects of neighborhood residence on child and adolescent outcomes. *Psychological Bulletin, 126,* 309–337.

Levine, R., & White, M. (1986). *Human conditions: The cultural basis for educational development.* New York: Routledge & Kegan Paul.

Levine, R., Dixon, S., LeVine, S., Richman, A., Leiderman, P. M., Keefer, C. H., & Brazelton, T. B. (1994). *Child care and culture: Lessons from Africa.* New York: Cambridge University Press.

Levine, S. C., Huttenlocher, J., Taylor, A., & Langrock, A. (1999). Early sex differences in spatial skill. *Developmental Psychology, 35,* 940–949.

Levine, S. C., Jordan, N. C., & Huttenlocher, J. (1992). Development of calculation abilities in young children. *Journal of Experimental Child Psychology, 53,* 72–103.

Levitin, D. J., & Bellugi, U. (1998). Musical abilities in individuals with Williams' syndrome. *Music Perception, 15(4),* 357–389.

Levitt, M. J., Guacci-Franco, N., & Levitt, J. L. (1993). Convoys of social support in childhood and early adolescence: Structure and function. *Developmental Psychology, 29,* 811–818.

Levy, G. D., Taylor, M. G., & Gelman, S. A. (1995). Traditional and evaluative aspects of flexibility in gender roles, social conventions, moral rules, and physical laws. *Child Development, 66,* 515–531.

Levy, Y. (1999). Early metalinguistic competence: Speech monitoring and repair behavior. *Developmental Psychology, 35,* 822–834.

Lew, A. R., Bremner, J. G., & Lefkovitch, L. P. (2000). The development of relational landmark use in six- to twelve-month old infants in a spatial orientation task. *Child Development, 71,* 1179–1190.

Lew, A. R., & Butterworth, G. (1997). The development of hand-mouth coordination in 2- to 5-month-old infants: Similarities with reaching and grasping. *Infant Behavior and Development, 20,* 59–69.

Lewis, M. (1983). On the nature of intelligence. In M. Lewis (Ed.), *Origins of intelligence.* New York: Plenum Press.

Lewis, M. (1989, April). *Self and self-conscious emotions.* Paper presented at the biennial meeting of the Society for Research in Child Development, Kansas City, MO.

Lewis, M. (1993). Early socioemotional predictors of cognitive competency at 4 years. *Developmental Psychology, 29,* 1036–1045.

Lewis, M., Alessandri, S., & Sullivan, M. (1992). Differences in shame and pride as a function of children's gender and task difficulty. *Child Development, 63,* 630–638.

Lewis, M., & Feiring, C. (1982). Some American families at dinner. In L. M. Laosa & I. E. Sigel (Eds.), *Families as learning environments for children.* New York: Plenum Press.

Lewis, M., Hitchcock, D. F. A., & Sullivan, M. W. (2004). Physiological and emotional reactivity to learning and frustration. *Infancy, 6,* 121–143.

Lewis, M. D., Lamm, C., Segalowitz, S. A., Stieben, J., & Zelazo, P. D. (2006). Neurophysiological correlates of emotion regulation in children and adolescents. *Journal of Cognitive Neuroscience, 18,* 1–17.

Lewis, M., & Michalson, L. (1983). *Children's emotions and moods: Developmental theory and measurement.* New York: Plenum Press.

Lewis, M., & Ramsay, D. (2002). Cortisol response to embarrassment and shame. *Child Development, 73,* 1034–1045.

Lewis, M., Sullivan, M. W., Stanger, C., & Weiss, M. (1989). Self development and self-conscious emotions. *Child Development, 60,* 146–156.

Lewis, T. L., Maurer, D., & Kay, D. (1978). Newborns' central vision: Whole or hole? *Journal of Experimental Child Psychology, 26,* 193–203.

Lewkowicz, D. J. (2000). The development of intersensory temporal perception: An epigenetic systems/limitations view. *Psychological Bulletin, 126,* 281–308.

Li, J. (2006). Self in learning: Chinese adolescents' goals and sense of agency. *Child Development, 77,* 482–501.

Li, X., Stanton, B., & Feigelman, S. (2000). Impact of perceived parental monitoring on adolescent risk behavior. *Journal of Adolescent Health, 27,* 49–56.

Liben, L. S., & Bigler, R. S. (2002). The developmental course of gender differentiation: Conceptualizing, measuring, and evaluating constructs and pathways. *Monographs of the Society for Research in Child Development, 67*(2, Serial no. 269).

Liben, L. S., & Downs, R. M. (1993). Understanding person-space-map relations: Cartographic and developmental perspectives. *Developmental Psychology, 29,* 739–752.

Liben, L. S., Susman, E. J., Finkelstein, J. W., Chinchilli, V. M., Kunselman, S., Schwab, J., et al. (2002). The effects of sex steroids on spatial performance: A review and an experimental clinical investigation. *Developmental Psychology, 38,* 236–253.

Lickliter, R., & Bahrick, L. E. (2000). The development of infant intersensory perception: Advantages of a comparative convergent-operations approach. *Psychological Bulletin, 126,* 260–280.

Lickona, T. (1976). Research on Piaget's theory of moral development. In T. Lickona (Ed.), *Moral development and behavior: Theory, research, and social issues* (pp. 219–240). New York: Holt, Rinehart & Winston.

Lieberman, D. (1985). Research on children and microcomputers: A review of utilization and effect studies. In M. Chen & W. Paisley (Eds.), *Children and microcomputers: Research on the newest medium.* Beverly Hills: Sage.

Lien, W., Klezovitch, O., Fernandez, T. E., Delrow, J., & Vasioukhin, V. (2006). E–catenin controls cerebral cortical size by regulating the hedgehog signaling pathway. *Science, 311,* 1609–1612.

Lightfoot, D. (1982). *The language lottery: Toward a biology of grammars.* Cambridge, MA: MIT Press.

Lillard, A. S. (1997). Other folks' theories of mind and behavior. *Psychological Science, 8,* 268–274.

Lillard, A. S. (1998). Ethnopsychologies: Cultural variation in theories of mind. *Psychological Bulletin, 123,* 3–32.

Limb, C. J., & Holmes, L. B. (1994). Anencephaly: Changes in prenatal detection and birth status, 1972 through 1990. *American Journal of Obstetrics and Gynecology, 170,* 1333–1338.

Lin, C. C., & Fu, V. R. (1990). A comparison of child-rearing practices among Chinese, immigrant Chinese, and Caucasian-American parents. *Child Development, 61,* 429–433.

Lindegren, M. L., Steinberg, S., & Byers, R. H. (2000). Epidemiology of HIV/AIDS in children. *Pediatric Clinics of North America, 47,* 1–20.

Lindsay, E. W., Mize, J., & Pettit, G. S. (1997). Differential play patterns of mothers and fathers of sons and daughters: Implications for children's gender role development. *Sex Roles, 37,* 643–661.

Linn, M. C., & Petersen, A. C. (1985). Emergence and characterization of sex differences in spatial ability: A meta-analysis. *Child Development, 56,* 1479–1498.

Linn, M. C., & Petersen, A. C. (1986). A meta-analysis of differences in spatial ability: Implications for mathematics and science achievement. In J. S. Hyde & M. C. Linn (Eds.), *The psychology of gender: Advances through meta-analysis.* Baltimore: Johns Hopkins University Press.

Linney, J. A., & Seidman, E. N. (1989). The future of schooling. *American Psychologist, 44,* 336–340.

Lips, H. M. (2004). The gender gap in possible selves: Divergence of academic self-views among high school and university students. *Sex Roles, 50,* 357–371.

Little, T. D., & Lopez, D. F. (1997). Regularities in the development of children's causality beliefs about school performance across six sociocultural contexts. *Developmental Psychology, 33,* 165–175.

Littleton, K., & Häkkinen, P. (1999). Learning together: Understanding the processes of computer-based collaborative learning. In P. Dillenbourg (Ed.), *Collaborative learning: Cognitive and computational approaches* (pp. 20–30). New York: Pergamon.

Littschwager, J. C., & Markman, E. M. (1994). Sixteen- and 24-month-olds' use of mutual exclusivity as a default assumption in second-label learning. *Developmental Psychology, 30,* 955–958.

Liu, H., Kuhl, P. K., & Tsao, F. (2003). An association between mothers' speech clarity and infants' discrimination skills. *Developmental Science, 6,* F1–F10.

Lobel, T. E., Gruber, R., Govrin, N., & Mashraki Pedhatzur, S. (2001). Children's gender-related inferences and judgments: A cross-cultural study. *Developmental Psychology, 37,* 839–846.

Locke, J. (1961). *An essay concerning human understanding.* London: J. M. Deut and Sons. (Original work published in 1690)

Locke, J. (1964). Some thoughts concerning education. In P. Gay (Ed.), *John Locke on education.* New York: Teacher's College. (Original work published in 1693).

Lockman, J. J., & Thelen, E. (1993). Developmental biodynamics: Brain, body, behavior connections. *Child Development, 64,* 953–959.

Loeb, R. C., Horst, L., & Horton, P. J. (1980). Family interaction patterns associated with self-esteem in preadolescent girls and boys. *Merrill-Palmer Quarterly, 26,* 203–217.

Loeber, R., & Hay, D. F. (1997). Key issues in the development of aggression and violence from childhood to early adulthood. *Annual Review of Psychology, 48,* 371–410.

Loehlin, J. C., Lindzey, G., & Spuhler, J. N. (1975). *Racial differences in intelligence.* San Francisco: W.H. Freeman.

Loewenstein, J., & Gentner, D. (2001). Spatial mapping in preschoolers: Close comparisons facilitate far mappings. *Journal of Cognition and Development, 2,* 189–219.

Lombroso, P. J. (2000). Genetics of childhood disorders: 16. Angleman syndrome: A failure to process. *Journal of the American Academy of Child and Adolescent Psychiatry, 39,* 931–933.

López-Camelo, J. S., Orioli, I. M., da Graça Dutra, M., Nazer-Herrera, J., Rivera, N., Ojeda, M. E., et al. (2005). Reduction of birth prevalence rates of neural tube defects after folic acid fortification in Chile. *American Journal of Medical Genetics: Part A, 135,* 120–125.

Lorch, E. P., Bellack, D. R., & Augsbach, L. H. (1987). Young children's memory for televised stories: Effects of importance. *Child Development, 58,* 453–463.

Lord, S. E., Eccles, J. S., & McCarthy, K. A. (1994). Surviving the junior high school transition: Family processes and self-perceptions as protective and risk factors. *Journal of Early Adolescence, 14,* 162–199.

Lorenz, J. M., Wooliever, D. E., Jetton, J. R., & Paneth, N. (1997). A quantitative review of mortality and developmental disability in extremely premature newborns. *Archives of Pediatric and Adolescent Medicine, 152,* 425–435.

Lorenz, K. Z. (1966). *On aggression* (M. K. Wilson, Trans.). New York: Harcourt, Brace, & World. (Original work published 1963)

Love, J. M., Harrison, L. , Sagi-Schwartz, A., van IJzendoorn, M. H., Ross, C., et al. (2003). Child care quality matters: How conclusions may vary with context. *Child Development, 74,* 1021–1033.

Love, J. M., Kisker, E. E., Ross, C., Raikes, H., Constantine, J., et al. (2005). The effectiveness of Early Head Start for 3-year-old children and their parents: Lessons for policy and programs. *Developmental Psychology, 41,* 885–901.

Lovdal, L. T. (1989). Sex role messages in television commercials: An update. *Sex Roles, 21,* 715–724.

Lu, G. C., Rouse, D. J., DuBard, M., Cliver, S., Kimberlin, D., & Hauth, J. C. (2001). The effect of the increasing prevalence of maternal obesity on prenatal morbidity. *American Journal of Obstetrics and Gynecology, 185,* 845–849.

Lubinski, D., Webb, R. M., Morelock, M. J., & Benbow, C. P. (2001). Top 1 in 10,000: A 10-year follow-up of the profoundly gifted. *Journal of Applied Psychology, 86,* 718–729.

Luciana, M., Conklin, H. M., Hooper, C. J., & Yarger, R. S. (2005). The development of nonverbal working memory and executive control processes in adolescents. *Child Development, 76,* 697–712.

Ludington-Hoe, S. M., & Swinth, J. Y. (1996). Developmental aspects of kangaroo care. *Journal of Obstetric and Gynecological Neonatal Nursing, 25,* 691–703.

Luecke-Aleksa, D. R., Anderson, D. R., Collins, P. A., & Schmitt, K. L. (1995). Gender constancy and television viewing. *Developmental Psychology, 31,* 773–780.

Luke, B., Avni, M., Min, L., & Misiumas, R. (1999). Work and pregnancy: The role of fatigue and the "second shift" on antenatal morbidity. *American Journal of Obstetrics and Gynecology, 181,* 1172–1179.

Lummis, M., & Stevenson, H. W. (1990). Gender differences in beliefs and achievement: A cross-cultural study. *Developmental Psychology, 26,* 254–263.

Luna, B., Garver, K. E., Urban, T. A., Lazar, N. A., & Sweeney, J. A. (2004). Maturation of cognitive processes from late childhood to adulthood. *Child Development, 75,* 1357–1372.

Luna, B., Thulborn, K. R., Munoz, D. P., Merriam, E. P., Garver, K. E., et al. (2001). Maturation of widely distributed brain function subserves cognitive development. *Neuroimage, 13,* 786–793.

Luria, A. R. (1961). *The role of speech in the regulation of normal and abnormal behavior.* New York: Liveright.

Luria, A. R. (1969). Speech and formation of mental processes. In M. Cole & I. Maltzman (Eds.), *A handbook of contemporary Soviet psychology.* New York: Basic Books.

Lussier, G., Deater-Deckard, K., Dunn, J., & Davies, L. (2002). Support across two generations: Children's closeness to grandparents following parental divorce and remarriage. *Journal of Family Psychology, 16,* 363–376.

Luster, T., & McAdoo, H. P. (1994). Factors related to the achievement and adjustment of young African American children. *Child Development, 65,* 1080–1994.

Luster, T., & McAdoo, H. P. (1996). Family and child influences on educational attainment: A secondary analysis of the High/Scope Perry Preschool data. *Developmental Psychology, 32,* 26–39.

Luthar, S. S., & Becker, B. E. (2002). Privileged but pressured? A study of affluent youth. *Child Development, 73,* 1593–1610.

Luthar, S. S., Cicchetti, D., & Becker, B. (2000). The construct of resilience: A critical evaluation and guidelines for future work. *Child Development, 71,* 543–562.

Luthar, S. S., & D'Avanzo, K. (1999). Contextual factors in substance use: A study of suburban and inner-city adolescents. *Development and Psychopathology, 11,* 845–867.

Luthar, S. S., & Latendresse, S. J. (2005). Children of the affluent: Challenges to well-being. *Current Directions in Psychological Science, 14,* 49–53.

Lutkenhaus, P., Bullock, M., & Geppert, U. (1987). Toddlers' actions: Knowledge, control, and the self. In F. Halisch & J. Kuhl (Eds.), *Motivation, intention, and volition.* Berlin: Springer.

Lykken, D. T. , McGue, M. Tellegen, A., & Bouchard, T. J., Jr. (1992). Emer-genesis: Genetic traits that may not run in families. *American Psychologist,* 47, 1565–1577.

Lyon, T. D., & Flavell, J. H. (1993). Young children's understanding of forgetting over time. *Child Development, 64,* 789–800.

Lyons-Ruth, K., Alpern, L., & Repacholi, B. (1993). Disorganized infant attachment classification and maternal psychosocial problems as predictors of hostile-aggressive behavior in preschool children. *Child Development, 64,* 572–585.

Lyons-Ruth, K., & Jacobvitz, D. (1999). Attachment disorganization: Unresolved loss, relational violence, and lapses in behavioral and attentional strategies. In J. Cassidy & P. R. Shaver (Eds.), *Handbook of attachment: Theory, research, and clinical applications* (pp. 520–554). New York: Guilford Press.

Lytton, H., & Romney, D. M. (1991). Parents' differential socialization of boys and girls: A meta-analysis. *Psychological Bulletin, 109,* 267–296.

Ma, H. K., & Cheung, C.-K. (1996). A cross-cultural study of moral stage structure in Hong Kong Chinese, English, and Americans. *Journal of Cross-Cultural Psychology, 27,* 700–713.

Maccoby, E. E. (1984). Socialization and developmental change. *Child Development, 55,* 317–328.

Maccoby, E. E. (1988). Gender as a social category. *Developmental Psychology, 24,* 755–765.

Maccoby, E. E. (1990). Gender and relationships: A developmental account. *American Psychologist, 45,* 513–520.

Maccoby, E. E. (2002). Gender and group process: A developmental perspective. *Current Directions in Psychological Science, 11,* 54–58.

Maccoby, E. E., & Jacklin, C. N. (1974). *The psychology of sex differences.* Stanford, CA: Stanford University Press.

Maccoby, E. E., & Jacklin, C. N. (1987). Gender segregation in childhood. In H. W. Reese (Ed.), *Advances in child development and behavior* (Vol. 20). Orlando, FL: Academic Press.

Maccoby, E. E., & Martin, J. A. (1983). Socialization in the context of the family: Parent-child interaction. In E. M. Hetherington (Ed.), *Handbook of child psychology: Vol. IV. Socialization, personality, and social development* (4th ed., pp. 1–101). New York: Wiley.

MacFarlane, J. A. (1975). Olfaction in the development of social preferences in the human neonate. In M. A. Hofer (Ed.), *Parent-infant interaction.* Amsterdam: Elsevier.

MacKinnon, C. E. (1988). Influences on sibling relations in families with married and divorced parents. *Journal of Social Issues, 9,* 469–477.

MacKinnon, C. E. (1989). Sibling interactions in married and divorced families: Influence of ordinal position, socioeconomic status, and play context. *Journal of Divorce, 12,* 221–251.

MacKinnon-Lewis, C., Rabiner, D., & Starnes, R. (1999). Predicting boys' social acceptance and aggression: The role of mother-child interactions and boys' beliefs about peers. *Developmental Psychology, 35,* 632–639.

MacKinnon-Lewis, C., Volling, B. L., Lamb, M. E., Dechman, K., Rabiner, D., & Curtner, M. E. (1994). A cross-contextual analysis of boys' social competence: From family to school. *Developmental Psychology, 30,* 325–333.

MacLusky, N. J., & Naftolin, F. (1981). Sexual differentiation of the nervous system. *Science, 211,* 1294–1303.

MacMillan, H. L., MacMillan, J. H., Offord, D. R., Griffith, L., & MacMillan, A. (1994). Primary prevention of child abuse and neglect: A critical review. Part I. *Journal of Child Psychology, Psychiatry, and Allied Disciplines, 35,* 835–856.

Madi, B. C., Sandall, J., Bennett, R., & MacLeod, C. (1999). Effects of female relative support in labor: A randomized controlled trial. *Birth, 26,* 4–8.

Madigan, S., Moran, G., & Pederson, D. R. (2006). Unresolved states of mind, disorganized attachment relationships, and disrupted interactions of adolescent mothers and their infants. *Developmental Psychology, 42,* 293–304.

Maffeis, C., Schutz, Y., Zaffanello, M., Piccoli, R., & Pinelli, L. (1994). Elevated energy expenditure and reduced energy intake in obese prepubertal children: Paradox of poor dietary reliability in obesity? *Journal of Pediatrics, 124,* 348–354.

Magnusson, D., Stattin, H., & Allen, V. (1986). Differential maturation among girls and its relations to social adjustment: A longitudinal perspective. In P. B. Baltes, D. L. Featherman, & R. M. Lerner (Eds.), *Life-span development and behavior* (Vol. 7). Hillsdale, NJ: Erlbaum.

Mahoney, J. L. (2000). School extracurricular activity participation as a moderator in the development of antisocial behavior patterns. *Child Development, 71,* 502–516.

Main, M., Kaplan, N., & Cassidy, J. (1985). Security in infancy, childhood, and adulthood: A move to the level of representation. In I. Bretherton & E. Waters (Eds.), *Growing points of attachment theory and research. Monographs of the Society for Research in Child Development, 50*(1–2, Serial No. 209).

Main, M., & Solomon, J. (1986). Discovery of a disorganized/disoriented attachment pattern. In T. B. Brazelton & M. W. Yogman (Eds.), *Affective development in infancy.* Norwood, NJ: Ablex.

Malatesta, C. Z., Culver, C., Tesman, J. R., & Shepard, B. (1989). The development of emotion expression during the first two years of life. *Monographs of the Society for Research in Child Development, 54*(1–2, Serial No. 219).

Malina, R. M. (1980). Biosocial correlates of motor development during infancy and early childhood. In L. S. Greene & F. E. Johnstone (Eds.), *Social and biological predictors of nutritional status, physical growth, and neurological development.* New York: Academic Press.

Malone, F. D., Canick, J. A., Ball, R. H. Nyberg, D. A., Comstock, C. H., Bukowski, R., et al. (2005). First-trimester or second-trimester screening, or both, for Down's syndrome. *New England Journal of Medicine, 353,* 2001–2011.

Mandler, J. M. (1988). How to build a baby: On the development of an accessible representational system. *Cognitive Development, 3,* 113–136.

Mandler, J. M. (1998). Representation. In W. Damon (Series Ed.) & D. Kuhn & R. S. Siegler (Vol. Eds.), *Handbook of child psychology: Vol. 2. Cognition, perception, and language* (5th ed., pp. 255–308). New York: Wiley.

Mandler, J. M. (2004). *The foundations of mind: The origins of the conceptual system.* New York: Oxford University Press.

Mandler, J. M., Fivush, R., & Reznick, J. S. (1987). The development of contextual categories. *Cognitive Development, 2,* 339–354.

Mandler, J. M., & McDonough, L. (1993). Concept formation in infancy. *Cognitive Development, 8,* 291–318.

Mandler, J. M., & McDonough, L. (1998). Studies in inductive inference in infancy. *Cognitive Psychology, 37,* 60–96.

Mandler, J. M., & McDonough, L. (2000). Advancing downward to the basic level. *Journal of Cognition and Development, 1,* 379–403.

Mangelsdorf, S. C., Plunkett, J. W., Dedrick, C. F., Berlin, M., Meisels, S. J., McHale, J. L., & Dichtellmiller, M. (1996). Attachment security in very low birth weight infants. *Developmental Psychology, 32,* 914–920.

Mannarino, A. P. (1978). Friendship patterns and self-concept development in preadolescent males. *Journal of Genetic Psychology, 133,* 105–110.

Maratsos, M. P. (1983). Some current issues in the study of the acquisition of grammar. In J. H. Flavell & E. M. Markman (Eds.), *Handbook of child psychology: Vol. III. Cognitive development* (4th ed., pp. 707–786). New York: Wiley.

Maratsos, M. P. (1989). Innateness and plasticity in language acquisition. In M. L. Rice & R. L. Schiefelbusch (Eds.), *The teachability of language.* Baltimore: Paul H. Brookes.

Marcus, G. F. (1996). Why do children say "breaked"? *Current Directions in Psychological Science, 5,* 81–85.

Marcus, G. F., Pinker, S., Ullman, M., Hollander, M., Rosen, T. J., & Xu, F. (1992). Overregularization in language acquisition. *Monographs of the Society for Research in Child Development, 57*(4 Serial No. 228).

Marcus, G. F., Vijayan, S., Bandi Rao, S., & Vishton, P. M. (1998). Rule learning by seven-month-old infants. *Science, 283,* 77–80.

Marean, G. C., Werner, L. A., & Kuhl, P. K. (1992). Vowel categorization by very young infants. *Developmental Psychology, 28,* 395–405.

Mareschal, D., & Johnson, S. P. (2002). Learning to perceive object unity: A connectionist account. *Developmental Science, 5,* 151–172.

Markman, E. M. (1987). How children constrain the possible meanings of words. In U. Neisser (Ed.), *Concepts and conceptual development: Ecological and intellectual factors in categorization.* Cambridge, UK: Cambridge University Press.

Markman, E. M. (1990). Constraints children place on word meanings. *Cognitive Science, 14,* 57–77.

Markman, E. M., & Hutchinson, J. E. (1984). Children's sensitivity to constraints on word meaning: Taxonomic versus thematic relations. *Cognitive Psychology, 16,* 1–27.

Markman, E. M., & Wachtel G. F. (1988). Children's use of mutual exclusivity to constrain the meanings of words. *Cognitive Psychology, 20,* 121–157.

Marlier, L., & Schaal, B. (2005). Human newborns prefer human milk: Conspecific milk odor is attractive without postnatal exposure. *Child Development, 76,* 155–168.

Marlier, L., Schaal, B., & Soussignan, R. (1998). Neonatal responsiveness to the odor of amniotic and lacteal fluids: A test of perinatal chemosensory continuity. *Child Development, 69,* 611–623.

Marr, D. B., & Sternberg, R. J. (1987). The role of mental speed in intelligence: A triarchic perspective. In P. A. Vernon (Ed.), *Speed of information-processing and intelligence.* Norwood, NJ: Ablex.

Marsh, H. W., Craven, R., & Debus, R. (1998). Structure, stability, and development of young children's self-concepts: A multicohort-multioccasion study. *Child Development, 69,* 1030–1053.

Marshall, N. (2004). The quality of early child care and children's development. *Current Directions in Psychological Science, 13,* 165–168.

Marshall, S. (1995). Ethnic socialization of African American children: Implications for parenting, identity development, and academic achievement. *Journal of Youth and Adolescence, 24,* 377–396.

Martin, C. L. (1995). Stereotypes about children with traditional and nontraditional gender roles. *Sex Roles, 33,* 727–751.

Martin, C. L., Eisenbud, L., & Rose, H. (1995). Children's gender-based reasoning about toys. *Child Development, 66,* 1453–1471.

Martin, C. L., & Fabes, R. A. (2001). The stability and consequences of young children's same-sex peer interactions. *Developmental Psychology, 37,* 431–446.

Martin, C. L., & Halverson, C. F. (1981). A schematic processing model of sex typing and stereotyping in children. *Child Development, 52,* 1119–1134.

Martin, C. L., & Halverson, C. F. (1987). The roles of cognition in sex role acquisition. In D. B. Carter (Ed.), *Current conceptions of sex roles and sex typing: Theory and research* (pp. 123–137). New York: Praeger.

Martin, C. L. , & Ruble, D. N. (1997). A developmental perspective of self-construals and sex differences: Comment on Cross and Madson (1997). *Psychological Bulletin, 122,* 45–50.

Martin, J., Martin, D. C., Lund, C. A., & Streissguth, A. P. (1977). Maternal alcohol ingestion and cigarette smoking and their effects on newborn conditioning. *Alcoholism: Clinical and Experimental Research, 1,* 243–247.

Martinez de Villarreal, L., Perez, J. Z., Vazquez, P. A., Herrera, P. H., Campos Mdel, R., Lopez, R. A., et al. (2002). Decline of neural tube defects after a folic acid campaign in Nuevo Leon, Mexico. *Teratology, 66,* 249–256.

Marvin, R. S. (1977). An ethological-cognitive model for the attenuation of mother-child attachment behavior. In T. M. Alloway, L. Krames, & P. Pliner (Eds.), *Advances in the study of communication and affect: Vol. 3. The development of social attachments.* New York: Plenum Press.

Masataka, N. (1996). Perception of motherese in a signed language by 6-month-old infants. *Developmental Psychology, 32,* 874–879.

Mason, C. A., Cauce, A. M., Gonzales, N., & Hiraga, Y. (1996). Neither too sweet nor too sour: Problem peers, maternal control, and problem behavior in African American adolescents. *Child Development, 67,* 2115–2130.

Massaro, D. W., & Cowan, N. (1993). Information processing models: Microscopes of mind. In L. W. Porter & M. R. Rosenzweig (Eds.), *Annual Review of Psychology, 34,* 383–425.

Masten, A. S., & Coatsworth, J. D. (1998). The development of competence in favorable and unfavorable environments: Lessons from research on successful children. *American Psychologist, 53,* 205–220.

Masur, E. F. (1982). Mothers' responses to infants' object-related gestures: Influences on lexical development. *Journal of Child Language, 9,* 23–30.

Matas, L., Arend, R. A., & Sroufe, L. A. (1978). Continuity of adaptation in the second year: The relationship between quality of attachment and later competence. *Child Development, 49,* 547–556.

Mathews, T. J., Honein, M. A., & Erickson, J. D. (2002). Spina bifida and anencephaly prevalence—United States. *MMWR Recommendations and Reports,* Rep 51(RR-13), pp. 9–11.

Matias, R., & Cohn, J. F. (1993). Are max-specified infant facial expressions during face-to-face interaction consistent with differential emotions theory? *Developmental Psychology, 29,* 524–531.

Mattson, S. N., Riley, E. P., Gramling, L., Delis, D. C., & Jones, K. L. (1997). Heavy prenatal alcohol exposure with or without physical features of fetal alcohol syndrome leads to IQ deficits. *Journal of Pediatrics, 131,* 718–721.

Mattys, S. L., & Jusczyk, P. W. (2001). Do infants segment words or recurring contiguous patterns? *Journal of Experimental Psychology: Human Perception and Performance, 27,* 644–655.

Matusov, E., Bell, N., & Rogoff, B. (2002). Schooling as cultural process: Working together and guidance by children from schools differing in collaborative practices. In R. V. Kail & H. W. Reese (Eds.), *Advances in child development* (Vol. 29, pp. 129–160). San Diego: Academic Press.

Maurer, D. (1983). The scanning of compound figures by young infants. *Journal of Experimental Child Psychology, 35,* 437–448.

Maurer, D., Lewis, T. L., Brent, H. P., & Levin, A. V. (1999). Rapid improvement in the acuity of infants after visual input. *Science, 286,* 108–110.

May, D. C., Kundert, D. K., & Brent, D. (1995). Does delayed school entry reduce later grade retentions and use of special education services? *Remedial and Special Education, 16,* 288–294.

Mayberry, R. I., & Nicoladis, E. (2000). Gesture reflects language development: Evidence from bilingual children. *Current Directions in Psychological Science, 9,* 192–196.

McAnarney, E. R. (1987). Young maternal age and adverse neonatal outcome. *American Journal of Diseases of Children, 141,* 1053–1059.

McAnarney, E. R., & Stevens-Simon, C. (1990). Maternal psychological stress/depression and low birth weight. *American Journal of Diseases of Children, 144,* 789–792.

McArdle, J. J., Ferrer Caja, E., Hamagami, F., & Woodcock, R. W. (2002). Comparative longitudinal structural analyses of the growth and decline of multiple intellectual abilities over the life span. *Developmental Psychology, 38,* 115–142.

McBride, W. G. (1961). Thalidomide and congenital abnormalities. *Lancet, 2,* 1358.

McCall, R. B. (1979). *Infants.* Cambridge, MA: Harvard University Press.

McCall, R. B., Parke, R. D., & Kavanaugh, R. D. (1977). Imitation of live and televised models in children one to three years of age. *Monographs of the Society for Research in Child Development, 42*(3, Serial No. 171).

McCartney, K., Harris, M. J., & Bernieri, F. (1990). Growing up and growing apart: A developmental meta-analysis of twin studies. *Psychological Bulletin, 107,* 226–237.

McCartney, K., & Nelson, K. (1981). Children's use of scripts in story recall. *Discourse Processes, 4,* 59–70.

McCartney, K., Scarr, S., Phillips, D., & Grajek, S. (1985). Day care as intervention: Comparisons of varying quality programs. *Journal of Applied Developmental Psychology, 6,* 247–260.

McCarty, M. E., Clifton, R. K., Ashmead, D. H., Lee, P., & Goubet, N. (2001) How infants use vision for grasping objects. *Child Development, 72,* 973–987.

McClelland, D. C. (1973). Testing for competence rather than for "intelligence." *American Psychologist, 28,* 1–14.

McClintock, M. K., & Herdt, G. (1996). Rethinking puberty: The development of sexual attraction. *Current Directions in Psychological Science, 5,* 178–183.

McCord, J. (1977). A comparative study of two generations of native Americans. In R. F. Meier (Ed.), *Theory in criminology* (pp. 83–92). Beverly Hills, CA: Sage.

McCormick, M. C. (1997). The outcomes of very low birth weight infants: Are we asking the right questions? *Pediatrics, 99,* 869–875.

McCormick, M. C., McCarton, C., Tonascia, J., & Brooks-Gunn, J. (1993). Early educational intervention for very low birth weight infants: Results from the Infant Health and Development Program. *Journal of Pediatrics, 123,* 527–533.

McDermott, S., & Greenberg, B. (1984). Parents, peers and television as determinants of Black children's esteem. In R. Bostrom (Ed.), *Communication yearbook* (Vol. 8, pp. 164–177). Beverly Hills, CA: Sage.

McDonald, M. A., Sigman, M., Espinosa, M. P., & Neumann, C. G. (1994). Impact of temporary food shortage on children and their mothers. *Child Development, 65,* 404–415.

McGhee, P. E. (1979). *Humor: Its origin and development.* San Francisco: W.H. Freeman.

McGinniss, M. J., & Kaback, M. M. (2002). Heterozygote testing and carrier screening. In D. L. Rimoin, J. M. Connor, R. E. Pyeritz, & B. R. Korf (Eds.), *Emery and Rimoin's principles and practice of medical genetics* (4th ed., Vol. 1, pp. 752–762). London: Churchill Livingston.

McGraw, M. B. (1935). *Growth: A study of Johnny and Jimmy.* New York: Appleton-Century-Crofts.

McGraw, M. B. (1939). Swimming behavior of the human infant. *Journal of Pediatrics, 15,* 485–490.

McGregor, J. A., & French, J. I. (1991). *Chlamydia trachomatis* infection during pregnancy. *American Journal of Obstetrics and Gynecology, 165,* 1782–1789.

McGue, M. (1999). The behavioral genetics of alcoholism. *Current Directions in Psychological Science, 8,* 109–115.

McGue, M., Elkins, I., Walden, B., & Iacono, W. G. (2005). Perceptions of parent-adolescent relationship: A longitudinal investigation. *Developmental Psychology, 41,* 971–984.

McGuire, J. (1988). Gender stereotypes of parents with two-year-olds and beliefs about gender differences in behavior. *Sex Roles, 19,* 233–240.

McGuire, K. D., & Weisz, J. R. (1982). Social cognition and behavior correlates of preadolescent chumship. *Child Development, 53,* 1478–1484.

McGuire, P. K., Robertson, D. A. T., David, A. S., Kitson, N., Frackowiak, R. S. J., & Frith, C. D. (1997). Neural correlates of thinking in sign language. *NeuroReport, 8,* 695–697.

McGurk, H., & MacDonald, J. (1976). Hearing lips and seeing voices. *Nature* (London), *264,* 746–748.

McHale, S. M., Crouter, A. C., McGuire, S. A., & Updegraff, K. A. (1995). Congruence between mothers' and fathers' differential treatment of siblings: Links with family relations and children's well-being. *Child Development, 66,* 116–128.

McHale, S. M., Crouter, A. C., & Tucker, C. J. (1999). Family context and gender role socialization in middle childhood: Comparing boys to girls and sisters to brothers. *Child Development, 70,* 990–1004.

McHale, S. M., Crouter, A. C., & Tucker, C. J. (2001). Free-time activities in middle childhood: Links with adjustment in early adolescence. *Child Development, 72,* 1764–1778.

McHale, S. M., Kim, J., Whiteman, S., & Crouter, A. C. (2004). Links between sex-typed time use in middle childhood and gender development in early adolescence. *Developmental Psychology, 40,* 868–881.

McHale, S. M., Shanahan, L., Updegraff, K. A., Crouter, A. C., & Booth, A. (2004). Developmental and individual differences in girls' sex-typed activities in middle childhood and adolescence. *Child Development, 75,* 1575–1593.

McHale, S. M., Updegraff, K. A., Jackson-Newsom, J., Tucker, C. J., & Crouter, A. C. (2000). When does parents' differential treatment have negative implications for siblings? *Social Development, 9,* 149–172.

McIlhaney, J. S., Jr. (2000). Sexually transmitted infection and teenage sexuality. *American Journal of Obstetrics and Gynecology, 183,* 334–339.

McKenna, J., & McDade, T. (2005). Why babies should never sleep alone: A review of the co-sleeping controversy in relation to SIDS, bedsharing and breast feeding. *Paediatric Respiratory Reviews, 6,* 134–152.

McKey, R. H., Condelli, L., Granson, H., Barrett, B., McConkey, C., & Plantz, M. (1985). *The impact of Head Start on children, families and communities* (Final report of the Head Start Evaluation, Synthesis and Utilization Project). Washington, DC: U.S. Government Printing Office.

McKusick, V. A., & Amberger, J. S. (2002). Morbid anatomy of the human genome. In D. L. Rimoin, J. M. Connor, R. E. Pyeritz, & B. R. Korf (Eds.), *Emery and Rimoin's principles and practice of medical genetics* (4th ed., Vol. 1, pp. 174–298). London: Churchill Livingston.

McLoyd, V. C. (1990). The impact of economic hardship on black families and children: Psychological distress, parenting, and socioemotional development. *Child Development, 61,* 311–346.

McLoyd, V. C. (1998). Changing demographics in the American population: Implications for research on minority children and adolescents. In V. C. McLoyd & L. Steinberg (Eds.), *Studying minority adolescents* (pp. 3–28). Mahwah, NJ: Erlbaum.

McLoyd, V. C., Epstein Jayaratne, T., Ceballo, R., & Borquez, J. (1994). Unemployment and work interruption among African American single mothers: Effects on parenting and adolescent socioemotional functioning. *Child Development, 65,* 562–589.

McManus, I. C., & Bryden, M. P. (1991). Geschwind's theory of cerebral lateralization: Developing a formal, causal model. *Psychological Bulletin, 110,* 237–253.

Mead, G. H. (1934). *Mind, self, and society.* Chicago: University of Chicago Press.

Medin, D. L. (1989). Concepts and conceptual structure. *American Psychologist, 44,* 1469–1481.

Meichenbaum, D. (1977). *Cognitive-behavior modification: An integrative approach.* New York: Plenum Press.

Meins, E. (1998). The effects of security of attachment and maternal attribution of meaning on children's linguistic acquisitional style. *Infant Behavior and Development, 21,* 237–252.

Mekos, D., Hetherington, E. M., & Reiss, D. (1996). Sibling differences in problem behavior and parental treatment in nondivorced and remarried families. *Child Development, 67,* 2148–2165.

Meltzoff, A. N. (1995). What infant memory tells us about infantile amnesia: Long-term recall and deferred imitation. *Journal of Experimental Child Psychology, 59,* 497–515.

Meltzoff, A. N., & Moore, M. K. (1999). Persons and representation: Why infant imitation is important for theories of human development. In J. Nadel & G. Butterworth (Eds.), *Imitation in infancy* (pp. 9–35). Cambridge, UK: Cambridge University Press.

Mennella, J. A., & Beauchamp, G. K. (1996). The human infant's response to vanilla flavors in mother's milk and formula. *Infant Behavior and Development, 19,* 13–19.

Mennella, J. A., Griffin, C. E., & Beauchamp, G. K. (2004). Flavor programming during infancy. *Pediatrics, 113,* 840–845.

Mennella, J. A., Pepino, M. Y., & Reed, D. R. (2005). Genetic and environmental determinants of bitter perception and sweet preferences. *Pediatrics, 115,* 216–222.

Merimee, T. J., Zapf, J., & Froesch, E. R. (1981). Dwarfism in the Pygmy: An isolated deficiency of insulin-like Growth Factor I. *New England Journal of Medicine, 305,* 965–968.

Mervis, C. B. (2003). Williams syndrome: 15 years of psychological research. *Developmental Neuroscience, 23,* 1–12.

Messer, D. J. (1981). The identification of names in maternal speech to infants. *Journal of Psycholinguistic Research, 10,* 69–77.

Messer, S. C., & Gross, A. M. (1995) Childhood depression and family interaction: A naturalistic observation study. *Journal of Clinical Child Psychology, 24,* 77–88.

Messinger, D. S., & Fogel, A. (1998). Give and take: The development of conventional infant gestures. *Merrill-Palmer Quarterly, 44,* 566–590.

Messinger, D. S., Fogel, A., & Dickson, K. L. (1999). What's in a smile? *Developmental Psychology, 35,* 701–708.

Messinger, D. S., Fogel, A., & Dickson, K. L. (2001). All smiles are positive, but some smiles are more positive than others. *Developmental Psychology, 37,* 642–653.

Meyer, M., & Fienberg, S. (1992). *Assessing evaluation studies: The case of bilingual education strategies.* Washington, DC: National Academy Press.

Meyer, M. B., & Tonascia, J. A. (1977). Maternal smoking, pregnancy complications, and perinatal mortality. *American Journal of Obstetrics and Gynecology, 128,* 494–502.

Michel, G. F. (1988). A neuropsychological perspective on infant sensorimotor development. In C. Rovee-Collier & L. P. Lipsitt (Eds.), *Advances in infancy research* (Vol. 5). Norwood, NJ: Ablex.

Michelsson, K., Sirvio, P., & Wasz-Hockert, D. (1977). Pain cry in fullterm asphyxiated newborn infants correlated with late findings. *Acta Paediatrica Scandinavica, 66,* 611–616.

Miech, R. A., Kumanyika, S. K., Stettler, N., Link, B. G., Phelan, J. C., & Chang, V. W. (2006). Trends in the association of poverty with overweight among US adolescents, 1971–2004. *Journal of the American Medical Association, 295,* 2385–2393.

Milgram, N. A. (1998). Children under stress. In T. H. Ollendick & M. Hersen (Eds.), *Handbook of child psychopathology* (3rd ed., pp. 505–533). New York: Plenum.

Miller, A. L., Volling, B. L., & McElwain, N. L. (2000). Sibling jealousy in a triadic context with mothers and fathers. *Social Development, 9,* 433–457.

Miller, B. C., Benson, B., & Galbraith, K. A. (2001). Family relationships and adolescent pregnancy risk: A research synthesis. *Developmental Review, 21,* 1–38.

Miller, B. C., Fan, X., Christensen, M., Grotevant, H. D., & van Dulmen, M. (2000). Comparison of adopted and nonadopted adolescents in a large, nationally representative sample. *Developmental Psychology, 71,* 1458–1473.

Miller, J. G. (1999). Cultural Psychology: Implications for basic psychological theory. *Psychological Science, 10,* 85–91.

Miller, J. M., Jr., & Boudreaux, M. C. (1999). A study of antenatal cocaine use—chaos in action. *American Journal of Obstetrics and Gynecology, 180,* 1427–1431.

Miller, L. T., & Vernon, P. A. (1996). Intelligence, reaction time, and working memory in 4- to 6-year-old children. *Intelligence, 22,* 155–190.

Miller, N. B., Cowan, P. A., Cowan, C. P., Hetherington, E. M., & Clingempeel, W. G. (1993). Externalizing in preschoolers and early adolescents: A cross-study replication of a family model. *Developmental Psychology, 29,* 3–18.

Miller, N., & Maruyama, G. (1976). Ordinal position and peer popularity. *Journal of Personality and Social Psychology, 33,* 123–131.

Miller, P. A., Eisenberg, N., Fabes, R. A., & Shell, R. (1996). Relations of moral reasoning and vicarious emotion to young children's prosocial behavior toward peers and adults. *Developmental Psychology, 32,* 210–219.

Miller, W. L., & Levine, L. S. (1987). Molecular and clinical advances in congenital adrenal hyperplasia. *Journal of Pediatrics, 111,* 1–17.

Miller-Jones, D. (1989). Culture and testing. *American Psychologist, 44,* 360–366.

Mills, D. L., Coffey-Corina, S. A., & Neville, H. J. (1993). Language acquisition and cerebral specialization in 20-month-old infants. *Journal of Cognitive Neuroscience, 5,* 317–334.

Mills, D. L., Coffey-Corina, S. A., & Neville, H. J. (1994). Variability in cerebral organization during primary language acquisition. In G. Dawson & K. W. Fischer (Eds.), *Human behavior and the developing brain* (pp. 427–455). New York: Guilford.

Mills, D. L., Coffey-Corina, S., & Neville, H. J. (1997). Language comprehension and cerebral specialization from 13 to 20 months. *Developmental Neuropsychology, 13,* 397–445.

Mills, R. S. L., & Grusec, J. E. (1989). Cognitive, affective, and behavioral consequences of praising altruism. *Merrill-Palmer Quarterly, 35,* 299–326.

Mills, R. S. L., & Rubin, K. H. (1993). Socialization factors in the development of social withdrawal. In K. H. Rubin & J. B. Asendorpf (Eds.), *Social withdrawal, inhibition, and shyness in childhood* (pp. 117–148). Hillsdale, NJ: Erlbaum.

Minuchin, P. P. (1988). Relationships within the family: A systems perspective on development. In R. A. Hinde & J. Stevenson-Hinde (Eds.), *Relationships within families: Mutual influences.* Oxford: Clarendon Press.

Minuchin, P. P., & Shapiro, E. K. (1983). The school as a context for social development. In E. M. Hetherington (Ed.), *Handbook of child psychology: Vol. IV. Socialization, personality, and social development* (pp. 197–274). New York: Wiley.

Mischel, H. N., & Mischel, W. (1983). The development of children's knowledge of self-control strategies. *Child Development, 54,* 603–619.

Mischel, W. (1966). A social learning view of sex differences in behavior. In E. E. Maccoby (Ed.), *The development of sex differences.* Stanford, CA: Stanford University Press.

Mischel, W., Ebbesen, E. B., & Zeiss, A. R. (1972). Cognitive and attentional mechanisms in delay of gratification. *Journal of Personality and Social Psychology, 21,* 204–218.

Mischel, W., Shoda, Y., & Rodriguez, M. L. (1989). Delay of gratification in children. *Science, 244,* 933–938.

Mitchell, E. A., & Milerad, J. (1999). *Smoking and sudden infant death syndrome.* Paper series prepared for International Consultation on Environmental Tobacco Smoke and Child Health. Geneva, Switzerland. Retrieved October 21, 2002, from www5.who.int/tobacco/repository/tld67/mitchell.pdf

Mitchell, E. A., Thach, B. T., Thompson, J. M. D., Williams, S. (1999). Changing infants' sleep position increases risk of sudden infant death syndrome. *Archives of Pediatrics and Adolescent Medicine, 153,* 1136–1141.

Mitchell, E. A., Tuohy, P. G., Brunt, J. M., Thompson, J. M. D., Clements, M. S., Stewart, A. W., et al. (1997). Risk factors for sudden infant death syndrome following the prevention campaign in New Zealand: A prospective study. *Pediatrics, 100,* 835–840.

Mittendorf, R., Williams, M. A., Berkey, C. S., & Cotter, P. F. (1990). The length of uncomplicated human gestation. *Obstetrics and Gynecology, 75,* 929–932.

Mittendorf, R., Williams, M. A., Berkley, C. S., Lieberman, E., & Monson, R. R. (1993). Predictors of human gestational length. *American Journal of Obstetrics and Gynecology, 168,* 480–484.

Mix, K. S., Huttenlocher, J., & Levine, S. C. (2002). *Quantitative development in infancy and early childhood*: London, Oxford University Press.

Mix, K. S., Levine, S. C., & Huttenlocher, J. (1999). Early fraction calculation ability. *Developmental Psychology, 35,* 164–174.

Miyake, A., Friedman, N. P., Rettinger, D. A., Shah, P., & Hegarty, M. (2001). How are visuospatial working memory, executive functioning, and spatial abilities related? A latent variable analysis. *Journal of Experimental Psychology: General, 130,* 621–640.

Miyake, K., Chen, S., & Campos, J. J. (1985). Infant temperament, mother's mode of interaction, and attachment in Japan: An interim report. In I. Bretherton & E. Waters (Eds.), *Growing points of attachment theory and research. Monographs of the Society for Research in Child Development, 50*(1–2, Serial No. 209).

Moely, B. E., Olson, F. A., Halwes, T. G., & Flavell, J. H. (1969). Production deficiency in young children's clustered recall. *Developmental Psychology, 1,* 26–34.

Moffat, R., & Hackel, A. (1985). Thermal aspects of neonatal care. In A. Gottfried & J. Gaiter (Eds.), *Infant stress under intensive care.* Baltimore: University Park Press.

Moffitt, T. E. (1993). Life-course-persistent and adolescence-limited antisocial behavior: A developmental taxonomy. *Psychological Review, 100,* 674–701.

Moldavsky, M., Lev, D., & Lerman-Sagie, T. (2001). Behavioral phenotypes of genetic syndromes: A reference guide to physicians. *Journal of the American Academy of Adolescent Psychiatry, 40,* 749–761.

Mondloch, C. J., Lewis, T. L., Budreau, D. R., Maurer, D., Dannemiller, J. L., Stephens, B. R., & Kleiner-Gathercoal, K. A. (1999). Face perception during early infancy. *Psychological Science, 10,* 419–422.

Monfries, M. M., & Kafer, N. F. (1987). Neglected and rejected children: A social-skills model. *Journal of Psychology, 121,* 401–407.

Montague, D. P. F., & Walker-Andrews, A. S. (2001). Peekaboo: A new look at infants' perception of emotion expressions. *Developmental Psychology, 37,* 826–838.

Moon, C., Cooper, R. P., & Fifer, W. P. (1993). Two-day-olds prefer their native language. *Infant Behavior and Development, 16,* 494–500.

Moon, R. Y., & Biliter, W. M. (2001). Infant sleep position policies in licensed child care centers after Back to Sleep campaign. *Pediatrics, 106,* 576–580.

Moon, R. Y., Patel, K. M., & McDermott Shaefer, S. J. (2000). Sudden infant death syndrome in child care settings. *Pediatrics, 106,* 295–300.

Moore, K. L., & Persaud, T. V. N. (1998). *Before we are born: Essentials of embryology and birth defects* (5th ed.). Philadelphia: W.B. Saunders.

Moore, K. L., & Persaud, T. V. N. (2003). *The developing human: Clinically oriented embryology.* Philadelphia: Saunders.

Morison, P., & Masten, A. S. (1991). Peer reputation in middle childhood as a predictor of adaptation in adolescence: A seven-year follow-up. *Child Development, 62,* 991–1007.

Morrelli, G., Rogoff, B., Oppenheim, D., & Goldsmith, D. (1992). Cultural variation in infants' sleeping arrangements: Questions of independence. *Developmental Psychology, 28,* 604–613.

Morris, R., & Kratchowill, T. (1983). *Treating children's fears and phobias.* New York: Pergamon Press.

Morrison, F. J., Griffith, E. M., & Alberts, D. M. (1997). Nature-nurture in the classroom: Entrance age, school readiness, and learning in children. *Developmental Psychology, 33,* 254–262.

Morrison, F. J., Smith, L., & Dow-Ehrensberger, M. (1995). Education and cognitive development: A natural experiment. *Developmental Psychology, 31,* 789–799.

Morrongiello, B. A. (1984). Auditory temporal pattern perception in 6- and 12-month-old infants. *Developmental Psychology, 20,* 441–448.

Morrongiello, B. A., Fenwick, K. D., & Chance, G. (1990). Sound localization acuity in very young infants: An observer-based testing procedure. *Developmental Psychology, 26,* 75–84.

Morrongiello, B. A., Fenwick, K. D., & Chance, G. (1998). Crossmodal learning in newborn infants: Inferences about properties of auditory-visual events. *Infant Behavior and Development, 21,* 543–554.

Moses, L. J., Baldwin, D. A., Rosicky, J. G., & Tidball, G. (2001). Evidence for referential understanding in the emotions domain at twelve and eighteen months. *Child Development, 72,* 718–735.

Mosko, S., Richard, C., & McKenna, J. (1997). Infant arousals during mother-infant bed sharing: Implications for infant sleep and sudden infant death syndrome research. *Pediatrics, 100,* 841–849.

Moss, E., Rousseau, D., Parent, S., St.-Laurent, D., & Saintonge, J. (1998). Correlates of attachment at school age: Maternal reported stress, mother-child interaction, and behavior problems. *Child Development, 69,* 1390–1405.

Mosteller, F. (1995, Summer/Fall). The Tennessee study of class size in the early school grades. *The Future of Children, 5*(2), pp. 113–127.

Mostow, A. J., Izard, C. E., Fine, S., & Trentacosta, C. J. (2002). Modeling emotional, cognitive, and behavioral predictors of peer acceptance. *Child Development, 73,* 1775–1787.

MTA Cooperative Group. (1999). A 14-month randomized clinical trial of treatment strategies for attention-deficit/hyperactivity disorder: Multimodal treatment study of children with ADHD. *Archives of General Psychiatry, 56,* 1073–1086.

Mullen, M. K. (1994). Earliest recollections of childhood: A demographic analysis. *Cognition, 52,* 55–79.

Mullen, M. K., & Yi, S. (1995). The cultural context of talk about the past: Implications for the development of autobiographical memory. *Cognitive Development, 10,* 407–419.

Mumme, D. L., & Fernald, A. (2003). The infant as onlooker: Learning from emotional reactions observed in a television scenario. *Child Development, 74,* 221–237.

Munakata, Y. (2001). Task dependency in infant behavior: Toward an understanding of the processes underlying cognitive development. In F. Lacerda & C. von Hofsten & M. Heimann (Eds.), *Emerging cognitive abilities in early infancy* (pp. 29–52). Mahwah, NJ: Erlbaum.

Munakata, Y. (2006). Information processing approaches to development. In W. Damon & R. M. Lerner (Editors-in-Chief) & D. M. Kuhn & R. S. Siegler (Vol. Eds.), *Handbook of child psychology: Vol. 2. Cognition, perception, and language* (6th ed., pp. 426–463). Hoboken, NJ: Wiley.

Munroe, R. H., Shimmin, H. S., & Munroe, R. L. (1984). Gender understanding and sex role preference in four cultures. *Developmental Psychology, 20,* 673–682.

Musher-Eizenman, D. R., Holub, S. C., Barnhart Miller, A., Goldstein, S. E., & Edwards-Leeper, L. (2004). Body size stigmatization in preschool children: The role of control attributions. *Journal of Pediatric Psychology, 29,* 613–620.

Mussen, P. H., & Jones, M. C. (1957). Self-conceptions, motivations, and interpersonal attitudes of late and early maturing boys. *Child Development, 28,* 243–256.

Mussen, P. H., & Jones, M. C. (1958). The behavior inferred motivations of late and early maturing boys. *Child Development, 29,* 61–67.

Mustanski, B. S., Viken, R. J., Kaprio, J., Pulkkinen, L., & Rose, R. J. (2004). Genetic and environmental influences on pubertal development: Longitudinal data from Finnish twins at ages 11 and 14. *Developmental Psychology, 40,* 1188–1198.

Myers, J., Jusczyk, P. W., Kemler Nelson, D. G., Charles-Luce, J., Woodward, A. L., & Hirsh-Pasek, K. (1996). Infants' sensitivity to word boundaries in fluent speech. *Journal of Child Language, 23,* 1–30.

Nachmias, M., Gunnar, M., Mangelsdorf, S., Parritz, R., & Buss, K. (1996). Behavioral inhibition and stress reactivity: Moderating role of attachment security. *Child Development, 67,* 508–522.

Nahmias, A. J., Keyserling, H. L., & Kernick, G. M. (1983). Herpes simplex. In J. S. Remington & J. O. Klein (Eds.), *Infectious diseases of the fetus and newborn infant.* Philadelphia: W.B. Saunders.

Naigles, L. (1990). Children use syntax to learn verb meanings. *Journal of Child Language, 17,* 357–374.

Naito, M., & Miura, H. (2001). Japanese children's numerical competencies: Age- and schooling-related influences on the development of number concepts and addition skills. *Developmental Psychology, 37,* 217–230.

Najarian, S. P. (1999). Infant cranial molding deformation and sleep position: Implications for primary care. *Journal of Pediatric Health Care, 13,* 173–177.

Nakamura, K. (2001). The acquisition of polite language by Japanese children. In K. E. Nelson, A. Aksu-Koc, & C. E. Johnson (Eds.), *Children's language: Developing narrative and discourse competence* (Vol. 10, pp. 93–112). Mahwah, NJ: Erlbaum.

Namy, L. L., & Waxman, S. R. (1998). Words and gestures: Infants' interpretations of different forms of symbolic reference. *Child Development, 69,* 295–308.

Nathanielsz, P. W. (1996). The timing of birth. *American Scientist, 84,* 562–569.

National Center for Education Statistics. (1999). *Service-learning and community service in K–12 public schools.* U.S. Department of Education, NCES 1999–043.

National Center for Education Statistics. (2001a). *Child care.* Retrieved on December 20, 2002, from childstats.gov/ac2002/indicators.asp?IID=43&id=1

National Center for Education Statistics. (2001b). *Student jobs and volunteer service.* U.S. Department of Education, NCES 2001–485.

National Center for Education Statistics. (2005). *Internet access in U. S. public schools and classrooms: 1994–2003.* Retrieved February 21, 2006, from nces.ed.gov/surveys/frss/publications/2005015/.

National Center for Education Statistics. (2006). *Fast facts: What are the most prevalent forms of child care?* Retrieved September 4, 2006 from http://nces.ed.gov/fastfacts/display.asp?id=4.

National Center for Health Statistics. (2005a). *Health, United States, 2005.* Hyattsville, MD: U.S. Government Printing Office.

National Center for Health Statistics. (2005b). *Teen births.* Retrieved October 1, 2005, from www.cdc.gov/nchs/fastats/teenbirth.htm.

National Center for Education Statistics. (2006). *Fast facts: What are the most prevalent forms of child care?* Retrieved September 4, 2006 from www.nces.ed.gov/fastfacts/display.asp?id=4.

National Clearinghouse for English Language Acquisition. (2002). Retrieved November 8, 2002 from ncela.gwu.edu/states/stateposter.pdf

National Human Genome Research Institute. (2003). 50 years of DNA: From double helix to health: A celebration of the genome. Retrieved May 3, 2006, from www.genome.gov/10005139.

National Institute of Mental Health. (1996). *Attention deficit hyperactivity disorder* (NIH Publication No. 96–3572). Washington, DC: U.S. Government Printing Office.

National Institute of Mental Health. (2002). *Suicide facts.* Retrieved December 12, 2002, from www.nimh.nih.gov/research/suifact.htm

National Institute on Drug Abuse. (1995). *Drug use among racial/ethnic minorities.* Bethesda, MD: Author:

National Institute on Drug Abuse. (2003). *Drug abuse among racial/ethnic minorities.* Bethesda, MD: Author

National Research Council and Institute of Medicine. (2001). *Nontechnical strategies to reduce children's exposure to inappropriate material on the Internet: Summary of a workshop* (Joah G. Iannotta, Ed.). Washington, DC: National Academies Press.

National Research Council and Institute of Medicine. (2002a). *Community programs to promote youth development* (J. Eccles & J. A. Gootman, Eds.). Washington, DC: National Academies Press.

National Research Council and Institute of Medicine. (2002b). *Deadly lessons: Understanding lethal school violence* (M. H. Moore, C. V. Petrie, A. A. Braga, & B. L. McLaughlin, Eds.). Washington, DC: National Academies Press.

National Research Council and Institute of Medicine, Committee on Family and Work Policies. (2003). *Working families and growing kids: Caring for children and adolescents.* Washington, DC: National Academies Press.

National Research Council, Committee on Mapping and Sequencing the Human Genome. (1988). *Mapping and sequencing the human genome.* Washington, DC: National Academy Press.

Nazzi, T., Bertoncini, J., & Mehler, J. (1998). Language discrimination by newborns: Towards an understanding of the role of rhythm. *Journal of Experimental Psychology: Human Perception and Performance, 24,* 756–766.

Nazzi, T., & Gopnik, A. (2001). Linguistic and cognitive abilities in infancy: When does language become a tool for categorization? *Cognition, 80,* B11–B20.

Nazzi, T., Kemler Nelson, D. G., Jusczyk, P. W., & Juczyk, A. M. (2000). Six-month-olds' detection of clauses embedded in contiguous speech: Effects of prosodic well-formedness. *Infancy, 1,* 123–147.

Needham, A. (2001). Object recognition and object segregation in 4.5-month-old infants. *Journal of Experimental Child Psychology, 78,* 3–24.

Needham, A., & Baillargeon, R. (1998). Effects of prior experience in 4.5-month-old infant's object segregation. *Infant Behavior and Development, 21,* 121–149.

Needham, A., & Modi, A. (2000). Infant's use of prior experiences with objects in object segregation: Implications for object recognition in infancy. In H. W. Reese (Ed.), *Advances in child development and behavior* (Vol. 27, pp. 100–135). San Diego: Academic Press.

Needleman, H. L., & Bellinger, D. (Eds.) (1994). *Prenatal exposure to toxicants: Developmental consequences.* Baltimore: Johns Hopkins University Press.

Neiderhiser, J. M., Reiss, D., Hetherington, E. M., & Plomin, R. (1999). Relationships between parenting and adolescent adjustment over time: Genetic and environmental contributions. *Developmental Psychology, 35,* 680–692.

Neimark, E. D. (1979). Current status of formal operations research. *Human Development, 22,* 60–67.

Neisser, U. (Ed.). (1998). *The rising curve: Long-term gains in IQ and related measures.* Washington, DC: American Psychological Association.

Neisser, U., Boodoo, G., Bouchard, T. J., Jr., Boykin, A. W., Brody, N., Ceci, S. J., et al. (1996). Intelligence: Knowns and unknowns. *American Psychologist, 51,* 77–101.

Nelson, C. A. (1995). The ontogeny of human memory: A cognitive neuroscience perspective. *Developmental Psychology, 31,* 723–738.

Nelson, C. A. (1999). Change and continuity in neurobehavioral development: Lessons from the study of neurobiology and neural plasticity. *Infant Behavior and Development, 22,* 415–429.

Nelson, C. A., & Monk, C. S. (2001). The use of event-related potentials in the study of cognitive development. From C. A. Nelson & M. Luciano (Eds.), *Handbook of developmental cognitive neuroscience* (pp. 125–136). Cambridge, MA: MIT Press.

Nelson, C. A., Thomas, K. M., & de Haan, M. (2006). Neural bases of cognitive development. In W. Damon & R. M. Lerner (Editors-in-Chief) & D. M. Kuhn & R. S. Siegler (Vol. Eds.), *Handbook of child psychology: Vol. 2. Cognition, perception, and language* (6th ed., pp. 3–57). Hoboken, NJ: Wiley.

Nelson, E. E., & Panksepp, J. (1998). Brain substrates of infant-mother attachment: Contributions of opioids, oxytocin, and norepinephrine. *Neuroscience and Biobehavioral Reviews, 22,* 437–452.

Nelson, K. (1973). Structure and strategy in learning to talk. *Monographs of the Society for Research in Child Development, 38*(1–2, Serial No. 149).

Nelson, K. (1993a). Events, narratives, memory: What develops? In C. A. Nelson (Ed.), *Memory and affect in development. The Minnesota symposia on child psychology* (Vol. 26, pp. 1–24). Hillsdale, NJ: Erlbaum.

Nelson, K. (1993b). The psychological and social origins of autobiographical memory. *Psychological Science, 4,* 7–14.

Nelson, K., & Fivush, R. (2004). The emergence of autobiographical memory: A social cultural developmental theory. *Psychological Review, 111,* 486–511.

Nelson, K., & Gruendel, J. (1981). Generalized event representations: Basic building blocks of cognitive development. In M. E. Lamb & A. L. Brown (Eds.), *Advances in developmental psychology* (Vol. 1). Hillsdale, NJ: Erlbaum.

Nemeth, M. (1997, August 19). Looking for moral anchors. *Maclean's, 109,* 17–18.

Neu, M. (1999). Parents' perception of skin-to-skin care with their preterm infants requiring assisted ventilation. *Journal of Obstetric, Gynecologic, and Neonatal Nursing, 28,* 157–164.

Neville, H., Mehler, J., Newport, E., Werker, J. F., & McClelland, J. (2001). Language. *Developmental Science, 4,* 293–312.

Newcomb , A. F., & Bagwell, C. L. (1995). Children's friendship relations: A meta-analytic review. *Psychological Bulletin, 117,* 306–347.

Newcomb, A. F., Bukowski, W. K., & Bagwell, C. L. (1999). Knowing the sounds: Friendship as a developmental context. In W. A. Collins & B. Laursen (Eds.), *Minnesota symposia on child psychology: Vol. 30. Relationships as developmental contexts* (pp. 63–84). Mahwah, NJ: Erlbaum.

Newcombe, N., & Huttenlocher, J. (1992). Children's early ability to solve perspective-taking problems. *Developmental Psychology, 28,* 635–643.

Newcombe, N. S., & Huttenlocher, J. (2006). Development of spatial cognition. In W. Damon & R. M. Lerner (Editors-in-Chief) & D. M. Kuhn & R. S. Siegler (Vol. Eds.), *Handbook of child psychology: Vol. 2. Cognition, perception, and language* (6th ed., pp. 734–776). Hoboken, NJ: Wiley.

Newport, E. L. (1977). Motherese: The speech of mothers to young children. In N. J. Castellan, D. B. Pisoni, & G. Potts (Eds.), *Cognitive theory* (Vol. 2). Hillsdale, NJ: Erlbaum.

Newport, E. L. (1990). Maturational constraints on language learning. *Cognitive Science, 14,* 11–28.

Newton, N. (1955). *Maternal emotions.* New York: P. B. Hoeber.

NICHD Early Child Care Research Network. (1997). The effects of infant child care on infant-mother attachment security: Results of the NICHD study of early child care. *Child Development, 68,* 860–879.

NICHD Early Child Care Research Network. (1998). Relations between family predictors and child outcomes: Are they weaker for children in child care? *Developmental Psychology, 34,* 1119–1128.

NICHD Early Child Care Research Network. (2000a). Factors associated with fathers' caregiving activities and sensitivity to young children. *Journal of Family Psychology, 14,* 200–219.

NICHD Early Child Care Research Network. (2000b). The relations of child care to cognitive and language development. *Child Development, 71,* 960–980.

NICHD Early Child Care Research Network. (2001a). Child care and children's peer interaction at 24 and 36 months: The NICHD study of early child care. *Developmental Psychology, 72,* 1478–1500.

NICHD Early Child Care Research Network. (2001b). Child-care and family predictors of preschool attachment and stability from infancy. *Developmental Psychobiology, 37,* 847–862.

NICHD Early Child Care Research Network. (2002). Child-care structure —> Process —> Outcome: Direct and indirect effects of child-care quality on young children's development. *Psychological Science, 13,* 199–206.

NICHD Early Child Care Research Network. (2003a). Does amount of time spent in child care predict socioemotional adjustment during the transition to kindergarten? *Child Development, 74,* 976–1005.

NICHD Early Child Care Research Network. (2003b). Does quality of child care affect child outcomes at age 4½? *Developmental Psychology, 39,* 451–469.

Nikken, P., & Peeters, A. L. (1988). Children's perceptions of television reality. *Journal of Broadcasting and Electronic Media, 32,* 417–423.

Ninio, A., & Bruner, J. S. (1978). The achievement and antecedents of labelling. *Journal of Child Language, 5,* 1–15.

Nix, R. L., Pinderhughes, E. E., Dodge, K. A., Bates, J. E., Pettit, G. S., & McFadyen-Ketchum, S. A. (1999). The relation between mothers' hostile attribution tendencies and children's externalizing problems: The mediating role of mother's harsh discipline practices. *Child Development, 70,* 896–909.

Nolen-Hoeksma, S. (2001). Gender differences in depression. *Current Directions in Psychological Science, 10,* 173–176.

Noll, R. B., Vannatta, K., Koontz, K., Kalinyak, K., Bukowski, W. M., & Davies, W. H. (1996). Peer relationships and emotional well-being of youngsters with sickle cell disease. *Child Development, 67,* 423–436.

Norbeck, J. S., & Tilden, V. P. (1983). Life stress, social support, and emotional disequilibrium in complications of pregnancy: A prospective, multivariate study. *Journal of Health and Social Behavior, 24,* 30–46.

Northrup, H., & Volcik, K. A. (2000). Spina bifida and neural tube defects. *Current Problems in Pediatrics, 30,* 317–332.

Novak, G. (1996). *Developmental psychology: Dynamic systems and behavioral analyses.* Reno, NV: Context Press.

Nucci, L. (2001). *Education in the moral domain.* New York: Cambridge University Press.

Nucci, L. P., & Turiel, E. (1978). Social interactions and the development of social concepts in preschool children. *Child Development, 49,* 400–407.

Nucci, L. P., & Turiel, E. (1993). God's word, religious rules, and their relation to Christian and Jewish children's concepts of morality. *Child Development, 64,* 1475–1491.

Nugent, J. K., Lester, B. M., Greene, S. M., Wieczorek-Doering, D., & O'Mahony, P. (1996). The effects of maternal alcohol consumption and cigarette smoking during pregnancy on acoustic cry analysis. *Child Development, 67,* 1806–1815.

Oakes, L. M., Coppage, D. J., & Dingel, A. (1997). By land or by sea: The role of perceptual similarity in infants' categorization of animals. *Developmental Psychology, 33,* 396–407.

Oakland, T. D. (1982). Nonbiased assessment in counseling: Issues and guidelines. *Measurement and Evaluation in Guidance, 15,* 107–116.

Oakley, D., Murray, M. E., Murtland, T., Hayashi, R., Andersen, H. F., Mayes, F., & Rooks, J. (1996). Comparisons of outcomes of maternity care by obstetricians and certified nurse-midwives. *Obstetrics and Gynecology, 88,* 923–929.

Ochs, E. (1988). *Culture and language development: Language acquisition and language socialization in a Samoan village.* New York: Cambridge University Press.

Ochs, E. (1990). Indexicality and socialization. In J. W. Stigler, R. A. Shweder, & G. Herdt (Eds.), *Cultural psychology.* Cambridge, UK: Cambridge University Press.

O'Connor, T. G., & Croft, C. M. (2001). A twin study of attachment in preschool children. *Child Development, 72,* 1501–1511.

O'Connor, T. G., Caspi, A., DeFries, J. C., & Plomin, R. (2000). Are associations between parental divorce and children's adjustment genetically mediated? An adoption study. *Developmental Psychology, 36,* 429–437.

Ogbu, J. U. (1974). *The next generation: An ethnography of education in an urban neighborhood.* New York: Academic Press.

Ogbu, J. U. (1994). From cultural differences to differences in cultural frame of reference. In P. M. Greenfield & R. R. Cocking (Eds.), *Cross-cultural roots of minority child development* (pp. 365–391). Hillsdale, NJ: Erlbaum.

Oldershaw, L., Walters, G. C., & Hall, D. K. (1986). Control strategies and noncompliance in abusive mother-child dyads: An observational study. *Child Development, 57,* 722–732.

Olson, R. K. (1994). Language deficits in "specific" reading disability. In M. A. Gernsbacher (Ed.), *Handbook of psycholinguistics* (pp. 895–916). New York: Academic Press.

Olson, S. L., Bayles, K., & Bates, J. E. (1986). Mother-child interaction and children's speech progress: A longitudinal study of the first two years. *Merrill Palmer Quarterly, 32,* 1–20.

Olweus, D. (1993a). Bullies on the playground: The role of victimization. In C. H. Hart (Ed.), *Children on playgrounds* (pp. 85–128). Albany: State University of New York Press.

Olweus, D. (1993b). *Bullying at school: What we know and what we can do.* Oxford, UK: Blackwell.

Olweus, D. (1994). Bullying at school: Long-term outcomes for the victims and an effective school-based intervention program. In L. R. Huesmann (Ed.), *Aggressive behavior: Current perspectives* (pp. 97–130). New York: Plenum.

Olweus, D. (1997). Tackling peer victimization with a school-based intervention program. In D. P. Frye & K. Bjorkqvist (Eds.), *Cultural variation in conflict resolution: Alternatives to violence* (pp. 215–231). Mahwah, NJ: Erlbaum.

O'Neil, R., Parke, R. D., & McDowell, D. J. (2001). Objective and subjective features of children's neighborhoods: Relations to parental regulatory strategies and children's social competence. *Applied Developmental Psychology, 22,* 135–155.

Orlebeke, J. F., Knol, D. L., & Verhulst, F. C. (1999). Child behavior problems increased by maternal smoking during pregnancy. *Archives of Environmental Health, 54,* 15–19.

Ornoy, A., Michailevskay, V., Lukashov, I., Barttamburger, R., & Harel, S. (1996). The developmental outcome of children born to heroin-dependent mothers, raised at home or adopted. *Child Abuse & Neglect, 20,* 385–396.

Ornstein, P. A., & Naus, M. J. (1978). Rehearsal processes in children's memory. In P. A. Ornstein (Ed.), *Memory development in children.* Hillsdale, NJ: Erlbaum.

Ornstein, P. A., Naus, M. J., & Liberty, C. (1975). Rehearsal and organizational processes in children's memory. *Child Development, 46,* 818–830.

Orobio de Castro, B., Veerman, J. W., Koops, W., Bosch, J. D., & Monshouwer, H. J. (2002). Hostile attribution of intent and aggressive behavior: A meta-analysis. *Child Development, 73,* 916–934.

O'Shea, T. M., Klinepeter, K. L., Goldstein, D. J., Jackson, B. W., & Dillard, R. G. (1997). Survival and developmental disability in infants with birth weights of 501 to 800 grams, born between 1979 and 1994. *Pediatrics, 100,* 982–986.

Osterling, J., & Dawson, G. (1994). Early recognition of children with autism: A study of first birthday home videotapes. *Journal of Autism and Developmental Disorders, 24,* 247–257.

Ounsted, C., Oppenheimer, R., & Lindsay, J. (1974). Aspects of bonding failure: The psychopathology and psychotherapeutic treatment of families of battered children. *Developmental Medicine and Child Neurology, 16,* 447–452.

Overman, W. H., Bachevalier, J., Schuhmann, E., & McDonough-Ryan, P. (1997). Sexually dimorphic brain-behavior development. In N. Krasnegor, G. R. Lyon, & P. S. Goldman-Rakic (Eds.), *Development of the prefrontal cortex: Evolution, neurobiology, and behavior* (pp. 337–357). Baltimore: Paul H. Brookes.

Overton, W. F. (2006). Developmental psychology: Philosophy, concepts, methodology. In W. Damon & R. M. Lerner (Editors-in-Chief) & R. M. Lerner (Vol. Ed.), *Handbook of child psychology: Vol. 1. Theoretical models of human development* (6th ed., pp. 18–88). Hoboken, NJ: Wiley.

Owen, M. T., & Cox, M. J. (1988). Maternal employment and the transition to parenthood. In A. E. Gottfried & A. W. Gottfried (Eds.), *Maternal employment and children's development: Longitudinal research.* New York: Plenum Press.

Ozer, E. J., & Weinstein, R. S. (2004). Urban adolescents' exposure to community violence: The role of support, school safety, and social constraints in a school-based sample of boys and girls. *Journal of Clinical Child and Adolescent Psychology, 33,* 463–476.

Palacios, J. (1996). Proverbs as images of children and childrearing. In C. P. Hwang, M. E. Lamb, & I. E. Sigel (Eds.), *Images of childhood* (pp. 75–98). Mahwah, NJ: Erlbaum.

Palmer, S. E., & Kimchi, R. (1986). The information processing approach to cognition. In T. J. Knapp & L. C. Robertson (Eds.), *Approaches to cognition: Contrasts and controversies.* Hillsdale, NJ: Erlbaum.

Paltrow, L. M., Cohen, D. W., & Carey, C. A. (2000). *Year 2000 overview: Governmental responses to pregnant women who use alcohol and other drugs.* Philadelphia, PA: Women's Law Project, National Advocates for Pregnant Women.

Papoušek, H., Papoušek, M., & Koester, L. S. (1986). Sharing emotionality and sharing knowledge: A microanalytic approach to parent-infant communication. In C. E. Izard & P. B. Read (Eds.), *Measuring emotions in infants and children* (Vol. 2). Cambridge, UK: Cambridge University Press.

Papoušek, M. (1992). Early ontogeny of vocal communication in parent-infant interactions. In H. Papoušek, U. Jürgens, & M. Papoušek (Eds.), *Nonverbal vocal communication: Comparative and developmental approaches.* Cambridge, UK: Cambridge University Press.

Parke, R. D., & Collmer, C. W. (1975). Child abuse: An interdisciplinary analysis. In E. M. Hetherington (Ed.), *Review of child development research* (Vol. 5, pp. 509–590). Chicago: University of Chicago Press.

Parke, R. D., MacDonald, K. B., Beitel, A., & Bhavnagri, N. (1988). The role of the family in the development of peer relationships. In R. D. Peters & R. J. McMahon (Eds.), *Social learning and systems approaches to marriage and the family.* New York: Brunner/Mazel.

Parke, R. D., & O'Leary, S. (1976). Father-mother-infant interaction in the newborn period: Some findings, some observations, and some unresolved issues. In K. F. Riegel & J. Meacham (Eds.), *The developing individual in a changing world: Vol. 2. Social and environmental issues.* The Hague: Mouton.

Parke, R. D., & O'Neil, R. (1999). Social relationships across contexts: Family-peer linkages. In W. A. Collins & B. Laursen (Eds.), *Minnesota Symposia on Child Psychology: Vol. 30. Relationships as developmental contexts* (pp. 211–239). Mahwah, NJ: Erlbaum.

Parke, R. D., & Slaby, R. G. (1983). The development of aggression. In E. M. Hetherington (Ed.), *Handbook of child psychology: Vol. IV. Socialization, personality, and social development* (4th ed., pp. 547–641). New York: Wiley.

Parker, J. G., & Asher, S. R. (1987). Peer relations and later personal adjustment: Are low-accepted children at risk? *Psychological Bulletin, 102,* 357–389.

Parker, J. G., & Asher, S. R. (1993). Friendship and friendship quality in middle childhood: Links with peer group acceptance and feelings of loneliness and social dissatisfaction. *Developmental Psychology, 29,* 611–621.

Parker, J. G., & Gottman, J. M. (1989). Social and emotional development in a relational context: Friendship interaction from early childhood to adolescence. In T. M. Berndt & G. W. Ladd (Eds.), *Peer relations in childhood.* New York: Wiley.

Parker, J. G., & Seal, J. (1996). Forming, losing, renewing, and replacing friendships: Applying temporal parameters to the assessment of children's friendship experiences. *Child Development, 67,* 2248–2268.

Parkhurst, J. T., & Asher, S. R. (1992). Peer rejection in middle school: subgroup differences in behavior, loneliness, and interpersonal concerns. *Developmental Psychology, 28,* 231–241.

Parsons, J. E. (1980). Psychosexual neutrality: Is anatomy destiny? In J. E. Parsons (Ed.), *The psychobiology of sex differences and sex roles* (pp. 3–29). New York: Hemisphere.

Parten, M. B. (1932). Social participation among pre-school children. *Journal of Abnormal and Social Psychology, 32,* 243–269.

Pascalis, O., de Schonen, S., Morton, J., Deruelle, C., & Fabre-Grenet, M. (1995). Mother's face recognition by neonates: A replication and an extension. *Infant Behavior and Development, 18,* 79–85.

Pass, R. F. (1987). Congenital and perinatal infections due to viruses and toxoplasma. In N. Kretchmer, E. J. Quilligan, & J. D. Johnson (Eds.), *Prenatal and perinatal biology and medicine: Vol. 2. Disorder, diagnosis, and therapy.* New York: Harwood Academic Publishers.

Patterson, C. J. (2000). Family relationships of lesbians and gay men. *Journal of Marriage and the Family, 62,* 1052–1069.

Patterson, G. R. (1982). *A social learning approach: Vol. 3. Coercive family process.* Eugene, OR: Castalia.

Patterson, G. R. (1986). Performance models for antisocial boys. *American Psychologist, 41,* 432–444.

Patterson, G. R., & Fleischman, M. J. (1979). Maintenance of treatment effects: Some considerations concerning family systems and follow-up data. *Behavior Therapy, 10,* 168–185.

Patterson, G. R., & Reid, J. B. (1973). Intervention for families of aggressive boys: A replication study. *Behavior Research and Therapy, 11,* 383–394.

Patterson, G. R., Reid, J. B., & Dishion, T. J. (1992). *A social learning approach: IV. Antisocial boys.* Eugene, OR: Castalia.

Patterson, G. R., Reid, J. B., Jones, R. R., & Conger, R. E. (1975). *A social learning approach: Vol. 1. Families with aggressive children.* Eugene, OR: Castalia.

Patterson, M. L., & Werker, J. F. (2003). Two-month-old infant match phonetic information in lips and voice. *Developmental Science, 6,* 191–196.

Paus, T. (2004). Mapping brain maturation and cognitive development during adolescence. *Trends in Cognitive Sciences, 9,* 60–68.

Paxton, S. J., Wertheim, E. H., Gibbons, K., Szmukler, G. I., Hillier, L., & Petrovich, J. L. (1991). Body image satisfaction, dieting beliefs, and weight loss behaviors in adolescent girls and boys. *Journal of Youth and Adolescence, 20,* 362–379.

Peak, K., & Del Papa, F. S. (1993). Criminal justice enters the womb: Enforcing the "right" to be born drug-free. *Journal of Criminal Justice, 21,* 245–263.

Pearce, M. J., Jones, S. M., Schwab-Stone, A. E., & Ruchkin, V. (2003). The protective effects of religiousness and parent involvement on the development of conduct problems among youth exposed to violence. *Child Development, 74,* 1682–1696.

Pederson, D. R., Gleason, K. E., Moran, G., & Bento, S. (1998). Maternal attachment representations, maternal sensitivity, and the infant-mother attachment relationship. *Developmental Psychology, 34,* 925–933.

Peisner-Feinberg, E. S., Burchinal, M., Clifford, R., Culkin, M., Howes, C., Kagan, S., & Yazejian, N. (2001). The relation of preschool child-care quality to children's cognitive and social developmental trajectories through second grade. *Child Development, 72,* 1534–1553.

Pelaez-Nogueras, M., Field, T., Gewirtz, J. L., Cigales, M., Gonzalez, A., Sanchez, A., & Richardson, S. C. (1997). The effects of systematic stroking versus tickling and poking on infant behavior. *Journal of Applied Developmental Psychology, 18,* 169–178.

Pellegrini, A. D., & Smith, P. K. (1998). Physical activity play: The nature and function of a neglected aspect of play. *Child Development, 69,* 577–598.

Peltonen, L., & McKusick, V. A. (2001). Dissecting human disease in the postgenomic era. *Science, 291,* 1224–1229.

Peña, M., Maki, A., Kovacic, D., Dehaene-Lambertz, G., Koizumi, H., Bouquet, F., et al. (2003). Sounds and silence: An optical topography study of language recognition at birth. *Proceedings of the National Academy of Science, 100,* 11702–11705.

Penn, A. A., & Shatz, C. J. (2002). Principles of endogenous and sensory activity-dependent brain development. In H. Langercrantz, M. Hanson, P. Evrard, & C. Rodeck (Eds.), *The newborn brain: Neuroscience and clinical applications.* Cambridge, U.K: Cambridge University Press.

Penn, Schoen, & Berland Associates. (2000, September). *Web savvy and safety: How kids and parents differ in what they know, whom they trust.* Retrieved November 27, 2002, from www.microsoft.com/PressPass/press/2000/Nov00/SafetyWebsitesPR.asp

Pennington, B. F. (1998). Dimensions of executive functions in normal and abnormal development. In N. A. Krasnegor, G. R. Lyon, & P. S. Goldman-Rakic (Eds.), *Development of the prefrontal cortex: Evolution, neurobiology, and behavior* (pp. 265–281). Baltimore, MD: Brookes.

Pennisi, E. (2001). The human genome: News. *Science, 291,* 1177–1180.

Perner, J., & Ruffman, T. (1995). Episodic memory and autonoetic consciousness: Developmental evidence and a theory of childhood amnesia. *Journal of Experimental Child Psychology, 59,* 516–548.

Perozynski, L., & Kramer, L. (1999). Parental beliefs about managing sibling conflict. *Developmental Psychology, 35,* 489–499.

Perry, D. G., & Bussey, K. (1979). The social learning theory of sex differences: Imitation is alive and well. *Journal of Personality and Social Psychology, 37,* 1699–1712.

Pérusse, L., & Chagnon, Y. C. (1997). Summary of human linkage and association studies. *Behavior Genetics, 27,* 359–372.

Petersen, A. C. (1980). Biopsychosocial processes in the development of sex-related differences. In J. Parsons (Ed.), *The psychobiology of sex differences and sex roles* (pp. 31–55). New York: Hemisphere.

Petersen, A. C. (1988). Adolescent development. *Annual Review of Psychology, 39,* 583–607.

Petersen, A. C., & Hamburg, B. (1986). Adolescence: A developmental approach to problems and psychopathology. *Behavior Therapy, 13,* 480–499.

Petersen, A. C., Compas, B. E., Brooks-Gunn, J., Stemmler, M., Ey, S., & Grant, K. E. (1993). Depression in adolescence. *American Psychologist, 48,* 155–168.

Peterson, C. A., & Siegal, M. (1999). Representing inner worlds: Theory of mind in autistic, deaf, and normal hearing children. *Psychological Science, 10,* 126–129.

Peterson, C. C., Wellman, H. M., & Liu, D. (2005). Steps in theory-of-mind development for children with deafness and autism. *Child Development, 76,* 502–517.

Peterson, C., & Whalen, N. (2001). Five years later: Children's memory for medical emergencies. *Applied Cognitive Psychology, 15,* S7–S24.

Peterson, G. W., & Rollins, B. C. (1987). Parent-child socialization. In M. B. Sussman & S. K. Steinmetz (Eds.), *Handbook of marriage and the family.* New York: Plenum Press.

Peterson, R. P., Johnson, D. W., & Johnson, R. T. (1991). Effects of cooperative learning on perceived status of male and female pupils. *Journal of Social Psychology, 131,* 717–735.

Petitto, L. A., Holowka, S., Sergio, L. E., & Ostry, D. (2001). Language rhythms in baby hand movements. *Nature, 413,* 35–36.

Petitto, L. A., & Marentette, P. F. (1991). Babbling in the manual code: Evidence for the ontogeny of language. *Science, 251,* 1493–1496.

Pettit, G. S. (2004). Violent children in developmental perspective: Risk and protective factors and the mechanisms through which they (may) operate. *Current Directions in Psychological Science, 13,* 194–197.

Pettit, G. S., Bates, J. E., Dodge, K. A., & Meece, D. W. (1999). The impact of after-school peer contact on early adolescent externalizing problems is moderated by parental monitoring, neighborhood safety, and prior adjustment. *Child Development, 70,* 768–778.

Pettit, G. S., Clawson, M. A., Dodge, K. A. & Bates, J. E. (1996). Stability and change in peer-rejected status: The role of child behavior, parenting, and family ecology. *Merrill-Palmer Quarterly, 42,* 267–294.

Pettit, G. S., Laird, R. D., Dodge, K. A., Bates, J. E., & Criss, M. M. (2001). Antecedents and behavior-problem outcomes of parental monitoring and psychological control in early adolescence. *Child Development, 72,* 583–598.

Pew Internet & American Life Project (2005). Generations on line. Retrieved June 7, 2006 from www.pewinternet.org/pdfs/PIP_Generations_Memo.pdf.

Phelps, E., & Damon, W. (1989). Problem solving with equals: Peer collaboration as a context for learning mathematics and spatial concepts. *Journal of Educational Psychology, 81,* 639–646.

Phenylketonuria. (2000, October 16–18). Phenylketonuria (PKU): Screening and management. *NIH Consensus Statement, 17,* 1–33.

Phillips, D. (1984). The illusion of incompetence among academically competent children. *Child Development, 55,* 2000–2016.

Phinney, J. S. (1990). Ethnic identity in adolescents and adults: Review of research. *Psychological Bulletin, 108,* 499–514.

Phinney, J. S., Ferguson, D. L., & Tate, J. D. (1997). Intergroup attitudes among ethnic minority adolescents: A causal model. *Child Development, 68,* 955–969.

Phinney, J. S., & Rosenthal, D. A. (1992). Ethnic identity in adolescence: Process, context and outcome. In G. R. Adams, T. P. Gullotta, & R. Montemayor (Eds.), *Adolescent identity formation.* Newbury Park, CA: Sage.

Piaget, J. (1929). *The child's conception of the world.* London: Routledge & Kegan Paul.

Piaget, J. (1952a). *The child's conception of number.* New York: W. W. Norton.

Piaget, J. (1952b). *The origins of intelligence in children.* New York: W. W. Norton.

Piaget, J. (1954). *The construction of reality in the child.* New York: Basic Books.

Piaget, J. (1962). *Play, dreams, and imitation in childhood.* New York: W. W. Norton.

Piaget, J. (1965). *The moral judgment of the child.* New York: Free Press. (Original work published 1932)

Piaget, J. (1971). *Biology and knowledge: An essay on the relationship between organic regulations and cognitive processes.* Chicago: University of Chicago Press.

Piaget, J., & Inhelder, B. (1956). *The child's conception of space.* London: Routledge & Kegan Paul.

Pick, A. D. (1965). Improvement of visual and tactual discrimination. *Journal of Experimental Psychology, 69,* 331–339.

Pick, H. L., Jr. (1987). Information and the effects of early perceptual experience. In N. Eisenberg (Ed.), *Contemporary topics in developmental psychology.* New York: Wiley.

Pick, H. L., Jr. (1992). Eleanor J. Gibson: Learning to perceive and perceiving to learn. *Developmental Psychology, 28,* 787–794.

Pickens, J. (1994). Perception of auditory-visual distance relations by 5-month-old infants. *Developmental Psychology, 30,* 537–544.

Pickens, J., & Field, T. (1993). Facial expressivity in infants of depressed mothers. *Developmental Psychology, 29,* 986–988.

Piecuch, R. E., Leonard, C. H., & Cooper, B. A. (1998). Infants with birth weight 1,000–1,499 grams born in three time periods: Has outcome changed over time? *Clinical Pediatrics, 37,* 537–546.

Pierce, J. W., & Wardle, J. (1997). Cause and effect beliefs and self-esteem of overweight children. *Journal of Child Psychology and Psychiatry, 38,* 645–650.

Pike, A., McGuire, S., Hetherington, E. M., Reiss, D., & Plomin, R. (1996). Family environment and adolescent depressive symptoms and antisocial behavior: A multivariate genetic analysis. *Developmental Psychology, 32,* 590–603.

Pillemer, D. B. (1998). *Momentous events, vivid memories.* Cambridge, MA; Harvard University Press.

Pillemer, D. B., & White, S. H. (1989). Childhood events recalled by children and adults. In H. W. Reese (Ed.), *Advances in child development and behavior* (Vol. 21, pp. 297–340). San Diego: Academic Press.

Pineau, A., & Streri, A. (1990). Intermodal transfer of spatial arrangement of the component parts of an object in infants aged 4–5 months. *Perception, 19,* 795–804.

Pinker, S. (1984). *Language learnability and language development.* Cambridge, MA: Harvard University Press.

Pinker, S. (1987). The bootstrapping problem in language acquisition. In B. MacWhinney (Ed.), *Mechanisms of language acquisition.* Hillsdale, NJ: Erlbaum.

Pinyerd, B. J. (1992). Assessment of infant growth. *Journal of Pediatric Health Care, 6,* 302–308.

Pipe, M., Gee, S., Wilson, J. C., & Egerton, J. M. (1999). Children's recall 1 or 2 years after an event. *Developmental Psychology, 35,* 781–789.

Platt, L. D., Koch, R., Hanley, W. B., Levy, H. L., Matalon, R., Rouse, B., et al. (2000). The International Study of Pregnancy Outcome in Women with Maternal Phenylketonuria: Report of a 12-year study. *American Journal of Obstetrics and Gynecology, 182,* 326–333.

Pleck, E. H., & Pleck, J. H. (1997). Fatherhood ideals in the United States: Historical dimensions. In M. E. Lamb (Ed.), *The role of the father in child development* (3rd ed., pp. 33–48). New York: Wiley.

Plomin, R., DeFries, J. C., & Fulker, D. (1988). The Colorado Adoption Project. In R. Plomin, J. C. DeFries, & D. Fulker (Eds.), *Nature and nurture during infancy and early childhood* (pp. 37–76). Cambridge, UK: Cambridge University Press.

Plomin, R., DeFries, J. C., McClearn, G. E., & McGuffin, P. (2001). *Behavioral genetics* (4th ed.). New York: Worth.

Plomin, R., Owen, M. J., & McGuffin, P (1994). The genetic basis of complex human behaviors. Science, 264, 1733–1739.

Plomin, R., Reiss, D., Hetherington, E. M., & Howe, G. W. (1994). Nature and nurture: Genetic contributions to measures of the family environment. *Developmental Psychology, 30,* 32–43.

Plomin, R., & Rutter, M. (1998). Child development, molecular genetics, and what to do with genes once they are found. *Child Development, 69,* 1223–1242.

Polka, L. M., & Werker, J. F. (1994). Developmental changes in perception of nonnative vowel contrasts. *Journal of Experimental Psychology: Human Perception and Performance, 20,* 421–435.

Pollak, S. D., Cicchetti, D., Hornung, K., & Reed, A. (2000). Recognizing emotion in faces: Developmental effects of child abuse and neglect. *Developmental Psychology, 36,* 679–688.

Pollard, I. (2000). Substance abuse and parenthood: Biological mechanisms–bioethical challenges. *Women & Health, 30,* 1–24.

Pollitt, E. (1994). Poverty and child development: Relevance of research in developing countries to the United States. *Child Development, 65,* 283–295.

Pollitt, E. (1996). Timing and vulnerability in research on malnutrition and cognition. *Nutrition Reviews, 54,* S49-S55.

Pollock, L. A. (1983). *Forgotten children: Parent-child relations from 1500–1900.* Cambridge, UK: Cambridge University Press.

Pomerantz, E. M., Ruble, D. N., Frey, K. S., & Greulich, F. (1995). Meeting goals and confronting conflict: Children's changing perceptions of social comparison. *Child Development, 66,* 723–738.

Pomerleau, A., Bolduc, D., Malcuit, G., & Cossette, L. (1990). Pink or blue: Environmental gender stereotypes in the first two years of life. *Sex Roles, 22,* 359–367.

Poole, D. A., & Lindsay, D. S. (2002). Reducing child witnesses' false reports of misinformation from parents. *Journal of Experimental Child Psychology, 81,* 117–140.

Poole, D. A., & White, L. T. (1991). Effects of question repetition on the eyewitness testimony of children and adults. *Developmental Psychology, 27,* 975–986.

Poole, D. A., & White, L. T. (1993). Two years later: Effects of question repetition and retention interval on the eyewitness testimony of children and adults. *Developmental Psychology, 29,* 844–853.

Pope, A. W., & Bierman, K. L. (1999). Predicting adolescent peer problems and antisocial activities: The relative roles of aggression and dysregulation. *Developmental Psychology, 35,* 335–346.

Pope, S., & Kipp, K. K. (1998). The development of efficient forgetting: Evidence from directed-forgetting tasks. *Developmental Review, 18,* 86–123.

Porges, S. W., Doussard-Roosevelt, J. A., & Maiti, A. K. (1994). Vagal tone and the physiological regulation of emotion. In N. A. Fox (Ed.), The development of emotion regulation: Biological and behavioral considerations. *Monographs of the Society for Research in Child Development, 59*(2–3, Serial No. 240).

Porter, F. L., Grunau, R. E., & Anand, K. J. S. (1999). Long-term effects of pain in infants. *Journal of Developmental and Behavioral Pediatrics, 20,* 253–261.

Porter, R. H., Balogh, R. D., & Makin, J. W. (1988). Olfactory influences on mother-infant interaction. In C. Rovee-Collier & L. P. Lipsitt (Eds.), *Advances in infancy research* (Vol. 5). Norwood, NJ: Ablex.

Posada, G., Gao, Y., Wu, F., Posada, R., Tascon, M., Schoelmerich, A., et al. (1995). The secure-base phenomenon across cultures: Children's behaviors, mothers' preferences, and experts' concepts. In E. Waters, B. E. Vaughn, G. Posada, & K. Kondo-Ikemura (Eds.), *Caregiving, cultural, and cognitive perspectives on secure-base behavior and working models: New growing points of attachment theory and research. Monographs of the Society for Research in Child Development, 60* (Nos. 2–3, Serial No. 244).

Post, R. M., & Weiss, S. R. B. (1997). Emergent properties of neural systems: How focal molecular neurobiological alterations can affect behavior. *Development and Psychopathology, 9,* 907–929.

Poulin-Dubois, D., Lepage, A., & Ferland, D. (1996). Infants' concept of animacy. *Cognitive Development, 11,* 19–36.

Poulin-Dubois, D., Serbin, L. A., & Derbyshire, A. (1998). Toddlers' intermodal and verbal knowledge about gender. *Merrill-Palmer Quarterly, 44,* 338–354.

Poulin-Dubois, D., Serbin, L. A., Eichstedt, J. A., Sen, M. G., & Beissel, C. F. (2002). Men don't put on make-up: Toddlers' knowledge of the gender stereotyping of household activities. *Social Development, 11,* 166–181.

Povinelli, D. (2001). The self: Elevated in consciousness and extended in time. In C. Moore & K. Lemmon (Eds.), *The self in time* (pp. 75–95). Mahwah, NJ: Erlbaum.

Power, T. G., & Chapieski, M. L. (1986). Childrearing and impulse control in toddlers: A naturalistic investigation. *Developmental Psychology, 22,* 271–275.

Powers, S. I., Hauser, S. T., & Kilner, L. A. (1989). Adolescent mental health. *American Psychologist, 44,* 200–208.

Prader, A. (1978). Catch-up growth. *Postgraduate Medical Journal, 54,* 133–146.

Pratt, M. W., Green, D., MacVicar, J., & Bountrogianni, M. (1992). The mathematical parent: Parental scaffolding, parenting style, and learning outcomes in long-division mathematics homework. *Journal of Applied Developmental Psychology, 13,* 17–34.

Premack, D. (1971). Language in chimpanzee? *Science, 172,* 808–822.

Pressley, M., & Levin, J. R. (1977). Task parameters affecting the efficacy of a visual imagery learning strategy in younger and older children. *Journal of Experimental Child Psychology, 24,* 53–59.

Preyer, W. (1888–1889). *The mind of the child* (H. W. Brown, Trans.). New York: Appleton. (Original work published in 1882)

Pride, P. G., Drugan, A., Johnson, M. P., Isada, N. B., & Evans, M. I. (1993). Prenatal diagnosis: Choices women make about pursuing testing and acting on abnormal results. *Clinical Obstetrics and Gynecology, 36,* 496–509.

Proffitt, D. R., & Bertenthal, B. I. (1990). Converging operations revisited: Assessing what infants perceive using discrimination measures. *Perception & Psychophysics, 47,* 1–11.

Pulkkinen, L. (1982). Self-control and continuity from childhood to adolescence. In P. B. Baltes & O. G. Brim (Eds.), *Life-span development and behavior* (Vol. 4, pp. 63–105). New York: Academic Press.

Purcell, P., & Stewart, L. (1990). Dick and Jane in 1989. *Sex Roles, 22,* 177–185.

Putallaz, M. (1987). Maternal behavior and children's sociometric status. *Child Development, 58,* 324–340.

Quinn, P. C., Eimas, P. D., & Rosenkranz, S. L. (1993). Evidence for representations of perceptually similar natural categories by 3-month-old and 4-month-old infants. *Perception, 22,* 463–475.

Radin, N. (1981). The role of the father in cognitive, academic, and intellectual development. In M. E. Lamb (Ed.), *The role of the father in child development.* New York: Wiley.

Radin, N. (1994). Primary-caregiving fathers in intact families. In A. E. Gottfried & A. W. Gottfried (Eds.), *Redefining families: Implications for children's development* (pp. 11 – 49). NY: Plenum Press.

Radke-Yarrow, M., & Zahn-Waxler, C. (1984). Roots, motives, and patterns of children's prosocial behavior. In E. Staub, D. Bar-Tel, J. Karylowski, & J. Reykowski (Eds.), *Development and maintenance of prosocial behavior.* New York: Plenum Press.

Radke-Yarrow, M., Zahn-Waxler, C., & Chapman, M. (1983). Children's prosocial dispositions and behavior. In E. M. Hetherington (Ed.), *Handbook of child psychology: Vol. IV. Socialization, personality, and social development* (4th ed., pp. 469–545). New York: Wiley.

Radziszewska, B., Richardson, J. L., Dent, C. W., & Flay, B. R. (1996). Parenting style and adolescent depressive symptoms, smoking, and academic achievement: Ethnic, gender, and SES differences. *Journal of Behavioral Medicine, 19,* 289–305.

Radziszewska, B., & Rogoff, B. (1988). Influence of adult and peer collaborators on children's planning skills. *Developmental Psychology, 24,* 840–848.

Radziszewska, B., & Rogoff, R. (1991). Children's guided participation in planning imaginary errands with skilled adult or peer partners. *Developmental Psychology, 27,* 381–389.

Rallison, M. L. (1986). *Growth disorders in infants, children, and adolescents.* New York: Wiley.

Ram, A., & Ross, H. S. (2001). Problem-solving, contention, and struggle: How siblings resolve a conflict of interests. *Child Development, 72,* 1710–1722.

Ramey, C. T., Bryant, D. M., & Suarez, T. M. (1987). Early intervention: Why, for whom, how, at what cost? In N. Gunzenhauser (Ed.), *Infant stimulation: For whom, what kind, when, and how much?* (Johnson & Johnson Baby Products Company Pediatric Round Table Series No. 13). Skilman, NJ: Johnson & Johnson.

Ramey, C. T., Bryant, D. M., Wasik, B. H., Sparling, J. J., Fendt, K. H., & LaVange, L. M. (1992). Infant Health and Development Program for low birth weight, premature infants: Program elements, family participation, and child intelligence. *Pediatrics, 89,* 454–465.

Ramey, C. T., & Campbell, F. A. (1981). Educational intervention for children at risk for mild retardation: A longitudinal analysis. In P. Mittler (Ed.), *Frontiers of knowledge in mental retardation: Vol. 1. Social, educational, and behavioral aspects.* Baltimore: University Park Press.

Ramey, C. T., Lee, M. W., & Burchinal, M. R. (1989). Developmental plasticity and predictability: Consequences of ecological change. In M. H. Bornstein & N. A. Krasnegor (Eds.), *Stability and continuity in mental development: Behavioral and biological perspectives.* Hillsdale, NJ: Erlbaum.

Ramey, C. T., & Ramey, S. L. (1998). Early intervention and early experience. *American Psychologist, 53,* 109–120.

Rao, N., & Stewart, S. M. (1999). Cultural influences on sharer and recipient behavior: Sharing in Chinese and Indian preschool children. *Journal of Cross-Cultural Psychology, 30,* 219–241.

Rapport, M. D. (1995). Attention-deficit hyperactivity disorder. In M. Hersen & R. T. Ammerman (Eds.), *Advanced abnormal psychology* (pp. 353–373). Hillsdale, NJ: Erlbaum.

Raven, J. C. (1962). *Coloured progressive matrices.* London: H. K. Lewis and Co.

Reece, E. A., Hobbins, J. C., Mahoney, M. J., & Petrie, R. H. (1995). *Handbook of medicine of the fetus & mother.* Philadelphia: J. B. Lippincott.

Reese, E., & Fivush, R. (1993). Parental styles for talking about the past. *Developmental Psychology, 29,* 596–606.

Reese, E., Haden, C. A., & Fivush, R. (1993). Mother-child conversations about the past: Relationships of style and memory over time. *Cognitive Development, 8,* 403–430.

Regan, P. C., Durvasula, R., Howell, L., Ureno, O., & Rea, M. (2004). Romance seems to be alive and well during the high school years. *Social Behavior and Personality, 32,* 667–676.

Reilly, J. J., & Dorosty, A. R. (1999). Epidemic of obesity in UK children. *Lancet, 354,* 1874–1875.

Reisman, J. E. (1987). Touch, motion, and proprioception. In P. Salapatek & L. Cohen (Eds.), *Handbook of infant perception: From sensation to perception* (Vol. 1). Orlando, FL: Academic Press.

Reiss, D., Neiderhiser, J. M., Hetherington, E. M., & Plomin, R. (2000). *The relationship code: Deciphering genetic and social patterns in adolescent development.* Cambridge, MA: Harvard University Press.

Reissland, N. (1988). Neonatal imitation in the first hour of life: Observations in rural Nepal. *Developmental Psychology, 24,* 464–469.

Remafedi, G., French, S., Story, M., Resnick, M. D., & Blum, R. (1998). The relationship between suicide risk and sexual orientation: Results of a population-based study. *American Journal of Public Health, 88,* 57–60.

Renshaw, P. D. & Brown, P. J. (1993). Loneliness in middle childhood: Concurrent and longitudinal predictors. *Child Development, 64,* 1271–1284.

Resnick, L. B. (1986). The development of mathematical intuition. In M. Perlmutter (Ed.), *Perspectives on intellectual development: The Minnesota symposia on child psychology* (Vol. 19). Hillsdale, NJ: Erlbaum.

Resnick, L. B. (1995). Inventing arithmetic: Making children's intuitions work at school. In C. A. Nelson (Ed.), *Basic and applied perspectives on learning, cognition, and development. Minnesota Symposia on Child Psychology* (Vol. 28, pp. 75–101). Mahwah, NJ: Erlbaum.

Resnick, L. B., & Singer, J. A. (1993). Protoquantitative origins of ratio reasoning. In T. P. Carpenter, E. Fennema, & T. A. Romberg (Eds.), *Rational numbers: An integration of research* (pp. 107–130). Hillsdale, NJ: Erlbaum.

Reyna, V. F., & Brainerd, C. J. (1995). Fuzzy-trace theory: An interim synthesis. *Learning and Individual Differences, 7,* 1–75.

Reynolds, A. J., Ou, S., & Topitzes, J. W. (2004). Paths of effects of early childhood intervention on educational attainment and delinquency: A confirmatory analysis of the Chicago Child-Parent Centers. *Child Development, 75,* 1299–1328.

Reynolds, A. J., Temple, J. A., Robertson, D. L., & Mann, E. A. (2001). Long-term effects of an early childhood intervention on educational achievement and juvenile arrest: A 15-year follow-up of low income children in public schools. *Journal of the American Medical Association, 285,* 2339–2346.

Reznick, J. S., & Goldfield, B. A. (1992). Rapid change in lexical development in comprehension and production. *Developmental Psychology, 28,* 406–413.

Rheingold, H. L., & Cook, K. V. (1975). The contents of boys' and girls' rooms as an index of parents' behavior. *Child Development, 46,* 459–463.

Rice, K. G. (1990). Attachment in adolescence: A narrative and meta-analytic review. *Journal of Youth and Adolescence, 19,* 511–538.

Rice, M. L. (1983). The role of television in language acquisition. *Developmental Review, 3,* 211–224.

Rice, M. L., Huston, A. C., Truglio, R., & Wright, J. (1990). Words from "Sesame Street": Learning vocabulary while viewing. *Developmental Psychology, 26,* 421–428.

Rice, M. L., & Woodsmall, L. (1988). Lessons from television: Children's word learning when viewing. *Child Development, 59,* 420–429.

Richards, H. G., Frentzen, B., Gerhardt, K. J., McCann, M. E., & Abrams, R. M. (1992). Sound levels in the human uterus. *Obstetrics and Gynecology, 80,* 186–190.

Richards, J. E., & Holley, F. B. (1999). Infant attention and the development of smooth pursuit tracking. *Developmental Psychology, 35,* 856–867.

Richards, M. H., Crowe, P. A., Larson, R., & Swarr, A. (1998). Developmental patterns and gender differences in the experience of peer companionship during adolescence. *Child Development, 69,* 154–163.

Richards, M. H., & Duckett, E. (1994). The relationship of maternal employment to early adolescent daily experience with and without parents. *Child Development, 65,* 225–236.

Rimoin, D. L., Connor, J. M., Pyeritz, R. E., & Korf, B. R. (2002). Nature and frequency of genetic disease. In D. L. Rimoin, J. M. Connor, R. E. Pyeritz, & B. R. Korf (Eds.), *Emery and Rimoin's principles and practice of medical genetics* (4th ed., Vol. 1, pp. 55–59). London: Churchill Livingston.

Ris, M. D., Williams, S. E., Hunt, M. M., Berry, H. K., & Leslie, N. (1994). Early-treated phenylketonuria: Adult neuropsychologic outcome. *Journal of Pediatrics, 124,* 388–392.

Robbins, W. J., Brody, S., Hogan, A. G., Jackson, C. M., & Green, C. W. (Eds.). (1928). *Growth.* New Haven: Yale University Press.

Roberts, D. F., & Foehr, U. G. (2004). *Kids and media in America.* New York: Cambridge University Press.

Roberts, D. F., Foehr, U. G., & Rideout, V. (2005). *Generation M: Media in the lives of 8- to 18-year-olds.* Menlo Park, CA: Kaiser Family Foundation.

Roberts, D. F., Foehr, U. G., Rideout, V. J., & Brodie, M. (1999). *Kids and media at the new millennium: A comprehensive national analysis of children's media use.* Menlo Park, CA: The Henry J. Kaiser Family Foundation.

Roberts, L. (1991). Does the egg beckon sperm when the time is right? *Science, 252,* 214.

Roberts, W., & Strayer, J. (1996). Empathy, emotional expressiveness, and prosocial behavior. *Child Development, 67,* 449–470.

Robin, D. J., Berthier, N. E., & Clifton, R. K. (1996). Infants' predictive reaching for moving objects in the dark. *Developmental Psychology, 32,* 824–835.

Robinson, A., & Clinkenbeard, P. R. (1998). Giftedness: An exceptionality examined. *Annual Review of Psychology, 49,* 117–139.

Robinson, J. L., Kagan, J., Reznick, J. S., & Corley, R. (1992). The heritability of inhibited and uninhibited behavior: A twin study. *Developmental Psychology, 28,* 1030–1037.

Robinson, J. L., Zahn-Waxler, C., & Emde, R. N. (1994). Patterns of development in early empathic behavior: Environmental and child constitutional influences. *Social Development, 3,* 125–145.

Robinson, T. N. (2001). Television viewing and childhood obesity. *Pediatric Clinics of North America, 48,* 1017–1026.

Robinson, T. N., Chang, J. Y., Haydel, K. F., & Killen, J. D. (2001). Overweight concerns and body dissatisfaction among third-grade children: The impacts of ethnicity and socioeconomic status. *Journal of Pediatrics, 138,* 181–187.

Rochat, P. (1993). Hand-mouth coordination in the newborn: Morphology, determinants, and early development of a basic act. In G. J. P. Savelsbergh (Ed.), *The development of coordination in infancy* (pp. 265–288). Amsterdam, The Netherlands: Elsevier.

Rochat, P. (2001). *The infant's social world.* Cambridge, MA: Harvard University Press.

Rochat, P., & Goubet, N. (1995). Development of sitting and reaching in 5- to 6-month-old infants. *Infant Behavior and Development, 18,* 53–68.

Rochat, P., & Morgan, R. (1995). Spatial determinants in perception of self-produced leg movements by 3- to 5-month-old infants. *Developmental Psychology, 31,* 626–636.

Rochat, P., & Morgan, R. (1998). Two functional orientations of self-exploration in infancy. *British Journal of Developmental Psychology, 16,* 139–154.

Rochat, P., & Striano, T. (1999). Social-cognitive development in the first year. In P. Rochat (Ed.), *Early social cognition: Understanding in the first months of life* (pp. 3–34). Mahwah, NJ: Erlbaum.

Rochat, P., & Striano, T. (2002). Who's in the mirror? Self-other discrimination in specular images by four- and nine-month-old infants. *Child Development, 73,* 35–46.

Roffwarg, H. P., Muzio, J. N., & Dement, W. C. (1966). Ontogenetic development of the human sleep-dream cycle. *Science, 152,* 604–619.

Rogeness, G. A., & McClure, E. B. (1996). Development and neurotransmitter-environmental interactions. *Development and Psychopathology, 8,* 183–199.

Rogoff, B. (1981). Schooling and the development of cognitive skills. In H. C. Triandis & A. Heron (Eds.), *Handbook of cross-cultural psychology: Developmental psychology* (Vol. 4). Boston: Allyn & Bacon.

Rogoff, B. (1998). Cognition as a collaborative process. In W. Damon (Series Ed.) & D. Kuhn & R. S. Siegler (Vol. Eds.), *Handbook of child psychology: Vol. 2. Cognition, perception, and language* (5th ed., pp. 679–744). New York: Wiley.

Rogoff, B., Mistry, J., Göncü, A., & Mosier, C. (1993). Guided participation in cultural activity by toddlers and caregivers. *Monographs of the Society for Research in Child Development, 58*(8, Serial No. 236).

Roid, G. (2003). *Stanford-Binet Intelligence Scales.* Boston: Houghton Mifflin.

Rönnqvist, L., & von Hofsten, C. (1994). Neonatal finger and arm movements as determined by a social and an object context. *Early Development & Parenting, 3,* 81–94.

Rosch, E., Mervis, C. B., Gray, W. D., Johnson, D. M., & Boyes-Braem, P. (1976). Basic objects in natural categories. *Cognitive Psychology, 8,* 382–439.

Roschelle, J. M., Pea, R. D., Hoadley, C. M., Gordin, D. N., & Means, B. M. (2000, Fall/Winter). Changing how and what children learn in school with computer-based technologies. *Future of Children, 10*(2), 76–101.

Rose, A. J., & Asher, S. R. (1999). Children's goals and strategies in response to conflicts within a friendship. *Developmental Psychology, 35,* 69–79.

Rose, A. J., & Asher, S. R. (2004). Children's strategies and goals in response to help-giving and help-seeking tasks within a friendship. *Child Development, 75,* 749–763.

Rose, A. J., Swenson, L. P., & Waller, E. M. (2004). Overt and relational aggression and perceived popularity: Developmental differences in concurrent and prospective relations. *Developmental Psychology, 40,* 378–387.

Rose, S. A., Feldman, J. F., & Jankowski, J. J. (2001). Visual short-term memory in the first year of life: Capacity and recency effects. *Developmental Psychology, 37,* 539–549.

Rose, S. A., Gottfried, A. W., & Bridger, W. H. (1981). Cross-modal transfer in 6-month-old infants. *Developmental Psychology, 17,* 661–669.

Rosen, K. S., & Burke, P. B. (1999). Multiple attachment relationships within families: Mothers and fathers with two young children. *Developmental Psychology, 35,* 436–444.

Rosenberg, K. R., & Trevathen, W. R. (2001, November). The evolution of human birth. *Scientific American, 285,* 72–77.

Rosengren, K. S., Gelman, S. A., Kalish, C. W., & McCormick, M. (1991). As time goes by: Children's early understanding of growth in animals. *Child Development, 62,* 1302–1320.

Rosenkoetter, L. I. (1973). Resistance to temptation: Inhibitory and disinhibitory effects of models. *Developmental Psychology, 8,* 80–84.

Rosenthal, R., & Jacobson, L. (1968). *Pygmalion in the classroom: Teacher expectation and pupils' intellectual development.* New York: Holt, Rinehart & Winston.

Ross, G. S. (1980). Categorization in infancy. *Developmental Psychology, 16,* 391–396.

Roth, J., & Brooks-Gunn, J. (2000). What do adolescents need for healthy development? Implications for youth policy. *Social Policy Report, 14,* 3–19.

Rothbart, M. K. (1986). Longitudinal home observations of infant temperament. *Developmental Psychology, 22,* 356–365.

Rothbart, M. K., Ahadi, S. A., & Evans, D. E. (2000). Temperament and personality: Origins and outcomes. *Journal of Personality and Social Psychology, 78,* 122–135.

Rothbart, M. K., Ahadi, S. A., & Hershey, K. L. (1994). Temperament and social behavior in childhood. *Merrill-Palmer Quarterly, 40,* 21–39.

Rothbart, M. K., & Bates, J. E. (2006). Temperament. In W. Damon & R. M. Lerner (Editors-in-Chief) & N. Eisenberg (Vol. Ed.), *Handbook of child psychology: Vol. 3. Social, emotional, and personality development* (6th ed., pp. 99–166). Hoboken, NJ: Wiley.

Rothbart, M. K., Derryberry, D., & Posner, M. I. (1994). A psychobiological approach to the development of temperament. In J. E. Bates & T. D. Wachs (Eds.), *Temperament: Individual differences at the interface of biology and behavior* (pp. 83–116). Washington, DC: American Psychological Association.

Rothbaum, F., Weisz, J., Pott, M., Miyake, K., & Morelli, G. (2000). Attachment and culture: Security in the United States and Japan. *American Psychologist, 55,* 1093–1104.

Rothberg, A. D., & Lits, B. (1991). Psychosocial support for maternal stress during pregnancy: Effect on birth weight. *American Journal of Obstetrics and Gynecology, 165,* 403–407.

Rouse, B., Matalon, R., Koch, R., Azen, C., Levy, H., Hanley, W., et al. (2000). Maternal phenylketonuria syndrome: Congenital heart defects, microcephaly, and developmental outcomes. *Journal of Pediatrics, 136,* 57–61.

Rousseau, J. J. (1895). *Émile or treatise on education* (W. H. Payne, Trans.). New York: Appleton. (Original work published 1762)

Rovee-Collier, C. (1999). The development of infant memory. *Current Directions in Psychological Science, 8,* 80–85.

Rovee-Collier, C. K. (1987). Learning and memory in infancy. In J. D. Osofsky (Ed.), *Handbook of infant development* (2nd ed., pp. 98–148). New York: Wiley.

Rovee-Collier, C. K., & Hayne, H. (1987). Reactivation of infant memory: Implications for cognitive development. In H. W. Reese (Ed.), *Advances in child development and behavior* (Vol. 20, pp. 185–238). San Diego, CA: Academic Press.

Rovee-Collier, C., Schechter, A., Shyi, G. C. W., & Shields, P. (1992). Perceptual identification of contextual attributes and infant memory retrieval. *Developmental Psychology, 28,* 307–318.

Rovee-Collier, C. K., & Shyi, G. (1992). A functional and cognitive analysis of infant long-term retention. In M. L. Howe, C. J. Brainerd, & V. F. Reyna (Eds.), *Development of long-term retention* (pp. 3–55). New York: Springer-Verlag.

Rowe, D. C., Jacobson, K. C., & Van den Oord, E. J. C. G. (1999). Genetic and environmental influences on vocabulary IQ: Parental education level as moderator. *Child Development, 70,* 1151–1162.

Rozin, P. (1990). Development in the food domain. *Developmental Psychology, 26,* 555–562.

Rubin, K. H. (1993). The Waterloo Longitudinal Project: Correlates and consequences of social withdrawal from childhood to adolescence. In K. H. Rubin & J. B. Asendorpf (Eds.), *Social withdrawal, inhibition, and shyness in childhood* (pp. 291–314). Hillsdale, NJ: Erlbaum.

Rubin, K. H., & Asendorpf, J. B. (1993). Social withdrawal, inhibition, and shyness in childhood: Conceptual and definitional issues. In K. H. Rubin & J. B. Asendorpf (Eds.), *Social withdrawal, inhibition, and shyness in childhood* (pp. 3–17). Hillsdale, NJ: Erlbaum.

Rubin, K. H., Bukowski, W., & Parker, J. G. (1998). Peer interactions, relationships, and groups. In W. Damon (Series Ed.) & N. Eisenberg (Vol. Ed.), *Handbook of child psychology. Vol. 3. Social, emotional, and personality development* (5th ed., pp. 619–700). New York: Wiley.

Rubin, K. H., Burgess, K. B., Dwyer, K. M., & Hastings, P. D. (2003). Predicting preschoolers' externalizing behaviors from toddler temperament, conflict, and maternal negativity. *Developmental Psychology, 39,* 164–176.

Rubin, K. H., Fein, G. G., & Vandenberg, B. (1983). Play. In E. M. Hetherington (Ed.), *Handbook of child psychology: Vol. IV. Socialization, personality, and social development* (4th ed., pp. 693–744). New York: Wiley.

Rubin, K. H., Hymel, S., & Mills, R. S. L. (1989). Sociability and social withdrawal in childhood: Stability and outcomes. *Journal of Personality, 57,* 238–255.

Rubin, K. H., & Krasnor, L. R. (1986). Social-cognitive and social behavioral perspectives on problem-solving. In M. Perlmutter (Ed.), *The Minnesota symposia on child psychology: Vol. 18. Cognitive perspectives on children's social and behavioral development.* Hillsdale, NJ: Erlbaum.

Rubin, K. H., Lynch, D., Coplan, R., Rose-Krasnor, L., & Booth, C. L. (1994). "Birds of a feather…": Behavioral concordances and preferential personal attraction in children. *Child Development, 65,* 1778–1785.

Rubin, K. H., Maioni, T. L., & Hornung, M. (1976). Free play behaviors in middle- and lower-class preschoolers: Parten and Piaget revisited. *Child Development, 47,* 414–419.

Ruble, D. N. (1983). The development of social-comparison processes and their role in achievement-related self-socialization. In E. T. Higgins, D. Ruble, & W. W. Hartup (Eds.), *Social cognition and social development: A sociocultural perspective.* Cambridge, UK: Cambridge University Press.

Ruble, D. N. (1987). The acquisition of self-knowledge: A self-socialization perspective. In N. Eisenberg (Ed.), *Contemporary topics in developmental psychology.* New York: Wiley.

Ruble, D. N., Boggiano, A. K., Feldman, N. S., & Loebl, J. H. (1980). Developmental analysis of the role of social comparison in self-evaluation. *Developmental Psychology, 16,* 105–115.

Ruble, D. N., & Brooks-Gunn, J. (1982). The experience of menarche. *Child Development, 53,* 1557–1566.

Ruble, D. N., Eisenberg, R., & Higgins, E. T. (1994). Developmental changes in achievement evaluation: Motivational implications of self-other differences. *Child Development, 65,* 1095–1110.

Ruble, D. N., & Flett, G. L. (1988). Conflicting goals in self-evaluative information seeking: Developmental and ability level analyses. *Child Development, 59,* 97–106.

Ruble, D. N., Martin, C. L., & Berenbaum, S. A. (2006). Gender development. In W. Damon & R. M. Lerner (Editors-in-Chief) & N. Eisenberg (Vol. Ed.), *Handbook of child psychology: Vol. 3. Social, emotional, and personality development* (6th ed., pp. 858–932). Hoboken, NJ: Wiley.

Rudolph, K. D., Caldwell, M., & Conley, C. S. (2005). Need for approval and children's well-being. *Child Development, 76,* 309–323.

Rudolph, K. D., & Hammen, C. (1999). Age and gender as determinants of stress exposure, generation, and reactions in youngsters: A transactional perspective. *Child Development, 70,* 660–677.

Rudolph, K. D., Hammen, C., & Burge, D. (1995). Cognitive representations of self, family, and peers in school-age children: Links with social competence and sociometric status. *Child Development, 66,* 1385–1402.

Rudolph, K. D., Lambert, S. F., Clark, A. G., & Kurlakowsky, K. D. (2001). Negotiating the transition to middle school: The role of self-regulatory processes. *Child Development, 72,* 929–946.

Ruff, H. A., & Kohler, C. J. (1978). Tactual visual transfer in 6-month-old infants. *Infant Behavior and Development, 1,* 259–264.

Ruff, H. A., & Rothbart, M. K. (1996). *Attention and early development: Themes and variations.* New York: Oxford University Press.

Ruffman, T., Slade, L., & Crowe, E. (2002). The relation between children's and mothers' mental state language and thoery-of-mind understanding. *Child Development, 73,* 734–751.

Rumbaugh, D. M., Gill, T. V., & von Glasersfeld, E. C. (1973). Reading and sentence completion by a chimpanzee (*Pan*). *Science, 182,* 731–733.

Runyan, D. K., Hunter, W. M., Socolar, R. R. S., Amaya-Jackson, L., English, D., Landsverk, J., et al. (1998). Children who prosper in unfavorable environments: The relationship to social capital. *Pediatrics, 101,* 12–18.

Rutter, M. (1983). School effects on pupil progress: Research findings and policy implications. *Child Development, 54,* 1–29.

Rutter, M. (1986). Meyerian psychobiology, personality development, and the role of life experiences. *American Journal of Psychiatry, 143,* 1077–1087.

Rutter, M. (1990). Psychosocial resilience and protective mechanisms. In J. Rolf, A. S. Masten, D. Cicchetti, K. H. Neuchterlein, & S. Weintraub (Eds.), *Risk and protective factors in the development of psychopathology* (pp. 79–101). New York: Cambridge University Press.

Rutter, M. (1991). Age changes in depressive disorders: Some developmental considerations. In J. Garber & K. A. Dodge (Eds.), *The development of emotion regulation and dysregulation* (pp. 273–300). Cambridge, UK: Cambridge University Press.

Rutter, M. (2002). Nature, nurture, and development: From evangelism through science toward policy and practice. *Child Development, 73,* 1–21.

Rutter, M. (2003). Commentary: Causal processes leading to antisocial behavior. *Developmental Psychology, 39,* 372–378.

Rutter, M., & Garmezy, N. (1983). Developmental psychopathology. In E. M. Hetherington (Ed.), *Handbook of child psychology: Vol. IV. Socialization, personality, and social development* (4th ed., pp. 775–911). New York: Wiley.

Rutter, M., & Madge, N. (1976). *Cycles of disadvantage.* London: Heinemmann.

Rutter, M., & Silberg, J. (2002). Gene-environment interplay in relation to emotional and behavioral disturbance. *Annual Review of Psychology, 53,* 463–490.

Rutter, M., Silberg, J., O'Connor, T., & Simonoff, E. (1999a). Genetics and child psychiatry: I. Advances in quantitative and molecular genetics. *Journal of Child Psychology and Psychiatry, 40,* 3–18.

Rutter, M., Silberg, J., O'Connor, T., & Simonoff, E. (1999b). Genetics and child psychiatry: II. Empirical research findings. *Journal of Child Psychology and Psychiatry, 40,* 19–55.

Ryan, R. M., & Grolnick, W. S. (1986). Origins and pawns in the classroom: Self-report and projective assessments of individual differences in children's perceptions. *Journal of Personality and Social Psychology, 50,* 550–558.

Saarni, C. (1998). Issues of cultural meaningfulness in emotional development. *Developmental Psychology, 34,* 647–652.

Saarni, C. (1999). *The development of emotional competence.* New York: Guilford.

Saarni, C., Campos, J. J., Camras, L. A., & Witherington, D. (2006). Emotional development: Action, communication, and understanding. In W. Damon & R. M. Lerner (Editors-in-Chief) & N. Eisenberg (Vol. Ed.), *Handbook of child psychology: Vol. 3. Social, emotional, and personality development* (6th ed., pp. 226–299). Hoboken, NJ: Wiley.

Saarni, C., Mumme, D. L., & Campos, J. L. (1998). Emotional development: Action, communication, and understanding. In W. Damon (Series Ed.) & N. Eisenberg (Vol. Ed.), *Handbook of child psychology: Vol. 3, Social, emotional, and personality development* (5th ed., pp. 237–309). New York: Wiley.

Sachs, S. (2001, August 15). Clinic's pitch to Indian emigres: It's a boy. *New York Times,* pp. A1, B6.

Sadker, M. & Sadker, D. (1994). *Failing at fairness: How America's schools cheat girls.* New York: Charles Scribner's Sons.

Sadler, T. M. (2004). *Langman's medical embryology* (9th ed.). Philadelphia: Lippincott Williams & Wilkins.

Saffran, J. R. (2001). Words in a sea of sounds: The output of infant statistical learning. *Cognition, 81,* 149–169.

Saffran, J. R., Aslin, R. N., & Newport, E. (1996). Statistical learning by 8-month-olds. *Science, 274,* 1926–1928.

Saffran, J. R., & Griepentrog, G. J. (2001). Absolute pitch in infant auditory learning: Evidence for developmental reorganization. *Developmental Psychology, 37,* 74–85.

Saffran, J. R., Loman, M. M., & Robertson, R. R. W. (2000). Infant memory for musical experiences. *Cognition, 77,* B15–B23.

Saffran, J. R., Werker, J. F., & Werner, L. A. (2006). The infant's auditory world: Hearing, speech, and the beginnings of language. In W. Damon & R. M. Lerner (Editors-in-Chief) & D. M. Kuhn & R. S. Siegler (Vol. Eds.), *Handbook of child psychology: Vol. 2. Cognition, perception, and language* (6th ed., pp. 58–108). Hoboken, NJ: Wiley.

Sagi, A., Lamb, M. E., Lewkowicz, K. S., Shoham, R., Dvir, R., & Estes, D. (1985). Security of infant-mother, -father, and -metapelet attachments among kibbutz-reared Israeli children. In I. Bretherton & E. Waters (Eds.), *Growing points of attachment theory and research. Monographs of the Society for Research in Child Development, 50*(1–2, Serial No. 209).

Sagi, A., Van IJzendoorn, M. H., Aviezer, O., Donnell, F., & Mayseless, O. (1994). Sleeping out of home in a kibbutz communal arrangement: It makes a difference for mother-child attachment. *Child Development, 65,* 991–1004.

Saigal, S., Hoult, L. A., Streiner, D. L., Stoskopf, B. L., & Rosenbaum, P. L. (2000). School difficulties at adolescence in a regional cohort of children who were extremely low birth weight. *Pediatrics, 105,* 325–331.

Sakala, C. (1993). Midwifery care and out-of-hospital birth settings: How do they reduce unnecessary cesarean section births? *Social Science and Medicine, 37,* 1233–1250.

Salapatek, P. (1975). Pattern perception in early infancy. In L. B. Cohen & P. Salapatek (Eds.), *Infant perception: From sensation to cognition* (Vol. 1). New York: Academic Press.

Salzinger, S., Feldman, R. S., Hammer, M., & Rosario, M. (1993). The effects of physical abuse on children's social relationships. *Child Development, 64,* 169–187.

Samarapungavan, A. (1992). Children's judgments in theory choice tasks: Scientific rationality in childhood. *Cognition, 45,* 1–32.

Sameroff, A. J. (1972). Learning and adaptation in infancy: A comparison of models. In H. W. Reese (Ed.), *Advances in child development and behavior* (Vol. 7). New York: Academic Press.

Sameroff, A. J. (1994). Developmental systems and family functioning. In R. D. Parke & S. G. Kellam (Eds.), *Exploring family relationships with other social contexts* (pp. 199–214). Hillsdale, NJ: Erlbaum.

Sameroff, A. J. (2005). The science of infancy: Academic, social, and political agendas. *Infancy, 7,* 219–242.

Sameroff, A. J., & Chandler, P. J. (1975). Reproductive risk and the continuum of caretaking casualty. In F. D. Horowitz (Ed.), *Review of child development research* (Vol. 4, pp. 187–244). Chicago: University of Chicago Press.

Sampson, P. D., Streissguth, A. P., Bookstein, F. L., Little, R. E., Clarren, S. K., Dehaene, P., et al. (1997). The incidence of fetal alcohol syndrome and the prevalence of alcohol-related neurodevelopmental disorder. *Teratology, 56,* 317–326.

Sampson, R. J., Raudenbush, S. W., & Earls, F. (1997). Neighborhoods and violent crime: A multilevel study of collective efficacy. *Science, 277,* 918–924.

Samuels, M., & Samuels, N. (1996). *The new well pregnancy book.* New York: Simon & Schuster.

Samuelson, L. K., & Smith, L. B. (1998). Memory and attention make smart word learning: An alternative account of Akhtar, Carpenter, and Tomasello. *Child Development, 69,* 94–104.

Samuelson, L. K., & Smith, L. B. (2000). Children's attention to rigid and deformable shape in naming and non-naming tasks. *Child Development, 71,* 1555–1570.

Sandberg, D. E., Brook, A. E., & Campos, S. P. (1994). Short stature: A psychosocial burden requiring growth hormone therapy? *Pediatrics, 94,* 832–840.

Sandberg, D. E., Meyer-Bahlburg, H. F., Ehrhardt, A. A., & Yager, T. J. (1993). The prevalence of gender-atypical behavior in elementary school. *Journal of the American Academy of Child and Adolescent Psychiatry, 32,* 306–314.

Sandberg, E. H., & Huttenlocher, J. (2001). Advanced spatial skills and advance planning: Components of 6-year-olds' navigational map use. *Journal of Cognition and Development, 2,* 51–70.

Sanders, C. E., Field, T. M., Diego, M., & Kaplan, M. (2000). The relationship of Internet use to depression and social isolation among adolescents. *Adolescence, 35,* 237–242.

Santrock, J. W., & Sitterle, K. A. (1987). Parent-child relationships in stepmother families. In K. Pasley & M. Ihinger-Tallman (Eds.), *Remarriage and stepparenting: Current research and theory.* New York: Guilford Press.

Saudino, K. J. (1997). Moving beyond the heritability question: New directions in behavioral genetic studies of personality. *Current Directions in Psychological Science, 6,* 86–90.

Savage, D. D., Becher, M., de la Torre, A. J., & Sutherland, R. J. (2002). Dose-dependent effects of prenatal ethanol exposure on synaptic plasticity and learning in mature offspring. *Alcoholism: Clinical and Experimental Research, 26,* 1752–1758.

Savage-Rumbaugh, E. S., Murphy, J., Sevcik, R. A., Brakke, K. E., Williams, S. L., & Rumbaugh, D. M. (1993). Language comprehension in ape and child. *Monographs of the Society for Research in Child Development, 58*(3–4, Serial No. 233).

Sawin, D. B., & Parke, R. D. (1979). The effects of interagent inconsistent discipline on children's aggressive behavior. *Journal of Experimental Child Psychology, 28,* 525–538.

Saxe, G. B., Guberman, S. R., & Gearhart, M. (1987). Social processes in early number development. *Monographs of the Society for Research in Child Development, 52* (2, Serial No. 216).

Saxton, M. (1997). The contrast theory of negative input. *Journal of Child Language, 24,* 139–161.

Scaramella, L. V., Conger, R. D., & Simons, R. L. (1999). Parental protective influences and gender-specific increases in adolescent internalizing and externalizing problems. *Journal of Research on Adolescence, 9,* 111–141.

Scaramella, L. V., Conger, R. D., Spoth, R., & Simons, R. L. (2002). Evaluation of a social contextual model of delinquency: A cross-study replication. *Child Development, 73,* 175–195.

Scarborough, H. S., & Dobrich, W. (1993). On the efficacy of reading to preschoolers. *Developmental Review, 14,* 245–302.

Scarr, S. (1992). Developmental theories for the 1990s: Development and individual differences. *Child Development, 63,* 1–19.

Scarr, S. (1993). Biological and cultural diversity: The legacy of Darwin for development. *Child Development, 64,* 1333–1353.

Scarr, S., & McCartney, K. (1983). How people make their own environments: A theory of genotype environment effects. *Child Development, 54,* 424–435.

Scarr, S., & Weinberg, R. A. (1976). IQ test performance of black children adopted by white families. *American Psychologist, 31,* 726–739.

Scarr, S., & Weinberg, R. A. (1977). Intellectual similarities within families of both adopted and biological children. *Intelligence, 1,* 170–191.

Scarr, S., & Weinberg, R. A. (1978). The influence of "family background" on intellectual attainment. *American Sociological Review, 43,* 674–692.

Scarr, S., & Weinberg, R. A. (1983). The Minnesota adoption studies: Genetic differences and malleability. *Child Development, 54,* 260–267.

Schachar, R., Mota, V., Logan, G. D., Tannock, R., & Klim, P. (2000). Confirmation of an inhibitory control deficit in attention-deficit/hyparactivity disorder. *Journal of Abnormal Child Psychology, 28,* 227–235.

Schachter, F. F. (1982). Sibling deidentification and split-parent identification: A family tetrad. In M. E. Lamb & B. Sutton-Smith (Eds.), *Sibling relationships: Their nature and significance across the life-span.* Hillsdale, NJ: Erlbaum.

Schaffer, H. R., & Emerson, P. E. (1964). The development of social attachments in infancy. *Monographs of the Society for Research in Child Development, 29*(3, Serial No. 94).

Schauble, L. (1996). The development of scientific reasoning in knowledge-rich contexts. *Developmental Psychology, 32,* 102–119.

Scheper-Hughes, N. (1992). *Death without weeping: The violence of everyday life in Brazil.* Berkeley: University of California Press.

Schieffelin, B. B., & Ochs, E. (1983). A cultural perspective on the transition from prelinguistic to linguistic communication. In R. M. Golinkoff (Ed.), *The transition from prelinguistic to linguistic communication.* Hillsdale, NJ: Erlbaum.

Schlegel, A., & Barry, H. III. (1991). *Adolescence: An anthropological inquiry.* New York: Free Press.

Schlinger, H.D., Jr. (1992). Theory in behavior analysis: An application to child development. *American Psychologist, 47,* 1396–1410.

Schmitt, K. L., Anderson, D. R., & Collins, P. A. (1999). Form and content: Looking at visual features of television. *Developmental Psychology, 35,* 1156–1167.

Schmuckler, M. A., & Fairhall, J. L. (2001). Visual-proprioceptive intermodal perception using point light displays. *Child Development, 72,* 949-962.

Schneider, B. H., Atkinson, L., & Tardif, C. (2001). Child-parent attachment and children's peer relations: A quantitative review. *Developmental Psychology, 37,* 86–100.

Schneider, W. (2000). Research on memory development: Historical trends and current themes. *International Journal of Behavioral Development, 24,* 407–420.

Schneider, W., & Lockl, K. (2002). The development of metacognitive knowledge in children and adolescents. In B. L. Schwartz & T. J. Perfect (Eds.), *Applied metacognition* (pp. 224–260). Cambridge, UK: Cambridge University Press.

Schneider-Rosen, K., Braunwald, K., Carlson, V., & Cicchetti, D. (1985). Current perspectives on attachment theory: Illustrations from the study of maltreated infants. In I. Bretherton & E. Waters (Eds.), *Growing points of attachment theory and research. Monographs of the Society for Research in Child Development, 50*(1–2, Serial No. 209).

Scholmerich, A., Fracasso, M. P., Lamb, M. E., & Broberg, A. (1995). Interactional harmony at 7- and 10-months-of-age predicts security of attachment as measured by Q-sort ratings. *Social Development, 4,* 62–74.

Schore, A. N. (1994). *Affect regulation and the origin of the self: The neurobiology of emotional development.* Hillsdale, NJ: Erlbaum.

Schore, A. N. (1996). The experience-dependent maturation of a regulatory system in the orbital prefrontal cortex and the origin of developmental psychopathology. *Development and Psychopathology, 8,* 59–87.

Schreck, R., & Silverman, N. (2002). Fetal loss. In D. L. Rimoin, J. M. Connor, R. E. Pyeritz, & B. R. Korf (Eds.), *Emery and Rimoin's principles and practice of medical genetics* (4th ed., Vol. 1, pp. 982–997). London: Churchill Livingston.

Schulenberg, J., Asp, C. E., & Petersen, A. (1984). School from the young adolescent's perspective: A descriptive report. *Journal of Early Adolescence, 4,* 107–130.

Schulting, A. B., Malone, P. S., & Dodge, K. A. (2005). The effect of school-based kindergarten transition policies and practices on child academic outcomes. *Developmental Psychology, 41,* 860–871.

Schwartz, D., Chang, L., & Farver, J. M. (2001). Correlates of victimization in Chinese children's peer groups. *Developmental Psychology, 37,* 520–532.

Schwartz, D., Dodge, K. A., & Coie, J. D. (1993). The emergence of chronic peer victimization in boys' play groups. *Child Development, 64,* 1755–1772.

Schwartz, D., Dodge, K. A., Pettit, G. S., Bates, J. E., & Conduct Problems Prevention Research Group. (2000). Friendship as a moderating factor in the pathway between early harsh home environment and later victimization in the peer group. *Developmental Psychology, 36,* 646–662.

Scott, K. D., Berkowitz, G., & Klaus, M. (1999). A comparison of intermittent and continuous support during labor: A meta-analysis. *American Journal of Obstetrics and Gynecology, 180,* 1054–1059.

Scoville, R. (1983). Development of the intention to communicate: The eye of the beholder. In L. Feagans, C. Garvey, & R. Golinkoff (Eds.), *The origins and growth of communication.* Norwood, NJ: Ablex.

Scriver, C. R., Beaudet, A. L., Sly, W. S., & Valle, D. (2001). *The metabolic and molecular bases of inherited disease* (8th ed., Vol. 1). New York: McGraw-Hill.

Sebanc, A. M. (2003). The friendship features of preschool children: Links with prosocial behavior and aggression. *Social Development, 12,* 249–268.

Secker-Walker, R. H., Vacek, P. M., Flynn, B. S., & Mead, P. B. (1997). Smoking in pregnancy, exhaled carbon monoxide, and birth weight. *Obstetrics and Gynecology, 89,* 648–653.

Segall, M. H., Campbell, D. T., & Herskovits, M. J. (1966). *The influence of culture on perception.* New York: Bobbs-Merrill.

Seidman, E., Allen, L., Aber, J. L., Mitchell, C., & Feinman, J. (1994). The impact of school transitions in early adolescence on the self-system and perceived social context of poor urban youth. *Child Development, 65,* 507–522.

Seitz, V., & Apfel, N. H. (1994). Effects of a school for pregnant students on the incidence of low-birthweight deliveries. *Child Development, 65,* 666–676.

Selman, R. L. (1980). *The growth of interpersonal understanding: Developmental and clinical analysis.* New York: Academic Press.

Selzer, J. A. (1991). Relationships between fathers and children who live apart: The father's role after separation. *Journal of Marriage and the Family, 53,* 79–101.

Senghas, A., & Coppola, M. (2001). Children creating language: How Nicaraguan Sign Language acquired a spatial grammar. *Psychological Science, 12,* 323–328.

Serbin, L. A., Connor, J. M., & Iler, I. (1979). Sex-stereotyped and nonstereotyped introductions of new toys in the preschool classroom: An observational study of teacher behavior and its effects. *Psychology of Women Quarterly, 4,* 261–265.

Serbin, L. A., O'Leary, K. D., Kent, R. N., & Tonick, I. J. (1973). A comparison of teacher response to the preacademic and problem behavior of boys and girls. *Child Development, 44,* 796–804.

Serbin, L. A., Poulin-Dubois, D., Colburne, K. A., Sen, M. G., & Eichstedt, J. A. (2001). Gender stereotyping in infancy: Visual preferences for and knowledge of gender-stereotyped toys in the second year. *International Journal of Behavioral Development, 25,* 7–15.

Serbin, L. A., Powlishta, K. K., & Gulko, J. (1993). The development of sex typing in middle childhood. *Monographs of the Society for Research in Child Development, 58* (No. 2, Serial No. 232).

Serbin, L. A., Tonick, I. J., & Sternglanz, S. H. (1977). Shaping cooperative cross-sex play. *Child Development, 48,* 924–929.

Shachar, H., & Sharan, S. (1994). Talking, relating, and achieving: Effects of cooperative learning and whole-class instruction. *Cognition and Instruction, 12,* 313–353.

Shah, N. R., & Bracken, M. B. (2000). A systematic review and meta-analysis of prospective studies on the association between maternal cigarette smoking and preterm delivery. *American Journal of Obstetrics and Gynecology, 182,* 465–472.

Shahar, S. (1990). *Childhood in the Middle Ages.* London: Routledge.

Shannon, J. D., Tamis-LeMonda, C. S., & Margolin, A. (2005). Father involvement in infancy: Influences of past and current relationships. *Infancy, 8,* 21–41.

Shantz, C. (1983). Social cognition. In J. H. Flavell & E. M. Markman (Eds.), *Handbook of child psychology: Vol. III. Cognitive development* (4th ed., pp. 495–555). New York: Wiley.

Sharma, A. R., McGue, M. K., & Benson, P. L. (1998). The psychological adjustment of United States adopted adolescents and their nonadopted siblings. *Child Development, 69,* 791–802.

Sharon, T. (2005). Made to symbolize: Intentionality and children's early understanding of symbols. *Journal of Cognition and Development, 6,* 163–178.

Sharp, D., Cole, M., & Lave, C. (1979). Education and cognitive development: The evidence from experimental research. *Monographs of the Society for Research in Child Development, 44*(1–2, Serial No. 178).

Shatz, M., & Gelman, R. (1973). The development of communication skills: Modification in the speech of young children as a function of listener. *Monographs of the Society for Research in Child Development, 38*(5, Serial No. 152).

Shaw, E., & Darling, J. (1985). *Strategies of being female.* Brighton, UK: Harvester Press.

Shepard, L. A., & Smith, M. L. (1986). Synthesis of research on school readiness and kindergarten retention. *Educational Leadership, 44,* 78–86.

Sherif, M., Harvey, O. J., White, B. J., Hood, W. R., & Sherif, C. W. (1961). *Inter-group conflict and cooperation: The Robber's Cave experiment.* Norman: University of Oklahoma Press.

Shinskey, J. L., & Munakata, Y. (2001). Detecting transparent barriers: Clear evidence against the means-end deficit account of search failures. *Infancy, 2,* 395–404.

Shoda, Y., Mischel, W., & Peake, P. K. (1990). Predicting adolescent cognitive and self-regulatory competencies from preschool delay of gratification: Identifying diagnostic conditions. *Developmental Psychology, 26,* 978–986.

Shonk, S. M., & Cicchetti, D. (2001). Maltreatment, competency deficits, and risk for academic and behavioral maladjustment. *Developmental Psychology, 37,* 3–17.

Shore, R. (1997). *Rethinking the brain: New insights into early development.* New York: Families and Work Institute.

Shostak, M. (1981). *Nisa: The life and words of a !Kung woman.* Cambridge, MA: Harvard University Press.

Shrum, W., & Cheek, N. H. (1987). Social structure during the school years: Onset of the degrouping process. *American Sociological Review, 52,* 218–223.

Shwalb, B. J., Shwalb, D. W., & Shoji, J. (1994). Structure and dimensions of maternal perceptions of Japanese infant temperament. *Developmental Psychology, 30,* 131–141.

Shwe, H. I., & Markman, E. M. (1997). Young children's appreciation of the mental impact of their communicative signals. *Developmental Psychology, 33,* 630–636.

Shweder, R., Goodnow, J., Hatano, G., LeVine, R., Markus, H., & Miller, P. (2006). The cultural psychology of development: One mind, many mentalities. In W. Damon & R. M. Lerner (Editors-in-Chief) & R. M. Lerner (Vol. Ed.), Handbook of child psychology: Vol. 1. Theoretical models of human development (6th ed., pp. 716–792). Hoboken, NJ: Wiley.

Shweder, R. A., Mahapatra, M., & Miller, J. G. (1987). Culture and moral development. In J. Kagan & S. Lamb (Eds.), *The emergence of morality in young children.* Chicago: University of Chicago Press.

Siegal, M. (1988). Children's knowledge of contagion and contamination as causes of illness. *Child Development, 59,* 1353–1359.

Siegel, L. S. (1993). Phonological processing deficits as the basis of a reading disability. *Developmental Review, 13,* 246–257.

Siegel, L. S. (1998). Phonological processing deficits and reading disabilities. In J. L. Metsala & L. C. Ehri (Eds.), *Word recognition in beginning literacy* (pp. 191–160). Mahwah, NJ: Erlbaum.

Siegler, R. S. (1989). Mechanisms of cognitive development. In M. R. Rosenzweig & L. W. Porter (Eds.), *Annual Review of Psychology, 40,* 353–379.

Siegler, R. S. (1994). Cognitive variability: A key to understanding cognitive development. *Current Directions in Psychological Science, 3,* 1–5.

Siegler, R. S. (1996). *Emerging minds: The process of change in children's thinking.* New York: Oxford University Press.

Siegler, R. S. (1997). Concepts and methods for studying cognitive change. In E. Amsel & K. A. Renninger (Eds.), *Change and development: Issues of theory, method, and application* (pp. 77–97). Mahwah, NJ: Erlbaum.

Siegler, R. S. (1998). *Children's thinking* (3rd ed.). Upper Saddle River, NJ: Prentice-Hall.

Siegler, R. S., & Crowley, K. (1991). The microgenetic method: A direct means for studying cognitive development. *American Psychologist, 46,* 606–620.

Siegler, R. S., & Ellis, S. (1996). Piaget on childhood. *Psychological Science, 7,* 211–215.

Siegler, R. S., & Jenkins, E. (1989). *How children discover new strategies.* Hillsdale, NJ: Erlbaum.

Siegler, R. S., & Richards, D. D. (1982). The development of intelligence. In R. J. Sternberg (Ed.), *Handbook of human intelligence.* Cambridge, UK: Cambridge University Press.

Siegler, R. S., & Robinson, M. (1982). The development of numerical understandings. In H. W. Reese & L. P. Lipsitt (Eds.), *Advances in child development and behavior* (Vol. 16). New York: Academic Press.

Siegler, R. S., & Shrager, J. (1984). Strategy choices in addition and subtraction: How do children know what to do? In C. Sophian (Ed.), *Origins of cognitive skills.* Hillsdale, NJ: Erlbaum.

Siegler, R. S., & Stern, E. (1998). Conscious and unconscious strategy discoveries: A microgenetic analysis. *Journal of Experimental Psychology: General, 127,* 377–397.

Signorella, M. L. (1987). Gender schemata: Individual differences and context effects. In L. S. Liben & M. L. Signorella (Eds.), *New directions for child development: No. 38. Children's gender schemata.* San Francisco: Jossey-Bass.

Signorielli, N., & Bacue, A. (1999). Recognition and respect: A content analysis of prime-time television characters across three decades. *Sex Roles, 40,* 527–544.

Silberstein, L., Gardner, H., Phelps, E., & Winner, E. (1982). Autumn leaves and old photographs: The development of metaphor preferences. *Journal of Experimental Child Psychology, 34,* 135–150.

Silk, J. S., Steinberg, L., & Morris, A. S. (2003). Adolescents' emotion regulation in daily life: Links to depressive symptoms and problem behavior. *Child Development, 74,* 1869–1880.

Silver, L. M. (1998, September 21). A quandary that isn't: Picking a baby's sex won't lead to disaster. *Time,* p. 83.

Simcock, G., & Hayne, H. (2002). Breaking the barrier? Children fail to translate their preverbal memories into language. *Psychological Science, 13,* 225–231.

Simmons, R. G., & Blyth, D. A. (1987). *Moving into adolescence: The impact of pubertal change and school context.* Hawthorne, NY: Aldine de Gruyter.

Simmons, R. G., Blyth, D. A., & McKinney, K. L. (1983). The social and psychological effects of puberty on white females. In J. Brooks-Gunn & A. C. Petersen (Eds.), *Girls at puberty.* New York: Plenum Press.

Simmons, R. G., Blyth, D. A., Van Cleave, E. F., & Bush, D. M. (1979). Entry into early adolescence: The impact of school structure, puberty, and early dating on self-esteem. *American Sociological Review, 44,* 948–967.

Simmons, R. G., Burgeson, R., Carlton-Ford, S., & Blyth, D. A. (1987). The impact of cumulative change in early adolescence. *Child Development, 58,* 1220–1234.

Simner, M. L. (1971). Newborn's response to the cry of another infant. *Developmental Psychology, 5,* 136–150.

Simon, T. J., Hespos, S. J., & Rochat, P. (1995). Do infants understand simple arithmetic? A replication of Wynn (1992). *Cognitive Development, 10,* 253–269.

Simons, R., Chao, W., Conger, R., & Elder, G. H. (2001). Quality of parenting as a mediator of the effect of childhood defiance on adolescent friendship choices and delinquency. *Journal of Marriage and Family, 63,* 63–79.

Sinclair, D. (1985). *Human growth after birth* (4th ed.). New York: Oxford University Press.

Singer, J. D., Fuller, B., Keiley, M. K., & Wolf, A. (1998). Early child-care selection: Variation by geographic location, maternal characteristics, and family structure. *Developmental Psychology, 34,* 1129–1144.

Singer, L. M., Brodzinsky, D. M., Ramsay, D., Steir, M., & Waters, E. (1985). Mother-infant attachment in adoptive families. *Child Development, 56,* 1543–1551.

Singer, L. T., Arendt, R., Minnes, S., Salvator, A., Siegel, A. C., & Lewis, B. A. (2001). Developing language skills of cocaine-exposed infants. *Pediatrics, 107,* 1057–1064.

Singer, L. T., Salvator, A., Guo, S., Collin, M., Lilien, L., & Baley, J. (1999). Maternal psychological distress and parenting after the birth of a very low-birth-weight infant. *Journal of the American Medical Association, 281,* 799–805.

Singh, L. Morgan, J. L., & Best, C. T. (2002). Infants listening preferences. Baby talk or happy talk? *Infancy, 3,* 365–394.

Sininger, Y. S., Doyle, K. J., & Moore, J. K. (1999). The case for early identification of hearing loss in children: Auditory system development, experimental auditory deprivation, and development of speech and hearing. *Pediatric Clinics of North America, 46,* 1–14.

Siqueland, E. R., & Lipsitt, L. P. (1966). Conditioned head turning in human newborns. *Journal of Experimental Child Psychology, 4,* 356–376.

Sireteanu, R. (1999). Switching on the infant brain. *Science, 286,* 59–61.

Skinner, B. F. (1953). *Science and human behavior.* New York: Macmillan.

Skinner, B. F. (1971). *Beyond freedom and dignity.* New York: Knopf.

Skinner, B. F. (1974). *About behaviorism.* New York: Knopf.

Skinner, E. A., & Belmont, M. J. (1993). Motivation in the classroom: Reciprocal effects of teacher behavior and student engagement across the school year. *Journal of Educational Psychology, 85,* 571–581.

Skinner, E. A., Zimmer-Gembeck, M. J., & Connell, J. P. (1998). Individual differences and the development of perceived control. *Monographs of the Society for Research in Child Development, 63*(2–3, Serial No. 254).

Skodak, M., & Skeels, H. M. (1949). A final follow-up study of one hundred adopted children. *Pedagogical Seminary and Journal of Genetic Psychology, 75,* 85–125.

Slaby, R. G., & Frey, K. S. (1975). Development of gender constancy and selective attention to same-sex models. *Child Development, 46,* 849–856.

Slade, A., Belsky, J., Aber, J. L., & Phelps, J. L. (1999). Mothers' representations of their relationships with their toddlers: Links to adult attachment and observed mothering. *Developmental Psychology, 35,* 611–619.

Slater, A., Quinn, P. C., Brown, E., & Hayes, R. (1999). Intermodal perception at birth: Intersensory redundancy guides newborn infant's learning of arbitrary auditory-visual pairings. *Developmental Science, 2,* 333–338.

Slater, A., Rose, D., & Morison, V. (1984). New-born infants' perception of similarities and differences between two- and three-dimensional stimuli. *British Journal of Developmental Psychology, 3,* 211–220.

Slater, A., Von der Schulenburg, C., Brown, E., Badenoch, M., Butterworth, G., Parsons, S., & Samuels, C. (1998). Newborn infants prefer attractive faces. *Infant Behavior and Development, 21,* 345–354.

Slaughter-Defoe, D. T., Nakagawa, K., Takanishi, R., & Johnson, D. J. (1990). Toward cultural/ecological perspectives on schooling and achievement in African- and Asian-American children. *Child Development, 61,* 363–383.

Slavin, R. E. (1990). *Cooperative learning: Theory, research, and practice.* Englewood Cliffs, NJ: Prentice Hall.

Slomkowski, C., & Dunn, J. (1996). Young children's understanding of other people's beliefs and feelings and their connected communication with friends. *Developmental Psychology, 32,* 442–447.

Smetana, J. G. (1988). Concepts of self and social conventions: Adolescents' and parents' reasoning about hypothetical and actual family conflicts. In M. R. Gunnar & W. A. Collins (Eds.), *The Minnesota symposia on child psychology: Vol. 21. Development during the transition to adolescence.* Hillsdale, NJ: Erlbaum.

Smetana, J. G., & Braeges, J. L. (1990). The development of toddlers' moral and conventional judgments. *Merrill-Palmer Quarterly, 36,* 329–346.

Smetana, J. G., Campione-Barr, N., & Daddis, C. (2004). Longitudinal development of family decision making: Defining healthy behavioral autonomy for middle-class African American adolescents. *Child Development, 75,* 1418–1434.

Smetana, J. G., Metzger, A., Gettman, D. C., & Campione-Barr, N. (2006). Disclosure and secrecy in adolescent-parent relationships. *Child Development, 77,* 201–217.

Smetana, J. G., Schlagman, N., & Adams, P. W. (1993). Preschool judgments about hypothetical and actual transgressions. *Child Development, 64,* 202–214

Smilkstein, G., Helsper-Lucas, A., Ashworth, C., Montano, D., & Pagel, M. (1984). Prediction of pregnancy complications: An application of the biopsychosocial model. *Social Sciences & Medicine, 18,* 315–321.

Smith, D. (2001). Harassment in the hallways. *Monitor in Psychology.* Retrieved July 24, 2006 from apa.org/monitor/sep01/harassment.html.

Smith, L. B. (1989). From global similarities to kinds of similarities: The construction of dimensions in development. In S. Vosniadou & A. Ortony (Eds.), *Similarity and analogical reasoning.* New York: Cambridge University Press.

Smith, L. B. (1995). Self-organizing processes in learning to learn words: Development is not induction. In C. A. Nelson (Ed.), *Basic and applied perspectives on learning, cognition, and development. The Minnesota symposia in child psychology* (Vol. 28). Mahwah, NJ: Erlbaum.

Smith, L. B. (1999a). Children's noun learning: How general learning processes make specialized learning mechanisms. In B. MacWhinney (Ed.), *The emergence of language* (pp. 277–303). Mahwah, NJ: Erlbaum.

Smith, L. B. (1999b). Do infants possess innate knowledge structures? The con side. *Developmental Science, 2,* 133–144.

Smith, L. B., Thelen, E., Titzer, R., & McLin, D. (1999). Knowing in the context of acting: The task dynamics of the A-not-B error. *Psychological Review, 106,* 235–260.

Smith, P., Perrin, S., Yule, W., & Rabe-Hesketh, S. (2001). War exposure and maternal reactions in the psychological adjustment of children from Bosnia-Hercegovina. *Journal of Child Psychology and Psychiatry, 42,* 395–404.

Smith, R. (1999, March). The timing of birth. *Scientific American, 280,* 68–75.

Smith, T. E. (1988). Parental control techniques: Relative frequencies and relationships with situational factors. *Journal of Family Issues, 9,* 155–176.

Snarey, J. R. (1985). Cross-cultural universality of social-moral development: A critical review of Kohlbergian research. *Psychological Bulletin, 97,* 202–232.

Snow, C. E. (1977). The development of conversation between babies and mothers. *Journal of Child Language, 4,* 1–22.

Snow, C. E. (1984). Parent-child interaction and the development of communicative ability. In R. L. Schiefelbusch & J. Pickar (Eds.), *The acquisition of communicative competence.* Baltimore: University Park Press.

Snow, C. E. (1987). Relevance of the notion of a critical period to language acquisition. In M. H. Bornstein (Ed.), *Sensitive periods in development.* Hillsdale, NJ: Erlbaum.

Snow, C. E. (1993). Families as social contexts for literacy development. In C. Daiute (Ed.), *The development of literacy through social interaction. New Directions for Child Development. No. 61* (pp. 11–24). San Francisco: Jossey-Bass.

Snow, C. E., & Kang, J. Y. (2006). Becoming bilingual, biliterate, and bicultural. In W. Damon & R. M. Lerner (Editors-in-Chief) & K. A. Renninger & I. E. Sigel (Vol. Eds.), *Handbook of child psychology: Vol. 4. Child psychology in practice* (6th ed., pp. 75–102). Hoboken, NJ: Wiley.

Snow, D. (2006). Regression and reorganization of intonation between 6 and 23 months. *Child Development, 77,* 281–296.

Snyder, J., Reid, J., & Patterson, G. (2003). A social learning model of child and adolescent antisocial behavior. In B. B. Lahey, T. E. Moffitt, & A. Caspi (Eds.), *Causes of conduct disorder and juvenile delinquency* (pp. 27–48). New York: Guilford.

Sobal, J., & Stunkard, A. J. (1989). Socioeconomic status and obesity: A review of the literature. *Psychological Bulletin, 105,* 260–275.

Society for Research in Child Development. (1996). Ethical standards for research with children. In *Directory of members.* Ann Arbor, MI: Author.

Society for Research in Child Development. (2002). *About the society.* Retrieved September 23, 2002, from www.srcd.org/index.html

Sodian, B., Zaitchik, D., & Carey, S. (1991). Young children's differentiation of hypothetical beliefs from evidence. *Child Development, 62,* 753–766.

Soenens, B., Vansteenkiste, M., Luyckx, K., & Goossens, L. (2006). Parenting and adolescent problem behavior: An integrated model with adolescent self disclosure and perceived parental knowledge as intervening variables. *Developmental Psychology, 42,* 305–318.

Sophian, C., Garyantes, D., & Chang, C. (1997). When three is less than two: Early developments in children's understanding of fractional quantities. *Developmental Psychology, 33,* 731–744.

Sorce, J. F., Emde, R. N., Campos, J., & Klinnert, M. D. (1985). Maternal emotional signaling: Its effect on the visual cliff behavior of 1-year-olds. *Developmental Psychology, 21,* 195–200.

Southwick, S. M., Yehuda, R., & Charney, D. S. (1997). Neurobiological alterations in PTSD: Review of the clinical literature. In C. S. Fullerton & R. J. Ursano (Eds.), *Posttraumatic stress disorder: Acute and long-term responses to trauma and disaster* (pp. 241–266). Washington, DC: American Psychiatric Press.

Spear, L. P. (2000). Neurobehavioral changes in adolescence. *Current Directions in Psychological Science, 9,* 111–114.

Spear, L. P. (2003). Neurodevelopment during adolescence. In D. Cicchetti & E. F. Walker (Eds.), *Neurodevelopmental mechanisms in psychopathology* (pp. 62–83). Cambridge, UK: Cambridge University Press.

Spear, L. S. (2000). The adolescent brain and age-related behavioral manifestations. *Neuroscience and Biobehavioral Reviews, 24,* 417–463.

Spears, W., & Hohle, R. (1967). Sensory and perceptual processes in infants. In Y. Brackbill (Ed.), *Infancy and early childhood.* New York: Free Press.

Spehr, M., Gisselmann, G., Poplawski, A., Riffell, J. A., Wetzel, C. H., Zimmer, R. K., & Hatt, H. (2003) Identification of a testicular odorant receptor mediating human sperm chemotaxis. *Science, 299,* 2054–2058.

Spelke, E. S. (1976). Infants' intermodal perception of events. *Cognitive Psychology, 8,* 553–560.

Spelke, E., Breinlinger, K., Macomber, J., & Jacobson, K. (1992). Origins of knowledge. *Psychological Review, 99,* 605–632.

Spelke, E., & Hespos, S. (2001). Continuity, competence, and the object concept. In E. Dupoux (Ed.), *Language, brain, and cognitive development: Essays in honor of Jacques Mehler* (pp. 325–340). Cambridge, MA: MIT Press.

Spelke, E. S., & Newport, E. L. (1998). Nativism, empiricism, and the development of knowledge. In W. Damon (Series Ed.) & R. Lerner (Vol. Ed.), *Handbook of child psychology: Vol. 1. Theoretical models of human development* (5th ed., pp. 275–340). New York: Wiley.

Spelke, E. S., & Owsley, C. J. (1979). Intermodal exploration and knowledge in infancy. *Infant Behavior and Development, 2,* 13–27.

Spence, M. J., & Freeman, M. S. (1996). Newborn infants prefer the maternal low-pass filtered voice, but not the maternal whispered voice. *Infant Behavior and Development, 19,* 199–212.

Spencer, J. P., Smith, L. B., & Thelen, E. (2001). Tests of a dynamic systems account of the A-not-B error: The influence of prior experience on the spatial memory abilities of two-year-olds. *Child Development, 72,* 1327–1346.

Spencer, J. P., Vereijken, B., Diedrich, F. J., & Thelen, E. (2000). Posture and the emergence of manual skills. *Developmental Science, 3,* 216–233.

Spinrad, T. L., Eisenberg, N., Harris, H., Hanish, L., Fabes, R. A., et al. (2004). The relation of children's everyday nonsocial peer play behavior to their emotionality, regulation, and social functioning. *Developmental Psychology, 40,* 67–80.

Spinrad, T. L., Stifter, C. A., Donelan-McCall, N., & Turner, L. (2004). Mothers' regulation strategies in response to toddlers' affect: Links to later emotion self-regulation. *Social Development, 13,* 40–55.

Spitz, H. H. (1986). *The raising of intelligence.* Hillsdale, NJ: Erlbaum.

Spitz, R. (1946a). Anaclitic depression. *Psychoanalytic Study of the Child, 2,* 313–342.

Sprauve, M. E. (1996) Substance abuse and HIV in pregnancy. *Clinical Obstetrics and Gynecology, 39,* 316–332.

Spreen, O., Risser, A. H., & Edgell, D. (1995). *Developmental neuropsychology.* New York: Oxford University Press.

Spreen, O., Tupper, D., Risser, A., Tuokko, H., & Edgell, D. (1984). *Human developmental neuropsychology.* New York: Oxford University Press.

Sroufe, L. A. (1983). Infant-caregiver attachment and patterns of adaptation in preschool: The roots of maladaptation and competence. In M. Perlmutter (Ed.), *The Minnesota symposia on child psychology: Vol. 16. Development and policy concerning children with special needs.* Hillsdale, NJ: Erlbaum.

Sroufe, L. A. (1996). *Emotional development: The organization of life in the early years.* New York: Cambridge University Press.

Sroufe, L. A., Egeland, B., & Carlson, E. A. (1999). One social world: The integrated development of parent-child and peer relationships. In W. A. Collins & B. Laursen (Eds.), *Minnesota symposia on child psychology: Vol. 30. Relationships as developmental contexts* (pp. 241–261). Mahwah, NJ: Erlbaum.

Staffieri, J. R. (1967). A study of social stereotypes of body image in children. *Journal of Personality and Social Psychology, 7,* 101–104.

Stagno, S., & Cloud, G. A. (1994). Working parents: The impact of day care and breast-feeding on cytomegalovirus infections in offspring. *Proceedings of the National Academy of Science, USA, 91,* 2384–2389.

Stams, G. J. M., Juffer, F., & van IJzendoorn, M. H. (2002). Maternal sensitivity, infant attachment, and temperament in early childhood predict adjustment in middle childhood: The case of adopted children and their biologically unrelated parents. *Developmental Psychology, 38,* 806–821.

Stanovich, K. E. (1993). A model for studies of reading disability. *Developmental Review, 13,* 225–245.

Stansbury, K., & Gunnar, M. R. (1994). Adrenocortical activity and emotion regulation. In N. A. Fox (Ed.), The development of emotion regulation: Biological and behavioral considerations. *Monographs of the Society for Research in Child Development, 59*(2–3, Serial No. 240).

Stanwood, G. D., & Levitt, P. (2001). The effects of cocaine on the developing nervous system. In C. A. Nelson & M. Luciana (Eds.), *Handbook of developmental cognitive neuroscience* (pp. 519–536). Cambridge, MA: MIT Press.

Stark, R. E. (1986). Prespeech segmental feature detection. In P. Fletcher & M. Garman (Eds.), *Language acquisition: Studies in first language development.* Cambridge, UK: Cambridge University Press.

Statistics Canada. (1999). Retreived January 13, 2003, from http:\\www.statcan.ca

Statistics Canada. (2005). *Visible minority population, by age group (2001 Census).* Retrieved October 27, 2005 from www40.statcan.ca/l01/cst01/demo50a.htm.

Stätten, H., & Kerr, M. (2000). Parental monitoring: A reinterpretation. *Child Development, 71,* 1072–1085.

Steele, C. M., & Aronson, J. (1995). Stereotype threat and the intellectual test performance of African Americans. *Journal of Personality and Social Psychology, 69,* 797–811.

Steele, H., Steele, M., & Fonagy, P. (1996). Associations among attachment classifications of mothers, fathers, and their infants. *Child Development, 67,* 541–555.

Stein, J. H., & Reiser, L. W. (1994). A study of white middle-class adolescent boys' responses to "semenarche" (the first ejaculation). *Journal of Youth and Adolescence, 23,* 373–384.

Stein, L. K. (1999). Factors influencing the efficacy of universal newborn hearing screening. *Pediatric Clinics of North America, 46,* 95–105.

Stein, N. (1995). Sexual harassment in the school: The public performance of gendered violence. *Harvard Educational Review, 65,* 145–162.

Stein, N., & Cappello, D. (1999). *Gender violence/Gender justice: An interdisciplinary teaching guide for teachers of English, literature, social studies, psychology, health, peer counseling, and family and consumer sciences (grades 7–12).* Wellesley, MA: Wellesley College Center for Research on Women.

Steinberg, L. (1996). *Beyond the classroom: Why school reform has failed and what parents need to do.* New York: Simon & Schuster.

Steinberg, L. (2001). We know some things: Adolescent-parent relationships in retrospect and prospect. *Journal of Research on Adolescence, 11,* 1–19.

Steinberg, L., Elmen, J. D., & Mounts, N. S. (1989). Authoritative parenting, psychosocial maturity, and academic success among adolescents. *Child Development, 60,* 1424–1436.

Steinberg, L., Greenberger, E., Garduque, L., & McAuliffe, S. (1982). High school students in the labor force: Some costs and benefits to schooling and learning. *Educational Evaluation and Policy Analysis, 4,* 363–372.

Steinberg, L., Lamborn, S. D., Darling, N., Mounts, N. S., & Dornbusch, S. (1994). Over-time changes in adjustment and competence among adolescents from authoritative, authoritarian, indulgent, and neglectful families. *Child Development, 65,* 754–770.

Steiner, J. E. (1979). Human facial expressions in response to taste and smell stimulation. In H. W. Reese & L. P. Lipsitt (Eds.), *Advances in child development and behavior* (Vol. 13). New York: Academic Press.

Stern, D. N. (1974). The goal and structure of mother-infant play. *Journal of the American Academy of Child Psychiatry, 13,* 402–421.

Sternberg, K. J., Lamb, M. E., Greenbaum, C., Cichetti, D., Dawud, S., Cortes, R. M., et al. (1993). Effects of domestic violence on children's behavior problems and depression. *Developmental Psychology, 29,* 44–52.

Sternberg, R. J. (1981). A componential theory of intellectual giftedness. *Gifted Child Quarterly, 25,* 86–93.

Sternberg, R. J. (1982). *Intelligence applied.* New York: Harcourt.

Sternberg, R. J. (1985). *Beyond IQ: A triarchic theory of human intelligence.* Cambridge, UK: Cambridge University Press.

Sternberg, R. J. (1986). Triarchic theory of intellectual giftedness. In R. J. Sternberg & J. E. Davidson (Eds.), *Conceptions of giftedness* (pp. 223–243). Cambridge, UK: Cambridge University Press.

Sternberg, R. J. (1995). Testing common sense. *American Psychologist, 50,* 912–927.

Sternberg, R. J. (1998). Applying the triarchic theory of human intelligence in the classroom. In R. J. Sternberg & W. M. Williams (Eds.), *Intelligence, instruction, and assessment: Theory into practice* (pp. 1–15). Mahwah, NJ: Erlbaum.

Sternberg, R. J. (2001). Successful intelligence: Understanding what Spearman had rather than what he studied. In J. M. Collis & S. Messick (Eds.), *Intelligence and personality: Bridging the gap in theory and measurement* (pp. 347–373). Mahwah, NJ: Erlbaum.

Sternberg, R. J., Conway, B. E., Ketron, J. L., & Bernstein, M. (1981). People's conceptions of intelligence. *Journal of Personality and Social Psychology, 41,* 37–55.

Sternberg, R. J., & Frensch, P. A. (1993). Mechanisms of transfer. In D. K. Detterman & R. J. Sternberg (Eds.), *Transfer on trial: Intelligence, cognition, and instruction* (pp. 25–38). Norwood, NJ: Ablex.

Sternberg, R. J., & Kaufman, J. C. (1998). Human abilities. *Annual Review of Psychology, 49,* 479–502.

Sternberger, J. (1992). A performance constraint on compensatory lengthening in child phonology. *Language and Speech, 35,* 207–218.

Stetsenko, A., Little, T. D., Gordeeva, T., Grasshof, M., & Oettingen, G. (2000). Gender effects in children's beliefs about school performance: A cross-cultural study. *Child Development, 71,* 517–527.

Stetsenko, A., Little, T. D., Oettingen, G., & Baltes, P. B. (1995). Agency, control, and means-ends beliefs about school performance in Moscow children: How similar are they to beliefs of western children? *Developmental Psychology, 31,* 285–299.

Stevenson, D. K., et al. (1998). Very low birth weight outcomes of the National Institute of Child Health and Human Development Neonatal Research Network, January 1993 through December 1994. *American Journal of Obstetrics and Gynecology, 179,* 1632–1639.

Stevenson, H. W., Chen, C., & Lee, S. (1993). Mathematics achievement of Chinese, Japanese, and American children: Ten years later. *Science, 259,* 53–58.

Stevenson, H. W., Lee, S., & Stigler, J. W. (1986). Mathematics achievement of Chinese, Japanese, and American children. *Science, 231,* 693–699.

Stevenson, H. W., Stigler, J. W., Lee, S., Lucker, G. W., Kitamura, S., & Hsu, C. (1985). Cognitive performance and academic achievement of Japanese, Chinese, and American children. *Child Development, 56,* 718–734.

Stevenson, J., Asherson, P., Hay, D., Levy, F., Swanson, J., Thapar, A., & Willcutt, E. (2005). Characterizing the ADHD phenotype for genetic studies. *Developmental Science, 8,* 115–121.

Stevenson-Hinde, J., & Shouldice, A. (1995). Maternal interactions and self-reports related to attachment classifications at 4.5 years. *Child Development, 66,* 583–596.

Stice, E., Presnell, K., & Bearman, S. K. (2001). Relation of early menarche to depression, eating disorders, substance abuse, and comorbid psychopathology among adolescent girls. *Developmental Psychology, 37,* 608–619.

Stice, E., & Whitenton, K. (2002). Risk factors for body dissatisfaction in adolescent girls: A longitudinal investigation. *Developmental Psychology, 38,* 669–678.

Stifter, C. A., Fox, N. A., & Porges, S. W. (1989). Facial expressivity and vagal tone in five- and ten-month-old infants. *Infant Behavior and Development, 12,* 127–137.

Stigler, J. W., Lee, S., & Stevenson, H. W. (1987). Mathematics classrooms in Japan, Taiwan, and the United States. *Child Development, 58,* 1272–1285.

Stigler, J. W., Smith, S., & Mao, L.-W. (1985). The self-perception of competence by Chinese children. *Child Development, 56,* 1259–1270.

Stipek, D., & Hoffman, J. M. (1980). Children's achievement related expectancies as a function of academic performance histories and sex. *Journal of Educational Psychology, 72,* 861–865.

Stipek, D., Recchia, S., & McClintic, S. (1992). Self-evaluation in young children. *Monographs of the Society for Research in Child Development, 57*(1, Serial No. 226).

Stoel-Gammon, C., & Otomo, K. (1986). Babbling development of hearing-impaired and normally hearing subjects. *Journal of Speech and Hearing Disorders, 51,* 33–41.

Stolberg, A. L., & Anker, J. M. (1984). Cognitive and behavioral changes in children resulting from parental divorce and consequent environmental changes. *Journal of Divorce, 8,* 184–197.

Stoolmiller, M. (2001). Synergistic interaction of child manageability problems and parent-discipline tactics in predicting future growth in externalizing behavior for boys. *Developmental Psychology, 37,* 814–825.

Stormshak, E. A., Bellanti, C. J., Bierman, K. L., & the Conduct Problems Prevention Group. (1996). The quality of sibling relationships and the development of social competence and behavioral control in aggressive children. *Developmental Psychology, 32,* 79–89.

Strasburger, V. C. (1993). Children, adolescents, and the media: Five crucial issues. Adolescent Medicine: State of the Art Review, 4, 479–493.Stratton, K. R., Howe, C. J., & Battaglia, F. C. (Eds.). (1996). *Fetal alcohol syndrome: Diagnosis, epidemiology, prevention and treatment.* Washington, DC: National Academy Press.

Straus, M. A., & Donnelly, D. A. (1993). Corporal punishment of adolescents by American parents. *Youth and Society, 24,* 419–442.

Straus, M. A., & Stewart, J. H. (1999). Corporal punishment by American parents: National data on prevalence, chronicity, severity, and duration, in relation to child and family characteristics. *Clinical Child and Family Psychology Review, 2,* 55–70.

Strauss, R. (1999). Childhood obesity. *Current Problems in Pediatrics, 29,* 5–29.

Streiner, D. L., Saigal, S., Burrows, E., Stoskopf, B., & Rosenbaum, P. (2001). Attitudes of parents and health care professionals toward active treatment of extremely premature infants. *Pediatrics, 108,* 152–157.

Streissguth, A. P., Barr, H. M., Bookstein, F. L., Sampson, P. D., & Olson, H. C. (1999). The long-term neurocognitive consequences of prenatal alcohol exposure: A 14-year study. *Psychological Science, 10,* 186–190.

Streissguth, A. P., Bookstein, F. L., Sampson, P. D., & Barr, H. M. (1995). Attention: Prenatal alcohol and continuities of vigilence and attentional problems from 4 through 14 years. *Development and Psychopathology, 7,* 419–446.

Streissguth, A. P., Sampson, P. D., Barr, H. M., Bookstein, F. L., & Olson, H. C. (1994). The effects of prenatal exposure to alcohol and tobacco: Contributions from the Seattle Longitudinal Prospective Study and implications for public policy. In H. L. Needleman & D. Bellinger (Eds.), *Prenatal exposure to toxicants: Developmental consequences* (pp. 148–183). Baltimore: Johns Hopkins University Press.

Streissguth, A. P., Treder, R., Barr, H. M., Shepard, T., Bleyer, A., & Martin, D. (1984). Prenatal aspirin and offspring IQ in a large group. *Teratology, 29,* 59A–60A.

Stricker, J. M., Miltenberger, R. G., Garlinghouse, M. A., Deaver, C. M., & Anderson, C. A. (2001). Evaluation of an awareness enhancement device for the treatment of thumb sucking in children. *Journal of Applied Behavior Analysis, 34,* 77–80.

Strough, J., & Berg, C. A. (2000). Goals as a mediator of gender differences in high-affiliation dyadic conversations. *Developmental Psychology, 36,* 117–125.

Strutt, G. F., Anderson, D. R., & Well, A. D. (1975). A developmental study of the effects of irrelevant information on speeded classification. *Journal of Experimental Child Psychology, 20,* 127–135.

Styne, D. M. (2001). Childhood and adolescent obesity. *Pediatric Clinics of North America, 48,* 832–862.

Suarez-Orozco, C., & Suarez-Orozco, M. (1996). *Transformations: Migration, family life and achievement motivation among Latino adolescents.* Palo Alto, CA: Stanford University Press.

Subrahmanyam, K., & Greenfield, P. M. (1998). Computer games for girls: What makes them play? In J. Cassell & H. Jenkins (Eds.), *From Barbie to Mortal Kombat: Gender and computer games* (pp. 46–71). Cambridge, MA: MIT Press.

Subrahmanyam, K., Greenfield, P., Kraut, R., & Gross, E. (2001). The impact of computer use on children's and adolescents' development. *Journal of Applied Developmental Psychology, 22,* 7–30.

Subrahmanyam, K., Kraut, R. E., Greenfield, P. M., & Gross, E. F. (2000, Fall/Winter). The impact of computer use on children's activities and development. *Future of Children, 10*(2), 123–144.

Subrahmanyam, K., Smahel, D., & Greenfield, P. (2006). Connecting developmental constructions to the Internet: Identity presentation and sexual exploration in online teen chat rooms. *Developmental Psychology, 42,* 395-406.

Sugarman, S. (1982). Developmental change in early representational intelligence: Evidence from spatial classification strategies and related verbal expressions. *Cognitive Psychology, 14,* 410–449.

Sugarman, S. (1983). *Children's early thought: Developments in classification.* New York: Cambridge University Press.

Sullivan, H. S. (1953). *The interpersonal theory of psychiatry.* New York: W. W. Norton.

Sullivan, T. N., Kung, E. M., & Farrell, A. D. (2004). Relation between witnessing violence and drug use initiation among rural adolescents: Parental monitoring and family support as protective factors. *Journal of Clinical and Adolescent Psychology, 33,* 488–498.

Sun, L. C., & Roopnarine, J. L. (1996). Mother-infant, father-infant interaction and involvement in childcare and household labor among Taiwanese families. *Infant Behavior and Development, 19,* 121–129.

Super, C. M. (1976). Environmental effects on motor development: The case of "African infant precocity." *Developmental Medicine and Child Neurology, 18,* 561–567.

Super, C. M., & Harkness, S. (1982). The infant's niche in rural Kenya and metropolitan America. In L. Adler (Ed.), *Cross-cultural research at issue*(pp. 247–255). New York: Academic Press.

Super, C. M., & Harkness, S. (1997). The cultural structuring of child development. In J. W. Berry (Ed.), *Handbook of cross-cultural psychology: Vol. 2. Basic processes and human development* (2nd ed., pp. 1–39). Boston: Allyn & Bacon.

Sutton-Smith, B., & Rosenberg, B. G. (1970). *The sibling.* New York: Holt, Rinehart & Winston.

Swain, I. U., Zelazo, P. R., & Clifton, R. K. (1993). Newborn infants' memory for speech sounds retained over 24 hours. *Developmental Psychology, 29,* 312–323.

Swanson, H. L., Mink, J., & Bocian, K. M. (1999). Cognitive processing deficits in poor readers with symptoms of reading disabilities and ADHD: More alike than different? *Journal of Educational Psychology, 91,* 321–333.

Szkrybalo, J., & Ruble, D. N. (1999). "God made me a girl": Sex-category constancy judgments and explanation revisited. *Developmental Psychology, 35,* 392–402.

Taddio, A., Goldbach, M., Ipp, M., Stevens, B., & Koren, G. (1995). Effect of neonatal circumcision on pain responses during vaccination in boys. *Lancet, 345,* 291–292.

Tager-Flusberg, H. (1985). Putting words together: Morphology and syntax in the preschool years. In J. B. Gleason (Ed.), *The development of language.* Columbus, OH: Charles E. Merrill.

Takahashi, K. (1990). Are the key assumptions of the Strange Situation procedure universal? A view from Japanese research. *Human Development, 33,* 23–30.

Takei, W. (2001). How do deaf infants attain first signs? *Developmental Science, 4,* 71–78.

Tallal, P., Miller, S. L., Bedi, G., Byma, G., Wang, X., Nagarajan, S. S., et al. (1996). Language comprehension in language-learning impaired children improved with acoustically modified speech. *Science, 271,* 81–84.

Tallal, P., Miller, S. L., Jenkins, W. M., & Merzenich, M. M. (1997). The role of temporal processing in developmental language-based learning disorders: Research and clinical implications. In B. Blachman (Ed.), *Foundations of reading acquisition and dyslexia: Implications for early intervention* (pp. 49–66). Mahwah, NJ: Erlbaum.

Tam, C. W. Y., & Stokes, S. F. (2001). Form and function of negation in early developmental Cantonese. *Journal of Child Language, 28,* 373–391.

Tamis-LeMonda, C. S., Bornstein, M. H., & Baumwell, L. (2001). Maternal responsiveness and children's achievement of language milestones. *Child Development, 72,* 748–767.

Tanapat, P., Hastings, N. B., & Gould, E. (2001). Adult neurogenesis in the hippocampal formation. In C. A. Nelson & M. Luciana (Eds.), *Handbook of developmental cognitive neuroscience* (pp. 93–105). Cambridge, MA: MIT Press.

Tanner, J. M. (1978). *Fetus into man: Physical growth from conception to maturity.* Cambridge, MA: Harvard University Press.

Tanner, J. M. (1990). *Foetus into man: Physical growth from conception to maturity* (rev. ed.). Cambridge, MA: Harvard University Press.

Tannock, R., & Martinussen, R. (2001). Reconceptualizing ADHD. *Educational Leadership, 59,* 20–25.

Tappin, D., Ecob, R., & Brooke, H. (2005). Bedsharing, roomsharing and sudden infant death syndrome in Scotland. *Journal of Pediatrics, 147,* 32–37.

Taras, H. L., Sallis, J. F., Patterson, T. L., Nader, P. R., & Nelson, J. A. (1989). Television's influence on children's diet and physical activity. *Journal of Developmental and Behavioral Pediatrics, 10,* 176–180.

Tardieu, M., Mayaux, M.-J., Seibel, N., Funck-Brentano, I., Straub, E., Teglas, J. P., & Blanche, S. (1995). Cognitive assessment of school-age children infected with maternally transmitted human immunodeficiency virus type 1. *Journal of Pediatrics, 126,* 375–379.

Tardif, T. (1996). Nouns are not always learned before verbs: Evidence from Mandarin speakers' early vocabularies. *Developmental Psychology, 32,* 492–504.

Tardif, T., Gelman, S. A., & Xu, F. (1999). Putting the "noun bias" in context: A comparison of English and Mandarin. *Child Development, 70,* 620–635.

Tardif, T., & Wellman, H. M. (2000). Acquisition of mental state language in Mandarin-speaking and Cantonese-speaking children. *Developmental Psychology, 36,* 25–43.

Taubes, G. (1998). As obesity rates rise, experts struggle to explain why. *Science, 1998,* 1367–1368.

Taylor, H. G., Klein, N., & Hack, M. (2000). School-age consequences of birth-weight less than 750g: A review and update. *Developmental Neuropsychology, 17,* 289–321.

Taylor, H. G., Klein, N., Minich, N. M., & Hack, M. (2001). Long-term family outcomes for children with very low birth weights. *Archives of Pediatrics & Adolescent Medicine, 155,* 155–161.

Taylor, R. D. (1996). Adolescents' perceptions of kinship support and family management practices: Association with adolescent adjustment in African American families. *Developmental Psychology, 32,* 687–695.

Teller, D. Y. (1998). Spatial and temporal aspects of infant color vision. *Vision Research, 38,* 3275–3282.

Tenenbaum, H. R., & Leaper, C. (2002). Are parents' gender schemas related to their children's gender-related cognitions? A meta-analysis. *Developmental Psychology, 38,* 615–630.

Teratology Society. (2005). *Teratology primer.* Reston, VA: Author.

Terman, L. M. (1916). *The measurement of intelligence.* Boston: Houghton Mifflin.

Terman, L. M. (1925). *Genetic studies of genius: Vol. 1. Mental and physical traits of a thousand gifted children.* Stanford, CA: Stanford University Press.

Terman, L. M. (1954). The discovery and encouragement of exceptional talent. *American Psychologist, 9,* 221–238.

Terman, L. M., & Oden, M. H. (1959). *Genetic studies of genius: Vol. 4. The gifted group at midlife.* Stanford, CA: Stanford University Press.

Terrace, H. S., Pettito, L. A., Sanders, R. J., & Bever, T. G. (1979). Can an ape create a sentence? *Science, 206,* 891–900.

Terrance, C., Logan, A. & Peters, D. (2004). Perceptions of peer sexual harassment among high school students. *Sex Roles, 51,* 479–490.

Teti, D. M., & Gelfand, D. M. (1991). Behavioral competence among mothers of infants in the first year: The mediational role of maternal self-efficacy. *Child Development, 62,* 918–929.

Teti, D. M., Gelfand, D. M., Messinger, D. S., & Isabella, R. (1995). Maternal depression and the quality of early attachment: An examination of infants, preschoolers, and their mothers. *Developmental Psychology, 31,* 364–376.

Teti, D. M., Sakin, J. W., Kucera, E., & Corns, K. M. (1996). And baby makes four: Predictors of attachment security among preschool age firstborns during the transition to siblinghood. *Child Development, 67,* 579–596.

Thabet, A. A., & Vostanis, P. (2000). Posttraumatic stress disorder reactions in children of war: A longitudinal study. *Child Abuse & Neglect, 24,* 291–298.

Tharp, R. G. (1989). Psychocultural variables and constants: Effects on teaching and learning in schools. *American Psychologist, 44,* 349–359.

Thelen, E. (1996). The improvising infant: Learning about learning to move. In M. R. Merrens & G. G. Brannigan (Eds.), *The developmental psychologists: Research adventures across the life span* (pp. 21–36). New York: McGraw-Hill.

Thelen, E., Skala, K. D., & Kelso, J. A. S. (1987). The dynamic nature of early coordination: Evidence from bilateral leg movements in young infants. *Developmental Psychology, 23,* 179–186.

Thelen, E., & Smith, L. B. (1994). *A dynamic systems approach to the development of cognition and action.* Cambridge, MA: MIT Press.

Thelen, E., & Smith, L. B. (2006). Dynamic systems theories. In W. Damon & R. M. Lerner (Editors-in-Chief) & R. M. Lerner (Vol. Ed.), *Handbook of child psychology: Vol. 1. Theoretical models of human development* (6th ed., pp. 258–312). Hoboken, NJ: Wiley.

Thelen, E., & Ulrich, B. D. (1991). Hidden skills: A dynamic systems analysis of treadmill stepping during the first year. *Monographs of the Society for Research in Child Development, 56*(1, Serial No. 223).

Thierry, K. L., & Spence, M. J. (2002). Source-monitoring training facilitates preschoolers' eyewitness memory performance. *Developmental Psychology, 38,* 428–437.

Thiessen, E. D., Hill, E. A., & Saffran, J. R. (2005). Infant-directed speech facilitates word segmentation. *Infancy, 7,* 53–71.

Thoman, A. (1993). Obligation and option in the premature nursery. *Developmental Review, 13,* 1–30.

Thomas, D. G., & Lykins, M. S. (1995). Event-related potential measures of 24-hour retention in 5-month-old infants. *Developmental Psychology, 31,* 946–957.

Thompson, C. (1982). Cortical activity in behavioural development. In J. W. T. Dickerson & H. McGurk (Eds.), *Brain and behavioural development.* London: Surrey University Press.

Thompson, R. A. (1990). Vulnerability in research: A developmental perspective on risk research. *Child Development, 61,* 1–16.

Thompson, R. A. (1994). Emotion regulation: A theme in search of definition. In N. A. Fox (Ed.), *The development of emotion regulation. Monographs of the Society for Research in Child Development, 59* (Nos. 2–3, Serial No. 240).

Thompson, R. A. (1996). Attachment and emotional development: From clinic to research to policy. In M. R. Merrens & G. G. Brannigan (Eds.), *The developmental psychologists: Research adventures across the life span* (pp. 69–87). New York: McGraw-Hill.

Thompson, R. A. (2006). The development of the person: Social understanding, relationships, conscience, self. In W. Damon & R. M. Lerner (Editors-in-Chief) & N. Eisenberg (Vol. Ed.), *Handbook of child psychology: Vol. 3. Social, emotional, and personality development* (6th ed., pp. 24–98). Hoboken, NJ: Wiley.

Thompson, R. A., & Nelson, C. A. (2001). Developmental science and the media: Early brain development. *American Psychologist, 56,* 5–15.

Thompson, V. D. (1974). Family size: Implicit policies and assumed psychological outcomes. *Journal of Social Issues, 30,* 93–124.

Thorn, F., Gwaizda, J., Cruz, A. V., Bauer, J. A., & Held, R. (1994). The development of eye alignment, convergence and sensory binocularity in young infants. *Investigative Ophthalmology and Visual Science, 35,* 544–553.

Thornton, S. (1999). Creating the conditions for cognitive change: The interaction between task structures and specific strategies. *Child Development, 70,* 588–603.

Thurstone, L. L. (1938). *Primary mental abilities.* Chicago: University of Chicago Press.

Tieger, T. (1980). On the biological basis of sex differences in aggression. *Child Development, 51,* 943–963.

Tietjen, A. M. (1986). Prosocial moral reasoning among children and adults in a Papua New Guinea society. *Developmental Psychology, 22,* 861–868.

Tincoff, R., & Jusczyk, P. W. (1999). Some beginnings of word comprehension in 6-month-olds. *Psychological Science, 10,* 172–175.

Toda, S., & Fogel, A. (1993). Infant response to the still-face situation at 3 and 6 months. *Developmental Psychology, 29,* 532–538.

Toda, S., Fogel, A., & Kawai, M. (1990). Maternal speech to three-month-old infants in the United States and Japan. *Journal of Child Language, 17,* 279–294.

Tolmie, J. L. (2002). Down syndrome and other autosomal trisomies. In D. L. Rimoin, J. M. Connor, R. E. Pyeritz, & B. R. Korf (Eds.), *Emery and Rimoin's principles and practice of medical genetics* (4th ed., Vol. 1, pp. 1129–1183). London: Churchill Livingston.

Tolson, J. M., & Urberg, K. A. (1993). Similarity between adolescent best friends. *Journal of Adolescent Research, 8,* 274–288.

Tomasello, M. (1995). Understanding the self as social agent. In P. Rochat (Ed.), *The self in infancy: Theory and research* (pp. 449–460). Amsterdam: North Holland-Elsevier.

Tomasello, M. (1998). Uniquely primate, uniquely human. *Developmental Science, 1,* 1–16.

Tomasello, M. (2000). Do young children have adult syntactic competence? *Cognition, 74,* 209–253.

Tomasello, M., Akhtar, N., Dodson, K., & Rekau, L. (1997). Differential productivity in young children's use of nouns and verbs. *Journal of Child Language, 24,* 373–387.

Tomasello, M., & Brooks, P. (1998). Young children's earliest transitive and intransitive contructions. *Cognitive Linguistics, 8,* 375–395.

Tomasello, M., & Brooks, P. J. (1999). Early syntactic development: A construction grammar approach. In M. Barrett (Ed.), *The development of language* (pp. 161–190). Hove, UK: Psychology Press.

Tomasello, M., Conti-Ramsden, G., & Ewert, B. (1990). Young children's conversations with their mothers and fathers: Differences in breakdown and repair. *Journal of Child Language, 17,* 115–130.

Tomasello, M., & Farrar, M. J. (1986). Joint attention and early language. *Child Development, 57,* 1454–1463.

Tomasello, M., Strosberg, R., & Akhtar, N. (1996). Eighteen-month-old children learn words in non-ostensive contexts. *Journal of Child Language, 23,* 157–176.

Tongsong, T., Wanapirak, C., Sirivatanapa, P., Piyamongkol, W., Sirichotiyakul, S. & Yampochai, A. (1998). Amniocentesis-related fetal loss: A cohort study. *Obstetrics and Gynecology, 92,* 64–67.

Tough, S. C., Greene, C. A., Svenson, L. W., & Belik, J. (2000). Effects of in vitro fertilization on low birth weight, preterm delivery, and multiple birth. *Journal of Pediatrics, 136,* 618–622.

Touwen, B. C. L. (1974). The neurological development of the infant. In J. A. Davis & J. Dobbing (Eds.), *Scientific foundations of paediatrics.* Philadelphia: W.B. Saunders.

Trainor, L. J. (1996). Infant preferences for infant-directed versus non-infant-directed play songs and lullabies. *Infant Behavior and Development,* 19, 83–92.

Trainor, L. J., & Heinmiller, B. M. (1998). The development of evaluative responses to music: Infants prefer to listen to consonance over dissonance. *Infant Behavior and Development, 21,* 77–88.

Trehub, S. E., Bull, D., & Thorpe, L. A. (1984). Infants' perception of melodies: The role of melodic contour. *Child Development, 55,* 821–830.

Trehub, S. E., Thorpe, L. A., & Morrongiello, B. A. (1985). Infants' perception of melodies: Changes in a single tone. *Infant Behavior and Development, 8,* 213–223.

Trehub, S. E., Unyk, A. M., & Trainor, L. J. (1993). Maternal singing in cross-cultural perspective. *Infant Behavior and Development, 16,* 285–295.

Treiber, F., & Wilcox, S. (1980). Perception of a "subjective" contour by infants. *Child Development, 51,* 915–917.

Trevarthen, C., & Aitken, K. J. (2001). Infant intersubjectivity: Research, theory, and clinical applications. *Journal of Child Psychology & Psychiatry & Allied Disciplines, 42,* 3–48.

Trevathen, W. R. (1987). *Human birth: An evolutionary perspective.* New York: Aldine de Gruyter.

Tronick, E. Z. (1987). The Neonatal Behavioral Assessment Scale as a biomarker of the effects of environmental agents on the newborn. *Environmental Health Perspectives, 74,* 185–189.

Tronick, E. Z., Als, H., Adamson, L., Wise, S., & Brazelton, T. E. (1978). The infant's response to entrapment between contradictory messages in face-to-face interaction. *Journal of the American Academy of Child Psychiatry, 17,* 1–13.

Tronick, E. Z., & Cohn, J. F. (1989). Infant-mother face-to-face interaction: Age and gender differences in coordination and the occurrence of miscoordination. *Child Development, 60,* 85–92.

Tronick, E. Z., Ricks, M., & Cohn, J. F. (1982). Maternal and infant affective exchange: Patterns of adaptation. In T. Field & A. Fogel (Eds.), *Emotion and early interaction.* Hillsdale, NJ: Erlbaum.

Troseth, G. L. (2003). TV guide: Two-year-old children learn to use video as a source of information. *Developmental Psychology, 39,* 140–150.

Tröster, H., & Brambring, M. (1993). Early motor development in blind infants. *Journal of Applied Developmental Psychology, 14,* 83–106.

True, M. M., Pisani, L., & Oumar, F. (2001). Infant-mother attachment among the Dogon of Mali. *Child Development, 72,* 1451–1466.

Trzesniewski, K. H., Brent Donnellan, M. B., Moffitt, T. E., Robins, R. W., Poulton, R., & Caspi, A. (2006). Low self-esteem during adolescence predicts poor health, criminal behavior, and limited economic prospects during adulthood. *Developmental Psychology, 42,* 382–290.

Tschopp, C., Viviani, P., Reicherts, M., Bullinger, A., Rudaz, N., Mermoud, C., & Safran, A. B. (1999). Does visual sensitivity improve between 5 and 8 years? A study of automated visual field examination. *Vision Research, 39,* 1107–1119.

Tucker, D. M. (1981). Lateral brain function, emotion, and conceptualization. *Psychological Bulletin, 89,* 19–46.

Tucker, G. R., & d'Anglejan, A. (1972). An approach to bilingual education: The St. Lambert experiment. In M. Swain (Ed.), *Bilingual schooling: Some experiences in Canada and the United States.* Ontario: Ontario Institute for Studies in Education.

Turiel, E. (1998). The development of morality. In W. Damon (Series Ed.) & N. Eisenberg (Vol. Ed.), *Handbook of child psychology: Vol. 3. Social, emotional, and personality development* (5th ed., pp. 863–932). New York: Wiley.

Turiel, E. (2006). The development of morality. In W. Damon & R. M. Lerner (Editors-in-Chief) & N. Eisenberg (Vol. Ed.), *Handbook of child psychology: Vol. 3. Social, emotional, and personality development* (6th ed., pp. 789–857). Hoboken, NJ: Wiley.

Turiel, E., & Wainryb, C. (1994). Social reasoning and the varieties of social experiences in cultural contexts. In H. Reese (Ed.), *Advances in child development and behavior* (Vol. 25, pp. 289–326).

Turkheimer, E., Goldsmith, H. H., & Gottesman, I. I. (1995). Commentary. *Human Development, 38,* 142–153.

Turner, R. A., Irwin, C. E., & Millstein, S. G. (1991). Family structure, family processes, and experimenting with substances during adolescence. *Journal of Research on Adolescence, 1,* 93–106.

Turner, S. M., & Mo, L. (1984). Chinese adolescents' self-concept as measured by the Offer Self-Image Questionnaire. *Journal of Youth and Adolescence, 13,* 131–142.

Turner-Bowker, D. M. (1996). Gender stereotyped descriptors in children's picture books: Does "Curious Jane" exist in the literature? *Sex Roles, 35,* 461–488.

Twenge, J. M., & Crocker, J. (2002). Race and self-esteem: Meta-analyses comparing Whites, Blacks, Hispanics, Asians, and American Indians and comment on Gray-Little and Hafdahl (2000). *Psychological Bulletin, 128,* 371–408.

Ullian, E. M., Sapperstein, S. K., Christopherson, K. S., & Barres, B. A. (2001). Control of synapse number by glia. *Science, 291,* 657–661.

Underwood, L. E. (1991, March/April). Normal adolescent growth and development. *Nutrition Today,* pp. 11–16.

Underwood, M. K., Schockner, A. E., & Hurley, J. C. (2001). Children's responses to same- and other-gender peers: An experimental investigation with 8-, 10-, and 12-year-olds. *Developmental Psychology, 37,* 362–372.

UNICEF. (2002). *The State of the World's Children 2002.* Retrieved November 27, 2002, from www.unicef.org/sowc02/

United Nations. (2001, October). *Population and vital statistics report* (Series A, Vol. 53, No. 4). New York: Author.

United Nations. (2005). *Population and vital statistics report.* Retrieved October 2, 2005, from unstats.un.org/unsd/demographic/products/vitstats/seriesa2.htm.

U.S. Bureau of the Census. (2001). *Statistical abstract of the United States* (121st ed.). Washington, DC: U.S. Government Printing Office.

U.S. Bureau of the Census. (2005a). *National population estimates—characteristics.* Retrieved October 27, 2005 from www.census.gov/popest/national/asrh/NC-EST2004-asrh.html.

U.S. Bureau of the Census. (2005b). *Statistical abstract of the United States, 2006: The national data book* (125th ed.). Washington, DC: U.S. Government Printing Office. Retrieved October 30, 2005, from www.census.gov/prod/2004pubs/04statab/labor.pdf.

U.S. Department of Education. (1993). *National excellence: A case for developing America's talent.* Washington, DC: Office of Educational Research and Improvement.

U.S. Department of Education. (1996). *1996 trends in academic programs.* Washington, DC: U.S. Government Printing Office.

U.S. Department of Health and Human Services. (2004). *What you need to know about mercury in fish and shellfish.* Retrieved May 10, 2006, from www.cfsan.fda.gov/~dms/admehg3.html.

U.S. Department of Health and Human Services. (2005). *Child maltreatment 2003.* Washington, DC: U.S. Government Printing Office.

U.S. Department of Justice. (2005). *Juvenile victimization and offending, 1993–2003.* Bureau of Justice Special Report, NCJ 209468.

Urberg, K. A., Degirmencioglu, S. M., Tolson, J. M., & Halliday-Scher, K. (1995). The structure of adolescent peer networks. *Developmental Psychology, 31,* 540–547.

Uttal, D. H., & Wellman, H. M. (1989). Young children's representation of spatial information acquired from maps. *Developmental Psychology, 25,* 128–138.

Uttal, D. H., Gregg, V. H., Tan, L. S., Chamberlin, M. H., & Sines, A. (2001). Connecting the dots: Children's use of a systematic figure to facilitate mapping and search. *Developmental Psychology, 37,* 338–350.

Valdez-Menchaca, M. C., & Whitehurst, G. J. (1992). Accelerating language development through picture book reading: A systematic extension to Mexican day care. *Developmental Psychology, 28,* 1106–1114.

Valeski, T. N., & Stipek, D. J. (2001). Young children's feelings about school. *Child Development, 72,* 1198–1213.

Valian, V. (1986). Syntactic categories in the speech of young children. *Developmental Psychology, 22,* 562–579.

Valk, A. (2000). Ethnic identity, ethnic attitudes, self-esteem, and esteem toward others among Estonian and Russian adolescents. *Journal of Adolescent Research, 15,* 637–651.

Valsiner, J. (2006). Developmental epistemology and implications for methodology. In W. Damon & R. M. Lerner (Editors-in-Chief) & R. M. Lerner (Vol. Ed.), *Handbook of child psychology: Vol. 1. Theoretical models of human development* (6th ed., pp. 166–209). Hoboken, NJ: Wiley.

Van Balen, F. (1998). Development of IVF children. *Developmental Review, 18,* 30–46.

van den Boom, D. C. (1994). The influence of temperament and mothering on attachment and exploration: An experimental manipulation of sensitive responsiveness among lower-class mothers with irritable infants. *Child Development, 65,* 1457–1477.

van den Boom, D. C. (1995). Do first-year intervention effects endure? Follow-up during toddlerhood of a sample of Dutch irritable infants. *Child Development, 66,* 1798–1816.

van den Boom, D. C., & Hoeksma, J. B. (1994). The effects of infant irritability on mother-infant interaction: A growth-curve analysis. *Developmental Psychology, 30,* 581–590.

Van IJzendoorn, M. H. (1995). Adult attachment representations, parental responsiveness and infant attachment: A meta-analysis on the predictive validity of the Adult Attachment Interview. *Psychological Bulletin, 117,* 387–403.

van IJzendoorn, M. H., Moran, G., Belsky, J., Pederson, D., Bakermans Kranenburg, M. J., & Kneppers, K. (2000). The similarity of siblings' attachments to their mother. *Child Development, 71,* 1086–1098.

van IJzendoorn, M. H., & Sagi, A. (1999). Cross-cultural patterns of attachment. In J. Cassidy & P. R. Shaver (Eds.), *Handbook of attachment: Theory, research, and clinical applications* (pp. 713–734). New York: Guilford Press.

Van Rooy, C., Stough, C., Pipingas, A., Hocking, C., & Silberstein, R. B. (2001). Spatial working memory and intelligence: Biological correlates. *Intelligence, 29,* 275–292.

Vandell, D. L. (2000). Parents, peers, and other socializing influences. *Developmental Psychology, 36,* 699–710.

Vandell, D. L., & Mueller, E. C. (1980). Peer play and friendships during the first two years. In H. C. Foot, A. J. Chapman, & J. R. Smith (Eds.), *Friendship and social relations in children.* New York: Wiley.

Vandell, D. L., & Ramanan, J. (1992). Effects of early and recent maternal employment on children from low-income families. *Child Development, 63,* 938–949.

Vandell, D. L., & Wilson, K. S. (1982). Social interaction in the first year of life: Infants' social skills with peers versus mother. In K. H. Rubin & H. S. Ross (Eds.), *Peer relationships and social skills in childhood.* New York: Springer-Verlag.

Vandell, D. L., Wilson, K. S., & Buchanan, N. R. (1980). Peer interaction in the first year of life: An examination of its structure, content, and sensitivity to toys. *Child Development, 51,* 481–488.

Vandenberg, S. G., & Vogler, G. P. (1985). Genetic determinants of intelligence. In B. B. Wolman (Ed.), *Handbook of intelligence.* New York: Wiley.

Varni, J. W. (1983). *Clinical behavioral pediatrics: An interdisciplinary biobehavioral approach.* New York: Pergamon Press.

Vaughn, B. E., Kopp, C. B., & Krakow, J. B. (1984). The emergence and consolidation of self-control from eighteen to thirty months of age: Normative trends and individual differences. *Child Development, 55,* 990–1004.

Vaughn, B. E., Taraldson, B., Crichton, L., & Egeland, B. (1980). Relationships between neonatal behavioral organization and infant behavior during the first year of life. *Infant Behavior and Development, 3,* 78–89.

Vernon, P. A. (1983). Speed of information processing and general intelligence. *Intelligence, 7,* 53–70.

Verschueren, K., & Marcoen, A. (1999). Representation of self and socioemotional competence in kindergartners: Differential and combined effects of attachment to mothers and fathers. *Child Development, 70,* 183–201.

Vihman, M. M. (1998). Early phonological disorders. In J. E. Bernthal & N. W. Bankson (Eds.), *Articulation and phonological development* (4th ed., pp. 63–110). Boston: Allyn & Bacon.

Vinter, A., & Perruchet, P. (2000). Implicit learning in children is not related to age: Evidence from drawing behavior. *Child Development, 71,* 1223–1240.

Vohr, B. R., Wright, L. L., Dusick, A. M., Mele, L., Verter, J., Steichen, J. J., et al. (2000). Neurodevelopmental and functional outcomes of extremely low birth weight infants in the National Institute of Child Health and Human Development Neonatal Research Network, 1993–1994. *Pediatrics, 105,* 1216–1226.

Volling, B. L., MacKinnon-Lewis, C., Rabiner, D., & Baradaran, L. P. (1993). Children's social competence and sociometric status: Further exploration of aggression, social withdrawal, and peer rejection. *Development and Psychopathology, 5,* 459–483.

von Hofsten, C., & Rönnqvist, L. (1993). The structuring of neonatal arm movement. *Child Development, 64,* 1046–1057.

von Hofsten, C., & Rosander, K. (1997). Development of smooth pursuit tracking in young infants. *Vision Research, 37,* 1799–1810.

Vorhees, C. V. (1986). Principles of behavioral teratology. In E. P. Riley & C. V. Vorhees (Eds.), *Handbook of behavioral teratology.* New York: Plenum Press.

Vouloumanos, A., & Werker, J. F. (2004). Tuned to the signal: The privileged status of speech for young infants. *Developmental Science, 3,* 270–276.

Voyer, D., Voyer, S., & Bryden, M. P. (1995). Magnitude of sex differences in spatial abilities: A meta-analysis and consideration of critical variables. *Psychological Bulletin, 117,* 250–270.

Vuchinich, S., Hetherington, E. M., Vuchinich, R. A., & Clingempeel, W. G. (1991). Parent-child interaction and gender differences in early adolescents' adaptation to stepfamilies. *Developmental Psychology, 27,* 618–626.

Vuyk, R. (1981). *Overview and critique of Piaget's genetic epistemology 1965–1980* (Vols. 1 & 2). New York: Academic Press.

Vygotsky, L. S. (1962). *Thought and language* (E. Hanfmann & G. Vakar, Trans.). Cambridge, MA: MIT Press.

Vygotsky, L. S. (1978). *Mind in society: The development of higher psychological processes.* Cambridge, MA: Harvard University Press.

Wachs, T. D., & Combs, T. T. (1995). The domains of infant mastery motivation. In R. H. McTurk & G. A. Morgan (Eds.), *Mastery motivation: Origins, conceptualizations, and applications* (pp. 147–164). Norwood, NJ: Ablex.

Waddington, C. H. (1971). Concepts of development. In E. Tobach, L. R. Aronson, & E. Shaw (Eds.), *The biopsychology of development.* San Diego, CA: Academic Press.

Wadhwa, P. D., Sandman, C. A., Porto, M., Dunkel-Schetter, C., & Garite, T. J. (1993). The association between prenatal stress and infant birth weight and gestational age at birth: A prospective investigation. *American Journal of Obstetrics and Gynecology, 169,* 858–865.

Wagner, B. M., & Phillips, D. A. (1992). Beyond beliefs: Parent and child behaviors and children's perceived academic competence. *Child Development, 63,* 1380–1391.

Wagner, L. (2001). Aspectual influences on early tense comprehension. *Journal of Child Language, 28,* 661–681.

Wagner, M. E., Schubert, H. J. P., & Schubert, D. S. P. (1985). Family size effects: A review. *Journal of Genetic Psychology, 146,* 65–78.

Wahlstrom, K. (2002). Changing times: Findings from the first longitudinal study of later high school start times. *NASSP Bulletin, 86,* 3–21.

Wainright, J. L., Russell, S. T., & Patterson, C. J. (2004). Psychosocial adjustment, school outcomes, and romantic relationships of adolescents with same-sex parents. *Child Development, 75,* 1886–1898.

Wainryb, C., Shaw, L. A., Laupa, M., & Smith, K. R. (2001). Children's, adolescents', and young adults' thinking about different types of disagreements. *Developmental Psychology, 37,* 373–386.

Walden, T. A., & Smith, M. C. (1997). Emotion regulation. *Motivation and Emotion, 21,* 7–25.

Waldenström, U. (1999). Experience of labor and birth in 1111 women. *Journal of Psychosomatic Research, 47,* 471–482.

Waldrop, M. F., & Halverson, C. F. (1975). Intensive and extensive peer behavior: Longitudinal and cross-sectional analyses. *Child Development, 46,* 19–26.

Walk, R. D. (1968). Monocular compared to binocular depth perception in human infants. *Science, 162,* 473–475.

Walker, E. F. (2002). Adolescent neurodevelopment and psychopathology. *Current Directions in Psychological Science, 11,* 24–28.

Walker, L. J. (1984). Sex differences in the development of moral reasoning: A critical review. *Child Development, 55,* 677–691.

Walker, L. J. (1989). A longitudinal study of moral reasoning. *Child Development, 60,* 157–166.

Walker, L. J. (1991). Sex differences in moral reasoning. In W. M. Kurtines & J. L. Gewirtz (Eds.), *Handbook of moral behavior and development: Vol. 2. Research* (pp. 333–364). Hillsdale, NJ: Erlbaum.

Walker, L. J. (1996). Is one sex morally superior? In M. R. Merrens & G. G. Brannigan (Eds.), *The developmental psychologists: Research adventures across the life span.* New York: McGraw-Hill.

Walker, L., Hennig, K. H., & Krettenauer, T. (2000). Parent and peer contexts for children's moral reasoning development. *Child Development, 71,* 1033–1048.

Walker, L. J., & Pitts, R. C. (1998). Naturalistic conceptions of moral maturity. *Developmental Psychology, 34,* 403–419.

Walker-Andrews, A. S., Bahrick, L. E., Raglioni, S. S., & Diaz, I. (1991). Infant's bimodal perception of gender. *Ecological Psychology, 3,* 55–75.

Walker-Andrews, A. S., & Lennon, E. M. (1985). Auditory-visual perception of changing distance by human infants. *Child Development, 56,* 544–548.

Wallerstein, J. S., Corbin, S. B., & Lewis, J. M. (1988). Children of divorce: A ten-year study. In E. M. Hetherington & J. Arasteh (Eds.), *Impact of divorce, single-parenting, and stepparenting on children* (pp. 198–214). Hillsdale, NJ: Erlbaum.

Wallerstein, J. S., & Kelly, J. B. (1980). *Surviving the breakup: How children and parents cope with divorce.* New York: Basic Books.

Walsh, B. T., & Devlin, M. J. (1998). Eating disorders: Progress and problems. *Science, 280,* 1387–1390.

Wang, Q. (2004). The emergence of cultural self-constructs: Autobiographical memory and self-description in European American and Chinese children. *Developmental Psychology, 40,* 3–15.

Ward, L. M. (2004). Wading through stereotypes: Positive and negative associations between media use and Black adolescents' conceptions of self. *Developmental Psychology, 40,* 284–294.

Ward, S., Reale, G., & Levinson, D. (1972). Children's perceptions, explanations, and judgments of television advertising. In E. A. Rubenstein, G. A. Comstock, & J. P. Murray (Eds.), *Television and social behavior: Vol. 4. Television in day-to-day life: Patterns of use.* Washington, DC: U.S. Government Printing Office.

Wark, G. R., & Krebs, D. L. (1996). Gender and dilemma differences in real-life moral judgment. *Developmental Psychology, 32,* 220–230.

Warkany, J., & Schraffenberger, E. (1947). Congenital malformations induced in rats by roentgen rays. *American Journal of Roentgenology and Radium Therapy, 57,* 455–463.

Warren, S. L., Huston, L., Egeland, B., & Sroufe, L. A. (1997). Child and adolescent anxiety disorders and early attachment. *Journal of the American Academy of Child and Adolescent Psychiatry, 36,* 637–644.

Wass, T. S., Persutte, W. H., & Hobbins, J. C. (2001). The impact of prenatal alcohol exposure on frontal cortex development in utero. *American Journal of Obstetrics and Gynecology, 185,* 737–742.

Waterhouse, L., Fein, D., & Modahl, C. (1996). Neurofunctional mechanisms in autism. *Psychological Review, 103,* 457–489.

Waters, E., & Deane, K. E. (1985). Defining and assessing individual differences in attachment relationships: Q-methodology and the organization of behavior in infancy and early childhood. In I. Bretherton & E. Waters (Eds.), *Growing points of attachment theory and research. Monographs of the Society for Research in Child Development, 50* (1–2, Serial No. 209).

Waters, E., Wippman, J., & Sroufe, L. A. (1979). Attachment, positive affect, and competence in the peer group: Two studies in construct validation. *Child Development, 50,* 821–829.

Watson, A. C., Nixon, C. L., Wilson, A., & Capage, L. (1999). Social interaction skills and theory of mind in young children. *Developmental Psychology, 35,* 386–391.

Watson, J. B. (1930). *Behaviorism.* New York: W. W. Norton.

Watson, J. S. (1971). Cognitive-perceptual development in infancy: Settings for the seventies. *Merrill-Palmer Quarterly, 17,* 139–152.

Watson, J. S., & Ramey, C. T. (1972). Reactions to response-contingent stimulation in early infancy. *Merrill-Palmer Quarterly, 18,* 219–227.

Waxman, S. R., & Booth, A. E. (2000). Principles that are invoked in the acquisition of words, but not facts. *Cognition, 77,* B33–B43.

Weber-Fox, C. M., & Neville, H. J. (1996). Maturational contraints on functional specializations for language processing: ERP and behavioral evidence in bilingual speakers. *Journal of Cognitive Neuroscience, 8,* 231–256.

Wechsler, D. (1991). *Wechsler intelligence scale for children—Third edition: Manual.* New York: The Psychological Corporation.

Weinberg, M. K., & Tronick, E. Z. (1994). Beyond the face: An empirical study of infant affective configurations of facial, vocal, gestural, and regulatory behaviors. *Child Development, 65,* 1503–1515.

Weinberg, W. K., Tronick, E. Z., Cohn, J. F., & Olson, K. L. (1999). Gender differences in emotional expressivity and self-regulation during early infancy. *Developmental Psychology, 35,* 175–188.

Weinberger, S. E., & Weiss, S. T. (1988). Pulmonary diseases. In G. N. Burrow & T. F. Ferris (Eds.), *Medical complications of pregnancy* (3rd ed., pp. 448–484). Philadelphia: W.B. Saunders.

Weiner, B., & Handel, S. J. (1985). A cognition-emotion-action sequence: Anticipated emotional consequences of causal attributions and reported communication strategy. *Developmental Psychology, 21,* 102–107.

Weinfield, N. S., Ogawa, J. R., & Sroufe, L. A. (1997). Early attachment as a pathway to adolescent peer competence. *Journal of Research on Adolescence, 7,* 241–265.

Weisner, T. S. (1996). Why ethnography should be the most important method in the study of human development. In A. C. R. Jessor & R. A. Shweder (Eds.), *Ethnography and human development* (pp. 305–324). Chicago: University of Chicago Press.

Weiss, L. H., & Schwarz, J. C. (1996). The relationship between parenting types and older adolescents' personality, academic achievement, adjustment, and substance abuse. *Child Development, 67,* 2101–2114.

Weitzman, L. J. (1985). *The divorce revolution: The unexpected social and economic consequences for women and children in America.* New York: Free Press.

Weitzman, M., Gortmaker, S., & Sobol, A. (1992). Maternal smoking and behavior problems of children. *Pediatrics, 90,* 342–349.

Welch-Ross, M. K. (1995). An integrative model of the development of autobiographical memory. *Developmental Review, 15,* 338–365.

Welch-Ross, M. K., & Schmidt, C. R. (1996). Gender-schema development and children's constructive story memory: Evidence for a developmental model. *Child Development, 67,* 820–835.

Wellman, H. M. (1977). The early development of intentional memory. *Human Development, 20,* 86–101.

Wellman, H. M. (1990). *The child's theory of mind.* Cambridge, MA: MIT Press.

Wellman, H. M., Cross, D., & Watson, J. (2001). Meta-analysis of theory-of-mind development: The truth about false belief. *Child Development, 72,* 655–684.

Wellman, H. M., & Estes, D. (1986). Early understanding of mental entities: A reexamination of childhood realism. *Child Development, 57,* 910–923.

Wellman, H. M., & Lempers, J. D. (1977). The naturalistic communicative abilities of two-year-olds. *Child Development, 48,* 1052–1057.

Wellman, H. M., & Liu, D. (2004). Scaling of theory-of-mind tasks. *Child Development, 75,* 523–541.

Welsh, M. C. (2002). Developmental and clinical variations in executive functions. In D. L. Molfese & V. J. Molfese (Eds.), *Developmental variations in learning: Applications to social, executive function, language, and reading skills* (pp. 139–185). Mahwah, NJ: Erlbaum.

Wenglinsky, H. (1998). *Does it compute? The relationship between educational technology and student achievement in mathematics.* Princeton, NJ: Educational Testing Service.

Wentzel, K. R. (2002). Are effective teachers like good parents? Teaching styles and student adjustment in early adolescence. *Child Development, 73,* 287–301.

Wentzel, K. R., & Erdley, C. A. (1993). Strategies for making friends: Relations to social behavior and peer acceptance in early adolescence. *Developmental Psychology, 29,* 819–826.

Werker, J. F., & Desjardins, R. N. (1995). Listening to speech in the 1st year of life: Experiential influences on phoneme perception. *Current Directions in Psychological Science, 4,* 76–81.

Werker, J. F., & Lalonde, C. E. (1988). Cross-language speech perception: Initial capabilities and developmental change. *Developmental Psychology, 24,* 672–683.

Werker, J. F., & Tees, R. C. (1984). Cross-language speech perception: Evidence for perceptual reorganization during the first year of life. *Infant Behavior and Development, 7,* 49–63.

Werner, E. E. (1972). Infants around the world: Cross-cultural studies of psychomotor development from birth to two years. *Journal of Cross-Cultural Psychology, 3,* 111–134.

Werner, E. E. (1995). Resilience in development. *Current Directions in Psychological Science, 4,* 81–85.

Wertsch, J. V. (1985). *Vygotsky and the social formation of mind.* Cambridge, MA: Harvard University Press.

Wertsch, J. V., & Tulviste, P. (1992). L. S. Vygotsky and contemporary developmental psychology. *Developmental Psychology, 28,* 548–557.

Wertz, D. C., & Fletcher, J. C. (1993). Feminist criticism of prenatal diagnosis: A response. *Clinical Obstetrics and Gynecology, 36,* 541–567.

Wertz, D. C., & Fletcher, J. C. (1998). Ethical and social issues in prenatal sex selection: A survey of geneticists in 37 nations. *Social Science & Medicine, 46,* 255–273.

West, T. A., & Bauer, P. J. (1999). Assumptions of infantile amnesia: Are there differences between early and later memories? *Memory, 7,* 257–278.

Westinghouse Learning Corporation. (1969). *Impact of Head Start: Evaluation of the effects of Head Start on children's cognitive and affective development.* Washington, DC: Clearinghouse for Federal, Scientific, and Technical Information.

Wexler, K. (1982). A principle theory for language acquisition. In E. Wanner & L. Gleitman (Eds.), *Language acquisition: The state of the art* (pp. 288–315). Cambridge: Cambridge University Press.

Whalen, C. K., Jamner, L. D., Henker, B., Delfino, R. J., & Lozano, J. M. (2002). The ADHD Spectrum and everyday life: Experience sampling of adolescent moods, activities, smoking, and drinking. *Child Development, 73,* 209–227.

Whalen, R. E. (1984). Multiple actions of steroids and their antagonists. *Archives of Sexual Behavior, 13,* 497–502.

Whitaker, R. C., Wright, J. A., Pepe, M. S., Seidel, K. D., & Dietz, W. H. (1997). Predicting obesity in young adulthood from childhood and parental obesity. *New England Journal of Medicine, 337,* 869–873.

White, B. Y., & Fredriksen, J. R. (1998). Inquiry, modeling, and metacognition: Making science accessible to all students. *Cognition and Instruction, 16*(63), 90–91.

White, R. W. (1959). Motivation reconsidered: The concept of competence. *Psychological Review, 66,* 297–333.

Whitehurst, G. J., Arnold, D. S., Epstein, J. N., Angell, A. L., Smith, M., & Fischel, J. E. (1994). A picture book reading intervention in day care and home for children from low-income families. *Developmental Psychology, 30,* 679–689.

Whitehurst, G. J., & Fischel, J. E. (2000). Reading and language impairments in conditions of poverty. In D. V. M. Bishop & L. B. Leonard (Eds.), *Speech and language impairments in children: Causes, characteristics, intervention and outcome* (pp. 53–71). Hove, UK: Psychology Press.

Whiteman, S. D., & Buchanan, C. M. (2002). Mothers' and children's expectations for adolescence: The impact of perceptions of an older sibling's experience. *Journal of Family Psychology, 16,* 157–171.

Whiting, B. B., & Edwards, C. P. (1988). *Children of different worlds.* Cambridge, MA: Harvard University Press.

Whiting, B. B., & Whiting, J. W. M. (1975). *Children of six cultures: A psychocultural analysis.* Cambridge, MA: Harvard University Press.

Whitlock, J. L., Powers, J. L., & Eckenrode, J. (2006). The virtual cutting edge: The Internet and adolescent self-injury. *Developmental Psychology, 42,* 407–417.

Wichstrøm, L. (1999). The emergence of gender difference in depressed mood during adolescence: The role of intensified gender socialization. *Developmental Psychology, 35,* 232–245.

Widom, C. S. (1989). The cycle of violence. *Science, 244,* 160–166.

Wigfield, A., & Eccles, J. S. (1994). Children's competence beliefs, achievement values, and general self-esteem: Changes across elementary and middle school. *Journal of Early Adolescence, 14,* 107–138.

Willats, P. (1990). Development of problem-solving strategies in infancy. In D. F. Bjorklund (Ed.), *Children's strategies: Contemporary views of cognitive development* (pp. 23–66). Hillsdale, NJ: Erlbaum.

Williams, J. E., & Best, D. L. (1982). *Measuring sex stereotypes: A thirty nation study.* Beverly Hills, CA: Sage.

Williams, J. M., & Currie, C. (2000). Self-esteem and physical development in early adolescence: Pubertal timing and body image. *Journal of Early Adolescence, 20,* 120–149.

Williams, L. J., Rasmussen, S. A., Flores, A., Kirby, R. S., & Edmonds, L. D. (2005). Decline in the prevalence of spina bifida and anencephaly by race/ethnicity: 1995–2002. *Pediatrics, 116,* 580–586.

Willig, A. C., & Ramirez, J. D. (1993). The evaluation of bilingual education. In M. B. Arias & U. Casanova (Eds.), *Bilingual education: Politics, practice, research.* Chicago: National Society for the Study of Education.

Willinger, M., Ko, C.-W., Hoffman, H. J., Kessler, R. C., & Corwin, M. J. (2000). Factors associated with caregivers' choice of infant sleep position, 1994–1998: The National Infant Sleep Position Study. *Journal of the American Medical Association, 283,* 2135–2142.

Willinger, M., Ko, C-W., Hoffman, H. J., Kessler, R. C., & Corwin, M. J. (2003). Trends in infant bed sharing in the United States, 1993–2000: The National Infant Sleep Position Study. *Archives of Pediatrics & Adolescent Medicine, 157,* 43–49.

Wilson, B. J., & Weiss, A. J. (1992). Developmental differences in children's reactions to a toy advertisement linked to a toy-based cartoon. *Journal of Broadcasting and Electronic Media, 36,* 371–394.

Wilson, J. G. (1977). Current status of teratology: General principles and mechanisms derived from animal studies. In J. G. Wilson & F. C. Fraser (Eds.), *Handbook of teratology: Vol. 1. General principles and etiology.* New York: Plenum Press.

Wilson, M. N. (1986). The black extended family: An analytical consideration. *Developmental Psychology, 22,* 246–258.

Wimmer, H., & Perner, J. (1983). Beliefs about beliefs: Representation and constraining function of wrong beliefs in young children's understanding of deception. *Cognition, 13,* 103–128.

Winner, E. (1979). New names for old things: The emergence of metaphoric language. *Journal of Child Language, 6,* 469–491.

Winner, E. (1996). *Gifted children: Myths and realities.* New York: Basic Books.

Winner, E. (1997). Exceptionally high intelligence and schooling. *American Psychologist, 52,* 1070–1081.

Winner, E. (2000). The origins and ends of giftedness. *American Psychologist, 55,* 159–169.

Winsler, A., Carlton, M. P., & Barry, M. J. (2000). Age-related changes in preschool children's systematic use of private speech in a natural setting. *Journal of Child Language, 27,* 665–687.

Winsler, A., Diaz, R. M., Atencio, D. J., McCarthy, E. M., & Chabay, L. A. (2000). Verbal self-regulation over time in preschool children at risk for attention and behavior problems. *Journal of Child Psychology and Psychiatry, 41,* 875–886.

Winsler, A., & Naglieri, J. (2003). Overt and covert verbal problem–solving strategies: Developmental trends in use, awareness, and relations with task performance in children aged 5 to 17. *Child Development, 74,* 659–678.

Winstead, B. A. (1986). Sex differences in same-sex friendships. In V. J. Derlaga & B. A. Winstead (Eds.), *Friendship and social interaction.* New York: Springer-Verlag.

Wolchik, S. A., West, S. G., Westover, S., Sandler, I. N., Martin, A., Lustig, J., et al. (2002). The children of divorce parenting intervention: Outcome evaluation of an empirically based program. In T. A. Revenson & A. R. D'Augelli (Eds.), *A quarter century of community psychology: Readings from the American Journal of Community Psychology* (pp. 409–444). New York: Kluwer Academic/Plenum Publishers.

Wolfe, D. A. (1985). Child-abusive parents: An empirical review and analysis. *Psychological Bulletin, 97,* 462–482.

Wolfe, D. A., Fairbank, J., Kelly, J. A., & Bradlyn, A. S. (1983). Child abusive parents' physiological responses to stressful and non-stressful behavior in children. *Behavioral Assessment, 5,* 363–371.

Wolfe, D. A., Sas, L., & Wekerle, C. (1994). Factors associated with the development of post-traumatic stress disorder among child victims of sexual abuse. *Child Abuse and Neglect, 18,* 37–50.

Wolff, P. H. (1969). The natural history of crying and other vocalizations in early infancy. In B. Foss (Ed.), *Determinants of infant behavior* (Vol. 4). London: Methuen.

Wolff, P. H. (1987). *The development of behavioral states and the expression of emotions in early infancy.* Chicago: University of Chicago Press.

Wolfner, G. D., & Gelles, R. J. (1993). A profile of violence toward children: A national study. *Child Abuse and Neglect, 17,* 197–212.

Wolfson, A. R., & Carskadon, M. A. (1998). Sleep schedules and daytime functioning in adolescents. *Child Development, 69,* 875–887.

Wood, D. J., Bruner, J. S., & Ross, G. (1976). The role of tutoring in problem solving. *Journal of Child Psychology and Psychiatry, 17,* 89–100.

Woolfe, T., Want, S. C., & Siegal, M. (2002). Signposts to development: Theory of mind in deaf children. *Child Development, 73,* 768–778.

Worobey, J. (1985). A review of Brazelton-based interventions to enhance parent-infant interaction. *Journal of Reproductive and Infant Psychology, 3,* 64–73.

Wright, J. C., Huston, A. C., Murphy, K. C., St. Peters, M., Piñon, M., Scantlin, R., & Kotler, J. (2001). The relations of early television viewing to school readiness and vocabulary of children from low-income families: The Early Window Project. *Child Development, 72,* 1347–1366.

Wright, J. C., Huston, A. C., Reitz, A. L., & Piemyat, S. (1994). Young children's perceptions of television reality: Determinants and developmental differences. *Developmental Psychology, 30,* 229–239.

Wright, K. (1998, May). Human in the age of mechanical reproduction. *Discover, 19,* pp. 79–84.

Wright, M. O., & Masten, A. S. (2005). Resilience processes in development. In S. Goldstein & R. B. Brooks (Eds.), *Handbook of resilience in children* (pp. 17–37). New York: Klewar/Plenum.

Wynn, K. (1992a). Addition and subtraction by human infants. *Nature, 358,* 749–750.

Wynn, K. (1992b). Children's acquisition of the number words and the counting system. *Cognitive Psychology, 24,* 220–251.

Wynn, K. (1998). Psychological foundations of number: Numerical competence in human infants. *Trends in Cognitive Science, 2,* 296–303.

Xu, F., & Spelke, E. S. (2000). Large number discrimination in 6-month-olds. *Cognition, 74,* B1–B11.

Yakovlev, P. I., & Lecours, A. R. (1967). The myelogenetic cycles of regional maturation of the brain. In A. Minkowski (Ed.), *Regional development of the brain in early life.* Oxford: Blackwell.

Yale, M. E., Messinger, D. S., Cobo-Lewis, A. B., Oller, D. K., & Eilers, R. E. (1999). An event-based analysis of the coordination of early child vocalizations and facial actions. *Developmental Psychology, 35,* 505–513.

Yarrow, L. J., Goodwin, M. S., Manheimer, H., & Milowe, I. D. (1973). Infancy experiences and cognitive and personality development at 10 years. In L. J. Stone, H. T. Smith, & L. B. Murphy (Eds.), *The competent infant: Research and commentary.* New York: Basic Books.

Yates, M., & Youniss, J. (1996a). Community service and political-moral identity in adolescents. *Journal of Research on Adolescence, 6,* 271–284.

Yates, M., & Youniss, J. (1996b). A developmental perspective on community service in adolescence. *Social Development, 5,* 85–111.

Yogman, M. W. (1982). Observations on the father-infant relationship. In S. H. Cath, A. R. Gurwitt, & J. M. Ross (Eds.), *Father and child: Developmental and clinical perspectives.* Boston: Little, Brown.

Yogman, M. W., Dixon, S., Tronick, E., Als, H., Adamson, L., Lester, B. M., & Brazelton, T. B. (1977, April). *The goals and structure of face-to-face interaction between infants and their fathers.* Paper presented at the biennial meeting of the Society for Research in Child Development, New Orleans.

Yonas, A., & Owsley, C. (1987). Development of visual space perception. In P. Salapatek & L. Cohen (Eds.), *Handbook of infant perception: From perception to cognition* (Vol. 2). Orlando, FL: Academic Press.

Yoon, P. W., Olney, R. S., Khoury, M. J., Sappenfield, W. M., Chavez, G. F., & Taylor, D. (1997). Contribution of birth defects and genetic diseases to pediatric hospitalizations. *Archives of Pediatrics & Adolescent Medicine, 151,* 1096–1103.

Young, S. K., Fox, N. A., & Zahn-Waxler, C. (1999). The relations between temperament and empathy in 2-year-olds. *Developmental Psychology, 35,* 1189–1197.

Youngblade, L. M., & Belsky, J. (1992). Parent-child antecedents of 5-year-olds' close friendships: A longitudinal analysis. *Developmental Psychology, 28,* 700–713.

Young-Browne, G., Rosenfeld, H. M., & Horowitz, F. D. (1977). Infant discrimination of facial expression. *Child Development, 48,* 555–562.

Younger, A., Gentile, C., & Burgess, K. (1993). Children's perceptions of social withdrawal: Changes across age. In K. H. Rubin & J. B. Asend-orpf (Eds.), *Social withdrawal, inhibition, and shyness in childhood* (pp. 215–235). Hillsdale, NJ: Erlbaum.

Younger, B. A. (2003). Parsing objects into categories: Infants' perception and use of correlated attributes. In D. H. Rakison & L. M. Oakes (Eds.), *Early category and concept development* (pp. 77–102). New York: Oxford University Press.

Youniss, J., McClellan, J., & Mazur, B. (2004). Voluntary service, peer group orientation, and civic engagement. *Journal of Adolescent Research, 16,* 456-468.

Youniss, J., McLellan, J., Su, Y., & Yates, M. (1999). The role of community service in identity development: Normative, unconventional, and deviant orientations. *Journal of Adolescent Research, 14,* 248–261.

Youniss, J., McLellan, J., & Yates, M. (1999). Religion, community service, and identity in American youth. *Journal of Adolescence, 22,* 243–253.

Yule, W. (1998). Posttraumatic stress disorder in children and its treatment. In T. W. Miller (Ed.), *Children of trauma: Stressful life events and their effects on children and adolescents* (pp. 219–243). Madison, CT: International Universities Press.

Yule, W. (2000). Emmanuel Miller lectures from pogroms to "ethnic cleansing": Meeting the needs of war affected children. *Journal of Child Psychology and Psychiatry, 41,* 695–702.

Yunger, J. L., Carver, P. R., & Perry, D. G. (2004). Does gender identity influence children's psychological well-being? *Developmental Psychology, 40,* 572–582.

Zagon, I. S., & McLaughlin, P. J. (1984). An overview of the neurobehavioral sequelae of perinatal opiod exposure. In J. Yanai (Ed.), *Neurobehavioral teratology.* New York: Elsevier.

Zahn-Waxler, C., Friedman, S. L., & Cummings, E. M. (1983). Children's emotions and behaviors in response to infants' cries. *Child Development, 54,* 1522–1528.

Zahn-Waxler, C., Radke-Yarrow, M., Wagner, E., & Chapman, M. (1992). Development of concern for others. *Developmental Psychology, 28,* 126–136.

Zajonc, R. B., Markus, H., & Markus, G. B. (1979). The birth order puzzle. *Journal of Personality and Social Psychology, 37,* 1325–1341.

Zaslow, M. J., Dion, M. R., Morrison, D. R., Weinfield, N., Ogawa, J., & Tabors, P. (1999). Protective factors in the development of preschool-age children of young mothers receiving welfare. In E. M. Hetherington (Ed.), *Coping with divorce, single parenting, and remarriage* (pp. 193–223). Mahwah, NJ: Erlbaum.

Zeanah, C. H., Smyke, A. T., Koga, S. F., Carlson, E., & The Bucharest Early Intervention Project. (2005). Attachment in institutionalized and community children in Romania. *Child Development, 76,* 1015–1028.

Zebrowitz, L. A., Kendall-Tackett, K., & Fafel, J. (1991). The influence of children's facial maturity on parental expectations and punishments. *Journal of Experimental Child Psychology, 52,* 221–238.

Zelazo, N. A., Zelazo, P. R., Cohen, K. M., & Zelazo, P. D. (1993). Specificity of practice effects on elementary neuromotor patterns. *Developmental Psychology, 29,* 686–691.

Zelazo, P. D., Helwig, C. C. & Lau, A. (1996). Intention, act, and outcome in behavioral prediction and moral judgment. *Child Development, 67,* 2478–2492.

Zelazo, P. R. (1983). The development of walking: New findings and old assumptions. *Journal of Motor Behavior, 15,* 99–137.

Zelazo, P. R. (1998). McGraw and the development of unaided walking. *Developmental Review, 18,* 449–471.

Zeskind, P. S. (1981). Behavioral dimensions and cry sounds of infants of differential fetal growth. *Infant Behavior and Development, 4,* 297–306.

Zhou, Q., Eisenberg, N., Losoya, S. H., Fabes, R. A., Reiser, M., Guthrie, I. K., et al. (2002). The relations of parental warmth and positive expressiveness to children's empathy-related responding and social functioning: A longitudinal study. *Developmental Psychology, 73,* 893–915.

Zhou, Q., Eisenberg, N., Wang, Y., & Reiser, M. (2004). Chinese children's effortful control and dispositional anger/frustration: Relations to parenting styles and children's social functioning. *Developmental Psychology, 40,* 352–366.

Zhu, J. L., Madsen, K. M., Vestergaard, M., Olesen, A. V., Basso, O., & Olsen, J. (2005). Paternal age and congenital malformations. *Human Reproduction, 20,* 3173–3177.

Ziegert, D. I., Kistner, J. A., Castro, R., & Robertson, B. (2001). Longitudinal study of young children's responses to challenging achievement situations. *Child Development, 72,* 609–624.

Zigler, E. (1967). Familial mental retardation: A continuing dilemma. *Science, 155,* 292–298.

Zigler, E., & Butterfield, E. C. (1968). Motivational aspects of changes in IQ test performance of culturally deprived nursery school children. *Child Development, 39,* 1–14.

Zill, N. (1988). Behavior, achievement, and health problems among children in stepfamilies: Findings from a national survey of child health. In E. M. Hetherington & J. D. Arasteh (Eds.), *Impact of divorce, single-parenting, and stepparenting on children.* Hillsdale, NJ: Erlbaum.

Zill, N. (1994). Understanding why children in stepfamilies have more learning and behavior problems than children in nuclear families. In A. Booth & J. Dunn (Eds.), *Stepfamilies: Who benefits? Who does not?* (pp. 97–106) Hillsdale, NJ: Erlbaum.

Zill, N., Morrison, D. R., & Coiro, M. J. (1993). Long-term effects of parental divorce on parent-child relationships, adjustment, and achievement in young adulthood. *Journal of Family Psychology, 7,* 1–13.

Zimet, G. D., Owens, R., Dahms, W., Cutler, M., Litvene, M., & Cuttler, L. (1997). Psychosocial outcome of children evaluated for short stature. *Archives of Pediatric and Adolescent Medicine, 151,* 1017–1023.

Zimmerman, M. A., Copeland, L. A., Shope, J. T., & Dielman, T. E. (1997). A longitudinal study of self-esteem: Implications for adolescent development. *Journal of Youth and Adolescence, 26,* 117–142.

Zucker, K. J., & Bradley, S. J. (2000). Gender identity disorder. In C. H. Zeanah, Jr. (Ed.), *Handbook of infant mental health* (2nd ed., pp. 412–424). New York: Guilford Press.

Zuckerman, B., & Bresnahan, K. (1991). Developmental and behavioral consequences of prenatal drug and alcohol exposure. *Pediatric Clinics of North America, 38,* 1387–1406.

CREDITS

Text Credits

Chapter 1: p. 8 *Figure 1.1* From Robert S. Siegler, *Emerging Minds: The Process of Change in Children's Thinking.* Copyright © 1996. Reprinted by Oxford University Press, England. **p. 29** *Figure 1.4* From Garabino, J., "Sociocultural Risk: Dangers to Competence," in C. Kopp and J. Krakow (Eds.), *Child Development in a Social Context.* Copyright © 1982. Reprinted by permission of Pearson Education, Inc.

Chapter 2: p. 44 *Figure 2.1* Adapted from Ram, A., & Ross, H. S. "Problem-solving, contention, and struggle: How siblings resolve a conflict of interests," *Child Development, 72,* 2001, p.1715 (Table 3). Reprinted with permission from the Society for Research in Child Development. **p. 50** *Figure 2.2* From Sheldrick, R.C. (2004). Social networks and degree of psychopathy among adolescent offenders (Doctoral dissertation, Temple University, 1990). Dissertation Abstracts International, 65, 1964. Reprinted by permission of the author. **p. 51** *Figure 2.3* From M. Gardner & L. Steinberg, "Peer influence on risk taking, risk preference, and risky decision making in adolescence and adulthood: An experimental study," *Developmental Psychology, 41,* pp. 625–635. Reprinted with permission of the publisher, American Psychological Association. **p. 54** From Gagnon, M. & Ladouceur, R., "Behavioral treatment of child stutterers: Replication and extension," *Behavior Therapy, 23,* 1992, pp. 113–129. Copyright 1992 by the Association for Advancement of Behavior Therapy. Reprinted by permission of the publisher. **p. 58** *Figure 2.7* From Cole, D. A., Maxwell, S. E., Martin, J. M., Peeke, L. G., Seroczynski, A. D., Tram, J. M., Hoffman, K. B., Ruiz, M. D., Jacquez, F., & Maschman, T., "The development of multiple domains of child and adolescent self-concept: A cohort sequential longitudinal design," *Child Development, 72,* 2001, p. 1735 (Figure 3). Reprinted with permission from the Society for Research in Child Development. **p. 60** *Figure 2.8* Data from R. S. Siegler & E. Stern, "Conscious and unconscious strategy discoveries: A microgenetic analysis," *Journal of Experimental Psychology, General, 127,* 1998, pp. 377–397. Reprinted with permission of the publisher, American Psychological Association.

Chapter 3: p. 72 *Figure 3.1* Adapted from Warren Isensee, *The Chronicle of Higher Education,* September 3, 1986. Reprinted by permission of Warren Isensee. **p. 100** *Table 3.5* Intelligence, Genes, and Success: Scientists Respond to The Bell Curve, 1997, pp. 45–70, "IQ and Degrees of Relatedness: Similarities of Genetically Related and Unrelated Individuals Who Live Together and Apart," B. Devlin, S. E. Feinberg, D. P. Resnick, & K. Roder (Eds.). With kind permission of Springer Science and Business Media, and the author.

Chapter 4: p. 120 *Figure 4.3* Reprinted from *The Developing Human* by Keith L. Moore, Ph.D. Copyright 1998, with permission from Elsevier. **p. 131** *Figure 4.4* Reprinted from Pediatric Clinics of North America, 47, Lindegren, Steinberg, & Byers, "Epidemiology of HIV/AIDS in children," pp. 1–20, Copyright 2000, with permission from Elsevier. **p. 133** *Table 4.4* From Reece, E. A., Hobbins, J. C., Mahoney, M. J., and Petrie, R. H., *Handbook of Medicine of the Fetus and the Mother.* Copyright © 1995. Reprinted by permission of Dr. Albert Reece. **p. 143** *Figure 4.7* From Brooks-Gunn, Kiebanov, Liaw, & Spiker, "Enha-ncing the Development of Low-Birthweight, Premature Infants: Changes in Cognition and Behavior Over the First Three Years," *Child Development, 64,* 736–754. Reprinted with permission from the Society for Research in Child Development. **p. 144** *Table 4.5* From V. Apgar, "A Proposal for a New Method of Evaluation of the Newborn Infant," *Anesthesia and Analgesia: Current Researches, 32,* 1953, 260–267. Reprinted by permission of Lippincott Williams & Wilkins.

Chapter 5: p. 156 *Figure 5.4* Illustration copyright 1998 John W. Karapelou. Reprinted by permission of John W. Karapelou. **p. 157** *Figure 5.5* Reprinted from *Neuropsychologia, 28,* Huttenlocher, P. R., "Morphometric Study of Human Cerebral Cortex Development," pp. 517–527, Copyright 1990, with permission from Elsevier. **p. 175** *Figure 5.8* Reprinted from *Infant Perception: From Sensation to Cognition,* Vol. 1 by L. B. Cohen and P. Salapatek (Eds.), "Pattern Perception in Early Infancy" by P. Salapatek, Copyright 1975, with permission from Elsevier.

Chapter 6: p. 191 *Figure 6.1* From Treiber et al., "Perception of a 'Subjective' Contour by Infants," *Child Development, 51,* 915–917. Reprinted by permission of Blackwell Publishing. **p. 192** *Figure 6.2* From V. M. Cassia, C. Turati, & F. Simon, "A nonspecific bias explains newborns' face preferences," *Psychological Science, 15,* 2004, pp. 379–383. Reprinted by permission of Blackwell Publishing. **p. 193** *Figure 6.3* Adapted from Spelke, E. S., "Perception of Unity, Persistence and Identity: Thoughts on Infants' Conceptions of Objects," in J. Mehler and R. Fox (Eds.), *Neonate Cognition: Beyond the Blooming, Buzzing Confusion,* 1985. Reprinted by permission. **p. 195** *Figure 6.4* From Adolph, K. E., "Specificity of learning: Why infants fall over a veritable cliff," *Psychological Science, 11,* 2000, p. 292. Reprinted by permission of Blackwell Publishing. **p. 203** *Figure 6.6* Adapted from Baillargeon, R. (1987). "Object Permanence in 3 1/2 – 4 1/2 month-old infants," *Developmental Psychology, 23,* pp. 655–664, 1987. Adapted with permission.**p. 204** *Figure 6.7* From Spelke, E., Breinlinger, K., Macomber, J., & Jacobson, K., "Origins of knowledge," *Psychological Review, 99,* pp. 605–632, 1992. Reprinted with permission. **p. 209** *Figure 6.9 Nature* by K. Wynn. Copyright 1992 by Nature Pubg Group. Reproduced with permission of Nature Pubg Group in the format Textbook via Copyright Clearance Center. **p. 210** *Figure 6.10* From J. F. Fagan, "Infant Recognition Memory: The Effects of Length ...," *Child Development, 45,* 1974, pp. 351–356. Reprinted by permission of Blackwell Publishing. **p. 213** *Figure 6.13* Adapted from Z. Chen, R. P. Sanchez, and T. Campbell, "From beyond to within their grasp: The rudiments of analogical problem solving in 10- and 13-month-olds," *Developmental Psychology, 33,* pp. 790–801, 1997. Adapted with permission. **p. 218** *Figure 6.14* Reprinted from *Infant Behavior & Development, 8,* Fernald, A., "Four-month-olds Prefer to Listen to Motherese," pp. 181–195, Copyright 1985, with permission from Elsevier. **p. 222** *Figure 6.15* From Bates, Thal, Fenson, Dale, Reznick, Reilley, & Hartung, "Developmental and Stylistic Variation in the Composition of Early Vocabulary," *Journal of Child Language, 21,* 1994, pp. 85–123. Reprinted with the permission of Cambridge University Press. **p. 223** *Figure 6.16* Adapted from Goldfield, B. A. & Reznick, J. S., "Early Lexical Acquisition: Rate, Content, & the Vocabulary Spurt," *Journal of Child Language, 17,* 1990, pp. 171–183. Reprinted with the permission of Cambridge University Press. **p. 226** *Table 6.2* Bayley Scales of Infant Development. Copyright © 1993, 1984, 1969 by Harcourt Assessment, Inc. Reproduced with permission. All rights reserved.

Chapter 7: p. 258 *Figure 7.3* Adapted from T. M. Field, "Affective Displays of High-Risk Infants During Early Interactions," in T. Field and A. Fogel (Eds.), *Emotion and Early Interaction,* 1982, p. 109. Reprinted by permission of Erlbaum, and the author.

p. 261 *Figure 7.4* From M. Nachmias, M. Gunnar, S. Mangelsdorf, R. Parritz, and K. Buss, "Behavioral inhibition and stress reactivity: Moderating role of attachment security," *Child Development, 67,* 1996, pp. 508–522. Reprinted by permission of the publisher, Blackwell.

Chapter 8: **p. 273** *Figure 8.1* From Brown and Pollitt, "Malnutrition, Poverty and Intellectual Development," *Scientific American, 274* (Feb. 1996), pp. 38–43. Reprinted by permission. **p. 276** *Figure 8.2* Adapted from Pick, A. D., "Improvement of Visual and Tactual Discrimination," *Journal of Experimental Psychology, 69,* 1965, pp. 331–339. Reprinted by permission of the author. **p. 277** *Figure 8.3* From Gopnik, A., & Rosati, A. (2001), "Duck or Rabbit? Reversing ambiguous figures and understanding ambiguous representations," *Developmental Science, 4,* pp. 175–183. Reprinted by permission of the publisher, Blackwell Publishing. **p. 287** *Figure 8.7* From *The Origins of Intellect: Piaget's Theory* (2nd ed.) by John L. Phillips. © 1975 by W.H. Freeman and Company. Used with permission of Worth Publishers. **p. 302** *Figure 8.8* From Kraus et al., "The Development of Communication," *Child Development, 40,* 255–266. Reprinted by permission of the publisher, Blackwell Publishing.

Chapter 9: **p. 313** *Figure 9.1* From Cole, Zahn-Waxler, & Smith, "Expressive Control During a Disappointment: Variations Related to Preschoolers' Behavior Problems," *Developmental Psychology, 30,* 1994, pp. 835–846. **p. 323** *Table 9.1* From C. L. Martin, "Stereotypes about Children with Traditional and Nontraditional Gender Roles," *Sex Roles, 33,* 1995, pp. 727–751. Reprinted with kind permission from Springer Science and Business Media. **p. 325** *Figure 9.2* Adapted from Hyde, J. S., Fennema, E., and Lamon, S. J., "Gender Differences in Mathematics Performance: A Meta-Analysis," *Psychological Bulletin, 107,* 139–155. Copyright © 1990. Published by American Psychological Association. Reprinted with permission. **p. 326** *Figure 9.3* From Linn, M. C. et al, "Emergence and Characterization of Sex Differences...," *Child Development, 56,* 1479–1498. Reprinted by permission of the publisher, Blackwell Publishing. **p. 330** *Figure 9.4* From Bussey, K., & Bandura, A. (1992), "Self-Regulatory Mechanisms Governing Gender Development, *Child Development, 63,* p. 1243. Reprinted by permission of the publisher, Blackwell Publishing. **p. 334** *Figure 9.5* From Jacklin, C. N. et al, "Social Behavior at 33 Months...," *Child Development, 49,* 557–569. Reprinted by permission of the publisher, Blackwell Publishing.

Chapter 10: **p. 343** *Figure 10.2* From M. B. Sussman & S. K. Steinmetz, *Handbook of Marriage and the Family,* 1999, figure by W. Peterson and B. C. Rollins. Reprinted with kind permission from Springer Science and Business Media. **p. 345** *Figure 10.3* Adapted from Maccoby, E. E., & Martin, J. A., "Socialization in the Context of the Family: Parent-Child Interaction," in Mussen, *Handbook of Child Psychology* (Vol. 4, 4th ed.). Copyright © John Wiley & Sons, Inc. Reprinted with permission of John Wiley. **p. 350** *Figure 10.5* Adapted from Dix, T. H., & Grusec, J. E., "Parent Attribution in the Socialization of Children," in I. E. Sigel (Ed.), *Parental Belief Systems: The Psychological Consequences For Children.* Copyright © 1985. Reprinted by permission of Lawrence Erlbaum. **p. 365** *Table 10.2* Reprinted from *Developmental Review,* Volume 1, R. Elardo, & R. H. Bradley, "The Home Observation of the Environment (HOME) Scale: A Review of Research," pp. 113–145, Copyright 1981, with permission from Elsevier.

Chapter 11: **p. 382** *Figure 11.3* Reprinted from *Current Problems in Pediatrics, 29,* R. Strauss, "Childhood Obesity," p. 11, Copyright 1999, with permission from Elsevier. **p. 389** *Figure 11.5* From "Memory Span: Sources of Individual and Developmental Differences," by F.N. Dempster, *Psychological Bulletin, 89,* pp. 63–100. Copyright © 1981. Published by American Psychological Association. Reprinted with permission. **p. 390** *Figure 11.6* From Ornstein, Naus, & Liberty, "Rehearsal and Organization Processes in Children's Memory," *Child Development, 46,* 1975, pp. 818–830. Reprinted by permission of the publisher, Blackwell Publishing. **p. 392** *Figure 11.7* From Eskritt, M., & Lee, K, "Remember where you last saw that card: Children's production of external symbols as a memory aid," *Developmental Psychology, 38,* 254–266. Copyright © 2002. Published by American Psychological Association. Reprinted with permission. **p. 407** *Figure 11.11* Raven's Progressive Matrices. Copyright © 1998 by Harcourt Assessment, Inc. Reproduced with permission. All rights reserved. **p. 409** *Figure 11.12* From Winsler, A., Carleton, M. P., & Barry, M. J., "Age-related changes in preschool children's systematic use of private speech in a natural setting," *Journal of Child Language, 27,* 2000, 665–687. Reprinted with the permission of Cambridge University Press.

Chapter 12: **p. 420** *Figure 12.2* From Harter, S. from *The Construction of the Self: A Developmental Perspective,* 1999, p. 131. Reprinted by permission of The Guilford Press. **p. 424** *Figure 12.3* From M. L. Kamins & C. S. Dweck, "Person versus process praise and criticism: Implications for contingent self-worth and coping," *Developmental Psychology, 35,* 1999, pp. 835–847. Reprinted with permission. **p. 426** *Figure 12.4* Adapted from Harter, S., "The Determinants and Mediational Role of Global Self-Worth in Children," in N. Eisenberg (Ed.), *Contemporary Topics In Developmental Psychology,* 1987, p. 227. Copyright © 1987 John Wiley & Sons, Inc. Reprinted with permission. **p. 432** *Figure 12.5* From Colby et al., "A Longitudinal Study of Moral Development," *Monographs, 48,* No. 1–2, Serial No. 200, 1983. Reprinted by permission of the publisher, Blackwell Publishing. **p. 441** *Figure 12.6* From Serbin, L. A., Powlishta, K. K., & Gulko, J. (1993), "The Development of Sex Typing in Middle Childhood," *Monographs of the Society for Research in Child Development, 58* (No. 2, Serial No. 32), p. 35. Reprinted by permission of the publisher, Blackwell Publishing.

Chapter 13: **p. 463** *Figure 13.3* Adapted from Linn, M. C., et al, "Emergence and Characterization of Sex Differences..." *Child Development, 56,* 1479–1498. Reprinted by permission of Blackwell Publishing. **p. 467** *Figure 13.4* From Cairns, R. B., & Cairns, B. D., *Lifelines and Risks: Pathways of Youth in Our Time,* 1994. Reprinted with the permission of Cambridge University Press. **p. 470** *Figure 13.5* From Renshaw, P. D., & Brown, P. J., "Loneliness in Middle Childhood: Concurrent and Longitudinal Predictors," *Child Development 64,* 1993, pp. 1271–1284. Reprinted by permission of Blackwell Publishing. **p. 474** *Figure 13.7* From Grolnick, W. S., Ryan, R. M., & Deci, E. L., "Inner Resources for School Achievement: Motivational Mediators of Children's Perceptions of Their Parents," *Journal of Educational Psychology, 83,* p. 515, 1991. Reprinted with permission. **p. 476** *Figure 13.8* From Kuklinski, M. R., & Weinstein, R. S. (2001), "Classroom and Developmental Differences in a Path Model of Teacher Expectancy Effects," *Child Development, 72,* pp. 1554–1578. Reprinted by permission of Blackwell Publishing. **p. 480** *Figure 13.9* Reprinted with permission from H. W. Stevenson, C. Chen, and S. Y. Lee, "Mathematics Achievement of Chinese, Japanese, and American Children: Ten Years Later," *Science, 259,* 1993, 53–58. Copyright 1993 AAAS. **p. 484** *Figure 13.10* From D. A. Cole, J. M. Martin, L. Peeke, A. D. Seroczynski, and J. Fier, "Children's over- and underestimation of academic competence: A longitudinal study of gender differences, depression, and anxiety," *Child Development, 70,* 1999, pp. 459–473. Reprinted by permission of Blackwell Publishing.

Chapter 14: **p. 501** *Figure 14.3* From Marshall, W. A., & Tanner, J. M., "Puberty," in Falkner & J. M. Tanner (Eds.), *Human Growth* (Vol. 2, 2nd ed.), 1986, p. 196. With kind permission of Springer

Science and Business Media. **p. 502** *Figure 14.4* From X. Ge, R. D. Conger, & G. H. Elder, Jr., "Coming of age too early: Pubertal influences on girls' vulnerability to psychological distress," *Child Development, 67,* 1996, p. 3394. Reprinted by permission of Blackwell Publishing. **p. 522** *Figure 14.7* Wechsler Intelligence Scale for Children - Third Edition. Copyright © 1990 by Harcourt Assessment, Inc. Reproduced with permission. All rights reserved. **p. 525** *Figure 14.8* From N. Ambady, M. Shih, A. Kim, and T. L. Pittinsky, "Stereotype susceptibility in children: Effects of identity activation on quantitative performance," *Psychological Science, 12,* **pp. 385–390.** Copyright © 2001. Reprinted by permission of Blackwell Publishing Ltd.

Chapter 15: **p. 532** *Figure 15.1* From R. Larson & M. Ham, "Stress and 'Storm and Stress' in Early Adolescence: The Relationship of Negative Effects with Dysphoric Affect," *Developmental Psychology, 29,* p. 136, 1993, published by American Psychological Association. Reprinted with permission. **p. 537** *Figure 15.2* From Harter, S., & Monsour, A., "Developmental Analysis of Conflict Caused by Opposing Attributes in the Adolescent Self-Portrait," *Developmental Psychology, 28,* pp. 251–260, 1992, published by American Psychological Association. Reprinted with permission. **p. 542** *Figure 15.3* From S. E. French, E. Seidman, L. Allen, & J. L. Aber, "The development of ethnic identity during adolescence," *Developmental Psychology, 42,* pp. 1–10, 2006, published by American Psychological Association. Reprinted with permission.

Chapter 16: **p. 555** *Figure 16.1* From Mason, C. A., Cauce, A. M., Gonzales, N., & Hiraga, Y. "Neither Too Sweet Nor Too Sour: Problem Peers, Maternal Control, and Problem Behavior in African American Adolescents," *Child Development, 67,* pp. 2115–2130. Copyright © 1996. Reprinted by permission. **p. 557** *Figure 16.2* From Nicholas Zill, Ph.D., "Understanding Why Children in Stepfamilies Have More Learning and Behavior Problems Than Children in Nuclear Families," in A. Booth & J. Dunn (Eds.), *Stepfamilies: Who Benefits? Who Does Not?* Copyright © 1994. Reprinted by permission. **p. 561** *Figure 16.3* Adapted from Berndt, "Developmental Changes in Conformity to Peers and Parents," *Developmental Psychology, 15,* 1979, pp. 608–616. Reprinted by permission of the American Psychological Association.

Photo Credits

Research Applied to Parenting/Education features: © Royalty-Free Getty Images.

Chapter 1: **p. 1** © Gavriel Jecan/Corbis. **p. 2** © Richard Koek/Taxi/Getty Images. **p. 7** © Don Smetzer/Stone/Getty Images. **p. 9** © Mark Richards/PhotoEdit. **p. 11** © Sean Sprague/The Image Works. **p. 12** Erich Lessing/Art Resource. **p. 14** Archives of the History of American Psychology - The University of Akron. **p. 16** Photo courtesy of Mitzi M. Wertheim. **p. 18** © Laura Dwight. **p. 21** © Bill Anderson/Photo Researchers. **p. 25** © Erik Homburger/Stock Montage. **p. 28** © Earl & Nazima Kowall/Corbis. **p. 30** © Elizabeth Harris/Stone/Getty Images. **p. 33** Thomas McAvoy/Time & Life Pictures/Getty Images.

Chapter 2: **p. 39** © Ariel Skelley/Corbis. **p. 41** © Spencer Grant/PhotoEdit. **p. 42** © Laura Dwight. **p. 45** © Royalty-Free/Corbis. **p. 56 (left and right)** © Elizabeth Crews. **p. 61** © Lindsay Hebberd/Corbis.

Chapter 3: **p. 69** © Royalty-Free/Corbis. **p. 73** *Figure 3.2* © CNRI/Science Photo Library/Photo Researchers. **p. 82** Photo property of Williams Syndrome Association, Inc. **p. 83** © Rosenan/Custom Medical Stock Photo. **p. 8.5** *Figure 3.7* Billie Carstens/Denver Children's Hospital. **p. 87** © Laura Dwight. **p. 91** © B. E. Barnes/PhotoEdit. **p. 95** © Rachel Epstein/The Image Works. **p. 99** © Larry Williams/Corbis. **p. 103** © Robert Brenner/PhotoEdit.

Chapter 4: **p. 109** © Dave LaBelle/The Image Works. **p. 111** © David Philips/SS/Photo Researchers. **p. 121** © George Steinmetz. **p. 132** © David Young-Wolff/PhotoEdit. **p. 135** © Jessie Casson/Corbis. **p. 136** © Jules Perrier/Corbis. **p. 137** © Jules Perrier/Corbis. **p. 142** © Lisa Spindler Photography Inc./Photonica/Getty Images. **p. 145** © Elizabeth Crews.

Chapter 5: **p. 149** © Laurence Monneret/Stone/Getty Images. **p. 150** © Myrleen Ferguson Cate/PhotoEdit. **p. 153** Courtesy of Dr. Joy Hirsch, Head, The Functional MRI Laboratory, Memorial Sloan-Kettering Cancer Center, New York. **p. 155** © Oliver Meckes/Ottawa/Photo Researchers. **p. 159** © Morgan McCauley/Corbis. **p. 163** © Laura Dwight. **p. 164** © Lionel Delevingne/Stock Boston. **p. 168** © Myrleen Ferguson Cate/PhotoEdit. **p. 172** *Figure 5.7* Nadja Reissland. **p. 178** *Figure 5.9* © PhotoDisc/Getty Images. **p. 181** *Figure 5.10* Steiner, J.E. (1979). Human facial expressions in response to taste and smell stimulation. In H. W. Reese & L. P. Lipsitt (eds.), Advances in child development and behavior (Vol. 13, pp. 257–295). New York: Academic Press.

Chapter 6: **p. 188** © Elizabeth Crews. **p. 192** *Figure 6.2* Cassia et al. A nonspecific bias explains newborns' face preferences. *Psychological Science 15* 379–383. **p. 202** © Laura Dwight/PhotoEdit. **p. 206** *Figure 6.8* Adele Diamond. **p. 211** *Figure 6.11* Courtesy of Carolyn Rovee-Collier. **p. 221** © Laura Dwight. **p. 225** © Bruce Dale/National Geographic Society Image Collection.

Chapter 7: **p. 236** © Caroline Penn/Panos Pictures. **p. 243** *Figure 7.1* Reprinted with permission from Field, T. M., Woodson, R., Greenberg, R., & Cohen, D. (1982). Discrimination and imitation of facial expressions by neonates. *Science, 218,* 179–181. Copyright 1982 American Association for the Advancement of Science. **p. 249** Harlow Primate Laboratory, University of Wisconsin. **p. 253** © Laura Dwight/PhotoEdit. **p. 262** © Laura Dwight/PhotoEdit. **p. 263** © Ron Dahlquist/SuperStock.

Chapter 8: **p. 269** © Laura Dwight. **p. 280** © Laura Dwight. **p. 282** *Figure 8.6* Mandler, J. M. (1997). Development of categorization: Perceptual and conceptual categories. In G. Bremner, A. Slater, & G. Butterworth (Eds.), *Infant development: Recent advances.* East Sussex, UK: Psychology Press. Reprinted by permission of Psychology Press Limited, Hove, UK. **p. 284** © Myrleen Ferguson Cate/PhotoEdit. **p. 294** © Michael Newman/PhotoEdit.

Chapter 9: **p. 308** © Laura Dwight. **p. 310** © David Young-Wolff/PhotoEdit. **p. 311** © Tony Freeman/PhotoEdit. **p. 312** © Laura Dwight. **p. 319** © Laura Dwight/Corbis. **p. 321** © Elizabeth Crews. **p. 324** © Syracuse Newspapers /Gary Walts/The Image Works.

Chapter 10: **p. 340** © Digital Vision/Getty Images. **p. 342** © Bob Daemmrich/The Image Works. **p. 346** © A. Inden/zefa/Corbis. **p. 347** © Goodman/Photo Researchers. **p. 356** © Philip & Karen Smith/Stone/Getty Images. **p. 361** © Cindy Charles/PhotoEdit. **p. 362** © Paul Conklin.

Chapter 11: **p. 377** Kevin Taylor/Alamy. **p. 380** © David Young-Wolff/PhotoEdit. **p. 381** © Ariel Skelley/Corbis. **p. 396** © Syracuse Newspapers/Michelle Gabel/The Image Works. **p. 400** © Rachel Epstein/The Image Works. **p. 402** © Royalty-Free/Corbis. **p. 406** *Figure 11.10 Nature* by K. H. S. Kim, N. R. Relkin, K. Lee, J. Hirsch. Copyright 1997 by Nature Publishing Group (Permission). Reproduced with permission of Nature Publishing Group (Permission) in the format Textbook via Copyright Clearance Center.

Chapter 12: p. 414 BananaStock/Alamy. **p. 416** © Royalty-Free/Corbis. **p. 421** © Rachel Epstein/The Image Works. **p. 433** © R. Lord/The Image Works. **p. 438** © Sean Sprague/The Image Works. **p. 441** © Hazel Hankin/Stock Boston. **p. 442** © Bob Daemmrich.

Chapter 13: p. 448 © Elizabeth Crews. **p. 450** © Victor Englebert. **p. 451** © Geri Engberg/The ImageWorks. **p. 458** © Bob Daemmrich/Stock Boston. **p. 466** © Tony Freeman/PhotoEdit. **p. 467 (left)** © Laura Dwight. **(right)** © Myrleen Ferguson Cate/PhotoEdit. **p. 476** © Elizabeth Crews/The Image Works.

Chapter 14: p. 495 © Larry Dale Gordon/The Image Bank/Getty Images. **p. 496** © Suzanne Arms/The Image Works. **p. 504** © Laura Dwight. **p. 509** © Michael Newman/PhotoEdit. **p. 510** © Elizabeth Crews. **p. 512** © Ted Horowitz/Corbis.

Chapter 15: p. 530 © Richard Hutchings/Corbis. **p. 540** © M. Fredericks/The Image Works. **p. 544** © Jeff Greenberg/The Image Works. **p. 546** © Jonathan Nourok/PhotoEdit. **p. 547** Steve Skjold/Alamy.

Chapter 16: p. 551 Dynamic Graphics Group/Creatas/Alamy. **p. 553** © SW Productions/PhotoDisc/Getty Images. **p. 560** © Robin Nelson/PhotoEdit. **p. 569** © Charles Gupton/Corbis. **p. 570** © Jeff Greenberg/PhotoEdit.

Name Index

Subject Index